Lecture Notes in Computer Science 14310

The series Lecture Notes in Computer Science (LNCS), including its subseries Lecture Notes in Artificial Intelligence (LNAI) and Lecture Notes in Bioinformatics (LNBI), has established itself as a medium for the publication of new developments in computer science and information technology research, teaching, and education.

LNCS enjoys close cooperation with the computer science R & D community, the series counts many renowned academics among its volume editors and paper authors, and collaborates with prestigious societies. Its mission is to serve this international community by providing an invaluable service, mainly focused on the publication of conference and workshop proceedings and postproceedings. LNCS commenced publication in 1973.

Shlomi Dolev · Baruch Schieber
Editors

Stabilization, Safety, and Security of Distributed Systems

25th International Symposium, SSS 2023
Jersey City, NJ, USA, October 2–4, 2023
Proceedings

Editors
Shlomi Dolev
Ben-Gurion University of the Negev
Be'er Sheva, Israel

Baruch Schieber
New Jersey Institute of Technology
Newark, NJ, USA

ISSN 0302-9743 ISSN 1611-3349 (electronic)
Lecture Notes in Computer Science
ISBN 978-3-031-44273-5 ISBN 978-3-031-44274-2 (eBook)
https://doi.org/10.1007/978-3-031-44274-2

This Springer imprint is published by the registered company Springer Nature Switzerland AG
The registered company address is: Gewerbestrasse 11, 6330 Cham, Switzerland

Paper in this product is recyclable.

Preface

The papers in this volume were presented at the *25th International Symposium on Stabilization, Safety, and Security of Distributed Systems (SSS)*, held on October 2–4, 2023, at NJIT, the Institute for Future Technologies in Jersey City, New Jersey.

SSS is an international forum for researchers and practitioners in the design and development of distributed systems with a focus on systems that are able to provide guarantees on their structure, performance, and/or security in the face of an adverse operational environment.

SSS started as a workshop dedicated to self-stabilizing systems, and the first two editions were held in 1989 and 1995, in Austin (USA) and Las Vegas (USA), respectively. From then, the workshop was held biennially until 2005 when it became an annual event. It broadened its scope and attracted researchers from other communities. In 2006, the name of the conference was changed to the International Symposium on Stabilization, Safety, and Security of Distributed Systems (SSS).

This year the Program Committee was organized into five tracks, reflecting major trends related to the conference: *(i)* Track A. Self-Stabilizing Systems: Theory and Practice, *(ii)* Track B. Distributed and Concurrent Computing: Foundations, Fault-Tolerance and Scalability, *(iii)* Track C. Cryptogrophy and Security, *(iv)* Track D. Dynamic, Mobile and Nature-Inspired Computing Mobile Agents, and *(v)* Distributed Databases.

We received 78 submissions. Each submission was double-blind review by at least three program committee members with the help of external reviewers. Out of the 78 submitted papers, 4 were (reviewed) invited papers, and 32 papers were selected as regular papers. The proceedings also included 8 brief announcements. Selected papers from the symposium will be published in a special issue of the journal *Theoretical Computer Science (TCS)*.

This year, we were very fortunate to have three distinguished keynote speakers: Maurice Herlihy, Alfred Spector, and Moti Yung. We were happy to award the best student paper award to Orestis Alpos and Christian Cachin for their paper "Do Not Trust in Numbers: Practical Distributed Cryptography with General Trust."

We are grateful to the Program Committee and the External Reviewers for their valuable and insightful comments. We also thank the members of the Steering Committee for their invaluable advice. Last but not least, on behalf of the Program Committee, we thank all the authors who submitted their work to SSS 2023.

October 2023

Shlomi Dolev
Baruch Schieber

Organization

General Chairs

Shlomi Dolev	Ben-Gurion University of the Negev, Israel
Baruch Schieber	New Jersey Institute of Technology, USA

Publicity Chairs

Nisha Panwar	Augusta University, USA
Volker Turau	University of Hamburg, Germany

Organization Chairs

Elke David	Ben-Gurion University of the Negev, Israel
Selenny Fabre	New Jersey Institute of Technology, USA
Rosemary Franklin	Ben-Gurion University of the Negev, Israel

Steering Committee

Anish Arora	Ohio State University, USA
Shlomi Dolev	Ben-Gurion University of the Negev, Israel
Sandeep Kulkarni	Michigan State University, USA
Toshimitsu Masuzawa	Osaka University, Japan
Franck Petit	Sorbonne Université, France
Sébastien Tixeuil (Chair)	Sorbonne Université, France
Elad Michael Schiller	Chalmers University of Technology, Sweden

Advisory Committee

Sukumar Ghosh	University of Iowa, USA
Mohamed Gouda	University of Texas at Austin, USA
Ted Herman	University of Iowa, USA

In Memory Of

Ajoy Kumar Datta
Edsger W. Dijkstra

Program Committee

Track A. Self-Stabilizing Systems: Theory and Practice

Lelia Blin (Co-chair)	Sorbonne Université - LIP6, France
Yuichi Sudo (Co-chair)	Hosei University, Japan
Janna Burman	LISN, Université Paris-Saclay, France
Ho-Lin Chen	National Taiwan University, Taiwan
Swan Dubois	Sorbonne Université, France
Anaïs Durand	Université Clermont Auvergne, France
Ryota Eguchi	Nara Institute of Science and Technology, Japan
Yuval Emek	Technion Institute of Technology, Israel
Chryssis Georgiou	University of Cyprus, Cyprus
Sayaka Kamei	Hiroshima University, Japan
Alexey Gotsman	IMDEA Software Institute, Spain
Yonghwan Kim	Nagoya Institute of Technology, Japan
Mikhail Nesterenko	Kent State University, USA
Mor Perry	Academic College of Tel Aviv-Yaffo, Israel
Tomasz Jurdziński	University of Wroclaw, Poland
Sayaka Kamei	Hiroshima University, Japan
Dariusz Kowalski	Augusta University, USA
Anissa Lamani	Université de Strasbourg, France
Othon Michail	University of Liverpool, UK
Alessia Milani	Aix-Marseille Université/LIS CNRS UMR 7020, France
Miguel Mosteiro	Pace University, USA
Mikhail Nesterenko	Kent State University, USA
Nicolas Nicolaou	University of Cyprus, Cyprus
Franck Petit	LiP6 CNRS-INRIA UPMC Sorbonne Université, France
Giuseppe Prencipe	Università di Pisa, Italy
Sergio Rajsbaum	Universidad Nacional Autónoma de México, Mexico
Ivan Rapaport	DIM and CMM (UMI 2807 CNRS), Universidad de Chile, Chile
Christopher Thraves	Universidad de Concepción, Chile

Lewis Tseng	Boston College, USA
Sara Tucci-Piergiovanni	Sapienza University of Rome, Italy
Volker Turau	Hamburg University of Technology, Germany
Giovanni Viglietta	JAIST, Japan
Prudence Wong	University of Liverpool, UK
Yukiko Yamauchi	Kyushu University, Japan

Track B. Distributed and Concurrent Computing: Foundations, Fault-Tolerance and Scalability

Michel Raynal (Co-chair)	IRISA, France
Achour Mostefaoui (Co-chair)	Nantes Université, France
Sergio Arevalo-Viñuales	Polytechnic University of Madrid, Spain
Quentin Bramas	ICUBE, Université de Strasbourg, France
Armando Castaneda	UNAM, Mexico
Hugues Fauconnier	IRIF Université Paris-Diderot, France
Carole Delporte-Gallet	University Paris Diderot, France
Vincent Gramoli	University of Sydney and Redbelly Network, Australia
Raimundo Macêdo	LASID/DCC/UFBA, Brazil
Fernando Pedone	Università della Svizzera Italiana, Italy
Paolo Romano	Lisbon University and INESC-ID, Portugal
Gadi Taubenfeld	Interdisciplinary Center Herzliya, Israel
Corentin Travers	LIS, Université d'Aix-Marseille, France
Lewis Tseng	Boston College, USA
Garg Vijay	UT Austin, USA
Jennifer Welch	Texas A&M University, USA

Track C. Cryptography and Security

Chandrasekaran Pandurangan (Co-chair)	Indian Institute of Technology Madras, India
Reza Curtmola (Co-chair)	NJIT, USA
Moti Yung (Co-chair)	Columbia University and Google, USA
Yinzhi Cao	Johns Hopkins University, USA
Ashish Choudhury	IIIT Bangalore, India
Jonathan Katz	GMU, USA
Anish Mathuria	DA-IICT, India
Sourav Mukhopadhyay	Indian Institute of Technology, Kharagpur, India
Dhiman Saha	Indian Institute of Technology Bhilai, India
Somitra Sanadhya	IIT Jodhpur, India
Qiang Tang	University of Sydney, Australia

Aishwarya Thiruvengadam	IIT Madras, India
Susanne Wetzel	Stevens Institute of Technology, USA

Track D. Dynamic, Mobile and Nature-Inspired Computing Mobile Agents

Paola Flocchini (Co-chair)	University of Ottawa, Canada
Nicola Santoro (Co-chair)	Carleton University, Canada
Subhash Bhagat	IIT Jodhpur, India
Joshua Daymude	Arizona State University, USA
Stéphane Devismes	MIS Lab, UR 4290, France
Giuseppe Di Luna	Sapienza University of Rome, Italy
Anissa Lamani	University of Strasbourg, France
Euripides Markou	University of Thessaly, Greece
Toshimitsu Masuzawa	Osaka University, Japan
Krishnendu Mukhopadhyaya	Indian Statistical Institute, India
Alfredo Navarra	University of Perugia, Italy
Giuseppe Prencipe	University of Pisa, Italy
Gokarna Sharma	Kent State University, USA
Koichi Wada	Hosei University, Japan

Track E. Distributed Databases

Sharad Mehrotra (Co-chair)	University of California at Irvine, USA
Shantanu Sharma (Co-chair)	New Jersey Institute of Technology, USA
Engin Arslan	University of Nevada, Reno, USA
Johes Bater	Tufts University, USA
Senjuti Basu Roy	New Jersey Institute of Technology, USA
Dong Deng	Rutgers University, USA
Sara Foresti	Università degli Studi di Milano, Italy
Himanshu Gupta	IBM India, India
Peeyush Gupta	Couchbase, USA
Suyash Gupta	University of California, Berkeley, USA
Rihan Hai	TU Delft, The Netherlands
Vagelis Hristidis	University of California, Riverside, USA
Thomas Hütter	University of Salzburg, Austria
Raghav Kaushik	Microsoft Research, USA
Avinash Kumar	Google, USA
Sujaya Maiyya	University of Waterloo, Canada
Keshav Murthy	Couchbase, USA
Vincent Oria	New Jersey Institute of Technology, USA
Sarvesh Pandey	Banaras Hindu University, India
Nisha Panwar	Augusta University, USA

Primal Pappachan	Pennsylvania State University, USA
Stefano Paraboschi	Università di Bergamo, Italy
Romila Pradhan	Purdue University, USA
Uday Kiran Rage	University of Aizu, Japan
Indrajit Ray	Colorado State University, USA
Indrakshi Ray	Colorado State University, USA
Mohammad Sadoghi	University of California, Davis, USA
Pierangela Samarati	Università degli Studi di Milano, Italy
Hiteshi Sharma	Microsoft, USA
Lidan Shou	Zhejiang University, China
Roee Shraga	Northeastern University, USA
Tarique Siddiqui	Microsoft Research, USA
Rekha Singhal	TCS, India
Dimitrios Theodoratos	New Jersey Institute of Technology, USA
Roberto Yus	University of Maryland, Baltimore County, USA

External Reviewers

Ananya Appan	SAP Labs, India
Kaustav Bose	Flatiron Construction, USA
Abhinav Chakraborty	Indian Statistical Institute, India
Anirudh Chandramouli	Bar-Ilan University, Israel
Serafino Cicerone	University of L'Aquila, Italy
Alain Cournier	Université de Picardie Jules Verne, France
Shantanu Das	Laboratoire d'Informatique et Systèmes, France
Alessia Di Fonso	University of L'Aquila, Italy
Gabriele Di Stefano	University of L'Aquila, Italy
Mitch Jacovetty	Kent State University, USA
Yoshiaki Katayama	Osaka University, Japan
Yonghwan Kim	Nagoya Institute of Technology, Japan
Ajay Kshemkalyani	University of Illinois at Chicago, USA
Manish Kumar	Bar-Ilan University, Israel
Kaushik Mondal	Indian Institute of Technology, Bombay, India
Shyam Murthy	IIIT Bangalore, India
Debasish Pattanayak	Université du Québec en Outaouais, Canada
Sachit Rao	IIIT Bangalore, India
Robert Streit	University of Texas at Austin, USA

Sponsors

In cooperation with

Contents

Exploring Worst Cases of Self-stabilizing Algorithms Using Simulations

Erwan Jahier[1(✉)], Karine Altisen[1], and Stéphane Devismes[2]

[1] Univ. Grenoble Alpes, CNRS, Grenoble INP, VERIMAG, Grenoble, France
erwan.jahier@univ-grenoble-alpes.fr

[2] Université de Picardie Jules Verne, MIS, Amiens, France

Abstract. Self-stabilization qualifies the ability of a distributed system to recover after transient failures. SASA is a simulator of self-stabilizing algorithms written in the atomic-state model, the most commonly used model in the self-stabilizing area.

A simulator is, in particular, useful to study the time complexity of algorithms. For example, one can experimentally check whether existing theoretical bounds are correct or tight. Simulations are also useful to get insights when no bound is known.

In this paper, we use SASA to investigate the worst cases of various well-known self-stabilization algorithms. We apply classical optimization methods (such as local search, branch and bound, Tabu list) on the two sources of non-determinism: the choice of initial configuration and the scheduling of process activations (daemon). We propose a methodology based on heuristics and an open-source tool to find tighter worst-case lower bounds.

1 Introduction

Usually, simulator engines are employed to test and find flaws early in the design process. Another popular usage of simulators is the empirical evaluation of average-case time complexity via simulation campaigns [3,6,9]. In this paper, we propose to investigate how to build worst-case executions of self-stabilizing algorithms using a simulator engine. For that purpose, we will apply classical optimization methods and heuristics on the two sources of non-determinism: the choice of the initial configuration and the scheduling of process activations. To that goal, we consider SASA [9], an open-source and versatile simulator dedicated to self-stabilizing algorithms written in the atomic-state model, the most commonly used model in self-stabilization. In this model, in one atomic step, a process can read its state and that of its neighbors, perform some local computations, and update its state accordingly. Local algorithms are defined as set of rules of the form ⟨*Guard*⟩ → ⟨*Statement*⟩. The guard is a Boolean predicate on the states of the process and its neighbors. The statement is a list of assignments

This work has been partially funded by the ANR project SkyData (ANR-22-CE25-0008-01).

S. Dolev and B. Schieber (Eds.): SSS 2023, LNCS 14310, pp. 1–17, 2023.
https://doi.org/10.1007/978-3-031-44274-2_1

on all or a part of the process' variables. A process is said to be enabled if the guard of at least one of its rules evaluates to true. Executions proceed in atomic steps in which at least one enabled process *moves*, *i.e.*, executes an enabled rule.

Self-stabilization [15] qualifies the ability of a distributed system to recover within finite time after transient faults. Starting from an arbitrary configuration, a self-stabilizing algorithm makes the system eventually reach a so-called *legitimate* configuration from which every possible execution suffix satisfies the intended specification. Self-stabilizing algorithms are mainly compared according to their *stabilization time*, *i.e.*, the maximum time, starting from an arbitrary configuration, before reaching a legitimate configuration. The stabilization time of algorithms written in the atomic-state model is commonly evaluated in terms of rounds, which measure the execution time according to the speed of the slowest processes. Another crucial issue is the *number of moves* which captures the number of local state updates. By definition, the stabilization time in moves exhibits the amount of computations an algorithm needs to recover a correct behavior. Hence, the move complexity is rather a measure of work than a measure of time: minimizing the number of state modifications allows the algorithm to use less communication operations and communication bandwidth [16].

In the atomic-state model, the asynchrony of the system is materialized by the notion of *daemon*. This latter is an adversary that decides which enabled processes move at each step. The most general daemon is the *distributed unfair* one. It only imposes the progress in the execution, *i.e.*, while there are enabled processes, at least one moves during the next step. Algorithms stabilizing under such an assumption are highly desirable because they work under any daemon assumption. Finally, since it does not impose fairness among process activations, the stabilization time of every self-stabilizing algorithm working under the distributed unfair daemon is necessarily finite in terms of moves.[1]

There are many self-stabilizing algorithms proven under the distributed unfair daemon [6,11,13,19]. However, analyses of the stabilization time in moves remain rather unusual and this is sometime an important issue. Indeed, several self-stabilizing algorithms working under a distributed unfair daemon have been shown to have an exponential stabilization time in moves in the worst case [6] for silent self-stabilizing leader election algorithms given in [11,13,14] for the BFS spanning tree construction of Huang and Chen [22], and [20] for the silent self-stabilizing algorithm they proposed in [19].

Methods and Contributions. Exhibiting worst-case executions in terms of stabilization time in moves is usually a difficult task since the executions of numerous interconnected processes involve many possible interleavings in executions. The combinatorics induced by such distributed executions is sometime hard to capture in order to prove a relevant lower bound. Hence, we propose here to use the simulator engine SASA to give some insights about worst-case scenarios. By judiciously exploring the transition system, we can expect to quickly find bad scenarios that can be generalized afterwards to obtain tighter bounds.

[1] The (classical) weakly fair daemon, for example, does not provide such a guarantee.

We consider here self-stabilizing algorithms working under the unfair daemon. Hence, the subgraph of the transition system induced by the set of illegitimate configurations is a directed acyclic graph (DAG). This subgraph can be huge and also dense since from a given configuration we may have up to $2^n - 1$ possible directed edges, where n is the number of nodes. Note that worst-case scenarios in moves are frequently central [5,6]: at each step, exactly one process moves. Therefore, and because it limits the number of possible steps from a configuration to at most n, we focus in the experiments on central schedulers – even if the methods presented in the article actually work for other unfair daemons.

Even with this restriction, the space to explore remains huge. Since worst cases depend on the initial configuration and the scheduling of moves, we propose exploration heuristics targeting these two sources of non-determinism. The goal is to get some insights on algorithms upper bounds, or to assess how tight known upper bounds are.

One of the proposed heuristics relies on so-called *potential functions*. A potential function is a classical technique used to prove convergence (and stabilization) of algorithms: it provides an evaluation of any configuration and decreases along all paths made of illegitimate configurations. We use them to guide the state space exploration, and to use classical optimization techniques (branch and bound). Note that potential functions usually give a rough upper bound on the stabilization time. Again, our approach allows to refine such a bound.

We also propose heuristics based on local search to speed-up the finding of worst-case initial configurations. All those heuristics are implemented into the open-source simulator SASA, and conclusive experiments on well-known self-stabilization algorithms are performed.

Related Work. SASA [9] is an open-source and versatile simulator dedicated to self-stabilizing algorithms written in the atomic-state model. All important concepts used in the model are available in SASA: simulations can be run and evaluated in moves, atomic steps, and rounds. Classical daemons are available: central, locally central, distributed, and synchronous daemons. Every level of anonymity can be considered, from fully anonymous to (partially or fully) identified. Finally, distributed algorithms can be either uniform (all nodes execute the same local algorithm) or non-uniform. SASA can be used to perform batch simulations which can use test oracles to check expected properties. For example, one can check that the stabilization time in rounds is upper bounded by a given function. The distribution provides several facilities to achieve batch-mode simulation campaigns. Simulations can also be run interactively, step by step (forward or backward), for debugging purposes.

Only a few other simulators dedicated to self-stabilization in locally shared memory models, such as the atomic-state model, have been proposed. None of them offers features to deal with worst-case scenarios. Flatebo and Datta [18] propose a simulator of the atomic-state model to evaluate leader election, mutual exclusion, and ℓ-exclusion algorithms on restricted topologies, mainly rings. This simulator has limited facilities including classical daemons and evaluation of stabilization time in moves only. It is not available anymore. Müllner *et al.* [24] present a simulator of the register model, a computational model which is close to the atomic-state model. This simulator does not allow to evaluate stabilization time. Actually, it focuses on three fault tolerance measures initially devoted to masking fault-tolerant systems (namely, reliability, instantaneous availability, and limiting availability [25]) to evaluate them on self-stabilizing systems. These measures are still uncommon today in analyses of self-stabilizing algorithms. The simulator proposed by Har-Tal [21] allows to run self-stabilizing algorithms in the register model on small networks (around 10 nodes). It proposes a small amount of facilities, *i.e.*, the execution scheduling is either synchronous, or controlled step by step by the user. Only the legitimacy of the current configuration can be tested. It provides neither batch mode, nor debugging tools. Evcimen *et al.* describe in [17] a simulation engine for self-stabilizing algorithms in message passing. Their simulator uses heavy mechanisms to implement this model, such as queue of events, threads, and fault injection. In the Evcimen *et al.*'s simulator, the execution scheduler can be only fully asynchronous. Being corner cases, central and synchronous executions are very useful to find bugs or to exhibit a worst-case scenario.

Several other studies deal with the empirical evaluation of self-stabilizing algorithms [1–3]. However, these studies focus on the average-case time complexity. Note that SASA has been also used to tackle average-case stabilization times through simulation campaigns [9].

2 Exploring Daemons

For a given topology T and an initial configuration c_{init}, the stabilization time in moves of an algorithm A depends on the choices made by the daemon at each step. Finding a worst-case stabilization time requires to explore all the illegitimate configurations of the transition system. Hence, we define $\mathcal{R}(A, T, c_{init})$ as the transition system where all legitimate configurations are collapsed into one node, as illustrated in Fig. 1. As the size of $\mathcal{R}(A, T, c_{init})$ grows exponentially, we need exploration heuristics. The goal of those heuristics is to build a scheduling of actions and thus to implement a daemon. We call *exhaustive daemon* the algorithm that builds a central daemon by exploring $\mathcal{R}(A, T, c_{init})$ until finding a longest path; we also use *random daemons* which, at each configuration, pick the next move uniformly at random.

Greedy Daemons. In self-stabilization, a *potential function* ϕ maps configurations to the set of natural integers and satisfies the following two properties: (1) if $\phi(c)$ is minimum, then c is legitimate; (2) ϕ is decreasing over illegitimate configurations, *i.e.*, for every execution $c_0, \dots c_i, c_{i+1}, \dots$, for every $i \geq 0$, if c_i is illegitimate, then $\phi(c_i) > \phi(c_{i+1})$. Exhibiting such a function is a classical technique to prove the self-stabilization of an algorithm. The idea here is to use potential functions during simulations, and define *greedy daemons* that always choose configurations that maximize ϕ. As shown by the experiments we perform below, for most algorithms, greedy daemons find longer *paths* in $\mathscr{R}(A, T, c_{init})$ than random ones – but not necessarily the longest.

Cutting Exploration Branches. Using a greedy daemon is of course a heuristic that can miss the longest path. To find it, we need to backtrack (branch) in the exploration of $\mathscr{R}(A, T, c_{init})$. A first simple optimization is the following: (1) perform a greedy traversal of $\mathscr{R}(A, T, c_{init})$ to get a lower bound on the maximum number of moves to stabilization; (2) then, during the remaining of the exploration, all configurations which depth (*i.e.*, the distance to c_{init}) plus its potential is less than or equal to the known lower bound will never lead to a longer path: the corresponding branches can then be cut (bound) without missing the worst-case. This can reduce a lot the number of steps necessary to explore exhaustively $\mathscr{R}(A, T, c_{init})$; see experiments below.

Perfect Potential Functions. Given an algorithm, a topology and an initial configuration, we say that the potential function is *perfect* if the corresponding greedy traversal finds in n moves a legitimate configuration when the potential of the initial configuration is n (*i.e.*, if it decreases by one at each move). In such cases, which are easy to detect during simulations, it is useless to continue the search as no better (longer) path can be found.

Tabu List. A classical optimization used to explore graphs is to maintain a (tabu) list of visited nodes in order to avoid to revisit the same node twice. A classical heuristic to prevent this list to grow too much is to keep only the more recently visited nodes. When a configuration α in the tabu list is reached, the length of the path associated to α just need to be updated. This often reduces drastically the exploration time measured in terms of number of visited edges of $\mathscr{R}(A, T, c_{init})$.

Promising Daemons. Consider Fig. 1; according to the values of ϕ, a greedy daemon would choose the path $c_{init} - c_5 - c_6 - \mathscr{C}_s$. In order to search for a better solution, one could backtrack to the last choice point (c_5), which amounts to perform a depth-first traversal of $\mathscr{R}(A, T, c_{init})$.

As $\mathscr{R}(A, T, c_{init})$ can be huge, exploring it exhaustively can be very long, and the use of a timeout is necessary in practice. In this context, it is better to explore the most promising configurations first. The next configurations that would be explored by a depth-first traversal would be c_7 or c_8; but they do not look promising, as their potential is 2 – which means that at most two more moves would be needed to reach the set of legitimate configurations $\mathscr{C}_s$, and will not lead to big improvements.

By taking into account the depth d in $\mathscr{R}(A, T, c_{init})$ and the potential ϕ, we can choose to backtrack to a more promising configuration. In order to have a choice criterion, we can remark that so far (once the greedy daemon found a path of length 3), each move consumed $18/3 = 6$ of the initial potential; we denote

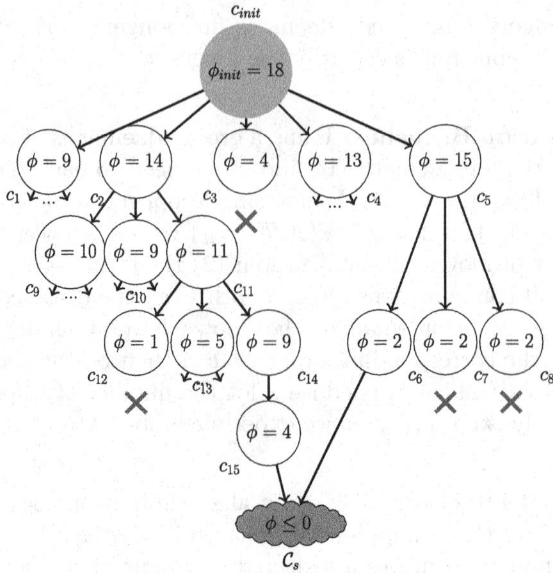

Fig. 1. Selected nodes in the graph $\mathscr{R}(A, T, c_{init})$ (Color figure online)

by s_ϕ this quantity. By choosing the configuration which maximizes the *promise* computed by $d + \phi/s_\phi$, we can hope to do better than a simple depth-first-search and find better solutions first. We now detail the behavior of this heuristic on the $\mathscr{R}(A, T, c_{init})$ of Fig. 1.

1. At the beginning, from c_{init}, we need to consider configurations that all have the same depth (c_1, c_2, c_3, c_4, c_5); the one with the highest promise is therefore the one with the highest potential, c_5.
2. c_7 and c_8 are thus added to the set of configurations to be considered (c_6 has already been visited during the initial greedy traversal), but their promises $(2 + 2/6 = 2.33)$ are lower than the promise of c_2 $(1 + 14/6 = 3.34)$.
3. c_2 is therefore selected, which adds c_9, c_{10}, c_{11} in the configurations set to be explored.
4. c_{11} has a promise of $2 + 11/6 = 3.83$, and is thus preferred over c_4, which has a promise of $1 + 13/6 = 3.17$.
5. Then c_{14} $(3 + 9/6 = 4.5)$ and c_{15} $(4 + 4/6 = 4.67)$ are selected, a new path of length 5 is found and s_ϕ is updated.

At this stage, all configurations for which the sum of the depth and the potential is smaller or equal than 5 can be cut (*cf.* red crosses in Fig. 1).

This algorithm is an heuristic in the sense that it sometimes finds the worst-case faster, but the exploration remains exhaustive as only branches that cannot lead to a worst-case are cut. Another exploration heuristics would have been to select configurations according to the sum of their depth and their potential. But using such a heuristic would delay the discovering of new longest paths (in step 4 above, c_4 would have been chosen over c_{11}), which in turn would prevent to cut branches. More generally, favoring depth over breadth allows to find longer paths sooner, which allows to cut more branches sooner and speed up the exhaustive exploration – which make this idea interesting even without using timeouts.

When No Potential Function is Available. Finding a potential function can be challenging for some algorithms. But note that any function that is able to approximate accurately enough the distance between a configuration and the set of legitimate configurations could be used to guide the exploration of $\mathscr{R}(A, T, c_{init})$ with the heuristics described above. The result of an exhaustive exploration using such a *pseudo-potential function* should be interpreted with care using the optimization described so far since the actual best solution can be missed.

Benchmark Algorithms. Those ideas have been implemented in SASA. We propose to experiment them on the following set of algorithms:

1. `token` is the first token ring algorithm proposed by Dijkstra [15]. It stabilizes to a legitimate configuration from which a unique token circulates in the ring. We use the potential function given in [5].
2. `coloring`is a vertex coloring algorithm [7]. The potential function, proposed in [7], counts the number of conflicting nodes.
3. `te-a5sf` consists of the two last layers of the algorithm given in Chapter 7 of [7] to illustrate some algorithm composition. It consists of a bottom-up computation followed by a top-down computation of the rooted tree. Its potential function is inspired from the general method proposed in [8].
4. `k-clust` computes sub-graphs (clusters) of radius at most k [12] in rooted trees. Its potential function is made of the sum of enabled node levels in the tree, as described in [4].
5. `st-algo1` computes a spanning tree (the first of the 2 algorithms proposed in [23]). Its potential function, also given in [23], consists of counting the number of correctly directed edges.
6. `unison` is a clock synchronization algorithm that stabilizes to a configuration from which clocks of neighboring nodes differ from at most one [10]. To the best of our knowledge, no potential function has been ever proposed for this algorithm. We use instead a pseudo-potential function that consists of counting the number of nodes that are not synchronized.

Simulations are performed on different topologies: directed rings (noted diring), random rooted trees (rtree), Erdős-Rényi random graphs (er), lines, grids and stars; in the sequel, the size of those graphs (in number of nodes) is noted aside the graph name. For example, diring5 denotes a directed ring with 5 nodes.

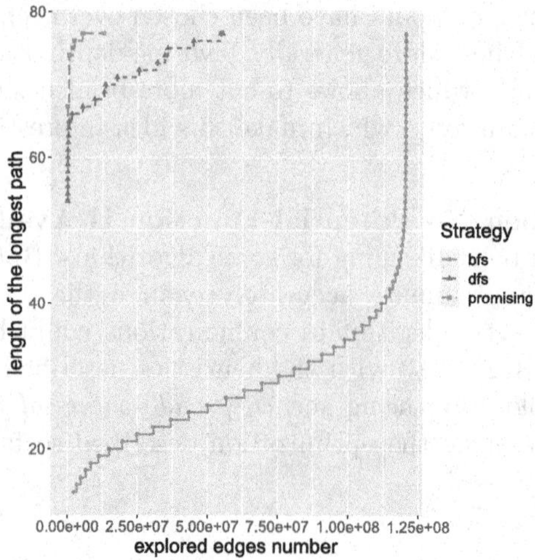

Fig. 2. Comparing exhaustive exploration strategies on `te-a5sf`/rtree5.

Finding Longest Paths First. The motivation for defining promising daemons is to find the longest paths as soon as possible during the exploration. In order to assess our design choices, we have conducted an experiment where, during a simulation of the `te-a5sf` algorithm on a rooted tree of size 5 under the promising daemon, we store the number of edges explored in $\mathscr{R}(A, T, c_{init})$ each time a new longest path is found. Figure 2 shows the result of this experiment together with the result obtained with a Depth-First Search (DFS) and a Breadth-First Search (BFS) exploration using the same parameters. One can see on Fig. 2 that indeed, on this particular example at least, the promising heuristic is better than a DFS exploration: the longest paths are discovered sooner, which allows to cut more branches and leads to less explored edges (less than 12 millions versus more than 55 millions for DFS and 120 millions for BFS) to perform the exhaustive exploration. Notice that it is just an heuristic, that sometimes gives better result, and sometimes doesn't.

Measuring the Effect of Branch Cuts and Tabu Lists. We ran the promising heuristic (values are similar with a Depth-First Search) with and without the optimizations of branch-cuts and tabu list.

Table 1 contains the results of the following experiments. We chose small enough topologies to get a result in a reasonable amount of time when computing without optimization (we use random rooted trees for `unison`, as for `k-clust` and `te-a5sf`). For a given algorithm and once the topology is fixed, an experiment consists of picking an initial configuration uniformly at random and running a simulation on it with four different sets of options. Column 2 contains the number of edges explored during the simulation using a promising daemon with no optimization at all. Column 3 contains the gain factor compared to the values of Column 2 using the branch-cuts *and* the tabu list optimizations. Column 4 (resp. 5) contains the same gain factor but using only the branch-cuts (resp. the tabu list) optimization. Each number in this table is the average of x experiments that were performed with different initial configurations picked at random. It is given (at the right-hand-side of the $\pm$ symbol) with the bounds of the corresponding confidence interval at 95% ($1.96 \times \sigma/\sqrt{x}$, where σ is the standard deviation). In order to get a tight enough interval, experiments were repeated from $x = 200$ to $x = 100\,000$ times.

Table 1. Measuring the effect of branch-cuts and tabu list.

algo/topology	no optimization edges number	cut + tabu gain factor	cut gain factor	tabu gain factor
`token`/diring5	$1\,400 \pm 100$	11 ± 0.7	11 ± 0.7	6 ± 0.3
`token`/diring6	$4 \cdot 10^6 \pm 2 \cdot 10^6$	$8\,500 \pm 4\,000$	$4\,700 \pm 3\,000$	$2\,200 \pm 800$
`k-clust`/rtree5	380 ± 30	5.4 ± 0.3	2.9 ± 0.1	4 ± 0.2
`k-clust`/rtree6	$2\,900 \pm 70$	18 ± 0.4	5.6 ± 0.2	12 ± 0.2
`k-clust`/rtree7	$2 \cdot 10^4 \pm 2 \cdot 10^3$	58 ± 5	7 ± 0.8	39 ± 3
`k-clust`/rtree8	$7 \cdot 10^5 \pm 8 \cdot 10^4$	850 ± 90	59 ± 20	400 ± 30
`te-a5sf`/rtree3	$2\,800 \pm 7$	12 ± 0.02	3 ± 0	10 ± 0.01
`te-a5sf`/rtree4	$6 \cdot 10^6 \pm 6 \cdot 10^4$	$2\,000 \pm 10$	6.2 ± 0.05	$1\,800 \pm 10$
`unison`/rtree3	12 ± 0.1	1.2 ± 0	1.2 ± 0	1.1 ± 0
`unison`/rtree4	$3\,900 \pm 100$	76 ± 2	73 ± 2	13 ± 0.3
`unison`/rtree5	$4 \cdot 10^7 \pm 1 \cdot 10^7$	$3 \cdot 10^5 \pm 2 \cdot 10^5$	$3 \cdot 10^5 \pm 2 \cdot 10^5$	$1 \cdot 10^4 \pm 7 \cdot 10^3$

Table 1 shows that, on those algorithms and topologies, the optimization gain factor grows exponentially with the topology size. It also shows that the two optimizations are complementary in the sense that their effects are cumulative.

Note that we do not show any result for `coloring` nor `st-algo1` since their potential functions are perfect which makes promising exploration useless.

Daemons Comparison. Given an algorithm and a topology with a particular initial configuration, the simplest way to search for the longest path is to perform several simulations using a random daemon. In order to assess the idea of using more elaborated methods based on a potential function and use greedy or promising daemons, we ran another set of simulations. Note that, as for the random daemon, we have performed several runs of the greedy one since it also has a random behavior with SASA: indeed, when several choices lead to the same potential, one is chosen uniformly at random. On the contrary, the promising daemon only needs to be run once.

The results obtained with those three kinds of daemons are provided in Table 2. This table is obtained, for each algorithm and topology, by repeating 1 000 times the following experiment:

1. choose an initial configuration I;
2. run once the promising daemon on I and report the resulting move number in column 2;
3. run n_1 (resp. n_2) times the algorithm on I with a greedy (resp. random) daemon and report the maximum move number in column 3 (resp. column 4). The numbers of simulations n_1 and n_2 are chosen in such a way that the same amount of CPU time budget is used for the three daemons.

Table 2 the shows average values for those 1 000 experiments, as well as the corresponding 95% confidence interval bounds. The last column indicates the total wall-clock simulation time.

Table 2. The longest path obtained with different daemons.

algo/topology	Promising	Greedy	Random	time
`coloring`/er11	4.6 ± 0.1	4.6 ± 0.1	4.2 ± 0.08	28 m
`st-algo1`/er20	24 ± 0.4	24 ± 0.4	23 ± 0.4	1 h
`k-clust`/rtree14	24 ± 0.3	22 ± 0.3	18 ± 0.2	3 h
`token`/diring12	69 ± 0.8	66 ± 0.8	28 ± 0.4	47 m
`te-a5sf`/rtree5	32 ± 0.07	30 ± 0.05	22 ± 0.1	1 h

The potential functions of `coloring` and `st-algo1` being perfect, the result is the same for greedy and promising daemons. Moreover, they do not significantly improve the result of the random daemon.

For `token`, `k-clust`, and `te-a5sf`, greedy daemons give better results than random ones, but fail to find the best solution given by the promising daemon.

The case of `unison` and its pseudo-potential function requires a special attention. Indeed, as previously noticed, the promising daemon with the branch-cut optimization is not exhaustive. This is why the results of the experimentation of this algorithm is in a different table (Table 3), which has an extra column (Column 2) that contains the result of the promising daemon run without this optimization. We can observe that the promising daemon finds much better solutions than the greedy daemon, provided that the cut optimization is inhibited. The greedy daemon is itself much better than the random daemon on most topologies. Note that the greedy daemon sometimes does better than the promising daemon (*e.g.*, on `grid16`), which seems counter-intuitive as the promising daemon starts its exploration by a greedy search. This can be explained since greedy daemons have randomness, and in Column 4, each experiment consists of several (n_1) simulations.

Table 3. The longest path obtained with different daemons for `unison`.

algo/topology	Promising no cut	Promising	Greedy	Random	time
`unison`/ring10	42 ± 2	27 ± 0.3	26 ± 0.2	18 ± 0.4	19 m
`unison`/er11	83 ± 4	35 ± 0.6	39 ± 0.6	22 ± 0.5	6 h
`unison`/grid16	59 ± 1	37 ± 0.5	40 ± 0.3	29 ± 0.4	29 h
`unison`/chain10	75 ± 2	36 ± 0.4	37 ± 0.4	19 ± 0.3	3 h
`unison`/rtree10	55 ± 3	27 ± 0.6	24 ± 0.7	19 ± 0.4	7 h
`unison`/star8	23 ± 0.6	15 ± 0.3	16 ± 0.4	14 ± 0.2	4 h

3 Exploring Initial Configurations

For a given topology, the stabilization time is also impacted by the choice of the initial configuration. Here again, simulations can help to experimentally figure out the worst case, and check whether the known bounds are tight.

3.1 Assessing Initial Configurations

Given an initial configuration I, a way to evaluate its ability to lead to worst case stabilization time is to exhaustively explore $\mathscr{R}(A, T, c_I)$ and seek for the longest path. Of course this is costly[2], in particular if we want to do that on a large number of configurations. Using a greedy or a random daemon to approximate this configuration evaluation would be cheaper, but how could we know if a *good* configuration, that leads to a long path, for a random or a greedy daemon, is also

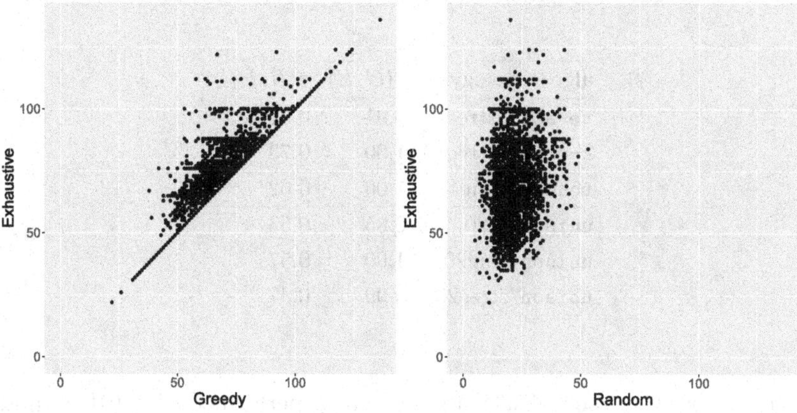

Fig. 3. Comparing configuration evaluation methods by running simulations of `token` on a directed ring of size 12.

[2] Even using the optimizations of Sect. 2.

a good configuration w.r.t. an exhaustive exploration? In other words, are the results of those different evaluations methods correlated? In order to get some insights on this question, we study this hypothesis experimentally, by running simulations using those three different daemons, and looking at the resulting stabilization time.

Figure 3 shows the result of such an experiment on the `token` algorithm over a directed ring of size 12. Each of the 1 000 points in both graphics is computed by running a simulation from a different random configuration; its abscissa corresponds to the stabilization time (in moves) obtained using a greedy (left) and a random (right) daemon; its ordinate corresponds to the stabilization time obtained using a promising (and thus exhaustive) daemon. One can notice that on this set of simulations, the worst case obtained by the greedy daemon (rightmost point of the left-hand-side graphics) is also the worst case for the exhaustive daemon (topmost point), whereas it is not the case for the worst case of the random daemon (*cf.* the rightmost point of the right-hand-side graphics). In order to synthesize this analysis numerically, we propose the following experiment. Given an algorithm A and a topology T:

- choose n initial configurations of the system at random;
- for each configuration j, measure (by simulations) the stabilization time R_j, G_j, and E_j using respectively a random, a greedy and an exhaustive daemon;
- let j_r, j_g, j_e be the index of the maximum of the sets $\{R_j\}_j$, $\{G_j\}_j$, and $\{E_j\}_j$ respectively; compute $\tau(R, E) = E_{j_r}/E_{j_e}$ and $\tau(G, E) = E_{j_g}/E_{j_e}$ to estimate the loss ratio that one gets by approximating the exhaustive daemon based evaluation of a configuration by a random and a greedy daemon.

Table 4. Measuring the correlation between worst cases obtained with various daemons

algo/topology	$\tau(G, E)$	$\tau(R, E)$
`te-a5sf`/rtree5	0.91	0.91
`k-clust`/rtree10	1.00	0.73
`token`/diring12	1.00	0.62
`unison`/er20	0.85	0.53
`unison`/ring20	1.00	0.57
`unison`/rtree20	0.99	0.47

Table 4 shows the result of such an experiment performed with 10 000 random initial configurations. We did not use the `coloring` nor the `st-algo1`, as greedy and exhaustive (with perfect ϕ) daemons produce the same results. One can observe that the worst cases obtained with exhaustive daemon-based evaluation and the greedy daemon-based one are indeed very well correlated. It is therefore interesting to approximate exhaustive daemons with greedy ones during the search of worst-case initial configuration.

When no potential function is available, using random daemons may be a stopgap, even if the correlation between random and exhaustive daemons is weaker. The exhaustive exploration of the daemons state space can then always be done, but without the branch-cut optimization. Smaller topologies should thus be considered.

3.2 Local Search

We can define a notion of distance between two configurations, for instance by counting the number of node states that differ (Hamming distance), and by which amount they differ (using a user-defined function). One practical question to find efficiently worst-case configurations is then the following: do close configurations lead to similar stabilization time in moves? If the answer is yes, it means that it should be interesting to perform a so-called *local search*, which consists of:

1. choosing a configuration I;
2. choosing a configuration I' that is close to I;
3. evaluating I by running a simulation (using, *e.g.*, a greedy daemon);
4. continuing in step 1 with the configuration I' if it leads to a higher stabilization time than I, and with I otherwise.

It is difficult to answer to such a question in the general case, as the answer might differ on the algorithm or on the topology. Once again, simulations can be useful to get insights.

SASA implements the local search described above. The SASA API requires the user to define a distance between two states, so that SASA can compute the configuration neighborhood. In order to take advantage of multi-core architectures, SASA tries several neighbors at each step, and puts them into a priority queue. The number of elements that are tried at each step depends on the number of cores that are used. The priority in the queue is computed by launching a simulation from the corresponding initial configuration (and any daemon available in SASA can be used).

An Experiment to Compare Global and Local Search. In order to assess the idea of using local search to speed up the discovery of worst-case initial configurations, we ran another experiment on a set of algorithms and topologies. For each experiment, we use 10 000 initial configurations. Each experiment has been repeated between 100 and 1 000 times, in order to obtain 95% confidence intervals (at the right-hand-side of the $\pm$ sign) that are small enough.

The result of those experiments is provided in Table 5. The second column contains moves numbers obtained by taking the maximum number of moves (the bigger, the better) among the ones obtained by running a greedy daemon on 10 000 random initial configurations. The values between square brackets correspond to the simulation indices $j \in [1, 10\,000]$ where the worst cases occur, in

Table 5. Comparing global and local searches of the initial configuration: number of moves [simulation index]

algo/topology	global		local	
`coloring`/er20	17 ± 0.1	$[3\,200 \pm 500]$	17 ± 0.2	$[1\,100 \pm 100]$
`token`/diring12	130 ± 0.6	$[4\,400 \pm 300]$	140 ± 1	$[3\,800 \pm 300]$
`k-clust`/rtree10	25 ± 0.2	$[3\,700 \pm 600]$	26 ± 0.1	$[1\,900 \pm 400]$
`st-algo1`/er20	44 ± 0.3	$[4\,200 \pm 500]$	60 ± 0.03	$[1\,600 \pm 100]$
`te-a5sf`/rtree5	31 ± 0	$[100 \pm 20]$	31 ± 0.02	$[330 \pm 100]$
`unison`/er20	99 ± 0.6	$[4\,800 \pm 200]$	150 ± 3	$[3\,800 \pm 200]$

average (the smaller, the better). The third column contains the same information as the second one, except that configurations are chosen via a local search, as described above.

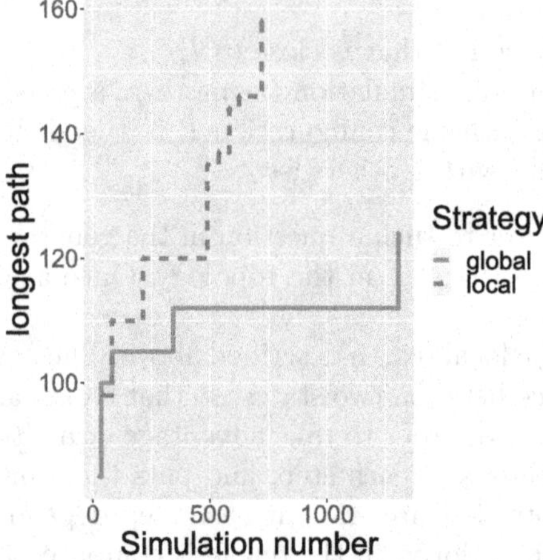

Fig. 4. One of the simulations performed for generating Table 5: `token`/diring12.

For `token`/diring12, `st-algo1`/er20, and `unison`/er20, we can observe in Table 5 that the local search is better, as we obtain better worst cases using less initial configurations. For `coloring`/er20 and `k-clust`/rtree10, the resulting worst cases are similar, but they are obtained quicker. For `te-a5sf`/rtree5 on the other hand, the global search is slightly better.

Figure 4 details those results on one of the (thousands of) experiments that were run to compute the values in Table 5 in the particular case of `token`/diring12. The more we try initial configurations (in abscissa) the longer path we find (in ordinate). On this figure, we can see the local search approach winning on both counts: higher worst cases that are found using less initial configurations.

4 Conclusion

In this paper, we present a methodology based on heuristics and an open-source tool [9] to find or refine worst-case stabilization times of self-stabilizing algorithms implemented in the atomic-state model using simulations.

We show how potential functions, designed for proving algorithm termination, can also be used to improve simulation worst cases, using greedy or exhaustive explorations of daemon behaviors. We propose a heuristic to speed up the exhaustive exploration and to potentially find the best solution early in the exploration process, which is a desirable property when timeouts are used. We experimentally show several results of practical interests.

- When a potential function is available, it can significantly speed up the search of the worst case.
- When no potential function is available, the use of a pseudo-potential function can still enhance the worst-case search.
- Local search can speed up the search for worst-case initial configurations.
- The worst cases obtained by greedy daemons are correlated (on the algorithms and topologies we tried) to the ones of (more costly) exhaustive daemons. This means that we can use greedy daemons to search for worst-case initial configurations, and then use an exhaustive daemon only on the resulting configuration.
- The same result can be observed, to a lesser extent, for random daemons. This is interesting as it allows to apply this idea on algorithms that have no known potential (nor pseudo-potential) function.

Future Work. On the algorithms and topologies we have considered, local searches are always better than global (*i.e.*, fully random) searches, except for the `te-a5sf`/rtree4, where the same worst case is found, but a little bit faster. Cases were global searches give better results certainly exist, if the local search starts in a configuration that is far from the ones that produce the worst cases. In such a case, it is easy to combine both heuristics, and to start the local search with the best result found by the global one. Another classical heuristic to combine local and global search would be to perform simulated-annealing.

References

1. Adamek, J., Farina, G., Nesterenko, M., Tixeuil, S.: Evaluating and optimizing stabilizing dining philosophers. J. Parallel Distrib. Comput. **109**, 63–74 (2017)
2. Adamek, J., Nesterenko, M., Tixeuil, S.: Evaluating practical tolerance properties of stabilizing programs through simulation: the case of propagation of information with feedback. In: Richa, A.W., Scheideler, C. (eds.) SSS 2012. LNCS, vol. 7596, pp. 126–132. Springer, Heidelberg (2012). https://doi.org/10.1007/978-3-642-33536-5_13

3. Aflaki, S., Bonakdarpour, B., Tixeuil, S.: Automated analysis of impact of scheduling on performance of self-stabilizing protocols. In: Pelc, A., Schwarzmann, A.A. (eds.) SSS 2015. LNCS, vol. 9212, pp. 156–170. Springer, Cham (2015). https://doi.org/10.1007/978-3-319-21741-3_11
4. Altisen, K., Corbineau, P., Devismes, S.: A framework for certified self-stabilization. Log. Methods Comput. Sci. **13**(4) (2017)
5. Altisen, K., Corbineau, P., Devismes, S.: Certification of an exact worst-case self-stabilization time. Theor. Comput. Sci. **941**, 262–277 (2023)
6. Altisen, K., Cournier, A., Devismes, S., Durand, A., Petit, F.: Self-stabilizing leader election in polynomial steps. Inf. Comput. **254**(Part 3), 330–366 (2017)
7. Altisen, K., Devismes, S., Dubois, S., Petit, F.: Introduction to Distributed Self-Stabilizing Algorithms, Volume 8 of Synthesis Lectures on Distributed Computing Theory (2019)
8. Altisen, K., Devismes, S., Durand, A.: Acyclic strategy for silent self-stabilization in spanning forests. In: Izumi, T., Kuznetsov, P. (eds.) SSS 2018. LNCS, vol. 11201, pp. 186–202. Springer, Cham (2018). https://doi.org/10.1007/978-3-030-03232-6_13
9. Altisen, K., Devismes, S., Jahier, E.: SASA: a SimulAtor of self-stabilizing algorithms. Comput. J. **66**(4), 796–814 (2022)
10. Couvreur, J.-M., Francez, N., Gouda, M.G.: Asynchronous unison (extended abstract). In: ICDCS 1992 (1992)
11. Datta, A.K., Larmore, L.L., Vemula, P.: An o(n)-time self-stabilizing leader election algorithm. J. Parallel Distrib. Comput. **71**(11), 1532–1544 (2011)
12. Datta, A.K., Devismes, S., Heurtefeux, K., Larmore, L.L., Rivierre, Y.: Competitive self-stabilizing k-clustering. Theor. Comput. Sci. **626**, 110–133 (2016)
13. Datta, A.K., Larmore, L.L., Vemula, P.: Self-stabilizing leader election in optimal space under an arbitrary scheduler. Theor. Comput. Sci. **412**(40), 5541–5561 (2011)
14. Devismes, S., Johnen, C.: Silent self-stabilizing BFS tree algorithms revisited. J. Parallel Distrib. Comput. **97**, 11–23 (2016)
15. Dijkstra, E.W.: Self-stabilizing systems in spite of distributed control. Commun. ACM **17**(11), 643–644 (1974)
16. Dolev, S., Gouda, M.G., Schneider, M.: Memory requirements for silent stabilization. Acta Informatica **36**(6), 447–462 (1999). https://doi.org/10.1007/s002360050180
17. Evcimen, H.T., Arapoglu, O., Dagdeviren, O.: SELFSIM: a discrete-event simulator for distributed self-stabilizing algorithms. In: International Conference on Artificial Intelligence and Data Processing (2018)
18. Flatebo, M., Datta, A.K.: Simulation of self-stabilizing algorithms in distributed systems. In: Annual Simulation Symposium (1992)
19. Christian, G., Nicolas, H., David, I., Colette, J.: Disconnected components detection and rooted shortest-path tree maintenance in networks. In: Felber, P., Garg, V. (eds.) SSS 2014. LNCS, vol. 8756, pp. 120–134. Springer, Cham (2014). https://doi.org/10.1007/978-3-319-11764-5_9
20. Glacet, C., Hanusse, N., Ilcinkas, D., Johnen, C.: Disconnected components detection and rooted shortest-path tree maintenance in networks. J. Parallel Distrib. Comput. **132**, 299–309 (2019)
21. Har-Tal, O.: A simulator for self-stabilizing distributed algorithms (2000). https://www.cs.bgu.ac.il/~projects/projects/odedha/html/
22. Huang, S.-T., Chen, N.-S.: A self-stabilizing algorithm for constructing breadth-first trees. Inf. Process. Lett. **41**(2), 109–117 (1992)

23. Kosowski, A., Kuszner, Ł: A self-stabilizing algorithm for finding a spanning tree in a polynomial number of moves. In: Wyrzykowski, R., Dongarra, J., Meyer, N., Waśniewski, J. (eds.) PPAM 2005. LNCS, vol. 3911, pp. 75–82. Springer, Heidelberg (2006). https://doi.org/10.1007/11752578_10
24. Müllner, N., Dhama, A., Theel, O.E.: Derivation of fault tolerance measures of self-stabilizing algorithms by simulation. In: Annual Simulation Symposium (2008)
25. Trivedi, K.S.: Probability and Statistics with Reliability, Queuing and Computer Science Applications, 2nd edn. Wiley, Hoboken (2002)

Model Checking of Distributed Algorithms Using Synchronous Programs

Erwan Jahier[1(✉)], Karine Altisen[1], Stéphane Devismes[2], and Gabriel B. Sant'Anna[3]

[1] Univ. Grenoble Alpes, CNRS, Grenoble INP, VERIMAG, Grenoble, France
erwan.jahier@univ-grenoble-alpes.fr
[2] Université de Picardie Jules Verne, MIS, Amiens, France
[3] BRy Tecnologia, Florianópolis, Brazil

Abstract. The development of trustworthy self-stabilizing algorithms requires the verification of some key properties with respect to the formal specification of the expected system executions. The atomic-state model (ASM) is the most commonly used computational model to reason on self-stabilizing algorithms. In this work, we propose methods and tools to automatically verify the self-stabilization of distributed algorithms defined in that model. To that goal, we exploit the similarities between the ASM and computational models issued from the synchronous programming area to reuse their associated verification tools, and in particular their model checkers. This allows the automatic verification of all safety (and bounded liveness) properties of any algorithm, regardless of any assumptions on network topologies and execution scheduling.

1 Introduction

Designing a distributed algorithm, checking its validity, and analyzing its performance is often difficult. Indeed, locality of information and asynchrony of communications imply numerous possible interleavings in executions of such algorithms. This is even more exacerbated in the context of fault-tolerant distributed computing, where failures, occurring at unpredictable times, have a drastic impact on the system behavior. Yet, in this research area, correctness and complexity analyses are usually made by pencil-and-paper proofs. As progress is made in distributed fault-tolerant computing, systems become more complex and require stronger correctness properties As a consequence, the combinatorics in the proofs establishing functional and complexity properties of these distributed systems constantly increases and requires ever more subtle arguments. In this context, computer-aided tools such as simulators, proof assistants, and model checkers are appropriate, and sometimes even mandatory, to help the design of a solution and to increase the confidence in its soundness.

Simulation tools [3,4] are interesting to test and find flaws early in the design process. However, simulators only partially cover the set of possible executions

This work has been partially funded by the ANR project SkyData (ANR-22-CE25-0008-01).

S. Dolev and B. Schieber (Eds.): SSS 2023, LNCS 14310, pp. 18–35, 2023.
https://doi.org/10.1007/978-3-031-44274-2_2

and so are not suited to formally establish properties. In contrast, proof assistants [24] offer strong formal guarantees. However, they are semi-automatic in the sense that the user must write the proof in a formal language specific to the software, which then mechanically checks it. Usually, proof assistants require a considerable amount of effort since they often necessitate a full reengineering of the initial pencil-and-paper proof. Finally, and contrary to the two previous methods, model checking [9] allows a complete and fully automatic verification of the soundness of a distributed system for a given topology.

We consider model checking for self-stabilization, a versatile lightweight fault-tolerant paradigm [2,11]. A self-stabilizing algorithm makes the system eventually reach a so-called *legitimate* configuration from which every possible execution satisfies the intended specification, regardless of its configuration – the initial one, or any configuration resulting from a finite number of transient faults. Our goal is to automatically verify the self-stabilization of distributed algorithms written in the atomic-state model (ASM), the most commonly used model in the area. To that end, we exploit the similarities between the ASM and computational models issued from formal methods based on synchronous programming languages [15], such as LUSTRE [16], to reuse their associated verification tools, in particular model checkers such as KIND2 [5]. This allows the automatic verification of all safety (and bounded liveness) properties of any algorithm, regardless the assumptions made on network topologies and the asynchrony of the execution model (daemons).

Contribution. We propose a language-based framework, named SALUT, to verify the self-stabilization of distributed algorithms written in ASM. In particular, we implement a translation from the network topology to a LUSTRE program, this latter calling upon an API designed to encode the algorithm. The verification then comes down to a state-space exploration problem performed by the model checker KIND2 [5]. Our proposal is modular and flexible thanks to a clear separation between the description of algorithms, daemons (which are also programmable), topologies, and properties to check. As a result, our framework is versatile and induces more simplicity by maximizing the code reuse. For example, using classical daemons (*e.g.*, synchronous, distributed, central) and standard network topologies (*e.g.*, rings, trees, random graphs) provided in the framework, the user just has to encode the algorithm and the properties to verify.

We demonstrate the versatility and scalability of our method by verifying many different self-stabilizing algorithms of the literature, solving both static and dynamic tasks in various contexts in terms of topologies and daemons. In particular, we include the common benchmarks (namely, Dijkstra's K-state algorithm [11], Ghosh's mutual exclusion [14], Hoepman's ring-orientation [18]) studied by the state-of-the-art, yet ad hoc, approaches [6,7,26] for comparison purposes. Our results show that the versatility of our solution does not come at the price of sacrificing too much efficiency in terms of scalability and verification time.

Related Work. Pioneer works on verification of distributed self-stabilizing algorithm have been led by Lakhnech and Siegel [23,25]. They propose formal frameworks to open the possibility of computer-aided-verification machinery. However, these two preliminary works do not propose any toolbox to apply and validate their approach.

In 2001, Tsuchiya *et al.* [26] proposed to use the symbolic model checker NuSMV [8]. They validate their approach by verifying several self-stabilizing algorithms defined in ASM under the central and distributed daemon assumptions. These case studies are representative since they cover various settings in terms of topologies and problem specifications. Yet, their approach is not generic since it mixes in the same user-written SMV file the description of the algorithm, the expected property, and the topology.

In 2006, Whittlesey-Harris and Nesterenko [27] modeled in SPIN [19] a specific yet practical self-stabilizing application, namely the fluids and combustion facility of the international space station, to automatically verify it. A few experimental results are given, but no analysis or comparison with [26] is given.

Chen *et al.* [6] focus on the bottlenecks, in particular related to fairness issues, involved by the verification of self-stabilizing algorithms. They also use the NuSMV [8] model checker. Chen and Kulkarni [7] use SMT solvers to verify stabilizing algorithms [12]. They apply bounded model-checking techniques to determine whether a given algorithm is stabilizing. They highlight trade-offs between verification with SMT solvers and the previously mentioned works on symbolic model checking [6,26]. Approaches in [6,7] are limited in terms of versatility and code reuse since, by construction, the verification is restricted to the central daemon, and again the whole system modeling is ad hoc and stored in to a single user-written file.

SASA [3] is an open-source tool dedicated to the simulation of self-stabilizing algorithms in the ASM. It provides all features needed to test, debug and evaluate self-stabilizing algorithms (such as an interactive debugger with graphical support, predefined daemons and custom test oracles). The SASA simulation facilities can actually be used with SALUT. The main difference is that algorithms should be written in OCAML rather than in LUSTRE – which is more convenient as LUSTRE is a more constrained language (it targets critical systems) and has a less rich programming environment. On the other hand, with SASA, one can only perform simulations.

Roadmap. The rest of the paper is organized as follows. Sections 2 and 3 respectively present the ASM and a theoretical model that grounds the synchronous programming paradigm. Section 4 proposes a general way of embedding the ASM into a synchronous programming model. Section 5 shows how to take advantage of this embedding to formulate ASM algorithm verification problems. Section 6 describes a possible implementation of this general framework using the LUSTRE language and Sect. 7 explains how to use the LUSTRE toolbox to perform automatic verifications in practice. Section 8 presents some experimentation results. We make concluding remarks in Sect. 9.

2 The Atomic-State Model

A distributed system is a finite set of processes, each equipped with a *local algorithm* working on a finite set of local variables. Processes can communicate with other processes through communication links that define the network topology. In the ASM model [11], communications are abstracted away as follows: each process can read its variables and those of its neighbors or predecessors (depending on whether or not communication links are bidirectional) and can only write to its own variables. The local algorithm of a process is given as a collection of guarded actions of the following form: $\langle label \rangle :: \langle guard \rangle \hookrightarrow \langle statement \rangle$. The label is only used to identify the action. The guard is a Boolean predicate involving variables the process can read. The statement describes modifications of the process variables. An action is *enabled* if its guard evaluates to true. A process can execute an action (its statement) only if the action is enabled. By extension, a process is said to be enabled when at least one of its action is enabled. An example of distributed algorithm is given in Fig. 1.

Inputs: K, a positive integer $\geq n$; and $q.Pred$, the predecessor in the ring
Variables: $v \in \{0, ..., K-1\}$
Actions for non-root processes:
$T_p :: q.v \neq q.Pred.v \hookrightarrow q.v \leftarrow q.Pred.v$
Actions for the root:
$T_{root} :: q.v = q.Pred.v \hookrightarrow q.v \leftarrow (q.v+1)\ mod\ K$

Fig. 1. The Dijkstra's K-state algorithm for n-size rooted unidirectional rings [11].

The semantics of a distributed system in the ASM is defined as follows. A *configuration* consists of the set of values of all process states, the state of each process being defined by the values its variables. An *execution* is a sequence of configurations, two consecutive configurations being linked by a *step*. The system *atomically* steps into a different configuration when at least one process is enabled. In this case, a non-empty set of enabled nodes is activated by an adversary, called *daemon*, which models the asynchronism of the system. Each activated process executes the statement of one of its enabled actions, producing the next configuration of the execution. Many assumptions can be made on such a daemon. Daemons are usually defined as the conjunction of their spreading and fairness properties [2]. In this paper, we consider four classical spreading properties: central, locally central, synchronous, and distributed. A central daemon activates only one process per step. A locally central daemon never activates two neighbors simultaneously. At each step, the synchronous daemon activates all enabled processes. A distributed daemon activates at least one process, maybe more, at each step. Every daemon we deal with in this paper is considered to be unfair, meaning that it might never select an enabled process unless it is the only remaining one.

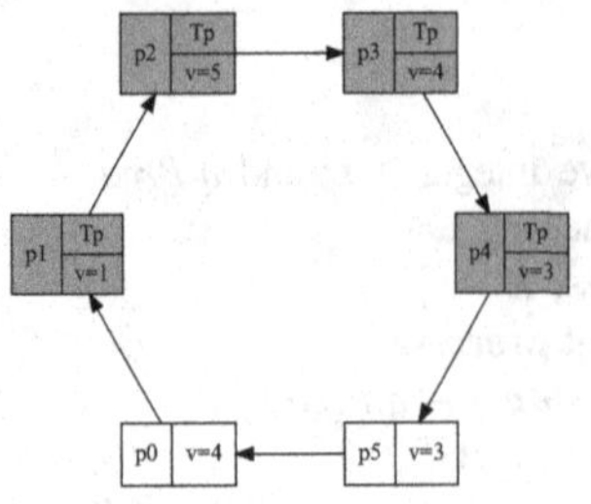

Fig. 2. Unidirectional ring of six processes rooted at *p0*.

Figure 2 displays an example of distributed system where the algorithm of Fig. 1 runs. This algorithm is executed on a rooted unidirectional ring. By rooted, we mean that all processes except one, the root (here, *p0*), executes the same local algorithm. In the figure, each enabled process, given in color, is decorated by the enabled action label (top-right). In the current configuration, processes from *p1* to *p4* are enabled because their v-variable is different from that of their predecessor; see Action T_p. The root process, *p0*, is disabled since its v-variable is different from that of its predecessor; see Action T_{root}. So, the daemon has to chose any non-empty subset of $\{p1, p2, p3, p4\}$ to be activated. In the present case, each activated process will copy its predecessor value during the step; see Action T_p.

A distributed system is meant to execute under a set of assumptions, which are in particular related by the topology (in the above example, a rooted unidirectional ring) and the daemon (in the above example, the distributed daemon) and to achieve a given specification (in the above example, the token circulation). Under a given set of assumptions, a distributed system is said to be *self-stabilizing* w.r.t. a specification if it reaches a set of configurations, called the *legitimate* configurations, satisfying the following three properties: Correctness: every execution satisfying the assumptions and starting from a legitimate configuration satisfies the specification; Closure: every execution satisfying the assumptions and starting from a legitimate configuration only contains legitimate configurations; Convergence: every execution satisfying the assumptions eventually reaches a legitimate configuration.

3 The Synchronous Programming Model

We now briefly present the main concepts grounding the *synchronous programming paradigm* [15] that are used in the sequel. At top level, a synchronous program can be activated periodically (time-triggered) or sporadically (event-triggered). A program execution is therefore made of a sequence of *steps.* To perform such a step, the environment has to provide inputs. The step itself consists in (1) computing outputs, as a function of the inputs and the internal state of the program, and (2) updating the program internal state.

The specific feature of synchronous programs is the way internal components interact when composed: one step of the whole composition consists of a "simultaneous" step of all the components, which communicate atomically with each other. Moreover, programs have a formal *deterministic* semantics: this enables to validate the program using testing and formal verification.

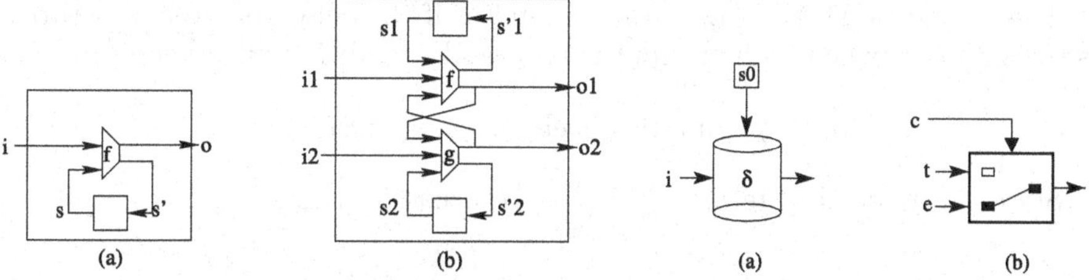

Fig. 3. General scheme of a synchronous node (a) and synchronous composition (b).

Fig. 4. Delay (a) and if-then-else (b) synchronous nodes.

Following the presentation in [15], a *synchronous node*[1] is a straightforward generalization of synchronous circuits (Mealy machines) that work with arbitrary datatypes: such a machine has a memory (a state) and a combinational part, and that computes the output and the next state as a function of the current input and the current state. The general dataflow scheme of a synchronous node is depicted in Fig. 3a: it has a vector of inputs, i, and a vector of outputs, o; its internal state variable is denoted by s. A step of the node is defined by a function made of two parts, $f = (f_o, f_s)$: f_o (resp. f_s) computes the output (resp. the next state, s') from the current input and the current state:

$$o = f_o(i, s) \qquad s' = f_s(i, s)$$

The behavior of the node is the following: it starts in some initial state s_0. In a given state s, it deterministically reacts to an input valuation i by returning the output $o = f_o(i, s)$ and by updating its state by $s' = f_s(i, s)$ for the next reaction. Those nodes can be composed, by plugging one's outputs to the other's inputs, as long as those wires do not introduce any combinational loop. The general scheme of the (synchronous) composition between two nodes is shown in Fig. 3b, where the step is computed by

$$o_1 = f_o(i_1, o_2, s_1) \qquad o_2 = g_o(i_2, o_1, s_2) \qquad s'_1 = f_s(i_1, o_2, s_1) \qquad s'_2 = g_s(i_2, o_1, s_2)$$

and either the result of $f_o(i_1, o_2, s_1)$ should not depend on o_2 or the result of $g_o(i_2, o_1, s_2)$ should not depend on o_1.

We now introduce two simple synchronous nodes that are used in the sequel. The first one is a single delay node, noted δ (Fig. 4a): it receives an input i of some generic type τ and returns its input delayed by one step; it has a state variable s of type τ. A step of δ is computed by:

$$f_o^\delta(i, s) = s \qquad f_s^\delta(i, s) = i$$

[1] Here, what we name a (ASM) process is also often called a node in the literature; we have chosen to call it a process to avoid confusion with synchronous nodes.

The second node (see Fig. 4b) is a stateless if-then-else operator: it returns its second input when its first input is true, and its third input otherwise:

$$f_o^{ite}(c,t,e) = \text{if } c \text{ then } t \text{ else } e \qquad f_s^{ite}(c,t,e) = \_$$

Since this node is stateless, $f_s^{ite}(c,t,e)$ returns nothing.

4 From ASM Processes to Synchronous Nodes

The ASM and synchronous programming models have a lot in common, in particular with respect to the atomicity of steps: all nodes of the program (resp. all processes of the network) react at the same logical instant, using the same global configuration; moreover, at the end of a global step, all nodes (resp. processes) outputs are broadcasted away instantaneously to define the new configuration. Another important similarity is the way the non-determinism is handled. As a synchronous program is deterministic, non-determinism is handled by adding external inputs – often called *oracles* in the programming language community. On the other hand, in the ASM, non-determinism due to asynchronism is modeled by daemons. For those reasons, using synchronous programs (and their associate toolboxes) is very natural to simulate and formally verify ASM algorithms.

We now explain how to encode ASM processes into synchronous nodes. In a network of n processes, each process is mapped to a synchronous node. This node contains two inner nodes encoding the ASM guarded actions of the process (see Fig. 5): (1) `enable`, whose inputs are the states the process can read (the predecessors in the graph); this node has a single output, a Boolean array, which elements are true if and only if the corresponding processes guards are enabled; (2) `step`, with the same inputs as `enable`, and that outputs a new state (as computed by the statement of the enabled action); this state is used as the new value of the corresponding process state if the daemon chooses to activate the process; the previous value is used otherwise.

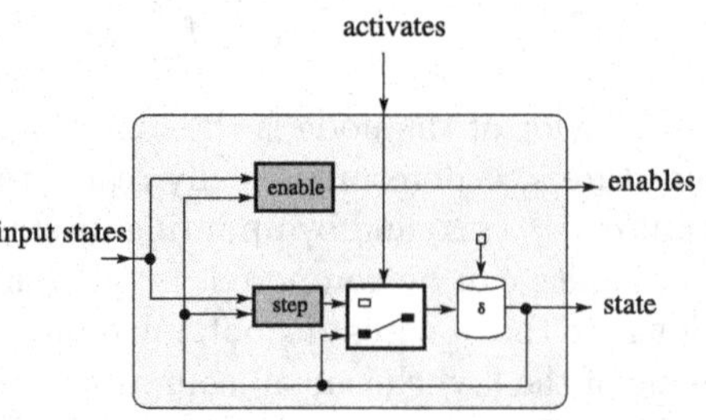

Fig. 5. Formalizing an ASM process as a synchronous node.

The communication links in the network topology are translated into data wires in the synchronous model. For each process, the `state` output wire of its node instance is plugged onto some other node instances, corresponding to its neighbors, as defined by the network topology – see the left-most node in Fig. 6.

5 ASM Algorithms Verification via Synchronous Observers

Once we have a formal model (made of synchronous nodes) of the process local algorithms and the network, it is possible to automatically verify some properties using so-called *synchronous observers* [17]: the desired properties can be expressed by the means of another synchronous node that observes the behavior of the outputs and returns a Boolean that states whether configurations sequences are correct.

Classically, the assumptions of the environment of the system under verification is also formalized by a synchronous observer; here, those assumptions are handled by the daemon, which decides which processes should be activated among the enabled ones. Therefore, the assumption observer is named daemon; it has $2 \times n$ input wires: n `activate` wires and n `enable` wires, one each per process; it outputs a Boolean whose value states whether the assumption made on the daemon (*e.g.*, synchronous, distributed, central) is satisfied. Those classical daemon assumptions, encoded as synchronous nodes, are provided as a library [1].

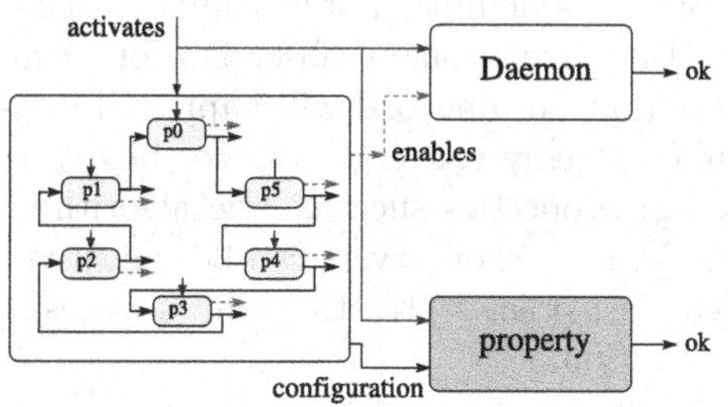

Fig. 6. Verifying a property using synchronous observers.

The verification of a given *property* then consists in checking that the synchronous composition of the synchronous nodes encoding the processes topology, the daemon observer, and the property observer never causes the latter to return false while the daemon observer has always returned true; this boils down to a state-space exploration problem. The composition is illustrated in Fig. 6, where a property is checked against ASM algorithms running on the network of Fig. 2. For the sake of clarity, we have omitted some wires: the processes output wires from left-to-right holding the `state` values are plugged into the `configuration` wire of the property node; the processes output wires from left-to-right holding the `enables` values are plugged into the `enables` wire of the daemon node; the processes input wires from up-to-down holding the `activation` values, that are also used as inputs for the daemon observer, are plugged into the corresponding processes.

In order to prove the closure property of the self-stabilization definition (Sect. 2), which states that an algorithm never steps from a legitimate to an illegitimate configuration, one can use the observer of Fig. 7. It checks that if the previous configuration (computed by the δ node) was legitimate, then so is the current one.

Similarly to the closure property, one can formalize classical convergence theorems, such as, "if $K \geq n$ and the daemon is distributed, then the stabilization time of the algorithm of Fig. 1 is at most $2n-3$ rounds"[2] (Theorem 6.37 of [2]). For some ASM algorithms, called *silent*, the legitimate configurations are the terminal ones, where no process is enabled. But for other algorithms, such as the one presented in Sect. 2, a definition of legitimacy needs to be provided.

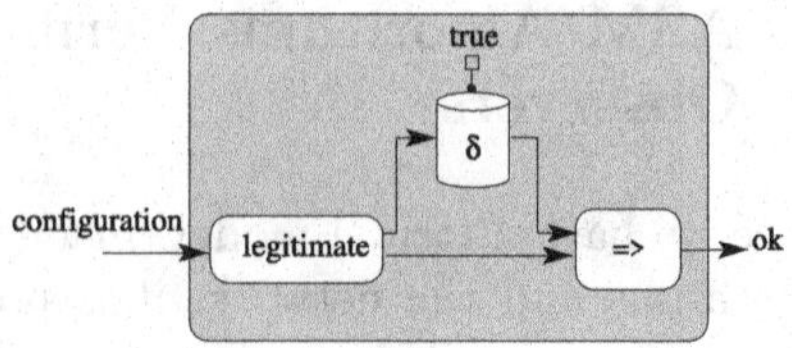

Fig. 7. The closure property Observer.

Using synchronous observers, one can just specify *safety properties*, which state that nothing bad will happen. Liveness properties, such as "the algorithm will eventually converge", cannot be expressed. But stronger (and equally interesting) properties such as "the algorithm will converge in at most $f(n)$ steps" can. Moreover, observers can be executed and used during simulations to implement test oracles [21]: this allows to test the whole model at first hand, before verification.

6 SALUT: Self-stabilizing Algorithms in LUsTre

In this section, we describe SALUT, a framework that implements the ideas presented so far. In order to implement such a framework, one has to (*i*) chose a format to describe the network, (*ii*) chose a language to implement synchronous nodes, (*iii*) propose an API for that language to define `enable` and `step` functions, and (*iv*) implement a translator from the format chosen in (*i*) to the language chosen in (*ii*).

Network Description. We have chosen to base the network description on DOT [13]: the rationale for choosing DOT was that many visualization tools and graph editors support the DOT format and many bridges from one and to another graph syntax exist. DOT *graphs* are defined as sets of *nodes* and *edges*. Graphs, nodes, and edges can have *attributes* specified by name-value pairs, so that we can take advantage of DOT attributes to (1) associate nodes with their algorithms, (2) optionally associate nodes with their initial states, and (3) associate graphs with parameters.

LUSTRE, a Language to Implement Synchronous Nodes. LUSTRE is a dataflow synchronous programming language designed for the development and verification of critical reactive systems [16]. It combines the synchronous model – where the system reacts instantaneously to a flow of input events at a precise discrete time scale – with the dataflow paradigm – which is based on block diagrams, where blocks are parallel operators concurrently computing their own output and possibly maintaining some states. Choosing LUSTRE to implement the

[2] A *round* is a time unit that captures the execution time according to the speed of the slowest processes; see [2] for a formal definition.

synchronous nodes of Sect. 3 is natural as they were designed to model LUSTRE programs in the first place [17]. Moreover, two LUSTRE model checkers are freely available to perform formal verifications (*cf.* Sect. 7).

A LUSTRE API to Define ASM Algorithms. The LUSTRE API for SALUT follows the formalization of Sect. 4. For each algorithm, one needs to define the process state datatype. Then, for each local algorithm, one needs to define a LUSTRE version of the enable and step nodes – the 2 left-most inner nodes of Fig. 5.

For Dijkstra's algorithm of Fig. 1, the state of each process is an integer and there is one action for the root process and one action for non-root processes:

```
type state = int;
const actions_number = 1;
```

The `root_enable` and `root_step` are implemented in Listing 1 and 2 for the root process. Their interfaces (Lines 1–2) are the same for all nodes and all algorithms.

```
1 function root_enable <<const d: int>>(st:state; ngbrs:neigh^d)
2 returns (enabled: bool^actions_number);
3 let
4   enabled = [ st = state (ngbrs[0]) ];
5 tel ;
```

Listing 1. The Lustre `enable` for the root process

Enable nodes take as inputs the state of the process (of type `state`) and an array containing the states the process has access to – namely, the ones of its neighbors. Such states are provided as an array of size `d`, where `d` is the degree of the process. As in LUSTRE, array sizes should be compile-time constants, the `d` parameter is provided as a static parameter (within «»). Type `neigh` contains information about every process neighbors, in particular its state, accessed using the `state` getter (see Line 4 of Listing 1). Enable nodes return an array of Booleans of size `actions_number`, stating for each action whether it is enabled or not.

The K-state algorithm of the root process is enabled when the process state value is equal to that of its predecessor (Line 4 of Listing 1), as stated in the guard of the root action in Fig. 1. In LUSTRE, stateless nodes are declared as `function` (Line 1 of Listing 1 and 2) and square brackets (`[index]`) gives access to the content of the array at a particular `index`.

```
1 function root_step <<const d: int>>(st: state; ngbrs: neigh^d; a:action)
2 returns (new: state);
3 let
4    new = (st + 1) mod k;
5 tel;
```

Listing 2. The Lustre `step` node for the root process

Step nodes have the same input parameters as enable ones, plus the active action label (see `a` in Listing 2, Line 1). It returns the new value of the process state (Line 2). The node body (Line 4) is a direct encoding of the statement of the root action given in Fig. 1. The predefined node `mod` computes the modulo operation. For this algorithm, there is only one possible action, so the argument `a` is not used.

The `enable` and `step` nodes are similarly implemented for the non-root processes (see [20] for the complete implementation).

The SALUT Translator. All the nodes required to describe the ASM algorithms are then generated automatically from the network topology using a DOT to LUSTRE translator. The two nodes, `enable` and `step`, are the only LUSTRE programs that need to be provided. SALUT generates from the DOT file a node, called `topology` (the leftmost node in Fig. 6). In particular, SALUT takes care of wiring the `enable` and the `step` node instances to the right processed and the right values of the degree `d` parameter, that can vary from one node instance to another.

7 Automatic Formal Verification

We have seen that properties on ASM algorithms can be proven using synchronous observers (*cf.* Fig. 6). By defining such observers in LUSTRE, we can perform the verification of these properties automatically using existing verification tools for LUSTRE such as KIND2 [5]. Technically, to use such a tool, one just needs to point out a node Boolean variable. Then, the tool will try to prove that the designated variable is always `true` for all possible sequences of the node inputs, by performing a symbolic state space exploration. Hence, one just needs to encode the desired properties into a Boolean, as done in the `verify` node given in Listing 3. This section is devoted to the explanation of this listing.

```
const n = card;   -- processes number extracted from the dot file
const worst_case = n*(n-1) + (n-4)*(n+1) div 2 + 1; -- in steps

node verify(active: bool^1^n; init_config: state^n)
returns (ok: bool);
var
  config: state^n;
  enabled: bool^1^n; -- 1 since the algorithm has only 1 rule per process
  enabled1: bool^n;    -- enabled projection
  legitimate, round: bool;
  closure, converge_cost, converge_wc: bool;
  steps, cost, round_nb: int;
let
  config, enabled, round, round_nb = topology(active, init_config);
  assert(true -> daemon_is_central<<1,n>>(active, pre enabled));
  enabled1 = map<<nary_or<<1>>,n>> (enabled); -- projection
  legitimate = nary_xor<<n>>(enabled1);
  closure = true -> (pre(legitimate) => legitimate);
  cost = cost(enabled, config);
  converge_cost = (true -> legitimate or pre(cost)>cost);
  steps = 0 -> (pre(steps) + 1); -- 0, 1, 2, ...
  converge_wc = (steps >= worst_case) => legitimate;
  ok = closure and converge_cost and converge_wc;
tel;
```

Listing 3. LUSTRE formalization of some properties of the K-state algorithm.

This node is a particular instance of Fig. 6. The information related to process enabling (`enabled` variable in Listing 3) and activation (`active`) are contained into 2-dimensional Boolean arrays. The first dimension is used to deal with algorithms that are made of several guarded actions (here only one is used). The second dimension is used to deal with topologies that have more than one process.

According to the current configuration and an array of Booleans `active` indicating which processes have been activated by the daemon, the `topology` node computes a new configuration `config`, which is an integer array of size n, and a matrix of Booleans `enabled` of size `1` × `n` to indicate which processes are enabled (Line 14). The `topology` node also outputs elements relative to round computation, which are not used here. At the first step, the current configuration returned by Node `topology` is the initial one, i.e., its argument `init_config`; for all other steps, the configuration is computed by `topology` from the previous configuration (which is stored as an internal memory in `topology`, cf. Fig. 5) and the process activations. At every step, the set of enabled processes is computed according to the configuration. The verification tools will try to prove that, *e.g.*, `ok` is always true for all possible values of its inputs, namely for every initial configuration, and all process activation scheduling.

Daemon Assumptions. As already mentioned, in order to fully encode the ASM algorithms, we need to express assumptions about the daemon; In LUSTRE, this can be done through the `assert` directive (Line 15). Here, a central daemon is used (the node `daemon_is_central` not shown here): it checks that, at each step, only enabled nodes can be activated, and that exactly one can be activated. Note that such a property is not checked at the first instant (`true->...`[3]) since `pre(enabled)`, which returns the previous value of `enabled`, is undefined at that instant.

Closure. The node `verify` should also define the properties involved in the definition of self-stabilization; see Sect. 2. The first expressed property is the closure: once the system has reached a legitimate configuration, it remains in legitimate configurations forever. The definition of a legitimate configuration is done with the variable `legitimate` in Line 17, which checks that exactly one process is enabled using a XOR operator (*n.b.*, `nary_xor` is a node that returns `true` if and only if exactly one element of its input Boolean array is `true`). Then, the definition of closure is given in Line 18 and is a direct implementation of Fig. 7. Again, this property is not checked at the first instant when `pre(legitimate)` is undefined.

[3] The `->` infix binary operator returns the value of its left-hand-side argument at the first instant, and the one of its right-hand-side argument for all the remaining instants.

Convergence. We now focus on the convergence part. For algorithms with an available *potential function*, that quantifies how far a configuration is from the set of legitimate configurations, we can check whether this function is decreasing; see the Boolean `convergence_cost` and Lines 19–20 (the `cost` node is not shown here). The existence of a decreasing function guarantees the convergence. Note that once a legitimate configuration is reached, the potential function does not necessarily decrease anymore. This is the kind of subtleties that a verification tool can spot (and have actually spotted) easily.

Alternatively, we can take advantage of known upper bounds for the convergence time, being tight or not. In our case, we use Theorem 6.30 of [2] (Line 2). Then, we can check this bound, and so the convergence, by stating that once the upper bound is reached, the configuration should be legitimate; see the variable `steps` that counts the number of steps elapsed since the beginning of the execution and the Boolean `convergence_wc` that checks the property (Lines 21–22).

8 Experimentations

One of the key advantages of our approach is that topologies, daemons, algorithms, and properties to check are described separately, contrary to the related work [6,7,26] where they are mixed into a single user-written SMV [8] or Yices [12] file. More precisely:

1. SALUT automatically translates into LUSTRE any topology described in the DOT language (for which many graph generators exist).
2. Classical daemons, *i.e.*, synchronous, distributed, central, and locally central, are generically modeled in LUSTRE so that they can be used for any number of nodes and actions (using 2-dimension arrays). Other daemons can be modeled similarly.
3. To model-check an algorithm, one thus just need to model its guarded actions, using the API described in Sect. 6. Actually, we have done it for several different algorithms: the Dijkstra's K-state algorithm [11] whose LUSTRE encoding is made of 37 lines of code (loc), the Ghosh's mutual exclusion [14] (50 loc), a Bread-First Search spanning tree construction [2] (80 loc), a synchronous unison [2] (40 loc); a k-clustering (with k = 2) algorithm [10] (130 loc), a vertex-coloring algorithm [2] (30 loc), and the Hoepman's ring orientation [18] (110 loc).
4. For all those algorithms, we have encoded the closure property and a convergence property based on a known upper bound. We also have encoded a convergence property based on a potential function, when available.

Once an algorithm and the properties to verify are written in LUSTRE,[4] we can model-check them using any daemon and any topology. Of course, not all combinations make sense, *e.g.*, the Dijkstra's K-state algorithm only works on rooted

[4] The LUSTRE code of those examples is given in the SALUT git repository [1].

unidirectional rings and the synchronous unison only works under a synchronous daemon. Still, a lot of combinations are possible. Table 1 presents results for a small subset of them.

Table 1. The maximum topology size that can be handled within an hour.

Algorithm	LUSTRE prog size for WC-conv (ϕ-conv) in loc	Topology	Daemon	Max topo size for WC-conv (ϕ-conv) in processes nb
K-state	7 (86)	rooted unidirectional ring	synchronous	48 (15)
			central	6 (8)
			distributed	6 (8)
Ghosh	8	"ring-like"	central	18
			distributed	16
Coloring	6 (8)	ring	central	10 (55)
		random		11 (26)
Sync unison	6	random	synchronous	40
		ring		17
BFS sp. tree	7	tree	distributed	8
k-clustering	30 (20)	rooted tree	distributed	9 (10)
Hoepman	6	odd-size ring	central	7

Table 1 summarizes experiments made with the KIND2 [5] model checker[5] to prove some properties against the corresponding algorithm encoding. Columns 1, 3, and 4 respectively contain the algorithm name, the topology,[6] and the daemon used for the experiment. Column 2 contains the number of lines of LUSTRE code used to encode the worst-case-based convergence property, apart from the main node declarations (and in parentheses the number of lines to encode the potential function property, when available). Column 5 contains the maximal number of processes for which we get a (positive) result in less than 1 h[7] (and ditto for the potential-based convergence in parentheses).

The topology sizes we can handle are quite small, but large enough to spot faults in algorithms, expected properties, or their LUSTRE encoding. Potential functions, when available, sometimes allow to check bigger topologies; indeed, we are able to check in less than one hour a ring of 55 processes using the potential function of the coloring algorithm, whereas using the worst-case-based convergence, we are only able to check the algorithm convergence on rings of

[5] We use kind2 v1.9.0 with the following command line option: `--smt_solver Bitwuzla --enable BMC --enable IND --timeout 3600` and `uint8` for representing integers, except for K-state/synchronous where `uint16` is necessary (indeed, for $n > 13$, $WC > 256$).

[6] Random graphs were generated using the Erdős-Rényi model.

[7] We used a multi-core server, where each core is made of Intel(R) Xeon(R) Gold 6330 CPU @ 2.00 GHz. Note that KIND2 is able to use several cores in parallel.

Table 2. Measuring the time to prove the convergence of the K-state algorithm.

topology size	Yices (SMT) encoding of [7]	SALUT+KIND2 (SMT)	"SALUT"+NuSMV (BDD)	NuSMV (BDD) encoding of [6]	NuSMV (BDD) encoding of [26]
5	200 (from [7])	6	0	0	0
6	–	190	0	0	0
7		–	2	0	1
8			10	3	4
9			60	80	10
10			600	20	20
11			–	650	40
12				2800	180
13				–	2500

size 10. The closure property is much cheaper to model-check. For instance, in less than an hour, we are able to check the Dijkstra's K-state algorithm on a unidirectional rooted ring made of 45 processes.

Performance Comparison. Table 2 reports the time (in seconds) necessary to check the convergence of the K-state algorithm under a central daemon, using different topology sizes, different solvers, and different problem encodings. We note "-" when the timeout of one hour is reached. All experiments were conducted on the same computer, except for the second column. Indeed, the exact encoding was not provided in the article, so we simply report the number from Table 3 of [7]. Column 3 shows the result of the proposed framework. Column 4 of Table 2 shows the result of a NuSMV program that was not automatically generated by SALUT, but that mimics the corresponding generated Lustre code (discussed below). Columns 5 and 6 show the result of a direct encoding of the problem in NuSMV as described in [26] and [6], respectively.

On this algorithm (and on the Ghosh's algorithm), the encoding performed using the BDD-based solver NuSMV give better performances. Therefore, this allows to handle topologies with a little bit more nodes. However:

- it seems unlikely that a problem occurring on topologies of size 10 can never occur on ones of size 6;
- nothing guarantees that it would be the case for all algorithms; and
- the BDD-encoding is limited to finite domains.

Moreover, using our proposal to target (for example) NuSMV should be not too difficult. Indeed, once completely expanded (using the `-ec` of the Lustre V6 compiler), the Lustre program provided to KIND2 is actually very close to a NuSMV program. In order to try that idea out, we wrote a NuSMV program that mimics the Lustre code coming from the Dijkstra's K-state (and measured its performance in Column 4 of Table 2).

As far as SMT-based verification is concerned, the proposed framework used with the KIND2 model checker (which delegates the solving part to external SMT solvers) does not seem to pay the price of genericity, as we get performances that have the same order of magnitude. Indeed, for the K-state and the Ghosh algorithms convergence under a central daemon, and using a timeout of one hour as we did in Table 1, Chen *et al.* [7] report to model-check topologies of size 5 and 14, respectively. We are able to handle slightly bigger topologies (6 and 18, respectively). But the difference is not significant and our numbers were obtained using a more recent computer.

9 Conclusion

This work presents an open-source framework that takes advantage of synchronous languages and model-checking tools to formally verify self-stabilizing algorithms. The encoding of the topology is automatically generated. Generic daemons are provided and cover the most commonly used cases (synchronous, distributed, central, and locally central). One just needs to formalize (in Lustre) the ASM actions and the properties to verify.[8] The article and its companion open-source repository contain many algorithm encoding examples, as well as examples of checkable properties including stabilization time upper bounds that can be expressed using steps, moves, or rounds.

It is worth noting that SALUT has been developed as a natural extension of SASA [3], an open-source simulator dedicated to self-stabilizing algorithms defined in the ASM. The integration of verification tools in the SASA suite is interesting from a technical and methodological point of view as it offers a unified interface for both simulating and verifying algorithms. In future works, it would be interesting to complete this suite with bridges to proof assistants to obtain, in the spirit of TLA+ [22], an exhaustive toolbox for computed-aided validation of self-stabilizing algorithms.

References

1. The SASA source code repository. https://gricad-gitlab.univ-grenoble-alpes.fr/verimag/synchrone/sasa
2. Altisen, K., Devismes, S., Dubois, S., Petit, F.: Introduction to Distributed Self-Stabilizing Algorithms. Synthesis Lectures on Distributed Computing Theory, vol. 8 (2019)
3. Altisen, K., Devismes, S., Jahier, E.: SASA: a simulator of self-stabilizing algorithms. Comput. J. **66**(4), 796–814 (2023)
4. Casteigts, A.: Jbotsim: a tool for fast prototyping of distributed algorithms in dynamic networks. In: SIMUtools, pp. 290–292 (2015)
5. Champion, A., Mebsout, A., Sticksel, C., Tinelli, C.: The KIND 2 model checker. In: Chaudhuri, S., Farzan, A. (eds.) CAV 2016. LNCS, vol. 9780, pp. 510–517. Springer, Cham (2016). https://doi.org/10.1007/978-3-319-41540-6_29

[8] During a 4-weeks internship, a first-year student has been able to learn LUSTRE, the SALUT framework, and encode and verify 3 of the 7 algorithms presented in this article.

6. Chen, J., Abujarad, F., Kulkarni, S.S.: Towards scalable model checking of self-stabilizing programs. J. Parallel Distrib. Comput. **73**(4), 400–410 (2013)
7. Chen, J., Kulkarni, S.: SMT-based model checking for stabilizing programs'. In: Frey, D., Raynal, M., Sarkar, S., Shyamasundar, R.K., Sinha, P. (eds.) ICDCN 2013. LNCS, vol. 7730, pp. 393–407. Springer, Heidelberg (2013). https://doi.org/10.1007/978-3-642-35668-1_27
8. Cimatti, A., et al.: NuSMV 2: an opensource tool for symbolic model checking. In: Brinksma, E., Larsen, K.G. (eds.) CAV 2002. LNCS, vol. 2404, pp. 359–364. Springer, Heidelberg (2002). https://doi.org/10.1007/3-540-45657-0_29
9. Clarke, E.M., Emerson, E.A., Sifakis, J.: Model checking: algorithmic verification and debugging. Commun. ACM **52**(11), 74–84 (2009)
10. Datta, A.K., Devismes, S., Heurtefeux, K., Larmore, L.L., Rivierre, Y.: Competitive self-stabilizing k-clustering. Theor. Comput. Sci. **626**, 110–133 (2016)
11. Dijkstra, E.W.: Self-stabilizing systems in spite of distributed control. Commun. ACM (1974)
12. Dutertre, B.: Yices 2.2. In: Biere, A., Bloem, R. (eds.) CAV 2014. LNCS, vol. 8559, pp. 737–744. Springer, Cham (2014). https://doi.org/10.1007/978-3-319-08867-9_49
13. Gansner, E.R., North, S.C.: An open graph visualization system and its applications to software engineering. Softw. Pract. Exper. **30**(11), 1203–1233 (2000)
14. Ghosh, S.: Binary self-stabilization in distributed systems. IPL **40**(3), 153–159 (1991)
15. Halbwachs, N., Baghdadi, S.: Synchronous modelling of asynchronous systems. In: Sangiovanni-Vincentelli, A., Sifakis, J. (eds.) EMSOFT 2002. LNCS, vol. 2491, pp. 240–251. Springer, Heidelberg (2002). https://doi.org/10.1007/3-540-45828-X_18
16. Halbwachs, N., Caspi, P., Raymond, P., Pilaud, D.: The synchronous data flow programming language LUSTRE. Proc. IEEE **79**(9), 1305–1320 (1991)
17. Halbwachs, N., Lagnier, F., Raymond, P.: Synchronous observers and the verification of reactive systems. In: Nivat, M., Rattray, C., Rus, T., Scollo, G. (eds.) AMAST 1993, pp. 83–96. Springer, London (1994). https://doi.org/10.1007/978-1-4471-3227-1_8
18. Hoepman, J.-H.: Uniform deterministic self-stabilizing ring-orientation on odd-length rings. In: Tel, G., Vitányi, P. (eds.) WDAG 1994. LNCS, vol. 857, pp. 265–279. Springer, Heidelberg (1994). https://doi.org/10.1007/BFb0020439
19. Holzmann, G.J., Peled, D.: An improvement in formal verification. In: Hogrefe, D., Leue, S. (eds.) Formal Description Techniques VII. IAICT, pp. 197–211. Springer, Boston (1995). https://doi.org/10.1007/978-0-387-34878-0_13
20. Jahier, E.: Verimag Tools Tutorials: Tutorials related to SASA. https://www-verimag.imag.fr/vtt/tags/sasa/
21. Jahier, E., Djoko-Djoko, S., Maiza, C., Lafont, E.: Environment-model based testing of control systems: case studies. In: Ábrahám, E., Havelund, K. (eds.) TACAS 2014. LNCS, vol. 8413, pp. 636–650. Springer, Heidelberg (2014). https://doi.org/10.1007/978-3-642-54862-8_55
22. Kuppe, M.A., Lamport, L., Ricketts, D.: The TLA+ toolbox. In: F-IDE@FM (2019)
23. Lakhnech, Y., Siegel, M.: Deductive verification of stabilizing systems. In: WSS (1997)
24. Paulson, L.C.: Natural deduction as higher-order resolution. J. Log. Prog. **3**, 237–258 (1986)

25. Siegel, M.: Formal verification of stabilizing systems. In: Ravn, A.P., Rischel, H. (eds.) FTRTFT 1998. LNCS, vol. 1486, pp. 158–172. Springer, Heidelberg (1998). https://doi.org/10.1007/BFb0055345
26. Tsuchiya, T., Nagano, S., Paidi, R.B., Kikuno, T.: Symbolic model checking for self-stabilizing algorithms. IEEE TPDS **12**(1), 81–95 (2001)
27. Whittlesey-Harris, R.S., Nesterenko, M.: Fault-tolerance verification of the fluids and combustion facility of the international space station. In: ICDCS, p. 5 (2006)

The Fence Complexity of Persistent Sets

Gaetano Coccimiglio[1(✉)], Trevor Brown[1(✉)], and Srivatsan Ravi[2(✉)]

[1] University of Waterloo, Waterloo, ON N2L 3G1, Canada
{gccoccim,trevor.brown}@uwaterloo.ca
[2] University of Southern California, Los Angeles, CA 90007, USA
srivatsr@usc.edu

Abstract. We study the psync complexity of concurrent sets in the non-volatile shared memory model. Flush instructions are used in non-volatile memory to force shared state to be written back to non-volatile memory and must typically be accompanied by the use of expensive fence instructions to enforce ordering among such flushes. Collectively we refer to a flush and a fence as a psync. The safety property of strict linearizability forces crashed operations to take effect before the crash or not take effect at all; the weaker property of durable linearizability enforces this requirement only for operations that have completed prior to the crash event. We consider lock-free implementations of list-based sets and prove two lower bounds. We prove that for any durable linearizable lock-free set there must exist an execution where some process must perform at least one redundant psync as part of an update operation. We introduce an extension to strict linearizability specialized for persistent sets that we call strict limited effect (SLE) linearizability. SLE linearizability explicitly ensures that operations do not take effect after a crash which better reflects the original intentions of strict linearizability. We show that it is impossible to implement SLE linearizable lock-free sets in which read-only (or search) operations do not flush or fence. We undertake an empirical study of persistent sets that examines various algorithmic design techniques and the impact of flush instructions in practice. We present concurrent set algorithms that provide matching upper bounds and rigorously evaluate them against existing persistent sets to expose the impact of algorithmic design and safety properties on psync complexity in practice as well as the cost of recovering the data structure following a system crash.

Keywords: Strict linearizability · Durable linearizability · Lower bounds · Persistent sets · Non-volatile memory

1 Introduction

Byte-addressable Non-Volatile Memory (NVM) is now commercially available, thus accelerating the need for efficient *persistent* concurrent data structure algorithms. We consider a model in which systems can experience full system crashes.

S. Dolev and B. Schieber (Eds.): SSS 2023, LNCS 14310, pp. 36–51, 2023.
https://doi.org/10.1007/978-3-031-44274-2_3

When a crash occurs the contents of volatile memory are lost but the contents of NVM remain persistent. Following a crash a recovery procedure is used to bring the data structure back to a consistent state using the contents of NVM. In order to force shared state to be written back to NVM the programmer is sometimes required to explicitly *flush* shared objects to NVM by using *explicit flush* and *persistence fence* primitives, the combination of which is referred to as a *psync* [21]. While concurrent sets have been extensively studied for volatile shared memory [14], they are still relatively nascent in non-volatile shared memory. This paper presents a detailed study of the psync complexity of *concurrent sets* in theory and practice.

Algorithmic Design Choices for Persistent Sets. The recent trend is to persist less data structure state to minimize the cost of writing to NVM. For example, the Link-Free and SOFT [21] persistent list-based sets do not persist any *pointers* in the data structure. Instead they persist the *keys* along with some other metadata used after a crash to determine if the key is in the data structure. This requires at most a single psync for update operations; however, not persisting the structure results in a more complicated recovery procedure.

A manuscript by Israelevitz and nine other authors presented a seminal in depth study of the performance characteristics of real NVM hardware [16]. Their results may have played a role in motivating the trend to persist as little as possible and reduce the number of fences. In particular, they found (Fig. 8 of [16]) that the latency to write 256 bytes and then perform a psync is at least 3.5x the latency to write 256 bytes and perform a flush but no persistence fence. Moreover, they found that NVM's write bandwidth could be a severe bottleneck, as a write-only benchmark (Fig. 9 of [16]) showed that NVM write bandwidth *scaled negatively* as the number of threads increased past four, and was approximately *9x lower* than volatile write bandwidth with 24 threads. A similar study of real NVM hardware was presented by Peng et al. [17].

While these results are compelling, it is unclear whether these latencies and bandwidth limitations are a problem for concurrent sets in practice. As it turns out, the push for *persistence-free* operations and synchronization mechanisms that minimize the amount of data persisted, and/or the number of *psyncs*, has many consequences, and the balance may favour incurring increased psyncs in some cases.

Contributions. Concurrent data structures in volatile shared memory typically satisfy the *linearizability* safety property, NVM data structures must consider the state of the persistent object following a full system crash. The safety property of *durable-linearizability* satisfies linearizability and following a crash, requires that the object state reflect a consistent operation subhistory that includes operations that had a response before the crash [15]. (i) We prove that for any durable-linearizable lock-free set there must exist an execution in which some process must perform at least one *redundant* psync as part of an update operation (Sect. 2). Informally, a redundant psync is one that does not change the contents of NVM. Our result is orthogonal to the lower bound of Cohen et al. who showed that the minimum number of psyncs per update for a durable-linearizable lock-free object is one [7]. However, Cohen et al. did not consider redundant psyncs. We show that redundant psyncs cannot be completely avoided in all concurrent executions: there exists an execution where n processes are concurrently performing update operations and $n-1$ processes perform a redundant psync. (ii) Our first result also applies to *SLE linearizability*, which we define to serve as a natural extension of the safety property of *strict linearizability* specifically for persistent sets. Originally defined by Aguilera and Frølund [1], strict linearizability forces crashed operations to be linearized before the crash or not at all. Strict linearizability was not originally defined for models in which the system can recover following a crash. To better capture the intentions of strict linearizability in the context of persistent concurrent sets, we introduce SLE linearizability to realize the intuition of Aguilera and Frølund for persistent concurrent sets. SLE linearizability is defined to explicitly enforce *limited effect* for persistent sets.

(iii) We prove that it is impossible to implement SLE linearizable lock-free sets in which read-only operations neither flush nor execute persistence fences, but it is possible to implement strict linearizable and durable linearizable lock-free sets with persistence-free reads (Sect. 2). (iv) We study the empirical costs of persistence fences in practice. To do this, we present matching upper bounds to our lower bound contributions (i) and (ii). Specifically, we describe a new technique for implementing persistent concurrent sets with persistence-free read-only operations called the extended link-and-persist technique and we utilize this technique to implement several persistent sets (Sect. 3). (v) We evaluate our upper bound implementations against existing persistent sets in a systemic empirical study of persistent sets. This study exposes the impact of algorithmic design and safety properties on persistence fence complexity in practice and the cost of recovering the data structure following a crash (Sect. 4).

The relationship between performance, psync complexity, recovery complexity and the correctness condition is subtle, even for seemingly simple data types like sorted sets. In this paper, we delve into the details of algorithmic design choices in persistent data structures to begin to characterize their impact.

2 Lower Bounds

Persistency Model and Safety Properties. We assume a full system crash-recovery model (all processes crash together). When a crash occurs all processes are returned to their initial states. After a crash a recovery procedure is invoked, and only after that can new operations begin.

Modifications to base objects first take effect in the volatile shared memory. Such modifications become persistent only once they are flushed to NVM. Base objects in volatile memory are flushed asynchronously by the processor (without the programmer's knowledge) to NVM arbitrarily. We refer to this as a *background flush*. We consider *background flushes* to be atomic. The programmer can also *explicitly* flush base objects to NVM by invoking *flush* primitives, typically accompanied by *persistence fence* primitives. An *explicit flush* is a primitive on a base object and is non-blocking, i.e., it may return *before* the base object has been written to persistent memory. An *explicit flush* by process p is guaranteed to have taken effect only after a subsequent *persistence fence* by p. An explicit flush combined with a persistence fence is referred to as a *psync*. We assume that psync events happen independently of RMW events and that psyncs do not change the configuration of volatile shared memory (other than updating the program counter). Note that on Intel platforms a RMW implies a fence, however, a RMW does not imply a flush before that fence, and therefore does not imply a psync.

In this paper, we consider the *set* type: an object of the set type stores a set of integer values, initially empty, and exports three operations: `insert`(v), `remove`(v), `contains`(v) where $v \in \mathbb{Z}$. A *history* is a sequence of invocations and responses of operations on the set implementation. We say a history is well-formed if no process invokes a new operation before the previous operation returns. Histories H and H' are *equivalent* if for every process p_i, $H|i = H'|i$.

A history H is durable linearizable, if it is well-formed and if $ops(H)$ is linearizable where $ops(H)$ is the subhistory of H containing no crash events [15].

Aguilera and Frølund defined strict linearizability for a model in which individual processes can crash and did not allow for recovery [1]. Berryhill et al. adapted strict linearizability for a model that allows for recovery following a system crash [2]. A history H is *strict linearizable* with respect to an object type τ if there exists a sequential history S equivalent to a *strict completion of* H, such that (1) $\rightarrow_{H^c} \subseteq \rightarrow_S$ and (2) *S is consistent with the sequential specification of τ*. A strict completion of H is obtained from H by inserting matching responses for a subset of pending operations after the operation's invocation and before the next crash event (if any), and finally removing any remaining pending operations and crash events.

Psync Complexity. It is likely that an implementation of persistent object will have many similarities to a volatile object of the same abstract data type. For this reason, when comparing implementations of persistent objects we are mostly interested in the overhead required to maintain a consistent state in persistent memory. Specifically, we consider psync complexity.

Programmers write data to persistent memory through the use of psyncs. A psync is an expensive operation. Cohen et al. [7] prove that update operations in a durable linearizable lock-free algorithm must perform at least one psync. In some implementations of persistent objects, reads also must perform psyncs. There is a clear focus in existing literature on minimizing the number of psyncs per data structure operation [9,11,21]. These factors suggest that psync complexity is a useful metric for comparing implementations of persistent objects.

Lower Bounds for Persistent Sets. We now present the two main lower bounds in this paper, but the full proofs are only provided in the full version of the paper [5] due to space constraints.

Impossibility of Persistence-Free Read-Only Searches. The key goal of the original work of Aguilera and Frølund [1] was to enforce *limited effect* by requiring operations to take effect before the crash or not at all. Limited effect requires that an operation takes effect within a limited amount of time after it is invoked. The point at which an operation takes effect is typically referred to as its *linearization point* and we say that the operation *linearizes* at that point. Rephrasing the intuition, when crashes can occur, limited effect requires that operations that were pending at the time of a crash linearize prior to the crash or not at all.

Strict linearizability is defined in terms of histories, which abstract away the real-time order of events. As a result, strict linearizability does not allow one to argue anything about the ordering of linearization points of operations that were pending at the time of a crash relative to the crash event. Thus, strict linearizability cannot and does not prevent operations from taking effect during the *recovery procedure* or even after the recovery procedure (which can occur for example in implementations that utilize linearization helping [4]). Strict linearizability only requires that at the time of a crash, pending operations *appear* to take effect prior to the crash. Although we are not aware of a formal proof of this, we conjecture in the full system crash-recovery model, durable linearizable objects are strict linearizable for some suitable definition of the recovery procedure. This is because we can always have the recovery procedure *clean-up* the state of the object returning it to a state such that the resulting history of any possible extension will satisfy strict linearizability. We note this conjecture as further motivation towards re-examining the way in which the definition of strict linearizability has been adapted for the full system crash-recovery model.

To this end, we define the concept of a *key write* to capture the intentions of Aguilera and Frølund in the context of sets by defining *Strict limited effect* (SLE) linearizability for sets as follows: a history satisfies SLE linearizability iff the history satisfies strict linearizability and for all operations with a key write, if the operation is pending at the time of a crash, the key write of the operation must occur before the crash event. In the strict completion of a history this is equivalent to requiring that the key write is always between the invocation and response of the operation. This is because the order of key writes relative to a crash event is fixed which means if the write occurs after the crash event then a strict completion of the history could insert a response for the operation only prior to the key write (at the crash) and this response cannot be reordered after the key write.

We show that it is impossible to implement a SLE linearizable lock-free set for which read-only searches do not perform any explicit flushes or persistence fences.

Theorem 1. *There exists no SLE linearizable lock-free set with* persistence-free *read-only searches.*

Redundant Psync Lower Bound for Durable Linearizable Sets. After modifying a base object only a single psync is required to ensure that it is written to persistent memory. Performing multiple psyncs on the same base object is therefore unnecessary and wasteful. We refer to these unnecessary psyncs as *redundant* psyncs. We show that for any durably linearizable lock-free set there must exist an execution in which n concurrent processes are invoking n concurrent update operations and n-1 processes each perform at least one redundant psync. At first glance one may think that this result is implied by the lower bound of Cohen et al. [7]. Cohen et al. show that for any lock-free durable linearizable object, there exists an execution wherein every update operation performs at least one persistence fence. Cohen et al. make no claims regarding redundant psyncs. Our result demonstrates that durable linearizable lock-free objects cannot completely avoid redundant psyncs.

Theorem 2. *In an n-process system, for every durable linearizable lock-free set implementation I, there exists an execution of I wherein n processes are concurrently performing update operations and n-1 processes perform a redundant psync.*

3 Upper Bounds

Briding the Gap Between Theory and Practice. The lower bounds presented in the previous section offer insights into the theoretical limits of persistent sets for both durable linearizability and SLE linearizability. While these lower bounds demonstrate a clear separation between durable and SLE linearizability, it is unclear whether or not we can observe any meaningful separation in practice. In order to answer this question we would like to compare durable and SLE linearizable variants of the same persistent set implementation. To this end, we extended the Link-and-Persist technique [9] to allow for persistence-free searches and use our extension to implement several persistent linked-list. We also add persistence helping to SOFT [21]. We explain both in detail next.

Notable Persistent Set Implementations. We briefly describe above mentioned existing implementations of persistent sets. We only focus on hand-crafted implementations since they generally perform better in practice compared to transforms or universal constructions [11,12].

David et al. describe a technique for implementing durable linearizable link-based data structures called the Link-and-Persist technique [9]. Using the Link-and-Persist technique, whenever a link in the data structure is updated, a single bit mark is applied to the link which denotes that it has not been written to persistent memory. The mark is removed after the link is written to persistent memory. We refer to this mark as the *persistence bit.* This technique was also presented by Wang et al. in the same year [19]. Wei et al. presented a more general technique which does not steal bits from data structure links [20].

The Link-Free algorithm of Zuriel et al. does not persist data structure links [21]. Instead, the Link-Free algorithm persists metadata added to every node.

Zuriel et al. designed a different algorithm called SOFT (Sets with an Optimal Flushing Technique) offering persistence-free searches. The SOFT algorithm does not persist data structure links and instead persists metadata added to each node. The major difference between the Link-Free algorithm and SOFT is that SOFT uses two different representations for every key in the data structure where only one representation is explicitly flushed to persistent memory.

Recovery Complexity. After a crash, a recovery procedure is invoked to return the objects in persistent memory back to a consistent state. Prior work has utilized a sequential recovery procedure [8,9,12,21]. A sequential recovery procedure is not required for correctness but it motivates the desire for efficient recovery procedures. No new data structure operations can be invoked until the recovery procedure has completed. Ideally we would like to minimize this period of downtime represented by the execution of recovery procedure. For the upper bounds in the this section, we use the asymptotic time complexity of the recovery procedure as another metric for comparing durable linearizable algorithms.

Extended Link-and-Persist. We choose to extend the Link-and-Persist technique of David et al. because it is quite simple and it represents the state of the art for hand-crafted algorithms that persist the links of a data structure. Moreover, unlike the algorithms in [21], the Link-and-Persist technique can be used to implement persistent sets without compromising recovery complexity. We build on the Link-and-Persist technique by extending it to allow for persistence-free searches and improved practical performance. Cohen et al. noted that persistence-free searches rely on the ability to linearize successful update operations at some point after the CPE of the operation [7]. In our case, this means that searches must be able to determine if the pointer is not persistent because of an `Insert` operation or a `Remove` operation. This is not possible with the original Link-and-Persist technique. We address this with two changes.

First, we require that a successful update operation, π_u, is linearized after its *Critical Persistence Event* (or CPE). Intuitively, the CPE represents the point after which the update will be recovered if a crash occurs. Specifically, if a volatile data structure would linearize π_u at the success of a RMW on a pointer v then we require that π_u is linearized at the success of the RMW that sets the persistence bit in v. If a search traverses a pointer, v, marked as not persistent the search can always be linearized prior to the concurrent update which modified v.

Secondly, since successful updates are linearized after their CPE, if the response of search operation depends on data that is linked into the data structure by a pointer marked as not persistent then the search must be able to access the last persistent value of that pointer. To achieve this, we add a pointer field to every node which we call the *old field.* A node will have both an *old field* and a pointer to its successor (*next pointer*) which effectively doubles the size of every data structure link. The *old field* will point to the last persistent value of the successor pointer while the successor pointer is marked as not persistent. In practice, the *old field* must be initialized to `null` then updated to a non-`null` value when the corresponding successor pointer is modified to a new value that needs to be persisted. Note that modifications like flagging or marking do not always need to be persisted; this depends on the whether or not the update can complete while the flagged or marked pointers are still reachable via a traversal from the root of the data structure. The easiest way to correctly update the *old field* is to update the successor pointer and the *old field* atomically using a hardware implementation of double-wide compare-and-swap (DWCAS) namely the cmpxchg16b instruction on Intel. Alternatively, a regular single-word compare-and-swap (SWCAS) can be used but this requires adding extra volatile memory synchronization to ensure correctness. For some data structures such as linked-lists using only SWCAS might also require adding an extra psync to updates. To allow searches to distinguish between pointers that are marked as not persistent because of a `remove` versus those that are not persistent because of an `insert` we require that the *old field* is always updated to a non-`null` value whenever a `remove` operation unlinks a node. `Insert` operations that modify the data structure must flag either the *old field* or the corresponding successor to indicate that the pointer marked as not persistent was last updated by an insert. When using SWCAS to update the *old field* this flag must be on the successor pointer.

With our extension if the response of a search operation depends on data linked into the data structure via a pointer marked as not persistent it can be linearized prior to the concurrent update operation that modified the pointer and it can use the information in the *old field* to determine the correct response which does not require performing any psyncs. If the search finds that the update was an insert it simply returns `false`. If the update was a remove but the search was able to find the value that it was looking for then it can return `true` since that key will be in persistent memory. If the update was a remove but the search was not able to find the value that it was looking for then it can check the if the node pointed to by the `old field` contains the value. As with the original, our extension still requires that an operation π will ensure that the CPE of any other operation which π depends on has occurred. π must also ensure that its own CPE has occurred before it returns. Another requirement which was not explicitly stated by David et al. is that operations must ensure that any data that a data structure link can point to is written to persistent memory before the link is updated to point to that data.

Our extension can be used to implement several link-based sets including trees and hash tables. Data structures implemented using our extension provide durable linearizability, however the use of persistence-free searches is optional. If the data structure does not utilize persistence-free searches then it would provide SLE linearizability (requiring only a change in the correctness proof).

Augmenting LF and SOFT. SOFT represents the state of the art for hand-crafted algorithms that do not persist the links of a data structure. The SOFT algorithm provides durable linearizability. For comparison, we added persistence helping for all operations of a persistent linked-list implemented using SOFT (thereby removing persistence-free searches) to achieve a SLE linearizable variant. We refer to this variant as SOFT-SLE. We also modified the implementation of the Link-Free algorithm. While the original Link-Free algorithm does not explicitly persist data structure links, it still allocates the links from persistent memory. We can achieve better performance by allocating the links from volatile memory. To emphasize the difference we refer to this as LF-V2.

3.1 Our Persistent List Implementations

In order to compare our extension to existing work we provide several implementations of persistent linked-lists which utilize our extended-link-and-persist approach. We choose to implement and study linked lists because they generally do not require complicated volatile synchronization.

```
def PersistenceFreeContains(key) :
    p = head, pNext = p.next, curr = UnmarkPtr(pNext)
    while true :
        if curr.key ≤ key : break
        p = curr, pNext = p.next
        curr = UnmarkPtr(pNext)
    hasKey = curr.key==key
    if IsDurable(ptNext) : return hasKey
    old1 = p.old, pNext2 = p.next, old2 = p.old
    pDiff = pNext≠pNext2, oldDiff = old1≠old2
    if pDiff or oldDiff or old1==null : return hasKey
    if IsIFlagged(old1) : return false
    if hasKey : return true
    return UnmarkPtr(old1).key==key
```

Algorithm 1. Pseudocode for the persistence-free contains function of our Physical-Delete (PD) list. The volatile synchronization is based on the list of Fomitchev and Ruppert.

We refer to our implementations as PD (Physical-Delete), PD-S (SWCAS implementation of PD), LD (Logical-Delete) and LD-S (SWCAS implementation of LD). The names refer to the synchronization approach and primitive. Our implementations use two different methods for achieving synchronization in volatile memory. Specifically we use one based on the Harris list [13] and another based on the work of Fomitchev and Ruppert [10]. The former takes a lazy approach to deletion that relies on marking for logical deletion and helping. As a result, marked pointers must be written to persistent memory which requires an extra psync. The latter does not take a lazy approach to deletions but still relies on helping and requires extra volatile memory synchronization through the use of marking and flagging. Fortunately, we do not need to persist marked or flagged pointers with this approach. Figure 1 shows an example of an update operation in the PD list implementation. We also implement separate variants using 2 different synchronization primitives, DWCAS and SWCAS. Table 1 summarizes some of the details of these approaches. We assume that the size of the *key* and *value* fields allow a single node to fit on one cache line meaning a *flush* on any field of the node guarantees that all fields are written to persistent memory. The assumption that the data we want to persist fits on a single cache line is common. David et al., Zuriel et al. and several others have relied on similar assumptions [8,9,18,21]. It is possible that our persistent list could be modified to allow for the case where nodes do not fit onto a single cache line by adopting a strategy similar to [6].

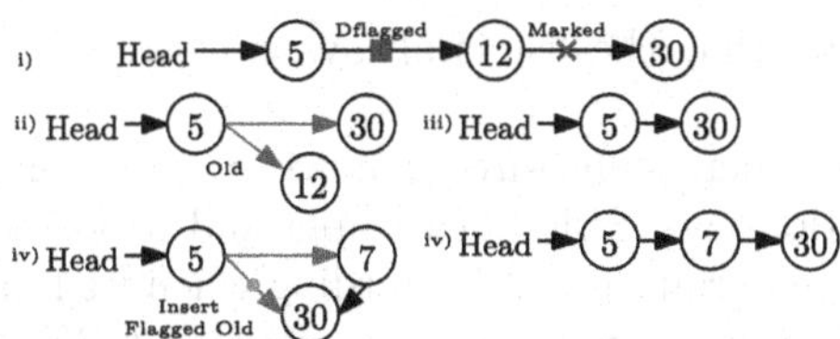

Fig. 1. Steps to execute an `insert(7)` operation in our PD list implementation. Blue pointers indicate non-durable pointers (with persistence bits set to 0). i) Initially we have three nodes. The node containing 5 has a pending delete flag (Dflagged) and the node containing 12 is marked for deletion. We traverse to find a key ≥7. ii) Help finish the pending `Remove` via DWCAS to unlink marked node and set old pointer. iii) Flush and set persistence bit via DWCAS (clearing old pointer). iv) Via DWCAS insert 7 and set old pointer. The old pointer is flagged to indicate a pending insert. v) Flush and set persistence bit via DWCAS.

Search Variants. As part of our persistent list, we implement 4 variants of the `contains` operation: persist all, asynchronous persist all, persist last and persistence free. We focus on the latter two since the others are naive approaches that perform many redundant psyncs.

Persist Last (PL). If the pointer into the terminal node of the traversal is marked as not persistent then write it to persistent memory and set its persistence bit via a CAS. This variant is the most similar to the searches in the linked list implemented using the original Link-and-Persist technique.

Persistence Free (PF). If the pointer into the terminal node of the traversal performed by the search is marked as not persistent then use the information in the *old field* of the node's predecessor to determine the correct return value without performing any persistence events. Since we do not need to set the durability bit of any link, this variant does not perform any writes and never performs a psync. Algorithm 1 shows the pseudocode for the persistence-free search of the PD list. For simplicity we abbreviate some of the bitwise operations with named functions. Specifically, *UnmarkPtr* which removes any marks or flags, *IsDurable* which checks if the pointer is marked as persistent and *IsIflagged* which checks if the pointer was flagged by an `insert`.

Theorem 3. *The PD, PD-S, LD, and LD-S lists are durable linearizable and lock-free.*

We prove Theorem 3 in the full version of the paper. We can also show that our list implementations are durable linearizable by considering a volatile abstract set (the keys in the list that are reachable in volatile memory) and a persistent abstract set (the keys in the list that are reachable in persistent memory). By identifying, for each operation, the points at which these sets change, we can show that updates change the volatile abstract set prior to changing the persistent abstract set and that each update changes the volatile abstract set exactly once. It follows that the list is always consistent with some persistent abstract set.

If we never invoke a persistence-free `contains` operation then we can prove that the implementations are SLE linearizable and lock-free. Doing so simply requires that we change our arguments regarding when we linearize update operations such that the linearization point is not after the CPE. Note that of the set implementations that we discuss, those that have persistence-free searches are examples of implementations which are strict linearizable but not SLE linearizable. These implementations require that the recovery procedure or operations invoked after a crash take steps which effectively linearize operations. This is because following a crash, one cannot tell the difference between an operation that has progressed far enough to allow some future operation to help linearize it and an operation that was already linearized.

Table 1. Our Novel Persistent List Details.

Name	Synch. Approach	Synch. Primitive	Min Psyncs Per Insert/Remove	
PD	Fomitchev	DWCAS	1	1
PD-S	Fomitchev	SWCAS	2	1
LD	Harris	DWCAS	1	2
LD-S	Harris	SWCAS	2	2

4 Evaluation

We present an experimental analysis of our persistent list compared to existing persistent lists on various workloads. We test our variants of the `contains` operation separately meaning no run includes more than one of the variants.[1] To distinguish between our implementations of the `contains` operation we prefix the names of our persistent list algorithms with the abbreviation of a `contains` variant (for example PFLD refers to one of our persistent lists which utilized only Persistence-Free searches and the Logical-Deletion algorithm). Due to space constraints we only present the best performing implementations of our persistent list. We test the performance of these lists in terms of throughput (operations per second). We also examine the psync behaviour of these algorithms. Specifically, we track the number of psyncs that are performed by searches and the number of psyncs that are performed by update operations.

All of the experiments were run on a machine with 48 cores across 2 Intel Xeon Gold 5220R 2.20GHz processors which provides 96 available threads (2 threads per core and 24 cores per socket). The system has a 36608K L3 cache, 1024K L2 cache, 64K L1 cache and 1.5 TB of NVRAM. The NVRAM modules

[1] Source code: https://gitlab.com/Coccimiglio/setbench.

installed on the system are Intel Optane DCPMMs. We utilize the same benchmark as [3] for conducting the empirical tests. Keys are accessed according to a uniform distribution. We prefill the lists to 50% capacity before collecting measurements. Each test consisted of ten iterations where each individual test ran for ten seconds. The graphs show the average of all iterations. Libvmmalloc was the persistent memory allocator used for all algorithms.

Throughput. Figure 2 shows the throughput of our best persistent list variants compared to the existing algorithms. Since the DWCAS implementation of our list out performed the SWCAS implementation we compare only our DWCAS implementations. SOFT performs best when there is high contention in read dominant workloads and consistently best for non-read dominant workloads.

Lesson Learned: Persisting more information in update operations is generally more costly but persistence free searches do not seem to provide major performance improvements.

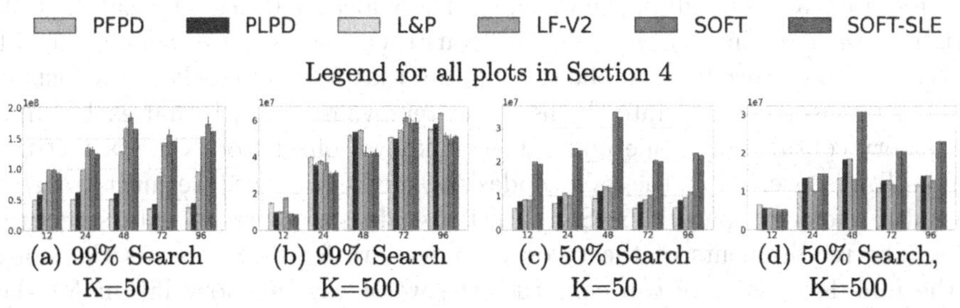

(a) 99% Search K=50 (b) 99% Search K=500 (c) 50% Search K=50 (d) 50% Search, K=500

Fig. 2. Persistent list throughput. X-axis: number of concurrent threads. Y-axis: operations/second. K is the list size.

Psync Behaviour. The recent trend to persist less data structure state has influenced implementations of persistent objects focused on minimizing the amount of psyncs required per operation. We know that SLE linearizable algorithms cannot have persistence-free searches. From [7] we also know that update operations require at least 1 psync. Of the persistent lists that we consider, the persistent lists from [21] are unique in that the maximum number of psyncs per update operation is bounded. To better understand the cost incurred by psyncs, we track the number of psyncs performed by read-only operations (searches) and the number of psyncs performed by update operations. Note that for updates this includes unsuccessful updates which might not need to perform a psync. Figure 3 shows the average number of psyncs per search and the average number of psyncs per update operation. We observe that searches rarely perform a psync in any of the algorithms that do not have persistence-free searches. On average, update operations do not perform more than the minimum number of required psyncs.

Lesson Learned: Algorithmic techniques such as *persistence bits* for reducing the number of psyncs are highly effective. On average, there are very few redundant psyncs in practice.

Recovery. It is not practical to force real system crashes in order to test the recovery procedure of any algorithm. It is possible that one could simulate a system crash by running the recovery procedure as a standalone algorithm on an artificially created memory configuration. This is problematic because the recovery procedure of a durable linearizable algorithm is often tightly coupled to some specific memory allocator (this is true of the existing algorithms that we consider). This makes a fair experimental analysis of the recovery procedure difficult. It is easier to describe the worst case scenario for recovering the data structure for each of the algorithms. To be specific, we describe the worst case persistent memory layout produced by the algorithm noting how this relates to the performance of the recovery procedure.

The Link-Free list does not persist data structure links. As a result, there is no way to efficiently discover all valid nodes meaning the recovery procedure might need require traversing all of the memory. The allocator utilized by Zuriel et al. partitions memory into *chunks*. We can construct a worse case memory layout for the recovery procedure as follows: Suppose that we completely fill persistent memory by inserting keys into the list. Now remove nodes such that each chunk of memory contains only one node at an unknown offset from the start of the chunk. To discover all of the valid nodes the recovery procedure must traverse the entire memory space. The SOFT list also does not persist data structure links. The requirements of the recovery procedure for SOFT list is the same as the Link-Free list. We can construct the worst case memory layout for the recovery procedure in the same way as we did for the Link-Free list yielding the same asymptotic time complexity. The Link-and-Persist list can utilize an empty recovery procedure. The actual recovery procedure for the list implemented by the authors of [9] does extra work related to memory reclamation.

We utilize DWCAS and asynchronous flush instructions to achieve a minimum of one psync per `insert` operation. There are some subtleties with this implementation that result in a recovery complexity which is $O(N+n)$ for a list containing N nodes and a maximum of n concurrent processes. Implementations that use SWCAS (or DWCAS allowing for a minimum of two psyncs per `insert`) can utilize an empty recovery procedure.

Lesson Learned: If structure is persisted, recovery can be highly efficient. Without any persisted structure, recovery must traverse large regions (or even all) of shared memory.

SLE Linearizable vs. Durable Linearizable Sets. We have seen that there exists a theoretical separation between SLE linearizable and durable linearizable objects. For persistent lists we observe that this separation does not lead to significant performance differences in practice. 4 of the algorithms (Fig. 2) are SLE linearizable. Specifically, our PLPD list, the L&P list, LF list, and SOFT-SLE. The SOFT list and our PFPD list which both use persistence-free

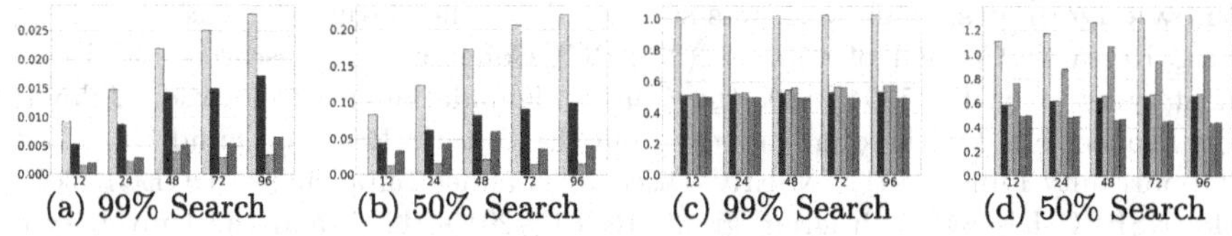

Fig. 3. Psync Behaviour. X-axis: number of concurrent threads. (a), (b) Y-axis: average psyncs/search, (c), (d) Y-axis: average psyncs/update. List size is 50.

searches are durable linearizable. The high cost of a psync and the impossibility of persistence-free searches in a SLE linearizable lock-free algorithm would suggest that the SLE linearizable algorithms that we test should perform noticeably worse. In practice, it is true that for most of the tested workloads, the algorithms that have persistence-free searches perform best (primarily SOFT). However, for many workloads, performance of SLE linearizable algorithms are comparable to the durable linearizable algorithms. In fact, for some workloads, the SLE linearizable lists perform better than the durable linearizable alternatives.

Lesson Learned: SLE linearizable algorithms can be fast in practice, despite theoretical tradeoffs.

5 Discussion

We prove that update operations in durable linearizable lock-free sets will perform at least one redundant psync. We motivate the importance of ensuring limited effect for sets and defined strict limited effect (SLE) linearizability for sets. We prove that SLE linearizable lock-free sets cannot have persistence-free reads. We implement several persistent lists and evaluate them rigorously. Our experiments demonstrate that SLE linearizable lock-free sets can achieve comparable or better performance to durable linearizable lock-free sets despite the theoretical separation. For the algorithms and techniques that we examined, supporting persistence-free reads is what separates the durable linearizable sets from the SLE linearizable. However, the SLE linearizable sets rarely perform a psync during a read. For those researchers that value ensuring limited effect for sets but are unsure about the performance implications, we recommend beginning with SLE linearizable implementations since a SLE linearizable implementation may not have much overhead and it may be sufficient for the application. Our work also exposes that psync complexity is not a good predictor of performance in practice, thus motivating need for better metrics to compare persistent objects.

In this work we focused specifically on sets because we wanted to understand the psync complexity of a relatively simple data structure like sets. We think that there is clear potential to generalize our theoretical results to other object types or classes of object types and perform similar empirical analysis of persistent algorithms for those objects, thus bridging the gap between theory and practice.

Acknowledgements. This work was supported by: the Natural Sciences and Engineering Research Council of Canada (NSERC) Collaborative Research and Development grant: CRDPJ 539431-19, the Canada Foundation for Innovation John R. Evans Leaders Fund with equal support from the Ontario Research Fund CFI Leaders Opportunity Fund: 38512, NSERC Discovery Launch Supplement: DGECR-2019-00048, NSERC Discovery Program grant: RGPIN-2019-04227, and the University of Waterloo.

References

1. Aguilera, M.K., Frolund, S.: Strict linearizability and the power of aborting. Technical report, HP Laboratories Palo Alto (2003)
2. Berryhill, R., Golab, W.M., Tripunitara, M.: Robust shared objects for non-volatile main memory. In: 19th International Conference on Principles of Distributed Systems, OPODIS 2015, Rennes, France, 14–17 December 2015, pp. 20:1–20:17 (2015)
3. Brown, T., Prokopec, A., Alistarh, D.: Non-blocking interpolation search trees with doubly-logarithmic running time. In: Proceedings of the 25th ACM SIGPLAN Symposium on Principles and Practice of Parallel Programming, pp. 276–291 (2020)
4. Censor-Hillel, K., Petrank, E., Timnat, S.: Help! In: Proceedings of the 2015 ACM Symposium on Principles of Distributed Computing, PODC 2015, Donostia-San Sebastián, Spain, 21–23 July 2015, pp. 241–250 (2015)
5. Coccimiglio, G., Brown, T., Ravi, S.: The fence complexity of persistent sets (2023). https://mc.uwaterloo.ca/pubs/fence_complexity/fullpaper.pdf. Full version of this paper
6. Cohen, N., Friedman, M., Larus, J.R.: Efficient logging in non-volatile memory by exploiting coherency protocols. Proc. ACM Program. Lang. **1**(OOPSLA), 1–24 (2017)
7. Cohen, N., Guerraoui, R., Zablotchi, I.: The inherent cost of remembering consistently. In: Proceedings of the 30th on Symposium on Parallelism in Algorithms and Architectures, pp. 259–269 (2018)
8. Correia, A., Felber, P., Ramalhete, P.: Persistent memory and the rise of universal constructions. In: Proceedings of the Fifteenth European Conference on Computer Systems, pp. 1–15 (2020)
9. David, T., Dragojevic, A., Guerraoui, R., Zablotchi, I.: Log-free concurrent data structures. In: 2018 USENIX Annual Technical Conference (USENIX ATC 2018), pp. 373–386 (2018)
10. Fomitchev, M., Ruppert, E.: Lock-free linked lists and skip lists. In: Proceedings of the Twenty-Third Annual ACM Symposium on Principles of Distributed Computing, pp. 50–59 (2004)
11. Friedman, M., Ben-David, N., Wei, Y., Blelloch, G.E., Petrank, E.: NVTraverse: in NVRAM data structures, the destination is more important than the journey. In: Proceedings of the 41st ACM SIGPLAN Conference on Programming Language Design and Implementation, pp. 377–392 (2020)
12. Friedman, M., Petrank, E., Ramalhete, P.: Mirror: making lock-free data structures persistent. In: Proceedings of the 42nd ACM SIGPLAN International Conference on Programming Language Design and Implementation, pp. 1218–1232 (2021)
13. Harris, T.L.: A pragmatic implementation of non-blocking linked-lists. In: Welch, J. (ed.) DISC 2001. LNCS, vol. 2180, pp. 300–314. Springer, Heidelberg (2001). https://doi.org/10.1007/3-540-45414-4_21

14. Herlihy, M., Shavit, N.: The Art of Multiprocessor Programming. Morgan Kaufmann (2008)
15. Izraelevitz, J., Mendes, H., Scott, M.L.: Linearizability of persistent memory objects under a full-system-crash failure model. In: Gavoille, C., Ilcinkas, D. (eds.) DISC 2016. LNCS, vol. 9888, pp. 313–327. Springer, Heidelberg (2016). https://doi.org/10.1007/978-3-662-53426-7_23
16. Izraelevitz, J., et al.: Basic performance measurements of the Intel Optane DC persistent memory module. arXiv preprint arXiv:1903.05714 (2019)
17. Peng, I.B., Gokhale, M.B., Green, E.W.: System evaluation of the Intel Optane byte-addressable NVM. In: Proceedings of the International Symposium on Memory Systems, pp. 304–315 (2019)
18. Ramalhete, P., Correia, A., Felber, P.: Efficient algorithms for persistent transactional memory. In: Proceedings of the 26th ACM SIGPLAN Symposium on Principles and Practice of Parallel Programming, pp. 1–15 (2021)
19. Wang, T., Levandoski, J., Larson, P.A.: Easy lock-free indexing in non-volatile memory. In: 2018 IEEE 34th International Conference on Data Engineering (ICDE), pp. 461–472. IEEE (2018)
20. Wei, Y., Ben-David, N., Friedman, M., Blelloch, G.E., Petrank, E.: Flit: a library for simple and efficient persistent algorithms. arXiv preprint arXiv:2108.04202 (2021)
21. Zuriel, Y., Friedman, M., Sheffi, G., Cohen, N., Petrank, E.: Efficient lock-free durable sets. Proc. ACM Program. Lang. **3**(OOPSLA), 1–26 (2019)

Brief Announcement: Understanding Self-stabilizing Node-Capacitated Overlay Networks Through Simulation

Winfred Afeaneku[1], Andrew Berns[1(✉)], Weston Kuchenberg[1], Sara Leisinger[1], and Cedric Liu[2]

[1] Department of Computer Science, University of Northern Iowa, Cedar Falls, IA, USA
andrew.berns@uni.edu

[2] Cedar Falls High School, Cedar Falls, IA, USA

Abstract. Overlay networks, where connections are made over logical links composed of zero or more physical links, are a popular paradigm in modern distributed computing. The use of logical links allows the creation of a variety of network topologies with desirable properties such as low degree and low diameter, regardless of the (usually) fixed physical topology. Many of these overlay networks operate in unfriendly environments where transient faults are commonplace. Self-stabilizing overlay networks present one way to manage these faults. In particular, self-stabilizing overlay networks can guarantee that the desired network topology is created when starting from *any* weakly-connected initial state.

To date, work on self-stabilizing overlay networks has assumed the network has either unbounded bandwidth, or that the bandwidth constraints are placed on the communication links themselves. In practice, however, the bandwidth constraints are actually capacities on the *nodes*: adding and deleting logical links does not change the fixed physical links being used. In this work, we describe the node-capacitated model for self-stabilizing overlay networks. To better understand this new model, we created a simulation and ran it numerous times while adjusting various parameters. We discuss this simulation and several experiments. Finally, we propose future directions for self-stabilizing node-capacitated overlay networks.

Keywords: topological stabilization · self-stabilizing overlay networks · node-capacitated model

1 Introduction

Overlay networks, where connections are made over logical links composed of zero or more physical links, are a firmly entrenched paradigm in modern comput-

This project is funded in part by the Louis Stokes Alliance for Minority Participation (LSAMP).

S. Dolev and B. Schieber (Eds.): SSS 2023, LNCS 14310, pp. 52–56, 2023.
https://doi.org/10.1007/978-3-031-44274-2_4

ing. From data centers with hundreds of servers to Internet-embedded applications of millions of nodes around the globe, overlay networks provide a means to manage the complexity of physical networks, allowing engineers to build logical topologies with desirable properties like low degree and low diameter, regardless of the limitations of the actual physical network.

Many of these overlay networks are deployed in fault-prone environments where transient faults are likely to perturb the system away from a legal configuration. *Self-stabilizing overlay networks* are one proposed mechanism for dealing with these fault-prone environments, promising to restore the overlay network to a legal configuration after *any* transient fault.

One limitation of existing work on self-stabilizing overlay networks, however, has been the unrealistic treatment of communication bandwidth. Existing work assumes either unlimited bandwidth on each edge, or limits bandwidth per overlay edge. In reality, each logical link of the overlay network is likely using the same physical links for a particular node. Adding additional logical links, then, does not increase the bandwidth as the physical network is unchanged. A more appropriate model would be to limit the size and number of messages a *node* can send and receive, called a *node-capacitated* model. In this brief announcement, we present the start of our work using simulations to understand the node-capacitated model for self-stabilizing overlay networks.

2 The Node-Capacitated Overlay Network Model

We model our distributed system as a graph $G = (V, E)$, with node set V representing the set of nodes ($|V| = n$), and undirected edge set E representing communication links between these nodes. We assume a synchronous message passing model where computation proceeds in rounds. In every round, each node will (i) receive messages sent to it in the previous round, (ii) perform local computation and (potentially) update its state, and (iii) send messages to its neighbors.

In the overlay network model, communication links are logical links that can be modified by program actions. This means the network topology can change as nodes add and delete edges. We will limit edge creation to the "introduction" process mentioned in Feldmann, Scheideler, and Schmid [1]. In this process, a node u may ask a neighboring node v to add the edge (v, w) if the edges (u, v) and (u, w) exist. The goal is for program actions to add and delete edges until a legal configuration is reached. A legal configuration (or *target topology*) is defined by a predicate over all nodes' state (which includes edges in the overlay network model). For this work, the legal configuration is a completely-connected network, a topology we call CLIQUE.

In the node-capacitated overlay network model, each node has a capacity for sending and receiving messages. This capacity limits both the number and size of messages sent and received by a node. In this capacitated model, a node u may send only a fixed number of messages in each round, regardless of how many logical links the node has. While a node capacity can be any fixed value, a common choice is to allow every node to send and receive $\mathcal{O}(\log(n))$ messages of size $\mathcal{O}(\log(n))$ in every round, for a total of $\mathcal{O}(\log^2(n))$ bits per round.

The goal for our self-stabilizing algorithms is for them to reach a legal configuration after any transient fault, a process which can be modeled by assuming an arbitrary initial state eventually reaches a legal configuration (and remains legal thereafter). We assume the graph starts in a weakly-connected configuration and, for simplicity, a node's neighborhood only contains links to valid and responding nodes. Each node executes program actions to update their local state, which includes edges. After some time, the system will reach a legal configuration and remain in a legal configuration thereafter. We call the time required to reach a legal configuration the *convergence time*, which we measure in rounds.

As a final comment regarding the model, note that we do not require our algorithms to be *silent* – that is, we do not require the state of the system to remain fixed once a legal configuration is reached. In the node-capacitated model with a target topology of CLIQUE, it is impossible for a node to know the state of all of its neighbors at once, meaning a node must in some way be constantly communicating with its neighbors.

3 Simulation

Our simulator works by creating a random graph, running an algorithm to build CLIQUE, and detecting termination.

Graph Creation. The simulation begins by creating a graph of a specified number of nodes n. It then repeatedly adds n edges between pairs of randomly-selected nodes, checking to see if the network is connected after each set of n edges are added. Once the graph is connected, the simulation moves on to the execution phase.

Algorithm Execution. Once the graph is connected, the simulation begins executing the algorithm round by round. In a round, each node executes the following steps:

1. At the beginning of a round, the node randomly selects a number of messages that were received in the previous round to be delivered. These messages each "introduce" the node to another node in the network: the receiving node adds an edge to the node specified in the message (provided an edge does not already exist).
2. After processing the messages, the node then creates new messages and sends them to the appropriate nodes. These messages are created by randomly selecting two distinct neighbors v and w and "introducing" v and w, thus creating the edge (v, w) (provided the message is not dropped from being over capacity and that the edge (v, w) does not already exist).

3. The simulation then checks to see if a legal topology has been created. For our target topology (CLIQUE), this check is as simple as checking to see if all nodes have n neighbors (including an edge to one's self). If the target topology has not been built, the simulation continues with the next round.

Termination. As discussed above, after every simulated round, we check the current graph to see if a legal configuration is reached. Once the legal configuration is detected, the simulation terminates while outputting to standard out the number of nodes in the simulation, the node capacities, the node message sending limit, the number of rounds required to reach a legal configuration, the total number of messages sent, and the total number of messages received.

4 Results and Discussion

Using our simulator, we ran a series of experiments to see how changes to network parameters affected performance. We found, for instance, that the convergence time was linear in the number of nodes. We describe two other interesting experiments and their results below.

4.1 Convergence Time vs. Node Capacity

For our second experiment, we tested the role node capacity has on convergence time. For this, we fixed the network size n at 1500 and varied the node capacity (and message sending limit) from 5 to 1500. The results are given in Fig. 1.

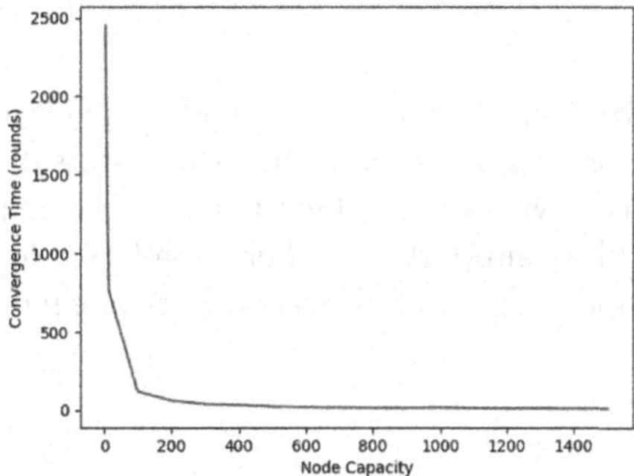

Fig. 1. Convergence Time vs. Node Capacity.

4.2 Convergence Time vs. Message Sending Limit

Give there seemed to be very few messages lost during our algorithm's execution, we thought it would be interesting to also examine the relationship between the message sending limit and the convergence time. Perhaps the messages were not getting lost but convergence was taking extraordinarily long. To check this, we fixed the network size n at 1500 and the node capacity at 111 (again approximately $\log^2(n)$) and varied the message sending limit from 5 to 110 (again covering from $\log(n)$ to $\log^2(n)$). The results of our experiment are plotted in Fig. 2.

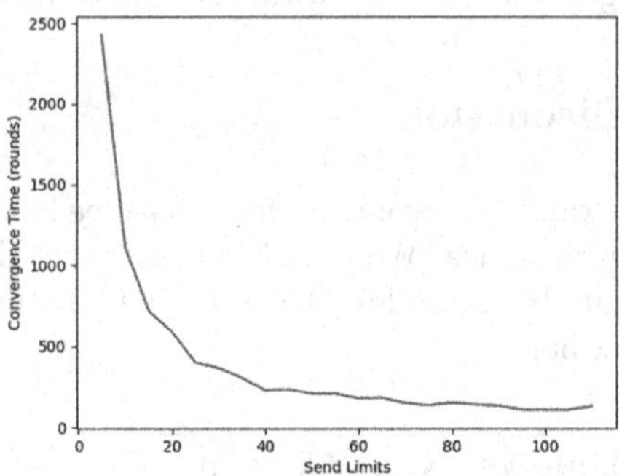

Fig. 2. Convergence Time vs. Message Sending Limit.

5 Conclusion

In this paper we have introduced a new node-capacitated model for self-stabilizing overlay networks and also described the results of several experiments we ran using a simulation we created. Our future work hopes to complete the simulator, including adding support for other target topologies, and using it to learn more about the node-capacitated overlay network model.

References

1. Feldmann, M., Scheideler, C., Schmid, S.: Survey on algorithms for self-stabilizing overlay networks. ACM Comput. Surv. **53**(4), 1–24 (2020). https://doi.org/10.1145/3397190

Brief Announcement: Byzantine-Tolerant Detection of Causality in Synchronous Systems

Anshuman Misra and Ajay D. Kshemkalyani(✉)

University of Illinois at Chicago, Chicago, IL 60607, USA
{amisra7,ajay}@uic.edu

Abstract. It was recently proved that the causality or the happens before relation between events in an asynchronous distributed system cannot be detected in the presence of Byzantine processes [Misra and Kshemkalyani, NCA 2022]. This result holds for the multicast, unicast, and broadcast modes of communication. This prompts us to examine whether the causality detection problem can be solved in synchronous systems in the presence of Byzantine processes. We answer this in the affirmative by outlining two approaches. The first approach uses Replicated State Machines (RSM) and vector clocks. Another approach is based on a transformation from Byzantine failures to crash failures for synchronous systems.

Keywords: Byzantine fault-tolerance · Happens before · Causality · Synchronous system · Message Passing

1 Introduction

The "happens before" or the causality relation, denoted $\rightarrow$, between events in a distributed system was defined by Lamport [6]. Given two events e and e', the *causality detection* problem asks to determine whether $e \rightarrow e'$.

There is a rich literature on solutions for solving the causality detection problem between events. See [4,5,9,15,17] for an overview of some approaches such as tracking causality graphs, scalar clocks, vector clocks [3,8], and variants of logical clocks such as hierarchical clocks, plausible clocks, dotted version vectors, Bloom clocks, interval tree clocks and resettable encoded vector clocks. Some of these variants track causality accurately while others introduce approximations as trade-offs to save on the space and/or time and/or message overheads. Schwarz and Mattern [17] stated that the quest for the holy grail of the ideal causality tracking mechanism is on. This literature above assumed that processes are correct (non-faulty). The causality detection problem for a system with Byzantine processes was recently introduced and studied in [11].

A related problem is the causal ordering of messages. Under the Byzantine failure model, causal ordering has recently been studied in [10,12,13].

S. Dolev and B. Schieber (Eds.): SSS 2023, LNCS 14310, pp. 57–61, 2023.
https://doi.org/10.1007/978-3-031-44274-2_5

Contributions. It was recently proved that the problem of detecting causality between a pair of events cannot be solved in an asynchronous system in the presence of Byzantine processes, irrespective of whether the communication is via unicasts, multicasts, or broadcasts [11]. In the multicast mode of communication, each send event sends a message to a group consisting of a subset of the set of processes in the system. Different send events can send to different subsets of processes. Communicating by unicasts and communicating by broadcasts are special cases of multicasting. It was shown in [11] that in asynchronous systems with even a single Byzantine process, the unicast and multicast modes of communication are susceptible to false positives and false negatives, whereas the broadcast mode of communication is susceptible to false negatives but no false positives. A false positive means that $e \not\to e'$ whereas $e \to e'$ is perceived/detected. A false negative means than $e \to e'$ whereas $e \not\to e'$ is perceived/detected. The impossibility result for asynchronous systems prompts us to examine whether the causality detection problem can be solved in synchronous systems in the presence of Byzantine processes. We answer in the affirmative for unicasts, multicasts, and broadcasts by outlining two approaches in this brief announcement. The results are summarized in Table 1.

Table 1. Solvability of causality detection between events under different communication modes in Byzantine-prone asynchronous and synchronous systems. FP is false positive, FN is false negative. $\overline{FP}/\overline{FN}$ means no false positive/no false negative is possible.

Mode of communication	Detecting "happens before" in asynchronous systems	Detecting "happens before" in synchronous systems
Multicasts	Impossible [11] FP, FN	Possible $\overline{FP}, \overline{FN}$
Unicasts	Impossible [11] FP, FN	Possible $\overline{FP}, \overline{FN}$
Broadcasts	Impossible [11] $\overline{FP}, FN$	Possible $\overline{FP}, \overline{FN}$

2 System Model

The distributed system is modelled as an undirected complete graph $G = (P, C)$. Here P is the set of processes communicating in the distributed system. Let $|P| = n$. C is the set of (logical) FIFO communication links over which processes communicate by message passing. The processes may be Byzantine [7,14]. The distributed system is assumed to be synchronous [2].

Let e_i^x, where $x \geq 1$, denote the x-th event executed by process p_i. An event may be an internal event, a message send event, or a message receive event. Let the state of p_i after e_i^x be denoted s_i^x, where $x \geq 1$, and let s_i^0 be the initial state. The execution at p_i is the sequence of alternating events and resulting states, as $\langle s_i^0, e_i^1, s_i^1, e_i^2, s_i^2 \ldots \rangle$. The sequence of events $\langle e_i^1, e_i^2, \ldots \rangle$ is called the execution history at p_i and denoted E_i. Let $E = \bigcup_i \{E_i\}$ and let $T(E)$ denote the set of all events in (the set of sequences) E. The *happens before* [6] relation, denoted $\rightarrow$, is an irreflexive, asymmetric, and transitive partial order defined over events in a distributed execution that is used to define causality. The *causal past* of an event e is denoted as $CP(e)$ and defined as the set of events $\{e' \in T(E) \mid e' \rightarrow e\}$.

3 Problem Formulation and a Brief Overview of Solutions

The problem formulation is analogous to that in [11]. An algorithm to solve the causality detection problem collects the execution history of each process in the system and derives causal relations from it. E_i is the *actual* execution history at p_i. For any causality detection algorithm, let F_i be the execution history at p_i as perceived and collected by the algorithm and let $F = \bigcup_i \{F_i\}$. F thus denotes the execution history of the system as perceived and collected by the algorithm. Analogous to $T(E)$, let $T(F)$ denote the set of all events in F. Analogous to the definition of $\rightarrow$ on $T(E)$ [6], the *happens before* relation can be defined on $T(F)$ instead of on $T(E)$.

Let $e1 \rightarrow e2|_E$ and $e1 \rightarrow e2|_F$ be the evaluation (1 or 0) of $e1 \rightarrow e2$ using E and F, respectively. Byzantine processes may corrupt the collection of F to make it different from E. We assume that a correct process p_i needs to detect whether $e_h^x \rightarrow e_i^*$ holds and e_i^* is an event in $T(E)$. If $e_h^x \notin T(E)$ then $e_h^x \rightarrow e_i^*|_E$ evaluates to *false*. If $e_h^x \notin T(F)$ (or $e_i^* \notin T(F)$) then $e_h^x \rightarrow e_i^*|_F$ evaluates to *false*. We assume an oracle that is used for determining correctness of the causality detection algorithm; this oracle has access to E which can be any execution history such that $T(E) \supseteq CP(e_i^*)$.

Byzantine processes may collude as follows.

1. To delete e_h^x from F_h or in general, record F as any alteration of E such that $e_h^x \rightarrow e_i^*|_F = 0$, while $e_h^x \rightarrow e_i^*|_E = 1$, or
2. To add a fake event e_h^x in F_h or in general, record F as any alteration of E such that $e_h^x \rightarrow e_i^*|_F = 1$, while $e_h^x \rightarrow e_i^*|_E = 0$.

Without loss of generality, we have that $e_h^x \in T(E) \cup T(F)$. Note that e_h^x belongs to $T(F) \setminus T(E)$ when it is a fake event in F.

Definition 1. *The causality detection problem $CD(E, F, e_i^*)$ for any event $e_i^* \in T(E)$ at a correct process p_i is to devise an algorithm to collect the execution history E as F at p_i such that $valid(F) = 1$, where*

$$valid(F) = \begin{cases} 1 \text{ if } \forall e_h^x, e_h^x \rightarrow e_i^*|_E = e_h^x \rightarrow e_i^*|_F \\ 0 \text{ otherwise} \end{cases}$$

When 1 is returned, the algorithm output matches the actual (God's) truth and solves *CD* correctly. Thus, returning 1 indicates that the problem has been solved correctly by the algorithm using F. 0 is returned if either

- $\exists e_h^x$ such that $e_h^x \rightarrow e_i^*|_E = 1 \wedge e_h^x \rightarrow e_i^*|_F = 0$ (denoting a false negative), or
- $\exists e_h^x$ such that $e_h^x \rightarrow e_i^*|_E = 0 \wedge e_h^x \rightarrow e_i^*|_F = 1$ (denoting a false positive).

In our first solution, we use the Replicated State Machine (RSM) approach [16] and vector clocks in the algorithm for causality detection. We can show that F at a correct process can be made to exactly match E, hence there is no possibility of a false positive or of a false negative. The RSM approach works only in synchronous systems. In a system with n application processes, the RSM-based solution uses $3t+1$ process replicas per application process, where t is the maximum number of Byzantine processes that can be tolerated in a RSM. Thus, there can be at most nt Byzantine processes among a total of $(3t+1)n$ processes partitioned into n RSMs of $3t+1$ processes each, with each RSM having up to t Byzantine processes. By using $(3t+1)n$ processes and the RSM approach to represent n application processes, the malicious effects of Byzantine process behaviors are neutralized.

Another approach is as follows. A generic transformation from Byzantine failures to crash failures for synchronous systems can be applied [1], this requires $t < n/3$. The possibility of correct Byzantine-tolerant causality detection would be implied by the possibility of correct crash-tolerant causality detection.

References

1. Bazzi, R.A., Neiger, G.: Simplifying fault-tolerance: providing the abstraction of crash failures. J. ACM **48**(3), 499–554 (2001). https://doi.org/10.1145/382780.382784
2. Dwork, C., Lynch, N.A., Stockmeyer, L.J.: Consensus in the presence of partial synchrony. J. ACM **35**(2), 288–323 (1988). https://doi.org/10.1145/42282.42283
3. Fidge, C.J.: Logical time in distributed computing systems. IEEE Comput. **24**(8), 28–33 (1991). https://doi.org/10.1109/2.84874
4. Kshemkalyani, A.D.: The power of logical clock abstractions. Distrib. Comput. **17**(2), 131–150 (2004). https://doi.org/10.1007/s00446-003-0105-9
5. Kshemkalyani, A.D., Shen, M., Voleti, B.: Prime clock: encoded vector clock to characterize causality in distributed systems. J. Parallel Distrib. Comput. **140**, 37–51 (2020). https://doi.org/10.1016/j.jpdc.2020.02.008
6. Lamport, L.: Time, clocks, and the ordering of events in a distributed system. Commun. ACM **21**(7), 558–565 (1978)
7. Lamport, L., Shostak, R.E., Pease, M.C.: The Byzantine generals problem. ACM Trans. Program. Lang. Syst. **4**(3), 382–401 (1982)
8. Mattern, F.: Virtual time and global states of distributed systems. In: Parallel and Distributed Algorithms, pp. 215–226. North-Holland (1988)
9. Misra, A., Kshemkalyani, A.D.: The bloom clock for causality testing. In: Goswami, D., Hoang, T.A. (eds.) ICDCIT 2021. LNCS, vol. 12582, pp. 3–23. Springer, Cham (2021). https://doi.org/10.1007/978-3-030-65621-8_1
10. Misra, A., Kshemkalyani, A.D.: Causal ordering in the presence of Byzantine processes. In: 28th IEEE International Conference on Parallel and Distributed Systems (ICPADS), pp. 130–138. IEEE (2022). https://doi.org/10.1109/ICPADS56603.2022.00025

11. Misra, A., Kshemkalyani, A.D.: Detecting causality in the presence of Byzantine processes: there is no holy grail. In: 21st IEEE International Symposium on Network Computing and Applications (NCA), pp. 73–80 (2022). https://doi.org/10.1109/NCA57778.2022.10013644
12. Misra, A., Kshemkalyani, A.D.: Solvability of Byzantine fault-tolerant causal ordering problems. In: Koulali, M.A., Mezini, M. (eds.) NETYS 2022. LNCS, vol. 13464, pp. 87–103. Springer, Cham (2022). https://doi.org/10.1007/978-3-031-17436-0_7
13. Misra, A., Kshemkalyani, A.D.: Byzantine fault-tolerant causal ordering. In: 24th International Conference on Distributed Computing and Networking (ICDCN), pp. 100–109. ACM (2023). https://doi.org/10.1145/3571306.3571395
14. Pease, M.C., Shostak, R.E., Lamport, L.: Reaching agreement in the presence of faults. J. ACM **27**(2), 228–234 (1980). https://doi.org/10.1145/322186.322188
15. Pozzetti, T., Kshemkalyani, A.D.: Resettable encoded vector clock for causality analysis with an application to dynamic race detection. IEEE Trans. Parallel Distrib. Syst. **32**(4), 772–785 (2021). https://doi.org/10.1109/TPDS.2020.3032293
16. Schneider, F.B.: Implementing fault-tolerant services using the state machine approach: a tutorial. ACM Comput. Surv. **22**(4), 299–319 (1990)
17. Schwarz, R., Mattern, F.: Detecting causal relationships in distributed computations: in search of the holy grail. Distrib. Comput. **7**(3), 149–174 (1994)

Invited Paper: Time Is Not a Healer, but It Sure Makes Hindsight 20:20

Eli Gafni[1] and Giuliano Losa[2(✉)]

[1] University of California, Los Angeles, USA
eli@ucla.edu
[2] Stellar Development Foundation, San Francisco, USA
giuliano@stellar.org

Abstract. In the 1980s, three related impossibility results emerged in the field of distributed computing. First, Fischer, Lynch, and Paterson demonstrated that deterministic consensus is unattainable in an asynchronous message-passing system when a single process may crash-stop. Subsequently, Loui and Abu-Amara showed the infeasibility of achieving consensus in asynchronous shared-memory systems, given the possibility of one crash-stop failure. Lastly, Santoro and Widmayer established the impossibility of consensus in synchronous message-passing systems with a single process per round experiencing send-omission faults.

In this paper, we revisit these seminal results. First, we observe that all these systems are equivalent in the sense of implementing each other. Then, we prove the impossibility of consensus in the synchronous system of Santoro and Widmayer, which is the easiest to reason about. Taking inspiration from Volzer's proof pearl and from the Borowski-Gafni simulation, we obtain a remarkably simple proof.

We believe that a contemporary pedagogical approach to teaching these results should first address the equivalence of the systems before proving the consensus impossibility within the system where the result is most evident.

1 Introduction

In their famous 1983 paper, Fischer, Lynch, and Paterson [10] (hereafter referred to as FLP) established that deterministic consensus is unattainable in an asynchronous message-passing system where one process may fail by stopping. As a foundational result in distributed computing and one of the most cited works in the field, it is crucial to teach this concept in an accessible manner that highlights the core reason for the impossibility. However, we believe that the original FLP proof is too technical for this purpose and that its low-level system details can obscure the essence of the proof.

In our quest to simplify the FLP proof, we revisit the subsequent extensions and improvements of the FLP result, including Loui and Abu-Amara's asynchronous shared-memory proof [14] and Santoro and Widmayer's impossibility

S. Dolev and B. Schieber (Eds.): SSS 2023, LNCS 14310, pp. 62–74, 2023.
https://doi.org/10.1007/978-3-031-44274-2_6

proof for synchronous systems with one process failing to send some of its messages per round [18]. The latter paper was titled "Time is not a healer," which inspired our own title.

While the impossibility of consensus was demonstrated in all of these systems, the proofs did not rely on reductions, but instead rehashed FLP's valency-based argument. This should have suggested that there are reductions between those models. In this work, we use elementary simulation algorithms to show that the aforementioned systems can indeed implement each other, and thus it suffices to prove consensus impossible in just one of them.

We then reconsider the impossibility proof in the system that is the easiest to reason about: the synchronous system of Santoro and Widmayer. In this system, we present a new and remarkably simple proof of the impossibility of consensus, which we believe is of great pedagogical value.

Unlike Santoro and Widmayer, we avoid using a valency argument inspired by FLP. Instead, we draw ideas from the Borowski-Gafni [6] simulation of a 1-resilient system using two wait-free processes and from Volzer's [21] brilliant impossibility proof. Volzer's idea, which he used to simplify FLP in the original FLP model, is to compare runs with one missing process with fault-free runs.

Next, we give an overview of the technical contributions of the paper.

1.1 Four Equivalent Models

The paper considers four models:

- **The FLP model**. This is the original asynchronous message-passing model of FLP, in which at most one process may crash-stop.
- **The 1-resilient shared-memory model**. This is an asynchronous shared-memory system in which at most one process may crash-stop.
- **The 1-resilient fail-to-receive model** (abbreviated fail-to-receive). This is a synchronous, round-by-round message-passing system in which processes never crash, but every round, each process might fail to receive one of the messages sent to it.
- **The 1-resilient fail-to-send model** (abbreviated fail-to-send). This is a synchronous, round-by-round message-passing system in which processes never crash, but every round one process might fail to send some of its messages. This model was originally presented by Santoro and Widmayer [18].

Assuming we have $n > 2$ processes[1], all the models above solve the same colorless tasks[2]. To show this, we proceed in three steps, each showing that two models simulate each other in the sense of Attiya and Welch [3, Chapter 7]. We write $A \leq B$ when B simulates A (and therefore B is stronger than A), and $A \equiv B$ when A and B simulate each other. The three steps are the following.

---

[1] $n > 2$ is required for the ABD shared-memory simulation algorithm and by the get-core algorithm.

[2] See Sect. 2.1 for a discussion of colorless tasks.

1. FLP $\equiv$ 1-resilient shared memory is a well-known result. We can simulate the FLP model in 1-resilient shared memory by implementing message-passing communication using shared-memory buffers that act as mailboxes. In the other direction, we can use the ABD [2] shared-memory simulation algorithm to simulate single-writer single-reader registers and then apply standard register transformation to obtain multi-reader multi-writer registers [3, Chapter 10]. A rigorous treatment of the equivalence between asynchronous message passing and shared memory appears in Lynch's book [15, Chapter 17].
2. FLP $\equiv$ fail-to-receive. fail-to-receive $\leq$ FLP follows from a simple synchronizer algorithm that is folklore in the field (each process has a current round and waits to receive messages sent in the current round from $n-2$ other processes before moving to the next round). In the other direction, we need to guarantee that the messages of all processes except one are eventually delivered; to do so, we simply require processes to keep resending all their messages forever and to do a little bookkeeping do avoid wrongly delivering a message twice.
3. fail-to-receive $\equiv$ fail-to-send. fail-to-receive $\leq$ fail-to-send is trivial[3]. In the other direction, we present in Sect. 3.1 a simulation based on the get-core algorithm of Gafni [3, Chapter 14]. Although the simulation relies entirely on this known algorithm, this is a new result.

1.2 The New Impossibility Proof

Having shown that all four models above are equivalent, we show the impossibility of deterministic consensus in the model in which it is the easiest: the synchronous model of Santoro and Widmayer.

Inspired by Volzer [21], we restrict our attention to fault-free runs and runs in which one process remains silent. This allows us to inductively construct an infinite execution in which, every round r, making a decision depends on one process p_r: if p_r remains silent, then the decision is b_r, but if no messages are dropped, then the decision is $\overline{b_r} \neq b_r$. Both the initial and inductive steps of the construction follow from a straightforward application of the one-dimensional case of Sperner's lemma.

The proof is also constructive in the sense of Constable [8]: it suggests a sequential procedure that, given a straw-man consensus algorithm, computes an infinite nondeciding execution.

2 The Models

We consider a set $\mathcal{P}$ of n deterministic processes. Each process has a local state consisting of a read-only input register, an internal state, and a write-once output register. A configuration of the system is a function that maps each process to its local state. Initially, each input register contains an input value taken from a

[3] This is an instance of the following first-order logic tautology: $\exists y.\forall x.P(x,y) \rightarrow \forall x.\exists y.P(x,y)$.

set of inputs that is specific to the task being solved (e.g. 0 or 1 for consensus), each process is in its initial internal state, and each process has an empty output register.

The four models differ in how execution proceeds from an initial state. Regardless of the model, when a process writes v to its output register, we say that it outputs v. Moreover, we assume that a process never communicates with itself (e.g. a process does not send a message to itself).

The FLP Model. In the FLP model, processes communicate by message passing, and each process takes atomic steps that consist in a) optionally receiving a message, b) updating its local state, and optionally, if it has not done so before, its output register, and c) sending any number of messages.

Processes are asynchronous, meaning that they take steps in an arbitrary order and there is no bound on the number of steps that a process can take while another takes no steps. However, the FLP model guarantees that every process takes infinitely many steps and that every message sent is eventually received, except that at most one process may at any point fail-stop, after which it permanently stops taking steps.

The 1-Resilient Shared-Memory Model. In the 1-resilient shared-memory model, processes are asynchronous and communicate by atomically reading or writing multi-writer multi-reader shared-memory registers, and at most one process may fail-stop.

The 1-Resilient Fail-to-Send Model. In the 1-resilient fail-to-send model, processes also communicate by message passing, but execution proceeds in an infinite sequence of synchronous, communication-closed rounds. Each round, every process first broadcasts a unique message. Once every process has broadcast its message, each process receives all messages broadcast in the current round, in a fixed order, except that an adversary picks a unique process p and a set of processes P which do not receive the message broadcast by p. Finally, at the end of the round, each process updates its internal state and optionally, if it has not done so before, its output register, both as a function of its current local state and of the set of messages received in the current round before entering the next round. No process ever fails.

We write $c \xrightarrow{p,P} c'$ to indicate that, starting from configuration c at the beginning of a round, the adversary chooses the process p and drops the messages that p sends to the members of the set of processes P, and the round ends in configuration c'. Note that in $c \xrightarrow{p,P} c'$, it is irrelevant whether $p \in P$, since a process does not send a message to itself. Also note that, because the order in which messages are received is fixed, c' is a function of c, p, and P.

With this notation, an execution is an infinite sequence of the form

$$c_1 \xrightarrow{p_1,P_1} c_2 \xrightarrow{p_2,P_2} c_3 \xrightarrow{p_3,P_3} \dots$$

where, in c_1, each process has input 0 or 1, is in the initial internal state, and has an empty output register, and for every i, $p_i \in \mathcal{P}$ and $P_i \subseteq \mathcal{P}$. An example appears in Fig. 1.

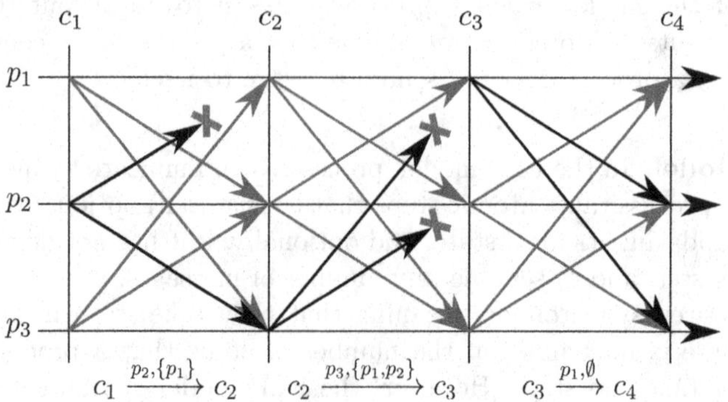

Fig. 1. An execution in the 1-resilient fail-to-send model. Each round, the messages of the process selected by the adversary are highlighted with a darker tone.

The 1-Resilient Fail-to-Receive Model. The 1-resilient fail-to-receive model is like the 1-resilient fail-to-send model, except that the specification of the adversary is different: each round, for every process p, the adversary may drop one of the messages addressed to p. So, contrary to the 1-resilient fail-to-send model, it is possible that different processes miss a message from a different process.

2.1 Simulations and Colorless Tasks

In Sect. 3, we show using simulation algorithms that the four models above all solve the same colorless tasks. We now informally define these notions.

Informally, a model A simulates a model B, noted $B \leq A$, when the communication primitives of model B, including the constraints placed on them, can be implemented using the communication primitives of model A. This corresponds to the notion of simulation defined by Attiya and Welch in their book [3, Chapter 7]. When models A and B both simulate each other, we write $A \equiv B$.

We define a colorless task as a relation Δ between the sets of inputs that the processes may receive and the set of outputs that they may produce. Note that we care only about sets of inputs or outputs, and not about which process received which input or produced which output. This is what makes a task colorless.

We say that an algorithm in a model solves a colorless tasks when, in every execution:

1. Every process that does not fail produces an output, and
2. If I is the set of inputs received by the processes and O is the set of outputs produced, then $(I, O) \in \Delta$.

For a more precise and rigorous treatment of tasks and colorless tasks, see Herlihy et al. [12, Chapter 4].

Note that, when solving a colorless task, a process can safely adopt the output of another process. This is important, e.g., to solve a colorless task T in the 1-resilient fail-to-receive model by simulating an algorithm that solves T in the FLP model: Because one process may not output in the FLP model (whereas all processes have to output in the 1-resilient fail-to-receive model), one process may need to adopt the output of another. For a colorless task, this is not a problem.

Informally, we have the following lemma:

Lemma 1. *For every two models A and B out of the four models of this section, if $B \leq A$ then A solves all the colorless tasks that B solves.*

We now define the consensus problem as a colorless task, independently of the model.

Definition 1. In the consensus problem, each process receives 0 or 1 as input and the outputs of the processes must satisfy the following properties:

Agreement No two processes output different values.

Validity If all processes receive the same input b, then no process outputs $b' \neq b$.

3 Model Equivalences

In this section, we show that the four models described in Sect. 2 all solve the same colorless tasks using simulations. We do not cover the two simulations between the 1-resilient shared-memory model and the FLP model, as this is done brilliantly by Lynch in her book [15, Chapter 17].

3.1 Fail-to-send ≡ fail-to-receive

fail-to-send ≤ fail-to-receive. The 1-resilient fail-to-send model is trivially a special case of the 1-resilient fail-to-receive model: one process p failing to send some of its messages is the same as some processes failing to receive from p. Thus, we have fail-to-send ≤ fail-to-receive.

fail-to-receive ≤ fail-to-send. In other direction, it is a-priori not obvious whether we can take a system in which each process may fail to receive from a different other process and simulate a system in which all processes may fail to receive from the same process. Surprisingly, if we have $n > 2$ processes, we can simulate the 1-resilient fail-to-send model in the 1-resilient fail-to-receive model.

We simulate each round of the 1-resilient fail-to-send model using an instance of the get-core algorithm of Gafni [3, Chapter 14], which takes 3 rounds of the 1-resilient fail-to-receive model which we call phases.

Each process p starts the first phase with a message that it wants to simulate the sending of and, at the end of the third round, it determines a set of messages to simulate the delivery of. To obtain a correct simulation, we must ensure that, each simulated round r, all processes receive all simulated messages sent in the round except for some messages of a unique process.

To simulate one round of the 1-resilient fail-to-send model, each process p does the following.

- In phase 1, p broadcasts its simulated message; then p waits until it receives $n-2$ messages before entering phase 2.
- In phase 2, p broadcasts a message containing the set of simulated messages it received in the first phase and then waits until it receives $n-2$ sets of simulated messages before entering phase 3.
- In phase 3, p broadcasts a message containing the union of all the sets of simulated messages it received in phase 2 and waits until it receives $n-2$ sets of simulated messages. Finally, p simulates receiving the union of all the sets of simulated messages it received in phase 3.

Lemma 2. *When $n > 2$, each simulated round, there is a set S of $n-1$ processes such that every process simulates receiving the messages of all members of S.*

Proof. Consider a simulated round. First, we show that there is a process p_l such that at least $n-2$ processes (different from p_l) hear from p_l in phase 2. Suppose towards a contradiction that, for every process p, there are no more than $n-3$ processes that hear from p in phase 2. Then, the total number of messages received in phase 2 is at most $n(n-3)$. However, in the 1-resilient fail-to-receive model, each process receives at least $n-2$ messages (since every process fails to receive at most one message), so at least $n(n-2)$ messages are received by the end of phase 2. Since $n(n-2) > n(n-3)$ for $n > 2$, this is a contradiction.

Next, consider the set S of at least $n-2$ processes different from p_l that p_l hears from in phase 1. Since p_l broadcasts the set of simulated messages received from S, by the above we see that at least $n-1$ processes (the members of S and p_l) have received all the simulated messages of the members of S by the end of phase 2. Thus, since $n-1 \geq 2$ and the adversary can only prevent each process from receiving one message, all processes receive the simulated messages of the members of S in phase 3. □

By Lemma 2, in each simulated round, all processes receive all messages sent in the round except for some messages of a unique process. Thus, the simulation algorithm faithfully simulates the 1-resilient fail-to-send model.

3.2 FLP ≡ fail-to-receive

fail-to-receive ≤ FLP. We simulate the 1-resilient fail-to-receive model in the FLP model using a simple synchronizer algorithm. Each process maintains a current round, initialized to 1, a simulated state, initially its initial state in the simulated model, and a buffer of messages, initially empty.

Each process p obeys the following rules.

- When p is in round r and it receives a round-r' message, p discards the message if $r' < r$ and otherwise buffers the message.
- When process p enters a round r, it broadcasts its round-r simulated message to all.
- When p is in round r and has $n-2$ round-r simulated messages in its buffer, it simulates receiving all those message and then increments its round number.

It is easy to see that this algorithm faithfully simulates $n-1$ processes executing in the 1-resilient fail-to-receive model (but not all n processes). One process may not be faithfully simulated if it fails because, by definition, no process fails in the 1-resilient fail-to-receive model. However, this does not matter because, in the FLP model, a failed processed does not have to output.

FLP $\leq$ fail-to-receive. The only difficulty in simulating the FLP model in the 1-resilient fail-to-receive model is that we have to ensure that every message sent in the simulated algorithm is eventually delivered, except for at most one process, despite the fact that messages can be lost in the 1-resilient fail-to-receive model.

To overcome this problem, it suffices that each process re-sends all its simulated messages forever. To ensure that messages that are sent multiple times in the simulated algorithm can be told apart from messages that are simply re-sent by the simulation algorithm, each process simply uses a strictly monotonic counter whose value is attached to simulated messages.

4 Impossibility of Consensus in the Fail-To-Send Model

In this section, we show that consensus is impossible in the 1-resilient fail-to-send model. To keep the proof constructive, we consider the pseudo-consensus problem, which is solvable, and we show that every pseudo-consensus algorithm has an infinite execution in which no process outputs. Since solving consensus implies solving pseudo-consensus, this shows that consensus is impossible.

The proof hinges on the notion of p-silent execution, which is just an execution in which the adversary drops every message of p.

Definition 2 (p-silent and 1-silent execution). We say that an execution e is p-silent, for a process p, when e is of the form $c_1 \xrightarrow{p,\mathcal{P}} c_2 \xrightarrow{p,\mathcal{P}} c_3 \xrightarrow{p,\mathcal{P}} \ldots$. We say that an execution is 1-silent when it is p-silent for some p.

Definition 3 (Pseudo-consensus). The pseudo-consensus problem relaxes the termination condition of the consensus problem by requiring outputs only in failure-free executions and 1-silent executions.

Note that pseudo-consensus is solvable, e.g. using a variant of the phase-king algorithm [4]. We now consider a pseudo-consensus algorithm.

Throughout the section, we say that a process decides b in an execution when it outputs b, and, when a process decides b in an execution, we also say that the execution decides b.

Definition 4 (p-dependent configuration). A configuration c is p-dependent when the decision in the failure-free execution from c is different from the decision in the p-silent execution from c.

Lemma 3. *If c is a p-dependent configuration, then no process has decided in c.*

Proof. Suppose by contradiction that a process has decided on a value v in c. Since c is p-dependent, there are two executions, starting from c, that decide differently. Thus, one of these executions decides a value $v' \neq v$. This contradicts the agreement property of pseudo-consensus. □

Definition 5 (Sequence of adjacent configurations). We say that a sequence of configurations $c_0, \ldots, c_m$ is a sequence of adjacent configurations when, for each $i \in 1..m$, the configurations c_{i-1} and c_i differ only in the local state of a single process noted p_i.

We are now ready to state and prove our main lemma:

Lemma 4. *Consider a sequence of adjacent configurations $c_0, \ldots, c_m$. Suppose that the failure-free decision from c_0 is different from the failure-free decision from c_m. Then there exists $k \in 0..m$ and a process p such that c_k is p-dependent.*

Proof. Suppose, without loss of generality, that the failure-free decision from c_0 is 0 while the failure-free decision from c_m is 1. Then, there must be $j \in 1..m$ such that the failure-free decision from c_{j-1} is 0 and the failure-free decision from c_j is 1 (this is the one-dimensional Sperner lemma).

We now have two cases. First, suppose that the p_j-silent decision from c_j is 0. Then, because the failure-free decision from c_j is 1, we conclude that c_j is p-dependent.

Second, suppose that the p_j-silent decision from c_j is 1. Note that, because c_{j-1} and c_j only differ in the local state of p_j, if p_j remains silent, then the decision is the same regardless of whether we start from c_{j-1} or c_j. Thus, the p_j-silent decision from c_{j-1} is also 1. We conclude that c_{j-1} is p_j-dependent. □

We now prove by induction that we can build an infinite execution consisting entirely of p-dependent configurations.

Lemma 5. *There exists a p-dependent initial configuration for some process p.*

Proof. Order the processes in an arbitrary sequence $p_1, \ldots, p_n$. Consider the sequence of initial configurations $c_0, \ldots, c_n$ where, for each configuration c_i and each process p_j, p_j has input 0 if and only if $j \geq i$. Note that the sequence

$c_0, \ldots, c_n$ is a sequence of adjacent configurations: for each $i \in 1..n$, configurations c_{i-1} and c_i differ only in the input of the process i. Moreover, by the validity property of consensus, the failure-free decision from c_0 is 0 and the failure-free decision from c_1 is 1. Thus, by Lemma 4, there exists a process p and $k \in 0..n$ such that c_k is p-dependent. □

Lemma 6. *Suppose that the configuration c is p-dependent. Then there exists a process q, a set of processes P, and a configuration c' such that $c \xrightarrow{p,P} c'$ and c' is q-dependent.*

Proof. Without loss of generality, assume that the p-silent decision from c is 0. Consider the configuration c' such that $c \xrightarrow{p,\mathcal{P}} c'$ (i.e. no process receives p's message in the transition from c to c'). There are two cases. First, suppose that the failure-free decision from c' is 1. Note that the p-silent decision from c' must be 0 because c' is the next configuration after c is the p-silent execution from c. Thus, c' is by definition p-dependent, and we are done with this case.

Second, suppose that the failure-free decision from c' is 0. Now order the processes in $\mathcal{P} \setminus \{p\}$ in a sequence $p_1, \ldots, p_{n-1}$. Consider the sequence of configurations $c_1, \ldots, c_n$ such that $c \xrightarrow{p,\mathcal{P}} c_1$ (so $c_1 = c'$), $c \xrightarrow{p,\mathcal{P}\setminus\{p_1\}} c_2$, $c \xrightarrow{p,\mathcal{P}\setminus\{p_1,p_2\}} c_3$, etc. until $c \xrightarrow{p,\emptyset} c_n$. In other words, no process receives the message from p in the transition from c to c_1; only p_1 receives p's message in the transition from c to c_2; only p_1 and p_2 receive p's message in the transition from c to c_3; etc. and all processes receive p's message in the transition from c to c_n. Figure 2 illustrates the situation when there are 3 processors.

Note that, for each $i \in 1..n-1$, configurations c_i and c_{i+1} only differ in p_i not having or having received p's message; thus, the sequence $c_1, \ldots, c_n$ is a sequence of adjacent configurations. Moreover, because $c_1 = c'$, the failure-free decision from c_1 is 0. Additionally, because c is p-dependent and the p-silent decision from c is 0, the failure-free decision from c_n is 1. Thus, we can apply Lemma 4, and we conclude that there exists a process q and $i \in 1..n$ such that c_i is q-dependent. □

Theorem 1. *Every pseudo-consensus algorithm has an infinite non-deciding execution.*

Proof. Using Lemmas 5 and 6, we inductively construct an infinite execution in which each configuration is p-dependent for some process p. By Lemma 3, every p-dependent configuration is undecided, and thus no process ever decides. □

Note that Lemma 6 would fail, and thus the whole proof would fail if, each round, the adversary were constrained to not remove all the messages of the selected process. This is because we would not be able to construct a sequence of adjacent configurations long enough to go from c_1 to c_n (we would be missing one configuration to reach c_n from c_1). In fact, as Santoro and Widmayer remark [18], if the adversary can only remove $n-2$ messages, a protocol proposed in earlier work of theirs solves consensus [19].

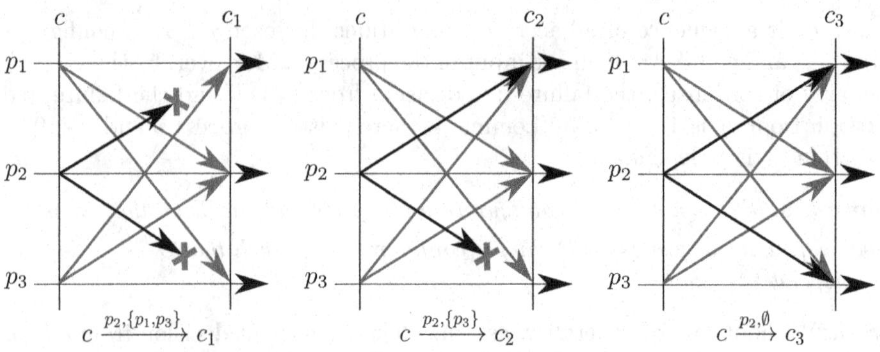

Fig. 2. Situation in the second case of the proof of Lemma 6, where $\mathcal{P} = \{p_1, p_2, p_3\}$ (so $n = 3$) and c is p_2-dependent. There must exist $q \in \mathcal{P}$ such that one of the configurations c_1, c_2, or c_3 is q-dependent.

5 Related Work

In 1983, Fischer, Lynch, and Paterson [9,10] first proved the impossibility of solving consensus deterministically in an asynchronous system in which one process may fail-stop. Following the FLP result, a number of other works proved similar impossibility results (for deterministic processes) in other models or improved some aspects of the FLP proof.

In 1987, Loui and Abu-Amara [14] showed that consensus is impossible in shared memory when one process may stop (also proved independently by Herlihy in 1991 [11]).

Santoro and Widmayer followed suit in 1989 with the paper "Time is not a healer" [18], showing, among other results, that, with message-passing communication, even synchrony does not help if, each round, one process may fail to send some of its messages [18, Theorem 4.1]. The proof of Santoro and Widmayer follows a valency-based argument inspired by the FLP proof. As we show in Sect. 3, this result is equivalent to the FLP result and could have been obtained by reduction.

In a pedagogical note, Raynal and Roy [16] observe that an asynchronous system with f crash failures and restricted to communication-closed rounds in which each process waits for $n - f$ processes before moving to the next round is equivalent, for task solvability, to the model of Santoro and Widmayer when, each round, each process fails to receive from f processes.

Inspired by Chandy and Misra [7], Taubenfeld [20] presents a proof of the FLP impossibility in an axiomatic model of sequences of events that avoids giving operational meaning to the events. This results in a more general and shorter proof.

In their textbook, Attiya and Welch [3] prove the FLP result by reduction to shared memory. They first prove that consensus is impossible for two processes and then use a variant of the BG simulation [6] to generalize to any number of processes. Lynch [15] also takes the shared memory route but proves the shared-memory impossibility using a bi-valency argument.

Volzer's proof pearl [21] gives an elegant, direct proof of the FLP impossibility in the asynchronous message-passing model. The main insight is to compare fault-free runs with runs in which one process does not participate. Reading Volzer's paper (in admiration) is the inspiration for the present paper. Bisping et al. [5] present a mechanically-checked formalization of Volzer's proof in Isabelle/HOL.

The latest development on the FLP proof, before the present work, is due to Constable [8]. Constable presents an impossibility proof in the FLP model that closely follows the FLP proof but that is constructive, meaning that we can extract from this proof an algorithm that, given an effectively non-blocking consensus procedure (in Constable's terminology), computes an infinite non-deciding execution. The proof of the present paper is also constructive in the same sense.

Finally, the idea of Santoro and Widmayer [18] to consider computability questions in a synchronous setting with message-omission faults inspired the development of the general message-adversary model of Afek and Gafni [1]; they present a message adversary equivalent to wait-free shared memory and use it to obtain a simple proof of the asynchronous computability theorem [6,13,17].

References

1. Afek, A., Gafni, E.: A simple characterization of asynchronous computations. Theor. Comput. Sci. **561**Part B, 88–95 (2015). ISSN 0304-3975. https://doi.org/10.1016/j.tcs.2014.07.022. http://www.sciencedirect.com/science/article/pii/S0304397514005659
2. Attiya, H., Bar-Noy, A., Dolev, D.: Sharing memory robustly in message-passing systems. J. ACM (JACM) **42**(1), 124–142 (1995). ISSN 0004-5411. https://doi.org/10.1145/200836.200869
3. Attiya, H., Welch, J.: Distributed Computing: Fundamentals, Simulations, and Advanced Topics, vol. 19. Wiley, Hoboken (2004)
4. Berman, P., Garay, J.A., Perry, K.J.: Towards optimal distributed consensus. In: FOCS, vol. 89, pp. 410–415 (1989)
5. Bisping, B., et al.: Mechanical verification of a constructive proof for FLP. In: Blanchette, J.C., Merz, S. (eds.) ITP 2016. LNCS, vol. 9807, pp. 107–122. Springer, Cham (2016). https://doi.org/10.1007/978-3-319-43144-4_7
6. Borowsky, E., Gafni, E.: Generalized FLP impossibility result for t-resilient asynchronous computations. In Proceedings of the Twenty-Fifth Annual ACM Symposium on Theory of Computing, STOC 1993, pp. 91–100 (1993). ACM. ISBN 978-0-89791-591-5. https://doi.org/10.1145/167088.167119
7. Chandy, M., Misra, J.: On the nonexistence of robust commit protocols (1985)
8. Constable, R.: Effectively nonblocking consensus procedures can execute forever-a constructive version of FLP (2011)
9. Fischer, M.J., Lynch, N.A., Paterson, M.S.: Impossibility of distributed consensus with one faulty process. **32**(2), 374–382 (1985). ISSN 0004-5411. https://doi.org/10.1145/3149.214121

10. Fischer, M.J., Lynch, N.A., Paterson, M.S.: Impossibility of distributed consensus with one faulty process. In: Proceedings of the 2nd ACM SIGACT-SIGMOD Symposium on Principles of Database Systems, PODS 1983, pp. 1–7 (1985). Association for Computing Machinery, ISBN 978-0-89791-097-2. https://doi.org/10.1145/588058.588060
11. Herlihy, M.: Wait-free synchronization. ACM Trans. Program. Lang. Syst. **13**(1), 124–149 (1991). ISSN 0164–0925. https://doi.org/10.1145/114005.102808
12. Herlihy, M., Kozlov, D., Rajsbaum, S.: Distributed Computing Through Combinatorial Topology. Morgan Kaufmann, Burlington (2013). ISBN 978-0-12-404578-1
13. Herlihy, M., Shavit, N.: The topological structure of asynchronous computability. J. ACM (JACM) **46**(6), 858–923 (1999)
14. Loui, M.C., Abu-Amara, H.H.: Memory requirements for agreement among unreliable asynchronous processes. Adv. Comput. Res. **4**(163), 31 (1987)
15. Lynch, N.A.: Distributed Algorithms. Morgan Kaufmann, Burlington (1996)
16. Raynal, M., Roy, M.: A note on a simple equivalence between round-based synchronous and asynchronous models. In: 11th Pacific Rim International Symposium on Dependable Computing (PRDC 2005), p. 4 (2005). https://doi.org/10.1109/PRDC.2005.10
17. Saks, M., Zaharoglou, F.: Wait-free k-set agreement is impossible: the topology of public knowledge. **29**(5):1449–1483 (2000). ISSN 0097–5397. https://doi.org/10.1137/S0097539796307698. https://epubs.siam.org/doi/abs/10.1137/S0097539796307698
18. Santoro, N., Widmayer, P.: Time is not a healer. In: Monien, B., Cori, R. (eds.) STACS 1989. LNCS, vol. 349, pp. 304–313. Springer, Heidelberg (1989). https://doi.org/10.1007/BFb0028994
19. Santoro, N., Widmayer, P.: Distributed function evaluation in the presence of transmission faults. In: Asano, T., Ibaraki, T., Imai, H., Nishizeki, T. (eds.) SIGAL 1990. LNCS, vol. 450, pp. 358–367. Springer, Heidelberg (1990). https://doi.org/10.1007/3-540-52921-7_85
20. Taubenfeld, G.: On the nonexistence of resilient consensus protocols. Inf. Process. Lett. **37**(5), 285–289 (1991)
21. Völzer, H.: A constructive proof for FLP. **92**(2), 83–87. http://www.sciencedirect.com/science/article/pii/S0020019004001887

Adding Pull to Push Sum for Approximate Data Aggregation

Saptadi Nugroho(✉), Alexander Weinmann, and Christian Schindelhauer

Albert-Ludwigs-Universität Freiburg, 79110 Freiburg im Breisgau, Germany
snugroho@informatik.uni-freiburg.de

Abstract. Kempe, Dobra, and Gehrke (2003) proposed the simple Push Sum protocol for averaging the value of nodes in a network: In every round, each node chooses a random neighbor node uniformly at random and sends half of its sum and weight to the chosen node. The Push Sum has the mass conservation property. It converges to the correct answer exponentially, which can be seen from the potential function that drops at least half in every round in expectation.

We evaluate the Push-Pull Sum protocol to distribute the data and calculate the mean value of all nodes. The Push-Pull Sum protocol complements the Push Sum protocol with the Pull Sum protocol. In the Pull Sum protocol, every caller node sends the pull request to the chosen node uniformly at random and itself. The node which gets the pull request will send its sum and weight divided by the number of pull requests to the caller nodes and itself.

In the Push-Pull Sum protocol, every node sends half its sum and half its weight to itself and its neighbor, chosen uniformly at random in each round. The callee node that receives the message from its neighbors will reply to the caller nodes and itself with half of its sum and weight divided by the number of nodes that send the message to the callee node. The Push-Pull Sum protocol and the Pull Sum protocol have mass conservation properties. We observed that the potential function decreases faster using the Push-Pull Sum protocol instead of the Push Sum protocol.

Keywords: Distributed algorithm · Communication protocol · Random call model · Approximation · Data aggregation

1 Introduction

The randomized rumor spreading in large-scale peer-to-peer sensor networks has been studied in past decades. Sensor nodes connected to a communication graph G_t can exchange data to compute the aggregation function for solving problems cooperatively [1]. The aggregation functions could be classified into algebraic (*average, variance*), distributive (*count, sum, max, min*), and holistic (*median*) [2]. The aggregation algorithm is categorized into structured, unstructured, and hybrid from the communication perspective [5,17]. In structured

S. Dolev and B. Schieber (Eds.): SSS 2023, LNCS 14310, pp. 75–89, 2023.
https://doi.org/10.1007/978-3-031-44274-2_7

communications, such as tree-based communication structures, the operation of aggregation algorithms will be affected by the network topology and routing scheme. In unstructured communication, such as rumor-based communication, aggregation algorithms can run independently from the structured network topology. The hybrid combines the use of structured and unstructured communications.

In randomized rumor spreading, every node chooses its neighbor randomly in each round for exchanging information [3,4]. Information that flows from one node to another can be differentiated between pull and push transmissions. The rumor is pushed when the caller node sends the rumor to the called node, while the rumor is pulled if the caller node receives the rumor from the called node [4,15]. Kempe et al. [4] developed the Push Sum protocol for averaging the value of nodes in a network. The Push Sum protocol converges to the correct aggregate of the ground truth because it has the mass conservation property. The Push-Pull strategy is a combination of the Push strategy and the Pull strategy [14]. The Push-Pull strategy disseminates the rumor faster than the Push strategy and the Pull Strategy [11].

Contribution. In this paper, we propose a data aggregation protocol that estimates the mean value using the Push-Pull Sum communication protocol. In the Push-Pull Sum protocol, every node sends the pair $\left(\frac{s_t}{2}, \frac{w_t}{2}\right)$ to the chosen node and itself. After the node receives $|R|$ requests from its neighbor, it sends the pair $\left(\frac{\frac{s_t}{2}}{|R|}, \frac{\frac{w_t}{2}}{|R|}\right)$ to itself and to the nodes that sent the request. The data sent to the node will be used as inputs for calculating an aggregation function. The Push-Pull Sum protocol converges to the correct aggregate of the ground truth. Regarding the time complexity, the Push-Pull Sum protocol has a lower Mean Squared Error (MSE) than the Push Sum protocol. Information sent in both directions between communication nodes using Push-Pull Sum protocol can significantly reduce the number of rounds.

2 Related Work

In the rumor-based communication model, the called node is selected uniformly and independently at random by the caller node. A push call occurs when the called node is randomly chosen to receive a data value x from the caller node. On the other hand, a pull call occurs when the called node sends a data value x to the caller node after receiving a request from the caller node [3,18].

The Push-Sum protocol is rumor-based communication. In each round, the caller node divides the weight in half $\frac{w_t}{2}$ and the sum in half $\frac{s_t}{2}$. Then the caller node chooses a called node at random to send the pair $(\frac{s_t}{2}, \frac{w_t}{2})$ to the called node and itself for estimating the average $f_{avg} = \frac{s_t}{w_t}$ [4].

The mass conservation that is not maintained in the communication protocols will cause the values to converge to the same value but not to the correct aggregate of the ground truth [4,16]. We assume no mass loss during the communication process. The Push-Sum protocol and the Pull-Sum protocol maintain the mass conservation property at all rounds.

In the Pull-Sum algorithm [12], the called node counts the number of requests $|R|$ received from the caller nodes in each round. Each weight w_t and the sum s_t are divided by the number of requests $|R|$ received. Then, the called node sends the pair $(\frac{s_t}{|R|}, \frac{w_t}{|R|})$ to the caller nodes and itself to estimate the average $f_{avg} = \frac{s_t}{w_t}$ [1].

In the restricted model of pull protocol, each called node responds to only one pull request chosen from many pull requests of the caller nodes and sends the data value x to the selected node in each round [6].

Frieze and Grimmet [10,13] proved that the number of rounds required to disseminate the rumor to n nodes is $\sigma_r = \log_2 n + \log_e n + o(\log n)$. Boris Pittel [10] showed a stronger result and proved that $\sigma_r = \log_2 n + \log_e n + O(1)$ is the number of rounds until all nodes have received the rumor.

3 Model

We consider n nodes connected by a static fully connected graph $G_t = (V, E_t \subseteq V \times V)$. In each round, every node sends messages to a random neighbor chosen independently with uniform probability. The nodes initially know the ground truth of the network size. Time is partitioned into synchronized rounds, where in each round, every node exchanges sum s and weight w to approximate the aggregation function f.

4 Algorithms

The Push-Pull Sum protocol inspired by the Push Sum protocol [4] and the Pull Sum protocol [1] converges to the true mean because it has a *mass conservation* property. Each node has a weight $w_{i,t}$ and a sum $s_{i,t}$. Initially, the weight $w_{i,0}$ is equal to 1 and the sum $s_{i,0}$ is equal to data input value $x_i \in \mathbb{R}_0^+$. The sum of all weights $\sum_i w_{i,t}$ at any round t is always equal to n [4], which is the number of nodes in the network.

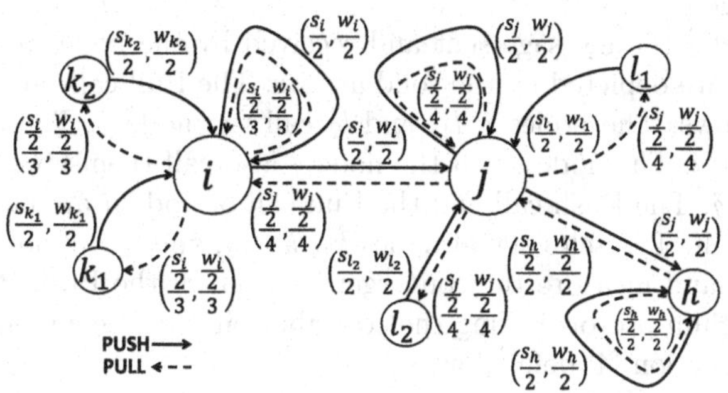

Fig. 1. Depiction of Push-Pull Sum Protocol.

Algorithm 1. Push-Pull Sum Protocol

procedure REQUESTDATA
  Choose a random neighbor node v
  Send $\left(\frac{s_{u,t}}{2}, \frac{w_{u,t}}{2}\right)$ to the chosen node v and the node u itself
end procedure
procedure RESPONSEDATA
  $R_{u,t} \leftarrow$ Set of the nodes calling u at a round t
  for all $i \in R_{u,t}$ **do**
    Reply to i with $\left(\frac{\frac{s_{u,t}}{2}}{|R_{u,t}|}, \frac{\frac{w_{u,t}}{2}}{|R_{u,t}|}\right)$
  end for
end procedure
procedure AGGREGATE
  $M_{u,t} \leftarrow \{(s_m, w_m)\}$ messages sent to u at a round $t-1$
  $s_{u,t} \leftarrow \sum_{m \in M_{u,t}} s_m$, $w_{u,t} \leftarrow \sum_{m \in M_{u,t}} w_m$
  $f_{avg} \leftarrow \frac{s_{u,t}}{w_{u,t}}$
end procedure

In every round of the communication process using the Push-Pull Sum protocol, each node will exchange information with other nodes in the network. Every node calls the AGGREGATE procedure at the beginning of every round t except the first round. Every node knows all messages sent to itself $M_{u,t} \leftarrow \{(s_m, w_m)\}$ at round $t-1$. The nodes calculate the sum $s_t \leftarrow \sum_{m \in M_{u,t}} s_m$ and the weight $w_t \leftarrow \sum_{m \in M_{u,t}} w_m$ for computing the approximate value of the mean $f_{avg} = \frac{s_t}{w_t}$.

After executing the AGGREGATE procedure, each node runs the REQUESTDATA procedure. The caller node u selects a neighbor node v randomly. No caller node chooses itself. The caller node u sends a pair $\left(\frac{s_{u,t}}{2}, \frac{w_{u,t}}{2}\right)$ to a chosen neighbor node v and the node u itself.

At the end of every round t, every node calls the RESPONSEDATA procedure. Each node counts the number of incoming calls $|R_{u,t}|$ from nodes which request information. The node u replies with $\left(\frac{\frac{s_{u,t}}{2}}{|R_{u,t}|}, \frac{\frac{w_{u,t}}{2}}{|R_{u,t}|}\right)$ to all caller nodes that have sent the message.

Figure 1 shows the message sent and received by the nodes in the network. The Push calls are depicted by the solid arrows. The Pull calls are described by the dashed arrows. The nodes i, l_1, and l_2 call the node j. The nodes k_1 and k_2 call the node i. The node i and the node j also call themselves. The node h called by node j. The Push call and the Pull call of node h are not shown. The node h calls itself. The self calls of nodes k_1, k_2, l_1, and l_2 are not shown.

We analyze and measure the convergence speed of the Push-Pull Sum protocol and Pull Sum protocol using the contribution vector component $v_{i,j,t}$ and the potential function [4] defined as:

$$\Phi_t = \sum_{i,j} \left(v_{i,j,t} - \frac{w_{i,t}}{n}\right)^2 \tag{1}$$

The potential function that drops to a lower value than the previous value implies good convergence and smaller errors. The proof of convergence using the potential function Φ_t in the Pull-Sum algorithm and the Push-Pull-Sum algorithm follows a similar structure as in the Push-Sum protocol [4].

The $v_{i,j,t}$ component of the contribution vector stores the fractional value of node j's contribution at a round t. The length of the contribution vector is equal to the size of the network n. Initially, the value of the $v_{i,j,0}$ component is equal to 1 for $i = j$ and 0 for all $i \neq j$ [4]. The sum of all node j's contributions at all nodes i $\sum_i v_{i,j,t}$ is equal to 1 at any round t [4].

Theorem 1. *Under the Push-Pull Sum protocol, the expected potential Φ_t decreases exponentially. The conditional expectation of Φ_{t+1} for the Push-Pull Sum protocol is $\mathbb{E}\left[\Phi_{t+1}|\Phi_t = \phi\right] = \left(\frac{2e-1}{4e} - \frac{1}{4n}\right)\phi$.*

Proof. Consider the values of contribution vector component and the weights received by the node i at time t. The node k chooses the node $f(k) = i$ as the target call for sending a message. The node i also sends half of its contribution vector component value and weight to a chosen neighbor l and itself. Let m_i and m_l denote the number of nodes choosing node i and node l, respectively. The node i receives the replied message from the node l. The contribution vector component and the weight of the node i at round $t+1$ are

$$v_{i,t+1} = \frac{\frac{1}{2}v_{i,j,t}}{m_i} + \frac{\frac{1}{2}v_{l,j,t}}{m_l} + \sum_{k:f(k)=i} \frac{1}{2}v_{k,j,t} \tag{2}$$

$$w_{i,t+1} = \frac{\frac{1}{2}w_{i,t}}{m_i} + \frac{\frac{1}{2}w_{l,t}}{m_l} + \sum_{k:f(k)=i} \frac{1}{2}w_{k,t} \tag{3}$$

The potential function of the next round Φ_{t+1} is defined as

$$\Phi_{t+1} = \sum_{i,j}\left(\frac{v_{i,j} - \frac{w_i}{n}}{2m_i} + \frac{v_{l,j} - \frac{w_l}{n}}{2m_l} + \sum_{k:f(k)=i}\frac{v_{k,j} - \frac{w_k}{n}}{2}\right)^2 \tag{4}$$

$$\begin{aligned}\Phi_{t+1} = &\sum_{i,j}\left(\frac{v_{i,j} - \frac{w_i}{n}}{2m_i}\right)^2 + \sum_{i,j}\left(\frac{v_{l,j} - \frac{w_l}{n}}{2m_l}\right)^2 + \sum_{i,j}\left(\frac{1}{2}\sum_{k:f(k)=i}\left(v_{k,j} - \frac{w_k}{n}\right)\right)^2\\ &+\sum_{i,j}\left(\frac{1}{2m_im_l}\left(v_{i,j} - \frac{w_i}{n}\right)\left(v_{l,j} - \frac{w_l}{n}\right)\right)\\ &+\sum_{i,j}\left(\frac{1}{2m_i}\left(v_{i,j} - \frac{w_i}{n}\right)\sum_{k:f(k)=i}\left(v_{k,j} - \frac{w_k}{n}\right)\right)\\ &+\sum_{i,j}\left(\frac{1}{2m_l}\left(v_{l,j} - \frac{w_l}{n}\right)\sum_{k:f(k)=i}\left(v_{k,j} - \frac{w_k}{n}\right)\right)\end{aligned} \tag{5}$$

In accordance with the mass conservation property, the sum of all node j's contribution at all nodes i $\sum_i v_{i,j,t}$ is equal to 1. The sum of all weights $\sum_i w_{i,t}$ is always equal to n at any round t [4], so the term $\sum_i \left(v_{i,j,t} - \frac{w_{i,t}}{n}\right)$ is equal to zero. We apply mass conservation to the potential function and resolve the term $\sum_{i,j} \left(\frac{1}{2}\sum_{k:f(k)=i}\left(v_{k,j} - \frac{w_k}{n}\right)\right)^2$, then we get:

$$\begin{aligned} \Phi_{t+1} = &\sum_{i,j} \frac{1}{4m_i^2}\left(v_{i,j} - \frac{w_i}{n}\right)^2 + \sum_{i,j,l} \frac{1}{4m_l^2}\left(v_{l,j} - \frac{w_l}{n}\right)^2 \\ &+ \frac{1}{4}\sum_{i,j}\sum_{k:f(k)=i}\left(v_{k,j} - \frac{w_k}{n}\right)^2 \\ &+ \frac{1}{4}\sum_{i,j}\sum_{\substack{k\neq k': \\ f(k)=f(k')=i}}\left(v_{k,j} - \frac{w_k}{n}\right)\left(v_{k',j} - \frac{w_{k'}}{n}\right) \end{aligned} \tag{6}$$

We let Φ_{t+1} consists of the terms $\Phi_{a,t+1}$, $\Phi_{b,t+1}$, $\Phi_{c,t+1}$, and $\Phi_{d,t+1}$ which will be analysed separately. The terms can now be written as follows:

$$\Phi_{a,t+1} = \sum_{i,j} \frac{1}{4m_i^2}\left(v_{i,j} - \frac{w_i}{n}\right)^2 \tag{7}$$

$$\Phi_{b,t+1} = \sum_{i,j,l} \frac{1}{4m_l^2}\left(v_{l,j} - \frac{w_l}{n}\right)^2 \tag{8}$$

$$\Phi_{c,t+1} = \frac{1}{4}\sum_{i,j}\sum_{k:f(k)=i}\left(v_{k,j} - \frac{w_k}{n}\right)^2 \tag{9}$$

$$\Phi_{d,t+1} = \frac{1}{4}\sum_{i,j}\sum_{k\neq k':f(k)=f(k')=i}\left(v_{k,j} - \frac{w_k}{n}\right)\left(v_{k',j} - \frac{w_{k'}}{n}\right) \tag{10}$$

The expectation of $\Phi_{a,t+1}$ is represented as

$$\begin{aligned} \mathbb{E}\left[\Phi_{a,t+1}|\Phi_t = \phi\right] = &\sum_{i,j}\left(v_{i,j} - \frac{w_i}{n}\right)^2 \\ &\frac{1}{4}\sum_{x=0}^{\infty}\frac{1}{(x+1)^2}\mathbb{P}\left[X = x\right]\mathbb{P}\left[f(i) = i\right] \end{aligned} \tag{11}$$

For a large n, we can use the Poisson distribution with $\lambda = 1$.

$$\mathbb{E}\left[\Phi_{a,t+1}|\Phi_t = \phi\right] = \phi\frac{1}{4}\sum_{x=0}^{\infty}\frac{e^{-1}}{(x+1)(x+1)!} \tag{12}$$

Abramowitz and Stegun [8] wrote the series expansions of exponential integral with $z > 0$ as follows:

$$Ei\left(z\right) = \gamma + ln(z) + \sum_{x=1}^{\infty}\frac{z^x}{xx!} \tag{13}$$

γ is Euler's constant [8]. Applying the series expansions of exponential integral for the expectation of $\Phi_{a,t+1}$ and $z = 1$ one gets:

$$\mathbb{E}\left[\Phi_{a,t+1}|\Phi_t = \phi\right] = \phi\frac{e^{-1}}{4}(Ei(1) - \gamma) \tag{14}$$

The expectation of $\Phi_{b,t+1}$ is defined as

$$\mathbb{E}\left[\Phi_{b,t+1}|\Phi_t = \phi\right] = \sum_{i,j,l}\left(v_{l,j} - \frac{w_l}{n}\right)^2 \frac{1}{4}\sum_{x=0}^{\infty}\frac{1}{(x+2)^2}\mathbb{P}\left[X = x\right]\mathbb{P}\left[f(l) = i\right] \tag{15}$$

For a large n, we can use the Poisson distribution with $\lambda = 1$.

$$\mathbb{E}\left[\Phi_{b,t+1}|\Phi_t = \phi\right] = \phi\frac{1}{4}\sum_{x=0}^{\infty}\frac{e^{-1}}{(x+2)(x+2)x!} \tag{16}$$

Applying the series expansions of exponential integral for the expectation of $\Phi_{b,t+1}$ one gets:

$$\mathbb{E}\left[\Phi_{b,t+1}|\Phi_t = \phi\right] = \phi\frac{e^{-1}}{4}\left(-Ei(1) - 1 + e + \gamma\right) \tag{17}$$

The expectation of $\Phi_{c,t+1}$ is further defined as

$$\mathbb{E}\left[\Phi_{c,t+1}|\Phi = \phi\right] = \frac{1}{4}\phi \tag{18}$$

The expectation of $\Phi_{d,t+1}$ is therefore

$$\mathbb{E}\left[\Phi_{d,t+1}|\Phi_t = \phi\right] = \frac{1}{4}\left(\sum_{i,j,k}\left(v_{i,j} - \frac{w_i}{n}\right)\left(v_{k,j} - \frac{w_k}{n}\right) - \sum_{j,k}\left(v_{k,j} - \frac{w_k}{n}\right)^2\right)\mathbb{P}\left[f(k) = f(k')\right] \tag{19}$$

$$\mathbb{E}\left[\Phi_{d,t+1}|\Phi_t = \phi\right] = -\frac{1}{4n}\sum_{j,k}\left(v_{k,j} - \frac{w_k}{n}\right)^2 \tag{20}$$

$$\mathbb{E}\left[\Phi_{d,t+1}|\Phi_t = \phi\right] = -\frac{1}{4n}\phi \tag{21}$$

The expectation of the potential function of the next round Φ_{t+1} is defined as

$$\mathbb{E}\left[\Phi_{t+1}|\Phi=\phi\right]=\mathbb{E}\left[\Phi(a)_{t+1}|\Phi_t=\phi\right]+\mathbb{E}\left[\Phi(b)_{t+1}|\Phi_t=\phi\right] \\ +\mathbb{E}\left[\Phi(c)_{t+1}|\Phi_t=\phi\right]+\mathbb{E}\left[\Phi(d)_{t+1}|\Phi_t=\phi\right] \tag{22}$$

$$\mathbb{E}\left[\Phi_{t+1}|\Phi=\phi\right]=\frac{1}{4e}(e-1)\phi+\frac{1}{4}\phi-\frac{1}{4n}\phi \tag{23}$$

$$\mathbb{E}\left[\Phi_{t+1}|\Phi=\phi\right]=\left(\frac{2e-1}{4e}-\frac{1}{4n}\right)\phi \tag{24}$$

Theorem 2. *Under the Pull Sum protocol, the conditional expectation of* Φ_{t+1} *is* $\mathbb{E}\left[\Phi_{t+1}|\Phi_t=\phi\right]=\frac{e-1}{e}\phi$.

Proof. Define $f(i)=k$ as the node k that is called by i in round t. Assume we know all $v_{i,j}$ and the random choices f of all nodes at time t. Let m_i and m_k be the number of pull calls received by node i and node k at time t, respectively. Then we can write the potential of the next round $t+1$ as:

$$\Phi_{t+1}=\sum_{i,j}\left(\frac{1}{m_i}\left(v_{i,j}-\frac{w_i}{n}\right)+\frac{1}{m_k}\left(v_{k,j}-\frac{w_k}{n}\right)\right)^2 \tag{25}$$

$$\Phi_{t+1}=\frac{1}{m_i^2}\sum_{i,j}\left(v_{i,j}-\frac{w_i}{n}\right)^2+\frac{1}{m_k^2}\sum_{i,j}\left(v_{k,j}-\frac{w_k}{n}\right)^2 \\ +\frac{2}{m_i m_k}\sum_{i,j,k}\left(v_{i,j}-\frac{w_i}{n}\right)\left(v_{k,j}-\frac{w_k}{n}\right) \tag{26}$$

We apply mass conservation to the potential function then we get:

$$\Phi_{t+1}=\frac{1}{m_i^2}\sum_{i,j}\left(v_{i,j}-\frac{w_i}{n}\right)^2+\frac{1}{m_k^2}\sum_{i,j}\left(v_{k,j}-\frac{w_k}{n}\right)^2 \tag{27}$$

The number of pull calls m_i at node i is at least one because every node calls itself. The number of calls m_k at node k is at least two calls because it has a self call and also receives a call from node i. Let $m_i=c_i+1$ and $m_k=c_k+2$, with c_i and c_k being approximated by Poisson random variables. Taking the expectation of Φ_{t+1} for Pull Sum protocol we get:

$$\mathbb{E}\left[\Phi_{t+1}|\Phi_t=\phi\right]=\sum_{i,j}\sum_{x=0}^{\infty}\frac{1}{(x+1)^2}\left(v_{i,j}-\frac{w_i}{n}\right)^2\mathbb{P}\left[c_i=x\right] \\ +\sum_{i,j,k}\sum_{x=0}^{\infty}\frac{1}{(x+2)^2}\left(v_{k,j}-\frac{w_k}{n}\right)^2\mathbb{P}\left[c_k=x\wedge f(i)=k\right] \tag{28}$$

For large n: c_i, c_k, and $f(i)$ can be considered independent and approximated by Poisson random variables with $\lambda = 1$.

$$\mathbb{E}\left[\Phi_{t+1}|\Phi_t = \phi\right] = \sum_{i,j}\left(v_{i,j} - \frac{w_i}{n}\right)^2 \sum_{x=0}^{\infty} \frac{1}{(x+1)(x+1)!}\frac{1}{e} + \sum_{i,j,k}\left(v_{k,j} - \frac{w_k}{n}\right)^2 \sum_{x=0}^{\infty} \frac{1}{(x+2)(x+2)}\frac{1}{ex!}\frac{1}{n} \tag{29}$$

$$= \frac{1}{e}\sum_{i,j}\left(v_{i,j} - \frac{w_i}{n}\right)^2 \sum_{x=1}^{\infty} \frac{1}{xx!} + \frac{1}{e}\sum_{i,j,k}\left(v_{k,j} - \frac{w_k}{n}\right)^2 \frac{1}{n}\sum_{x=1}^{\infty} \frac{1}{(x+1)(x+1)!} \tag{30}$$

Applying the series expansions of exponential integral for the expectation of Φ_{t+1} for Pull Sum protocol we get:

$$\mathbb{E}\left[\Phi_{t+1}|\Phi_t = \phi\right] = \frac{e-1}{e}\phi \tag{31}$$

The conditional expectation of Φ_{t+1} at round $t+1$ for Push Sum [4,9] is

$$\mathbb{E}\left[\Phi_{t+1}|\Phi_t = \phi\right] = \left(\frac{1}{2} - \frac{1}{4n}\right)\phi \tag{32}$$

5 Experiments and Analysis

Every node calculates the approximate mean value of all data inputs using the data samples retrieved from the other nodes during the communication process. The input data values of nodes used for the experiments are sampled independently at random from the uniform distribution between 0 and 100. We performed the simulation processes of communication protocols using PeerSim [7]. Every round, the observer calculates the Mean Squared Error (MSE) [1] between the ground truth average of all nodes' data inputs and the average value of each node. The MSE is computed by measuring the average squared error between the estimated node's mean value f_{avg} and the network's mean ground truth f_{gt}. The f_{avg} is computed during the aggregation process using communication protocols. The f_{gt} is calculated by the observer.

$$MSE = \frac{\sum_{i=1}^{n}\left(f_{gt} - f_{avg}\right)^2}{n} \tag{33}$$

Figure 2 shows the comparison of simulation results and the conditional expectation for the Push-Pull Sum protocol, the Pull Sum protocol, and the Push Sum protocol for network size 10^4 regarding the MSE and the time complexity defined by the number of rounds. This comparison of the communication protocol experiment is run 50 simulations to increase statistical significance. The Push-Pull Sum protocol has a lower MSE than that of the Push Sum protocol and the Pull Sum protocol in terms of rounds, while the Pull Sum protocol has a higher MSE than that of the Push Sum protocol.

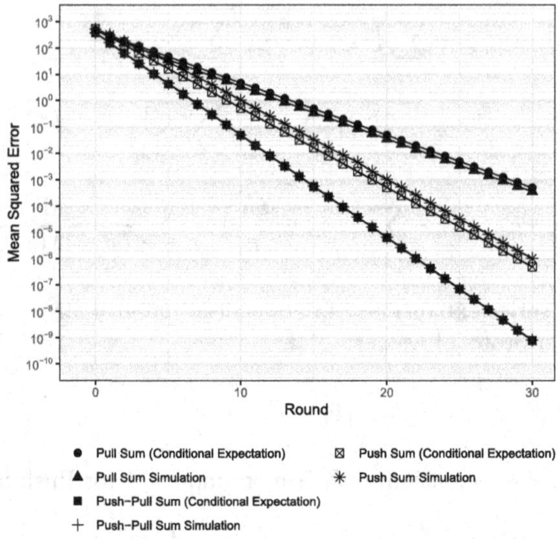

Fig. 2. Comparison of the communication protocol algorithms regarding the MSE and the round. Inputs are uniformly distributed and the number of nodes n is 10^4.

Figure 3 shows the comparison of simulation results and the conditional expectation for the Push-Pull Sum protocol, the Pull Sum protocol, and the Push Sum protocol for network size 10^4 regarding the MSE and the message complexity defined by the cumulative messages sent by nodes. The Push-Pull Sum protocol needs to send more messages than the Push Sum protocol to get a lower MSE, even though the number of rounds used by the Push-Pull Sum protocol is less. The dots in Fig. 3 depict the number of rounds. Overall, the MSE decreases as the number of rounds and the cumulative number of messages sent by nodes increase. The message complexity and the time complexity of the Push-Pull Sum and Push Sum protocols have a trade-off regarding the MSE.

The simulation results are very close to the conditional expectation of Φ_{t+1} results for the Push-Pull Sum protocol, the Pull Sum protocol, and the Push Sum protocol. The Push Sum, the Pull Sum, and the Push-Pull Sum communication protocols converge to the correct answer, which can be seen from the expected potential that decreases in every round. The Push-Pull Sum protocol converges faster than the Push Sum protocol and Pull Sum protocol to the ground truth. The proof will appear in the full version.

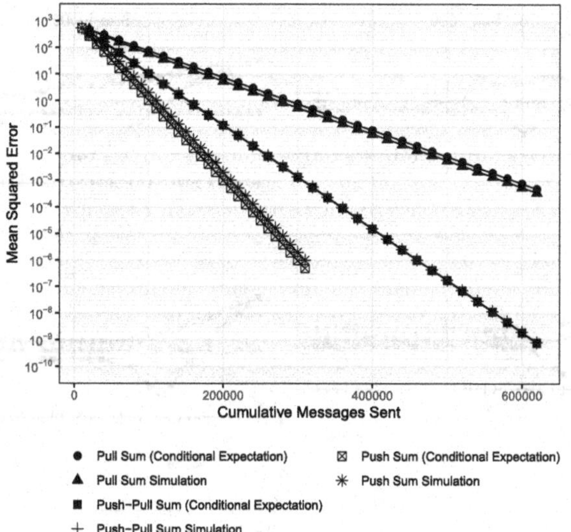

Fig. 3. Comparison of the communication protocol algorithms regarding the MSE and the cumulative message sent. Inputs are uniformly distributed and the number of nodes n is 10^4. The number of rounds is 30.

We observed the weight using communication protocols. The weight will influence the result of the estimated mean value calculated by the node. We let the node u is the only one informed node with the weight $w = 1$ at the beginning of the round, and all uninformed nodes, except the node u, have the weight $w = 0$. The informed nodes disseminate the information to the other nodes using the Push Sum protocol, Pull Sum protocol, and Push-Pull Sum protocol in rounds. In this case, the sum of all weights $\sum_i w_{i,t}$ at any round t is always equal to 1. The smallest weight in Proposition 1 could be analyzed.

Proposition 1. *Let w_t' be the smallest weight of any informed nodes at any round t. Then the smallest weight of informed nodes is not equal to 0 at any round.*

Proof. We let define the uninformed node with weight that is equal to 0 ($w_t = 0$). By induction, if the node gets information from other nodes, then the informed node will have the positive weight ($w_t > 0$). In the Push Sum protocol, Pull Sum protocol, and Push-Pull Sum protocol, there is no operation to change the weight from positive value to zero value during the dissemination process of weight. □

Based on the theorem by Boris Pittel [10], with constant probability, the random number of rounds until everybody receives the rumor is $\sigma_r = \log_2 n + \log_e n + O(1)$.

In the Push Sum protocol, the caller node divides the weight in half $\frac{w_t}{2}$ and sends it to the chosen neighbor and itself in each round t. Suppose the node v is the only one with the weight $w = 0$ at round σ_r. The node v gets the smallest

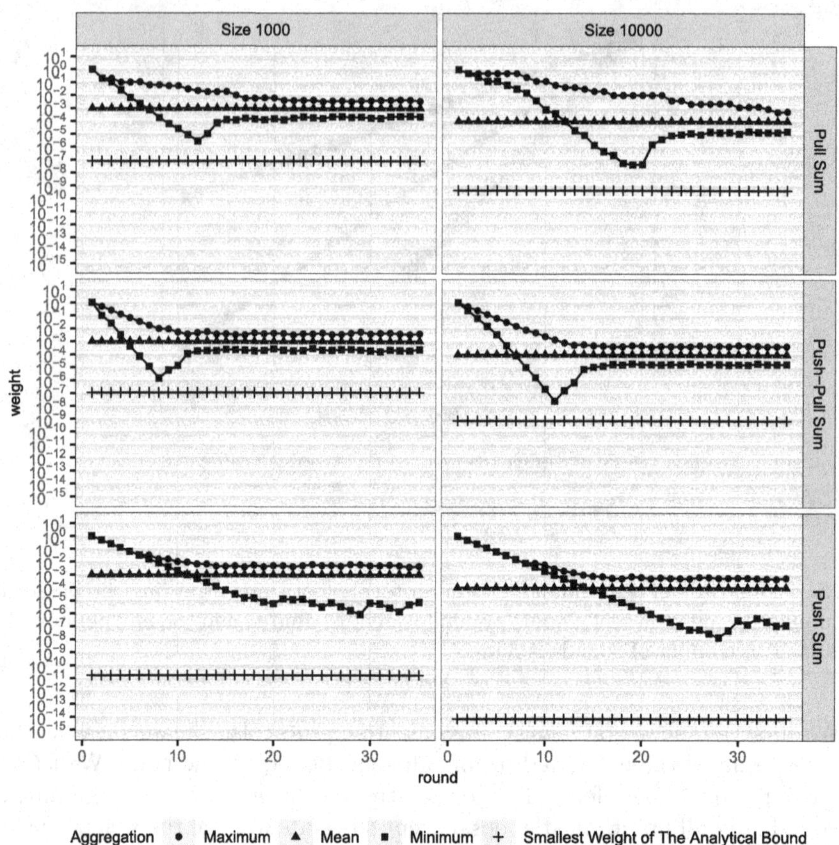

Fig. 4. Mean, maximum, minimum, and the smallest weight of nodes in the network.

weight at round σ_r from the node u which has not received the message from one of its neighbors, but the node u sent half weight $\frac{w_t}{2}$ to its neighbors (unlikely, but possible). All nodes have received the rumor after σ_r steps. In every round, the node v sends half weight $\frac{w_t}{2}$ to its neighbors, but the node v has the possibility of not getting the message from its neighbors until σ_r steps later. At round $2\sigma_r$, the node v has the smallest weight that will be sent to another node that already has a certain weight. The decrease in weight in each round follows the conditional expectation of Φ_{t+1} for the Push Sum protocol [4,9]. The smallest weight of the analytical bound of the Push Sum protocol with $\chi \geq 1$ and $c \geq 2$ at any round, with constant probability, is

$$w'_{t_{PushSum}} \geq \left(\frac{1}{2} - \frac{1}{4n}\right)^{c(\log_2 n + \log_e n + \chi)} \tag{34}$$

In the Pull Sum protocol, the caller node u will receive the weight $\frac{w_{v_t}}{|R|_v}$ from the chosen node v and the weight $\frac{w_{u_t}}{|R|_u}$ from itself. |R| is the number of requests received by a node. The node's weight could potentially be quite small because it receives many call requests or has yet to receive any rumors from its selected neighbors for a while (unlikely, but possible). The decrease in weight in each round follows the conditional expectation of Φ_{t+1} for Pull Sum protocol in Theorem 2. The smallest weight of the analytical bound of the Pull Sum protocol with $\chi \geq 1$ and $c \geq 2$ at any round, with constant probability, is

$$w'_{t_{PullSum}} \geq \left(\frac{e-1}{e}\right)^{c(\log_2 n + \log_e n + \chi)} \tag{35}$$

In the Push-Pull Sum protocol, the caller node u will receive the weight $\frac{w_k}{2}$ from nodes which choose node u, the weight $\frac{\frac{w_{v_t}}{2}}{|R|_v}$ from the chosen node v and the weight $\frac{\frac{w_{u_t}}{2}}{|R|_u}$ from itself at round t. The weight of node could be quite small because it has yet to receive any rumors from its chosen neighbors for a while (unlikely, but possible). The decrease in weight in each round follows the conditional expectation of Φ_{t+1} for the Push-Pull Sum protocol in Theorem 1. The smallest weight of the analytical bound of the Push-Pull Sum protocol with $\chi \geq 1$ and $c \geq 1$ at any round, with constant probability, is

$$w'_{t_{PushPullSum}} \geq \left(\frac{2e-1}{4e} - \frac{1}{4n}\right)^{c(\log_2 n + \log_e n + \chi)} \tag{36}$$

Figure 4 shows the informed node's minimum weight, maximum weight, and average weight of the informed nodes using the Pull Sum protocol, the Push-Pull Sum protocol, and the Push Sum protocol with different network sizes at different rounds. The communication protocols have the property of mass conservation. The smallest weight of the analytical bound in Fig. 4 refers to the analytical bound for the Push Sum protocol, the Pull Sum protocol, and the Push-Pull Sum protocol that are derived in Eq. 34, Eq. 35, and Eq. 36, respectively. The minimum weight in Fig. 4 refers to the smallest non-zero weight of the nodes that have received information in a round. We depict the analytical bound of the smallest weight in each round to show that the minimum weight will not exceed the theoretical smallest weight of the analytical bound value. In disseminating the message, the smallest weight of informed nodes at any round will not equal to zero because nodes will get the positive weight from other informed nodes. There is no operation to set the weight to zero value using the communication protocols. The uninformed node will get the message after the number of stages $\sigma_r = \log_2 n + \log_e n + O(1)$ with constant probability based on the theorem by Boris Pittel [10].

6 Conclusion

Push-Pull Sum protocol converges to the ground truth result because of the mass conservation property. The Push-Pull Sum protocol complements the Push Sum protocol with the Pull Sum protocol. Based on the conditional expectation, the

Push-Pull Sum protocol outperforms the Push Sum protocol and the Pull Sum protocol in terms of time complexity. Overall, the MSE decreases as the number of rounds and the cumulative number of messages sent by nodes increase. The message complexity and the time complexity of the Push-Pull Sum and the Push Sum protocols have a trade-off between the number of rounds and the number of messages regarding the MSE.

References

1. Nugroho, S., Weinmann, A., Schindelhauer, C.: Trade off between accuracy and message complexity for approximate data aggregation. In: 18th International Conference on Distributed Computing in Sensor Systems, DCOSS 2022, pp. 61–64, Marina del Rey, Los Angeles, CA, USA, 30 May 2022–01 June (2022). https://doi.org/10.1109/DCOSS54816.2022.00021
2. Kuhn, F., Locher, T., Wattenhofer, R.: Tight bounds for distributed selection. In: Proceedings of the Nineteenth Annual ACM Symposium on Parallel Algorithms and Architectures, SPAA 2007, pp. 145–153. Association for Computing Machinery, New York, NY, USA (2007). https://doi.org/10.1145/1248377.1248401
3. Karp, R., Schindelhauer, C., Shenker, S., Vocking, B.: Randomized rumor spreading. In: Proceedings 41st Annual Symposium on Foundations of Computer Science, pp. 565–574, Redondo Beach, CA, USA (2000). https://doi.org/10.1109/SFCS.2000.892324
4. Kempe, D., Dobra, A., Gehrke, J.: Gossip-based computation of aggregate information. In: Proceedings 44th Annual IEEE Symposium on Foundations of Computer Science, pp. 482–491, Cambridge, MA, USA (2003). https://doi.org/10.1109/SFCS.2003.1238221
5. Jesus, P., Baquero, C., Almeida, P.S.: A survey of distributed data aggregation algorithms. IEEE Commun. Surv. Tutorials J. **17**(1), 381–404 (2015). https://doi.org/10.1109/COMST.2014.2354398
6. Daum, S., Kuhn, F., Maus, Y.: Rumor spreading with bounded in-degree. Theor. Comput. Sci. J. **810**, 43–57 (2020). https://doi.org/10.1016/j.tcs.2018.05.041
7. Montresor, A., Jelasity, M.: PeerSim: a scalable P2P simulator. In: Proceedings of the IEEE Ninth International Conference on Peer-to-Peer Computing, pp. 99–100. Seattle, WA, USA (2009). https://doi.org/10.1109/P2P.2009.5284506
8. Abramowitz, M., Stegun, I.A.: Handbook of Mathematical Functions with Formulas, Graphs, and Mathematical Tables. Dover, New York (1964)
9. Kempe, D.: Structure and dynamics of information in networks (2021). http://david-kempe.com/teaching/structure-dynamics.pdf. Accessed 17 Oct 2022
10. Pittel, B.: On spreading a rumor. SIAM J. Appl. Math. **47**(1), 213–223 (1987). https://www.jstor.org/stable/2101696
11. Chierichetti, F., Lattanzi, S., Panconesi, A.: Rumor spreading in social networks. In: Albers, S., Marchetti-Spaccamela, A., Matias, Y., Nikoletseas, S., Thomas, W. (eds.) ICALP 2009. LNCS, vol. 5556, pp. 375–386. Springer, Heidelberg (2009). https://doi.org/10.1007/978-3-642-02930-1_31
12. Weinmann, A.: Simulation, evaluation, and analysis of data aggregation methods under different random call models suitable for time series data. Master thesis. University of Freiburg Faculty of Engineering Department of Computer Science Chair of Computer Networks and Telematics, Freiburg, Germany (2022)

13. Frieze, A.M., Grimmett, G.R.: The shortest-path problem for graphs with random arc-lengths. Discr. Appl. Math. **10**(1), 57–77 (1985). https://doi.org/10.1016/0166-218X(85)90059-9
14. Chierichetti, F., Giakkoupis, G., Lattanzi, S., Panconesi, A.: Rumor spreading and conductance. J. Assoc. Comput. Mach. **65**(4), 1–21 (2018). Article No.: 17. https://doi.org/10.1145/3173043
15. Daknama, R., Panagiotou, K., Reisser, S.: Robustness of randomized rumour spreading. Comb. Probab. Comput. **30**(1), 37–78 (2021). https://doi.org/10.1017/S0963548320000310
16. Casas, M., Gansterer, W.N., Wimmer, E.: Resilient gossip-inspired all-reduce algorithms for high-performance computing: potential, limitations, and open questions. Int. J. High Perform. Comput. Appl. **33**(2), 366–383 (2019). https://doi.org/10.1177/1094342018762531
17. Mahlmann, P.: Peer-to-peer networks based on random graphs. Dissertation (PhD). Fakultät für Elektrotechnik, Informatik und Mathematik, Universität Paderborn, Verlagsschriftenreihe des Heinz Nixdorf Instituts, Paderborn, Band 283, Paderborn (2010)
18. Schindelhauer, C.: Communication network problems (2002). http://archive.cone.informatik.uni-freiburg.de/pubs/Habil.pdf. Accessed 17 Oct 2022

Exploring Trade-Offs in Partial Snapshot Implementations

Nikolaos D. Kallimanis[1(✉)], Eleni Kanellou[2], Charidimos Kiosterakis[4], and Vasiliki Liagkou[3]

[1] ISI/Athena RC & University of Ioannina, Arta, Greece
nkallima@isi.gr

[2] ICS-FORTH, Heraklion, Greece
kanellou@ics.forth.gr

[3] University of Ioannina, Arta, Greece
liagkou@uoi.gr

[4] Department of Computer Science, University of Crete, Rethymnon, Greece
xarkio@gmail.com

Abstract. A snapshot object is a concurrent object that consists of m components, each storing a value from a given set. Processes can read-/modify the state of the object by performing *Update* and *Scan* operations. An *Update* operation gives processes the ability to change the value of a component, while a *Scan* operation returns a "consistent" view of all the components. In *single-scanner* snapshot objects, at most one *Scan* is performed at any given time (whilst supporting many concurrent *Update* operations). *Multi-scanner* snapshot objects support multiple concurrent *Scan* operations at any given time.

In this paper, we propose the λ-scanner snapshot, a variation of the snapshot object, which supports any fixed amount of $0 < \lambda \leq n$ different *Scan* operations being active at any given time. Whenever λ is equal to the number of processes n in the system, the λ-scanner object implements a multi-scanner object, while in case that λ is equal to 1, the λ-scanner object implements a single-scanner object. We present $\lambda - Snap$, a wait-free λ-scanner snapshot implementation that has a step complexity of $O(\lambda)$ for *Update* operations and $O(\lambda m)$ for *Scan* operations. For ease of understanding, we first provide $1 - Snap$, a simple single-scanner version of $\lambda - Snap$. The *Update* in $1 - Snap$ has a step complexity of $O(1)$, while the *Scan* has a step complexity of $O(m)$. This implementation uses $O(m)$ LL/SC registers. The space complexity of $\lambda - Snap$ is $O(\lambda m)$. $\lambda - Snap$ provides a trade-off between the step/space complexity and the maximum number of *Scan* operations that the system can afford to be active on any given point in time. The low space complexity that our implementations provide makes them more appealing in real system applications. Moreover, we provide *partial* $\lambda - Snap$, a slightly modified version of $\lambda - Snap$, which supports dynamic partial scan operations. This object supports modified *Scan* operations that can obtain a part of the snapshot object avoiding to read the whole set of components.

Keywords: Snapshots · concurrent objects · wait-free · dynamic snapshots

S. Dolev and B. Schieber (Eds.): SSS 2023, LNCS 14310, pp. 90–105, 2023.
https://doi.org/10.1007/978-3-031-44274-2_8

1 Introduction

At the heart of exploiting the potential that *multi-core CPUs* provide, are concurrent data structures, since they are essential building blocks of concurrent algorithms. The design of concurrent data structures, such as lists [25], queues [18,23], stacks [6,23], and even trees [8,12] is a thoroughly explored topic. Compared to sequential data structures, the concurrent ones can simultaneously be accessed and/or modified by more than one process. Ideally, we would like to have the best concurrent implementation, in terms of space and step complexity, of any given data structure. However, this cannot always be the case since the design of those data structures is a complex task.

In this work, we present a *snapshot object*, a concurrent object that consists of components which can be read and modified by any process. Such objects are used in numerous applications in order to provide a coherent "view" of the memory of a system. They are also used to design and validate various concurrent algorithms such as the construction of concurrent timestamps [14], approximate agreement [5], etc., and the ideas at their core can be further developed in order to implement more complex data structures [2]. Applications of snapshots also appear in sensor networks where snapshot implementations can provide a consistent view of the state of the various sensors of the network. Under certain circumstances, snapshots can even be used to simulate concurrent graphs, as seen e.g. in [20]. The graph data structure is widely used for the representation of transport networks [1], video-game design [9], automated design of digital circuits [19], making the study of snapshot objects pertinent even to these areas.

In order to be fault-tolerant against process failure, a concurrent object has to have strong progress guarantees, such as *wait-freedom*, which ensures that an operation invoked by any process that does not fail, returns a result after it executes a finite number of steps. We provide two wait-free algorithms, an algorithm for a *single-scanner* snapshot object, i.e. a snapshot object where only one process is allowed to read the values of the components, although any process may modify the values of components; and an algorithm for a λ-*scanner* snapshot object, where up to λ predefined processes may read the components of the object, while any process may change the value of any component. Note that λ should be lower than or equal to n, i.e. the number of processes in the system. In case λ is equal to n, we obtain a general multi-scanner snapshot object. Our implementation allows us to study trade-offs, since the increase of the value of λ leads to a linear increase of the space and step complexity. Our *Scan* operations can be modified to obtain partial snapshot implementations (see Sects. 3.1 and 4.1), that obtain the values of just a subset of the components.

$\lambda - Snap$ has a low space complexity of $O(\lambda m)$, where m is the number of the components of the snapshot object. This does not come with major compromises in terms of step complexity, since the step complexity of an *Update* operation is $O(\lambda)$, while that of a *Scan* operation is $O(\lambda m)$. As is common practice from many state-of-the-art implementations [13,24], we use registers of unbounded size, although the only unbounded value they store is a sequence number.

1.1 Related Work

Most of current multi-scanner snapshot implementations that use registers of relatively small size either have step complexity that is linear to the number of processes n [4,15] or the space complexity is linear to n [3,15–17,20]. An exception is the multi-scanner snapshot implementation presented by Fatourou and Kallimanis in [11], with $O(m)$ step complexity for *Scan* operations and $O(1)$ step complexity for *Update* operations. In contrast to $\lambda - Snap$, this snapshot implementation requires unrealistically large registers that contain a vector of m values as well as a sequence number, and does not support partial snapshots.

Similarly, the implementation by Bashari and Woelfel [7] nominally has a step complexity of $O(1)$ for *Scan* operations and a step complexity of $O(\log m)$ for Update operations. However, *Scan* operations do not return anything, and in order for a process to obtain the value of a particular component in the consistent view captured by a *Scan*, it has to use *Observe*, an auxiliary operation with complexity $O(\log m)$, thus resulting in a step complexity of $O(m \log m)$ to obtain the values of all m components of the snapshot. While the combination of *Scan* and *Observe* allow for a partial snapshot, Bashari and Woelfel's implementation allows for a single writer, contrary to ours which is multi-writer.

The step complexity of $\lambda - Snap$ is $O(\lambda m)$ for *Scan* and $O(\lambda)$ for *Update*, while it uses $O(\lambda m)$ LL/SC registers. In cases where λ is a relatively small constant, the number of registers can be reduced almost to $O(m)$, while the step complexity of *Scan* is almost linear to m and the step complexity of *Update* is almost constant. Compared to current single-scanner snapshot implementations (e.g. [10,11,13,17,22,24]), $\lambda - Snap$ allows for more than one *Scan* operation at each point of time by slightly worsening the step complexity. In the worst case where λ equals n, $\lambda - Snap$ uses a smaller amount of registers than [4,16,17,24]. To the best of our knowledge, $\lambda - Snap$ provides the first trade-off between the number of active scanners and the step/space complexity.

Riany et al. have presented in [24] an implementation of snapshot objects that uses $O(n^2)$ registers and achieves $O(n)$ and $O(1)$ step complexity for *Scan* and *Update* operations respectively. Attiya, Herlihy & Rachman present in [4] a snapshot object that has $O(n \log^2 n)$ step complexity for both *Scan* and *Update* operations, while it uses dynamic Test&Set registers.

Kallimanis and Kanellou [20] present a wait-free implementation of a graph object, which can be slightly modified to simulate a snapshot object with partial *Scan* operations. *Update* and *Scan* operations have step complexity of $O(k)$, where k is the number of active processes in a given execution. While the space complexity of $O(n + m)$ is low, the registers used are of unbounded size, since they have to be able to contain $O(n)$ integer values.

Imbs and Raynal [15] provide two implementations of a partial snapshot object. The first uses simpler registers than the second one, but it has a higher space complexity. Thus, we concentrate on the second implementation that achieves a step complexity of $O(nr)$ for *Scan* and $O(r_i n)$ for *Update*, where r_i is a value relative to the helping mechanism provided by *Update* operations. This implementation uses $O(n)$ Read/Write (RW) and LL/SC registers and provides a new helping mechanism by implementing the "write first, help later" technique. Attiya, Guerraoui and Ruppert [3] provide a partial snapshot algorithm that uses $O(m+n)$ CAS registers. The step complexity for *Update* is $O(r^2)$ and for *Scan* is $O(\overline{C}_S^2 r_{max}^2)$, where $\overline{C}_S$ is the number of active *Scan* operations, whose execution interval overlaps with the execution interval of S, and r_{max} is the maximum number of components that any *Scan* operation may read in any given execution. A summary of the above comparisons that follow a similar model as $\lambda - Snap$ is presented in Table 1.

Table 1. Known multi-scanner snapshot implementations.

Implementation	Partial	Regs type	Regs number	*Scan*	*Update*
λ-Snap		LL/SC & *RW*	$O(\lambda m)$	$O(\lambda m)$	$O(\lambda)$
partial λ-Snap	✓	LL/SC & *RW*	$O(\lambda m)$	$O(\lambda r)$	$O(\lambda)$
Attiya, et. al. [4]		dynamic Test&Set	unbounded	$O(n \log^2 n)$	$O(n \log^2 n)$
Fatourou & Kallimanis [11]		CAS & *RW*	$O(m)$	$O(m)$	$O(1)$
Jayanti [17]		CAS or LL/SC & *RW*	$O(mn^2)$	$O(m)$	$O(1)$
Jayanti [16]		CAS or LL/SC & *RW*	$O(mn^2)$	$O(m)$	$O(m)$
Riany et al. [24]		CAS or LL/SC & Fetch&Inc & *RW*	$O(n^2)$	$O(n)$	(1)
Kallimanis & Kanellou [20]	✓	CAS or LL/SC & *RW*	$O(n+m)$	$O(k)$	$O(k)$
D. Imbs & M. Raynal [15]	✓	LL/SC & *RW*	$O(n)$	$O(nr)$	$O(r_i n)$
Attiya, Guerraoui & Ruppert [3]	✓	CAS & *RW*	$O(n+m)$	$O(r^2)$	$O((\overline{C}_S)^2 r_{max}^2)$

We now compare $\lambda - Snap$ and $1 - Snap$ snapshot with other single-scanner algorithms and present a summary of their basic characteristics in Table 2.

In [11,13], Fatourou and Kallimanis present $T - Opt$, a single-scanner snapshot implementation with $O(1)$ step complexity for *Update* and $O(m)$ for *Scan*. Through trivial modifications to $T - Opt$, a partial snapshot implementation with $O(r)$ step complexity for *Scan* and $O(1)$ for *Update* could be derived. In contrast to $1 - Snap$, $T - Opt$ uses an unbounded number of registers. Moreover, RT and $RT - Opt$ presented in [11,13] do not support partial *Scan* operations.

In [17], Jayanti presents a single-scanner snapshot algorithm with $O(1)$ step complexity for *Update* and $O(m)$ for *Scan*, while it uses $O(m)$ LL/SC & *RW* registers. The algorithm of [17] could be easily modified to support partial *Scan* operations without having any negative impact on step and space complexity. Therefore, $1 - Snap$ and $\lambda - Snap$ (for $\lambda = 1$) match the step complexity of implementations presented in [11,13,17], which is $O(m)$ for *Scan* and $O(1)$ for *Update*. Notice that the single-scanner implementations of [11,13] use *RW* registers, while $1 - Snap$ and $\lambda - Snap$ use LL/SC registers. The partial versions of $1 - Snap$ and $\lambda - Snap$ (for $\lambda = 1$) have step complexity of *Scan* that is reduced to $O(r)$, where r is the amount of components the *Scan* operation wants to read.

Kirousis et al. [22] present a single-scanner snapshot that uses an unbounded number of registers and has unbounded time complexity for *Scan*. A register recycling technique is applied, resulting in a snapshot implementation with $O(mn)$ step complexity for *Scan* and $O(1)$ for *Update*. Riany et al. [24] present a single-scanner implementation which is a simplified variant of the algorithm presented in [22] and achieves $O(1)$ step complexity for *Update* and $O(n)$ for *Scan*. Through trivial modifications, a partial snapshot implementation could be derived. However, this implementation is a single-updater snapshot object, since it does not allow more than one processes to update the same component at each point of time. In [10,13], Fatourou and Kallimanis provide the *Checkmarking* algorithm that achieves $O(m^2)$ step complexity for both *Scan* and *Update*, while using $O(m)$ *RW* registers. It does however not support partial *Scan* operations.

Table 2. Known single-scanner snapshot implementations.

Implementation	Partial	Regs type	Regs number	*Scan*	*Update*
$1-Snap$		LL/SC & SW *RW*	$O(m)$	$O(m)$	$O(1)$
$1-Snap$ *(partial)*	✓	LL/SC & SW *RW*	$O(m)$	$O(r)$	$O(1)$
Checkmarking [10,13]		*RW*	$m+1$	$O(m^2)$	$O(m^2)$
$T-Opt$ [11,13](modified)	✓	*RW*	Unbounded	$O(m)$	$O(1)$
RT [11,13]		*RW*	$O(mn)$	$O(n)$	$O(1)$
$RT-Opt$ [11,13]		*RW*	$O(mn)$	$O(m)$	$O(1)$
Kirousis et al. [22]		*RW*	$O(mn)$	$O(mn)$	$O(1)$
Riany et al. [24]	✓	*RW*	$n+1$	$O(n)$	$O(1)$
Jayanti [17]	✓	LL/SC & *RW*	$O(m)$	$O(m)$	$O(1)$

2 Model

We consider a system consisting of n uniquely distinguishable processes modeled as sequential state machines, where processes may fail by crashing. The processes are asynchronous and communicate through shared *base objects*. A base object stores a value and provides a set of *primitives*, through which the object's value can be accessed and/or modified. A $Read-Write$ *register* R ($RWregister$), is a shared object that stores a value from a set and that supports the primitives: (i) $Write\,(R,v)$ that writes the value v in R, and returns *true*, and (ii) *Read*(R) that returns the value stored in R. An LL/SC *register* R is a shared object that stores a value from a set and supports the primitives: (i) $LL(R)$ which returns the value of R, and (ii) $SC(R,v)$ which can be executed by a process p only after the execution of an $LL(R)$ by the same process. An $SC(R,v)$ writes the value v in R only if the state of R hasn't changed since p executed the last $LL(R)$, in which case the operation returns *true*; it returns $false$ otherwise. An $LL/SC-Write$ *register* R is a shared object that stores a value from a set. It supports the same primitives as an LL/SC *register* as well as the primitive $Write(R,v)$ that writes the value v in R, and returns *true*.

A *shared object* is a data structure that can be accessed and/or modified by processes in the system through a set of *operations* that it provides. An *implementation* of a shared object uses base objects to store the state of the shared object and provides algorithms that use base objects to implement each operation of the shared object. An operation consists of an *invocation* by some process and terminates by returning a *response* to the process that invoked it.

Each process also has an internal state. A *configuration* C of the system is a vector that contains the state of each of the n processes and the value of each of the base objects at some point in time. In an *initial configuration*, the processes are in an *initial state* and the base objects hold an *initial value*. We denote an initial configuration by C_0. A *step* taken by a process consists either of a primitive to some base object or the response to that primitive. Operation invocations and responses are also considered steps. Each step is executed atomically.

An *execution* a is a (possibly infinite) sequence $C_o, e_1, C_1, e_2, C_2 \ldots,$ that alternates between configurations and steps, starting from an initial configuration C_o, where each C_k, $k > 0$, results from applying step e_k to configuration C_{k-1}. If C is a configuration that is present in a we write $C \in a$. An *execution interval* of a given execution a is a subsequence of a which starts with some configuration C_k and ends with some configuration C_l (where $0 \leq k < l$). An *execution interval* of an operation *op* is an execution interval with its first configuration being the one right after the step where *op* was invoked and last being the one right after the step where *op* responded. Given an execution a, we say that a configuration C_k *precedes* C_l if $k < l$. Similarly, step e_k precedes step e_l if $k < l$. A configuration C_k precedes the step e_l in a, if $k < l$. On the other hand, step e_l precedes C_k in a if $l \leq k$. Furthermore, *op* precedes *op'* if the step where *op* responds precedes the step where *op'* is invoked. Given two execution intervals I, I' of a, we say that I precedes I' if any configuration C contained in I precedes any configuration C' contained in I'. An operation *op* is called *concurrent* with an operation *op'* in a if there is at least one configuration $C \in a$, such that both *op* and *op'* are active in C. An execution a is called *sequential* if in any given $C \in a$ there is at most one active *op*. An execution a that is not *sequential* is called *concurrent*. Executions a and a' are *equivalent* if they contain the same operations and only those operations are invoked in both of them by the same process, which in turn have the same responses in a and a'.

An execution a is *linearizable* if it is possible to assign a linearization point, inside the execution interval of each operation *op* in a, so that the response of *op* in a is the same as its response would be in the equivalent sequential execution that would result from performing the operations in a sequentially, following the order of their linearization points. An implementation of a shared object is linearizable if all executions it produces are linearizable. An implementation IM of a shared object O is $wait-free$ if any operation *op*, of a process that does not crash in a, responds after a finite amount of steps. The maximum number of those steps is called *step complexity* of *op*.

A *snapshot* S is a shared object that consists of m components, each taking values from a set, that provides the following two primitives: (i) $Scan()$ which returns a vector of size m, containing the values of m components of the object, and (ii) *Update*(i, v) which writes the non $\perp$ value v on the $i-th$ component of the object. A *partial snapshot* S is a shared object that consists of m distinct components denoted by $c_o, c_1, \ldots, c_{m-1}$, each taking values from a set, that provides the following two primitives: (i) $PartialScan(A)$ which, given a set A that contains integer values ranging from 0 to $m-1$, returns for each $i \in A$ the value of the component c_i, and (ii) $Update(i, v)$ which writes the non $\perp$ value v on c_i. A snapshot implementation is $single - scanner$ if in any execution a produced by the implementation there is no $C \in a$ in which there are more than one active *Scan* operations, and it is $\lambda - scanner$ if there is no $C \in a$ in which there are more than λ active *Scan* operations.

3 1-Snap

In this section, we present the $1 - Snap$ snapshot object (see Listings 1.1-1.2). In $1 - Snap$, only a single, predefined process is allowed to invoke *Scan* operations, while any processes can invoke *Update* operations on any component. We provide $1 - Snap$ just for presentation purposes, since it is simpler than $\lambda - Snap$.

We start by presenting the high-level ideas of the implementation. $1 - Snap$ uses a shared integer *seq* for providing sequence numbers to operations with an initial value of 0. Given that only *Scan* operations write the *seq* register (line 10 and since in any configuration there is only one active *Scan*, the *seq* register can safely be *RW*. Each *Scan* operation increases the value of *seq* by one and uses this value as its sequence number (line 32). Each *Update* operation gets a sequence number by reading the value of *seq* (line 47). These sequence numbers give us the ability to order the operations of an execution, e.g., any operation *op* that is applied with a smaller sequence number than the sequence number of some other operation op' is considered to be applied before op'. Thus, an *Update* operation that is applied with a sequence number less than that written by some *Scan* 'precedes' this specific *Scan*, while an *Update* that has an equal or greater sequence number follows the this *Scan*. Thus, the increase of *seq* by a *Scan* specifies which *Update* operations will be visible and which will not.

$1 - Snap$ employs the *pre_values* and *values* shared vectors consisting of m registers each. The i-th register of the *values* array stores the current value of the i-th component. For helping *Scan* operations to return a consistent view, the i-th register of *pre_values* array preserves a previous value of the component and not the current one. Notably, maintaining an older value other than the current one for each component simplifies design of the snapshot object and the assignment of linearization points. Specifically, *Update* operations with a sequence number less than the sequence number of a *Scan* are safely linearized before the *Scan* and their value is preserved in *pre_values* and returned by the *Scan* (even if there are *Update* operations that have obliterate the contents of *value* and have a sequence number that is equal or greater than that of the *Scan*). Moreover, *Update* operations with a sequence number greater ore equal to the sequence number of a *Scan* are linearized after the *Scan* operation. A similar technique is employed in the snapshot implementations presented in [11]. However, the implementations of [11] use *Read/Write* registers instead of *LL/SC* and serious effort was put on recycling the *Read/Write* registers.

Listing 1.1. Data Structures of 1-Snap.

```
struct value_struct {
    val value;
    int seq;
    val proposed_value;
};
struct pre_value_struct {
    val value;
    int seq;
};

shared int seq;
shared ValueStruct values[0..m−1]=[<⊥,⊥,⊥>,...,<⊥,⊥,⊥>];
shared PreValueStruct pre_values[0..m−1]=[<⊥,⊥>,...,<⊥,⊥>];
private int view[0..m−1]=[⊥,⊥,...,⊥,⊥];
```

We now briefly describe *Update* operations. Each of the components has a state that alternates between *propose* state and *apply update* state, while the initial state of any component is *apply update*. The role of the *propose* state is to allow *Update* operations to propose a new value for a component (lines 17-21). In the *propose* state, more than two processes may try to propose a new value for a specific component. In this case, only one of the *Update* operations (i.e., the winner) will be proposed successfully and the remaining *Update* operations will be considered to have been obliterated by the winner *Update*. In the *apply update* state, *Update* operations try to preserve the current value of the component to the *pre_value* register, and save the proposed value of the component (written by the winner updater) to the appropriate *values* register. The code that handles the *apply update* state is provided by the *ApplyUpdate* (see Listing 1.2). Notably, the *ApplyUpdate* function is also executed by *Scan* operations in each of the component for helping any pending *Update* operations to finish their execution. Whenever an *Update* starts its execution, the state of a component could be either *apply update* or *propose*. In case that the state is in *apply update*, the *Update* should first help any other process to finish its execution and after that it will change the component's state to *propose*. For this reason the code for alternating the state of the component between *propose* and *apply update* states is executed twice (line 16).

We now turn our attention to *Scan* operations. As a first step, a *Scan* operation increases the value of *seq* by one and uses this value as its sequence number (line 32). Afterwards, for each component of the snapshot object (lines 33-41), *Scan* performs the following: Afterwards, for each component i, a *Scan* operation does the following steps:

1. It helps any pending *Update* on the component to finish it's execution by calling *ApplyUpdate* (line 34),
2. it reads the *values*[i] and *pre_values*[i] registers (lines 35, 36),
3. in case the sequence number read in *values*[i] is less than the sequence number of the *Scan*, the value read on *values*[i] should be returned; this value is written by an *Update* that is old enough and it should be safely linearized before the increment of *seq* by the *Scan*,

Listing 1.2. *Update* and *Scan* implementations of 1-Snap.

```
14 void Update(int j, val value){
15     ValueStruct up_value, cur_value;
16     for (int i=0; i<2; i++){
17         cur_value=LL(values[j]);
18         up_value=cur_value;
19         up_value.proposed_value=value;
20         if (cur_value.proposed_value==⊥){
21             if (SC(values[j], up_value)){
22                 ApplyUpdate(j);
23                 break;
24             }
25         }
26         ApplyUpdate(j);
27     }
28 }

29 pointer Scan(){
30     ValueStruct v1;
31     PreValue_struct v2;
32     seq=seq+1;
33     for (int j=0;j<m; j++){
34         ApplyUpdate(j);   // Help any other running Update
35         v1=values[j];
36         v2=pre_values[j];
37         if (v1.seq<seq)
38             view[j]=v1.value;
39         else
40             view[j]=v2.value;
41     }
42     return view[0..m-1];
43 }

44 void ApplyUpdate(int j) {
45     ValueStruct cur_value;
46     LL(values[j]);
47     cur_seq=seq;
48     for (t=0; t<2; t++) {
49         LL(pre_values[j]);
50         cur_value=values[j];
51         if (cur_value.seq<seq)
52             SC(pre_values[j],<cur_value.seq, cur_value.value>);
53     }
54     if (cur_value.proposed_value!=⊥)
55     SC(values[j],<cur_value.proposed_value, cur_seq, ⊥>);
56 }
```

4. otherwise the value read in *pre_values*[i] is returned, since the *value*[i] is written by an *Update* that should be linearized after the increment of *seq*.

Finally, *Scan* returns its copy of the snapshot object (line 42).

The correctness proof of $1 - Snap$ is provided in [21]. Listings 1.1-1.2 imply that $1 - Snap$ uses $O(m)$ registers.

Theorem 1. *$1-Snap$ is a wait-free linearizable concurrent single-scanner snapshot implementation that uses $O(m)$ registers, and it provides $O(1)$ step complexity to Update operations and $O(m)$ to Scan operations.*

Listing 1.3. Partial version of 1-Snap.

```
void PartialScan(A){
    seq=seq+1;
    for each j in A{
        ApplyUpdate(j);
        Read(j);
    }
}

val Read(j){
    ValueStruct v1;
    PreValue_struct v2;
    v1=values[j];
    v2=pre_values[j];
    if (v1.seq<seq) view[j]=v1.
        value;
    else view[j]=v2.value;
    return view[j];
}
```

3.1 A Partial Version of 1-Snap

The $1 - snap$ snapshot implementation can be trivially modified in order to implement a partial snapshot object (see Listing 1.3). In order to do that, a new function *Read* is introduced. This function is invoked by *PartialScan* operations in order to read the values of the components indicated by A, which a subset of the components of the snapshot object. For each component c_j that is contained in A, the *PartialScan* operation tries to help an *Update* operation that wants to update the value of c_j by invoking the *ApplyUpdate*. Afterwards, it reads the value of c_j by invoking the *Read* function.

4 λ-Snap

We now present the $\lambda - Snap$ snapshot object (see Listings 1.4-1.6). In $\lambda - Snap$, only a predefined set of $1 \leq \lambda \leq n$ processes are allowed to invoke *Scan* operations, while all processes can perform *Update* operations on any component.

We start by presenting the high-level ideas of the implementation. Similarly to $1-Snap$, each *Scan* and *Update* operation gets a sequence number by reading the shared register *seq*. However, in $\lambda - Snap$ *seq* is a shared *LL*/*SC* register (line 14), which takes integer values and only *Scan* operations are able to increase its value by one (lines 36-47). The reason is that in contrast to $1 - Snap$, *Scan* operations in $\lambda - Snap$ get sequence numbers in a more complex way (lines 36-47) that resembles a consensus protocol. Notably, more than one *Scan* operations may get the same sequence number. However, for all *Scan* operations that get the same sequence number, the following hold: (1) their execution intervals are overlapping, (2) the increment of the *seq* register using *LL*/*SC* instructions takes place inside the execution interval of all of them, and (3) all these *Scan* operations are eventually linearized at the same point of the increment of register *seq* (see [21] for the correctness of $\lambda - Snap$). We remark that assigning the same sequence number to overlapping *Scan* operations greatly simplifies the algorithm's design and correctness proof (i.e., assignment os linerization points). Similarly to $1 - Snap$, an *Update* operation U that has been applied with a sequence number greater or equal to the sequence number of some *Scan* S operation, is not visible to S. Since U is not visible to S, U is linearized after S.

Similarly to $1 - Snap$, $\lambda - Snap$ employs the *pre_values* and *values* shared vectors consisting of m registers each (see Listing 1.4). In the i-th register of the *values* array, the current value of the i-th component is stored. To help *Scan* operations return a consistent view, the *pre_values* array stores previous values of the components. However, in $\lambda - Snap$, the *pre_values* array is 2D (i.e., $\lambda \times m$) since it has to preserve at most λ older values per component (i.e., one per scanning process). Moreover, each process S_p that is able to execute *Scan* operations, owns the i-th register of *s_table* array (line 17) that stores the sequence number gotten by S_p and the *write_enable* bit. The *write_enable* bit indicates if S_p wants or not to increase *seq* and gives the ability to running scanners to help each other while getting sequence numbers.

As a first step, S_p tries to increase the value of *seq* by executing the consensus-like protocol of lines 36-47 and gets a sequence number. Recall that more than one *Scan* operations may get the same sequence number. Afterwards, for each component i, S_p does the following steps:

1. It helps any pending *Update* on the component to finish it's execution by calling *ApplyUpdate*,
2. it reads the *values*[i] and *pre_values*[p][i] registers,
3. in case the sequence number read in *values*[i] is less than the sequence number of s_p, the value read on *values*[i] should be returned; this value is written by an *Update* that is old enough and it should be safely linearized before the increment of *seq* by S_p,
4. otherwise the value read in *pre_values*[p][i] is returned, since the *value*[i] is written by an *Update* that should be linearized after the increment of *seq*.

Finally, S_p returns its copy of the snapshot object (line 57).

In general, *Update* operations in $\lambda - Snap$ operate similar to those of $1 - Snap$. The main differentiation is that the *pre_values* array is 2D (i.e., $\lambda \times m$) since it has to preserve λ older values at most (one per scanning process). Specifically, whenever an *Update* updates the i-th component, it performs the following:

Listing 1.4. Data structures of λ-Snap.

```
1  struct ValueStruct {
2      val value;
3      val proposed_value;
4      int seq;
5  };
6  struct PreValueStruct {
7      val value;
8      int seq;
9  };
10 struct ScanStruct {
11     int seq;
12     boolean write_enable;
13 };

14 shared int seq;
15 shared ValueStruct values[0..m-1]=[<⊥,⊥,⊥>,...,<⊥,⊥,⊥>];
16 shared PreValueStruct pre_values[0..λ-1][0..m-1]=[<⊥,⊥>,...,<⊥,⊥>];
17 shared ScanStruct s_table[0..λ-1]=[<⊥,0>,<⊥,0>,...,<⊥,0>];
18 private int view[0..m-1]=[⊥,⊥,...,⊥,⊥];
```

Listing 1.5. *Scan* and *Update* implementation of λ-Snap.

```
void Update(int j, val value){
    ValueStruct up_value, cur_value;
    for (i=0; i<2; i++){
        cur_value=LL(values[j]);
        up_value=cur_value;
        up_value.proposed_value=value;
        if (cur_value.proposed_value==⊥){
            if (SC(values[j],up_value)){
                ApplyUpdate(j);
                break;
            }
        }
        ApplyUpdate(j);
    }
}

pointer Scan(){ // Executed by process S_p with id p
    s_table[p]=<1,seq>;
    for (i=0;i<3;i++){
        cur_seq=LL(seq);
        for (j=0;j<λ;j++){
            cur_s_table=LL(s_table[j]);
            if(cur_s_table.seq<seq+2 && cur_s_table.write_enable==1){
                cur_s_table.write_enable=0;
                cur_s_table.seq=seq+2;
                SC(s_table[j],cur_s_table);
            }
        }
        SC(seq,cur_seq+1);
    }
    for (j=0;j<m;j++){
        ApplyUpdate(j);
        v1=values[j];
        v2=pre_values[p][j];
        if (v1.seq<s_table[p].seq)
            view[j]=v1.value;
        else
            view[j]=v2.value;
    }
    return view[0..m-1];
}
```

1. it reads the current value of the component on register *values*[*i*] (line 62),
2. it gets a sequence number by reading *seq* (line 63),
3. for each scanner S_p, it stores the in *pre_values*[*p*][*i*] the current value of the *i*-th component if the sequence number of S_p (stored in *s_table*[*p*]) is greater or equal to that stored in *values*[*i*] (lines 64-74), and
4. it tries to update component value with an *SC* instruction.

4.1 A Partial Version of λSnap

We now present a slightly modified version of $\lambda - Snap$ (see Listing 1.7) that implements a partial snapshot object. The data structures used in this version remain the same as in $\lambda - Snap$ (Listing 1.4). Furthermore, the pseudocode of *Update* and *ApplyUpdate* function remain the same as shown in Listings 1.5 and 1.6. A new function, *Read*, is introduced (Listing 1.7), which is invoked by *PartialScan* operations in order to read the values of the snapshot object.

Listing 1.6. *ApplyUpdate* function of λ-Snap.

```
void ApplyUpdate(int j) {
    ValueStruct cur_value;
    PreValueStruct cur_pre_value, proposed_pre_value;
    cur_value=LL(values[j]);
    cur_seq=seq;
    for (i=0; i<λ; i++) {
        for (t=0; t<2; t++) {
            cur_pre_value=LL(pre_values[i][j]);
            cur_value=values[j];
            if (cur_value.seq<s_table[j].seq){
                proposed_pre_value.seq=cur_value.seq;
                proposed_pre_value.value=cur_value.value;
                SC(pre_values[i][j], proposed_pre_value);
            }
        }
    }
    if (cur_value.proposed_value!=⊥) {
        cur_value.value=cur_value.proposed_value;
        cur_value.seq=cur_seq;
        cur_value.proposed_value=⊥;
        SC(values[j], cur_value);
    }
}
```

Listing 1.7. *Update* and *Scan* implementations for the partial version of λ-Snap.

```
1  pointer PartialScan(set A) {
2      s_table[p_id]={1,seq};
3      for (i=0; i<3; i++) {
4          cur_seq=LL(seq);
5          for (j=0;j<λ;j++) {
6              cur_s_table=LL(s_table[j]);
7              if(cur_s_table.seq<seq+2 && cur_s_table.write_enable==1) {
8                  cur_s_table.write_enable=0;
9                  cur_s_table.seq=seq+2;
10                 SC(s_table[j],cur_s_table);
11             }
12         }
13         SC(seq,cur_seq+1);
14     }
15     for each j in A {
16         ApplyUpdate(j);
17         Read(j);
18     }
19 }

20 val Read(int j){
21     ValueStruct v1=values[j];
22     PreValueStruct v2=pre_values[j];
23     if (v1.seq<seq) view[j]=v1.value;
24     else view[j]=v2.value;
25     return view[j];
26 }
```

The only modification in this version of $\lambda - Snap$ is that the $PartialScan$ operations do not read all the components of the snapshot, they only read the components of set A. For each component j contained in A (the set of components that a $Scan$ wants to read), the $PartialScan$ operation tries to help $Update$ operations on the j-th component by invoking *ApplyUpdate* (lines 15–18). Then, it reads the value of the j-th component by invoking the *Read* function.

Both partial $\lambda - Snap$ and non-partial $\lambda - Snap$ have the same step complexity of $Update$ operations, and the same space complexity. However, partial $\lambda - Snap$ provides a step complexity of $O(\lambda r)$ for $Scan$ operations, where r is the number of components that the $PartialScan$ operation reads.

The correctness proof of $\lambda - Snap$ is provided in [21]. Listings 1.4-1.6 imply that $\lambda - Snap$ uses $1 + m + \lambda m + \lambda$ LL/SC $write$ registers. Thus, it follows that its space complexity is $O(\lambda m)$.

Theorem 2. *$\lambda - Snap$ is a wait-free linearizable concurrent λ-scanner snapshot implementation that uses $O(\lambda m)$ registers, and it provides $O(\lambda)$ step complexity to $Update$ operations and $O(\lambda m)$ to $Scan$ operations.*

5 Discussion

This work proposes the $\lambda - Snap$ snapshot object and its implementations. If λ is equal to 1, then λ - *Snap snapshot* simulates a single-scanner snapshot object, while if λ is equal to the maximum number of processes, then it simulates a multi-scanner snapshot object. To the best of our knowledge, there is no known solution that supports a preset amount of $Scan$ operation that run concurrently.

$1 - Snap$ solves the single-scanner flavor of snapshot problem. Although, we only allow one process with a certain id to invoke $Scan$ operations, this is a restriction that can be easily lifted. The system can support invocations of $Scan$ operations by any process, although only one process can be active in any given configuration. In this case, our algorithm would be correct only in executions that at most one $Scan$ is active in any given configuration of the execution.

A λ - *Snap snapshot* can efficiently applied in systems where only a preset amount of processes want to execute $Scan$ operations. Especially in systems that the amount of processes that may want to invoke a $Scan$ operation is small enough, our algorithm has almost the same performance as a single-scanner snapshot object. For example, in a sensor network, where many sensors are communicating with a small amount of monitor devices. In this case, sensors essentially perform $Update$ operations while monitor devices invoke $Scan$ operations.

Acknowledgments. This work is funded by the project "Immersive Virtual, Augmented and Mixed Reality Center of Epirus" (MIS 5047221) implemented under the Action "Reinforcement of the Research and Innovation Infrastructure", funded by the Operational Programme "Competitiveness, Entrepreneurship and Innovation" (NSRF 2014-2020) and co-financed by Greece and the European Union (European Regional Development Fund). We further thankfully acknowledge the support of the European Commission and the Greek General Secretariat for Research and Innovation under the EuroHPC Research and Innovation Programme through project EUROCC2 (Grant Agreement No 101101903).

References

1. Añez, J., De La Barra, T., Pérez, B.: Dual graph representation of transport networks. Transp. Res. Part B: Methodological **30**(3), 209–216 (1996)

2. Aspnes, J., Herlihy, M.: Wait-free data structures in the asynchronous pram model. In: Proceedings of the Second Annual ACM Symposium on Parallel Algorithms and Architectures, pp. 340–349. SPAA 1990, ACM, New York, NY, USA (1990)
3. Attiya, H., Guerraoui, R., Ruppert, E.: Partial snapshot objects. In: Proceedings of the Twentieth Annual Symposium on Parallelism in Algorithms and Architectures, pp. 336–343. SPAA 2008, ACM, New York, NY, USA (2008)
4. Attiya, H., Herlihy, M., Rachman, O.: Atomic snapshots using lattice agreement. Distrib. Comput. **8**(3), 121–132 (1995)
5. Attiya, H., Lynch, N., Shavit, N.: Are wait-free algorithms fast? J. ACM **41**(4), 725–763 (1994)
6. Bar-Nissan, G., Hendler, D., Suissa, A.: A dynamic elimination-combining stack algorithm. CoRR abs/1106.6304 (2011). http://arxiv.org/abs/1106.6304
7. Bashari, B., Woelfel, P.: An efficient adaptive partial snapshot implementation. In: Proceedings of the 2021 ACM Symposium on Principles of Distributed Computing, pp. 545–555. PODC 2021, ACM, New York, NY, USA (2021)
8. Brown, T., Ellen, F., Ruppert, E.: A general technique for non-blocking trees. In: Proceedings of the 19th ACM SIGPLAN Symposium on Principles and Practice of Parallel Programming, pp. 329–342. PPoPP 2014, ACM, New York, NY, USA (2014)
9. Bulitko, V., Björnsson, Y., Sturtevant, N.R., Lawrence, R.: Real-time heuristic search fo Pathfinding in Video Games. In: González-Calero, P., Gómez-Martín, M. (eds.) Artificial Intelligence for Computer Games, pp. 1–30. Springer, New York (2011). https://doi.org/10.1007/978-1-4419-8188-2_1
10. Fatourou, P., Kallimanis, N.D.: Single-scanner multi-writer snapshot implementations are fast! In: Proceedings of the Twenty-fifth Annual ACM Symposium on Principles of Distributed Computing, pp. 228–237 (2006)
11. Fatourou, P., Kallimanis, N.D.: Time-optimal, space-efficient single-scanner snapshots & multi-scanner snapshots using CAS. In: Proceedings of the Twenty-Sixth Annual ACM Symposium on Principles of Distributed Computing, pp. 33–42. PODC 2007, ACM, New York, NY, USA (2007)
12. Fatourou, P., Kallimanis, N.D.: Highly-efficient wait-free synchronization. Theor. Comput. Sys. **55**(3), 475–520 (2014)
13. Fatourou, P., Kallimanis, N.D.: Lower and upper bounds for single-scanner snapshot implementations. Distrib. Comput. **30**(4), 231–260 (2017)
14. Gawlick, R., Lynch, N., Shavit, N.: Concurrent timestamping made simple. In: Dolev, D., Galil, Z., Rodeh, M. (eds.) Theor. Comput. Syst., pp. 171–183. Springer, Berlin Heidelberg, Berlin, Heidelberg (1992)
15. Imbs, D., Raynal, M.: Help when needed, but no more: efficient read/write partial snapshot. J. Parallel Distrib. Comput. **72**(1), 1–12 (2012)
16. Jayanti, P.: F-arrays: implementation and applications. In: Proceedings of the Twenty-First Annual Symposium on Principles of Distributed Computing, pp. 270–279. PODC 2002, ACM, New York, NY, USA (2002)
17. Jayanti, P.: An optimal multi-writer snapshot algorithm. In: Proceedings of the Thirty-Seventh Annual ACM Symposium on Theory of Computing, pp. 723–732. STOC 2005, ACM, New York, NY, USA (2005)
18. Jayanti, P., Petrovic, S.: Logarithmic-time single deleter, multiple inserter wait-free queues and stacks. In: Sarukkai, S., Sen, S. (eds.) FSTTCS 2005. LNCS, vol. 3821, pp. 408–419. Springer, Heidelberg (2005). https://doi.org/10.1007/11590156_33
19. Johannes, F.M.: Partitioning of VLSI circuits and systems. In: Proceedings of the 33rd Annual Design Automation Conference, pp. 83–87. DAC 1996, ACM, New York, NY, USA (1996)

20. Kallimanis, N.D., Kanellou, E.: Wait-free concurrent graph objects with dynamic traversals. In: 19th International Conference on Principles of Distributed Systems (OPODIS 2015). Leibniz International Proceedings in Informatics (LIPIcs), vol. 46, pp. 1–17. Dagstuhl, Germany (2016)
21. Kallimanis, N.D., Kanellou, E., Kiosterakis, C.: Efficient partial snapshot implementations (2020)
22. Kirousis, L.M., Spirakis, P., Tsigas, P.: Reading many variables in one atomic operation: solutions with linear or sublinear complexity. IEEE Trans. Parallel Distrib. Syst. **5**(7), 688–696 (1994)
23. Kogan, A., Petrank, E.: Wait-free queues with multiple enqueuers and dequeuers. ACM SIGPLAN Not. **46**, 223–234 (2011)
24. Riany, Y., Shavit, N., Touitou, D.: Towards a practical snapshot algorithm. Theoret. Comput. Sci. **269**(1), 163–201 (2001)
25. Timnat, S., Braginsky, A., Kogan, A., Petrank, E.: Wait-free linked-lists. In: Baldoni, R., Flocchini, P., Binoy, R. (eds.) OPODIS 2012. LNCS, vol. 7702, pp. 330–344. Springer, Heidelberg (2012). https://doi.org/10.1007/978-3-642-35476-2_23

Brief Announcement: Non-blocking Dynamic Unbounded Graphs with Wait-Free Snapshot

Gaurav Bhardwaj(✉), Sathya Peri, and Pratik Shetty

Indian Institute of Technology, Hyderabad, India
{CS19RESCH11003,ai21mtech12005}@iith.ac.in, sathya_p@cse.iith.ac.in

Abstract. In this paper, we have implemented a dynamic unbounded concurrent graph which can perform the add, delete or lookup operations on vertices and edges concurrently and are linearizable. In addition to these operations, we also have a wait-free graph snapshot method. To the best of our knowledge, we are the first to develop a wait-free graph snapshot algorithm.

Keywords: Graphs · Snapshot · Lock-Free · Wait-Free

1 Introduction

Graph data structure have several real-life applications such as blockchains, maps, machine learning applications, biological networks, social networks, etc. A paired entity relation in a graph displays the relationship and structure between the objects. Social networks, for instance, use graphs to depict user relationships, which aids in making suggestions, spotting trends, and forecasting user behaviour. Over other data structures like linked lists, hash tables, trees, etc., graphs have a significant advantage in terms of application domains, making graph problem solving a major area of research.

Due to these practical applications, there has been a lot of interest on concurrent graph implementations [1,2,5]. Most of these implementations support two kinds of operations: (a) *graph-point* methods, which are adding/removing/looking-up vertices/edges on the graph. These operations can be considered as operating on one (or two) vertex points of interest. (b) *graph-set* method(s), which involves taking a partial or complete snapshot of the graph. graph-set operation consider and collect several vertices. We use the term graph-set and snapshot interchangeably.

It has been observed that constructing (partial) snapshots of a dynamic, concurrent graph efficiently is an important problem which can be used for various graph analytics operations as shown by [1]. Among the various concurrent graph structures proposed in the literature, none support *wait-free*[1] snapshot construction for unbounded graphs.

[1] A progress condition in which every thread invoking a method will complete in finite number of steps [4].

S. Dolev and B. Schieber (Eds.): SSS 2023, LNCS 14310, pp. 106–110, 2023.
https://doi.org/10.1007/978-3-031-44274-2_9

1.1 Our Contribution

This paper addresses this shortcoming by developing a concurrent graph structure that supports wait-free snapshot construction while the graph-point methods are lock-free. To illustrate the usefulness of the snapshot constructed, we use it to compute analytics operations Betweenness Centrality (BC) and Diameter (DIA).

Our solution is an extension of Chatterjee et al.'s [2] concurrent framework for unbounded graphs. We extend their graph-point methods for constructing a wait-free snapshot of the graph, which is based on the snapshot algorithm of Petrank and Timnat [6] developed for iterators.

2 Preliminaries and ADT

We created a concurrent lock-free graph data structure that maintains the vertices and edges in an adjacency list format inspired by Chatterjee et al's [2] implementation. The adjacency lists are maintained as lock-free linked lists.

In addition to the graph-point methods of [2], our implementation supports the following graph-set methods:

1. **Snapshot**: Given a graph G, returns a consistent state of the graph.
2. **Diameter**: Given a graph G, returns the shortest path with respect to the total number of edges traversed for two farthest nodes from all pair of vertices $u, v \in V$.
3. **Betweenness Centrality**: Given a graph G, returns a vertex which lies most frequently in the shortest path of all pair of vertices $u, v \in V$.

2.1 The Abstract Data Type (ADT)

We define an *ADT* $\mathcal{A}$ to be the collection of operations: $\mathcal{A}$ = ADDVERTEX, REMOVEVERTEX, CONTAINSVERTEX, ADDEDGE, REMOVEEDGE, CONTAINSEDGE, SNAP, BETWEENCENTRALITY, DIAMETER.

1. ADDVERTEX (v): adds a vertex v to V ($V \leftarrow V \cup v$) if $v \notin V$ and returns `VERTEXADDED`. If $v \in V$ then returns `VERTEX ALREADY PRESENT`.
2. REMOVEVERTEX (v): removes a vertex v from V if $v \in V$ and returns `VERTEXREMOVED`. If $v \notin V$ then returns `VERTEX NOT PRESENT`.
3. CONTAINSVERTEX (v): returns `VERTEX PRESENT` if $v \in V$ otherwise returns `VERTEX NOT PRESENT`.
4. ADDEDGE (u,v): returns `VERTEX NOT PRESENT` if $u \notin V \vee v \notin V$. If edge $e(u, v) \in E$, it returns `EDGE PRESENT` otherwise, it adds an edge $e(u, v)$ to E ($E \leftarrow E \cup e(u.v)$) and returns `EDGE ADDED`.
5. REMOVEEDGE (u,v): returns `VERTEX NOT PRESENT` if $u \notin V \vee v \notin V$. If edge $e(u, v) \notin E$, it returns `EDGE NOT PRESENT`; otherwise, it removes the edge $e(u, v)$ from E ($E \leftarrow E - e(u, v)$) and returns `EDGE REMOVED`.
6. CONTAINSEDGE (u,v): returns `VERTEX NOT PRESENT` if $u \notin V \vee v \notin V$. If edge $e(u, v) \notin E$, it returns `EDGENOTPRESENT` otherwise, it returns `EDGE PRESENT`.

7. SNAP: returns the previously described consistent snapshot of the graph.
8. BETWEENCENTRALITY: returns the Between Centrality of Graph G as described above.
9. DIAMETER: returns Diameter of graph G as mentioned above.

3 Design and Algorithm

We utilised the same graph structure of adjacency lists with lock-free linked lists as Chatterjee et al. [2] employed. We have separated the operations into two categories for clarity: a) graph-point operation and b) graph-set operation. Graph-point operations are comparable to those implemented by Chatterjee et al. [2], with modest adjustments to allow for more advanced wait-free graph analytics procedures. Graph-set operation necessitates a consistent snapshot of the graph, which is inspired by Timnak and Shavit's [7] iterative wait-free snapshot approach.

3.1 Graph Point Operations

We used the lock-free linked list [3] structure for defining the graph's nodes and edges. Vertices are linked lists, and each vertex is connected to the edge linked list. We modified the graph-point operation compared to the version of Chatterjee et al. [2] because we forward the value to the concurrent ongoing snapshot operation for each graph-point operation. When a point operation reads or updates a vertex or an edge, the value is forwarded to the concurrent snapshot operation for the consistent snapshot.

3.2 Graph Snapshot Operation

Timnak inspires our graph snapshot and Shavit's [7] iterator snapshot algorithm. We used the same forwarding principle, where we forward the value as reports to the snapshot operation if some concurrent snapshot operation occurs. The snapshot procedure initially gathers all the graph elements by traversing all its components. Meanwhile, all concurrent graph-point operations transfer the values of the element they act on to the snapshot method. After gathering all the data, items from the graph are added or removed based on the reports obtained during that period to generate a consistent picture.

4 Experiments and Results

Platform Configuration: We conducted our experiments on a system with Intel(R) Xeon(R) Gold 6230R CPU packing 52 cores with a clock speed of 2.10 GHz. There are two logical threads for each core, each core with a private 32 KB L1 and 1024 KB L2 cache. The 36608KB L3 cache is shared across the cores. The system has 376 GB of RAM and 1 TB of hard disk. It runs on a 64-bit Linux operating system.

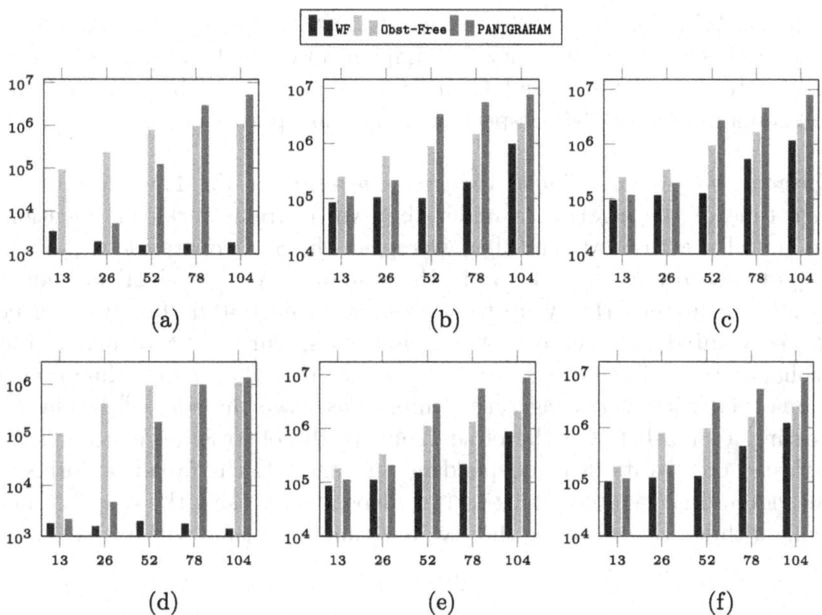

Fig. 1. Performance of our implementation compared to its counterparts. x-axis: Number of threads. y-axis: Average Time taken in microseconds.(a) Read Heavy workload with snapshot, (b) Read Heavy workload with Diameter, (c) Read Heavy workload with Betweenness Centrality, (d) Update Heavy with snapshot, (e) Update Heavy with Diameter, (f) Update Heavy with Betweenness Centrality.

Experimental Setup: All implementations are in C++ without garbage collection. We used Posix threads for multi-threaded implementation. We initially populated the graph with uniformly distributed synthetic data of 10K nodes and 20K edges for the experiments. In all our experiments, we have considered all the point operations AddVertex, RemoveVertex, ContainsVertex, AddEdge, RemoveEdge, ContainsEdge from ADT and one of the graph analytics operations from Snap, BetweenCentrality and Diameter. The evaluation metric used is the average time taken to complete each operation. We measure the average time w.r.t increasing spawned threads.

Workload Distribution : The distribution is over the following ordered set of Operations (AddVertex, RemoveVertex, ContainsEdge, AddEdge, RemoveEdge, ContainsEdge, and Critical Operation(Snap/ Diameter/ BetweenCentrality).

1. Read Heavy Workload : 3%, 2%, 45%, 3%, 2%, 45% , 2%
2. Update Heavy Workload: 12%, 13%, 25%, 13%, 12%, 25% , 2%

Algorithms : We compare our wait-free Snap/ Diameter/ BetweenCentrality approaches to the obstruction-free implementation of the same operations using Chatterjee et al. [2], and Chatterjee et al. [1]. We have named them `Obst-Free` and `PANIGRAHAM`, respectively, and our approach as `WF`.

Performance for various Graph Analytics Operation In Fig. 1, we compare the average time of the algorithms under the two different workloads mentioned above. Initially, with Snap, and then we replace the Snap operation with Diameter and BetweenCentrality. In the case of Snap, our algorithm outperforms all its counterparts by up to two orders of magnitude because if a new thread is required to execute Snap, it assists the current Snap if it is there and collaboratively finds the Snap. Thus we see that the average time remains the same even with increasing active threads as more threads will be involved in creating a snapshot. On the other hand, in the obstruction-free algorithm, each thread creates its own independent Snapshot. Each thread performs the Diameter and BetweenCentrality independently using the snapshot in all three algorithms. Hence we see the Average time increasing with threads.

References

1. Chatterjee, B., Peri, S., Sa, M., Manogna, K.: Non-blocking dynamic unbounded graphs with worst-case amortized bounds. In: International Conference on Principles of Distributed Systems (2021)
2. Chatterjee, B., Peri, S., Sa, M., Singhal, N.: A simple and practical concurrent non-blocking unbounded graph with linearizable reachability queries. In: ICDCN 2019, Bangalore, India, 04–07 January 2019, pp. 168–177 (2019)
3. Harris, T.L.: A pragmatic implementation of non-blocking linked-lists. In: Welch, J. (ed.) DISC 2001. LNCS, vol. 2180, pp. 300–314. Springer, Heidelberg (2001). https://doi.org/10.1007/3-540-45414-4_21
4. Herlihy, M., Shavit, N.: On the nature of progress. In: OPODIS, pp. 313–328 (2011)
5. Kallimanis, N.D., Kanellou, E.: Wait-free concurrent graph objects with dynamic traversals. In: OPODIS, pp. 1–27 (2015)
6. Petrank, E., Timnat, S.: Lock-free data-structure iterators. In: Afek, Y. (ed.) DISC 2013. LNCS, vol. 8205, pp. 224–238. Springer, Heidelberg (2013). https://doi.org/10.1007/978-3-642-41527-2_16
7. Timnat, S., Braginsky, A., Kogan, A., Petrank, E.: Wait-free linked-lists. In: OPODIS, pp. 330–344 (2012)

Byzantine Fault-Tolerant Causal Order Satisfying Strong Safety

Anshuman Misra and Ajay D. Kshemkalyani[✉]

University of Illinois at Chicago, Chicago, IL 60607, USA
{amisra7,ajay}@uic.edu

Abstract. Causal ordering is an important building block for distributed software systems. It was recently proved that it is impossible to provide causal ordering – liveness and strong safety – using a deterministic non-cryptographic algorithm in the presence of even a single Byzantine process in an asynchronous system for unicast, multicast, and broadcast modes of communication. Strong safety is critical for real-time distributed collaborative software such as multiplayer gaming and social media networks. In this paper, we solve the causal ordering problem under the strong safety condition in the presence of Byzantine processes by relaxing the problem specification in two ways. First, we propose a deterministic algorithm for causal ordering of unicasts in a synchronous system that also uses threshold cryptography. Second, we propose a (probabilistic) algorithm based on randomization for causal ordering of multicasts in an asynchronous system that also uses threshold cryptography. These algorithms complement the previous impossibility result for the asynchronous system.

Keywords: Causal Order · Message Passing · Byzantine Fault-Tolerance · Distributed Systems · Multicast

1 Introduction

Many distributed applications rely on causal ordering of messages for correct semantics [2,14,15]. Algorithms for providing causal ordering have been proposed over nearly the last four decades. Causal ordering requires that liveness (each message sent by a correct process to another correct process is eventually delivered) and strong safety (if the send event for message m_1 happens before the send event for message m_2 and both messages are sent to the same correct process(es), no correct process delivers m_2 before m_1) are satisfied.

It was recently proved that it is impossible to provide causal ordering – liveness and strong safety – (using a deterministic algorithm) in the presence of even a single Byzantine process in an asynchronous system for unicast, multicast, and broadcast modes of communication in a system model that does not allow cryptography [21,22]. In light of this result, algorithms for Byzantine-tolerant causal ordering under the synchronous system model that satisfy liveness and

S. Dolev and B. Schieber (Eds.): SSS 2023, LNCS 14310, pp. 111–125, 2023.
https://doi.org/10.1007/978-3-031-44274-2_10

a weaker notion of safety, namely *weak safety*, wherein there is path from the send event of m_1 to the send event of m_2 passing through only correct processes, were proposed [19,21]. These algorithms were for unicast, multicast, as well as broadcast modes of communication. For the broadcast mode of communication, a Byzantine-tolerant causal ordering algorithm for asynchronous systems was proposed in [1] – this satisfies liveness and weak safety but no strong safety as shown in [21]. Previously, a probabilistic algorithm based on atomic (total order) broadcast and cryptography for secure causal atomic broadcast (liveness and strong safety) in an asynchronous system was proposed [5]. This logic used acknowledgements and effectively processed the atomic broadcasts serially. More recently for the client-server configuration, two protocols for crash failures and a third for Byzantine failure of clients based on cryptography were proposed for secure causal atomic broadcast [9]. The third made assumptions on latency of messages, and hence works only in a synchronous system.

Main Contributions: The impossibility result given in [22] showed a reduction from consensus to causal ordering, and the FLP impossibility result for consensus [11] implied the impossibility of causal ordering using a deterministic algorithm in an asynchronous system. Solving consensus is equivalent to or mutually reducible to solving the atomic broadcast problem [24], and both are impossible using deterministic algorithms in an asynchronous system. In this paper, we overcome the impossibility result of [21,22] mentioned above. We solve the causal ordering problem in the presence of Byzantine processes by relaxing the system assumptions in two ways.

1. First, we weaken the asynchrony assumption and propose an algorithm to solve the causal ordering problem under the strong safety condition for unicasts in a synchronous system that also uses threshold cryptography.
2. Second, we propose an algorithm based on atomic broadcast in an asynchronous system having Byzantine processes; the algorithm also uses threshold cryptography. Solving consensus is equivalent to or mutually reducible to solving the atomic broadcast problem [6,18], and both are impossible using deterministic algorithms in an asynchronous system. However, atomic broadcasts, i.e., total order broadcasts, can be solved (in the presence of Byzantine processes) only using probabilistic algorithms in an asynchronous system [5,7,12,16]. Our second algorithm for causal ordering uses a source-order preserving total order broadcast primitive as a lower layer interface. It uses threshold cryptography similar to the way it is used in [5] for secure causal atomic broadcast but does not use acknowledgements and is not constrained to process the atomic broadcasts serially, thus there is no concurrency inhibition. Our algorithm is presented for the multicast mode of communication and we show how it can be modified to unicast and broadcast modes which are special cases of multicast mode.

Our algorithms complement the previous impossibility result for the asynchronous system. The main contribution of this paper is to develop efficient causal ordering algorithms that provide *strong safety* in the presence of Byzantine processes. These algorithms bypass the impossibility result proved in [21,22], which states that it is impossible to provide Byzantine-tolerant strong safety in the absence of cryptographic protocols. This is a critical result from the perspective of real-world distributed applications because weak safety cannot guarantee correct functioning of applications. For example, in a multiplayer online gaming scenario utilizing a weak safety protocol for causal ordering, Byzantine players can order their events ahead of correct players' events despite having causal dependencies on the correct players' events leading to unfair advantages in gameplay. However, by using a strong safety causal ordering algorithm, the gaming application can ensure fair gameplay. Similar situations can arise in social media networks (message ordering presented to users in a single message thread), collaborative group editing of documents (updates to documents need to ensure causality across updates regardless of whether the update comes from a correct/Byzantine user) among other distributed applications.

Outline: Section 2 gives the system model. Section 3 reviews some basic cryptography used in our algorithms. Section 4 reviews the specifications of Byzantine-tolerant reliable multicast/broadcast and Byzantine-tolerant atomic broadcast. Section 5 gives the algorithm for Byzantine-tolerant causal order of unicasts in a synchronous system. Section 6 gives the algorithm for Byzantine-tolerant causal order of multicasts in an asynchronous system. Section 7 concludes.

2 System Model

This paper deals with a distributed system having Byzantine processes which are processes that can misbehave [17,23]. A correct process behaves exactly as specified by the algorithm whereas a Byzantine process may exhibit arbitrary behaviour including crashing at any point during the execution. A Byzantine process cannot impersonate another process or spawn new processes.

The distributed system is modelled as an undirected graph $G = (P, H)$. Here P is the set of processes communicating asynchronously in the distributed system. Let n be $|P|$. H is the set of FIFO logical communication links over which processes communicate by message passing. G is a complete graph.

The system is first assumed to be synchronous, i.e., there is a known fixed upper bound δ on the message latency, and a known fixed upper bound ψ on the relative speeds of processors [10]. We provide a deterministic causal ordering unicast algorithm for this system model. Next, we assume an asynchronous system, i.e., there is no upper bound δ on the message latency, nor any upper bound ψ on the relative speeds of processors [10]. We provide a non-deterministic causal ordering multicast algorithm for this system model.

Definition 1. *The happens before relation $\rightarrow$ on messages consists of the following rules:*

1. *The set of messages delivered from any $p_i \in P$ by a process is totally ordered by $\rightarrow$.*
2. *If p_i sent or delivered message m before sending message m', then $m \rightarrow m'$.*

3. *If* $m \rightarrow m'$ *and* $m' \rightarrow m''$, *then* $m \rightarrow m''$.

Let R denote the set of messages in the execution.

Definition 2. *The causal past of message* m *is denoted as* $CP(m)$ *and defined as the set of messages in* R *that causally precede message* m *under* $\rightarrow$.

The correctness of Byzantine causal order unicast/multicast/broadcast is specified on $(R, \rightarrow)$ for strong safety.

Definition 3. *A causal ordering algorithm for unicast/multicast/broadcast messages must ensure the following:*

1. ***Strong Safety:*** $\forall m' \in CP(m)$ *such that* m' *and* m *are sent to the same (correct) process(es), no correct process delivers* m *before* m'.
2. ***Liveness:*** *Each message sent by a correct process to another correct process will be eventually delivered.*

3 Some Cryptographic Basics

We utilize non-interactive threshold cryptography as a means to guarantee strong safety [25]. Threshold cryptography consists of an initialization function to generate keys, message encryption, sharing decrypted shares of the message and finally combining the decrypted shares to obtain the original message from ciphertext. The following functions are used in a threshold cryptographic scheme:

Definition 4. *The dealer executes the generate() function to obtain the public key* PK, *Verification key* VK *and the private keys* SK_1, SK_2, ... , SK_n.

The dealer shares private key SK_i with each process p_i while PK and VK are publicly available.

Definition 5. *When process* p_i *wants to send a message* m *to* p_j, *it executes* $E(PK, m, L)$ *to obtain* C_m. *Here* C_m *is the ciphertext corresponding to* m, E *is the encryption algorithm and* L *is a label to identify* m. p_i *then broadcasts* C_m *to the system of processes.*

Definition 6. *When process* p_l *receives ciphertext* C_m, *it executes* $D(SK_l, C_m)$ *to obtain* σ_l^m *where* D *is the decryption share generation algorithm and* σ_l^m *is* p_l*'s decryption share for message* m.

When process p_j receives a cipher message C_m intended for it, it has to wait for k decryption shares to arrive from the system to obtain m. The value of k depends on the security properties of the system. It derives the message from the ciphertext as follows:

Definition 7. *When process* p_j *wants to generate the original message* m *from ciphertext* C_m, *it executes* $C(VK, C_m, S)$ *where* S *is a set of* k *decryption shares for* m *and* C *is the combining algorithm for the* k *decryption shares that gives* m.

The following function V is used to verify the authenticity of a decryption share:

Definition 8. *When a decryption share σ is received for message m, the Share Verification Algorithm is used to ascertain whether σ is authentic:*
$V(VK, C_m, \sigma) = 1$ *if σ is authentic,* $V(VK, C_m, \sigma) = 0$ *if σ is not authentic.*

4 Reliable Broadcast and Atomic (Total Order) Broadcast Properties

The multicast algorithm for asynchronous systems that we propose assumes access to a BA_broadcast primitive that provides Byzantine-tolerant total order and delivers a broadcast message via BA_deliver.

Definition 9. *Byzantine-tolerant atomic (total order) broadcast provides the following guarantees [7,8,12,13,16,24]:*

1. *(BAB-Validity:) If a correct process* BA_deliver*s a message m from sender-(m), then sender(m) must have* BA_broadcast *m.*
2. *(BAB-Termination-1:) If a correct process* BA_broadcast*s a message m, then it eventually* BA_deliver*s m.*
3. *(BAB-Agreement or BAB-Termination-2:) If a correct process* BA_deliver*s a message m from a possibly faulty process, then all correct processes eventually* BA_deliver *m.*
4. *(BAB-Integrity:) For any message m, every correct process* BA_deliver*s m at most once.*
5. *(BAB-Total-Order:) If correct processes p_i and p_j both* BA_deliver *messages m and m', then p_i* BA_deliver*s m before m' if and only if p_j* BA_deliver*s m before m'.*

This total order primitive also provides source-FIFO order [13], i.e., if a process BA_broadcasts m before m', then m is BA_delivered before m' at all correct processes. As it is impossible to provide Byzantine-tolerant total order using a deterministic algorithm in an asynchronous system due to its equivalence to consensus [5,24], we use a probabilistic algorithm such as in [5,7,12,16].

Byzantine Reliable Broadcast (BRB) [3,4] is invoked via BR_broadcast and delivered via BR_deliver. It is defined similar to Definition 9 minus BAB-Total-Order.

We propose a causal order multicast algorithm for asynchronous systems. In a multicast, a message is sent to a subset of processes forming a process group. Different multicast send events can send to different process groups. Byzantine-tolerant causal multicast is invoked as BC_multicast(m, G), where G is the multicast group, and delivers a message through BC_deliver(m). Based on the reliability properties proposed in the literature for Byzantine Reliable Broadcast [3,4] and Byzantine Causal Broadcast [1], we define Byzantine Causal Multicast as follows.

Definition 10. *Byzantine Causal Multicast satisfies the following properties:*

1. *(BCM-Validity:) If a correct process p_i* BC_delivers *message m from sender(m) to group G, then sender(m) must have* BC_multicast *m to G and $p_i \in G$.*
2. *(BCM-Termination-1:) If a correct process* BC_multicasts *a message m to G, then some correct process in G eventually* BC_delivers *m.*
3. *(BCM-Agreement or BCM-Termination-2:) If a correct process in G* BC_delivers *a message m from a possibly faulty process, then all correct processes in G will eventually deliver m.*
4. *(BCM-Integrity:) For any message m, every correct process in G* BC_delivers *m at most once.*
5. *(BCM-Causal-Order:) If $m \rightarrow m'$, m is sent to G, m' is sent to G', then no correct process in $G \cap G'$* BC_delivers *m' before m.*

BCM-Causal-Order is the Strong Safety property of Definition 3 whereas BCM-Termination-1 and BCM-Agreement imply the liveness property of Definition 3.

Definition 11. *A Byzantine-tolerant causal multicast algorithm must satisfy BCM-Validity, BCM-Termination-1, BCM-Agreement, BCM-Integrity, and BCM-Causal-Order.*

5 Causal Order Unicast in a Synchronous System

In Algorithm 1 we present a causal ordering algorithm guaranteeing strong safety and liveness in the presence of t Byzantine processes for synchronous systems. Algorithm 1 is inherently asynchronous, because it does not assume the expensive and binding notion of rounds. Algorithm 1 requires that key generation and distribution has been accomplished by a trusted dealer prior to start of execution. Therefore, all processes have access to global PK (public key), VK (verification key) and have a local SK_i (secret key). Algorithm 1 assumes that the network provides an upper bound δ on the message transmission time. Algorithm 1 has to prevent Byzantine processes from implementing the following actions:

1. Reading the contents of an incoming message prior to delivering it and sending an outgoing message based on the contents of the undelivered message with the intention of causing a strong safety violation.
2. Sending a message to a correct process with the intention of preventing further messages getting delivered at that process, causing a liveness attack.

When p_i wants to unicast a message m to p_j, it encrypts m with PK and broadcasts the ciphertext C_m along with p_j's id (j) and a globally unique message id id_m to the system. p_j requires $(t+1)$ unique decryption shares from processes in the system to obtain m from C_m. Upon receiving a ciphertext C_m, all processes compute their respective decryption shares σ_x^m. Upon receiving C_m, p_j inserts C_m into its FIFO delivery queue and broadcasts a request for decryption shares.

If the required number of decryption shares do not arrive within $(3\delta + 1)$ time units, p_j will delete C_m from its delivery queue preventing liveness attacks by Byzantine processes. This will be formally proved in Theorem 1.

When a process p_k receives p_j's request for its decryption share for m, it first checks to make sure that p_j is indeed the recipient of m. If that is the case, p_k waits for $(\delta + 1)$ time units and sends σ_k^m to p_j. Once p_j receives the required number of decryption shares, it decrypts C_m and replaces it with m in its delivery queue. When C_m is both decrypted and m is at the head of the queue, it gets delivered when the application is ready to process the next message. The intuitive reasoning for preservation of strong safety by Algorithm 1 is as follows: Since correct processes wait for $(\delta+1)$ time units before sending their decryption shares, a Byzantine process p_k can read a message m at least $(\delta + 1)$ time units after receiving C_m. Hence, any message m' such that $m \rightarrow m'$ that p_k sends to process p_l will arrive at p_l at least 1 time unit after any m'' sent to p_l, where $m'' \rightarrow m \rightarrow m'$. Hence m' will be after m'' in the delivery queue at p_l. This is formally proved in Theorem 2. Algorithm 1 can tolerate upto t Byzantine failures, where the total number of processes, $n > 2t$.

Each message m has a globally unique identifier id_m assigned by the sender. In the Algorithm 1 pseudo-code, technically C_m, σ_i^m, S should be C_{id_m}, $\sigma_i^{id_m}$, S_{id_m} respectively; however to simplify the presentation, we use the first version while keeping in mind that the data structure is to be associated with a particular id_m.

Theorem 1. *All messages sent by a correct process to another correct process via unicast following Algorithm 1 will eventually be delivered even in the presence of Byzantine processes.*

Proof. Consider message m sent by p_i to p_j. p_i executes $broadcast(C_m, j, id_m)$ at line 3, ensuring that all processes receive C_m and compute their respective decryption shares at line 5. Once p_j receives C_m, it pushes C_m into a FIFO queue, starts a timer of $(3\delta + 1)$ time units at lines 6–8. p_j then broadcasts a request for decryption shares to all processes at line 9. The maximum latency for an individual response to this request is the sum of (i) the maximum of the maximum time it takes for the request sent at line 9 to arrive (δ) at a receiver and the maximum time it takes for the broadcast of line 3 to reach the receiver (δ), (ii) the waiting time at the receiver of this request $(\delta + 1)$, and (iii) the maximum latency of the response to p_j (δ). Therefore, p_j will receive decryption share σ_x^m from each correct process p_x within $\max(\delta, \delta) + (\delta + 1) + \delta = (3\delta + 1)$ time units. Since there are at least $(t + 1)$ correct processes, p_j is guaranteed to receive the required $(t + 1)$ decryption shares in line 16 before message m times out (lines 20–22). Therefore, C_m is guaranteed to be decrypted and m is guaranteed to be present in Q (lines 16–19).

A ciphertext $C_{m'}$ present ahead of m in Q at p_j is one of the following:

1. $C_{m'}$ was sent by a Byzantine process p_l. In this case, the required number of decryption shares for $C_{m'}$ in lines 16–20 may not arrive within $(3\delta + 1)$ time

Algorithm 1: Secure Causal Unicast in a Synchronous System

Data: Each process has access to PK (global public key) and VK (global verification key) as well as a local secret key SK_i. Each process maintains a FIFO queue Q for incoming application messages.

1 **when** p_i needs to send application message m to p_j:
2 $C_m = E(PK, m, id_m)$
3 $broadcast(C_m, j, id_m)$

4 **when** $\langle C_m, recipient, id_m \rangle$ arrives at p_i:
5 $\sigma_i^m = D(SK_i, C_m)$
6 **if** $recipient = i$ **then**
7 $\quad Q.push(C_m)$
8 $\quad$ start *timer* set to $3\delta + 1$ for message m
9 $\quad broadcast(request, id_m)$ to $\forall p_x$

10 **when** p_i receives $\langle request, id_m \rangle$ from p_j
11 **if** *C_m has not arrived at p_i* **then**
12 $\quad$ wait for min(δ time units, arrival of C_m) in a non-blocking manner
13 **if** *C_m has arrived $\wedge$ p_j is the recipient of message m* **then**
14 $\quad$ wait for $(\delta + 1)$ time units in a non-blocking manner
15 $\quad$ send(σ_i^m) to p_j

16 **when** p_i receives $(t + 1)$ valid $\langle \sigma_x^m \rangle$ messages:
17 Store $(t + 1)$ decryption shares in set S
18 $m = C(VK, C_m, S)$
19 replace C_m in Q with m

20 **when** any C_m times out in Q:
21 **if** *less than $(t + 1)$ valid decryption shares corresponding to m have arrived* **then**
22 $\quad Q.delete(C_m)$

23 **when** the application is ready to process a message at p_i:
24 **if** *$Q.head()$ is decrypted* **then**
25 $\quad m = Q.pop()$
26 $\quad$ deliver m

units since starting the timer for $C_{m'}$. In this case $C_{m'}$ will be deleted from the queue in lines 20–22, thus ensuring progress.

2. $C_{m'}$ was sent by a correct process p_k. Therefore, within $(3\delta + 1)$ time units since its insertion in Q at p_j, $C_{m'}$ will be decrypted and m' will be present in Q ready to be delivered as p_k and correct processes will follow the protocol.

Combining points 1 and 2, m is guaranteed to reach the head of Q and eventually be delivered in lines 23–26. □

Corollary 1. *Algorithm 1 guarantees liveness.*

Theorem 2. *If $m_1 \rightarrow m_2$ and both messages are sent to the same correct destination process, then Algorithm 1 guarantees that m_2 is not delivered before m_1.*

Proof. Consider messages m_1 and m_2 sent to a correct process p_k where $m_1 \rightarrow m_2$. In order for p_k to ensure causal delivery of m_1 with respect to m_2 (lines 23–26), C_{m_1} must be enqueued in Q before C_{m_2} in lines 4–9. One of the following scenarios must hold:

1. The same process p_i sent both m_1 and m_2. Due to FIFO channels, C_{m_1} will arrive before C_{m_2} at p_k and as a result, get enqueued in Q before C_{m_2}.
2. p_i sent m_1 and p_j sent m_2. As $m_1 \rightarrow m_2$, there must be at least one message hop along the message chain from the sending of m_1 to the sending of m_2. Let the last message along this message chain, which was delivered to p_j, be m^*. A lower bound on the duration between the sending of m_1 and the sending of m_2 is $(\delta + 1)$. This is because C_{m^*} must have resided in the Q at p_j at least for $(\delta + 1)$ time units, the duration that p_j's request is delayed by the correct processes before they send p_j their decryption shares for C_{m^*}, before C_{m^*} is decrypted and delivered to p_j.
   As m_2 is sent at least $(\delta + 1)$ time units after m_1 is sent to the common destination p_k, even if C_{m_1} takes the full δ time units to reach p_k and C_{m_2} takes 0 time units to reach p_k, C_{m_1} will be queued ahead of C_{m_2} in Q at p_k.

As C_{m_1} is enqueued ahead of C_{m_2} in Q at p_k, causal delivery of m_1 with respect to m_2 is guaranteed. □

Corollary 2. *Algorithm 1 guarantees strong safety.*

Corollary 3. *Algorithm 1 satisfies Definition 3 for causal order unicasting.*

Note that the broadcasts in lines 3 and 9 can be replaced by a multicast to a group of size k as long as the upper bound on the number of Byzantine processes in the group satisfies $k \geq 2t + 1$.

Algorithm 1 for unicasts can be adapted for multicast to groups, each group being identified by G_{id_m}, with straightforward modifications (such as replacing j by G_{id_m} in line 3 and replacing "$recipient = i$" by "$i \in G_{id_m}$" in line 6). This adaptation guarantees liveness and strong safety but does not provide the reliability properties (BCM-Validity, BCM-Termination-1, BCM-Agreement, BCM-Integrity). To satisfy these, one could replace the regular broadcast in line 3 by a Byzantine Reliable Broadcast primitive BR_broadcast. However, two messages sent by a process via BR_broadcast are not guaranteed to be delivered in the order they were sent (thus even FIFO order is not guaranteed) [20] or in a total order. Hence, we need to use a different approach for providing reliable causal multicast. A different approach that invokes FIFO-total order broadcast via BA_broadcast, for asynchronous systems in given in Sect. 6. This algorithm in Sect. 6 is a probabilistic algorithm because its BA_broadcast cannot be implemented in an asynchronous system deterministically.

6 Causal Order Multicast for an Asynchronous System

In Algorithm 2 we present a causal ordering algorithm guaranteeing strong safety and liveness in the presence of Byzantine processes for asynchronous systems. Algorithm 2 is a non-deterministic algorithm, complementing the result in [21,22]. Similar to Algorithm 1, Algorithm 2 requires that key generation and distribution has been accomplished by a trusted dealer prior to start of execution. Therefore, all processes have access to global PK (public key), VK (verification key) and have a local SK_i (secret key). In addition to this, all multicast groups share a unique symmetric key for encryption and decryption of messages intended for them. Algorithm 2 *double encrypts* each message, first with the group key (K_G) and then with the system key (PK) and invokes a source-order preserving atomic broadcast on the resulting ciphertext. Upon receiving the ciphertext, all processes compute their respective decryption shares and the recipients of the multicast message enqueue the ciphertext in their respective FIFO delivery queues and broadcast a request to the system for decryption shares. Upon receiving the required number of valid and unique decryption shares, the ciphertext is decrypted to obtain the ciphertext encrypted with the group key. When this ciphertext reaches the head of the delivery queue it is decrypted with the group key to obtain the original message and delivered to the application. The number of Byzantine failures that Algorithm 2 can tolerate is dependent on the tolerance of the atomic broadcast primitive used. The requirement for atomic broadcast is typically $n > 3t$.

Each message m has a globally unique identifier id_m assigned by the sender. In the Algorithm 2 pseudo-code, technically C_m, C'_m, σ_i^m, S should be C_{id_m},C'_{id_m}, $\sigma_i^{id_m}$, S_{id_m} respectively; however to simplify the presentation, we use the first version while keeping in mind that the data structure is to be associated with a particular id_m.

Lemma 1. *(***Process Order:***) If a process* BA_broadcast*s* m_1 *before it* BA_-broadcast*s* m_2*, i.e.,* $m_1 \rightarrow m_2$*, and if some correct process is* BA_deliver*ed* m_1 *and* m_2*, then all correct processes are* BA_deliver*ed* m_1 *before* m_2*.*

Proof. Follows from the source-FIFO ordering property of BA_broadcast. □

Lemma 2. *(***Message Order:***) If a (correct or Byzantine) process* BA_broadcast*s message* m_2 *after it* BA_deliver*s, decrypts, and dequeues* m_1*, i.e.,* $m_1 \rightarrow m_2$*, then no correct process* BA_deliver*s* m_2 *before it* BA_deliver*s* m_1*.*

Proof. When a process p_x BA_delivers, decrypts, and dequeues m_1, it must have received a decryption share $\sigma_x^{m_1}$ from at least one correct process p_c which implies that at least one correct process p_c must have already BA_delivered m_1. By BAB-Agreement, all correct processes BA_deliver m_1. The correct process p_c will necessarily never have BA_delivered m_2 before it has BA_delivered m_1. From the BAB-Agreement property, if m_2 is BA_delivered to any correct process, it will necessarily be BA_delivered to all correct processes including p_c. At p_c, m_2 will be BA_delivered after m_1. Therefore by the BAB-Total-Ordering property, m_2 will be BA_delivered after m_1 at all correct processes. □

Algorithm 2: Asynchronous Secure Causal Multicast

Data: Each process has access to PK (global public key) and VK (global verification key) as well as a local secret key SK_i. Each process maintains a FIFO queue Q for incoming application messages. All processes in a multicast group G locally store the group key K_G.

1 **when** p_i has to send m to G_{id_m} via BC_multicast(m, G_{id_m}):
2 $C'_m = Enc(K_{G_{id_m}}, m)$
3 $C_m = E(PK, C'_m, id_m)$
4 BA_broadcast(C_m, G_{id_m}, id_m)

5 **when** $\langle C_m, G_{id_m}, id_m \rangle$ arrives at p_i via BA_deliver():
6 $\sigma_i^m = D(SK_i, C_m)$
7 **if** $p_i \in G_{id_m}$ **then**
8     $Q.push(C_m)$
9     $broadcast(request, id_m)$ to $\forall p_x$

10 **when** p_i receives $\langle request, id_m \rangle$ from p_j:
11 **while** *C_m has not arrived at p_i* **do**
12   wait in a non-blocking manner
13 **if** $p_j \in G_{id_m}$ **then**
14   send(σ_i^m) to p_j

15 **when** p_i receives $(t+1)$ valid $\langle \sigma_x^m \rangle$ messages:
16 Store $(t+1)$ decryption shares in set S
17 $C'_m = C(VK, C_m, S)$
18 replace C_m in Q with C'_m

19 **when** the application is ready to process a message at p_i:
20 **if** *$Q.head()$ has been decrypted using decryption shares* **then**
21     $C'_m = Q.pop()$
22     $m = Dec(K_{G_{id_m}}, C'_m)$ using group key $K_{G_{id_m}}$
23   BC_deliver(m)

Theorem 3. *Algorithm 2 guarantees BCM-Validity, BCM-Termination-1, BCM-Agreement, BCM-Integrity and BCM-Causal-Order in the presence of Byzantine processes.*

Proof. 1. (BCM-Validity:) An incoming message m at a correct process p_i sent to group G_{id_m} is enqueued, double-decrypted, dequeued and BC_delivered only if (i) p_i belongs to G_{id_m}, and (ii) the (double-encrypted) message was BA_delivered. This follows from the pseudo-code. As m was BA_delivered, by BAB-Validity, it must also have been BA_broadcast by $sender(m)$ with parameter G_{id_m}. Therefore, a message m can be BC_delivered at p_i only if it is BC_multicasted in lines 1–4 by $sender(m)$ to G_{id_m} via BA_broadcast after double-encryption and $p_i \in G_{id_m}$.

2. (BCM-Termination-1:) Consider message m BC_multicast by a correct process p_i to group G_{id_m}. p_i executes BA_broadcast(C_m, G_{id_m}, id_m) at line 4, ensuring via its properties of BAB-Termination-1 and BAB-Agreement that all correct processes receive C_m via BA_deliver and compute their respective decryption shares at lines 5–6. Once $p_j \in G_{id_m}$ receives C_m via BA_deliver, it pushes C_m into a FIFO queue at lines 5–9. p_j then broadcasts a request for decryption shares to all processes at line 9. p_j will receive decryption share σ_x^m from each correct process p_x eventually, once p_x has also BA_delivered C_m and computed its decryption share. Since there are $(2t+1)$ correct processes, p_j is guaranteed to receive the required $(t+1)$ decryption shares in line 15. Therefore, C_m is guaranteed to be decrypted and C'_m is guaranteed to be present in Q (lines 15–18). The encryption of m using the group key $K_{G_{id_m}}$ in line 2 and its corresponding decryption in line 22 ensures that only members of group G_{id_m} can access the content of C'_m.
   A ciphertext $C_{m'}$ present ahead of C'_m in Q at p_j may have been sent via BA_broadcast by a Byzantine process or by a correct process. Irrespective of this, as $C_{m'}$ has been BA_delivered to (correct) process p_j, by the BAB-Agreement property of BA_broadcast it ($C_{m'}$) would also have been BA_delivered to all at least $2t+1$ correct processes p_x which would compute their decryption share $\sigma_x^{m'}$ in line 6 and reply to p_j's request broadcast in line 9 with the decryption share $\sigma_x^{m'}$ in line 14. Thus p_j is guaranteed to get $(t+1)$ decryption shares and decrypt $C_{m'}$ to $C'_{m'}$ which can then get popped from Q after its double-decryption using its group key $K_{G_{id_{m'}}}$. This allows C'_m to be at *head*(Q) and get processed when popped (lines 19 to 23). Therefore, any message enqueued in the delivery queue will eventually reach the head of the queue. This means m is guaranteed to reach the head of Q and eventually be BC_delivered in lines 19–23 ensuring BCM-Termination-1.
3. (BCM-Agreement:) If a correct process $p_i \in G_{id_m}$ BC_delivers a message m, it means that C_m was BA_delivered in lines 5–9. By the BAB-Agreement property of BA_broadcast, this means that all correct processes in the system BA_deliver C_m, compute their respective decryption shares and push C_m in their respective delivery queues if they are part of G_{id_m}. Therefore, if there exists another correct process $p_j \in G_{id_m}$, it will receive C_m via BA_delivery and insert C_m in its delivery queue. From the reasoning for BCM-Termination-1 given in the above item, we know that any message enqueued in the delivery queue eventually reaches the head of the queue. Therefore, C_m will eventually reach the head of the queue. Additionally, between lines 10–18, p_j will receive $(t+1)$ decryption shares required to decrypt C_m in the queue since there are $(2t+1)$ correct processes in the system. Therefore, m is guaranteed to be BC_delivered at p_i and any correct p_j in G_{id_m} in lines 19–23, thereby guaranteeing BCM-Agreement.
4. (BCM-Integrity:) By the BAB-Integrity property of BA_broadcast a message is BA_delivered at most once at a correct process. Therefore any incoming message will be enqueued (lines 5–9) and dequeued from the delivery queue

(lines 19–23) at most once at a correct process. Hence, any given message m will be BC_delivered at most once at a correct process.

5. (BCM-Causal-Order:) Consider multicast messages m and m' sent by p_x and p_y to groups containing a correct process p_k, where $m \longrightarrow m'$. Then there must exist a message chain $\langle m_0, m_1, m_2, \ldots m_{z-1}, m_z = m' \rangle$ such that (i) m_0 was sent (via BA_broadcast) by $p_{i_0} = p_x$ after it sent m (via BA_broadcast), (ii) m_{a-1} for $a \in [1, z]$ was BA_delivered, decrypted, and dequeued (BC_delivered) by p_{i_a} before p_{i_a} sent m_a (by executing BA_broadcast), and (iii) $p_{i_z} = p_y$.
Let p_k BA_deliver m and m'. Further, all correct processes BA_deliver m_{a-1} and m_a, for $a \in [1, z]$. By Lemma 1 (*Process Order*), $m \longrightarrow m_0$ and all correct processes will BA_deliver m_0 after m. By Lemma 2 (*Message Order*), $m_{b-1} \longrightarrow m_b$, for $b \in [1, z]$, hence all correct processes will BA_deliver m_{b-1} before m_b. Hence by transitivity, it follows that all correct processes will BA_deliver m before $m_z = m'$. As p_k is a common member of multicast groups addressed by m and m', it will enqueue m, i.e., C_m, before m', i.e., $C_{m'}$ in Q. This ensures that m will be dequeued and delivered before m', thus satisfying BCM-Causal-Order.

□

Corollary 4. *Algorithm 2 guarantees Byzantine-tolerant causal order multicast as per Definition 11.*

Since Algorithm 2 guarantees BCM-Termination-1 and BCM-Agreement, it implicitly guarantees liveness. Algorithm 2 explicitly guarantees Strong Safety because it guarantees BCM-Causal-Order.

Corollary 5. *Algorithm 2 satisfies Definition 3 for causal order multicasting.*

6.1 Adaptations to Special Cases

Asynchronous System, Unicast: The encryption in line 2 and corresponding decryption in line 22 are done using the symmetric key K_{ij} when p_i is sending to p_j. In line 4, the second parameter of BA_broadcast is j and in line 5, the second parameter of the delivered message is *recipient*. Line 7 tests if $p_i = recipient$. Line 13 tests if p_j is the recipient of message m.

Asynchronous System, Broadcast: Lines 2 and 22 can be deleted as the group contains all processes and there is no need to encrypt with the group key.

Synchronous System; Multicast, Unicast, and Broadcast: Algorithm 2 directly applies to a multicast in a synchronous system. The difference is that the BA_broadcast which is necessarily a probabilistic algorithm in the asynchronous system now becomes a deterministic algorithm. The special cases of unicast and broadcast in an asynchronous system likewise work in a synchronous system with the probabilistic BA_broadcast now becoming a deterministic BA_broadcast. Due to the high message complexity and latency of this version of unicast in a synchronous system, Algorithm 1 is more efficient for unicast.

7 Discussion

We conjecture that it is impossible to provide strong safety in Byzantine-tolerant causal order for multicasts, (unicasts, or broadcasts) in synchronous systems without using cryptographic techniques, complementing the impossibility result [21,22] for asynchronous systems. This is because in isolation, a Byzantine process is free to delete true dependencies of its messages on messages that it sends out. By using cryptographic techniques, this advantage is nullified by making the Byzantine process dependent on correct processes to decipher and read incoming messages. This makes sure that a Byzantine process cannot falsify/delete causal dependencies because it no longer operates in isolation and requires cooperation of one or more correct processes in reading and sending messages.

In this paper, we have extended previous work that provided weak safety of causal order unicasts/multicasts to now provide strong safety with the use of threshold encryption for both synchronous and asynchronous systems. The causal ordering algorithm for asynchronous systems is non-deterministic, while the algorithm for synchronous systems is deterministic. The synchronous algorithm for unicasts (Algorithm 1) has a low cost with message complexity $O(n)$ point-to-point messages per application message, but assumes assistance from the network in terms of an upper bound on message latency. The asynchronous algorithm for multicasts (Algorithm 2) has a higher message cost of at least $O(n^2)$ (depending on the implementation of the BA_broadcast primitive [7,12,16]) plus $O(n \cdot |G|)$ point-to-point messages per multicast to group G, but does not assume any support from the network. Depending on the application requirements and constraints, either of the two algorithms can be used for causal ordering.

References

1. Auvolat, A., Frey, D., Raynal, M., Taïani, F.: Byzantine-tolerant causal broadcast. Theoret. Comput. Sci. **885**, 55–68 (2021)
2. Birman, K.P., Joseph, T.A.: Reliable communication in the presence of failures. ACM Trans. Comput. Syst. (TOCS) **5**(1), 47–76 (1987)
3. Bracha, G.: Asynchronous byzantine agreement protocols. Inf. Comput. **75**(2), 130–143 (1987)
4. Bracha, G., Toueg, S.: Asynchronous consensus and broadcast protocols. J. ACM (JACM) **32**(4), 824–840 (1985)
5. Cachin, C., Kursawe, K., Petzold, F., Shoup, V.: Secure and efficient asynchronous broadcast protocols. IACR Cryptol. ePrint Arch, p. 6 (2001)
6. Chandra, T.D., Toueg, S.: Unreliable failure detectors for reliable distributed systems. J. (JACM) **43**(2), 225–267 (1996)
7. Correia, M., Neves, N.F., Veríssimo, P.: From consensus to atomic broadcast: time-free byzantine-resistant protocols without signatures. Comput. J. **49**(1), 82–96 (2006)
8. Défago, X., Schiper, A., Urbán, P.: Total order broadcast and multicast algorithms: taxonomy and survey. ACM Comput. Surv. **36**(4), 372–421 (2004)

9. Duan, S., Reiter, M.K., Zhang, H.: Secure causal atomic broadcast, revisited. In: 2017 47th Annual IEEE/IFIP International Conference on Dependable Systems and Networks (DSN), pp. 61–72. IEEE (2017)
10. Dwork, C., Lynch, N.A., Stockmeyer, L.J.: Consensus in the presence of partial synchrony. J. ACM **35**(2), 288–323 (1988)
11. Fischer, M.J., Lynch, N.A., Paterson, M.: Impossibility of distributed consensus with one faulty process. J. ACM **32**(2), 374–382 (1985)
12. Gągol, A., Leśniak, D., Straszak, D., Świętek, M.: Aleph: efficient atomic broadcast in asynchronous networks with byzantine nodes. In: Proceedings of the 1st ACM Conference on Advances in Financial Technologies, pp. 214–228 (2019)
13. Hadzilacos, V., Toueg, S.: A modular approach to fault-tolerant broadcasts and related problems. Technical report 94–1425, p. 83. Cornell University (1994)
14. Kshemkalyani, A.D., Singhal, M.: Necessary and sufficient conditions on information for causal message ordering and their optimal implementation. Distributed Comput. **11**(2), 91–111 (1998)
15. Kshemkalyani, A.D., Singhal, M.: Distributed Computing: Principles, Algorithms, and Systems. Cambridge University Press, Cambridge (2011)
16. Kursawe, K., Shoup, V.: Optimistic asynchronous atomic broadcast. In: Caires, L., Italiano, G.F., Monteiro, L., Palamidessi, C., Yung, M. (eds.) ICALP 2005. LNCS, vol. 3580, pp. 204–215. Springer, Heidelberg (2005). https://doi.org/10.1007/11523468_17
17. Lamport, L., Shostak, R.E., Pease, M.C.: The byzantine generals problem. ACM Trans. Program. Lang. Syst. **4**(3), 382–401 (1982)
18. Milosevic, Z., Hutle, M., Schiper, A.: On the reduction of atomic broadcast to consensus with byzantine faults. In: 2011 IEEE 30th International Symposium on Reliable Distributed Systems, pp. 235–244. IEEE (2011)
19. Misra, A., Kshemkalyani, A.D.: Causal ordering in the presence of byzantine processes. In: 28th IEEE International Conference on Parallel and Distributed Systems, ICPADS, pp. 130–138. IEEE (2022)
20. Misra, A., Kshemkalyani, A.D.: Causal ordering properties of byzantine reliable broadcast primitives. In: Colajanni, M., Ferretti, L., Pardal, M.L., Avresky, D.R. (eds.) 21st IEEE International Symposium on Network Computing and Applications, NCA 2022, pp. 115–122. IEEE (2022)
21. Misra, A., Kshemkalyani, A.D.: Solvability of byzantine fault-tolerant causal ordering problems. In: Koulali, M., Mezini, M. (eds.) NETYS 2022. LNCS, vol. 13464, pp. 87–103. Springer, Cham (2022). https://doi.org/10.1007/978-3-031-17436-0_7
22. Misra, A., Kshemkalyani, A.D.: Byzantine fault-tolerant causal ordering. In: 24th International Conference on Distributed Computing and Networking, ICDCN 2023, Kharagpur, India, January 4–7, 2023, pp. 100–109. ACM (2023)
23. Pease, M.C., Shostak, R.E., Lamport, L.: Reaching agreement in the presence of faults. J. ACM **27**(2), 228–234 (1980)
24. Raynal, M.: Fault-Tolerant Message-Passing Distributed Systems: An Algorithmic Approach. Springer, Cham (2018). https://doi.org/10.1007/978-3-319-94141-7
25. Shoup, V., Gennaro, R.: Securing threshold cryptosystems against chosen ciphertext attack. J. Cryptol. **15**(2), 75–96 (2002)

Improved Paths to Stability for the Stable Marriage Problem

Vijay K. Garg(✉) and Changyong Hu

The University of Texas at Austin, Austin, USA
{garg,colinhu9}@ece.utexas.edu

Abstract. The stable marriage problem has wide applications in distributed computing such as the placement of virtual machines in a distributed system. The stable marriage problem requires one to find a marriage with no blocking pair. Given a matching that is not stable, Roth and Vande Vate have shown that there exists a sequence of matchings that leads to a stable matching in which each successive matching is obtained by satisfying a blocking pair. The sequence produced by Roth and Vande Vate's algorithm is of length $O(n^3)$ where n is the number of men (and women). In this paper, we present an algorithm that achieves stability in a sequence of matchings of length $O(n^2)$. We also give an efficient algorithm to find the stable matching closest to the given initial matching under an appropriate distance function between matchings.

Keywords: Stable Matching · Nearest Stable Matching

1 Introduction

The Stable Matching Problem [4] has wide applications in distributed computing such as the placement of virtual machines in a distributed system [9] or the placement of files in a distributed system. It has applications in many other numerous fields such as economics and resource allocation with multiple books and survey articles [3,6–8,10]. In the standard version of the problem, there are n men and n women each with their totally ordered preference list. The goal is to find a matching between men and women such that there is no blocking pair, i.e., there is no pair of a woman and a man such that they are not married to each other but prefer each other over their partners. The standard Gale-Shapley (GS) algorithm produces such a matching starting from an empty matching with the deferred acceptance proposal algorithm that takes $O(n^2)$ proposals. The algorithm produces the man-optimal stable matching.

In many applications, it is useful to consider the initial state of the system as an arbitrary assignment of men to women and then to find a path to a stable matching. For example, suppose that we consider a system in which there are more women than men and suppose that every man is matched to a unique

Supported by NSF CNS-1812349, CNS-1563544, and the Cullen Trust for Higher Education Endowed Professorship.

S. Dolev and B. Schieber (Eds.): SSS 2023, LNCS 14310, pp. 126–140, 2023.
https://doi.org/10.1007/978-3-031-44274-2_11

woman such that there is no blocking pair. Now, if a new man or a woman joins the system, it is more natural to start with the initial state as the existing assignment rather than the empty matching. In particular, if there is some cost associated with breaking up an existing couple, then we may be interested in the paths to stability that are of short lengths. Hence, this generalization allows one to consider *incremental* stable matching algorithms.

As another example, suppose that we have a stable matching. In a dynamic preference mechanism, a woman may change her list of preferences. The existing matching may not be stable under new preferences of the woman. Again, it is more natural to start with the existing matching and then to find a path to a stable matching under new preferences. Thus, the generalization allows one to consider a *dynamic* stable matching algorithm in which preferences of a man or a woman may change and the goal is to find a stable matching under new preferences.

Given a matching, a natural method to make progress towards a stable matching is as follows. The man and the woman in the blocking pair are married and their spouses are divorced. By marrying these divorcees, we get another matching. The reader is referred to the book [3] for a detailed discussion of algorithms that go from a matching to a stable matching. Knuth [8] showed that starting from any matching and iteratively satisfying a blocking pair may lead to a cycle. Abeledo and Rothblum [1] have shown that a cycle exists even if one chooses the best blocking pair to satisfy at each step. A pair (p, q') is the best blocking pair for p if for any other blocking pair (p, q) in M, p prefers q' to q. Indeed, it has been shown by Tamura [13] and independently by Tan and Su [14], that there are matchings for which it is not possible to reach a stable marriage by marrying off divorcees. However, if the divorcees are allowed to remain single, then one can achieve stability. The Roth and Vande Vate (RVV) mechanism [11] is the most well known method to determine a path to stability. Their algorithm introduces agents (men or women) incrementally and let them iteratively reach a stable matching. Given any matching M_0, the RVV mechanism produces a sequence of matchings $M_0, M_1, \ldots, M_t$ such that M_t is stable matching and for each k $(1 \leq k \leq t)$, M_k is obtained from M_{k-1} by satisfying a blocking pair. The value of t is at most $2n^3$ (assuming that the number of acceptable pairs is n^2).

In this paper, we analyze the path to stability from the perspective of traversal in the *proposal vector lattice*. Any man-saturating matching corresponds to a unique proposal vector but when the matching is incomplete there may be multiple proposal vectors corresponding to it. Working with proposal vectors instead of matching allows us to generate shorter sequences to a stable matching. In particular, we show that given any proposal vector G_0, there exists a sequence of proposal vectors $G_0, G_1, \ldots, G_t$ such that G_t corresponds to a stable matching and for each k $(1 \leq k \leq t)$, G_k is obtained from G_{k-1} by either increasing the choice number for one man (thereby worsening his match) or decreasing the choice number for one man (thereby improving his match). The value of t is at most $2m^2$ where m is the number of men. Our result can also be phrased in terms of matching as follows. Given any matching M_0, there exists a sequence of matching $M_0, M_1, \ldots, M_t$ such that M_t corresponds to a stable matching and for each k $(1 \leq k \leq t)$, M_k is obtained from M_{k-1} by either (1) marrying a man whose current partner is in a blocking pair (or, if he is single) to another woman who is agreeable to his proposal, or (2) by marrying a woman to her best blocking pair partner. The value of t is at most $2m^2$ where m is the number of men. Thus, this sequence is shorter than the RVV sequence by a factor of m.

We propose four algorithms in this paper for achieving stability (see Fig. 1). The first algorithm α is a generalization of the GS algorithm to find the man-optimal marriage. The GS algorithm starts with the matching that results when all men propose to their top choice. It then determines the man-optimal stable marriage in $O(n^2)$ moves. What if instead of the top choices, men propose to any arbitrary vector of women? In such a scenario, a woman cannot accept the first proposal she receives (as in the GS algorithm), because that may result in an unstable matching. Algorithm α gives the rules for advancing from an arbitrary proposal vector to end up in a stable marriage (whenever possible). Given any initial matching M_0, algorithm α produces a sequence of matchings ending in a stable marriage M_t such that the matching only improves from the perspective of women and gets only worse from the perspective of men. This sequence is of length $O(n^2)$. Since there may not exist any stable matching that is based only on improving from the women's perspective, algorithm α may return null in these cases (for example, when the initial matching M_0 assigns some man a partner who is ranked lower than in the man-pessimal matching). The set of stable matchings can be viewed as a sublattice of the lattice of all proposal vectors and the algorithm α can be viewed as upward traversal in this lattice from any arbitrary proposal vector to a proposal vector that corresponds to a stable matching.

One of the goals of the paper is to find a matching that is not too far from the original matching (or the initial proposal vector). Given any proposal vector I, the *regret* of a man is defined as the rank the woman he is assigned in I, i.e., if a man is assigned his k^{th} top choice in I then his regret is k. Given two proposal vectors I and M, we define the distance between I and M, $dist(I, M)$ as the sum of differences of regrets for all men in I and M, i.e. the L_1 distance between two vectors, $dist(I, M) = \|I - M\|_1$. Algorithm α guarantees that the stable matching M_t computed has the least distance of all stable matchings that are better than I from the women's perspective.

The second algorithm β does the downward traversal in the proposal lattice in search of a stable marriage. Algorithm β also takes an arbitrary proposal vector I as the starting point and results in a stable marriage whenever possible. It improves the matching from the perspective of men. When men and women are equal then such a traversal can be accomplished by switching the roles of men and women. However, in this paper we assume that the number of men m may be much smaller than the number of women w. All our algorithms have time complexity of $O(m^2 + w)$. Switching the roles of men and women is not feasible without increasing the complexity of our algorithms. Algorithm β guarantees that the stable matching M_t computed has the least distance of all stable matchings that are better than I from the men's perspective.

The third algorithm γ combines a downward traversal with an upward traversal to guarantee that irrespective of the initial matching I, there always exists a sequence of matchings that results in a stable matching. This sequence consists of two subsequences each of length $O(m^2)$ giving us the path to stability of length $O(m^2)$, thereby improving on the RVV mechanism. Intuitively, the RVV algorithm may traverse the lattice in the upward direction or downwards direction multiple times. In contrast, our algorithm γ traverses the proposal lattice once in the downward direction and then in the upward direction ending in a stable matching. It generates a sequence of proposal vectors that results in a stable matching with $O(m^2 + w)$ time complexity.

Our last algorithm δ finds the closest stable matching to the given initial proposal vector. Algorithm δ is based on a linear programming formulation of the stable marriage problem by Rothblum [12]. By appropriately defining the objective function to minimize the distance from the initial proposal vector, we get a polynomial time algorithm to find the closest stable marriage.

Our algorithms are also useful in the context of arriving at more egalitarian matchings than we get using the Gale-Shapley algorithm. If there are m men, instead of starting with the proposal vector $(1, 1, \ldots, 1)$, we may start with the proposal vector $(m/2, m/2, \ldots, m/2)$ to find a stable vector close to the center of the proposal lattice. Alternatively, we can also start with various proposal vectors chosen at random and obtain multiple stable matchings. Once we have multiple stable matchings, we can use Teo and Sethuraman's median stable matching theorem [15] to return the median stable matching.

We note here that the path to a stable matching from an unstable matching can be of different types. Given any blocking pair, the RVV algorithm is based on a *better response* dynamics. Under these dynamics, any blocking pair (p, q) for a matching M is chosen and they are matched. The partners of p and q in M, if any, are unmatched. An alternative approach based on *best response dynamics* is explored in [2]. Here, one side, say the set of women, is considered active and the other side is considered passive. An active agent of a blocking pair (p, q) in M plays the *best response* if p is matched to q' such that (p, q') is the best blocking pair for p. In other words, if there is any other blocking pair (p, q) in M, then p prefers q' to q. The paper [2] gives an example of a two sided market with three men and women in which *best response dynamics* can cycle. They also propose an algorithm to generate a sequence of $2mw$ best responses from any matching M that leads to a stable matching. Their algorithm has some similarities with our algorithm in that it also consists of two phases. In the first phase, only matched women can make best response moves whereas in the second phase all women can play the best response. However, a crucial difference from our algorithm is that we are interested in finding a matching that is close to the original matching (where the distance is defined based on the proposal lattice). The algorithm in [2] does not concern itself with the issue of the distance between matchings. In particular, under the *best response dynamics*, their algorithm has the tendency to get to the woman-optimal marriage irrespective of the initial matching. In contrast, our algorithms provide guarantees on the matching returned. For example, Algorithm α returns the proposal vector that has the least distance from I, the initial proposal vector of all the proposal vectors that are bigger than I.

The missing proofs in this paper are available in [5]

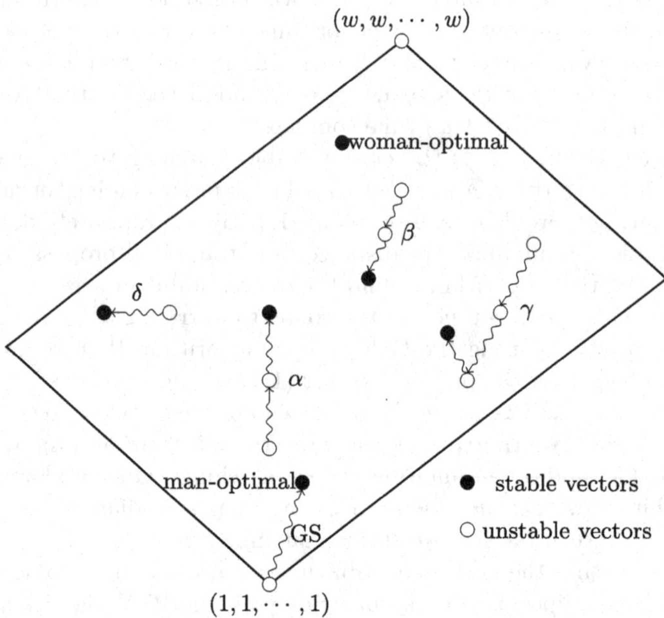

Fig. 1. A proposal lattice with various traversals. Algorithm GS always starts from the bottom of the lattice and finds the man-optimal vector. Algorithm α starts from any vector I and finds the smallest stable vector which is greater than or equal to I (if any exists). Algorithm β finds the largest stable vector which is less than or equal to I. Algorithm γ always converges to a stable vector. Algorithm δ finds a stable vector that is closest in Manhattan metric.

2 Proposal Vector Lattice

We consider stable marriage instances with m men numbered $1, 2, \ldots, m$ and w women numbered $1, 2, \ldots w$. We assume that the number of women w is at least m; otherwise, the roles of men and women can be switched. The variables $mpref$ and $wpref$ specify the men preferences and the women preferences, respectively. Thus, $mpref[i][k] = j$ iff woman j is the kth preference for man i. Figure 2 shows an instance of the stable matching problem.

We use the notion of a *proposal vector* for our algorithms. A (man) proposal vector, G, is of dimension m, the number of men. We view any vector G as follows: $(G[i] = k)$ if man i has proposed to his k^{th} preference, i.e. the woman given by $mpref[i][k]$. If $mpref[i][k]$ equals j, then $G[i]$ equals k corresponds to man i proposing to woman j. For convenience, let $\rho(G, i)$ denote the woman $mpref[i][G[i]]$. The vector $(1, 1, \ldots, 1)$ corresponds the proposal vector in which every man has proposed to his top choice. Similarly, $(w, w, \ldots, w)$ corresponds to the vector in which every man has proposed to his last choice. Our algorithms can also handle the case when the lists are incomplete, i.e., a man prefers staying alone to being matched to some women. However, for simplicity, we assume complete lists. It is clear that the set of all proposal vectors forms a distributive lattice under the natural less than order in which the meet and join are given by the component-wise minimum and the component-wise maximum, respectively. This lattice has w^m elements.

Given any proposal vector, G, there is a unique matching defined as follows: man i and $\rho(G, i)$ are matched in G if the proposal by man i is the best for that woman in G. A man p is unmatched in G if his proposal is not the best proposal for that woman in G. A woman q is unmatched in G if she does not receive any proposal in G; otherwise, she is matched with the best proposal for her in G.

A proposal vector G represents a *man-saturating matching* iff no woman receives more than one proposal in G. Formally, G is a man-saturating matching if $\forall i, j : i \neq j : \rho(G, i) \neq \rho(G, j)$. When the number of men equals the number women, a man-saturating matching is a perfect matching (all men and women are matched). When the number of men is less than the number of women, then G is a man-saturating matching if every man is matched (but some women are unmatched). We say that a matching M_1 (or a marriage) is less than another matching M_2 if the proposal vector for M_1 is less than that of M_2. Thus, the man-optimal marriage is the *least* stable matching in the proposal lattice and woman-optimal marriage is the *greatest* stable matching.

A proposal vector G may have one or more blocking pairs. A pair of man and woman (p, q) is a *blocking pair* in G iff $\rho(G, p)$ is not q, man p prefers q to $\rho(G, p)$, and woman q prefers p to any proposal she receives in G. Observe that this definition works even when woman q is unmatched, i.e. she has not received any proposals in G. In this case, woman q prefers p to staying alone, and p prefers q to $\rho(G, p)$.

A proposal vector G is a stable marriage (or a stable proposal vector) iff it is a man-saturating matching and there are no blocking pairs in G. The usual stable matching problem is to determine such a proposal vector given $mpref$ and $wpref$. The problem that we consider in this paper includes an additional input: the initial proposal vector, I. The goal is to traverse the proposal lattice starting from I to find a stable proposal vector G. In this paper, we use two different mechanisms—upward traversal and downward traversal—to reach a stable matching proposal vector.

Algorithm α uses upward traversal. Suppose that q is matched with p' in G and is part of the blocking pair (p, q). Instead of satisfying the blocking pair (p, q), we *move* p' to his next choice in his preference list. This move makes the proposal vector better from the women's perspective and worse from the men's perspective. By continuing in this manner if some man makes a proposal to q

who is even better than p, the blocking pair (p, q) gets eliminated. If no man better than p ever makes a proposal to q, then there is no proposal vector bigger than G that corresponds to a stable matching.

$mpref$		$wpref$	
m_1	$w_1\ w_2\ w_3$	w_1	$m_2\ m_1\ m_3$
m_2	$w_2\ w_3\ w_1$	w_2	$m_3\ m_2\ m_1$
m_3	$w_3\ w_1\ w_2$	w_3	$m_1\ m_3\ m_2$

Fig. 2. Stable Matching Problem with men preference list ($mpref$) and women preference list ($wpref$).

Algorithm β uses downward traversal in the proposal lattice. Let G be a proposal vector that is not stable. Of all the blocking pairs that q is part of, we choose the best blocking pair from q's perspective. Let (p, q) be such a blocking pair. We construct a proposal vector G' that *moves* man p to woman q by changing the proposal of man p from his current proposal to that for woman q and keeping all other proposals as before.

Since Algorithm α traverses the lattice upwards, any sequence of proposal vector it generates can be of length at most m^2. Similarly, Algorithm β also generates a sequence of length at most m^2. Algorithm γ combines one downward traversal and one upward traversal to go from any proposal vector to a stable matching proposal vector in a sequence of length at most $O(m^2)$.

We now describe Algorithms α, β and γ in detail.

3 Algorithm α

Given any initial proposal vector I, Algorithm α, finds a stable matching G such that $I \leq G$ whenever there exists such a stable matching. The initial proposal vector is arbitrary instead of the top choice for each man. This generalizes the GS algorithm which starts with $I = (1, 1, \ldots, 1)$. Observe that the GS algorithm does not work when the starting proposal vector is arbitrary. The GS algorithm requires men to make proposals and women to accept the best proposals they have received so far. If the starting proposal vector is a man-saturating matching but not stable, then each woman gets a unique proposal. All women would accept the only proposal received, but the resulting marriage would not be stable.

This instability may arise due to two reasons. First, it may arise when the number of women exceeds the number of men. If we start with the top choices of all men, then the GS algorithm would still return a man-optimal stable matching with the excess women unmatched. However, if we start from an arbitrary proposal vector, we can end up with all women getting unique proposals but there may exist an unmatched woman who is preferred by some man over his current match.

To tackle this problem, we first do a simple check on the initial proposal vector as given by the following Lemma. Let $numw(I)$ be the total number of unique women that have been proposed in all vectors that are less than or equal to I, i.e., $numw(I) = \#\{j \in [w] : \exists G \leq I, \exists i, \rho(G,i) = j\}$.

Lemma 1. *Let I be the initial proposal vector for any stable marriage instance with m men. There is no stable marriage for any proposal vector $G \geq I$ whenever $numw(I) > m$.*

Proof. Consider any proposal vector $G \geq I$. Since the total number of men is m, there is at least one woman q who has been proposed to in a vector less than G and who does not have any proposal in G. Suppose that proposal was made by man p. Then, man p prefers q to $\rho(G,p)$ and q prefers p to staying alone. □

Hence, in our algorithm we only consider I such that the total number of women proposed until I (in all vectors less than or equal to I) is at most m.

Instability may arise even when the number of men and women are equal. In Fig. 2, this situation would arise if we started with $I = (2,2,2)$. The initial proposal vector may be a perfect matching but not stable. A woman q may receive a unique proposal from a man p but she prefers p' who has made his proposal to q' even though p' prefers q to q'. Such a scenario cannot happen when men propose starting from the top choice and in the decreasing order as in the GS algorithm. However, now the starting vector is arbitrary and a blocking pair may exist in the man-saturating matching.

To address this problem, we define the notion of a *forbidden* man in a proposal vector.

Definition 1 (forbidden). *A man i is forbidden in G if either he is unmatched in G or matched to a woman in G who is part of a blocking pair. Formally, the predicate $forbidden(G,i)$ holds if there exists another man j such that either (1) both i and j have proposed to the same woman in G and that woman prefers j, or (2) $(j, \rho(G,i))$ is a blocking pair in G.*

We first show that

Lemma 2. *Let G be any proposal vector such that $numw(G) \leq m$. There exists a man i such that $forbidden(G,i)$ iff G is not a stable marriage.*

Algorithm α shown in Fig. 3 exploits the $forbidden(G,i)$ function to search for the stable marriage in the proposal lattice. The basic idea is that if a man i is forbidden in the current proposal vector G, then he must go down his preference list until he finds a woman who is either unmatched or prefers him to her current match. The while loop at line (1) iterates until none of the men are forbidden in G. If the while loop terminates then G is a stable marriage on account of Lemma 2. At line (2), man i advances on his preference list until his proposal is the most preferred proposal to the woman among all proposals that are made to her in any proposal vector less than or equal to G. If there is no such proposal,

input: A stable marriage instance, initial proposal vector I
output: smallest stable marriage greater than or equal to I (if one exists)
$forbidden(G, i)$ holds if i is unmatched or his partner forms a blocking pair in G.

(0) If $numw(I) > m$ then return null else $G := I$;
(1) **while** there exists a man i such that $forbidden(G, i)$
(2) let q be the next woman in the list of man i such that i has the most preferred proposal to q,
(3) if no such choice after $G[i]$ or the number of women proposed including q exceeds m then
return null; // "no stable matching exists"
(4) else $G[i]$:= choice that corresponds to woman q;
(5) **endwhile**;
(6) return G;

Fig. 3. Algorithm α that returns the least stable vector greater than or equal to the given proposal vector I.

then there does not exist any $G \geq I$ such that G is stable and in line (3), the algorithm returns null. Otherwise, the man makes that proposal at line (4).

For example, consider the initial proposal vector $G = (2, 2, 2)$ in Fig. 2. In this proposal vector, we have the matching $\{(m_1, w_2), (m_2, w_3), (m_3, w_1)\}$. While this is a man-saturating matching, it is not stable because it has blocking pairs. Consider the blocking pair (m_2, w_2) (because, m_2 prefers w_2 to w_3 and w_2 prefers m_2 to m_1). In an upward traversal, we advance the partner of the woman w_2 in the blocking pair, m_1, to his next choice. The next choice for m_1 is w_3. This results in w_3 rejecting m_2 and therefore m_2 moves to his next choice w_1. This proposal, in turn, results in w_1 rejecting m_3. Next, m_3 makes a proposal to w_2 and now (m_2, w_2) is not a blocking pair. The new proposal vector $(3, 3, 3)$ which corresponds to the matching $\{(m_1, w_3), (m_2, w_1), (m_3, w_2)\}$ is a stable matching with all women getting their top choices.

There are two main differences between the GS algorithm and Algorithm α. The first difference is the simple check on the number of women that have been proposed until G. We require $numw(G) \leq m$. Clearly, if the number of women is equal to the number of men, then $numw(G)$ can never exceed m and this check can be dropped.

The second difference is in the definition of $forbidden(G, i)$. In the standard GS algorithm, a man advances on his preference list only when he is unmatched, i.e., the woman he has proposed to is either matched with someone more preferable or receives a proposal from a more preferable man. Whenever the GS algorithm reaches a man-saturating matching, it is a stable matching. For any arbitrary I (for example, a man-saturating matching that is not stable), it is important to take blocking pairs in consideration as part of the forbidden predicate. This difference can be summarized as follows.

- *GS Algorithm*: A man proposes to the next woman on his preference list if he is currently unmatched.

- *Algorithm α*: A man i proposes to the next woman on his preference list if he is currently unmatched or matched with a woman q who is in a blocking pair.

Observe that if all men propose starting from their top choices, then the rule for Algorithm α becomes identical to that for the GS Algorithm.

To prove the correctness of the algorithm α, the following Lemma is crucial.

Lemma 3. *If $forbidden(G, i)$ holds, then there is no proposal vector H such that $(H \geq G)$ and $(G[i] = H[i])$ and H is a stable marriage.*

A consequence of Lemma 3 is that if $forbidden(G, i)$ holds, then it is safe to advance man i to the next choice without any danger of missing a proposal vector that is a stable marriage. We can now show the correctness of Algorithm α.

Theorem 1. *Algorithm α returns the least stable proposal vector $G \geq I$ in the proposal lattice whenever it exists. If there is no stable proposal vector greater than or equal to I, then the algorithm returns null.*

The following Corollary states that the stable marriage returned by Algorithm α has the least distance of all stable marriages greater than I.

Corollary 1. *Given any proposal vector I, Algorithm α returns the stable marriage greater than or equal to I with the least distance from I.*

Proof. Suppose that Algorithm α returns G and G' is any other stable marriage such that $I \leq G'$. From Theorem 1, we get that $I \leq G \leq G'$. It follows that the distance between I and G is less than or equal to the distance between I and G'. □

As another application of Algorithm α consider a scenario where we have a stable marriage and a new man joins the system (we can assume that initially the number of women were more than the number of men). Instead of running the GS from scratch, algorithm α can start from the existing proposal vector for existing men and the median choice for the new entrant. If the existing matching had certain desirable properties (e.g. fairness), then the new stable matching found would be close to the existing matching.

4 Algorithm β: Downward Traversal

We now give the dual of Algorithm α that does the downward traversal in the proposal vector lattice and returns the greatest stable marriage less than or equal to I. In the standard literature, one does not consider the dual of the GS algorithm to find the woman-optimal stable marriage. Just by switching roles of men and women from the man-optimal GS, we get the woman-optimal GS algorithm. We cannot employ this strategy because we had assumed that the

input: A stable marriage instance, initial proposal vector I
output: greatest stable marriage less than or equal to I if one exists

The predicate $rForbidden(G,i)$ holds if there exists a woman q such that q prefers i to all her proposals in any vector less than or equal to G, and i prefers q to $\rho(G,i)$.
L: proposal vector corresponding to man optimal stable marriage.
(1) for all i: $G[i] := \min(m, I[i])$;
(2) if $(\exists i : G[i] < L[i])$ **return** null; // no stable matching exists
(3) **while** (there exists a man i such that $rForbidden(G,i)$)
(4) $G[i]$:= rank of woman q s.t. q prefers i of all proposers in any vector less than G
(5) **endwhile**;
(6) return G;

Fig. 4. Algorithm β: An Algorithm that returns the woman-optimal marriage less than or equal to the given proposal vector I.

number of men is less than or equal to the number of women. Switching men and women violates this assumption.

In addition, the downward traversal of the proposal lattice gives different insights into the algorithm for finding a stable matching even when the number of men equals the number of women.

We first give a necessary condition for a stable marriage to exist that is less than or equal to I.

Lemma 4. *If $numw(I)$ (the number of unique women who have proposals in any vector less than or equal to I) is less than m, then there cannot be any stable proposal vector less than or equal to I.*

Proof. The claim follows because any proposal vector less than or equal to I cannot be a man-saturating matching if the number of unique women is less than m. □

If $numw(I) \geq m$, there may or may not be a proposal vector that corresponds to a stable marriage depending upon the women's preferences.

While traversing the proposal lattice in the downward direction, we use the predicate $rForbidden(G,p)$ (short for reverse-Forbidden) which uses the notion of *best blocking pair.*

Definition 2 (Best blocking pair). *A blocking pair (p,q) is the* best blocking pair *in G for q if for all blocking pairs (p',q) in G, the woman q prefers p to p'.*

Definition 3 (Forbidden). *A man p is* rForbidden *in G if there exists a woman q such that (p,q) is the best blocking pair in G for q.*

We first show that

Lemma 5. *Let G be any proposal vector such that $numw(G) \geq m$. There exists a man i such that $rForbidden(G,i)$ iff G is not a stable marriage.*

Proof. First suppose that there exists i such that $rForbidden(G, i)$. Then, there exists a woman q such that man i and woman q form a blocking pair for G. Hence G is not a stable marriage.

Conversely, assume that G is not a stable marriage. If G is not a man-saturating matching, then there exists at least one woman q who has not received any proposal in G but has received it earlier because $num(W) \geq m$. Of all such proposals to q let the most favorable proposal be from man i. Then, $rForbidden(G, i)$ holds. If G is a man-saturating matching, but not stable, then there exists at least one blocking pair. Therefore, there exists at least one best blocking pair. □

Analogous to upward traversal using forbidden predicate, we get that

Lemma 6. *Assume $numw(G) \geq m$. If $rForbidden(G, i)$ holds, then there is no stable proposal vector H such that $(H \leq G)$ and $(G[i] = H[i])$.*

Figure 4 shows a high-level description of a downward traversal of the proposal lattice. At line (1), we ensure that $G[i]$ is at most m because due to Lemma 1, we know that there cannot be any stable marriage in which any component exceeds m. At line (2), we first ensure that G is at least equal to L, the proposal vector corresponding to the man-optimal stable marriage. Otherwise, there cannot be a stable marriage vector less than or equal to G. At line (3) we pick i such that $rForbidden(G, i)$ holds. This means that there exists a woman q such that (i, q) is a best blocking pair. At line (4), we satisfy the pair (i, q) by decreasing $G[i]$ until $\rho(G, i) = q$. This step corresponds to a downward traversal in the proposal lattice. At line (6), when we exit from the while loop, we know that G must be a stable marriage on account of Lemma 5. This algorithm ensures that the match for any man can only improve.

For example of Algorithm β, consider the initial proposal vector $G = (2, 2, 2)$. The pair (m_2, w_2) is blocking. Of all the blocking pairs in G for w_2, m_2 is best. Even though w_2 prefers m_3 to m_2, the pair (m_3, w_2) is not blocking because m_3 is at his choice 2 in G and w_2 corresponds to his third choice. Since m_2 is the best blocking pair for w_2, we make m_2 propose to w_2. Hence, the new proposal vector is $(2, 1, 2)$. In this proposal vector, w_3 is unmatched and (m_3, w_3) is the best blocking pair for w_3. The new proposal vector is $(2, 1, 1)$. Now, w_1 is unmatched and her best blocking pair is (m_1, w_1). When m_1 proposes to w_1, we get the stable marriage proposal vector $(1, 1, 1)$. This corresponds to the man-optimal stable marriage.

5 Algorithm γ: Path to Stability

We now present an algorithm that gives a path from any proposal vector to a stable marriage vector. Note that depending on the initial proposal vector, both Algorithms α and β may return null. For example, when the number of men is equal to the number of women and the initial vector is greater than or incomparable to the woman-optimal vector, then the algorithm α will return null. Similarly,

```
input: A stable marriage instance, initial proposal vector I
output: a stable marriage M
G := I;
// Downward traversal
K := max(G, U); //Compute U using Algorithm β with the initial vector as [m, m, ..., m];
while there exists a man i such that rForbidden(K, i)
        K[i] := K[i] − 1; G[i] := G[i] − 1;
endwhile;
//Upward traversal
while there exists a man i such that forbidden(G, i)
    G[i] := G[i] + 1;
endwhile;
return G;
```

Fig. 5. Algorithm γ with $O(m^2 + w)$ complexity.

if the initial vector is less than or incomparable to the man-optimal vector, then the algorithm β returns null. If the initial vector is incomparable to both the man-optimal and the woman-optimal proposal vectors, then both algorithms α and β will return null. In the RVV setting, we need to combine a downwards traversal with an upwards traversal to go from an arbitrary proposal vector to a stable matching. There are two choices for combining these traversals—a downward traversal followed by an upwards traversal, or vice-versa. We will use the former approach. The RVV algorithm introduces men and women incrementally and does multiple upward and downward traversals.

The Algorithm γ is shown in Fig. 5. Given any arbitrary initial vector I, we first do a downward traversal to get to a proposal vector that is less than or equal to U, the largest possible stable marriage. If the initial vector is at most U, then this step is not necessary. U can be computed using Algorithm β by using a downward traversal starting from the vector $[m, m, \ldots, m]$. Our goal is to find blocking pairs in G such that by satisfying them we get to a proposal vector $G \leq U$. In contrast to algorithms in literature, we pick blocking pairs to satisfy carefully. Specifically, during the downward traversal, we satisfy only those men whose component in the proposal vector is beyond U. To find a sequence from I to G such that $G \leq U$, we first compute a vector K as $\max(U, G)$. We now invoke a downward traversal on K using $rForbidden$ function of algorithm β. Since Algorithm β returns the greatest stable marriage less than the initial proposal vector (in our case K), it finds as blocking pair only those men i such that $K[i] > U[i]$. By definition of $rForbidden$ any j such that $K[j]$ equals $U[j]$ can not satisfy $rForbidden(K, j)$ because U is a stable marriage.

Lemma 7. *Let* $K = max(G, U)$*. Then, for any* i*,* $rForbidden(K, i)$ *implies* $rForbidden(G, i)$*.*

Proof. Suppose i is not $rForbidden$ in G. This means that there exists a stable marriage H less than or equal to G such that $H[i] = G[i]$. Since G is less than or equal to K, we get that H is a stable marriage less than or equal to K. However, this implies that i is not *rForbidden* in K. □

Since i is *rForbidden* in G it is safe to decrement $G[i]$ in search for a stable marriage. By repeating this process, we generate a sequence of proposal vectors that makes G less than or equal to U. Note that consecutive proposal vectors generated in this phase differ in the proposals by at most one man. The downward traversal step can be viewed as invocation of Algorithm β on K such that whenever K is updated, G is updated as well. This downward traversal can be done in $O(m^2 + w)$ time. At the end of this step $G \leq U$, and we can start the second phase of the algorithm.

In the second phase, we do an upward traversal in which women improve their match. We use the function α to find the least stable marriage that is greater than or equal to G. In this phase, we satisfy blocking pairs by improving the match of women. Since the input to algorithm α is less than or equal to U, we are guaranteed to get a stable marriage at the end.

Hence, we have the following result.

Theorem 2. *Given any initial proposal vector I, there exists a sequence of proposal vectors $G_0, G_1, \ldots, G_t$ such that G_0 is equal to I, G_t corresponds to a stable matching and for each k ($1 \leq k \leq t$), G_k is obtained from G_{k-1} by either increasing the choice number for one man (thereby worsening his match) or decreasing the choice number for one man (thereby improving his match). The value of t is at most $2m^2$ where m is the number of men.*

This sequence can be obtained using algorithm γ that takes $O(m^2 + w)$ computation time given all the data structures (preference lists and rankings) in memory.

```
input: A stable marriage instance, initial proposal vector I
output: a stable marriage M
    compute U using Algorithm β with the initial vector as [m, m, ..., m];
    G := I;    K := max(G, U);
    while ∃ a man i such that (i, q) is a best blocking pair in K
        set K[i] and G[i] to the choice corresponding to woman q;
        generate a matching that satisfies the blocking pair (i, q);
    endwhile;

    while ∃ a man i s.t. i unmatched or (i, q) is a blocking pair in G
        set G[i] to the next woman q who would accept proposal from i;
        generate a matching that moves the man i from the current partner to q;
    endwhile;
    return G;
```

Fig. 6. Algorithm γ that generates a sequence of matchings.

Since the RVV Algorithm generates a sequence of matchings instead of proposal vectors, we show how to generate a sequence of matchings explicitly instead of proposal vectors in Fig. 6. The downward traversal is performed by using the best blocking pairs in K. The matching is generated from the proposal vector G as defined in Sect. 2. Observe that these matchings may not be men-saturating and therefore some men and women may be unmatched. The upward traversal is performed by matching those men who are either unmatched or matched to a woman in a blocking pair. Clearly, the length of the sequence of these matchings is at most $O(m^2)$.

References

1. Abeledo, H., Rothblum, U.G.: Paths to marriage stability. Discrete Appl. Math. **63**(1), 1–12 (1995)
2. Ackermann, H., Goldberg, P.W., Mirrokni, V.S., Röglin, H., Vöcking, B.: Uncoordinated two-sided matching markets. SIAM J. Comput. **40**(1), 92–106 (2011)
3. David, M.: Algorithmics of Matching Under Preferences, vol. 2. World Scientific, Singapore (2013)
4. Gale, D., Shapley, L.S.: College admissions and the stability of marriage. Am. Math. Monthly **69**(1), 9–15 (1962)
5. Garg, V.K., Hu, C. :Improved paths to stability for the stable marriage problem. arXiv (2023)
6. Gusfield, D., Irving, R.W.: The Stable Marriage Problem: Structure and Algorithms. MIT press, Cambridge (1989)
7. Iwama, K., Miyazaki, S.: A survey of the stable marriage problem and its variants. In: International Conference on Informatics Education and Research for Knowledge-Circulating Society, 2008. ICKS 2008, pp. 131–136. IEEE (2008)
8. Knuth, D.E.: Stable Marriage and its Relation to Other Combinatorial Problems: An Introduction to the Mathematical Analysis of Algorithms, vol. 10. American Mathematical Soc. (1997)
9. Maggs, B.M., Sitaraman, R.K.: Algorithmic nuggets in content delivery. ACM SIGCOMM Comput. Commun. Rev. **45**(3), 52–66 (2015)
10. Roth, A.E., Sotomayor, M.: Two-Sided Matching. Handbook of Game Theory with Economic Applications 1, 485–541 (1992)
11. Roth, A.E., Vate, J.H.V.: Random paths to stability in two-sided matching. Econometrica: J. Econometric Soc. **58**, 1475–1480 (1990)
12. Rothblum, U.G.: Characterization of stable matchings as extreme points of a polytope. Math. Program. **54**(1–3), 57–67 (1992)
13. Tamura, A.: Transformation from arbitrary matchings to stable matchings. J. Comb. Theory, Ser. A **62**(2), 310–323 (1993)
14. Tan, J.J., Su, W.C.: On the divorce digraph of the stable marriage problem. Proc. Natl Sci. Coun. Repub. China **19**, 342–354 (1995)
15. Teo, C.-P., Sethuraman, J.: The geometry of fractional stable matchings and its applications. Math. Oper. Res. **23**(4), 874–891 (1998)

Lattice Linearity of Multiplication and Modulo

Arya Tanmay Gupta(✉) and Sandeep S. Kulkarni(✉)

Computer Science and Engineering, Michigan State University, East Lansing, USA
{atgupta,sandeep}@msu.edu

Abstract. In this paper, we study the lattice linearity of multiplication and modulo operations. We demonstrate that these operations are lattice linear and the parallel processing algorithms that we study for both these operations are able to exploit the lattice linearity of their respective problems. This implies that these algorithms can be implemented in asynchronous environments, where the nodes are allowed to read old information from each other. These algorithms also exhibit snap-stabilizing properties, i.e., starting from an arbitrary state, the sequence of state transitions made by the system strictly follows its specification.

Keywords: lattice linear · modulo · multiplication · self-stabilization · asynchrony

1 Introduction

Development of parallel processing algorithms to solve problems is increasingly gaining interest. This is because computing machines are manufactured with multiprocessor chips as we face a bound on the rate of architectural development of individual microprocessors. Such algorithms, in general, require synchronization among their processing nodes. Without such synchronization, the nodes perform executions based on inconsistent values possibly resulting in substantial delay or potentially incorrect computation.

In this context, lattice theory has provided with very useful concepts. In lattice linear systems, a partial order is induced in the state space, which allows the nodes to perform executions asynchronously. Lattice linearity was utilized in modelling the problems (where there exists a predicate, naturally describing the problem, under which the global states form a lattice, called *lattice linear problems*) [5] and in developing algorithms (called *lattice linear algorithms*) which impose a lattice structure in problems (which are not lattice linear) [7,8]. Thus, the algorithms that traverse such a state transition system can allow the nodes to perform executions asynchronously while preserving correctness.

Lattice linearity allows inducing single or multiple lattices among the global states. If self-stabilization is required, then for every induced lattice, its supremum must be an optimal state. This way, it can be ensured that the system can traverse to an optimal state from an arbitrary state. We introduced eventually

S. Dolev and B. Schieber (Eds.): SSS 2023, LNCS 14310, pp. 141–156, 2023.
https://doi.org/10.1007/978-3-031-44274-2_12

lattice linear algorithms [7] and fully lattice linear algorithms [8] for non-lattice linear problems (we discuss more on this in Sect. 2 for the sake of completeness, but non-lattice linear problems are not the focus of this paper). These algorithms are self-stabilizing.

Many lattice linear problems do not allow self-stabilization [4–6]. While developing new algorithms for lattice linear and non-lattice linear problems is very interesting, it is also worthwhile to study if algorithms already present in the literature exploit lattice linearity of problems or if lattice linearity is present in existing algorithms. For example, lattice linearity was found to be exploited by Johnson's algorithm for shortest paths in graphs [5] and by Gale's top trading cycle algorithm for housing market [6].

In this paper, we study parallel implementations of two fundamental operations in mathematics: multiplication and modulo. We study algorithms for $n \times m$ and $n \mod m$ where n and m are *large* integers represented as binary strings.

The applications of integer multiplication include the computation of power, matrix products which has applications in a plethora of fields including artificial intelligence and game theory, the sum of fractions and coprime base. Modular arithmetic has applications in theoretical mathematics, where it is heavily used in number theory and various topics (groups, rings, fields, knots, etc.) in abstract algebra. Modular arithmetic also has applications in applied mathematics, where it is used in computer algebra, cryptography, chemistry and the visual and musical arts. In many of these applications, the value of the divisor is fixed.

A crucial observation is that these operations are lattice linear. Also, the algorithms that we study in this paper are capable of computing the correct answer even if the nodes are initialized in an arbitrary state. These properties are present in these operations as opposed to many other lattice linear problems where the lattice structure does not allow self-stabilization.

1.1 Contributions of the Paper

- We study the lattice linearity of modulo and multiplication operations. We demonstrate that these problems satisfy the constraints of lattice linear problems [5]. This implies that some of the algorithms for them are capable of benefiting from the property of lattice linearity.
- We also show that these algorithms exhibit properties that are similar to snap-stabilizing algorithms [1], i.e., starting from an arbitrary state, the sequence of state transitions made by the system strictly follows its specification, i.e., initializing in an arbitrary state, the nodes immediately start obtaining the values as expected with each action they execute.

1.2 Organization of the Paper

In Sect. 2, we describe the definitions and notations that we use in this paper. In Sect. 3, we discuss the related work. We study lattice linearity of the multiplication operation in Sect. 4. Then, in Sect. 5, we study the lattice linearity of the modulo operation. Finally, we conclude in Sect. 6.

2 Preliminaries

This paper focuses on multiplication and modulo operations, where the operands are n and m. In the computation $n \times m$ or $n \mod m$, n and m are the values of these numbers respectively, and $|n|$ and $|m|$ are the length of the bitstrings required to represent n and m respectively. If n is a bitstring, then $n[i]$ is the ith bit of n (indices start from 1). For a bitstring n, $n[1]$, for example, is the most significant bit of n and $n[|n|]$ is the least significant bit of n. $n[i:j]$ is the bitstring from i^{th} to j^{th} bit of n. For simplicity, we stipulate that n and m are of lengths in some power of 2. Since size of n and m may be substantially different, we provide complexity results that are of the form $O(f(n, m))$ in all cases.

We use the following string operations: (1) *append*(a, b), appends b to the end of a in $O(1)$ time, (2) $rshift(a, k)$, deletes rightmost k bits of a in $O(k)$ time, and (3) $lshift(a, k)$, appends k zeros to the right of a in $O(k)$ time.

2.1 Modeling Distributed Programs

$n \times m$ or $n \mod m$ are typically thought of as arithmetic operations. However, when n and m are large, we view them as algorithms. In this paper, we view them as parallel/distributed algorithms where the nodes collectively perform computations to converge to the final output. Next, we provide the relevant definitions of a parallel/distributed program that we utilize in this paper.

The parallel/distributed program consists of nodes where each node is associated with a set of variables. A *global state*, say s, is obtained by assigning each variable of each node a value from its respective domain. s is represented as a vector, where $s[i]$ itself is a vector of the variables of node i. S denotes the *state space*, which is the set of all global states that a given system can obtain.

Each node is associated with actions. Each action at node i checks the values of other nodes and updates its own variables. An *action* is of the form $g \longrightarrow a_c$, where g is the *guard* (a Boolean predicate involving variables of i and other nodes) and a_c is an instruction that updates the variables of i. We assume all actions to be executed atomically.

An algorithm A is *self-stabilizing* for the subset S_o of S where S is the set of all global states, iff (1) *convergence.* starting from an arbitrary state, any sequence of computations of A reaches a state in S_o, and (2) *closure.* any computation of A starting from S_o always stays in S_o. We assume S_o to be the set of optimal states: the system is deemed converged once it reaches a state in S_o. An algorithm is *snap-stabilizing* iff starting from an arbitrary state, it makes the system follow a sequence of state transitions as per the specification of that system.

2.2 Execution Without Synchronization

Typically, we view the *computation* of an algorithm as a sequence of global states $\langle s_0, s_1, \cdots \rangle$, where $s_{t+1}, t \geq 0$, is obtained by executing some action by one or more nodes in s_t. For the sake of discussion, assume that only node i executes in state s_t. The computation prefix uptil s_t is $\langle s_0, s_1, \cdots, s_t \rangle$. The state that the system traverses to after s_t is s_{t+1}. Under proper synchronization, i would evaluate its guards on the *current* local states of its neighbours in s_t.

To understand the execution in asynchrony, let $x(s)$ be the value of some variable x in state s. If i executes in asynchrony, then it views the global state that it is in to be s', where $x(s') \in \{x(s_0), x(s_1), \cdots, x(s_t)\}$. In this case, s_{t+1} is evaluated as follows. If all guards in i evaluate to false, then the system will continue to remain in state s_t, i.e., $s_{t+1} = s_t$. If a guard g evaluates to true then i will execute its corresponding action a_c. Here, we have the following observations: (1) $s_{t+1}[i]$ is the state that i obtains after executing an action in s', and (2) $\forall j \neq i$, $s_{t+1}[j] = s_t[j]$.

The model described above allows nodes to read old values of other nodes arbitrarily. In this paper, however, we require that the values of variables of other nodes are read/received in the order in which they were updated/sent.

2.3 Embedding a <-Lattice in Global States

Let s denote a global state, and let $s[i]$ denote the state of node i in s. First, we define a total order $<_l$; all local states of a node i are totally ordered under $<_l$. Using $<_l$, we define a partial order $<_g$ among global states as follows:

We say that $s <_g s'$ iff $(\forall i : s[i] = s'[i] \vee s[i] <_l s'[i]) \wedge (\exists i : s[i] <_l s'[i])$. Also, $s = s'$ iff $\forall i\ s[i] = s'[i]$. For brevity, we use $<$ to denote $<_l$ and $<_g$: $<$ corresponds to $<_l$ while comparing local states, and $<$ corresponds to $<_g$ while comparing global states. We also use the symbol '$>$' which is such that $s > s'$ iff $s' < s$. Similarly, we use symbols '$\leq$' and '$\geq$'; e.g., $s \leq s'$ iff $s = s' \vee s < s'$. We call the lattice, formed from such partial order, a *<-lattice*.

Definition 1. ***<-lattice***. Given a total relation $<_l$ that orders the states visited by i (for each i) the <-lattice corresponding to $<_l$ is defined by the following partial order: $s < s'$ iff $(\forall i\ \ s[i] \leq_l s'[i]) \wedge (\exists i\ \ s[i] <_l s'[i])$.

A <-lattice constraints how global states can transition among one another: state s can transition to state s' iff $s < s'$. In the <-lattice discussed above, we can define the meet and join of two states in the standard way: the meet (respectively, join), of two states s_1 and s_2 is a state s_3 where $\forall i$, $s_3[i]$ is equal to $min(s_1[i], s_2[i])$ (respectively, $max(s_1[i], s_2[i])$), where $\min(x, y) = min(y, x) = x$ iff $(x <_l y \vee x = y)$, and $\max(x, y) = \max(y, x) = y$ iff $(y >_l x \vee y = x)$. For s_1 and s_2, their meet (respectively, join) has a path to (respectively, is reachable from) both s_1 and s_2.

By varying $<_l$ that identifies a total order among the states of a node, one can obtain different lattices. A <-lattice, embedded in the state space, is useful for permitting the algorithm to execute asynchronously. Under proper constraints on the structure of <-lattice, convergence can be ensured.

2.4 Lattice Linear Problems

Next, we discuss *lattice linear problems*, i.e., the problems where the problem statement creates the lattice structure automatically. Such problems can be represented by a predicate that induces a lattice among the states in S.

In *lattice linear problems*, a problem P can be represented by a predicate $\mathcal{P}$ such that for any node i, if it is violating $\mathcal{P}$ in some state s, then it must change its state. Otherwise, the system will not satisfy $\mathcal{P}$. Let $\mathcal{P}(s)$ be true iff state s satisfies $\mathcal{P}$. A node violating $\mathcal{P}$ in s is called an *impedensable* node (an *impediment* to progress if does not execute, *indispensable* to execute for progress). Formally,

Definition 2. [5] ***Impedensable node.*** $\text{IMPEDENSABLE}(i, s, \mathcal{P}) \equiv \neg\mathcal{P}(s) \wedge (\forall s' > s : s'[i] = s[i] \implies \neg\mathcal{P}(s'))$.

Definition 2 implies that if a node i is impedensable in state s, then in any state s' such that $s' > s$, if the state of i remains the same, then the algorithm will not converge. Thus $\mathcal{P}$ induces a total order among the local states visited by a node, for all nodes. Consequently, the discrete structure that gets induced among the global states is a $<$-lattice, as described in Definition 1. Thus, any $<$-lattice among the global states is induced by a predicate $\mathcal{P}$ that satisfies Definition 2.

There can be multiple arbitrary lattices that can be induced among the global states. A system cannot guarantee convergence while traversing an arbitrary lattice. To resolve this, we design the predicate $\mathcal{P}$ such that it fulfils some properties, and guarantees reachability to an optimal state. $\mathcal{P}$ is used by the nodes to determine if they are impedensable, using Definition 2. Thus, $\mathcal{P}$ induces a $<_l$ relation among the local states, and as a result, a $<$-lattice among the global states. We say that $\mathcal{P}$ is *lattice linear* with respect to that $<$-lattice. Consequently, in any suboptimal global state, there will be at least one impedensable node. Formally,

Definition 3. [5] ***Lattice Linear Predicate.*** $\mathcal{P}$ is a lattice linear predicate with respect to a $<$-lattice induced among the global states iff $\forall s \in S : \neg\mathcal{P}(s) \Rightarrow \exists i : \text{IMPEDENSABLE}(i, s, \mathcal{P})$.

Now we complete the definition of lattice linear problems. In a lattice linear problem P, given any suboptimal global state, we can identify all and the only nodes which cannot retain their state. In this paper, we observe that the algorithms that we study exploit this nature of their respective problems. $\mathcal{P}$ is thus designed conserving this nature of the subject problem P.

Definition 4. Lattice linear problems. A problem P is lattice linear iff there exists a predicate $\mathcal{P}$ and a $<$-lattice such that

- P is deemed solved iff the system reaches a state where $\mathcal{P}$ is true, and
- $\mathcal{P}$ is lattice linear with respect to the $<$-lattice induced in S, i.e., $\forall s : \neg\mathcal{P}(s) \Rightarrow \exists i : \text{IMPEDENSABLE}(i, s, \mathcal{P})$.
- $\forall s : (\exists i : \text{IMPEDENSABLE}(i, s, \mathcal{P}) \Rightarrow (\forall s' : \mathcal{P}(s') \Rightarrow s'[i] \neq s[i]))$.

Remark: Certain problems are non-lattice linear problems. In such problems, there are instances in which the impedensable nodes cannot be distinctly determined, i.e., in those instances $\exists s : \neg\mathcal{P}(s) \Rightarrow (\exists s' : \forall i : \mathcal{P}(s') \wedge s[i] = s'[i])$.

Minimal dominating set (MDS) and several other graph theoretic problems are examples of such problems. (This can be illustrated through a simple instance of a 2 node connected network with nodes A and B, initially both in the dominating set. Here, MDS can be obtained without removing A. Thus, A is not impedensable. The same applies to B.) For such problems, $<$-lattices are induced algorithmically as an impedensable node cannot be distinctly determined naturally. Eventually lattice linear algorithms (introduced in [7]) and fully lattice linear algorithms (introduced in [8]) were developed for many such problems.

Problems such as stable marriage, job scheduling and market clearing price, as studied in [5], are lattice linear problems. In this paper, we study lattice structures that can be induced in multiplication and modulo: we show that multiplication and modulo are lattice linear problems. All the lattice structures that we study in this paper allow self-stabilization: the supremum of the lattice induced in the state space is the optimal state.

Definition 5. Self-stabilizing lattice linear predicate. Continuing from Definition 4, $\mathcal{P}$ is a self-stabilizing lattice linear predicate if and only if the supremum of the lattice that $\mathcal{P}$ induces is an optimal state, i.e., $\mathcal{P}(supremum(S)) = true$.

Note that $\mathcal{P}$ can also be true in states other than the supremum of the $<$-lattice.

Remark: A $<$-lattice, induced under $\mathcal{P}$, allows asynchrony because if a node, reading old values, reads the current state as s, then for the current state s', $s < s'$. So $\neg\mathcal{P}(s) \Rightarrow \neg\mathcal{P}(s')$ because $\textsc{Impedensable}(i, s, \mathcal{P})$ and $s[i] = s'[i]$.

3 Related Work

Lattice Linear Problems: The notion of representing problems through a predicate under which the states form a lattice was introduced in [5]. We call the problems for which such a representation is possible *lattice linear problems.* Lattice linear problems are studied in [4–6], where the authors have studied lattice linearity in, respectively, housing market problem and several dynamic programming problems. Many of these problems are not self-stabilizing.

Snap-Stabilization: The notion of snap-stabilization was introduced in [1]. The algorithms that we study in this paper make the system follow a sequence of states that are deterministically predictable because of the underlying lattice structure in the state space. Thus, they exhibit snap-stabilization. In general, self-stabilizing algorithms where lattice linearity is utilized are snap stabilizing.

Modulo: In [12], the authors have presented parallel processing algorithms for inverse, discrete roots, or a large power modulo a number that has only small prime factors. A hardware circuit implementation for mod is presented in [2].

In this paper, we present several parallel processing algorithms which are self-stabilizing. Some require critical preprocessing, and some do not. The general algorithm for modulo (Algorithm 2) utilizes the power of (sequential or parallel) modulo and multiplication operations on smaller operands.

Multiplication: In [3], the authors presented three parallel implementations of the Karatsuba algorithm for long integer multiplication on a distributed memory architecture. Two of the implementations have time complexity of $O(n)$ on $n^{\lg 3}$ processors. The third algorithm has complexity $O(n \lg n)$ on n processors.

In this paper, we study lattice linearity of parallelized Karatsuba algorithm.

4 Parallelized Karatsuba's Multiplication Operation

In this section, we study the lattice linearity of this algorithm that was presented in [3]. First we discuss the idea behind the sequential Karatsuba's algorithm, and then we elaborate on its lattice linearity.

4.1 Key Idea of the Sequential Karatsuba's Algorithm [10]

The input is a pair of bitstrings n and m. This algorithm is recursive in nature. As the base case, if the length of n and m equals 1 then, the multiplication result is trivial. When the length is greater than 1, we let $m = ab$ and $n = cd$, where a and b are half the length of m, and c and d are half the length of n. Here, ab, for example, represents concatenation of a and b, which equals m.

Let $z = 2^{|b|}$. $n \times m$ can be computed as $ac \times z^2 + (ad + bc) \times z + bd$. $ad + bc$ can be computed as $(a + b) \times (c + d) - ac - bd$. Thus, to compute $m \times n$, it suffices to compute 3 multiplications $a \times c$, $b \times d$ and $(a + b) \times (c + d)$. Hence, we can eliminate one of the multiplications. In the following section, we analyse the lattice linearity of the parallelization of this algorithm as described in [3].

4.2 The CM Parallelization [3] for Karatsuba's Algorithm

The Karatsuba multiplication algorithm involves dividing the input string into substrings and use them to evaluate the multiplication recursively. In the parallel version of this algorithm, the recursive call is replaced by utilizing another *children* nodes to treat those substrings. We elaborate more on this in the following paragraphs. Consequently, this algorithm induces a tree among the computing nodes. Every non-leaf node has three children. This algorithm works in two phases, top-down and bottom-up. This algorithm uses four variables to represent the state of each node i: $n.i$, $m.i$, $ans.i$ and $shift.i$ respectively.

In the sequential Karatsuba's algorithm, both of the input strings n and m are divided into two substrings each and the algorithm then runs recursively on three different input pairs computed from those excerpt bitstrings. In the parallel version, those recursive calls are replaced by *activating* three children nodes [3]. As a result of such parallelization, if there is no carry-forwarding due to addition, we require $\lg |n|$ levels, for which a total of $|n|^{\lg 3}$ nodes are required. However, if there is carry-forwarding due to additions, then we require $2 \lg |n|$ levels, for which a total of $|n|^{2 \lg 3}$ nodes are required.

In the top-down phase, if $|m.i| > 1$ or $|n.i| > 1$, then i writes (1) a and c to its left child, node $3i - 1$ ($m.(3i - 1) = a.i$ and $n.(3i - 1) = c.i$), (2) b and d to its middle child, node $3i$ ($m.(3i) = b.i$ and $n.(3i) = d.i$), and (3) $a+b$ and $c+d$ to its right child, node $3i+1$ ($m.(3i+1) = a.i + b.i$ and $n.(3i+1) = c.i + d.i$). If $|m.i| = |n.i| = 1$, i.e., in the base case, the bottom-up phase begins and node i sets $ans.i = m.i \times n.i$ that can be computed trivially since $|m.i| = |n.i| = 1$.

In the bottom-up phase, node i sets $ans.i = ans.(3i-1) \times z^2 + (ans.(3i+1) - (ans.(3i-1) + ans.(3i)) \times z + ans.(3i)$. Notice that multiplication by z and z^2 corresponds to bit shifts and does not need an actual multiplication. Consequently, the product of $m \times n$ for node i is computed by this algorithm.

With some book-keeping (storing the place values of most significant bits of $a+b$ and $c+d$), a node i only needs to write the rightmost $\frac{|m.i|}{2}$ and $\frac{|n.i|}{2}$ bits to its children. Thus, we can safely assume that when a node writes m and n to any of its children, then m and n of that child are of equal length and are of length in some power of 2. (If we do not do the book-keeping, the required number of nodes increases, this number is upper bounded by $|n|^{2\lg 3}$ as the number of levels is upper bounded by $2\lg|n|$; this observation was not made in [3].) However, we do not show the same in the algorithm for brevity. Thus this algorithm would require $2\lg|n|$ levels, i.e., $|n|^{2\lg 3}$ nodes.

Computation of shift.i: This algorithm utilizes $shift$ to compute z. A node i updates $shift.i$ by doubling the value of $shift$ from its children. A node i evaluates that it is impedensable because of an incorrect value of $shift.i$ by evaluating the following macro.

$$\textsc{Impedensable-Multiplication-Karatsuba-Shift}(i) \equiv$$
$$\begin{cases} |m.i| = 1 \wedge |n.i| = 1 \wedge shift.i \neq 0 \;\; OR \\ shift.(3i) = shift.(3i-1) = 0 \leq shift.(3i+1) \wedge shift.i \neq 1 \;\; OR \\ 0 < shift.(3i) = shift.(3i-1) \leq shift.(3i+1) \wedge shift.i \neq shift.(3i) * 2. \end{cases}$$

Computation of m.i and n.i: To ensure that the data flows down correctly, we declare a node i to be impedensable as follows.

$$\textsc{Impedensable-Multiplication-Karatsuba-TopDown}(i) \equiv$$
$$\begin{cases} i = 1 \wedge (m.i \neq m \vee n.i \neq n) \;\; OR \\ ((|m.i| > 1 \wedge |n.i| > 1) \wedge \\ (m.(3i-1) \neq m.i\left[1 : \frac{|m.i|}{2}\right] \;\; OR \\ n.(3i-1) \neq n.i\left[1 : \frac{|n.i|}{2}\right] \;\; OR \\ m.(3i) \neq m.i\left[\frac{|m.i|}{2} + 1 : |m.i|\right] \;\; OR \\ n.(3i) \neq n.i\left[\frac{|n.i|}{2} + 1 : |n.i|\right] \;\; OR \\ m.(3i+1) \neq m.i\left[1 : \frac{|m.i|}{2}\right] + m.i\left[\frac{|m.i|}{2} + 1 : |m.i|\right] \;\; OR \\ n.(3i+1) \neq n.i\left[1 : \frac{|n.i|}{2}\right] + n.i\left[\frac{|n.i|}{2} + 1 : |n.i|\right])). \end{cases}$$

Computation of ans.i: To determine if a node i has stored $ans.i$ incorrectly, it evaluates to be impedensable as follows.

$$\text{IMPEDENSABLE-MULTIPLICATION-KARATSUBA-BOTTOMUP}(i) \equiv$$
$$\begin{cases} |m.i| = 1 \wedge |n.i| = 1 \wedge ans.i \neq m.i \times n.i \quad OR \\ |m.i| > 1 \wedge |n.i| > 1 \wedge (ans.i \neq lshift(ans.(3i-1), shift.i) \\ \qquad +lshift(ans.(3i+1) - ans.(3i-1) - ans.(3i), shift.(3i)) \\ \qquad +ans.(3i+1)) \end{cases}$$

Thus, Algorithm 1 is described as follows:

Algorithm 1. *Parallel processing version of Karatsuba's algorithm.*

Rules for node i.

$$\text{IMPEDENSABLE-MULTIPLICATION-KARATSUBA-SHIFT}(i) \longrightarrow$$
$$\begin{cases} shift.i = 0 & \text{if } |m.i| = 1 \wedge |n.i| = 1 \wedge shift.i \neq 0. \\ shift.i = 1 & \text{if } shift.(3i) = shift.(3i-1) = 0 \\ & \quad \leq shift.(3i+1) \wedge shift.i \neq 1 \\ shift.i = shift.(3i) \times 2 & \text{otherwise} \end{cases}$$

$$\text{IMPEDENSABLE-MULTIPLICATION-KARATSUBA-TOPDOWN}(i) \longrightarrow$$
$$\begin{cases} m.i = m, n.i = n & \text{if } i = 1 \wedge (m.i \neq m \vee n.i \neq n). \\ m.(3i-1) = m.i\left[1 : \frac{|m.i|}{2}\right] & \text{if } m.(3i-1) \neq m.i\left[1 : \frac{|m.i|}{2}\right]. \\ n.(3i-1) = n.i\left[1 : \frac{|n.i|}{2}\right] & \text{if } n.(3i-1) \neq n.i\left[1 : \frac{|n.i|}{2}\right]. \\ m.(3i) = m.i\left[\frac{|m.i|}{2} + 1 : |m.i|\right] & \text{if } m.(3i) \neq m.i\left[\frac{|m.i|}{2} + 1 : |m.i|\right]. \\ n.(3i) = n.i\left[\frac{|n.i|}{2} + 1 : |n.i|\right] & \text{if } n.(3i) \neq n.i\left[\frac{|n.i|}{2} + 1 : |n.i|\right]. \\ m.(3i+1) = m.i\left[1 : \frac{|m.i|}{2}\right] & \\ \quad +m.i\left[\frac{|m.i|}{2} + 1 : |m.i|\right] & \text{if } m.(3i+1) \neq m.i\left[1 : \frac{|m.i|}{2}\right]. \\ & \quad +m.i\left[\frac{|m.i|}{2} + 1 : |m.i|\right]. \\ n.(3i+1) = n.i\left[1 : \frac{|n.i|}{2}\right] & \\ \quad +n.i\left[\frac{|n.i|}{2} + 1 : |n.i|\right] & \text{otherwise} \end{cases}$$

$$\text{IMPEDENSABLE-MULTIPLICATION-KARATSUBA-BOTTOMUP}(i) \longrightarrow$$
$$\begin{cases} ans.i = m.i \times n.i & \text{if } |m.i| = 1 \wedge |n.i| = 1 \\ ans.i = lshift(ans.(3i-1), shift.i) + & \\ \quad lshift(ans.(3i+1) - ans.(3i-1) & \\ \qquad -ans.(3i), shift.(3i)) + ans.(3i+1)) & \text{otherwise.} \end{cases}$$

Algorithm 1 converges in $O(|n|)$ time [3], and its work complexity is $O(n^{\lg 3})$, which is the time complexity of the sequential Karatsuba's algorithm [3].

Example 1. Figure 1 evaluates 100 × 100 following Algorithm 1. □

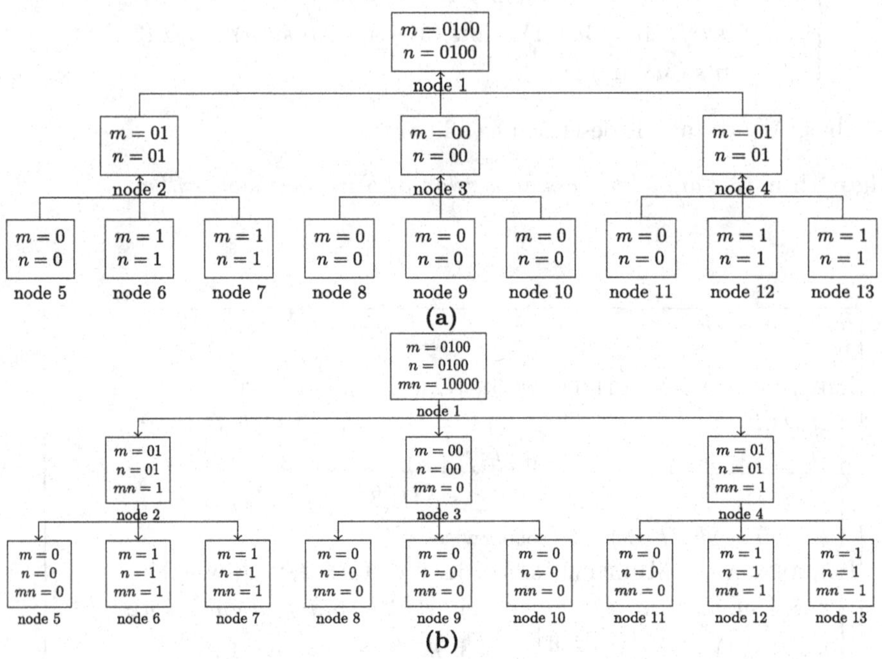

Fig. 1. Demonstration of multiplication of 100 and 100 in base 2: (a) top down (b) bottom up.

4.3 Lattice Linearity

Theorem 1. *Given the input bitstrings n and m, the predicate*

$$\forall i \neg(\textsc{Impedensable-Multiplication-Karatsuba-Shift}(i) \vee \\ \textsc{Impedensable-Multiplication-Karatsuba-TopDown}(i) \vee \\ \textsc{Impedensable-Multiplication-Karatsuba-BottomUp}(i))$$

is lattice linear on $|n|^{2\lg 3}$ computing nodes.

Proof. For the global state to be optimal, in this problem, we require node 1 to store the correct multiplication result in $ans.1$. To achieve this, each node i must have the correct value of $n.i$ and $m.i$, and their children must store correct values of n, m and i according to their $n.i$ and $m.i$ values. This in turn requires all nodes to store the correct $shift.i$ values.

Let us assume for contradiction that node 1 does not have the correct value of $ans.1 = n \times m$. This implies that (1) node 1 does not have an updated value in $n.1$ or $m.1$, or (2) node 1 has a non-updated value of $ans.1$, (3) node 1 has not written the updated values to $n.2$ & $m.2$ or $n.3$ & $m.3$ or $n.4$ & $m.4$, (4) node 1 has a non-updated value in $shift.1$, or (5) nodes 2, 3 or 4 have incorrect values in their respective n, m, ans or $shift$ variables. In cases (1),...,(4), node 1 is impedensable.

Recursively, this can be extended to any node i. Let node i has stored an incorrect value in $ans.i$ or $shift.i$. Let $i > 1$. Then (1) node i has a non-updated value in $shift.i$, $ans.i$, $n.i$ or $m.i$, or (2) (if $m.i > 1$ or $n.i > 1$) node i has not written updated values to $n.(3i-1)$ & $m.(3i-1)$ or $n.(3i)$ & $m.(3i)$ or $n.(3i+1)$ & $m.(3i+1)$, in which case node i is impedensable. In both these cases, node i is impedensable. It is also possible that at least one of the children of node i has incorrect values in its respective n, m, ans or $shift$ variables. From these cases, we have that given a global state s, where $s = \langle\langle n.1, m.1, ans.1\rangle, \langle n.2, m.2, ans.2\rangle, ..., \langle n.(|n|^{2\lg 3}), m.(|n|^{2\lg 3}), ans.(|n|^{2\lg 3})\rangle\rangle$, if s is impedensable, there is at least one node which is impedensable. This shows that if the global state is impedensable, then there exists some node i which is impedensable.

Next, we show that if some node is impedensable, then node 1 will not store the correct answer. Node 1 is impedensable if it has not read the correct value $m.1$ and $n.1$. Additionally, $\forall i : i \in [1 : n^{2\lg 3}]$ node i is impedensable if (1) it has non-updated values in $ans.i$ or $shift.i$, (2) i has not written the correct values to $ans.(3i-1)$ or $ans.(3i)$ or $ans.(3i+1)$. This implies that the parent of i will also store incorrect value in its ans or $shift$ variable. Recursively, we have that node 1 stores an incorrect value in $ans.1$. Thus, the global state is impedensable. $\square$

Corollary 1. *Algorithm 1 computes multiplication of two numbers with $n^{2\lg 3}$ nodes without synchronization.*

In Algorithm 1, we allow nodes to change values of other nodes, where parents update their children, which is generally not allowed in a distributed system. It can be transformed such that all nodes update themselves only, and will stay lattice linear, as follows. Nodes will copy n and m from their parents and update their own n and m values. With this change, the definition of IMPEDENSABLE-MULTIPLICATION-KARATSUBA-TOPDOWN(i) will change accordingly.

5 Parallel Processing Modulo Operation

In this section, we present a parallel processing algorithm to compute $n \mod m$ using $4 \times |n|/|m| - 1$ computing nodes. It induces a binary tree among the nodes based on their ids; there are $2 \times |n|/|m|$ nodes in the lowest level (level 1).

This algorithm starts from the leaves where all leaves compute, contiguously, a substring of n of length $|m|/2$ under modulo m. In the induced binary tree, the computed modulo result by sibling nodes at level ℓ is sent to the parent. Consecutively, those parents at level $\ell + 1$, contiguously, store a larger substring of n (double the bits as their children cover) under modulo m. We elaborate this procedure in this subsection. This algorithm uses three variables to represent the state of each node i: $shift.i$, $pow.i$ and $ans.i$.

Computation of *shift.i*: The variable $shift$ stores the required power of 2. At any node at level 1, $shift$ is 0. At level 2, the value of $shift$ at any node is $|m|/2$. At any higher level, the value of $shilft$ is twice the value of shift of its children. Impedensable-Log-Modulo-Shift, in this context, is defined below.

$$\text{IMPEDENSABLE-LOG-MODULO-SHIFT}(i) \equiv$$
$$\begin{cases} shift.i \neq 0 & \text{if } i \geq 2 \times |n|/|m| \\ shift.i \neq |m|/2 & \text{if } shift.(2i) = shift.(2i+1) = 0 \\ shift.i \neq 2 \times shift.(2i) & \text{if } shift.(2i) = shift.(2i+1) \geq |m| \end{cases}$$

Computation of *pow.i*: The goal of this computation is to set $pow.i$ to be $2^{shift.i} \mod m$, whenever $level.i \geq 2$. This can be implemented using the following definition for Impedensable-Log-Modulo-Pow.

$$\text{IMPEDENSABLE-LOG-MODULO-POW}(i) \equiv$$
$$\begin{cases} pow.i \neq 1 & \text{if } shift.i = 0 \\ pow.i \neq 2^{\frac{|m|}{2}} & \text{if } shift.i = |m|/2 \\ pow.i \neq (pow.(2i))^2 \mod m & \text{otherwise} \end{cases}$$

By definition, $pow.i$ is less than m. Also, computation of pow requires multiplication of two numbers that are bounded by $|m|$. Hence, this calculation can benefit from parallelization of Algorithm 1. However, as we will see later, the complexity of this algorithm (for modulo) is dominated by the modulo operation happening in individual nodes which is $O(|m|^2)$, we can use the sequential version of Karatsuba's algorithm for multiplication as well, without affecting the order of the time complexity of this algorithm.

Computation of *ans.i*: We split n into strings of size $\frac{|m|}{2}$, the number representing this substring is less than m. At the lowest level (level 1), $ans.i$ is set to the corresponding substring. At higher levels, $ans.i$ is set to $(pow.i \times ans.(2i) + ans.(2i+1)) \mod m$. This computation also involves multiplication of two numbers whose size is upper bounded by $|m|$. An impedensable node i from a non-updated $ans.i$ can be evaluated using Impedensable-Log-Modulo-Ans(i).

$$\text{IMPEDENSABLE-LOG-MODULO-ANS}(i) \equiv$$
$$\begin{cases} ans.i \neq n[(i - 2 \times \frac{|n|}{|m|}) \times \frac{|m|}{2} + 1 : (i - 2 \times \frac{|n|}{|m|} + 1) \times \frac{|m|}{2}] & \text{if } shift.i = 0 \\ ans.i \neq \text{MOD}(\text{SUM}(\text{MUL}(ans.(2i), pow.i), ans.(2i+1)), m) & \text{otherwise} \end{cases}$$

We describe the algorithm as Algorithm 2.

Algorithm 2. *Modulo computation by inducing a tree among the nodes.*

Rules for node i.

IMPEDENSABLE-LOG-MODULO-SHIFT$(i) \longrightarrow$

$$\begin{cases} shift.i = 0 & \text{if } i \geq 2 \times |n|/|m| \\ shift.i = \frac{|m|}{2} & \text{if } shift.(2i) = shift.(2i+1) = 0 \\ shift.i = 2 \times shift.(2i) & \text{if } shift.(2i) = shift.(2i+1) \geq |m| \end{cases}$$

IMPEDENSABLE-LOG-MODULO-POW$(i) \longrightarrow$

$$\begin{cases} pow.i = 1 & \text{if } shift.i = 0 \\ pow.i = 2^{\frac{|m|}{2}} & \text{if } shift.i = |m|/2 \\ pow.i = \text{MOD}(\text{MUL}(pow.i, pow.i), m) & \text{otherwise} \end{cases}$$

IMPEDENSABLE-LOG-MODULO-ANS$(i) \longrightarrow$

$$\begin{cases} ans.i = n[(i - 2 \times \frac{|n|}{|m|}) \times \frac{|m|}{2} + 1 : (i - 2 \times \frac{|n|}{|m|} + 1) \times \frac{|m|}{2}] & \text{if } shift.i = 0 \\ ans.i = \text{MOD}(\text{SUM}(\text{MUL}(ans.(2i), pow.i), ans.(2i+1)), m) & \text{otherwise} \end{cases}$$

Example 2. Figure 2 shows the computation of 11011 mod 11 as performed by Algorithm 2. □

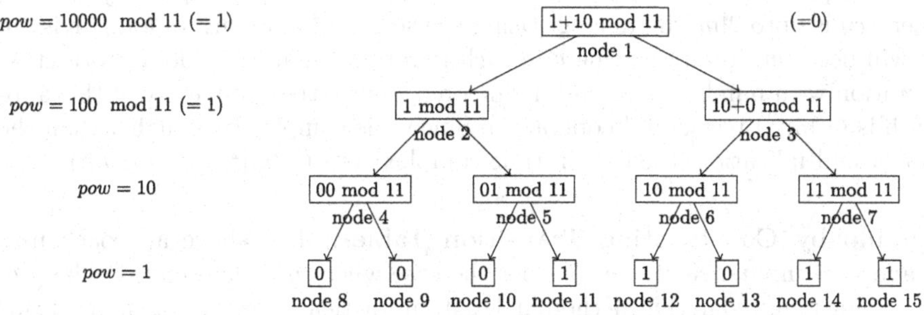

Fig. 2. Processing 11011 mod 11 following Algorithm 2.

5.1 Lattice Linearity

Theorem 2. *Given the input bitstrings n and m, the predicate*

$$\forall i \neg(\text{IMPEDENSABLE-LOG-MODULO-SHIFT}(i) \vee \\ \text{IMPEDENSABLE-LOG-MODULO-POW}(i) \vee \\ \text{IMPEDENSABLE-LOG-MODULO-ANS}(i))$$

is lattice linear on $4|n|/|m| - 1$ *computing nodes.*

Since the proof of this theorem is similar to the proof of Theorem 1, we provide this proof in the technical report of this paper [9].

Corollary 2. *Algorithm 2 computes multiplication of two numbers with* $4 \times |n|/|m|$ *nodes without synchronization.*

5.2 Time Complexity Analysis

Algorithm 2 is a general algorithm that uses the MOD(MUL($\cdots$)) and MOD(SUM($\cdots$)). For some given x, y and z values, MOD(MUL(x, y),z) (resp., MOD (SUM(x, y),z)) involves first the multiplication (resp., addition) of two input values x and y and then evaluating the resulting value under modulo z. These functions can be implemented in different ways. Choices for these implementations affect the time complexity. We consider two approaches for this as follows.

Modulo via Long Division. First, we consider the standard approach for computing MOD(MUL($\cdots$)) and MOD(SUM($\cdots$)). Observe that in Algorithm 2, if we compute MOD(MUL(x, y)) then $x, y < m$. Hence, we can use Karatsuba's parallelized algorithm from Sect. 4 where the input numbers are less than m. Using the analysis from Sect. 4, we have that each multiplication operation has a time complexity of $O(|n|)$.

Subsequently, to compute the mod operation, we need to compute $xy \mod m$ where xy is upto $2|m|$ digits long. Using the standard approach of long division, we will need $|m|$ iterations where in each iteration, we need to do a subtraction operation with numbers that $|m|$ digits long. Hence, the complexity of this approach is $O(|m|^2)$ per modulo operation. Since this complexity is higher than the cost of multiplication, the overall time complexity is $O(|m|^2 \times \lg(|n|/|m|))$.

Modulo by Constructing Transition Tables. The above approach uses m and n as inputs. Next, we consider the case where m is hardcoded. The preprocessing required in this method makes it impractical. However, we present this method to show lower bounds on the complexity of the modulo operation when m is hardcoded, and to show that there is a potential to reduce the complexity.

This approach is motivated by algorithms such as RSA [11] where the value of n changes based on the message to be encrypted/decrypted, but the value of m is fixed once the keys are determined. Thus, some pre-processing can potentially improve the performance of the modulo operation; we observe that certain optimizations are possible. While the time and space complexities required for preprocessing in this algorithm are high, thereby making it impractical, it demonstrates a gap between the lower and upper bound in the complexity.

If m is fixed, we can create a table δ_{sum} of size $m \times m$ where an entry at location (i, j) represents $i + j \mod m$ in $O(m^2)$ time. Using δ_{sum}, we can create another transition table δ_{mul} of size $m \times m$ where an entry at location (i, j) represents $i \times j \mod m$ in $O(m^2)$ time. Using δ_{mul}, the time complexity of a MOD(MUL($\cdots$)) operation becomes $O(1)$. Hence, the overall complexity of the modulo operation becomes $O(\lg(|n|/|m|))$.

6 Conclusion

Multiplication and modulo operations are among the fundamental mathematical operations. Fast parallel processing algorithms for such operations reduce the execution time of the applications which they are employed in. In this paper, we showed that these problems are lattice linear. In this context, we studied an algorithm by Cesari and Maeder [3] which is a parallelization of Karatsuba's algorithm for multiplication. We showed how to correctly implement this algorithm using $|n|^{\lg 3}$ nodes. In addition, we studied a parallel processing algorithm for the modulo operation.

The presence of lattice linearity in problems and algorithms allows nodes to execute asynchronously. This is specifically valuable in parallel algorithms where synchronization can be removed as is. These algorithms are snap-stabilizing, which means that even if the initial states of the nodes are arbitrary, the state transitions of the system strictly follow its specification. These are also self-stabilizing, i.e., the supremum states in the lattices induced under the respective predicates are the respective optimal states.

Utilizing these algorithms, a virtual machine, e.g., Java or Python, can utilize the available GPU power to compute the multiplication and modulo operations on big-number inputs. In this case, a synchronization primitive also does not need to be deployed. Thus a plethora of applications will benefit from the observations presented in this paper.

References

1. Bui, A., Datta, A.K., Petit, F., Villain, V.: State-optimal snap-stabilizing PIF in tree networks. In: Proceedings 19th IEEE International Conference on Distributed Computing Systems, pp. 78–85 (1999)
2. Butler, J.T., Sasao, T.: Fast hardware computation of X mod Z. In: 2011 IEEE International Symposium on Parallel and Distributed Processing Workshops and Phd Forum, pp. 294–297 (2011)
3. Cesari, G., Maeder, R.: Performance analysis of the parallel karatsuba multiplication algorithm for distributed memory architectures. J. Symb. Comput. **21**(4), 467–473 (1996)
4. Garg, V.: A lattice linear predicate parallel algorithm for the dynamic programming problems. In: 23rd International Conference on Distributed Computing and Networking, ICDCN 2022, New York, NY, USA, pp. 72–76. Association for Computing Machinery (2022)
5. Garg, V.K.: Predicate detection to solve combinatorial optimization problems. In: Scheideler, C., Spear, M. (eds.) SPAA 2020: 32nd ACM Symposium on Parallelism in Algorithms and Architectures, Virtual Event, USA, 15–17 July 2020, pp. 235–245. ACM (2020)
6. Garg, V.K.: A lattice linear predicate parallel algorithm for the housing market problem. In: Johnen, C., Schiller, E.M., Schmid, S. (eds.) SSS 2021. LNCS, vol. 13046, pp. 108–122. Springer, Cham (2021). https://doi.org/10.1007/978-3-030-91081-5_8

7. Gupta, A.T., Kulkarni, S.S.: Extending lattice linearity for self-stabilizing algorithms. In: Johnen, C., Schiller, E.M., Schmid, S. (eds.) SSS 2021. LNCS, vol. 13046, pp. 365–379. Springer, Cham (2021). https://doi.org/10.1007/978-3-030-91081-5_24
8. Gupta, A.T., Kulkarni, S.S.: Brief announcement: fully lattice linear algorithms. In: Devismes, S., Petit, F., Altisen, K., Di Luna, G.A., Fernandez Anta, A. (eds.) SSS 2022. LNCS, vol. 13751, pp. 341–345. Springer, Heidelberg (2022). https://doi.org/10.1007/978-3-031-21017-4_24
9. Gupta, A.T., Kulkarni, S.S.: Lattice linearity of multiplication and modulo. CoRR/2302.07207 (2023)
10. Karatsuba, A., Ofman, Y.: Multiplication of many-digital numbers by automatic computers. In: Doklady Akademii Nauk SSSR, vol. 14, no. 145, pp. 293–294 (1962)
11. Rivest, R.L., Shamir, A., Adleman, L.: A method for obtaining digital signatures and public-key cryptosystems. Commun. ACM **21**(2), 120–126 (1978)
12. Zeugmann, T.: Highly parallel computations modulo a number having only small prime factors. Inf. Comput. **96**(1), 95–114 (1992)

The Fagnano Triangle Patrolling Problem
(Extended Abstract)

Konstantinos Georgiou[1(✉)], Somnath Kundu[2], and Paweł Prałat[1]

[1] Department of Mathematics, Toronto Metropolitan University, Toronto, ON, Canada
{konstantinos,pralat}@torontomu.ca

[2] Department of Computer Science, Toronto Metropolitan University, Toronto, ON, Canada
somnath.kundu@torontomu.ca

Abstract. We investigate a combinatorial optimization problem that involves patrolling the edges of an acute triangle using a unit-speed agent. The goal is to minimize the maximum (1-gap) idle time of any edge, which is defined as the time gap between consecutive visits to that edge. This problem has roots in a centuries-old optimization problem posed by Fagnano in 1775, who sought to determine the inscribed triangle of an acute triangle with the minimum perimeter. It is well-known that the orthic triangle, giving rise to a periodic and cyclic trajectory obeying the laws of geometric optics, is the optimal solution to Fagnano's problem. Such trajectories are known as Fagnano orbits, or more generally as billiard trajectories. We demonstrate that the orthic triangle is also an optimal solution to the patrolling problem.

Our main contributions pertain to new connections between billiard trajectories and optimal patrolling schedules in combinatorial optimization. In particular, as an artifact of our arguments, we introduce a novel 2-gap patrolling problem that seeks to minimize the visitation time of objects every three visits. We prove that there exist infinitely many well-structured billiard-type optimal trajectories for this problem, including the orthic trajectory, which has the special property of minimizing the visitation time gap between any two consecutively visited edges. Complementary to that, we also examine the cost of dynamic, sub-optimal trajectories to the 1-gap patrolling optimization problem. These trajectories result from a greedy algorithm and can be implemented by a computationally primitive mobile agent.

Keywords: Patrolling · Triangle · Fagnano Orbits · Billiard Trajectories

1 Introduction

Patrolling refers to the perpetual monitoring, protection, and supervision of a domain or its perimeter using mobile agents. In a typical patrolling problem involving one mobile agent, the agent must move through a given domain in order to monitor or check specific locations or objects. The objective is to find a trajectory that satisfies certain constraints and/or that addresses quantitative objectives, such as minimizing the total distance traveled or maximizing the frequency of visits to certain areas. The purpose of

The full version of this paper appears on arXiv [20].

S. Dolev and B. Schieber (Eds.): SSS 2023, LNCS 14310, pp. 157–171, 2023.
https://doi.org/10.1007/978-3-031-44274-2_13

patrolling could be to detect any intrusion attempts, monitor for possible faults or to identify and rescue individuals or objects in a disaster environment, and for this reason, such problems arise in a variety of real-world applications, such as security patrol routes, autonomous robot navigation, and wildlife monitoring. Overall the subject of patrolling has seen a growing number of applications in Computer Science, including Infrastructure Security, Computer Games, perpetual domain-surveying, and monitoring in 1D and 2D geometric domains.

In addition to its practical applications, patrolling has emerged (not as a combinatorial optimization problem) in the context of theoretical physics. In particular, the problem of finding periodic trajectories in billiard systems has been a topic of interest for many years. A billiard system is a model of a particle or a waveform moving inside a domain (typically polygonal, but also elliptical, convex, or even non-convex region) and reflecting off its boundaries according to the laws of elastic collision. The problem of finding periodic trajectories in a billiard system is equivalent to finding a closed path in the domain that satisfies certain geometric conditions.

One important example of a periodic trajectory in billiard systems is the so-called Fagnano orbit on acute triangles, a periodic, closed (and piece-wise linear) curve that visits the three edges of an acute triangle. Fagnano orbits, named after the Italian mathematician Giulio Fagnano who first studied them in the mid-18th century, arise as solutions to the optimization problem which asks for the shortest such curve. In this work we explore further connections between billiard trajectories and patrolling as a combinatorial optimization problem. In particular, we are asking what are the patrolling strategies for the edges of an acute triangle that optimize standard frequency-related objectives are. Our findings demonstrate that a family of Fagnano orbits are actually optimal solutions to the corresponding combinatorial optimization problems, revealing this way deeper connections between the seemingly disparate areas of combinatorial patrolling and billiard trajectories.

2 Related Work

Patrolling problems are a fundamental class of problems in computational geometry, combinatorial optimization, and robotics that have attracted significant research interest in recent years. Due to their practical applications, they have received extensive treatment in the realm of robotics, see for example [1,6,14,15,22,31,41], as well as surveys [3,23,35]. When patrolling is seen as part of infrastructure security, it leads to a number of optimization problems [27], with one particular example being the identification of network failures or web pages requiring indexing [31].

Combinatorial trade-offs of triangle edge visitation costs have been explored in [19]. In contrast, the current work pertains to the cost associated with the perpetual monitoring of the triangle edges by a single unit speed agent. Numerous variations of similar patrolling problems have been explored in computational geometry, which vary depending on the application domain, patrolling specifications, agent restrictions, and computational abilities. Many efficient algorithms have been developed for several of these variants, utilizing a range of techniques from graph theory, computational geometry, and optimization, see survey [10] for some recent developments. Some examples of studied domains include the bounded line segment [25], networks [41], polygonal regions [38], trees [11], disconnected boundaries of one dimensional curves [8], arbitrary polygonal environments [33] (with a reduction to graphs), or even 3-dimensional environments [16].

Identifying optimal patrolling strategies can be computationally hard [12], while even in seemingly easy setups the optimal trajectories can be counter-intuitive [26]. The addition of combinatorial specifications has given rise to multiple intriguing variations, including the requirement of uneven coverage [7,34] or waiting times [13], the presence of high-priority segments [32], and patrolling with distinct speed agents [9]. Patrolling has also been studied extensively from the perspective of distributed computing [30], while the class of these problems also admit a game-theoretic interpretation between an intruder and a surveillance agent [2,18].

Maybe not surprisingly, the optimal patrolling trajectories that we derive are in fact billiard-type trajectories, that is, periodic and cyclic trajectories obeying the standard law of geometric optics, and which are referred to as Fagnano orbits specifically when the underlying billiard/domain is triangular. Fagnano orbits have been studied extensively both experimentally [28] and theoretically [39]. Billiard-type trajectories have been explored in equilateral triangles [4], obtuse triangles [21], as well as polygons [40]. More recently, there have been studies on ellipses [17] and general convex bodies [24], or even fractals [29] and polyhedra [5], with the list of domains or trajectory specifications still growing.

3 Main Definitions and Results

A patrolling schedule S (or simply a schedule) for triangle Δ with edges (line segments) $E = \{\alpha, \beta, \gamma\}$ is an infinite sequence $\{s_i\}_{i \geq 0}$, where each s_i is on a line segment of E that we also denote by $e(s_i)$, i.e. $e(s_i) \in E$ for each $i \geq 0$. When $e(s_i) = \delta \in E$ we say that segment δ and point s_i are visited at step i of the schedule. We will only be studying *feasible schedules*, i.e. schedules for which eventually all segments in E are visited (and infinitely often).

For simplicity, our notation above is tailored to points s_i that are not vertices of Δ. When s_i is a vertex of Δ we assume that both incident edges are visited. We also think of schedule S as the trajectory of a unit speed agent, and hence we refer to the time between the visitation of $s_j, s_{j+\ell}$ as the summation of the lengths of segments $s_{j+i}s_{j+i+1}$ over $i \in \{0, \ldots, \ell - 1\}$.

A schedule S is called:

- *cyclic* if $\{e(s_0), e(s_1), e(s_2)\} = E$ and $e(s_{i+3}) = e(s_i)$, for every $i \geq 0$, and
- *k-periodic* (for $k \geq 3$) if $s_{i+k} = s_i$, for every $i \geq 0$.

For any segment $\delta \in E$ we define its *t-gap sequence*, $g^t(\delta)$, that records the visitation time gaps of δ over every $t+1$ consecutive visitations. In particular, $t = 1$ corresponds to the standard *idle time* considered previously, and that measures the additional time it takes for each object to be revisited, after each visitation. Formally, let $e(s_j) = e(s_{j'}) = \delta$ and suppose that points $s_j, s_{j'}$ are the k-th and $(k+t)$-th visitation of δ, respectively. Then the time between the visitations of $s_j, s_{j'}$ is exactly the value of k-th element of sequence $g^t(\delta)$. From this definition, it is also immediate that $(g^t(\delta))_i = \sum_{i=1}^{t} (g^1(\delta))_i$.

The *t-gap* $G^t(\delta)$ of $\delta \in E$ is defined as $\sup_i (g^t(\delta))_i$, while the *t-gap* G^t of schedule S for edges E (hence for input triangle Δ) is defined as $\max_{\delta \in E} G^t(\delta)$. When it is clear from the context, we will abbreviate G^1 simply by G.

3.1 Main Contributions and More Terminology

In this section we summarize our main contributions, pertaining to the optimal 1-gap and 2-gap patrolling schedules of acute triangles. Due to space limitations, any omitted proofs from the following sections can be found in the full version of the paper on arXiv [20].

As a warm-up, we first give a self-contained proof of optimality for 1-gap patrolling schedules, restricted to cyclic and 3-periodic schedules. In order to present our result, we remind the reader of the so-called *orthic triangle*, a pedal-type triangle of an acute triangle Δ, which is a triangle inscribed in Δ whose vertices are the projections of the Δ's orthocenter (intersection of altitudes) to its three edges. Note also the any 3-periodic cyclic schedule corresponds to a triangle inscribed in Δ. The next theorem, given first by Fagnano in 1775, is proven in Sect. 4, where we also introduce some key concepts for our follow-up main contributions.

Theorem 1 (Fagnano's Theorem). *The optimal* 1*-gap* 3*-periodic cyclic patrolling schedule of a triangle* Δ *is its orthic triangle.*

Towards our goal to provide the optimal 1-gap schedules, we find all (infinitely many) optimal 2-gap cyclic schedules, which are in fact billiard-type trajectories. We prove the next theorem in Sect. 6.

Theorem 2. *There are infinitely many optimal* 2*-gap cyclic schedules of a triangle* Δ*, that include also the orthic triangle. Every* 2*-gap optimal schedule is* 6*-periodic and has value equal to 2 times the perimeter of the orthic triangle. Moreover, each optimal schedule is made up of segments that are parallel to the edges of the orthic triangle.*

Then in Sect. 7 we derive our main contribution.

Theorem 3. *The optimal* 1*-gap schedule of a triangle* Δ *is its orthic triangle.*

In the same section we also quantify the 1-gap cost of the orthic triangle, and we compare it to the optimal 2-gap schedules. Indeed, we ask which of the optimal 2-gap schedules minimizes the maximum time in-between the visitation of any two edges of Δ (and not of the same edge), and we prove that the orthic schedule is again the optimal, in this multi-objective optimization problem.

From our previous contributions, we conclude that a mobile agent whose task is to 1-gap optimally patrol a triangle Δ needs to be able to compute the base points of Δ's altitudes. Therefore, a natural question is whether we can obtain efficient solutions with a primitive agent. In Sect. 8 we show the following result.

Theorem 4. *There is a greedy-type schedule that converges to a 3-periodic cyclic schedule whose 1-gap cost is off from the 1-gap optimal cyclic schedule by a factor $\gamma \in [1, \gamma_0]$, where $\gamma_0 = \sqrt{2}/2 + 1/2$, and γ admits a closed formula as a function of the angles of the given triangle.*

It will follow from our analysis that our greedy algorithm will be nearly optimal for any acute triangle with one arbitrarily small angle, and it will be the worst off from the optimal solution when the given triangle is a right isosceles.

4 The 1-Gap Optimal 3-Periodic Cyclic Schedule

There are many proofs known for the fact that inscribed triangle with the shortest perimeter is its orthic triangle. In the language of triangle patrolling, the statement is equivalent to that the optimal 1-gap 3-periodic cyclic schedule of a triangle is its orthic triangle, articulated in Theorem 1.

The next complementary lemma effectively provides a formula for the optimal 1-gap cost of cyclic 3-periodic schedules.

Lemma 1. *Let p be the perimeter of an acute triangle. Then, the perimeter of its orthic triangle is given by* $2p\left(\frac{1}{\sin(B)\sin(C)} + \frac{1}{\sin(A)\sin(C)} + \frac{1}{\sin(A)\sin(B)}\right)^{-1}$.

5 Technical Properties of the Orthic Patrolling Schedule

In this section we explore a number of technical properties associated with the orthic patrolling schedule, which will be the cornerstone of our main results. All observations in this section refer to Fig. 1 which we explain gradually as we present our findings.

Our starting point is triangle ABC with edges $\alpha \geq \beta \geq \gamma$, and hence the same relation holds for the opposite angles. We also depict the base points K, L, K of altitudes corresponding to A, B, C respectively. It follows that inscribed triangle KLM is the orthic triangle.

We apply a number of reflections of triangle ABC as follows: we obtain reflection C_1 of C around AB, reflection B_1 of B around AC_1, reflection A_1 of A around B_1C_1, reflection C_2 of C_1 around A_1B_1, and reflection B_2 of B_1 around A_1C_2. We refer to the resulting triangles as the *reflected triangles*.

Lemma 2. *The line passing through B_2, C_2 is parallel to line passing through BC.*

Proof. We consider the slope of several line segments relevant to BC. We have the following observations pertaining to counterclockwise rotation of line segments about one of their endpoints. The rotation of BC about B by angle $2B$ gives segment BC_1. The rotation of BC_1 about C_1 by angle $3C$ gives segment C_1A_1. The rotation of C_1A_1 about A_1 by angle $3A$ gives segment A_1B_2. Finally, the rotation of A_1B_2 about B_2 by angle B gives segment B_2C_2.

It follows that segment B_2C_2 follows by repeated rotation of angle $2B+3C+3A+B = 3(A+B+C) = 6\pi$. Since 6π is a multiple of π we conclude the claim. □

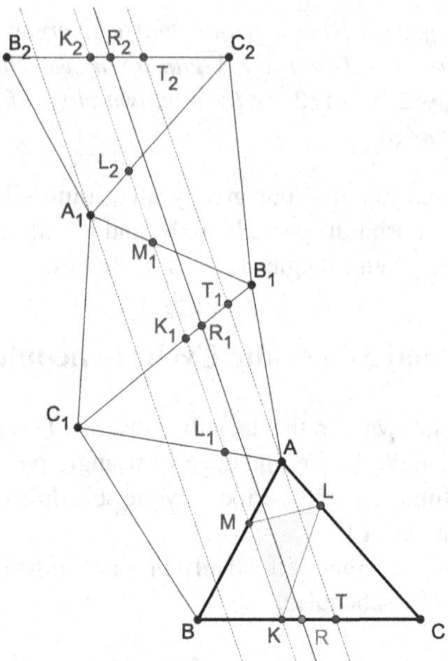

Fig. 1. The orthic channel (stripe enclosed between the red dotted lines) as it is obtained by 5 triangle reflections. (Color figure online)

Next we provide an alternative representation of the orthic trajectory.

Lemma 3. *The line passing through MK (green dotted line in Fig. 1) passes through the following points:* L_1 *on* AC_1, K_1 *on* B_1C_1, M_1 *on* A_1B_1, L_2 *on* A_1C_2, *and* K_2 *on* B_2C_2. *Moreover, points* L_1, K_1, M_1, L_2, K_2 *are the bases of corresponding altitudes in the series of the reflected triangles.*

Proof. By the proof of Theorem 1, the orthic triangle KLM can be obtained by considering the image K_1 of K (on B_1C_1) along the same reflections that resulted into the reflected triangles. Now consider the intersections M, L_1 of KK_1 with AB, AC_1, respectively. It follows that CM and C_1M are altitudes in triangles ABC, ABC_1, and BL_1 and B_1L_1 are altitudes in triangles ABC_1, AB_1C_1. In particular, it follows that K, M, L_1, K_1 are collinear.

The same argument applies if we start from triangle AB_1C_1 and invoke the same reflections starting from the third one, in the series that gave us the reflected triangles. It follows that by extending line KK_1 we intersect segment A_1B_1 at a point M_1, and segment A_1C_2 at a point L_2, where C_1M_1 and C_2M_1 are altitudes in triangles $A_1B_1C_1$, and B_1L_2 is altitudes in triangles $A_1B_1C_2$. Hence, L_2, M_1, K_1, L_1, M, K are also collinear.

Finally, we observe that the base K_2 of altitude A_1K_2 is obtained as the reflection of K_1 using the last two reflections of the series of reflections that gave us the reflected triangles. It follows that K_2 is also collinear with L_2 and M_1 concluding our argument. □

It follows from Lemma 3 that the orthic trajectory along two cycles of the patrolling schedule can also be described by the line segment K_1K_2. We refer to the line passing through K, K_2 as the *orthic line*. Alternatively, we showed that all points within segment K_1K_2 lie within the reflected triangles. Our observation justifies that the following concept is well-defined.

Definition 1. The *orthic channel* is defined by two lines ℓ_1, ℓ_2 parallel to the orthic line of maximum distance, and with the following properties: ℓ_1, ℓ_2 intersect segments BC and B_2C_2 and all points on lines ℓ_1, ℓ_2 in-between segments BC and B_2C_2 lie within the reflected triangles.

Similar reflection-induced channels were studied in [36,37], while the orthic-channel that we use was also observed experimentally in [28]. Next we formalize its usefulness.

Lemma 4. *Any line parallel to the orthic line within the orthic channel gives rise to a cyclic* 6*-periodic patrolling schedule with* 2*-gap cost equal to twice the orthic perimeter.*

Proof. Consider an arbitrary line, parallel to the orthic line, that intersects line segments BC, B_1C_1, B_2C_2 at points R, R_1, R_2 respectively, see Fig. 1. We observe that $KK2$ is parallel to RR_2, and by Lemma 2 we have that K_2R_2 is parallel to KR. Therefore, KRR_2K_2 is a parallelogram with $KR = KR_2$.

We conclude that R_2 is the reflection of R using the same reflections that obtained K_2 from K. But then, it follows RR_2 corresponds to cyclic 6-periodic patrolling schedule of 2-gap cost equal to $RR_2 = KK_2 = KK_1 + K_1K2 = 2KK1$, as promised. □

Next we identify all cyclic 6-periodic patrolling schedules of the same 2-gap costs. We note that in the following lemma we make explicit use of that the repeated reflections were done first along the smallest two edges.

Lemma 5. *The lines identifying the orthic channel are the two lines parallel to the orthic line, one passing through A and one passing through A_1.*

Proof. Consider a line parallel to the orthic line passing through A, and intersecting BC at T and the line passing through B_1C_1 at point T_1. We will show that T_1 lies in the segment K_1B_1.

First we claim that $KT = K_1T_1$. To see why, recall that KK_1 is parallel to TT_1. It is enough to show that KTT_1K_1 is an isosceles trapezoid. Indeed, note that angle AT_1C_1 (read counterclockwise) equals angle KK_1C (because TT_1 is parallel to KK_1), and angle KK_1C equals angle BKM (because KK_1 corresponds to the orthic trajectory that results from reflections). Finally, angle BKM equals angle BTT_1, because TT_1 is parallel to KK_1. Overall, this shows that indeed, angles KTT_1 and TT_1K_1 are equal, showing that KTT_1K_1 is an isosceles trapezoid as claimed.

We conclude that in order to show that T_1 lies within segment K_1B_1 it is enough to show that $KT < KB$. Equivalently, it is enough to show that the middle point of BT lies within segment BK. To see why recall that AT is parallel to MK. Moreover, because angle A is at least as large as angle B (that is our initial reflections where done using the largest edge last), it follows that the base M of altitude CM is closer to A than to B. Effectively, this shows that $BM \geq AB/2$, and hence $BK \geq BT/2$ as wanted.

Now let the extension of TT_1 intersect the line passing through B_2C_2 at point T_2. From the parallelogram KTT_2K_2 we have that $KT = K_2T_2$, and hence T_2 lies within segment K_2C_2, and by construction is it clear than T_1T_2 intersect segments A_1B1 and A_1C_2. This shows that indeed the line passing throught AT is one of the extreme lines of the orthic channel.

The proof follows by observing that we can repeat the same argument, starting from triangle $A_1B_2C_2$ and applying the reverse list of reflections that gave us the reflected triangles (where ABC would be the final reflected triangle, and note that these reflections would still be first with respect to the two smallest edges). Indeed, we can consider line, parallel to the orthic line, and passing through A_1, which by the same argument that line is the other extreme line of the orthic channel. □

6 The Optimal 2-Gap Cyclic Schedules

In this section we prove Theorem 2. We do so by proving that the cyclic 6-periodic patrolling schedule of Lemma 4 are the 2-gap optimal cyclic schedules of cost twice the perimeter of the orthic triangle.

Indeed, as per our result, any line parallel to the orthic line within the orthic channel (whose boundaries are given in Lemma 5) gives rise to a cyclic 6-periodic schedules that we call *sub-orthic* schedules. We depict such a sub-orthic schedule in Fig. 2.

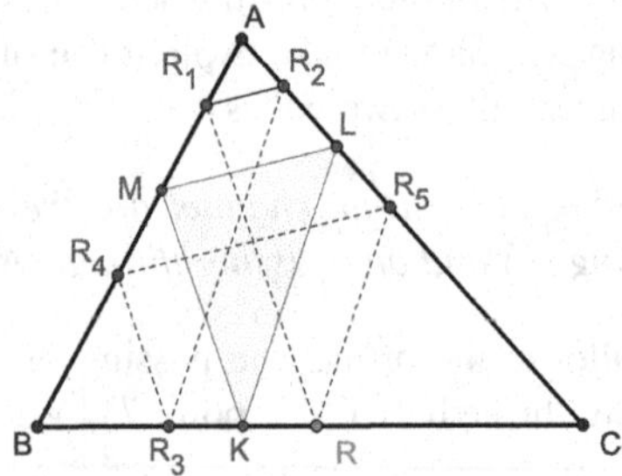

Fig. 2. A sub-orthic trajectory example.

In order to show that any sub-orthic trajectory is 2-gap optimal, we consider a new patrolling problem on input triangle ABC with a limited visitation horizon. In particular, in the $2k$-*limited* patrolling problem the goal is to find a cyclic trajectory that starts from edge BC (the largest edge) ends after $2k$ visitations of BC and is of minimum total length. Given triangle ABC, we denote by v_k the cost of the optimal solution to the $2k$-*limited* patrolling problem. The following is immediate from our definitions.

Observation 5. *For every $k \geq 1$, the optimal cyclic 2-gap solution has cost at least v_k/k.*

Now recall that by Lemma 4, any sub-orthic trajectory has 2-gap cost equal to twice the orthic triangle. Hence, Theorem 2 is a corollary of the following lemma.

Lemma 6. *The value of* $\lim_{k\to\infty} v_k/k$ *equals twice the perimeter of the orthic triangle.*

Proof. In order to visualize the $2k$*-limited* patrolling problem we apply repeatedly (k times) the gadget induced by the reflected triangles of Sect. 5, see also Fig. 3 for an example when $k = 2$.

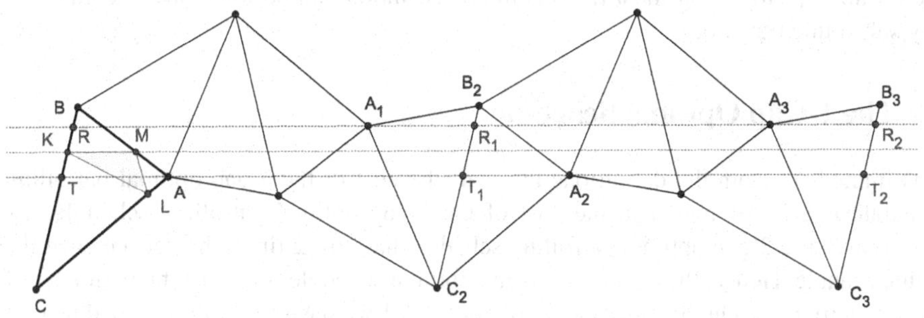

Fig. 3. Two applications of reflections.

Indeed, the gadget of the reflected triangles defines B_2C_2 which is parallel to BC. One more reflection of A_1 about B_2C_2 results into triangle $A_2B_2C_2$ whose edges are piecewise parallel to the edges of ABC, hence the same reflection sequence, applied on $A_2B_2C_2$ defines B_3C_3 parallel to B_2C_2 and so on.

This way, we define a sequence of parallel segments B_kC_k. Now consider the orthic channel of ABC identified by lines passing through R, A_1 and T, A (as per Lemma 5). Consider also the corresponding points R_k, T_k that these two lines intersect segments B_kC_k.

By the definition of the $2k$-limited patrolling problem, its optimal schedule (with cost v_k) is the shortest trajectory that starts from BC and ends at B_kC_k. Since the orthic channel stays within all reflected triangles, the optimal solution to the $2k$-limited patrolling problem is the shortest line segment with endpoints within RT and R_kT_k. Observe that the shortest such segment is the shortest diagonal of parallelogram RTT_kR_k. Now as k grows, one side RT of these parallelograms stays constant, while the length of both diagonals tend (in the limit) to the length of $RR_k = TT_k$ which are also equal to k times the 2-gap cost of any sub-orthic trajectory, and hence are equal to $2k$ times the orthic perimeter. □

Note that the orthic trajectory is one among the sub-orthic trajectories, and hence optimal too to the 2-gap patrolling problem (among cyclic algorithms). In the following lemma we show that the orthic trajectory is also the optimal solution to a multi-objective optimization problem.

Lemma 7. *Among all 2-gap optimal sub-orthic trajectories, the one that minimizes the visitation gap between any two (not necessarily same) edges is the orthic trajectory.*

Proof. Consider an arbitrary sub-orthic trajectory $RR_1R_2R_3R_4R_5R$, see Fig. 2. Note that the sub-orthic schedule is made up of segments that are piecewise parallel to the segments of the orthic trajectory, and any of the orthic line segments lies in the middle of any of the two parallel segments of the sub-orthic schedule.

In particular we have RR_1, R_3R_4 are parallel to MK, as well as R_1R2, R_4R_5 are parallel to ML, and RR_5, R_2R_3 are parallel to KL. Moreover, $MK \leq \max\{RR_1, R_3R_4\}, ML \leq \max\{R_1R2, R_4R_5\}$, and $KL \leq \max\{RR_5, R_2R_3\}$. It follows that maximum visitation gap $\max\{MK, ML, KL\}$ between any two edges in the orthic trajectory is at most the maximum visitation gap between any two edges in any sub-orthic trajectory. □

7 The 1-Gap Optimal Schedule

It is immediate from the definitions that half the cost of the 2-gap optimal patrolling schedule is a lower bound to the cost of the 1-gap optimal patrolling schedule. By Theorem 2, the 2-gap optimal patrolling schedule has cost 2 times the perimeter of the orthic triangle. Hence, the cost of the 1-gap optimal schedule is at least the perimeter of the orthic triangle. On the other hand, by Theorem 1 we have a patrolling schedule (the orthic trajectory) with 1-gap cost equal to the orthic perimeter. Therefore, we obtain the following immediate corollary.

Corollary 1. *The optimal* 1*-gap cyclic schedule of a triangle* Δ *is its orthic triangle.*

The purpose of this section is to prove Theorem 3, that is to strengthen the statement of Corollary 1 by showing that the optimal 1-gap schedule is actually cyclic. We do so by showing how to modify an arbitrary schedule into a cyclic schedule, without increasing its 1-gap cost. Effectively, the next lemma implies Theorem 3.

Lemma 8. *There is a* 1*-gap optimal schedule that is cyclic.*

Proof. Consider an arbitrary schedule $S = \{s_i\}_i$ that is not cyclic. We show how to construct a new schedule that is cyclic and 3-periodic, without increasing its 1-gap. Indeed, since S is not cyclic, and after renaming edges, there are two consecutive visitations of edge α so that both edges β, γ are visited in between, with at least one of them being visited more than once. In other words, for some $k, \ell \in \mathbb{N}$, $\ell \geq 4$ we have that $e(s_k) = e(s_{k+\ell}) = \alpha$, $e(s_{k+1}) = e(s_{k+3}) = \beta$ and $e(s_{k+2}) = \gamma$.

In what follows we denote by s_is_j the distance between points s_i, s_j. Then, we see that for the 1-gap cost G of S, we have that

$$
\begin{aligned}
G = \max_{\delta \in E} G(\delta) \geq G(\alpha) \geq \sum_{i=0}^{\ell-1} s_{k+i}s_{k+i+1} \\
\geq & s_ks_{k+1} + s_{k+1}s_{k+2} + s_{k+2}s_{k+3} + s_{k+3}s_{k+\ell} \\
\geq & 2\min\{s_ks_{k+1} + s_{k+1}s_{k+2}, s_{k+2}s_{k+3} + s_{k+3}s_{k+\ell}\},
\end{aligned}
$$

where the second to last inequality is due to the triangle inequality.

Now we consider two different cyclic and 3-periodic schedules, S', S'', with 1-gap costs G', G'', respectively, and we show that $\min\{G', G''\} \leq G$. The first schedule is $S' = s_k, s_{k+1}, s_{k+2}, s_k, s_{k+1}, s_{k+2}, s_k, s_{k+1}, s_{k+2}, \ldots$, and the second schedule is $S'' = s_{k+2}, s_{k+3}, s_{k+\ell}, s_{k+2}, s_{k+3}, s_{k+\ell}, s_{k+2}, s_{k+3}, s_{k+\ell} \ldots$. Since both S', S'' are cyclic and periodic, we have that $G' = G'(\alpha) = G'(\beta) = G'(\gamma)$ and $G'' = G''(\alpha) = G''(\beta) = G''(\gamma)$. In particular, using the triangle inequalities again, we have

$$G' = s_k s_{k+1} + s_{k+1} s_{k+2} + s_{k+2} s_k \leq 2(s_k s_{k+1} + s_{k+1} s_{k+2})$$
$$G'' = s_{k+2} s_{k+3} + s_{k+3} s_{k+\ell} + s_{k+\ell} s_{k+2} \leq 2(s_{k+2} s_{k+3} + s_{k+3} s_{k+\ell}).$$

But then, $\min\{G', G''\} \leq 2 \min\{s_k s_{k+1} + s_{k+1} s_{k+2}, s_{k+2} s_{k+3} + s_{k+3} s_{k+\ell}\} \leq G$, as wanted. □

8 The Greedy Cyclic Algorithm

In this section we prove Theorem 4 that is we describe a patrolling schedule that converges to a 3-periodic cyclic schedule whose 1-gap cost is off from the 1-gap optimal cyclic schedule by a factor $\gamma \in [1, 1.20711]$. It will follow from our analysis that our greedy algorithm will be nearly optimal for any acute triangle with one arbitrarily small angle, and it will be the worst off from the optimal solution when the given triangle is a right isosceles.

We proceed by the description of a greedy patrolling schedule. We assume that the patroller can remember the current and previously visited edges (not necessarily their points), as well as that it can compute (move along) the projection of its current position to any other edge. Formally, we label the three edges BC, AB, AC as $0, 1, 2$, respectively. The patrolling schedule starts from an arbitrary point p_0 on BC. For each $i \geq 1$, the patroller moves to point p_i, which is the projection of p_{i-1} onto edge $i \bmod 3$. Referring to triangle ABC as in Fig. 4, we note that the patrolling schedule induces a clockwise cyclic visitation of the given triangle. An immediate corollary of our results will imply that also the corresponding counterclockwise cyclic visitation induces the same 1-gap cost.

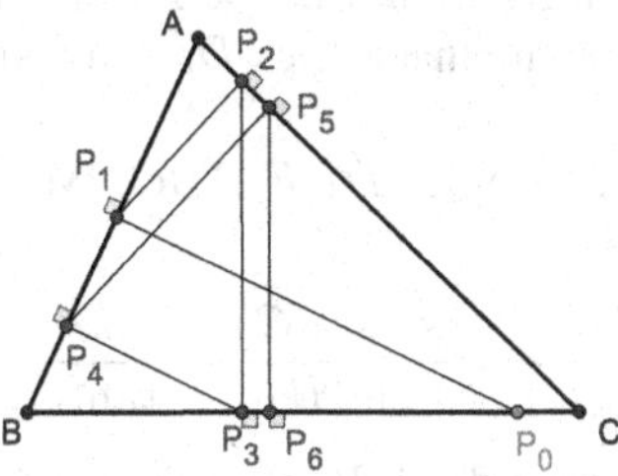

Fig. 4. Six iterations of the greedy patrolling schedule that starts from point p_0 of edge BC.

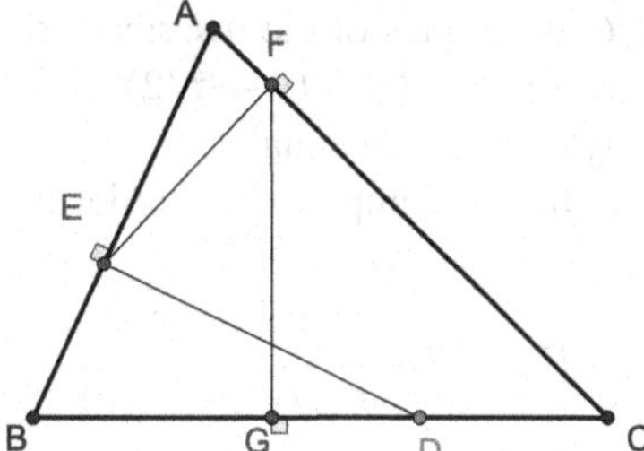

Fig. 5. One iteration of the greedy patrolling schedule, stating from point D 1 iteration.

Lemma 9. *On input acute triangle ABC, and for any starting point, the greedy algorithm converges to a cyclic 3-periodic schedule that has 1-gap cost $p \cdot \frac{\sin(A)\sin(B)\sin(C)}{1+\cos(A)\cos(B)\cos(C)}$, where p is the perimeter of triangle ABC.*

Proof. Consider an arbitrary iteration of the greedy algorithm and a point D on BC, see Fig. 5. After 3 consecutive steps, the patroller has moved to the projection E of D onto AB, its projection F on AC and to its projection G back on BD. To simplify calculations, assume also that AB has length 1. Below, we derive a relation between BG and BD.

First we note that $AF = \cos(A)AE = \cos(A)(\gamma - BE) = \cos(A)(\gamma - \cos(B)BD)$. Then, we use the derived formula for AF to calculate

$$BG = 1 - CG = 1 - \cos(C)CF = 1 - \cos(C)(\beta - AF) = 1 - \cos(C)\left(\beta - \cos(A)(\gamma - \cos(B)BD)\right).$$

It follows that there exists a constant c, independent of points G, D, such that $BG = c - \cos(A)\cos(B)\cos(C)BD$. If we denote by d_i the distance of a point on the greedy patrolling schedule at the i-th visitation of edge BC, the previous argument shows that for the same constant c, we have $d_{i+1} = c - \cos(A)\cos(B)\cos(C)d_i$.

Since $|\cos(A)\cos(B)\cos(C)| < 1$, it follows that $\lim_{i\to\infty} d_i$ exists and its value is obtained when in the previous argument points D, G coincide, see Fig. 6.

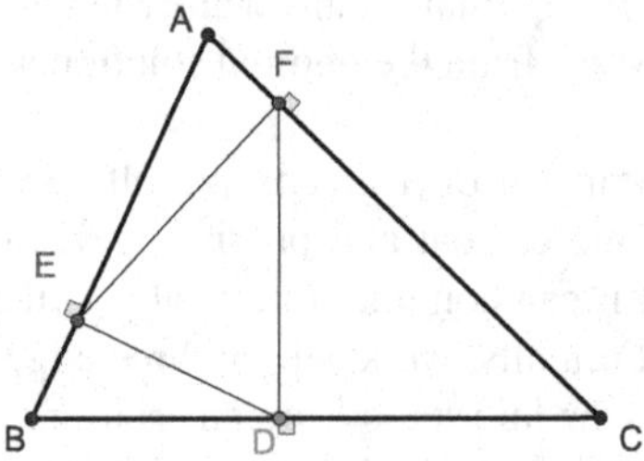

Fig. 6. The limiting cyclic 3-periodic trajectory of the (clockwise) greedy algorithm.

We proved that inscribed triangle DEF is the limiting patrolling schedule of the greedy algorithm, which is indeed a cyclic 3-periodic schedule. Next we calculate its cost. To this end, we claim that triangles DEF and ABC are similar. By denoting by F, E, G the angles of the inscribed triangle, and looking at right triangle FD we have $F = \pi - \pi/2 - (\pi - C - \pi/2) = C$. Similarly we obtain that angles D, B are equal, and angles E, A are equal.

Finally we compute the similarity ratio $k < 1$ of triangles DEF, ABC. We have that

$$\alpha = BD + D\frac{ED}{\sin(B)} + \frac{DF}{\tan(c)} = \frac{k\gamma}{\sin(B)} + \frac{k\alpha}{\tan(C)} = \frac{k\alpha\sin(C)}{\sin(B)} + \frac{k\alpha}{\tan(C)},$$

where the last equality follows from the sin Law in triangle ABC. But then, solving for k and simplifying the trigonometric expressions yields $k = \frac{\sin(A)\sin(B)\sin(C)}{1+\cos(A)\cos(B)\cos(C)}$. It follows that the 1-gap cost of the induced patrolling schedule is equal to the perimeter of triangle DEF which equals k times the perimeter of ABC as claimed. □

We are now ready to prove Theorem 4. An immediate corollary of Lemma 9 is that the (limiting) cost of the greedy algorithm is the same also for the corresponding counter-clock wise trajectory. Moreover, the ratio between its cost and the optimal 1-gap cost, as per Lemma 1, is given by

$$\frac{\sin(A)\sin(B)\sin(C)}{2(1+\cos(A)\cos(B)\cos(C))}\left(\frac{1}{\sin(B)\sin(C)}+\frac{1}{\sin(A)\sin(C)}+\frac{1}{\sin(A)\sin(B)}\right)$$
$$=\frac{\sin(A)+\sin(B)+\sin(C)}{2(1+\cos(A)\cos(B)\cos(C))}.$$

The latter expression, over all non-obtuse triangles, is maximized when any of the angles A, B, C is a right angle, and the other two are equal, that is for the right isosceles, in which case the ratio becomes $\frac{1}{2}\left(\sqrt{2}+1\right)$. In the other extreme case, it is also easy to show that the ratio tends to 1 if any of the angles tends to 0 (hence the other two tend to $\pi/2$), while also for the equilateral triangle, the ratio becomes $2\sqrt{3}/3$.

9 Discussion

In this work we demonstrated the connection between billiard-type trajectories and optimal patrolling schedules in combinatorial optimization. Specifically, we introduced and solved the problem of patrolling the edges of an acute triangle using a unit-speed agent with the goal of minimizing the maximum 1-gap and 2-gap idle time of any edge. We show that billiard-type trajectories are optimal solution to these combinatorial patrolling problems.

Our findings point to several future directions. One natural extension of our work is to generalize the patrolling problem to arbitrary polygons with one or more agents. Moreover, the introduction of the novel 2-gap patrolling problem suggests the investigation of optimal solutions for more complex frequency requirements or time restrictions, especially with the presence of multiple patrolling agents or multiple objects to be patrolled. In that direction, it would be interesting to examine how our results extend to patrolling 3 or more arbitrary line segments on the plane, as subsets of the edges of convex polygones with one or more agents.

References

1. Almeida, A., et al.: Recent advances on multi-agent patrolling. In: Bazzan, A.L.C., Labidi, S. (eds.) SBIA 2004. LNCS (LNAI), vol. 3171, pp. 474–483. Springer, Heidelberg (2004). https://doi.org/10.1007/978-3-540-28645-5_48
2. Alpern, S., Morton, A., Papadaki, K.: Patrolling games. Oper. Res. **59**(5), 1246–1257 (2011)
3. Basilico, N.: Recent trends in robotic patrolling. Curr. Robot. Rep. **3**(2), 65–76 (2022)
4. Baxter, A.M., Umble, R.: Periodic orbits for billiards on an equilateral triangle. Amer. Math. Monthly **115**(6), 479–491 (2008)
5. Bedaride, N.: Periodic billiard trajectories in polyhedra. arXiv preprint arXiv:1104.1051 (2011)
6. Chevaleyre, Y.: Theoretical analysis of the multi-agent patrolling problem. In: IAT, pp. 302–308 (2004)

7. Chuangpishit, H., Czyzowicz, J., Gąsieniec, L., Georgiou, K., Jurdziński, T., Kranakis, E.: Patrolling a path connecting a set of points with unbalanced frequencies of visits. In: Tjoa, A.M., Bellatreche, L., Biffl, S., van Leeuwen, J., Wiedermann, J. (eds.) SOFSEM 2018. LNCS, vol. 10706, pp. 367–380. Springer, Cham (2018). https://doi.org/10.1007/978-3-319-73117-9_26
8. Collins, A., et al.: Optimal patrolling of fragmented boundaries. In: Blelloch, G.E., Vöcking, B. (eds.) 25th ACM Symposium on Parallelism in Algorithms and Architectures, SPAA 2013, Montreal, QC, Canada, 23–25 July 2013, pp. 241–250. ACM (2013)
9. Czyzowicz, J., Georgiou, K., Kranakis, E., MacQuarrie, F., Pajak, D.: Distributed patrolling with two-speed robots (and an application to transportation). In: Vitoriano, B., Parlier, G.H. (eds.) ICORES 2016. CCIS, vol. 695, pp. 71–95. Springer, Cham (2017). https://doi.org/10.1007/978-3-319-53982-9_5
10. Czyzowicz, J., Georgiou, K., Kranakis, E.: Patrolling. In: Flocchini, P., Prencipe, G., Santoro, N. (eds.) Distributed Computing by Mobile Entities: Current Research in Moving and Computing. LNCS, vol. 11340, pp. 371–400. Springer, Cham (2019). https://doi.org/10.1007/978-3-030-11072-7_15
11. Czyzowicz, J., Kosowski, A., Kranakis, E., Taleb, N.: Patrolling trees with mobile robots. In: Cuppens, F., Wang, L., Cuppens-Boulahia, N., Tawbi, N., Garcia-Alfaro, J. (eds.) FPS 2016. LNCS, vol. 10128, pp. 331–344. Springer, Cham (2017). https://doi.org/10.1007/978-3-319-51966-1_22
12. Damaschke, P.: Two robots patrolling on a line: integer version and approximability. In: Gąsieniec, L., Klasing, R., Radzik, T. (eds.) IWOCA 2020. LNCS, vol. 12126, pp. 211–223. Springer, Cham (2020). https://doi.org/10.1007/978-3-030-48966-3_16
13. Damaschke, P.: Distance-based solution of patrolling problems with individual waiting times. In: Müller-Hannemann, M., Perea, F. (eds.) ATMOS 2021. OASIcs, vol. 96, pp. 14:1–14:14. Schloss Dagstuhl - Leibniz-Zentrum für Informatik (2021)
14. Elmaliach, Y., Agmon, N., Kaminka, G.A.: Multi-robot area patrol under frequency constraints. Ann. Math. Artif. Intell. **57**(3–4), 293–320 (2009)
15. Elmaliach, Y., Shiloni, A., Kaminka, G.A.: A realistic model of frequency-based multi-robot polyline patrolling. In: AAMAS (1), pp. 63–70 (2008)
16. Freda, L., et al.: 3D multi-robot patrolling with a two-level coordination strategy. Auton. Robots **43**(7), 1747–1779 (2019)
17. Garcia, R.: Elliptic billiards and ellipses associated to the 3-periodic orbits. Am. Math. Mon **126**(6), 491–504 (2019)
18. Garrec, T.: Continuous patrolling and hiding games. Eur. J. Oper. Res. **277**(1), 42–51 (2019)
19. Georgiou, K., Kundu, S., Prałat, P.: Makespan trade-offs for visiting triangle edges. In: Flocchini, P., Moura, L. (eds.) IWOCA 2021. LNCS, vol. 12757, pp. 340–355. Springer, Cham (2021). https://doi.org/10.1007/978-3-030-79987-8_24
20. Georgiou, K., Kundu, S., Pralat, P.: The Fagnano triangle patrolling problem. CoRR, abs/2307.13153 (2023)
21. Halbeisen, L., Hungerbühler, N.: On periodic billiard trajectories in obtuse triangles. SIAM Rev. **42**(4), 657–670 (2000)
22. Hazon, N., Kaminka, G.A.: On redundancy, efficiency, and robustness in coverage for multiple robots. Robot. Auton. Syst. **56**(12), 1102–1114 (2008)
23. Huang, L., Zhou, M., Hao, K., Hou, E.S.H.: A survey of multi-robot regular and adversarial patrolling. IEEE CAA J. Autom. Sinica **6**(4), 894–903 (2019)
24. Karasev, R.N.: Periodic billiard trajectories in smooth convex bodies. Geom. Funct. Anal. **19**(2), 423–428 (2009)
25. Kawamura, A., Kobayashi, Y.: Fence patrolling by mobile agents with distinct speeds. Distrib. Comput. **28**(2), 147–154 (2015)

26. Kawamura, A., Soejima, M.: Simple strategies versus optimal schedules in multi-agent patrolling. Theoret. Comput. Sci. **839**, 195–206 (2020)
27. Kranakis, E., Krizanc, D.: Optimization problems in infrastructure security. In: Garcia-Alfaro, J., Kranakis, E., Bonfante, G. (eds.) FPS 2015. LNCS, vol. 9482, pp. 3–13. Springer, Cham (2016). https://doi.org/10.1007/978-3-319-30303-1_1
28. Lafargue, C., et al.: Localized lasing modes of triangular organic microlasers. Phys. Rev. E **90**(5), 052922 (2014)
29. Lapidus, M.L., Niemeyer, R.G.: Families of periodic orbits of the koch snowflake fractal billiard (2011)
30. Lee, S.K., Fekete, S.P., McLurkin, J.: Structured triangulation in multi-robot systems: coverage, patrolling, voronoi partitions, and geodesic centers. Int. J. Robot. Res. **35**(10), 1234–1260 (2016)
31. Machado, A., Ramalho, G., Zucker, J.-D., Drogoul, A.: Multi-agent patrolling: an empirical analysis of alternative architectures. In: Simão Sichman, J., Bousquet, F., Davidsson, P. (eds.) MABS 2002. LNCS (LNAI), vol. 2581, pp. 155–170. Springer, Heidelberg (2003). https://doi.org/10.1007/3-540-36483-8_11
32. Morales-Ponce, O.: Optimal patrolling of high priority segments while visiting the unit interval with a set of mobile robots. In: Mukherjee, N., Pemmaraju, S.V. (eds.) ICDCN 2020: 21st International Conference on Distributed Computing and Networking, Kolkata, India, 4–7 January 2020, pp. 10:1–10:10. ACM (2020)
33. Pasqualetti, F., Franchi, A., Bullo, F.: On optimal cooperative patrolling. In: CDC, pp. 7153–7158. IEEE (2010)
34. Piciarelli, C., Foresti, G.L.: Drone swarm patrolling with uneven coverage requirements. IET Comput. Vis. **14**(7), 452–461 (2020)
35. Portugal, D., Rocha, R.: A survey on multi-robot patrolling algorithms. In: Camarinha-Matos, L.M. (ed.) DoCEIS 2011. IAICT, vol. 349, pp. 139–146. Springer, Heidelberg (2011). https://doi.org/10.1007/978-3-642-19170-1_15
36. Schwartz, R.E.: Obtuse triangular billiards i: near the (2, 3, 6) triangle. Exp. Math. **15**(2), 161–182 (2006)
37. Schwartz, R.E.: Obtuse triangular billiards ii: one hundred degrees worth of periodic trajectories. Exp. Math. **18**(2), 137–171 (2009)
38. Tan, X., Jiang, B.: Minimization of the maximum distance between the two guards patrolling a polygonal region. Theor. Comput. Sci. **532**, 73–79 (2014)
39. Troubetzkoy, S.: Dual billiards, fagnano orbits, and regular polygons. Am. Math. Mon. **116**(3), 251–260 (2009)
40. Vorobets, Y.B., Gal'perin, G.A., Stepin, A.M.: Periodic billiard trajectories in polygons: generating mechanisms. Russ. Math. Surv. **47**(3), 5 (1992)
41. Yanovski, V., Wagner, I.A., Bruckstein, A.M.: A distributed ant algorithm for efficiently patrolling a network. Algorithmica **37**(3), 165–186 (2003)

Invited Paper: Monotonicity and Opportunistically-Batched Actions in Derecho

Ken Birman[1(✉)], Sagar Jha[1], Mae Milano[2], Lorenzo Rosa[1,3], Weijia Song[1], and Edward Tremel[4]

[1] Cornell University, Ithaca, USA
ken@cs.cornell.edu
[2] UC Berkeley, Berkeley, USA
[3] University of Bologna, Bologna, Italy
[4] Augusta University, Augusta, USA

Abstract. Our work centers on a programming style in which a system separates data movement from control-data exchange, streaming the former over hardware-implemented reliable channels, while using a new form of distributed shared memory to manage the latter. Protocol decisions and control actions are expressed as *monotonic predicates* over the control data guarding protocol actions. Provable invariants about the protocol are expressed as *effectively-common knowledge*, which can be derived from the monotonic predicates in effect during a particular membership epoch. The methodology enables a natural style of code that is easy to reason about, and it runs efficiently on modern hardware. We used this approach to create Derecho, an optimal Paxos-based data replication library that sets performance records, and we believe it is broadly applicable to the construction of reliable distributed systems on high-bandwidth networks.

1 The Design of RDMA-Friendly Protocols

We are interested in distributed systems in which data transfers are streamed asynchronously by a layer independent of the one used for coordination, and in which peers asynchronously exchange control data. The approach makes it possible for the control layer to be implemented using *monotonic deduction*. We start by sketching the overall approach, after which subsections discuss the framework in greater detail.

In any setting, high performance requires developers to match their protocols to the hardware. The hardware of greatest interest for our work is a type of network that offers remote direct memory access (RDMA), a technology with which a process can reliably read or write the memory of another process asynchronously and without locking (the underlying mechanism involves message-passing between the RDMA network interface cards). RDMA is far faster than TCP/IP, achieving data rates of 100–200 Gbps and latencies as low as 0.75 μs.

S. Dolev and B. Schieber (Eds.): SSS 2023, LNCS 14310, pp. 172–190, 2023.
https://doi.org/10.1007/978-3-031-44274-2_14

Despite its use of RDMA networking hardware, our target environment can still be modeled in a traditional way. It supports concurrently active processes, interconnected by asynchronous networks and experiencing infrequent crash (halting) failures. Network failures do not partition the data center: a severe disruption will either shut down a group of machines or the entire data center.

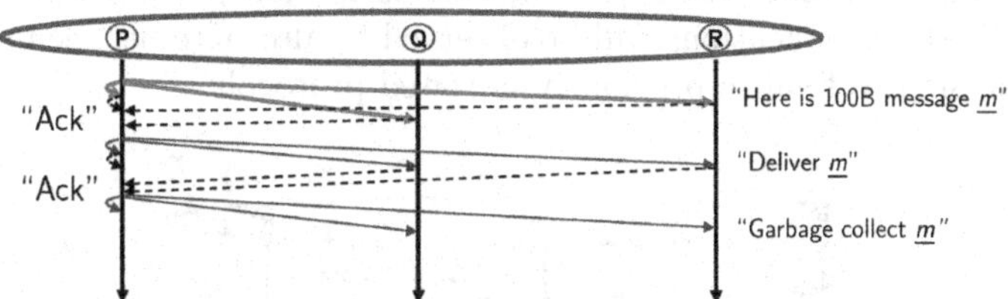

Fig. 1. An event triggers a 2PC that sends data (green) in its first phase, then waits for acknowledgments (dashed) before sending commit messages (red). Efficiency is low: the full run of the protocol does not end until after all the replies are collected and the commit has been successfully sent. On a 100 Gbps RDMA network, each small message takes 0.75 µs to arrive, which means the entire interaction takes 4.5 µs to deliver 100B of data. This uses only 0.02% of the available bandwidth. (Color figure online)

It is natural to wonder whether protocols such as 2-phase commit, atomic multicast, leader election, and replicated logging can take full advantage of RDMA. A first finding is that RDMA is not simply a faster replacement for TCP/IP: Although RDMA can mimic TCP/IP [15], higher-level protocols that treat RDMA as if it was TCP/IP gain little speedup. The central issue is latency: RDMA bandwidth can be 10x-20x better than that of TCP, yet its one-way latencies are not very different, causing a bottleneck (Fig. 1).

What sorts of protocol-engineering steps are needed to fully leverage ultra-fast networking? A system can load-balance updates, allowing them to be initiated by all members of the application. Each member could transmit a sequence or stream of actions, which potentially enables batching multiple operations per message. It may be feasible to have multiple threads per member, and hence transmit multiple data streams per member. Peers can send in a one-to-all manner, enabling decentralized decision-making. As illustrated in Fig. 2, which illustrates a system streaming atomic multicasts, such steps are indeed helpful. Yet (and this is also shown in the figure) data flow is likely to remain bursty. There are limits on how many threads we can have, or how evenly we can spread the workload. Batching is a wonderful idea, but it delays messages, and sooner or later, a partial batch may need to be sent. The network remains lightly used and throughput is limited.

The limiting factor turns out to be the disproportionately high delay noted above: RDMA delay is low compared with a protocol such as IP, and yet can seem high when we consider how much data could have been transmitted during one RDMA round-trip time. Pausing data transmission to exchange control information, even for a single RTT, will substantially reduce throughput. A second issue involves the unpredictable scheduling of endpoint applications: if a new message arrives but the receiver cannot process it immediately, the sender will be left waiting.

Lacking a mechanism to reduce the impact of delay, protocol instances will wait for acknowledgments or commit messages. This will trigger a rapid accumulation of protocol state until resource exhaustion forces the entire system to pause. As a result, applications will be observed to alternate between streaming data and pausing to finalize previously-initiated protocols.

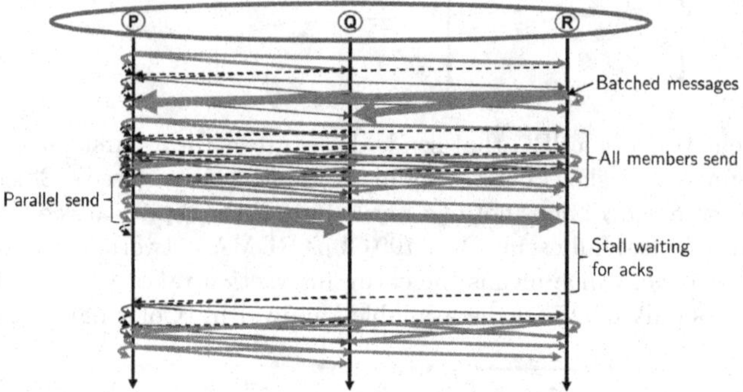

Fig. 2. Techniques such as parallel streaming and batching can improve network utilization, yet there is still idle time in the run due to round-trip delays that stall senders.

Our project first encountered this set of challenges when we created Derecho, a platform intended as a supporting framework for a new generation of cloud computing applications [12]. Derecho centers on data replication supported by a self-managed (virtually synchronous) version of Paxos. We decided to build entirely new protocols from the ground up. Our first step was to separate the data transportation layer ("data plane") of the system from the one handling control data ("control plane"), as seen in Fig. 3, giving each an independent communication channel. Now we can continuously stream, improving concurrency: members send data messages as updates are initiated. On the receiving side, these incoming messages trigger state updates, which are reflected in continuously exchanged streams of control data.

Consider a situation in which a receiver participating in some protocol experiences some form of delay. Data piles up briefly, but then the delay ends and streaming resumes. It will be common for a sequence of pending data messages or control events to become available as a group (for example, a series of data messages may have all become deliverable). We use the term *opportunistically batched* to refer to an action that can be applied to the whole group of messages rather one by one, hopefully enabling the receiver to quickly catch up and amortizing overheads. Opportunistic batching contrasts with sender-side batching, in which senders deliberately delay messages to group them into fixed-sized

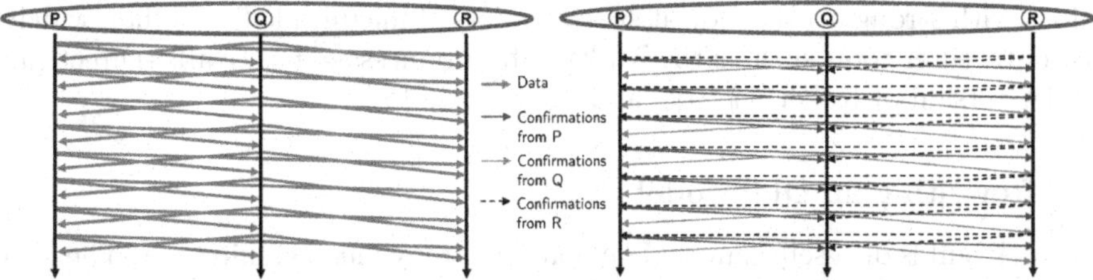

Fig. 3. By separating data plane (left) from control (right), we can design protocols that stream data in a continuous and reliable manner, achieving much higher efficiencies.

batches, delaying messages even when doing so is unnecessary. At RDMA speeds, opportunistic batching is an unqualified improvement: it copes with inevitable delays yet doesn't introduce any of its own. Moreover, the technique turns out to be especially suited to the one-sided RDMA write hardware we use, in which the receiver asynchronously discovers that some section of its memory has changed, rather than being explicitly notified each time a new message arrives.

We now need to address two questions. One centers on the best way to stream data messages reliably while preserving sender order. We describe our work on this problem in [4,13], and will not repeat that material here.

The second question involves the streaming of control data, and is the main focus of this paper. Derecho innovates by reexpressing the concept of a stream of control messages. Rather than viewing such a stream as a series of small messages, we focus on the actual values, and ask whether a stream of control-variable updates can be transmitted using the form of shared memory enabled by RDMA, in which one process is granted permission to asynchronously write into some memory region in a second process.

Our central idea was to focus on *monotonic* control data: given a variable such as a messages-received counter, which only increases, new values can overwrite older ones. For example, suppose that process a sends message x with id 17 and then message y with id 18. Process b receives and acknowledges x by writing 17 into a location in the memory of a using a one-sided RDMA write. Now y arrives, and b overwrites the acknowledgment variable. If a observes 17 first and reacts to this control event, then observes 18 and reacts to it, it is as if we sent two acknowledgment messages from b to a. But if a experiences a small delay and sees the counter jump from 16 to 18, it can *infer* that 17 was previously reported. In effect, the observed value (18) covers the range [1 ... 18]. A single RDMA-shared-memory counter has replaced a stream of acknowledgment messages.

Derecho's entire control plane is monotonic, and this even includes sequences of complex objects, such as proposed membership updates: we guard such an object by a counter and adopt a round-robin model in which we can send some number of objects without delaying. This approach let us eliminate the lock-step dependency on round-trip messages carrying acknowledgments and commits. Jointly, such steps enable the dramatic performance improvements described in [12]: the system is able to replicate data and coordinate distributed actions with strong consistency at speeds orders of magnitude faster than widely used datacenter tools such as the Kafka pub/sub message bus, Kafka-Direct (an RDMA version of Kafka [17,21]), and Zookeeper [14].

1.1 Revisiting an Old Model

Our work builds on a self-managed virtual synchrony membership layer. The idea of building systems that manage their own membership was introduced in the 1985–1987 period [5–7]. Whereas classic protocols struggle to deal with failures, virtual synchrony replaces both liveness and failure-tolerance with a subsuming concept of "dynamic membership."

Processes must *join* the system upon starting and cannot exchange messages with members until they are admitted to the current membership (the current *view*). Upon sensing a possible failure, any member can request exclusion of members *suspected* of having failed from the current view. No process will accept or send messages to a suspected peer, and it will promptly be dropped from the view. This establishes an *epoch* model, in which each epoch starts with a new view, performs protocol actions for a period of time, then ends when the membership management system learns of a new join or failure event. The membership service will pause the active message-sending protocols, assist in cleanup to terminate any that were incomplete when paused, then switch to a new view which initiates a new epoch. Should a full shutdown occur, restart is similar: the membership service forms what will become the first view, repairs any persisted state that was damaged by the failure, and then can initiate the first epoch of the new run. Should any of these steps be impossible (for example, if persisted data is inaccessible due to crashes), the system refuses to restart and a human operator would need to repair the problem, for example by loading the missing data from a backup.

By trusting suspicions and immediately excluding the impacted processes from the view, virtual synchrony systems wall off potentially malfunctioning group members. The policy assumes that the rate of mistaken suspicions will be low, but that assumption is valid in today's cloud data centers. Importantly, protocols such as atomic multicast [6] or Paxos replicated logs [18] are simplified by this model because each instance runs in a single epoch. In effect, we separate functionality: a protocol has a normal failure-free logic component and a distinct view-change component used to clean up when a failure disrupts execution, as we detail immediately below. Finally, the protocol has a component responsible for reissuing requests (while preserving the sender message ordering) in the event that cleanup rolled the partially completed messaging protocol back rather than terminating it by rolling forward and delivering messages. The overall structure must still guarantee atomicity and ordering (linearizability [11]), but these needs do not arise all at once.

Derecho, like other virtual synchrony systems (e.g. [1]), uses a leader-based membership protocol, where age-ranking determines the leader succession sequence in case of failure; the leader initiates a view change when it learns of a new join or failure. However, Derecho's membership protocol is specifically designed to use monotonic logic. The new views proposed by leaders form a monotonic sequence, each building on the prior one. Views must be accepted in order, and each proposal must individually be accepted by every non-suspected member. Additionally, the set of healthy (non-suspected) members that accept a proposal must include a majority of members from both the current view and from each proposed new view up to and including the new proposal. If some new membership event occurs while the protocol is running, the leader extends the list of proposals with follow-on proposals. Similar to the split of data plane from control plane, we can think of the sequence of proposals as a data plane, streaming from leader to participants, and the proposal acceptances as a control plane streaming from participants back to the leader.

We do not wish for this sequence of proposals to ever roll back, or for a proposal to be lost at some members and yet to commit at others. With this in mind, when a new leader suspects the older leaders and prepares to take over, it first queries every non-suspected member it knows of. In doing so, its own suspicions are immediately shared, and it learns any suspicions or proposals known to any of those processes. We can then prove that if the system remains live, any proposal witnessed by a majority of a view will eventually be adopted, and that any proposal that could have been adopted will be learned by the new leader. Conversely, if the system loses majority (i.e. observes that a majority of processes are suspected), it will shut itself down.

Why go to such lengths to make this protocol monotonic? The central issue revolves around the unpredictable sequencing of events that system members can experience and the importance of avoiding logical partitioning, in which one system splits into two separate subsystems that each consider themselves to be in charge. Members might advance at different rates, but due to monotonicity they learn of the same views in the same order. Indeed, protocols in which we think of the peers as reasoning and leveraging monotonicity to take actions based on monotonic deductions are a hallmark of virtual synchrony and arise extensively in the Derecho protocols. In some ways this should not be surprising: one could have made a similar remark about the Isis Toolkit and its protocols in 1987 [5]. Others have reached very similar conclusions. Elaborating the CALM methodology for BLOOM (a distributed computing language based on Datalog [2]), a 2013 paper by Ameloot *et. al.* argues that monotonicity (combined with occasional consensus) is complete for distributed computing in a logically-founded deductive style [3].

1.2 Effectively-Common Knowledge

Any developer of a non-trivial distributed system eventually encounters a protocol that is difficult to prove correct. With fault-tolerant systems one issue is the exponentially large state space that must be considered: distributed runs in which at each instant, any message that could be in flight might be received, but also in which any participant might fail. Focusing on our own Derecho protocols, the most challenging aspects to prove correct are associated with runs in which the failures could include the initial leader or even a series of leaders, each of which could have made proposals and perhaps even received adequate quorums to commit some of them. This forces the developer to formalize the concept of a run, to express the "healthy majority in each view" policy rigorously, and then to demonstrate that all of this yields a single perceived sequence of views that will never partition.

The creation of a proof is ultimately an exercise in logical reasoning, and is increasingly supported by proof checking systems (we have direct experience with Ivy [22] and have experimented with Coq [8]). Highly visible proofs include the Dafny proof for IronFleet [10]; Paxos proofs in TLA+ [19] and recent proofs of a number of protocols using the DistAlgo specification language [20,23]. The question now arises: does our monotonic protocol specification align well with formal reasoning?

Not every style of network is conducive to easy correctness proofs. For example, protocols expressed using exchanges of unreliable point-to-point messaging (UDP) are notoriously hard to reason about. UDP does guarantee that a corrupted message will not be delivered, but messages can be lost, delivered out of order, replayed, or arrive after very long delays. The already large state space becomes daunting.

It turns out (and this is one of our main contributions) that a virtually-synchronous monotonic programming style, implemented over RDMA with its hardware-supported reliability features, dramatically simplifies proof tasks. Logicians refer to information that is simply accepted and trusted by all members of a set as *common knowledge* [9], leading us to use the term *effectively-common knowledge* for per-epoch data such as the membership view and other application-specific information that might be piggybacked along with the view.

Common knowledge can be understood as data that all active members of a system possess and trust. Every process knows the information, and also knows that every other process has the identical information. This type of "I know that you know" inference can be iterated to arbitrary degree. Effectively-common knowledge is information tied to the epoch. It introduces facts known to every current member, and that every member can assume that its peers also know, again iterated to arbitrary degree.

An example of effectively-common knowledge employed in Derecho is the message delivery ordering used in an epoch. The ordering rule cannot be anticipated before the epoch begins: it depends on the membership and the anticipated message sending patterns in a group, and neither of these is known *a priori*. By attaching the ordering rule to the view, Derecho can be flexible and adapt this rule as needed, while allowing each member to assume for the duration of the view that every other member knows the same ordering rule. The alternative, used in the classic Paxos protocol, involves a "competition" for each message delivery slot, since members can disagree about delivery ordering. That policy forces the classic Paxos to use just the kind of round-trip message passing we are trying to avoid due to its sensitivity to delay.

Why not just call epoch knowledge "common knowledge?" The issue is that common knowledge cannot be gained while a protocol is running (a main result in [9]). Effectively-common knowledge, in contrast, is easily generated: we simply need to create a new epoch.

Appendix A offers some classic examples of common knowledge, showing how seemingly minor changes to a problem statement can make a protocol "impossible" to implement. Appendix B then goes to highlight the connection to formal verification using automated proof systems.

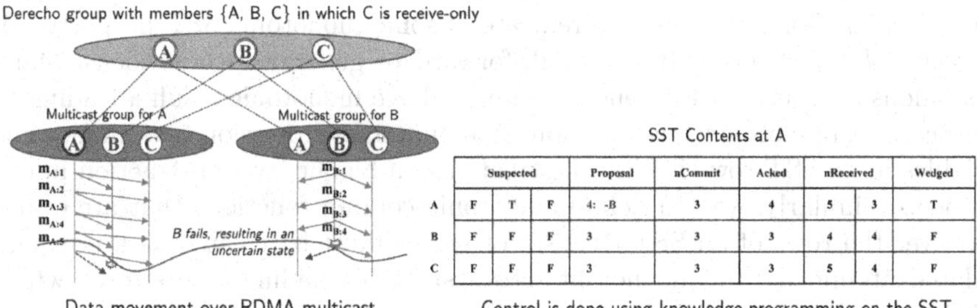

	Suspected			Proposal	nCommit	Acked	nReceived		Wedged
A	F	T	F	4: -B	3	4	5	3	T
B	F	F	F	3	3	3	4	4	F
C	F	F	F	3	3	3	5	4	F

Fig. 4. The shared state table abstraction offers a convenient representation of monotonic protocol control data. In the example shown, processes a and b are streaming atomic multicasts to a group that also includes c; each has an SST replica and uses it to share control information with its peers (see [12] for details).

2 Deep Dive: Shared State Table

As discussed in Sect. 1, Derecho separates its protocols into a data plane and a control plane. The central abstraction used for representing and exchanging control data is the *shared state table* or SST (Fig. 4). This table is a replicated data structure created afresh for each epoch. Every process in the epoch possesses a copy, within which it owns and can update one row. These updates are then asynchronously written to its peers using one-sided RDMA write operations, which are reliable but lock-free (Fig. 5). The effect is that updates arrive continuously, streaming in an all-to-all pattern.[1] Updates to a row arrive in order, but different peers can see updates to *different* rows in different orders. If we were to pause the updates, all SST replicas would converge, but during normal execution we only do this while switching from epoch to epoch.

Unnoticed updates are a common phenomenon in Derecho, in part because each process has a single predicate thread. When a process starts up, each protocol registers one or more predicated actions: a tuple consisting of the boolean

[1] All-to-all exchange of control state would scale poorly in many settings, but no issue arises because Derecho is sharded: most activity occurs in tiny subgroups with just 2 or 3 members. We have experimented with far larger subgroups without problems. Future systems deploying Derecho in immense subgroups might need to exchange control data in a different manner, but the underlying principle of asynchronous updates and monotonic deduction of system state would still apply.

function to test and the logic to run if that test evaluates to true. The SST predicate thread then starts up and loops, evaluating predicates one by one like a long list of if statements. By the time a predicate is rechecked, the underlying data may have advanced multiple times, in which case the triggered logic will catch up by processing several events as a batch.

Derecho's use of monotonicity plays into this dynamic. Not only is the underlying data monotonic, but many aggregating operations over monotonic data are as well: obvious examples are *min* and *max*. This leads us to define *predicate monotonicity*: P is a monotonic predicate of some monotonic SST property x if $\forall y > x : \ P(y) \Rightarrow P(x)$. It is straightforward to generalize these ideas. Many expressions computed over monotonic inputs have monotonic results, leading to the idea of a monotonic row function: A monotonic expression over monotonic variables in an SST row that can be treated as a higher level abstraction in our protocols. Similarly, we can define monotonic column functions that are evaluated over the rows of an SST. If a set of values must be treated as a unit and updated atomically, but do not fit into a single cache-line (the size at which RDMA writes are atomic), we first update the values, then update some form of guard, such as a "version counter" (which is a monotonic variable). Any participant that sees the updated guard will see the full set of preceding updates, since writes are applied in sender order.

When we set out to create Derecho's virtual synchrony view update protocol, it turned out to remarkably easy to express the algorithm in this manner. Given the epoch mechanism, we then designed simple atomic multicast (very similar to protocol II in vertical Paxos) and durable replicated log update protocols (very similar to classic Paxos in a failure-free run, with the quorum size set to the full current membership of the group, and the read quorum size set to 1). Again, the methodology led us directly to simple, highly efficient solutions.

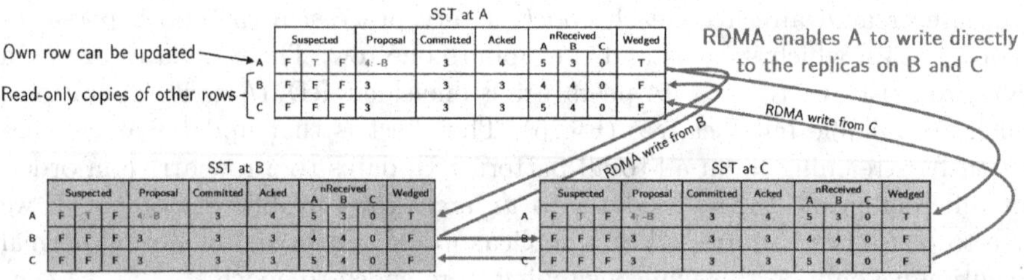

Fig. 5. After updating a row, an SST participant uses RDMA to asynchronously "push" the new data to the remote replicas. These push operations are lock-free and uncoordinated hence the updates are not totally ordered. However, if one process does two push operations with the same target, the updates respect the sender order.

3 Using Logic to Reason About Protocols

A knowledge perspective formalizes a way of describing protocols such as Paxos that most of us use when reasoning about them. For example, consider the first stage of a Paxos protocol [18]. The leader (a) sends a proposed update for a specified slot and ballot number. At the moment of sending it, only a knows the contents. Upon receiving such a message, participant b learns the contents. Because a is the sender, b now also knows that a knows the contents, but would not yet be safe to deliver the message: a and b might both fail, and perhaps no other member has a copy. In the terminology of Paxos, we would say that the update is not yet *stable*. Later, when a process is finally able to deduce that all other processes have a copy (know the contents), it can conclude that the update has stabilized. Depending on the particular Paxos protocol used, some steps can involve all-to-all control-data exchanges. With these versions of Paxos, if process c discovers that message m has become stable, c may also be able to deduce that eventually every healthy process will arrive at this same conclusion.

A knowledge logic introduces operators to represent the idea of reasoning about information directly available to processes in a system (facts), together with indirect knowledge paths: process a may know that process b knows some fact f. For example, if a sends a message to b, initially a has no information about when b will have received that message. Later, b acknowledges the message, and a now is said to *know* that b *knows* any facts carried in the message, etc. This leads to a hierarchy of knowledge: $K_a(f)$ if *a knows f*, $K_a(K_b(f))$, etc. If the set of participants is known, we write $K_a^1(f)$ to denote that a *knows* that every member *knows* f. In a similar sense, K^n denotes the n-fold property that every process knows, that every process knows, ... (n times), that some fact holds. K^* denotes common knowledge: a fact for which K^n holds for all values of n.

To make this concrete, here is an example from Derecho's atomic multicast protocol. Using asynchronous monotonic deduction over the SST, we employ a provably-correct safety deduction to detect the condition that *all messages from m to n can safely be delivered, in a round-robin order that also respects the sender FIFO ordering.* If a member has nothing to send, it sends a *null multicast.* Even under heavy load, this rule is fast: Experiments showed that the delay from sending a multicast to delivery is often as small as $1.5us$: double the one-way RDMA latency on our hardware. Moreover, this same pattern arose in several stages of our protocols, and it lends itself to opportunistic batching.

4 Implications for Other Systems

The success of the effectively-common knowledge model as an enabling tool for Derecho's asynchronous, monotonic control plane surprised even the development team. We were led to adopt this model by the sequence of insights laid out in the paper: first the recognition that asynchronous streaming is the key to high performance on modern networks supporting RDMA, then that this pattern is easy to achieve for data streams but much more challenging with control data. This then led us to the insight that monotonic control data could stream quite efficiently if the applications consuming the data are able to reason using a monotonic deductive style, in which missing an update or two poses no difficulty at all because the next deductive inference simply "catches up" on a batch of events rather than just one. Opportunistic batching doesn't impact protocol complexity but it does change the "constants." Fewer messages are needed, and when one process falls slightly behind it can catch up quickly.

The power of this sequence of steps became clear when we realized that our Paxos protocol achieves theoretical lower bounds proved by Keidar and Schraer [16]. No proof was required: Keidar and Schraer express their bounds in terms of the number of message exchanges required to safely deliver an atomic multicast or a similar update. A colleague of ours at the University of Surrey, Professor Gregory Chockler, offered to review the specification of the Derecho protocol and undertook to count the exchanges of information that occur through the intermediary of the Derecho SST. He pointed out that the number of remote RDMA writes performed by Derecho matches the bound they derived. Interestingly, this is actually a worst case for Derecho: because of batching, Derecho will sometimes omit some writes, performing one write at the end of a batch of message receives. When this happens, we actually do even better than the lower bound! On the other hand, opportunistic batch sizes are limited, so the speedup is at best a constant factor.

Seemingly, simply by setting out to express the control plane of Derecho as an asynchronous stream of monotonic information, we stumbled upon an optimal Paxos implementation. This is particularly striking because, to our knowledge, no prior Paxos is optimal in the Keidar and Schraer sense. Yet we did not set out to achieve this property: it emerged from our methodology. Thus while the idea of effectively-common knowledge may be somewhat esoteric, the pragmatic value of the overall methodology is evident. It forces a new mindset, and this mindset turns out to align closely with the "right" way to think about protocols.

Recalling our 2PC examples from the introduction, it makes sense that monotonic SST-based protocols can achieve optimal behavior. Suppose that a is using a 2PC to stream reliable multicasts to b, c, etc. Clearly, a 2PC can commit as soon as the required set of acknowledgments are received, which we express as an aggregation query over the SST. Process a, looping through a series of SST predicates, will reevaluate this query again and again, reacting as soon as the needed property is observed. Nonetheless, a's discovery of message stability may Snot occur instantly when b performs its RDMA write to acknowledge reception. After all, a also has other work to do and the predicate thread might not get a chance to reevaluate the predicate "instantly" in a real-time sense. But our opportunistic batching approach allows a to sense that the commit property was achieved for this 2PC instance the very next time the aggregation query is performed – and because of monotonicity, a simultaneously detects stability for any other instances that have reached the same knowledge level! Thus, the detection of safety occurs as early as possible and covers all the 2PC instances that are now committable, as a batch.

We have come to believe that distributed protocols are best visualized from an information-theoretic perspective in which the protocol developer asks what knowledge is gained from each deductive inference performed by the system, and what knowledge is communicated in each message or remote RDMA write. We begin to express safety properties as knowledge predicates: K^1 knowledge being the case required for most steps of Paxos (for example, "when process p deduces that all peers have received message m, it learns that m cannot be lost and hence that it is safe to advance to the next protocol stage"). Monotonicity makes the SST compact, while also guiding the developer towards opportunistic batching.

This methodology could usefully be applied in other settings that depend on strong consistency or other forms of strong guarantees. Databases and transaction systems are an obvious candidate to consider, but it is notable that even modern ML training systems provide fault-tolerance and exactly-once semantics (many MapReduce frameworks adopt this approach). Microsoft's Azure storage fabric is strongly consistent, and the AWS S3 infrastructure recently added strong consistency as well. The same sequence of reasoning and development that yielded Derecho would be a promising basis for work that could lead to speedups in all of these cases.

5 Conclusion

Our paper is an outgrowth of work on Derecho, a system created at Cornell to support distributed application development. The paper focuses on *effectively-common knowledge*, defining this concept, discussing its value (illustrated by an unusually efficient message-ordering policy), and describing its implementation. The approach lends itself to a style of monotonic exchange of state information that enables opportunistically batched decision-making, and is particularly efficient in systems supporting RDMA hardware.

Acknowledgements. The authors are very grateful to Luis Rodriguez, who read an earlier draft of this paper and suggested many ways that it could be improved. The SSS 2023 reviewers were incredibly helpful. Our work was funded, in part, by grants from AFRL under its SWEC program, Microsoft Research and Siemens, and the experiments summarized here used hardware generously provided by NVIDA and its Mellanox subsidiary.

Appendices

The two appendices in this section provide additional detail going beyond the material in the body of the paper. Neither is needed to understand our main contributions. Appendix A offers two examples of common knowledge, drawing on examples from [9]. Appendix B discusses the connection between effectively-common knowledge and a tactic used when formally verifying protocols using provers that can fully automate subproofs provided that they are fully expressed in a decidable fragment of first-order logic (often, the subset that the Z3 SMT solver can handle). We considered but decided against including an appendix on RDMA (this kind of hardware has been actively discussed for at least a decade, and there is an excellent Wikipedia article covering the one-sided write feature we used), and on virtual synchrony (well known to the community since 1987).

Appendix A: Common Knowledge

A.1 Impossibility of Outdoor Dining in Seattle

Two friends work in Seattle, a city known for cloud cover and damp weather, but when the sun pops out they would prefer to meet outside. The complication is that both sometimes attend meetings in rooms lacking phone reception. A first idea is that if one of them notices that the weather is fine, they will text the other, who will confirm, and then they can meet outside for lunch.

"But wait", says one to the other. "If I text you, but receive no reply, I will have to assume that my text was not received. In that case I would wait for you here, in the cafeteria." "In fact," replies the other, "I would have the symmetric problem: even if I do receive your text, I wouldn't know that you received my confirmation, and would have no choice but to wait for you in here in the cafeteria. And if you confirm my confirmation, that doesn't help either!"

This is very strange. After all, once the intial text is confirmed, and the confirmation is confirmed, both are aware that it is a sunny day. Yet no matter how many messages they exchange, they do not converge to the identical state. An inductive analysis always leads to the cafeteria: their "default" option.

Both fall silent: the impossibility of meeting outside for lunch now being apparent. "Well," says one, "if the weather is nice I'll just send you a text and will be out here. No need to confirm. If you can't make it, I'll understand!"

This first example illustrates that (1) Posed in this manner, logicians can only base "symmetric" decisions on existing common knowledge. (2) No matter how many messages are exchanged knowledge asymmetry cannot be eliminated. Of course, in real life we don't need common knowledge (and sometimes, things happen, and we can't join the lunch crowd).

Discussion: The insight to take from this first story is that distributed systems in which information must be observed (by some process) and then learned (by other processes) embody an asymmetry. When formalized, their members will never all be in the identical knowledge state, and attempts to achieve symmetry lead to unbounded yet ineffective exchanges of messages.

In what way is this relevant to distributed computing? The main and perhaps only importance relates to specification and proof. It is very easy to write a specification that unintentionally requires common knowledge. However, such a statement must either be implied from the initial conditions (and hence vacuous), or if not, cannot be achieved by any protocol. A proof assistant can check the logic of a given proof, or even find certain kinds of proofs or counterexamples on its own, but will not signal this type of specification error. Thus a seemingly innocent mistake can lead to an impossible-to-prove specification. The person tasked with carrying out the proof would either give up or, more likely, abandon parts of the task. This last scenario should worry us: it suggests that there could be "proved correct" systems for critical tasks that actually ignore parts of the protocols used.

Effectively-common knowledge is in fact not identical to the form of common knowledge of the kind Halpern and Moses considered in [9]. With effectively-common knowledge, we consider a modular system in which one module implements epochs, and the other modules run within epochs and simply trust the view and any annotations as if they were common knowledge. We carry out separate proofs for the two modules, then compose one system from the two modules. Our proof coverage is stronger, and the developer never confronts what would otherwise be an infeasible task.

A.2 The Inscription on the Cake was a Lie!

On Carol's birthday, her friends come to play outside before lunch. It being Seattle, all are quite muddy when they enter the kitchen. "In this house we have a rule!", proclaims her father, Ted. "No dessert for anyone who has a dirty face!". His wording is ill-chosen, because no child likes to wash their face, and every child optimistically believes their own face to be clean until proven otherwise. None moves a hair, although all the children see one-another's dirty faces. Increasingly annoyed, Ted repeats himself a few times. But even after n repetitions (n being the number of children), no child has washed. Ted puts the cake to the side and sends them all to wash up.

Later he relents after Carol explains the inductive proof that justified their action. She first addresses $n = 1$. "Daddy, just the other day this happened. You told me I would need to wash if my face was dirty, but I was hoping it was clean." "Carol, " replies Ted, "all you needed to do was to look in the mirror." "But Daddy, the mirror is too high!". Ted is forced to acknowledge that Carol would have had no way to deduce that her face must have been dirty.

"Now Daddy, consider $n = 2$. Timmy and I come in, both dirty. You remind us of the rule. But neither of us likes to wash our faces, and anyway, Timmy is mean and would love for me to not get cake and have to watch him enjoying it. And I feel the same! So we both look at each other, and I see that Timmy's face is dirty, and he sees that mine is dirty, and neither of us moves." Ted replies, "Yes Carol, but now your logic fails. I repeated myself." "You did, Daddy. But I was hoping my face was clean. Timmy hoped that his was clean. So our decision not to go and wash up was consistent with one of us believing that neither of our faces was dirty, even if it also consistent with one in which both of us had dirty faces. You didn't give us enough information!"

At the next party, when the children come in from playing, Ted first says "Well, I see some very dirty faces here!" and then repeats the household rule n times. On the nth repetition, all the children simultaneously rush to the sink and wash up. Beaming, Ted unveils a cake which is inscribed: "K^* is necessary and sufficient!" The children groan: A typical Seattle "dad joke."

Later, Carol corners her dad. "Daddy, that was embarrassing! What if one of my friends hadn't heard you clearly at the start!" Ted realizes that this is a valid criticism: was his initial statement genuinely common knowledge?

Discussion: Here, we illustrate another peculiarity of common knowledge. Even in classic problems such as muddy children, it is debatable that common knowledge is really being introduced dynamically. To the extent that this does occur, some form of assertion of trust is required: the participants trust that the mechanism that shared the new common knowledge is completely reliable.

An epoch-based virtual synchrony system has an advantage here: to switch from epoch j to epoch j, members definitely must receive and "install" the new view together with any additional data annotating it. Thus for process a to interact with process b as members of epoch j, it genuinely is the case that both have replicas of the new view. By proving that the group membership cannot partition into two logically distinct views, we arrive at guarantee that the annotation can be treated like common knowledge. Ted, for example, waited until all the children were present and then assumed they would understand him.

A.3 Other Forms of Effectively-Common Knowledge

The example we offered in Sect. 1.2 focused on message ordering. What would be other uses for effectively-common knowledge?

A good place to start is with an old, classic, database partitioning scenario. When ATM machines were first introduced, they depended on dialup modems that were not always able to establish a connection (a flurry of ATM use could overload the central modem pool, leading to persistent busy signals). To fix the issue, banks introduced the idea of a "primary ATM". Perhaps, Carol almost always uses the ATM machine at the intersection of Main Street and Old Market Avenue. The bank could give that ATM "ownership" of some of Carol's current balance. For a withdrawal up to this limit, the ATM could authorize that transaction without first phoning the main office. Of course, the bank's other ATMs would not be able to access Carol's full balance: the bank has locked down this portion of her balance. But schemes were then proposed for dynamically adapting the policy.

More broadly, effectively-common knowledge arises in situations where some form of policy will span a dynamically varying set of participants. If the participant set was non-varying, we don't really need effectively-common knowledge: totally ordered multicast would suffice. But if the set of participants changes and simultaneously we need a policy that depends on a nondeterministic decision or attribute of the members, it is hard to avoid an effectively-common knowledge model.

Our insight is that virtual synchrony epochs can be viewed as virtualizing many otherwise intractable behaviors and unachievable guarantees. Within an epoch, failures "do not occur", hence protocols do not need to be fault-tolerant. Instead they can simply trust the view. And then when we realized that it would be faster to preagree on multicast delivery order in Derecho, we simply annotated the view with the ordering policy to use. The fully generalized case simply allows the application itself to provide additional annotations, which it can then treat as effectively-common knowledge once the epoch begins.

Appendix B: Higher-Order Protocol Components

Effective common knowledge in the context of virtually synchronous epochs enables a deductive strategy also seen in protocol verification. This statement may feel like a non-sequitor: any protocol exchanges messages to gain information, and is designed to achieve a state in which it is safe to take whatever action the protocol embodies. Yet we do not normally think of formal reasoning of the kind used in protocol verification as offering ideas that can be directly useful in protocol design.

Developers of complex protocols have always struggled to prove them correct. Today this burden is much reduced: Provers such as Dafny, TLA+ and Ivy are widely used to check the correctness of protocols [10,19,22]. DistAlgo, a specification and proof framework, goes even further, allowing rigorously specified protocols to be proved correct and even generating an executable verified code instance [20]. Less widely appreciated is that they struggle to overcome a significant expressivity limit. Today's most popular provers operate by taking a specification and reducing it to a decidable logic formula expressed entirely in first order logic. The basic tactic is to form a conjunction of protocol invariants, invert it, and then use Z3 (an SMT solver) to search for a counterexample. If Z3 terminates, either it exhibits a counterexample and the protocol is not correct, or it finds none and the protocol is proved. If Z3 fails to terminate, the developer modifies assertions and then tries again. If a protocol is buggy, this yields a concrete example of how the bug can be triggered.

The expressivity issue stems from the inability of first-order logic to capture and hence verify higher order properties, such as conditions that need to be expressed over traces, or progress conditions. However, encountering such an issue is not a dead end. In such systems it is also possible for a developer to *combine hand-created higher order proofs with first order automated checking.*

To see how this is done, we should start by noting that first-order provers normally support modularization of protocol proofs, allowing the user to isolate and reason about a component of the protocol without simultaneously reasoning about the rest of the system. An example of this might involve a "sub-protocol" for forming a collection of processes into a ring: an example relevant to our running example, which used a ring to define the round-robin order used in Derecho message delivery.

It may be surprising to realize that a ring is an example of a system property that cannot be expressed in a first order logic. The central issue is that first-order logics are limited to boolean variables, relations that take boolean inputs and output a boolean result, logical conjunctions and (with significant limitations) existential quantifiers. This model is not strong enough to define the natural numbers, or to talk about the natural order on the natural numbers, and for the same reason, it is not strong enough to express some properties that depend on protocol traces that represent runs. And, to be very specific, first order logic cannot verify a protocol that organizes a set of nodes into a ring.

Yet this is simply a limitation of first-order logic. There are many logics within which we do have access to the natural numbers, can reason about orderings and other properties, and can define a ring. For example, on a ring every process has a predecessor, a successor. Call these $pred(a)$ and $succ(a)$ for process a. Both are unique, and moreover there exists some integer k such that $pred^k(a) = a$ and $succ^k(a) = a$. The issue is that to the extent that Dafny and Ivy proofs are checked by Z3, we accept that it will be infeasible to verify protocol modules that maintain properties such as the ring one. There would be no problem doing this in a higher-order logic such as the one used in Coq, but the task will be much less automated: a human would need to carry out the proof, and perform many steps by hand.

The usual work-around is to provide a second proof framework in which a human developer can express higher order questions and carry out higher order proofs of protocol fragments that rely on higher order logic. To integrate such proofs into the first-order layer, they then need a way to export artifacts from these proofs back into first-order logic (and keep in mind: this cannot involve extending first order logic, which is a fixed and unchangeable aspect of the methodology).

The solution leverages the fact that first order logic can express relations: functions on first-order variables that perform some kind of logical computation and return true or false. We simply treat the higher order protocol as an uninterpreted black box that outputs relations magically populated with the correct content. Our higher order protocol component can be proved to correctly construct these relations. Then, having completed this proof, we can simply declare that "there exists a relation with the following properties", using first-order logic to define those properties. In this way, the higher-order artifact can be reasoned about rigorously, then used as a tool by the first-order relation. This is how first-order systems deal with properties such as the ordering on the natural numbers.

Thus, from the perspective of the first order logic, $succ$, $succ^k$, $pred$, $pred^k$ and k are relations, but uninterpreted ones populated "elsewhere". To reason about how they are constructed we use the higher-order prover. But if we simply need to describe a step in which a protocol takes some action, such as a node a passing a message to its successor, we can use an existential quantifier to assert that there exists a node b such that $succ(a) = b$, and this uses only first-order logic, because the verifier doesn't actually need to compute a value for a or b: it treats the logic statement as a universal property. The same is true for the assertion that in a ring, $\exists k: \ succ^k(a) = a$. This statement is true for all rings, and for all members, and hence the first-order prover can make use of it without needing specific values.

Our realization was that these higher order objects and properties are a bit like effectively-common knowledge: the first-order layer of the protocol simply trusts that they exist and were properly created. By packaging effectively-common knowledge as an annotation to the view, we simplify the use of this idea. The developer writes software to run in the membership leader and able to compute any desired annotations for the next membership view. One would potentially need to prove that module correct, in the higher-order logic. Having done so, the output of the module becomes effectively-common knowledge and can be treated as a well-known fact by processes running during the epoch. In effect, we compartmentalize an otherwise complicated, error-prone task.

We are not claiming that such steps magically make proofs trivial. In the case of Derecho, we are still faced with doing manual higher-order proofs for many properties. As an example, the termination condition for Derecho's virtually synchronous view update protocol is a fixed-point: eventually either the system shuts down, or reaches a point where (1) some process believes itself to be the leader, and (2) it suspects every higher-ranked process, and (3) it gains consent for some sequence of membership updates, (4) that consent is obtained from a majority of the most recently active view, and from a majority of members of each proposed view, and (5) no process in the last of these proposed views suspects the leader. This is clearly not expressible in first-order logic, nor is it a trivial proof goal even when expressed in higher-order logic. Yet it is a *feasible* proof goal, and yields a progress condition for Derecho. We can even express optimality assertions as higher-order statements.

References

1. Agarwal, D.A., Moser, L.E., Melliar-Smith, P.M., Budhia, R.K.: The Totem multiple-ring ordering and topology maintenance protocol. ACM Trans. Comput. Syst. **16**(2), 93–132 (1998). https://doi.org/10.1145/279227.279228
2. Alvaro, P., Conway, N., Hellerstein, J.M., Marczak, W.R.: Consistency analysis in bloom: a CALM and collected approach. In: Conference on Innovative Data Systems Research (2011)
3. Ameloot, T.J., Neven, F., Van Den Bussche, J.: Relational transducers for declarative networking. J. ACM **60**(2) (2013). https://doi.org/10.1145/2450142.2450151
4. Behrens, J., Jha, S., Birman, K., Tremel, E.: RDMC: a reliable RDMA multicast for large objects. In: 2018 48th Annual IEEE/IFIP International Conference on Dependable Systems and Networks (DSN), Luxembourg City, Luxembourg, pp. 71–82. IEEE (2018). https://doi.org/10.1109/DSN.2018.00020
5. Birman, K., Joseph, T.: Exploiting virtual synchrony in distributed systems. In: SOSP 1987, Austin, Texas, USA, pp. 123–138. ACM (1987). https://doi.org/10.1145/41457.37515
6. Birman, K.: Guide to Reliable Distributed Systems: Building High-Assurance Applications and Cloud-Hosted Services. Texts in Computer Science. Springer, London (2012). https://doi.org/10.1007/978-1-4471-2416-0
7. Birman, K.P.: Replication and fault-tolerance in the ISIS system. SIGOPS Oper. Syst. Rev. **19**(5), 79–86 (1985). https://doi.org/10.1145/323627.323636
8. Coquand, T., Huet, G.: Constructions: a higher order proof system for mechanizing mathematics. In: Buchberger, B. (ed.) EUROCAL 1985. LNCS, vol. 203, pp. 151–184. Springer, Heidelberg (1985). https://doi.org/10.1007/3-540-15983-5_13
9. Halpern, J.Y., Moses, Y.: Knowledge and common knowledge in a distributed environment. J. ACM **37**(3), 549–587 (1990). https://doi.org/10.1145/79147.79161

10. Hawblitzel, C., et al.: IronFleet: proving safety and liveness of practical distributed systems. Commun. ACM **60**(7), 83–92 (2017). https://doi.org/10.1145/3068608
11. Herlihy, M.P., Wing, J.M.: Linearizability: a correctness condition for concurrent objects. ACM Trans. Program. Lang. Syst. **12**(3), 463–492 (1990). https://doi.org/10.1145/78969.78972
12. Jha, S., et al.: Derecho: fast state machine replication for cloud services. ACM Trans. Comput. Syst. (TOCS) **36**(2), 1–49 (2019)
13. Jha, S., Rosa, L., Birman, K.P.: Spindle: techniques for optimizing atomic multicast on RDMA. In: 2022 IEEE 42nd International Conference on Distributed Computing Systems (ICDCS), pp. 1085–1097 (2022). https://doi.org/10.1109/ICDCS54860.2022.00108
14. Junqueira, F., Reed, B.: ZooKeeper: Distributed Process Coordination, 1st edn. O'Reilly Media Inc., Sebastopol (2013)
15. Kashyap, V.: IP over InfiniBand (IPoIB) architecture. Technical report (2006)
16. Keidar, I., Shraer, A.: Timeliness, failure-detectors, and consensus performance. In: Proceedings of the Twenty-fifth Annual ACM Symposium on Principles of Distributed Computing, PODC 2006, Denver, Colorado, USA, pp. 169–178. ACM (2006). https://doi.org/10.1145/1146381.1146408
17. Kreps, J., Narkhede, N., Rao, J., et al.: Kafka: a distributed messaging system for log processing. In: Proceedings of the NetDB, vol. 11, pp. 1–7 (2011)
18. Lamport, L.: The part-time parliament. ACM Trans. Comput. Syst. **16**(2), 133–169 (1998). https://doi.org/10.1145/279227.279229
19. Lamport, L., Matthews, J., Tuttle, M., Yu, Y.: Specifying and verifying systems with TLA+. In: Proceedings of the 10th Workshop on ACM SIGOPS European Workshop, EW 10, Saint-Emilion, France, pp. 45–48. Association for Computing Machinery (2002). https://doi.org/10.1145/1133373.1133382
20. Liu, Y.A., Stoller, S.D., Lin, B., Gorbovitski, M.: From clarity to efficiency for distributed algorithms. In: Proceedings of the ACM International Conference on Object Oriented Programming Systems Languages and Applications, OOPSLA 2012, Tucson, Arizona, USA, pp. 395–410. ACM (2012). https://doi.org/10.1145/2384616.2384645
21. Network-Based Computing Laboratory at the Ohio State University: RDMA-based Apache Kafka (RDMA-kafka). https://hibd.cse.ohio-state.edu/kafka
22. Padon, O., McMillan, K.L., Panda, A., Sagiv, M., Shoham, S.: Ivy: safety verification by interactive generalization. SIGPLAN Not. **51**(6), 614–630 (2016). https://doi.org/10.1145/2980983.2908118
23. Shivam, K., Paladugu, V., Liu, Y.: Specification and runtime checking of Derecho, a protocol for fast replication for cloud services. In: Proceedings of the 2023 Workshop on Advanced Tools, Programming Languages, and PLatforms for Implementing and Evaluating Algorithms for Distributed Systems, ApPLIED 2023, Orlando, Florida. ACM (2023). https://doi.org/10.1145/3584684.3597275

Robust Overlays Meet Blockchains

On Handling High Churn and Catastrophic Failures

Vijeth Aradhya[1(✉)], Seth Gilbert[1], and Aquinas Hobor[1,2]

[1] National University of Singapore, Singapore, Singapore
{varadhya,seth.gilbert}@comp.nus.edu.sg
[2] University College London, London, UK
a.hobor@cs.ucl.ac.uk

Abstract. Blockchains have become ubiquitous in the world of robust decentralized applications. A crucial requirement for implementing a blockchain is a reliable "overlay network" providing robust communication among the participants. In this work, we provide communication-efficient and churn-optimal (barring log factors) Byzantine-resilient algorithms for maintaining blockchain networks. Our approach utilizes an interesting "cross-layer optimization" wherein the overlay network relies on the blockchain that is built on top of it. An important contribution is a tight "half-life" analysis on the *amount of churn* that can be tolerated, where peers have bandwidth restrictions. Moreover, by leveraging synergies between the blockchain and the overlay network, we can provide non-trivial recovery guarantees from unexpected *catastrophic failures*, which include a large class of connectivity issues such as denial-of-service, or exponentially unlikely lucky streaks for Byzantine peers, etc.

1 Introduction

A network formed by *logical* links among entities, wherein a logical link may consist of many *physical* links, is called an overlay network. Blockchains, distributed ledgers, and most other distributed services rely on overlays to facilitate communication. For example, cryptocurrencies such as Bitcoin [25] rely on a peer-to-peer network for fast and efficient communication among the peers.

However, existing overlay networks used by blockchains are insecure. In recent years, there have been attacks on the network connectivity provided by overlays, exploiting several aspects such as unsafe peer storage and connection policies [15, 22], weak network synchronization [33], and churn [34]. Moreover, such network partitioning attacks form the basis of other powerful attacks such as double spending, reducing effective honest resources, and selfish mining [10,28].

V. Aradhya and S. Gilbert acknowledge the support by Singapore MOE Tier 2 Grant MOE-T2EP20122-0014.

S. Dolev and B. Schieber (Eds.): SSS 2023, LNCS 14310, pp. 191–206, 2023.
https://doi.org/10.1007/978-3-031-44274-2_15

In this work, we make connections between blockchains and robust overlays for distributed hash table, resulting in improvements for both systems, including efficient joining, guaranteed reliability, and the ability to recover from bad situations. We exploit a form of "cross-layer optimization", where the overlay maintenance protocols use the blockchain for global coordination, and the blockchain, in turn, uses the efficient overlay for its communication. We provide a new Byzantine-resilient algorithm for maintaining an efficient overlay that tolerates near-optimal rates of churn. There are four key aspects in which our work improves on existing solutions by augmenting the overlay with a blockchain.

Table 1. Comparison under different performance metrics.

	Join latency (in rounds)	Join comm. complexity	Network size variation	Recovery (catastr- ophic failures)
Group spreading [4]	$O(\log N)$	$O(\log^3 N)$	✗	✗
S-Chord [12]	$O(\log N)$	$O(\log^3 N)$	✗	✗
Cuckoo rule [5]	$O(\log N)$	$O(\log^3 N)$	✗	✗
NOW [14]	$O(\log^4 N)$	$O(\log^6 N)$	✓	✗
This work	$O(1)$	$O(\log^3 N)$	✓	✓

1. **Joining.** Byzantine peers can strategically join and leave to affect the overlay connectivity. This leads to Byzantine join-leave attacks [4], where Byzantine peers repeatedly rejoin the system. Thus, the join protocol is crucial to maintain the properties of the overlay. Unfortunately, existing solutions to such join-leave attacks can be expensive, both from latency and message complexity perspective [4,5,12,14].
2. **Bootstrapping and Churn Analysis.** Often, the problem of securely introducing a new peer to the system is unfortunately swept under the hood (both in theory and practice). This is, in fact, crucial to the robustness of join algorithms. This is also a reason for the lack of a thorough analysis on the churn tolerance of a system. A fundamental question in dynamic systems, where peers can join and leave, is how long do peers necessarily have to remain in the system so that it works properly? We answer this question in the context of blockchain networks, where the peers have limited bandwidth. We provide a "half-life" analysis of churn, showing that our overlay design achieves near-optimal churn.
3. **Changes in Network Size.** Early solutions [4,5,12] for join-leave attacks assumed that the network size changes by at most a constant factor. Those solutions maintained highly structured (routable) topologies, making it hard to shrink and expand the overlay if the network size were to polynomially change over time. A crucial property of the design in [14] is being able to efficiently adapt to such changes. We show that the peers can consistently

be in consensus on key parameters of the overlay (via the blockchain), which results in a simple and efficient way to adapt to changes in network size.
4. **Recovery.** Existing solutions are "brittle" in that if Byzantine peers overwhelm a part of the overlay, then it is difficult to recover the original properties of the overlay. This situation can occur over time as these protocols (with probabilistic guarantees) are run indefinitely. Moreover, open distributed systems are vulnerable to denial-of-service attacks, for e.g., the Gnutella network, while resilient to random failures, could be split into a large number of disconnected components after a targeted attack [36]. We combine several ideas, i.e., limited lifetime for a peer [4], fault-tolerant topologies [8], and blockchain consensus, to quickly and efficiently recover from a large class of connectivity issues, termed as "catastrophic failures" (cf. Sect. 6).

Our Approach

The standard approach for fault tolerance in overlays is *replication* (e.g., [5,11, 27]). Thus, our starting point is a virtual network, specifically a hypercube, in which each vertex of the hypercube is implemented in a replicated fashion by a small set of peers which are collectively termed as a *committee.* Such replication ensures that there are sufficient number of honest peers in each committee.

Typically, replication in dynamic overlays subjected to churn and Byzantine faults requires considerable coordination among peers. Our insight is that this coordination can be solved via the blockchain itself by storing small amounts of auxiliary data on the blocks to achieve the necessary synchronization. For e.g., our committees do not need to run a consensus algorithm, perform random walks, or do any other sort of coordination (unlike in [4,5,12,14]). This is similar to a recent trend exploiting on-chain information to simplify and facilitate off-chain distributed algorithms, see, e.g., payment channel networks (e.g., [31]) or dynamic sharding [38].

A key observation is that blockchains are publicly available, i.e., their contents can be read by anyone. Specifically, a recent copy of the blockchain is available at all times, and this provides an entry point to the service (e.g., blockchain explorers [6,7]). This allows new peers to easily join the network, avoiding more centralized solutions [20]. This paves the way for *explicitly* designing a secure and dynamic bootstrapping service that tolerates churn and Byzantine faults.

An existing model that captures a similar idea is a "public bulletin board" [24]. A blockchain differs from a typical bulletin board in three ways: (1) the amount of auxiliary information in a block must be small, (2) the rate at which information can be shared is limited by the block interval, and (3) the network may never be fully synchronized where each peer holds the same chain. Thus, one of our contributions is to carefully distill the properties provided by the blockchain in a way that the overlay algorithms can be concisely described while not losing track of real-world implementations.

Our goal is to *minimally* use the space on a block for maintaining the overlay. Specifically, each block stores the identity of only one peer in the overlay. To maintain a virtual hypercube with at most N peers, we rely on a set of about

$\widetilde{\Theta}(\sqrt{N})$ of the most recent blocks which store a set of about $\widetilde{\Theta}(\sqrt{N})$ peers, which we refer to collectively as a *directory*. Each peer in the directory is responsible for a subset of the committees, and keeps track of the members of those committees.

If the adversary can generate unlimited (Sybil) identities, and if the system has churn, then over time, the adversary can take over honest peers' connections. As in many blockchains, we rely on proof-of-work to mitigate such attacks. The peers can *simultaneously* mine both identities and blocks *without* spending extra computational resources by using the 2-for-1 PoW technique [13,30]. While we focus on proof-of-work for concreteness, our overlay design can similarly be made to work with blockchains based on a different resource constraint.

Churn. A primary goal of this paper is to understand the limits of the *rate* of churn. We adopt the *half-life* approach to churn rate for honest peers: if there are H peers in the system, then over a specific interval of time, the half-life, at most $H/2$ new peers can join or at most $H/2$ peers can depart. This allows for highly bursty behavior, with large numbers of concurrent joins and departures. We provide a lower bound for the feasible half-life that depends on the rate of churn and the bandwidth constraints.

As new blocks are added to the blockchain, and as existing blocks age, the members of the directory change, handing off information from old directory members to new directory members in a controlled process. Similarly, when the number of peers changes significantly, the size of the virtual hypercube has to change, migrating information to new directory members. Such information exchanges need to be carefully managed to avoid Byzantine interference.

Recovery. Finally, the blockchain is not just an alternative interface for new peers to join, it also aids the overlay to recover from catastrophic failures (e.g., a constant fraction of committees and their corresponding directory members are instantly corrupted). As long as most of the committees and directory are still functioning properly, our observation is that the overlay operates sufficiently well to continue installing new blocks, to continue replacing directory and committee members, and restoring the fully correct operation of the overlay, i.e., to ensure that there are again sufficient number of honest peers in every committee. To show recovery properties, we not only rely on fault-tolerant properties of the overlay topology (e.g., [3,8,11]), but also prove that the overlay can reliably and efficiently adapt to large network size variations *during* recovery.

Summary. We exploit the blockchain for securely bootstrapping peers and (global) coordination among peers (e.g., agreement on new topology, etc.). We summarize our contributions (that hold with high probability), in the context of a network with at most N peers, where the average block interval is β.

1. We design protocols to maintain a hypercubic overlay of committees for a polynomial number of rounds, where the half-life is $\alpha = \Theta(\beta\sqrt{N}\log N)$, the network size can vary polynomially over time, and each peer sends/receives only $O(\log^3 N)$ messages per round.
2. We show that when catastrophic failures occur, the overlay recovers (i.e., retains its original properties) within a constant number of half-lives.

3. We give a lower bound, barring log-factors, for half-life, $\alpha = \widetilde{\Omega}(\sqrt{\beta N})$, showing that it is impossible to tolerate higher rates of churn, even if peers share a public bulletin board that can be used for joining.

2 Related Works

An in-depth related work exposition can be found in the full version [1].

Early Designs. Fiat and Saia [11] design an overlay based on bipartite expanders where at least $(1 - \epsilon)N$ peers can efficiently communicate with at least $(1 - \epsilon)N$ peers for a small constant ϵ. Their topology is fixed; [35] modified it to handle a restricted form of churn. Datar [8] built a content addressable network over multi-hypercube, having fault-tolerance against adversarial deletion similar to [11], improving on the communication and storage costs. However, the design is not resilient against Byzantine failures. Many overlays were designed to be robust against random failures, where each peer (independently) has a bounded probability of being Byzantine [9,16,18,26].

Join-Leave Attacks. DHTs are typically made robust by replication of each data item over a small group, e.g., a logarithmic number of peers, of which a majority are honest [11,16,26,35]. Alas, Byzantine peers can often repeatedly join and leave until they overwhelm a particular group.

Awerbuch and Scheideler [4] showed that a hypercubic topology can be maintained (with logarithmic redundancy and honest majority) over polynomial number of join/leave events, where each peer simulates $O(\log N)$ nodes and every node has a limited lifetime, if at most $O(1/\log N)$ fraction of the nodes can be Byzantine. Subsequent works tolerate a linear fraction of Byzantine faults. Fiat et al. [12] used the k-rotation rule [37]; Awerbuch and Scheideler [5] introduced the cuckoo rule; Guerraoui et al. [14] exploit random walks to maintain clusters. Jaiyeola et al. [17] use the limited lifetime method and $O(\log\log N)$ redundancy to show that at least $(1 - o(1))N$ peers can reach at least $(1 - o(1))N$ peers. This line of work either assumes static "gateway peers" with unlimited bandwidth or access to random peers for bootstrapping new peers. Moreover, their join algorithms are rather complicated and expensive (see Table 1).

Recently, Augustine et al. [2] designed a Byzantine-resilient overlay network (for a fixed network size) using the idea of a "dynamic whiteboard" to incorporate new peers into the system. But their algorithms cannot be adapted in our case, which is optimized for integration with blockchains. They use a constant-degree expander topology; whereas we rely on a (fault-tolerant) routable topology, and prove that the overlay can recover from catastrophic failures.

Blockchain Overlays. Kadcast [32] builds on Kademlia [23] and proposes a structured broadcast protocol for disseminating blocks. It is unclear how this protocol performs with respect to high churn and Byantine faults. In Perigree [21], a peer retains the "best" subset of neighbours after regular intervals, and connects to a small set of random peers to explore potentially better-connected peers. But Perigree may actually be prone to eclipse attacks because the adversary can monopolize a peer's connections by providing well-connected neighbors.

3 Model

Entities. A peer is a real-world entity, and can be: (1) honest, following the protocol, or (2) Byzantine, arbitrarily deviating from the protocol. A peer can control multiple *identities*. The *network size* is the total number of peers. The *maximum* network size is denoted by N. Byzantine peers always constitute at most a ρ fraction of the network size. They know the network topology at any time (but they cannot modify or delete messages sent by honest peers).

Communication. Each peer maintains a set of *neighbouring* peers that it is *connected* with. The system proceeds in synchronous *rounds*; in each round, a message that is sent at the beginning of a round by a peer is assumed to reach its neighbours by the end of that round.

Computational Restriction. The peers have a *hash power* constraint, i.e., each peer owns one unit of hash power that allows the peer to query a hash function (modelled as a random oracle) q times in a round [13,29]. (If an entity has more hash power, then it is viewed as a coalition of peers.) For any given input, the hash function provides a (fixed) random output of length $\kappa = \Theta(\log N)$.

Blockchain. If the overlay has at least $\mu_n(1-\rho)n$ honest peers[1] with a diameter of at most $2\log N$, and there are at most ρn Byzantine peers, for appropriate constants $\rho < \mu_n < 1$, where n is the *current* number of peers, then the blockchain is guaranteed to provide the following properties [29,30] for honest peers. (In this work, our goal is to provably maintain an overlay with such properties.)

Safety. There exists a *confirmed chain*[2] C_u^r for any honest peer u in round r having the following properties: (i) Δ-Synchronization: If $|C_u^r|$ is honest peer u's confirmed chain length at round r, then by round $r + \Delta$, every honest peer's confirmed chain length is at least $|C_u^r|$; (ii) Consistency: C_u^r is a prefix of $C_u^{r'}$ for any round $r' \geq r$. At any round r, if $|C_u^r| \leq |C_v^r|$, then C_u^r is a prefix of C_v^r, and for a large enough constant μ_s, $|C_u^r| - |C_v^r| \leq \mu_s$.

Liveness. For large enough T and constant μ_b, any consecutive $T \geq \Omega(1)$ blocks are included in any confirmed chain in $[T\beta/\mu_b, T\mu_b\beta]$ rounds; β is the average block interval.

δ-Approximate Fairness. Any set of honest peers controlling a ϕ fraction of hash power is guaranteed to get at least a $(1-\delta)\phi$ fraction of the blocks in any $\Omega(\kappa/\delta)$ length segment of the chain.

Public Availability. There exists an introduction service $\mathcal{I}$ that provides a local copy of an existing honest peer's chain.

Churn. We consider the standard "partially oblivious" adversary [4,5,12,14] that specifies the join/leave sequence σ for honest peers in advance. However,

[1] We consider a (large) subset of honest peers because the network can get split into multiple components during a catastrophic failure (cf. Sect. 6).

[2] The interpretation of confirmed chain is typically blockchain-specific; for example, Bitcoin deems a block to be confirmed if it is at least 6 blocks deep.

it can choose to adaptively join/leave Byzantine peers. In particular, after the first i events in σ are executed, the adversary can either choose to join/leave a Byzantine peer or initiate the $(i+1)^{\text{th}}$ event in σ.

Churn Rate. We consider the *half-life* measure [19] to model the churn rate for honest peers. At any given round r, the halving time is the number of rounds taken for half the number of honest peers (which were alive at round r) to leave the network; the doubling time is the number of rounds required for the number of honest peers to double. An *epoch*, denoted by α, is defined as the smallest halving time or doubling time over all rounds in the execution. Furthermore, we assume that the epoch is much greater than the average block generation interval; in other words, $\alpha \gg \beta \log N$.

Change of Network Size. The network size can change by a factor of at most 2 in any epoch. It can thus polynomially vary over time; the number of peers at any round r, $N_r \in [N^{1/y}, N]$ for any constant $y > 1$.

4 Overlay Design and Algorithms (Stable Network Size)

We first describe our overlay algorithm for a fixed network size of $\Theta(N)$. Two key parameters are the epoch length α (half-life) and the "directory size" $\mathcal{B}$. We will observe that α should roughly be the time it takes $\tilde{\Theta}(\sqrt{N})$ blocks to be added, and $\mathcal{B}$ (number of blocks in a directory) should be about $\tilde{\Theta}(\sqrt{N})$.

Nodes. Each peer generates and controls $\Theta(\log N)$ (virtual) identities, known as *nodes* in the overlay. Each peer participates (sends and receives messages) via its nodes. All peers are required to perform proof-of-work to generate nodes. Each node has a *lifetime* after which it will be considered invalid.

Directory. Every node is initially a "non-directory" node. Some nodes also become directory nodes: a peer that adds a block to the blockchain promotes one of its nodes to a directory node, adding the identity of the promoted directory node, along with its network address, to the new block.

Committees. We maintain a hypercubic network of *committees*; each vertex corresponds to a committee. There are $\mathcal{C} = N$ committees, each consisting of $\Theta(\log N)$ nodes. If two committees are adjacent in the hypercube, then every pair of nodes in those committees are neighbors. Logarithmic redundancy ensures that a sufficient fraction of peers are honest so that the hypercube structure is maintained. Each committee is identified by a (unique) committee ID. As a peer may control multiple nodes, it may be present in multiple committees.

Limited Lifetime. Byzantine peers can repeatedly rejoin until their nodes get placed (by chance) in desired committees, potentially resulting in honest nodes having mostly Byzantine neighbors. A standard solution is to limit the lifetime of nodes, forcing them to rejoin (e.g., [4]). To avoid too much induced churn, the lifetime should be large, but not so large as to allow Byzantine join-leave attacks. Thus, we set the node lifetime to be $\Theta(\alpha/\beta)$ blocks, i.e., a constant number of half-lives. This ensures that at most a constant fraction of any honest peer's neighbours are Byzantine. Moreover, limited node lifetime is important for providing time bounds on recovery from catastrophic failures (see Sect. 6).

We now provide further details on the overlay maintenance. The technical difficulty lies in enabling directory nodes to help honest nodes join, while respecting the bandwidth constraints—even as the adversary may try to flood some directory nodes with requests. Figure 1 gives an overview of our design.

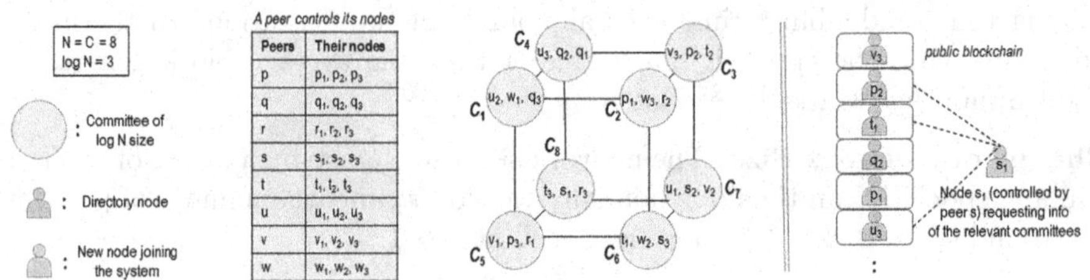

Fig. 1. High-level overview of our design for 8 peers.

Directories

A directory on the blockchain comprises of $\mathcal{B}$ consecutive "buckets", and each bucket consists of consecutive $\lambda_d \log^2 N$ blocks, where λ_d is a suitable constant. Each block refers to one directory node, so a directory refers to $\mathcal{K} = \mathcal{B}\lambda_d \log^2 N$ directory nodes. (The chain is divided into buckets from the beginning.)

There must always be enough honest directory nodes in each bucket, despite churn. By the blockchain fairness assumption, $\Theta(\log^2 N)$ bucket size is sufficient to ensure $\Omega(\log N)$ honest peers per bucket at any time.

Directory Responsibilities. Each bucket is *responsible* for a set of committees, i.e., directory nodes in that bucket help new nodes join those committees. There are two main *functions* of a directory node. (1) A directory node *stores* information about the nodes in its committees. (2) A directory node *sends* that information to new joining nodes and to neighboring committees. There exists a predetermined mapping $[\mathcal{C}] \rightarrow [\mathcal{B}]$ from committees to buckets, specifying which bucket manages a given committee, such that each bucket is responsible for (almost) the same number of committees.

Phases of a Bucket. We describe the phases of buckets and its directory nodes (and the transitions between phases), which determine the nodes' functions over time: (1) *Infant.* A bucket in which at least one block (out of $\lambda_d \log^2 N$) is confirmed, but not all the $\lambda_d \log^2 N$ blocks are confirmed. The directory nodes neither store entry information, nor respond to any requests. If all $\lambda_d \log^2 N$ blocks of the bucket are confirmed in the blockchain, then the bucket transitions to middle-aged. (2) *Middle-aged.* These directory nodes store new node entry information as they receive it, and reply to requests. If the bucket is not among the most recent (confirmed) $\mathcal{B}$ buckets, then the bucket transitions to veteran phase. (3) *Veteran.* These directory nodes do not store new nodes' entry information, but they do reply to requests with committee information already known to them. If the bucket is not among the most recent (confirmed) $\mathcal{B}_{act}$ buckets (to be defined), then it shifts to dead phase. (4) *Dead.* These directory nodes (as in the infant phase) neither store any new node information, nor respond to requests. During the transitions, there is a delay of Δ rounds to ensure that the confirmed chains of honest peers reach the same required height.

Active Directory. The *active directory*, also known as *bootstrapping service*, is the most recent $\mathcal{B}_{act}$ consecutive (confirmed) buckets. The most recent $\mathcal{B}$ consecutive buckets, forming an entire directory, are middle-aged. The rest of the buckets, forming one or more directories, are veteran. The number of blocks and number of buckets in an active directory are denoted as $\mathcal{K}_{act}$ and $\mathcal{B}_{act}$ respectively. An example of an active directory is illustrated in Fig. 2.

New nodes figure out the sequence of buckets in the active directory (using the blockchain and committee-directory mapping), and contact the relevant buckets to get the required committees' entry information for joining the network.

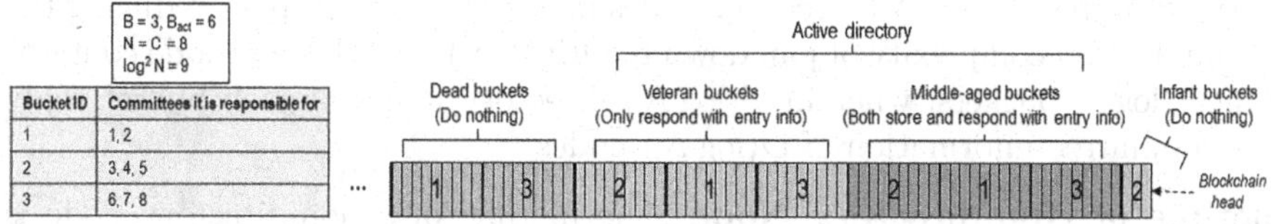

Fig. 2. An illustration of buckets (and their blocks with directory nodes), represented by their IDs, in different phases.

Node Joins and Lifetimes

A new node must provide a *proof-of-work* for joining the network, and directory nodes only interact with a new node if its proof is valid.

Proof for Joining. Let N_c be a nonce, $\hat{\mathrm{B}}_l$ be the hash of the latest confirmed block B_l, and *net_addr* be the network address of the peer. Then, the peer evaluates, $P_{join} = \mathbf{H}(\hat{\mathrm{B}}_l \parallel net\_addr \parallel N_c)$, where $\mathbf{H}$ is the (pseudorandom) hash function, to join the network through a new node. If $P_{join} < T_{join}$, where T_{join} is the *mining target* for joining, then the node is said to be a "valid" node, which means that the peer would be able to communicate with the bootstrapping service to register that node, and join the network. A directory node rejects the proof if B_l is not among the most recent μ_s blocks in its confirmed chain.

Joining the Network. A node's *entry information* constitutes its network address, the nonce N_c and the block number of the block that was used while mining for that node. We now describe the steps taken by a peer p to generate and join a new node q into the network. (1) It first produces a proof for joining. The leftmost $\log N$ bits of P_{join} represent the ID of the (random) committee, denoted by c, to which this new node would belong to. Let C_{rel} be the set of committees neighboring c in the hypercube, including c. (2) Peer p sends its entry information to all directory nodes in the middle-aged bucket responsible for committee c. (3) Peer p requests information, sampling $\Theta(\log N)$ nodes uniformly in each bucket responsible for committee c and requesting information on each of its neighbors in the hypercube. The directory nodes respond with the relevant entry information. (4) Peer p appropriately sends messages to handle Δ-synchrony. Let b_1 and b_2 be the first and $(\mathcal{B}+1)^{\text{th}}$ confirmed buckets (i.e., most recent middle-aged and veteran buckets). If the number of blocks confirmed after bucket b_1 is at most μ_s, and if b_1 is responsible for committee c, then p send its entry information to all nodes in b_2. (5) To complete the join, node q takes the union of valid entry information received in responses (as the adversary can only under-represent the nodes in a committee). It then sends its entry information to the nodes in each neighboring committee in the hypercube.

The key observation is that a constant fraction of directory nodes in a bucket are honest and available at any time, due to logarithmic redundancy in buckets and blockchain fairness. Thus, it is sufficient for the new node needs to hear back information from $O(\log N)$ directory nodes in each bucket (Step 3), reducing the communication complexity of join down to $O(\log^3 N)$, i.e., the new node contacts at most $\log N$ buckets, wherein $O(\log N)$ directory nodes in each bucket reply with committee information of $O(\log N)$ nodes.

Lifetime of Non-directory Node. The lifetime of a non-directory node is $T_l = \Theta(\alpha/\beta)$ blocks. The node u that had joined at block number b_l (which can be checked in its proof for joining) is considered invalid after block $b_l + T_l$ is confirmed, at which point the peer stops controlling that node u, and all other nodes that had node u as a neighbour remove u from their neighbour list.

Lifetime of Directory Node. If a node is promoted to a directory node, then it obtains another life (separate from the non-directory life). The directory node is considered to be alive for T_{dl} blocks from the block in which it is embedded in. We set T_{dl} to be $\Theta(\alpha/\beta)$ blocks, where $T_l < T_{dl}$. This time is chosen to be sufficiently long for the directory node to reach the veteran phase, and then for the lifetimes of all the non-directory nodes in its committee to fail (i.e., an additional T_l blocks), i.e., $T_{dl} > (1+\mathcal{B})\lambda_d \log^2 N + T_l$.

Node Generation Rate. The mining target T_{join} is set such that, in each epoch, the expected number of valid nodes that can be generated during an epoch is equal to $\Theta(N \log N)$. Each committee has $\Theta(\log N)$ nodes at any time because in every epoch, about $\Theta(N \log N)$ nodes join, while a similar number of them leave due to limited lifetime (set to be a constant number of epochs).

Directory Size and Half-Life (Relation between $\mathcal{B}$ and α)

First, the lifetime of a non-directory node is $\Theta(\alpha/\beta)$ blocks, so $\mathcal{B} \leq \Theta\left(\frac{\alpha}{\beta \log^2 N}\right)$, so that the node can fully participate in a directory's life cycle.

Due to node generation rate, the system must have bandwidth for $\Theta(N \log N)$ nodes to join in any α (consecutive) rounds. As a new node sends a join request to all directories within the active directory (both middle-aged and veteran), it suffices to focus on the number of join requests handled by one directory.

Due to the proof-of-work mechanism, we can ensure that the join requests are load-balanced across the rounds in an epoch. Let λ_{jr} be the highest number of join requests that can be handled by a bucket per round. For any directory, we calculate the total number of join requests that need to be handled in any round as $\mathcal{B}\lambda_{jr} \geq \Theta\left(\frac{\beta N \log^2 N}{\alpha}\right)$, where LHS is the total number of join requests that can be handled in a round, and RHS represents the minimum number of join requests that need to be handled in a round. The extra β factor is due to a possible precomputation attack, where an adversary sends join requests computed over the last μ_s confirmed blocks, and the extra $\log N$ factor is due to new nodes contacting $O(\log N)$ buckets while joining. These extra multiplicative factors ensure that the communication complexity per peer per round is $O(\log^3 N)$.

Ideally, we want to minimize α to handle maximum churn. Solving the above constraints, with bandwidth cost of $O(\log^3 N)$ messages per round for a peer, we find that $\alpha = \Theta(\beta\sqrt{N} \log N)$ and $\mathcal{B} = \Theta(\sqrt{N}/\log N)$. In Sect. 7, we show that this value of α is close to optimal.

Analysis Overview

We present the key lemmas and theorems for stable network size. The complete analysis can be found in the full version [1]. Consider a connectivity property called *partition resilience*, where (1) each committee has $O(\log N)$ nodes and $\Omega(\log N)$ honest peers, (2) every pair of honest nodes in each committee are connected, and (3) each honest node is connected to $\Omega(\log N)$ honest peers in each neighbouring committee. An epoch e is said to be *bandwidth-adequate* if each peer needs to send/receive $O(\log^3 N)$ messages for overlay maintenance in any round. The active directory is said to be *robust* if each bucket has $\Omega(\log^2 N)$ honest nodes that store entry information of all nodes in the relevant committees.

First, we see that no peer gets too many join requests due to load balancing, random committee assignment (via hash function), and random sampling:

Lemma 1. *Each peer receives $O(\log^2 N)$ join requests and information requests in any round in an epoch with high probability.*

Next, we argue that if the bandwidth is not exceeded, then the active directory is properly constructed and has the correct information to process join requests:

Lemma 2. *The active directory is* robust *in the epoch with high probability, if the last $\Theta(\beta T_{dl}/\alpha)$ epochs are* bandwidth-adequate.

Together, these lemmas imply that all joins are successful, ensuring the overlay is well-connected with each committee having sufficient number of honest peers:

Theorem 1. *The network is* partition-resilient *for polynomial number of rounds with high probability.*

5 Extension to Dynamic Network Size

We briefly discuss how to augment the protocols described in Sect. 4 to handle polynomial variation in network size over time. These techniques are an extension of the previous idea—see the full version [1] for the details.

The main problem caused by changing numbers of peers is that the system needs to adapt to maintain logarithmic redundancy. If the number of committees remains fixed, while the number of peers decreases, then each peer would need to simulate too many nodes at any time in order for the system to maintain $\Theta(\log N)$ nodes in every committee, exhausting the peer's bandwidth. And if the network size keeps increasing, then some peers may not be able to participate in the network all the time because they may take too long to generate nodes. Therefore, we adapt the size of the hypercube and the number of committees.

The key insight is that the blockchain can facilitate the necessary coordination to switch to a new topology. The first step is to efficiently estimate the network size, every constant number of epochs. Each node keeps track of new nodes that joined its committee in a span of fixed number of blocks. Then, all the nodes of a (random) committee (determined by a hash function) broadcast that count along with the entry information of new nodes that joined that committee (as evidence of the count) to everyone. This sampled change in committee size allows peers to estimate the size of the network. This information is then included on the blockchain to ensure that all peers agree on it.

Each peer then uses this estimate to determine whether the dimension of the hypercube is changing and number of committees in the new hypercube. Again, the information is placed on the blockchain to ensure agreement.

At that point, if necessary, the dimension of the hypercube is changed. During dimension change, the new hypercube is constructed while the old one is kept around to ensure connectivity. The directory goes into a "split state" for about one epoch, serving committees in the current hypercube and also constructing committees in the next hypercube. New nodes also get placed in the next hypercube, as well as the old one. Until each committee in the next hypercube has a sufficient number of new (honest) nodes, the overlay operates in the old hypercube. The directory then stops serving committees in the old hypercube, and the network adopts the new hypercube for broadcasting blocks.

6 Recovery

Catastrophic failures model a large class of connectivity issues, e.g., denial-of-service attacks or low probability events. We say that a *bucket fails* if $> 1/2$ of its honest peers are *corrupted*; a *committee fails* if it has $< 20 \log N$ honest peers, or if the bucket responsible for it has failed. The *corruption* could be Byzantine, or simply crashing, if honest peers leave faster than allowed by the churn model.

Consider an "(ϵ, δ)-catastrophic failure" where at most ϵ fraction of committees and/or buckets may have failed, and in total, at most δ fraction of honest peers get corrupted (for small constants ϵ and δ), while there still exists a connected network of honest peers of linear size and logarithmic diameter for which bootstrapping can be securely done. Such failures model exceptional scenarios that occur in practice wherein the network is split into multiple components, resulting in considerable wastage of honest peers' hash power over time.

Recovery. Our goal is to provably show that the network *recovers* from such catastrophic failures in a short period of time. Here, we naturally define recovery as the event at which the overlay retains its original properties.

There are two basic requirements for the overlay to recover from a catastrophic failure. First, a large fraction of honest peers can continue to run the blockchain protocol (ensuring the blockchain provides the same guarantees), albeit some honest peers may end up unable to participate fully (i.e., effective honest hash power is reduced) for a brief period of time. Secondly, the introduction service is not affected by the failure, i.e., it continues to return the chain of an honest peer in the largest connected component of honest peers.

The high-level intuition for recovery is to replace the entire active directory by a new one (that has no bucket failures), which will reliably facilitate new honest node joins. After a catastrophic failure, there is a large connected component of sufficient number of honest peers with a low diameter, that is responsible for the progress of the blockchain. First, this component should get replenished with new (honest) peers amidst churn, maintaining the required proportion. Then, the coordination protocols such as network size estimation, etc., must work for that component *during* recovery. Specifically, we rely on the fault-tolerance of the overlay topology [8] and properties of bipartite expanders [11] for showing that changing dimensions after a catastrophic failure does not inhibit recovery.

For a wide range of failures, the overlay, augmented with a blockchain, can exhibit a novel recovery property. The security arguments in existing designs for join-leave attacks [4,5,12,14,17] heavily rely on honest majority in committees. In the full version [1], we show the inherent difficulty of such localized algorithms to recover from committee failures, e.g., a small number of committees having malicious majority, can keep maintaining the majority over time.

Theorem 2. *If the network experiences (ϵ, δ)-catastrophic failure, then it becomes partition-resilient within $O(1)$ epochs with high probability.*

7 Lower Bound for Half-Life

In dynamic overlays, there is always a problem of bootstrapping a new peer, i.e., how does a new peer contact an existing peer within the network? A bootstrapping service $\mathcal{S}$ should have two properties: (i) *Secure:* the service responds with the identity of at least one honest peer in the network; and (ii) *Bandwidth-constrained:* Each peer communicates at most $\tilde{O}(1)$ bits in any round.

We show that there are unavoidable trade-offs in implementing such a service. Notably, the overlay algorithm described in this paper satisfies these basic service requirements—and so it is also subject to these inevitable trade-offs.

Let N be the number of peers in the network, and assume peers are honest. Assume network addresses require $\Omega(\log N)$ bits, i.e., there is no encoding scheme to compress network addresses. Peers can write $O(\log N)$ bit messages to a publicly visible *bulletin board* (e.g., [24]). An arbitrary peer is selected to write to the board at every β rounds. The bulletin board is the only interface through which the peers can disseminate information to the public.

We prove the following theorem by analyzing the number of bits of useful information on the bulletin board, compared to the number of identifiers needed to support the bandwidth required for all joins. Our theorem depends only on the minimum requirement that to complete a join operation, a newly joining node must receive at least one message from an existing member of the network.

Theorem 3. *Any dynamic system that implements a bootstrapping service S using a public bulletin board can support a half-life of only $\widetilde{\Omega}(\sqrt{\beta N})$.*

References

1. Aradhya, V., Gilbert, S., Hobor, A.: OverChain: building a robust overlay with a blockchain. arXiv preprint arXiv:2201.12809 (2022)
2. Augustine, J., Bhat, W.G., Nair, S.: Plateau: a secure and scalable overlay network for large distributed trust applications. In: Devismes, S., Petit, F., Altisen, K., Di Luna, G.A., Fernandez Anta, A. (eds.) Stabilization, Safety, and Security of Distributed Systems. LNCS, vol. 13751, pp. 69–83. Springer, Cham (2022). https://doi.org/10.1007/978-3-031-21017-4_5
3. Augustine, J., Chatterjee, S., Pandurangan, G.: A fully-distributed scalable peer-to-peer protocol for byzantine-resilient distributed hash tables. In: Proceedings of the 34th ACM Symposium on Parallelism in Algorithms and Architectures, pp. 87–98 (2022)
4. Awerbuch, B., Scheideler, C.: Group spreading: a protocol for provably secure distributed name service. In: Díaz, J., Karhumäki, J., Lepistö, A., Sannella, D. (eds.) ICALP 2004. LNCS, vol. 3142, pp. 183–195. Springer, Heidelberg (2004). https://doi.org/10.1007/978-3-540-27836-8_18
5. Awerbuch, B., Scheideler, C.: Towards a scalable and robust DHT. Theory Comput. Syst. **45**(2), 234–260 (2009)
6. BitInfoCharts: Bitcoin Explorer (2023). https://bitinfocharts.com/bitcoin/explorer/
7. Blockchain.com: Explorer (2023). https://www.blockchain.com/explorer
8. Datar, M.: Butterflies and peer-to-peer networks. In: Möhring, R., Raman, R. (eds.) ESA 2002. LNCS, vol. 2461, pp. 310–322. Springer, Heidelberg (2002). https://doi.org/10.1007/3-540-45749-6_30
9. Dolev, D., Hoch, E.N., van Renesse, R.: Self-stabilizing and byzantine-tolerant overlay network. In: Tovar, E., Tsigas, P., Fouchal, H. (eds.) OPODIS 2007. LNCS, vol. 4878, pp. 343–357. Springer, Heidelberg (2007). https://doi.org/10.1007/978-3-540-77096-1_25

10. Eyal, I., Sirer, E.G.: Majority is not enough: bitcoin mining is vulnerable. In: Christin, N., Safavi-Naini, R. (eds.) FC 2014. LNCS, vol. 8437, pp. 436–454. Springer, Heidelberg (2014). https://doi.org/10.1007/978-3-662-45472-5_28
11. Fiat, A., Saia, J.: Censorship resistant peer-to-peer networks. Theory Comput. **3**(1), 1–23 (2007). (previously appearing in SODA 2002)
12. Fiat, A., Saia, J., Young, M.: Making chord robust to byzantine attacks. In: Brodal, G.S., Leonardi, S. (eds.) ESA 2005. LNCS, vol. 3669, pp. 803–814. Springer, Heidelberg (2005). https://doi.org/10.1007/11561071_71
13. Garay, J., Kiayias, A., Leonardos, N.: The bitcoin backbone protocol: analysis and applications. In: Oswald, E., Fischlin, M. (eds.) EUROCRYPT 2015. LNCS, vol. 9057, pp. 281–310. Springer, Heidelberg (2015). https://doi.org/10.1007/978-3-662-46803-6_10
14. Guerraoui, R., Huc, F., Kermarrec, A.M.: Highly dynamic distributed computing with byzantine failures. In: Proceedings of the 2013 ACM Symposium on Principles of Distributed Computing, pp. 176–183 (2013)
15. Heilman, E., Kendler, A., Zohar, A., Goldberg, S.: Eclipse attacks on bitcoin's peer-to-peer network. In: 24th USENIX Security Symposium, pp. 129–144 (2015)
16. Hildrum, K., Kubiatowicz, J.: Asymptotically efficient approaches to fault-tolerance in peer-to-peer networks. In: Fich, F.E. (ed.) DISC 2003. LNCS, vol. 2848, pp. 321–336. Springer, Heidelberg (2003). https://doi.org/10.1007/978-3-540-39989-6_23
17. Jaiyeola, M.O., Patron, K., Saia, J., Young, M., Zhou, Q.M.: Tiny groups tackle byzantine adversaries. In: 2018 IEEE International Parallel and Distributed Processing Symposium (IPDPS), pp. 1030–1039. IEEE (2018)
18. Johansen, H.D., Renesse, R.V., Vigfusson, Y., Johansen, D.: Fireflies: a secure and scalable membership and gossip service. ACM Trans. Comput. Syst. (TOCS) **33**(2), 1–32 (2015)
19. Liben-Nowell, D., Balakrishnan, H., Karger, D.: Analysis of the evolution of peer-to-peer systems. In: Proceedings of the Twenty-First Annual Symposium on Principles of Distributed Computing, pp. 233–242 (2002)
20. Loe, A.F., Quaglia, E.A.: You shall not join: a measurement study of cryptocurrency peer-to-peer bootstrapping techniques. In: Proceedings of the 2019 ACM SIGSAC Conference on Computer and Communications Security, pp. 2231–2247 (2019)
21. Mao, Y., Deb, S., Venkatakrishnan, S.B., Kannan, S., Srinivasan, K.: Perigee: efficient peer-to-peer network design for blockchains. In: Proceedings of the 39th Symposium on Principles of Distributed Computing, pp. 428–437 (2020)
22. Marcus, Y., Heilman, E., Goldberg, S.: Low-resource eclipse attacks on ethereum's peer-to-peer network. Cryptology ePrint Archive, Report 2018/236 (2018)
23. Maymounkov, P., Mazières, D.: Kademlia: a peer-to-peer information system based on the XOR metric. In: Druschel, P., Kaashoek, F., Rowstron, A. (eds.) IPTPS 2002. LNCS, vol. 2429, pp. 53–65. Springer, Heidelberg (2002). https://doi.org/10.1007/3-540-45748-8_5
24. Mitzenmacher, M.: How useful is old information? IEEE Trans. Parallel Distrib. Syst. **11**(1), 6–20 (2000)
25. Nakamoto, S.: Bitcoin: a peer-to-peer electronic cash system (White Paper) (2008). https://bitcoin.org/bitcoin.pdf
26. Naor, M., Wieder, U.: A simple fault tolerant distributed hash table. In: Kaashoek, M.F., Stoica, I. (eds.) IPTPS 2003. LNCS, vol. 2735, pp. 88–97. Springer, Heidelberg (2003). https://doi.org/10.1007/978-3-540-45172-3_8

27. Naor, M., Wieder, U.: Novel architectures for p2p applications: the continuous-discrete approach. ACM Trans. Algorithms (TALG) **3**(3), 34-es (2007)
28. Nayak, K., Kumar, S., Miller, A., Shi, E.: Stubborn mining: generalizing selfish mining and combining with an eclipse attack. In: 2016 IEEE European Symposium on Security and Privacy (EuroS&P), pp. 305–320. IEEE (2016)
29. Pass, R., Seeman, L., Shelat, A.: Analysis of the blockchain protocol in asynchronous networks. In: Coron, J.-S., Nielsen, J.B. (eds.) EUROCRYPT 2017. LNCS, vol. 10211, pp. 643–673. Springer, Cham (2017). https://doi.org/10.1007/978-3-319-56614-6_22
30. Pass, R., Shi, E.: Fruitchains: a fair blockchain. In: Proceedings of the ACM Symposium on Principles of Distributed Computing, pp. 315–324 (2017)
31. Poon, J., Dryja, T.: The bitcoin lightning network: Scalable off-chain instant payments (2016). https://lightning.network/lightning-network-paper.pdf
32. Rohrer, E., Tschorsch, F.: Kadcast: a structured approach to broadcast in blockchain networks. In: Proceedings of the 1st ACM Conference on Advances in Financial Technologies, pp. 199–213 (2019)
33. Saad, M., Anwar, A., Ravi, S., Mohaisen, D.: Revisiting nakamoto consensus in asynchronous networks: a comprehensive analysis of bitcoin safety and chainquality. In: Proceedings of the 2021 ACM SIGSAC Conference on Computer and Communications Security, pp. 988–1005 (2021)
34. Saad, M., Chen, S., Mohaisen, D.: Syncattack: double-spending in bitcoin without mining power. In: Proceedings of the 2021 ACM SIGSAC Conference on Computer and Communications Security, pp. 1668–1685 (2021)
35. Saia, J., Fiat, A., Gribble, S., Karlin, A.R., Saroiu, S.: Dynamically fault-tolerant content addressable networks. In: Druschel, P., Kaashoek, F., Rowstron, A. (eds.) IPTPS 2002. LNCS, vol. 2429, pp. 270–279. Springer, Heidelberg (2002). https://doi.org/10.1007/3-540-45748-8_26
36. Saroiu, S., Gummadi, P.K., Gribble, S.D.: Measurement study of peer-to-peer file sharing systems. In: Multimedia Computing and Networking 2002, vol. 4673, pp. 156–170. International Society for Optics and Photonics (2001)
37. Scheideler, C.: How to spread adversarial nodes? Rotate! In: Proceedings of the Thirty-Seventh Annual ACM Symposium on Theory of Computing, pp. 704–713 (2005)
38. Tennakoon, D., Gramoli, V.: Dynamic blockchain sharding. In: 5th International Symposium on Foundations and Applications of Blockchain 2022 (FAB 2022). Schloss Dagstuhl-Leibniz-Zentrum für Informatik (2022)

Disconnected Agreement in Networks Prone to Link Failures

Bogdan S. Chlebus[1], Dariusz R. Kowalski[1], Jan Olkowski[2](✉), and Jędrzej Olkowski[3]

[1] School of Computer and Cyber Sciences, Augusta University, Georgia, USA
[2] University of Maryland, College Park, MD, USA
olkowski@umd.edu
[3] Wydział Matematyki, Mechaniki i Informatyki, Uniwersytet Warszawski,Warszawa, Poland

Abstract. We consider deterministic distributed algorithms for reaching agreement in synchronous networks of arbitrary topologies. Links are bi-directional and prone to failures while nodes stay non-faulty at all times. A faulty link may omit messages. Agreement among nodes is understood as holding in each connected component of a network obtained by removing faulty links – we call it a "disconnected agreement". We introduce the concept of stretch, which is the number of connected components of a network, obtained by removing faulty links, minus 1 plus the sum of diameters of connected components. We define the concepts of "fast" and "early-stopping" algorithms for disconnected agreement by referring to stretch. We consider trade-offs between the knowledge of nodes, the size of messages, and the running times of algorithms. A network has n nodes and m links. We give a general disconnected agreement algorithm operating in $n+1$ rounds that uses messages of $\mathcal{O}(\log n)$ bits. Let λ be an unknown stretch occurring in an execution; we give an algorithm working in time $(\lambda+2)^3$ and using messages of $\mathcal{O}(n \log n)$ bits. We show that disconnected agreement can be solved in the optimal $\mathcal{O}(\lambda)$ time, but at the cost of increasing message size to $\mathcal{O}(m \log n)$. We also design an algorithm that uses only $\mathcal{O}(n)$ non-faulty links and works in time $\mathcal{O}(nm)$, while nodes start with their ports mapped to neighbors and messages carry $\mathcal{O}(m \log n)$ bits. We prove lower bounds on the performance of disconnected-agreement solutions that refer to the parameters of evolving network topologies and the knowledge available to nodes.

Keywords: Network · Synchrony · Omission link failures · Agreement · Time complexity · Message size · Link use

1 Introduction

We introduce a variant of agreement and present deterministic distributed algorithms for this problem in synchronous networks. Nodes represent processing

D. R. Kowalski—This work is partially supported by the NSF grant number 2131538.

S. Dolev and B. Schieber (Eds.): SSS 2023, LNCS 14310, pp. 207–222, 2023.
https://doi.org/10.1007/978-3-031-44274-2_16

units and links model bi-directional communication channels between pairs of nodes. Links are prone to failures but nodes stay operational at all times. A faulty link may not convey a message transmitted at a round. A link that has omitted a message manifested its faultiness and is considered *unreliable* until the end of the execution. We model a network with link failures as evolving through a chain of sub-networks, obtained by removing unreliable links.

We study agreement that allows nodes in different connected components of the network, obtained by removing unreliable links, to decide on different values but still requires nodes within a connected component to decide on the same value.

We use a network's dynamic attribute, called "stretch", which is an integer determined by the number of connected components and their diameters (see Sect. 2 for formal definition). The purpose of using stretch is to consider scalability of disconnected agreement solutions to networks evolving through link failures.

Table 1. A summary of the given deterministic distributed algorithms for disconnected agreement and their respective performance bounds. Bound Λ is known in Sect. 3. The dagger symbol † indicates the asymptotic optimality of the respective upper bound.

algorithm/section	time	message size	# links	knowledge	lower bound
FAST-AGREEMENT/Sect. 3	Λ †	$\mathcal{O}(\log n)$	$\mathcal{O}(m)$	Λ known	time $\lambda \leq \Lambda$
SM-AGREEMENT/Sect. 4	$n+1$	$\mathcal{O}(\log n)$	$\mathcal{O}(m)$	minimal	time λ
LM-AGREEMENT/Sect. 5	$(\lambda+2)^3$	$\mathcal{O}(n \log n)$	$\mathcal{O}(m)$	minimal	time λ
ES-AGREEMENT/Sect. 6	$\lambda+2$ †	$\mathcal{O}(m \log n)$	$\mathcal{O}(m)$	minimal	time λ
OL-AGREEMENT/Sect. 7	$\mathcal{O}(nm)$	$\mathcal{O}(m \log n)$	$2n$ †	neighbors known	# links $\Omega(n)$

A Summary of the Results. We introduce the problem of disconnected agreement and give deterministic algorithms for this problem in synchronous networks with links prone to failures. Let n denote the number of nodes and m the number of links in an initial network. An upper bound on stretch, denoted Λ, could be given to all nodes, with an understanding that faults occurring in an execution are restricted such that the actual stretch never surpasses Λ. An algorithm solving disconnected agreement with a known upper bound Λ on the stretch is considered "fast" if it runs in time $\mathcal{O}(\Lambda)$. A fast solution to disconnected agreement is discussed in Sect. 3. We also show a lower bound which demonstrates that, for each natural number λ and an algorithm solving disconnected agreement in networks prone to link failures, there exists a network that has stretch λ and such that each execution of the algorithm on this network takes at least λ rounds. In Sect. 4, we show how to solve disconnected agreement in $n+1$ rounds with short messages of $\mathcal{O}(\log n)$ bits in networks where nodes have minimal knowledge. We give an algorithm relying on minimal knowledge working in time $(\lambda+2)^3$ and using linear messages[1] of $\mathcal{O}(n \log n)$ bits, where λ is an unknown stretch

[1] We call a message 'linear' if it could carry at most $O(n)$ ids (each id has $O(\log n)$ bits).

occurring in an execution; this algorithm is presented in Sect. 5. A disconnected agreement solution is considered "early-stopping" if it operates in time proportional to the unknown stretch actually occurring in an execution. In Sect. 6, we develop an early-stopping solution to disconnected agreement relying on minimal knowledge that employs messages of $\mathcal{O}(m \log n)$ bits. We propose to count the number of reliable links used by a communication algorithm during its execution as its performance metric. To make this performance measure meaningful, the nodes need to start knowing their neighbors, in having a correct mapping of communication ports to neighbors. In Sect. 7, we give a solution to disconnected agreement that uses at most an asymptotically optimum number $2n$ of reliable links and works in $\mathcal{O}(nm)$ rounds, without knowing the size n of the network. We then show a separation result in Sect. 7: if the nodes start with their ports not mapped on neighbors, then any disconnected agreement solution has to use $\Omega(m)$ links in some networks of $\Theta(m)$ links, for all numbers n and m such that $n \leq m \leq n^2$. A summary of algorithms with their performance bounds and optimality is in Table 1. Full paper is available in [8].

The Previous Work on Agreement in Networks. Dolev [10] studied Byzantine consensus in networks with faulty nodes and gave connectivity conditions sufficient and necessary for a solution to exist; see also Fischer et al. [11], and Hadzilacos [12]. Khan et al. [13] considered a related problem in the model with restricted Byzantine faults, in particular, in the model requiring a node to broadcast identical messages to all neighbors at a round. Tseng and Vaidya [20] presented necessary and sufficient conditions for the solvability of consensus in directed graphs under the models of crash and Byzantine failures. For recent advancements, we refer the reader to [4,7,9,19,21,22].

Next, we discuss previous work on solving consensus in networks undergoing topology changes, malfunctioning links and transmission failures.

Kuhn et al. [15] considered Δ-coordinated binary consensus in undirected graphs, whose topology could change arbitrarily from round to round, as long it stayed connected; here Δ is a parameter that bounds from above the difference in times of termination for any two nodes. Paper [15] showed how to solve Δ-coordinated binary consensus in $\mathcal{O}(\frac{nD}{D+\Delta} + \Delta)$ rounds using message of $\mathcal{O}(m^2 \log n)$ size without a prior knowledge of the network's diameter D. Comparing to our work, the paper [15] assumes that network connectivity is maintained and the Δ-coordination property imposes additional constrains on the algorithms.

Biely et al. [2] considered reaching agreement and k-set agreement in networks when communication is modeled by directed-graph topologies controlled by adversaries, with the goal to identify constraints on adversaries to make the considered problems solvable. Paper [2] solved k-set agreement in time $\mathcal{O}(3D + H)$ and using messages of $\mathcal{O}(nD \log n)$ size, where D denotes the dynamic source diameter and H denotes the dynamic graph depth, and the code of algorithm includes D. Some of our solutions can be faster and use smaller messages in this setting, since $D = E = \Lambda \geq \lambda$; for example, in dynamic networks in which $Dn = \omega(m)$.

Kuhn et al. [14] considered dynamic networks in which the network topology changes from round to round such that in every $T \geq 1$ consecutive rounds there exists a stable connected spanning subgraph, where T is a parameter. Paper [14] gave an algorithm that implements any computable function of the initial inputs, working in $\mathcal{O}(n + n^2/T)$ time with messages of $\mathcal{O}(\log n + d)$ size, where d denotes the size of input values. That solution is similar to our $\mathcal{O}(n)$ time algorithm, but it assumes the existence of a spanning connected subgraph throughout an execution, and T must be $\Omega(n)$ to result in time $\mathcal{O}(n)$, while our algorithm adjusts to disjoint connected components as they occur.

Other related work includes: agreement in complete networks in the presence of dynamic transmission failures, cf., [6,16,17]; almost-everywhere agreement [1]; approximate consensus [5]; and other models with transient failures [3,18].

2 Preliminaries

We model distributed systems as collections of nodes that communicate through a wired communication network. Executions of distributed algorithms are synchronous, in that they are partitioned into global rounds coordinated across the whole network. There are n nodes in a network. Each node has a unique *name* used to determine its identity; a name can be encoded by $\mathcal{O}(\log n)$ bits.

Links connecting pairs of nodes serve as bi-directional communication channels. If at least one message is transmitted by a link in an execution then this link is *used* and otherwise it is *unused* in this execution. A link may fail to deliver a message transmitted through it at a round; once such omission happens for a link, it is considered *unreliable*. The functionality of an unreliable link is unpredictable, in that it may either deliver a transmitted message or fail to do it. A link that has never failed to deliver a message by a given round is *reliable* at this round. A path in the network is *reliable* at a round if it consists only of links that are reliable at this round. Nodes and links of a network can be interpreted as a simple graph, with nodes serving as vertices and links as undirected edges. A network at the start of an execution is represented by some *initial graph* G, which is simple and connected. An edge representing an unreliable link is removed from the graph G at the first round it fails to deliver a transmitted message. A graph representing the network evolves through a sequence of its sub-graphs and may become partitioned into multiple connected components. Once an algorithm's execution halts, we stop this evolution of the initial graph G. An evolving network, and its graph representation G, at the first round after all the nodes have halted in an execution is denoted by G_F.

We precisely define the algorithmic problem of interest as follows. Each node p starts with an initial value $\texttt{input}_p$. We assume two properties of such input values. One is that an input value can be represented by $\mathcal{O}(\log n)$ bits. The other is that input values can be compared, in the sense of belonging to a domain with a total order. In particular, finitely many initial input values contain a maximum one. We say that a node *decides* when it produces an output by setting a dedicated variable to a decision value. The operation of deciding is irrevocable. An algorithm *solves disconnected agreement* in networks with links prone to failures if the following three properties hold in all executions:

Termination: every node eventually decides.
Validity: each decision value is among the input values.
Agreement: when a node p decides then its decision value is the same as these of the nodes that have already decided and to which p is connected by a reliable path at the round of deciding.

If a message sent by a node executing a disconnected agreement solution carries a constant number of node names and a constant number of input values then the size of such a message is $\mathcal{O}(\log n)$ bits, due to our assumptions about encoding names and input values. Messages of $\mathcal{O}(\log n)$ bits are called *short.* If a message carries $\mathcal{O}(n)$ node names and $\mathcal{O}(n)$ input values then the size of such a message is $\mathcal{O}(n \log n)$ bits. We call messages of $\mathcal{O}(n \log n)$ bits *linear.*

Let H be a simple graph. If H is connected then $\text{diam}(H)$ denotes the diameter of H. Suppose H has k connected components $C_1, \ldots, C_k$, where $k \geq 1$, and let $d_i = \text{diam}(C_i)$ be the diameter of component C_i. The *stretch of* H is defined as a number $k - 1 + \sum_{i=1}^{k} d_i$. The stretch of a connected graph equals its diameter, because then $k = 1$. The stretch of H can be interpreted as the maximum diameter of a graph obtained from H by adding $k - 1$ edges such that the obtained graph is connected. The maximum stretch of a graph with n vertices is $n - 1$, which occurs when every vertex is isolated or, more generally, when each connected component is a line of nodes.

We say that an algorithm relies on *minimal knowledge* if each node knows its unique name and can identify a port through which a message arrives and can assign a port for a message to be transmitted through.

A disconnected-agreement algorithm in a synchronous network with links prone to failures is *early stopping* if it runs in a number of rounds proportional to the unknown stretch λ actually occurring. Such an algorithm is *fast* if it runs in a number of rounds proportional to an upper bound on stretch Λ, assuming this bound is known to all the nodes.

3 Fast Agreement

We present a fast algorithm solving disconnected agreement, assuming that a bound Λ on stretch is known to all nodes. The algorithm is called FAST-AGREEMENT; its pseudocode is given in Fig. 1.

Theorem 1. *Consider an execution of algorithm* FAST-AGREEMENT (Λ) *in a network. If the stretch of the network never gets greater than* Λ *then the algorithm solves disconnected agreement in* Λ *rounds using messages of* $\mathcal{O}(\log n)$ *bits.*

We next focus on lower bounds on the number of rounds of any algorithm.

```
algorithm Fast-Agreement (Λ)

1. initialize candidate ← input_p
2. repeat Λ times
       if the current value of candidate has not been sent before then
           send candidate to all neighbors
       receive messages from all neighbors
       if a value greater than candidate has just been received
           then set candidate to the maximum value just received
3. decide on candidate
```

Fig. 1. A pseudocode of algorithm Fast-Agreement for a node p. The parameter Λ represents an upper bound on stretches, which is known to all nodes.

Lemma 1. *For any algorithm $\mathcal{A}$ solving disconnected agreement in networks prone to link failures, and for positive integers D and $n \geq 2D$, there exists a network G with n nodes and with diameter D such that some execution of $\mathcal{A}$ on G takes at least D rounds with no link failures.*

Corollary 1. *For any algorithm $\mathcal{A}$ solving disconnected agreement in networks prone to link failures, and for any even positive integer n, there exists a network G with n nodes such that some execution of $\mathcal{A}$ on G takes at least $\frac{n}{2}$ rounds with no link failures.*

Theorem 2. *For any natural number $\lambda \leq \Lambda$ and an algorithm $\mathcal{A}$ solving disconnected agreement in networks prone to link failures, there exists a network G that has stretch at most λ and such that each execution of $\mathcal{A}$ on G takes at least λ rounds.*

4 General Agreement with Short Messages

We present a general disconnected-agreement algorithm using short messages of $\mathcal{O}(\log n)$ bits. Algorithm Fast-Agreement presented in Sect. 3, which also employs messages of $\mathcal{O}(\log n)$ bits, relies on an upper bound on stretch Λ that is a part of code, and if the actual stretch in an execution goes beyond Λ then an execution of algorithm Fast-Agreement may not be correct. We assume in this section that nodes rely on minimal knowledge only and the given algorithm is correct for arbitrary patterns of link failures and the resulting stretches. The algorithm terminates in at most $n+1$ rounds, while the number of nodes n is not known. The running time is asymptotically optimal in case there are no failures, by Corollary 1 in Sect. 3.

The algorithm is called SM-Agreement, its pseudocode is in Fig. 2.

Theorem 3. *Algorithm* SM-Agreement *solves disconnected agreement in $n+1$ rounds relying on minimal knowledge and using short messages of $\mathcal{O}(\log n)$ bits.*

```
algorithm SM-AGREEMENT
```

1. initialize: $\texttt{Inputs}$ to empty list, $\texttt{round} \leftarrow 1$; append $(\texttt{name}_p, \texttt{input}_p)$ to $\texttt{Inputs}$
2. **for** each port α **do**
   initialize set $\texttt{Channel}[\alpha]$ to empty ; send $(\texttt{name}_p, \texttt{input}_p)$ through α
3. **for** each port α **do**
   if a pair $(\texttt{name}_q, \texttt{input}_q)$ received through α **then**
   add $(\texttt{name}_q, \texttt{input}_q)$ to $\texttt{Channel}[\alpha]$; append $(\texttt{name}_q, \texttt{input}_q)$ to $\texttt{Inputs}$
4. **repeat**
   (a) **for** each port α **do**
   if some item in $\texttt{Inputs}$ is not in $\texttt{Channel}[\alpha]$ **then**
   let x be the first such an item ; send x through α ; add x to $\texttt{Channel}[\alpha]$
   (b) **for** each port α **do**
   if a pair $(\texttt{name}_q, \texttt{input}_q)$ was just received through α **then**
   add $(\texttt{name}_q, \texttt{input}_q)$ to $\texttt{Channel}[\alpha]$; append $(\texttt{name}_q, \texttt{input}_q)$ to $\texttt{Inputs}$
   (c) $\texttt{round} \leftarrow \texttt{round} + 1$
   until $\texttt{round} > |\texttt{Inputs}|$
5. decide on the maximum input value in $\texttt{Inputs}$

Fig. 2. A pseudocode for a node p. The operation of adding an item to a set is void if the item is already in the set. The operation of appending an item to a list is void if the item is already in the list. The notation $|\texttt{Inputs}|$ means the number of items in the list $\texttt{Inputs}$. For a port α, the set $\texttt{Channel}[\alpha]$ contains pairs of the format (node's name, node's input) that the node p has either received or sent through the port α.

5 Agreement with Linear Messages

The goal of this section is to develop an algorithm whose running time scales well to the stretch actually occurring in an execution. We are ready to use messages longer than short ones used in the previous sections, and will use linear messages of $\mathcal{O}(n \log n)$ bits. Nodes are to rely on the minimal knowledge only: each node knows its own name and can distinguish ports by their communication functionality. The size of linear messages imposes constrains on the design of algorithms, and the obtained algorithm is not early stopping, but its running time is polynomial in λ. Our algorithm is called LM-Agreement, its pseudocode is in Fig. 3.

Every node maintains a counter of round numbers, incremented when a round begins. In each round, a node p generates a new timestamp r equal to the current value of the round counter, and forms a pair $(\texttt{name}_p, r)$, which we call a *timestamp pair* of node p. Such timestamp pairs are sent to the neighbors, to be forwarded through the network. Each node p stores a timestamp pair with the latest timestamp for a node it has ever received a timestamp pair from, and sends all such pairs to the neighbors in every round. An execution of the algorithm at a node is partitioned into *epochs*, each epoch being a contiguous interval of rounds. Epochs are not coordinated among nodes, and each node governs its own epochs. The first epoch begins at round zero, and for the following epochs, the last round of an epoch is remembered in order to discern timestamp pairs sent in the following epochs. For the purpose of monitoring progress of discovering the nodes in the connected component during an epoch, each node maintains a separate collection of timestamp pairs, which we call *pairs serving the epoch*. This collection stores only timestamp pairs sent in the current epoch, a pair with the greatest timestamp per node which originally generated the pair. The *status of a node q at a node p* during an epoch can be either absent, updated, or stale. If the node p does not have a timestamp pair for q serving the epoch then q is *absent* at p. If at a round of an epoch the node p either adds a timestamp pair serving the epoch for an absent node q or replaces a timestamp pair of a node q by a new timestamp pair with a greater timestamp than the previously held one, then q is *updated* at this round. If the node p has a timestamp pair for a node q serving the epoch but does not replace it at a round with a different timestamp pair to make it updated, then q is *stale* at this round.

---

algorithm LM-AGREEMENT

---

1. initialize: **candidate**$_p$ ← **input**$_p$, **round** ← 0, **Timestamps** ← ∅, **Nodes** ←⊥
2. **repeat**
   (a) **epoch** ← **round**, **PreviousNodes** ← **Nodes**, **EpochTimestamps** ← ∅
   (b) **repeat**
      i. **round** ← **round** + 1
      ii. add pair (**name**$_p$, **round**) to sets **Timestamps** and **EpochTimestamps**
      iii. **for** each port **do**
         A. send **Timestamps** and (this-is-candidate, **candidate**$_p$) through the port
         B. receive messages coming through the port
      iv. **for** each received pair (this-is-candidate, x) **do**
         if $x >$ **candidate**$_p$ **then** assign **candidate**$_p$ ← x
      v. **for** each received timestamp pair (**name**$_q$, y) **do**
         A. add (**name**$_q$, y) to **Timestamps** if this is a good update
         B. **if** $y >$ **epoch then** add (**name**$_q$, y) to **EpochTimestamps** if this is a good update
   (c) **until** epoch stabilized at the round
   (d) set **Nodes** to the set of first coordinates of timestamp pairs in **EpochTimestamps**
3. **until** **PreviousNodes** = **Nodes**
4. send (this-is-decision, **candidate**$_p$) through each port
5. decide on **candidate**$_p$

Fig. 3. A pseudocode for a node p. Each iteration of the main repeat-loop (2) makes an epoch. Symbol ⊥ denotes a value different from any actual set of nodes, so the initialization of **Nodes** to ⊥ in line (1) guarantees execution of at least two epochs. A *good update* of a timestamp pair for a node q either adds a first such a pair for q or replaces a present pair for q with one with a greater timestamp. At each round, p checks to see if a message of the form (this-is-decision, z) has been received, and if so then p forwards this message through each port, then decides on z, and halts.

We say that an epoch of a node p *stabilizes* at a round if either no new node has its status changed from absent to updated at p or no node gets its range changed at p. If an epoch stabilizes at a round, then the epoch ends. During an epoch, a node p builds a set of names of nodes from which it has received timestamp pairs serving this epoch. A similar set produced in the previous epoch is also stored. As an epoch ends, p compares the two sets. If they are equal then p stops executing epochs, decides on the maximum input value ever learned about, notifies the neighbors of the decision, and halts.

Each node p uses a variable $\texttt{candidate}_p$, which it initializes to $\texttt{input}_p$. Node p creates a pair (this-is-candidate, $\texttt{candidate}_p$), which we call a *candidate pair of* p. Nodes keep forwarding their candidate pairs to the neighbors continually. If a node p receives a candidate pair of some other node with a value x such that $x > \texttt{candidate}_p$ then p sets its $\texttt{candidate}_p$ to x. An execution concludes with deciding by performing instruction (5). Just before deciding, a node notifies the neighbors of the decision. Once a notification of a decision is received, the recipient forwards the decision to its neighbors, decides on the same value, and halts.

The variable `round` is an integer counter of rounds, which is incremented in each iteration of the inner repeat loop by executing instruction (2(b)i). The round counter is used to generate timestamps. The variable `Timestamps` stores timestamp pairs that p has received and forwards to its neighbors. The variable `EpochTimestamps` stores timestamp pairs serving the current epoch, which have been generated after the beginning of the current epoch. Each set `Timestamps` and `EpochTimestamps` stores at most one timestamp pair per node, the one with the greatest received timestamp. Each iteration of the inner repeat loop (2b) implements one round of sending and collecting messages through all the ports by executing instruction (2(b)iii). The inner repeat loop (2b) ends as soon as the epoch stays stable at a round, which is represented by condition (2c). The variable `Nodes` stores the names of nodes from which timestamp pairs serving the epoch have been received. The variable `Nodes` is calculated at the end of an epoch by instruction (2d). The set of nodes in `Nodes` at the end of an epoch is stored as `PreviousNodes` at the start of the next epoch. The main repeat loop (2) stops to be iterated as soon as the set of names of nodes stored in `Nodes` stays the same as the set stored in `PreviousNodes`, which is checked by condition (3).

Theorem 4. *Algorithm* LM-AGREEMENT *solves disconnected agreement in* $(\lambda + 2)^3$ *rounds, relying on minimal knowledge and using* $\mathcal{O}(n \log n)$ *bit messages.*

6 Early Stopping Agreement

We give an early-stopping disconnected agreement algorithm whose running time performance $\mathcal{O}(\lambda)$ scales optimally to the stretch λ occurring in an execution by the time of halting. Nodes rely only on the minimal knowledge, similarly as in algorithms SM-AGREEMENT (in Sect. 4) and LM-AGREEMENT (in Sect. 5), but messages carry $\mathcal{O}(m \log n)$ bits. This size is greater than that of short messages with $\mathcal{O}(\log n)$ bits in algorithm SM-AGREEMENT and linear messages with $\mathcal{O}(n \log n)$ bits in algorithm LM-AGREEMENT.

Algorithm ES-AGREEMENT

---

1. initialize: `Nodes` ← {$\texttt{name}_p$}, `Inputs` ← {($\texttt{name}_p$, $\texttt{input}_p$)}, `Links` ← ∅, `Unreliable` ← ∅
2. **for** each port **do**
   (a) send $\texttt{name}_p$ through this port
   (b) **if** $\texttt{name}_q$ received through this port **then**
      i. assign $\texttt{name}_q$ to the port as a name of the neighbor
      ii. add $\texttt{name}_q$ to `Nodes`; add edge {$\texttt{name}_p$, $\texttt{name}_q$} to `Links`
3. **while** there is an unsettled node in p's connected component in the snapshot **do**
   for each neighbor q **do**
      i. send sets `Nodes`, `Links`, `Unreliable`, `Inputs` to q
      ii. **if** a message from q was just received **then**
         update the sets `Nodes`, `Links`, `Unreliable`, `Inputs`
            by adding new elements included in this message from q
      else add edge {$\texttt{name}_p$, $\texttt{name}_q$} to `Unreliable`
4. **for** each neighbor q **do** send sets `Nodes`, `Links`, `Unreliable`, `Inputs` to q
5. decide on the maximum input value at the second coordinate of a pair in `Inputs`

Fig. 4. A pseudocode for a node p. A node q is considered unsettled by p if it is in the same connected component as p, according to the snapshot at p, and there is no pair of the form ($\texttt{name}_q$, ?) in $\texttt{Inputs}_p$.

The algorithm is called ES-AGREEMENT, its pseudocode is given in Fig. 4. The pseudocode refers to a number of variables that we introduce next. A set variable `Nodes` at a node p stores the names of all the nodes that the node p has ever learned about, and a set variable `Links` stores the links known by p to have transmitted messages successfully at least once, a link is represented as a set of two names of nodes at the endpoints of the link. A set variable `Unreliable` stores the edges representing links known to have failed. Knowledge about failures can be acquired in two ways: either directly, when a neighbor is expected to send a message at a round and no message arrives through the link, or indirectly, contained in a snapshot received from a neighbor. A node stores all known initial input values of nodes q as pairs ($\texttt{name}_q$, $\texttt{input}_q$) in a set variable `Inputs`. The nodes keep notifying their neighbors of the values of some of their private variables during iterations of the while loop in instruction (3) in Fig. 4. A node iterates this loop until all vertices in the connected component of the node are settled, which is sufficient to decide. Once a node is ready to decide, it forwards its snapshot to all the neighbors for the last time, decides on the maximum input value in some pair in `Inputs`, and halts. An execution of the algorithm starts with each node announcing its name to all its neighbors, by executing the instruction (2) in Fig. 4. This allows every node to discover its neighbors and map its ports to the neighbors' names. A node does not send its input in the first round of communication. A node sends its snapshot to the neighbors for the first time at the second round, by instruction (3) in the pseudocode in Fig. 4. A node p has heard of a node q if $\texttt{name}_q$ is in the set $\texttt{Nodes}_p$.

A node p has settled node q once the pair ($\texttt{name}_q$, $\texttt{input}_q$) is in $\texttt{Inputs}_p$ and the node q belongs to the connected component of p according to its snapshot.

Theorem 5. *Algorithm* ES-AGREEMENT *is an early stopping solution of disconnected agreement that relies on minimal knowledge, terminates within* $\lambda + 2$ *rounds and uses messages carrying* $\mathcal{O}(m \log n)$ *bits.*

7 Optimizing Link Use

We present an algorithm solving disconnected agreement that uses the optimal number $\mathcal{O}(n)$ of links and messages of $\mathcal{O}(m \log n)$ bits. We depart from the model of minimal knowledge of the previous sections and assume that nodes know their neighbors at the outset, in having names of the corresponding neighbors associated with all their ports. We complement the algorithm by showing that using $\mathcal{O}(n)$ links is only possible when each node starts with a mapping of ports on its neighbors, because otherwise $\Omega(m)$ is a lower bound on the link use.

The general idea of the algorithm is to have nodes build their maps of the network that include the connected component of each node. An approximation of the map at a node evolves through a sequence of snapshots of the vicinity of the node. Such a snapshot helps to coordinate choosing links through which messages are sent to extend the current snapshot to a bigger one. Input values could be a part of node attributes of the vertices on such a map. A node categorizes its incident links as either passive, active or unreliable; these are exclusive categories that evolve in time. An *active* link is used to send messages through it, so a node categorizes an incident link as active once it receives a message through it. Initially, one link incident to a node is considered as active by the node, and all the remaining incident links are considered passive. A link is *passive* at a round if none of its endpoint nodes has ever attempted a transmission through this link. A node transmits through an active port at every round, unless the node decides and halts. It follows that if a node p considers a link active, which connects it to a neighbor q, then q considers the link active as well, possibly with a delay of one round. Similarly, if a node p considers a link passive, which connects it to a neighbor q, then q considers the link passive as well, possibly for one round longer than p. A node p detects a failure of an active link and begins to consider it unreliable after the link fails to deliver a message to p as it should. For an active link connecting a node p with q, once p considers the link unreliable then q considers the link unreliable as well, possibly with a delay of one round. The *state of a node p at a round* consists of its name, the input value, and a set of its neighbors, with each incident link categorized as either passive, active, or unreliable, representing this categorization of links by the node p at the round. Links start as passive, except for one incident link per node initialized as active, then they may become active, and finally they may become unreliable.

A snapshot of the network at a node represents the node's knowledge of its connected component in the network restricted to the active edges and the states of its nodes. Formally, a *snapshot of network* at a node p at a round is a collection

algorithm OL-AGREEMENT

1. initialize: `Unreliable` $\leftarrow \emptyset$, `Active` $\leftarrow \{\{p, q\}\}$ where q is some neighbor,
   `Passive` $\leftarrow$ set of links to p's neighbors, except for the neighbor q used in `Active`,
   `state` $\leftarrow$ ($\mathtt{name}_p$, $\mathtt{input}_p$, `Active`, `Passive`, `Unreliable`),
   `round` $\leftarrow 0$, `timestamp` $\leftarrow$ (`state`, `round`)
2. **repeat**
   (a) `epoch` $\leftarrow$ `round`, `Snapshot` $\leftarrow$ {`state`}
   (b) **repeat**
      i. `round` $\leftarrow$ `round` $+ 1$, add `timestamp` to set `Timestamps`
      ii. **for** each incident link α **do**
         A. **if** α is in `Active` **then** send `Timestamps` through α
         B. **if** α is mature in `Active` and no message received through α **then** move α to `Unreliable`
         C. **if** a message received through α **then** place α in `Active`
      iii. **for** each received timestamp pair (`state`, y) **do**
         A. add (`state`, y) to `Timestamps`
         B. **if** $y >$ `epoch` **then** add `state` to `Snapshot`
   (c) **until** the active connected component is settled
   (d) if the active connected component is extendible then
      i. identify an outgoing edge as a connector
      ii. if the connector is incident to p then place it in `Active`
3. **until** the active connected component is enclosed
4. set $\mathtt{candidate}_p$ to the maximum input value in `Snapshot`
5. send pair (this-is-decision, $\mathtt{candidate}_p$) through each active incident link
6. decide on $\mathtt{candidate}_p$

Fig. 5. A pseudocode for a node p. In each round, node p checks to see if a pair of the form (`decision`, z) has been received, and if so then p forwards this pair through each active port, decides on z, and halts.

of states of some nodes that p has received and stores. A snapshot allows to create a map of a portion of the network, which is a graph with the names of nodes as vertices and the edges representing links. This map can include the input values of some nodes, should they become known. A connected component of a node with other nodes reachable by active links is a part of such a map. Formally, the *active connected component* of a node p at a round is a connected component, of the vertex representing p, in a graph that is a map of the network according to the snapshot of p at the round with only active links represented by edges.

A node p sends a summary of its knowledge of the states of nodes in the network to the neighbors through all its active links at each round. If p receives a message with such knowledge from a neighbor, then p updates its knowledge and the snapshot by incorporating the newly learned information. At each round, a node p determines its active connected component based on the current snapshot. We say that *a node p has heard of a node q* if the $\mathtt{name}_q$ occurs in the snapshot at p; the node p may either store some q's state or q's name may belong to a state of some other node that p stores. A node p considers another node q *settled* if p

has q's state in its snapshot. A node p considers its active connected component *settled* if p has settled all the nodes in its active connected component. If a node p has heard about another node q such that q does not belong to the node p's active connected component, but it is connected to a node r in the active connected component by a passive link, then the node p considers the link connecting q to r as *outgoing*. If there is an outgoing link in p's active connected component then p considers its active connected component *extendible*, otherwise p considers its active connected component *enclosed*.

The algorithm is called OL-Agreement, its pseudocode is in Fig. 5. Each node stores links it knows as unreliable in a set `Unreliable`, initialized to the empty set. Each node stores links it considers active in a set `Active`, initialized to some incident link. Each node stores passive links in a set `Passive`, which a node initializes to the set of all incident links except for the one initially activated link. All nodes maintain a variable `round` as a counter of rounds. In each round, a node creates a *timestamp pair*, which consists of its current state and the value of the round counter used as a timestamp. A node p stores timestamp pairs in a set `Timestamps`. For each node q different from p, a node p stores a timestamp pair for q if such a pair arrived in messages and only one pair with the largest timestamp. These variables are initialized by instruction (1) in Fig. 5.

The initialization is followed by iterating a loop performed by instruction (2) in the pseudocode in Fig. 5. The purpose of an iteration is to identify a new settled active connected component; we call an iteration *epoch*. An epoch is determined by the round in which it started, remembered in the variable `epoch` by instruction (2a). The knowledge of an active connected component of a node p identified in an epoch is stored in a set `Snapshot`, which is initialized at the outset of an epoch to the p's state by instruction (2a). This knowledge is represented as a collection of states of nodes that arrived to p in timestamp pairs, with timestamps indicating that they were created after the start of the current epoch, as verified by instruction (2(b)iiiB). The main part of an epoch is implemented as an inner repeat loop (2b). An iteration of this loop implements a round of communication with neighbors through active links and updating the state by instruction (2(b)ii).

An incident link in `Active` is *mature* if either it became active because a message arrived through it or p made it active spontaneously at some round i and the current round is at least $i + 2$. If a mature active link fails to deliver a message then p moves it to `Unreliable`. A set variable `Timestamps` stores timestamp pairs that a node sends in each message and updates after receiving messages at a round. A set variable `Snapshot` is used to construct an active connected component. `Snapshot` is rebuilt in each epoch, starting only with the current p's state. We separate storing timestamp pairs in a set `Timestamps` used for communication from storing states in `Snapshot` to build an active connected component, to facilitate a proper advancement of epochs in other nodes. We say that node p *completes the survey* of the network by a round if p has settled all the nodes in its active connected component according to the snapshot of this round. If the active connected component is extendible, then p identifies a *connector* which is an outgoing edge to be made active. We may identify an outgoing edge that is minimal with respect to the lexicographic order among all the outgoing links for a settled active connected component to be designated as a connector. If a connector is a link incident to p then p moves it to the set `Active`, by instruction (2d).

Theorem 6. *Algorithm* OL-AGREEMENT *solves disconnected agreement in $\mathcal{O}(nm)$ rounds with fewer than $2n$ links used at any round and sending messages of $\mathcal{O}(m \log n)$ bits.*

Lower Bounds for Link Usage. We now consider a setting in which the destinations of ports are not initially known to nodes. For any positive integers n and m such that $m = \mathcal{O}(n^2)$, we design a graph $\mathcal{G}(n,m)$ with $\Theta(n)$ vertices and $\Theta(m)$ edges, which makes any disconnected agreement solution to use $\Theta(m)$ links even if the nodes know the parameters n and m. We drop the parameters n and m from the notation $\mathcal{G}(n,m)$, whenever they are fixed and understood from context, and simply use $\mathcal{G}$. Consider any positive integers n and m such that $m = \mathcal{O}(n^2)$. Let graph $\mathcal{G}$ consist of two identical parts G_1 and G_2 as its subgraphs. The parts are $\lceil \frac{m}{n} \rceil$-regular graphs of $\lceil \frac{n}{2} \rceil$ vertices each. Without loss of generality, we can assume that the number $\lceil \frac{m}{n} \rceil$ is even, to guarantee that such regular graphs exist. Graph $\mathcal{G}$ is obtained by connecting G_1 and G_2 with $\lceil \frac{n}{2} \rceil$ edges such that each vertex from G_1 has exactly one neighbor in G_2. By the construction, graph $\mathcal{G}$ has $2\lceil \frac{n}{2} \rceil = \Theta(n)$ vertices and $(\lceil \frac{m}{n} \rceil + 1)\lceil \frac{n}{2} \rceil = \Theta(m)$ edges. Let us assume now that the destinations of outgoing links are not initially known to the nodes. This means that ports can be associated with neighbors's names only after receiving messages through them. The following holds even if n, m can be a part of code.

Theorem 7. *For any disconnected agreement algorithm $\mathcal{A}$ relying on minimal knowledge and positive integer numbers n and m such that $n \le m$ and $m \le n^2$, there exists a network $\mathcal{G}(n,m)$ with $\Theta(n)$ nodes and $\Theta(m)$ links and an execution of algorithm $\mathcal{A}$ on $\mathcal{G}(n,m)$ that uses $\Theta(m)$ links.*

Theorem 8. *Let $\mathcal{A}$ be a disconnected agreement algorithm that uses $\mathcal{O}(n)$ reliable links concurrently when executed in networks with n nodes. For all natural numbers n and $\lambda \le n$, there exists a network $\mathcal{G}$ with the stretch λ on which some execution of algorithm $\mathcal{A}$ takes $\Omega(n)$ rounds.*

Corollary 2. *If a disconnected agreement algorithm uses $\mathcal{O}(n)$ reliable links concurrently at any time, when executed in networks of n nodes, then this algorithm cannot be early stopping.*

8 Conclusion

We introduced the problem of disconnected agreement in the model of networks with links prone to failures such that faulty links may omit messages. This problem is of different nature than consensus or k-set agreement problems, which are typically considered in connected communication network, see the full version of the paper [8] for a related discussion. We measure the communication efficiency of algorithms by the size of individual messages or the number of non-faulty links used. This approach allows to demonstrate apparent trade-offs between running time and communication. One could study dependencies of the running time and the total number of messages exchanged or the total number of bits in messages sent by nodes executing disconnected-agreement algorithms. Another possible future direction of work concerns more severe link faults, for example such that result in delivering forged messages. Studying stretch of specific families of evolving networks is an open problem of independent interest.

References

1. Augustine, J., Pandurangan, G., Robinson, P., Upfal, E.: Towards robust and efficient computation in dynamic peer-to-peer networks. In: SODA 2012 (2012)
2. Biely, M., Robinson, P., Schmid, U., Schwarz, M., Winkler, K.: Gracefully degrading consensus and k-set agreement in directed dynamic networks. Theoret. Comput. Sci. **726**, 41–77 (2018)
3. Biely, M., Schmid, U., Weiss, B.: Synchronous consensus under hybrid process and link failures. Theoret. Comput. Sci. **412**(40), 5602–5630 (2011)
4. Castañeda, A., Fraigniaud, P., Paz, A., Rajsbaum, S., Roy, M., Travers, C.: Synchronous t-resilient consensus in arbitrary graphs. In: Proceeding of the 21st International Symposium on Stabilization, Safety, and Security of Distributed Systems (SSS) (2019)
5. Charron-Bost, B., Függer, M., Nowak, T.: Approximate consensus in highly dynamic networks: the role of averaging algorithms. In: ICALP 2015 (2015)
6. Charron-Bost, B., Schiper, A.: The heard-of model: computing in distributed systems with benign faults. Distrib. Comput. **22**, 49–71 (2009)
7. Chlebus, B.S., Kowalski, D.R., Olkowski, J.: Fast agreement in networks with Byzantine nodes. In: Proceedings of the 34th International Symposium on Distributed Computing (DISC). LIPIcs, vol. 179, pp. 30:1–30:18 (2020)
8. Chlebus, B.S., Kowalski, D.R., Olkowski, J., Olkowski, J.: Disconnected agreement in networks prone to link failures. CoRR abs/2102.01251 (2021)
9. Choudhury, A., Garimella, G., Patra, A., Ravi, D., Sarkar, P.: Crash-tolerant consensus in directed graph revisited (extended abstract). In: SIROCCO 2018 (2018)
10. Dolev, D.: The Byzantine generals strike again. J. Algorithms **3**(1), 14–30 (1982)
11. Fischer, M.J., Lynch, N.A., Merritt, M.: Easy impossibility proofs for distributed consensus problems. Distrib. Comput. **1**(1), 26–39 (1986)
12. Hadzilacos, V.: Connectivity requirements for Byzantine agreement under restricted types of failures. Distrib. Comput. **2**(2), 95–103 (1987)
13. Khan, M.S., Naqvi, S.S., Vaidya, N.H.: Exact Byzantine consensus on undirected graphs under local broadcast model. In: Proceedings of the ACM Symposium on Principles of Distributed Computing (PODC), pp. 327–336. ACM (2019)
14. Kuhn, F., Lynch, N.A., Oshman, R.: Distributed computation in dynamic networks. In: STOC (2010)
15. Kuhn, F., Moses, Y., Oshman, R.: Coordinated consensus in dynamic networks. In: Proceedings of the 30th Annual ACM Symposium on Principles of Distributed Computing (PODC 2011), pp. 1–10. ACM (2011)

16. Perry, K.J., Toueg, S.: Distributed agreement in the presence of processor and communication faults. IEEE Trans. Software Eng. **12**(3), 477–482 (1986)
17. Santoro, N., Widmayer, P.: Time is not a healer. In: Monien, B., Cori, R. (eds.) STACS 1989. LNCS, vol. 349, pp. 304–313. Springer, Heidelberg (1989). https://doi.org/10.1007/BFb0028994
18. Schmid, U., Weiss, B., Keidar, I.: Impossibility results and lower bounds for consensus under link failures. SIAM J. Comput. **38**(5), 1912–1951 (2009)
19. Tseng, L.: Recent results on fault-tolerant consensus in message-passing networks. In: Suomela, J. (ed.) SIROCCO 2016. LNCS, vol. 9988, pp. 92–108. Springer, Cham (2016). https://doi.org/10.1007/978-3-319-48314-6_7
20. Tseng, L., Vaidya, N.H.: Fault-tolerant consensus in directed graphs. In: Proceedings of ACM Symposium on Principles of Distributed Computing (PODC), pp. 451–460 (2015)
21. Tseng, L., Vaidya, N.H.: A note on fault-tolerant consensus in directed networks. SIGACT News **47**(3), 70–91 (2016)
22. Winkler, K., Schmid, U.: An overview of recent results for consensus in directed dynamic networks. Bull. EATCS **128** (2019)

Where Are the Constants? New Insights on the Role of Round Constant Addition in the SymSum Distinguisher

Sahiba Suryawanshi(✉) and Dhiman Saha(✉)

de.ci.phe.red Lab, Department of Computer Science & Engineering, Indian Institute of Technology, Bhilai 492015, India
{sahibas,Dhiman}@iitbhilai.ac.in

Abstract. The current work makes a systematic attempt to describe the effect of *the relative order of round constant (*RCon*) addition in the round function of an SPN cipher* on its algebraic structure. The observations are applied to the SymSum distinguisher, introduced by Saha *et al.* in FSE 2017 which is one of the best distinguishers on the SHA3 hash function reported in literature. Results show that certain ordering (referred to as Type-LCN) of RCon makes the distinguisher less effective but it still works with some limitations. Results in the form of new SymSum distinguishers are reported on concrete Type-LCN constructions - NIST LWC competition finalist Xoodyak-Hash and its internal permutation Xoodoo. New linear structures are also reported on Xoodoo that augment the distinguisher to penetrate more rounds. Final results include SymSum distinguishers on 7 rounds of Xoodoo and 5 rounds of Xoodyak-Hash with complexity 2^{128} and 2^{32}, respectively. All practical distinguishers have been verified. The characterization encompassing the algebraic structure and effect of RCon provided by the current work improves the understanding of SymSum in general and constitutes one of the first such result on Xoodyak-Hash and Xoodoo.

Keywords: Higher Order Derivative · SPN cipher · SymSum Distinguisher · ZeroSum Distinguisher · Xoodoo · Xoodyak-Hash

1 Introduction

Substitution-Permutation Networks (SPN) have emerged as one of the most popular cipher design strategies for modern Symmetric-key cryptography. Since Rijndael [14], which is an SPN design, was announced as the winner of the AES [3] competition, SPN based crypto primitives have gained a lot of attention. Security evaluation of symmetric-key crypto has widely benefited from public cryptanalysis, which forms the cornerstone of trust on such constructions since they are not *provably* secure as their asymmetric counterparts. Public competitions like eSTREAM [5], CAESAR [1] and the National Institute of Standards and Technology Lightweight Cryptography Competition (NIST-LWC) [2] have largely

S. Dolev and B. Schieber (Eds.): SSS 2023, LNCS 14310, pp. 223–239, 2023.
https://doi.org/10.1007/978-3-031-44274-2_17

contributed into the evolution of SPN strategy both from design and cryptanalysis perspectives. Among various cryptanalysis strategies employed, devising distinguishers targets the most fundamental requirement of a crypto primitive - *non-randomness*. A very popular technique to make such distinguishers is based on higher-order differential cryptanalysis [4] and relies on computing what is known as the ZeroSum. It is based on the higher-order derivatives principle, stating that the $(d+1)^{th}$ order derivative of a d–degree function leads to a zero function. This is evidenced by obtaining a zero XOR-Sum for 2^{d+1} computations of function on a $(d+1)$–dimensional subspace.

A very interesting demonstration of the ZeroSum idea was by Aumasson *et al.* on the internal permutation (Keccak-f) of the hash function Keccak [9] which went on to be the winner of the NIST SHA3 [8] competition. The idea constituted what is referred to as the inside-out technique that allows to devise the ZeroSum property from the middle round of the permutations and extending in either direction. This work spawned a rich body of results [10,11,15,17] including full-round ZeroSum distinguishers. However, the reliance on the inside-out strategy implied that the results were inapplicable on the Keccak/SHA3 hash function. In FSE 2017, Saha *et al.* came up with the idea of the SymSum distinguisher [22] which was more efficient than ZeroSum by a factor of 4 and constituted the most efficient distinguishing attack on SHA3 at that time. SymSum exploited the fact that RCon were added after the non-linear operation in the SHA3 round function. Augmenting this with symmetry preserving property of the round sub-operations, $(d-1)^{th}$–fold vectorial derivatives (Refer Definition 1) over symmetric input subspaces led to what the authors called as the *Symmetric-Sum* or SymSum. Suryawanshi *et al.* extended the SymSum distinguisher using linearization to reach higher number of rounds [23].

The current work uncovers new insights on effect of RCon addition on algebraic structure in the light of SymSum. This systematic attempt tries to formalize the SPN structure that leads to SymSum-like properties. In doing so, we classify SPN designs in three classes: Type-LNC,Type-LCN and Type-CLN based on the relative order of RCon addition with regards to substitution and permutation layers. Our research reveals that while Type-LNC is captured by results reported on SHA3 by Saha *et al.*, linearization used by Suryawanshi *et al.* actually maps to Type-CLN. However, analysis of a Type-LCN SPN construction is furnished for the first time in the current work. The findings of work are finally verified in the form of new SymSum distinguishers on a concrete Type-LCN SPN design and NIST-LWC finalist - Xoodyak-Hash [13] and its internal permutation Xoodoo.

Related Work. Despite being a relatively new design by the same team who designed Keccak, both Xoodoo and Xoodyak have had a fair share of distinguishing attacks. In 2020, Liu *et al.* proposed a full-round ZeroSum distinguishing attack on Xoodoo [19]. Since then, other researchers have introduced new distinguishing attacks on round-reduced Xoodoo, such as using rotational cryptanalysis reported by Liu *et al.* in [20], a functional distinguisher introduced by Bellini and Minematsu in [6], and a higher-order differential-linear distinguisher presented by Hu *et al.* in [18]. Moreover, Dunkelman *et al.* introduced a distinguishing attack using differential-linear cryptanalysis on Xoodyak in [16].

Along with the theoretical analysis of the three types of SPN constructions state above, the current work makes an in-depth study of the round-function of XOODOO to mount SYMSUM on both XOODOO and XOODYAK-HASH. We report that the XOODOO state is symmetric in multiple dimensions (Refer Definition 3) leading to distinguishers in two different axes. This is a stark difference with KECCAK-f, where symmetry is only in the z–axis. We also report linear structures in the XOODOO round-function that allow the SYMSUM property with lesser complexity. Overall, using XOODOO and XOODYAK-HASH, we successfully verify our theoretical result on Type-LCN SPN primitives which states that for Type-LCN ordering of RCON, SYMSUM outperforms ZEROSUM by a factor of 2. Final results constitute distinguishers on 5 rounds of XOODYAK-HASH and 7 rounds of XOODOO with complexities of 2^{16} and 2^{128}, respectively. Table 1 summarizes our results.

Table 1. Summary of the results, here DoF is degree of freedom

#Rounds	XOODOO			XOODYAK-HASH		
	ZEROSUM	SYMSUM	Remark	ZEROSUM	SYMSUM	Remark
1	2^1	2^0	Only 1 input required	2^3	2^0	Only 1 input required
2	2^1	2^0	Only 1 input required	2^5	2^4	SYMSUM
3	2^5	2^4	SYMSUM+ 1R Linearization	2^9	2^8	SYMSUM
4	2^9	2^8	SYMSUM+ 1R Linearization + Insideout	2^{17}	2^{16}	SYMSUM
5	2^{17}	2^{16}	SYMSUM+ 1R Linearization	2^{33}	2^{32}	SYMSUM
6	2^{33}	2^{32}	SYMSUM+ 1R Linearization + Insideout	2^{65}	-	Exceed DoF
7	2^{129}	2^{128}	SYMSUM	2^{129}	-	Exceed DoF
8	2^{257}	-	Exceed DoF	-	-	Exceed

Organization: Here is the structure of the paper: Sect. 2 provides an overview of the m-fold vectorial derivative. Section 3 explores the impact of reordering the RCON on the algebraic structure of SPN cipher. Finally, in Sect. 4, we apply our study practically to XOODOO/XOODYAK-HASH and discuss the linearization technique for XOODOO, including their complexity and DoF. Section 5 presents experimental evidence supporting our claims and in Sect. 6, we conclude the paper. The Appendix includes brief details of XOODOO and XOODYAK-HASH.

2 Preliminaries

This work relies on the idea m–fold Boolean vectorial derivatives, which allow differentiation with respect to a specific subspace. While simple Boolean derivatives capture change in a function w.r.t a change in value of a single variable, vectorial derivatives capture simultaneous change in set of variables [21]. Higher order vectorial derivatives use multiple such disjoint partitions. Saha *et al.* used this operator in [22] and is restated below.

Definition 1 (m-Fold Vectorial Derivative [21,22]**).** *Let* $\{\mathbf{x_1}, \mathbf{x_2}, \cdots, \mathbf{x_m}, \mathbf{x_{m+1}}\}$ *be* $(m+1)$ *partitions of Boolean variables* $(x_1, x_2, \cdots, x_n)$ *and* $f(\mathbf{x_1}, \mathbf{x_2}, \cdots, \mathbf{x_m}, \mathbf{x_{m+1}}) = f(x_1, x_2, \cdots, x_n) = f(\mathbf{x})$ *a Boolean function of* n *variables, then*

$$\left.\frac{\partial^m f}{\partial \mathbf{x_m} \cdots \partial \mathbf{x_2} \partial \mathbf{x_1}}\right|_{\substack{(\mathbf{x_1}, \mathbf{x_2}, \cdots, \mathbf{x_m}) \\ =(\mathbf{c_1}, \mathbf{c_2}, \cdots, \mathbf{c_m})}} = \frac{\partial}{\partial \mathbf{x_m}} \left(\cdots \left(\frac{\partial}{\partial \mathbf{x_2}} \left(\left. \frac{\partial f}{\partial \mathbf{x_1}} \right|_{\mathbf{x_1}=\mathbf{c_1}} \right) \right|_{\mathbf{x_2}=\mathbf{c_2}} \right) \cdots \right) \Bigg|_{\mathbf{x_m}=\mathbf{c_m}}$$

is the **m***-***fold vectorial derivative** *of the Boolean function* $f(\mathbf{x_1}, \mathbf{x_2}, \cdots, \mathbf{x_m}, \mathbf{x_{m+1}})$ *with regards to the* m *partitions* $\{\mathbf{x_1}, \mathbf{x_2}, \cdots, \mathbf{x_m}\}$.

$$\left.\frac{\partial^m f}{\partial \mathbf{x_m} \cdots \partial \mathbf{x_2} \partial \mathbf{x_1}}\right|_{\substack{(\mathbf{x_1}, \mathbf{x_2}, \cdots, \mathbf{x_m}) \\ =(\mathbf{c_1}, \mathbf{c_2}, \cdots, \mathbf{c_m})}} = \bigoplus_{\substack{\{\mathbf{x_1}, \mathbf{x_2}, \cdots, \mathbf{x_m}\} \in \mathbf{C} \\ \mathbf{x_{m+1}}=\mathbf{c_{m+1}}}} f(\mathbf{x_1}, \mathbf{x_2}, \cdots, \mathbf{x_m}, \mathbf{x_{m+1}}) \tag{1}$$

$$\text{where, } \mathbf{C} = \begin{bmatrix} c_1, & c_2, & \cdots, & c_{m-1}, & c_m \\ c_1, & c_2, & \cdots, & c_{m-1}, & \overline{c_m} \\ c_1, & c_2, & \cdots, & \overline{c_{m-1}}, & c_m \\ c_1, & c_2, & \cdots, & \overline{c_{m-1}}, & \overline{c_m} \\ \vdots & \vdots & \ddots & \vdots & \vdots \\ \overline{c_1}, & \overline{c_2}, & \cdots, & \overline{c_{m-1}}, & \overline{c_m} \end{bmatrix}_{2^m \times m} \qquad \mathbf{c_i} \in \mathbb{F}_2^{|\mathbf{x_i}|}$$

3 Investigating Commutativity of Round-Constant Addition with the Linear and Non-linear Operation

SPN is a round-based iterative function that in a generic form consists of combination of linear ($\mathcal{L}$) and non-linear operations ($\mathcal{N}$) along-with RCon addition ($\mathcal{C}$) which is aimed to reduce any symmetry which might eventually develop in the internal state. Though RCon addition is essentially a linear operation, we look at it in isolation for reasons that will be apparent soon. Our aim is to study the algebraic structure of SPN ciphers considering the position of RCon addition relative to the ordered pair $(\mathcal{L}, \mathcal{N})$ implying 3 possibilities: $(\mathcal{L}, \mathcal{N}, \texttt{RCon})$, $(\mathcal{L}, \texttt{RCon}, \mathcal{N})$ and $(\texttt{RCon}, \mathcal{L}, \mathcal{N})$. We respectively classify SPN ciphers into 3 categories: Type-LNC, Type-LCN and Type-CLN. Our investigation introduces the algebraic structure of these ciphers which is based on the nature of the monomials that appear in their Algebraic Normal Form (ANF) and classify[1] them into 3 types: Type-I monomials are free from any RCon, Type-II monomials involve both RCon and state variables and Type-III monomials consist only of constant terms. To illustrate Type-I, Type-II and Type-III monomials, we use following example.

Example 1. Let us consider an arbitrary Boolean function f with the ANF: $f = x_1x_2x_3x_4 + x_1x_3x_4c_2 + x_1x_4x_5 + x_2x_4c_1c_4 + c_1c_2c_3 + c_2c_4$, where c_i is a constant.

$$\begin{aligned} f &= x_1x_2x_3x_4 + x_1x_3x_4c_2 + x_1x_4x_5 + x_2x_4c_1c_4 + c_1c_2c_3 + c_2c_4 \\ &= \overbrace{(x_1x_2x_3x_4 + x_1x_4x_5)}^{f_{\text{Type-I}}} + \overbrace{(x_1x_3x_4c_2 + x_2x_4c_1c_4)}^{f_{\text{Type-II}}} + \overbrace{(c_1c_2c_3 + c_2c_4)}^{f_{\text{Type-III}}} \end{aligned}$$

Throughout the section, we use $X = \{x_1, x_2, \ldots x_n\}$ to denote the state variables for the initial state of the cipher while $C = \{c_1, c_2, \ldots c_m\}$ denote RCon

[1] Note that this classification was introduced in [22].

added at various rounds. λ denotes algebraic degree of non-linear component $\mathcal{N}$. In the following subsections, we analyze the algebraic structure of Type-LNC, Type-LCN and Type-CLN SPN cipher.

3.1 Algebraic Structure of Type-LNC SPN Cipher

Type-LNC function is obtained by iterating $\mathcal{C} \circ \mathcal{N} \circ \mathcal{L}$ sequence. After 1 round, resulting polynomial takes form $\sum_{k} \prod_{x_i \in \mathbf{x}_k \subset X} x_i + \sum_{c_j \in \mathbf{c}_r \subset C} c_j$ where $|\mathbf{x}_k| \leq \lambda, \forall k$. Thus, algebraic degree (d°) of monomials is upper bounded by λ. This also implies that for a Type-LNC cipher, no Type-II monomials are generated after the first round. It is only after second round that Type-II monomials may be generated. Also after the second round (d°_{max}Type-I $- d^\circ_{max}$Type-II $\leq \lambda$). Thus difference in the highest degrees *always* persists even at higher rounds. In [22], Saha *et al.* utilized this property to develop SymSum distinguisher. The basic idea was to use $m-$fold vectorial derivatives to eliminate Type-II monomials thereby arriving at a RCon independent function. When derivatives were computed over specially selected symmetric subspaces, the output sum was deterministically symmetric i.e. SymSum. However, the analysis furnished in [22] was only limited to Type-LNC design SHA3. In the current work we give it a more generalized treatment and study SymSum property for other variants Type-LCN and Type-CLN.

3.2 Algebraic Structure of Type-LCN SPN Cipher

We can obtain the Type-LCN function by iterating the $\mathcal{N} \circ \mathcal{C} \circ \mathcal{L}$ sequence. The algebraic form of the resulting function after one iteration is given below.

$$\sum_{k} \prod_{x_i \in \mathbf{x}_k \subset X} x_i + \sum \prod_{\substack{x_m \in \mathbf{x}_m \subset X \\ c_l \in \mathbf{c}_l \subset C}} x_m c_l + \sum_{r} \prod_{c_j \in \mathbf{c}_r \subset C} c_j \tag{2}$$

Analyzing this polynomial easily reveals that the highest degrees of Type-I, Type-II and Type-III monomials are λ, $\lambda - 1$ and 0, respectively. Here we can see that the highest degree of RCon independent monomials is greater than RCon dependent monomials. Our work studies the case when RCon addition precedes non-linear (or both linear and non-linear) operations. We argue that SymSum remains more effective than ZeroSum distinguisher by a factor of 2, even after switching the operations. In addition, we offer a theoretical validation for our argument using similar approach as in [22], making it more comprehensible. To support our claim, we rely on Theorem 1 that builds upon the following Lemma.

Lemma 1. *Let $\mathcal{F}$ be a* SPN *round function with $\mathcal{N} \circ \mathcal{C} \circ \mathcal{L}$ components, where $\mathcal{C}$, $\mathcal{N}$ and $\mathcal{L}$ represent the non-linear, round-constant addition and linear components, respectively. Then, we can express the function $\mathcal{F}$ as:*

$$\mathcal{F} = \mathcal{G} + C \times \mathcal{H} + C,$$

where $d^\circ\mathcal{F} = d^\circ\mathcal{G} > d^\circ\mathcal{H}$, $\mathcal{G}, \mathcal{H} : \mathbb{F}_2^n \rightarrow \mathbb{F}_2^n$ and C is a constant

Proof. Function $\mathcal{F}^{n_r}$, which consists of n_r rounds, can be expressed as follows:

$$\begin{aligned}\mathcal{F} &= (\mathcal{N} \circ \mathcal{C}_{n_r} \circ \mathcal{L}) \circ \cdots \circ (\mathcal{N} \circ \mathcal{C}_2 \circ \mathcal{L}) \circ (\mathcal{N} \circ \mathcal{C}_1 \circ \mathcal{L}) \\ &= \Big[(\mathcal{N} \circ \mathcal{C}_{n_r} \circ \mathcal{L}) \circ \cdots \circ (\mathcal{N} \circ \mathcal{C}_2 \circ \mathcal{L})) \circ (\mathcal{N} \circ \mathcal{C}_1)\Big] \circ \mathcal{L} \qquad (3)\end{aligned}$$

The monomials that contain RCon are unaffected[2] by the linear function $\mathcal{L}$ in the first round due to the order of operations illustrated in Eq. (3). To distinguish monomials, we need to segregate them. The $\mathcal{F}^{n_r}$ function in n_r round SPN can be expressed as: $\mathcal{F}^{n_r} = \mathcal{F}^{n_r}_{\text{Type-I}} + \mathcal{F}^{n_r}_{\text{Type-II}} + \mathcal{F}^{n_r}_{\text{Type-III}}$

Let us examine degree of monomials $d^\circ\mathcal{F}^{n_r} = max(d^\circ\mathcal{F}^{n_r}_{\text{Type-I}}, d^\circ\mathcal{F}^{n_r}_{\text{Type-II}}, d^\circ\mathcal{F}^{n_r}_{\text{Type-III}})$ Now, let us pursue the inductive proof. Note that $d^\circ\mathcal{F}_{\text{Type-III}} = 0$ by definition.

Base Case: For $n_r = 1$, the degrees of monomials are:

$$\begin{aligned}d^\circ\mathcal{F}_{\text{Type-I}} &\leq \lambda \text{ (degree of non-linear layer)} \\ d^\circ\mathcal{F}_{\text{Type-II}} &\leq \lambda - 1 \text{ (Due to } \mathit{Exp}\text{ (2))}\end{aligned}$$

Thus, highest degree $d^\circ\mathcal{F}_{\text{Type-I}} > d^\circ\mathcal{F}_{\text{Type-II}}$. Thus, statement holds for $n_r = 1$.

Inductive Hypothesis: Assume that Lemma is true for $n_r = k$, then $d^\circ\mathcal{F}^k = d^\circ\mathcal{F}^k_{\text{Type-I}}$ (maximum degree of SPN function $\mathcal{F}$ is $k\lambda$) and $d^\circ\mathcal{F}^k_{\text{Type-I}} > d^\circ\mathcal{F}^k_{\text{Type-II}}$

Inductive Step: Let $n_r = k+1$ then $\mathcal{F}^{k+1} = \mathcal{N} \circ \mathcal{C}^{k+1} \circ \mathcal{L} \circ \mathcal{F}^k$

$$\begin{aligned}d^\circ\mathcal{F}^{k+1}_{\text{Type-I}} &= d^\circ(\mathcal{N} \circ \mathcal{C}^{k+1} \circ \mathcal{L}) + d^\circ\mathcal{F}^k_{\text{Type-I}} \\ &> d^\circ(\mathcal{N} \circ \mathcal{C}^{k+1} \circ \mathcal{L}) + d^\circ\mathcal{F}^k_{\text{Type-II}} \;\; (\because d^\circ\mathcal{F}^k_{\text{Type-I}} > d^\circ\mathcal{F}^k_{\text{Type-II}}) \\ &> d^\circ\mathcal{F}^{k+1}_{\text{Type-II}}\end{aligned}$$

Hence, by induction, the Lemma holds $\forall n_r \in \mathbb{N}$. □

As a result, we obtain $d^\circ\mathcal{F}^{n_r} = d^\circ\mathcal{F}^{n_r}_{\text{Type-I}} > d^\circ\mathcal{F}^{n_r}_{\text{Type-II}}$, which indicates that even after swapping the non-linear operation with RCon addition, the highest degree monomial of $\mathcal{F}$ is of Type-I. Obtaining an upper bound on the maximum degree of the Type-II and understanding how it relates to the highest degree of the Type-I from Lemma 1 establishes the following:

Theorem 1. *The upper-bound on the degree of Type-II monomials is given by the following expression:* $d^\circ\mathcal{F}^{n_r}_{\text{Type-II}} \leq d^\circ\mathcal{F}^{n_r} - 1$

Proof. The proof is very similar to the proof of Lemma 1.

Lemma 2. *The* $d^\circ\mathcal{F}$*–fold vectorial derivative of* $\mathcal{F}^{n_r}$ *is a function which is unaffected by the* RCon.

This follows logically from Theorem 1 that $d^\circ\mathcal{F}$–fold vectorial derivative of $\mathcal{F}^{n_r}$ will give function without Type-II or Type-III monomials. Lemma 2, thus, leads us toward obtaining a RCon independent function. Later in this work, we demonstrate practical application of this Lemma in form of new SymSum distinguishers on real-world Type-LCN primitives namely Xoodoo and Xoodyak-Hash.

[2] In terms of the change in algebraic degree.

3.3 Algebraic Structure of Type-CLN SPN Cipher

Type-CLN is generated by iteratively applying the $\mathcal{N} \circ \mathcal{L} \circ \mathcal{C}$ sequence. When we apply $\mathcal{N} \circ \mathcal{L} \circ \mathcal{C}$ once, we get a polynomial of the following form.

$$\sum \prod_{\substack{x_u \in \mathbf{x}_w \subset X \\ c_v \in \mathbf{c}_s \subset C}} (x_u + c_v) = \sum_k \prod_{x_i \in \mathbf{x}_k \subset X} x_i + \sum \prod_{\substack{x_m \in \mathbf{x}_m \subset X \\ c_l \in \mathbf{c}_l \subset C}} x_m c_l + \sum_r \prod_{c_j \in \mathbf{c}_r \subset C} c_j \quad (4)$$

It easy to see that Eq. 4 is same as Eq. 2. Thus $\mathcal{N} \circ \mathcal{L} \circ \mathcal{C} \equiv \mathcal{N} \circ \mathcal{C} \circ \mathcal{L}$ in terms of the algebraic structure implying that $\mathcal{L} \circ \mathcal{C} \equiv \mathcal{C} \circ \mathcal{L}$ or alternatively $\mathcal{C}$ and $\mathcal{L}$ satisfy the commutative property. As a result, similar to the Type-LCN scenario, we can deduce that for Type-CLN, the highest degrees of Type-I, Type-II and Type-III monomials are λ, $\lambda - 1$ and 0, respectively. Thus Type-CLN follows all the properties of Type-LCN.

4 Concrete Applications of Type-LNC Xoodoo/Xoodyak-Hash

This section will explore how the concepts discussed in the preceding sections can be applied practically, specifically focusing on XOODOO/XOODYAK (brief description of XOODOO/XOODYAK is given in the Appendix A). To accomplish this, we will investigate the behaviour of XOODOO/ XOODYAK under symmetric-inputs. We will also analyze the benefits of utilizing SYMSUM over ZEROSUM distinguisher after deploying it on XOODOO/XOODYAK-HASH.

4.1 Multi-dimensional-Symmetric State

XOODOO is a permutation that operates on a 3-D array of 384 bits $(4 \times 3 \times 32)$ and applies a round function to the input state for a specified number of rounds (n_r), denoted as $X^{n_r} = \text{XOODOO}[384, n_r]$. S defines the internal state of X^{n_r}. In order to capture the notion of symmetry in the internal state of XOODOO/XOODYAK-HASH we will use the following definitions.

Definition 2. *Symmetric-Half-State* (SHS)*: A state that can be split into two identical halves is SHS. A SHS in* XOODOO *has a size of* 192 *bits and can be split in two directions:* H_{S_z} *along the z-axis with size* $4 \times 3 \times 16$ *and* H_{S_x} *along the x-axis with size* $2 \times 3 \times 32$.

Definition 3. *Multi-Dimensional-Symmetric State* (MDSS): *Each member of* $S^{\#}$ *is referred to as Multi-Dimensional-Symmetry if* $S^{\#}$ *is the set of all states in which both the conditions satisfy:*

$$H_{S_{x_1}} = H_{S_{x_2}} \textit{ and } H_{S_{z_1}} = H_{S_{z_2}} \quad (5)$$

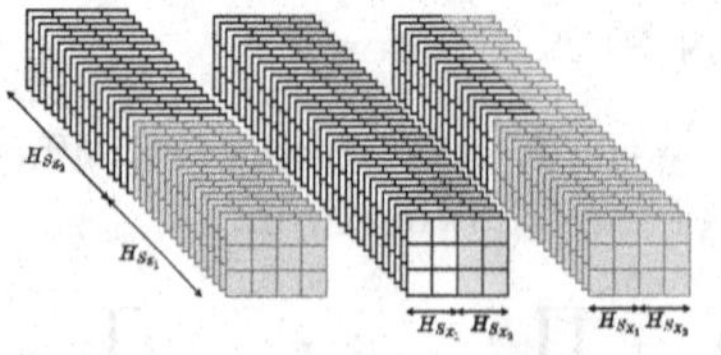

(a) Symmetry along z, x and both axes

8BED	8BED	**EC14**	EC14	**8BED**	8BED	**EC14**	EC14
5453	5453	**D705**	D705	**5453**	5453	**D705**	D705
51FF	51FF	**25D6**	25D6	**51FF**	51FF	**25D6**	25D6

(b) Self-Symmetric State with $H_{S_{z_1}}$ is shown in black and $H_{S_{z_2}}$ is shown in blue and $H_{S_{x_2}}$ is highlighted in yellow

Fig. 1. Exhibiting Self-Symmetric State (Color figure online)

Figure 1a depicts three symmetric states, each with unique symmetric characteristics. The leftmost state shows symmetry along the z–axis, where $H_{S_{z_1}}$ (red) is identical to $H_{S_{z_2}}$ (white). Similarly, state in the center has symmetry in x–axis in which first two sheets (white) are same as the other two (blue). The right-most state has symmetry in both x and z axes, with first 16 slices being identical to the last 16 slices and the first two columns in each slice being the same as the next two. This state is an example of MDSS in two directions. When symmetry is in one of the directions (x–axis or z–axis), it is clear from Definitions 2 that $|S^x| = |S^z| = 2^{192}$, where S^x and S^z have all states that have symmetry in the x–axis and z–axis, respectively, one of the examples is illustrated Table 2. When symmetry is in both the x–axis and z–axis, then $|S^{\#}| = 2^{96}$ (by Definition 3); one of the examples is given in Table 1b.

Table 2. Depicting the Self-Symmetric State in the x–axis with $H_{S_{x_1}}$ (black) and $H_{S_{x_2}}$ (blue) and the z–axis $H_{S_{z_1}}$ (black) and $H_{S_{z_2}}$ (highlighted in yellow).

Symmetry in z-axis				Symmetry in x-axis							
FFFA6482	DEEE4E3B	FFFA6482	DEEE4E3B	8BED	8BED	EC14	EC14	3B68	3B68	EF3F	EF3F
C2F49C55	F04F94D1	C2F49C55	F04F94D1	5453	5453	D705	D705	0C7F	0C7F	970A	970A
571AAB4A	335CD3F0	571AAB4A	335CD3F0	51FF	51FF	25D6	25D6	48A0	48A0	B154	B154

4.2 Distinguishing Attack Using Symmetric Property in Xoodoo

This section explores the behaviour of symmetry in Xoodoo. When a symmetric state is fed into Xoodoo, the output after one round displays near-symmetry because the ι function introduces asymmetry in some bits. As a result, we get an output symmetry of over 70% for up to two rounds. However, as the number of rounds increases, the symmetry diminishes from the third round. This property enables us to identify round-reduced Xoodoo. Therefore, with just one message, we can distinguish round-reduced Xoodoo up to two rounds.

Corollary 1. *The highest degree of a monomial including round-constant for n_r rounds of the* Xoodoo *permutation is $d^\circ \mathcal{K}^{n_r} - 1$.*

Proof. The XOODOO design $\mathcal{F}$ expresses as $\mathcal{F} = \mathcal{L}_2 \circ \mathcal{N} \circ \mathcal{C} \circ \mathcal{L}_1$, with linear components $\mathcal{L}_1$ and $\mathcal{L}_2$, non-linear component $\mathcal{N}$ and constant addition component $\mathcal{C}$. $\mathcal{F}^{n_r}$, the XOODOO-permutation in n_r rounds, unwraps as follows:

$$\begin{aligned}\mathcal{F} &= (\mathcal{L}_2 \circ \mathcal{N} \circ \mathcal{C}_{n_r} \circ \mathcal{L}_1) \circ \cdots \circ (\mathcal{L}_2 \circ \mathcal{N} \circ \mathcal{C}_2 \circ \mathcal{L}_1) \circ (\mathcal{L}_2 \circ \mathcal{N} \circ \mathcal{C}_1 \circ \mathcal{L}_1)\\ &= (\mathcal{L}_2 \circ \mathcal{N}) \circ \mathcal{C}_{n_r} \circ (\mathcal{L}_1 \circ \mathcal{L}_2) \circ \cdots \circ (\mathcal{L}_1 \circ \mathcal{L}_2) \circ \mathcal{N} \circ \mathcal{C}_2 \circ (\mathcal{L}_1 \circ \mathcal{L}_2) \circ \mathcal{N} \circ \mathcal{C}_1 \circ \mathcal{L}_1\\ &= (\mathcal{N}^{'} \circ \mathcal{C}_{n_r} \circ \mathcal{L}^{'}) \circ (\mathcal{N} \circ \mathcal{C}_{n_r-1} \circ \mathcal{L}^{'}) \circ \cdots \circ (\mathcal{N} \circ \mathcal{C}_2 \circ \mathcal{L}^{'}) \circ (\mathcal{N} \circ \mathcal{C}_1 \circ \mathcal{L}_1)\end{aligned}$$

Here, the composition of two linear functions always is a linear function denoted by $\mathcal{L}^{'}$(where $\mathcal{L}^{'} = \mathcal{L}_1 \circ \mathcal{L}_2$). Also, a nonlinear function followed by a linear function is a nonlinear function $\mathcal{N}^{'}$(where $\mathcal{N}^{'} = \mathcal{L}_2 \circ \mathcal{N}$). Therefore, one round of the XOODOO permutation can represent $\mathcal{N} \circ \mathcal{C} \circ \mathcal{L}$. Thus by Theorem 1, $d^\circ \mathcal{K}^{n_r} - 1$ is the highest degree of RCON dependent monomial for n_r rounds. □

Proposition 1. *While computing the d°XOODOO–fold vectorial derivative of the XOODOO's self-symmetric input states, the symmetric property will be maintained.*

As RCON addition disturbs symmetry, by Proposition 1 the symmetry will be preserved while computing (d°XOODOO)–fold vectorial derivative of XOODOO using self-symmetric inputs. However, this property is not assured for $m <$ (d°XOODOO). The experimental result for the theoretical claim is given in Sect. 5.

Degree of Freedom: There are 2^{384} ways to generate XOODOO states, but it must meet at least one of the two conditions from Eqs. (5) to produce a symmetric state. Thus, the maximum number of symmetric states is 2^{192} due to 192 conditions. By Corollary 1, (d°XOODOO)–fold vectorial derivatives are required for the symmetric state of XOODOO. Therefore, this distinguisher can be used on round-reduced XOODOO up to 7 rounds with complexity 2^{128}.

4.3 Extending the Distinguisher on Xoodoo Using Linearization

This section formalizes the idea of linearizing XOODOO for one round, inspired by the linear structure of KECCAK, proposed by Guo *et al.* in [17]. XOODOO's non-linear function χ acts on the column as $x_i \oplus (x_{i+1} \oplus 1) x_{i+2}$, where $i, i+1, i+2 \in \{0, 1, 2\}$. Thus to linearize χ, we must take at most one variable in a column. Moreover, to handle θ diffusion, we need to maintain state parity which can be achieved by following constraints.

$$A_{(0,0,*)} \oplus A_{(1,0,*)} = C_0 \quad (6)$$

$$A_{(0,2,*)} \oplus A_{(1,2,*)} = C_2 \quad (7)$$

Here, C_0 and C_1 are constants, lane $A_{(x,y,*)}$ is located at coordinate (x, y) and $*$ represents the entire lane of 32 bits. Equation (6) and (7) ensure a constant parity for the first and third sheet, respectively. Figure 2a illustrates the idea of linearizing XOODOO. The size of each cell in the figure is 1 byte for a clearer demonstration. The lanes with white cells are constant, while those with grey

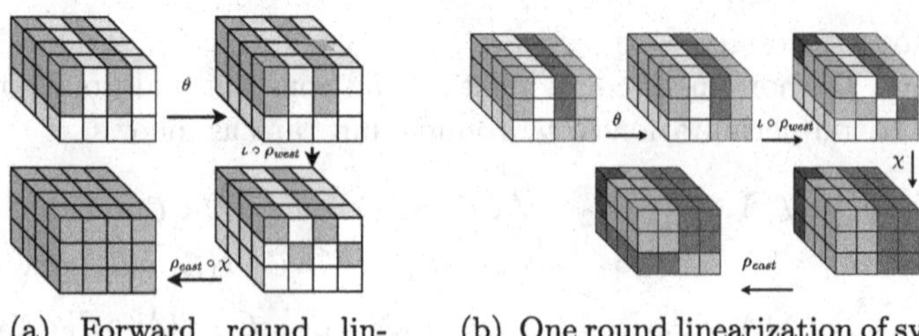

(a) Forward round linearization with 2^{64} DoF.

(b) One round linearization of symmetric state with 2^{32} DoF.

Fig. 2. Showing one round linearization of Xoodoo which is represented in bytes rather than in bits for brevity.

cells have an algebraic degree of 1, which meet the requirements of Eq. (6) and (7) to deal with θ.

Due to those conditions after θ, the number of elements with algebraic degree 1 remain the same. ι function does not affect degrees. However, for the subsequent operation, ρ_{west}, the bit positions change, aiding in maintaining the input to χ. As we can see in the Fig. 2a, the input to χ should have only linear terms in each column to maintain linearity of the state after χ. ρ_{east} does not impact the degree, only alters the positions.

Degree of Freedom: To linearize the state, we can take at most one bit in each column to handle χ. Thus total variable we can take is 128. These variables should satisfy 64 constraints to handle θ. As a result, we can have $2^{128-64} = 2^{64}$ such states that maintain the linearity for 1 round. Therefore, the degrees of freedom of such states is 2^{64}.

Linearization in Symmetric States: Both x and z axes can provide symmetry to the Xoodoo input. To linearize the symmetric input state, we need to apply the following equations.

$$A_{(x,*,*)} \oplus A_{(x+2,*,*)} = 0 \text{ where } x \in \{0,1\} \quad (8)$$

$$A_{(*,*,z)} \oplus A_{(*,*,z+16)} = 0 \text{ where } z \in \{0,1,\ldots,15\} \quad (9)$$

$$A_{(0,0,*)} \oplus A_{(1,0,*)} = C_0 \quad (10)$$

Here, $*$ in above equations represents all; more specifically, $*$ represents $x \in \{0,1,2,3\}; y \in \{0,1,2\}$; and $z \in \{0,1,\ldots,31\}$ on the x, y, and z axis, respectively. Here either Eq. (8) or Eq. (9) is used to provide symmetry in the direction of x or z axis and Eq. (10) handles θ for linearization.

Figure 2b depicts an overview of one round of linearization for symmetric input to Xoodoo, with the symmetry shown along x–axis. Here, purple and grey bytes are equal. Similarly, white and pink bytes are equal. White and pink cells are constants, and grey and purple cells have an algebraic degree 1. The initial state satisfies conditions stated in Eq. (8) and (10), ensuring that the plane's parity will be constant. As a result, the symmetry of the state is preserved after

θ. The symmetry is destroyed due to ι at lane $(0, 0)$ and the asymmetry induced due to ι is further propagated by χ as depicted in dark gray. Consequently, there is only one variable in each column. Thus, the highest degree of the state remains 1 after one round.

Lemma 3. *Lemma 1 holds under linearization.*

If the SPN round function $\mathcal{F}$ were to be linearized for l_r rounds, revised $\mathcal{F}'$ could be represented as:

$$\begin{aligned}\mathcal{F}' &= (\mathcal{N} \circ \mathcal{C}_{n_r} \circ \mathcal{L}) \circ (\mathcal{N} \circ \mathcal{C}_{n_r-1} \circ \mathcal{L}) \circ \cdots \circ (\mathcal{N} \circ \mathcal{C}_{n_r-l_r} \circ \mathcal{L}) \\ &\quad \circ (\mathcal{L}' \circ \mathcal{C}_{l_r} \circ \mathcal{L}) \circ \cdots \circ (\mathcal{L}' \circ \mathcal{C}_1 \circ \mathcal{L}) \\ &= \Big[(\mathcal{N} \circ \mathcal{C}_{n_r} \circ \mathcal{L}) \circ (\mathcal{N} \circ \mathcal{C}_{n_r-1} \circ \mathcal{L}) \circ \cdots \circ (\mathcal{N} \circ \mathcal{C}_{n_r-l_r} \circ \mathcal{L}) \\ &\quad \circ (\mathcal{L}' \circ \mathcal{C}_{l_r} \circ \mathcal{L}) \circ \cdots \circ (\mathcal{L}' \circ \mathcal{C}_1)\Big] \circ \mathcal{L} \end{aligned} \tag{11}$$

Here $\mathcal{L}'$ is a linearized version of $\mathcal{N}$. The lemma mentioned above can be trivially proved, by observing Eq. (11)

Theorem 2. *For an iterated SPN round function $\mathcal{F}$, the relationship between the upper bound on degree of Type-I and Type-II monomials will remain same after linearization such that: $d^\circ \mathcal{F}^{n_r}_{\textsf{Type-II}} \leq d^\circ \mathcal{F}^{n_r}_{\textsf{Type-I}} - 1$*

Lemma 1, Lemma 3, and Theorem 2 can be used to easily prove this Theorem.

Corollary 2. *With l_r linearized rounds $d^\circ \mathcal{F}$-fold vectorial derivative of $\mathcal{F}$ is a function which is independent of round constants.*

The symmetry will be retained by Corollary 2 when computing the d°Xoodoo-fold vectorial derivative of linearized Xoodoo with self-symmetric inputs. Section 5 provides the experimental outcome for theoretical claim.

Degree of Freedom: There are 2^{384} Xoodoo states, that can be generated, out of which 2^{192} symmetric states are possible. Nevertheless, due to the 32 conditions given in Eq. (10) that must be fulfilled to achieve 1-round linearization, it drops to $2^{192-32} = 2^{160}$. Thus, 2^{160} is the DoF for these states. Since there are four lanes of variables, each with a size of 32, we have 128 variables while fixing the constants. Due to symmetry, half of the variables should be same as the others because of Eq. (8) and (9) (one of them). However, for 1 round of linearization of Xoodoo, 32 conditions are required. As a result, we can have $2^{128-64-32} = 2^{32}$ states that maintain 1-round linearization while the input to Xoodoo is symmetric. Therefore, DoF of such states is 2^{32}.

Linearization in Backward Direction: The inside-out technique is widely recognized in the most well-known classical distinguishing attack ZeroSum to attack any permutation since it can start from the middle and move in both directions. We have also explored linearization in the backward direction, as shown in Fig. 3a. Instead of four lanes, we can use a single plane, as shown in the figure. Furthermore, this linearization method can be applied to symmetric states, as illustrated in Fig. 3b.

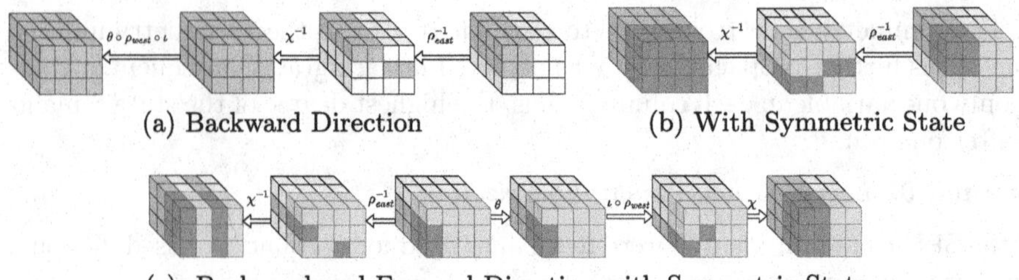

(a) Backward Direction (b) With Symmetric State

(c) Backward and Forward Direction with Symmetric State

Fig. 3. Linearization of Xoodoo

Extending SymSum Distinguisher in Xoodoo: Using the linearization technique symmetry property described in the preceding section can be extended to 1 additional round. We explain our approach by assuming symmetry along the x–axis. However, other directions can also be applied. To linearize 1-round along with fulfilling the essential condition for self-symmetry of Xoodoo, the input set must satisfy the following criteria (for details, see Sect. 4.3):

1. To maintain the input symmetry state should satisfy: $H_{S_{x_1}} = H_{S_{x_2}}$.
2. The constraint for linearization is $A_{(0,0,*)} \oplus A_{(1,0,*)} = C$ where $*$ define the whole lane, and C is a 32 bit constant.

Given the circumstances mentioned above, this state has a dimension of 32. As a result, this strategy can be used up to 6-round with a complexity of 2^{32}. Furthermore, there are 160 constant bits, each with a value of either 0 or 1. So, we can construct 2^{160} of such sets using various fixed values. Using linearization and inside-out technique, we have 16 degree of freedom. As a result, we can attack up to 10 (4–round backward + 1–round backward linearization + 1–round forward linearization + 4–round forward) rounds with complexity 2^{16}. To simultaneously visualize the linearization in a backward and forward direction, refer to Fig. 3c.

4.4 Adapting the Distinguisher on Xoodyak-Hash

Xoodyak combines the Cyclist mode of operation with the Xoodoo permutation, which is responsible for preparing the data before inputting it into Xoodoo and computing output according to required operation. For example, when calculating the digest in hash and keyed hash modes, domain separator value is set to `0x01` and `0x03`, respectively. Similarly, in other modes, the domain separator values differ. However, this study focuses on Xoodyak-Hash mode, which absorbs at most 16 bytes at a time, and `0x01` is added as a padding bit to indicate the end of input. Thus, to ensure input state is symmetric, we need to input 15 bytes with a fixed value of `0x01`. However, since we cannot control the capacity bytes and the Cyclist mode adds domain separator in the capacity portion of the state, our state *cannot* become fully symmetric and there will always be an asymmetric byte in the state. Table 3 shows the input state before and after the Cyclist mode. Xoodyak-Hash exhibits near-symmetry in its output when input has a

Table 3. Input to XOODYAK-HASH and intermediate state after cyclist operation

Input to Cyclist				input to XOODOO			
0E2E0E2E	0AAE0AAE	0C440C44	018001	0E2E0E2E	0AAE0AAE	0C440C44	01800180
00000000	00000000	00000000	00000000	00000000	00000000	00000000	00000000
00000000	00000000	00000000	00000000	00000000	00000000	00000000	00000080

near-symmetric state, but the symmetry is lost as the number of rounds increase. This property allows us to distinguish round-reduced XOODYAK-HASH with just one input message. The operations that disturb symmetry are RCON addition and domain separator. However, by Corollary 1, d°XOODOO–vectorial derivative of XOODOO is independent of round-constant addition, allowing us to observe near-symmetry in the (d°XOODOO)–fold vectorial derivative of XOODYAK-HASH when using near-symmetric input states. Experimental results conforming to the theoretical justifications are presented in Sect. 5.

Degree of Freedom: There are 2^{128} ways to generate XOODYAK-HASH states, but only those satisfying at least one condition from Eq. (3) result in a symmetric state. There are a maximum of 2^{64} symmetric states due to 64 conditions for symmetry generation. However, one additional condition is needed to handle the padding byte, limiting the number of possible states to 2^{56}. Therefore, DoF for XOODYAK-HASH symmetric states is 2^{56}, and Corollary 1 requires (d°XOODOO) vectorial derivatives. This distinguisher can be used on round-reduced XOODOO up to 5 rounds with a complexity of 2^{32}.

5 Experimental Verification

This section provides experimental proof for supporting the previous claims by demonstrating 1-round linearization of 4-rounds XOODOO. The degree for 4-rounds is reduced to $2^{4-1} = 8$ due to 1-round linearization, and in line with Corollary 2, vectorial derivative of the 8th order will possess the SYMSUM property. Figure 1 shows input state for XOODOO.

Table 4. Representing XOODOO/XOODYAK-HASH state and output Sum

<table>
<tr><td colspan="16">XOODYAK-HASH State</td></tr>
<tr><td colspan="8">Input State</td><td colspan="8">Output Sum</td></tr>
<tr><td>*E35</td><td>*E35</td><td>*041</td><td>*041</td><td>*9B6</td><td>*9B6</td><td>*B80</td><td>*B80</td><td>B68E</td><td>B68E</td><td>B68E</td><td>B68E</td><td>B68E</td><td>B68E</td><td>B68E</td><td>B68E</td></tr>
<tr><td>0000</td><td>0000</td><td>0000</td><td>0000</td><td>0000</td><td>0000</td><td>0000</td><td>0000</td><td>8C51</td><td>8C51</td><td>8C51</td><td>8C51</td><td>8C51</td><td>8C51</td><td>8C51</td><td>8C51</td></tr>
<tr><td>0000</td><td>0000</td><td>0000</td><td>0000</td><td>0000</td><td>0000</td><td>0000</td><td>0080</td><td>CA4F</td><td>CA4F</td><td>CA4F</td><td>CA4F</td><td>CA4F</td><td>CA4F</td><td>CA4F</td><td>CA4F</td></tr>
<tr><td colspan="16">XOODOO State</td></tr>
<tr><td colspan="8">Input State</td><td colspan="8">Output Sum</td></tr>
<tr><td colspan="2">********</td><td colspan="2">7E5B9440</td><td colspan="2">********</td><td colspan="2">7E5B9440</td><td colspan="2">B9D83814</td><td colspan="2">96F1AF94</td><td colspan="2">B9D83814</td><td colspan="2">96F1AF94</td></tr>
<tr><td colspan="2">††††††††</td><td colspan="2">24A2A799</td><td colspan="2">††††††††</td><td colspan="2">24A2A799</td><td colspan="2">A33C141F</td><td colspan="2">AB79F93C</td><td colspan="2">A33C141F</td><td colspan="2">AB79F93C</td></tr>
<tr><td colspan="2">14DA894E</td><td colspan="2">4642ACED</td><td colspan="2">14DA894E</td><td colspan="2">4642ACED</td><td colspan="2">B7ECCBF7</td><td colspan="2">5A5C712F</td><td colspan="2">B7ECCBF7</td><td colspan="2">5A5C712F</td></tr>
</table>

Table 4 shows the input state subspace of XOODYAK-HASH. Here the subspace is generated by setting all possible values to * while maintaining the symmetry in the z–axis. The text in black is dependent on the text in blue, which means that the first 16 slices are identical to the next 16 slices. This can be visualized by left most figure in Fig. 1a. While for the linearized Xoodoo state, the subspace is generated by setting all possible values to $*$ and $\dagger$ to maintain the parity of columns while maintaining the symmetry in the x–axis, which means that the first two sheets are identical to the next two sheets. In Table 4, text in blue is identical to blacktext, which can be visualized by the middle figure in Fig. 1a.

6 Conclusion

The current work thoroughly investigated the algebraic structure of SPN cipher with varying RCon ordering relative to the linear and non-linear layers of an SPN round-function. We also showed how our findings can be used in practice by mounting the SymSum distinguisher on Xoodoo/Xoodyak-Hash while achieving one of the most efficient distinguishers reported on Xoodyak-Hash so far - 5 rounds with 2^{32}. We demonstrated how symmetry propagation in Xoodoo/Xoodyak-Hash allows us to identify attacks with only one symmetric state for up to two rounds. Furthermore, regardless of the degree of nonlinear operation, we provided theoretical proof that the SymSum distinguisher outperforms the ZeroSum distinguisher by a factor of two. Finally, we applied linearization on Xoodoo, which resulted in a 10–round SymSum distinguisher with a complexity of 2^{16} leveraging the inside-out technique. Our research expands the understanding of SPN ciphers with regards to the relation of their algebraic structure and the influence of RCon on the highest degree monomials which we believe provides valuable insights for designing future cryptographic algorithms.

Acknowledgment. The first author receives financial assistance through the TCS Research Scholarship Programme (TCS RSP) thanks to the support of Tata Consultancy Services (TCS). We also thank Darunjeet Bag for his support with this research.

A Xoodoo Permutation [12]

Daemen *et al.* presented Xoodoo, a 48-byte cryptographic permutation at ToSC 2018, inspired by Keccak [9] and Gimli [7]. It operates on a $3D$ array of size $4 \times 3 \times 32$, where row, column, and lane refer to $1D$ arrays in the x, y, and z directions respectively. Slices, sheets, and planes illustrate the $2D$ arrays in (x, y), (y, z), and (x, z) planes. These arrays are 12–bits, 96–bits, and 128–bits in size. Figure 4 depicts all the terms described above.

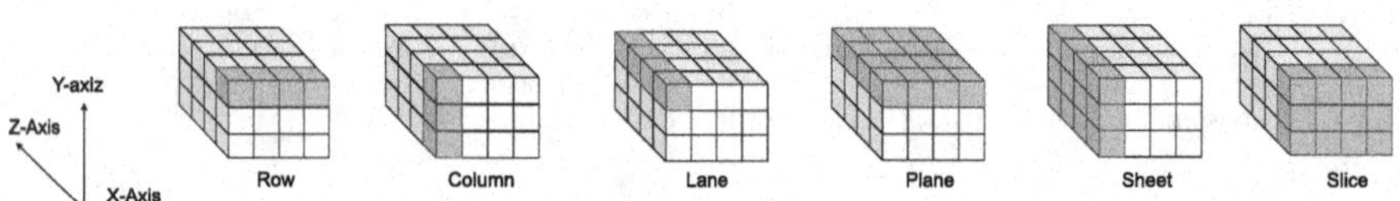

Fig. 4. The state displayed is of size 3×4×4 bytes, achieved by combining 8 cells into 1 for brevity, resulting in each cell of the state being of size 1 byte.

The XOODOO permutation is a sequence of iterations on a $3D$ XOODOO state using five different mappings: $X = \rho_{east} \circ \chi \circ \iota \circ \rho_{west} \circ \theta$. The θ mapping is responsible for diffusing the state linearly, while ρ_{west} and ρ_{east} rotate the bits of the planes in the x and z directions by specific values for each plane. Depending on the round number, the ι mapping adds a unique RCON to the first lane of plane A_0. The only non-linear function that operates on the plane is χ. All the sub-functions of the XOODOO round-function are listed below.

$$\theta : \begin{cases} A_y & = A_y \oplus E \text{ where } y \in \{0,1,2\} \\ E & = P \lll (1,5) \oplus P \lll (1,14) \\ P & = A_0 \oplus A_1 \oplus A_2 \end{cases}$$

$$\rho_{west} : \begin{cases} A_1 & = A_1 \lll (1,0) \\ A_2 & = A_2 \lll (0,11) \end{cases}$$

$$\iota : \begin{cases} A_0 = A_0 \oplus RC_i \end{cases}$$

$$\chi : \begin{cases} A_y & = A_y \oplus B_y \text{ where } y \in \{0,1,2\} \\ B_y & = \sim A_{y+1 \bmod 3} \cdot A_{y+2 \bmod 3} \end{cases}$$

$$\rho_{east} : \begin{cases} A_1 & = A_1 \lll (0,1) \\ A_2 & = A_2 \lll (2,8) \end{cases}$$

B Xoodyak-Hash [13]

XOODYAK-HASH, one of the ten NIST-LWC finalists, is a versatile cryptographic primitive combining sponge structure and XOODOO permutation based on an operational mode termed Cyclist. The number of rounds in XOODYAK-HASH is 12, which provides the designed primitive with a sufficient safety margin against all potential attacks. Both hash and keyed modes are available in XOODYAK-HASH. The block sizes for the hash, the input, and the output in keyed modes are set, respectively, by the R_{hash}, R_{kin}, and R_{kout} block sizes to the mode of operation Cyclist, which depends on cryptographic permutation.

The hash mode consumes input strings and squeezes digests. Depending on the input string length, the absorbing function is called more than once because it can only absorb up to 16 bytes at once, and depending on the data absorbed so far, Squeeze(l) outputs an l-byte, where $l = 128$ bits. The XOODYAK-HASH offers 128-bit security and, as a result, it generates 256-bits (32 bytes) of the digest by performing considerable squeeze operations, as seen in Fig. 5

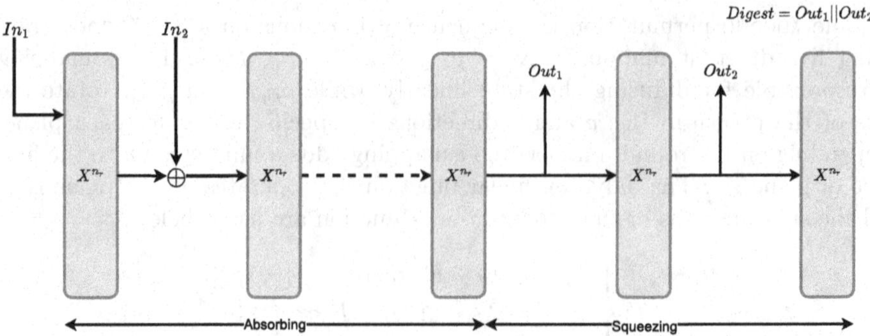

Fig. 5. This construction absorbs a variable input size and produces a 32-byte digest.

References

1. Caesar: Competition for authenticated encryption: security, applicability, and robustness. http://competitions.cr.yp.to/caesar.html
2. NIST Lwc: National institute of standards and technology lightweight cryptographic. https://csrc.nist.gov/Projects/lightweight-cryptography/finalists
3. Dworkin, M.J., Barker, E.B., Nechvatal, J.R., Foti, J.: Advanced encryption standard (AES) (2001). https://doi.org/10.6028/NIST.FIPS.197
4. Aumasson, J.P., Meier, W.: Zero-sum distinguishers for reduced Keccak-f and for the core functions of Luffa and Hamsi. In: Rump Session of Cryptographic Hardware and Embedded Systems-CHES 2009, p. 67 (2009)
5. Babbage, S., et al.: The eSTREAM portfolio. Citeseer (2008). https://www.ecrypt.eu.org/stream/
6. Bellini, E., Makarim, R.H.: Functional cryptanalysis: application to reduced-round Xoodoo. IACR Cryptology ePrint Archive, p. 134 (2022)
7. Bernstein, D.J., et al.: Gimli: a cross-platform permutation. In: Fischer, W., Homma, N. (eds.) CHES 2017. LNCS, vol. 10529, pp. 299–320. Springer, Cham (2017). https://doi.org/10.1007/978-3-319-66787-4_15
8. Bertoni, G., Daemen, J., Peeters, M., Assche, G.V.: The Keccak SHA-3 submission. Submission to NIST (Round 3) (2011). http://keccak.noekeon.org/Keccak-submission-3.pdf
9. Bertoni, G., Daemen, J., Peeters, M., Van Assche, G.: Keccak. In: Johansson, T., Nguyen, P.Q. (eds.) EUROCRYPT 2013. LNCS, vol. 7881, pp. 313–314. Springer, Heidelberg (2013). https://doi.org/10.1007/978-3-642-38348-9_19
10. Boura, C., Canteaut, A.: A zero-sum property for the Keccak-f permutation with 18 rounds. In: ISIT, pp. 2488–2492. IEEE (2010)
11. Boura, C., Canteaut, A., De Cannière, C.: Higher-order differential properties of Keccak and *Luffa*. In: Joux, A. (ed.) FSE 2011. LNCS, vol. 6733, pp. 252–269. Springer, Heidelberg (2011). https://doi.org/10.1007/978-3-642-21702-9_15
12. Daemen, J., Hoffert, S., Assche, G.V., Keer, R.V.: The design of Xoodoo and Xoofff. IACR Trans. Symmetric Cryptol. **2018**(4), 1–38 (2018)
13. Daemen, J., Hoffert, S., Peeters, M., Assche, G.V., Keer, R.V.: Xoodyak, a lightweight cryptographic scheme. IACR Trans. Symmetric Cryptol. **2020**(S1), 60–87 (2020)

14. Daemen, J., Rijmen, V.: The block cipher Rijndael. In: Quisquater, J.-J., Schneier, B. (eds.) CARDIS 1998. LNCS, vol. 1820, pp. 277–284. Springer, Heidelberg (2000). https://doi.org/10.1007/10721064_26
15. Duan, M., Lai, X.: Improved zero-sum distinguisher for full round Keccak-f permutation. IACR Cryptology ePrint Archive, p. 23 (2011)
16. Dunkelman, O., Weizman, A.: Differential-linear cryptanalysis on Xoodyak. In: NIST Lightweight Cryptography Workshop (2022)
17. Guo, J., Liu, M., Song, L.: Linear structures: applications to cryptanalysis of round-reduced Keccak. In: Cheon, J.H., Takagi, T. (eds.) ASIACRYPT 2016. LNCS, vol. 10031, pp. 249–274. Springer, Heidelberg (2016). https://doi.org/10.1007/978-3-662-53887-6_9
18. Hu, K., Peyrin, T.: Revisiting higher-order differential(-linear) attacks from an algebraic perspective - applications to Ascon, Grain v1, Xoodoo, and ChaCha. IACR Cryptology ePrint Archive, p. 1335 (2022)
19. Liu, F., Isobe, T., Meier, W., Yang, Z.: Algebraic attacks on round-reduced Keccak/Xoodoo. IACR Cryptology ePrint Archive, p. 346 (2020)
20. Liu, Y., Sun, S., Li, C.: Rotational cryptanalysis from a differential-linear perspective. In: Canteaut, A., Standaert, F.-X. (eds.) EUROCRYPT 2021. LNCS, vol. 12696, pp. 741–770. Springer, Cham (2021). https://doi.org/10.1007/978-3-030-77870-5_26
21. Posthoff, C., Steinbach, B.: Logic Functions and Equations: Binary Models for Computer Science. Springer, New York (2004). https://doi.org/10.1007/978-1-4020-2938-7
22. Saha, D., Kuila, S., Chowdhury, D.R.: SymSum: symmetric-sum distinguishers against round reduced SHA3. IACR Trans. Symmetric Cryptol. **2017**, 240–258 (2017)
23. Suryawanshi, S., Saha, D., Sachan, S.: New results on the `SymSum` distinguisher on round-reduced `SHA3`. In: Nitaj, A., Youssef, A. (eds.) AFRICACRYPT 2020. LNCS, vol. 12174, pp. 132–151. Springer, Cham (2020). https://doi.org/10.1007/978-3-030-51938-4_7

Invited Paper: Detection of False Data Injection Attacks in Power Systems Using a Secured-Sensors and Graph-Based Method

Gal Morgenstern[1(✉)], Lital Dabush[1], Jip Kim[2], James Anderson[3], Gil Zussman[3], and Tirza Routtenberg[1]

[1] Ben Gurion University of the Negev, 84105 Beer-Sheva, Israel
galmo@post.bgu.ac.il
[2] KENTECH, Naju-si, South Korea
[3] Columbia University, New York, NY, USA

Abstract. False data injection (FDI) attacks pose a significant threat to the reliability of power system state estimation (PSSE). Recently, graph signal processing (GSP)-based detectors have been shown to enable the detection of well-designed cyber attacks named unobservable FDI attacks. However, current detectors, including GSP-based detectors, do not consider the impact of secured sensors on the detection process; thus, they may have limited power, especially in the low signal-to-noise ratio (SNR) regime. In this paper, we propose a novel FDI attack detection method that incorporates both knowledge of the locations of secured sensors and the GSP properties of power system states (voltages). We develop the secured-sensors-and-graph-Laplacian-based generalized likelihood ratio test (SSGL-GLRT) that integrates the secured data and the graph smoothness properties of the state variables. Furthermore, we introduce a generalization of the method that allows the use of different high-pass GSP filters together with prior knowledge of the locations of the secured sensors. Then, we develop the SSGL-GLRT for a distributed PSSE based on the alternating direction method of multipliers (ADMM). Numerical simulations demonstrate that the proposed method significantly improves the probability of detecting FDI attacks compared to existing GSP-based detectors, achieving an increase of up to 30% in the detection probability for the same false alarm rate by integrating secured sensor location information.

Keywords: Graph signal processing (GSP) · false data injection (FDI) attack detection · secured sensors · power system state estimation (PSSE) · cyber-physical systems · distributed detection

1 Introduction

Smart grids integrate traditional power system components with advanced information and communication technology (ICT), providing critical cyber-physical

S. Dolev and B. Schieber (Eds.): SSS 2023, LNCS 14310, pp. 240–258, 2023.
https://doi.org/10.1007/978-3-031-44274-2_18

infrastructure [43]. However, this also makes them vulnerable to cyber attacks [40–42], particularly false data injection (FDI) attacks, where an attacker corrupts measurements and injects fake information into the system. FDI attacks may inflict severe damage that ranges from economic consequences to the destruction of grid devices [14,23,24,47,48] by influencing the critical power system state estimation (PSSE) process, which provides grid monitoring signals for power system operations [26,27]. PSSE is typically equipped with residual-based bad data detection (BDD) capabilities and, therefore can identify faulty data and random faults [27]. However, a well-designed, unobservable FDI attack can bypass the conventional residual-based BDD [21,25]. Therefore, developing advanced tools to detect unobservable FDI attacks is crucial to maintaining high power supply quality and stable system operation.

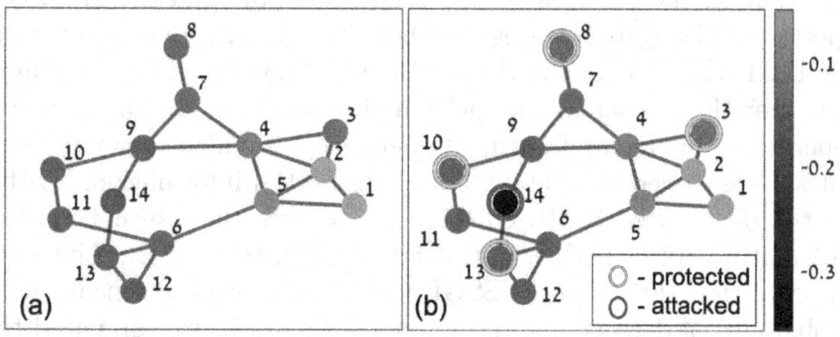

Fig. 1. Graph representation of IEEE 14-bus system. The node color represents the value of the states (voltage phases). In (a), the grid is not under attack, whereas in (b), node 14 is attacked (red circle), and nodes $\{3, 8, 10, 13\}$ are protected (green circles). It can be seen that the unattacked grid state is much smoother than the attacked grid state, i.e., the states of connected buses tend to be similar. (Color figure online)

In the past decade, various methods have been proposed for the detection of unobservable FDI attacks. Some methods utilize a set of protected measurements or synchronized phasor measurement units [2,6,19,20]. Specifically, these works aim to find the best locations for the protected sensors. Machine learning-based methods have been proposed, but they require a large, stationary, and reliable database of data, which is often not available [10,12,18,44]. Sparse methods were proposed in [28,34]. However, these methods impose assumptions on the stationary and structural characteristics of the system loads, such as the lack of correlation with the system topology and the sparse nature of the attack in the time domain, which may not be true in real-world situations. Additionally, previous studies, such as [17,31,46], investigated the use of BDD and cyber attacks to compromise the distributed PSSE. Furthermore, graph signal processing (GSP) methods have been demonstrated to be useful for the detection of failures, topology changes, and FDI attacks [4,5,9,11,29,33,37,38]. Despite this, incorporating information on secured sensor locations into FDI detection designs has not yet been explored either in centralized or in distributed frameworks. Additionally, the use of GSP properties for FDI detection remains at a preliminary stage and has not been fully investigated.

In this study, we present a novel approach for the detection of unobservable FDI attacks in power systems in the presence of secured sensors that are assumed to be immune to adversarial cyber attacks. These sensors with secured measurements can be obtained by additional validation processes by methods such as encryption, continuous monitoring, and separation from the Internet [20]. Our approach leverages the fact that the system states are known to be smooth graph signals [8,9,33], as illustrated in Fig. 1. Moreover, our approach is distinguished from existing GSP-based detectors by its ability to incorporate prior knowledge on the locations of the secured sensors. We formulate the hypothesis testing for this setting and derive the secured-sensors-and-graph-Laplacian-based generalized likelihood ratio test (SSGL-GLRT) that incorporates both the information on the locations of the secured-sensors and the graph smoothness properties of the system states. Furthermore, we introduce a generalization of the SSGL-GLRT by replacing the graph smoothness measure with any high-pass graph filter. The considered model can also accommodate distributed power system operation. In this approach, the network is divided into interconnected areas that are controlled separately, but share partial information. To this end, we derive the distributed SSGL-GLRT, that utilizes the alternating detection method of multipliers (ADMM) optimization algorithm in [3]. The numerical results indicate that the proposed SSGL-GLRT with secured sensors achieves a higher probability of detection and a lower false alarm rate, compared to existing methods, in the presence of secured sensors. This is due to the fact that the SSGL-GLRT exploits the graph smoothness property of the states as well as the knowledge of unattacked measurements.

In the following, vectors and matrices are denoted by boldface lowercase and uppercase letters, respectively. The mth element of the vector $\mathbf{a}$ and the $(m,q)^{\text{th}}$ element of the matrix $\mathbf{A}$ are denoted by a_m and $A_{m,q}$, respectively. Similarly, $\mathbf{a}_\Lambda$ is a subvector of $\mathbf{a}$ with the elements indexed by Λ. The matrix $\mathbf{I}$ and the vector $\mathbf{0}$ denote the identity matrix and the zero vector, respectively, with appropriate dimensions, and $||\cdot||$ denotes the Euclidean l_2-norm of vectors.

2 Model

The power system is represented by an undirected weighted graph, $\mathcal{G}(\mathcal{V},\xi)$, where $\mathcal{V}$ is the set of N nodes (bus and/or generators), and ξ is the set of edges (transmission lines) between the nodes. In this graph representation of the power system, it can be shown that the nodal admittance matrix is a graph Laplacian matrix. The (k,l)th element of $\mathbf{B}$ is given by [27]

$$B_{k,l} = \begin{cases} -\sum_{n\in\mathcal{N}_k} b_{k,n}, & k = l \\ b_{k,l}, & (k,l)\in\xi \\ 0, & \text{otherwise} \end{cases}, \quad \forall k,l = 1,\dots,N, \tag{1}$$

where $\mathcal{N}_k$ is the set of buses connected to bus k and $b_{k,n} < 0$ is the susceptance of line $(k, n) \in \xi$.

The power system is governed by the nonlinear power flow equations, which are often approximated by the linearized DC model [27]. We consider the attacked and noisy DC model:

$$\mathbf{z} = \mathbf{H}\boldsymbol{\theta} + \mathbf{a} + \mathbf{e}, \tag{2}$$

where the active power measurements, $\mathbf{z} \in \mathbb{R}^M$, are corrupted by an additive FDI attack, $\mathbf{a} \in \mathbb{R}^M$, and by measurement noise, $\mathbf{e} \in \mathbb{R}^M$, which is assumed to be a zero-mean Gaussian vector with covariance matrix $\mathbf{R}$. The matrix $\mathbf{H} \in \mathbb{R}^{M \times N}$ is a known full-rank matrix, which is determined by the network topology and by the admittance matrix [27]. It should be noted that the matrix $\mathbf{B}$ from (1) is a submatrix of $\mathbf{H}$ from (2) that is associated with the power injection meters. Finally, the system states, i.e., the voltage phases, are denoted by $\boldsymbol{\theta} \in \mathbb{R}^N$.

In the GSP literature, signals measured over the nodes of the graph are assumed to be smooth w.r.t. the Laplacian matrix [7,15,22,35,39,45,49]. In the context of power systems, it was shown in [4,9,32] that the system states are smooth graph signals, i.e.

$$TV_{\mathcal{G}}(\boldsymbol{\theta}) \stackrel{\triangle}{=} \boldsymbol{\theta}^T \mathbf{B} \boldsymbol{\theta} \leq \varepsilon_1, \tag{3}$$

where $\varepsilon_1 > 0$ is small relative to all other parameters in the system. By substituting (1) in (3), we obtain

$$TV_{\mathcal{G}}(\boldsymbol{\theta}) = \frac{1}{2} \sum_{k=1}^{N} \sum_{n \in \mathcal{N}_k} B_{k,n} (\theta_k - \theta_n)^2. \tag{4}$$

Roughly speaking, the smoothness property in (3), also referred to as graph total variation (TV), implies that the signal values (states in power systems) associated with the end nodes of edges with high weights in the graph (buses with large susceptance values) tend to be similar. In particular, the voltage angles of connected buses are similar.

The FDI attack, $\mathbf{a} \in \mathbb{R}^M$, is considered to be an unobservable FDI attack [25], i.e. it satisfies

$$\mathbf{a} = \mathbf{H}\mathbf{c}, \tag{5}$$

where $\mathbf{c} \in \mathbb{R}^N$ is an arbitrary vector. As a result, the attack $\mathbf{a}$ is in the range of $\mathbf{H}$. It is known that the attack described in (5) surpasses classical BDD methods [21].

3 GSP-Based FDI Detection with Secured Sensors

In this section, we design the SSGL-GLRT for detecting unobservable FDI attacks in the presence of secured measurements. In particular, it is assumed that a subset of the measurements is more reliable as these measurements are equipped with additional protection measures, e.g. encryption, continuous monitoring, and separation from the Internet [20]. This set of protected sensors may encompass generator nodes, which are typically highly secured, and/or specific locations that were chosen based on a defense policy against FDI attacks. The SSGL-GLRT is based on the generalized likelihood ratio test (GLRT). Specifically, we consider the following hypothesis test associated with the model from Sect. 2:

$$\begin{cases} \mathcal{H}_0 : \mathbf{a} = \mathbf{0} \\ \mathcal{H}_1 : \mathbf{a} \neq \mathbf{0}. \end{cases}$$

To this end, we derive the secured-sensors-and-graph-Laplacian-based maximum likelihood estimator (SSGL-ML) of the states in Subsect. 3.1. Subsequently, we use the SSGL-ML to derive the SSGL-GLRT in Subsect. 3.2, and discuss its properties in Subsect. 3.3.

3.1 SSGL-MLE

As stated at the beginning of this section, a subset of measurements, $\Lambda \subset \{1, \ldots, M\}$, is assumed highly secured. From the point of view of an adversary, this assumption implies that the measurements in the subset Λ cannot be attacked:

$$\mathbf{a}_\Lambda = \mathbf{0}. \tag{6}$$

From the defender's perspective, we assume that constraint (6) is relaxed and replaced by the following assumption:

$$||\mathbf{a}_\Lambda||^2 = ||\mathbf{Ma}||^2 \leq \varepsilon_2, \tag{7}$$

where ε_2 is small relative to the other parameters in the system and $\mathbf{M}$ is a diagonal mask matrix with the diagonal elements

$$M_{i,i} = \begin{cases} 1 & i \in \Lambda \\ 0 & i \notin \Lambda. \end{cases}$$

Assumption (7) implies that the attack, $\mathbf{a}$, has relatively small absolute values over the sensors in the set $\Lambda \subset \mathcal{M}$. This assumption permits flexibility in the case where some sensors in the set Λ are affected by random bad data (not originated by an attack), and makes the system more robust to small misspecifications or perturbations of Λ.

The SSGL-ML is a PSSE method with prior knowledge about the locations of the secured measurements and the graph smoothness properties of the system states [4,9,33]. The SSGL-ML is solved by maximizing the following regularized log-likelihood function over the system state variables $\boldsymbol{\theta}$ and the FDI attack $\mathbf{a}$:

$$\begin{aligned} \mathcal{Q}^{SSGL}(\boldsymbol{\theta}, \mathbf{a}) = &- (\mathbf{z} - \mathbf{H}\boldsymbol{\theta} - \mathbf{a})^T \mathbf{R}^{-1} (\mathbf{z} - \mathbf{H}\boldsymbol{\theta} - \mathbf{a}) \\ &- \mu_1 \boldsymbol{\theta}^T \mathbf{B} \boldsymbol{\theta} - \mu_2 ||\mathbf{Ma}||^2, \end{aligned} \tag{8}$$

where $\mu_1 > 0$ and $\mu_2 > 0$ are regularization parameters. These parameters enable the system operator to adjust the importance of each of the regularization functions. Note that the log-likelihood function in (8) is a concave function (see Appendix), and thus, the solution to the SSGL-ML is obtained by solving the normal equations. This function is equivalent to the standard PSSE log-likelihood function with two additional regularization terms:

R.1 Graph-Laplacian regularization ($\mu_1 \boldsymbol{\theta}^T \mathbf{B} \boldsymbol{\theta}$): A graph smoothness regularization term that incorporates the smoothness of the states in (3). This allows us to make a distinction between the system states, which are considered smooth, and the non-smooth FDI attack.

R.2 Secured-sensors regularization ($\mu_2 ||\mathbf{Ma}||^2$): An energy regularization function that incorporates the information on the locations of the secured sensors by using (7). This allows further distinction between the signal $\mathbf{H}\boldsymbol{\theta}$, which is a non-sparse signal with energy across all sensor positions, and the low-energy attack.

We now derive the SSGL-ML for the state vector, $\boldsymbol{\theta}$, and the attack vector, $\mathbf{a}$, based on the regularized log-likelihood function in (8). Later, these estimators will be used for deriving the GLRT in Subsect. 3.2. We first consider the null hypothesis, $\mathcal{H}_0$, i.e. there is no attack ($\mathbf{a} = \mathbf{0}$). By substituting $\mathbf{a} = \mathbf{0}$ in (8), we obtain that under hypothesis $\mathcal{H}_0$, the SSGL-ML of $\boldsymbol{\theta}$ is

$$\begin{aligned}\hat{\boldsymbol{\theta}}^{\text{SSGL-ML}}_{|\mathcal{H}_0} &= \arg\min_{\boldsymbol{\theta}\in\mathbb{R}^N} -\mathcal{Q}^{SSGL}(\boldsymbol{\theta}, \mathbf{a} = \mathbf{0}) \\ &= \arg\min_{\boldsymbol{\theta}\in\mathbb{R}^N} (\mathbf{z} - \mathbf{H}\boldsymbol{\theta})^T \mathbf{R}^{-1} (\mathbf{z} - \mathbf{H}\boldsymbol{\theta}) + \mu_1 \boldsymbol{\theta}^T \mathbf{B} \boldsymbol{\theta} \\ &= \mathbf{K}^{\boldsymbol{\theta}} \mathbf{z}, \end{aligned} \tag{9}$$

where the gain matrix is given by

$$\mathbf{K}^{\boldsymbol{\theta}} \triangleq (\mathbf{H}^T \mathbf{R}^{-1} \mathbf{H} + \mu_1 \mathbf{B})^{-1} \mathbf{H}^T \mathbf{R}^{-1}. \tag{10}$$

The SSGL-ML estimator in (9)–(10) coincides with the GSP weighted least squares (GSP-WLS) estimator from [4].

Under hypothesis $\mathcal{H}_1$, when it is known that $\mathbf{a} \neq \mathbf{0}$, the SSGL-ML for both $\boldsymbol{\theta}$ and $\mathbf{a}$ is given by

$$(\hat{\boldsymbol{\theta}}^{\text{SSGL-ML}}_{|\mathcal{H}_1}, \hat{\mathbf{a}}^{\text{SSGL-ML}}_{|\mathcal{H}_1}) = \arg\min_{\boldsymbol{\theta}\in\mathbb{R}^N, \mathbf{a}\in\mathbb{R}^M} -\mathcal{Q}^{SSGL}(\boldsymbol{\theta}, \mathbf{a}). \tag{11}$$

Since $-\mathcal{Q}^{SSGL}(\boldsymbol{\theta}, \mathbf{a})$ from (8) is convex (see Appendix), the estimators of $\boldsymbol{\theta}$ and $\mathbf{a}$ can be computed by the following normal equations:

$$\mathbf{a} = \mathbf{K}^{\mathbf{a}} (\mathbf{z} - \mathbf{H}\boldsymbol{\theta}) \tag{12}$$

$$\boldsymbol{\theta} = \mathbf{K}^{\boldsymbol{\theta}} (\mathbf{z} - \mathbf{a}), \tag{13}$$

where $\mathbf{K}^{\boldsymbol{\theta}}$ is defined in (10) and

$$\mathbf{K}^{\mathbf{a}} = (\mathbf{R}^{-1} + \mu_2 \mathbf{M})^{-1} \mathbf{R}^{-1}. \tag{14}$$

Substituting (12) into (13) results in

$$\hat{\boldsymbol{\theta}}^{\text{SSGL-ML}}_{|\mathcal{H}_1} = \mathbf{A}^{\theta}\mathbf{z}, \tag{15}$$

where

$$\mathbf{A}^{\theta} \triangleq (\mathbf{I} - \mathbf{K}^{\theta}\mathbf{K}^{\text{a}}\mathbf{H})^{-1}\mathbf{K}^{\theta}(\mathbf{I} - \mathbf{K}^{\text{a}}). \tag{16}$$

Substituting (15) in (12) results in

$$\hat{\mathbf{a}}^{\text{SSGL-ML}}_{|\mathcal{H}_1} = \mathbf{K}^{\text{a}}(\mathbf{I} - \mathbf{H}\mathbf{A}^{\theta})\mathbf{z}. \tag{17}$$

The MLEs of $\boldsymbol{\theta}$ and $\mathbf{a}$ given in (9), (15), and (17), are used in the next subsection to derive the SSGL-GLRT.

3.2 SSGL-GLRT

The SSGL-GLRT is the difference between the regularized log-likelihood function from (8) under $\mathcal{H}_1$ and under $\mathcal{H}_0$ [16]:

$$T^{\text{SSGL-GLRT}}(\mathbf{z}) = \mathcal{Q}^{SSGL}(\hat{\boldsymbol{\theta}}^{\text{SSGL-ML}}_{|\mathcal{H}_1}, \hat{\mathbf{a}}^{\text{SSGL-ML}}_{|\mathcal{H}_1}) - \mathcal{Q}^{SSGL}(\hat{\boldsymbol{\theta}}^{\text{SSGL-ML}}_{|\mathcal{H}_0}, \mathbf{0}). \tag{18}$$

By using (15) and (17), we obtain

$$\begin{aligned} \mathcal{Q}^{SSGL}(\hat{\boldsymbol{\theta}}^{\text{SSGL-ML}}_{|\mathcal{H}_1}, \hat{\mathbf{a}}^{\text{SSGL-ML}}_{|\mathcal{H}_1}) = &- (\mathbf{z} - \mathbf{H}\mathbf{A}^{\theta}\mathbf{z} - \mathbf{K}^{\text{a}}(\mathbf{I} - \mathbf{H}\mathbf{A}^{\theta})\mathbf{z})^T\mathbf{R}^{-1} \\ &\times (\mathbf{z} - \mathbf{H}\mathbf{A}^{\theta}\mathbf{z} - \mathbf{K}^{\text{a}}(\mathbf{I} - \mathbf{H}\mathbf{A}^{\theta})\mathbf{z}) \\ &- \mu_1(\mathbf{A}^{\theta}\mathbf{z})^T\mathbf{B}\mathbf{A}^{\theta}\mathbf{z} - \mu_2||\mathbf{M}\mathbf{K}^{\text{a}}(\mathbf{I} - \mathbf{H}\mathbf{A}^{\theta})\mathbf{z}||^2. \end{aligned} \tag{19}$$

Similarly, using (9), we obtain

$$\begin{aligned} \mathcal{Q}^{SSGL}(\hat{\boldsymbol{\theta}}^{\text{SSGL-ML}}_{|\mathcal{H}_0}, \mathbf{0}) = &- (\mathbf{z} - \mathbf{H}\mathbf{K}^{\theta}\mathbf{z})^T\mathbf{R}^{-1}(\mathbf{z} - \mathbf{H}\mathbf{K}^{\theta}\mathbf{z}) \\ &- \mu_1(\mathbf{K}^{\theta}\mathbf{z})^T\mathbf{B}\mathbf{K}^{\theta}\mathbf{z}. \end{aligned} \tag{20}$$

Substituting (19) and (20) in (18), results in

$$T^{\text{SSGL-GLRT}}(\mathbf{z}) = \mathbf{z}^T\mathbf{G}\mathbf{z}, \tag{21}$$

where

$$\begin{aligned} \mathbf{G} \triangleq\, &(\mathbf{I} - \mathbf{H}\mathbf{K}^{\theta})^T\mathbf{R}^{-1}(\mathbf{I} - \mathbf{H}\mathbf{K}^{\theta}) - (\mathbf{I} - \mathbf{H}\mathbf{A}^{\theta})^T(\mathbf{I} - \mathbf{K}^{\text{a}})^T\mathbf{R}^{-1} \\ &\times (\mathbf{I} - \mathbf{K}^{\text{a}})(\mathbf{I} - \mathbf{H}\mathbf{A}^{\theta}) + \mu_1((\mathbf{K}^{\theta})^T\mathbf{B}\mathbf{K}^{\theta} - (\mathbf{A}^{\theta})^T\mathbf{B}\mathbf{A}^{\theta}) \\ &- \mu_2(\mathbf{I} - \mathbf{H}\mathbf{A}^{\theta})^T(\mathbf{K}^{\text{a}})^T\mathbf{M}\mathbf{K}^{\text{a}}(\mathbf{I} - \mathbf{H}\mathbf{A}^{\theta}). \end{aligned} \tag{22}$$

The SSGL-GLRT in (21) is a weighted energy detector, where the weight matrix $\mathbf{G}$ in (22) is composed of five components: The first and second components evaluate the estimation accuracy of the SSGL-ML under hypotheses $\mathcal{H}_0$ and $\mathcal{H}_1$, respectively, w.r.t. the input measurements. The third and fourth components evaluate the smoothness of the estimated state vector under hypotheses

$\mathcal{H}_0$ and $\mathcal{H}_1$, respectively. Finally, the fifth component evaluates the compliance of the estimated attack with the assumption in (7).

The computational complexity of the detector proposed in (21)–(22) can be separated into two parts: the online and offline operations. Online, it is required to compute (21) given the $M \times M$ matrix $\mathbf{G}$ and the $M \times 1$ vector $\mathbf{z}$. In this case, the number of multiplications is in order of $O(M^2)$ when $\mathbf{G}$ is dense and unstructured. Offline, it is required to calculate the matrix $\mathbf{G}$ defined in (22). In this case, the most demanding procedure is the inverse of $\mathbf{R}$, which is an $M \times M$ matrix. Thus, the computational complexity is in order of $O(M^3)$ when $\mathbf{R}$ is dense and unstructured.

3.3 Special Cases

In the following, we present a few special cases of the SSGL-GLRT.

C.1 No regularization ($\mu_1 = \mu_2 = 0$): By substituting $\mu_1 = 0$ and $\mu_2 = 0$ in (10) and (14), we obtain

$$\mathbf{K}^{\boldsymbol{\theta}} = \mathbf{K} \triangleq (\mathbf{H}^T\mathbf{R}\mathbf{H})^{-1}\mathbf{H}^T\mathbf{R}^{-1}$$

and $\mathbf{K}^{\mathrm{a}} = \mathbf{I}$, respectively. Substituting these results and $\mu_1 = \mu_2 = 0$ in (22), results in

$$\mathbf{G} = (\mathbf{I} - \mathbf{H}\mathbf{K})^T\mathbf{R}^{-1}(\mathbf{I} - \mathbf{H}\mathbf{K}). \tag{23}$$

By substituting (23) in (21), one obtains the $J(\boldsymbol{\theta})$-test [27]:

$$T^{\mathrm{BDD}}(\mathbf{z}) = \mathbf{z}^T(\mathbf{I} - \mathbf{H}\mathbf{K})^T\mathbf{R}^{-1}(\mathbf{I} - \mathbf{H}\mathbf{K})\mathbf{z}. \tag{24}$$

It is known that the BDD detector in (24) cannot detect unobservable FDI attacks as defined in (5) (see e.g. [21,25]).

C.2 Only Laplacian-based regularization ($\mu_1 > 0$, $\mu_2 = 0$): When $\mu_2 = 0$, similarly to in **C.1**, we obtain that $\mathbf{K}^{\mathrm{a}} = \mathbf{I}$. By substituting this result and $\mu_2 = 0$ into (16), we get $\mathbf{A}^{\boldsymbol{\theta}} = \mathbf{0}$. Thus, in this case, (22) is reduced to

$$\mathbf{G} = (\mathbf{I} - \mathbf{H}\mathbf{K}^{\boldsymbol{\theta}})^T\mathbf{R}^{-1}(\mathbf{I} - \mathbf{H}\mathbf{K}^{\boldsymbol{\theta}}) + \mu_1(\mathbf{K}^{\boldsymbol{\theta}})^T\mathbf{B}\mathbf{K}^{\boldsymbol{\theta}}. \tag{25}$$

Finally, substitution of (25) in (21) results in

$$\begin{aligned} T^{\text{GL-GLRT}}(\mathbf{z}) =& \mathbf{z}^T(\mathbf{I} - \mathbf{H}\mathbf{K}^{\boldsymbol{\theta}})^T\mathbf{R}^{-1}(\mathbf{I} - \mathbf{H}\mathbf{K}^{\boldsymbol{\theta}})^T\mathbf{z} \\ &+ \mu_1\mathbf{z}^T(\mathbf{K}^{\boldsymbol{\theta}})^T\mathbf{B}\mathbf{K}^{\boldsymbol{\theta}}\mathbf{z}, \end{aligned} \tag{26}$$

which is the graph-Laplacian-regularized GLRT (GL-GLRT) from [5]: that only considers the prior on the smoothness of the states.

C.3 Only secured-sensors-based regularization ($\mu_1 = 0$, $\mu_2 > 0$): By substituting $\mu_1 = 0$ in (10) and (16) we obtain $\mathbf{K}^{\boldsymbol{\theta}} = \mathbf{K}$ and

$$\mathbf{A}_2^{\boldsymbol{\theta}} \triangleq (\mathbf{I} - \mathbf{K}\mathbf{K}^{\mathrm{a}}\mathbf{H})^{-1}\mathbf{K}(\mathbf{I} - \mathbf{K}^{\mathrm{a}}).$$

By substituting these results in (22), we obtain the weighting matrix for this case:

$$\begin{aligned}\mathbf{G} = &-(\mathbf{I}-\mathbf{H}\mathbf{A}_2^\theta)^T(\mathbf{I}-\mathbf{K}^\mathbf{a})^T\mathbf{R}^{-1}(\mathbf{I}-\mathbf{K}^\mathbf{a})(\mathbf{I}-\mathbf{H}\mathbf{A}_2^\theta)\\ &-\mu_2(\mathbf{I}-\mathbf{H}\mathbf{A}_2^\theta)^T(\mathbf{K}^\mathbf{a})^T\mathbf{M}\mathbf{K}^\mathbf{a}(\mathbf{I}-\mathbf{H}\mathbf{A}_2^\theta)\\ &+(\mathbf{I}-\mathbf{H}\mathbf{K})^T\mathbf{R}^{-1}(\mathbf{I}-\mathbf{H}\mathbf{K}).\end{aligned}$$

The resulting detector only takes into account the prior information of the secured measurements. However, this detector is not practical because if Λ does not include all measurements, i.e. some measurements are not secured, then $(\mathbf{I}-\mathbf{K}\mathbf{K}^\mathbf{a}\mathbf{H})$ is not invertible. Moreover, by substituting (13) in (12) and then substituting $\mathbf{K}^\theta=\mathbf{K}$ we see that (17) can also be written as

$$\hat{\mathbf{a}}^{\text{SS-ML}}_{|\mathcal{H}_1} = (I-\mathbf{K}^\mathbf{a}\mathbf{H}\mathbf{K})^{-1}\mathbf{K}^\mathbf{a}(\mathbf{I}-\mathbf{H}\mathbf{K})\mathbf{z}.$$

This indicates that for unobservable attacks, $\mathbf{a}=\mathbf{H}\mathbf{c}$, we obtain that $\hat{\mathbf{a}}^{\text{SS-ML}}_{|\mathcal{H}_1}$ is the same for input $\mathbf{z}$ and its corrupted version $\mathbf{z}+\mathbf{H}\mathbf{c}$, because

$$(\mathbf{I}-\mathbf{H}\mathbf{K})\mathbf{H}\mathbf{c} = \mathbf{H}\mathbf{c}-\mathbf{H}\mathbf{c} = \mathbf{0}.$$

Hence, this detector is not effective against unobservable FDI attacks (Table 1).

Table 1. Classification of the different GLRTs based on the regularization functions used.

Detector	Regularization term	
	Secured sensors	Graph Laplacian
SSGL-GLRT	v	v
GL-GLRT	x	v
PP-GLRT	v	x
BDD	x	x

3.4 General Graph High Pass Filter (GHPF)

The SSGL-GLRT exploits the smoothness property of the states in (3). Other approaches in [9,32] are built upon the idea that the states can be thought of as graph signals with low energy in the high-frequency range of the graph spectrum, as defined in the GSP literature [39]. Similarly, we can generalize the proposed SSGL-GLRT as follows. Since the states can be considered low-pass graph signals [32], the smoothness term, $\boldsymbol{\theta}^T\mathbf{B}\boldsymbol{\theta}$, can be replaced by any term of the form

$$\boldsymbol{\theta}^T\mathbf{U}_B f(\boldsymbol{\Phi}_B)\mathbf{U}_B^T\boldsymbol{\theta}, \tag{27}$$

where $\mathbf{U}_B$ and $\boldsymbol{\Phi}_B$ are the eigenvector and eigenvalue matrices of $\mathbf{B}$, i.e. $\mathbf{B} = \mathbf{U}_B\boldsymbol{\Phi}_B\mathbf{U}_B^T$. The graph filter $f(\cdot)$ is assumed to be a nonnegative analytic function, defined by its graph frequency response [30], $f(\boldsymbol{\Phi}) = \text{diag}(f(\phi_1),\ldots,f(\phi_N))$. Roughly speaking, $f(\boldsymbol{\Phi})$ is a GHPF if the frequency response $f(\phi_n)$ increases as the eigenvalue ϕ_n increases. Thus, using the GHPF in (27) results in a penalty on signal content in the high graph frequencies that can be used to detect outliers/anomalies w.r.t. the graph [36], or, in our case, FDI attacks. The practical implementation results in the same SSGL-GLRT, where $\mathbf{B}$ is replaced by $\left(\mathbf{U}_B f(\boldsymbol{\Phi}_B)\mathbf{U}_B^T\right)$ everywhere.

For example, using the graph frequency response

$$f(\phi_n) = \sqrt{\phi_n}, \quad n = 1,\ldots,N$$

in (27), results in the smoothness criterion $\boldsymbol{\theta}^T\mathbf{B}\boldsymbol{\theta}$ used in the CP-GLRT. An alternative GHPF is the following ideal-GHPF:

$$f^{\text{GHPF}}(\phi_n) = \begin{cases} 0 & \phi_n \leq \phi_{cut} \\ 1 & \phi_n > \phi_{cut} \end{cases}, \quad n = 1,\ldots,N, \tag{28}$$

where ϕ_{cut} is the cutoff frequency. This GHPF is used for FDI detection in [9,33], but without using protected measurements.

4 Distributed Detection

In the previous section, we derived the SSGL-GLRT for the centralized approach in which a single control center operates the system. However, a centralized approach may incur impractical computational and communication load, increased vulnerability, and disclosure of the internal system structure. Therefore, in this section, we discuss the modification of the SSGL-GLRT, and a special case, the GL-GLRT, for distributed frameworks. Our derivation is based on the distributed PSSE approach described in [17], in which the PSSE is performed with measurements corrupted by bad data. This section is organized as follows. In Subsect. 4.1, we review the distributed PSSE from [17]. Then, in Subsect. 4.2, we derive the proposed distributed SSGL-GLRT and GL-GLRT detectors.

4.1 Distributed PSSE

We consider an interconnected power system comprising L control areas. The measurement model for the lth area, based on the DC power flow model given in (2), can be expressed as

$$\mathbf{z}_l = \mathbf{H}_l\boldsymbol{\theta}_l + \mathbf{a}_l + \mathbf{e}_l, \quad l = 1,\ldots,L, \tag{29}$$

where $\boldsymbol{\theta}_l \in \mathbb{R}^{N_l\times 1}$ represents the subset of interconnected power system states (i.e. a subvector of $\boldsymbol{\theta}$) associated with the measurements in $\mathbf{z}_l$, $\mathbf{H}_l \in \mathbb{R}^{M_l\times N_l}$ is the appropriate submatrix topology matrix (a submatrix of $\mathbf{H}$), $\mathbf{a}_l \in \mathbb{R}^{M_l \times 1}$ is the attack on the sensors in the lth area (a submatrix of $\mathbf{H}$), and $\mathbf{e}_l \in \mathbb{R}^{M_l \times 1}$ represents the system noise in this area, modeled as a zero-mean Gaussian noise with covariance matrix $\mathbf{R}_q \in \mathbb{R}^{M_l \times M_l}$ (a submatrix of $\mathbf{R}$). The distributed PSSE can be written as the following optimization problem [17]:

$$\{\hat{\boldsymbol{\theta}}_l\}_{l=1}^{L} = \arg \min_{\substack{\boldsymbol{\theta}_l \\ l=1,\ldots,L}} \sum_{l=1}^{L} \mathcal{Q}_l \quad \text{s.t. } \boldsymbol{\theta}_l[l'] = \boldsymbol{\theta}_{l'}[l],\ \forall l' \in \mathcal{A}_l,\ \forall l, \tag{30}$$

where the cost function of the different areas, $\mathcal{Q}_l$, is jointly minimized subject to the constraint that the state vectors of each area partially overlap. Specifically, we assume that the state vector of area l includes all buses in that area and their first-order neighbors, and the set $\mathcal{A}_l$ includes all areas that share state variables with area l. The notation $\boldsymbol{\theta}_l[l']$ represents the subvector of $\boldsymbol{\theta}_l$ that includes all state variables shared with area l'.

The solution to (30) by the ADMM algorithm [3] consists of the following iterative steps [17]:

$$\boldsymbol{\theta}_l^{(t+1)} = \arg\min_{\boldsymbol{\theta}} \mathcal{Q}_l(\boldsymbol{\theta}_l) + \frac{\zeta}{2} \sum_{i=1}^{N_l} \mathbb{1}_{\{\mathcal{A}_l^i \neq \emptyset\}} |\mathcal{A}_l^i| (\boldsymbol{\theta}_l(i) - \mathbf{p}_l^{(t)}(i))^2, \tag{31a}$$

$$\mathbf{s}_l^{(t+1)}(i) = \frac{1}{|\mathcal{A}_l^i|} \sum_{l' \in \mathcal{A}_l^i} \boldsymbol{\theta}_{l'}^{(t+1)}[i],\ \forall i \text{ with } \mathcal{A}_l^i \neq \emptyset, \tag{31b}$$

$$\mathbf{p}_l^{(t+1)}(i) = \mathbf{p}_l^{(t)}(i) + \mathbf{s}_l^{(t+1)}(i) - \frac{\boldsymbol{\theta}_l^{(t)}(i) - \mathbf{s}_l^{(t)}(i)}{2},\ \forall i \text{ with } \mathcal{A}_l^i \neq \emptyset. \tag{31c}$$

Here, the auxiliary vectors $\mathbf{s}_l$ and $\mathbf{p}_l$ are used, and $\mathbb{1}_{(\cdot)}$ denotes the indicator function, which equals 1 if its condition is met and 0 otherwise. The set $\mathcal{A}_l^i$ represents the areas that share variable $\boldsymbol{\theta}_l(i)$ with area l. Additionally, the parameter ζ represents the user-defined step size. We use here the least squares cost function, $Q^{LS}(\theta) = (\mathbf{z} - \mathbf{H}\boldsymbol{\theta})^T \mathbf{R}^{-1} (\mathbf{z} - \mathbf{H}\boldsymbol{\theta})$, which can be modified for each area l to $Q_l^{LS}(\boldsymbol{\theta}) = (\mathbf{z}_l - \mathbf{H}_l\boldsymbol{\theta}_l)^T \mathbf{R}_l^{-1} (\mathbf{z}_l - \mathbf{H}_l\boldsymbol{\theta}_l)$. In this case, as shown in [17], the problem is solved using (31) while replacing (31a) with:

$$\boldsymbol{\theta}_l^{(t+1)} = (\mathbf{H}_l \mathbf{R}_l^{-1} \mathbf{H}_l + \zeta \mathbf{D}_l)^{-1} (\mathbf{R}_l^{-1} \mathbf{H}_l^T \mathbf{z}_l + \zeta \mathbf{D}_l \mathbf{p}_l^{(t)}), \tag{32}$$

where $\mathbf{D}_l$ is the diagonal matrix with the (i, i) entry $|\mathcal{A}_l^i|$. As for initialization, the state variables $\boldsymbol{\theta}_l$ are set to arbitrary values $\theta_l^{(0)}$, variables $\mathbf{s}_l^{(0)}$ are initialized as in (31b), and $\mathbf{p}_l^{(0)}(i)$ is initialized as $(\mathbf{x}_l^{(0)}(i) - \mathbf{s}_l^{(0)}(i))/2$. The ADMM iterative step converges when the objective function and constraints functions are convex, closed, and proper, and the augmented Lagrangian has a saddle point [3].

4.2 Distributed SSGL-GLRT and GL-GLRT

The cost function for the SSGL-ML in (8) is obtained by solving the standard PSSE, which is defined as an unconstrained LS problem along with two regular-

Algorithm 1: Distributed SS-GLRT in area l

Input: Fix detection threshold γ_l and step size ζ Set initial guess: $\boldsymbol{\theta}^{(0)}_{|\mathcal{H}_0,l}$, $\mathbf{s}_l^{(0)}$, and $\mathbf{p}_l^{(0)}$

for $t = 0, 1, \ldots$ **do**

  Update:

  $\boldsymbol{\theta}^{(t+1)}_{|\mathcal{H}_0,l} = (\mathbf{H}_l\mathbf{R}_l^{-1}\mathbf{H}_l + \mu_{1,l}\mathbf{B}_l + \zeta\mathbf{D}_l)^{-1}(\mathbf{R}_l^{-1}\mathbf{H}_l^T\mathbf{z}_l + \zeta\mathbf{D}_l\mathbf{p}_l^{(t)})$

  $\mathbf{s}_l^{(t+1)}(i) = \frac{1}{|\mathcal{A}_l^i|}\sum_{l' \in \mathcal{A}_l^i} \boldsymbol{\theta}^{(t+1)}_{|\mathcal{H}_0,l'}[i]$, $\forall i$ with $\mathcal{A}_l^i \neq \emptyset$

  $\mathbf{p}_l^{(t+1)}(i) = \mathbf{p}_l^{(t)}(i) + \mathbf{s}_l^{(t+1)}(i) - \frac{\boldsymbol{\theta}^{(t)}_{|\mathcal{H}_0,l}(i) - \mathbf{s}_l^{(t)}(i)}{2}$, $\forall i$ with $\mathcal{A}_l^i \neq \emptyset$

Set $\hat{\boldsymbol{\theta}}^{\text{SSGL-ML}}_{|\mathcal{H}_0,l} = \boldsymbol{\theta}^{(t+1)}_{|\mathcal{H}_0,l}$

Set initial guess: $\boldsymbol{\theta}^{(0)}_{|\mathcal{H}_1,l}$, $\mathbf{s}_l^{(0)}$, $\mathbf{p}_l^{(0)}$, and $\mathbf{a}^{(0)}_{|\mathcal{H}_1,l}$

for $t = 0, 1, \ldots$ **do**

  Update:

  $\boldsymbol{\theta}^{(t+1)}_{|\mathcal{H}_1,l} = (\mathbf{H}_l\mathbf{R}_l^{-1}\mathbf{H}_l + \mu_{1,l}\mathbf{B}_l + \zeta\mathbf{D}_l)^{-1}(\mathbf{R}_l^{-1}\mathbf{H}_l^T(\mathbf{z}_l - \mathbf{a}_l^{(t)}) + \zeta\mathbf{D}_l\mathbf{p}_l^{(t)})$

  $\mathbf{s}_l^{(t+1)}(i) = \frac{1}{|\mathcal{A}_l^i|}\sum_{l' \in \mathcal{A}_l^i} \boldsymbol{\theta}^{(t+1)}_{|\mathcal{H}_0,l'}[i]$, $\forall i$ with $\mathcal{A}_l^i \neq \emptyset$

  $\mathbf{p}_l^{(t+1)}(i) = \mathbf{p}_l^{(t)}(i) + \mathbf{s}_l^{(t+1)}(i) - \frac{\boldsymbol{\theta}^{(t)}_{|\mathcal{H}_0,l}(i) - \mathbf{s}_l^{(t)}(i)}{2}$, $\forall i$ with $\mathcal{A}_l^i \neq \emptyset$

  $\mathbf{a}^{(t+1)}_{|\mathcal{H}_1,l} = (\mathbf{R}_l^{-1} + \mu_{2,l}\mathbf{M}_l)^{-1}\mathbf{R}_l^{-1}(\mathbf{z}_l - \mathbf{H}_l\boldsymbol{\theta}_l^{(t+1)})$

Set $\hat{\boldsymbol{\theta}}^{\text{SSGL-ML}}_{|\mathcal{H}_1,l} = \boldsymbol{\theta}^{(t+1)}_{|\mathcal{H}_1,l}$ and $\hat{\mathbf{a}}^{\text{SSGL-ML}}_{|\mathcal{H}_1,l} = \mathbf{a}^{(t+1)}_{|\mathcal{H}_1,l}$

if $\mathcal{Q}_l^{SSGL}(\hat{\boldsymbol{\theta}}^{SSGL\text{-}ML}_{|\mathcal{H}_1,l}, \hat{\mathbf{a}}^{SSGL\text{-}ML}_{|\mathcal{H}_1,l}) - \mathcal{Q}_l^{SSGL}(\hat{\boldsymbol{\theta}}^{SSGL\text{-}ML}_{|\mathcal{H}_0,l}, \mathbf{0}) > \gamma_l$ **then**

  return "The area is under an FDI attack"

else

  return "The area is under normal operation"

ization terms. One term, $\mu_1\boldsymbol{\theta}^T\mathbf{B}\boldsymbol{\theta}$, imposes prior knowledge on the smoothness property of the state variables, as defined in (3). The other term, $\mu_2\|\mathbf{Ma}\|^2$, imposes prior knowledge on the secured sensors, as defined in (7). We modify the regularization terms to recast the optimization problem as the minimization of a regional cost function. Specifically, we introduce the local smoothness measure defined in [39], which is given by the inner summation of the global smoothness measure in (4):

$$S_i(\theta) = \sum_{j \in \mathcal{N}_i} B_{i,j}(\theta_i - \theta_j)^2, \tag{33}$$

where $\mathcal{N}_i$ is the first-order neighborhood of bus i. We measure the smoothness over each region by summing the local smoothness of all buses in that region, resulting in $\sum_{i=1}^{N_l} S_i(\boldsymbol{\theta})$. It can be verified that this sum satisfies

$$\sum_{i \in R} S_i(\boldsymbol{\theta}) = \boldsymbol{\theta}_l^T\mathbf{B}_l\boldsymbol{\theta}_l,$$

where $\mathbf{B}_l$ is the submatrix of $\mathbf{B}$ associated with the state variables in the lth region. Moreover, since the prior knowledge on the location of the secured sensors is local to each sensor, we modify the prior assumption in (34) for each area l to

$$\|\mathbf{M}_l \mathbf{a}_l\|^2 \leq \varepsilon_l, \tag{34}$$

where $\mathbf{M}_l$ is the $M_l \times M_l$ submatrix of the diagonal matrix $\mathbf{M}$ associated with the power measurements in the lth area. Using (29) and (33)–(34), we can modify the log-likelihood function in (8) to measure the cost function of the lth area as

$$\mathcal{Q}_l^{SSGL}(\boldsymbol{\theta}_l, \mathbf{a}_l) = -(\mathbf{z}_l - \mathbf{H}_l\boldsymbol{\theta}_l - \mathbf{a}_l)^T \mathbf{R}_l^{-1}(\mathbf{z}_l - \mathbf{H}_q\boldsymbol{\theta}_l - \mathbf{a}_l) - \mu_{1,l}\boldsymbol{\theta}_l^T \mathbf{B}_l \boldsymbol{\theta}_l - \mu_{2,l}\|\mathbf{M}_l\mathbf{a}_l\|^2. \tag{35}$$

As presented in Sect. 3.2, the SSGL-GLRT is a detector derived from (18). For the distributed case, the SSGL-GLRT can be adapted by defining L detectors, denoted as $T_l^{\text{SSGL-GLRT}}$, where each detection test is performed in the corresponding control center. These detectors are defined as follows:

$$T_l^{\text{SSGL-GLRT}} = \mathcal{Q}_l^{SSGL}(\hat{\boldsymbol{\theta}}_{|\mathcal{H}_1,l}^{\text{SSGL-ML}}, \hat{\mathbf{a}}_{|\mathcal{H}_1,l}^{\text{SSGL-ML}}) - \mathcal{Q}_l^{SSGL}(\hat{\boldsymbol{\theta}}_{|\mathcal{H}_0,l}^{\text{SSGL-ML}}, \mathbf{0}),\ l = 1, \ldots, L, \tag{36}$$

where $\hat{\boldsymbol{\theta}}_{|\mathcal{H}_1,l}^{\text{SSGL-ML}}$ and $\hat{\mathbf{a}}_{|\mathcal{H}_1,l}^{\text{SSGL-ML}}$ are the ML estimates for the state variables and the attack in the lth area under the $\mathcal{H}_1$ hypothesis, and $\hat{\boldsymbol{\theta}}_{|\mathcal{H}_0,l}^{\text{SSGL-ML}}$ are the ML estimates for the state variable in the lth area under the $\mathcal{H}_0$ hypothesis.

For hypothesis $\mathcal{H}_0$, we seek to estimate $\hat{\boldsymbol{\theta}}_{|\mathcal{H}_0,l}^{\text{SSGL-ML}}$, which is obtained by replacing $\mathcal{Q}_l(\boldsymbol{\theta}_l)$ in (31) with (35) when $\mathbf{a}_l$ is replaced with $\mathbf{0}$. Therefore, we can estimate $\hat{\boldsymbol{\theta}}_{|\mathcal{H}_0,l}^{\text{SSGL-ML}}$ by applying the results from (9)–(10) to (31), which results in replacing (31a) with

$$\boldsymbol{\theta}_{|\mathcal{H}_0,l}^{(t+1)} = (\mathbf{H}_l \mathbf{R}_l^{-1}\mathbf{H}_l + \mu_{1,l}\mathbf{B}_l + \zeta\mathbf{D}_l)^{-1}(\mathbf{R}_l^{-1}\mathbf{H}_l^T\mathbf{z}_l + \zeta\mathbf{D}_l\mathbf{p}_l^{(t)}). \tag{37}$$

Note that the inclusion of the term $\zeta\mathbf{D}_l$ is motivated by the same reasons as in (32). For hypothesis $\mathcal{H}_1$, we want to estimate $(\hat{\boldsymbol{\theta}}_{|\mathcal{H}_1,l}^{\text{SSGL-ML}}, \hat{\mathbf{a}}_{|\mathcal{H}_1,l}^{\text{SSGL-ML}})$, which is obtained by replacing $\mathcal{Q}_l(\boldsymbol{\theta}_l)$ in (31) with (35), a function of both $\boldsymbol{\theta}_l$ and $\mathbf{a}_l$. In this case, we can estimate $(\hat{\boldsymbol{\theta}}_{|\mathcal{H}_1,l}^{\text{SSGL-ML}}, \hat{\mathbf{a}}_{|\mathcal{H}_1,l}^{\text{SSGL-ML}})$ by applying the results from (9)–(14) to (31), which results in replacing (31a) with

$$\boldsymbol{\theta}_{|\mathcal{H}_1,l}^{(t+1)} = (\mathbf{H}_l \mathbf{R}_l^{-1}\mathbf{H}_l + \mu_{1,l}\mathbf{B}_l + \zeta\mathbf{D}_l)^{-1}(\mathbf{R}_l^{-1}\mathbf{H}_l^T(\mathbf{z}_l - \mathbf{a}_l^{(t)}) + \zeta\mathbf{D}_l\mathbf{p}_l^{(t)}) \tag{38}$$

and adding

$$\mathbf{a}_{|\mathcal{H}_1,l}^{(t+1)} = (\mathbf{R}_l^{-1} + \mu_{2,l}\mathbf{M}_l)^{-1}\mathbf{R}_l^{-1}(\mathbf{z}_l - \mathbf{H}_l\boldsymbol{\theta}_l^{(t+1)}). \tag{39}$$

Note that steps (31b)–(31c) are not modified, ensuring that the agreement between shared states is unrelated to the local functions $\mathcal{Q}_l$. Moreover, the inclusion of the term $\zeta\mathbf{D}_l$ is motivated by the same reasons as in (32) and (37). The distributed SS-GLRT is summarized in Algorithm 1.

Moreover, from (20) and (26) we observe that the GL-GLRT, which is a special case of the SSGL-GLRT, can be expressed as $T^{\text{GL-GLRT}} =$

Algorithm 2: Distributed GL-GLRT in area l

Input: Fix detection threshold γ_l and step size ζ Set initial guess: $\boldsymbol{\theta}^{(0)}_{|\mathcal{H}_0,l}$, $\mathbf{s}^{(0)}_l$, and $\mathbf{p}^{(0)}_l$

for $t = 0, 1, \ldots$ **do**
- Update:
- $\boldsymbol{\theta}^{(t+1)}_{|\mathcal{H}_0,l} = (\mathbf{H}_l\mathbf{R}_l^{-1}\mathbf{H}_l + \mu_{1,l}\mathbf{B}_l + \zeta\mathbf{D}_l)^{-1}(\mathbf{R}_l^{-1}\mathbf{H}_l^T\mathbf{z}_l + \zeta\mathbf{D}_l\mathbf{p}_l^{(t)})$
- $\mathbf{s}_l^{(t+1)}(i) = \frac{1}{|\mathcal{A}_l^i|}\sum_{l'\in\mathcal{A}_l^i}\boldsymbol{\theta}^{(t+1)}_{|\mathcal{H}_0,l'}[i]$, $\forall i$ with $\mathcal{A}_l^i \neq \emptyset$
- $\mathbf{p}_l^{(t+1)}(i) = \mathbf{p}_l^{(t)}(i) + \mathbf{s}_l^{(t+1)}(i) - \frac{\boldsymbol{\theta}^{(t)}_{|\mathcal{H}_0,l}(i) - \mathbf{s}_l^{(t)}(i)}{2}$, $\forall i$ with $\mathcal{A}_l^i \neq \emptyset$

Set $\hat{\boldsymbol{\theta}}^{\text{SSGL-ML}}_{|\mathcal{H}_0,l} = \boldsymbol{\theta}^{(t+1)}_{|\mathcal{H}_0,l}$ **if** $-\mathcal{Q}_l^{SSGL}(\hat{\boldsymbol{\theta}}^{SSGL\text{-}ML}_{|\mathcal{H}_0,l}, \mathbf{0}) > \gamma_l$ **then**
- **return** "The area is under an FDI attack"

else
- **return** "The area is under normal operation"

$\mathcal{Q}^{SSGL}(\hat{\boldsymbol{\theta}}^{\text{SSGL-ML}}_{|\mathcal{H}_0}, \mathbf{0})$. Similar to the SSGL-GLRT, the SSGL-GLRT can be adjusted for the distributed scenario by applying L detectors, represented as $T_l^{\text{GL-GLRT}}$, where each test is performed in the appropriate control center. These detectors are defined as

$$T_l^{\text{GL-GLRT}} = \mathcal{Q}_l^{SSGL}(\hat{\boldsymbol{\theta}}^{\text{SSGL-ML}}_{|\mathcal{H}_0,l}, \mathbf{0}),\ l = 1, \ldots, L,$$

where $\hat{\boldsymbol{\theta}}^{\text{SSGL-ML}}_{|\mathcal{H}_0,l}$ estimation is described in (37). The distributed GL-GLRT is summarized in Algorithm 2.

5 Simulations: IEEE 57-Bus Test Case

The performance of the SSGL-GLRT from (21) is evaluated and compared with the following detectors:

1. The $J(\boldsymbol{\theta})$ test in (24) [1], which is the conventional BDD method.
2. GSP-based methods: the GL-GLRT in (26). and the Ideal-GLRT introduced in [9,33].
3. The SSGL-GLRT obtained by using $\mathbf{B} = f^{\frac{1}{2}}(\boldsymbol{\Phi}_B)$ in (21), where $f(\boldsymbol{\Phi}_B) = 1 + 99 \times f^{\text{GHPF}}(\boldsymbol{\Phi}_B)$, which is the perturbed ideal GHPF defined in (28).

These methods were selected to demonstrate the advantage of incorporating both the physical and the GSP information. For the SSGL-GLRT, SS-Ideal-GLRT, GL-GLRT, and Ideal-GLRT, we chose the regularization parameter $\mu_1 = 900$; in addition, for the SSGL-GLRT and SS-Ideal-GLRT we also set $\mu_2 = 10$. We conducted 1,000 Monte-Carlo simulations based on the IEEE 57-bus test case network using the DC-PF model in (2) to evaluate performance. For each trial, we randomly drew the load demand from a Gaussian distribution with the mean set to the load values provided in the test case. We computed the system states

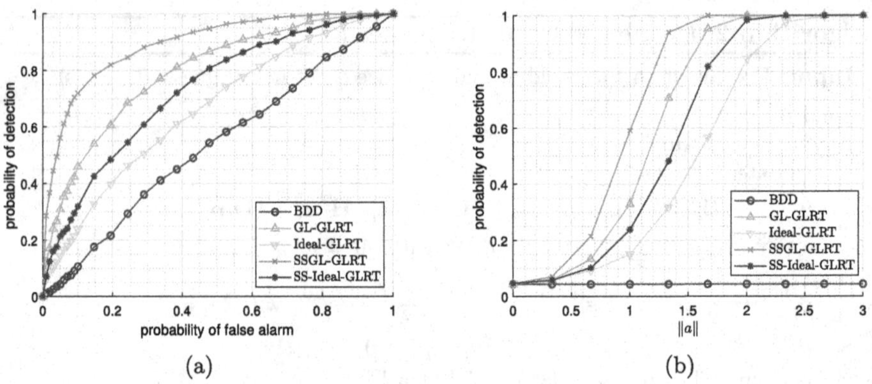

Fig. 2. The probability of detection is measured versus: (a) the probability of false alarm (ROC), and (b) the strength of the attack $||\mathbf{a}||$

using the Matpower command $runpf(\cdot)$ [50]. We set the noise covariance matrix to $\mathbf{R} = \sigma^2\mathbf{I}$ with $\sigma^2 = 0.01$. We generated an unobservable FDI attack using (5) with $c_{33} \neq 0$, and then normalized it to satisfy $||\mathbf{a}|| = 1$. In addition, we defined the set of secured sensors $\mathcal{S}$ by constraining 80 power measurements (36% of the total measurements) such that it was ensured that the state variables in the generator buses and their first-order neighbors are not affected by the attack. This set includes the power injection measurements in these buses and the power flow measurement in the lines entering these buses.

The performance of the different detectors is exhibited in Fig. 2. In Fig. 2(a), the receiver operating characteristic (ROC) curves demonstrate the balance between the probability of detection and the probability of false alarms. The results show that the proposed SSGL-GLRT outperforms all other detectors in terms of the probability of detection for any level of false alarm probability. In particular, the inclusion of prior information about protected measurements gives the SSGL-GLRT an advantage over the GL-GLRT. Similarly, the SS-Ideal-GLRT, which benefits from incorporating the additional information on the locations of the secured sensors, outperforms the Ideal-GLRT. The results also show that detectors based on the smoothness of the states, i.e., the SSGL-GLRT and GL-GLRT, perform better than those based on the graph-bandlimited assumption, i.e., the SS-Ideal-GLRT and Ideal-GHPF. This is because the smoothness assumption provides a better description of the states' behavior than the graph-bandlimited assumption. Finally, it can be seen that the that the conventional BDD method - the $J(\boldsymbol{\theta})$ test - has the same power as random chance ("coin flipping"). Thus, it cannot detect the unobservable FDI attack, as expected.

In Fig. 2(b) the detection probability is shown versus the attack strength, which is measured by $||\mathbf{a}||$. As expected, it can be seen that the detection probability of all the detectors except the BDD detector increases with an increase in $||\mathbf{a}||$. In a similar manner to Fig. 2(a), it can be observed that incorporating the additional information on the locations of the secured sensors improves the probability of detection, where the SSGL-GLRT and SS-Ideal-GLRT outperforms the GL-GLRT and the Ideal-GLRT, respectively. Moreover, it can be observed that the SSGL-GLRT shows the best performance. Finally, as expected, the BDD detector fails to detect the unobservable FDI attack for any selection of $||\mathbf{a}||$ presented.

6 Conclusions

We introduce SSGL-GLRT, which is a new detection method against FDI attacks based on the well-known GLRT. The SSGL-GLRT is derived while incorporating knowledge of secured sensors' locations and graph smoothness properties of power system state variables. We provide a generalization of the method that allows the use of different high-pass GSP filters instead of using the graph smoothness measure. Moreover, we also consider the case where the power system is operated in a distributed manner and provide the distributed SSGL-GLRT detector. Numerical simulation show that incorporating the knowledge of the locations of the secured sensors alongside the graph smoothness properties in the design of the detector significantly improves the detection capabilities against FDI attacks. Future work may focus on expanding the proposed detector to the alternating current (AC) power flow model, which is often used in power systems.

Acknowledgments. This work was supported in part by the Next Generation Internet (NGI) program, the Jabotinsky Scholarship from the Israel Ministry of Technology and Science, the Israel Ministry of National Infrastructure, Energy, National Research Foundation of Korea (NRF) grant funded by the Korean government (MSIT) (No. RS-2023-00210018), NSF grants CNS-2148128, EPCN-2144634, EPCN-2231350, and by the U.S. Department of Energy's Office of Energy Efficiency and Renewable Energy under the Solar Energy Technology Office Award Number DE-EE0008769. The views expressed herein do not necessarily represent the views of the U.S. Department of Energy or the United States Government.

Appendix: Concavity of $\mathcal{Q}(\boldsymbol{\theta}, \mathbf{a})$

In order to show that the function $\mathcal{Q}(\boldsymbol{\theta}, \mathbf{a})$ from (8) is a concave function w.r.t $\boldsymbol{\theta}$ and $\mathbf{a}$, we need to show that the Hessian matrix of the second-order partial derivatives of $-\mathcal{Q}(\boldsymbol{\theta}, \mathbf{a})$ is a positive semidefinite matrix. It can be seen that the Hessian matrix of $-\mathcal{Q}(\boldsymbol{\theta}, \mathbf{a})$ w.r.t. the vector $[\boldsymbol{\theta}^T, \mathbf{a}^T]^T$ is

$$\begin{pmatrix} \mathbf{H}^T\mathbf{R}^{-1}\mathbf{H} + \mathbf{B} & \mathbf{H}^T\mathbf{R}^{-1} \\ \mathbf{R}^{-1}\mathbf{H} & \mathbf{R}^{-1} + \mathbf{M} \end{pmatrix} = \begin{pmatrix} \mathbf{H}^T\mathbf{R}^{-1}\mathbf{H} & \mathbf{H}^T\mathbf{R}^{-1} \\ \mathbf{R}^{-1}\mathbf{H} & \mathbf{R}^{-1} \end{pmatrix} + \begin{pmatrix} \mathbf{B} & \mathbf{0} \\ \mathbf{0} & \mathbf{M} \end{pmatrix}.$$

The Hessian is a sum of two matrices. In the following, we show that each one of these matrices is positive semidefinite, which implies that the Hessian is a positive semidefinite matrix. First, it can be seen that the matrix $\begin{pmatrix} \mathbf{B} & \mathbf{0} \\ \mathbf{0} & \mathbf{M} \end{pmatrix}$ is a positive semidefinite matrix because it is a block diagonal matrix of two positive semidefinite matrices (see the definitions of $\mathbf{B}$ and $\mathbf{M}$ in (1) and (8), respectively). Second, the matrix $\begin{pmatrix} \mathbf{H}^T\mathbf{R}^{-1}\mathbf{H} & \mathbf{H}^T\mathbf{R}^{-1} \\ \mathbf{R}^{-1}\mathbf{H} & \mathbf{R}^{-1} \end{pmatrix}$ is a positive semidefinite matrix since it can be verified that its Schur complement,

$$\mathbf{H}^T\mathbf{R}^{-1}\mathbf{H} - \mathbf{H}^T\mathbf{R}^{-1}\mathbf{R}\mathbf{R}^{-1}\mathbf{H} = \mathbf{0},$$

is a positive semidefinite matrix [13].

References

1. Abur, A., Gomez-Exposito, A.: Power System State Estimation: Theory and Implementation. Marcel Dekker (2004)
2. Bi, S., Zhang, Y.J.: Graphical methods for defense against false-data injection attacks on power system state estimation. IEEE Trans. Smart Grid **5**(3), 1216–1227 (2014)
3. Boyd, S., Parikh, N., Chu, E., Peleato, B., Eckstein, J., et al.: Distributed optimization and statistical learning via the alternating direction method of multipliers. Found. Trends® Mach. Learn. **3**(1), 1–122 (2011)
4. Dabush, L., Kroizer, A., Routtenberg, T.: State estimation in partially observable power systems via graph signal processing tools. Sens. (MDPI) **23**(3), 1387 (2023)
5. Dabush, L., Routtenberg, T.: Detection of false data injection attacks in unobservable power systems by Laplacian regularization. In: IEEE Sensor Array and Multichannel Signal Processing Workshop (SAM), pp. 415–419 (2022)
6. Deng, R., Xiao, G., Lu, R.: Defending against false data injection attacks on power system state estimation. IEEE Trans. Ind. Informat. **13**(1), 198–207 (2015)
7. Dong, X., Thanou, D., Frossard, P., Vandergheynst, P.: Learning Laplacian matrix in smooth graph signal representations. IEEE Trans. Signal Process. **64**(23), 6160–6173 (2016)
8. Drayer, E., Routtenberg, T.: Detection of false data injection attacks in power systems with graph Fourier transform. In: Global Conference on Signal and Information Processing (GlobalSIP), pp. 890–894 (2018)
9. Drayer, E., Routtenberg, T.: Detection of false data injection attacks in smart grids based on graph signal processing. IEEE Syst. J. (2019)
10. Esmalifalak, M., Liu, L., Nguyen, N., Zheng, R., Han, Z.: Detecting stealthy false data injection using machine learning in smart grid. IEEE Syst. J. **11**(3), 1644–1652 (2017)
11. Hasnat, M.A., Rahnamay-Naeini, M.: A graph signal processing framework for detecting and locating cyber and physical stresses in smart grids. IEEE Trans. Smart Grid **13**(5), 3688–3699 (2022)
12. He, Y., Mendis, G.J., Wei, J.: Real-time detection of false data injection attacks in smart grid: a deep learning-based intelligent mechanism. IEEE Trans. Smart Grid **8**(5), 2505–2516 (2017)
13. Horn, R.A., Johnson, C.R.: Matrix Analysis, 2nd edn. Cambridge University Press, New York (2012)
14. Jia, L., Kim, J., Thomas, R.J., Tong, L.: Impact of data quality on real-time locational marginal price. IEEE Trans. Power Syst. **29**(2), 627–636 (2014)

15. Kalofolias, V.: How to learn a graph from smooth signals. J. Mach. Learn. Res. (JMLR) (2016)
16. Kay, S.M.: Fundamentals of Statistical Signal Processing: Detection Theory, vol. 2. Prentice Hall PTR, Englewood Cliffs (1998)
17. Kekatos, V., Giannakis, G.B.: Distributed robust power system state estimation. IEEE Trans. Power Syst. **28**(2), 1617–1626 (2012)
18. Kim, J., Bhela, S., Anderson, J., Zussman, G.: Identification of intraday false data injection attack on DER dispatch signals. In: 2022 IEEE International Conference on Communications, Control, and Computing Technologies for Smart Grids (SmartGridComm), pp. 40–46 (2022)
19. Kim, J., Tong, L.: On phasor measurement unit placement against state and topology attacks. In: SmartGridComm, pp. 396–401 (2013)
20. Kim, T.T., Poor, H.V.: Strategic protection against data injection attacks on power grids. IEEE Trans. Smart Grid **2**(2), 326–333 (2011)
21. Kosut, O., Jia, L., Thomas, R.J., Tong, L.: Malicious data attacks on smart grid state estimation: Attack strategies and countermeasures. In: 2010 First IEEE International Conference on Smart Grid Communications, pp. 220–225 (2010)
22. Kroizer, A., Routtenberg, T., Eldar, Y.C.: Bayesian estimation of graph signals. IEEE Trans. Signal Process. **70**, 2207–2223 (2022)
23. Liang, G., Zhao, J., Luo, F., Weller, S.R., Dong, Z.Y.: A review of false data injection attacks against modern power systems. IEEE Trans. Smart Grid **8**(4), 1630–1638 (2017)
24. Lin, J., Yu, W., Yang, X., Xu, G., Zhao, W.: On false data injection attacks against distributed energy routing in smart grid. In: International Conference on Cyber-Physical Systems, pp. 183–192. IEEE Computer Society (2012)
25. Liu, Y., Ning, P., Reiter, M.K.: False data injection attacks against state estimation in electric power grids. ACM Trans. Inf. Syst. Secur. **14**(1), 13 (2011)
26. Minot, A., Lu, Y.M., Li, N.: A distributed Gauss-Newton method for power system state estimation. IEEE Trans. Power Syst. **31**(5), 3804–3815 (2015)
27. Monticelli, A.: State Estimation in Electric Power Systems: A Generalized Approach, pp. 39–61, 91–101, 161–199. Springer, Boston (1999)
28. Morgenstern, G., Routtenberg, T.: Structural-constrained methods for the identification of unobservable false data injection attacks in power systems. IEEE Access **10**, 94169–94185 (2022)
29. Morgenstern, G., Kim, J., Anderson, J., Zussman, G., Routtenberg, T.: Protection against graph-based false data injection attacks on power systems (2023). https://arxiv.org/abs/2304.10801
30. Ortega, A., Frossard, P., Kovačević, J., Moura, J.M.F., Vandergheynst, P.: Graph signal processing: overview, challenges, and applications. Proc. IEEE **106**(5), 808–828 (2018)
31. Primadianto, A., Lu, C.N.: A review on distribution system state estimation. IEEE Trans. Power Syst. **32**(5), 3875–3883 (2016)
32. Ramakrishna, R., Scaglione, A.: Grid-graph signal processing (Grid-GSP): a graph signal processing framework for the power grid. IEEE Trans. Signal Process. **69**, 2725–2739 (2021)
33. Ramakrishna, R., Scaglione, A.: Detection of false data injection attack using graph signal processing for the power grid. In: 2019 IEEE Global Conference on Signal and Information Processing (GlobalSIP), pp. 1–5. IEEE (2019)
34. Routtenberg, T., Eldar, Y.C.: Centralized identification of imbalances in power networks with synchrophasor data. IEEE Trans. Power Syst. **33**(2), 1981–1992 (2017)

35. Rudin, L.I., Osher, S., Fatemi, E.: Nonlinear total variation based noise removal algorithms. Phys. D **60**(1–4), 259–268 (1992)
36. Sandryhaila, A., Moura, J.M.F.: Discrete signal processing on graphs: frequency analysis. IEEE Trans. Signal Process. **62**(12), 3042–3054 (2014)
37. Shaked, S., Routtenberg, T.: Identification of edge disconnections in networks based on graph filter outputs. IEEE Trans. Signal Inf. Process. Netw. **7**, 578–594 (2021)
38. Shereen, E., Ramakrishna, R., Dán, G.: Detection and localization of PMU time synchronization attacks via graph signal processing. IEEE Trans. Smart Grid **13**(4), 3241–3254 (2022)
39. Shuman, D.I., Narang, S.K., Frossard, P., Ortega, A., Vandergheynst, P.: The emerging field of signal processing on graphs: extending high-dimensional data analysis to networks and other irregular domains. IIEEE Signal Process. Mag. **30**(3), 83–98 (2013)
40. Soltan, S., Mazauric, D., Zussman, G.: Analysis of failures in power grids. IEEE Control Netw. Syst. **4**(2), 288–300 (2017)
41. Soltan, S., Yannakakis, M., Zussman, G.: Power grid state estimation following a joint cyber and physical attack. IEEE Trans. Control. Netw. Syst. **5**(1), 499–512 (2016)
42. Soltan, S., Yannakakis, M., Zussman, G.: React to cyber attacks on power grids. IEEE Trans. Netw. Sci. Eng. **6**(3), 459–473 (2018)
43. Sridhar, S., Hahn, A., Govindarasu, M.: Cyber-physical system security for the electric power grid. Proc. IEEE **100**(1), 210–224 (2011)
44. Veith, E., Fischer, L., Tröschel, M., Nieße, A.: Analyzing cyber-physical systems from the perspective of artificial intelligence. In: Proceedings of the 2019 International Conference on Artificial Intelligence, Robotics and Control, pp. 85–95 (2019)
45. Verdoja, F., Grangetto, M.: Graph Laplacian for image anomaly detection. Mach. Vision Appl. **31**(1–2), 11 (2020)
46. Vuković, O., Dán, G.: Security of fully distributed power system state estimation: detection and mitigation of data integrity attacks. IEEE J. Sel. Areas Commun. **32**(7), 1500–1508 (2014)
47. Xie, L., Mo, Y., Sinopoli, B.: Integrity data attacks in power market operations. IEEE Trans. Smart Grid **2**(4), 659–666 (2011)
48. Yuan, Y., Li, Z., Ren, K.: Quantitative analysis of load redistribution attacks in power systems. IEEE Trans. Parallel Distrib. Syst. **23**(9), 1731–1738 (2012)
49. Zhu, X., Kandola, J.S., Lafferty, J., Ghahramani, Z.: Graph kernels by spectral transforms (2006)
50. Zimmerman, R.D., Murillo-Sanchez, C.E., Thomas, R.J.: MATPOWER: steady-state operations, planning, and analysis tools for power systems research and education. IEEE Trans. Power Syst. **26**(1), 12–19 (2011)

KerberSSIze Us: Providing Sovereignty to the People

Ronald Petrlic(✉) and Christof Lange

Nuremberg Institute of Technology, 90489 Nuremberg, Germany
ronald.petrlic@th-nuernberg.de

Abstract. *Kerberos* is an old, yet widely used protocol for authentication and authorization in (local) network environments. *Self Sovereign Identity* (SSI), on the other hand, is a relatively new model for managing digital identities—not so widely used in practice yet but with a promising future. We are the first to propose to bring Kerberos and SSI together and thereby achieve the advantages of both worlds.

We come up with a concept to integrate SSI authentication in Kerberos by requiring only a few changes in the Kerberos ecosystem to enable application in practice. We implement our concept and show its feasibility.

With our proposed integration of SSI in Kerberos, we not only advance the usage of SSI in practice but we furthermore get rid of the main security problem of Kerberos: the usage of (weak) user passwords, and, thus, advance the overall security of Kerberos environments.

Keywords: Authentication · Kerberos · Self Sovereign Identity

1 Introduction

Kerberos is *the* protocol used for authentication and authorization in local networks. Developed at MIT decades ago, Kerberos has been further developed (an RFC search reveals 43 results and a Google Scholar search reveals thousands of papers and patents) and has become the de-facto standard for authentication and authorization in Windows Server network environments.

On the other side, a paradigm shift in user authentication is on the horizon: *Self-Sovereign Identity (SSI)* promises to give users full control over their digital identities and, thus, their personal data. In the future, we all might make use of SSI and get rid of data-collecting central identity providers like Meta or Google.

The goal of our work is to come up with an extension for Kerberos that supports the usage of SSI as an authentication method. Thereby, the advantages of SSI—like *Selective Disclosure* and *full control over one's own identity*—can be directly used in Kerberos. Moreover, the biggest weakness of Kerberos—the usage of passwords—is mitigated.

S. Dolev and B. Schieber (Eds.): SSS 2023, LNCS 14310, pp. 259–273, 2023.
https://doi.org/10.1007/978-3-031-44274-2_19

The rest of the paper is structured as follows. In Sect. 2 we give an overview of Kerberos and SSI. Then we point out the requirements for our solution in Sect. 3 before we present our concept in Sect. 4 and the implementation in Sect. 5. We evaluate our approach in Sect. 6. Finally, we present related work in Sect. 7.

2 Background

2.1 Kerberos

The current version of Kerberos is version 5, which is also the basis for the integration of Kerberos in Windows Active Directory domains.

There are four entities in the Kerberos protocol: *Client*, *Authentication Server (AS)*, *Ticket-Granting Service (TGS)*, and *Service.*

The AS and the TGS are two different entities, which are often implemented in one program (called *Key Distribution Center* (KDC))—both have access to the same database (in Windows network environments the Active Directory serves as the database for the storage of user and service keys). [1]

The client is a piece of software running on the user's system, allowing the user to authenticate and ask for permission to use a certain service. [2] The protocol flow is as follows.

1. The client contacts the AS, which is responsible for authenticating the user. If the user authentication is successful, the client receives a so-called *Ticket-Granting Ticket* (TGT). Therefore, AS_REQ and AS_REP messages are exchanged between the client and AS.
2. In the next step, the authorization takes place: the client contacts the TGS to receive a (service) *Ticket* that can later on be used to access a specific service.
3. The client uses the ticket to access the service.

Main Weakness: Usage of Passwords. In Kerberos, *passwords* are used both for authentication and key generation, entailing several risks. An attacker who gets ahold of a user's password can assume the victim's identity. As passwords are mostly chosen by users they are typically not very strong—increasing the probability of a successful attack.

An attacker may use an online or offline attack to retrieve a user's password. While the online attack entails a request by the attacker to the KDC for every try, and, thus, can be detected and prohibited, the offline attack is hard to detect and prohibit. In the offline attack, the attacker eavesdrops on the network communication and records the AS_REQ and AS_REP messages. Both messages include the user name in clear text. Moreover, there is a part that is encrypted with K_{Client}—the user key derived from the password. The attacker can now perform a dictionary attack, trying all possible user passwords and checking whether decryption provides a meaningful message and if so, having found the correct password. This attack shows that the strength of the password directly influences how well the messages are protected.

The users' keys are stored in the central database of the KDC. An attacker with access to the database can use the (symmetric) keys to read the encrypted communication and impersonate users. In the event of an attack, this means that all user passwords need to be changed.

Extensions. The pre-authentication framework provides extensibility for Kerberos. The messages that are exchanged with the KDC include a pre-authentication data field. Within this field, any data can be included. For standardization purposes, RFC 6113 determines functions and tools that provide information on how to develop new pre-authentication mechanisms. This allows for the facilitation of integration in existing software projects. Several such extensions that make use of this possibility have been developed in the past. [3]

One such extension is called *Flexible Authentication Secure Tunneling* (FAST). From a technical perspective, this is a new pre-authentication type that includes an encrypted component. This enables secure transmission of data between a client and the KDC (within a tunnel). This functionality is useful for new pre-authentication mechanisms, as data can be securely exchanged within FAST messages.

The key for the encryption is called armor key (K_{Armor}). This key is derived from the session key of the armor TGT and a sub-key of the user key. To retrieve the armor TGT, several methods are possible according to RFC 6113. One of them is the use of (anonymous[1]) PKINIT (Public Key Cryptography for Initial Authentication), another important Kerberos extension (RFC 4556) that enables authentication in Kerberos via asymmetric cryptography [5].

2.2 Self-Sovereign Identity (SSI)

With *Self-Sovereign Identity* (SSI) paradigm, users get control over their digital identities. This is in contrast to other identity management models used so far.

The basis for SSI is a new identifier that does not rely on a central trust authority. The *Decentralized Identifier* (DID), which can be created on one's own, identifies a subject (a person, organization, object, etc.). The DID is managed by a DID controller (in most cases the same person as the DID subject) who can cryptographically prove that he controls the DID. [6] Typically, a DID document, containing data like a public key or information about the initiation of a secure connection (i.e., an URL to the DID subject), is assigned to a DID. The DID and the corresponding DID document are typically stored on a verifiable data registry (VDR)—in most cases on a Blockchain [6,7].

Building upon (layer 1) DIDs, the *DID Communication Protocol* (DIDComm) is located on layer 2. DIDComm enables asynchronous and end-to-end encrypted connections between communication partners. DIDComm can be used independently of the transport mechanism (e.g., HTTP, Bluetooth, email, NFC,...). There are different ways how the communication initiation can be

[1] Anonymous PKINIT means that only the KDC is authenticated and the client stays anonymous [4].

achieved. The sending party might either know the recipient's DID (and can then look up the necessary data on the Blockchain—i.e., the URL of the recipient and its public key) or the sending party receives a communication invitation by scanning a QR code (and thereby retrieving the necessary data). The sending party's agent then encrypts and signs the message and sends it to the recipient—whose agent performs the decryption and signature check (the public key of the sender being retrieved through the sender's DID document on the Blockchain).

Another layer provides trust: On layer 3, we have so-called *Verifiable Credentials* (VCs), which can be used to vouch for certain facts, e.g. that a person is a student at a certain university. [8] VCs are the digital equivalent of ID documents. They are issued by an *issuer* and digitally stored by the *holder* in a wallet and can be shown to a *verifier* on demand. The individual statements about a subject are called claims. For the proof towards a verifier, a so-called *Verifiable Presentation* (VP) is created. VPs support *Selective Disclosure*, which enables sharing only particular claims and not the whole VC. There are two types of VCs: *W3C Verifiable Credentials* and *AnonCreds*. With W3C VCs a standard for the data model of VCs is determined. AnonCreds were developed earlier and have stronger protection of anonymity as a goal. Due to their widespread, they are the de-facto standard for zero-knowledge proof (ZKP) based credentials.

3 Requirement Analysis

Before we discuss the requirements in detail, we point out why the integration of SSI in Kerberos is advantageous, i.e., which improvements can be achieved.

Mitigation of the Password Risk: Passwords are completely removed with our Kerberos extension, as users only present verifiable credentials, thus, mitigating the main security risk of Kerberos. Moreover, the strength of the encryption in Kerberos is also improved as it does not depend on the strength of a user password anymore.

No Central Storage of User Keys: As the users and the KDC does not need a common secret anymore with our extension, there is no need for a central database with user keys anymore. This minimizes the risk of an attack and the compromising of user accounts.

DIDs and VCs Instead of CAs: The drawbacks of passwords could be eliminated by the PKINIT Kerberos extension. However, CAs are used as trusted third parties (TTPs) with the PKINIT extension to bind public keys to user names (introducing a potential single point of failure). With our extension, issuers (only) issue VCs that contain claims about a user behind a DID. The binding of DIDs to keys is done in a decentralized and independent way. The trust shifts from CAs to governance authorities. For our use case, the SSI architecture has the advantage that the keys of the DIDs can be rotated independently. Moreover, the number of issuers increases due to the separation of identity verification and public key verification [7] and VCs are more flexible than certificates (e.g., any attributes and any combinations of VCs in a VP are possible).

Data Minimization: By using selective disclosure, the user only needs to share the data of a VC that are needed for authentication and authorization.

Single Verification: A user can use a VC for authentication and authorization at different KDCs. There is no need for a second account, an exchange for a password, or additional verification. The KDC gets all the needed data for the login through VCs (or even claims from different VCs in a VP).

Increase of Comfort: The user does not need to remember a password with our extension but only needs to unlock his wallet and show the claims.

Integration in Existing Infrastructure: It is easier to keep the infrastructure for services by integrating SSI into an existing protocol than to change the overall architecture by migrating to SSI (i.e., get rid of IdP, adapt every single service, etc.). [9]. For our scenario, this means that the access to services is still done by using tickets (the infrastructure with kerberized services does not need to be adapted). Only the AS protocol is adapted so that SSI can be used as an additional login method in Kerberos.

3.1 Requirements

Functional Requirements

- FR1: The user can get a TGT with his SSI
- FR2: Claims can be extracted from a VC to enable authorization
- FR3: CAs get replaced by a decentralized solution
- FR4: The login at a Kerberos system shall be possible without prior registration at the KDC
- FR5: The KDC does not need to store a database with user keys
- FR6: The user only needs to share those data that are needed for authentication and authorization (selective disclosure)
- FR7: The access to services is still done via tickets, i.e. the existing infrastructure of kerberized services does not need to be modified

Non-functional Requirements

- NFR1: The wallet with the SSI does not need to be on the same device on which the login shall take place
- NFR2: The extension shall be compatible with Kerberos clients that do not support the extension

4 Concept

4.1 Assumptions

To be able to log in to a Kerberos system, a user needs credentials from a trustworthy issuer. With SSI, a governance framework is used to establish trust. [8]

4.2 Merging of Kerberos and SSI Components

Let us start the concept description with a high-level overview (shown in Fig. 1) of a merging of Kerberos and SSI and by discussing the difficulties in doing so.

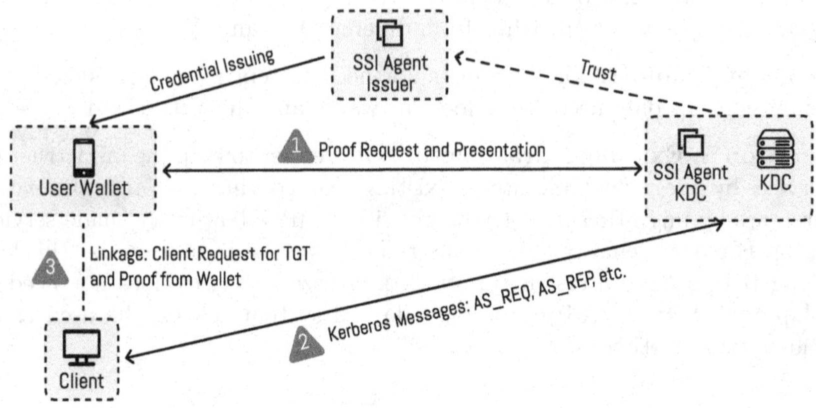

Fig. 1. Merging of Kerberos and SSI components.

As we can see in the overview, there is only a single change on the Kerberos side necessary: the KDC is extended by an SSI Agent. This implies a main change in responsibilities at the KDC as well: The KDC is not responsible for managing users any longer—instead, the SSI Agent verifies users' SSI credentials and provides the KDC with proper identity information. The account management of services at the KDC remains as it was.

It would be possible to extend the client with SSI capabilities, which would solve some challenges. We investigated this in detail but in the end, we came to the conclusion that this solution would have the disadvantage that the client software would need to be adapted and standard wallets could not be used. Thus, we will only focus on the solution where the client does not need to be adapted (except for the need to understand the new pre-authentication type).

Merging Kerberos and SSI is not straightforward and we can identify three significant challenges when doing so, which we will discuss now:

Challenge 1 (Transmission of the Proof): As shown in Fig. 1, the proof is directly exchanged between the user wallet and SSI Agent KDC. A possible protocol for the exchange of the proof is the *present proof protocol*[2].

Another option would be the aforementioned client extension with an SSI agent. [10] However, this would require that the wallet is able to forward credentials to other agents, a functionality not all wallets are equipped with. Moreover, the client agent would be involved in the proof process and could read the data.

[2] https://github.com/hyperledger/aries-rfcs/blob/main/features/0037-present-proof/README.md.

Challenge 2 (AS_REP Protection and KDC Authenticity): Parts of the message *AS_REP* are encrypted with K_{Client} in standard Kerberos. However, as there are no passwords from which the key could be derived any longer with our new extension, an alternative needs to be found. In standard Kerberos, the client knows that the KDC is authentic as only the KDC (and the client itself) knows the proper K_{Client}. The problem can be solved by using a FAST tunnel.

Challenge 3 (Connection of the client and the wallet): As stated for Challenge 1, the proof is directly sent from the user's wallet to the KDC's agent. However, the Kerberos message *AS_REQ* is sent from the client to the KDC. Thus, the KDC needs to link messages from two different sources.

We propose to use personalized DIDComm communication invitations to solve the problem: The KDC agent generates a communication invitation, which is then forwarded from the client to the user's wallet. When the user's wallet establishes a DIDComm communication via that invitation, the KDC agent determines the client via the connection ID [11].

4.3 Authorization

Authorizations can be extracted based on the user names from a central database in standard Kerberos. Another option is to transport them within the tickets.

In order to enable the full potential of SSI, we propose to write the claims to the TGT, resp. tickets. The user's DID is thereby used as the Kerberos username. During the login at a Kerberos system, the KDC agent sends a proof request to the user's wallet, which queries the role of the user. Afterward, when the client sends the *AS_REQ* message, the claims from the proof are written as authorization data into the TGT. When the TGT is used to get a ticket later on, the KDC transfers the authorization data from the TGT to the ticket. The service can then use the data for the authorization.

4.4 New Pre-authentication Type

As we decided to only extend the KDC with SSI functionality, it is not possible to securely communicate between the client and KDC via DIDComm-encrypted messages. We thus need an alternative for secure communication. We employ the FAST tunnel as described in Sect. 2 for that.

Another challenge for our extension is that KDCs do not hold state in Kerberos (which is a main design goal). KDCs can be replicated and two consecutive requests do not necessarily get to the same KDC [3].

We use new pre-authentication types: If the type *PA-SSI-REQUEST* is contained in the *AS_REQ* message, the KDC knows that the SSI extension shall be used.

If it is the first request, there is no cookie contained in the message and the KDC requests a new DIDComm invitation (coming with a Connection ID) from its SSI agent. The KDC then creates a Connection ID Cookie by encrypting the Connection ID with K_{KDC}. This ensures that no other party can create the cookie. The KDC then sends the invitation and the cookie back to the client as part of the new pre-authentication type *PA-SSI-INFO*.

If the Connection ID Cookie is contained in the *AS_REQ* message, the KDC decrypts it and retrieves the Connection ID. This serves as evidence that the client retrieved the invitation suitable to the Connection ID before. The Connection ID is then used to check whether a proof is available. If this is the case, the proof is retrieved and the data are used to generate the *AS_REP* message.

4.5 AS_REP Protection and KDC Authenticity

As an alternative to K_{Client}, the armor key is used to encrypt the message *AS_REP*. The KDC's authenticity is determined when retrieving the armor ticket. By using PKINIT, the signature of the KDC (as part of *AS_REP*) is validated with the KDC's certificate. The certificate needs to be issued by a CA trusted by the client.

4.6 Protocol in Detail

Now that we have discussed the design decisions and have the building blocks together, we can describe the whole protocol in detail.

Phase 1: Invitation for KDC SSI Agent

1. The user starts a new login attempt at a client. After the selection of a realm, an armor ticket is retrieved.
2. In order to signalize the KDC that the SSI extension shall be used, an *AS_REQ* message with the pre-authentication type *PA-SSI-REQUEST* is sent to the KDC. The FAST mechanism is used to encrypt the message with the armor key.
3. The KDC retrieves the request and notices the SSI pre-authentication element. The KDC then sends a request for a DIDComm invitation to its SSI agent. The SSI agent responds with a personalized invitation link and a corresponding Connection ID.
4. The KDC creates the Connection ID Cookie and forwards it (together with the invitation link) to the client via an encrypted error message. The error code is *MORE_PREAUTH_DATA_REQUIRED*.
5. The client presents the invitation link in the form of a QR code to the user.

Phase 2: Identity Proof

1. The user scans the QR code with his wallet. This causes the wallet to establish a DIDComm connection to the KDC SSI Agent. The KDC SSI Agent requests a proof request with the relevant attributes.
2. The wallet shows the user the proof request and the user chooses the proper credentials. After the user's confirmation, a proof presentation is sent to the KDC SSI Agent. All the advantages of SSI, like Selective Disclosure, can be used in this step.
3. The KDC SSI Agent retrieves and verifies the proof.

Phase 3: Ticket Retrieval

1. The user informs the client via a button that the proof has been submitted. The client then issues a new *AS_REQ* request with the type *PA-SSI-REQUEST* through the FAST tunnel. This time, the Connection ID Cookie is included.
2. The KDC extracts the cookie from the SSI pre-authentication element and decrypts it.
3. The KDC asks its SSI Agent whether a successful proof for the Connection ID is available.
4. If this is the case, the proof with the claims is forwarded to the KDC. The username and authorization data are set. The answer *AS_REP* is encrypted with the armor key and sent to the client. The login is finished. If there is no proof available, the client retrieves an error message.

5 Implementation

To demonstrate the functionality of our concept, we implemented a proof of concept (PoC). The system overview is shown in Fig. 2.

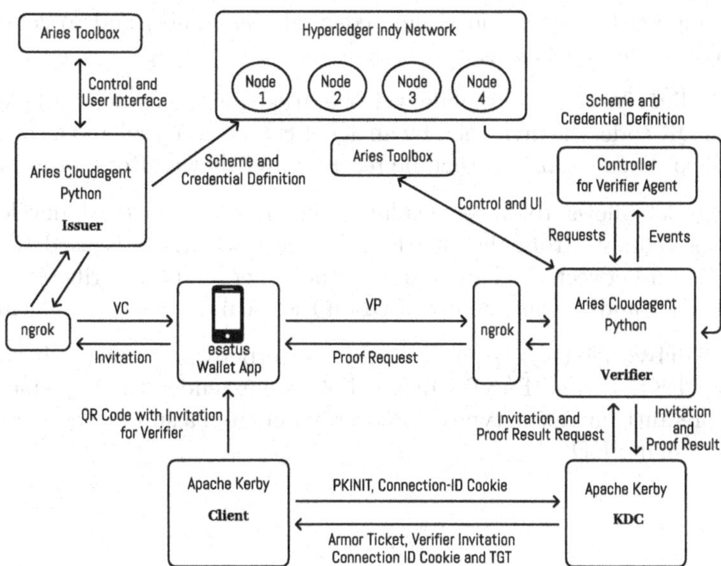

Fig. 2. PoC Implementation System Overview

5.1 Components

Indico DemoNet: The public permissioned Blockchain from the Hyperledger Indy project[3] is used for the SSI solution. The schemata and credential definitions are stored on the Blockchain by the issuer.

Aries Cloudagent Python: An agent is needed for the interaction with the Indy blockchain and other components in the SSI ecosystem. The Aries Cloudagent Python[4] (ACA-py), developed in the Hyperledger Aries project, is best suited for our purpose. The agent is controlled by a controller software that receives webhook events such as the initiation of a new DIDComm connection. For our PoC, two instances of ACA-py are used in docker containers[5]. One agent takes the role of the issuer and the other agent takes the role of the verifier.

Verifier Controller: The controller for the verifier agent is written in Kotlin and uses the library ktor[6], which enables the setup of an HTTP server and the initiation of HTTP requests. When a new DIDComm connection is initiated (from ACA-py), an event is triggered. The controller is informed through a webhook and instructs the agent (via a REST request) to send a proof request.

Aries Toolbox: The Aries Toolbox[7] provides a user interface that helps configure the Aries Cloudagent Python: invitations can be created, connections can be queried and credentials can be created and issued via the UI for example. We used the toolbox to create and issue credentials (as issuer) and to control the functionality of the verifier agent.

esatus Wallet: We use the mobile wallet esatus[8] for the credential holder. By scanning a QR code, the invitation by an agent can be accepted and a connection is established. Credentials can then be received and shown after a proof request.

ngrok: ngrok[9] allows to make available the host of the local development machine for requests from the Internet. In our PoC, ngrok is used to enable communication between the mobile wallet, the issuer, and the verifier—as in our PoC, the issuer and verifier are executed on the local development machine.

Apache Kerby: We chose Apache Kerby as Kerberos solution, as it supports anonymous PKINIT and FAST. For our PoC, we extended the implementation by a new pre-authentication type. Moreover, we created a sub-project for a demo client and a demo KDC.

[3] https://www.hyperledger.org/use/hyperledger-indy.
[4] https://github.com/hyperledger/aries-cloudagent-python.
[5] https://hub.docker.com/r/bcgovimages/aries-cloudagent.
[6] https://ktor.io.
[7] https://github.com/hyperledger/aries-toolbox.
[8] https://esatus.com/index.html%3Fp=7947.html.
[9] https://ngrok.com.

5.2 Issuance of Credentials

The user needs to have credentials in his wallet, which are used for the login to the Kerberos system. We used the Aries Toolbox to prepare a schema for the membership at a certain organization (including several attributes) and write the schema definition to the Indico DemoNet in the role of the issuer. Moreover, the issuer is bound to the schema by a credential definition.

We furthermore created an invitation QR code for the issuer, which is scanned by the user with his wallet. The code contains the endpoint, where the issuer can be reached (in our case: the URL of ngrok with the forwarding to the development machine), as well as the key material for the initiation of a secure connection. When the user confirms the connection initiation, the credential can be sent to the wallet after input of the claim values. After confirmation, the credential is stored in the wallet and can be used.

5.3 Start of the Login

The user starts the login at the Kerberos client. After the client sends the *AS_REQ* message, it receives the Connection ID Cookie and the invitation for the KDC SSI Agent (as part of an error message). The invitation is embedded into a QR code and shown on the screen. The client shows the notice that the identity needs to be proven and that a button click proceeds the login later on.

5.4 Proof of the Identity with VP

When the user scans the QR code with his esatus wallet, a DIDComm connection from the wallet to the verifier is established. The controller is informed about the new connection via a webhook. The controller then prepares the proof request, which can be different for every use case. Restrictions can be used to state conditions for the claims; for example, only credentials from certain issuers with certain fields (e.g. roles) can be accepted. When the wallet receives the proof request, the user is notified and sees which information shall be transmitted. From the available credentials, the suitable ones are selected automatically. The user sees whether he has the needed authorizations even before sending the data.

5.5 Receiving the TGT

After the proof is sent to the verifier through the wallet, the login at the client is continued. When the KDC receives the *AS_REQ* (this time with the Connection ID Cookie), the cookie is decrypted to receive the Connection ID. The verifier is then contacted and asked via a REST inquiry, whether verified proofs for the Connection ID are available. If a valid proof is available, the user has proven his identity, and the username claim from the proof is used as the username in the TGT. The other claims from the proof are also extracted and written into the authorization field of the TGT. Before the TGT is sent to the client, the KDC deletes the proof via a REST call to the KDC SSI Agent. This ensures that the identity needs to be proven again when the user wants to authenticate again.

6 Evaluation

Our concept fulfills all requirements stated in Sect. 3.

6.1 Security Evaluation

Authenticity, integrity, and confidentiality of the messages between the user wallet and the KDC SSI Agent are ensured by the DIDComm protocol.

For the exchange of messages between the client and the KDC, the client needs to receive an armor ticket in advance. As we use PKINIT, the authenticity and integrity of the message can be checked by validating the signature of the KDC. The confidentiality of the message is ensured by the asymmetric encryption of the key.

With a symmetric key that is derived from the armor ticket, a secure tunnel can be established. The Connection ID Cookie and the invitation link are secured through this tunnel. Authenticity and integrity are given, as only the client and the KDC have the common key.

Every message exchanged between the client and the KDC using FAST is independent of each other. The KDC does not hold any state. Only the possession of the cookie identifies a client. Thus, it is important that an attacker does not gain access to the cookie, as he could impersonate the client then.

The encryption of the cookie with K_{KDC} ensures that only the KDC can generate and read it. The cookie is only exchanged encrypted and, thus, an attacker cannot retrieve the cookie in plain text.

The KDC and its SSI Agent communicate within a closed network without access to external parties, ensuring authenticity, integrity, and confidentiality.

The transmission of the DIDComm invitation from the client to the user's wallet is done through a QR code scan. The pre-requisite is that the client is not compromised and the QR code is authentic.

Replay Attack. An attacker could record the proof presentation from the user's wallet to the KDC SSI Agent and later on replay the proof as a response to another proof request. To prevent this attack, a nonce is included in each request. Only if the same nonce is included in the answer, the proof is accepted [3].

Another attack surface is the *AS_REQ* and *AS_REP* messages. A recorded answer could be replayed to the client. This is prevented in standard Kerberos by including a nonce in the *AS_REQ* message [12]. Moreover, an armor ticket shall only be used once. Afterward, a new armor ticket is needed [3]. An *AS_REP* message secured with the old armor key cannot be used in a replay attack.

The Connection ID Cookie shall only be usable once for the receiving of a TGT. Otherwise, it would equal a ticket with an infinite lifetime. This is why the proof available for a specific Connection ID is deleted before issuing the TGT. If the cookie is used once again, the proof does not exist anymore and the user needs to authenticate with his SSI again.

6.2 Comparison to Standard Kerberos

The main advantage of our extension is that users do not need to choose strong Kerberos passwords for each realm. Instead, a single private key for identity verification is stored via DID and VC within the wallet. Moreover, the strength of the encryption depends on the strength of the user's password in standard Kerberos. As we employ FAST for Kerberos message exchange and asymmetric encryption for DIDComm, the encryption is stronger as longer keys are employed. Another advantage of our extension with regards to security is that no more encryption keys of users are stored in a central database, prone to attacks.

Without the extension, the user is supplied with an identity via his account. By using SSI, the user is in full control of his identity and can use privacy-preserving mechanisms such as Selective Disclosure. Moreover, the user knows exactly which data are shared. Registration at the KDC is not necessary beforehand, as users can show all necessary attributes via verifiable credentials.

As SSI is universal, users can access services across realm borders, without the need for a prior registration. This is one of the major advantages of our extension in terms of usability for users. The main difference to standard Kerberos cross-realm authentication is that the home KDC does not need to be contacted and the target KDC does not need to be registered beforehand at the home KDC, simplifying cross-realm service usage not only for users but also for administrators. In the indirect cross-realm trust model in standard Kerberos, each KDC in the authentication chain has access to the session key, enabling MITM attacks [13]. As the authenticity is directly proven towards the target KDC with our extension, an indirect trust model can be realized without security loss.

A drawback of our extension is that the complexity of the overall system is extended. A verifiable data registry, a user wallet and an SSI agent is needed, which increases the setup overhead.

7 Related Work

An SSI integration has been proposed for other authentication protocols in the past. Integration in the OAuth 2.0 protocol was presented by Hong et al. [14]. However, the authors propose to store personal data in smart contracts on the Ethereum blockchain, contradicting privacy protection. In our concept, no personal data are stored on the Blockchain; instead, personal data are only stored within the users' wallets securely. Grüner et al. [15] and Lux et al. [16] proposed concepts for SSI integration in OpenID and Yildiz et al. [11] proposed to integrate SSI in the SAML protocol. Kuperberg et al. [9] show in their study how SSI can be integrated into conventional software using established protocols. They investigate popular SSI implementations and check whether they work together with typical IAM protocols. They point out that there is no SSI support for Kerberos—a gap that we close with our paper.

As mentioned in Sect. 2, PKINIT is an extension to Kerberos that allows authentication via asymmetric cryptography. The KDC and the users are thereby certified by a certificate authority (CA). In contrast to our extension, a user account needs to be created in the KDC database with PKINIT. It would theoretically be possible to include attributes in certificates that are used for authorization. However, our approach based on SSI is more flexible as VCs are more flexible (any content and the combination of VCs to a VP is possible), and better privacy protection is possible by using Selective Disclosure and ZKPs.

Another extension to Kerberos was proposed by Zheng et al. [17]: Tokens, issued by token authorities and representing user identities, should be usable as identity proof towards a Kerberos system. The most common type of token is the JSON Web Token (JWT). The extension by Zheng et al. currently works with bearer tokens, which can be used by anyone who possesses them. The approach provides a bridge to OAuth 2.0. In contrast to our extension, users are not in full control of their data, though.

8 Conclusion and Outlook

We presented an approach to integrate SSI usage in Kerberos, requiring only minimal changes in the Kerberos ecosystem in order to foster its practicability.

The main advantage of our approach is that we can get rid of (insecure) user passwords that pose a real threat in Windows environments, which use Kerberos for authentication. Moreover, our approach enables practical cross-realm service usage without requiring prior user registration or registrations of KDCs in other realms, which would be needed in standard Kerberos environments.

We are the first to propose to use SSI authentication and authorization in Kerberos. We are very confident that this approach—besides the security advantages—fosters SSI usage as there is a direct use case due to the widespread penetration of Kerberos environments in practice. SSI provides full control over their identities to users—for the first time in identity management and users can benefit in terms of privacy protection by making use of selective disclosure.

In future work, we plan to extend our solution to provide accounting as well. This third "a" (besides authentication and authorization) in the AAA Kerberos protocol has been neglected in practice so far and our approach (being based on the Blockchain technology) can make this practicable.

A formal security analysis of our approach is left as future work.

References

1. Garman, J.: Kerberos: The Definitive Guide. O'Reilly Media, Sebastopol (2003)
2. Kohl, J.T., Neuman, B.C., Theodore, Y.: The evolution of the Kerberos authentication service (1994)
3. Hartman, S., Zhu, L.: A Generalized Framework for Kerberos Pre-Authentication. RFC 6113 (2011). https://www.rfc-editor.org/info/rfc6113
4. PKINIT configuration (2022). https://web.mit.edu/kerberos/www/krb5-latest/doc/admin/pkinit.html
5. Zhu, L., Tung, B.: Public key cryptography for initial authentication in Kerberos (PKINIT). RFC 4556 (2006)

6. Reed, D., Sabadello, M., Sporny, M., Guy, A.: Decentralized Identifiers (DIDs) v1.0 (2022). https://www.w3.org/TR/2022/RECdid-core-20220719/
7. Preukschat, A., Reed, D.: Self-Sovereign Identity. Manning Publications, Shelter Island (2021)
8. Introduction to Trust Over IP (2021). https://trustoverip.org/wp-content/uploads/Introduction-to-ToIP-V2.0-2021-11-17.pdf
9. Kuperberg, M., Klemens, R.: Integration of self-sovereign identity into conventional software using established IAM protocols: a survey. In: Roßnagel, H., Schunck, C.H., Mödersheim, S. (eds.) Open Identity Summit 2022, pp. 51–62. Gesellschaft für Informatik e.V., Bonn (2022)
10. Noble, G., Sporny, M., Zundel, B., Burnett, D., Hartog, K.D., Longley, D.: Verifiable Credentials Data Model v1.1 (2022). https://www.w3.org/TR/2022/REC-vc-data-model-20220303/
11. Yildiz, H., Ritter, C., Nguyen, L.T., Frech, B., Martinez, M.M., Küpper, A.: Connecting self-sovereign identity with federated and user-centric identities via SAML integration. In: 2021 IEEE Symposium on Computers and Communications (ISCC), pp. 1–7 (2021)
12. Neuman, C., Yu, T., Hartman, S., Raeburn, K.: RFC 4120: The Kerberos Network Authentication Service (V5), USA (2005)
13. Sakane, S., Kamada, K., Zrelli, S., Ishiyama, M.: Problem Statement on the Cross-Realm Operation of Kerberos. RFC, vol. 5868, pp. 1–13 (2010). https://doi.org/10.17487/RFC5868
14. Hong, S., Kim, H.: VaultPoint: a blockchain-based SSI model that complies with OAuth 2.0. Electronics **9**(8) (2020). https://www.mdpi.com/2079-9292/9/8/1231
15. Grüner, A., Mühle, A., Meinel, C.: An integration architecture to enable service providers for self-sovereign identity. In: 2019 IEEE 18th International Symposium on Network Computing and Applications (NCA), pp. 1–5 (2019)
16. Lux, Z.A., Thatmann, D., Zickau, S., Beierle, F.: Distributed-ledger-based authentication with decentralized identifiers and verifiable credentials. In: 2020 2nd Conference on Blockchain Research & Applications for Innovative Networks and Services (BRAINS), pp. 71–78. IEEE (2020)
17. Zheng, K., Jiang, W.: A token authentication solution for hadoop based on kerberos pre-authentication. In: 2014 International Conference on Data Science and Advanced Analytics (DSAA), pp. 354–360 (2014)

Hierarchical Identity-Based Inner Product Functional Encryption for Unbounded Hierarchical Depth

Anushree Belel(✉), Ratna Dutta, and Sourav Mukhopadhyay

Indian Institute of Technology Kharagpur, Kharagpur 721302, West Bengal, India
anubelel@gmail.com, {ratna,sourav}@maths.iitkgp.ac.in

Abstract. Cloud computing is becoming popular with emerging applications in big data analysis, online storage, e-commerce, social network, accounting, and management. As industries, organizations and individuals prefer to use the cloud for high speed, scalability, and easy accessibility, it is essential to protect data privacy and security. *Inner product functional encryption* (IPFE) with access control is a promising technique for protecting privacy of original data by specifying who can obtain inner product on encrypted data in the cloud. *Hierarchical identity-based* IPFE (HID-IPFE), proposed by Song et al. (Information Sciences 2021) is a variant in hierarchical environment that specifies which hierarchical identities are allowed to obtain the inner product on encrypted data. We have observed that the existing works on HID-IPFE fixes the maximum hierarchical identity depth at the Setup phase. It is not practical as the maximum hierarchy depth may increase. To resolve this issue, we introduce the technique of *unbounded hierarchical identity-based inner product functional encryption* (UHID-IPFE) that does not fix maximum hierarchy depth at the Setup phase to support unbounded hierarchy depth. We provide an instantiation of *selective chosen plaintext attack* (CPA) secure UHID-IPFE protocol based on hardness of the q-RW2 problem. We prove the security of our protocol by detailed security analysis in the existing security model. More interestingly, our scheme outperforms the previous HID-IPFE schemes in terms of storage and is the first scheme supporting unbounded hierarchy depth.

Keywords: Inner product functional encryption · Hierarchical identity · Unbounded depth

1 Introduction

Recent emerging applications of cloud services highlight the demand for a sophisticated method of encryption rather than traditional *public key encryption* (PKE). To fix *all-or-nothing* type access on encrypted data, plain PKE has been refined over the years into more advanced primitives like *identity-based encryption* [9], *attribute-based encryption* [8], and *predicate encryption* [16]. All these mechanisms can be unified into a novel primitive called *functional encryption* (FE) proposed by Boneh et al. [12] with applications in privacy-preserving

S. Dolev and B. Schieber (Eds.): SSS 2023, LNCS 14310, pp. 274–288, 2023.
https://doi.org/10.1007/978-3-031-44274-2_20

cloud computing such as IoT e-Health care systems [21], secure Digital Rights Management system [1], tax calculations in smart cities [23], electricity billing via smart meters [15], and many more. As realizing FE for general functions requires heavy-duty cryptographic tools, there is a tendency to sketch FE for specific functionalities like inner product, boolean formula, and keyword search [16].

Inner product functional encryption (IPFE) is a specific type of FE that computes inner product on encrypted data. IPFE produces secret keys $\mathsf{SK}_{\boldsymbol{y}}$ for arbitrary chosen vectors $\boldsymbol{y}$ which can be used to decrypt a ciphertext $\mathsf{CT}_{\boldsymbol{x}}$ corresponding to a vector $\boldsymbol{x}$ and recover the inner product $\langle \boldsymbol{x}, \boldsymbol{y} \rangle$ in contrast to the original message $\boldsymbol{x}$ as in standard PKE. IPFE has important applications for computing the weighted mean. For enhancing IPFE with access control so that only specific users with a predefined identity are able to obtain the inner product, Abdalla et al. [3] introduced the technique of *identity-based* IPFE (ID-IPFE). This notion allows encryptors to specify a recipient identity ID in ciphertext $\mathsf{CT}_{\boldsymbol{x},\mathsf{ID}}$. Every secret key $\mathsf{SK}_{\boldsymbol{y},\mathsf{ID}'}$ is associated with an identity ID'. A user owning secret key $\mathsf{SK}_{\boldsymbol{y},\mathsf{ID}'}$ can decrypt the ciphertext $\mathsf{CT}_{\boldsymbol{x},\mathsf{ID}}$ to get $\langle \boldsymbol{x}, \boldsymbol{y} \rangle$ only if $\mathsf{ID}' = \mathsf{ID}$. Song et al. [22] extended the notion of ID-IPFE for hierarchical identity by adding an extra Delegate algorithm in ID-IPFE. In this notion, a user with hierarchical identity $\widetilde{\mathsf{HID}}$ possessing secret key $\mathsf{SK}_{\boldsymbol{y},\widetilde{\mathsf{HID}}}$ can apply the algorithm Delegate to generate secret key $\mathsf{SK}_{\boldsymbol{y},\mathsf{HID}'}$ for a lower level user in the hierarchy with identity $\mathsf{HID}' = \widetilde{\mathsf{HID}} \cup \mathsf{ID}$, encryptor specifies recipient identity HID in $\mathsf{CT}_{\boldsymbol{x},\mathsf{HID}}$, a user can decrypt $\mathsf{CT}_{\boldsymbol{x},\mathsf{HID}}$ to obtain $\langle \boldsymbol{x}, \boldsymbol{y} \rangle$ if it owns $\mathsf{SK}_{\boldsymbol{y},\mathsf{HID}}$ or can derive $\mathsf{SK}_{\boldsymbol{y},\mathsf{HID}}$ from its secret key $\mathsf{SK}_{\boldsymbol{y}\widetilde{\mathsf{HID}}}$ ($\widetilde{\mathsf{HID}}$ being a prefix of HID). The technique of *hierarchical identity-based* IPFE (HID-IPFE) monitors hierarchical system where higher-level users in the hierarchy can produce secret keys for lower-level users in the hierarchy. This property is very useful in real-life applications as the structure of most commercial and industrial systems is hierarchical. For instance, consider Company A consisting of numerous sectors: Social media marketing, Digital marketing, Graphic designing, Web development, Client servicing, etc. Several experts are there in each sector, and many trainers work under each expert. This company has announced internship advertisement and asked participants to encrypt grades for the skills of previous experience, academics, and programming. Suppose that a fresher candidate Bob receives grades 75 for previous experience, 65 for academics, and 60 for programming from an assessment center. Thus, the plaintext of Bob can be considered as a vector $\boldsymbol{x} = (75, 65, 60)$. Suppose that Bob wants to join as an intern under trainer T working under expert E at the Digital marketing sector in Company A. Bob encrypts $\boldsymbol{x}$ using the recipient identity HID = "Company A, Digital marketing sector, Expert E, Trainer T". Now, the trainer T is granted secret key $\mathsf{SK}_{\boldsymbol{y},\mathsf{HID}}$ with respect to weight vector $\boldsymbol{y} = (40\%, 30\%, 30\%)$ which assigns weights 40%, 30% and 30% for previous experience, academics, and programming respectively. Bob wants that only trainer T or his superiors (Head of the Company A or Head of the Digital marketing sector or Expert E) who provided a secret key to trainer T should learn $\langle \boldsymbol{x}, \boldsymbol{y} \rangle$. The advanced primitive HID-IPFE can be utilized in this application.

Generally, HID-IPFE is composed of polynomial time algorithms (Setup, Encrypt, KeyGen, Delegate, Decrypt). While Setup is performed, a trusted entity takes as input security parameter, vector length, maximum hierarchical identity depth and generates a public key together with a master secret key. It declares the public key and holds the master secret key secret. An encryptor takes input public key, a recipient hierarchical identity HID (depth of HID is less than or equal to the maximum hierarchy depth), plaintext vector $\boldsymbol{x}$, and produces ciphertext $\mathsf{CT}_{\boldsymbol{x},\mathsf{HID}}$. The trusted entity issues secret key $\mathsf{SK}_{\boldsymbol{y},\mathsf{HID}'}$ to recipient hierarchical identity HID' (depth of HID' is less than or equal to the maximum hierarchy depth) for a vector $\boldsymbol{y}$ by invoking the algorithm KeyGen. A higher-level user in the hierarchy with identity $\widetilde{\mathsf{HID}}$ owning secret key $\mathsf{SK}_{\boldsymbol{y},\widetilde{\mathsf{HID}}}$ applies Delegate algorithm to produce secret key $\mathsf{SK}_{\boldsymbol{y},\mathsf{HID}'}$ for a lower-level user in the hierarchy with identity $\mathsf{HID}' = \widetilde{\mathsf{HID}} \cup \mathsf{ID}$. A decryptor performs the algorithm Decrypt on input public key, $\mathsf{CT}_{\boldsymbol{x},\mathsf{HID}}$, $\mathsf{SK}_{\boldsymbol{y},\mathsf{HID}'}$ to obtain the inner product $\langle \boldsymbol{x}, \boldsymbol{y} \rangle$ if $\mathsf{HID} = \mathsf{HID}'$. Here $\mathsf{SK}_{\boldsymbol{y},\mathsf{HID}'}$ is produced by either KeyGen for vector $\boldsymbol{y}$ and identity HID' or by Delegate algorithm on input identity $\widetilde{\mathsf{HID}}$ and $\mathsf{SK}_{\boldsymbol{y},\widetilde{\mathsf{HID}}}$ ($\widetilde{\mathsf{HID}}$ being a prefix of HID'). If $\mathsf{HID} = \mathsf{HID}'$, the earlier one represents the event that intended recipient acts as decryptor while the latter one represents the event that delegator acts as decryptor. In 2021, Song et al. [22] proposed this notion of HID-IPFE which is selective *chosen plaintext attack* (CPA) secure based on the hardness of the *q-decisional bilinear Diffie-Hellman Exponent* (DBDHE) problem in a symmetric bilinear setting. In 2023, Belel et al. [6] provided another construction of selective CPA secure HID-IPFE from the hardness of standard DBDH problem. Note that, both of these constructions take input maximum hierarchical identity depth in the Setup phase.

Table 1. Comparison of storage overhead, communication bandwidth and other property

Scheme	Storage			Communication	Maximum hierarchy depth	Assumption	Security
	$\lvert\mathsf{PK}\rvert$	$\lvert\mathsf{MSK}\rvert$	$\lvert\mathsf{SK}\rvert$	$\lvert\mathsf{CT}\rvert$			
Song et al. [22]	$\mathcal{O}(d+n)$	$\mathcal{O}(1)$	$\mathcal{O}(d+n)$	$\mathcal{O}(l+n)$	bounded	q-DBDHE	Selective
Belel et al. [6]	$\mathcal{O}(d+n)$	$\mathcal{O}(n)$	$\mathcal{O}(l+n)$	$\mathcal{O}(l+n)$	bounded	DBDH	Selective
Our	$\mathcal{O}(n)$	$\mathcal{O}(1)$	$\mathcal{O}(l+n)$	$\mathcal{O}(l+n)$	unbounded	q-RW2	Selective

$\lvert\mathsf{PK}\rvert$ = size of public key, $\lvert\mathsf{MSK}\rvert$ = size of master secret key, $\lvert\mathsf{SK}\rvert$ = size of secret key, $\lvert\mathsf{CT}\rvert$ = size of ciphertext, l = hierarchical identity depth, d = maximum hierarchical identity depth, n = vector length

Our Contribution. In this work, we address the trouble of practical deployment of the existing HID-IPFE schemes as the maximum depth of hierarchical identity is kept fixed in the Setup phase. In real-life applications, the maximum hierarchy depth may change over time. In that case, the Setup algorithm has to be done again which is problematic. This inherent issue motivates us to extend the notion of HID-IPFE that supports unbounded hierarchical depth. Our Setup algorithm does not take input the maximum hierarchy depth. At the time of encryption and key generation, any arbitrary length of hierarchical identity can be chosen. We call this notion *unbounded* HID-IPFE. Our UHID-IPFE protocol uses the technique of Ryu et al. [20] and is established to be secure against *selective* CPA attacker under q-type assumption in a symmetric bilinear setting. Specifically, we establish the following.

Theorem 1. *(Informal) Based on the hardness of the* q-RW2 *problem, our* UHID-IPFE = (Setup, Encrypt, KeyGen, Delegate, Decrypt) *protocol is secure against selective* CPA *adversary.*

We compare storage, communication bandwidth, and other features of our scheme with respect to the previous approach of Song et al. [22] and Belel et al. [6] in Table 1.

- In our construction, we use symmetric bilinear pairing similar to the work of Song et al. [22] while Belel et al. [6] use asymmetric bilinear setting. We emphasize that unlike the previous works [6,22], our public key size does not depend on the maximum hierarchy depth. The public key sizes ($|\mathsf{PK}|$) of [6,22] are linear to the maximum hierarchy depth d and length of vector n while our public key sizes ($|\mathsf{PK}|$) is only linear to the length of vector n. Our master secret key size ($|\mathsf{MSK}|$) is constant size (only 1) similar to [22] while that of [6] is linear to n. Our secret key size ($|\mathsf{SK}|$) is linear to n and the depth of hierarchical identity l (chosen at key generation time) is similar to [6] while that of [22] is linear to n and d (maximum hierarchy depth). Like the existing schemes, our ciphertext size is also linear to l and n. Thus, we obtain an HID-IPFE scheme supporting unbounded hierarchical depth without compromising storage and communication bandwidth.
- Our scheme achieves selective security against *chosen plaintext attack* (CPA) adversary in the existing security model under the hardness of the q-RW2 problem. Note that similar to the previous works our security proof against selective CPA adversary also follows the standard model without using any random oracles. Thus, our proposed UHID-IPFE scheme is also comparable with the previous HID-IPFE schemes in terms of security.

Related Work. In 2015, Abdalla et al. [2] formally introduced IPFE with direct applications in privacy-preserving approaches in cloud computing followed by a series of improved variants [5,7,13,17]. In 2020, Abdalla et al. [3] provided new IPFE schemes allowing users to insert access policy on the encrypted data. They provided two *identity-based* IPFE (IB-IPFE) protocols from the *learning with errors* (LWE) problem. One scheme combines the LWE based *identity-based encryption* (IBE) of Gentry et al. [14] with the LWE based IPFE of Agrawal et al. [5] and achieves adaptive security in the random oracle model while the other scheme integrates the LWE based IBE of Agrawal et al. [4] with the LWE based IPFE of Agrawal et al. [5] and achieves selective security in the standard model. They also proposed the notion of *attribute-based* IPFE (AB-IPFE) where ciphertext $\mathsf{CT}_{\boldsymbol{x},\mathsf{P}}$ is related to a predicate P and a vector $\boldsymbol{x}$, secret key $\mathsf{SK}_{\boldsymbol{y},\mathsf{att}}$ is related to a vector $\boldsymbol{y}$ and an attribute att, a decryptor possessing secret key $\mathsf{SK}_{\boldsymbol{y},\mathsf{att}}$ gets $\langle \boldsymbol{x}, \boldsymbol{y} \rangle$ if att satisfies predicate P. Their constructions are quite generic and combine the *decisional Diffie-Hellman* (DDH) based IPFE scheme of [5] with existing pairing based attribute-based encryption that makes use of the dual system encryption methodology. In 2020, Zhang et al. [25] provided an adaptively secure construction of IB-IPFE from hardness of the DBDH problem. In 2021, Song et al. [22] introduced *hierarchical identity-based* IPFE (HID-IPFE) and provided a selective secure construction of HID-IPFE from the hardness of the q-DBDHE assumption. In 2023, Belel et al. [6] came up with another selective secure HIB-IPFE protocol conditioned on the hardness of the DBDH assumption utilizing *hierarchical* IBE scheme of Boneh et al. [10]. In 2021, Pal et al. [18] provided construction of LWE based AB-IPFE integrating the LWE based *attribute-based encryption* (ABE) protocol of Boneh et al. [11] with LWE based IPFE protocol of [5]. In 2019, Sans et al. introduced the concept of *unbounded* IPFE that handles vectors of unbounded lengths and provided a selective secure construction of UIPFE based on the DBDH problem. In 2020, Tomida et al. [24] came up with two instantiations of UIPFE based on the *symmetric external Diffie-Hellman* (SXDH) problem.

2 Preliminaries

2.1 Notation

λ stands for the security parameter and $[n]$ denotes the set $\{1, 2, \ldots, n\}$. We use $x \xleftarrow{u} S$ to indicate that x is chosen uniformly from the set S. A map $f : \mathbb{N} \to \mathbb{R}$ is called a *negligible* function of n if it is $\mathcal{O}(n^{-c})$ for all $c > 0$ and we make use of the notation $\mathsf{negl}(n)$ for the negligible function of n. Let $\perp$ represent failure or null value and $\langle \cdot, \cdot \rangle$ stands for inner product of two vectors.

2.2 Unbounded Hierarchical Identity-Based Inner Product Functional Encryption

We initiate the study of a variant of Hierarchical Identity-based Inner Product Functional Encryption (HID-IPFE) supporting unbounded hierarchical depth following the work of Song et al. [22]. An unbounded HID-IPFE (UHID-IPFE) scheme comprises the algorithms HID-IPFE = (Setup, Encrypt, KeyGen, Delegate, Decrypt) as defined below.

- $\mathsf{Setup}\ (1^\lambda, n) \to (\mathsf{PK}, \mathsf{MSK})$: On input the security parameter λ, vector length n, a trusted entity executes this probabilistic algorithm to produce the public key PK and the master secret key MSK. It publishes PK and keeps MSK secret to itself.
- $\mathsf{Encrypt}\ (\mathsf{PK}, \mathsf{HID}_l, \boldsymbol{x}) \to \mathsf{CT}_{\boldsymbol{x},\mathsf{HID}_l}$: An encryptor takes as input the public key PK, a hierarchical identity $\mathsf{HID}_l = (\mathsf{ID}_1, \mathsf{ID}_2, \ldots, \mathsf{ID}_l)$ of depth $l \in \mathbb{N}$, a plaintext vector $\boldsymbol{x}$ of length n and computes the corresponding ciphertext $\mathsf{CT}_{\boldsymbol{x},\mathsf{HID}_l}$.

- $\mathsf{KeyGen}\ (\mathsf{PK}, \mathsf{MSK}, \mathsf{HID}_l, \boldsymbol{y}) \rightarrow \mathsf{SK}_{\boldsymbol{y},\mathsf{HID}_l}$: On input the public key PK, the master secret key MSK, a hierarchical identity $\mathsf{HID}_l = (\mathsf{ID}_1, \mathsf{ID}_2, \ldots, \mathsf{ID}_l)$ of depth $l \in \mathbb{N}$, a vector $\boldsymbol{y}$ of length n, the trusted entity runs this algorithm to generate a secret key $\mathsf{SK}_{\boldsymbol{y},\mathsf{HID}_l}$. It sends $\mathsf{SK}_{\boldsymbol{y},\mathsf{HID}_l}$ to the user with hierarchical identity HID_l via a secure channel between them.
- $\mathsf{Delegate}\ (\mathsf{PK}, \mathsf{HID}_l, \mathsf{SK}_{\boldsymbol{y},\mathsf{HID}_l}, \mathsf{ID}) \rightarrow \mathsf{SK}_{\boldsymbol{y},\mathsf{HID}_{l+1}}$: A user with hierarchical identity HID_l performs this algorithm taking input the public key PK, a secret key $\mathsf{SK}_{\boldsymbol{y},\mathsf{HID}_l}$ corresponding to its hierarchical identity HID_l of depth $l \in \mathbb{N}$ and vector $\boldsymbol{y}$ of length n, a sub-identity ID and generates a secret key $\mathsf{SK}_{\boldsymbol{y},\mathsf{HID}_{l+1}}$ associated with a level $l+1$ identity $\mathsf{HID}_{l+1} = \mathsf{HID}_l \cup \mathsf{ID}$ and vector $\boldsymbol{y}$.
- $\mathsf{Decrypt}\ (\mathsf{PK}, \mathsf{CT}_{\boldsymbol{x},\mathsf{HID}}, \mathsf{SK}_{\boldsymbol{y},\mathsf{HID}'}) \rightarrow \langle \boldsymbol{x}, \boldsymbol{y} \rangle /\ \perp$: On input the public key PK, ciphertext $\mathsf{CT}_{\boldsymbol{x},\mathsf{HID}}$, secret key $\mathsf{SK}_{\boldsymbol{y},\mathsf{HID}'}$, a decryptor obtains the inner product $\langle \boldsymbol{x}, \boldsymbol{y} \rangle$ or $\perp$.

Correctness. It is required for $(\mathsf{PK}, \mathsf{MSK}) \leftarrow \mathsf{Setup}\ (1^\lambda, n)$, $\mathsf{SK}_{\boldsymbol{y},\mathsf{HID}'} \leftarrow \mathsf{KeyGen}(\mathsf{PK}, \mathsf{MSK}, \mathsf{HID}', \boldsymbol{y}) / \mathsf{Delegate}\ (\mathsf{PK}, \widehat{\mathsf{HID}}, \mathsf{SK}_{\boldsymbol{y},\widehat{\mathsf{HID}}}, \mathsf{ID})$ where $\mathsf{HID}' = \widehat{\mathsf{HID}} \cup \mathsf{ID}$ ($\widehat{\mathsf{HID}}$ being a prefix of HID') , $\mathsf{CT}_{\boldsymbol{x},\mathsf{HID}} \leftarrow \mathsf{Encrypt}(\mathsf{PK}, \mathsf{HID}, \boldsymbol{x})$ output $\perp$ if $\mathsf{HID} \neq \mathsf{HID}'$. Else,

$$\mathsf{Decrypt}(\mathsf{PK}, \mathsf{CT}_{\boldsymbol{x},\mathsf{HID}}, \mathsf{SK}_{\boldsymbol{y},\mathsf{HID}'}) = \langle \boldsymbol{x}, \boldsymbol{y} \rangle$$

where $\langle \boldsymbol{x}, \boldsymbol{y} \rangle$ is from a fixed polynomial size range.

Security. The security game of UHID-IPFE between challenger $\mathcal{C}$ and *selective chosen plaintext attack* adversary $\mathcal{A}$ is described below.

- **Init**: $\mathcal{A}$ submits two challenge vectors $\boldsymbol{x}_0^\star$, $\boldsymbol{x}_1^\star$ ($\boldsymbol{x}_0^\star \neq \boldsymbol{x}_1^\star$) and a challenge hierarchical identity $\mathsf{HID}^\star$ to $\mathcal{C}$.
- **Setup**: $\mathcal{C}$ produces $(\mathsf{PK}, \mathsf{MSK}) \leftarrow \mathsf{Setup}(1^\lambda, n)$ and issues PK to $\mathcal{A}$.
- **Query phase 1**: $\mathcal{A}$ asks private key queries $\mathsf{SK}_{\boldsymbol{y},\mathsf{HID}}$ corresponding to vector $\boldsymbol{y}$ and hierarchical identity HID to $\mathcal{C}$ polynomially many times. We assume that $|\mathsf{HID}| \leq |\mathsf{HID}^\star|$ where the notation $|\mathsf{HID}|$ is used to denote the depth of the hierarchical identity HID. $\mathcal{C}$ answers with $\mathsf{SK}_{\boldsymbol{y},\mathsf{HID}} \leftarrow \mathsf{KeyGen}(\mathsf{PK}, \mathsf{MSK}, \mathsf{HID}, \boldsymbol{y})$ following the restriction that if $\langle \boldsymbol{x}_0^\star - \boldsymbol{x}_1^\star, \boldsymbol{y} \rangle \neq 0$, then HID should not be a prefix of the challenge hierarchical identity $\mathsf{HID}^\star$. If depth of the hierarchical identity $|\mathsf{HID}|$ is strictly greater than the challenge hierarchical identity $|\mathsf{HID}^\star|$, $\mathcal{C}$ first evaluates $\mathsf{SK}_{\boldsymbol{y},\mathsf{HID}''} \leftarrow \mathsf{KeyGen}(\mathsf{PK}, \mathsf{MSK}, \mathsf{HID}'', \boldsymbol{y})$ (HID'' being the prefix of HID with $|\mathsf{HID}''| = |\mathsf{HID}^\star|$), computes $\mathsf{SK}_{\boldsymbol{y},\mathsf{HID}}$ by applying algorithm $\mathsf{Delegate}$ $(|\mathsf{HID}| - |\mathsf{HID}^\star|)$ times beginning from $\mathsf{SK}_{\boldsymbol{y},\mathsf{HID}''}$ and sends $\mathsf{SK}_{\boldsymbol{y},\mathsf{HID}}$ to $\mathcal{A}$.
- **Challenge**: $\mathcal{C}$ randomly chooses a bit $\beta \in \{0, 1\}$, evaluates $\mathsf{CT}_{\boldsymbol{x}_\beta^\star,\mathsf{HID}^\star} \leftarrow \mathsf{Encrypt}(\mathsf{PK}, \mathsf{HID}^\star, \boldsymbol{x}_\beta^\star)$ and issues the challenge ciphertext $\mathsf{CT}_{\boldsymbol{x}_\beta^\star,\mathsf{HID}^\star}$ to $\mathcal{A}$.
- **Query phase 2**: Similar to Query phase 1.
- **Guess**: At last, $\mathcal{A}$ returns a guess β' and wins the game if $\beta' = \beta$.

Advantage of $\mathcal{A}$ is interpreted as:

$$\mathsf{Adv}^{s\mathsf{CPA}}_{\mathsf{UHID-IPFE},\mathcal{A}}(\lambda) = \left| \mathsf{Pr}[\beta' = \beta] - \frac{1}{2} \right|$$

A UHID-IPFE protocol is called selectively CPA-secure if

$$\mathsf{Adv}^{s\mathsf{CPA}}_{\mathsf{HID-IPFE},\mathcal{A}}(\lambda) \le \mathsf{negl}(\lambda)$$

The restriction imposed on the Query phase 1 is necessary. Otherwise, $\mathcal{A}$ will get $\mathsf{SK}_{\boldsymbol{y},\mathsf{HID}}$ for some pair $(\boldsymbol{y}, \mathsf{HID})$ where HID is a prefix of $\mathsf{HID}^\star$ and $\langle \boldsymbol{x}_0^\star, \boldsymbol{y}\rangle \neq \langle \boldsymbol{x}_1^\star, \boldsymbol{y}\rangle$. Then $\mathcal{A}$ applies the Delegate algorithm to produce $\mathsf{SK}_{\boldsymbol{y},\mathsf{HID}^\star}$ and compute $\langle \boldsymbol{x}_\beta^\star, \boldsymbol{y}\rangle$ by using the Decrypt algorithm on input $\mathsf{CT}_{\boldsymbol{x}_\beta^\star,\mathsf{HID}^\star}$ and $\mathsf{SK}_{\boldsymbol{y},\mathsf{HID}^\star}$. Finally, $\mathcal{A}$ returns a bit 1 if $\langle \boldsymbol{x}_\beta^\star, \boldsymbol{y}\rangle = \langle \boldsymbol{x}_1^\star, \boldsymbol{y}\rangle$ and returns a bit 0 if $\langle \boldsymbol{x}_\beta^\star, \boldsymbol{y}\rangle = \langle \boldsymbol{x}_0^\star, \boldsymbol{y}\rangle$. Hence, $\mathcal{A}$ easily wins the game.

2.3 Symmetric Bilinear Map and Hardness Assumption

Definition 1. (Symmetric Bilinear Map). *Let $\mathbb{G}, \mathbb{G}_t$ be multiplicative cyclic groups having prime order p with generators g, $e(g, g)$ respectively. A symmetric bilinear map $e : \mathbb{G} \times \mathbb{G} \to \mathbb{G}_t$ satisfies the following.*

1. *$e(g^a, h^b) = e(g, h)^{ab}$ $\forall g, h \in \mathbb{G}$ and $\forall a, b \in \mathbb{Z}_p$.*
2. *The mapping is non-degenerate and $e(g, g)$ is a generator of $\mathbb{G}_t$.*
3. *There exists efficient technique to calculate $e(g, h)$ for all $g, h \in \mathbb{G}$.*

we assume that there exists a group generator scheme $\mathcal{G}$ that on input security parameter λ outputs a tuple $(p, \mathbb{G}, \mathbb{G}_t, e)$ where p is a prime having $\Theta(\lambda)$ bits.

Definition 2. (q-RW2 Assumption) *[20]. Let $\mathbb{G}$, $\mathbb{G}_t$ be cyclic groups having prime order p and $e : \mathbb{G} \times \mathbb{G} \to \mathbb{G}_t$ be a symmetric bilinear map. Let $a, b, c, \{d_i\}_{i\in[q]} \xleftarrow{u} \mathbb{Z}_p$, g be an arbitrary generator of $\mathbb{G}$, $z_1 = (g,\ g^a,\ g^b,\ g^c,\ g^{(ac)^2},\ \{g^{d_i},\ g^{acd_i},\ g^{ac/d_i},\ g^{a^2cd_i},\ g^{b/d_i^2},\ g^{b^2/d_i^2}\}_{i\in[q]}, \{g^{acd_i/d_j}, g^{bd_i/d_j^2}, g^{abcd_i/d_j^2}, g^{(ac)^2d_i/d_j}\}_{i,j\in[q],i\neq j})$ and $z_2 \in \mathbb{G}_t$. Given (z_1, z_2), the q-RW2 problem decides if z_2 is $e(g, g)^{abc}$ or an arbitrary member of $\mathbb{G}_t$. Advantage of a differentiator $\mathcal{A}$ is interpreted as*

$$\mathsf{Adv}^{q-\mathsf{RW2}}_{\mathcal{A}}(\lambda) = |\mathsf{Pr}[\mathcal{A}(z_1, e(g, g)^{abc}) \to 1] - \mathsf{Pr}[\mathcal{A}(z_1, z_2) \to 1]|$$

This hardness assumption was first introduced by Rouselakis et al. [19] and was proven to be secure in the generic group model (GGM).

3 Construction of UHID-IPFE

Our UHID-IPFE = (Setup, Encrypt, KeyGen, Delegate, Decrypt) protocol has hierarchical identity space $\{0, 1\}^{\lambda l}$ for $l \in \mathbb{N}$, vector space $\mathbb{Z}_p^n$ and utilizes symmetric bilinear setting.

- $\mathsf{Setup}(1^\lambda, n) \to (\mathsf{PK}, \mathsf{MSK})$: A trusted entity on input security parameter λ, vector length n proceeds in following way.

- Generates a symmetric bilinear map $e : \mathbb{G} \times \mathbb{G} \to \mathbb{G}_t$ ($\mathbb{G}, \mathbb{G}_t$ being cyclic groups having prime order p) and arbitrarily selects generator g of $\mathbb{G}$. Let $\mathcal{T}$ be a subset of $\mathbb{Z}_p$ that specifies the polynomial range for the inner product value to be obtained at the end of decryption phase.
- Arbitrarily selects $u, v, h_1, h_2, \ldots, h_n \in \mathbb{G}$, $a, b \in \mathbb{Z}_p$ and specifies $g_1 = g^a, g_2 = g^b, \alpha = ab, w_i = e(g, h_i)^\alpha$ for $i \in [n]$.
- Specifies public key and master secret key as

$$\mathsf{PK} = (p, \mathbb{G}, \mathbb{G}_t, e, g, g_t = e(g,g), u, v, g_1, g_2, \{h_i\}_{i\in[n]}, \{w_i\}_{i\in[n]}), \mathsf{MSK} = \alpha$$

- It declares PK and holds MSK secret to itself.

– $\mathsf{Encrypt}(\mathsf{PK}, \mathsf{HID}_l, \boldsymbol{x}) \to \mathsf{CT}_{\boldsymbol{x},\mathsf{HID}_l}$: An encryptor takes as input

$$\mathsf{PK} = (p, \mathbb{G}, \mathbb{G}_t, e, g, g_t, u, v, g_1, g_2, \{h_i\}_{i\in[n]}, \{w_i\}_{i\in[n]}),$$

a recipient identity $\mathsf{HID}_l = (\mathsf{ID}_1, \mathsf{ID}_2, \ldots, \mathsf{ID}_l) \in \mathcal{I}^l$ where $\mathcal{I} = \{0,1\}^\lambda$, plain-text vector $\boldsymbol{x} = (x_1, x_2, \ldots, x_n) \in \mathbb{Z}_p^n$ and executes the subsequent steps.

- Selects $r, s_1, s_2, \ldots, s_l \xleftarrow{u} \mathbb{Z}_p$, extracts $g, g_t, u, v, g_1, \{w_i\}_{i\in[n]}$ from PK and evaluates

$$E_i = g_t^{x_i} w_i^r, i \in [n], C_0 = g^r, \{C_{k,1} = g^{s_k}, C_{k,2} = (u^{\mathsf{ID}_k} v)^{s_k} g_1^{-r}\}_{k\in[l]}$$

- Sets $\mathsf{CT}_{\boldsymbol{x},\mathsf{HID}_l} = (\mathsf{HID}_l, \{E_i\}_{i\in[n]}, C_0, \{C_{k,1}, C_{k,2}\}_{k\in[l]})$ and publishes $\mathsf{CT}_{\boldsymbol{x},\mathsf{HID}_l}$.

– $\mathsf{KeyGen}(\mathsf{PK}, \mathsf{MSK}, \mathsf{HID}_l, \boldsymbol{y}) \to \mathsf{SK}_{\boldsymbol{y},\mathsf{HID}_l}$: On input PK, MSK, $\mathsf{HID}_l = (\mathsf{ID}_1, \mathsf{ID}_2, \ldots, \mathsf{ID}_l) \in \mathcal{I}^l$ where $\mathcal{I} = \{0,1\}^\lambda$, a vector $\boldsymbol{y} = (y_1, y_2, \ldots, y_n) \in \mathbb{Z}_p^n$, the trusted authority proceeds as follows.

- Chooses $\gamma_1, \gamma_2, \ldots, \gamma_l \xleftarrow{u} \mathbb{Z}_p$, extracts $g, g_1, u, v, \{h_i\}_{i\in[n]}$ from PK, α from MSK and computes

$$D_0 = (h_1^{y_1} h_2^{y_2} \ldots h_n^{y_n})^\alpha \prod_{i=1}^{l} g_1^{\gamma_i}, \{D_{i,1} = (u^{\mathsf{ID}_i} v)^{-\gamma_i}, D_{i,2} = g^{\gamma_i}\}_{i\in[l]}$$

- Sets $\mathsf{SK}_{\boldsymbol{y},\mathsf{HID}_l} = (\mathsf{HID}_l, \boldsymbol{y}, D_0, \{D_{i,1}, D_{i,2}\}_{i\in[l]})$ and provides $\mathsf{SK}_{\boldsymbol{y},\mathsf{HID}_l}$ to user owning hierarchical identity HID_l via a safe channel.

– $\mathsf{Delegate}(\mathsf{PK}, \mathsf{HID}_l, \mathsf{SK}_{\boldsymbol{y},\mathsf{HID}_l}, \mathsf{ID}_{l+1}) \to \mathsf{SK}_{\boldsymbol{y},\mathsf{HID}_{l+1}}$: A user owning identity $\mathsf{HID}_l = (\mathsf{ID}_1, \mathsf{ID}_2, \ldots, \mathsf{ID}_l)$ proceeds as follows taking input PK, $\mathsf{SK}_{\boldsymbol{y},\mathsf{HID}_l} = (\mathsf{HID}_l, \boldsymbol{y}, D_0, \{D_{i,1}, D_{i,2}\}_{i\in[l]})$ corresponding to HID_l, vector $\boldsymbol{y}$ and a sub-identity ID_{l+1}.

- Chooses arbitrarily $\gamma_{l+1} \in \mathbb{Z}_p$, extracts g, g_1, u, v from PK, computes

$$D_0' = D_0 g_1^{\gamma_{l+1}}, \{D_{i,1}' = D_{i,1}, D_{i,2}' = D_{i,2}\}_{i\in[l]}, D_{l+1,1}' = (u^{\mathsf{ID}_{l+1}} v)^{-\gamma_{l+1}}, D_{l+1,2}' = g^{\gamma_{l+1}},$$

and sets a temporary delegated secret key

$$\mathsf{TSK}_{\boldsymbol{y},\mathsf{HID}_{l+1}} = (\mathsf{HID}_{l+1} = \mathsf{HID}_l \cup \mathsf{ID}_{l+1}, \boldsymbol{y}, D_0', \{D_{i,1}', D_{i,2}'\}_{i\in[l+1]})$$

- Chooses arbitrarily $\widehat{\gamma}_1, \widehat{\gamma}_2, \ldots, \widehat{\gamma}_{l+1} \in \mathbb{Z}_p$, extracts g, g_1, u, v from PK and computes

$$D_0'' = D_0' \prod_{i=1}^{l+1} g_1^{\widehat{\gamma}_i}, \{D_{i,1}'' = D_{i,1}'(u^{\mathsf{ID}_i} v)^{-\widehat{\gamma}_i}, D_{i,2}'' = D_{i,2}'\, g^{\widehat{\gamma}_i}\}_{i\in[l+1]}$$

- Specifies

$$\mathsf{SK}_{\boldsymbol{y},\mathsf{HID}_{l+1}} = (\mathsf{HID}_{l+1} = \mathsf{HID}_l \cup \mathsf{ID}_{l+1}, \boldsymbol{y}, D_0'', \{D_{i,1}'', D_{i,2}''\}_{i\in[l+1]})$$

corresponding to depth $(l+1)$ identity $\mathsf{HID}_{l+1} = \mathsf{HID}_l \cup \mathsf{ID}_{l+1} = (\mathsf{ID}_1, \mathsf{ID}_2, \ldots, \mathsf{ID}_l, \mathsf{ID}_{l+1})$ and vector $\boldsymbol{y}$.
- Issues $\mathsf{SK}_{\boldsymbol{y},\mathsf{HID}_{l+1}}$ to user owning identity HID_{l+1} via a safe channel.

– $\mathsf{Decrypt}(\mathsf{PK}, \mathsf{CT}_{\boldsymbol{x},\mathsf{HID}}, \mathsf{SK}_{\boldsymbol{y},\mathsf{HID}'}) \rightarrow \langle \boldsymbol{x}, \boldsymbol{y}\rangle / \perp$: On input PK, $\mathsf{CT} = (\mathsf{HID}, \{E_i\}_{i\in[n]}, C_0, \{C_{i,1}, C_{i,2}\}_{i\in[l]})$, $\mathsf{SK} = (\mathsf{HID}', \boldsymbol{y} = (y_1, y_2, \ldots, y_n), D_0, \{D_{i,1}, D_{i,2}\}_{i\in[l']})$ where depth of $\mathsf{HID}', \mathsf{HID}$ are l', l respectively, a decryptor executes the following steps.
  - If $\mathsf{HID}' \neq \mathsf{HID}$, outputs $\perp$.
  - Else, calculates

$$A_1 = \prod_{i=1}^{n} E_i^{y_i}, A_2 = \prod_{k=1}^{l} \{e(C_{k,1}, D_{k,1}) e(C_{k,2}, D_{k,2})\}, A_3 = e(C_0, D_0)$$

and retrieves

$$g_t^{\langle \boldsymbol{x},\boldsymbol{y}\rangle} = \frac{A_1}{A_2 A_3}$$

Finds specific $M \in \mathcal{T}$ such that $e(g,g)^{\langle \boldsymbol{x},\boldsymbol{y}\rangle} = e(g,g)^M$ and returns M.

Correctness. Let $\mathsf{HID} = \mathsf{HID}' = (\mathsf{ID}_1, \mathsf{ID}_2, \ldots, \mathsf{ID}_l)$ and KeyGen (PK, MSK, HID', $\boldsymbol{y}$) $\rightarrow \mathsf{SK}_{\boldsymbol{y},\mathsf{HID}'}$. Then we have

$$A_1 = \prod_{i=1}^{n} E_i^{y_i} = \prod_{i=1}^{n} g_t^{x_i y_i} w_i^{r y_i} = e(g,g)^{\sum_{i=1}^{n} x_i y_i} \prod_{i=1}^{n} e(g, h_i)^{\alpha r y_i}$$

$$\begin{aligned}
A_2 &= \prod_{k=1}^{l} \{e(C_{k,1}, D_{k,1}) e(C_{k,2}, D_{k,2})\} = \prod_{k=1}^{l} \{e\Big(g^{s_k}, (u^{\mathsf{ID}_k} v)^{-\gamma_k}\Big) e\Big((u^{\mathsf{ID}_k} v)^{s_k} g_1^{-r}, g^{\gamma_k}\Big)\} \\
&= \prod_{k=1}^{l} \{e(g, u^{\mathsf{ID}_k} v)^{-s_k \gamma_k} e(u^{\mathsf{ID}_k} v, g)^{s_k \gamma_k} e(g_1^{-r}, g^{\gamma_k})\} \\
&= \prod_{k=1}^{l} \{e(u^{\mathsf{ID}_k} v, g)^{-s_k \gamma_k} e(u^{\mathsf{ID}_k} v, g)^{s_k \gamma_k} e(g_1^{-r}, g^{\gamma_k})\} \\
&= \prod_{k=1}^{l} e(g_1^{-r}, g^{\gamma_k}) = \prod_{k=1}^{l} e(g, g_1)^{-r\gamma_k}
\end{aligned}$$

$$A_3 = e(C_0, D_0) = e(g^r, (h_1^{y_1} h_2^{y_2} \dots h_n^{y_n})^\alpha \prod_{k=1}^{l} g_1^{\gamma_k})$$
$$= e(g^r, (h_1^{y_1} h_2^{y_2} \dots h_n^{y_n})^\alpha) e(g^r, \prod_{k=1}^{l} g_1^{\gamma_k})$$
$$= e(g^r, \prod_{i=1}^{n} h_i^{\alpha y_i}) e(g^r, \prod_{k=1}^{l} g_1^{\gamma_k}) = \prod_{i=1}^{n} e(g, h_i)^{\alpha r y_i} \prod_{k=1}^{l} e(g, g_1)^{r\gamma_k}$$

$$\frac{A_1}{A_2 A_3} = \frac{e(g,g)^{\sum_{i=1}^{n} x_i y_i} \prod_{i=1}^{n} e(g, h_i)^{\alpha r y_i}}{\prod_{k=1}^{l} e(g, g_1)^{-r\gamma_k} \prod_{i=1}^{n} e(g, h_i)^{\alpha r y_i} \prod_{k=1}^{l} e(g, g_1)^{r\gamma_k}} = g_t^{\langle \boldsymbol{x}, \boldsymbol{y} \rangle}$$

Let $\mathsf{HID}' = \mathsf{HID} = (\mathsf{ID}_1, \mathsf{ID}_2, \dots, \mathsf{ID}_l)$ and $\mathsf{Delegate}(\mathsf{PK}, \widehat{\mathsf{HID}}, \mathsf{SK}_{\boldsymbol{y}, \widehat{\mathsf{HID}}}, \mathsf{ID}_l) \rightarrow \mathsf{SK}_{\boldsymbol{y}, \mathsf{HID}'} = (\mathsf{HID}', \boldsymbol{y}, D_0'', \{D_{i,1}'', D_{i,2}''\}_{i \in [l]})$ where $\widehat{\mathsf{HID}} = (\mathsf{ID}_1, \mathsf{ID}_2, \dots, \mathsf{ID}_{l-1})$, $\mathsf{HID}' = \widehat{\mathsf{HID}} \cup \mathsf{ID}_l$. Then we have

$$A_1 = \prod_{i=1}^{n} E_i^{y_i} = \prod_{i=1}^{n} g_t^{x_i y_i} w_i^{r y_i} = e(g,g)^{\sum_{i=1}^{n} x_i y_i} \prod_{i=1}^{n} e(g, h_i)^{\alpha r y_i}$$

$$A_2 = \prod_{k=1}^{l} \{e(C_{k,1}, D_{k,1}'') e(C_{k,2}, D_{k,2}'')\} = \prod_{k=1}^{l} \{e\Big(g^{s_k}, (u^{\mathsf{ID}_k} v)^{-\gamma_k - \widehat{\gamma}_k}\Big) e\Big((u^{\mathsf{ID}_k} v)^{s_k} g_1^{-r}, g^{\gamma_k + \widehat{\gamma}_k}\Big)\}$$
$$= \prod_{k=1}^{l} \{e(g, u^{\mathsf{ID}_k} v)^{s_k(-\gamma_k - \widehat{\gamma}_k)} e(u^{\mathsf{ID}_k} v, g)^{s_k(\gamma_k + \widehat{\gamma}_k)} e(g_1^{-r}, g^{\gamma_k + \widehat{\gamma}_k})\} = \prod_{k=1}^{l} e(g, g_1)^{-r(\gamma_k + \widehat{\gamma}_k)}$$

$$A_3 = e(C_0, D_0) = e(g^r, (h_1^{y_1} h_2^{y_2} \dots h_n^{y_n})^\alpha \prod_{k=1}^{l} g_1^{\gamma_k + \widehat{\gamma}_k}) = e(g^r, (h_1^{y_1} h_2^{y_2} \dots h_n^{y_n})^\alpha) e(g^r, \prod_{k=1}^{l} g_1^{\gamma_k + \widehat{\gamma}_k})$$
$$= e(g^r, \prod_{i=1}^{n} h_i^{\alpha y_i}) e(g^r, \prod_{k=1}^{l} g_1^{\gamma_k + \widehat{\gamma}_k})$$
$$= \prod_{i=1}^{n} e(g, h_i)^{\alpha r y_i} \prod_{k=1}^{l} e(g, g_1)^{r(\gamma_k + \widehat{\gamma}_k)}$$

$$\frac{A_1}{A_2 A_3} = \frac{e(g,g)^{\sum_{i=1}^{n} x_i y_i} \prod_{i=1}^{n} e(g, h_i)^{\alpha r y_i}}{\prod_{k=1}^{l} e(g, g_1)^{-r(\gamma_k + \widehat{\gamma}_k)} \prod_{i=1}^{n} e(g, h_i)^{\alpha r y_i} \prod_{k=1}^{l} e(g, g_1)^{r(\gamma_k + \widehat{\gamma}_k)}} = g_t^{\langle \boldsymbol{x}, \boldsymbol{y} \rangle}$$

4 Security Analysis

Theorem 2. *Our unbounded hierarchical identity-based inner product functional encryption* (UHID-IPFE) *is selectively* CPA *secure in the prescribed security model assuming that the* q-RW2 *problem is hard.*

Proof. Let $\mathcal{A}$ be an attacker against UHID-IPFE protocol with non-negligible advantage ϵ. We describe the procedure to build up a simulator $\mathcal{B}$ to solve the q-RW2 problem by communicating with $\mathcal{A}$.

- **Init**: Collecting the pair $z_1 = \Big(g, g^a, g^b, g^c, g^{(ac)^2}, \{g^{d_i}, g^{acd_i}, g^{ac/d_i}, g^{a^2cd_i}, g^{b/d_i^2}, g^{b^2/d_i^2}\}_{i\in[q]}, \{g^{acd_i/d_j}, g^{bd_i/d_j^2}, g^{abcd_i/d_j^2}, g^{(ac)^2d_i/d_j}\}_{i,j\in[q],i\neq j}\Big)$, $z_2 \in \mathbb{G}_t$ of q-RW2 problem, $\mathcal{B}$ has to find out if z_2 is $e(g,g)^{abc}$ or arbitrary member by interacting with $\mathcal{A}$. $\mathcal{A}$ provides two challenge vectors $\boldsymbol{x}_0^\star = (x_{0,1}^\star, x_{0,2}^\star, \ldots, x_{0,n}^\star)$, $\boldsymbol{x}_1^\star = (x_{1,1}^\star, x_{1,2}^\star, \ldots, x_{1,n}^\star)$ with $\boldsymbol{x}_0^\star \neq \boldsymbol{x}_1^\star$ and a challenge hierarchical identity $\mathsf{HID}^\star = (\mathsf{ID}_1^\star, \mathsf{ID}_2^\star, \ldots, \mathsf{ID}_{l^\star}^\star)$ ($l^\star \leq q$) to $\mathcal{B}$.
- **Setup**: $\mathcal{B}$ arbitrarily selects $u', v', \delta \in \mathbb{Z}_p$, sets $g_1 = g^a, g_2 = g^b$, $h_i = g^{\delta(x_{0,i}^\star - x_{1,i}^\star)}$ for $i \in [n]$, implicitly sets $\alpha = ab$ and computes

$$u = g^{u'} \prod_{i=1}^{l^\star} g^{b/d_i^2}, v = g^{v'} \prod_{i=1}^{l^\star} \left(g^{ac/d_i}(g^{b/d_i^2})^{-\mathsf{ID}_i^\star}\right), w_i = e(g_1, g_2)^{\delta(x_{0,i}^\star - x_{1,i}^\star)}, i \in [n]$$

  $\mathcal{B}$ issues

$$\mathsf{PK} = (p, \mathbb{G}, \mathbb{G}_t, e, g, g_t = e(g,g), u, v, g_1, g_2, \{h_i\}_{i\in[n]}, \{w_i\}_{i\in[n]})$$

  to $\mathcal{A}$ and implicitly sets $\mathsf{MSK} = \alpha = ab$.
- **Query Phase 1**: $\mathcal{A}$ asks secret key queries $\mathsf{SK}_{\boldsymbol{y},\mathsf{HID}}$ to $\mathcal{B}$ polynomially many times. For clarification, let the depth of the queried $\mathsf{HID} = (\mathsf{ID}_1, \mathsf{ID}_2, \ldots, \mathsf{ID}_l)$ be $l \leq l^\star$. (Note that if $l > l^\star$, the simulator $\mathcal{B}$ first computes KeyGen (PK, MSK, HID$''$, $\boldsymbol{y}$) $\rightarrow \mathsf{SK}_{\boldsymbol{y},\mathsf{HID}''}$ where HID$''$ is prefix of HID having $|\mathsf{HID}''| = |\mathsf{HID}^\star| = l^\star$, gets $\mathsf{SK}_{\boldsymbol{y},\mathsf{HID}}$ by performing algorithm Delegate continuously $(l - l^\star)$ beginning from $\mathsf{SK}_{\boldsymbol{y},\mathsf{HID}''}$ and provides $\mathsf{SK}_{\boldsymbol{y},\mathsf{HID}}$ to $\mathcal{A}$. This secret key is correctly simulated as the distribution of the secret key generated by algorithm Delegate is similar to that generated by algorithm KeyGen). For a query on $(\mathsf{HID}, \boldsymbol{y})$, $\mathcal{B}$ performs the tasks as described below.
  1. Checks whether $(\mathsf{HID}, \boldsymbol{y})$ has been queried previously, if yes then outputs 0.
  2. Checks if HID is the prefix of $\mathsf{HID}^\star$ and $\langle \boldsymbol{x}_0^\star - \boldsymbol{x}_1^\star, \boldsymbol{y}\rangle \neq 0$, if yes then outputs 0.
  3. If the previous checks passed but returned no output, it outputs 1.

  Now, $\mathcal{B}$ goes ahead in the following way.
  1. If the check outputs 0, $\mathcal{B}$ does not respond and attends the upcoming query from $\mathcal{A}$.
  2. If the check outputs 1 and $\langle \boldsymbol{x}_0^\star - \boldsymbol{x}_1^\star, \boldsymbol{y}\rangle \neq 0$, $\mathsf{HID} = (\mathsf{ID}_1, \mathsf{ID}_2, \ldots, \mathsf{ID}_l)$ is not a prefix of $\mathsf{HID}^\star = (\mathsf{ID}_1^\star, \mathsf{ID}_2^\star, \ldots, \mathsf{ID}_l^\star)$. So, at least one $\mathsf{ID}_j \in \mathsf{HID}$ $(1 \leq j \leq l)$ exists so that $\mathsf{ID}_j \notin \mathsf{HID}^\star$. $\mathcal{B}$ first evaluates $\mathsf{SK}_{\boldsymbol{y},\mathsf{HID}_j} = (\mathsf{HID}_j, \boldsymbol{y}, D_0, \{D_{i,1}, D_{i,2}\}_{i\in[j]})$ for $\mathsf{HID}_j = (\mathsf{ID}_1, \mathsf{ID}_2, \ldots, \mathsf{ID}_j)$. It selects randomly $\gamma_1, \gamma_2, \ldots, \gamma_{j-1}, \widetilde{\gamma}_j$, sets $\eta = \delta\langle \boldsymbol{x}_0^\star - \boldsymbol{x}_1^\star, \boldsymbol{y}\rangle$ and computes

$$D_0 = \prod_{i=1}^{l^\star}\{(g^{a^2cd_i})^{\frac{\eta}{\mathsf{ID}_j-\mathsf{ID}_i^\star}} g_1^{\widetilde{\gamma}_j}\}\prod_{i=1}^{j-1} g_1^{\gamma_i}.\{D_{i,1}=(u^{\mathsf{ID}_i}v)^{-\gamma_i}, D_{i,2}=g^{\gamma_i}\}_{i=1}^{j-1},$$

$$D_{j,1} = (g_2^{\eta}g^{-\widetilde{\gamma}_j})^{(u'\mathsf{ID}_j+v')}\prod_{i=1}^{l^\star}\Bigg[(g^{acd_i})^{\frac{-\eta(u'\mathsf{ID}_j+v')}{\mathsf{ID}_j-\mathsf{ID}_i^\star}}\{(g^{b^2/d_i^2})^{\eta}(g^{b/d_i^2})^{-\widetilde{\gamma}_j}$$
$$\prod_{\substack{\tau=1\\ \tau\neq i}}^{l^\star}(g^{abcd_i/d_j^2})^{\frac{-\eta}{\mathsf{ID}_j-\mathsf{ID}_\tau^\star}}\}^{\mathsf{ID}_j-\mathsf{ID}_i^\star}$$
$$\prod_{\tau=1}^{l^\star}(g^{(ac)^2d_\tau/d_i})^{\frac{-\eta}{\mathsf{ID}_j-\mathsf{ID}_\tau^\star}}(g^{ac/d_i})^{-\widetilde{\gamma}_j}\Bigg]$$

$$D_{j,2} = g_2^{-\eta}\prod_{i=1}^{l^\star}(g^{acd_i})^{\frac{\eta}{\mathsf{ID}_j-\mathsf{ID}_i^\star}} g^{\widetilde{\gamma}_j}$$

After that, $\mathcal{B}$ produces secret key for $\mathsf{HID} = (\mathsf{ID}_1, \mathsf{ID}_2, \ldots, \mathsf{ID}_l)$ by continuously using the $\mathsf{Delegate}$ algorithm $(l-j)$ times beginning from $\mathsf{SK}_{\boldsymbol{y},\mathsf{HID}_j} = (\mathsf{HID}_j, \boldsymbol{y}, D_0, \{D_{i,1}, D_{i,2}\}_{i\in[j]})$.
It can be verified that $\mathsf{SK}_{\boldsymbol{y},\mathsf{HID}_j} = (\mathsf{HID}_j, \boldsymbol{y}, D_0, \{D_{i,1}, D_{i,2}\}_{i\in[j]})$ as defined above is distributed properly.

3. If $\langle \boldsymbol{x}_0^\star - \boldsymbol{x}_1^\star, \boldsymbol{y}\rangle = 0$ and the check outputs 1, then $\mathcal{B}$ evaluates $\mathsf{SK}_{\boldsymbol{y},\mathsf{HID}} = (\mathsf{HID}, \boldsymbol{y}, D_0, \{D_{i,1}, D_{i,2}\}_{i\in[l]})$ by choosing arbitrarily $\gamma_1, \gamma_2, \ldots, \gamma_l \in \mathbb{Z}_p$ and computing $D_0 = \prod_{i=1}^{l} g_1^{\gamma_i}, \{D_{i,1} = (u^{\mathsf{ID}_i}v)^{-\gamma_i}, D_{i,2} = g^{\gamma_i}\}_{i\in[l]}$. Observe that $(h_1^{y_1}h_2^{y_2}\cdots h_n^{y_n})^{\alpha} = \prod_{i=1}^{n} g^{ab\delta(x_{0,i}^\star - x_{1,i}^\star)y_i} = g^{ab\delta\langle \boldsymbol{x}_0^\star-\boldsymbol{x}_1^\star,\boldsymbol{y}\rangle} = 1$ as $\langle \boldsymbol{x}_0^\star - \boldsymbol{x}_1^\star, \boldsymbol{y}\rangle = 0$. Hence

$$D_0 = (h_1^{y_1}h_2^{y_2}\ldots h_n^{y_n})^{\alpha}\prod_{i=1}^{l} g_1^{\gamma_i}, \{D_{i,1} = (u^{\mathsf{ID}_i}v)^{-\gamma_i}, D_{i,2} = g^{\gamma_i}\}_{i\in[l]}$$

similar to the real scheme. Hence distribution of $\mathsf{SK}_{\boldsymbol{y},\mathsf{HID}}$ is equivalent to that generated by KeyGen in real protocol.

- **Challenge**: $\mathcal{B}$ randomly chooses $\beta \in \{0,1\}$ and encrypts $\boldsymbol{x}_\beta^\star = (x_{\beta,1}^\star, x_{\beta,2}^\star, \ldots, x_{\beta,n}^\star)$ under $\mathsf{HID}^\star = (\mathsf{ID}_1^\star, \mathsf{ID}_2^\star, \ldots, \mathsf{ID}_{l^\star}^\star)$ to produce

$$\mathsf{CT}_{\boldsymbol{x}_\beta^\star,\mathsf{HID}^\star} = (\mathsf{HID}^\star, \{E_i\}_{i\in[n]}, C_0, \{C_{k,1}, C_{k,2}\}_{k\in[l^\star]})$$

where $E_i = g_t^{x^\star_{\beta,i}} z_2^{\delta(x^\star_{0,i}-x^\star_{1,i})}$ for $i \in [n]$, $C_0 = g^c$. For $k \in [l^\star]$, $C_{k,1} = g^{d_k}$,

$$C_{k,2} = (g^{d_k})^{u'\mathsf{ID}^\star_k+v'} \prod_{\substack{\tau=1\\ \tau\neq k}}^{l^\star} \{(g^{bd_k/d_\tau^2})^{\mathsf{ID}^\star_k-\mathsf{ID}^\star_\tau} g^{acd_k/d_\tau}\}$$

$$= [g^{u'\mathsf{ID}^\star_k+v'} \prod_{\tau=1}^{l^\star} \{(g^{b/d_\tau^2})^{\mathsf{ID}^\star_k-\mathsf{ID}^\star_\tau} g^{ac/d_\tau}\}]^{d_k} g^{-ac}$$

$$= (u^{\mathsf{ID}^\star_k} v)^{d_k} g^{-ac} \quad \left[\because u = g^{u'} \prod_{\tau=1}^{l^\star} g^{b/d_\tau^2}, v = g^{v'} \prod_{\tau=1}^{l^\star} \left(g^{ac/d_\tau} (g^{b/d_\tau^2})^{-\mathsf{ID}^\star_\tau}\right)\right]$$

$$= (u^{\mathsf{ID}^\star_k} v)^{d_k} g_1^{-c}$$

Implicitly setting $r = c$, $s_k = d_k$ for $k \in [l^\star]$, it can be seen that $\mathsf{CT}_{\boldsymbol{x}^\star_\beta,\mathsf{HID}^\star}$ is correctly simulated if $z_2 = e(g,g)^{abc}$ as for each $i \in [n]$,

$$g_t^{x^\star_{\beta,i}} w_i^c = g_t^{x^\star_{\beta,i}} e(g,h_i)^{\alpha c} = g_t^{x^\star_{\beta,i}} e(g, g^{\delta(x^\star_{0,i}-x^\star_{1,i})})^{abc}$$
$$= g_t^{x^\star_{\beta,i}} \{e(g,g)^{abc}\}^{\delta(x^\star_{0,i}-x^\star_{1,i})} = g_t^{x^\star_{\beta,i}} z_2^{\delta(x^\star_{0,i}-x^\star_{1,i})} = E_i$$

- **Query phase 2**: Same as Query phase 1.
- **Guess**: Finally, $\mathcal{A}$ returns a guess bit β' of β. If $\beta' = \beta$, the simulator $\mathcal{B}$ returns 1 to indicate that $z_2 = e(g,g)^{abc}$. Otherwise, $\mathcal{B}$ returns 0 implying that z_2 is a random element of $\mathbb{G}_t$.

Note that, if $z_2 = e(g,g)^{abc} e(g,g)^\psi$ where $\psi \xleftarrow{u} \mathbb{Z}_p^\star$ then we have

$$E_i = g_t^{x^\star_{\beta,i}} z_2^{\delta(x^\star_{0,i}-x^\star_{1,i})} = e(g,g)^{x^\star_{\beta,i}} \left(e(g,g)^{abc} e(g,g)^\psi\right)^{\delta_i} \quad [\delta_i = \delta(x^\star_{0,i} - x^\star_{1,i})]$$
$$= e(g,g)^{x^\star_{\beta,i}+\psi\delta_i} e(g,g)^{abc\delta_i} = g_t^{x^\star_{\beta,i}+\psi\delta_i} w_i^c$$

and hence the ciphertext which is simulated turns as encryption of $\boldsymbol{x}' = (x^\star_{\beta,1} + \psi\delta_1, x^\star_{\beta,2} + \psi\delta_2, \ldots, x^\star_{\beta,n} + \psi\delta_n)$ in place of the challenge vector $\boldsymbol{x}^\star_\beta = (x^\star_{\beta,1}, x^\star_{\beta,2}, \ldots, x^\star_{\beta,n})$. As ψ is selected arbitrarily, $\boldsymbol{x}' \neq \boldsymbol{x}^\star_\beta$ with high probability. $\mathcal{B}$ cannot simulate $\mathsf{CT}_{\boldsymbol{x}^\star_\beta,\mathsf{HID}^\star}$ if z_2 is an arbitrary element of $\mathbb{G}_t$. Thus, plaintext vector $\boldsymbol{x}^\star_\beta$ is hidden. So, $\Pr[\mathcal{B}(z_1,z_2) \to 1] = \frac{1}{2}$.

When $z_2 = e(g,g)^{abc}$, $\mathcal{B}$ provides properly simulated ciphertext. So, $\Pr[\mathcal{B}(z_1, e(g,g)^{abc}) \to 1] = \frac{1}{2} + \epsilon$. Hence $\mathcal{B}$ can resolve the q-RW2 problem with advantage

$$\mathsf{Adv}_{\mathcal{B}}^{q\text{-RW2}}(\lambda) = \left|\Pr[\mathcal{B}(z_1, e(g,g)^{abc}) \to 1] - \Pr[\mathcal{B}(z_1,z_2) \to 1]\right| = \left|\frac{1}{2} + \epsilon - \frac{1}{2}\right| = \epsilon$$

which is non-negligible.

5 Conclusion

In this work, we have provided the *first* construction of a *selective* CPA secure HID-IPFE scheme supporting unbounded hierarchical depth. We have explained that handling unbounded depth of hierarchical identity is necessary for practical applications. We obtain this property following the technique of Ryu et al. and analyze the security in the *standard* model based on the hardness of the q-RW2 problem. Furthermore, our design offers better result regarding storage compared to the previous works.

References

1. Abdalla, H., Xiong, H., Wahaballa, A., Ali, A.A., Ramadan, M., Qin, Z.: Integrating the functional encryption and proxy re-cryptography to secure DRM scheme. Int. J. Netw. Secur. **19**(1), 27–38 (2017)
2. Abdalla, M., Bourse, F., De Caro, A., Pointcheval, D.: Simple functional encryption schemes for inner products. Cryptology ePrint Archive (2015)
3. Abdalla, M., Catalano, D., Gay, R., Ursu, B.: Inner-product functional encryption with fine-grained access control. In: Moriai, S., Wang, H. (eds.) ASIACRYPT 2020. LNCS, vol. 12493, pp. 467–497. Springer, Cham (2020). https://doi.org/10.1007/978-3-030-64840-4_16
4. Agrawal, S., Boneh, D., Boyen, X.: Efficient lattice (H)IBE in the standard model. In: Gilbert, H. (ed.) EUROCRYPT 2010. LNCS, vol. 6110, pp. 553–572. Springer, Heidelberg (2010). https://doi.org/10.1007/978-3-642-13190-5_28
5. Agrawal, S., Libert, B., Stehlé, D.: Fully secure functional encryption for inner products, from standard assumptions. In: Robshaw, M., Katz, J. (eds.) CRYPTO 2016. LNCS, vol. 9816, pp. 333–362. Springer, Heidelberg (2016). https://doi.org/10.1007/978-3-662-53015-3_12
6. Belel, A., Dutta, R., Mukhopadhyay, S.: Hierarchical identity based inner product functional encryption for privacy preserving statistical analysis without Q-type assumption. In: Chen, J., He, D., Lu, R. (eds.) Emerging Information Security and Applications. CCIS, vol. 1641, pp. 108–125. Springer, Cham (2023). https://doi.org/10.1007/978-3-031-23098-1_7
7. Benhamouda, F., Bourse, F., Lipmaa, H.: CCA-secure inner-product functional encryption from projective hash functions. In: Fehr, S. (ed.) PKC 2017. LNCS, vol. 10175, pp. 36–66. Springer, Heidelberg (2017). https://doi.org/10.1007/978-3-662-54388-7_2
8. Bethencourt, J., Sahai, A., Waters, B.: Ciphertext-policy attribute-based encryption. In: 2007 IEEE Symposium on Security and Privacy (SP 2007), pp. 321–334. IEEE (2007)
9. Boneh, D., Boyen, X.: Secure identity based encryption without random oracles. In: Franklin, M. (ed.) CRYPTO 2004. LNCS, vol. 3152, pp. 443–459. Springer, Heidelberg (2004). https://doi.org/10.1007/978-3-540-28628-8_27
10. Boneh, D., Boyen, X.: Efficient selective identity-based encryption without random oracles. J. Cryptol. **24**, 659–693 (2011)
11. Boneh, D., et al.: Fully key-homomorphic encryption, arithmetic circuit ABE and compact garbled circuits. In: Nguyen, P.Q., Oswald, E. (eds.) EUROCRYPT 2014. LNCS, vol. 8441, pp. 533–556. Springer, Heidelberg (2014). https://doi.org/10.1007/978-3-642-55220-5_30

12. Boneh, D., Sahai, A., Waters, B.: Functional encryption: definitions and challenges. In: Ishai, Y. (ed.) TCC 2011. LNCS, vol. 6597, pp. 253–273. Springer, Heidelberg (2011). https://doi.org/10.1007/978-3-642-19571-6_16
13. Datta, P., Dutta, R., Mukhopadhyay, S.: Functional encryption for inner product with full function privacy. In: Cheng, C.-M., Chung, K.-M., Persiano, G., Yang, B.-Y. (eds.) PKC 2016. LNCS, vol. 9614, pp. 164–195. Springer, Heidelberg (2016). https://doi.org/10.1007/978-3-662-49384-7_7
14. Gentry, C., Peikert, C., Vaikuntanathan, V.: Trapdoors for hard lattices and new cryptographic constructions. In: Proceedings of the Fortieth Annual ACM Symposium on Theory of Computing, pp. 197–206 (2008)
15. Im, J.H., Kwon, H.Y., Jeon, S.Y., Lee, M.K.: Privacy-preserving electricity billing system using functional encryption. Energies **12**(7), 1237 (2019)
16. Katz, J., Sahai, A., Waters, B.: Predicate encryption supporting disjunctions, polynomial equations, and inner products. In: Smart, N. (ed.) EUROCRYPT 2008. LNCS, vol. 4965, pp. 146–162. Springer, Heidelberg (2008). https://doi.org/10.1007/978-3-540-78967-3_9
17. Kim, S., Lewi, K., Mandal, A., Montgomery, H., Roy, A., Wu, D.J.: Function-hiding inner product encryption is practical. In: Catalano, D., De Prisco, R. (eds.) SCN 2018. LNCS, vol. 11035, pp. 544–562. Springer, Cham (2018). https://doi.org/10.1007/978-3-319-98113-0_29
18. Pal, T., Dutta, R.: Attribute-based access control for inner product functional encryption from LWE. In: Longa, P., Ràfols, C. (eds.) LATINCRYPT 2021. LNCS, vol. 12912, pp. 127–148. Springer, Cham (2021). https://doi.org/10.1007/978-3-030-88238-9_7
19. Rouselakis, Y., Waters, B.: Practical constructions and new proof methods for large universe attribute-based encryption. In: Proceedings of the 2013 ACM SIGSAC Conference on Computer & Communications Security, pp. 463–474 (2013)
20. Ryu, G., Lee, K., Park, S., Lee, D.H.: Unbounded hierarchical identity-based encryption with efficient revocation. In: Kim, H., Choi, D. (eds.) WISA 2015. LNCS, vol. 9503, pp. 122–133. Springer, Cham (2016). https://doi.org/10.1007/978-3-319-31875-2_11
21. Sharma, D., Jinwala, D.: Functional encryption in IoT E-health care system. In: Jajodia, S., Mazumdar, C. (eds.) ICISS 2015. LNCS, vol. 9478, pp. 345–363. Springer, Cham (2015). https://doi.org/10.1007/978-3-319-26961-0_21
22. Song, G., Deng, Y., Huang, Q., Peng, C., Tang, C., Wang, X.: Hierarchical identity-based inner product functional encryption. Inf. Sci. **573**, 332–344 (2021)
23. Stan, O., Sirdey, R., Gouy-Pailler, C., Blanchart, P., BenHamida, A., Zayani, M.H.: Privacy-preserving tax calculations in smart cities by means of inner-product functional encryption. In: 2018 2nd Cyber Security in Networking Conference (CSNet), pp. 1–8. IEEE (2018)
24. Tomida, J., Takashima, K.: Unbounded inner product functional encryption from bilinear maps. Jpn. J. Ind. Appl. Math. **37**(3), 723–779 (2020). https://doi.org/10.1007/s13160-020-00419-x
25. Zhang, L., Wang, X., Chen, Y., Yiu, S.-M.: Adaptive-secure identity-based inner-product functional encryption and its leakage-resilience. In: Bhargavan, K., Oswald, E., Prabhakaran, M. (eds.) INDOCRYPT 2020. LNCS, vol. 12578, pp. 666–690. Springer, Cham (2020). https://doi.org/10.1007/978-3-030-65277-7_30

Brief Announcement: Efficient Probabilistic Approximations for *Sign* and *Compare*

Devharsh Trivedi(✉)

Stevens Institute of Technology, Hoboken, NJ 07030, USA
dtrived5@stevens.edu

Abstract. Fully Homomorphic Encryption (FHE) is a prime candidate for designing privacy-preserving schemes due to its cryptographic security guarantees. For word-wise FHE schemes, often, the complex functions need to be approximated as low-order polynomials. Meanwhile, Artificial Neural Networks (ANN) are known for their ability to approximate arbitrary functions. This paper presents an ANN-based probabilistic polynomial approximation approach using a Perceptron with linear activation in our publicly available Python library. Our approach can be used to generate approximation polynomials with desired degree terms. We further provide third and seventh-degree approximations for univariate $Sign(x) \in \{-1, 0, 1\}$ and $Compare(a - b) \in \{0, \frac{1}{2}, 1\}$ functions in the intervals $[-1, 1]$ and $[-5, -5]$. Finally, we empirically show that our polynomials improve up to 15% accuracy over Chebyshev's.

Keywords: python library · comparison approximation · private machine learning · fully homomorphic encryption

1 Introduction

Fully Homomorphic Encryption (FHE) is a cryptographic primitive that can perform arithmetic computations directly on encrypted data. This makes FHE a preferred candidate for privacy-preserving computation and storage [28,29]. FHE has received significant attention worldwide, which yielded many improvements since Gentry's scheme in 2009 [16]. As a result, FHE is used in many applications [1,3–5,20,26,30]. FHE can be classified as word-wise [6,7,15,17] and bit-wise [10,14] schemes as per the supported operations.

Word-wise FHE provides component-wise addition and multiplication of an encrypted array over $\mathbb{Z}_p$ for a positive integer $p > 2$ [6,15] or the field of complex numbers $\mathbb{C}$ [7]. These schemes allow for packing multiple data values into a single ciphertext and performing computations on these values in a Single Instruction Multiple Data (SIMD) [25] manner. Encrypted inputs are packed to different slots of ciphertext such that the operations carried over a single ciphertext are carried over each slot independently.

S. Dolev and B. Schieber (Eds.): SSS 2023, LNCS 14310, pp. 289–296, 2023.
https://doi.org/10.1007/978-3-031-44274-2_21

For word-wise FHE schemes, performing a non-polynomial operation such as *Sigmoid*, *Sign*(*Signum*), and *Compare* becomes difficult. As a compromise, the existing approaches using these schemes either approximate non-polynomial functions using a low-degree polynomial [19,21] or avoid using them [13].

Contrary to word-wise FHE schemes, bit-wise FHE provides basic operations in the forms of logic gates such as NAND [14] and Look-Up Table (LUT) [10, 11]. Bit-wise schemes encrypt their input in a bit-wise fashion such that each bit of the input is encrypted to a different ciphertext, and the operations are carried over each bit separately. While these schemes support arbitrary functions presented by boolean circuits, they are impractical for large circuit depth [9,12].

Our contributions in this paper can be summarized as follows:

- First, we propose to use Perceptron (basic block of Artificial Neural Network (ANN)) with linear activation for polynomial approximation of arbitrary functions and release the implementation as an open-source Python library.
- We propose to calculate *Compare* function by approximating *Sign*(*Signum*) as a parameterized *TanH* function for a word-wise FHE using our ANN based approximation scheme.
- We also approximate *Compare* directly as a parameterized *Sigmoid* in the intervals $[-1, 1]$ and $[-5, 5]$.
- Finally, we show that the polynomials generated using our scheme have lower estimation errors (losses) than *Chebyshev* polynomials of the same order.

2 Approximation Library

Complex (non-linear) functions like Sigmoid ($\sigma(x)$) and Hyperbolic Tangent ($\tanh x$) can be computed with FHE in an encrypted domain using piecewise-linear functions (a linear approximation of $\sigma(x) = 0.5 + 0.25x$ can be derived from the first two terms of Taylor series $\frac{1}{2} + \frac{1}{4}x$) or polynomial approximations like Taylor [18], Pade [2], Chebyshev [23], Remez [24], and Fourier [18] series. These deterministic approaches yield the same polynomial for the same function. In contrast, we propose to use ANN to derive the approximation polynomial probabilistically, where the coefficients are based on the initial weights and convergence of the ANN model.

While ANNs are known for their universal function approximation properties, they are often treated as a black box and used to calculate the output value. We propose to use a basic 3-layer perceptron (Fig. 1) consisting of an input layer, a hidden layer, and an output layer; both hidden and output layers having linear activations to generate the coefficients for an approximation polynomial of a given order. In this architecture, the input layer is dynamic, with the input nodes corresponding to the desired polynomial degrees. While having a variable number of hidden layers is possible, we fix it to a single layer with a single node to minimize the computation.

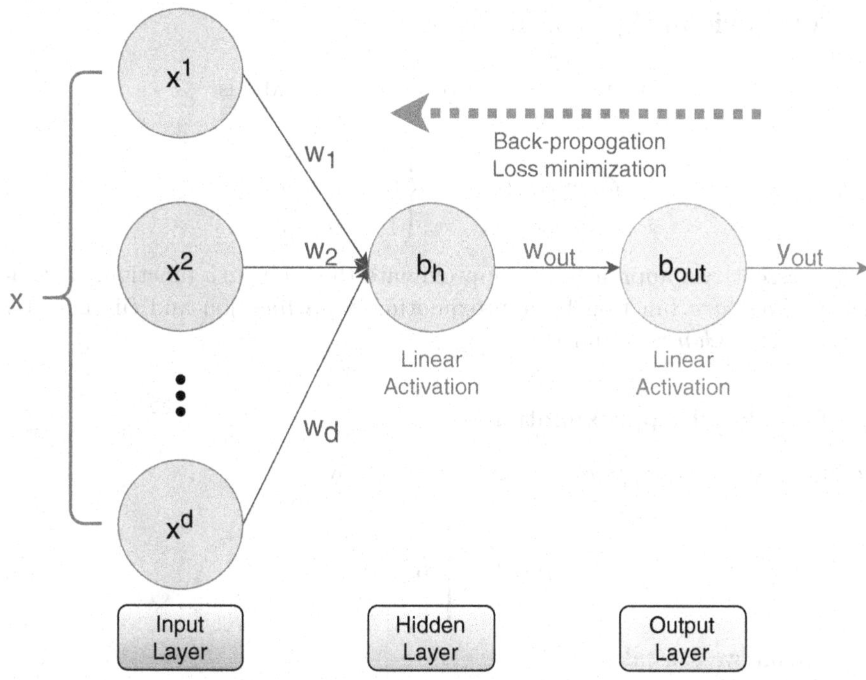

Fig. 1. Polynomial approximation using *ANN*

We show coefficient calculations for a third-order polynomial ($d = 3$) for a univariate function $f(x) = y$ for an input x, actual output y, and predicted output y_{out}. Input layer weights are

$$\{w_1, w_2, \ldots, w_d\} = \{w_1, w_2, w_3\} = \{x, x^2, x^3\}$$

and biases are $\{b_1, b_2, b_3\} = b_h$. Thus the output of the hidden layer is

$$y_h = w_1x + w_2x^2 + w_3x^3 + b_h$$

The predicted output is calculated by

$$\begin{aligned} y_{out} &= w_{out} \cdot y_h + b_{out} \\ &= w_1w_{out}x + w_2w_{out}x^2 + w_3w_{out}x^3 + (b_hw_{out} + b_{out}) \end{aligned} \tag{1}$$

where the layer weights $\{w_1w_{out}, w_2w_{out}, w_3w_{out}\}$ are the coefficients for the approximating polynomial of order-3 and the constant term is $b_hw_{out} + b_{out}$.

3 Comparison Approximation

The bi-variate *Compare* function of two variables a and b is

$$Compare(a,b) = \begin{cases} 0 & a < b \\ 0.5 & a = b \\ 1 & a > b \end{cases} \tag{2}$$

We present two approaches to approximate the *Compare* function. (i) Calculating *Compare* function by approximating *Sign* function and (ii) Directly approximating *Compare* function.

3.1 Calculated Approximation

The univariate $Sign(Signum)$ function is given by

$$Sign(x) = \begin{cases} -1 & x < 0 \\ 0 & x = 0 \\ 1 & x > 0 \end{cases} \tag{3}$$

Therefore we can calculate

$$Compare(a,b) = \frac{Sign(a-b)+1}{2} \tag{4}$$

The step function *Sign* in Eq. 3 can be approximated as a parameterized hyperbolic tangent

$$\tanh(x;k) = \frac{e^{kx} - e^{-kx}}{e^{kx} + e^{-kx}} \tag{5}$$

The higher value of the parameter k yields a higher precision. Thus we set $k = 9223372036854775807 = 2^{63} - 1$, which is the value of $sys.maxsize$ in Python 3. Now we can generate approximations using different methods.

Taylor series at $point = 0$ for Eq. 5 is given by

$$0 + 1.62800e^{17}x + 9.87590e^{36}x^2 - 1.51815e^{55}x^3 + \ldots \tag{6}$$

We present (low-order) Chebyshev polynomials of $degree = 3$ for the *Sign* function in Eq. 3 in the range $[-1, 1]$ and $[-5, 5]$.

$$c_1^3(x) = -2.16478x^3 + 2.93015x \tag{7}$$

$$c_5^3(x) = -0.0173183x^3 + 0.58603x \tag{8}$$

Chebyshev polynomials of seventh-order with odd coefficients in the interval $[-1, 1]$ and $[-5, 5]$ are given by

$$c_1^7(x) = -16.3135x^7 + 33.3593x^5 - 22.0877x^3 + 5.91907x \tag{9}$$

$$c_5^7(x) = -0.000208812x^7 + 0.010675x^5 - 0.176701x^3 + 1.18381x \quad (10)$$

We further approximate third-order polynomials with the proposed *ANN* method in the interval $[-1, 1]$ and $[-5, 5]$.

$$a_1^3(x) = -2.183534x^3 + 2.816129x - 0.017685238 \quad (11)$$

$$a_5^3(x) = -0.017504148x^3 + 0.5667412x + 0.000051538 \quad (12)$$

ANN approximation of *degree* = 7 with odd coefficients in the interval $[-1, 1]$ and $[-5, 5]$ are given by

$$a_1^7(x) = -15.559336x^7 + 30.594683x^5 - 19.622007x^3 + 5.366039x - 0.004171798 \quad (13)$$

$$a_5^7(x) = -0.00018785524x^7 + 0.009339935x^5 - 0.15198348x^3 + 1.0683376x - 0.0025376866 \quad (14)$$

3.2 Direct Approximation

The step function *Compare* in Eq. 2 can be approximated as a parameterized *Sigmoid* with input x and parameter k

$$\sigma(x; k) = \frac{1}{1 + e^{(-kx)}} \quad (15)$$

As explained earlier, we set $k = 2^{63} - 1$ to generate approximations. Taylor series at *point* = 0 for Eq. 15 is given by

$$0.5 + 4.66779e^{17}x + 2.97300e^{36}x^2 - 4.57019e^{54}x^3 + \ldots \quad (16)$$

We calculate Chebyshev polynomials of *degree* = $\{3, 7\}$ for the intervals $[-1, 1]$ and $[-5, 5]$.

$$c_1^3(x) = -1.08239x^3 + 1.46508x + 0.5 \quad (17)$$

$$c_5^3(x) = -0.00865914x^3 + 0.293015x + 0.5 \quad (18)$$

$$c_1^7(x) = -8.15673x^7 + 16.6797x^5 - 11.0438x^3 + 2.95953x + 0.5 \quad (19)$$

$$c_5^7(x) = -0.000104406x^7 + 0.00533749x^5 - 0.0883507x^3 + 0.591907x + 0.5 \quad (20)$$

We also generate odd-powered *ANN* polynomials using our approach for *degree* = 3 and the intervals $[-1, 1]$ and $[-5, 5]$.

$$a_1^3(x) = -1.0963224x^3 + 1.4150281x + 0.50884116 \quad (21)$$

$$a_5^3(x) = -0.008709235x^3 + 0.28203508x + 0.50143045 \quad (22)$$

7th-order *ANN* polynomials for the interval $[-1, 1]$ and $[-5, 5]$ are

$$a_1^7(x) = -7.795442x^7 + 15.27373x^5 - 9.812823x^3 + 2.6885476x + 0.5056917 \quad (23)$$

$$a_5^7(x) = -9.614773e - 05x^7 + 0.0047283764x^5 - 0.07679807x^3 + 0.5358904x + 0.4984604 \quad (24)$$

4 Conclusion

Chebyshev approximations of low order for FHE are widely used in many privacy-preserving tasks. We compare our ANN-based polynomials with Chebyshev and compare the accuracy through various loss functions such as MSLE, MAE, Huber, Hinge, and Logcosh. E.g., for *Compare* approximation with $degree = 7$ and interval $[-5, 5]$, we achieve an $\frac{ANN}{Chebyshev}$ loss ratio for $MAE = 0.8757$ (1 indicates equal losses), which is ≈13% improvement in accuracy.

Our publicly available Python library [27] supports Taylor, Remez, Fourier, Chebyshev, and ANN approximations. In the future, we would like to include other interpolation techniques, such as Lagrange and Power series. Also, comparing our scheme with composite (iterative) polynomials [8,22] would make an interesting study.

References

1. Angel, S., Chen, H., Laine, K., Setty, S.: PIR with compressed queries and amortized query processing. In: 2018 IEEE symposium on security and privacy (SP), pp. 962–979. IEEE (2018)
2. Baker, G.A., Baker Jr., G.A., Graves-Morris, P., Baker, S.S.: Pade Approximants: Encyclopedia of Mathematics and It's Applications, vol. 59. Cambridge University Press, Cambridge (1996)
3. Bos, J.W., Castryck, W., Iliashenko, I., Vercauteren, F.: Privacy-friendly forecasting for the smart grid using homomorphic encryption and the group method of data handling. In: Joye, M., Nitaj, A. (eds.) AFRICACRYPT 2017. LNCS, vol. 10239, pp. 184–201. Springer, Cham (2017). https://doi.org/10.1007/978-3-319-57339-7_11
4. Boudguiga, A., Stan, O., Sedjelmaci, H., Carpov, S.: Homomorphic encryption at work for private analysis of security logs. In: ICISSP, pp. 515–523 (2020)
5. Bourse, F., Minelli, M., Minihold, M., Paillier, P.: Fast homomorphic evaluation of deep discretized neural networks. In: Shacham, H., Boldyreva, A. (eds.) CRYPTO 2018, Part III. LNCS, vol. 10993, pp. 483–512. Springer, Cham (2018). https://doi.org/10.1007/978-3-319-96878-0_17
6. Brakerski, Z., Gentry, C., Vaikuntanathan, V.: (Leveled) fully homomorphic encryption without bootstrapping. ACM Trans. Comput. Theory (TOCT) **6**(3), 1–36 (2014)
7. Cheon, J.H., Kim, A., Kim, M., Song, Y.: Homomorphic encryption for arithmetic of approximate numbers. In: Takagi, T., Peyrin, T. (eds.) ASIACRYPT 2017, Part I. LNCS, vol. 10624, pp. 409–437. Springer, Cham (2017). https://doi.org/10.1007/978-3-319-70694-8_15

8. Cheon, J.H., Kim, D., Kim, D., Lee, H.H., Lee, K.: Numerical method for comparison on homomorphically encrypted numbers. In: Galbraith, S.D., Moriai, S. (eds.) ASIACRYPT 2019, Part II. LNCS, vol. 11922, pp. 415–445. Springer, Cham (2019). https://doi.org/10.1007/978-3-030-34621-8_15
9. Cheon, J.H., Kim, D., Park, J.H.: Towards a practical clustering analysis over encrypted data. IACR Cryptol. ePrint Arch. **2019**, 465 (2019)
10. Chillotti, I., Gama, N., Georgieva, M., Izabachène, M.: Faster fully homomorphic encryption: bootstrapping in less than 0.1 seconds. In: Cheon, J.H., Takagi, T. (eds.) ASIACRYPT 2016, Part I. LNCS, vol. 10031, pp. 3–33. Springer, Heidelberg (2016). https://doi.org/10.1007/978-3-662-53887-6_1
11. Chillotti, I., Gama, N., Georgieva, M., Izabachène, M.: Faster packed homomorphic operations and efficient circuit bootstrapping for TFHE. In: Takagi, T., Peyrin, T. (eds.) ASIACRYPT 2017, Part I. LNCS, vol. 10624, pp. 377–408. Springer, Cham (2017). https://doi.org/10.1007/978-3-319-70694-8_14
12. Chillotti, I., Gama, N., Georgieva, M., Izabachène, M.: TFHE: fast fully homomorphic encryption over the torus. J. Cryptol. **33**(1), 34–91 (2020)
13. Dathathri, R., et al.: CHET: an optimizing compiler for fully-homomorphic neural-network inferencing. In: Proceedings of the 40th ACM SIGPLAN Conference on Programming Language Design and Implementation, pp. 142–156 (2019)
14. Ducas, L., Micciancio, D.: FHEW: bootstrapping homomorphic encryption in less than a second. In: Oswald, E., Fischlin, M. (eds.) EUROCRYPT 2015, Part I. LNCS, vol. 9056, pp. 617–640. Springer, Heidelberg (2015). https://doi.org/10.1007/978-3-662-46800-5_24
15. Fan, J., Vercauteren, F.: Somewhat practical fully homomorphic encryption. Cryptology ePrint Archive (2012)
16. Gentry, C.: Fully homomorphic encryption using ideal lattices. In: Proceedings of the Forty-First Annual ACM Symposium on Theory of Computing, pp. 169–178 (2009)
17. Gentry, C., Sahai, A., Waters, B.: Homomorphic encryption from learning with errors: conceptually-simpler, asymptotically-faster, attribute-based. In: Canetti, R., Garay, J.A. (eds.) CRYPTO 2013, Part I. LNCS, vol. 8042, pp. 75–92. Springer, Heidelberg (2013). https://doi.org/10.1007/978-3-642-40041-4_5
18. George, A.: Mathematical Methods for Physicists. Academic Press, Cambridge (1985)
19. Gilad-Bachrach, R., Dowlin, N., Laine, K., Lauter, K., Naehrig, M., Wernsing, J.: Cryptonets: Applying neural networks to encrypted data with high throughput and accuracy. In: International Conference on Machine Learning, pp. 201–210. PMLR (2016)
20. Kim, M., Lauter, K.: Private genome analysis through homomorphic encryption. In: BMC Medical Informatics and Decision Making, vol. 15, pp. 1–12. BioMed Central (2015)
21. Kim, M., Song, Y., Wang, S., Xia, Y., Jiang, X., et al.: Secure logistic regression based on homomorphic encryption: Design and evaluation. JMIR Med. Inform. **6**(2), e8805 (2018)
22. Lee, E., Lee, J.W., No, J.S., Kim, Y.S.: Minimax approximation of sign function by composite polynomial for homomorphic comparison. IEEE Trans. Dependable Secure Comput. **19**(6), 3711–3727 (2021)
23. Press, W.H., Vetterling, W.T., Teukolsky, S.A., Flannery, B.P.: Numerical Recipes Example Book (FORTRAN). Cambridge University Press, Cambridge (1992)
24. Remez, E.Y.: Sur le calcul effectif des polynomes d'approximation de tschebyscheff. CR Acad. Sci. Paris **199**(2), 337–340 (1934)

25. Smart, N.P., Vercauteren, F.: Fully homomorphic SIMD operations. Des. Codes Crypt. **71**, 57–81 (2014)
26. Trama, D., Clet, P.E., Boudguiga, A., Sirdey, R.: Building blocks for LSTM homomorphic evaluation with TFHE. In: Dolev, S., Gudes, E., Paillier, P. (eds.) CSCML 2023. LNCS, vol. 13914, pp. 117–134. Springer, Cham (2023). https://doi.org/10.1007/978-3-031-34671-2_9
27. Trivedi, D.: GitHub - devharsh/chiku: polynomial function approximation library in Python. (2023). https://github.com/devharsh/chiku
28. Trivedi, D.: Privacy-preserving security analytics (2023). https://www.isaca.org/resources/news-and-trends/isaca-now-blog/2023/privacy-preserving-security-analytics
29. Trivedi, D.: The future of cryptography: performing computations on encrypted data. ISACA J. **1**(2023) (2023). https://www.isaca.org/resources/isaca-journal/issues/2023/volume-1/the-future-of-cryptography
30. Trivedi, D., Boudguiga, A., Triandopoulos, N.: SigML: supervised log anomaly with fully homomorphic encryption. In: Dolev, S., Gudes, E., Paillier, P. (eds.) CSCML 2023. LNCS, vol. 13914, pp. 372–388. Springer, Cham (2023). https://doi.org/10.1007/978-3-031-34671-2_26

Meeting Times of Non-atomic Random Walks

Ryota Eguchi[1(✉)], Fukuhito Ooshita[2], Michiko Inoue[1], and Sébastien Tixeuil[3]

[1] Nara Institute of Science and Technology, Ikoma, Japan
{ry.eguchi,kounoe}@is.naist.jp
[2] Fukui University of Technology, Fukui, Japan
f-oosita@fukui-ut.ac.jp
[3] Sorbonne Université, CNRS, LIP6, Institut Universitaire de France, Paris, France
Sebastien.Tixeuil@lip6.fr

Abstract. In this paper, we revisit the problem of classical *meeting times* of random walks in graphs. In the process that two tokens (called agents) perform random walks on an undirected graph, the meeting times are defined as the expected times until they meet when the two agents are initially located at different vertices. A key feature of the problem is that, in each discrete time-clock (called *round*) of the process, the scheduler selects only one of the two agents, and the agent performs one move of the random walk. In the adversarial setting, the scheduler utilizes the strategy that intends to *maximizing* the expected time to meet. In the seminal papers [5,11,18], for the random walks of two agents, the notion of *atomicity* is implicitly considered. That is, each move of agents should complete while the other agent waits. In this paper, we consider and formalize the meeting time of *non-atomic* random walks. In the non-atomic random walks, we assume that in each round, only one agent can move but the move does not necessarily complete in the next round. In other words, we assume that an agent can move at a round while the other agent is still moving on an edge. For the non-atomic random walks with the adversarial schedulers, we give a polynomial upper bound on the meeting times.

Keywords: meeting times · random walks · adversarial scheduler

1 Introduction

In the process that two tokens (called agents) perform random walks on an undirected graph, the classical *meeting times* are defined as the expected times until they meet when the two agents are initially located at different vertices [3, 5,11,17,18]. A key feature of the meeting times is that, in each discrete time-clock (called *round*) of the process, the scheduler selects only one of the two

This paper was supported by ANR project SAPPORO (Ref. 2019-CE25-0005-1). The full version of this article is available on arXiv.

S. Dolev and B. Schieber (Eds.): SSS 2023, LNCS 14310, pp. 297–311, 2023.
https://doi.org/10.1007/978-3-031-44274-2_22

agents, and the agent performs one move of the random walk[1]. Several schedulers are considered, namely, random scheduler where the scheduler selects an agent randomly; 'angel' scheduler with the intent of *minimizing* the expected time before the tokens meet; or adversarial scheduler with the intent of *maximizing* the expected time [18]. The schedulers have *strategies*. According to a strategy, a scheduler chooses an agent to move in the current configuration. Note that, the schedulers do not know the future moves of the agent, that is, it does not have any prior information about the random bits used by the agents. For the adversarial scheduler, Coppersmith et al. [5] show an upper-bound of the meeting times of each initial configuration, and after that, Tetali and Winkler [18] give the exact characterization of the meeting time of each initial configuration. (The specifications are presented in Subsect. 1.2.) The process they consider, however, assumes the *atomicity* of two independent random walks. That is, while an agent moves, the other agent has to wait until the move completes. Specifically, we define two random walks are *atomic*, if in each (atomic) round, (1) only one agent moves, and (2) at the next round, the moving agent completes the move and reaches the next vertex.

In this paper, we consider the *non-atomic* random walks of the two agents. In the non-atomic random walks, we assume that in each time step, (1) only one agent can move but (2) the move does not necessarily complete in the next round. In other words, we assume that an agent can be chosen to move at a round while the other agent b is still moving on an edge to the goal vertex. To define such behavior, we consider *subdivided graph* $\tilde{G}$ of the original graph $G = (V, E)$. The graph $\tilde{G}$ is produced by subdividing each edge $e \in E$ (that is, adding another vertex in the intermediate point of each edge). We say the vertices in V are *original vertices*, and the added vertices *intermediate vertices*. Intuitively, the situations in which an agent at some intermediate vertex in $\tilde{G}$ are interpreted as the ones in which the agent is traversing the corresponding edge in G. Therefore, the meetings at some intermediate vertex in $\tilde{G}$ are interpreted as the meetings in an edge in G.

Suppose that the two agents are initially located at original vertices $x, y \in V$ at round r. The non-atomic random walks under any scheduler proceed as follows: When the agent located at x is chosen to move, it determines to move to adjacent vertex $w \in N_G(x)$. Then, it moves to the intermediate vertex between x and w *with direction* from x to w at the current round r. So the next round $r+1$, the scheduler chooses an agent from the configuration that agents are located at y and intermediate vertex between x and w with direction from x to w. At the round $r + 1$, if the adversary chooses the agent in the intermediate vertex, then the agent reaches vertex w at round $r + 2$. Otherwise, if at round $r + 1$, the agent at y is chosen to move, it also reaches an intermediate vertex with the corresponding direction. In the executions, the scheduler repeatedly chooses one of the agents. For the non-atomicity, we do not impose any restrictions for

[1] In the literature, the term "meeting time" also be referred to represent the expected time to meet in the process that the two agents move randomly in each round [4,10, 13,15].

reaching the goals of original vertices from the moves of intermediate vertices. For example, in an extreme case, the adversary can only choose an agent once to locate the agent to the intermediate vertex, and after that, it can repeatedly move the other agent.

When an agent is located at an intermediate vertex, then the state of the agent is interpreted as traversing the corresponding edge in the original graph G. Also, similar to the atomic case, the agents do not return to the original vertex they left in the random walks. Therefore, when the agent located at an intermediate vertex is chosen to move, the direction for the move is kept. In other words, when the agent is located at an intermediate vertex between v and w with direction from v to w, then it must reach the vertex w (not v). Note also that, if the meetings can occur only when the agents are located at the same original vertex, then any meeting does not occur in the non-atomic random walks. For example, the scheduler at first moves an agent to the intermediate vertex and repeatedly moves another agent. By doing so, the agents never meet at the original vertices. Therefore, we need to allow the agents to meet in the intermediate vertices as well as the original vertices.Allowing agents to meet on intermediate vertices hints that previous results on random walks in the atomic case may be simply expanded to the non-atomic case. However, this is not the case:

- Considering a random walk on the subdivided graph (illustrated in part (a) of Fig. 1) does not take into account that in our setting, since agents may not return back to the original node they left when at an intermediate node.
- Considering a random walk on the directed graph induced by the intermediate node direction constraints (part (b) in Fig. 1) does not take into account that for two original neighboring vertices u and v, the intermediate vertices $\pi_{\{u,v\}}$ and $\pi_{\{v,u\}}$ must be a single vertex (otherwise, any meeting cannot occur at an intermediate node).

1.1 Our Contribution

The first contribution is the formalization of the meeting time of non-atomic random walks by two agents. For the formalization, we introduce the notion of non-atomic moves of agents in the subdivided graphs $\tilde{G}$. We then show that our definitions match the intuitions described above by formally proving the impossibility to meet when we restrict the meeting points to the original vertices in V. By the impossibility, we relax the assumption such that the agents can meet at the intermediate vertices as well as the original vertices. We assume that the agents can meet when they are located at the same intermediate vertex regardless of their direction. That is, they can meet if they are located at the same intermediate vertex in the same direction or opposite directions.

Then, we prove an upper bound of the meeting times of the non-atomic random walks. Specifically, based on the proof arguments in [5], we extend their proofs and show the following theorem. For the adversarial scheduler, let

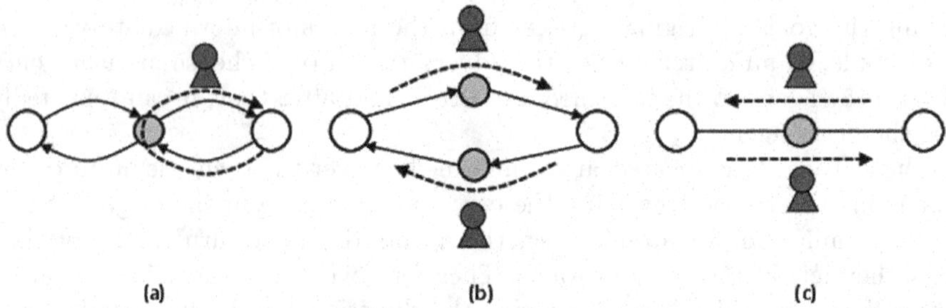

Fig. 1. In this figure, the white circles represent the original nodes, and the gray circles represent the intermediate nodes. The objects with a black circle combined with a triangle represent the agents. **(a)** (Color figure online) Random walks in the subdivided graphs. In this case, returning back to the original node they left is unavoidable. **(b)** Two intermediate nodes. In this case, the agents cannot meet when they enter the two intermediate nodes in different directions. **(c)** Our definition. The intermediate node is unique, and the agents have a direction as their state(Precise definition is presented in Sect. 2).

$\tilde{M}_G(x, y)$ denote the worst meeting time of non-atomic random walks from initial positions $x, y \in V$. Also, let $H(x, y)$ be the hitting time from x to y, which is the expected time to reach y from x by an agent for $x, y \in V$ in G.

Theorem 1. *For a pair of $x, y \in V$, suppose that the agents are initially located at vertices x, y and conduct the non-atomic random walks under the strategy of the adversarial scheduler. Then, there is a pair of vertices $t, u \in V$ such that*

$$\tilde{M}_G(x, y) \leq 2 \left(H(x, y) + H(y, u) - H(u, y) + d_u - 1 + \sum_{z \in N_G(u) \setminus t} H(z, u) \right)$$

holds, where d_u is the degree of the original vertex $u \in V$.

The vertices t, u in Theorem 1 are special in the sense that the state s_{tu} is *hidden*, whose precise definition appears in Subsect. 4.2. Also, since the hitting times have a polynomial upper bound of $O(n^3)$, Theorem 1 also shows the polynomial upper bound of $O(n^4)$ on the worst meeting times of the non-atomic random walks.

1.2 Related Work

The meeting times of (atomic) random walks were first presented by Israeli and Jalfon [11]. In the paper, they introduced a token-management scheme for self-stabilizing mutual exclusion. In the initial configuration of the scheme, multiple tokens (i.e., agents) can exist, and processors (i.e., vertices) send the tokens to their adjacent processors randomly. If some tokens move to the same processor, then the tokens are merged into one token. For the scheme, it is required that tokens eventually are eventually merged into one token. In particular, the authors showed that, in a ring of n vertices, the meeting time is $O(n^2)$, and also that, in general graphs, an exponential upper bound $O((\Delta - 1)^{D-1})$ exists, where Δ is the maximum degree of the graph, and D is the diameter of the graph.

Tetali and Winkler [17] proved the upper bound of the adversarial meeting times of random walks, specifically as follows. For any connected graph G, $M_G(x, y) \leq H(x, y) + H(y, z) - H(z, y)$ holds for the initial positions x, y, where z is special vertex called the *hidden* vertex. In more detail, z satisfies $H(z, v) \leq H(v, z)$ for each $v \in V$. Hence the meeting times M_G are upper bounded by at most twice the worst hitting time of the graph G in the worst adversarial settings. Then, Coppersmith, Tetali, and Winkler [5] showed another upper bound: the worst meeting time is upper bounded by $(\frac{4}{27} + o(1))n^3$ for any graphs and any initial positions.

Tetali and Winkler [18] provided the exact characterization of the meeting time of each initial configuration. The specification of the characterization is as follows: Let c be the vertex such that, for any vertex $v \in V$, $H(v, c) \leq H(c, v)$ holds. Let $q_G(w; x, y)$ denote the probability that agents initially located at x, y first meet at vertex w and let $Z(x)$ be another potential function that $Z(x) = H(c, x) - H(x, c)$. Then, they show $M_G(x, y) = \Phi(x, y) - \sum_{w \in V} q_G(w; x, y)[Z(z) - Z(w)]$, where $\Phi(x, y) = H(x, y) + H(y, z) - H(z, y)$ is introduced by Coppersmith, Tetali, and Winkle [5].

The meeting times of (atomic) random walks by k agents for $k \geq 2$ were examined by Bshouty et al. [3]. In the paper, they showed that the meeting times of multiple random walks have an upper bound in terms of the meeting times of fewer random walks. The meeting time of random walks by k agents is the expected number of rounds to merge the agents into one agent. Quantities related to a random walk in graphs such as hitting time, cover time, and commute time are well studied [2,8,12,16] and the interested reader can refer to the survey of Lovasz [14]. Interestingly, Brightwell and Winkler showed [2] that the worst hitting time among all graphs is $O(n^3)$, which appears in the so-called lollipop graphs. The relation between random walks in graphs and electrical networks has also been investigated [16].

The related problem concerning the meeting time of the non-atomic random walks is *asynchronous rendezvous* of two agents [1,6,7,9]. The asynchronous rendezvous problem is similar problem to the non-atomic meeting time, in the sense that the adversary controls the speed of the agents (or the rounds to reach the destination of a move). The notion of subdivided graphs was introduced to study asynchronous rendezvous by Bampas et al. [1].

1.3 Organization of Paper

In Sect. 2, we explain the definitions and notations for the meeting times of non-atomic random walks. In Sect. 3, we prove the impossibility that the agents cannot meet with the assumption that they are only assumed to meet in the original vertices. In Sect. 4, we show an upper bound for meeting times of non-atomic random walks. In Sect. 5, we examine the upper bound in several graph classes such as lines and rings, and complete graphs. Finally, we conclude this paper in Sect. 6.

2 Preliminaries

Let $G = (V(G), E(G))$ be a connected undirected graph with n vertices and m edges. Let $\tilde{G}$ denote the graph produced by subdividing each edge of G into two parts. Precisely, we define $\tilde{G} = (V(\tilde{G}), E(\tilde{G}))$. The vertex set is defined by $V(\tilde{G}) = V(G) \cup V_{intm}$, where $V_{intm} = \{\pi_{\{v,w\}} \mid (v, w) \in E(G)\}$. The edge set is defined by $E(\tilde{G}) = \{(v, \pi_{\{v,w\}}) \mid v \in V(G) \wedge \pi_{\{v,w\}} \in V_{intm}\}$. Note that $\pi_{\{v,w\}} = \pi_{\{w,v\}}$ holds. Also, we say vertices in $V(G)$ are *original vertices*, and vertices in V_{intm} are *intermediate vertices.*

Each state of an agent is an element from a set $V \cup S_{intm}$, where $S_{intm} = \{s_{xy} \mid \pi_{\{x,y\}} \in V_{intm}\}$. The state s_{xy} represents that the agent is located at $\pi_{\{x,y\}}$ and it has the direction from x to y. That is, in the original graph G, the agent with state s_{xy} is heading to the vertex y from x in the edge (x, y) in G. Note that for each $\pi_{\{v,w\}}$, there are two states s_{xy} and s_{yx}, and $s_{xy} \neq s_{yx}$ holds since the directions are different. The states from V represent that the current position of the agent is an original vertex of G. We call the states from V *original states.* We define states from S_{intm} are *intermediate states.* For each state s, we define the following bar operation: if $s \in V$, then $\overline{s} = s$, and if $s = s_{xy} \in S_{intm}$, then $\overline{s_{xy}} = s_{yx}$. Next, we define the adjacent states of each state. The set of adjacent states $N_{as}(s)$ for a state $s \in V \cup S_{intm}$ is defined that (1) $N_{as}(s) = \{s_{vw} \in S_{intm} \mid w \in N_G(v)\}$ if $s = v$ (original), and (2) $N_{as}(s) = \{w\}$ if $s = s_{vw} \in S_{intm}$ (intermediate). We also define $d_s = |N_{as}(s)|$. The set of configurations $\mathcal{C}$ is defined by $(V \cup S_{intm})^2$. The elements of a configuration correspond to the states of the two agents.

The computation proceeds in discrete time $r = 0, 1, 2, \ldots$, which is called *rounds.* In each round r, the adversary determines which agent moves for a configuration c in the round. The selected agent at state s moves to an adjacent state $s' \in N_{as}(s)$ in $\tilde{G}$ with probability $1/d_s$. Note that if the state is intermediate state s_{vw}, then the next state is uniquely determined to w. Note that even if we consider the non-atomic moves of the agents, these moves of the agents are assumed to be complete in the current round, and in the next round the moving agent should be at the next state in $V \cup S_{intm}$.

The adversary chooses an agent in the current configuration according to a strategy $S_{\tilde{G}}$ for a subdivided graph $\tilde{G}$. The strategy $S_{\tilde{G}}$ is a function $S_{\tilde{G}} : \mathcal{C} \to [0, 1]$, where $\mathcal{C}$ is a set of configurations. The expression $S_{\tilde{G}}(c) = p$ for $c = (s, s') \in (V \cup S_{intm})^2$ and $p \in [0, 1]$ represents that the adversary moves an agent in the state s with probability p (otherwise it moves the other agent in the state s') in the current configuration c.

We say that the agents meet, if the execution reaches a configuration $c = (s, s')$ such that $s = s'$ or $s = \overline{s'}$. In other words, the agents meet if they are located at the same original vertices or intermediate vertices regardless of the direction of the agents. We define $\tilde{M}_S(x, y)$ as the expected rounds for non-atomic random walks starting at initial position x, y to meet when the adversary adopts the strategy S. $\tilde{M}_G(x, y)$ denotes the worst meeting time of non-atomic random walks starting at $x, y \in V$ for all strategies in $\tilde{G}$.

3 Impossibility Results

In this section, using our definition we show the impossibility that the agents cannot meet when we restrict the meeting points to original vertices.

Theorem 2. *If the meeting cannot occur on intermediate vertices, there exists an adversarial strategy such that agents never meet at an original vertex.*

Proof. We specify the strategy as follows. For each $v \in V$ and each $s_{uv} \in S_{intm}$ for $u \in N_G(v)$, the strategy moves the agent at v with probability 1 in the configuration (v, s_{uv}), and moves agents arbitrary in other configurations. Obviously, to meet at an original vertex, the agents should reach the configuration (v, s_{uv}) for some v and s_{uv}. However, in the next configuration, the agents cannot meet by the strategy, since by the assumption of meeting, the agents at s_{vu} and s_{uv} cannot meet. □

Observe that weakening the power of the scheduler does not help. Even if the scheduler is 2-fair (in such a strategy, each agent is selected infinitely often, and between any two selections of an agent, any other agent is selected at most twice), it remains impossible to obtain meeting if they can only occur on original vertices. For example, consider an alternating strategy (the scheduler alternates between two consecutive activations of the two agents, except for the first activations in the strategy, where the first time an agent is activated, it is activated only once). Then, after the first activation, the first agent is on an intermediate node. After the second agent is activated, both agents are on intermediate nodes. Then, the first agent is activated twice, and both agents remain on intermediate nodes. The selection continues so that both agents are on intermediate nodes at the end of each activation.

4 An Upper Bound for Non-atomic Meeting Time

In this section, we show the upper bound for non-atomic meeting time. At first, we define the hitting times between states in $\tilde{G}$, which is a generalization of the hitting time between vertices in G. In the following, we say the generalized version of the hitting times *extended hitting times*. We also show a property of the extended hitting time, which we call triangle property in the following. It is also the generalized version of the triangle property shown in the arguments in [5]. In our argument, the property is generalized in a bit tricky way to hold the latter arguments. Using the generalized triangle property, we can prove the existence of special states called *hidden states* (Subsect. 4.2). The hidden states allow us to introduce a potential function $\tilde{\Phi}$ for a pair of states (Subsect. 4.3), and finally we show an upper bound on the non-atomic meeting times using the potential function $\tilde{\Phi}$.

4.1 Hitting Time of States and Triangle Property

For a pair of states s, s', we define that the extended hitting time $\tilde{H}(s, s')$ is the expected moves to reach the state s' from the state s by an agent in $\tilde{G}$. The moves of the agent are the same as the ones in the non-atomic moves in Sect. 2, specifically as follows: if its state s is in V, then it moves to $s_{sw} \in N_{as}(s)$ with probability $1/d_s$ for each $w \in N_G(v)$; If its state s is $s_{xy} \in S_{intm}$, then it moves to y as a move.

If $s, s' \in V$ holds, then $\tilde{H}(s, s')$ is twice of the value of the original hitting time $H(s, s')$ in G, that is, $\tilde{H}(s, s') = 2H(s, s')$. This is because, in the moves in $\tilde{G}$, the agent should move twice to traverse an edge corresponding to G. If the starting point is intermediate, that is, $s = s_{xy} \in S_{intm}$ and $s' \in V$, then we have $\tilde{H}(s_{xy}, s') = 1 + \tilde{H}(y, s') = 1 + 2H(y, s')$. The extended hitting time in this case can be also calculated by the original hitting time. The remaining case is that the goal state is an intermediate state, that is, $s' = s_{xy}$ for $s_{xy} \in S_{intm}$. In this case, to reach s_{xy} the agent should visit the original vertex x. Therefore, the following equality holds by the linearity of expectation: $\tilde{H}(s, s_{xy}) = \tilde{H}(s, x) + \tilde{H}(x, s_{xy})$. Therefore, we should calculate the value of $\tilde{H}(x, s_{xy})$ for any x and $s_{xy} \in N_{as}(x)$.

Lemma 1. *For each $x \in V$ and $s_{xy} \in S_{intm}$, we have*

$$\tilde{H}(x, s_{xy}) = 2d_x - 1 + \sum_{z \in N_G(x) \setminus \{y\}} \tilde{H}(z, x).$$

Proof. Let $\tilde{H}(x, s_{xy}) = T$. At vertex x, the agent reaches the state s_{xy} with the probability $1/d_x$. Otherwise, it moves z for $z \in N_G(x) \setminus \{y\}$ with the same probability with two moves. After the latter case, the agent should return to the vertex x for reaching the state s_{xy}. Therefore, the value can be written the following recursive formula:

$$T = \frac{1}{d_x}\left(1 + \sum_{z \in N_G(x) \setminus \{y\}} (2 + \tilde{H}(z, x) + T)\right).$$

Therefore we have

$$d_x \cdot T = 1 + 2d_x - 2 + \left(\sum_{z \in N_G(x) \setminus \{y\}} \tilde{H}(z, x)\right) + (d_x - 1) \cdot T$$

$$T = 2d_x - 1 + \sum_{z \in N_G(x) \setminus \{y\}} \tilde{H}(z, x).$$

□

Next, we prove the key property of the extended hitting times. Here we introduce the original triangle property of the original hitting times.

Lemma 2 (From [5]). *For any $x, y, z \in V$, we have*
$H(x, y) + H(y, z) + H(z, x) = H(x, z) + H(z, y) + H(y, x)$

Note that the left side of the equation is the expected time that a random walk starting at x visits y then visits z, and returns to x, similarly to the right side of the equation. While there may exist multiple generalizations of the property, we use the following generalization of the triangle property to establish the latter argument of our proof.

Lemma 3. *For states $x, y, z \in V \cup S_{intm}$, we have*
$\tilde{H}(x,\overline{y}) + \tilde{H}(y,\overline{z}) + \tilde{H}(z,\overline{x}) = \tilde{H}(x,\overline{z}) + \tilde{H}(z,\overline{y}) + \tilde{H}(y,\overline{x})$

Proof. To prove the lemma, we use the function $f : V \cup S_{intm} \to V$, where $f(v) = v$ for $v \in V$ and $f(s_{ab}) = a$ for $s_{ab} \in S_{intm}$. Using the function, we can rewrite the extended hitting time as follows: For states $s, s' \in V \cup S_{intm}$, $\tilde{H}(s,s') = \tilde{H}(s,f(s')) + \tilde{H}(f(s'),s')$. Using the function, we rewrite the left side of the equation in the lemma as

$$\begin{aligned}
\tilde{H}(x,\overline{y}) + &\tilde{H}(y,\overline{z}) + \tilde{H}(z,\overline{x}) \\
&= \tilde{H}(x,f(\overline{y})) + \tilde{H}(f(\overline{y}),\overline{y}) + \tilde{H}(y,f(\overline{z})) + \tilde{H}(f(\overline{z}),\overline{z}) \\
&\quad + \tilde{H}(z,f(\overline{x})) + \tilde{H}(f(\overline{x}),\overline{x}) \\
&= \tilde{H}(x,f(\overline{y})) + \tilde{H}(y,f(\overline{z})) + \tilde{H}(z,f(\overline{x})) \\
&\quad + \tilde{H}(f(\overline{x}),\overline{x}) + \tilde{H}(f(\overline{y}),\overline{y}) + \tilde{H}(f(\overline{z}),\overline{z}).
\end{aligned}$$

Similarly, for the right side of the equation, we have

$$\begin{aligned}
\tilde{H}(x,\overline{z}) + \tilde{H}(z,\overline{y}) + \tilde{H}(y,\overline{x}) &= \tilde{H}(x,f(\overline{z})) + \tilde{H}(z,f(\overline{y})) + \tilde{H}(y,f(\overline{x})) \\
&\quad + \tilde{H}(f(\overline{x}),\overline{x}) + \tilde{H}(f(\overline{y}),\overline{y}) + \tilde{H}(f(\overline{z}),\overline{z}).
\end{aligned}$$

Therefore it is sufficient to show that $\tilde{H}(x,f(\overline{y})) + \tilde{H}(y,f(\overline{z})) + \tilde{H}(z,f(\overline{x})) = \tilde{H}(x,f(\overline{z})) + \tilde{H}(z,f(\overline{y})) + \tilde{H}(y,f(\overline{x}))$. We then define another function $g : V \cup S_{intm} \to V$, which returns v if the input is $v \in V$, and b if it is $s_{ab} \in S_{intm}$. Similarly for f, we have $\tilde{H}(s,s') = \tilde{H}(s,g(s)) + \tilde{H}(g(s),s')$. Thus this proof is reduced to if the following equation holds: $\tilde{H}(g(x),f(\overline{y})) + \tilde{H}(g(y),f(\overline{z})) + \tilde{H}(g(z),f(\overline{x})) = \tilde{H}(g(x),f(\overline{z})) + \tilde{H}(g(z),f(\overline{y})) + \tilde{H}(g(y),f(\overline{x}))$. For the functions, it holds that $g(x) = f(\overline{x})$ and $g(x)$ is an original state. Therefore, the last equation holds by the original triangle property of Lemma 2. □

4.2 Hidden States

We define the following relation $\leq_{EHT}$ as follows: For any pair of states s, s', $s \leq_{EHT} s'$ holds if $\tilde{H}(s,\overline{s'}) \leq \tilde{H}(s',\overline{s})$ holds. It is also the extension of the relation $\leq_{HT}$ given in [5]. In the proofs of [5] the relation for the original hitting times is defined as follows: For any vertex $v, w \in V$, the relation $v \leq_{HT} w$ holds if $\tilde{H}(v,w) \leq \tilde{H}(w,v)$ holds. The main purpose of the relations is to prove the existence of the *hidden* vertex (or state). The hidden vertex in the original argument is the minimum vertex in the relation. It is proven by showing the relation is transitive. We also prove the extended relation $\leq_{EHT}$ is transitive, and prove the existence of the hidden state.

Lemma 4. *lemma The relation $\leq_{EHT}$ is transitive. As a consequence, there is a state $s \in V \cup S_{intm}$ such that for any $s' \in V \cup S_{intm}$, it holds that $s \leq_{EHT} s'$.*

Proof. It is sufficient to show that for any states $x, y, z \in V \cup S_{intm}$, if $x \leq_{EHT} y$ and $y \leq_{EHT} z$ holds, then we have $x \leq_{EHT} z$. By the assumption, we have $\tilde{H}(x, \overline{y}) \leq \tilde{H}(y, \overline{x})$ and $\tilde{H}(y, \overline{z}) \leq \tilde{H}(z, \overline{y})$. Applying the triangle property for the states x, y, z of Lemma 3, we have

$$\begin{aligned} \tilde{H}(x,\overline{y}) + \tilde{H}(y,\overline{z}) + \tilde{H}(z,\overline{x}) &= \tilde{H}(x,\overline{z}) + \tilde{H}(z,\overline{y}) + \tilde{H}(y,\overline{x}) \\ \tilde{H}(x,\overline{y}) - \tilde{H}(y,\overline{x}) + \tilde{H}(y,\overline{z}) - \tilde{H}(z,\overline{y}) &= \tilde{H}(x,\overline{z}) - \tilde{H}(z,\overline{x}) \\ \tilde{H}(x,\overline{z}) - \tilde{H}(z,\overline{x}) &\leq 0 \end{aligned}$$

Therefore it holds that $\tilde{H}(x, \overline{z}) \leq \tilde{H}(z, \overline{x})$, proving the lemma. □

Then, we show that the hidden state(s) is intermediate. For any original state $v \in V$, we show that $s_{wv} \leq_{EHT} v$ for any intermediate $s_{wv} \in S_{intm}$ for $w \in N_G(v)$. For any vertex v and any s_{wv}, we have $\tilde{H}(s_{wv}, \overline{v}) = \tilde{H}(s_{wv}, v) = 1$ by definition, and $\tilde{H}(v, \overline{s}_{wv}) = \tilde{H}(v, s_{vw}) = 2d_v - 1 + \sum_{z \in N_{as}(v)\setminus\{w\}} \tilde{H}(z, v)$. Since the graph $\tilde{G}$ is connected, we have $d_v \geq 1$. Hence it holds that $\tilde{H}(v, s_{vw}) \geq 1$. Therefore for v, s_{wv}, we have $s_{wv} \leq_{EHT} v$, as desired.

Proposition 1. *An intermediate state is hidden.*

4.3 Main Argument

Now we define a potential function $\tilde{\Phi}$. For each pair of states x, y and a hidden state s_{tu}, we set the function $\tilde{\Phi}(x, y) = \tilde{H}(x, \overline{y}) + \tilde{H}(y, \overline{s_{tu}}) - \tilde{H}(s_{tu}, \overline{y})$. The function is derived using the triangle property for states s, s', s_{tu} as follows:

$$\begin{aligned} \tilde{H}(x,\overline{y}) + \tilde{H}(y,\overline{s_{tu}}) + \tilde{H}(s_{tu},\overline{x}) &= \tilde{H}(x,\overline{s_{tu}}) + \tilde{H}(s_{tu},\overline{y}) + \tilde{H}(y,\overline{x}) \\ \tilde{H}(x,\overline{y}) + \tilde{H}(y,\overline{s_{tu}}) - \tilde{H}(s_{tu},\overline{y}) &= \tilde{H}(y,\overline{x}) + \tilde{H}(x,\overline{s_{tu}}) - \tilde{H}(s_{tu},\overline{x}) \end{aligned}$$

Therefore it holds that $\tilde{\Phi}(x, y) = \tilde{\Phi}(y, x)$. Also, since the states s_{tu} is hidden, we have that $\tilde{H}(z, \overline{s_{tu}}) - \tilde{H}(s_{tu}, \overline{z}) \geq 0$ for any state $z \in V \cup S_{intm}$. Thus we have the following proposition, which is implicitly used in Theorem 3.

Proposition 2. $\tilde{\Phi}(x, y) \geq 0$ *for any* $x, y \in V \cup S_{intm}$

Now we add some modifications for initial positions, define some notations, and present the preliminary propositions/lemmas for the main proof. At first, we extend the initial positions of the non-atomic meeting times, to the ones that include states from $V \cup S_{intm}$. That is, we define that the starting states of the agents include the intermediate states. In the following, we assume that any strategy S contains the intermediate states as initial positions. Next, we define the optimal (longest) and deterministic strategy. A strategy is deterministic, if for any pair $s, s' \in V \cup S_{intm}$, the moving agent is chosen with probability 1.

Also, an strategy S is optimal, if for any pair $s, s' \in V \cup S_{intm}$, it holds that $\tilde{M}_G(s, s') = \tilde{M}_S(s, s')$.

We also define a value of configurations called *destination value*. For a configuration (s_1, s_2), the value is defined according to the function g defined in the proof of Lemma 3. Recall that $g(s) = s$ if $s = v \in V$ and $g(s_{ab}) = b$ for $s_{ab} \in S_{intm}$. The destination value of the configuration (s_1, s_2) is defined as $d(s_1, s_2) = dist(s_1, g(s_1)) + dist(g(s_1), g(s_2)) + dist(s_2, g(s_2))$, where (1) $dist(s, g(s)) = 1$ if the state s is intermediate, and (2) $dist(s, g(s)) = 0$ if $s \in V$, and (3) for $s, s' \in V$, $dist(s, s')$ is the hop-distance of the vertices in $\tilde{G}$. Observe that $d(s_1, s_2) \geq d(g(s_1), g(s_2))$ holds.

To prove the existence of the optimal and deterministic strategy, we first show the following lemma. Let $S(x, y)$ be the strategy that maximizes the non-atomic meeting time starting at $x, y \in V \cup S_{intm}$, i.e., $\tilde{M}_{S(x,y)}(x, y) = \tilde{M}_G(x, y)$ holds. Its proof is deferred to the full paper.

Lemma 5. *For any $x, y \in V$, suppose that $S(x, y)$ moves the agent with the state x with positive probability $p > 0$. Then, we have that*

$$\tilde{M}_{S(x,y)}(x, y) = 1 + \frac{1}{d_x} \sum_{z \in N_{as}(x)} \tilde{M}_G(z, y).$$

Lemma 6. *For any G, there is an optimal and deterministic strategy S^*.*

Proof. Using $S(x, y)$, we define the strategy S^* as follows: If the strategy $S(x, y)$ moves the agent at x at initial configuration (x, y) with the probability strictly greater than 0, then the strategy S^* moves x at (x, y). Otherwise if $S(x, y)$ moves y with probability 1, then S^* moves y. The strategy S^* is created by conducting the above operation for all pairs of states (x, y). Obviously, the strategy is deterministic. We argue that such strategy S^* is optimal.

Towards the contradiction, suppose that S^* is not optimal. Then there is at least one pair of states x, y such that $\tilde{M}_G(x, y) - \tilde{M}_{S^*}(x, y) > 0$ holds. Let α be the maximum value of $\tilde{M}_G(x, y) - \tilde{M}_{S^*}(x, y)$ among such pairs. We choose a pair x, y such that they attain α and have the minimum destination value $d(x, y)$ among the pairs that attain the value α. It holds that $x \neq y$, since if $x = y$ then $\tilde{M}_G(x, x) = \tilde{M}_{S^*}(x, x) = 0$. Assume that in the strategy $S(x, y)$ the agent in the state x is moved with positive probability $p > 0$. Therefore, S^* moves the agent in the state x with probability one. Hence, by averaging the moves of the agent among the neighbors of the state x, we have

$$\tilde{M}_{S^*}(x, y) = 1 + \frac{1}{d_x} \left(\sum_{z \in N_{as}(x)} \tilde{M}_{S^*}(z, y) \right). \tag{1}$$

Using Lemma 5 and Equation (1), we can derive the following contradiction,

$$\begin{aligned}
\tilde{M}_{S(x,y)}(x,y) &= 1 + \frac{1}{d_x} \sum_{z \in N_{as}(x)} \tilde{M}_G(z,y) && \text{(by Lemma 5)} \\
&= 1 + \frac{1}{d_x} \sum_{z \in N_{as}(x)} \left(\tilde{M}_{S^*}(z,y) + \alpha(z,y)\right) \\
&< 1 + \frac{1}{d_x} \sum_{z \in N_{as}(x)} \left(\tilde{M}_{S^*}(z,y)\right) + \alpha \\
&= \tilde{M}_{S^*}(x,y) + \alpha && \text{(by Equation 1)} \\
&= \tilde{M}_G(x,y) = \tilde{M}_{S(x,y)}(x,y),
\end{aligned}$$

where $\alpha(z,y) = \tilde{M}_G(z,y) - \tilde{M}_{S(z,y)}(z,y)$. The strict inequality holds because of the (x,y) choice. That is, there is at least one adjacent state $z' \in N_{as}(x)$ such that $d(z,y) < d(x,y)$ by the definition of d. Therefore, at such a configuration (z',y) we have $\alpha(z',y) < \alpha$.

The other case is that in the strategy $S(x,y)$, the adversary moves the agent in the state y with probability 1. In this case, we can directly have $\tilde{M}_{S(x,y)}(x,y) = 1 + \frac{1}{d_y} \sum_{z \in N_{as}(y)} \tilde{M}_G(x,z)$. Also, $\tilde{M}_{S^*}(x,y) = 1 + \frac{1}{d_y} \left(\sum_{z \in N_{as}(y)} \tilde{M}_{S^*}(x,z)\right)$ holds. Therefore, we can derive a contradiction similarly, proving the lemma. □

For the extended hitting times, the following proposition holds.

Proposition 3. *For any pair of states $s_1, s_2 \in V \cup S_{intm}$ such that $s_1 \neq s_2$, we have*

$$\tilde{H}(s_1, s_2) = 1 + \frac{1}{d_{s_1}} \sum_{z \in N_{as}(s_1)} \tilde{H}(z, s_2).$$

Thus we have the following equations for the potential function $\tilde{\Phi}$, whose proof is deferred to the full paper.

Lemma 7. *For any pair of states s_1, s_2 such that $s_1 \neq s_2$, we have*

$$\tilde{\Phi}(s_1, s_2) = 1 + \frac{1}{d_{s_1}} \sum_{z \in N_{as}(s_1)} \tilde{\Phi}(z, s_2) = 1 + \frac{1}{d_{s_2}} \sum_{z \in N_{as}(s_2)} \tilde{\Phi}(z, s_1).$$

A similar proposition holds for the non-atomic meeting times.

Proposition 4. *For any pair of states s_1, s_2 such that $s_1 \neq s_2$ and an optimal and deterministic strategy S^*, suppose that the agent with state s_1 is moved in the configuration (s_1, s_2) by the strategy. Then, we have*

$$\tilde{M}_G(s_1, s_2) = 1 + \frac{1}{d_{s_1}} \sum_{z \in N_{as}(s_1)} \tilde{M}_G(z, s_2).$$

Otherwise, if the strategy moves the agent with state s_2*, then we have*

$$\tilde{M}_G(s_1, s_2) = 1 + \frac{1}{d_{s_2}} \sum_{z \in N_{as}(s_2)} \tilde{M}_G(z, s_1).$$

Note that these two cases exclusively hold, that is, both equations do not hold at a time. This fact holds since in the case that the adversary moves the agent x, we cannot take the average among the adjacent states of y.

Finally, we can claim the main argument.

Theorem 3. *Let* G *be any connected and undirected graph, and let* s_{tu} *be a hidden state of non-atomic random walks of* $\tilde{G}$*. Then, for every pair of states* x, y*, we have* $\tilde{M}_G(x, y) \leq \tilde{\Phi}(x, y)$*, where* $\tilde{\Phi}(x, y) = \tilde{H}(x, \overline{y}) + \tilde{H}(y, \overline{s_{tu}}) - \tilde{H}(s_{tu}, \overline{y})$.

Proof. To prove the theorem by contradiction, assume that there is a pair of states x, y such that $\tilde{M}_G(x, y) - \tilde{\Phi}(x, y) > 0$. Let β_{max} be the maximum value of such differences. Let $\beta(x, y)$ be the difference $\tilde{M}_G(x, y) - \tilde{\Phi}(x, y)$ at the configuration (x, y). We choose a configuration (x, y) such that it obtains minimum $d(x, y)$ among the configurations that achieve β_{max}. Without loss of generality, suppose that the strategy S^* moves the agent in the state x. Since $\tilde{M}_G(x, x) = 0$ and $\tilde{\Phi}(x, x) \geq 0$ by Proposition 2, it holds that $x \neq y$. Using the average argument, we have the following contradiction:

$$\begin{aligned}
\tilde{M}_G(x, y) &= \tilde{\Phi}(x, y) + \beta_{max} \\
&= 1 + \frac{1}{d_x} \sum_{z \in N_{as}(x)} \tilde{\Phi}(z, y) + \beta_{max} \\
&> 1 + \frac{1}{d_x} \sum_{z \in N_{as}(x)} \left(\tilde{\Phi}(z, y) + \beta(z, y)\right) \\
&= 1 + \frac{1}{d_x} \sum_{z \in N_{as}(x)} \tilde{M}_G(z, y) = \tilde{M}_G(x, y).
\end{aligned}$$

The second equality uses Lemma 7, and the last equality uses Proposition 4. The inequality is strict, since there is an adjacent state $z' \in N_{as}(x)$ such that $d(z', y) < d(x, y)$, therefore we have $\beta(z', y) < \beta_{max}$. □

5 Discussion

In this section, we examine the upper bounds for several graph classes, namely graphs with bounded degrees including lines and rings, and complete graphs. We also consider the general graphs. Let Δ be the maximum degree of the vertices in V, and $H_G = \max_{x,y \in V} H(x, y)$.

- In general graphs, we have the following upper bound. Since in the last summation of the upper bound of Theorem 1, the number of sums is upper bounded by the max degree of the initial positions x, y, we have the general upper bound of $O(\Delta H_G)$. Also, $H_G = O(n^3)$ holds for any graph G, which is shown by the paper [2], we have $O(\Delta n^3) = O(n^4)$. For the meeting time of atomic random walks, in the paper [17] the authors show that $M_G(x, y) = O(n^3)$ for any graph G and any initial positions x, y.

- For any graph G with bounded degrees for any initial position x, y, the meeting time $\tilde{M}(x, y)$ is bounded by $O(H_G)$. Especially in the lines and rings, since the hitting time $H(z, u)$ for $z \in N_G(u)$ is $O(n)$, we have $\tilde{M}_G(x, y) \leq 4H_G + O(n)$.
- The complete graphs are an instance in which the meeting times are different between atomic and non-atomic random walks. In the original (atomic) random walks, the meeting times for the complete graph with n vertices is $\Theta(n)$, while the one for the non-atomic random walk is $\Theta(n^2)$. For the original random walks, the $O(n)$-upper bound is derived by the original upper bound in [5]. Also, $\Omega(n)$-lower bound is given by the following strategy: for the agents starting at different vertices, the strategy repeatedly chooses the same agent until they meet. Obviously, the expected time to meet is $\Theta(n)$ with the adversary using the strategy. Since there is a strategy that obtains $\Theta(n)$ time to meet, the meeting time of the worst strategy is at least $\Omega(n)$. Similarly, in the non-atomic random walks, an $O(n^2)$ upper bound of the meeting time is given by calculating the potential function $\tilde{\Phi}$. Since any intermediate state is hidden by the symmetry of the topology, we can choose any intermediate state as a hidden state, suppose s_h. For any pair of intermediate states s_{ab}, s_{cd}, we have $\tilde{H}(s_{ab}, s_{cd}) = 1 + \tilde{H}(b, c) + \tilde{H}(c, s_{cd}) = O(n + \tilde{H}(c, s_{cd})) = O(n^2)$. Also, the upper bound is derived by the following strategy: we let the agents start at s_{ab} and s_h, and the strategy repeatedly moves the agent starting at s_{ab} until they meet. This takes expected $\Theta(n^2)$ time to meet, and as a consequence, the meeting time of the worst strategy is at least $\Omega(n^2)$.

6 Conclusion

In this paper, we revisit the adversarial meeting time of the random walks by two agents and consider the non-atomic version of the random walks. For the extended version of the random walks, we give a new upper bound of the worst-case expected time to meet in a given graph G. We also show for atomic and non-atomic random walks, the meeting times are different in the complete graphs.

References

1. Bampas, E., et al.: On asynchronous rendezvous in general graphs. Theoret. Comput. Sci. **753**, 80–90 (2019). https://doi.org/10.1016/j.tcs.2018.06.045
2. Brightwell, G., Winkler, P.: Maximum hitting time for random walks on graphs. Random Struct. Algorithms **1**(3), 263–276 (1990). https://doi.org/10.1002/rsa.3240010303

3. Bshouty, N.H., Higham, L., Warpechowska-Gruca, J.: Meeting times of random walks on graphs. Inf. Process. Lett. **69**(5), 259–265 (1999). https://doi.org/10.1016/S0020-0190(99)00017-4
4. Cooper, C., Elsässer, R., Ono, H., Radzik, T.: Coalescing random walks and voting on connected graphs. SIAM J. Discret. Math. **27**(4), 1748–1758 (2013). https://doi.org/10.1137/120900368
5. Coppersmith, D., Tetali, P., Winkler, P.: Collisions among random walks on a graph. SIAM J. Discret. Math. **6**(3), 363–374 (1993). https://doi.org/10.1137/0406029
6. Czyzowicz, J., Pelc, A., Labourel, A.: How to meet asynchronously (almost) everywhere. ACM Trans. Algorithms **8**(4), 1–14 (2012). https://doi.org/10.1145/2344422.2344427
7. De Marco, G., Gargano, L., Kranakis, E., Krizanc, D., Pelc, A., Vaccaro, U.: Asynchronous deterministic rendezvous in graphs. In: Jędrzejowicz, J., Szepietowski, A. (eds.) MFCS 2005. LNCS, vol. 3618, pp. 271–282. Springer, Heidelberg (2005). https://doi.org/10.1007/11549345_24
8. Feige, U.: A tight upper bound on the cover time for random walks on graphs. Random Struct. Algorithms **6**(1), 51–54 (1995). https://doi.org/10.1002/rsa.3240060106
9. Guilbault, S., Pelc, A.: Asynchronous rendezvous of anonymous agents in arbitrary graphs. In: Fernàndez Anta, A., Lipari, G., Roy, M. (eds.) OPODIS 2011. LNCS, vol. 7109, pp. 421–434. Springer, Heidelberg (2011). https://doi.org/10.1007/978-3-642-25873-2_29
10. Hassin, Y., Peleg, D.: Distributed probabilistic polling and applications to proportionate agreement. In: Wiedermann, J., van Emde Boas, P., Nielsen, M. (eds.) ICALP 1999. LNCS, vol. 1644, pp. 402–411. Springer, Heidelberg (1999). https://doi.org/10.1007/3-540-48523-6_37
11. Israeli, A., Jalfon, M.: Token management schemes and random walks yield self-stabilizing mutual exclusion. In: Proceedings of the Ninth Annual ACM Symposium on Principles of Distributed Computing, pp. 119–131 (1990)
12. Kahn, J.D., Linial, N., Nisan, N., Saks, M.E.: On the cover time of random walks on graphs. J. Theor. Probab. **2**, 121–128 (1989)
13. Kanade, V., Mallmann-Trenn, F., Sauerwald, T.: On coalescence time in graphs-when is coalescing as fast as meeting? ACM Trans. Algorithms **19**(2), 1–46 (2023). https://doi.org/10.1145/3576900
14. Lovász, L.: Random walks on graphs. Comb. Paul Erdos Eighty **2**, 1–46 (1993)
15. Oliveira, R.I., Peres, Y.: Random walks on graphs: new bounds on hitting, meeting, coalescing and returning. In: 2019 Proceedings of the Meeting on Analytic Algorithmics and Combinatorics, pp. 119–126 (2019). https://doi.org/10.1137/1.9781611975505.13
16. Tetali, P.: Random walks and the effective resistance of networks. J. Theor. Probab. **4**, 101–109 (1991)
17. Tetali, P., Winkler, P.: On a random walk problem arising in self-stabilizing token management. In: Proceedings of the Tenth Annual ACM Symposium on Principles of Distributed Computing, pp. 273–280. Association for Computing Machinery (1991). https://doi.org/10.1145/112600.112623
18. Tetali, P., Winkler, P.: Simultaneous reversible Markov chains. Comb. Paul Erdos Eighty **1** (1993)

Minimum Algorithm Sizes for Self-stabilizing Gathering and Related Problems of Autonomous Mobile Robots (Extended Abstract)

Yuichi Asahiro[1(✉)] and Masafumi Yamashita[2]

[1] Kyushu Sangyo University, Fukuoka, Japan
asahiro@is.kyusan-u.ac.jp
[2] Kyushu University, Fukuoka, Japan
masafumi.yamashita@gmail.com

Abstract. We investigate swarms of autonomous mobile robots in the Euclidean plane. Each robot has a target function to determine a destination point from the robots' positions. All robots in a swarm conventionally take the same target function. We allow the robots in a swarm to take different target functions, and investigate the effects of the number of distinct target functions on the problem-solving ability. Specifically, we are interested in how many distinct target functions are necessary and sufficient to solve some well-known problems which are not solvable when all robots take the same target function, regarding target function as a resource, like time and message, to solve a problem. The number of distinct target functions necessary and sufficient to solve a problem Π is called the *minimum algorithm size* (MAS) for Π. (The MAS is ∞, if Π is not solvable even for the robots with unique target functions.) We establish the MASs for solving the gathering and related problems from any initial configuration, i.e., in a self-stabilizing manner. Our results include: There is a family of the scattering problems cSCT ($1 \leq c \leq n$) such that the MAS for the cSCAT is c, where n is the size of the swarm. The MAS for the gathering problem is 2. It is 3, for the problem of gathering **all non-faulty** robots at a single point, regardless of the number ($< n$) of crash failures. It is however ∞, for the problem of gathering **all robots** at a single point, in the presence of at most one crash failure.

Keywords: Autonomous mobile robot · Minimum algorithm size · Scattering · Gathering · Pattern formation · Crash failure

1 Introduction

Swarms of anonymous oblivious mobile robots have been attracting many researchers over four decades, e.g., [1,3,9–12,15,21,22,26,27]. An anonymous

Due to space limitation, some proofs and contributions are deferred to full version [7].

S. Dolev and B. Schieber (Eds.): SSS 2023, LNCS 14310, pp. 312–327, 2023.
https://doi.org/10.1007/978-3-031-44274-2_23

oblivious mobile robot, which is represented by a point in the Euclidean space, looks identical and indistinguishable, lacks identifiers and communication devices, and operates in Look-Compute-Move cycles: When a robot starts a cycle, it identifies the multiset of the robots' positions, computes a destination point using a function called *target function* based only on the multiset identified, and then moves to the destination point. All papers listed above investigate swarms, provided that all robots composing a swarm take the same target function. It makes sense: Anonymous robots taking different target functions can behave, as if they had different identifiers. On the other hand, robots with different identifiers can behave, as if they took different target functions, even when they take the same one. The problems investigated cover from simple problems like the convergence and the gathering problems (e.g., [1,22]) to hard problems like the formation problem of a sequence of patterns and the gathering problem in the presence of Byzantine failures (e.g., [12,18]). It has turned out that a swarm of anonymous oblivious robots is powerful enough to solve sufficiently hard problems. At the same time, however, we have realized limitation of its problem-solving ability. For example, the gathering problem is, in general, not solvable even if the number of robots is 2 [26].

A promising idea to increase the problem-solving ability of a swarm is to allow robots to take different target functions. It is also natural, since almost all artificial distributed systems enjoy unique identifiers, e.g., serial numbers. This paper takes this approach, and investigates the effects of the number of distinct target functions on the problem-solving ability. Specifically, we are interested in how many distinct target functions are necessary and sufficient to solve some problems which are not solvable when all robots take the same target function.

Let $\mathcal{R}$ and Φ be a swarm of n robots, and a set of target functions such that $|\Phi| \leq n$, respectively. An *assignment* $\mathcal{A} : \mathcal{R} \to \Phi$ of target functions is a surjection from $\mathcal{R}$ to Φ, i.e., every target function is assigned to at least one robot. We call Φ an *algorithm*[1] of $\mathcal{R}$ for a problem Π, if $\mathcal{R}$ solves Π, regardless of the assignment $\mathcal{A}$ that $\mathcal{R}$ takes. (Thus, we cannot assume a particular assignment to design target functions.) The *minimum algorithm size* (MAS) for Π is the size $|\Phi|$ of algorithm Φ necessary and sufficient to solve Π. It is ∞, if Π is not solvable even for the robots with unique target functions. We then investigate the MASs of **self-stabilizing** algorithms for solving the gathering and related problems from **any** initial configuration. In what follows, an algorithm means a self-stabilizing algorithm, unless otherwise stated.

Motivations. We have investigated the time and the message complexities of distributed problems, considering time and message as important resources in the distributed computing. We regard target function as another resource. You will find the MASs of many problems are larger than 1 (but not ∞). The complexity of a problem is thus (at least partly) measured by its MAS. Also, an anonymous

[1] Here, we abuse a term "algorithm." Despite that an algorithm must have a finite description conventionally, a target function (and hence a set of target functions) may not, as defined in Sect. 2. To compensate the abuse, when we will show the existence of an algorithm, we insist on giving a finite procedure to compute it.

swarm with c distinct target functions can be regarded as a swarm with c distinct identifiers (and the same target function). Maintaining a large number of distinct identifiers not only is a centralized task, but also causes a substantial load. These motivate our theoretical work of establishing the MASs for problems.

Homonymous Distributed Systems. A distributed system is *homonymous*, if some processing elements (e.g., processors, processes, agents, or robots) may have the same identifier. Two extreme cases are anonymous systems and those whose identifiers are unique. The extreme cases have been investigated extensively. A relatively small number of researches on "properly" homonymous distributed system are known. Recall that we can identify an anonymous distributed system with c distinct local algorithms with a homonymous distributed system with c distinct identifiers.

Angluin [4] started investigation on anonymous computer networks in 1980, and a few researchers (e.g., [8,20,23]) followed her, to pursuit a purely distributed algorithm which does not rely on a central controller, in the spirit of the minimalist. Yamashita and Kameda [24] investigated the leader election problem on homonymous computer networks in 1989. Their main research topic was symmetry breaking, and they searched for a condition symmetry breaking becomes possible. A rough conclusion established is that symmetry breaking is impossible in general, but the probability that it is possible approaches to 1, as the number of processors increases, provided that the network topology is random, and identifiers, even if they are not unique, substantially increase the probability. The leader election problem on homonymous computer networks has also been investigated under several assumptions e.g., in [2,14,17,25].

Other research topics on homonymous computer networks include failure detectors [5] and the Byzantine agreement problem [13]. In [13], the authors showed that the Byzantine agreement problem is solvable if and only if $\ell \geq 3f + 1$ in the synchronous case, and it is solvable only if $\ell > \frac{n+3f}{2}$ in the partially synchronous case, where ℓ is the number of distinct identifiers and f is an upperbound on the number of faulty processors. Thus, the MAS of the Byzantine agreement problem is $3f + 1$ in the synchronous case.

Only a few researchers have investigated homonymous swarms of robots: Team assembly of heterogeneous robots, each dedicated to solve a subtask, is discussed in [19], and the compatibility of target functions is discussed in [6,11].

Contributions. We investigate the MASs for a variety of **self-stabilizing** problems, which are asked to solve problems from **any** initial configuration. The *c-scattering problem* (cSCT) is the problem of forming a configuration in which robots are distributed at least c different positions. The *scattering problem* is the nSCT. The *c-gathering problem* (cGAT) is the problem of forming a configuration in which robots are distributed at most c different positions. The *gathering problem* (GAT) is the 1GAT. The *pattern formation problem* (PF) for a given pattern G is the problem of forming a configuration P similar[2] to G.

[2] We say that one object is similar to another, if the latter is obtained from the former by a combination of scaling, translation, and rotation (but not by a reflection).

We also investigate problems in the presence of *crash failures*: A faulty robot can stop functioning at any time, becoming permanently inactive. A faulty robot may not cause a malfunction, forever. We cannot distinguish such a robot from a non-faulty one. The *f-fault tolerant c-scattering problem* (fFcS) is the problem of forming a configuration in which robots are distributed at c (or more) different positions, as long as at most f robots have crashed. The *f-fault tolerant gathering problem* (fFG) is the problem of gathering **all non-faulty robots** at a point, as long as at most f robots have crashed. The *f-fault tolerant gathering problem to f points* (fFGP) is the problem of gathering **all robots** (including faulty ones) at f (or less) points, as long as at most f robots have crashed.

Table 1 summarizes main results.

Table 1. For each problem Π, the MAS for Π, an algorithm for Π achieving the MAS (and the theorem/corollary/observation citation number establishing the result in parentheses) are shown.

problem Π	MAS	algorithm
cSCT ($1 \leq c \leq n$)	c	cSCTA (Thm. 1)
cGAT ($2 \leq c \leq n$)	1	2GATA (Cor. 1)
GAT	2	GATA (Thm. 3)
PF	n	PFA (Thm. 6)
fF1S ($1 \leq f \leq n-1$)	1	1SCTA (Obs. 1)
fF2S ($1 \leq f \leq n-2$)	$f+2$	$(f+2)$SCTA (Thm. 7)
$(n-1)$F2S	∞	– (Thm. 7)
fFcS ($c \geq 3$, $c+f-1 \leq n$)	$c+f-1$	$(c+f-1)$SCTA (Thm. 7)
fFcS ($c \geq 3$, $c+f-1 > n$)	∞	– (Thm. 7)
fFG ($1 \leq f \leq n-1$)	3	SGTA (Thm. 8)
fFGP ($1 \leq f \leq n-1$)	∞	– (Thm. 9)

Organization. After introducing the robot model and several measures in Sect. 2, we first establish the MAS for the cSCT in Sect. 3. Then the MASs for the cGAT and the PF are respectively investigated in Sects. 4 and 5. Sections 6 and 7 consider the MASs for the fFcS, the fFG, and the fFGP. Finally, we conclude the paper by giving open problems in Sect. 8.

2 Preliminaries

The Model. Consider a swarm $\mathcal{R}$ of n robots $r_1, r_2, \ldots, r_n$. Each robot r_i has its own unit of length and a local compass, which define an x-y local coordinate system Z_i: Z_i is right-handed and self-centric, i.e., the origin $(0,0)$ always shows the position of r_i. Robot r_i has the strong multiplicity detection capability, and can count the number of robots that reside at a point.

A *target function* ϕ is a function from $(R^2)^n$ to $R^2 \cup \{\bot\}$ for all $n \geq 1$ such that $\phi(P) = \bot$, if and only if $(0,0) \notin P$.[3] Here, $\bot$ is a special symbol to denote that $(0,0) \notin P$. Given a target function ϕ_i, r_i executes a Look-Compute-Move cycle when it is activated:

Look: r_i identifies the multiset P of the robots' positions in Z_i.
Compute: r_i computes $\boldsymbol{x}_i = \phi_i(P)$. Since $(0,0) \in P$, $\phi_i(P) \neq \bot$. (In case ϕ_i is not computable, we simply assume that $\phi_i(P)$ is given by an oracle.)
Move: r_i moves to $\boldsymbol{x}_i$, where it always reaches $\boldsymbol{x}_i$ before this Move phase ends.

We assume a discrete time $0, 1, \ldots$. At each time $t \geq 0$, a scheduler activates some unpredictable non-empty subset (that may be all) of robots. Then activated robots execute a cycle which starts at t and ends before (not including) $t+1$, i.e., $\mathcal{R}$ is semi-synchronous ($\mathcal{SSYNC}$).

Let Z_0 be the x-y global coordinate system. It is right-handed. The coordinate transformation from Z_i to Z_0 is denoted by γ_i. We use Z_0 and γ_i just for the purpose of explanation. They are not available to any robot r_i.

The position of robot r_i at time t in Z_0 is denoted by $\boldsymbol{x}_t(r_i)$. Then $P_t = \{\boldsymbol{x}_t(r_i) : 1 \leq i \leq n\}$ is a multiset representing the positions of all robots at time t, which is called the *configuration* of $\mathcal{R}$ at t.

Given an initial configuration P_0, an assignment $\mathcal{A}$ of a target function ϕ_i to each robot r_i, and an $\mathcal{SSYNC}$ schedule, the execution is a sequence $\mathcal{E} : P_0, P_1, \ldots, P_t, \ldots$ of configurations starting from P_0. Here, for all r_i and $t \geq 0$, if r_i is not activated at t, then $\boldsymbol{x}_{t+1}(r_i) = \boldsymbol{x}_t(r_i)$. Otherwise, if it is activated, r_i identifies $Q_t^{(i)} = \gamma_i^{-1}(P_t)$ in Z_i, computes $\boldsymbol{y} = \phi_i(Q_t^{(i)})$, and moves to $\boldsymbol{y}$ in Z_i. (Since $(0,0) \in Q_t^{(i)}$, $\boldsymbol{y} \neq \bot$.) Then $\boldsymbol{x}_{t+1}(r_i) = \gamma_i(\boldsymbol{y})$. We assume that the scheduler is fair: It activates every robot infinitely many times. Throughout the paper, we regard the scheduler as an adversary.

An $\mathcal{SSYNC}$ schedule is said to be *fully synchronous* ($\mathcal{FSYNC}$), if every robot r_i is activated every time instant $t = 0, 1, 2, \ldots$. A schedule which is not $\mathcal{SSYNC}$ is said to be *asynchronous* ($\mathcal{ASYNC}$). Throughout the paper, we assume that the scheduler is fair and $\mathcal{SSYNC}$, i.e., it always produces a fair $\mathcal{SSYNC}$ schedule.

Orders and Symmetries. Let $<$[4] be a lexicographic order on R^2. For distinct points $\boldsymbol{p} = (p_x, p_y)$ and $\boldsymbol{q} = (q_x, q_y)$, $\boldsymbol{p} < \boldsymbol{q}$, if either (i) $p_x < q_x$ or (ii) $p_x = q_x$ and $p_y < q_y$ holds. Let $\sqsubset$ be a lexicographic order on $(R^2)^n$. For distinct multisets of n points $P = \{\boldsymbol{p}_1, \boldsymbol{p}_2, \ldots, \boldsymbol{p}_n\}$ and $Q = \{\boldsymbol{q}_1, \boldsymbol{q}_2, \ldots, \boldsymbol{q}_n\}$, where for all $i = 1, 2, \ldots, n-1$, $\boldsymbol{p}_i \leq \boldsymbol{p}_{i+1}$ and $\boldsymbol{q}_i \leq \boldsymbol{q}_{i+1}$ hold, $P \sqsubset Q$, if there is an $i (1 \leq i \leq n-1)$ such that $\boldsymbol{p}_j = \boldsymbol{q}_j$ for all $j = 1, 2, \ldots, i-1$,[5] and

[3] Since Z_i is self-centric, $(0,0) \notin P$ means an error of eye sensor, which we assume will not occur.

[4] We use the same notation $<$ to denote the lexicographic order on R^2 and the order on R to save the number of notations.

[5] We assume $\boldsymbol{p}_0 = \boldsymbol{q}_0$.

$\boldsymbol{p}_i < \boldsymbol{q}_i$. The set of distinct points of P is denoted by $\overline{P} = \{\boldsymbol{q}_1, \boldsymbol{q}_2, \ldots, \boldsymbol{q}_m\}$, where $|P| = n$ and $|\overline{P}| = m$. We denote the multiplicity of $\boldsymbol{q}$ in P by $\mu_P(\boldsymbol{q})$, i.e., $\mu_P(\boldsymbol{q}) = |\{i : \boldsymbol{p}_i = \boldsymbol{q} \in P\}|$. We identify P with the pair $(\overline{P}, \mu_P)$, where μ_P is a labeling function to associate label $\mu_P(\boldsymbol{q})$ with each element $\boldsymbol{q} \in \overline{P}$.

Let G_P be the rotation group $G_{\overline{P}}$ of $\overline{P}$ about $\boldsymbol{o}_P$ preserving μ_P, where $\boldsymbol{o}_P$ is the center of the smallest enclosing circle of P. The order $|G_P|$ of G_P is denoted by k_P. We assume that $k_P = 0$, if $|\overline{P}| = 1$, i.e., if $\overline{P} = \{\boldsymbol{o}_P\}$. The symmetricity $\sigma(P)$ of P is $GCD(k_P, \mu_P(\boldsymbol{o}_P))$ [22]. See Fig. 1(1) for an example.

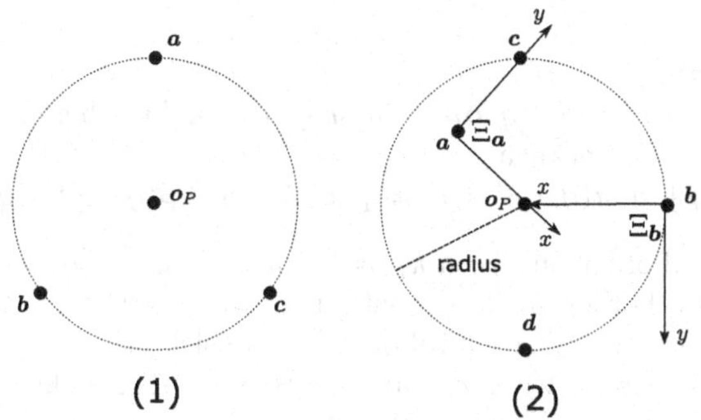

Fig. 1. (1) A configuration P, where $\overline{P} = \{\boldsymbol{o}_P, \boldsymbol{a}, \boldsymbol{b}, \boldsymbol{c}\}$. If $\mu_P(\boldsymbol{a}) = \mu_P(\boldsymbol{b}) = \mu_P(\boldsymbol{c}) = i$ for an integer $i > 0$, then $k_P = 3$. If (k_P=3 and) $\mu_P(\boldsymbol{o}_P) = 3j$ for an integer $j \geq 0$, then $\sigma(P) = 3$; otherwise, $\sigma(P) = 1$. (2) A configuration P, where $\overline{P} = \{\boldsymbol{o}_P, \boldsymbol{a}, \boldsymbol{b}, \boldsymbol{c}, \boldsymbol{d}\}$. In Z_0, $\boldsymbol{o}_P = (0,0)$, $\boldsymbol{a} = (-1/2, 1/2)$, $\boldsymbol{b} = (1,0)$, $\boldsymbol{c} = (0,1)$, $\boldsymbol{d} = (0,-1)$, and the radius of C is 1. Solid arrows represent directions of x- and y-axes of Ξ_a and Ξ_b, and have the unit length (the radius 1 of C). In Ξ_b, $\boldsymbol{o}_P, \boldsymbol{a}, \boldsymbol{b}, \boldsymbol{c}$, and $\boldsymbol{d}$ are $(1,0)$,$(3/2,-1/2)$,$(0,0)$,$(1,-1)$, and $(1,1)$, respectively, and thus $\gamma_b^{-1}(P) = V_P(\boldsymbol{b}) = \{(1,0), (3/2,-1/2), (0,0), (1,-1), (1,1)\}$.

We use both measures k_P and $\sigma(P)$. Suppose that P is a configuration in Z_0. When activated, a robot r_i identifies the robots' positions $Q^{(i)} = \gamma_i^{-1}(P)$ in Z_i in Look phase. Since P and $Q^{(i)}$ are similar, $k_P = k_{Q^{(i)}}$ and $\sigma(P) = \sigma(Q^{(i)})$ hold, i.e., all robots can consistently compute k_P and $\sigma(P)$.

On the contrary, robots cannot consistently compute lexicographic orders $<$ and $\sqsubset$. To see this fact, let $\boldsymbol{x}$ and $\boldsymbol{y}$ be distinct points in $\overline{P}$ in Z_0. Then both $\gamma_i^{-1}(\boldsymbol{x}) < \gamma_i^{-1}(\boldsymbol{y})$ and $\gamma_i^{-1}(\boldsymbol{x}) > \gamma_i^{-1}(\boldsymbol{y})$ can occur, depending on Z_i. Thus robots cannot consistently compare $\boldsymbol{x}$ and $\boldsymbol{y}$ using $>$. And it is the same for $\sqsubset$.

We introduce a total order $\succ$ on $\overline{P}$, in such a way that all robots can agree on the order, provided $k_P = 1$. A key trick behind the definition of $\succ$ is to use, instead of Z_i, an x-y coordinate system Ξ_i which is computable for any robot r_j from $Q^{(j)}$. Let $\Gamma_P(\boldsymbol{q}) \subseteq \overline{P}$ be the orbit of G_P through $\boldsymbol{q} \in \overline{P}$. Then $|\Gamma_P(\boldsymbol{q})| = k_P$ if $\boldsymbol{q} \neq \boldsymbol{o}_P$, and $\mu_P(\boldsymbol{q}') = \mu_P(\boldsymbol{q})$ if $\boldsymbol{q}' \in \Gamma_P(\boldsymbol{q})$. If $\boldsymbol{o}_P \in \overline{P}$, $\Gamma_P(\boldsymbol{o}_P) = \{\boldsymbol{o}_P\}$. Let $\Gamma_P = \{\Gamma_P(\boldsymbol{q}) : \boldsymbol{q} \in \overline{P}\}$. Then Γ_P is a partition of $\overline{P}$. Define an x-y coordinate system Ξ_q for each point $\boldsymbol{q} \in \overline{P} \setminus \{\boldsymbol{o}_P\}$. The origin of Ξ_q is $\boldsymbol{q}$, the unit distance is the radius of the smallest enclosing circle of P, the

x-axis is taken so that it goes through $\boldsymbol{o}_P$, and it is right-handed. Let $\gamma_{\boldsymbol{q}}$ be the coordinate transformation from $\Xi_{\boldsymbol{q}}$ to Z_0. Then the view $V_P(\boldsymbol{q})$ of $\boldsymbol{q}$ is defined to be $\gamma_{\boldsymbol{q}}^{-1}(P)$. Obviously $V_P(\boldsymbol{q}') = V_P(\boldsymbol{q})$ (as multisets), if and only if $\boldsymbol{q}' \in \Gamma_P(\boldsymbol{q})$. Let $View_P = \{V_P(\boldsymbol{q}) : \boldsymbol{q} \in \overline{P} \setminus \{\boldsymbol{o}_P\}\}$. See Fig. 1(2) for an example.

A robot r_i, in Compute phase, can compute from $Q^{(i)}$, for each $\boldsymbol{q} \in \overline{Q^{(i)}} \setminus \{\boldsymbol{o}_{Q^{(i)}}\}$, $\Xi_{\boldsymbol{q}}$, $V_{Q^{(i)}}(\boldsymbol{q})$, and $View_{Q^{(i)}}$. Since P and $Q^{(i)}$ are similar, by the definition of $\Xi_{\boldsymbol{q}}$, $View_P = View_{Q^{(i)}}$, which implies that all robots r_i can consistently compute $View_P$. We define $\succ_P$ on Γ_P using $View_P$. For any distinct orbits $\Gamma_P(\boldsymbol{q})$ and $\Gamma_P(\boldsymbol{q}')$, $\Gamma_P(\boldsymbol{q}) \succ_P \Gamma_P(\boldsymbol{q}')$, if one of the following conditions hold:

1. $\mu_P(\boldsymbol{q}) > \mu_P(\boldsymbol{q}')$.
2. $\mu_P(\boldsymbol{q}) = \mu_P(\boldsymbol{q}')$ and $dist(\boldsymbol{q}, \boldsymbol{o}_P) < dist(\boldsymbol{q}', \boldsymbol{o}_P)$ hold, where $dist(\boldsymbol{x}, \boldsymbol{y})$ is the Euclidean distance between $\boldsymbol{x}$ and $\boldsymbol{y}$.
3. $\mu_P(\boldsymbol{q}) = \mu_P(\boldsymbol{q}')$, $dist(\boldsymbol{q}, \boldsymbol{o}_P) = dist(\boldsymbol{q}', \boldsymbol{o}_P)$, and $V_P(\boldsymbol{q}) \sqsupset V_P(\boldsymbol{q}')$ hold.[6]

Then $\succ_P$ is a total order on Γ_P. If $k_P = 1$, since $\Gamma_P(\boldsymbol{q}) = \{\boldsymbol{q}\}$ for all $\boldsymbol{q} \in \overline{P}$, we regard $\succ_P$ as a total order on $\overline{P}$ by identifying $\Gamma_P(\boldsymbol{q})$ with $\boldsymbol{q}$. For a configuration P (in Z_0), from $Q^{(i)}$ (in Z_i), each robot r_i can consistently compute $k_P = k_{Q^{(i)}}$, $\Gamma_P = \Gamma_{Q^{(i)}}$ and $View_P = View_{Q^{(i)}}$, and hence $\succ_P = \succ_{Q^{(i)}}$. Thus, all robots can agree on, e.g., the largest point $\boldsymbol{q} \in \overline{P}$ with respect to $\succ_P$.

3 C-Scattering Problem

Let $\mathcal{P} = \{P \in (R^2)^n : (0,0) \in P,\ n \geq 1\}$. Since a target function returns $\perp$ when $(0,0) \notin P$, we regard $\mathcal{P}$ as the domain of a target function.

The *scattering problem* (SCT) is the problem to have the robots occupy distinct positions, starting from any configuration [15]. For $1 \leq c \leq n$, let the *c-scattering problem* (cSCT) be the problem of transforming any initial configuration to a configuration P such that $|\overline{P}| \geq c$. Thus, the nSCT is the SCT. An algorithm for the cSCT is an algorithm for the $(c-1)$SCT, for $2 \leq c \leq n$.

Consider a set cSCTA $= \{sct_1, sct_2, \ldots, sct_c\}$ of c target functions, where target function sct_i is defined as follows for any $P \in \mathcal{P}$.

[Target function sct_i]

1. If $|\overline{P}| \geq c$, then $sct_i(P) = (0,0)$ for $i = 1, 2, \ldots, c$.
2. If $|\overline{P}| = 1$, then $sct_1(P) = (0,0)$, and $sct_i(P) = (1,0)$ for $i = 2, 3, \ldots, c$.
3. If $2 \leq |\overline{P}| \leq c-1$, $sct_i(P) = (\delta/(2(i+1)), 0)$ for $i = 1, 2, \ldots, c$, where δ is the smallest distance between two (distinct) points in $\overline{P}$.

Theorem 1. *For any* $1 \leq c \leq n$, cSCTA *is an algorithm for the* cSCT. *The MAS for the* cSCT *is* c.

---

[6] Since $dist(\boldsymbol{o}_P, \boldsymbol{o}_P) = 0$, $V_P(\boldsymbol{q})$ is not compared with $V_P(\boldsymbol{o}_P)$ with respect to $\sqsupset$.

Proof. We omit the proof that cSCTA is a correct algorithm for the cSCT, and present only a proof that the MAS for the cSCT is at least c.

The proof is by contradiction. Suppose that the MAS for the cSCT is $m < c$ to derive a contradiction. Let $\Phi = \{\phi_1, \phi_2, \ldots, \phi_m\}$ be an algorithm for the cSCT. Consider the following situation:

1. All robots r_i $(1 \le i \le n)$ share the unit length and the direction of positive x-axis.
2. A target function assignment $\mathcal{A}$ is defined as follows: $\mathcal{A}(r_i) = \phi_i$ for $1 \le i \le m-1$, and $\mathcal{A}(r_i) = \phi_m$ for $m \le i \le n$.
3. All robots initially occupy the same location $(0,0)$. That is, $P_0 = \{(0,0), (0,0), \ldots, (0,0)\}$.
4. The schedule is $\mathcal{FSYNC}$.

Let $\mathcal{E} : P_0, P_1, \ldots$ be the execution of $\mathcal{R}$ starting from P_0, under the above situation. By an easy induction on t, all robots r_i $(m \le i \le n)$ occupy the same location, i.e., for all $t \ge 0$, $\boldsymbol{x}_t(r_m) = \boldsymbol{x}_t(r_{m+1}) = \cdots = \boldsymbol{x}_t(r_n)$. Since $|\overline{P_t}| \le m < c$ for all $t \ge 0$, a contradiction is derived. □

4 C-Gathering Problem

Let $P = \{\boldsymbol{p}_1, \boldsymbol{p}_2, \ldots, \boldsymbol{p}_n\} \in \mathcal{P}$, $\overline{P} = \{\boldsymbol{q}_1, \boldsymbol{q}_2, \ldots, \boldsymbol{q}_{m_P}\}$, $m_P = |\overline{P}|$ be the size of $\overline{P}$, $\mu_P(\boldsymbol{q})$ denote the multiplicity of $\boldsymbol{q}$ in P, $\boldsymbol{o}_P$ be the center of the smallest enclosing circle C_P of P, and $CH(P)$ be the convex hull of P.

The *c-gathering problem* (cGAT) is the problem of transforming any initial configuration to a configuration P such that $|\overline{P}| \le c$. The 1GAT is thus the *gathering problem* (GAT). An algorithm for the cGAT is an algorithm for the $(c+1)$GAT, for $1 \le c \le n-1$.

Under the $\mathcal{SSYNC}$ scheduler, the GAT from distinct initial positions is solvable (by an algorithm of size 1), if and only if $n \ge 3$ [22], and the GAT from any initial configuration is solvable (by an algorithm of size 1), if and only if n is odd [16]. The MAS for the GAT is thus at least 2. Gathering algorithms $\psi_{f-point(n)}$ (for $n \ge 3$ robots from distinct initial positions) in Theorem 3.4 of [22] and Algorithm 1 (for odd n robots from any initial positions) in [16] share the skeleton: Given a configuration P, if there is the (unique) "largest point" $\boldsymbol{q} \in \overline{P}$, then go to $\boldsymbol{q}$; otherwise, go to $\boldsymbol{o}_P$. Consider the following singleton 2GATA $= \{2gat\}$ of a target function $2gat$, which is a direct implementation of this strategy using $\succ_P$ as the measure to determine the largest point in $\overline{P}$.

[Target function 2gat]

1. If $m_P = 1$, or $m_P = 2$ and $k_P = 2$, i.e., $\mu_P(\boldsymbol{q}_1) = \mu_P(\boldsymbol{q}_2)$, then $2gat(P) = (0,0)$.
2. If $m_P \ge 2$ and $k_P = 1$, then $2gat(P) = \boldsymbol{q}$, where $\boldsymbol{q} \in \overline{P}$ is the largest point with respect to $\succ_P$.
3. If $m_P \ge 3$ and $k_P \ge 2$, then $2gat(P) = \boldsymbol{o}_P$.

Theorem 2. *Suppose that all robots take 2gat as their target functions. Then they transform any initial configuration P_0 to a configuration P satisfying that (1) $m_P = 1$, or (2) $m_P = 2$ and $k_P = 2$.*

Corollary 1. *The MAS for the* cGAT *is* 1, *for all* $2 \le c \le n$.

Corollary 2. 2GATA *solves the* GAT, *if and only if the initial configuration* P_0 *satisfies either* $m_{P_0} \neq 2$ *or* $k_{P_0} \neq 2$.

Corollary 2 has been obtained by some researchers: The GAT is solvable (for the robots with the same target function), if and only if n is odd [16]. Or more precisely, it is solvable, if and only if the initial configuration is not bivalent [9]. Note that the algorithm of [9] makes use of the Weber point and tolerates at most $n-1$ crashes.

Consider a set GATA $= \{gat_1, gat_2\}$ of target functions gat_1 and gat_2 defined as follows:

[Target function gat_1]

1. If $m = 1$, then $gat_1(P) = (0, 0)$.
2. If $m = 2$ and $k_P = 1$, or $m \ge 3$, $gat_1(P) = 2gat(P)$.
3. If $m = 2$ and $k_P = 2$, then $gat_1(P) = (0, 0)$.

[Target function gat_2]

1. If $m = 1$, then $gat_2(P) = (0, 0)$.
2. If $m = 2$ and $k_P = 1$, or $m \ge 3$, then $gat_2(P) = 2gat(P)$.
3. Suppose that $m = 2$ and $k_P = 2$. Let $\boldsymbol{q}$ ($\neq (0, 0)$) be the point in $\overline{P}$. Since $(0, 0) \in \overline{P}$, $\boldsymbol{q}$ is uniquely determined. If $\boldsymbol{q} > (0, 0)$, then $gat_2(P) = \boldsymbol{q}$. Else if $\boldsymbol{q} < (0, 0)$, then $gat_2(P) = 2\boldsymbol{q}$.

Theorem 3. GATA *is an algorithm for the* GAT. *The MAS for the* GAT *is, hence,* 2.

For a configuration P, let $-P = \{-\boldsymbol{p} : \boldsymbol{p} \in P\}$. A target function ϕ is said to be *symmetric* (with respect to the origin) if $\phi(P) = -\phi(-P)$ for all $P \in \mathcal{P}$. An algorithm Φ is said to be *symmetric* if every target function $\phi \in \Phi$ is symmetric. Target function $2gat$ is symmetric, but GATA is not a symmetric algorithm. Indeed, the next lemma holds.

Lemma 1. *There is no symmetric algorithm of size* 2 *for the* GAT.

There is however a symmetric gathering algorithm SGTA $= \{sgat_1, sgat_2, sgat_3\}$, where target functions $sgat_1, sgat_2$, and $sgat_3$ are defined as follows:

[Target function $sgat_1$]

1. If $m = 1$, then $sgat_1(P) = (0, 0)$.
2. If $m \ge 3$, or $m = 2$ and $k_P \neq 2$, then $sgat_1(P) = 2gat(P)$.
3. Suppose that $m = 2$ and $k_P = 2$. Let $\boldsymbol{q}$ ($\neq (0, 0)$) be the point in $\overline{P}$. Since $(0, 0) \in \overline{P}$, $\boldsymbol{q}$ is uniquely determined. Then $sgat_2(P) = -\boldsymbol{q}$.

[Target function $sgat_2$]

1. If $m = 1$, then $sgat_2(P) = (0, 0)$.
2. If $m \geq 3$, or $m = 2$ and $k_P \neq 2$, then $sgat_2(P) = 2gat(P)$.
3. Suppose that $m = 2$ and $k_P = 2$. Let $\boldsymbol{q}$ ($\neq (0, 0)$) be the point in $\overline{P}$. Since $(0, 0) \in \overline{P}$, $\boldsymbol{q}$ is uniquely determined. Then $sgat_2(P) = -2\boldsymbol{q}$.

[Target function $sgat_3$]

1. If $m = 1$, then $sgat_3(P) = (0, 0)$.
2. If $m \geq 3$, or $m = 2$ and $k_P \neq 2$, then $sgat_3(P) = 2gat(P)$.
3. Suppose that $m = 2$ and $k_P = 2$. Let $\boldsymbol{q}$ ($\neq (0, 0)$) be the point in $\overline{P}$. Since $(0, 0) \in \overline{P}$, $\boldsymbol{q}$ is uniquely determined. Then $sgat_3(P) = -3\boldsymbol{q}$.

Theorem 4. SGTA *solves the* GAT. *The MAS of symmetric algorithm for the* GAT *is* 3.

5 Pattern Formation Problem

Given a goal pattern $G \in (R^2)^n$ in Z_0, the *pattern formation problem* (PF) for G is the problem of transforming any initial configuration I into a configuration similar to G. The GAT is the PF for a goal pattern $G = \{(0, 0), (0, 0), \ldots, (0, 0)\} \in (R^2)^n$, and the SCT is reducible to the PF for a right n-gon.

Theorem 5 ([26]). *The* PF *for a goal pattern G is solvable (by an algorithm of size* 1*) from an initial configuration I such that $|I| = |\overline{I}|$, if and only if $\sigma(G)$ is divisible by $\sigma(I)$. The only exception is the* GAT *for two robots.*

Thus a pattern G is not formable from a configuration I by an algorithm of size 1, if $\sigma(G)$ is not divisible by $\sigma(I)$. In the following, we investigate an algorithm that solves the PF from any initial configuration I, for any G.

Lemma 2. *The MAS for the* PF *is at least n.*

Proof. If there were a pattern formation algorithm for a right n-gon with size $m < n$, it could solve the SCT, which contradicts to Theorem 1. □

Theorem 6. *The MAS for the* PF *is n.*

Proof. By Lemma 2, the MAS for the PF is at least n.

To show that the MAS for the PF is at most n, we propose a PF algorithm PFA of size n, and then give a sketch of its correctness proof.

A scattering algorithm nSCTA transforms any initial configuration I into a configuration P satisfying $P = \overline{P}$. We can modify nSCTA so that the resulting algorithm nSCTA* can transform any initial configuration I into a configuration P satisfying ($P = \overline{P}$ and) $\sigma(P) = 1$. On the other hand, there is a pattern formation algorithm (of size 1) for G which transforms any initial configuration

P satisfying ($P = \overline{P}$ and) $\sigma(P) = 1$ into a configuration similar to a goal pattern G (see, e.g., [26]). The pattern formation problem is thus solvable by executing nSCTA* as the first phase, and then such a pattern formation algorithm as the second phase, if we can modify these algorithms so that the robots can consistently recognize which phase they are working. Algorithm PFA takes this approach. Since the cases of $n \leq 3$ are trivial, we assume $n \geq 4$.

We say a configuration P is *good*, if P satisfies either one of the following conditions (1) and (2):

(1) $P = \overline{P}$, i.e., P is a set, and can be partitioned into two subsets P_1 and P_2 satisfying all of the following conditions:
  (1a) $P_1 = \{\boldsymbol{p}_1\}$ for some $\boldsymbol{p}_1 \in P$.
  (1b) $dist(\boldsymbol{p}_1, \boldsymbol{o}_2) \geq 10\delta_2$, where $\boldsymbol{o}_2$ and δ_2 are respectively the center and the radius of the smallest enclosing circle C_2 of $P \setminus \{\boldsymbol{p}_1\}$.

(2) The smallest enclosing circle C of P contains exactly two points $\boldsymbol{p}_1, \boldsymbol{p}_3 \in P$, i.e., $\overline{\boldsymbol{p}_1\boldsymbol{p}_3}$ forms a diameter of C. Consider a (right-handed) x-y coordinate system Z satisfying $\boldsymbol{p}_1 = (0,0)$ and $\boldsymbol{p}_3 = (31,0)$.[7] For $i = 1,2,3$, let C_i be the unit circle with center $\boldsymbol{o}_i$ (and radius 1 in Z), where $\boldsymbol{o}_1 = (0,0)$, $\boldsymbol{o}_2 = (10,0)$, and $\boldsymbol{o}_3 = (30,0)$. Let $P_i \subseteq P$ be the multiset of points included in C_i for $i = 1,2,3$. Then P is partitioned into three submultisets P_1, P_2, and P_3, i.e., $P \setminus (P_1 \cup P_2 \cup P_3) = \emptyset$, and P_1, P_2, and P_3 satisfy the following conditions:
  (2a) $P_1 = \{\boldsymbol{p}_1\}$.
  (2b) P_2 is a set (not a multiset).
  (2c) P_3 is a multiset that includes $\boldsymbol{p}_3$ as a member. It has a supermultiset P^* which is similar to G, and is contained in C_3, i.e., P_3 is similar to a submultiset $H \subseteq G$.

Let P be a good configuration. Then P satisfies exactly one of conditions (1) and (2), and $\boldsymbol{p}_1$ is uniquely determined in each case. We first define nSCTA* $= \{sct_i^* : i = 1,2,\ldots,n\}$, which is a slight modification of nSCTA.

[Target function sct_i^*]
(I) If P is good: $sct_i^*(P) = (0,0)$ for $i = 1,2,\ldots,n$.
(II) If P is not good:

1. For $i = 2,3,\ldots,n$:
   If $P \neq \overline{P}$, then $sct_i^*(P) = sct_i(P)$. Else if $P = \overline{P}$, then $sct_i^*(P) = (0,0)$.
2. For $i = 1$:
   (a) If $P \neq \overline{P}$, then $sct_1^*(P) = sct_i(P)$.
   (b) If $P = \overline{P}$ and $dist((0,0), \boldsymbol{o}) < 10\delta$, then $sct_1^*(P) = \boldsymbol{p}$. Here $\boldsymbol{o}$ and δ are, respectively, the center and the radius of the smallest enclosing circle of $P \setminus \{(0,0)\}$. If $\boldsymbol{o} \neq (0,0)$, $\boldsymbol{p}$ is the point such that $(0,0) \in \overline{\boldsymbol{op}}$ and $dist(\boldsymbol{p}, \boldsymbol{o}) = 10\delta$. If $\boldsymbol{o} = (0,0)$, $\boldsymbol{p} = (10\delta, 0)$.
   (c) If $P = \overline{P}$ and $dist((0,0), \boldsymbol{o}) \geq 10\delta$, then $sct_1^*(P) = (0,0)$.

[7] Note that Z is uniquely determined, and the unit distance of Z is $dist(\boldsymbol{p}_1, \boldsymbol{p}_3)/31$.

Then nSCTA* transforms any initial configuration P_0 to a good configuration P. We next explain how to construct a configuration similar to G from a good configuration P.

(I) Suppose that P satisfies condition (1) for a partition $\{P_1, P_2\}$, where $P_1 = \{\boldsymbol{p}_1\}$. If there is a point $\boldsymbol{q}$ such that $P_2 \cup \{\boldsymbol{q}\}$ is similar to G, then we move the robot at $\boldsymbol{p}_1$ to $\boldsymbol{q}$ to complete the formation.

Otherwise, let $\boldsymbol{p}_3$ be the point satisfying $\boldsymbol{o}_2 \in \overline{\boldsymbol{p}_1\boldsymbol{p}_3}$ and $dist(\boldsymbol{o}_2, \boldsymbol{p}_3) = 21\delta_2$, where $\boldsymbol{o}_2$ and δ_2 are, respectively, the center and the radius of the smallest enclosing circle C_2 of P_2. We choose a point $\boldsymbol{p}$ in P_2, and move the robot at $\boldsymbol{p}$ to $\boldsymbol{p}_3$. Note that the robot at $\boldsymbol{p}$ is uniquely determined, since $P_2 = \overline{P_2}$.

Then P is transformed into a configuration P' which is good, and satisfies condition (2) for partition $\{P_1, P_2 \setminus \{\boldsymbol{p}_2\}, \{\boldsymbol{p}_3\}\}$.

(II) Suppose that P satisfies condition (2) for a partition $\{P_1, P_2, P_3\}$, where $P_1 = \{\boldsymbol{p}_1\}$. Like the above case, we choose a point $\boldsymbol{p}$ in P_2, and move the robot at $\boldsymbol{p}$ to a point $\boldsymbol{q}$. Here $\boldsymbol{q}$ must satisfy that there is a superset P^* of $P_3 \cup \{\boldsymbol{q}\}$ which is contained in C_3, and is similar to G.

By repeating this transformation, a configuration P such that $|P_3| = n - 1$ and P_3 is similar to a submultiset of G is eventually obtained, when P_2 becomes empty. Then $\boldsymbol{p}_1$ can move to $\boldsymbol{q}$ to complete the formation.

To carry out this process, we need to specify (i) $\boldsymbol{p} \in P_2$ in such a way that all robots can consistently recognize it, and (ii) $\boldsymbol{p}_3$ in (I) and $\boldsymbol{q}$ in (II).

We define a point $\boldsymbol{p} \in P_2$. When $|P_2| = 1$, $\boldsymbol{p}$ is the unique element of P_2. When $|P_2| \geq 2$, let $P_{12} = P_1 \cup P_2$. Then $k_{P_{12}} = 1$ by the definition of $\boldsymbol{p}_1$. Since $k_{P_{12}} = 1$, $\succ_{P_{12}}$ is a total order on P_{12} (and hence on P_2), which all robots in P (in particular, in P_2) can compute. Let $\boldsymbol{p} \in P_2$ be the largest point in P_2 with respect to $\succ_{P_{12}}$. Since P_2 is a set, the robot r at $\boldsymbol{p}$ is uniquely determined, and r (or its target function) knows that it is the robot to move to $\boldsymbol{p}_3$ or $\boldsymbol{q}$.

We define the target points $\boldsymbol{p}_3$ and $\boldsymbol{q}$. It is worth emphasizing that r can choose the target point by itself, and the point is not necessary to share by all robots. Point $\boldsymbol{p}_3$ is uniquely determined. To determine $\boldsymbol{q}$, note that P_3 has a supermultiset P^* which is similar to G, and is contained in C_3. Thus r arbitrarily chooses such a multiset P^*, and takes any point in $P^* \setminus P_3$ as $\boldsymbol{q}$. (There may be many candidates for P^*. Robot r can choose any one, e.g., the smallest one in terms of $\sqsupset$ in its x-y local coordinate system.)

Using points $\boldsymbol{p}$, $\boldsymbol{p}_3$, and $\boldsymbol{q}$ defined above, we finally describe PFA $= \{pf_1, pf_2, \ldots, pf_n\}$ for a goal pattern G, where target functions $pf_i (i = 1, 2, \ldots, n)$ are defined as follows:

[Target function pf_i]

1. When P is not good: $pf_i(P) = sct_i^*(P)$.
2. When P is a good configuration satisfying condition (1):
   (2a) Suppose that there is a $\boldsymbol{q}$ such that $P_2 \cup \{\boldsymbol{q}\}$ is similar to G. Then $pf_i(P) = \boldsymbol{q}$ if $(0, 0) \in P_1$; otherwise, $pf_i(P) = (0, 0)$.
   (2b) Suppose that there is no point $\boldsymbol{q}$ such that $P_2 \cup \{\boldsymbol{q}\}$ is similar to G. Then $pf_i(P) = \boldsymbol{p}_3$ if $(0, 0)$ is the largest point in P_2 with respect to $\succ_{P_1 \cup P_2}$; otherwise, $pf_i(P) = (0, 0)$.

3. When P is a good configuration satisfying condition (2): $pf_i(P) = \boldsymbol{q}$ if $(0,0)$ is the largest point in P_2 with respect to $\succ_{P_1 \cup P_2}$; otherwise, $pf_i(P) = (0,0)$.

The correctness of PFA is clear from its construction. □

6 Fault Tolerant Scattering Problems

A fault means a crash fault in this paper. The *f-fault tolerant c-scattering problem* (fFcS) is the problem of transforming any initial configuration to a configuration P such that $|\overline{P}| \geq c$, as long as at most f robots have crashed.

Observation 1 *1.* 1SCTA *solves the* fF1S *for all* $1 \leq f \leq n$, *since* $|\overline{P}| \geq 1$ *for any configuration* P. *The MAS for the* fF1S *is thus* 1 *for all* $1 \leq f \leq n$.
2. The MAS for the nFcS *is* ∞ *for all* $2 \leq c \leq n$, *since* $|\overline{P_0}| = |\overline{P_t}| = 1$ *holds for all* $t \geq 0$, *if* $|\overline{P_0}| = 1$, *and all robots have crashed at time* 0.

Theorem 7. *Suppose that* $1 \leq f \leq n-1$ *and* $2 \leq c \leq n$.

1. *The MAS for the* fF2S *is* ∞, *if* $f = n-1$; *otherwise if* $1 \leq f \leq n-2$, *the MAS for the* fF2S *is* $f+2$. *Indeed,* $(f+2)$SCTA *solves the* fF2S, *if* $1 \leq f \leq n-2$.
2. *If* $3 \leq c \leq n$, *the MAS for the* fFcS *is* ∞, *if* $c+f-1 > n$; *otherwise if* $c+f-1 \leq n$, *the MAS for the* fFcS *is* $c+f-1$. *Indeed,* $(c+f-1)$SCTA *solves the* fFcS, *if* $c+f-1 \leq n$.

7 Fault Tolerant Gathering Problems

The f-fault tolerant c-gathering problem (fFcG) is the problem of gathering **all non-faulty robots** at c (or less) points, as long as at most f robots have crashed. *The f-fault tolerant c-gathering problem to c points* (fFcGP) is the problem of gathering **all robots** (including faulty ones) at c (or less) points, as long as at most f robots have crashed. When $c = 1$, fFcG is abbreviated as fFG, and fFcGP is abbreviated as fFGP when $c = f$. The fFcG is not harder than the fFcGP by definition. In general, the fFcGP is not solvable if $c < f$.

Theorem 8. SGTA *solves the* fFG *for all* $f = 1, 2, \ldots, n-1$. *The MAS for the* fFG *is* 3.

The fFGP is definitely not easier than the fFG by definition. You might consider that the difference of difficulty between them would be subtle. Indeed, it is not the case.

Theorem 9. *The* fFGP *is unsolvable for all* $f = 1, 2, \ldots, n-1$. *That is, the MAS for the* fFGP *is* ∞ *for all* $f = 1, 2, \ldots, n-1$.

Proof (sketch). Suppose that there is an algorithm Φ for the fFGP. We arbitrarily choose a configuration P_0 such that $m_0 > f$, and consider any execution $\mathcal{E} : P_0, P_1, \ldots$ from P_0, provided that no crashes occur, under a schedule $\mathcal{S}$ we specify as follows: For P_t, let A_t be a largest set of robots such that its activation does not yield a goal configuration. If there are two or more such largest sets, A_t is an arbitrary one. Then $\mathcal{S}$ activates all robots in A_t at time t, and the execution reaches P_{t+1}, which is not a goal configuration. (A_t may be an empty set.)

Then $|U| \leq f$ holds. Suppose that at t_0 all robots in U crash, and consider a schedule $\mathcal{S}'$ that activates A_t for all $0 \leq t \leq t_0 - 1$, and $A_t \cup U$ for all $t \geq t_0$. Then the execution $\mathcal{E}'$ starting from P_0 under $\mathcal{S}'$ is exactly the same as $\mathcal{E}$, and does not reach a goal configuration, despite that $\mathcal{S}'$ is fair; Φ is not an algorithm for the fFGP. It is a contradiction. □

It is interesting to see that the fF$(f+1)$GP, which looks to be the "slightest" relaxation of the fFGP ($= f$FfGP), is solvable by an easy algorithm 2GATA of size 1.

Theorem 10. 2GATA *solves both of the* fF2G *and the* fF$(f+1)$GP, *for all* $f = 1, 2, \ldots, n-1$. *The MASs for the* fF2G *and* fF$(f+1)$GP *are both* 1, *for all* $f = 1, 2, \ldots, n-1$.

8 Conclusions

There is a problem like the self-stabilizing gathering problem which is not solvable by a swarm of anonymous oblivious mobile robots when all robots take the same target function. For a problem Π, we have investigated the minimum algorithm size (MAS) for Π, which is the number of distinct target functions necessary and sufficient to solve Π from **any** initial configuration. To figure out the effects of the number of distinct target functions on the problem-solving ability, we have established the MASs for the gathering and related problems.

As mentioned in Sect. 1, we consider target function as a resource like time and message, and regard the MAS of a problem as a measure to measure the complexity of the problem. There is an apparent trade-off between the number of distinct target functions and the time complexity, but this topic has not been investigated in this paper, and is left as an interesting open problem.

In the real world, gathering objects needs energy (since entropy decreases), while scattering them does not (since entropy increases). Thus a natural guess would be that cGAT is harder than cSCT. On the contrary, we have showed that, for $2 \leq c \leq n$, the MAS is c for cSCT, while it is 1, for cGAT. Other main results are summarized in Table 1.

Finally, we conclude the paper by giving a list of some open problems.

1. What is the MAS for the gathering problem under the $\mathcal{ASYNC}$ scheduler?
2. What is the MAS for the pattern formation problem for a fixed G?
3. What is the MAS for the f-fault tolerant convergence problem to f points, for $f \geq 3$?

4. What is the MAS for the Byzantine fault tolerant gathering problem?
5. Characterize the problem whose MAS is 2.
6. Investigate trade-off between the number of distinct target functions and the time complexity.

Acknowledgments. This work is supported in part by JSPS KAKENHI Grant Numbers JP17K00024 and JP22K11915.

References

1. Agmon, N., Peleg, D.: Fault-tolerant gathering algorithms for autonomous mobile robots. In: 15th Annual ACM-SIAM Symposium on Discrete Algorithms, pp. 1063–1071(2004)
2. Altisen, K., Datta, A.K., Devismes, S., Durand, A., Larmore, L.L.: Election in unidirectional rings with homonyms. J. Parallel Distrib. Comput. **146**, 79–95 (2010)
3. Ando, H., Oasa, Y., Suzuki, I., Yamashita, M.: A distributed memoryless point convergence algorithm for mobile robots with limited visibility. IEEE Trans. Robot. Autom. **15**, 818–828 (1999)
4. Angluin, D.: Local and global properties in networks of processors. In: 12th ACM Symposium on Theory of Computing, pp. 82–93 (1980)
5. Arévalo, S., Anta, A.F., Imbs, D., Jiménez, E., Raynal, M.: Failure detectors in homonymous distributed systems (with an application to consensus). J. Parallel Distrib. Comput. **83**, 83–95 (2015)
6. Asahiro, Y., Yamashita, M.: Compatibility of convergence algorithms for autonomous mobile robots. In: Rajsbaum, S., Balliu, A., Daymude, J.J., Olivetti, D. (eds.) Structural Information and Communication Complexity. SIROCCO 2023. LNCS, vol. 13892, pp. 149–164. Springer, Cham (2023). https://doi.org/10.1007/978-3-031-32733-9_8
7. Asahiro, Y., Yamashita, M.: Minimum algorithm sizes for self-stabilizing gathering and related problems of autonomous mobile robots. arXiv: 2304.02212
8. Attiya, H., Snir, M., Warmuth, M.K.: Computing on the anonymous ring. J. ACM **35**(4), 845–875 (1988)
9. Bouzid, Z., Das, S., Tixeuil, S.: Gathering of mobile robots tolerating multiple crash faults. In: IEEE 33rd International Conference on Distributed Computing Systems, pp. 337–346 (2013)
10. Cieliebak, M., Flocchini, P., Prencipe, G., Santoro, N.: Distributed computing by mobile robots: gathering. SIAM J. Comput. **41**, 829–879 (2012)
11. Cord-Landwehr, A., et al.: A new approach for analyzing convergence algorithms for mobile robots. In: Aceto, L., Henzinger, M., Sgall, J. (eds.) ICALP 2011. LNCS, vol. 6756, pp. 650–661. Springer, Heidelberg (2011). https://doi.org/10.1007/978-3-642-22012-8_52
12. Das, S., Flocchini, P., Santoro, N., Yamashita, M.: Forming sequences of geometric patterns with oblivious mobile robots. Distrib. Comput. **28**, 131–145 (2015)
13. Delporte-Gallet, C., Fauconnier, H., Guerraoui, R., Kermarrec, A., Ruppert, E., Tran-The, H.: Byzantine agreement with homonyms. Distrib. Comput. **26**, 321–340 (2013)
14. Delporte-Gallet, C., Fauconnier, H., Tran-The, H.: Leader election in rings with homonyms. In: Noubir, G., Raynal, M. (eds.) NETYS 2014. LNCS, vol. 8593, pp. 9–24. Springer, Cham (2014). https://doi.org/10.1007/978-3-319-09581-3_2

15. Dieudonné, Y., Petit, F.: Scatter of weak mobile robots. Parallel Process. Lett. **19**(1), 175–184 (2009)
16. Dieudonné, Y., Petit, F.: Self-stabilizing gathering with strong multiplicity detection. Theor. Comput. Sci. **428**, 47–57 (2012)
17. Dobrev, S., Pelc, A.: Leader election in rings with nonunique labels. Fund. Inform. **59**(4), 333–347 (2004)
18. Flocchini, P.: Gathering. In: Flocchini, P., Prencipe, G., Santoro, N. (eds.) Distributed Computing by Mobile Entities. Lecture Notes in Computer Science, vol. 11340, pp. 63–82. Springer, Cham (2019). https://doi.org/10.1007/978-3-030-11072-7_4
19. Liu, Z., Yamauchi, Y., Kijima, S., Yamashita, M.: Team assembling problem for asynchronous heterogeneous mobile robots. Theor. Comput. Sci. **721**, 27–41 (2018)
20. Matias, Y., Afek, Y.: Simple and efficient election algorithms for anonymous networks. In: Bermond, J.-C., Raynal, M. (eds.) WDAG 1989. LNCS, vol. 392, pp. 183–194. Springer, Heidelberg (1989). https://doi.org/10.1007/3-540-51687-5_42
21. Prencipe, G.: Pattern formation. In: Flocchini, P., Prencipe, G., Santoro, N. (eds.) Distributed Computing by Mobile Entities. LNCS, vol. 11340, pp. 37–62. Springer, Cham (2019). https://doi.org/10.1007/978-3-030-11072-7_3
22. Suzuki, I., Yamashita, M.: Distributed anonymous mobile robots - formation and agreement problems. SIAM J. Comput. **28**, 1347–1363 (1999)
23. Yamashita, M., Kameda, T.: Computing on an anonymous network. In: 7th ACM Symposium on Principles of Distributed Computing, pp. 117–130(1988)
24. Yamashita, M., Kameda, T.: Electing a leader when processor identity numbers are not distinct (extended abstract). In: Bermond, J.-C., Raynal, M. (eds.) WDAG 1989. LNCS, vol. 392, pp. 303–314. Springer, Heidelberg (1989). https://doi.org/10.1007/3-540-51687-5_52
25. Yamashita, M., Kameda, T.: Leader election problem on networks in which processor identity numbers are not distinct. IEEE Trans. Parallel Distrib. Syst. **10**(9), 878–887 (1999)
26. Yamashita, M., Suzuki, I.: Characterizing geometric patterns formable by oblivious anonymous mobile robots. Theor. Comput. Sci. **411**, 2433–2453 (2010)
27. Yamauchi, Y., Uehara, T., Kijima, S., Yamashita, M.: Plane formation by synchronous mobile robots in the three-dimensional Euclidean space. J. ACM **64**, 1–43 (2017)

Separation of Unconscious Colored Robots

Hirokazu Seike[1] and Yukiko Yamauchi[2(✉)]

[1] Graduate School of ISEE, Kyushu University, Fukuoka, Japan
[2] Faculty of ISEE, Kyushu University, Fukuoka, Japan
yamauchi@inf.kyushu-u.ac.jp

Abstract. We introduce a new mobile robot model, called *unconscious* colored robots, where each robot is given a color and can observe the colors of robots except itself. We consider the *separation problem* that requires the robots to be separated according to their colors. We consider two variants; the separation-into-points problem requires the robots with the same color gather at one point and the separation-into-circles problem requires the robots with the same color form a circle concentric with the smallest enclosing circle of the entire robots. We first show that the separation-into-points problem is not always solvable due to symmetry of an initial configuration. We then present a distributed algorithm for the separation-into-circles problem by oblivious semi-synchronous unconscious colored robots with two colors. The proposed algorithm requires that there are at least three robots of the same color and the total number of robots is larger than five.

Keywords: Mobile robots · externally visible color · separation

1 Introduction

Distributed coordination of autonomous mobile robots has been extensively studied for more than 25 years. The robots are points moving on a 2D Euclidean space. They are *anonymous* (indistinguishable), *oblivious* (state-less), and *uniform* (executing a common algorithm). They are not equipped with communication capabilities and have no access to the global coordinate system. Each robot repeats a *Look-Compute-Move cycle*, where it observes the positions of other robots in its local coordinate system (Look), computes its next position and movement by a common algorithm (Compute), and moves to the next position (Move). One of the most challenging properties of the mobile robot systems is their homogeneity. That is, the combination of anonymity, uniformity and locality results in the impossibility of symmetry breaking. Existing literature shows that the computational power of a mobile robot system is determined by the symmetry of its initial configuration, i.e., rotational symmetry of the positions and local coordinate systems of the robots [7,8,11,13]. For example, starting from an initial configuration, where the robots form a regular polygon, they cannot form a line. The *symmetricity* of a set of points is in general the number of rotation operations that yields the same set of points. When the center

S. Dolev and B. Schieber (Eds.): SSS 2023, LNCS 14310, pp. 328–343, 2023.
https://doi.org/10.1007/978-3-031-44274-2_24

of the smallest enclosing circle (SEC) of the points is contained in the set of points, the symmetricity is defined to be one, because the robot on the center can break the symmetry by slightly moving away. It has been shown that the set of formable shapes can be characterized by the symmetricity of an initial configuration irrespective of obliviousness [13] and asynchrony [7,11].

Heterogeneous mobile robot systems have been introduce for the partitioning problem and the team assembling problem. Sugihara and Suzuki proposed a partitioning algorithm for mobile robots when given a small number of leaders controlled externally [10]. Partitioning is achieved by the leaders moving in different directions and non-leader robots following their neighbors. Liu et al. introduced the *colored robots*, each of which is given a color [8]. The color of a robot is observed by all robots, but the robots with the same color are still indistinguishable. Hence, robots can behave differently according to their colors. The colors of the robots can be considered as the difference in their abilities or equipment, such as CPUs, programs, sensors, robot arms, and so on. The *team assembling* problem requires the robots to form small teams according to a given specification on the number of robots of each color in a team [8]. The authors present a necessary and sufficient condition on the team specifications for the colored robots to separate into teams according to a given specification.

In this paper, we introduce a new colored robot model. A colored robot is *unconscious* if it can observe the colors of other robots but cannot observe its own color. Although the robots may have unique colors, they are still uniform in the sense that they execute a common algorithm. The color of a robot can be considered as externally visible properties that the robot itself cannot recognize, such as the degree of damage, failure, residual resource, and so on. We then newly introduce the *separation problem*, that requires the unconscious colored robots to separate according to their colors. We recognize two variants of the separation problem; the *separation-into-points* problem requires the robots with the same color to form a point, and the *separation-into-circles* problem requires the robots with the same color to form a circle concentric with the smallest enclosing circle of the entire robots. The gathering points or circles must be distinct for different colors. Hence, these separation problems require the unconscious colored robots behave differently according to their colors.

We first show that the robots cannot always solve the separation-into-points problem due to the symmetry of an initial configuration. We then propose a distributed algorithm for the separation-into-circles problem for two colors, say blue and red, for oblivious semi-synchronous robots. We assume that there are more than two red robots and the total number of robots is larger than five. The proposed algorithm first makes the robots form a regular polygon (thus, a uniform circle on the SEC) and then each blue robot is informed to enter the interior of the SEC by its clockwise neighbor approaching it. Finally, the blue robots form a circle concentric with the SEC.

Related Work. Symmetry of an initial configuration of a robot system is a source of many impossibilities in distributed coordination of mobile robots irrespective of the degree of synchronization among the robots. There are three synchronization models; the *asynchronous* (ASYNC) model, the *semi-synchronous* (SSYNC) model, and the *fully-synchronous* (FSYNC) model. In the FSYNC model, the robots synchronously execute a Look-Compute-Move cycle at each time step. In the SSYNC model, non-empty subset of the robots synchronously execute a Look-Compute-Move cycle at each time step. In the ASYNC model, there is no assumption on the timing of Look-Compute-Move cycles, but the length of each cycle is finite. For example, anonymous robots on the same point (also called *multiplicity*) cannot separate themselves by a deterministic algorithm irrespective of the synchronization model. In the worst case, these robots may have identical local coordinate system, execute the common algorithm synchronously, and thus the computed next position is always the same. This worst-case FSYNC execution occurs in the SSYNC model and the ASYNC model. The *pattern formation problem* requires the robots to form a target pattern from an initial configuration. It has been shown that oblivious ASYNC robots can form a target pattern T from an initial configuration I if and only if the symmetricity of I divides that of T except the target pattern of a single point for two robots [7,11,13]. The target patterns with the highest symmetricity are a uniform circle and a single multiplicity point. Flocchini et al. showed that more than four oblivious ASYNC robots do not need an agreement on the clockwise direction (i.e., chirality) for forming a regular polygon [6]. Cieliebak et al. showed that more than two oblivious ASYNC robots can form a single point without chirality [2]. The point formation problem for two robots is called the *rendezvous problem*, and it is unsolvable in the SSYNC (thus, the ASYNC) model [11].

One of the most important related robot models is the *luminous robot model* introduced by Das et al. [4]. A luminous robot is equipped with a *light* that can take different colors and each robot can change the color of its light as a result of computation. There are three types of lights; the *internally visible light* is visible only to the robot with the light, and the *externally visible light* is visible to all robots except the robot with the light. Finally, the internally and externally visible light is visible to all robots. The internally visible light serves as a local memory at a robot and an externally visible light is a communication mechanism among the robots. The minimum requirement on the number of colors shows the necessary size of local memory or necessary message size. Existing literature shows that luminous robots can solve problems that non-luminous robots cannot solve including the rendezvous problem [4,9,12], formation of sequence of patterns [3], and collision-less solutions for mutual visibility [5]. Das et al. proposed simulation algorithms for luminous robots to overcome asynchrony [4]. Buchin et al. showed the relationship between the classes of solvable problems by the robots equipped with the three different types of lights [1]. The unconscious colored robot model is analogous to the externally visible lights, however a colored robot cannot change its color.

2 Preliminary

We consider a set of anonymous mobile robots $R = \{r_1, r_2, \dots, r_n\}$, where r_i is used just for notation. Each robot r_i is a point in the 2D Euclidean space and $p_i(t)$ denotes its position at time t in the global coordinate system Z_0. The *color* c_i of robot r_i is selected from a set C of colors and r_i does not know c_i. Let R_j be the robots with color $j \in C$. Then, we have $R_j \cap R_k = \emptyset$ for two different colors $j, k \in C$, and $\bigcup_{j \in C} R_j = R$. The *configuration* of the robots at time t is a multiset $P(t) = \{(p_1(t), c_1), (p_2(t), c_2), \dots, (p_n(t), c_n)\}$. We call the point occupied by more than one robots a *multiplicity*.

Each robot r_i repeats a *Look-Compute-Move* cycle. In a look phase, r_i observes the positions and colors of all robots except c_i in its local coordinate system. Let $Z_i(t)$ be the local coordinate system of r_i at time t, which is a right-handed orthogonal coordinate system with the origin $p_i(t)$, an arbitrary unit length, and arbitrary directions and orientations of x-y axes.[1] Then, the result of a Look is $Z_i(t)[P(t) \setminus \{(p_i(t), c_i)\} \cup \{(p_i(t), \perp)\}]$ at some time t. The robots are equipped with the *multiplicity detection ability*, i.e., r_i can observe whether a point in its observation is occupied by a single robot or more than one robots. When a point is occupied by robots with different colors, r_i can observe all colors of the robots at the point but does not know the number of robots for each color. The robots are *oblivious*, i.e., in a compute phase, r_i computes its next position and moving track by a common deterministic algorithm ψ and the input to ψ is the observation of the preceding look phase. In a move phase, r_i moves along the result of the compute phase. We assume *non-rigid movement*; r_i may stop en route after moving the minimum moving distance δ (in Z_0), whose value is not known to r_i. When the length of the moving track is shorter than δ, r_i stops at the destination.

The robots are *semi-synchronous*, i.e., at each time step $t = 0, 1, 2, \dots$ a non-empty subset of robots are activated and execute a Look-Compute-Move cycle with each of the look, compute, and move phases executed synchronously. We assume that each robot executes infinite number of cycles to guarantee fairness and progress. We call the sequence of configurations $P(0), P(1), P(2), \dots$ an *execution* of algorithm ψ from an initial configuration $P(0)$. We may have more than one executions from $P(0)$ due to the activation of the robots and non-rigid movement.

The *smallest enclosing circle* (SEC) of a set of points is the smallest circle that contains all points in its interior and on its boundary. Let $C(P)$ be the SEC of a configuration P and $c(P)$ be the center of $C(P)$.

A problem for a robot system is defined by a set of *terminal configurations*. When any execution of algorithm ψ from an initial configuration $P(0)$ reaches a terminal configuration, we say ψ solves the problem from $P(0)$.

The *separation problem* requires the robots to geometrically separate according to their colors. The *separation-into-points* problem requires the robots to form points for each color. That is, for each color $j \in C$, the robots in R_j gather at a single point and these $|C|$ gathering points must be different. The *separation-into-circles* problem requires the robots to form circles concentric with the SEC

[1] In this paper, we only need that the robots agree on the clockwise direction. Thus, not only the origin but also the unit length and x-y axes of a local coordinate system may change over time.

of the entire robots for each color. That is, for each color $j \in C$, the robots in R_j are on a concentric circle and these $|C|$ concentric circles must be different.

In the following, when we consider two colors (i.e., $|C| = 2$), we call one color red and the other blue.

3 Separation into Points

We first show that separation-into-points problem cannot be solved from an arbitrary initial configuration. We use the colored symmetricity defined in [8]. Given a set P of colored points, we consider the decomposition of P into regular monochromatic k-gons centered at $c(P)$. That is, each regular k-gon consists of the robots with the same color. The maximum value of such k is the *colored symmetricity* of P, denoted by $\rho(P)$. A point is a regular 1-gon centered at $c(P)$ and a pair of points is a regular 2-gon when their midpoint is $c(P)$. However, when P contains $c(P)$, we define $\rho(P)$ as one. When $\rho(P)$ is larger than one, we say P *has rotational symmetry.*

Theorem 1. *The separation-into-points problem cannot be solved by a deterministic algorithm when the initial configuration has rotational symmetry irrespective of the synchronization model.*

Due to the page limitation, we show a sketch of the proof. When an initial configuration I has rotational symmetry, the robots are divided into regular $\rho(I)$-gons each of which is centered at $c(I)$ and formed by more than one robots with the same color. In the worst case, these $\rho(I)$ robots cannot break their symmetry, and the possible gathering point is $c(I)$. Hence, when I contains robots with different colors, they cannot be separated into points according to their colors.

Next, we consider the case where $R_j = \emptyset$ for some $j \in C$.

Theorem 2. *The separation-into-points problem for three robots with two colors (i.e., $|C| = 2$) cannot be solved by a deterministic algorithm.*

Proof. Consider the separation-into-points problem for three robots when $|C| = 2$. Assume that there exists an algorithm A for the separation-into-points problem in the SSYNC model. Thus, there exists an execution of A for three blue robots, where the terminal configuration is reached by a single blue robot moving to a point of multiplicity formed by two blue robots. Thus, a robot is navigated by A to a multiplicity point when it observes a multiplicity formed by two blue robots. Now, consider a terminal configuration for two blue robots and one red robot. That is, the two blue robots form a multiplicity and one red robot is at another point. In this case, A guides the red robot to move to the multiplicity. Hence, A never solves the separation-into-points problem for two blue robots and one red robot. Consequently, there exists no algorithm that solves the separation-into-points problem for three robots. □

When we assume that there exists at least one red robot and one blue robot, the following simple algorithm solves the separation-into-points problem for three

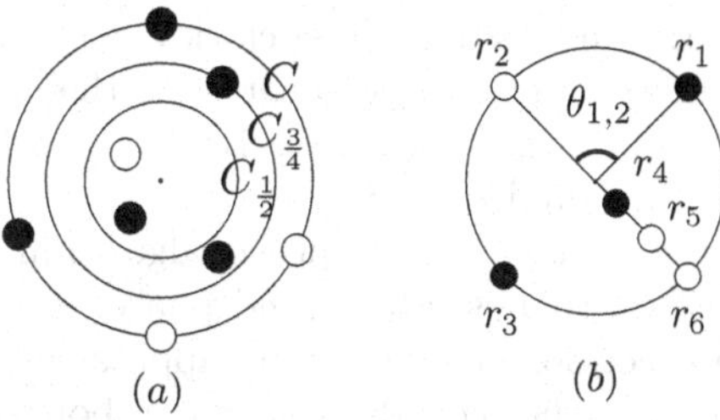

Fig. 1. Concentric circles and robots on the SEC. A small black circle represents a blue robot and a small white circle represents a red robot. (a) Smallest enclosing circle C and its concentric circles $C_{1/2}$ and $C_{3/4}$. (b) The successor of r_1 is r_2, and its predecessor is r_6. The angle between r_1 and r_2 is $\theta_{1,2}$. The three robots r_4, r_5, and r_6 are on a radius, where r_4 is the head and r_6 is the tail.

robots: If a robot observes one blue robot and one red robot, then it moves to the Weber point of the three robots. Otherwise (i.e., the robot observes two robots with the same color), if it is on the Weber point of the three robots, it leaves the current position.

4 Separation into Circles for Two Colors

In this section, we propose a distributed algorithm for the separation-into-circles problem for two colors. We assume that there are more than two red robots and the total number of robots is larger than five.

4.1 Overview of the Proposed Algorithm

The proposed algorithm consists of three phases. The first phase makes n robots form a regular n-gon on the SEC, say C, of an initial configuration. The second phase makes the blue robots move to the interior of C. Finally, in the third phase, the blue robots form a circle concentric with C. In the following, we use "initial configuration" and "terminal configuration" for each of the three phases.

During any execution of the proposed algorithm, the robots keep SEC C of an initial configuration. We consider the radius of C as the unit distance and C_ℓ denotes the concentric circle with radius ℓ. When a robot r_i is on a circle C' concentric with C, we call C' the *concentric circle* of r_i. See Fig. 1(a) as an example. In the third phase, the blue robots spread over $C_{1/2}$.

When robot r_i is on C, its *successor* is the first robot that appears on C in the counter-clockwise direction. If r_i is a successor of r_j, r_j is the *predecessor* of r_i. Predecessors and successors are defined for the robots on C. For each robot r_i, r_i's *radius* is the radius of C containing r_i. The *(central) angle* $\theta_{i,j}$ between a pair of robots r_i and r_j is the counter-clockwise angle from r_i's radius to r_j's radius and we say r_j is *at angle* $\theta_{i,j}$ from r_i. If $\theta_{i,j}$ is equal to or smaller than some value ϕ, we say r_j is *within angle* ϕ from r_i. See Fig. 1(b) as an example.

We sometimes use negative angles to address clockwise angles. When a radius of C contains some robots, we call the robot nearest to the center c of C the *head* and the robot farthest from c the *tail*. In Fig. 1(b), r_4 is a head and r_6 is a tail of a radius containing r_4, r_5, and r_6.

The most challenging part of the proposed algorithm is sending the blue robots to the interior of C, that is, the second phase. A predecessor of a blue robot informs its blue successor of its color by approaching it at angle $2\pi/4n$. In an initial configuration of the second phase, the robots form a regular n-gon on C. Then, C is cut into arcs by the blue robots on C whose successor is a red robot. We call these blue robots the *blue leaders*. Each arc starts from a blue leader, spans clockwise, and ends at the position of the predecessor of the first red robot (but not containing the predecessor). For a blue leader r_i, we call the robots that appear on r_i's arc (except r_i) the *followers* of r_i. See Fig. 2(a) as an example. By definition, the followers are blue robots and one last red robot. The predecessor of the last follower is either a blue leader or a red robot. Intuitively, in the second phase, the blue leader and its followers line up on the blue leader's radius, which we call the *aligning radius*. However, each robot cannot determine whether it is a blue leader or a follower by itself due to unconsciousness. Instead, when robot r_i is a blue leader, its predecessor, say r_j, approaches r_i at angle $2\pi/4n$ and informs that r_i is a blue leader. Then, r_i moves to $C_{1/2}$ along its radius and r_j becomes a new blue leader. After that, r_j proceeds to the endpoint of the aligning radius. If r_j is blue, r_j's predecessor approaches r_j. By repeating this procedure, the last follower robot, which is a red robot, reaches the endpoint of the aligning radius and the second phase for this arc finishes. Figure 2 shows an execution of the second phase.

However, when the arc of a blue leader is longer than π, this procedure may change C. We say a blue leader's arc is *long* when it is longer than π, otherwise *short*. When a blue leader's arc is long, the aligning radius is selected so that C is kept unchanged. We will show the detail in Sect. 4.3.

We then give an overview of the other two phases. The first phase and the third phase do not use the colors of the robots. The first phase makes the robots form a regular n-gon on C. It first divides C into congruent *sectors* so that each sector contains the same number of robots. The arc of each sector starts at a robot on C and spreads counterclockwise. We call this robot on the starting point a *sector leader*. The robots on the sector leader's radius belong to this sector, and the robots on the other border radius do not. There may exist more than one such sector decompositons but the robots select the one that maximizes the number of sectors. For example, in Fig. 3(a), there are four robots on the SEC, but only two of them divide the robots into sectors containing equal number of robots. Further ties are broken by the observations at sector leaders as explained in Sect. 4.2. The target regular n-gon is embedded so that its corners overlap the sector leaders. Then, non-leader robots can agree on a matching between their positions and the corners of the regular n-gon and each of them moves to its matched corners first along its concentric circle, then along its radius. See Fig. 3 as an example.

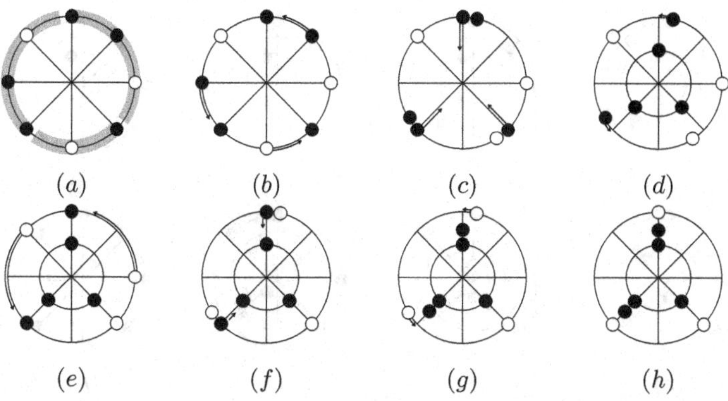

Fig. 2. The second phase for short arcs. (a) Arcs cut by the blue leaders. (b) The first followers move. (c) The blue leaders are informed and move toward $C_{1/2}$. (d) The new blue leaders move to the endpoint of their aligning radii. (e) The first followers move. (f) New blue leaders enter the interior of C. (g) Last followers move. (h) A terminal configuration of the second phase.

In the third phase, the blue robots in the interior of C spread on $C_{1/2}$. Figure 4 shows an execution of the third phase.

Due to unconsciousness, some robots may execute an algorithm for a wrong phase or perform wrong movements. For example, consider an initial configuration shown in Fig. 5, where all robots except the red robot r_5 can recognize that they are not in the second phase, but r_5 cannot. In this case, the proposed algorithm must allow r_5 to execute the algorithm for the second phase as if it is blue, otherwise the proposed algorithm never moves r_5 in a configuration shown in Fig. 2(c). In each look phase, a robot considers two possibilities for the current observation, one is the case where its color is blue and the other is the case where it is red. Then, the robot optimistically chooses the one which goes ahead of the other. There is at most one robot that executes the algorithm for a wrong phase, but such movement stops in finite steps due to the SSYNC model, while other robots execute the algorithm for the correct phase. Then, all robots eventually execute the algorithm for the current phase.

4.2 First Phase

The goal of the first phase is to form a regular n-gon on the SEC of an initial configuration P. Let $C = C(P)$ and $c = c(P)$. In this first phase, the robots do not use their colors. Rather, they use only their positions.

For a configuration P, its *sector decomposition* is a set of non-overlapping sectors of C that satisfies, (i) the arc of a sector starts at a robot on C (i.e., a sector leader) and spreads counter-clockwise, (ii) all sectors are the same size, and (iii) all sectors contain the same number of robots. A robot on an starting border radius of a sector belongs to the sector, and a robot on the other

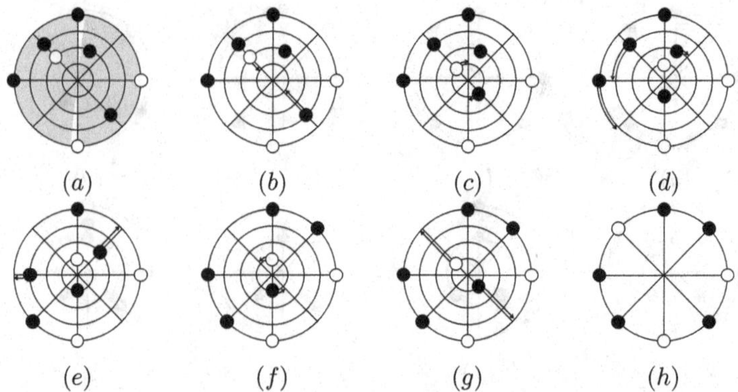

Fig. 3. The first phase. (*a*) Two sector leaders and their sectors. (*b*) The sector supporters move to $C_{1/4}$, then (*c*) to the leaders' radii. (*d*) The sector members move along their concentric circles, then (*e*) along their radii to C. (*f*) The sector supporters move to the radii of their destinations, then (*g*) to C. (*h*) A terminal configuration of the first phase.

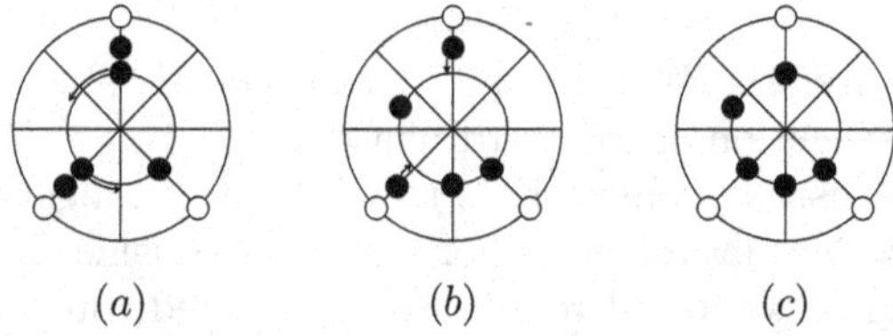

Fig. 4. The third phase for short arcs. (*a*) Blue head robots spread on $C_{1/2}$. (*b*) New blue head robots reach $C_{1/2}$. (*b*) A terminal configuration for the third phase.

border radius of a sector does not. There may exist more than one sector decompositions, and we select the one that maximize the number of sectors. When a sector decomposition divides C into k sectors, we call the decomposition *k-sector decomposition.* When there exist more than one k-sector decompositions, we select one of them based on the *polar view* of sector leaders. The polar view of a sector leader is the sequence of polar coordinates of all robots except the leader itself in the increasing order. The polar axis is the radius of the leader and each point is represented as (θ, r), where θ is the angle between the leader and the robot and r is the distance from c. We have $(\theta, r) < (\theta', r')$ when $\theta < \theta'$ or $\theta = \theta'$ and $r < r'$. Thus, in the polar view of a sector leader, robots appear in the increasing order of their angles with respect to the sector leader's axis. The first phase chooses the sector decomposition that contains a sector leader with the lexicographically minimum polar view. Clearly, all robots can agree on this sector decomposition because they can compute the polar view of any robots on C.

We first consider the case where C is divided into $k(\geq 2)$ sectors. The target regular n-gon is embedded so that its corners overlap the sector leaders.

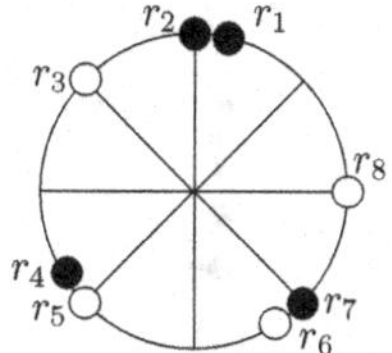

Fig. 5. Optimistic choice of the current phase at r_5.

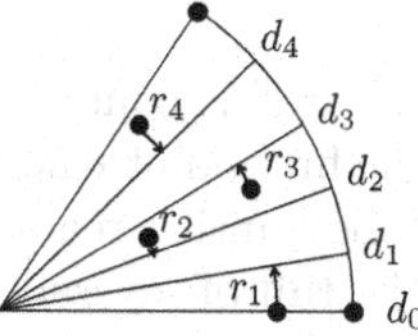

Fig. 6. Destinations in the first phase

Thus, each arc of a sector contains n/k corners. We focus on one sector. Let $d_0, d_1, \ldots, d_{n/k-1}$ be these corners in the counter-clockwise direction and let $r_1, r_2, \ldots, r_{n/k-1}$ be the first $n/k - 1$ robots in the polar view of the sector leader. We call r_1 the *sector supporter* and $r_2, \ldots, r_{n/k-1}$ the *sector members.* The sector leader is at d_0, and the final destination of r_i in the first phase is d_i. See Fig. 6 as an example.

The first phase starts by sending r_1 to the radius of the sector leader. It first moves to the interior of $C_{1/4}$ along its radius and then moves clockwise along its concentric circle. By definition, no robot is on this moving track. The selection of the sector decomposition does not change by this movement, because one of the sector leaders keep the minimum polar view.

We call the sector formed by the radius of a sector member r_i and that of its destination d_i the *moving sector* of r_i. We have the following properties. Due to the page limitation, we omit the proof.

Lemma 1. *For a sector of a k-sector decomposition of a configuration P, let $r_1, r_2, \ldots, r_{n/k-1}$ be the first $n/k - 1$ robots in the polar view of the sector leader and $d_0, d_1, d_2, \ldots, d_{n/k-1}$ be the corners of the regular n-gon embedded by the sector leaders. Then, we have the following properties.*

1. *For any pair of robots r_i and r_j, r_i's moving sector does not overlap r_j's moving sector if their moving directions are opposite.*
2. *For any pair of robots r_i and r_j, r_i's moving sector covers r_j's moving sector if and only if they are on the same radius.*

Each sector member first moves toward the radius of the destination corner along its concentric circle. The sector members move cautiously, that is, they avoid any overlap of their radii, thus any change in their ordering in the polar view of the sector leader. Because each robot can compute the matching of all

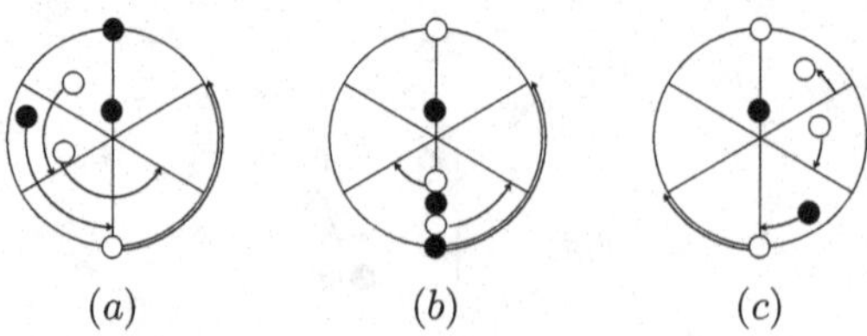

Fig. 7. Movement on the concentric circles in a single sector.

robots, they walk as follows; If my radius contains no other robot, I move along my concentric circle just before the first point where my concentric circle overlaps a moving sector of some other robot until I reach the radius of my destination. Otherwise, I will move if I am the tail of my radius in the same way. After the robot reaches the radius of its destination, it moves to C along its radius. By Lemma 1, this cautious walk makes no collision among the robots.

When the number of sectors (i.e., the value of k) is one, the sector supporter is the first robot in the polar view of the single sector leader that does not change C when it leaves the current position. Then, the robot first moves to the interior of $C_{1/4}$ along its radius and then to the radius of its leader along $C_{1/4}$. By definition, no other robot is on this moving track. During this movement, the sector leader may change, but due to SSYNC execution, the robots start with the new sector leader. The regular n-gon is embedded so that one of its corners overlaps the sector leader. Some sector members on C may collapse C by the first movement. Figure 7 shows some examples. In this case, such robot r_i waits until all robots that can move finish their movements. By the second property of Lemma 1, when r_i moves counter-clockwise, the robots whose destinations are $d_1, d_2, \ldots, d_\ell$ can move without waiting for r_i to move, where d_ℓ is the last destination that appears before r_i's position on C. This observation can be also applied to the case where r_i moves clockwise. Thus, after these robots move to C, the movement r_i does not collapse C.

4.3 Second Phase

An initial configuration of the second phase is a regular n-gon. The goal of the second phase is to make for each blue leader's arc the blue leader and followers line up on one radius. On an arc of a blue leader r_i, when the followers $r_{i_1}, r_{i_2}, \ldots$ appear clockwise, we say r_{i_k} is the kth follower of r_i. As already explained, when all arcs are short, the procedure is easy to understand. The first follower informs the blue leader to move to the interior of C by approaching the blue leader, and the blue leader moves along its radius toward $C_{1/2}$. Once the blue leader leaves C the first follower moves counter-clockwise to the previous blue leader's position. Now, the first follower becomes a new blue leader and it will be informed by the new first follower. By repeating this, the robots on a short arc line up on the aligning radius.

When a robot enters the interior of C, its destination is the *first midpoint*, which is the intersection of its radius and $C_{1/2}$ if there is no other robot on its radius, otherwise it is the mid point between it and the nearest robot on its radius. The robot may stop before it reaches the first midpoint due to nonrigid movement.

When a regular n-gon formed in the first phase has a long arc, the proposed algorithm fold the long arc so that the red robots keep C in a terminal configuration of the second phase. However, each follower of a long arc cannot determine whether it is on a long arc or not due to unconsciousness. The proposed algorithm makes the blue leader inform the followers that they are on a long arc. We say a blue leader of a long arc is *locked* if it is at angle $-2\pi/8n$ from its original position and its blue predecessor is at angle $-2\pi/8n$. A blue leader becomes locked by moving $2\pi/8n$ clockwise after it is informed by its predecessor. Hence, robot r_i can recognize that it is a follower of a long arc when there is a locked blue leader and the counter-clockwise arc from r_i to the blue leader contains only blue robots. Then the followers of a long arc lines up a radius at the *folding point*, which is defined when its blue leader is locked. The *blue arc* of a robot is the arc starting from the robot, spans clockwise, and ends at the predecessor of the first red robot. The folding point of a long arc is the first follower whose blue arc is equal to or shorter than π. When the first follower is at the folding point, the folding point is defined to be the position of the second follower. By the assumption on the number of red robots, this keeps the SEC unchanged. Then, the blue robots that resides on the arc from the folding point to the second follower first lines up the radius of the folding point. After that, the blue leader and its first follower enters the interior of C. Then, the new blue leader is the robot on the folding point. The remaining robots on the long arc joins one by one the radius on the folding point in the same way as the short arcs. Finally the last follower reaches the folding point. Figure 8 shows an example of the second phase for a long arc.

4.4 Third Phase

An initial configuration of the third phase is a terminal configuration of the second phase, where all red robots are on C, while all blue robots are on the radii of red robots except the locked leader and its first follower.

From this configuration, the robots scatter on $C_{1/2}$. For each radius of a red robot, if it contains blue robots, $r_1, r_2, \ldots, r_k$, these robots move counter-clockwise on $C_{1/2}$. Let r_ℓ be the first robot that appears on $C_{1/2}$ in the counter-clockwise direction. Then, r_1 moves to the point which divides the arc of $C_{1/2}$ between $r_1 r_\ell$ into half. After r_1 reaches its destination, r_2 proceeds to $C_{1/2}$ and circulates on it to the point computed in the same way with respect to r_1. By repeating this procedure, the blue robots can scatter on $C_{1/2}$.

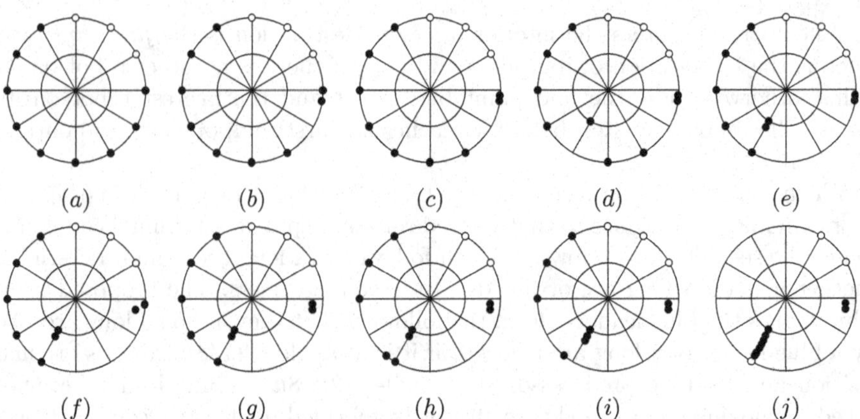

Fig. 8. The second phase with a long arc. (*a*) Initial configuration. (*b*) The blue leader is informed. (*c*) The blue leader is locked. (*d*) The follower on the folding point enters the interior of SEC. (*e*) The second and third followers join the aligning radius. (*f*) The first follower enters the interior of SEC. (*g*) The blue leader enters the interior of SEC. (*h*) The new blue leader is informed. (*i*) The new blue leader enters the interior of SEC. (*j*) By repeating the same procedure as short arcs, the second and later followers line up the radius at the folding point.

4.5 Combining the Phases

We show how to combine the three phases. Let $\mathcal{C}_{j,k}$ be the set of all possible configurations of j blue robots and k red robots. We divide $\mathcal{C}_{j,k}$ into three classes, that is, class $\mathcal{C}2_{j,k}$ is the set of configurations that appear in the second phase, and class $\mathcal{C}3_{j,k}$ is that in the third phase. Then, $\mathcal{C}1_{j,k} = \mathcal{C}_{j,k} \setminus (\mathcal{C}2_{j,k} \cup \mathcal{C}3_{j,k})$. The robots are expected to execute the algorithm for the ith phase when their configuration is in $\mathcal{C}i_{j,k}$. As already explained in Sect. 4.1, each robot considers two possibilities for the current observation, one is the case where its color is blue and the other is the case where it is red. Then, the robot optimistically chooses the one which goes ahead of the other.

We then show how each robot checks the membership of a current configuration. Class $\mathcal{C}2_{j,k}$ and class $\mathcal{C}3_{j,k}$ are defined by the conditions on the blue leader's arcs. Although, the blue leader changes during the execution of the second phase, by the algorithm the robots can recognize the original blue leader. The conditions for each arc in $\mathcal{C}2_{j,k}$ is defined as follows.

- $C2-1$. The robots are placed every $2\pi/n$ on the arc.
- $C2-2$. The blue robots are forming a line on the aligning radius.
- $C2-3a$. If the blue leader's arc was short in an initial configuration of the second phase, all blue robots are on an aligning arc and a red robot is at the end of the arc.
- $C2-3b$. If the blue leader's arc was long in an initial configuration of the second phase, its blue leader and the first follower is in the interior of SEC

and the other blue robots are on an aligning arc and a red robot is at the end of the arc.
- $C2-3c$. All red robots are on the SEC.

Intuitively, the conditions corresponds to the progress of the proposed algorithm. When the second phase starts, each arc satisfies $C2-1$, and during the execution, it satisfies $C2-2$. Eventually each arc satisfies either $C2-3a$ or C_2-3b. The terminal configuration of the second phase is a configuration where all blue leaders' arcs satisfy $C2-3a$ or $C2-3b$ while red robots satisfy $C2-3c$ at the same time. The execution of the proposed algorithm progresses in each arc without any synchronization. Thus, $\mathcal{C}2_{j,k}$ is a set of all configurations where each blue leader's arc satisfies one of the configurations.

The conditions for each arc in $\mathcal{C}3_{j,k}$ is defined as follows.

- $C3-1$. All blue robots are on the aligning radius and the red robot is on the endpoint.
- $C3-2$. The blue robots are moving to their destinations on $C_{1/2}$.
- $C3-3a$. The blue robots have reached their destinations on $C_{1/2}$.
- $C3-3b$. All red robots are on the SEC.

Then, $\mathcal{C}3_{j,k}$ is a set of all configurations where each blue leader's arc satisfies one of the above configurations while the red robots satisfy $C3-3b$. A configuration is a terminal configuration of the third phase if all blue leaders' arcs satisfy $C3-3a$ while red robots satisfy $C3-3c$ at the same time.

We have the following theorem. Due to the page limitation, we omit the proof.

Theorem 3. *Oblivious SSYNC unconscious colored robots can solve the separation-into-circles problem when there exists more than two red robots and the total number of robots is larger than five.*

Consequently, each robot eventually recognizes its color. We finally note that at least three red robots are necessary to keep the smallest enclosing circle in the second phase. The total number of robots is also a requirement from the second phase. Consider the case where two succeeding red robots and three succeeding blue robots on C form a regular pentagon and execute the second phase. Then the blue locked robots cannot enter the interior of the SEC because it changed the SEC. If there are six robots containing three red robots, even when the robots with the same color appears successively on SEC, the SEC cannot be changed by the proposed algorithm.

5 Conclusion

In this paper, we newly introduced the unconscious colored robot model and the separation problem. We first showed that the separation-into-points problem cannot be always solved due to the symmetry in the initial configuration. We then proposed a distributed algorithm for the separation-into-circles problem by the oblivious SSYNC unconscious colored robots. The proposed algorithm is designed for a robot system with two colors, and it can be easily extended to more than two colors due to the SSYNC model. That is, in the first stage, the robots of color c_1 is placed on the SEC and in the ith stage, the robots of color c_i is separated on the $C_{1/2^i}$.

There are many interesting open problems for the unconscious colored robots and the separation problem. One of the most important direction is a separation algorithm for the ASYNC model, where uncertain movement due to obsolete observation of the ASYNC model and unconsciousness of colors must be carefully treated. Second, solutions for small number of robots is open. Third, solving the separation problem for all robot systems including the one lacking some colors might be difficult as discussed in Sect. 3. Finally, any parallel solution can speed up the separation procedure.

Acknowledgments. This work was supported by JSPS KAKENHI Grant Number JP18H03202.

References

1. Buchin, K., Flocchini, P., Kostitsyna, I., Peters, T., Santoro, N., Wada, K.: On the computational power of energy-constrained mobile robots: algorithms and cross-model analysis. In: Parter, M. (ed.) SIROCCO 2022. LNCS, vol. 13298, pp. 42–61. Springer, Cham (2022). https://doi.org/10.1007/978-3-031-09993-9_3
2. Cieliebak, M., Flocchini, P., Prencipe, G., Santoro, N.: Distributed computing by mobile robots: gathering. SIAM J. Comput. **41**(4), 829–879 (2012)
3. Das, S., Flocchini, P., Prencipe, G., Santoro, N.: Synchronized dancing of oblivious chameleons. In: Ferro, A., Luccio, F., Widmayer, P. (eds.) FUN 2014. LNCS, vol. 8496, pp. 113–124. Springer, Cham (2014). https://doi.org/10.1007/978-3-319-07890-8_10
4. Das, S., Flocchini, P., Prencipe, G., Santoro, N., Yamashita, M.: Autonomous mobile robots with lights. Theoret. Comput. Sci. **609**(1), 171–184 (2016)
5. Di Luna, G.A., Flocchini, P., Gan Chaudhuri, S., Poloni, F., Santoro, N., Viglietta, G.: Mutual visibility by luminous robots without collisions. Inf. Comput. **254**(3), 392–418 (2017)
6. Flocchini, P., Prencipe, G., Santoro, N., Viglietta, G.: Distributed computing by mobile robots: uniform circle formation. Distrib. Comput. **30**, 413–457 (2017)
7. Fujinaga, N., Yamauchi, Y., Ono, H., Kijima, S., Yamashita, M.: Pattern formation by oblivious asynchronous mobile robots. SIAM J. Comput. **44**(3), 740–785 (2015)
8. Liu, Z., Yamauchi, Y., Kijima, S., Yamashita, M.: Team assembling problem for asynchronous heterogeneous mobile robots. Theoret. Comput. Sci. **721**, 27–41 (2018)
9. Okumura, T., Wada, K., Défago, X.: Optimal rendezvous L-algorithms for asynchronous mobile robots with external-lights. In: Proceedings of the 22nd International Conference on Principles of Distributed Systems (OPODIS 2018), pp. 24:1–24:16 (2018)
10. Sugihara, K., Suzuki, I.: Distributed algorithms for formation of geometric patterns with many mobile robots. J. Robot. Syst. **13**, 127–139 (1996)

11. Suzuki, I., Yamashita, M.: Distributed anonymous mobile robots: formation of geometric patterns. SIAM J. Comput. **28**(4), 1347–1363 (1999)
12. Terai, S., Wada, K., Katayama, Y.: Gathering problems for autonomous mobile robots with lights. Theoret. Comput. Sci. **941**, 241–261 (2023)
13. Yamashita, M., Suzuki, I.: Characterizing geometric patterns formable by oblivious anonymous mobile robots. Theoret. Comput. Sci. **411**(26–28), 2433–2453 (2010)

Forbidden Patterns in Temporal Graphs Resulting from Encounters in a Corridor

Michel Habib[1], Minh-Hang Nguyen[1], Mikaël Rabie[1(✉)], and Laurent Viennot[2]

[1] Université Paris Cité, CNRS, IRIF, 75013 Paris, France
{michel.habib,minh-hang.nguyen,mikael.rabie}@irif.fr
[2] Université Paris Cité, CNRS, Inria, IRIF, 75013 Paris, France
laurent.viennot@irif.fr

Abstract. In this paper, we study temporal graphs arising from mobility models where some agents move in a space and where edges appear each time two agents meet. We propose a rather natural one-dimensional model.

If each pair of agents meets exactly once, we get a simple temporal clique where each possible edge appears exactly once. By ordering the edges according to meeting times, we get a subset of the temporal cliques. We introduce the first notion of forbidden patterns in temporal graphs, which leads to a characterization of this class of graphs. We provide, thanks to classical combinatorial results, the number of such cliques for a given number of agents.

Our characterization in terms of forbidden patterns can be extended to the case where each edge appears at most once. We also provide a forbidden pattern when we allow multiple crossings between agents, and leave open the question of a characterization in this situation.

Keywords: Temporal graphs · mobility models · forbidden patterns · mobile clique

1 Introduction

1.1 Motivation

Temporal graphs arise when the edges of a graph appear at particular points in time (see e.g. [4,11,14]). Many practical graphs are indeed temporal from social contacts, co-authorship graphs, to transit networks. A very natural range of models for temporal graphs comes from mobility. When agents move around a space, we can track the moments when they meet each other and obtain a temporal graph. We ask how to characterize temporal graphs resulting from such a mobility model.

A classical model used for mobile networks is the unit disk graph where a set of unit disks lie in the plane, and two disk are linked when they intersect. When the disks are moving, we obtain a so-called dynamic unit disk graph [19],

S. Dolev and B. Schieber (Eds.): SSS 2023, LNCS 14310, pp. 344–358, 2023.
https://doi.org/10.1007/978-3-031-44274-2_25

and the appearance of links then forms a temporal graph. We consider a one-dimensional version where the disks are moving along a line or equivalently a narrow corridor of unit width. This could encompass practical settings such as communicating cars on a single road. In particular, if each car has constant speed, each pair of cars encounters each other at most once. We further restrict to the sparse regime where each disk intersects at most one other disk at a time. In other words, the edges appearing at any given time always form a matching. This restriction, called local injectivity, has already been considered in the study of simple temporal cliques [5] which are temporal graphs where an edge between any pair of nodes appears exactly once.

When two agents can communicate when they meet, one can ask how information can flow in the network. The appropriate notion of connectivity then arises from temporal paths which are paths where edges appear one after another along the path. A temporal spanner can then be defined as a temporal subgraph that preserves connectivity. An interesting question concerning temporal graphs is to understand which classes of temporal graphs have temporal spanners of linear size. Although some temporal graphs have only $\Theta(n^2)$-size temporal spanners [2], simple temporal cliques happen to have $O(n \log n)$-size temporal spanners [5], and it is conjectured that they could even have linear size spanners. Indeed, a natural question is whether temporal graphs resulting from a mobility model can have sparse spanners. In particular, do temporal cliques arising from our 1D model have temporal spanners of linear size?

1.2 Our Contribution

Our main contribution is a characterization of the simple temporal cliques that result from this 1D model. A simple temporal clique can only arise when agents start out in a certain order along the corridor and end up in the opposite order after crossing each other exactly once. We provide a characterization of such temporal cliques in terms of forbidden ordered patterns on three nodes. This characterization leads directly to an $O(n^3)$-time algorithm for testing whether an ordering of the n nodes of a temporal clique is appropriate and allows to exclude these patterns. Interestingly, an $O(n^2)$-time algorithm allows to find such an appropriate initial ordering of the nodes from the list of the edges of the clique ordered by appearance time. Moreover, we can actually check in $O(n^2)$ time that this order excludes the forbidden patterns to obtain an overall linear-time recognition algorithm, since we have $n(n-1)/2$ edges in our graphs.

Another way of looking at this problem is sorting through adjacent transpositions an array A, where n elements are initially stored in reverse order. At each step, we choose an index i such that $A[i] > A[i+1]$ and swap the two elements at positions i and $i+1$. The array is guaranteed to be sorted in increasing order after $T = n(n-1)/2$ steps, since the permutation of the elements in A has initially T inversions while each step decreases this number by one. Note that this is reminiscent of bubble sorting, which indeed operates according to a sequence of such transpositions. This naturally connects our 1D model to the notion of reduced decompositions of a permutation [17]. A classical combinatorial result gives a formula for the number of temporal cliques with n nodes resulting from our 1D model.

As far as we know, we introduce the first definition of forbidden patterns in a temporal graph. Our definition is based on the existence of an order on the nodes (which actually corresponds to their initial order along the line). A forbidden pattern is a temporal subgraph with a relative ordering of its nodes, and with a forbidden relative ordering of its edges according to their time labels.

In addition, we show that our temporal cliques do contain temporal spanners of linear size (with exactly $2n - 3$ edges) by enlightening a convenient temporal subgraph that considers only the edges having, as one of their endpoints, one of the two extreme agents in the initial order along the line.

Finally, we consider some generalizations. First, what happens if each edge appears at most once. We provide the forbidden patterns to add to characterize that situation. Second, we consider what might be a forbidden pattern definition if edges can occur multiple times, that is when some pairs of agents can cross each other multiple times.

1.3 Related Works

Dynamic Unit Disk Graph. A closely related work concerns the detection of dynamic unit disk graphs on a line [18,19]. An algorithm is proposed to decide whether a continuous temporal graph can be embedded in the line along its evolution, such that the edges present at each time instant correspond to the unit disk graph within the nodes according to their current position in the embedding at that time. The sequence of edge events (appearance or disappearance) is processed online one after another, relying on a PQ-tree to represent all possible embeddings at the time of the current event according to all events seen so far. It runs within a logarithmic factor from linear time. Our model is tailored for discrete time and assumes that two nodes cross each other when an edge appears between them. This is not the case in the dynamic unit disk graph model: an edge can appear during a certain period of time between two nodes even if they don't cross each other. The PQ-tree approach can probably be adapted to our model for a more general recognition of the temporal graphs it produces. Note that our characterization leads to a faster linear-time algorithm for recognizing simple temporal cliques arising from our model.

Temporal Graph. Temporal graphs (also known as dynamic, evolving or time-varying networks) can be informally described as graphs that change with time, and are an important topic in both theory and practice when there are many real-world systems that can be modelled as temporal graphs, see [11]. The problem of temporal connectivity has been considered, by Awerbuch and Even [1], and studied more systematically in [12].

Forbidden Patterns. Since the seminal papers [6,15], many hereditary graph classes have been characterized by the existence of an order of the vertices that avoids some pattern, i.e. an ordered structure. These include bipartite graphs, interval graphs, chordal graphs, comparability graphs and many others. In [10], it is proved that any class defined by a set of forbidden patterns on three nodes can be recognized in $O(n^3)$ time. This was later improved in [7] with a full characterization of the 22 graph classes that can be defined with forbidden patterns on three nodes. An interesting extension to forbidden circular structures is given in [9]. The growing interest in forbidden patterns in the study of hereditary graph classes is partly supported by the certification that such an ordering avoiding the patterns provides a recognition algorithm in the YES case.

Reduced Decomposition. The number of reduced decompositions of a permutation of n elements is studied in [16]. An explicit formula is given for the reverse permutation $n, n-1, \ldots, 1$ based on the hook length formula [3,8].

1.4 Roadmap

In Sect. 2, we introduce the notions that we will use throughout the paper. In particular, we provide the definitions of temporal graphs and 1D mobility models. Section 3 provides our main results: a characterization of mobility cliques through forbidden patterns, the number of cliques of a given size, a detection algorithm, and a linear size spanner of the graph. Section 4 handles the case where each pair crosses at most once, by providing the patterns needed. Section 5 provides a forbidden pattern in the case where pairs can cross each other several times. Finally, we raise some open questions and perspectives in Sect. 6.

2 Preliminaries and Mobility Model

In this section, we introduce the definitions and notations we will use through the paper. In particular, we first define formally temporal graphs and forbidden patterns. We then introduce the mobility model and related combinatoric concepts.

2.1 Temporal Graphs and Forbidden Patterns

Informally, a temporal graph is a graph with a fixed vertex set and whose edges change with time. A *temporal graph* can be formally defined as a pair $\mathcal{G} = (G, \lambda)$ where $G = (V, E)$ is a graph with vertex set V and edge set E, and $\lambda : E \to 2^{\mathbb{N}}$ is a labeling assigning to each edge $e \in E$ a non-empty set $\lambda(e)$ of discrete times when it appears. We note $uv \in E$ the edge between the pair of vertices (or nodes) u and v. If λ is locally injective in the sense that adjacent edges have disjoint sets of labels, then the temporal graph is said to be *locally injective.* If λ is additionally *single valued* (i.e. $|\lambda(e)| = 1$ for all $e \in E$), then (G, λ) is said to be simple [5]. The maximum time label $T = \max \cup_{e \in E} \lambda(e)$ of an edge is called the *lifetime* of (G, λ). In the sequel, we will mostly restrict ourselves to simple temporal graphs and even require the following restriction of locally injective. A temporal graph is *incremental* if at most one edge appears in each time step, that is $\lambda(e) \cap \lambda(f) = \emptyset$ for any distinct $e, f \in E$.

A (strict) *temporal path* is a sequence of triplets $(u_i, u_{i+1}, t_i)_{i \in [k]}$ such that $(u_1, \ldots, u_{k+1})$ is a path in G with increasing time labels where its edges appear: formally, for all $i \in [k]$, we have $u_i u_{i+1} \in E$, $t_i \in \lambda(u_i u_{i+1})$ and $t_i < t_{i+1}$. Note that our definition corresponds to the classical strict version of temporal path as we require time labels to strictly increase along the path[1]. A temporal graph is *temporally connected*, if every vertex can reach any other vertex through a temporal path. A *temporal subgraph* (G', λ') of a temporal graph (G, λ) is a temporal graph such that G' is a subgraph of G and λ' satisfies $\lambda'(e) \subseteq \lambda(e)$ for all $e \in E'$. A *temporal spanner* of $\mathcal{G}$ is a temporal subgraph $\mathcal{H}$ preserving temporal connectivity, that is there exists a temporal path from u to v in $\mathcal{H}$ whenever there exists one in $\mathcal{G}$.

A representation $\mathcal{R}$ of a temporal graph $\mathcal{G} = ((V, E), \lambda)$ is defined as an ordered list of $M = |\lambda| = \sum_{e \in E} |\lambda(e)|$ triplets $\mathcal{R} = (u_1, v_1, t_1), \ldots, (u_M, v_M, t_M)$ where each triplet (u_i, v_i, t_i) indicates that edge $u_i v_i$ appears at time t_i. We additionally require that the list is sorted by non-decreasing time. In other words, we have $\lambda(uv) = \{t_i : \exists i \in [M], (u, v_i, t_i) \in \mathcal{R}\}$ for all $uv \in E$. Note that any incremental temporal graph $\mathcal{G}$ has a unique representation denoted by $\mathcal{R}(\mathcal{G})$. Indeed, its temporal connectivity only depends on the ordering in which edges appear, we can thus assume without loss of generality that we have $\cup_{e \in E} \lambda(e) = [T]$ where T is the lifetime of $((V, E), \lambda)$ (we use the notation $[T] = \{1, \ldots, T\}$). Given two incremental temporal graphs $\mathcal{G} = ((V, E), \lambda)$ and $\mathcal{G}' = ((V', E'), \lambda')$, an *isomorphism* from $\mathcal{G}$ to $\mathcal{G}'$ is a one-to-one mapping $\phi : V \to V'$ such that, for any $u, v \in V$, $uv \in E \Leftrightarrow \phi(u)\phi(v) \in E'$ (ϕ is a graph isomorphism), and their representation $\mathcal{R}(\mathcal{G}) = (u_1, v_1, t_1), \ldots, (u_M, v_M, t_M)$ and $\mathcal{R}(\mathcal{G}') = (u'_1, v'_1, t'_1), \ldots, (u'_M, v'_M, t'_M)$ have same length $M = |\lambda| = |\lambda'|$ and are temporally equivalent in the sense that edges appear in the same order: $u'_i v'_i = \phi(u_i)\phi(v_i)$ for all $i \in [M]$. When such an isomorphism exists, we say that $\mathcal{G}$ and $\mathcal{G}'$ are *isomorphic*.

A *temporal clique* is a temporal graph (G, λ) where the set of edges is complete, and where we additionally require the temporal graph to be incremental and λ to be single valued. Notice that it is a slight restriction compared to the definition of [5] which requires (G, λ) to be locally injective rather than incremental. However, we do not lose in generality as one can easily transform any locally injective temporal graph into an incremental temporal graph with same temporal connectivity (we simply stretch time by multiplying all time labels by n^2 and arbitrarily order edges with same original time label within the corresponding interval of n^2 time slots in the stretched version). With a slight abuse of notation, we then denote the label of an edge uv by $\lambda(uv) \in \mathbb{N}$.

A *temporal pattern* is defined as an incremental temporal graph $\mathcal{H} = (H, \lambda)$. An incremental temporal graph $\mathcal{G} = (G, \lambda')$ *excludes* $\mathcal{H}$ when it does not have any temporal subgraph $\mathcal{H}'$ which is isomorphic to $\mathcal{H}$. A temporal pattern *with forbidden edges* is a temporal pattern $\mathcal{H} = (H, \lambda)$ together with a set $F \subseteq V \times V \setminus E$ of forbidden edges in $H = (V, E)$. An incremental temporal graph

[1] The interested reader can check that the two notions of strict temporal path and non-strict temporal path are the same in locally injective temporal graphs.

$\mathcal{G} = ((V', E'), \lambda')$ *excludes* $\mathcal{H}$ when it does not have any temporal subgraph $\mathcal{H}'$ which is isomorphic to (H, λ') through an isomorphism ϕ respecting non-edges, that is any pair of nodes $u, v \in V'$ which is mapped to a forbidden edge $\phi(u)\phi(v) \in F$, we have $uv \notin E'$.

An *ordered temporal graph* is a pair $(\mathcal{G}, \pi)$, where $\mathcal{G}$ is a temporal graph and π is an ordering of its nodes. Similarly, an *ordered temporal pattern* $(\mathcal{H}, \pi)$ is a temporal pattern $\mathcal{H}$ together with an ordering π of its node. An ordered incremental temporal graph $(\mathcal{G}, \pi')$ *excludes* $(\mathcal{H}, \pi)$ when it does not have any temporal subgraph $\mathcal{H}'$ which is isomorphic to $\mathcal{H}$ through an isomorphism ϕ preserving relative orderings, that is $\pi(\phi(u)) < \pi(\phi(v))$ whenever $\pi'(u) < \pi'(v)$. We then also say that the ordering π' *excludes* $(\mathcal{H}, \pi)$ *from* $\mathcal{G}$, or simply excludes $(\mathcal{H}, \pi)$ when $\mathcal{G}$ is clear from the context. We also define an ordered temporal pattern with forbidden edges similarly as above.

2.2 1D-Mobility Model

We introduce here the notion of temporal graph associated to mobile agents moving along a line that is an one-dimensional space. Consider n mobile agents in an oriented horizontal line. At time $t_0 = 0$, they initially appear along the line according to an ordering π_0. These agents move in the line and can cross one another as time goes on. We assume that a crossing is always between exactly two neighboring agents, and a single pair of agents cross each other at a single time. By ordering the crossings, we have the kth crossing happening at time $t_k = k$.

A *1D-mobility schedule* from an ordering $\pi_0 = a_1, \ldots, a_n$ of n agents is a sequence $x = x_1, \ldots, x_T$ of crossings within the agents. Each crossing x_t is a pair uv indicating that agents u and v cross each other at time t. Note that their ordering π_t at time t is obtained from π_{t-1} by exchanging u and v, and it is thus required that they appear consecutively in π_{t-1}. To such a schedule, we can associate a temporal graph $\mathcal{G}_{\pi_0,x} = ((V, E), \lambda)$ such that:

- $V = \{a_1, \ldots, a_n\}$,
- $E = \{uv : \exists t \in [T], x_t = uv\}$,
- for all $uv \in E$, $\lambda(uv) = \{t : x_t = uv\}$.

We are interested in particular by the case where all agents cross each other exactly once as the resulting temporal graph is then a temporal clique which is called *1D-mobility temporal clique*. More generally, we say that an incremental temporal graph $\mathcal{G}$ *corresponds to a 1D-mobility schedule* if there exists some ordering π of its vertices and a 1D-mobility schedule x from π such that the identity is an isomorphism from $\mathcal{G}$ to $\mathcal{G}_{\pi,x}$. It is then called a *1D-mobility temporal graph*.

2.3 Reduced Decomposition of a Permutation

Our definition of mobility model is tightly related to the notion of reduced decomposition of a permutation [17]. Let $\mathcal{S}_n$ denote the symmetric group on n

elements. We represent a permutation $w \in S_n$ as a sequence $w = w(1), \dots, w(n)$ and define its length $l(w)$ as the number of inverse pairs in w, i.e. $l(w) = |\{i, j : i < j, w(i) > w(j)\}|$. A *sub-sequence* w' of w is defined by its length $k \in [n]$ and indices $1 \leq i_1 < \dots < i_k \leq n$ such that $w' = w(i_1), \dots, w(i_k)$.

A *transposition* $\tau = (i, j)$ is the transposition of i and j, that is $\tau(i) = j$, $\tau(j) = i$ and $\tau(k) = k$ for $k \in [n] \setminus \{i, j\}$. It is an *adjacent* transposition when $j = i+1$. Given a permutation w and an adjacent transposition $\tau = (i, i+1)$, we define the *right product* of w by τ as the composition $w\tau = w \circ \tau$. Note that $w' = w\tau$, as a sequence, is obtained from w by exchanging the numbers in positions i and $i+1$ as we have $w'(i) = w(\tau(i)) = w(i+1)$, $w'(i+1) = w(\tau(i+1)) = w(i)$ and $w'(k) = w(k)$ for $k \neq i, j$. A *reduced decomposition* of a permutation $w \in S_n$ with length $l(w) = l$, is a sequence of adjacent transpositions $\tau_1, \tau_2, \dots, \tau_l$ such that we have $w = \tau_1 \dots \tau_l$. Counting the number of reduced decompositions of a permutation has been well studied (see in particular [16]).

The link with our 1D-mobility model is the following. Consider a 1D-mobility schedule x from an ordering π_0. Without loss of generality we assume that agents are numbered from 1 to n. Each ordering π_t is then a permutation. If agents u and v cross at time t, i.e. $x_t = uv$, and their positions in π_{t-1} are i and $i+1$, we then have $\pi_t = \pi_{t-1}\tau_t$ where $\tau_t = (i, i+1)$. If each pair of agents cross at most once, then one can easily see that the schedule x of crossings corresponds to a reduced decomposition $\tau_1, \dots, \tau_T$ of $\pi_0^{-1}\pi_T = \tau_1 \cdots \tau_T$ as the ending permutation is $\pi_T = \pi_0\tau_1 \cdots \tau_T$. Note that this does not hold if two agents can cross each other more than once as the length of the schedule can then be longer than the length of $\pi_0^{-1}\pi_T$.

Interestingly, another decomposition is obtained by interpreting the crossing $x_t = uv$ at time t as the transposition (u, v). We then have $\pi_t = x_t\pi_{t-1}$ for each time t, and finally obtain $\pi_T = x_T \cdots x_1\pi_0$. Note that given an arbitrary sequence of transpositions $x_1, \dots, x_T$, it is not clear how to decide whether there exists an ordering π_0 and a corresponding sequence of *adjacent* transpositions $\tau_1, \dots, \tau_T$ such that $x_t \cdots x_1\pi_0 = \pi_0\tau_1 \cdots \tau_t$ for all $t \in [T]$. This is basically the problem we address in the next section.

3 1D-Mobility Temporal Cliques

3.1 Characterization

Consider the ordered temporal patterns from Fig. 1 with respect to the initial ordering of the nodes in a 1D-mobility schedule x producing a temporal clique $\mathcal{G}_x$. One can easily see that the upper-left pattern cannot occur in $\mathcal{G}_x$ within three agents a, b, c appearing in that order initially: a and c cannot cross each other as long as b is still in-between them, while the pattern requires that edge ac appears before ab and bc. A similar reasoning prevents the presence of the three other patterns. It appears that excluding these four patterns suffices to characterize 1D-mobility temporal cliques, as stated bellow.

Theorem 1. *A temporal clique is a 1D-mobility temporal clique if and only if there exists an ordering of its nodes that excludes the four ordered temporal patterns of Fig. 1.*

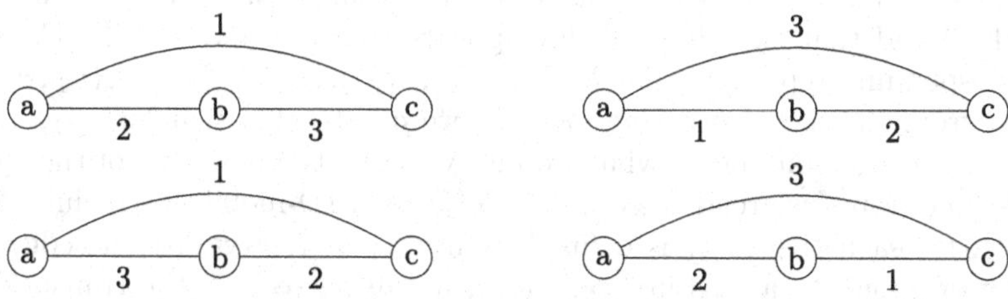

Fig. 1. Ordered forbidden patterns in an ordered 1D-mobility temporal clique. Each pattern is ordered from left to right and has associated ordering a, b, c.

Let $\mathcal{C}$ denote the class of temporal cliques which have an ordering excluding the four ordered temporal patterns of Fig. 1. We first prove that any 1D-mobility temporal clique is in $\mathcal{C}$:

Proposition 1. *For any 1D-mobility schedule x from an ordering π of n agents such that $\mathcal{G}_{\pi,x} = ((V, E), \lambda)$ is a temporal clique, the initial ordering π excludes the four patterns of Fig. 1.*

This proposition is a direct consequence of the following lemma.

Lemma 1. *Consider three nodes $a, b, c \in V$ such that time $\lambda(ac)$ happens in-between $\lambda(ab)$ and $\lambda(bc)$, i.e. $\lambda(ac)$ is the median of $\{\lambda(ab), \lambda(ac), \lambda(bc)\}$, then b is in-between a and c in the initial ordering, i.e. either a, b, c or c, b, a is a sub-sequence of π.*

Proof. For the sake of contradiction, suppose that b is not in-between a and c initially. At time $\min\{\lambda(ab), \lambda(bc)\}$, it first crosses a or c, and it is now in-between a and c. As a and c cannot cross each other as long as b lies in-between them, the other crossing of b with a or c should thus occur before $\lambda(ac)$, implying $\max\{\lambda(ab), \lambda(bc)\} < \lambda(ac)$, in contradiction with the hypothesis. The only possible initial orderings of these three nodes are thus a, b, c and c, b, a. □

One can easily check that the above Lemma forbids the four patterns of Fig. 1. Indeed, in each pattern, the edge of label 2 that appears in-between the two others in time, is adjacent to the middle node while it should link the leftmost and rightmost nodes. Proposition 1 thus follows.

We now show that forbidding these four patterns fully characterizes 1D-mobility temporal cliques. For that purpose, we construct a mapping from ordered temporal cliques in $\mathcal{C}$ to the set $R(w_n)$ of all reduced decompositions of w_n where $w_n = n, n-1, \ldots, 1$ is the permutation in S_n with longest length.

Lemma 2. *Any temporal clique $\mathcal{G} \in \mathcal{C}$ having an ordering π excluding the four patterns of Fig. 1, can be associated to a reduced decomposition $f(\mathcal{G}, \pi)$ of w_n. Moreover, the representation $\mathcal{R}(\mathcal{G})$ of $\mathcal{G}$ corresponds to a 1D-mobility schedule starting from π and $\mathcal{G}$ is a 1D-mobility temporal clique.*

Proof. Recall that, up to isomorphism, we can assume that $\mathcal{G}$ has lifetime $T = n(n-1)/2$ and that exactly one edge appears at each time $t \in [T]$. Consider the corresponding representation $\mathcal{R}(\mathcal{G}) = (u_1, v_1, 1), (u_2, v_2, 2), \ldots, (u_T, v_T, T)$. Starting from the initial ordering $\pi_0 = \pi$, we construct a sequence $\pi_1, \ldots, \pi_T$ of orderings corresponding to what we believe to be the positions of the agents at each time step if we read the edges in $\mathcal{R}(\mathcal{G})$ as a 1D-mobility schedule. More precisely, for each $t \in T$, π_t is defined from π_{t-1} as follows. As the edge $u_t v_t$ should correspond to a crossing $x_t = u_t v_t$, it can be seen as the transposition exchanging u_t and v_t so that we define $\pi_t = x_t \pi_{t-1}$. Equivalently, we set $\tau_t = (i, j)$ where i and j respectively denote the indexes of u_t and v_t in π_{t-1}, i.e. $\pi_{t-1}(i) = u_t$ and $\pi_{t-1}(j) = v_t$. We then also have $\pi_t = \pi_{t-1}\tau_t$.

Our main goal is to prove that $f(\mathcal{G}, \pi) := \tau_1, \ldots, \tau_T$ is the desired reduced decomposition of w_n. For that, we need to prove that u_t and v_t are indeed adjacent in $\pi_{t-1} = \pi_0\tau_1 \cdots \tau_{t-1} = x_{t-1} \cdots x_1 \pi_0$. For the sake of contradiction, consider the first time t when this fails to be. That is $\tau_1, \ldots, \tau_{t-1}$ are indeed adjacent transpositions, edge uv appears at time t, i.e. $uv = u_t v_t$, and u, v are not consecutive in π_{t-1}. We assume without loss of generality that u is before v in π_0, i.e. u, v is a sub-sequence of π_0. We will mainly rely on the following observation:

Consider two nodes x, y such that x is before y in π_0, then x is before y in π_{t-1} if and only edge xy appears at t or later, i.e. $\lambda(xy) \geq t$.

The reason comes from the assumption that $\tau_1, \ldots, \tau_{t-1}$ are all adjacent transpositions: as long as only x or y is involved in such a transposition, their relative order cannot change. The above observation thus implies in particular that u is still before v in π_{t-1}. Now, as u and v are not consecutive in π_{t-1}, there must exist an element w between elements u and v in π_{t-1}. We consider the two following cases:

Case 1. w was already in-between u and v in π_0, that is u, w, v is a sub-sequence of π_0. As the relative order has not changed between these three nodes, we have $\lambda(uw) > t$ and $\lambda(wv) > t$ as their appearing time is distinct from $t = \lambda(uv)$. This is in contradiction with the exclusion of the two patterns on the left of Fig. 1.

Case 2. w was not in-between u and v in π_0. Consider the case where u, v, w is a sub-sequence of π_0. From the observation, we we deduce that $\lambda(vw) < t$ and $\lambda(uw) > t$, which contradicts with the exclusion of the bottom-right pattern of Fig. 1. The other case where w, u, v is a sub-sequence of π_0 is symmetrical and similarly leads to a contradiction with the exclusion of the top-right pattern of Fig. 1.

We get a contradiction in all cases and conclude that $\tau_1, \ldots, \tau_T$ are all adjacent transpositions. This implies that x is indeed a valid 1D-mobility schedule from π. As x is defined according to the ordering of edges in $\mathcal{R}(\mathcal{G})$ by appearing time, $\mathcal{G}$ is obviously isomorphic to $\mathcal{G}_{\pi,x}$.

Additionally, as each pair of elements occurs exactly in one transposition, the permutation $\tau_1 \cdots \tau_T$ has length $T = n(n-1)/2$ and must equal w_n. The decomposition $f(\mathcal{G}, \pi) = \tau_1, \ldots, \tau_T$ is thus indeed a reduced decomposition of w_n. □

Theorem 1 is a direct consequence of Proposition 1 and Lemma 2.

3.2 Recognition Algorithm

The full version provides an algorithm that decides if a clique belongs to $\mathcal{C}$, and provides an ordering of the nodes that avoids the patterns if it is the case. The algorithm runs in $O(n^2)$ time, which is linear in the size of the description of the clique.

The main idea of the algorithm relies on Lemma 1 which allows to detect within a triangle which node should be in-between the two others in any ordering avoiding the patterns by checking the three times at which the edges of the triangle appear.

First we try to compute an ordering of the vertices. To do that, we use a subroutine that provides the two nodes that should be at the extremities of some given subset V of nodes. It outputs these two nodes by excluding repeatedly a node out of some triplets again and again until only two nodes are left, using Lemma 1 to identify which one is in the middle.

We deduce the two extremities a and z of V, keep a as the first element. We then repeat $n-2$ times: add back z to the remaining nodes, compute the extremities. If z is one of the extremities, remove the other element and add it to the ordering. Otherwise, return $\perp$ as a contradiction has been found (z must always be an extremity if we have a 1D-mobility temporal clique).

We then need to check that each edge indeed switches two consecutive nodes one after another in the 1D-mobility model. To do that, we represent the sequence of permutations starting from π the initial ordering, and check that each switch, according to the edges sorted by time label, corresponds to an exchange between two consecutive nodes. If at some point, we try to switch non consecutive elements, we return *False*, otherwise at the end we proved that we had a 1D-mobility temporal clique and return *True*.

3.3 Counting

We now provide the exact number $|\mathcal{C}|$ of 1D-mobility temporal cliques with n nodes. The proof appears in the full version of the article, using combinatoric results from [8,16].

Proposition 2. *The number of 1D-mobility temporal cliques with n nodes is*

$$|\mathcal{C}| = \frac{|R(w_n)|}{2} = \frac{1}{2} \frac{\binom{n}{2}!}{1^{n-1} 3^{n-2} \cdots (2n-3)^1}.$$

3.4 Temporal Spanner

In this subsection, we show that any 1D-mobility temporal clique has a spanner of $\mathcal{G}$ of size $(2n-3)$. Moreover, this spanner has diameter 3, and provides a new structure for (sub)spanners compared to the ones introduced in [5], see Fig. 2 below.

Theorem 2. *Given a 1D-mobility temporal clique $\mathcal{G}$, let $\mathcal{H}$ be the temporal subgraph of $\mathcal{G}$ consisting in the $(2n-3)$ edges that are adjacent with either v_1 or vertex v_n. $\mathcal{H}$ is a temporal spanner of $\mathcal{G}$.*

Proof. Let us consider the edge (v_1, v_n, t) that corresponds to the crossing of the initial two extremities on the line. When this happens, we have two sets: V_L (resp. V_R) corresponding to the agents being at the left of v_1 (resp. right of v_n) at time t. Before t, we got all edges of the form v_1v_l with $v_l \in V_L$ and of the form v_rv_n with $v_r \in V_R$. After t, we get all edges of the form v_1v_r with $v_r \in V_R$ and of the form v_lv_n with $v_l \in V_L$. Figure 2 shows how we get each path between a pair of vertices. □

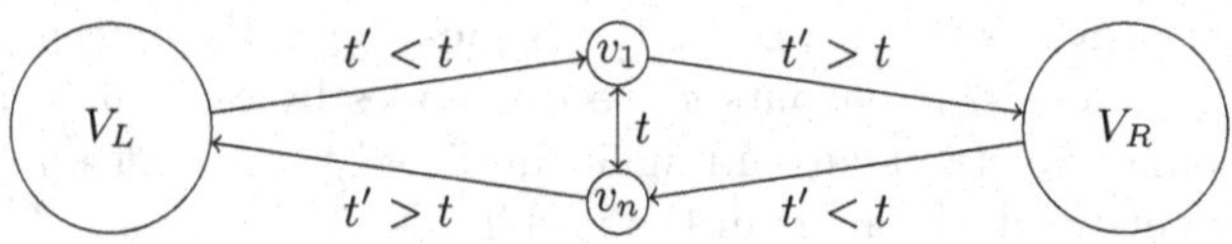

Fig. 2. Relative order of edge-labelling between the sets V_L, V_R and the two vertices v_1 and v_n. Edges are here to show how connectivity paths are used

4 Mobility Graph with at Most One Crossing

In this section, we consider the case where each pair of agents cross each other at most once. We provide a characterization with the addition of the forbidden patterns of Fig. 3 which includes non-edges corresponding of the non-crossings.

Theorem 3. *A single valued incremental temporal graph is a 1D-mobility temporal graph if and only if there exists an ordering of its nodes that excludes the ordered temporal patterns of Figs. 1 and 3.*

Proposition 3. *For any mobility schedule x of n agents where each pair of agents cross at most once producing a incremental single valued temporal graph $\mathcal{G}_x = ((V, E), \lambda)$, the initial ordering π of the agents excludes the patterns of Figs. 1 and 3.*

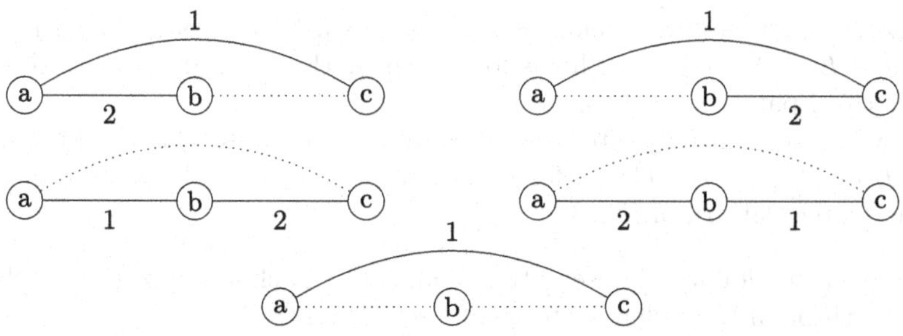

Fig. 3. Ordered forbidden patterns with forbidden edges in the 1D-mobility model when each pair of agents cross at most once. The ordering associated to each pattern is a, b, c.

Proof. Lemma 1 gives us the proof for the patterns of Fig. 1. About the patterns of Fig. 3, we have the following observations. Pick three nodes a, b, c such that a, b, c is a sub-sequence of π and there exists two agents among them which do not cross each other. If b and c do not cross each other, and a crosses b and c, then a crosses b before crossing agent c (top left pattern). If b and c do not cross each other, and a does not cross b, then a does not cross c (bottom pattern). If a and b do not cross, similarly, π excludes the top right pattern and the bottom pattern. If a and c do not cross each other, then b cannot cross both a and c (two patterns in the second row). □

Lemma 3. *Any incremental single valued temporal graph $\mathcal{G}$ having an ordering π excluding the patterns of Figs. 1 and 3 can be associated to a mobility schedule x of n agents where each pair of agents cross at most once.*

Proof. Starting from the initial ordering $\pi_0 = \pi$, we define a sequence $\pi_1, \ldots, \pi_T$, of orderings, corresponding to what, we believe, to be the positions of the agents at each time step if we read the edges of $\mathcal{G}$ by increasing time label as a mobility schedule. More precisely, for each $t \in T$, π_t is defined from π_{t-1} as follows. Consider the edge $uv = \lambda^{-1}(t)$ appearing at time t in $\mathcal{G}$. We define τ_t as the transposition exchanging u and v in w_{t-1}. Equivalently, we set $\tau_t = (i, j)$ where i and j respectively denote the indexes of u and v in π_{t-1}, i.e. $\pi_{t-1}(i) = u$ and $\pi_{t-1}(j) = v$. We then set $\pi_t = \pi_{t-1}\tau_t$.

We need to proof that u_t and v_t are indeed adjacent in π_{t-1}. Consider the first time t when this fails to be. That is $\tau_1, \ldots, \tau_{t-1}$ are adjacent transpositions, edge uv appears at time t, i.e. $uv = u_t v_t$, and u, v are not consecutive in π_{t-1}. It implies that there exists another node w such that in π_{t-1}, the relative ordering amongs the three vertices is u_t, w, v_t. We consider the temporal subgraph, $\mathcal{H}$, induced by the three vertices u_t, w, v_t. We get to a contradiction by proving that any order on those nodes in π_0 will imply that $\mathcal{H}$ is a forbidden pattern.

Case 1. w was already in-between u_t and v_t in π_0. It implies that ($u_t w \notin E$ or $\lambda(u_t w) > t$) and ($v_t w \notin E$ or $\lambda(v_t w) > t$). This is forbidden by the two left patterns of Fig. 1, the two top patterns and the last pattern of Fig. 3.

Case 2. w was initially before u_t and v_t in π_0. It implies that $\lambda(u_tw) < t$, and $v_tw \notin E$ or $\lambda(v_tw) > t$. This is forbidden by the top right pattern of Fig. 1 and the third pattern of Fig. 3.

Case 3. w was initially after u_t and v_t in π_0. It implies that $\lambda(v_tw) < t$, and $u_tw \notin E$ or $\lambda(u_tw) > t$. This is forbidden by the bottom right pattern of Fig. 1 and the fourth pattern of Fig. 3. □

We make the following observation thanks to the characterization of classes of graphs through forbidden patterns of size 3 from [7].

Proposition 4. *The set of graphs that can be associated to a mobility schedule x of n agents where each pair of agents cross at most once is contained in the set of permutation graphs.*

Proof. First we can note that in the 5 patterns of Fig. 3, the last three do not depend on the time labels, either by symmetry (3, 4) or because there is only one label on the pattern (5). Using [7], we know that the corresponding class of graph is the permutation graphs, i.e. they are comparability graph and their complement also. Therefore this class is included in permutation graphs. □

It should be noted that if we consider only patterns of Fig. 3 ignoring the labels of the 2 first patterns, this corresponds exactly to the particular case of trivially perfect graphs [7].These graphs are also known as comparability graphs of trees or quasi-threshold graphs.

5 Multi-crossing Mobility Model

In this section, we consider schedules where a pair of agents can cross each other more than once. Each edge can have multiple times. Hence, the previous patterns have no more sense, as they concern only 0 or 1 crossing. We do not have a characterization of the class through forbidden patterns. However, we provide an unordered pattern by introducing the notion of *sliding windows*: given two time limits $T_1 < T_2$, if each edge on each pair of some subset of nodes appear at most once, we can forbid a pattern. In particular, with this definition, we get the following result:

Theorem 4. *Any temporal graph associated to a 1D-mobility schedule must exclude the pattern of Fig. 4 in any of its single-valued sliding window.*

Proof. Let assume that there exists some 1D-mobility schedule which produces a temporal graph where the pattern of Fig. 4 on some nodes a, b, c and d. Thanks to Lemma 1 applied to 3 nodes, we know from the largest label which node is in between two others. We deduce that, at time T_1, b is between a and c, d is between b and c, and d in between a and b. There is no way to order a, b, c and d with regards to those constrains. □

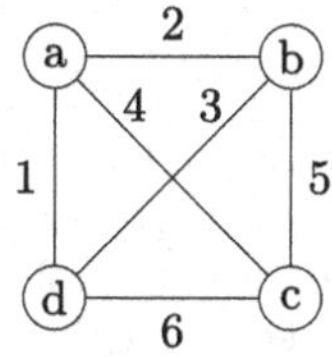

Fig. 4. A forbidden structure in multi-crossing mobility graphs.

Even though we have a forbidden pattern, we cannot characterize this class only with single valued patterns. For example, we could not detect a subgraph with the pattern of Fig. 4 where an edge is multiplied. More precisely, if we have $\lambda_{[T_1,T_2]}(cd) = \{5, 6, 7\}$ and $\lambda_{[T_1,T_2]}(bc) = \{8\}$, this cannot happen in a 1D-mobility schedule for the same reason, but it does not have any forbidden pattern in some subinterval.

6 Conclusion and Perspectives

In this paper, we have introduced the first notion of forbidden patterns in temporal graphs. In particular, this notion allowed us to describe a new class of temporal cliques corresponding to a mobility problem of agents crossing each other exactly once on a line. This new class of temporal cliques has spanners of size $2n-3$, following the conjecture from [5]. The mobility description allows the agents to adapt their speed to ensure that each crossing occurs in the correct order. A first open question is: can any 1D mobility temporal clique be the result of crossings if the agents move at constant speed, choosing wisely the distance at which they start? We can note that, for each crossing to occur from a starting situation, we would need to sort the agents by increasing speed from left to right.

Another question that arises is: can we find a mobility model on more dimensions that also provides a temporal clique that could be studied?

Our patterns only consider single times on the edges. One perspective is to figure out how to describe forbidden patterns on edges such that λ provides more than one time slot. Considering sub-intervals where λ gives at most one value is a possibility, but we multi-crossing section showed that it would not be enough to describe all forbidden patterns. This raises another question: is there a way to fully describe multi-crossing mobility model with forbidden patterns?

Our work can also be seen as a characterization of square integers matrices in terms of patterns, perhaps it could be generalized to a study of well-structured matrices as in the seminal work of [13] on Robinsonian matrices which are closely related to interval graphs.

Acknowledgement. This work was supported by ANR project TEMPOGRAL (ANR-22-CE48-0001). The second author has received funding from the European Union's Horizon 2020 research and innovation programme under the Marie Skłodowska-Curie grant agreement No 945332.

References

1. Awerbuch, B., Even, S.: Efficient and reliable broadcast is achievable in an eventually connected network. In: Proceedings of the Third Annual ACM Symposium on Principles of Distributed Computing, pp. 278–281 (1984)
2. Axiotis, K., Fotakis, D.: On the size and the approximability of minimum temporally connected subgraphs. In: Chatzigiannakis, I., Mitzenmacher, M., Rabani, Y., Sangiorgi, D. (eds.) 43rd International Colloquium on Automata, Languages, and Programming, ICALP 2016, 11–15 July 2016, Rome, Italy. LIPIcs, vol. 55, pp. 149:1–149:14. Schloss Dagstuhl - Leibniz-Zentrum für Informatik (2016). https://doi.org/10.4230/LIPIcs.ICALP.2016.149
3. Bandlow, J.: An elementary proof of the hook formula. Electron. J. Combin. R45 (2008)
4. Casteigts, A., Flocchini, P., Quattrociocchi, W., Santoro, N.: Time-varying graphs and dynamic networks. IJPEDS **27**(5), 387–408 (2012)
5. Casteigts, A., Peters, J.G., Schoeters, J.: Temporal cliques admit sparse spanners. J. Comput. Syst. Sci. **121**, 1–17 (2021)
6. Damaschke, P.: Forbidden ordered subgraphs. In: Bodendiek, R., Henn, R. (eds.) Topics in Combinatorics and Graph Theory: Essays in Honour of Gerhard Ringel, pp. 219–229. Springer, Heidelberg (1990). https://doi.org/10.1007/978-3-642-46908-4_25
7. Feuilloley, L., Habib, M.: Graph classes and forbidden patterns on three vertices. SIAM J. Discret. Math. **35**(1), 55–90 (2021)
8. Frame, J.S., Robinson, G.D.B., Thrall, R.M.: The hook graphs of the symmetric group. Can. J. Math. **6**, 316–324 (1954)
9. Guzmán-Pro, S., Hell, P., Hernández-Cruz, C.: Describing hereditary properties by forbidden circular orderings. Appl. Math. Comput. **438**, 127555 (2023)
10. Hell, P., Mohar, B., Rafiey, A.: Ordering without forbidden patterns. In: Schulz, A.S., Wagner, D. (eds.) ESA 2014. LNCS, vol. 8737, pp. 554–565. Springer, Heidelberg (2014). https://doi.org/10.1007/978-3-662-44777-2_46
11. Holme, P., Saramäki, J.: Temporal networks. Phys. Rep. **519**(3), 97–125 (2012)
12. Kempe, D., Kleinberg, J., Kumar, A.: Connectivity and inference problems for temporal networks. In: Proceedings of the Thirty-Second Annual ACM Symposium on Theory of Computing, pp. 504–513 (2000)
13. Laurent, M., Seminaroti, M., Tanigawa, S.: A structural characterization for certifying Robinsonian matrices. Electron. J. Comb. **24**(2), 2 (2017)
14. Michail, O.: An introduction to temporal graphs: an algorithmic perspective. Internet Math. **12**(4), 239–280 (2016)
15. Skrien, D.J.: A relationship between triangulated graphs, comparability graphs, proper interval graphs, proper circular-arc graphs, and nested interval graphs. J. Graph Theory **6**(3), 309–316 (1982)
16. Stanley, R.P.: On the number of reduced decompositions of elements of coxeter groups. Eur. J. Comb. **5**(4), 359–372 (1984)
17. Tenner, B.E.: Reduced decompositions and permutation patterns. J. Algebraic Combin. **24**(3), 263–284 (2006). https://doi.org/10.1007/s10801-006-0015-6
18. Villani, N.: Dynamic unit disk graph recognition. Master's thesis, Université de Bordeaux (2021). https://perso.crans.org/vanille/share/satge/report.pdf
19. Villani, N., Casteigts, A.: Some thoughts on dynamic unit disk graphs. Algorithmic Aspects of Temporal Graphs IV (2021). https://www.youtube.com/watch?v=yZRNLjbfxxs. Satellite workshop of ICALP

Uniform k-Circle Formation by Fat Robots

Bibhuti Das(✉) and Krishnendu Mukhopadhyaya

Advanced Computing and Microelectronics Unit, Indian Statistical Institute, Kolkata, India
dasbibhuti905@gmail.com

Abstract. In this paper, we study the *uniform k-circle formation* by a swarm of mobile robots with dimensional extent. For some $k > 0$, the *k-circle formation* problem asks the robots to form disjoint circles. Each circle must be centered at one of the pre-fixed points given in the plane. Each circle should contain exactly k distinct robot positions. The *k-circle formation* problem has already been studied for punctiform robots in the plane. In this paper, the robots are represented by transparent unit disks in the plane. They are autonomous, anonymous, homogeneous, and silent. The robots are oblivious and execute Look-Compute-Move (LCM) cycle under a fair asynchronous scheduler. The direction and orientation of one of the axes are agreed upon by the robots. In this setting, we have characterized all the initial configurations and values of k for which the *uniform k-circle formation* problem is deterministically unsolvable. For the remaining configurations and values of k, a deterministic distributed algorithm has been proposed that solves the *uniform k-circle formation* problem within finite time.

Keywords: Distributed Computing · k-Circle Formation · Fat Robots · Asynchronous · Oblivious

1 Introduction

In the field of distributed computing by a swarm of mobile robots [1], the research focuses on the computational and complexity issues for an autonomous multi-robot system. The study aims at identifying sets of minimal capabilities for the robots to accomplish a given task. Some of the well-studied problems in this research area are *gathering* [2,3], *pattern formation* [4–8], etc. In this paper, we are interested in studying the *k-circle formation* problem [9,10] which is a special kind of *pattern formation* problem. For some $k > 0$, the *k-circle formation* problem requires the robots to form disjoint circles with exactly k distinct robot positions. Also, each circle must be centered at one of the pre-fixed points given in the plane. The problem is theoretically interesting as it has both the components of *partitioning* [11,12] and *circle formation* [13–16]. In addition, Bhagat et al. [9] showed that if the *k-circle formation* problem can be solved in a deterministic

S. Dolev and B. Schieber (Eds.): SSS 2023, LNCS 14310, pp. 359–373, 2023.
https://doi.org/10.1007/978-3-031-44274-2_26

manner, then the robots can also deterministically solve the *k-epf* problem, which is a more general version of the *embedded pattern formation* [7,8]).

Bhagat et al. [9,10] investigated the *k-circle formation* problem for punctiform robots where the formed circles were non-uniform. In the real world, a robot cannot possibly be dimensionless. Czyzowicz et al. [3] considered unit disk robots in the plane. In this current paper, we have investigated the *uniform k-circle formation* problem in a more realistic model where the robots have a dimensional extent. They are represented by unit disks in the Euclidean plane.

The assumption on the dimension of a robot introduces additional challenges to solve the *uniform k-circle formation* problem. A point robot can always pass through the gap between any two points in the plane. It can compute a path in the plane that lies at an infinitesimal distance from another robot. In comparison, a fat robot cannot do so due to its dimensional extent. A fat robot would act as a physical barrier for the other robots. If a robot is punctiform, then either it lies on a circle or it does not. However, for a fat robot, there are two scenarios (e.g., the unit disk intersects the circle or the center of the unit disk lies on the circle) when a robot can be said to lie on a circle. Also, the robots need to compute a suitable radius for the circles so that k robots can be accommodated without any overlapping. Therefore, the solution proposed by Bhagat et al. [9,10] would fail to work for fat robots.

Our Contributions: This paper studies the *uniform k-circle formation* problem for a swarm of transparent fat robots in the Euclidean plane. The activations of the robots are determined by a fair asynchronous scheduler. The following results are shown under the assumption of one-axis agreement:

1. All the initial configurations and values of k for which the *uniform k-circle formation* problem is deterministically unsolvable are characterized.
2. A deterministic distributed algorithm is proposed that solves the *uniform k-circle formation* problem within finite time.

1.1 Related Works

The *partitioning* problem [11] and the *team assembling* problem [12] are very closely related to the *k-circle formation* problem. To solve the *partitioning* problem the robots must divide into multiple groups. Each group should contain equal number of robots. The robots in each group also need to converge to a small area. For a swarm of heterogeneous robots, Liu et al. [12] studied the *team assembling* problem which asks the robots to form multiple teams, each team containing a pre-fixed number of robots of different kinds. For a given set of pre-fixed pattern points, the *embedded pattern formation* problem [7,8] requires the robots to transform a given configuration into one in which each pattern point is occupied by a single robot.

Another very closely related problem to *k-circle formation* problem is the *circle formation* problem. The *circle formation* problem [13–16] asks the robots to position themselves on a circle centered at a point, which is not defined a priori, within finite time. Biswas et al. [17] studied the formation of multiple uniform circles by fat robots under synchronous scheduler without fixed points. Jiang et al. [18] proposed a decentralized algorithm for repeating pattern formation by a multi-robot system. Cicerone et al. [19] introduced molecular oblivious robots (MOBLOT): similar to the way atoms combine to form molecules, in the MOBLOT model, simple robots can move to form more complex computational units, having an extent and different capabilities with respect to robots. In this model, they investigated matter formation by molecular oblivious robots and provided a necessary condition for its solvability, which relies on symmetricity.

For an arbitrary number of fat robots, Agathangelou et al. [20] solved the *gathering* problem. Bose et al. [21] studied the *arbitrary pattern formation* problem for opaque fat robots with externally visible lights that can assume a constant number of pre-defined colors. Sharma et al. [22] investigated the *complete visibility* problem for opaque fat robots.

2 The Model, Notations and Definitions

Consider $m > 0$ pre-fixed points in the plane. Let $F = \{f_1, f_2, \dots, f_m\}$ represent the set of fixed points. The center of gravity of F is denoted by F_c. For some $k > 0$, we have considered $n = km$ mobile robots. The robots are represented by transparent unit disks in the Euclidean plane. $R = \{R_1, R_2, \dots, R_n\}$ denotes the set of all the robots in the plane. $R_i(t)$ represents the centre of R_i at time t. $R(t) = \{R_1(t), R_2(t), \dots, R_n(t)\}$ denotes the set of all the robot centers at time t. $U_i(t)$ denotes the unit disk centered at $R_i(t)$. The configuration at time t is denoted by $C(t) = (R(t), F)$. In this paper, the robots are assumed to have an agreement on the orientation and direction of the y-axis. Let F_y denote the set of fixed points on the y-axis. Also, let $R_y(t)$ represent the set of robots whose center lies on the y-axis at time t. The robots consider F_c as the origin. They do not have any agreement on a common chirality (agreement on the global clockwise or counter-clockwise direction). They are assumed to be: *autonomous* (no centralized controller), *anonymous* (no unique identifier), *oblivious* (no memory of past actions), *silent* (no explicit direct communication), and *homogeneous* (run the same algorithm). The robots are not allowed to overlap each other. They have *unlimited visibility*, i.e., they can observe the entire plane.

Robots can either be in an active state or an idle state. Initially, all the robots are considered to be static. An active robot executes Look-Compute-Move (LCM) cycle. In its *look* phase, a robot observes the current configuration in its own local coordinate system. In the *compute* phase, a robot computes a destination point based on its observation in its look phase. A robot moves towards its destination point in its *move* phase and exhibits non-rigid motion. In non-rigid movements, a robot may be stopped by an adversary before reaching its destination point. However, to guarantee finite-time reachability, there exists a fixed but unknown $\delta > 0$ so that the robots are guaranteed to move by at least δ distance towards its destination point. If the destination point is located within δ distance, it is guaranteed that the robot will reach it. A robot is unable to differentiate between static and moving robots.

It is assumed that the robots are activated by a fair asynchronous (ASYNC) scheduler. Each robot is activated an infinite number of times, and its LCM cycle is completed within a finite amount of time. They do not have any global concept of time. Each LCM cycle has a finite but unbounded duration.

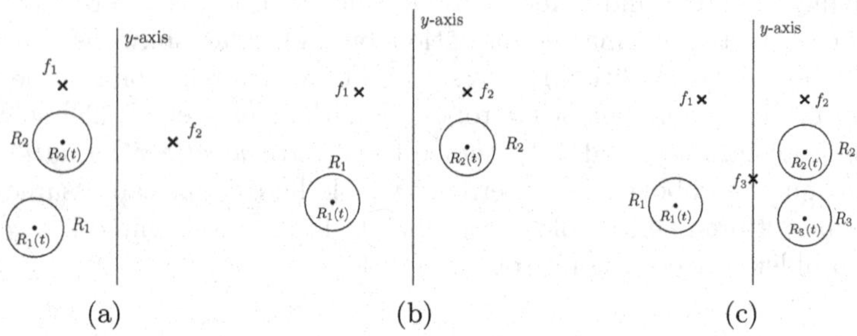

Fig. 1. Disks represent robot positions, small black circles represent center of a robot and crosses represent fixed points. (a) $\mathcal{I}_1$-configuration. (b) $\mathcal{I}_2$-configuration. (c) $\mathcal{I}_3$-configuration.

Let $y(p_i)$ represent the y-coordinate of a point p_i in the plane. If the robots could make an agreement on the positive x-axis direction, then $x(p_i)$ represents the x-coordinate of p_i. Otherwise, $x(p_i)$ denotes the distance of p_i from the y-axis. $\gamma(p_i) = (x(p_i), y(p_i))$ is called the rank of point p_i. A point p_j is said to have lower rank than p_i, if either $y(p_j) < y(p_i)$ or $y(p_j) = y(p_i)$ and $x(p_j) < x(p_i)$. In its *look* phase, a robot perceives the ranks of all the robots and fixed points as its configuration view. Two distinct robots are said to be symmetric about the y-axis if their centers have the same rank. Similarly, if two fixed points have the same rank, then they are said to be symmetric. $C(t)$ is said to be symmetric if $R(t) \cup F$ is symmetric about the y-axis. As $R(t) \cup F$ can be ordered with respect to the y-axis, the presence of rotational symmetries can be overlooked.

All the configurations can be partitioned into the following disjoint classes:

1. $\mathcal{I}_1-$ F is asymmetric about the y-axis (Fig. 1(a)).
2. $\mathcal{I}_2-$ F is symmetric about the y-axis and $F_y = \emptyset$ (Fig. 1(b)).
3. $\mathcal{I}_3-$ F is symmetric about the y-axis and $F_y \neq \emptyset$ (Fig. 1(c)).

Since the partition is based upon fixed points, the robots can easily identify the class of a configuration by observing the fixed points.

The radii of the circles are assumed to be homogeneous. Let $r > 0$ denote the radius of a circle. The choice of the value of r is arbitrary. However, it must be ensured that k robots can be placed on a circle without overlapping. The minimum radius for a circle for fat robots is achieved when there are no gaps between any two adjacent robots on the circle. When $k = 1$, we assume that the radius is one unit. For $k > 1$, let $\alpha = \dfrac{2\pi}{k}$ and a be the mid-point of the line segment $\overline{R_1(t)R_2(t)}$ (Fig. 2).

We have, $\sin\frac{\alpha}{2} = \frac{\overline{R_2(t)a}}{\overline{R_2(t)f}} = \frac{1}{r} \implies r = \frac{1}{\sin\frac{\alpha}{2}}$.

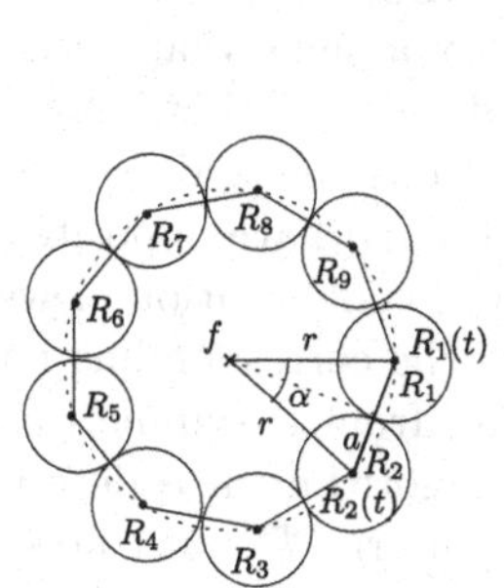

Fig. 2. The minimum radius required to form a circle containing exactly k robots.

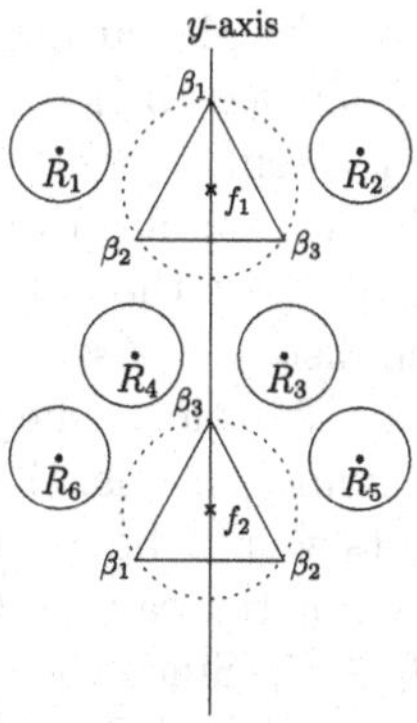

Fig. 3. An example of a configuration satisfying the impossibility criterion (Theorem 1).

Let $\mathcal{P}_i$ denote the regular k-gon centered at $f_i \in F$ with $\{\beta_1, \beta_2, \ldots, \beta_k\}$ as the set of vertices such that $d(\beta_i, \beta_j) = 2$, where $i \in \{1, 2, \ldots, k\}$ and $j = i + 1 \mod k$. We assume that the minimum distance between any two fixed points is greater than or equal to $2(r + 1)$. This would always ensure that even if two adjacent k-gons are rotated, the formation of disjoint circles without any overlapping of robots would be guaranteed.

Let $C(f_i, r)$ denote the circle centered at $f_i \in F$. If $R_i(t)$ lies on a circle, then R_i is said to lie on that circle. Depending on the number of robots on $C(f_i, r)$, the fixed point f_i can be catagorized as one of the following types: *unsaturated* (number of robots $< k$), *saturated* (number of robots $= k$), and *oversaturated* (number of robots $> k$).

The Uniform k-Circle Formation Problem: $C(t)$ for some $t \geq 0$ is said to be a *final* configuration, if it satisfies the following conditions:

i) $\forall R_i \in R$, $R_i(t) \in C(f_j, r)$ for some $f_j \in F$,
ii) $|C(f_i, r) \cap R(t)| = k$, $\forall f_i \in F$, and
iii) All k robots located on the same circle form a regular k-gon.

For a given *initial* configuration, the robots are required to transform and remain in a *final* configuration to solve *uniform k-circle formation* problem.

3 Impossibility Results

Theorem 1. *Let $C(0)$ be a given initial configuration. If k is some odd integer and $C(0) \in \mathcal{I}_3$, such that the following conditions hold:*

i) $R(0)$ is symmetric about the y-axis, and
ii) $R_y(0) = \emptyset$,

then the uniform k-circle formation problem is deterministically unsolvable.

Proof. If possible, let algorithm $\mathcal{A}$ solve the *uniform k-circle formation* problem. Suppose $\phi(R_i)$ denotes the symmetric image of R_i. Assume that the robots are activated under a semi-synchronous[1] scheduler. Also, assume that both R_i and $\phi(R_i)$ are activated simultaneously. It is assumed that the robots move at the same constant speed without any transient stops. Consider that R_i and $\phi(R_i)$ travel the same distance. Assume that both R_i and $\phi(R_i)$ have opposite notions of positive x-axis direction. They would have identical configuration views. Since the robots are homogeneous, their destinations and the corresponding paths for their movements would be mirror images. Starting from a symmetric configuration, the symmetry cannot be broken by any algorithm in a deterministic manner. Let $f_i \in F_y$. Since the configuration is symmetric, $\mathcal{P}_i$ must be symmetric about the y-axis. As k is odd, $\mathcal{P}_i$ must have a vertex on the y-axis. We have $R_y(0) = \emptyset$. Thus, moving a robot R_i to the y-axis would mean moving $\phi(R_i)$ to the same point. However, overlapping of the robots is not allowed. Hence, the *uniform k-circle formation* problem is deterministically unsolvable. □

Let $\mathcal{I}$ denote set of all the initial configurations and $\mathcal{U}$ be the set of all the configurations satisfying impossibility criterion presented in Theorem 1 (Fig. 3).

4 Algorithm

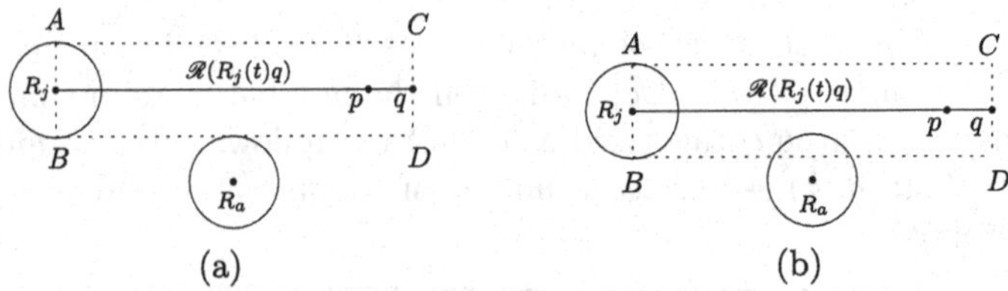

Fig. 4. (a) $\mathscr{R}(R_j(t)q)$ is empty. (b) $\mathscr{R}(R_j(t)q)$ is non-empty

In this section, we present a distributed algorithm that deterministically solves the *uniform k-circle formation* problem for $C(0) \in \mathcal{I} \setminus \mathcal{U}$. An active robot would execute the proposed algorithm *AlgorithmFatRobot* unless the current configuration is a *final* configuration.

Definition 1. *Let p be the destination point of R_j and q be the point such that $p \in \overline{R_j(t)q}$ and $d(p,q) = 1$. The rectangular strip ABCD (Figs. 4(a) and*

[1] Time is divided into global rounds within the semi-synchronous (SSYNC) scheduler. A subset of robots is activated in each round. An active robot completes its LCM cycle in the round in which it becomes active.

4(b)) between $R_j(t)$ and q having width of two units is denoted by $\mathscr{R}(R_j(t)q)$. If $\nexists R_i \in R$ such that $U_i(t)$ intersects $\mathscr{R}(R_j(t)q)$, then $\mathscr{R}(R_j(t)q)$ is said to be empty (Fig. 4(a)). Otherwise, it is said to be non-empty (Fig. 4(b)). If $\mathscr{R}(R_j(t)q)$ is empty, then R_j is said to have a free path for movement towards p.

Half-planes: Let $\mathcal{H}_1$ and $\mathcal{H}_2$ denote the two open half-planes delimited by the y-axis. F_i denotes the set of fixed points in $\mathcal{H}_i \in \{\mathcal{H}_1, \mathcal{H}_2\}$. $C_i(t) = (R(t), F_i)$ represents the part of the configuration consisting of $R(t) \cup F_i$, where $i \in \{1, 2\}$. $C_3(t) = (R(t), F_y)$ denotes the part of the configuration consisting of $R(t) \cup F_y$. In $\mathcal{H}_1$, the positive x-axis direction is considered along the perpendicular direction away from the y-axis. Similarly, the positive x-axis direction in $\mathcal{H}_2$ is the perpendicular direction away from the y-axis.

Definition 2. *If k is some odd integer and $C(t) \in \mathcal{I}_3$, then $C(t)$ is said to be an unsafe configuration. A pivot position is defined for an unsafe configuration. Suppose $f \in F_y$ be the topmost fixed point. Let $\rho_1 \in \mathcal{H}_1$ be the point such that $\rho_1 \in C(f, r)$ and $x(\rho_1) - x(f) = \frac{1}{2}$ unit distance. Similarly, let ρ_2 be such a point in $\mathcal{H}_2$. The points ρ_1 and ρ_2 are said to be pivot positions. A robot placed on a pivot position is said to be a pivot robot.*

4.1 Overview

During the execution of *AlgorithmFatRobot* (Sect. 4.5), the robots decide their strategy depending on the class of the initial configuration. Due to its dimensional extent, a robot can only start to move towards its destination point if it has a free path for movement. An overview of the *AlgorithmFatRobot* is described below:

1. If $C(0) \in \mathcal{I}_1$ or $C(0)$ is an *unsafe* configuration, then the robots agree upon the positive x-axis direction. In case, $C(0) \in \mathcal{I}_1$ the x-axis agreement is based on fixed points only. If $C(0)$ is an *unsafe* configuration, then the robots would execute *PivotSelection* (Sect. 4.3). This is the procedure by which a *pivot* robot would be selected and placed in a *pivot* position. The *pivot* robot would remain fixed at the *pivot* position. The *pivot* position is selected by ensuring that the configuration will remain asymmetric once the *pivot* robot is placed. In this case, the x-axis agreement is based on the *pivot* position.
2. The robots would execute *CircleFormation* (Sect. 4.4) for a unique fixed point (or for two fixed points when there is no global x-axis agreement). Such a fixed point is said to be a *target* fixed point. The robots would accomplish the formation of circles by executing the procedure *CircleFormation*.

During the execution of the *AlgorithmFatRobot*, the robots would move downwards by the execution of procedure *DownwardMovement* (Sect. 4.2).

4.2 *DownwardMovement*

DownwardMovement is the procedure in *AlgorithmFatRobot* by which the robots would move downwards. Assume that R_j has been selected for downward movement by one unit. R_j would move one unit vertically downwards by the execution of the procedure *DownwardMovement*. However, if the *pivot* robot falls in its path, then it cannot move downwards. In such a case, it would move one unit horizontally. First, some new notations and definitions are introduced.

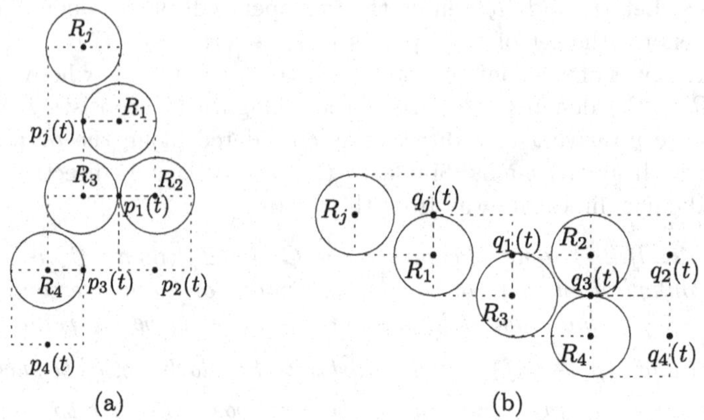

Fig. 5. (a) $M_j(t) = \{R_1, R_2, R_3, R_4\}$. As $U_1(t)$ intersects $\mathscr{R}(R_j(t)p_j(t))$, $R_1 \in M_j(t)$. Also, $U_2(t)$ and $U_3(t)$ intersect $\mathscr{R}(R_1(t)p_1(t))$, $R_2 \in M_j(t)$ and $R_3 \in M_j(t)$. $U_4(t)$ intersects $\mathscr{R}(R_3(t)p_3(t))$ and $R_4 \in M_j(t)$. (b) $N_j(t) = \{R_1, R_2, R_3, R_4\}$. As $U_1(t)$ intersects $\mathscr{R}(R_j(t)q_j(t))$, $R_1 \in N_j(t)$. $U_3(t)$ intersects $\mathscr{R}(R_1(t)q_1(t))$ and $R_3 \in N_j(t)$. Also, $U_2(t)$ and $U_4(t)$ intersect $\mathscr{R}(R_3(t)q_1(t))$, $R_2 \in N_j(t)$ and $R_4 \in N_j(t)$.

Suppose $VL_j(t)$ denotes the vertical line passing through $R_j(t)$. Let $p_j(t) \in VL_j(t)$ be the point such that $\gamma(R_j(t)) > \gamma(p_j(t))$ and $d(R_j(t), p_j(t)) = 2$. Define the set $M_j(t)$ as follows:

1. **Base case:** If $\mathscr{R}(R_j(t)p_j(t))$ is empty, then $M_j(t) = \emptyset$. Else, $M_j(t) = \{R_a \mid U_a(t)\ \textit{intersects}\ \mathscr{R}(R_j(t)p_j(t))\}$.
2. **Constructor case:**
$M_j(t) = M_j(t) \cup \{R_b \mid U_b(t)\ \textit{intersects}\ \mathscr{R}(R_i(t)p_i(t))\ \textit{for some}\ R_i \in M_j(t)\}$.

The set $M_j(t)$ contains all the robots that must be moved downwards before R_j can move one unit vertically downwards (Fig. 5(a)). Let $HL_j(t)$ denote the horizontal line passing through $R_j(t)$. In case, R_j is selected for horizontal movement, let $q_j(t) \in HL_j(t)$ be the point such that $\gamma(R_j(t)) < \gamma(q_j(t))$ and $d(R_j(t), q_j(t)) = 2$. Define the set $N_j(t)$ as follows:

1. **Base case:** If $\mathscr{R}(R_j(t)q_j(t))$ is empty, then $N_j(t) = \emptyset$. Else, $N_j(t) = \{R_a \mid U_a(t)\ \textit{intersects}\ \mathscr{R}(R_j(t)q_j(t))\}$.
2. **Constructor case:**
$N_j(t) = N_j(t) \cup \{R_b \mid U_b(t)\ \textit{intersects}\ \mathscr{R}(R_i(t)q_i(t))\ \textit{for some}\ R_i \in N_j(t)\}$.

The set $N_j(t)$ contains all the robots that must be moved horizontally so that $\mathscr{R}(R_j(t)q_j(t))$ becomes empty (Fig. 5(b)). During the execution of the procedure *DownwardMovement*(R_j), the following cases are to be considered:

1. $M_j(t) = \emptyset$. R_j would start moving towards $p_j(t)$ along $\overline{R_j(t)p_j(t)}$.
2. $M_j(t) \neq \emptyset$. There are two possible cases:
   (a) $M_j(t)$ contains the *pivot* robot. If $N_j(t) = \emptyset$, then R_j moves towards $q_j(t)$ along $\overline{R_j(t)q_j(t)}$. Otherwise, let $R_a \in N_j(t)$ be such that $d(R_j(t), R_a(t)) = \max_{R_k \in N_j(t)} d(R_j(t), R_k(t))$. R_a moves towards $q_a(t)$ along $\overline{R_a(t)q_a(t)}$. There may be multiple such robots which would perform the required movement.
   (b) $M_j(t)$ does not contain the *pivot* robot. Let $R_a \in M_j(t)$ be such that $\gamma(R_a(t)) \leq \min_{R_k \in M_j(t)} \gamma(R_k(t))$. R_a moves towards $p_a(t)$ along $\overline{R_a(t)p_a(t)}$. If there are multiple such robots, then all of them would perform the required vertical movement.

4.3 *PivotSelection*

PivotSelection is the procedure in *AlgorithmFatRobot* by which a robot would be placed at one of the *pivot* positions. Let R_a be the robot that is located at the closest distance from the *pivot* position ρ_1. If there are multiple such robots, then select the topmost one. In case there is a tie, select the one closest to the y-axis. Similarly, consider R_b to be the robot that is located closest to ρ_2. The following cases are to be considered:

1. $d(R_a(t), \rho_1) \neq d(R_b(t), \rho_2)$. Without loss of generality, let $d(R_a(t), \rho_1) < d(R_b(t), \rho_2)$. The robot R_a would start moving towards ρ_1 along $\overline{R_a(t)\rho_1}$.
2. $d(R_a(t), \rho_1) = d(R_b(t), \rho_2)$ and $R_y(t) = \emptyset$. Since $C(t) \notin \mathcal{U}$, it must be asymmetric about the y-axis. Let R_l be the topmost asymmetric robot. If there are multiple such robot then select the one which is at the closest distance from the y-axis. Without loss of generality, assume that $R_l \in \mathcal{H}_1$. The robot R_a would start moving towards ρ_1 along $\overline{R_a(t)\rho_1}$.
3. $d(R_a(t), \rho_1) = d(R_b(t), \rho_2)$ and $R_y(t) \neq \emptyset$. There are two possible cases:
   (i) $C(t)$ is asymmetric. In this case, the robots will perform the required actions similarly as in case 2.
   (ii) $C(t)$ is symmetric. First, consider the case when $\exists R_a \in R_y(t)$ that can be moved horizontally half a unit away from the y-axis. If there are multiple such robots, select the topmost one. R_a would move horizontally half a unit away from the y-axis. Next, consider the case when there are no such robots on the y-axis. Let $R_a \in R_y(t)$ be the robot that has the minimum rank. *DownwardMovement*(R_a) would be executed.

4.4 *CircleFormation*

CircleFormation is the procedure in *AlgorithmFatRobot* by which the robots would accomplish the formation of a circle. Let f_i be a *target* fixed point. The selection of the regular k-gon $\mathcal{P}_i$ is discussed below:

1. The robots have global x-axis agreement or $f_i \notin F_y$. $\mathcal{P}_i$ denotes the regular k-gon centered at f_i with β_i as one of the vertices. If $f_i \in F_y$ and $C(t)$ is an *unsafe* configuration, then the center of *pivot* robot position is considered as one the vertices of $\mathcal{P}_i$.

2. The robots do not have any global x-axis agreement and $f_i \in F_y$. Let $\beta_1 \in \mathcal{H}_1$ be the point on $C(f_i, r)$ such that it is at one unit distance from the y-axis. Since there are two such points in $\mathcal{H}_1$, select the one that has the highest rank. Similarly, let β_2 be such a point in $\mathcal{H}_2$. $\mathcal{P}_i$ denotes the regular k-gon centered at f_i with β_1 and β_2 as vertices.

The following additional notations and terminologies are introduced:

1. $A_i(t) = \{R_j \mid R_j(t) \in C(f_a, r) \text{ } where \text{ } f_a \in F \text{ } be \text{ } such \text{ } that \text{ } \gamma(f_a) \geq \gamma(f_i)\}$.
2. $f_l \in F$ denotes a fixed point such that $\gamma(f_l) \leq \gamma(f_j)$, $\forall f_j \in F$.
3. R_j is said to satisfy condition $C1$ if it is not the *pivot* robot.
4. R_j is said to satisfy condition $C2$ if $y(R_j(t)) \geq y(f_l) - (r+1)$.
5. $B_i(t) = \{R_j \mid R_j \notin A_i(t) \text{ } and \text{ } it \text{ } satisfies \text{ } C1 \text{ } and \text{ } C2\}$.
6. Let $\beta_a \in \mathcal{P}_i$ be the empty vertex that has the highest rank. Assume that R_j has been selected for moving towards β_a. If $\mathscr{R}(R_j(t), \beta_a)$ is non-empty, then let $a_j \in HL_j(t)$ denote the point that lies at the closest distance from R_j such that $\mathscr{R}(R_j(t) = a_j, \beta_a)$ is empty.

Definition 3. *$C(f_i, r)$ is called a perfect circle, if the following conditions hold:*

1. *If $R_j(t) \in C(f_i, r)$, then $R_j(t) = \beta_k$ for some $\beta_k \in \mathcal{P}_i$.*
2. *If $R_j(t) \in C(f_i, r)$ and $R_j(t) = \beta_k \in \mathcal{P}_i$, then $\nexists$ $\beta_j \in \mathcal{P}_i$ such that $\gamma(\beta_k) < \gamma(\beta_j)$ and β_j is not occupied.*

If $R_j \in C(f_i, r)$ be such that one of the above conditions is not satisfied, then it is said to be an imperfect robot. A circle is said to be imperfect if it contains an imperfect robot.

During an execution of $CircleFormation(C(t), f_i)$, an active robot considers the following cases:

1. **The robots have global x-axis agreement or $f_i \notin F_y$.** The following cases are to be considered:
   (a) $|B_i(t)| > 1$. Let $R_j \in B_i(t)$ be the robot that has the maximum rank. The robots would execute $DownwardMovement(R_j)$.
   (b) $|B_i(t)| = 1$. Let $\beta_c \in \mathcal{P}_i$ be the empty vertex that has the maximum rank. Let $R_j \in B_i(t)$. If $\mathscr{R}(R_j(t)\beta_c)$ is empty, then R_j would start moving towards β_c. Otherwise, $DownwardMovement(R_j)$ would be executed.
   (c) $|B_i(t)| = 0$ **and $C(f_i, r)$ is *imperfect*.** Let $\beta_c \in \mathcal{P}_i$ be the empty vertex that has the maximum rank. Let $R_j \in C(f_i, r)$ be such that $\gamma(R_j(t)) < \gamma(\beta_c)$ and $d(R_j(t), \beta_c)$ is minimum. If there is a tie, select the one that has the maximum rank. R_j would start moving towards β_c along $\overline{R_j(t)\beta_c}$.
   (d) $|B_i(t)| = 0$ **and $C(f_i, r)$ is *perfect*.** Let $\beta_c \in \mathcal{P}_i$ be the empty vertex that has the maximum rank. Let $R_j \in R(t) \setminus A_i(t)$ be such that $d(R_j(t), \beta_c)$ is minimum. If there is a tie, select the one that has the maximum rank. If $\mathscr{R}(R_j(t)\beta_c)$ is empty, then R_j would start moving towards β_c along $\overline{R_j(t)\beta_c}$. Else, R_j would start moving towards a_j along $\overline{R_j(t)a_j}$.

   Fig. 6 depicts the transformations among the above-mentioned cases.

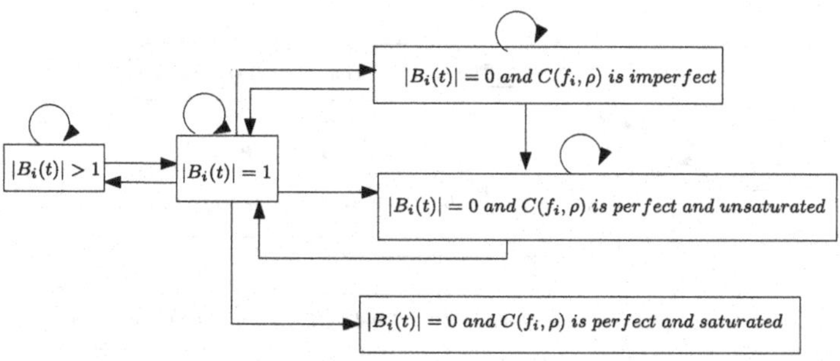

Fig. 6. A flow chart showing the transformations among the various cases during an execution of *CircleFormation* when the robots have a global x-axis agreement or the *target* fixed point does not belong to F_y.

2. **The robots do not have any global x-axis agreement and $f_i \in F_y$.** The following cases are to be considered:
   (a) $|B_i(t)| > 2$. Let $R_j \in B_i(t)$ be the robot that has the maximum rank. The robots would execute $DownwardMovement(R_j)$.
   (b) $0 < |B_i(t)| \leq 2$. Let $\beta_a \in \mathcal{H}_1$ be the empty vertex of $\mathcal{P}_i$ that has the highest rank. Similarly, let β_b be such a vertex in $\mathcal{H}_2$. Assume that R_j and R_k are the robots that are at the closest distance from β_a and β_b, respectively. If $\mathscr{R}(R_j(t)\beta_a)$ is empty, then R_j would start moving towards β_a. Otherwise, $DownwardMovement(R_j)$ would be executed. Similarly, if $\mathscr{R}(R_k(t)\beta_b)$ is empty, then R_k would start moving towards β_b. Otherwise, $DownwardMovement(R_k)$ would be executed.
   (c) $|B_i(t)| = 0$ **and** $C(f_i, r)$ **is *imperfect*.** Let $\beta_a \in \mathcal{H}_1$ be the empty vertex of $\mathcal{P}_i$ that has the highest rank. Similarly, let β_b be such a vertex in $\mathcal{H}_2$. Let $R_j \in C(f_i, r)$ be such that $\gamma(R_j(t)) < \gamma(\beta_a)$ and $d(R_j(t), \beta_a)$ is minimum. If there is a tie, select the one that has the maximum rank. Let R_k be such an robot for the vertex β_b. R_j would move towards β_a along $\overline{R_j(t)\beta_a}$. Similarly, R_k would move towards β_b along $\overline{R_k(t)\beta_b}$.
   (d) $|B_i(t)| = 0$ **and** $C(f_i, r)$ **is *perfect*.** Let $\beta_a \in \mathcal{H}_1$ be the empty vertex of $\mathcal{P}_i$ that has the highest rank. Similarly, let β_b be such a vertex in $\mathcal{H}_2$. Let $R_j \in R(t) \setminus A_i(t)$ such that $d(R_j(t), \beta_a)$ is minimum. If there is a tie, select the one that has the maximum rank. Assume that R_k be such a robot for β_b. If $\mathscr{R}(R_j(t)\beta_a)$ is empty, then R_j would start moving towards β_a along $\overline{R_j(t)\beta_a}$. Otherwise, R_j would move towards a_j along $\overline{R_j(t)a_j}$. Similarly, R_k would select its destination point and move towards it.

   If $R_j = R_k$ for any of the above cases, then R_j would select the *target* fixed point that lies at the closest distance from it. If there is a tie, it would select one of the *target* fixed point arbitrarily. Figure 7 depicts the transformations among the above mentioned cases.

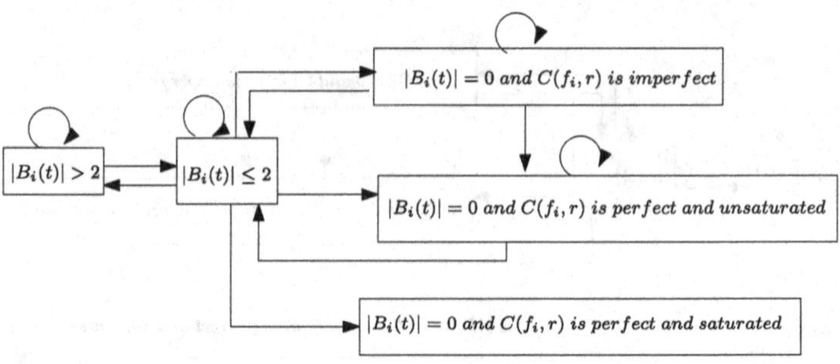

Fig. 7. A flow chart showing the transformations among the various cases during an execution of *CircleFormation* when the robots do not have any global x-axis agreement and the *target* fixed point belongs to F_y.

4.5 *AlgorithmFatRobot*

AlgorithmFatRobot is the proposed deterministic distributed algorithm that solves the *uniform k-circle formation* problem within finite time. If $C(t)$ is a *non-final* configuration, then *AlgorithmFatRobot*$(C(t))$ would be executed. Consider the following cases:

1. $C(t) \in \mathcal{I}_1$. Since F is asymmetric, the fixed points can be ordered. Let f be the topmost asymmetric fixed point. In case there are multiple such fixed points, select the one that has the minimum rank. The direction from the y-axis towards f is considered to be the positive x-axis direction. This is a global agreement. Let $f_i \in C(t)$ be the *unsaturated* fixed point that has the maximum rank. f_i is selected as the *target* fixed point. The robots would execute *CircleFormation*$(C(t), f_i)$.
2. $C(t) \in \mathcal{I}_2$. Let $f_a \in C_1(t)$ be the *unsaturated* fixed point that has the maximum rank. f_i is selected as the *target* fixed point in $C_1(t)$. Similarly, the robots would select a unique *target* fixed point (say f_b) in $C_2(t)$. The robots would execute *CircleFormation*$(C_1(t), f_a)$ and *CircleFormation*$(C_2(t), f_b)$.
3. $C(t) \in \mathcal{I}_3$. In this case, $F_y \neq \emptyset$. The following cases are to be considered:
   (a) **k is even and $C(t)$ is not an *unsafe* configuration.** Consider the following cases:
      (i) **$\exists f \in F_y$ such that f is *unsaturated*.** Let $f_j \in F_y$ be the topmost *unsaturated* fixed point. f_j is selected as the *target* fixed point. They would execute *CircleFormation*$(C_3(t), f_j)$.
      (ii) **$\forall f \in F_y$, f is *saturated*.** Let $f_a \in C_1(t)$ be the *unsaturated* fixed point that has the maximum rank. f_a is selected as the *target* fixed point in $C_1(t)$. Since the fixed points in $C_1(t)$ are orderable, f_a is unique. Similarly, the robots would select a unique *target* fixed point (say f_b) in $C_2(t)$. The robots would execute *CircleFormation*$(C_1(t), f_a)$ and *CircleFormation*$(C_2(t), f_b)$.
   (b) **$C(t)$ is an *unsafe* configuration.** If none of the *pivot* positions have been occupied, then the robots would execute *PivotSelection*$(C(t))$.

Next, consider the case when one of the *pivot* positions has been occupied. The direction from the y-axis towards the *pivot* robot is considered as the positive x-axis direction. This is a global agreement. Next, the algorithm proceeds similarly to the case when $C(t) \in \mathcal{I}_1$.

5 Correctness

In this section, the correctness of *AlgorithmFatRobot* is discussed. During an execution of *AlgorithmFatRobot*, the following points must be ensured:

1. *Solvability:* At time $t > 0$, $C(t) \notin \mathcal{U}$.
2. *Progress:* The *uniform k-circle formation* is solved within finite time.

Lemma 1. *If $C(0) \in \mathcal{I}_1 \cup \mathcal{I}_2 \cup \mathcal{I}_3$ and $C(0) \in \mathscr{I} \setminus \mathcal{U}$, then at any arbitrary point of time $t \geq 0$ during an execution of AlgorithmFatRobot, $C(t) \notin \mathcal{U}$.*

During an execution of algorithm *AlgorithmFatRobot*, a robot will move by either *PivotSelection* or *DownwardMovement* or *CircleFormation*.

Progress of First Kind: For some $R_j \in C(t)$, consider an execution of procedure *DownwardMovement*(R_j). Define $k_1(t) = d(R_j(t), p_j(t))$ and $k_2(t) = d(R_j(t), q_j(t))$. In case $|M_j(t)| > 0$, let $R_a \in M_j(t)$ be a robot that has the minimum rank. Define $d_1(t) = d(R_a(t), p_a(t))$. If $|M_j(t)| = 0$, then assume that $d_1(t) = 0$. Similarly, if $|N_j(t)| > 0$ then assume that $R_b \in N_j(t)$ be a robot that lies at the farthest distance from $R_j(t)$. Let $d_2(t) = d(R_b(t), q_a(t))$. If $|N_j(t)| = 0$, then assume that $d_2(t) = 0$. Define $W_1(t) = (k_1(t), |M_j(t)|, d_1(t))$ and $W_2(t) = (k_2(t), |N_j(t)|, d_2(t))$. In the time interval t to t', $W_i(t') < W_i(t)$ where $i \in \{1, 2\}$ if $W_i(t')$ is lexicographically smaller than $W_i(t)$. During an execution of *DownwardMovement*, the configuration is said to have *progress* of first kind in the time interval t to t' if either $W_1(t') < W_1(t)$ or $W_2(t') < W_2(t)$.

Lemma 2. *During the execution of DownwardMovement(R_j) for some $R_j \in C(t)$, let $t' > t$ be the point of time at which each robot has completed at least one LCM cycle. Progress of first kind is ensured in the time interval t to t'.*

Lemma 3. *Let $C(t) \in \mathcal{I}_3$ be an unsafe configuration. The pivot robot would be placed within finite time by the execution of PivotSelection$(C(t))$.*

Progress of Second Kind: Suppose R_j has been selected for movement towards a vertex $\beta_k \in \mathcal{P}_i$ during an execution *CircleFormation*$(C(t), f_i)$. For the configurations without any global x-axis agreement, there might be two such moving robots. In that case, both the robots would move towards different vertices of $\mathcal{P}_i$. First, consider the case when there is only one such robot. Let $n_i(t) = k - |C(f_i, r) \cap R(t)|$. Suppose $n(t)$ denotes the number of *unsaturated* fixed points. Let

$$E_j(t) = \begin{cases} d(R_j(t), \beta_k) & \mathscr{R}(R_j(t)\beta_k) \text{ is empty} \\ d(R_j(t), a_j) & \mathscr{R}(R_j(t)\beta_k) \text{ is non-empty} \end{cases}$$

Let $Z_j(t) = (n(t), n_i(t), E_j(t))$. In case there are two such moving robots, assume that R_a is the other robot that starts moving towards a vertex $\beta_b \in \mathcal{P}_i$. Similarly, define $E_a(t)$ and $Z_a(t) = (n(t), n_i(t), E_a(t))$. In the time interval t to t', $Z_i(t') < Z_i(t)$, where $i \in \{j, a\}$ if $Z_i(t')$ is lexicographically smaller than $Z_i(t)$. During an execution of $AlgorithmFatRobot$, the configuration is said to have *progress* of second kind in the time interval t to t', if either $Z_j(t') < Z_j(t)$ or $Z_a(t') < Z_a(t)$.

Lemma 4. *Let $C(t)$ be a given configuration. During the execution of the procedure $CircleFormation$, let $t' > t$ be an arbitrary point of time at which all the robots have completed at least one LCM cycle. In the time between t and t', either progress of first kind or progress of second kind is guaranteed.*

Lemma 5. *Let $C(0)$ be a given initial configuration. During the execution of $AlgorithmFatRobot$ collision-free movement is ensured by the robots.*

Theorem 2. *If $C(0) \in \mathscr{I} \setminus \mathcal{U}$, then the uniform k-circle formation problem is deterministically solvable by the execution of $AlgorithmFatRobot$.*

Conclusions

In this paper, we have investigated the *uniform k-circle formation* problem for transparent fat robots under asynchronous scheduler. The problem can be considered under various types of restricted visibility models, namely, obstructed visibility and limited visibility range. We have assumed that the robots have one-axis agreement. Another direction for future work would be to study the problem without the assumption of one-axis agreement.

References

1. Flocchini, P., Prencipe, G., Santoro, N. (eds.): Distributed Computing by Mobile Entities, Current Research in Moving and Computing, LNCS, vol. 11340. Springer, Cham (2019). https://doi.org/10.1007/978-3-030-11072-7
2. Cohen, R., Peleg, D.: Convergence properties of the gravitational algorithm in asynchronous robot systems. SIAM J. Comput. **34**(6), 1516–1528 (2005)
3. Czyzowicz, J., Gasieniec, L., Pelc, A.: Gathering few fat mobile robots in the plane. Theor. Comput. Sci. **410**(6–7), 481–499 (2009)
4. Suzuki, I., Yamashita, M.: Distributed anonymous mobile robots: formation of geometric patterns. SIAM J. Comput. **28**(4), 1347–1363 (1999)
5. Flocchini, P., Prencipe, G., Santoro, N., Widmayer, P.: Arbitrary pattern formation by asynchronous, anonymous, oblivious robots. Theor. Comput. Sci. **407**(1), 412–447 (2008)
6. Cicerone, S., Di Stefano, G., Navarra, A.: Asynchronous arbitrary pattern formation: the effects of a rigorous approach. Distrib. Comput. **32**(2), 91–132 (2019)
7. Fujinaga, N., Ono, H., Kijima, S., Yamashita, M.: Pattern formation through optimum matching by oblivious CORDA robots. In: Lu, C., Masuzawa, T., Mosbah, M. (eds.) OPODIS 2010. LNCS, vol. 6490, pp. 1–15. Springer, Heidelberg (2010). https://doi.org/10.1007/978-3-642-17653-1_1

8. Cicerone, S., Di Stefano, G., Navarra, A.: Embedded pattern formation by asynchronous robots without chirality. Distrib. Comput. **32**(4), 291–315 (2019)
9. Bhagat, S., Das, B., Chakraborty, A., Mukhopadhyaya, K.: k-circle formation and k-epf by asynchronous robots. Algorithms **14**(2), 62 (2021)
10. Das, B., Chakraborty, A., Bhagat, S., Mukhopadhyaya, K.: k-circle formation by disoriented asynchronous robots. Theor. Comput. Sci. **916**, 40–61 (2022)
11. Efrima, A., Peleg, D.: Distributed algorithms for partitioning a swarm of autonomous mobile robots. Theor. Comput. Sci. **410**(14), 1355–68 (2009)
12. Liu, Z., Yamauchi, Y., Kijima, S., Yamashita, M.: Team assembling problem for asynchronous heterogeneous mobile robots. Theor. Comput. Sci. **721**, 27–41 (2018)
13. Flocchini, P., Prencipe, G., Santoro, N., Viglietta, G.: Distributed computing by mobile robots: uniform circle formation. Distrib. Comput. **30**(6), 413–457 (2017)
14. Dieudonné, Y., Labbani-Igbida, O., Petit, F.: Circle formation of weak mobile robots. ACM Trans. Auton. Adapt. Syst. (TAAS) **3**(4), 1–20 (2008)
15. Feletti, C., Mereghetti, C., Palano, B.: Uniform circle formation for swarms of opaque robots with lights. In: Izumi, T., Kuznetsov, P. (eds.) SSS 2018. LNCS, vol. 11201, pp. 317–332. Springer, Cham (2018). https://doi.org/10.1007/978-3-030-03232-6_21
16. Dutta, A., Gan Chaudhuri, S., Datta, S., Mukhopadhyaya, K.: Circle Formation by asynchronous fat robots with limited visibility. In: Ramanujam, R., Ramaswamy, S. (eds.) ICDCIT 2012. LNCS, vol. 7154, pp. 83–93. Springer, Heidelberg (2012). https://doi.org/10.1007/978-3-642-28073-3_8
17. Biswas, M., Rahaman, S., Mondal, M., Gan Chaudhuri, S.: Multiple uniform circle formation by fat robots under limited visibility. In: 24th International Conference on Distributed Computing and Networking, pp. 311–317 (2023)
18. Jiang, S., Liang, J., Cao, J., Wang, J., Chen, J., Liang, Z.: Decentralized algorithm for repeating pattern formation by multiple robots. In: 2019 IEEE 25th International Conference on Parallel and Distributed Systems (ICPADS), pp. 594–601. IEEE (2019)
19. Cicerone, S., Di Fonso, A., Di Stefano, G., Navarra, A.: MOBLOT: molecular oblivious robots. In: Proceedings of the 20th International Conference on Autonomous Agents and MultiAgent Systems, pp. 350–358 (2021)
20. Agathangelou, C., Georgiou, C., Mavronicolas, M.: A distributed algorithm for gathering many fat mobile robots in the plane. In: Proceedings of the 2013 ACM Symposium on Principles of Distributed Computing, 2013, pp. 250–259 (2013)
21. Bose, K., Adhikary, R., Kundu, M.K., Sau, B.: Arbitrary pattern formation by opaque fat robots with lights. In: Changat, M., Das, S. (eds.) CALDAM 2020. LNCS, vol. 12016, pp. 347–359. Springer, Cham (2020). https://doi.org/10.1007/978-3-030-39219-2_28
22. Sharma, G., Alsaedi, R., Busch, C., Mukhopadhyay, S.: The complete visibility problem for fat robots with lights. In: Proceedings of the 19th International Conference on Distributed Computing and Networking, pp. 1–4 (2018)

Brief Announcement: Rendezvous on a Known Dynamic Point in a Finite Unoriented Grid

Pritam Goswami(✉), Avisek Sharma, Satakshi Ghosh, and Buddhadeb Sau

Jadavpur University, 188, Raja S.C. Mallick Rd, Kolkata 700032, India
{pritamgoswami.math.rs,aviseks.math.rs,satakshighosh.math.rs, buddhadeb.sau}@jadavpuruniversity.in

Abstract. In this paper, we have considered two fully synchronous $\mathcal{OBLOT}$ robots having no agreement on coordinates entering a finite unoriented grid through a door vertex at a corner, one by one. There is a resource that can move around the grid synchronously with the robots until it gets co-located with at least one robot. Assuming the robots can see and identify the resource, we consider the problem where the robots must meet at the location of this dynamic resource within finite rounds. We name this problem "Rendezvous on a Known Dynamic Point".

Here, we have provided an algorithm for the two robots to gather at the location of the dynamic resource. We have also provided a lower bound on time for this problem and showed that with certain assumptions on the waiting time of the resource on a single vertex, the algorithm provided is time optimal. We have also shown that it is impossible to solve this problem if the scheduler considered is semi-synchronous.

Keywords: Rendezvous · Finite Grid · Unoriented Grid · Dynamic Resource · Oblivious Robots

1 Introduction

Gathering (first introduced in [2]) is a classical problem studied in swarm robotics, where multiple computational entities (robots) need to move to a single point to exchange information. Rendezvous is a special case of gathering where only two robots are involved. The main motivation for gathering is to meet at a single point where the robots can exchange information. Now, let the information be stored at a single point or a set of points called resources in the environment, and the robots need to be on one of those resources to exchange information. In that case, the robots must gather at one of those specific points to exchange information. Now the question is, "What happens if the resource is also mobile?". This has been the main motivation behind the paper.

Now, it is quite obvious that the environment should be a bounded region; otherwise, it would be impossible to reach the resource. Also, for a bounded

S. Dolev and B. Schieber (Eds.): SSS 2023, LNCS 14310, pp. 374–379, 2023.
https://doi.org/10.1007/978-3-031-44274-2_27

region in a plane, finitely many point robots can't meet at the location of the resource, as there are infinitely many empty points where the resource can move to avoid the meeting. Thus, it is natural to consider this problem for a bounded network. A finite grid is a widely used network in various fields and has many real-life applications. For that reason, we have considered a finite grid as the environment in this work.

This work assumes that two fully synchronous robots enter a finite, unoriented grid one by one through a door at a corner of the grid. They know the current location of the meeting point (i.e., they can see and identify the resource). A deterministic and distributed algorithm has been provided that solves the rendezvous problem on a known dynamic meeting point within $O(T_f \times (m+n))$ rounds, where T_f is the upper bound of the number of consecutive rounds the meeting point (i.e., the resource) can stay at a single vertex alone and $m \times n$ is the dimension of the grid. We have also shown that for solving rendezvous on a known dynamic point on a finite grid of dimension $m \times n$ at least $\Omega(m+n)$ epochs are necessary, and proved that solving rendezvous on a known dynamic point on a finite grid is impossible if the scheduler considered is semi-synchronous, so a fully synchronous scheduler has been considered in this work.

2 Model and Problem Definition

2.1 Model

Let $G = (V, E)$ be a graph embedded on an euclidean plane where $V = \{(i, j) \in \mathbb{R}^2 : i, j \in \mathbb{Z}, 0 \leq i < n, 0 \leq j < m\}$ and there is an edge $e \in E$ between two vertices, say (i_1, j_1) and (i_2, j_2), only if either $i_1 = i_2$ and $|j_1 - j_2| = 1$ or $j_1 = j_2$ and $|i_1 - i_2| = 1$. We call this graph a finite grid of dimension $m \times n$. Though the graph is defined here using coordinates, the robots have no perception of these coordinates, which makes this grid unoriented. A corner vertex is a vertex of G of degree two. A vertex is called a boundary if either the degree of that vertex is three or the vertex is a corner. G has four corner vertices, among which exactly one corner vertex has a door. This vertex having a door is called the *door vertex*. Robots can enter the grid by entering through that door one by one. There is a movable resource (which we can think of as another robot doing some other task in the environment), initially placed arbitrarily at a vertex g_0 (g_0 is not the door) of G. The resource moves synchronously with the robots. i.e., in a round, if the resource moves, it must move to one of its adjacent vertices. The resource can stay at a single vertex for infinitely many consecutive rounds only if it is co-located with at least one robot. Otherwise, it cannot stay alone at a single vertex for more than T_f consecutive rounds. Also, it is assumed that the resource cannot cross a robot on an edge without colliding. On such a collision, the colliding robot carries the resource to the robot's destination vertex and terminates.

We consider the weakest $\mathcal{OBLOT}$ robot model. In this model, the robots are considered to be points. They do not have persistent memory and communication capabilities. A robot can distinguish if a vertex is on the boundary or a corner of the grid. Also, a robot can identify the door only if it is on the door vertex. A robot can distinguish the resource. Also, the robots are capable of detecting whether a vertex contains one or more entities (i.e., robot and resource). This capability is known as weak multiplicity detection. Each robot has its own local coordinate system, but they do not agree on any global coordinate system.

The robots operate in a LOOK-COMPUTE-MOVE (LCM) cycle upon activation. In LOOK operation, it gets the position of the other robot and the resource as input. Then in COMPUTE operation, it runs the algorithm and gets an output. The output is a vertex, which can be its current position or any one of the adjacent vertices. Finally, during MOVE operation, the robot moves to the output vertex.

After completion of MOVE operation, the robot becomes idle until it is activated again. In this paper, we assume that the activation of robots is controlled by a fully synchronous ($\mathcal{FSYNC}$) scheduler. In this type of scheduler, the time can be divided into global rounds of equal duration, and at the beginning of each round, all robots are activated.

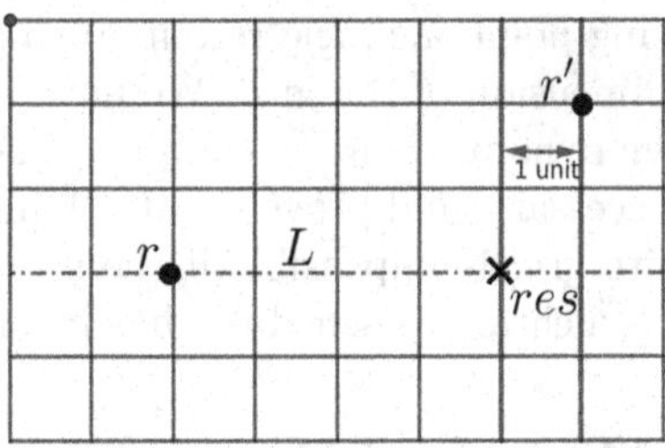

Fig. 1. Diagram of an INITGATHER CONFIGURATION

We now define a special type of configuration called INITGATHER CONFIGURATION (Fig. 1) which will be needed to describe the algorithm.

Definition 1 (InitGather Configuartion). *A configuration $\mathcal{C}$ is called a* INITGATHER CONFIGUARTION *if:*

1. *two robots, r and r', are not on the same grid line.*
2. *there is a robot r such that r and the resource res are on a grid line (say L).*
3. *the perpendicular distance of the other robot r' to the line passing through res and perpendicular to L is at most one.*

2.2 Problem Definition

Let G be a finite grid of dimension $m \times n$. Suppose there is a doorway in a corner of the grid through which two synchronous robots r_1 and r_2 can enter the grid. The robots can only identify the door if they are located on it. Consider a movable resource that is placed arbitrarily on a vertex of G. Both robots can see the resource. The resource will become fixed if at least one of r_1 or r_2 is on the same vertex as the resource. Now the problem is to design a distributed algorithm such that, after a finite execution, both robots gather at the vertex of the resource.

3 Some Results and Overview of the Algorithm

We start this section by describing some results. The first obvious observation is that for a $m \times n$ grid, at least $\Omega(m + n)$ rounds must be needed to solve this problem. Now we will discuss the impossibility result in the next theorem. which justifies our assumption of considering a fully synchronous scheduler for the algorithm to work.

Theorem 1. *No algorithm can solve the problem of rendezvous on a known dynamic point on a finite grid of dimension $m \times n$ if the scheduler is semi-synchronous.*

We now describe the algorithm DYNAMIC RENDEZVOUS which solves the proposed problem under a fully synchronous scheduler. The main idea of the algorithm is to push the resource towards a corner before meeting it. The algorithm DYNAMIC RENDEZVOUS is executed in three phases. ENTRY PHASE, BOUNDARY PHASE and GATHER PHASE. The pseudocode of the algorithm is given below.

Algorithm 1: Dynamic Rendezvous

```
Input: A configuration C.
Output: A destination point of robot r.
if a robot, say r, is at a corner ∧ no robot terminates ∧ (there is no other robot on the
  grid ∨ another robot is adjacent to r ) then
    Execute ENTRY PHASE;
else
    if C is INITGATHER CONFIGURATION then
        Execute GATHER PHASE;
    else
        Execute BOUNDARY PHASE;
```

ENTRY PHASE: The robots move in the grid one by one through the door vertex and moves to an empty adjacent vertex of the door vertex. This phase ends when the two robots are located on the two adjacent vertices of the door vertex.

BOUNDARY PHASE: This phase starts after the ENTRY PHASE and terminates when the configuration becomes an INITGATHER CONFIGURATION. The main idea behind forming an INITGATHER CONFIGURATION is that it is easy to contain the resource in a bounded region while decreasing the area of the region eventually with such a configuration. This is necessary for the robots to meet the resource. Also in the next phase (called GATHER PHASE), when the robots leave their corresponding boundary, they lose the direction agreement. The INITGATHER CONFIGURATION helps the robots agree on a direction to move in.

Now, before describing this phase, let us define the distance of the resource *res* from the robot r as $dist(r)$. This phase starts after ENTRY PHASE. During this phase, if a robot r sees that no robots are terminated and for both the robots r and r', $dist(r)$ and $dist(r')$ are not zero, and if the vertex v along its boundary towards the resource is not a corner, then r moves to v only if it sees r' is also not adjacent to a corner. On the other hand, if r' is adjacent to a corner, then r moves to v only if $dist(r) \neq 1$. r also moves to v if $dist(r') = 0$ and $dist(r) > 1$. If a robot already terminates in this phase by meeting the resource, the other robot will then move to the meeting node via the shortest path, avoiding corners. If no robots terminate, we ensure that eventually the robots form an INITGATHER CONFIGURATION and then start the next phase.

Gather Phase: This phase is executed if the configuration is an InitGather Configuration.The main idea behind this phase is that the robots move, maintaining the InitGather Configuration and push the resource to a corner. During this phase, if the robot r is on the same line, say L, along with the resource res, then r moves along L towards res only if r is not adjacent to res or if res is at a corner and both r and r' are adjacent to res. On the other hand, if r is not on the same line as res, then r' must be on the same line as L along with res. In that case, r moves parallel to L towards res. In the worst case, if no robot terminates, in the penultimate configuration, the resource will be located at a corner, and the robots will be located on two adjacent vertices of that corner. In this configuration, the robots finally move and meet the resource at the corner. Now we have the following theorem that ensures the correctness of the algorithm Dynamic Rendezvous

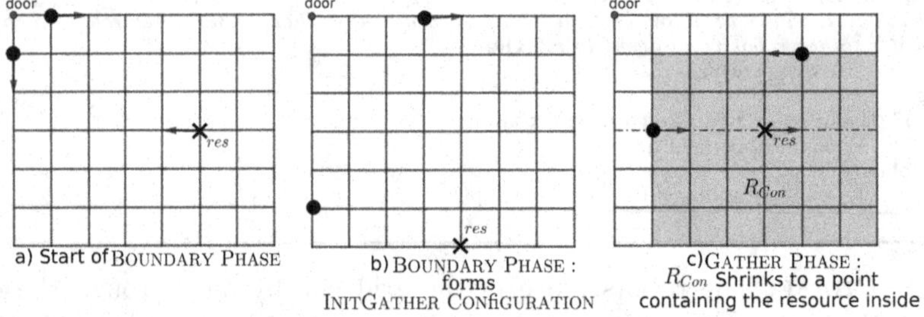

Fig. 2. a) After Entry Phase terminates robots start Boundary Phase. **b)** Robots forms InitGather Configuration to terminate Boundary Phase. **c)** Robots in Gather Phase moves such a way that res stays inside the shaded region called R_{Con} and it decrease to a point eventually.

Theorem 2. *Algorithm* Dynamic Rendezvous *terminates within* $O(T_f \times (m+n))$ *rounds.*

So if we assume T_f is constant then our algorithm becomes time optimal.

For the pseudo code of each of the phases along with detailed description and correctness proofs, check the full version of the paper [1].

4 Conclusion

The gathering is a classical problem. To the best of our knowledge, this is the first work that considers a known but dynamic gathering point. In this work, we have shown that it is impossible to solve this problem on a finite grid with two robots if the scheduler is semi-synchronous. So assuming a fully synchronous scheduler, we have provided a deterministic and distributed algorithm called Dynamic Rendezvous that solves the problem in $O(T_f \times (m+n))$ rounds. T_f

is the maximum number of consecutive rounds the resource can stay at a single vertex alone, and $m \times n$ is the dimension of the grid. In the future, it would be interesting to model this problem on different graphs and find out the minimum number of robots necessary to solve the problem on those graphs under different schedulers.

Acknowledgement. The first and second authors are supported by UGC, the Government of India. The third author is supported by the West Bengal State Government Fellowship Scheme.

References

1. Goswami, P., Sharma, A., Ghosh, S., Sau, B.: Rendezvous on a known dynamic point on a finite unoriented grid (2023). https://arxiv.org/abs/2301.08519
2. Suzuki, I., Yamashita, M.: Distributed anonymous mobile robots: formation of geometric patterns. SIAM J. Comput. **28**(4), 1347–1363 (1999). https://doi.org/10.1137/S009753979628292X

Brief Announcement: Crash-Tolerant Exploration by Energy Sharing Mobile Agents

Quentin Bramas[1(✉)], Toshimitsu Masuzawa[2], and Sébastien Tixeuil[3,4]

[1] ICUBE, Strasbourg University, CNRS, Strasbourg, France
bramas@unistra.fr

[2] Graduate School of Information Science and Technology, Osaka University, Osaka, Japan

[3] Sorbonne University, CNRS, LIP6, Paris, France

[4] Institut Universitaire de France, Paris, France

Abstract. This paper examines the exploration of a weighted graph by two mobile agents, where the energy cost of traversing an edge is equal to the edge weight. Agents located at the same position (potentially on an edge) can freely transfer energy, but one agent may unpredictably crash and cease operation. Two settings are considered: asynchronous, with no bound on the relative speed of the agents, and synchronous, with synchronized clocks and equal speeds. The study focuses ring networks and investigates the conditions for complete edge exploration based on the initial energy levels of the agents.

1 Introduction

Swarm robotics has led to numerous studies on the abilities of groups of autonomous mobile robots, or agents, with limited individual capabilities. These agents work together to accomplish complex tasks such as pattern formation, object clustering and assembly, search, and exploration. Collaboration offers several advantages, including faster task completion, the possibility of fault tolerance, and lower construction costs and energy efficiency compared to larger, more complex agents.

This paper examines the collective exploration of a known edge-weighted graph by mobile agents starting at arbitrary nodes. The goal is for every edge to be traversed by at least one agent, with edge weights representing their lengths. Each agent has a battery with an initial energy level, which may vary between agents. Moving a distance of x depletes an agent's battery by x.

A recently explored mechanism for collaboration among agents is the ability to share energy, allowing one agent to transfer energy to another when they meet. This capability opens up new possibilities for tasks that can be accomplished with the same initial energy levels. Energy-sharing capabilities enable graph exploration in situations where it would otherwise be impossible. On the other hand, an exploration algorithm with energy sharing must assign trajectories to

S. Dolev and B. Schieber (Eds.): SSS 2023, LNCS 14310, pp. 380–384, 2023.
https://doi.org/10.1007/978-3-031-44274-2_28

agents to collectively explore the entire graph and schedule achievable energy transfers, and is therefore more complex to design.

This paper introduces the possibility of an agent crashing, or ceasing to operate indefinitely and unpredictably. An exploration algorithm must now consider not only the feasibility of energy sharing, but also the feasibility of any plan that accounts for an agent crashing at any point in its prescribed algorithm.

Related Works. Energy transfer by mobile agents was previously considered by Czyzowicz et al. [1]. Agents travel and spend energy proportional to distance traversed. Some nodes have information acquired by visiting agents. Meeting agents may exchange information and energy. They consider communication problems where information held by some nodes must be communicated to other nodes or agents. They deal with data delivery and convergecast problems for a centralized scheduler with full knowledge of the instance. With energy exchange, both problems have linear-time solutions on trees. For general undirected and directed graphs, these problems are NP-complete.

Most related to our paper are the works by Czyzowicz et al. [2] and Sun et al. [3]. On the one hand, Czyzowicz et al. [2] study the collective exploration of a known n-node edge-weighted graph by k mobile agents with limited energy and energy transfer capability. The goal is for every edge to be traversed by at least one agent. For an n-node path, they give an $O(n+k)$ time algorithm to find an exploration strategy or report that none exists. For an n-node tree with ℓ leaves, they provide an $O(n+\ell k^2)$ algorithm to find an exploration strategy if one exists. For general graphs, deciding if exploration is possible by energy-sharing agents is NP-hard, even for 3-regular graphs. However, it's always possible to find an exploration strategy if the total energy of agents is at least twice the total weight of edges; this is asymptotically optimal. Sun et al. [3] examines circulating graph exploration by energy-sharing agents on an arbitrary graph. They present the necessary and sufficient energy condition for exploration and an algorithm to find an exploration strategy if one exists. The exploration requires each node to have the same number of agents before and after.

Our Contribution. We consider the problem of exploring every weighted edge of a given graph by a team of two mobile agents. To fully traverse an edge of weight x, the agent must spend energy x. Two agents located at the same location (possibly on an edge) may freely transfer energy in an arbitrary manner. However, we introduce the possibility for an agent to fail unpredictably and stop operating forever (that is, crashing).

In this context, we consider two settings: asynchronous (where no bound on the relative speed of the agents is known, so one agent cannot wait at a meeting point for another agent a bounded amount of time and deduce that the other agent is crashed, as it may just be arbitrarily slow), and synchronous (where the two agents have synchronized clocks and move at the exact same speed). We consider ring shaped networks, and study the necessary and sufficient conditions for full edge exploration solvability, depending on the initial energies allocated to each agent.

2 Model

Our model is similar to that proposed by Czyzowicz et al. [2], except that we simplify the edge weights to be strictly positive integers rather than real numbers. Also, we consolidate the model to accommodate agent crashes.

We are given a weighted graph $G = (V, E)$ where V is a set of n nodes, E is a set of m edges, and each edge $e_i \in E$ is assigned a positive integer $w_i \in \mathbb{N}^+$, denoting its weight (or length). We have k mobile agents (or agents) $r_0, r_1, \ldots, r_{k-1}$ respectively placed at some of the nodes $s_0, s_1, \ldots s_{k-1}$ of the graph. We allow more than one agents to be located in the same place. Each mobile agent (or agent for short) r_i initially possesses a specific amount of energy equal to en_i for its moves. An agent has the ability to travel along the edges of graph G in any direction. It can pause its movement if necessary and can change its direction either at a node or while traveling along an edge. The energy consumed by a moving agent is equal to the distance x it moved. An agent can move only if its energy is greater than zero. Now, the distance between two agents is the smallest amount of energy needed for them to meet at some point.

In our setting, agents can share energy with each other. When two agents, r_i and r_j, meet at a point (possibly in an edge) in the graph, r_i can take some energy from r_j. If their energy levels at the time of meeting are en'_i and en'_j, then r_i can take an amount of energy $0 < en \leq en'_j$ from r_j. After the transfer, their energy levels will be $en'_i + en$ and $en'_j - en$, respectively.

Each agent adheres to a pre-established trajectory until encountering another agent. At this point, the agent determines if it acquires energy, and calculates its ensuing trajectory. The definition of a trajectory depends on the synchrony model:

- **In the synchronous model**, a trajectory is a sequence of pairs $((u_0, t_0),$ $(u_1, t_1), \ldots)$, where u_i is a node, and t_i denotes the time at which the agent should reach u_i. For each $i \geq 0$, $t_i < t_{i+1}$, and u_{i+1} is either equal to u_i (*i.e.*, the agent waits at u_i between t_i and t_{i+1}), or is adjacent to u_i (*i.e.*, the agent leaves u_i at time t_i and arrives at u_{i+1} at time t_{i+1}). For simplicity, we assume in our algorithm that the moving speed in always one (it takes time d to travel distance d, so if $u_i \neq u_{i+1}$ and the weight between u_i and u_{i+1} is w, then $t_{i+1} - t_i = w$).
- **In the asynchronous model**, a trajectory is just a sequence of nodes $(u_0, u_1, u_2, \ldots)$, u_{i+1} being adjacent to u_i for each $i \geq 0$, and the times at which it reaches the nodes are determined by an adversary.

In other words, in the synchronous model, the agent controls its speed and its waiting time at nodes. The computation of the trajectory and the decision to echange energy is based on a localized algorithm (that is, an algorithm executed by the agent). Time can be divided into discrete rounds that correspond to the time instants where at least two agents meet. In a given execution, the configuration at round t is denoted C_t.

Localized Algorithm. A *localized algorithm* f_i executed by an agent r_i at time t takes as input the *past* of r_i and its collocated agents, and returns *(i)* a trajectory

$traj_i$, and *(ii)* the amount of energy $take_{i,j}$ taken from each collocated agent r_j. The past $Past_i(t)$ of Agent r_i at round t corresponds to the path already traversed by r_i union the past of all the previously met agents. More formally:

$$Past_i(t) = \{path_i(t)\} \cup \{Past_j(t') \mid r_i \text{ met } r_j \text{ at round } t' \leq t\}$$

A set of localized algorithms is *valid* for a given initial configuration c, if for any execution starting from c, agents that are ordered to move have enough energy to do so, and when an agent r_i takes energy from an agent r_j at round t, then r_j does not take energy from r_i at the same time.

In this paper, we introduce the possibility of agent crashes. At any point in the execution, an agent r_i may crash and stop operating forever. However, if r_i's remaining energy $en_i' > 0$, other agents meeting r_i may take energy from r_i for any purpose. Now, a set of localized algorithms is t-crash-tolerant if it is valid even in executions where at most t agents crash. We are interested in solving the following general problem of t-crash-tolerant collaborative exploration:

Crash-tolerant Collaborative Exploration. Given a weighted graph $G = (V, E)$ and k mobile agents $r_0, r_1, \ldots, r_{k-1}$ together with their respective initial energies $en_0, en_1, \ldots, en_{k-1}$ and positions $s_0, s_1, \ldots, s_{k-1}$ in the graph, find a valid set of localized algorithms that explore (or cover) all edges of the graph despite the unexpected crashes of at most $t < k$ agents.

3 Crash-Tolerant Algorithms for Two Energy-Sharing Agents in Ring Shaped Networks

Our algorithms are presented as a set of rules. Each rule is composed of a condition (that must be true to execute the rule action) and an action (the rest of the rule, that is executed when the condition is satisfied). Each action can be a move; an alternation of actions, depending on a Boolean condition ; or a waiting instruction (in the synchronous setting). There are two possible moves towards a target point p, one to move clockwise ($\circlearrowright (p)$) and the other to move counterclockwise ($(p) \circlearrowleft$). The Boolean condition $p_1 \prec p_2$ is true if and only if the point p_1 is closer than the point p_2.

Let $G = (V, E)$ be a ring graph. ℓ denotes the total weight of G, and d, resp. m, the weight of the shortest, resp. longest, path from r_0 to r_1. Consider that agents r_0 and r_1 are initially located at nodes s_0 and s_1 respectively. Without loss of generality, we can assume the shortest path from r_0 to r_1 is along the counterclockwise direction.

Asynchronous Rings. We show that an algorithm exists if and only if the following condition is satisfied: c_1: $(en_0 \geq d) \wedge (en_1 \geq d) \wedge (en_0 + en_1 \geq 2\ell)$. In this case the localized algorithms are the following:

r_0: $(r_1) \circlearrowleft$; $(s_0) \circlearrowleft$ r_1: $\circlearrowright (r_0)$; $\circlearrowright (s_1)$

In the above algorithms, when two agent meet, they share energy so that both have the same amount.

Lemma 1. *If condition c_1 holds, then if at most one agent crashes, two asynchronous agents executing localized algorithms prescribed above explore the entire ring. Otherwise, if c_1 does not hold, the problem is not solvable.*

Synchronous Rings. When the agents are synchronous, we show that one of the following conditions must be satisfied:

$$c_1 : (en_0 \geq d) \wedge (en_1 \geq d) \wedge (en_0 + en_1 \geq \ell + m)$$
$$c_2 : (en_0 \geq m) \wedge (en_1 \geq m) \wedge (en_0 + en_1 \geq \max(\ell + d, \ell + \tfrac{m}{2}))$$

For each condition, the corresponding actions are as follows:

Action a_1

r_0 : $(r_1)\curvearrowright$; $(s_0)\curvearrowright$

r_1 :
wait d *time units* r_0 **then**
| $(s_0)\curvearrowright$
timeout
| $\curvearrowleft(r_0)$
| **if** * **then** $s_0 \prec s_1$ $\curvearrowleft(s_0)$; $\curvearrowleft$ (s_1)
| **else** * $(s_1)\curvearrowright$; $(s_0)\curvearrowright$
end

Action a_2:

r_0 : $\curvearrowleft(r_1)$; $\curvearrowleft(s_0)$

r_1 :
wait m *time units* r_0 **then**
| $\curvearrowleft(s_0)$
timeout
| $(r_0)\curvearrowright$
| **if** * **then** $s_0 \prec s_1$ $(s_0)\curvearrowright$; $(s_1)\curvearrowright$
| **else** * $\curvearrowleft(s_1)$; $\curvearrowleft(s_0)$
end

In the above algorithms, when two agent meet, if the other agent is not crashed (yet), the agents share energy so that both have the same amount. Otherwise, if an agent r is crashed, then the other agent takes all the remaining energy from r.

Lemma 2. *If condition c_1, resp. c_2, holds, then if at most one agent crashes, two synchronous agents executing localized algorithms prescribed by action a_1, resp. a_2, explore the entire ring. If both conditions c_1 and c_2 are not satisfied, then the problem is not solvable.*

References

1. Czyzowicz, J., Diks, K., Moussi, J., Rytter, W.: Communication problems for mobile agents exchanging energy. In: Suomela, J. (ed.) SIROCCO 2016. LNCS, vol. 9988, pp. 275–288. Springer, Cham (2016). https://doi.org/10.1007/978-3-319-48314-6_18
2. Czyzowicz, J., et al.: Graph exploration by energy-sharing mobile agents. In: Jurdziński, T., Schmid, S. (eds.) SIROCCO 2021. LNCS, vol. 12810, pp. 185–203. Springer, Cham (2021). https://doi.org/10.1007/978-3-030-79527-6_11
3. Sun, X., Kitamura, N., Izumi, T., Masuzawa, T.: Circulating exploration of an arbitrary graph by energy-sharing agents. In: Proceedings of the 2023 IEICE General Conference, pp. 1–2 (2023)

Time-Optimal Geodesic Mutual Visibility of Robots on Grids Within Minimum Area

Serafino Cicerone[1], Alessia Di Fonso[1], Gabriele Di Stefano[1], and Alfredo Navarra[2(✉)]

[1] Dipartimento di Ingegneria e Scienze dell'Informazione e Matematica, Università degli Studi dell'Aquila, L'Aquila, Italy
{serafino.cicerone,alessia.difonso,gabriele.distefano}@univaq.it

[2] Dipartimento di Matematica e Informatica, Università degli Studi di Perugia, Perugia, Italy
alfredo.navarra@unipg.it

Abstract. For a set of robots disposed on the Euclidean plane, Mutual Visibility is often desirable. The requirement is to move robots without collisions so as to achieve a placement where no three robots are collinear. For robots moving on graphs, we consider the Geodesic Mutual Visibility (GMV) problem. Robots move along the edges of the graph, without collisions, so as to occupy some vertices that guarantee they become pairwise geodesic mutually visible. This means that there is a shortest path (i.e., a "geodesic") between each pair of robots along which no other robots reside. We study this problem in the context of square grids for robots operating under the standard Look-Compute-Move model. We add the further requirement to obtain a placement of the robots so as that the final bounding rectangle enclosing all the robots is of minimum area. This leads to the $\mathrm{GMV}_{\mathsf{area}}$ version of the problem. We show that $\mathrm{GMV}_{\mathsf{area}}$ can be solved by a time-optimal distributed algorithm for synchronous robots sharing chirality.

Keywords: Autonomous mobile robots · Oblivious robots · Mutual visibility · Grids

1 Introduction

One of the basic primitives required within the distributed computing for autonomous robots moving in the Euclidean plane is certainly the *Mutual Visibility*. Robots are required to move without collisions, i.e., no two robots must reach the same position at the same time, in order to achieve a configuration where no three robots are collinear.

Mutual Visibility has been largely investigated in the recent years in many forms, subject to different assumptions. We are interested in autonomous, identical and homogeneous robots operating in cyclic operations dictated by the well-known Look-Compute-Move model [11,12,15]. When activated, in one cycle a

The work has been supported in part by project SICURA – CUP C19C20000520004, and by the Italian National Group for Scientific Computation (GNCS-INdAM).

S. Dolev and B. Schieber (Eds.): SSS 2023, LNCS 14310, pp. 385–399, 2023.
https://doi.org/10.1007/978-3-031-44274-2_29

robot takes a snapshot of the current global configuration (`Look`) in terms of relative robots' positions, according to its own local coordinate system. Successively, in the `Compute` phase, it decides whether to move toward a specific direction, and in case it moves (`Move`).

Concerning Mutual Visibility, in [3], robots are assumed to be synchronous, i.e., they are always all active and perform each computational cycle within a same amount of time; in [6,13,17], semi-synchronous robots are considered, i.e., they are not always all active but all active robots perform their computational cycles within a same amount of time, after which a new subset of robots can be activated; in [1,4,5,13,16–18], asynchronous robots are considered, where each robot can be activated at any time and the duration of its computational cycle is finite but unknown. In most of the work, robots are assumed to have limited visibility but endowed with visible and persistent lights. More recently, in [1,18] robots are constrained to move along the edges of a graph embedded in the plane instead of freely moving in the plane. Still, Mutual Visibility is defined according to the collinearity of the robots in the plane.

The Complete Visitability problem concerns robots moving on the nodes of a graph that must rearrange themselves so that each robot has a path to all others without an intermediate node occupied by any other robot. In [2] this problem is introduced and studied in infinite square and hexagonal grids embedded in the plane. In [8], the Geodesic Mutual Visibility problem (GMV, for short) has been introduced. Two robots on a graph are defined to be mutually visible if there is a shortest path (i.e., a "geodesic") between them, along which no other robots reside. GMV requires that within finite time the robots reach, without collisions, a configuration where they all are in geodesic mutual visibility, i.e., they are pairwise mutually visible. In [8], GMV has been investigated when the underlying graph is a tree. The motivation for introducing GMV comes by the fact that once the problem is solved, robots can communicate in an efficient and "confidential" way, by exchanging messages through the vertices of the graph that are not occupied by other robots. Furthermore, once GMV is solved, a robot can reach any other one along a shortest path without collisions.

The geodesic mutual visibility has been investigated in [14] from a pure graph-theoretical point of view, to understand how many robots, at most, can potentially be placed within a graph G in order to guarantee GMV. The corresponding number of robots has been denoted by $\mu(G)$. It is shown that computing $\mu(G)$ in a general graph G is NP-complete, whereas there are exact formulas for special graph classes like paths, cycles, trees, block graphs, cographs, and grids [9,14].

In this paper, we solve GMV for robots moving on square grids embedded in the plane. Furthermore, we add the requirement to obtain a placement of the robots such that the final minimum bounding rectangle enclosing all the robots is of minimum area (this area-constrained problem is denoted as $\text{GMV}_{\mathsf{area}}$). First, we provide a time-optimal algorithm that is able to solve $\text{GMV}_{\mathsf{area}}$ in finite grid graphs. Furthermore, we provide useful hints to extend the algorithm to infinite square grids. The algorithm works for synchronous robots endowed with chirality (i.e., a common handedness), but without any explicit means of communication nor memory of past events, i.e., robots are oblivious and without lights.

2 The Robot Model and the Addressed Problem

An OBLOT system is composed by a set $R = \{r_1, r_2, \ldots, r_n\}$ of robots, that live and operate in graphs. Robots are viewed as points (they are **dimensionless**). They have the following basic properties: **identical** (indistinguishable from their appearance), **anonymous** (they do not have distinct ids), **autonomous** (they operate without a central control or external supervision), **homogeneous** (they all execute the same algorithm), **silent** (they have no means of direct communication of information to other robots), and **disoriented** (each robot has its own local coordinate system - LCS) but they share a common handedness, i.e., *chirality* is assumed. A robot is capable of observing the positions (expressed in its LCS) of all the robots. We consider synchronous robots whose behavior follows the sequential phases that form a so-called computational `LCM` cycle:

- `Wait`. The robot is idle. A robot cannot stay indefinitely idle.
- `Look`. The robot obtains a snapshot of the positions of all the other robots expressed in its own LCS.
- `Compute`. The robot performs a local computation according to a deterministic algorithm $\mathcal{A}$ (i.e., the robot executes $\mathcal{A}$), which is the same for all robots, and the output is a vertex among its neighbors or the one where it resides.
- `Move`. The robot performs a *nil* movement if the destination is its current location otherwise it instantaneously moves on the computed neighbor.

Robots are **oblivious**, that is they have no memory of past events. This implies that the `Compute` phase is based only on what determined in their current cycle (in particular, from the snapshot acquired in the current `Look` phase). A data structure containing all the information elaborated from the current snapshot represents what later is called the **view** of a robot. Since each robot refers to its own LCS, the view cannot exploit absolute orienteering but it is based on relative positions of robots. Hence, if symmetries occur, then symmetric robots have the same view. In turn, (i) the algorithm cannot distinguish between symmetric robots (even when placed in different positions), and (ii) symmetric robots perform the same movements. As chirality is assumed, and we are considering square grids embedded in the plane as field of movement, the only possible symmetries are rotations of 90 or 180°.

The topology where robots are placed on is represented by a simple, undirected, and connected graph $G = (V, E)$. A function $\lambda : V \to \mathbb{N}$ represents the number of robots on each vertex of G, and we call $C = (G, \lambda)$ a **configuration** whenever $\sum_{v \in V} \lambda(v)$ is bounded and greater than zero. A vertex $v \in V$ such that $\lambda(v) > 0$ is said *occupied*, *unoccupied* otherwise.

THE GMV PROBLEM.

- *Given a configuration $C = (G, \lambda)$ where each robot lies on a different vertex of the graph G, design a deterministic distributed algorithm working under the* `LCM` *model that, starting from C, brings all robots on distinct vertices – without generating collisions, in order to obtain the geodesic mutual visibility.*

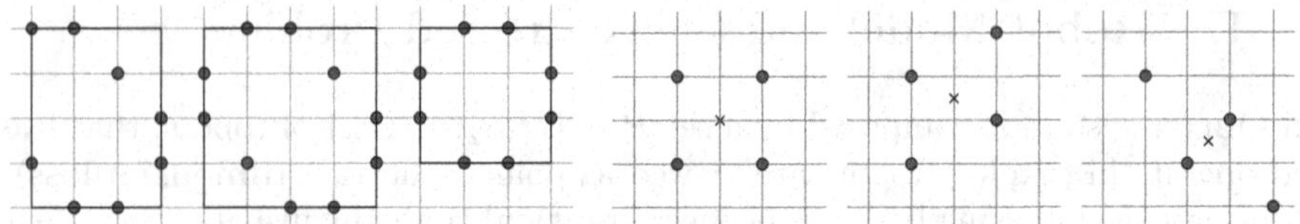

Fig. 1. *(first three)* Examples of $mbr(R)$; *(last three)* Examples for the notion of center of three rotational configurations: in order, $tc(C_1) = 1$, $tc(C_2) = 2$, and $tc(C_3) = 3$.

We study this problem in the context of square grids. We add the further requirement to obtain a placement of the robots such that the final minimum bounding rectangle enclosing all the robots is of **minimum area**. This area-constrained GMV problem is denoted as $\text{GMV}_{\mathsf{area}}$. We then provide a time-optimal algorithm – simply denoted as $\mathcal{A}$, that is able to solve $\text{GMV}_{\mathsf{area}}$ in finite grid graphs. Then, we provide some hints on how to extend the approach to infinite grids.

3 Notation and Preliminary Concepts

Let $C = (G, \lambda)$ be a configuration, with $G = (V, E)$. $R = \{r_1, r_2, \ldots, r_n\}$ denotes the set of robots located on C. As usual, $d(u, v)$ denotes the distance in G between two vertices $u, v \in V$. We extend the notion of distance to robots: given $r_i, r_j \in R$, $d(r_i, r_j)$ represents the distance between the vertices in which the robots reside. $D(r)$ denotes the sum of distances of $r \in C$ from any other robot, that is $D(r) = \sum_{r_i \in C} d(r, r_i)$. A square tessellation of the Euclidean plane is the covering of the plane using squares of side length 1, called tiles, with no overlaps and in which the corners of squares are identically arranged. Let S be the infinite lattice formed by the vertices of the square tessellation. The graph called infinite **grid graph**, and denoted by G_∞, is such that its vertices are the points in S and its edges connect vertices that are distance 1 apart. In what follows, G denotes a finite grid graph formed by $M \cdot N$ vertices (i.e., informally generated by M "rows" and N "columns"). By $mbr(R)$, we denote the **minimum bounding rectangle** of R, that is the smallest rectangle (with sides parallel to the edges of G) enclosing all robots (cf. Fig. 1). Note that $mbr(R)$ is unique. By $c(R)$, we denote the center of $mbr(R)$.

Symmetric configurations. As chirality is assumed, we already observed that the only possible symmetries that can occur in our setting are rotations of 90 or 180°. A rotation is defined by a center c and a minimum angle of rotation $\alpha \in \{90, 180, 360\}$ working as follows: if the configuration is rotated around c by an angle α, then a configuration coincident with itself is obtained. The **order** of a configuration is given by $360/\alpha$. A configuration is **rotational** if its order is 2 or 4. The **symmetricity** of a configuration C, denoted as $\rho(C)$, is equal to its order, unless its center is occupied by one robot, in which case $\rho(C) = 1$. Clearly, any asymmetric configuration C implies $\rho(C) = 1$.

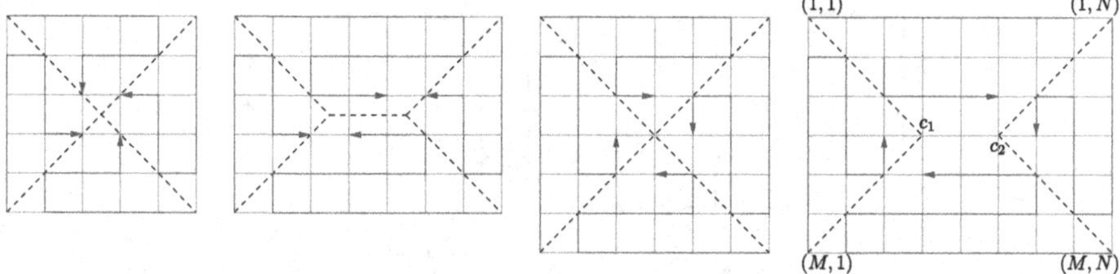

Fig. 2. Examples of special-paths with respect to different configurations.

The **type of center** of a rotational configuration C is denoted by $tc(C)$ and is equal to 1, 2, or 3 according whether the center of rotation is on a vertex, on a median point of an edge, or on the center of a square of the tessellation forming a grid, respectively (cf. Fig. 1).

THE VIEW OF ROBOTS. In $\mathcal{A}$, robots encode the perceived configuration into a binary string called **lexicographically smallest string** and denoted as $LSS(R)$ (cf. [7,12]). To define how robots compute the string, we first analyze the case in which $mbr(R)$ is a square: the grid enclosed by $mbr(R)$ is analyzed row by row or column by column starting from a corner and proceeding clockwise, and 1 or 0 corresponds to the presence or the absence, respectively, of a robot for each encountered vertex. This produces a string assigned to the starting corner, and four strings in total are generated. If $mbr(R)$ is a rectangle, then the approach is restricted to the two strings generated along the smallest sides. The lexicographically smallest string is the $LSS(R)$. Note that, if two strings obtained from opposite corners along opposite directions are equal, then the configuration is rotational, otherwise it is asymmetric. The robot(s) with **minimum view** is the one with minimum position in $LSS(R)$. The first three configurations shown in Fig. 1 can be also used for providing examples about the view. In particular: in the first case, we have $\rho(C) = 1$ and $LSS(R) =$ 0110 1001 1000 0100 0011; in the second case, we have $\rho(C) = 2$ and $LSS(R) =$ 00110 01001 10001 10010 01100; in the last case, we have $\rho(C) = 4$ and $LSS(R) =$ 0110 1001 1001 0110.

REGIONS. Our algorithm assumes that robots are assigned to **regions** of $mbr(R)$ as follows (cf. Fig. 2). If $mbr(R)$ is a square, the four regions are those obtained by drawing the two diagonals of $mbr(R)$ that meet at $c(R)$. If $mbr(R)$ is a rectangle, then from each of the vertices positioned on the shorter side of $mbr(R)$ starts a line at 45° toward the interior of $mbr(R)$ - these two pairs of lines meet at two points (say $c_1(R)$ and $c_2(R)$) which are then joined by a segment.

In each of the four regions, it is possible to define a **special-path** that starts from a corner v and goes along most of the vertices in the region. To simplify the description of such a path, assume that $mbr(R)$ coincides with a sub-grid with M rows and N columns, and the vertices are denoted as (i, j), with $1 \leq i \leq M$ and $1 \leq j \leq N$. The special-path that starts at $(1, 1)$ is made of a sequence of "traits" defined as follows: the first trait is $(1,1), (1,2), \ldots, (1, N-1)$, the second is $(2, N-1), (2, N-2), \ldots, (2, 3)$, the third is $(3, 3), (3, 4), \ldots, (3, N-3)$, and

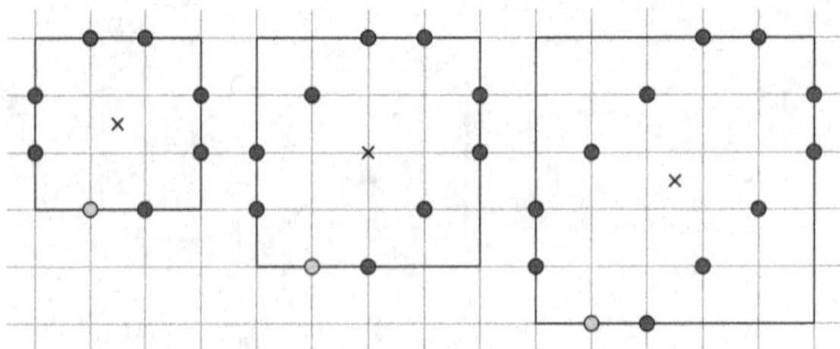

Fig. 3. Patterns F for asymmetric input configurations with $n = 8, 10, 12$ robots. For $n = 7, 9, 11$, the position represented in light gray is not considered in F. (Color figure online)

so on. This process ends after $\lfloor \min\{M, N\}/2 \rfloor$ traits are formed in each region, and the special-path is obtained by composing, in order, the traits defined in each region (see the red lines in Fig. 2).

4 A Resolving Algorithm for $\mathrm{GMV}_{\mathsf{area}}$

In this section, we present a resolution algorithm for the $\mathrm{GMV}_{\mathsf{area}}$ problem, when the problem concerns $n \geq 7$ fully synchronous robots endowed with chirality and moving on a finite grid graph G with $M, N \geq \lceil n/2 \rceil$ rows and columns. Note that, the constraint depends on the fact that on each row (or column) it is possible to place at most two robots, otherwise the outermost robots on the row (or column) are not in mutual visibility.

Our approach is to first design a specific algorithm $\mathcal{A}_{\mathsf{asym}}$ that solves $\mathrm{GMV}_{\mathsf{area}}$ only for **asymmetric configurations**. Later, we will describe (1) how $\mathcal{A}_{\mathsf{asym}}$ can be extended to a general algorithm $\mathcal{A}$ that also handles symmetric configurations, and (2) how, in turn, $\mathcal{A}$ can be modified into an algorithm $\mathcal{A}_{\infty}$ that solves the same problem for each input configuration defined on infinite grids.

THE PATTERN FORMATION APPROACH. $\mathcal{A}_{\mathsf{asym}}$ follows the "pattern formation" approach. In the general pattern formation problem, robots belonging to an initial configuration C are required to arrange themselves in order to form a configuration F which is provided as input. In [10] it is shown that F can be formed if and only if $\rho(C)$ divides $\rho(F)$. Hence, here we show some patterns that can be provided as input to $\mathcal{A}_{\mathsf{asym}}$ so that:

1. $\rho(C)$ divides $\rho(F)$;
2. if $\rho(C) \in \{2, 4\}$ then $tc(C) = tc(F)$;
3. the positions specified by F solve $\mathrm{GMV}_{\mathsf{area}}$.

The first requirement trivially holds since we are assuming that C is asymmetric and hence $\rho(C) = 1$. The second is required since the center of symmetric configuration is an invariant for synchronous robots. Concerning the last requirement, in Fig. 3 we show some examples for F when $7 \leq n \leq 12$. In [14], it is shown how F is defined for any n and it is also proved that the elements in these patterns always solve GMV for the grid G. Finally, since in F there are two robots per row and per column, and since in $mbr(F)$ all the rows and columns are occupied (for n even), it can be easily observed that F solves $\text{GMV}_{\textsf{area}}$.

4.1 High Level Description of the Algorithm

The problem $\text{GMV}_{\textsf{area}}$ is divided into a set of sub-problems that are simple enough to be thought as "tasks" to be performed by (a subset of) robots.

As a first sub-problem, the algorithm $\mathcal{A}_{\textsf{asym}}$ selects a single robot, called guard r_g, to occupy a corner of the grid G. As robots are disoriented (only sharing chirality), the positioning of the guard allows the creation of a common reference system used by robots in the successive stages of the algorithm. Given chirality, the position of r_g allows robots to identify and enumerate rows and columns. r_g is not moved until the final stage of the algorithm and guarantees that the configuration C is kept asymmetric during the movements of the other robots. Given the common reference system, all robots agree on the embedding of the pattern F, which is realized by placing the corner of F with the maximum view in correspondence with the corner of G in which r_g resides. This sub-problem is solved by tasks T_{1a}, T_{1b}, or T_{1c}. In task T_2, the algorithm moves the robots so as to obtain the suitable number of robots for each row according to pattern F, that is, two robots per row. The only exception comes when n is odd, in which case the last row will require just one robot. During task T_3, robots move toward their final target along rows, except for r_g. When T_3 ends, $n-1$ robots are in place according to the final pattern F. During task T_4, r_g moves from the corner of G toward its final target, placed on a neighbor vertex, hence leading to the final configuration in one step.

4.2 Detailed Description of the Tasks

In this section, we detail each of the tasks.

TASK T_1. Here the goal is to select a single robot r_g to occupy a corner of the grid G. This task is divided into three sub-tasks based on the number of robots occupying the perimeter – and in particular the corners, of G. Let RS be the number of robots on the sides of G, and let RC be the number of robots on the corners of G.

Task T_{1a} starts when there are no robots on the perimeter of G and selects the robot r_g such that $D(r)$ is maximum, with r of minimum view in case of ties. The planned move is m_{1a}: *r_g moves toward the closest side of G.* At the end of the task, r_g is on the perimeter of G.

Task T_{1b} activates when the following precondition holds:

$$\texttt{pre}_{1b} \equiv RS \geq 1 \wedge RC = 0.$$

In this case, there is more than one robot on the perimeter of G but none on corners. The task selects the robot r_g located on a side of G closest to a corner

Algorithm 1. MoveAlong special-path

```
Input: a configuration C
1: if p = 0 then
2:     Let S be the occupied special-path whose first robot has the minimum view.
3:     move: all the robots on a special-subpath and not on S move toward the neighbor
       vertex along the special-path.
4: if p = 1 then
5:     Let I be the fully-occupied special-path
6:     move: all the robots on a special-subpath and not on I move toward the neighbor
       vertex along the special-path
7: if p = 2 then
8:     move: the robot on a corner of G, with an empty neighbor, moves toward it.
```

of G, with the minimum view in case of ties, to move toward a corner of G. Move m_{1_b} is defined as follows: r_g *moves toward the closest corner of* G – arbitrarily chosen if more than one. At the end of task T_{1b}, a single robot r_g occupies a corner of the grid G. Task T_{1c} activates when the following precondition holds:

$$\mathtt{pre}_{1c} \equiv RC > 1.$$

In this case, all the robots on the corners but one move away from the corners. The moves are specified by Algorithm 1. This algorithm uses some additional definitions. In particular, a special-path is said **occupied** if there is a robot on its corner. A special-path is said to be **fully-occupied** if robots are placed on all its vertices. Given an occupied special-path P, a special-subpath is a fully occupied sub-path of P starting from the corner of P. Finally, p denotes the number of fully-occupied special-paths.

At line 1, the algorithm checks if there are no fully-occupied special-paths. In this case, there are at least two occupied special-paths. The robot, occupying the corner, with minimum view, is elected as guard r_g. The move is designed to empty all the other corners of G except for the one occupied by r_g. In each occupied special-paths, but the one to which r_g belongs to, the robots on the corners, and those in front of them along the special-paths until the first empty vertex, move forward along the special-path. At line 4, there is exactly one fully-occupied special path. Therefore, robots on the fully-occupied special-path are kept still. Concerning the other occupied special-paths, the robots on corners, and those in front of them until the first empty vertex, move forward along the special-path. At line 7 there are more than one fully-occupied special-path. In fact, this can occur only for a 4×4 grid G with two fully-occupied special-paths located on two successive corners of G. Therefore, there is a single robot r, on a corner of G, with an empty neighbor. Then, r moves toward that neighbor.

Note that, Algorithm 1 is designed so that, in a robot cycle, a configuration is obtained where exactly one corner of G is occupied.

Task T_2. In task T_2, the algorithm moves the robots to place the suitable number of robots for each row according to the pattern F, starting from the first row, while possible spare rows remain empty. At the end of the task, for each row corresponding to those of the pattern F, there are two robots, except when the number of robots n is odd, in which case in the last row is placed a single robot. The position of r_g allows robots to identify the embedding of F and hence the corresponding rows and columns. We assume, without loss of generality, that r_g is positioned on the upper-right corner of G. r_g identifies the first row. In this task, we define $c(r)$ and $l(r)$ the column and the row, respectively, where robot r resides. Columns are numbered from left to right, therefore $l(r_g) = 1$ and $c(r_g) = N$. Let t_l be the number of targets on row l in F, let $(t_1, t_2, \ldots, t_M)$ be the vector of the number of targets, and let $(\overline{r_1}, \overline{r_2}, \ldots, \overline{r_M})$ be the number of robots on each of the M rows of G.

For each row l, the algorithm computes the number of exceeding robots above and below l wrt the number of targets, to determine the number of robots that need to leave row l. Given a row l, let R_l be the number of robots on rows from 1 to $l-1$, and let R'_l be the number of robots on rows from $l+1$ to M. Accordingly, let T_l and T'_l be the number of targets above and below the line l, respectively. We define the subtraction operation $\dot{-}$ between two natural numbers a and b as $a \dot{-} b = 0$ if $a < b$, $a \dot{-} b = a - b$, otherwise. Concerning to the number of targets, given a row l, let B_l be the number of exceeding robots above l, l included, and let A_l be the number of exceeding robots below l, l included. Formally, $B_l = (R_l + \overline{r_l}) \dot{-} (T_l + t_l)$ and $A_l = (R'_l + \overline{r_l}) \dot{-} (T'_l + t_l)$.

Let $RD_l = \overline{r_l} - (\overline{r_l} \dot{-} B_l)$ be the number of robots that must move downward and $RU_l = \overline{r_l} - (\overline{r_l} \dot{-} A_l)$ be the number of robots that must move upward from row l. Task T_2 activates when precondition $\texttt{pre}_2$ becomes true:

$$\texttt{pre}_2 \equiv RC = 1 \wedge \exists\ l \in 1, \ldots, M : B_l \neq 0 \vee A_l \neq 0.$$

The precondition identifies the configuration in which the guard r_g is placed on a corner of G and there is at least a row in which there is an excess of robots. We define **outermost** a robot that resides on the first or the last column of G. Let U_l (D_l, resp.) be a set of robots on row l chosen to move upward (downward, resp.) and let U (D, resp.) be the list of sets U_l (D_l, resp.) with $l \in \{1, \ldots, M\}$. The robots that move upward or downward are chosen as described in Algorithm 2.

For each row l, at lines 4–7, the algorithm computes the number of exceeding robots B_l, A_l, and the number RD_l and RU_l of robots that must leave the row. Then, it checks whether the number M of rows of G is greater than the number k of rows of F. The algorithm selects RD_l robots to move downward, starting from the first column, and A_l robots to move upward, starting from the N-th column. Line 11 deals with the case in which $M = k$, the algorithm selects RD_l robots to move downward, starting from the second column and RU_l robots to move upward, starting from the $N-1$ column. This avoids the selection of robots that may move in one of the corners of G. At line 14, the algorithm checks if a robot r selected to move upward on row 2, occupies vertex $(2, 1)$. In the positive case, r is removed from U_2. This avoids r to move to a corner of G. At line 15, the algorithm returns the sets U of robots chosen to move upward for each row, and the sets D of robots chosen to move downward. Given a robot r on a row l, let *AlignedUp* (*AlignedDown*, resp.) be the boolean variable that is true when

Algorithm 2. SelectRobots

Input: $C' = (C \setminus r_g)$
Let $U = \{U_1, U_2, \ldots, U_M\}$ be a list of empty sets
Let $D = \{D_1, D_2, \ldots, D_M\}$ be a list of empty sets
for all $l \in (1 \ldots m)$ **do**
    $B_l \leftarrow (R_l + \overline{r_l}) \dot{-} (T_l + t_l)$
    $A_l \leftarrow (R'_l + \overline{r_l}) \dot{-} (T'_l + t_l)$
    $RD_l \leftarrow \overline{r_l} - (\overline{r_l} \dot{-} B_l)$
    $RU_l \leftarrow \overline{r_l} - (\overline{r_l} \dot{-} A_l)$
    if $M > \lceil n/2 \rceil$ **then**
        Let U_l be the set of RU_l robots of row l selected from right
        Let D_l be the set of RD_l robots of row l selected from left
    else
        Let U_l be the set of RU_l robots of row l from right and not outermost
        Let D_l be the set of RD_l robots of row l from left and not outermost
if $U_2 = \{r\}$ and $l(r) = 2$ and $c(r) = 1$ **then** $U_2 = \emptyset$
return U, D

there exists another robot r' such that $U_{l+1} = \{r'\}$ ($D_{l-1} = \{r'\}$, resp.) and $c(r) = c(r')$ holds. Let $t(r)$ be the target of a robot r defined as follows:

$$t(r) = \begin{cases} (l(r)+1, c(r)) & \text{if } r \in D_l \\ (l(r)-1, c(r)) & \text{if } r \in U_l \\ (l(r), c(r)-1) & \text{if } (\mathit{AlignedUp} \text{ or } \mathit{AlignedDown}) \text{ and } c(r) \geq N/2 \\ (l(r), c(r)+1) & \text{if } (\mathit{AlignedUp} \text{ or } \mathit{AlignedDown}) \text{ and } c(r) < N/2 \\ (2,2) & \text{if } RU_2 = 1 \text{ and } \exists! \text{ r on } l_2 \mid c(r) = 1 \text{ and } l(r) = 2 \\ (l(r), c(r)) & \mathit{otherwise} \end{cases} \quad (1)$$

The first two cases reported in the definition of Eq. (1) identify the target of robot r when is selected to move downward (upward, resp.). The target of r is one row below (above, resp.) its current position and on the same column. The third and the fourth cases refer to the occurrence in which there is a robot r_1, positioned in the same column of r, that is selected to move upward or downward. Then, the target of r is on a neighboring vertex, on the same row, closer to the center of G. The fifth case reports the target of a robot r when positioned on the second row and first column, and one robot is required to move on the first row. To avoid occupying a corner of G, the target of r is the neighboring vertex to r on its same row. In all other cases, the target of a robot r is its current position. Robots move according to Algorithm 3.

Each robot runs Algorithm 3 independently. At line 1, a robot calls procedure SelectRobots on $C' = \{C \setminus r_g\}$ and acquires the sets of robots selected to move upward and downward, respectively. At lines 2–3, a robot computes the targets of all the robots. At line 4, the robot checks if it is not selected to move upward and if any couple of robots have the same target. This test avoids collisions. Possible conflicting moves are shown in Fig. 4.(b). Two robots can have the same target when they are in the same column at distance two and the robot with

Algorithm 3. MoveRobot

Input: a configuration C, guard r_g
$U, D =$ SelectRobots($C \setminus r_g$)
for all robots r **do**
  Compute $t(r)$
if $r \notin U_{l(r)}$ or $\forall\, r_1, r_2,\, t(r_1) \neq t(r_2)$ **then**
  move to $t(r)$

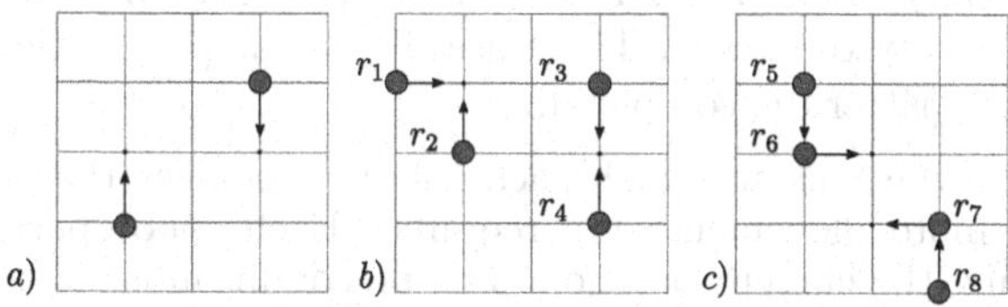

Fig. 4. The three possibile movement combinations as described in task T_2. Grey circles represent robots, arrows the direction of movements, small dots are robot targets. (Color figure online)

the smallest row index is selected to move downward, while the other upward. An example is shown in Fig. 4.(b) for robots r_3 and r_4. The only other possibile collision is for the robot r_1 having $t(r_1) = (2, 2)$ (case five in Eq. (1)). There might be a robot r_2 with $l(r_2) = 3$ and $c(r_2) = 2$ selected to move upward. This configuration is shown in Fig. 4.(b). In all these cases, to avoid any collision, the upward movement is performed only when there are no robots having the same target, otherwise the robot stays still. Each conflict is resolved in a robot cycle since downward and side movements are always allowed.

Figure 4 shows the three types of possible movements performed by robots. Robots move concurrently without collisions. Figure 4.(a) shows robots moving downward or upward and having different targets. Figure 4.(b) shows two robots having the same target. To resolve the conflict, the upward movement is stopped for a cycle. Figure 4.(c) shows the cases in which a robot is selected to move upward (r_8) or downward (r_5) on a target vertex that is already occupied by another robot (r_7, r_6 respectively). Robots r_5 and r_8 perform their move while r_6 and r_7 move on a neighboring vertex on the same row and closer to the center of G. Since movements are concurrent (robots are synchronous), collisions are avoided.

TASK T_3. This task is designed to bring $n-1$ robots to their final target except for r_g. This task activates when task T_2 is over, therefore $\texttt{pre}_3$ holds:

$$\texttt{pre}_3 \equiv RC = 1 \wedge \forall \text{ row } l : (B_l = 0 \wedge A_l = 0).$$

Given the embedding of F on G, in each row l, there are t_l targets and $\overline{r_l}$ robots, with $t_l{=}\overline{r_l}$, therefore robots identify their final target and move toward it without collisions. Given the particular shape of F, there are at most two targets per row, therefore we can state the move m_3 as follows: *for each row, the rightmost robot moves toward the rightmost target and the leftmost robot moves toward the leftmost target except for* r_g.

TASK T_4. During task T_4, the guard r_g moves from the corner of G and goes toward its final target. This task activates when $\texttt{pre}_4$ holds:

$$\texttt{pre}_4 \equiv n - 1 \text{ robots but } r_g \text{ match their final target.}$$

The corresponding move is called m_4 and is defined as follows: r_g *moves toward its final target.* The embedding of F guarantees that the final target of r_g is on its neighboring vertex on row 1. Therefore, in one step, r_g reaches its target. After task T_4, the pattern is completed.

TASK T_5. This is the task in which each robot recognizes that the pattern is formed and no more movements are required. Each robot performs the null movement keeping the current position. The precondition is

$$\texttt{pre}_5 \equiv F \text{ is formed.}$$

4.3 Formalization of the Algorithm

The algorithm has been designed according to the methodology proposed in [11]. Table 1 summarizes the decomposition into tasks for $\mathcal{A}_{\mathsf{asym}}$. To detect which task must be accomplished in any configuration observed during an execution, a **predicate** P_i is assigned to task T_i, for each i. P_i is defined as follows:

$$P_i = \texttt{pre}_i \wedge \neg(\texttt{pre}_{i+1} \vee \texttt{pre}_{i+2} \vee \ldots \vee \texttt{pre}_5).$$

The predicate is evaluated in the `Compute` phase, based on the view acquired during the `Look` phase. As soon as the robots recognize that a task T_i must be accomplished, move m_i – associated with that task, is performed by a subset of designed entities. In the `Compute` phase, each robot evaluates – for the perceived configuration and the provided input – the preconditions starting from $\texttt{pre}_5$ and proceeding in the reverse order until a true precondition is found. In case all predicates $P_5, P_4, \ldots, P_{1b}$ are evaluated false, then task T_{1a}, whose precondition is simply `true`, is performed. It follows that the provided algorithm $\mathcal{A}_{\mathsf{asym}}$ can be used by each entity in the `Compute` phase as follows:

- *if an entity executing the algorithm detects that predicate* P_i *holds, then it simply performs move* m_i *associated with* T_i.

4.4 Main Result

In the following, we state our main result in terms of time required by the algorithm to solve the problem $\text{GMV}_{\mathsf{area}}$. Time is calculated using the number of required `LCM` cycles given that robots are synchronous. Let L be the side of the smallest square that can contain both the initial configuration and target configuration. Note that, any algorithm requires at least $O(L)$ `LCM` cycles to solve $\text{GMV}_{\mathsf{area}}$. Our algorithm solves $\text{GMV}_{\mathsf{area}}$ in $O(L)$ `LCM` cycles which is time optimal. Our result is stated in the following theorem:

Table 1. Phases of the algorithm: the first column reports a summary of the task's goal, the second column reports the task's name, the third column reports the precondition to enter each task, the last column reports the transitions among tasks.

sub-problems	*task*	*precondition*	*transitions*
Placement of the guard robot	T_{1a}	true	T_{1b}
	T_{1b}	$RS \geq 1 \wedge RC = 0$	T_2, T_3, T_4
	T_{1c}	$RC > 1$	T_2, T_3, T_4
Bringing t_l robots or each row	T_2	$RC = 1 \wedge \exists\, l \in \{1 \ldots m\} : B_l \neq 0 \vee A_l \neq 0$	T_3, T_4
Bring $n-1$ robots to final target	T_3	$RC = 1 \wedge \forall$ row l $(B_l = 0 \wedge A_l = 0)$	T_4
Bring the guard robot to final target	T_4	$n-1$ robots on final target	T_5
Termination	T_5	F formed	T_5

Theorem 1. *$\mathcal{A}_{\mathsf{asym}}$ is a time-optimal algorithm that solves* GMV$_{\mathsf{area}}$ *in each asymmetric configuration C defined on a finite grid.*

The correctness of $\mathcal{A}_{\mathsf{asym}}$ is obtained by proving all the following properties: (1) for each task T_i, the transitions from T_i are exactly those declared in Table 1, (2) each transition occurs within finite time, (3) possible cycles among transitions are traversed a finite number of times, (4) the algorithm is collision-free. Actually, as the transitions reported in Table 1 do not constitute cycles, requirement (3) is automatically satisfied. Concerning the time required by $\mathcal{A}_{\mathsf{asym}}$, tasks T_{1a}, T_{1b} require $O(L)$ `LCM` cycle; T_{1c} requires one `LCM` cycle; T_2 and T_3 require at most $O(L)$ `LCM` cycles, and T_4 one `LCM` cycle.

5 Symmetric Configurations and Infinite Grids

In this section, we discuss (1) how $\mathcal{A}_{\mathsf{asym}}$ can be extended to a general algorithm $\mathcal{A}$ able to handle also symmetric configurations, and (2) how, in turn, $\mathcal{A}$ can be modified into an algorithm $\mathcal{A}_\infty$ that solves the same problem defined on the infinite grid G_∞.

We first explain how to solve symmetric initial configurations with $\rho(C) = 1$, then those with $\rho(C) \in \{2, 4\}$. If C is a symmetric configuration with $\rho(C) = 1$, then there exists a robot r_c located at the center c of C, and for $C' = \{C \setminus r_c\}$, $\rho(C') \in \{2, 4\}$. To make the configuration asymmetric, $\mathcal{A}$ moves r_c out of c. To this end, when r_c has an empty neighbor – arbitrarily chosen if more than one, then it moves toward it. Otherwise, all robots having either the same row or the same column as r_c move away from c to an empty vertex if it exists and a neighbor of r_c will eventually be emptied. If all the vertices on the same row and column of r_c are occupied, then all other vertices except one (if any) must be empty. Therefore the neighbor robots of r_c move toward a vertex placed on the right wrt c, if empty. After the synchronous move of all these robots, r_c has empty neighbors and it moves toward one of them, hence making the configuration asymmetric. Then, $\mathcal{A}_{\mathsf{asym}}$ runs on C and GMV$_{\mathsf{area}}$ is solved.

Consider now C with $\rho(C) \in \{2, 4\}$. Since robots in C are synchronous, irrespective of the algorithm operating on C, the center c of C is invariant, therefore robots agree on the embedding of F by identifying its center with c. F is suitably selected so that $\rho(F) = \rho(C)$, $tc(F) = tc(C)$, and the placement of robots in F solves $\text{GMV}_{\mathsf{area}}$. According to the embedding of F, robots also agree on how to subdivide G into $\rho(F)$ "sectors", i.e., regions of G which are equivalent wrt rotations. Since each sector contains a sub-configuration that is asymmetric wrt the whole configuration, then $\mathcal{A}$ instantiates $\mathcal{A}_{\mathsf{asym}}$ in each sector: a guard robot is chosen in each sector and the definitions of functions A_l, B_l, RD_l, and RU_l guarantee that the algorithm works in a sector of G since the number of exceeding robots is computed wrt the number of targets of F. Algorithm $\mathcal{A}_{\mathsf{asym}}$ requires slight adaptations to deal with sectors, e.g., concerning the movement of the guards toward their final target.

Concerning infinite grids, in order to obtain algorithm $\mathcal{A}_\infty$, it is sufficient to make small changes to tasks T_{1a}, T_{1b}, and T_4. In $\mathcal{A}_{\mathsf{asym}}$, task T_{1a} selects a single robot r_g to occupy a corner of G. Since G_∞ does not have corners, $\mathcal{A}_\infty$ selects r_g as in T_{1a} and then moves it to a distance $\mathcal{D} \geq 3 \cdot \max\{w(C'), w(F)\}$, where $C' = \{C \setminus r_g\}$, and $w(C')$, $w(F)$ are the longest sides of $mbr(C')$ and $mbr(F)$, respectively. In task T_{1b}, r_g must be chosen as the robot with distance $\mathcal{D}$ from C', and it moves toward a corner of C. In T_2, the first row is identified as the first row of C' occupied by a robot, approaching C' from r_g. The embedding on F is achieved by matching the corner of F with the maximum view in correspondence with the corner of C' on the first row and having the same column of r_g. Tasks T_2 and T_3 are unchanged, while in task T_4, r_g takes $\mathcal{D}$ `LCM` cycles to move toward its final target in F.

6 Conclusion

We have studied the Geodesic Mutual Visibility problem in the context of robots moving along square grids according to the `LCM` model. The considered robots are synchronous, oblivious and sharing chirality. We have shown that this problem can be solved by a time-optimal distributed algorithm even when a further optimality constraint is considered: when robots reach the geodesic mutual visibility, the bounding rectangle enclosing all the robots must have minimum area.

This work opens a wide research area concerning GMV on other graph topologies or even on general graphs. However, difficulties may arise in moving robots in presence of symmetries or without chirality. Then, the study of GMV in asymmetric graphs or graphs with a limited number of symmetries deserves main attention. Other directions concern the investigation on semi-synchronous or asynchronous environments.

References

1. Adhikary, R., Bose, K., Kundu, M.K., Sau, B.: Mutual visibility by asynchronous robots on infinite grid. In: Gilbert, S., Hughes, D., Krishnamachari, B. (eds.) ALGOSENSORS 2018. LNCS, vol. 11410, pp. 83–101. Springer, Cham (2019). https://doi.org/10.1007/978-3-030-14094-6_6

2. Aljohani, A., Poudel, P., Sharma, G.: Complete visitability for autonomous robots on graphs. In: International Parallel and Distributed Processing Symposium (IPDPS), pp. 733–742. IEEE (2018)
3. Bhagat, S.: Optimum algorithm for the mutual visibility problem. In: Rahman, M.S., Sadakane, K., Sung, W.-K. (eds.) WALCOM 2020. LNCS, vol. 12049, pp. 31–42. Springer, Cham (2020). https://doi.org/10.1007/978-3-030-39881-1_4
4. Bhagat, S., Gan Chaudhuri, S., Mukhopadhyaya, K.: Mutual visibility for asynchronous robots. In: Censor-Hillel, K., Flammini, M. (eds.) SIROCCO 2019. LNCS, vol. 11639, pp. 336–339. Springer, Cham (2019). https://doi.org/10.1007/978-3-030-24922-9_24
5. Bhagat, S., Mukhopadhyaya, K.: Optimum algorithm for mutual visibility among asynchronous robots with lights. In: Spirakis, P., Tsigas, P. (eds.) SSS 2017. LNCS, vol. 10616, pp. 341–355. Springer, Cham (2017). https://doi.org/10.1007/978-3-319-69084-1_24
6. Bhagat, S., Mukhopadhyaya, K.: Mutual visibility by robots with persistent memory. In: Chen, Y., Deng, X., Lu, M. (eds.) FAW 2019. LNCS, vol. 11458, pp. 144–155. Springer, Cham (2019). https://doi.org/10.1007/978-3-030-18126-0_13
7. Cicerone, S., Di Fonso, A., Di Stefano, G., Navarra, A.: Arbitrary pattern formation on infinite regular tessellation graphs. Theor. Comput. Sci. **942**, 1–20 (2023)
8. Cicerone, S., Di Fonso, A., Di Stefano, G., Navarra, A.: The geodesic mutual visibility problem for oblivious robots: the case of trees. In: Proceedings of the 24th International Conference on Distributed Computing and Networking (ICDCN), pp. 150–159. ACM (2023)
9. Cicerone, S., Di Stefano, G., Klavzar, S.: On the mutual visibility in cartesian products and triangle-free graphs. Appl. Math. Comput. **438**, 127619 (2023)
10. Cicerone, S., Di Stefano, G., Navarra, A.: Solving the pattern formation by mobile robots with chirality. IEEE Access **9**, 88177–88204 (2021)
11. Cicerone, S., Di Stefano, G., Navarra, A.: A structured methodology for designing distributed algorithms for mobile entities. Inf. Sci. **574**, 111–132 (2021)
12. D'Angelo, G., Di Stefano, G., Klasing, R., Navarra, A.: Gathering of robots on anonymous grids and trees without multiplicity detection. Theor. Comput. Sci. **610**, 158–168 (2016)
13. Di Luna, G.A., Flocchini, P., Chaudhuri, S.G., Poloni, F., Santoro, N., Viglietta, G.: Mutual visibility by luminous robots without collisions. Inf. Comput. **254**, 392–418 (2017)
14. Di Stefano, G.: Mutual visibility in graphs. Appl. Math. Comput. **419**, 126850 (2022)
15. Flocchini, P., Prencipe, G., Santoro, N. (eds.): Distributed Computing by Mobile Entities, Current Research in Moving and Computing, LNCS, vol. 11340. Springer, Cham (2019). https://doi.org/10.1007/978-3-030-11072-7
16. Poudel, P., Aljohani, A., Sharma, G.: Fault-tolerant complete visibility for asynchronous robots with lights under one-axis agreement. Theor. Comput. Sci. **850**, 116–134 (2021)
17. Sharma, G., Busch, C., Mukhopadhyay, S.: Mutual visibility with an optimal number of colors. In: Bose, P., Gąsieniec, L.A., Römer, K., Wattenhofer, R. (eds.) ALGOSENSORS 2015. LNCS, vol. 9536, pp. 196–210. Springer, Cham (2015). https://doi.org/10.1007/978-3-319-28472-9_15
18. Sharma, G., Vaidyanathan, R., Trahan, J.L.: Optimal randomized complete visibility on a grid for asynchronous robots with lights. Int. J. Netw. Comput. **11**(1), 50–77 (2021)

Privacy in Population Protocols with Probabilistic Scheduling

Talley Amir(✉) and James Aspnes

Yale University, New Haven, CT 06511, USA
{talley.amir,james.aspnes}@yale.edu

Abstract. The population protocol model [3] offers a theoretical framework for designing and analyzing distributed algorithms among limited-resource mobile agents. While the original population protocol model considers the concept of anonymity, the issue of privacy is not investigated thoroughly. However, there is a need for time- and space-efficient privacy-preserving techniques in the population protocol model if these algorithms are to be implemented in settings handling sensitive data, such as sensor networks, IoT devices, and drones. In this work, we introduce several formal definitions of privacy, ranging from assuring only plausible deniability of the population input vector to having a full information-theoretic guarantee that knowledge beyond an agent's input and output bear no influence on the probability of a particular input vector. We then apply these definitions to both existing and novel protocols. We show that the `Remainder`-computing protocol from [10] (which is proven to satisfy output independent privacy under adversarial scheduling) is not information-theoretically private under probabilistic scheduling. In contrast, we provide a new algorithm and demonstrate that it correctly and information-theoretically privately computes `Remainder` under probabilistic scheduling.

Keywords: Mobile ad-hoc networks · Population protocols · Information-theoretic privacy

1 Introduction

Various issues arise when applying the theoretical population protocol model to real-world systems, one of the most critical of which is that of preserving privacy. The motivation for furthering the study of privacy within population protocols is to better adapt these algorithms to the real-world systems that they aim to model, such as sensor networks, systems of IoT devices, and swarms of drones, all of which handle sensitive data. Previous research in private population protocols only considers adversarial scheduling, which makes generous assumptions about our obliviousness to the scheduler's interaction choices and offers only very weak criteria for satisfying the definition of "privacy". In this work, we further refine these definitions considering a realistic range of threat models and security concerns under arbitrary schedules.

S. Dolev and B. Schieber (Eds.): SSS 2023, LNCS 14310, pp. 400–413, 2023.
https://doi.org/10.1007/978-3-031-44274-2_30

1.1 Related Work

Research in private computation within ad hoc networks is distributed (pun intended) over multiple academic fields. We limit our review of the literature to works that most closely relate to the theoretical model we study in this paper.

Population Protocols. Privacy was introduced to the population protocol model in [10], where the authors define a notion of privacy called *output independent privacy* and provide protocols satisfying this definition for computing the semilinear predicates. Output independent privacy basically states that for any input vector and execution yielding a particular sequence of observations at an agent, there exists a different input vector and execution yielding the same sequence of observations at that agent. The practicality of this definition relies on adversarial scheduling, which allows the schedule of interactions to delay pairs of agents from interacting for an unbounded number of steps. Due to adversarial scheduling, the *existence* of an execution is sufficient to achieve plausible deniability: Agents have no metric for estimating time elapsed nor approximating how many interactions in which another agent has participated. Therefore, the observed state of an agent cannot be used to infer the agent's input as it may have deviated from its original state over the course of many interactions. However, if instead the scheduler is probabilistic, then there arises the issue of data leakage from inferring the population's interaction patterns.

Sensor Networks. Population protocols are designed to model sensor networks, but there is a large body of literature on sensor networks that is not connected to the population protocol model. The capacity of agents in the domain of sensor networks is much larger than is assumed in population protocols; in particular, much of the privacy-preserving algorithms in this area involve encryption, which requires linear state space in the size of the population.

In recent years, viral exposure notification via Bluetooth has become a popular area of study [7,9], and one that demands verifiable privacy guarantees due to widespread laws governing protected health data. However, the solutions in [7,9] require centralization and high storage overhead. The closely related problem of anonymous source detection is studied in [5,6]; however, these works require superconstant state space and only address this one task. Other research in wireless sensor networks investigates private data aggregation, which most closely resembles the goal of our research [8,12,15]. As before, these works require high computation and local memory as they implement their solutions using homomorphic encryption. Where alternative methods are used to avoid relying on encryption, a specialized network topology is needed for success [14] or only specific functions are computable [15].

While far from comprehensive, this sample of related works suggests that much of the research on privacy in wireless sensor networks is either limited by network topology or relies on computationally intensive encryption. For this reason, our goal is to develop privacy-preserving solutions for data aggregation in population protocols, bearing in mind the resource restrictions of the model.

1.2 Contribution

In this work, we study the privacy of population protocols in the random scheduling model. We demonstrate how existing privacy definitions fail under certain modelling assumptions, give new precise definitions of privacy in these settings, and offer a novel protocol in the uniform random scheduling population protocol model satisfying the new privacy definitions. In this work, we restrict our focus to computing the `Remainder` predicate. The proofs of all claims in this publication can be found in the extended version of our paper [1].

2 Preliminaries

A **population protocol** $\mathcal{P}$ is a tuple $(Q, \delta, \Sigma, \mathcal{I}, O, \mathcal{O})$ consisting of **state set** Q, **transition function** δ, **input set** Σ, **input function** $\mathcal{I}$, **output set** O, and **output function** $\mathcal{O}$ [3]. Protocols are run by a population, which consists of a set of n agents $\{A_j\}_{j=1}^n$ each with some input $i_j \in \Sigma$. At the start of the protocol, each agent converts its input to a state in Q via $\mathcal{I} : \Sigma \to Q$. In the early population protocol literature, $\mathcal{I}$ is only ever considered to be a deterministic function; however, in this work, we extend the model to allow for $\mathcal{I}$ to be randomized. The transition function $\delta : Q^2 \to Q^2$ designates how the agents update their states upon interacting with each other in pairs. As a shorthand for saying $\delta(q_1, q_2) = (q_1', q_2')$, we write $q_1, q_2 \to q_1', q_2'$ where δ is implied. The protocol aims to compute some function (whose output is in the output set O) on the initial inputs of the agents in the population. An agent's output value is a function of the agent's state, determined by $\mathcal{O} : Q \to O$.

The collection of agents' inputs is denoted as a vector $I \in \Sigma^n$, where each index of I reflects the input of a particular agent in the population. Adopting terminology from [10], we refer to I as an **input vector**. When the size of the state space is $O(1)$, the protocol cannot distinguish between two agents in the same state nor with the same input; therefore, we may want to refer to the multiset of input values in the input vector I, denoted multiset(I). After converting these inputs to elements of Q, the global state of the population is called a **configuration** and is represented as a vector $C \in Q^n$, where the i-th entry of the vector denotes the state of the i-th agent. Abusing notation, we say that $\mathcal{I}(I) = \langle \mathcal{I}(i_j) \rangle_{j=1}^n$ is the configuration resulting from applying the input function $\mathcal{I}$ to each of the agent inputs in $I = \langle i_j \rangle_{j=1}^n$.

Agents update their states via interactions with one another which are performed at discrete intervals, called **steps**. At each step, an ordered pair of agents (A_i, A_j) is selected from the population by the **scheduler**. To distinguish between the two agents in the ordered pair, we call the first agent the **Initiator** and the second the **Responder**. When an interaction takes place, the two selected agents update their states according to the transition function δ which may change the counts of states in the population, thereby updating the configuration. Let $\mathcal{C}$ be the configuration space, or the set of all possible configurations for a population of n agents with state space Q. We say that a configuration $D \in \mathcal{C}$ is **reachable** from $C \in \mathcal{C}$ via δ if there exists some series of ordered agent pairs such that starting from C, if the configuration is updated according to δ on those ordered pairs, then the resulting configuration is D [3]. If D is reachable from C, then we write $C \to D$. The infinite sequence of configurations resulting from the scheduler's infinite choice of interaction pairs is called an **execution**. An execution of a protocol is said to **converge** at a step τ when, for every step $t > \tau$, the output of each agent's state at t is the same as it is at τ (i.e. the output of every agent converges to some value and never changes thereafter). A stronger notion of termination is for a protocol to **stabilize**, meaning that after reaching some configuration C^*, the only configurations reachable from C^* result in the same outputs at every agent as in C^*. Abusing notation, we say $\mathcal{O}(C) = \lambda$ (or, the output of the *configuration* is λ) if $\mathcal{O}(q_j) = \lambda$ for every $q_j \in C$.

The goal of the population is to compute some function Φ on the input vector I, which means that the population eventually stabilizes towards a set of configurations $\mathcal{D} \subseteq \mathcal{C}$ for which $\mathcal{O}(D) = \Phi(I)$ for all $D \in \mathcal{D}$. The results of our work are commensurable with those of [10] which demonstrate that the semilinear predicates, which can be expressed using `Threshold` and `Remainder`, can be computed with output independent privacy under adversarial scheduling. Our work focuses on `Remainder`, defined for population protocols as follows:

Definition 1. *Given positive integers k and n, non-negative integer $r < k$, and input vector $I \in \mathbb{Z}_k^n$, let* `Remainder`$(I) = $ TRUE *iff* $\sum_{j=1}^{n} i_j \equiv r \pmod{k}$.

The scheduler determines the pair of agents that interact at each step. The scheduler's choice of agent pairs may either be adversarial or probabilistic. An **adversarial scheduler** chooses pairs of agents to interact at each step as it desires, subject to a fairness condition. The condition used most commonly is called **strong global fairness**, and it states that if some configuration C occurs infinitely often, and $C \to C'$, then C' must occur infinitely often as well [3]. This means that if some configuration *can* occur, it eventually *must* occur, even if the adversarial scheduler wishes to delay its occurrence indefinitely. In works adopting adversarial scheduling, it can be claimed that a protocol eventually stabilizes to the correct answer, but not how quickly. A random or **probabilistic scheduler** instead selects pairs of agents to interact with one another according to some fixed probability distribution (usually uniform) over the ordered pairs of agents. Although population protocols consider interactions to occur in sequence, the systems they model typically consist of agents participating in interactions in parallel. As such, a natural estimation of **parallel time** is to divide the total number of interactions by n, as this roughly estimates the expected number of interactions initiated by a particular agent in the population.[1]

Our work crucially relies on distinguishing between an externally visible component of the agent state and a concealable secret state. Adopting notation from [2], we let S be the **internal state** space and M the set of **messages** which can be sent between the agents. Since each agent has both an internal and external state component, the total state space is then the Cartesian product of these sets $Q = S \times M$. This means that δ is instead a function computed

[1] Under *non-uniform* random scheduling, this notion of time no longer applies.

locally at each agent according to its own state and the "message received" by its interacting partner $\delta : S \times M \times M \times \{\mathsf{Initiator}, \mathsf{Responder}\} \rightarrow S \times M$. This new mapping enforces the restriction that an agent can only use its received message to update its own state, and it does not observe the update to its interacting partner's state. For convenience, we use the original shorthand notation $\langle s_0, m_0\rangle, \langle s_1, m_1\rangle \rightarrow \langle s_0', m_0'\rangle, \langle s_1', m_1'\rangle$ to reflect the agents' state changes, where it is understood that the state update of A_b is computed independently of s_{1-b}.

3 Adversarial Model

In order to evaluate the extent to which private information can be learned by an observer in a population protocol, we must define the nature of the observer and its capabilities. In this work, we consider the agent inputs to be private information. We will consider the observer to take the form of an agent interacting in the protocol, meaning that it can observe the population only as other agents do, i.e., by participating in interactions as they are slated by the scheduler. However, we do not preclude the possibility that the observer may have greater computational capabilities than ordinary honest agents, and may therefore infer additional information from its observed history of interactions. We assume that the observer is **semi-honest**, meaning that it must adhere to the protocol rules exactly, but may try to infer additional knowledge from the system [11]. As such, the observer can only gather knowledge by interacting with other agents as prescribed by the transition function δ.

Since an observer presents as an agent in the population, we can imagine that multiple adversaries may infiltrate the system. However, we restrict that each observer be **non-colluding**, meaning that it cannot communicate with other nodes in the network besides participating in the protocol interactions honestly. This is because otherwise we could imagine that an observer may disguise itself as multiple agents in the population making up any fraction of the system. Although not studied within this work, it is of interest to find bounds on the fraction of agents that can be simulated by the observer in any network and still successfully hide honest agents' inputs. Notice that the restriction that the observer is both semi-honest and non-colluding is equivalent to assuming that there is only one such agent in the population, because from the point of view of the observer, all other agents appear to be honest.

Finally, we allow a distinction between externally visible messages and internally hidden states as in [2] to allow agents to conceal a portion of their states toward the end goal of achieving privacy. The distinction between messages and the internal state will be crucial to studying privacy in the population model as without it, there is no mechanism for hiding information from an observer.

4 Definitions of Input Privacy

In this section, we examine definitions of privacy in population protocols under adversarial and probabilistic scheduling given our specified adversarial model.

4.1 Output Independent Privacy

The privacy-preserving population protocol from [10] operates under the adversarial scheduling model and uses constant state-space. Therefore, [10] demonstrates privacy in the context of computing semilinear predicates only. The authors offer a formal definition of input privacy under these circumstances called **output independent privacy**, defined as follows:

> "A population protocol has this property if and only if there is a constant n_0 such that for any agent p and any inputs I_1 and I_2 of size at least n_0 in which p has the same input, and any execution E_1 on input I_1, and any T, there exists an execution E_2 on input I_2, such that the histories of p's interactions up to T are identical in E_1 and E_2".

Essentially, this definition states that a semi-honest process p cannot tell whether the input vector is I_1 or I_2 given its sequence of observations because either input could have yielded the same observations under an adversarial scheduler.

Output independent privacy is a successful measure in [10] because the scheduling in that work is assumed to be adversarial, therefore no inference can be made about the interaction pattern. The authors leverage this to achieve privacy which is best framed as "plausible deniability" – an agent may directly observe another agent's input, but the unpredictability of the scheduler disallows the observer to claim with certainty that the observed value is indeed the input.

This argument breaks down when the scheduler is probabilistic because now an agent can infer a probability distribution on the interaction pattern, and thus also infer a probability distribution on the input value of the agent's interacting partner. In light of this insight, we now introduce novel definitions for the purpose of assessing privacy in population protocols with probabilistic scheduling.

4.2 Definitions of Privacy Under Probabilistic Schedules

Consider an agent $\mathcal{A}$ with initial state $q_0^{\mathcal{A}} = (s_0^{\mathcal{A}}, m_0^{\mathcal{A}})$. Given its sequence of observed messages and the role (Initiator or Responder) played by $\mathcal{A}$ in each interaction, $\mathcal{A}$ can deterministically compute each of its subsequent state updates. Let's call these messages (observed by $\mathcal{A}$) $o_1^{\mathcal{A}}, o_2^{\mathcal{A}}, o_3^{\mathcal{A}}, ...,$ and denote by $q_\varepsilon^{\mathcal{A}} = \delta(\rho_\varepsilon^{\mathcal{A}}, s_{\varepsilon-1}^{\mathcal{A}}, m_{\varepsilon-1}^{\mathcal{A}}, o_\varepsilon^{\mathcal{A}}) = (s_\varepsilon^{\mathcal{A}}, m_\varepsilon^{\mathcal{A}})$ the updated state of $\mathcal{A}$, originally in state $q_{\varepsilon-1}^{\mathcal{A}} = (s_{\varepsilon-1}^{\mathcal{A}}, m_{\varepsilon-1}^{\mathcal{A}})$, upon interacting as $\rho_\varepsilon^{\mathcal{A}} \in \{\mathsf{Initiator}, \mathsf{Responder}\}$ with another agent with message $o_\varepsilon^{\mathcal{A}}$ in its ε-th interaction. Adopting notation from [11], we denote the **view** of an agent $\mathcal{A}$ participating in protocol $\mathcal{P}$ in an execution E by $\mathsf{view}_{\mathcal{A}}^{\mathcal{P}}(E) = \langle i_{\mathcal{A}}; q_0^{\mathcal{A}}; (\rho_1^{\mathcal{A}}, o_1^{\mathcal{A}}), (\rho_2^{\mathcal{A}}, o_2^{\mathcal{A}}), ...\rangle$. This view consists of $\mathcal{A}$'s input, the initial state of $\mathcal{A}$, and a list of $\mathcal{A}$'s interactions over the course of the execution, from which every subsequent state of $\mathcal{A}$ can be computed.[2]

Let $\boldsymbol{view}_{\mathcal{A}^{\mathcal{P}}(C)}$ be a random variable representing the view of agent $\mathcal{A}$ drawn uniformly from all realizable executions starting from configuration C resulting

[2] For randomized δ, we assume $\mathcal{A}$ has a fixed tape of random bits that it uses to update its state, so $\mathcal{A}$ can still reconstruct its entire view from the specified information.

from the possible randomness used by the scheduler. Similarly, let $\boldsymbol{view}_{\mathcal{A}}^{\mathcal{P}}(\boldsymbol{I})$ be a random variable representing the view of agent $\mathcal{A}$ drawn from all possible executions starting from any configuration C in the range of $\mathcal{I}(I)$ according to the probability distribution given by the randomness of $\mathcal{I}$. In general, we use the convention that random variables appear in mathematical boldface.

Privacy, like many other security-related key terms, has a wide range of technical interpretations. As such, we now offer several distinct formal definitions of privacy in the population model.

Plausible Deniability. Perhaps the weakest form of privacy we can possibly define is that of *plausible deniability*, meaning that an adversary always doubts its guess of an agent's input value (even if it has unbounded resources). This is not a novel concept [10,13], but in the context of input vector privacy for probabilistic population protocols, we define this notion as follows:

Let $\mathcal{M}_\lambda = \{\text{multiset}(I) : \Phi(I) = \lambda\}$ be the set of all distinct multisets of inputs whose corresponding input vector evaluates to λ,[3] and let $\mathcal{M}_\lambda^\kappa = \{\text{multiset}(I) : \text{multiset}(I) \in \mathcal{M}_\lambda \wedge \kappa \in \text{multiset}(I)\}$ be the set of all distinct multisets of inputs outputting λ which contain at least one input equal to κ.

Definition 2. *Let $\mathcal{P}$ be a population protocol on n agents with input set Σ and let $\mathcal{D}$ be any probability distribution on input vectors in Σ^n. Then $\mathcal{P}$ is* ***weakly private*** *if for every distribution $\mathcal{D}$ on Σ^n, every non-colluding semi-honest unbounded agent $\mathcal{A}$ in a population of size n executing $\mathcal{P}$, and for any view $V = \langle i; q; \{(\rho_\varepsilon^{\mathcal{A}}, o_\varepsilon^{\mathcal{A}})\}\rangle$ with output λ (as determined from the view V) and with $|\mathcal{M}_\lambda^i| > 1$, there exist I_1 and I_2 in $\mathcal{S}_\lambda$ such that*

1. *both* $\text{multiset}(I_1)$ *and* $\text{multiset}(I_2)$ *are elements of* $\mathcal{M}_\lambda^i$,
2. $\text{multiset}(I_1) \neq \text{multiset}(I_2)$, *and*
3. $\Pr(\boldsymbol{view}_{\mathcal{A}}^{\mathcal{P}}(\boldsymbol{I_1}) = V) = \Pr(\boldsymbol{view}_{\mathcal{A}}^{\mathcal{P}}(\boldsymbol{I_2}) = V)$,

where the probabilities in the final condition are taken over $\mathcal{D}$, the randomness of $\mathcal{I}$, and the uniform randomness of the scheduler.

In plain English, Definition 2 says that any agent participating in the protocol cannot simply guess the "most likely" input vector because for each such vector, pending certain circumstances, there exists a distinct input vector yielding the same views for that agent with the same probabilities. This definition differs from output independent privacy [10] in that it considers adversarial strategies for guessing the input vector which rely on distributional data collected from interactions with other agents.

The condition $|\mathcal{M}_\lambda^i| > 1$ necessitates that weak privacy may only hold for multisets of inputs for which plausible deniability is even possible. For example, if the output of the computation for the `Or` predicate is 0, then there is only one possible multiset of inputs that could have yielded this outcome, so there is no denying what the input vector must have been (namely, the all-zero vector).

[3] Recall that agents in the same state are indistinguishable by the protocol; therefore, Φ must map any input vectors with the same multiset of inputs to the same output.

Information-Theoretic Input Privacy. A stronger notion of privacy is one that claims that an observer cannot narrow down the possibility of input vectors at all based on its observations. This prompts our next definition.

Let $\mathcal{P}$ be a population protocol with input set Σ and let $\mathcal{D}$ be a probability distribution on input vectors in Σ^n. Let $\boldsymbol{I} \sim \mathcal{D}$ be a random variable representing the selected input vector. Additionally, let $\boldsymbol{i_\mathcal{A}}$ and $\boldsymbol{\lambda_\mathcal{A}}$ be random variables representing the input and output at agent $\mathcal{A}$, and let $\textbf{\textit{view}}^{\mathcal{P}}_{\mathcal{A}}(\boldsymbol{i}, \boldsymbol{\lambda})$ be a random variable representing the view of agent $\mathcal{A}$ participating in an honest execution of $\mathcal{P}$ that is consistent with a fixed input i at $\mathcal{A}$ and observed output λ.

Definition 3. *Protocol $\mathcal{P}$ satisfies **information-theoretic input privacy** if for every non-colluding semi-honest unbounded agent $\mathcal{A}$ and every input $i \in \Sigma$, output $\lambda \in O$, view V, input vector $I \in S_\lambda$, and distribution $\mathcal{D}$ on Σ^n,*

$$Pr(\boldsymbol{I} = I \mid \textbf{\textit{view}}^{\mathcal{P}}_{\mathcal{A}}(\boldsymbol{i}, \boldsymbol{\lambda}) = V) = Pr(\boldsymbol{I} = I \mid \boldsymbol{i_\mathcal{A}} = i, \boldsymbol{\lambda_\mathcal{A}} = \lambda),$$

where V is consistent with input i and output λ.

The above definition essentially states that conditioned on knowing one's own input and the output of the computation, the rest of the agent's view in the protocol's computation gives no advantage in guessing the input vector.

We offer another definition of privacy called **input indistinguishability** in the extended version of this paper that is independent of our main results.

Intuitively, it is straightforward to see that information-theoretic privacy is the strongest of the definitions discussed in this section (proof in full paper):

Theorem 1. *If $\mathcal{P}$ is information-theoretically private, then $\mathcal{P}$ also satisfies output independent privacy, weak privacy, and input indistinguishability.*

5 Private `Remainder` with Adversarial Scheduling

As a means for comparison, we analyze the `Remainder` protocol from [10], shown in Algorithm 1. The protocol does not distinguish between internal state space and message space, so the entirety of each agent's state is seen by its interacting partner. The agent states are tuples (v, f), initially $(i_j, 1)$, where v is the value of the agent and f is a flag bit denoting whether or not the agent has decided its output yet. The protocol accumulates the total sum (modulo k) of all agents' inputs by transferring values in units rather than in full in a single interaction. As shown in (M1), the protocol subtracts 1 (modulo k) from one of the inputs and adds it to the other input, maintaining the invariant that the sum of all the values in the population is the same at each step. Because all computations are done modulo k, (M1) can be repeated indefinitely. Transitions (M2) and (M3) handle the flag bit (where $*$ is a wildcard that can match any value), ensuring that (M1) occurs an unbounded but finite number of times. The output values are $\{\bot_0, \bot_1\}$, denoting that the predicate is FALSE or TRUE, respectively. The protocol converges when all but one agent has $\bot_0$ or $\bot_1$ as their value.

$$(v_1, 1), (v_2, 1) \rightarrow (v_1 + 1, 1), (v_2 - 1, 1) \quad \text{(M1)}$$
$$(*, 1), (*, *) \rightarrow (*, 0), (*, *) \quad \text{(M2)}$$
$$(*, 0), (*, 1) \rightarrow (*, 1), (*, 1) \quad \text{(M3)}$$
$$(v_1, 0), (v_2, 0) \rightarrow (v_1 + v_2, 0), (0, 0) \quad \text{(M4)}$$
$$(v_1, 0), (0, 0) \rightarrow (v_1, 0), (\bot_0, 0) \quad \text{(M5)}$$
$$(\bot_i, *), (*, 1) \rightarrow (0, 0), (*, 1) \quad \text{(M6)}$$
$$(r, 0), (\bot_i, 0) \rightarrow (r, 0), (\bot_1, 0) \quad \text{(M7)}$$
$$(v_1, 0), (\bot_i, 0) \rightarrow (v_1, 0), (\bot_0, 0), \text{ if } v_1 \neq r \quad \text{(M8)}$$

Algorithm 1: Output Independent Private Remainder [10]

The crux of the proof that Algorithm 1 satisfies output independent privacy focuses on transition (M1). When an adversarial process p interacts with an honest agent A in state (v, f), p cannot know how close v is to A's original input because, for $n \geq 3$, we can construct multiple executions wherein A has value v upon interacting with p. For example, we can construct an execution where some agent B transfers as many units to A via (M1) as needed to get A's value to be v, and as long as p and B do not interact with each other before p interacts with A, p's view is the same in this execution.

However, output independent privacy does not successfully carry over to the random scheduling model because we can no longer construct *any* execution "fooling" the process p, as some such executions are of very low probability. For instance, the probability that agents A and B interact v' times in a row, during which time p does not interact with B at all, becomes small for large values of v'. This means that it is less probable that an agent's value will deviate from its original input value early on in the execution.

6 Private Remainder with Probabilistic Scheduling

In this section, we introduce a novel algorithm for information-theoretically privately computing Remainder in the population protocol model with probabilistic scheduling. Our algorithm is inspired by the famous example of cryptographically secure multiparty computation of Remainder in a ring network. We refer to this algorithm as RingRemainder, and it works as follows:

There are n agents $A_1, ..., A_n$ arranged in a circle. Agent A_1 performs the leader's role, which is to add a uniformly random element $r \in \mathbb{Z}_k$ to their input and pass the sum (modulo k) to agent A_2. For each remaining agent A_i, upon receiving a value from A_{i-1}, A_i adds its own input to that value and passes the resulting sum to $A_{i+1 \pmod n}$. When A_1 receives a value from A_n, it subtracts r and broadcasts the result to everyone. Suppose the agents have inputs $i_1, ..., i_n$. Then A_1 sends $m_1 = i_1 + r$ to A_2, A_2 sends $m_2 = i_1 + r + i_2$ to A_3, and so on, until A_n sends $m_n = r + \sum_{j=1}^{n} i_j$ to A_1. Thus, the value broadcast to all agents $m_n - r$ is exactly equal to $\sum_{j=1}^{n} i_j$, the sum of the agents' inputs modulo k.

Assuming honest participants and secure pairwise communication, this protocol achieves information-theoretic input privacy (see extended paper for proof).

We now adapt this scheme to compute `Remainder` in the population model with information-theoretic privacy.

Algorithm Overview. Our protocol simulates the transfer of information exactly as in RingRemainder. We assume that the protocol has an initial leader with a special token that circulates the population. Each time an agent receives the token and some accompanying value, it adds its input to that value and passes the sum, along with the token, to another agent. This means the current owner of the token holds the aggregate sum of the agents' inputs who previously held the token. When an agent passes the token to another agent, it labels itself as "visited" so as to ensure that its input is included in the sum exactly one time. Once the token has visited all of the agents, it is returned to the leader (along with the total sum of all of the agents' inputs). In order to achieve this functionality, there are two crucial obstacles we must overcome:

First, we need a mechanism for securely transferring a message between two agents such that no other agent learns the message except the sender and the intended recipient. This task is nontrivial because population protocols do not allow agents to verify a condition before transmitting a message in an interaction; it is assumed that the message exchange and state update occur instantaneously. To do this, we provide a secure peer-to-peer transfer subroutine in Sect. 6.1.

Second, we need a way to determine whether or not every agent in the population has been visited by the token. When this happens, we want the final token owner to pass the token back to the leader so that the leader can remove the randomness it initially added to the aggregate that has been passed among the agents. We must try to prevent passing the aggregate back to the leader before all inputs have been incorporated into the aggregate as this would cause some agents to be excluded from the computation. In order to achieve this, we use the probing protocol from [4] which we describe in further detail in Sect. 6.2.

Leveraging these two subroutines, we design our main algorithm for computing `Remainder` with information-theoretic privacy in Sect. 6.3.

6.1 Secure Peer-to-Peer Transfer

In order for our algorithm to guarantee input privacy, the communication of the intermediate sums between any two agents must remain secure. Here we introduce a novel secure peer-to-peer transfer protocol, defined as follows:

Definition 4. *Let M be a message space, $\mathcal{D}$ be some distribution on M, and I be any fixed input vector in Σ^n. A* ***secure peer-to-peer transfer routine*** *is a protocol $\mathcal{P}$ that transfers data $m \xleftarrow{\mathcal{D}} M$ from one agent* Sender *to another* Receiver *such that there exist PPT algorithms W_1, W_2 where*

$$\Pr\left(W_1(\textit{\textbf{view}}^{\mathcal{P}}_{\mathsf{Sender}}(\boldsymbol{I})) = m\right) = \Pr\left(W_2(\textit{\textbf{view}}^{\mathcal{P}}_{\mathsf{Receiver}}(\boldsymbol{I})) = m\right) = 1$$

$$\langle \mu, (r, \mathfrak{S})\rangle, \langle *, (*, \bar{\mathfrak{u}})\rangle \to \langle \mu, (r', \mathfrak{S})\rangle, \langle *, (*, \bar{\mathfrak{u}})\rangle \quad \text{(S1)}$$
$$\langle \mu, (r, \mathfrak{S})\rangle, \langle *, (*, \mathfrak{u})\rangle \to \langle \bot, (\mu - r, \mathfrak{S}')\rangle, \langle r, (*, \mathfrak{R})\rangle \quad \text{(S2)}$$
$$\langle \bot, (x, \mathfrak{S}')\rangle, \langle y, (*, \mathfrak{R})\rangle \to \langle \bot, (\bot, \bar{\mathfrak{u}})\rangle, \langle x + y, (*, \mathfrak{S})\rangle \quad \text{(S3)}$$

Algorithm 2: Population Protocol for Secure P2P Transfer

and for all $i : A_i \notin \{\textsf{Sender}, \textsf{Receiver}\}$ and PPT algorithm W'

$$\Pr\left(W'(\textbf{\textsf{view}}^{\mathcal{P}}_{A_i}(\boldsymbol{I})) = m\right) = \Pr(m \overset{\mathcal{D}}{\leftarrow} M)$$

In other words, a secure peer-to-peer transfer routine allows a Sender to transfer a message m to a Receiver such that only Sender and Receiver are privy to m and all other agents cannot guess m with any advantage over knowing only the *a priori* distribution on the message space.

Our Algorithm 2 satisfies this definition: Each agent's state $\langle \mu, (r, L)\rangle$ consists of a hidden secret μ, and a public randomness value r and label L. The goal of the protocol is to pass a secret message from one agent (marked as Sender with label $\mathfrak{S}$, of which there may only be one in the population) to another agent meeting some specified criteria labeled by $\mathfrak{u}$, of which there may be any number (including zero). Until the Sender meets an agent with label $\mathfrak{u}$, it refreshes its randomness at each interaction to ensure that the randomness it transmits to the Receiver is uniform (S1). When the Sender finally meets some agent with $\mathfrak{u}$, it marks that agent as the Receiver and transmits r; it also updates its own token to $\mathfrak{S}'$ to remember that it has met and labeled a Receiver (S2). Then, the Sender waits to meet the Receiver again, at which point it gives it a message masked with the randomness it sent in the previous interaction and marks itself with the label $\bar{\mathfrak{u}}$ to signify the end of the transmission (S3). By the end of the protocol, exactly one agent is selected as the Receiver and stores μ internally. The protocol has state space $(\mathbb{Z}_k \cup \{\bot\})^2 \times \{\mathfrak{S}, \mathfrak{S}', \mathfrak{R}, \mathfrak{u}, \bar{\mathfrak{u}}\}$, which for constant k is of size $O(1)$. As such, we conclude (and prove in the extended paper):

Theorem 2. *Algorithm 2 is a secure peer-to-peer transfer routine.*

6.2 Probing Protocol

In order to adapt RingRemainder to the population protocol model, we need a way to detect when every agent has been included in the aggregation so the final sum can be passed back to the leader. To do this, we use a probe.

A **probing protocol**, or **probe**, is a population protocol that detects the existence of an agent in the population satisfying a given predicate [4]. In essence, the probe (initiated by the leader) sends out a 1-signal through a population of agents in state 0. If the 1-signal reaches an agent satisfying the predicate, that agent initiates a 2-signal which spreads back to the leader by epidemic. Higher number epidemics overwrite lower ones, so if some agent in the population satisfies π then the leader eventually sees the 2-signal. The probe, used in conjunction with the phase clock from the same work [4], allows the leader to detect the presence of an agent satisfying π in $O(n \log n)$ interactions using $O(1)$ states with probability $1 - n^{-c}$ for any fixed constant $c > 0$.

We define the "output" of the protocol (computed only at the leader) to be 0 for states 0 and 1, and 1 for state 2 (i.e. the leader's probe outputs 1 if and only if some agent in the population satisfies π). At the start of each round of the phase clock, agents reset their value to 0 and the leader initiates a new probe. Both the probe and the phase clock states are components of the message space, and the transitions for these subroutines are independent of the transitions for the main protocol, so we consider the two "protocols" to be taking place in parallel.

6.3 `Remainder` with Information-Theoretic Privacy

We provide here a novel algorithm which computes `Remainder` and achieves *information-theoretic input privacy* in the population protocol model with high probability, assuming a uniform random scheduler.

First, each agent applies the input function $\mathcal{I}$ to their input as follows:

$$\mathcal{I}(i_j, \ell) = \begin{cases} \langle i_j + r^0, (r^j, \mathfrak{S}, 1, Z = Z_0)\rangle & \ell = 1 \\ \langle i_j, (r^j, \mathfrak{u}, 0, Z = Z_0)\rangle & \ell = 0 \end{cases}$$

where r^j is drawn uniformly at random from $\mathbb{Z}_k$ for $j \in \{0, 1, ..., n\}$, and Z (initialized to Z_0) is a probe subroutine (including its associate phase clock). The input function assumes an initial leader, specified by $\ell = 1$. The components of the state $\langle \mu, (r, L, \ell, Z)\rangle$ are μ (the hidden internal component of the state called the **secret**), r (the **mask**), L (the agent's **label**), ℓ (the **leader bit**), and Z (the **probe**). The transitions describing the protocol can be found in Algorithm 3.

The general structure of the transitions from the secure peer-to-peer transfer protocol in Algorithm 2 is used to send the intermediate sums in (R1), (R2), and (R3). However, instead of just storing the message received, the Receiver computes the sum of the message and its own input and stores the result internally. Each subsequent Sender searches the population for an agent whose input has not yet been incorporated into the sum (signified by the $\mathfrak{u}$ state). When no one in the population has $\mathfrak{u}$ anymore, the probe detects this and outputs 1 at the leader from this point onward.

Although not shown, each interaction also performs an update to the probing subroutine by advancing the phase clock and probe at both agents in the interaction. When the probe begins to output 1, with high probability every agents' label is set to $\bar{\mathfrak{u}}$, alerting the leader to set its label to $\mathfrak{u}$. This makes the leader the only agent able to be the next Receiver. When the leader receives the final value stored at the Sender, the leader can place the answer into a separate portion of the external state (not shown in Algorithm 3) so that all other agents can copy it, which takes $O(n^2 \log n)$ additional steps with high probability. The leader must also have an additional component to its *hidden* state which stores the randomness used in its initial message transfer (also not shown in Algorithm 3).

$$\langle *, (r, \mathfrak{S}, *, *)\rangle, \langle *, (*, \bar{\mathfrak{u}}, *, *)\rangle \rightarrow \langle *, (r', \mathfrak{S}, *, *)\rangle, \langle *, (*, \bar{\mathfrak{u}}, *, *)\rangle \quad \text{(R1)}$$

$$\langle u, (r, \mathfrak{S}, *, *)\rangle, \langle v, (*, \mathfrak{u}, *, *)\rangle \rightarrow \langle \perp, (u - r, \mathfrak{S}', *, *)\rangle, \langle v + r, (*, \mathfrak{R}, *, *)\rangle \quad \text{(R2)}$$

$$\langle *, (x, \mathfrak{S}', *, *)\rangle, \langle y, (*, \mathfrak{R}, *, *)\rangle \rightarrow \langle *, (\perp, \bar{\mathfrak{u}}, *, *)\rangle, \langle x + y, (*, \mathfrak{S}, *, *)\rangle \quad \text{(R3)}$$

$$\langle \perp, (\perp, \bar{\mathfrak{u}}, 1, 1)\rangle, \langle *, (*, *, *, *)\rangle \rightarrow \langle \perp, (\perp, \mathfrak{u}, 1, 1)\rangle, \langle *, (*, *, *, *)\rangle \quad \text{(R4)}$$

Algorithm 3: Information-Theoretically Private `Remainder`

The correctness and privacy guarantees of Algorithm 3 are stated below (see extended paper for proofs):

Theorem 3. *For any fixed $c > 0$, Algorithm 3 computes* `Remainder` *in a population of size n in $\Theta(n^3 \log n)$ steps with probability at least $1 - n^{-c}$.*

Theorem 4. *When Algorithm 3 correctly computes the* `Remainder` *predicate, it satisfies information-theoretic input privacy.*

If the protocol fails due to a phase clock error in the probing subroutine, we actually do not know how much information is leaked by the protocol, though we suspect it to be limited. We designate this as outside of the scope of this work and only make claims about privacy when the protocol succeeds. Note that it is impossible to achieve information-theoretic privacy with probability 1 in asynchronous distributed systems because there is always the possibility of premature termination due to indefinite exclusion of agents from the protocol.

7 Conclusion

In this work, we offer various new security definitions in population protocols, such as multiple definitions of privacy which accommodate a range of threat models and scheduling assumptions, and a formal definition of secure peer-to-peer communication. We also develop algorithms solving secure pairwise communication in the model and information-theoretically private computation of the `Remainder` predicate. In order to show that we can achieve information-theoretic privacy (with high probability) for all semilinear predicates, as in [10], similar algorithms for computing `Threshold` and `Or` are also needed. We leave these problems as open for future work.

References

1. Amir, T., Aspnes, J.: Privacy in population protocols with probabilistic scheduling (2023). https://arxiv.org/abs/2305.02377
2. Amir, T., Aspnes, J., Doty, D., Eftekhari, M., Severson, E.: Message complexity of population protocols. In: 34th International Symposium on Distributed Computing (DISC 2020). Leibniz International Proceedings in Informatics (LIPIcs), vol. 179, pp. 6:1–6:18. Schloss Dagstuhl-Leibniz-Zentrum für Informatik, Dagstuhl, Germany (2020). https://doi.org/10.4230/LIPIcs.DISC.2020.6

3. Angluin, D., Aspnes, J., Diamadi, Z., Fischer, M.J., Peralta, R.: Computation in networks of passively mobile finite-state sensors. Proc. Annu. ACM Symp. Principles Distrib. Comput. **18**, 235–253 (2006). https://doi.org/10.1007/s00446-005-0138-3
4. Angluin, D., Aspnes, J., Eisenstat, D.: Fast computation by population protocols with a leader. Distrib. Comput. **21**, 183–199 (2006). https://doi.org/10.1007/s00446-008-0067-z
5. Aspnes, J., Diamadi, Z., Gjøsteen, K., Peralta, R., Yampolskiy, A.: Spreading alerts quietly and the subgroup escape problem. In: Roy, B. (ed.) ASIACRYPT 2005. LNCS, vol. 3788, pp. 253–272. Springer, Heidelberg (2005). https://doi.org/10.1007/11593447_14
6. Blazy, O., Chevalier, C.: Spreading alerts quietly: new insights from theory and practice. In: Proceedings of the 13th International Conference on Availability, Reliability and Security. ARES 2018, Association for Computing Machinery, New York, NY, USA (2018). https://doi.org/10.1145/3230833.3230841
7. Canetti, R., et al.: Privacy-preserving automated exposure notification. IACR Cryptology ePrint Archive **2020**, 863 (2020)
8. Castelluccia, C., Mykletun, E., Tsudik, G.: Efficient aggregation of encrypted data in wireless sensor networks. In: The Second Annual International Conference on Mobile and Ubiquitous Systems: Networking and Services, pp. 109–117 (2005)
9. Chan, J., et al.: PACT: privacy sensitive protocols and mechanisms for mobile contact tracing (2020)
10. Delporte-Gallet, C., Fauconnier, H., Guerraoui, R., Ruppert, E.: Secretive birds: privacy in population protocols. In: Tovar, E., Tsigas, P., Fouchal, H. (eds.) OPODIS 2007. LNCS, vol. 4878, pp. 329–342. Springer, Heidelberg (2007). https://doi.org/10.1007/978-3-540-77096-1_24
11. Lindell, Y.: How to simulate it – a tutorial on the simulation proof technique. In: Tutorials on the Foundations of Cryptography. ISC, pp. 277–346. Springer, Cham (2017). https://doi.org/10.1007/978-3-319-57048-8_6
12. Liu, C.X., Liu, Y., Zhang, Z.J., Cheng, Z.Y.: High energy-efficient and privacy-preserving secure data aggregation for wireless sensor networks. Int. J. Commun Syst **26**(3), 380–394 (2013). https://doi.org/10.1002/dac.2412
13. Monshizadeh, N., Tabuada, P.: Plausible deniability as a notion of privacy. In: 2019 IEEE 58th Conference on Decision and Control (CDC), pp. 1710–1715 (2019). https://doi.org/10.1109/CDC40024.2019.9030201
14. Setia, P.K., Tillem, G., Erkin, Z.: Private data aggregation in decentralized networks. In: 2019 7th International Istanbul Smart Grids and Cities Congress and Fair (ICSG), pp. 76–80 (2019). https://doi.org/10.1109/SGCF.2019.8782377
15. Taban, G., Gligor, V.D.: Privacy-preserving integrity-assured data aggregation in sensor networks. In: Proceedings of the 2009 International Conference on Computational Science and Engineering - Volume 03, pp. 168–175. CSE 2009, IEEE Computer Society, USA (2009). https://doi.org/10.1109/CSE.2009.389

Dispersion of Mobile Robots in Spite of Faults

Debasish Pattanayak[1], Gokarna Sharma[2(✉)], and Partha Sarathi Mandal[3]

[1] Université du Québec en Outaouais, Gatineau, Canada
[2] Kent State University, Kent, OH, USA
gsharma2@kent.edu
[3] Indian Institute of Technology Guwahati, Guwahati, India
psm@iitg.ac.in

Abstract. We consider the problem of *dispersion* that asks a group of $k \leq n$ mobile robots to relocate autonomously on an anonymous n-node m-edge graph of maximum degree Δ such that each node contains at most one robot. We consider the case where the robots may *crash* at any time. The objective is to minimize (or provide trade-off between) the time to achieve dispersion and the memory requirement at each robot. Following the literature, we consider the synchronous setting where time is measured in rounds. We present two deterministic algorithms for arbitrary graphs under *local communication* model in which only the robots at the current node can communicate. The presented algorithms are interesting since they trade-off one metric for the sake of another metric. Specifically, the first algorithm solves dispersion in $O(\min\{m, k\Delta\})$ rounds with $O(k \log(k + \Delta))$ bits memory at each robot, independent of the number of robot crashes $f \leq k$, whereas the second algorithm solves dispersion in $O(\min\{m, k\Delta\} \cdot (\ell + f))$ rounds with $O(\log(k + \Delta))$ bits memory at each robot; ℓ denotes the number of nodes with multiple robots positioned in the initial configuration. Both of the algorithms work without a priori knowledge on graph parameters m and Δ as well as problem parameters ℓ, k, and f. To the best of our knowledge, these are the first such bounds for dispersion under crash faults.

1 Introduction

How to disperse autonomous mobile robots or agents in a given region is a problem of significant interest in distributed robotics [15,16]. Recently, this problem has been formulated by Augustine and Moses Jr. [1] in a graph setting as follows: Given any arbitrary initial configuration of $k \leq n$ robots positioned on the nodes of an anonymous n-node m-edge graph G of maximum degree Δ, the robots reposition autonomously to reach a configuration where each robot is positioned on a distinct node of the graph; which we call the DISPERSION problem. See Fig. 1 for an example. This problem has many practical applications, e.g., in relocating self-driving electric cars (robots) to recharging stations (nodes), assuming that the cars have smart devices to communicate with each other to find a free/empty charging station [1,19,20,23]. This problem is also important due to its relationship to many other coordination problems including exploration, scattering, and load balancing, and self-deployment [1,19,20,23].

S. Dolev and B. Schieber (Eds.): SSS 2023, LNCS 14310, pp. 414–429, 2023.
https://doi.org/10.1007/978-3-031-44274-2_31

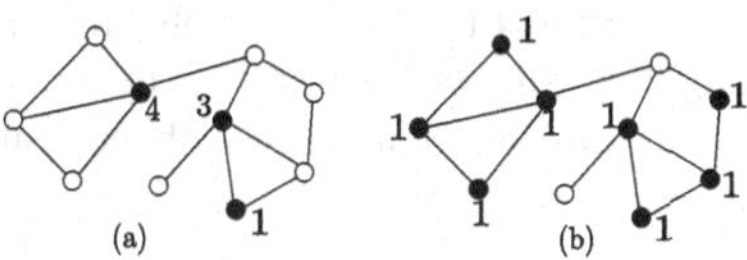

Fig. 1. The DISPERSION problem of $k = 8$ robots on a 10-node graph: (a) The initial configuration; (b) The final configuration with each node having at most one robot. Integers near nodes denote robot counts on those nodes.

The main objective is to simultaneously minimize (or provide trade-off between) two performance metrics that are fundamental to the problem: (i) *time* to achieve dispersion and (ii) *memory* requirement at each robot. DISPERSION has been studied significantly in a long series of works recently [1,7,14,17,19–24,26–28], considering both specific (such as trees) and arbitrary graphs as well as static and dynamic natures of the graphs [22]. However, most of these works focus consider fault-free robots, except [4,29] which provide partial solution under crash faults, assuming either (i) all k robots start initially from a single node ($\ell = 1$) or (ii) the algorithm is provided with a priori knowledge on graph as well as problem parameters m, Δ, ℓ, k, f, where $f \leq k$ denotes the number of robot crash faults. Under faults, DISPERSION is said to be achieved when $k - f$ non-faulty robots are positioned on $k - f$ different nodes of G. The following question naturally arises:

Starting from any arbitrary initial configuration and without a priori knowledge on parameters m, Δ, ℓ, k, f, is it possible to solve DISPERSION *on an anonymous graph G when $f \leq k$ robots may experience crash fault?*

In this paper, we answer this question in the affirmative providing two deterministic algorithms that solve DISPERSION on any anonymous graph, with robots starting from any initial configuration and without a priori knowledge on parameters m, Δ, ℓ, k, f.

Contributions. Graph G is anonymous, connected, undirected, and port-labeled, i.e., nodes have no unique IDs and hence are indistinguishable but the ports (leading to incident edges) at each node have unique labels in the range $[1, \delta]$, where δ is the degree of that node. The robots are distinguishable, i.e., they have unique IDs in the range $[1, k^{O(1)}]$. Nodes are memory-less but robots have memory. The setting is *synchronous* – all robots are activated in a round and they perform their operations in synchronized rounds. Runtime is measured in rounds (or steps). Additionally, we consider the standard *local communication* model, where the robots can only communicate with other co-located robots at the same node of G. We say that $f \leq k$ robots may experience crash fault at any time, meaning that they remain stationary, the information, if any, stored by them is lost, they lose their communication capability, and hence they can be treated as if they are vanished from the system. In the initial configuration, the robots may be positioned on one or more nodes. If the robots are on k different nodes in the initial configuration, DISPERSION is already achieved. Therefore, the interesting cases are those initial configurations in which the k robots are on $< k$ different nodes. Therefore, a graph node may have zero, one, or more robots in any initial configuration.

Table 1. Algorithms solving DISPERSION for $k \leq n$ robots on an anonymous n-node m-edge graph of maximum degree Δ for $f \leq k$ robot crashes. $^{\dagger}\ell$ is the number of multiplicity nodes in the initial configuration. Theorem 1 should be compared with the result of [24] whereas Theorem 2 should be compared with the second result of [4].

Algorithm	Memory/robot (in bits)	Time (in rounds)	$\ell^{\dagger}$	Faults	Knowledge of m, Δ, ℓ, k, f
Lower bound	$\Omega(\log(k+\Delta))$ [19]	$\Omega(k)$ [19]	$\ell \geq 1$	Fault-free	No
[24]	$\Theta(\log(k+\Delta))$	$O(\min\{m, k\Delta\})$	$\ell \geq 1$	Fault-free	No
[29]	$\Theta(\log(k+\Delta))$	$O(\min\{m, k\Delta\} \cdot f)$	$\ell = 1$	Crash	No
[4]	$\Theta(\log(k+\Delta))$	$O(k^2)$	$\ell = 1$	Crash	No
[4]	$\Theta(\log(k+\Delta))$	$O(\min\{m, k\Delta, k^2\} \cdot (\ell+f))$	$\ell > 1$	Crash	Yes
Theorem 1	$O(k\log(k+\Delta))$	$O(\min\{m, k\Delta\})$	$\ell \geq 1$	Crash	No
Theorem 2	$\Theta(\log(k+\Delta))$	$O(\min\{m, k\Delta\} \cdot (\ell+f))$	$\ell \geq 1$	Crash	No

We have the following two results for DISPERSION in any arbitrary anonymous graph G. Table 1 outlines and compares them with the best previous results.

- There is a deterministic algorithm that solves DISPERSION tolerating $f \leq k$ crash faults in $O(\min\{m, k\Delta\})$ rounds with $O(k\log(k+\Delta))$ bits memory at each robot.
- There is a deterministic algorithm that solves DISPERSION tolerating $f \leq k$ crash faults in $O(\min\{m, k\Delta\} \cdot (\ell+f))$ rounds with $O(\log(k+\Delta))$ bits memory at each robot, where ℓ the number of nodes with multiple robots in the initial configuration.

The results are interesting and provide time-memory trade-offs. The time bound in the first result is optimal for constant degree graphs (given the $\Omega(k)$ lower bound) but memory is $O(k)$ factor away from the optimal, whereas the memory bound in the second result is optimal given the memory lower bound $\Omega(\log(k+\Delta))$ even for the fault-free case but the time bound is $O(\ell+f)$ factor away from the time bound in the first result. In other words, time (memory) is sacrificed for better memory (time).

We now discuss how our results compare with two previous works [4,29] that considered crash faults. Chand *et al.* [4] provided an $O(k^2)$-round algorithm for $\ell = 1$, and for $\ell > 1$, provided an $O(\min\{m, k\Delta, k^2\} \cdot (\ell+f))$-round algorithm. The algorithm for $\ell > 1$ is designed under the assumption that the robots have a priori knowledge on the graph and problem parameters m, Δ, ℓ, k, f. Compared to their result for $\ell = 1$, the time bound in our algorithm is better when $\Delta \leq k$ for even $\ell > 1$. Compared to their result for $\ell > 1$, both of our algorithms work without such assumption. Pattanayak *et al.* [29] provided an $O(\min\{m, k\Delta\} \cdot f)$-round algorithm only for $\ell = 1$. Compared to their result, both of our algorithms work for $\ell = 1$ as well as $\ell > 1$.

Challenges and Techniques. The well-known depth first search (DFS) traversal was heavily used to solve DISPERSION [1,14,17,19–21,23,24,28]. If all k robots are positioned initially on a single node, the DFS traversal finishes in $\min\{4m-2n+2, 4k\Delta\}$ rounds solving DISPERSION [1,19,20]. If k robots are initially on k different nodes, DISPERSION is solved in a single round. However, if not all of them are on a single node, then the robots on nodes with multiple robots need to reposition to reach to free nodes and settle. The natural approach is to run DFS traversals in parallel to minimize time. The challenge arises when two or more DFS traversals meet before all robots settle. When this happens, the robots that have not settled yet need to find free nodes. For this, they may need to re-traverse the already traversed part of the graph by the DFS traversal. With $O(\log(k + \Delta))$ bits memory per robot, this re-traversal was shown to add an $O(\ell)$ multiplicative factor [1, 19], which has been progressively improved to an $O(\log \ell)$ factor [20, 32] to finally an $O(1)$ factor [24]. Therefore, even in the case of two or more DFS traversals meet, DISPERSION can be solved in $O(\min\{4m-2n+2, 4k\Delta\})$ rounds, independent of ℓ. With $O(k \log(k + \Delta))$ bits memory per robot, it has been shown by Augustine and Moses Jr. [1] that multiple meeting DFSs can be synchronized with $O(1)$ factor overhead, solving the problem in $O(\min\{4m-2n+2, 4k\Delta\})$ rounds. Therefore, the time result of [24] matched [1] with only $O(\log(k + \Delta))$ bits memory per robot. However, all these results were obtained considering fault-free robots.

The natural question is can the time bound of $O(\min\{4m - 2n + 2, 4k\Delta\})$ rounds be obtained in the case of robot crash faults. Indeed, our first result shows that the time bound of $O(\min\{4m - 2n + 2, 4k\Delta\})$ rounds can be obtained with $O(k \log(k + \Delta))$ bits memory at each robot even when $f \leq k$ robots crash. The idea behind this result is highly non-trivial. In the fault-free case, having the $O(k \log(k + \Delta))$ bits memory allows for each robot to track k different DFS traversals. A robot runs its DFS traversal until it reaches an empty node, at some round t, on which it settles if it is the highest ID robot among the robots that are on that node, at that round t. Others continue their DFS traversals. Since there are k robots, all robots must find an empty node to settle within $O(\min\{4m - 2n + 2, 4k\Delta\})$ rounds. However, in the crash fault case, the information of all the DFS traversals stored at the settled robot r_v at some node v will be lost when it crashes. Therefore, the neighbor nodes of v need to be visited to recover the information that was lost from r_v. However, there might be the case that one or multiple neighbors may also have crashed and this might create problem on how to recover the information correctly. We modified the DFS traversal developing a novel technique so that the DFS information can be recovered visiting the first non-crashed robot towards the root node of the DFS tree and the total time to recover this information is proportional to $O(\min\{4m-2n+2, 4k\Delta\})$ rounds, giving in overall the $O(\min\{4m-2n+2, 4k\Delta\})$ rounds time bound, independent of ℓ tolerating any number $f \leq k$ of robot crashes.

Our second result asks what can be done w.r.t. time when only $O(\log(k + \Delta))$ bits memory is provided to each robot. Recall that, in the fault-free case, Kshemkalyani and Sharma [24] obtained $O(\min\{4m - 2n + 2, 4k\Delta\})$ rounds time bound with $O(\log(k + \Delta))$ bits memory at each robot. However, in the fault case, it turned out to be difficult to recover the lost DFS information maintained by a robot r_v settled at a node v. This is partly due to the fact that with $O(\log(k + \Delta))$ bits memory at each robot, only information related to $O(1)$ DFSs can be tracked/recovered. Therefore, we extend the result of Pattanayak *et al.* [29] for the case of $\ell = 1$ to $\ell > 1$ along the lines of the $O(k \log(k + \Delta))$ bits memory algorithm we designed as the first result in this paper (Theorem 1). Recall that, [29] showed $O(\min\{m, k\Delta\} \cdot f)$ rounds time bound with $O(\log(k + \Delta))$ bits memory at each robot for the case of $\ell = 1$. They used the technique of starting a new DFS traversal as soon as a crash was detected. They showed that for $f \leq k$ crashes, $f+1$ such DFS traversals may be initiated throughout the execution of the algorithm, which will finish in total time $O(\min\{m, k\Delta\} \cdot f)$ rounds, since for the fault-free case, the single DFS traversal finishes in $O(\min\{m, k\Delta\})$ rounds. We borrow the idea of [29] and extend it to the case of $\ell > 1$ developing a synchronization mechanism so that all ℓ different DFS traversals finish in $O(\min\{m, k\Delta\} \cdot (\ell + f))$ rounds. We observe that there are total $\ell + f$ different DFS traversals initiated throughout the execution. The trivial analysis would only give $O(\min\{m, k\Delta\} \cdot \ell \cdot f)$ rounds time bound but we proved that if there is no crash for the duration of $O(\min\{m, k\Delta\})$ rounds, then the number of total DFS traversals decrease by at least 1. Therefore, since there are total $(\ell + f)$ DFS traversals, they finish in $O(\min\{m, k\Delta\} \cdot (\ell + f))$ rounds.

Related Work. The most relevant results to this paper are listed in Table 1 as well as the established results. The best previously known fault-free result is due to Kshemkalyani and Sharma [24] which solves DISPERSION in $O(\min\{m, k\Delta\})$ rounds with $O(\log(k+\Delta))$ bits memory at each robot. This time is optimal for constant-degree graphs (i.e., $\Delta = O(1)$) given the time lower bound of $\Omega(k)$ [19]. Additionally, the memory is optimal given the lower bound of $\Omega(\log(k + \Delta))$ [19,23]. Under robots crash faults, there are two existing results due to Pattanayak *et al.* [29] and Chand *et al.* [4]. Pattanayak *et al.* [29] solved DISPERSION for the case of $\ell = 1$ in $O(\min\{m, k\Delta\} \cdot f)$ rounds with $O(\log(k + \Delta))$ memory bits at each robot for $f \leq k$ robot crashes. Chand *et al.* [4] solved DISPERSION for $\ell = 1$ in $O(k^2)$ rounds and for $\ell > 1$ in $O(\min\{m, k\Delta, k^2\} \cdot (\ell + f))$ rounds with $O(\log(k + \Delta))$ bits memory at each robot under the assumption that the graph and problem parameters n, m, Δ, k, f are known to the algorithm. Our results do not have that assumption.

DISPERSION was studied in a graph setting intensively [1,4,7,14,17–24,26,32]. The majority of works considered the faulty-free case, except [27,28] which considered Byzantine faults (in which robots might act arbitrarily) and [4,29] which considered crash faults (where robots stop working). The majority of the works considered the local communication model, except Kshemkalyani *et al.* [23] where they considered the *global communication* model – robots can communicate irrespective of their positions on the graph. Most of the works considered static graphs, except Kshemkalyani *et al.* [22] which considered in dynamic graphs. Moreover, most of the works presented deterministic algorithms except [7,26] where randomness is used to minimize memory requirement for the $\ell = 1$ case. DISPERSION is considered by providing an alternative measure to communication capability of co-located robots in [14] and putting an additional constraint that no two adjacent nodes can contain robots in the final configuration in [18]. The majority of the studies considered DISPERSION in arbitrary graphs but special graph cases were also considered: grid [21], ring [1,28], and trees [1,23].

Additionally, DISPERSION is closely related to graph exploration by mobile robots or agents. The exploration problem has been quite extensively studied for specific as well as arbitrary graphs, e.g., [2,5,9,13,25]. Another problem related to DISPERSION is the scattering of robots. This problem has been studied for rings [10,31] and grids [3]. Recently, Poudel and Sharma [30] provided a $\Theta(\sqrt{n})$-time algorithm for uniform scattering on a grid [8]. DISPERSION is also related to the load balancing problem, where a given load has to be (re-)distributed among several nodes. This problem has been studied quite heavily in graphs, e.g., [6,33]. Note that all these studies do not consider faults. We refer readers to [11,12] for recent developments in these topics.

Roadmap. The model, formal problem definition, and preliminaries are given in Sect. 2. The first $O(\min\{m, k\Delta\})$-round $O(k\log(k+\Delta))$-bit memory algorithm is described in Sect. 3. The second $O(\min\{m, k\Delta\}\cdot(\ell+f))$-round $O(\log(k+\Delta))$-bit memory algorithm is described in Sect. 4. Finally, we conclude the paper in Sect. 5 with a short discussion. Some proofs are omitted due to space constraints.

2 Model and Preliminaries

Graph. Let $G = (V, E)$ represent an arbitrary, connected, unweighted, undirected, anonymous graph with n nodes and m edges, i.e., $|V| = n$ and $|E| = m$. The nodes lack identifiers but, at any node $v \in V$, its incident edges are uniquely identified by a *label* (aka port number) in the range $[1, \delta_v]$, where δ_v is the *degree* of v. The *maximum degree* of G is $\Delta := \max_{v\in V}\delta_v$. We assume that there is no correlation between two port numbers of an edge. Any number of robots are allowed to move along an edge at any time. The graph nodes do not have memory, i.e., they can not store information.

Robots. Let $\mathcal{R} := \{r_1, r_2, \ldots, r_k\}$ be a set of $k \leq n$ robots residing on the nodes of G. No robot can reside on the edges of G, but multiple robots can occupy the same node. A node with multiple robots is called a multiplicity node. Each robot has a unique $\lceil\log k\rceil$-bit ID taken from $[1, k^{O(1)}]$. We denote a robot r_i's ID by $r_i.ID$ with $r_i.ID = i$. When a robot moves from node u to node v in G, it is aware of the port of u it used to leave u and the port of v it used to enter v. Furthermore, it is assumed that each robot is equipped with memory to store information.

Communication Model. There are two communication models: local and global. In the local model, a robot can only communicate with other robots co-located at a node. In the global model, a robot can communicate with any other robot, not necessarily co-located. This paper considers the local model.

Time Cycle. At any time, a robot $r_i \in \mathcal{R}$ could be active or inactive. When r_i becomes active, it performs the "Communicate-Compute-Move" (CCM) cycle as follows.

- *Communicate:* For each robot $r_j \in \mathcal{R}$ that is at some node v_i, another robot r_i at v_i can observe the memory of r_j. Robot r_i can also observe its own memory.
- *Compute:* r_i may perform an arbitrary computation using the information observed during the "communicate" portion of that cycle. This includes determination of a port to use to exit v_i and the information to store in the robot r_j that is at v_i.
- *Move:* At the end of the cycle, r_i writes new information (if any) in the memory of a robot r_k at v_i, and exits v_i using the computed port to reach to a neighbor of v_i.

Faults. We consider *crash* faults. Robots may be susceptible to fault at any point in time during execution. The robot which experiences a crash fault at some time t stops interaction after t, i.e., the robot stops communicating, giving the perception that it has vanished from the system. Robot r_i will not have any information on whether $r_j \neq r_i$ is faulty and also does not have information on the number of faulty robots f.

Time and Memory Complexity. We consider the synchronous setting where every robot performs each CCM cycle in synchrony becoming active in every CCM cycle.

Therefore, time is measured in *rounds* (a cycle is a round). Another important parameter is memory. Memory comes from a single source – the number of bits stored at each robot. We assume that the execution starts at round 1. We denote the initial configuration (in the beginning of round 1) by C_{init}. We divide C_{init} into two categories:

- ***rooted*** – all $k \leq n$ robots are initially on a single node ($\ell = 1$).
- ***general*** – $k \leq n$ robots are initially on multiple nodes ($1 < \ell \leq k/2$).

Dispersion. The DISPERSION problem can be formally defined as follows.

Definition 1. (DISPERSION). Given an n-node anonymous graph $G = (V, E)$ having $k \leq n$ robots, out of which $f \leq k$ may experience crash faults, positioned initially arbitrarily on the nodes of G, the robots reposition autonomously to reach a configuration where each non-faulty robot is on a distinct node of G and stay stationary thereafter.

The initial configuration may have $\ell < k$ multiplicity nodes. A *settled* robot at a node u stays stationary at u. Another robot can settle at u, after the settled robot crashes. A node can have at most one settled robot at one time.

3 $O(\min\{m, k\Delta\})$-Round Algorithm

In this section, we present a deterministic algorithm for DISPERSION with a runtime of $O(\min\{m, k\Delta\})$ rounds that tolerates $f \leq k$ crash faults using $O(k \log(k + \Delta))$ bits memory per robot. This is the first algorithm that achieves this time bound for the crash robot faults even when $\ell > 1$, matching the time bound for the fault-free case [24] (recall ℓ is the number of multiplicity nodes in the initial configuration).

First, we describe the high-level idea behind the algorithm. In the detailed description, we start with fault-free scenario and then extend that to handle crash faults.

High-level Overview of the Algorithm. The objective of a robot is to find an empty node such that it can settle at that node. If there are multiple robots, the highest ID robot among them settles and it remains at that node thenceforth. An unsettled robot executes the algorithm until it settles. The algorithm consists of four phases: *forward*, *backtrack*, *retrace*, and *revert*. The forward and backtrack phases are as in the standard DFS traversal of a graph. The two phases retrace and revert are the new phases added to handle the crash faults once they are detected in the forward phase. In the forward phase, a robot explores new nodes; on encountering an already visited node, backtrack phase begins, and it returns to the last node on its path with unvisited ports. The forward and backtrack phases are sufficient if there are no crashes. In these two phases, the robot builds and maintains a list to keep track of the visited nodes and the parent-child relationship among them using settled robots as identifiers and port numbers as parent pointers. If a settled robot crashes at some node, and an exploring robot reaches that node in backtrack phase, then it is sufficient for the exploring robot to recognize the newly settled robot at that node and update the robot ID in the list in its memory. However, if a crash is not handled properly in the forward phase, there is a possibility that the parent pointers may form a cycle and thus leading to failure of backtrack and hence the DFS traversal. Thus, the phases retrace and revert are necessary to recover the parent-children relationship among the nodes in case of robot crashes. The DFS traversal is maintained by a robot in its memory and it produces a tree, i.e., the DFS tree. The algorithm always starts in the forward phase.

On crash detection in the forward phase, retrace and revert phases are used. In the retrace phase, the robot retraces its path from the current node to an ancestor in the DFS tree that has not crashed. If no such non-crashed ancestor is found during retrace phase, it can recognize that it has reached the root of the DFS traversal due to the absence of a parent pointer and hence it can start the revert phase. In the revert phase, the robot returns to the head of the DFS tree following the reverse of the path it has taken in the retrace phase to the non-crashed ancestor. In some cases, the retrace phase is implicit if the robot reaches to a non-crashed ancestor in the forward phase itself (the crash detection happens due to the non-crashed ancestor), then it immediately starts the revert phase. We call this fault-tolerant algorithm `DFS_recover` since this algorithm uses a technique to recover the correct DFS traversal once a crash is detected. Note that the DFS recovery is done in the memory of each robot based on the information it is storing about the DFS traversal (more on this in the detailed description). Therefore, the recovery procedure does not ask robot to revisit previously explored parts of the graph. In other words, the DFS traversal state is in the memory of each robot. Figure 2 (top) shows the diagram of the state transitions between the phases. The second to bottom of Fig. 2 show respectively the conditions which make a phase (forward, backtrack, retrace, and revert, respectively) to either stay in that phase or transition to another.

Detailed Description of the Algorithm. We first describe the DISPERSION process of the robots in a fault-free scenario and then extend it to handle crash faults. Recall that, in the fault-free scenario, each robot only needs forward and backtrack phases. We explain how the robot keeps track of information in each of the phases and correctly maintains the DFS tree it has traversed.

The Datastructure at Each Robot: To achieve this, each robot maintains a list P of its own that describes its path as a sequence of visited nodes with specific information. An element of the list P corresponding to node u is a quadruple $\sigma_u = (p_u^{in}, r_u.ID, r_u.depth, p_u^{out})$, where p_u^{in} is the port number via which it enters u, $r_u.ID$ is the ID of the settled robot r_u at u, $r_u.depth$ is the depth of u, and p_u^{out} is the port via which it exits u. The robot r_i also maintains $r_i.phase$ (indicating the phase of r_i), $r_i.depth$ (indicating the depth of r_i at the current node), and $r_i.trace$ (a stack of robot IDs used in the retrace and revert phases).

Intuitively, the list P contains elements corresponding to a node u if it is visited by an edge traversal of the DFS tree. The list P has at most two entries corresponding to each edge of the DFS tree. If the robot r_i visiting node u contains $r_u.ID$ in its list P, it can determine the following from list P. Let σ_u and σ'_u be the first and last element of P with $r_u.ID$. Now, $r_u.parent$ is p_u^{in} in σ_u, and $r_u.recent$ is $p_u^{out'}$ in σ'_u. The top robot in the stack $r_i.trace$ is called r_{top}. A *fully-visited* node is a node u with all of its ports visited. A node contains unvisited ports if it is not fully-visited. The *head* of the DFS is the node with unvisited ports at the highest depth. To determine the head of the DFS in P, a robot starts at the last element of P and moves in reverse order until it finds a node with unvisited ports. We call this element of P as σ_{head} and the corresponding robot as r_{head}.

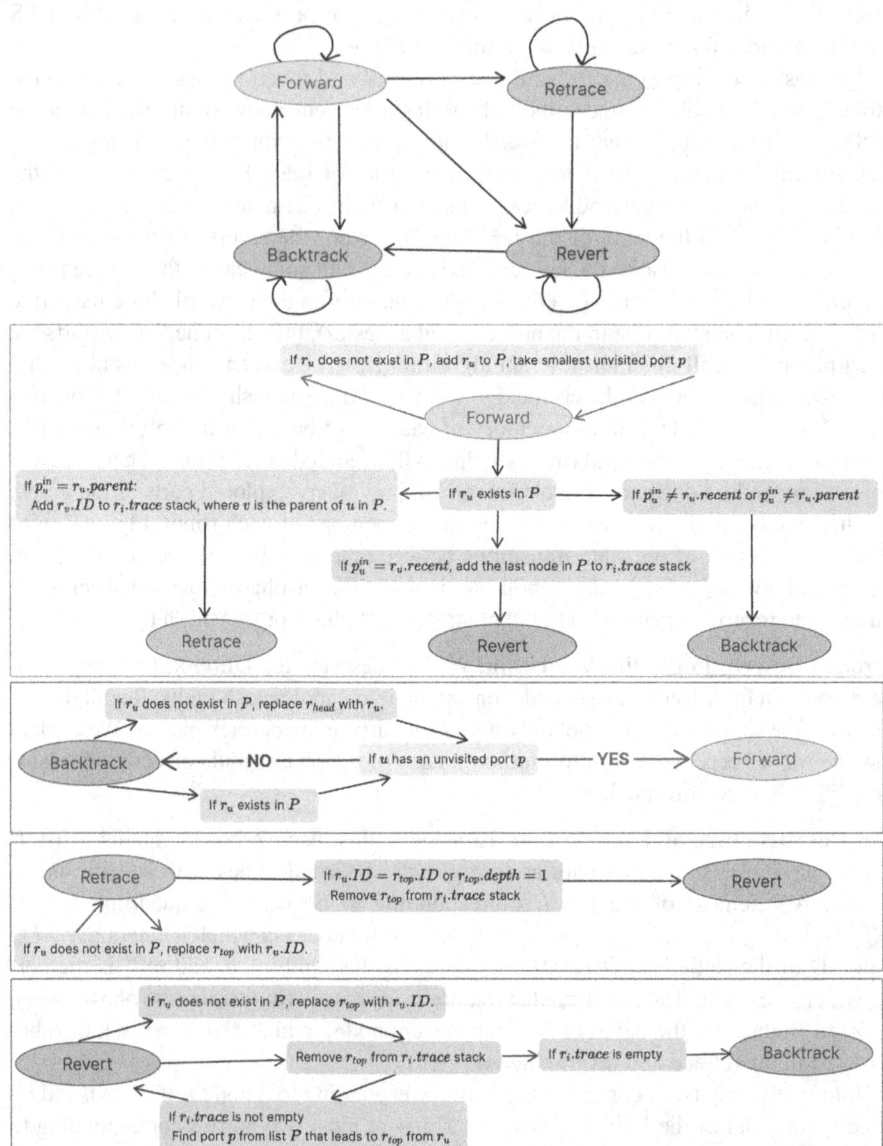

Fig. 2. The top figure shows an illustration of the transitions between the four phases (forward, backtrack, retrace, and revert) of the $O(\min\{m, k\Delta\})$-time algorithm `DFS_recover` and each of the subsequent figures show the conditions that trigger transition of the algorithm from one state to another for each of the states in the order forward, backtrack, retrace, and revert, respectively. The algorithm always starts with the forward phase. In each scenario, the robot r_i visits a node u with settled robot r_u.

Finding the Smallest Unvisited Port: To find the smallest unvisited port at node u with settled robot r_u, a robot goes through all the elements of P with $r_u.ID$ and checks if port p was taken for each p in $[1, \delta_u]$ in increasing order, where $p \neq r_u.parent$. This is enough to run the forward and backtrack phases correctly.

We would like the readers to keep note on the following robot behavior, which will be common to all phases in our algorithm. When the robot r_i reaches a node u, if u does not have a settled robot and r_i has the highest ID among the unsettled robots at u, it settles at u and finishes its execution. Otherwise, the robot with the highest ID among the unsettled robots at u settles at u. For the rest of the section, we describe the following phases from the perspective of the last robot to settle among all the robots.

Initialization: Algorithm `DFS_recover` starts at round 1. In round 1, the robot r_i initializes with $r_i.phase = forward$ at node v with $p_v^{in} = \perp$ ($\perp$ indicates that no parent pointer exists for the root node of the DFS traversal). The current depth $r_i.depth$ is initialized to 1. Let r_v be the settled robot at v. The robot r_i adds the quadruple $(\perp, r_v.ID, r_i.depth, 1)$ to the list P. Initially, $r_i.trace$ is empty.

In round $t \geq 2$, suppose r_i visits node u from port p_u^{in}. Let r_u be the settled robot at u. We are ready to describe the algorithm `DFS_recover`. We first describe `DFS_recover` for the fault-free execution and then the crash-fault execution.

Fault-Free DFS. We describe the action of the robots in the fault-free scenario. Recall that in the fault-free scenario, only forward and backtrack phases are enough.

Forward Phase: In this case, r_i checks if an element σ_u with r_u exists in P.

1. If σ_u does not exist in P, then r_i adds the quadruple $(p_u^{in}, r_u.ID, r_i.depth, p_u^{out})$ to the list P, where p_u^{out} is the smallest unvisited port at u. The robot r_i increases $r_i.depth$ by 1 and leaves u via port p_u^{out}.
2. If σ_u exists in P, then $r_i.phase = backtrack$. The robot r_i reduces $r_i.depth$ by 1 and leaves u via port p_u^{in}.

Backtrack Phase: The robot r_i finds the last element σ_u containing r_u in P. By design, $\sigma_u = \sigma_{head}$.

1. The robot r_i finds the smallest unvisited port p at u. The robot r_i adds the quadruple $(p_u^{in}, r_u.ID, r_i.depth, p)$ to P, sets $r_i.phase = forward$, increases $r_i.depth$ by 1, and leaves u via port p.
2. If there are no unvisited ports, then u is fully-visited, and $p = r_u.parent$. The robot r_i adds the quadruple $(p_u^{in}, r_u.ID, r_i.depth, p)$ to the list P, sets $r_i.phase = backtrack$, reduces $r_i.depth$ by 1, and leaves u via port p.

Since r_i keeps an element in P for each edge traversal of the DFS tree, it merges the last two elements of P if they are of the same robot r_u. Let $\sigma_u = (p_u^{in}, r_u.ID, r_i.depth, p_u^{out})$ and $\sigma_u' = (p_u^{in'}, r_u.ID, r_i.depth, p_u^{out'})$ be the last two elements of P. Robot r_i merges them by replacing them with $(p_u^{in}, r_u.ID, r_i.depth, p_u^{out'})$. Note that this merging happens for each leaf of the DFS tree.

Crash Detection. We identify that there are faults in each of the phases as follows.

1. In the forward phase, a fault can be identified if the robot r_i visits a node u with a settled robot r_u either from port $r_u.parent$ or $r_u.recent$.
   (a) If it visits from $r_u.parent$, this means the parent robot of r_u has crashed, allowing r_i to visit u in the forward phase from the parent port.
   (b) If it visits from the $r_u.recent$ port, this means the most recent child of r_u has crashed, since otherwise, this port would be taken only in the backtrack phase.
2. If r_i leaves a node u with a settled robot r_u from the parent pointer in either the retrace or backtrack phase to reach node v with a settled robot r_v in P, and the robot ID does not match, then there is a crash.
3. If r_i reaches a node in the revert phase where r_{top} (the robot at the top of the stack $r_i.trace$) does not match, then there is a crash.

We are now ready to we discuss the fault-tolerant algorithm.

Crash-Fault DFS. The algorithm in this case includes the forward, backtrack, retrace, and revert phases, designed to handle crash faults.

Crash-Tolerant Forward Phase: Suppose robot r_i visits node u with settled robot r_u from port p_u^{in}, and r_u is present in the list P. The robot operates as follows:

1. If $p_u^{in} = r_u.parent$, robot r_i sets its phase to retrace, locates the parent r_v of r_u in P, adds $r_v.ID$ to $r_i.trace$, and leaves via port p_u^{in}.
2. If $p_u^{in} = r_u.recent$, robot r_i sets its phase to revert, locates the recent child r_w of r_u, adds $r_w.ID$ to $r_i.trace$, and leaves via p_u^{in}.

Retrace Phase: Robot r_i retraces the path from the DFS head to a non-crashed ancestor or until depth reaches 1, utilizing stack $r_i.trace$. If $r_u.ID \neq r_{top}.ID$, r_i replaces r_{top} in P with r_u, changes $r_{top}.ID = r_u.ID$, pushes $r_v.ID$ onto $r_i.trace$ where v is the parent of u in P, and leaves u via $r_u.parent$. If $r_u.ID = r_{top}.ID$ or $r_{top}.depth = 1$, r_i switches to the revert phase, pops the top of $r_i.trace$, and leaves via p_u^{in}.

Revert Phase: Robot r_i returns to the DFS head, following the path in the stack. If $r_u.ID \neq r_{top}.ID$, r_i replaces instances of r_{top} in P with r_u. Pop the top of the stack $r_i.trace$. Now, based on the stack's state:

1. If $r_i.trace$ is empty, r_i sets its phase to backtrack, leaves via p_{last}^{in} where r_{last} is the robot in the last element of P, and removes the last element from P.
2. If $r_i.trace$ is not empty, r_i finds port p leading to the new r_{top} from r_u and leaves via port p.

Crash-Tolerant Backtrack Phase: At node u, robot r_i identifies the DFS head r_{head} from σ_{head} in P. If $r_u.ID \neq r_{head}.ID$, implying robot r_{head} has crashed, r_i replaces all instances of $r_{head}.ID$ with $r_u.ID$ in P and proceeds with the crash-free backtrack phase.

Example: Figure 3 illustrates the robot's behavior, starting at node a. As the robot moves through the graph, it updates the list P with corresponding entries for each visited node. When the robot encounters a crashed robot, it initiates the retrace and revert phases to handle the fault, as demonstrated in the example.

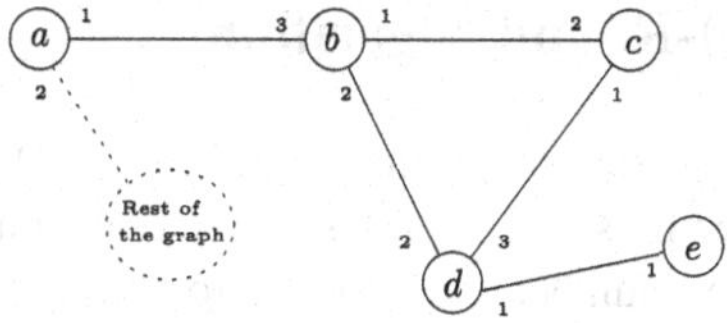

Fig. 3. Example of the crash-tolerant forward phase.

In the example, robot r_i begins at node a and visits nodes b, c, d, and e, before returning to node d. During this traversal, P stores entries for robots r_a, r_b, r_c, r_d, and r_e. When robot r_b crashes and is replaced by robot r'_b, robot r_i does not immediately detect the crash. It adds r'_b to P and moves to node c. At node c, r_i recognizes that it has already visited the node and that it arrived from $r_c.parent$. It then enters the retrace phase, adds $r_b.ID$ to $r_i.trace$, and leaves via $r_c.parent$.

At node b, robot r_i replaces all instances of r_b with r'_b in P, adds $r_a.ID$ to $r_i.trace$, and moves to node a. At node a, r_i completes the retrace phase, enters the revert phase, and removes the top of the stack $r_i.trace$. Since the stack is not empty, it finds the port p of r_a that leads to r'_b from P. Robot r_i then follows the path in the revert phase, reaching node b. Since the stack $r_i.trace$ is empty, it follows p^{in}_{last} to reach node d. Then, the robot continues executing the algorithm in the backtrack phase.

3.1 Analysis of the Algorithm

In the list P, we define the parent pointer for a robot r_u as the p^{in}_u for the first occurrence of r_u. We construct a graph G' starting at the root, taking the first occurrence of a new robot r and the corresponding previous robot in P as its parent. We show that the graph G' is a tree with distinct robot IDs. Due to space constraints, we omit the proofs.

Lemma 1. *The parent pointer graph G' constructed from P is a tree.*

We show that a node becomes fully-visited as long as the robots do not crash.

Lemma 2. *A node is fully-visited only once for each settled robot.*

Now, we show that the crashes can be recovered in time proportional to the number of crashes detected. This is an important lemma which is crucial on establishing the claimed time bound.

Lemma 3. *Crash detection and recovery takes $O(f)$ rounds for f crashes.*

Finally, we have the following theorem for the algorithm of this section.

Theorem 1. *Algorithm* `DFS_recover` *achieves* DISPERSION *in $O(\min\{m, k\Delta\})$ rounds using $O(k \log(k + \Delta))$ bits memory at each robot.*

Proof. (sketch). Each robot performs its own crash-free DFS traversal in at most $O(\min\{m, k\Delta\})$ rounds and it can recover from f crashes in at most $O(f)$ rounds where $f < k$. □

4 $O(\min\{m, k\Delta\})$-Round Algorithm

In this section, we present a deterministic algorithm for DISPERSION with runtime $O(\min\{m, k\Delta\} \cdot (\ell + f))$ rounds that tolerates $f \leq k$ crash faults using $O(\log(k + \Delta))$ bits memory per robot. The bounds are analogous to the algorithm by Chand *et al.* [4] but in contrast to [4] the knowledge on m, Δ, ℓ, k, f is not required in our algorithm.

High-level Idea of the Algorithm. $O(\log(k + \Delta))$ bits memory per robot is in fact optimal for DISPERSION even in the fault-free case [19]. To achieve DISPERSION under this lower memory bound, we extend the idea of DFS traversal as in [29]. Unlike the previous section, the robots do not maintain a list P to keep track of the traversal. Instead, each group of unsettled robots start a DFS traversal with a DFS ID that consists of a tuple $(round\_no, r_{dfshead}.ID)$, where $r_{dfshead}$ is the robot with highest ID among them and that settles at the node. A settled robot r_u at node u maintains a DFS ID $r_u.DFSID$ for a DFS traversal. It also maintains $r_u.parent$ and $r_u.recent$ corresponding to the DFS ID. The algorithm follows the crash-free forward and backtrack phases with crash detection. Every time a crash is detected, the unsettled robots at the DFS head begin a new DFS traversal with the current round number in the DFS ID. Since we assume synchronous rounds and simultaneous start for all robots, the round number is consistent across all robots in the graph. The DFS IDs are ordered lexicographically and the higher DFS ID has higher priority compared to the lower one. We call this algorithm `DFS_new`, as it starts a new DFS traversal for each detected crash. By the hierarchy among the DFS IDs, a DFS traversal that begins later has higher priority.

Detailed Description of the Algorithm. We begin the description with the variables stored at each robot. The forward and backtrack phases are same as the crash-free algorithm in the previous section. We describe here the details of meeting between two DFS traversals. In the previous section, since each robot maintained their own traversal, there was no need for involvement of the settled robot. However, here the settled robot keeps track of the DFS traversal and hence it needs to update its memory according to the changes in the DFS traversal.

Initialization: A group of unsettled robots at a node u begin a DFS traversal. The highest ID robot r_u among them settles at the node u, and it takes the DFS ID consisting of $(1, r_u.ID)$. It sets $r_u.parent = \perp$ and $r_u.recent = 1$. Other unsettled robots at u also set the same DFS ID and leave u via port number 1.

The forward and backtrack phases work similarly to the previous section. As long as the exploring robots meet a settled robot at v with the same DFS ID, they backtrack to the previous node u by p_v^{in} and find the smallest unvisited port at u.

Determining the Smallest Unvisited Port: In the backtrack phase, the exploring robot(s) has to determine the smallest unvisited port at a settled robot r_u. The settled robot keeps track of the recent and parent ports. The ports at each node are visited in an increasing order excluding the parent. If $(r_u.recent = \delta_u)$ or $(r_u.recent = \delta_u - 1$ and $r_u.parent = \delta_u)$, then u does not have unvisited ports, and the next port to take is $r_u.parent$ in the backtrack phase. Otherwise, we can determine the smallest unvisited port of u as $r_u.recent + 1$ (if $r_u.recent + 1 \neq r_u.parent$) or $r_u.recent + 2$ and continue in the forward phase.

Merging DFS Traversals. When r_i visits u with a settled robot r_u in the forward phase and $r_i.DFSID \neq r_u.DFSID$, we have two cases.

(i) $r_i.DFSID > r_u.DFSID$: In this case, the r_i has the higher DFS ID. Thus the node u becomes part of the same DFS traversal as r_i. Now, r_u becomes a settled robot of $r_i.DFSID$; r_u updates its DFS ID as $r_u.DFSID \leftarrow r_i.DFSID$ and $r_u.parent = p_u^{in}$. The robot r_i leaves node u via smallest unvisited port p_u^{out} at u in the forward phase. Since r_u essentially behaves like a newly settled robot of $r_i.DFSID$, $p_u^{out} = 1$ if $p_u^{in} \neq 1$ or $p_u^{out} = 2$ if $p_u^{in} = 1$. Now, r_u also updates the recent pointer to $r_u.recent = p_u^{out}$.

(ii) $r_i.DFSID < r_u.DFSID$: In this case, the DFS traversal that r_i is part of becomes subsumed by the DFS traversal of $r_u.DFSID$. Then, r_i updates its DFS ID as $r_i.DFSID \leftarrow r_u.DFSID$. Now, it follows $r_u.recent$ in the forward phase.

Crash Detection: A crash is detected during the forward phase if a robot r_i encounters a settled robot r_u possessing the same DFS ID, arriving either from the $r_u.recent$ or $r_u.parent$ port. In the backtrack phase, the detection of a crash occurs under two conditions: either if $r_u.DFSID < r_i.DFSID$ or if $p_u^{in} \neq r_u.recent$ when $r_u.DFSID = r_i.DFSID$. Upon crash detection at round t, unsettled robots at node u initialize a fresh DFS traversal. The new DFS ID is set as $(t, r_k.ID)$, where r_k is the unsettled robot with the highest ID present at u. Concurrently, the settled robot r_u adopts the newly generated DFS ID as its own. This initiates a new DFS traversal during the forward phase with r_u as the root.

Analysis of the Algorithm. We prove that this algorithm correctly performs dispersion and show the time and memory requirements. Intuitively, the correctness follows from the fact that the DFS traversal with the highest ID starts at round t such that no crash is detected after t. Since it is the highest ID DFS traversal, it continues without crash detection and achieves DISPERSION. The details are omitted due to space constraints.

Theorem 2. *Algorithm* `DFS_new` *achieves* DISPERSION *in* $O(\min\{m, k\Delta\} \cdot (\ell + f))$ *rounds using* $O(\log(k + \Delta))$ *bits memory at each robot.*

Proof. (sketch). Algorithm `DFS_new` creates at most $(\ell + f)$ DFS traversals, each of which may take at most $O(\min\{m, k\Delta\})$ rounds when active and $O(k)$ rounds of inactivity when unsettled robots join the DFS traversal. □

5 Concluding Remarks

In this paper, we have presented two deterministic algorithms for DISPERSION of $k \leq n$ mobile robots in any n-node arbitrary anonymous graph tolerating $f \leq k$ robot crash faults. The algorithms are interesting since they provide trade-offs on two fundamental performance metrics, time and memory per robot. The first (second) algorithm achieves improved time (memory) complexity with $O(k)$ ($O(f)$) factor more memory (time) compared to the second (first) algorithm. For the future work, it would be interesting to see whether memory in the first algorithm (or time in the second algorithm) can be improved keeping time (or memory in the second algorithm) as is.

References

1. Augustine, J., Moses Jr., W.K.: Dispersion of mobile robots: a study of memory-time trade-offs. In: ICDCN, pp. 1:1–1:10 (2018)
2. Bampas, E., Gasieniec, L., Hanusse, N., Ilcinkas, D., Klasing, R., Kosowski, A.: Euler tour lock-in problem in the rotor-router model. In: Keidar, I. (ed.) DISC 2009. LNCS, vol. 5805, pp. 423–435. Springer, Heidelberg (2009). https://doi.org/10.1007/978-3-642-04355-0_44
3. Barriere, L., Flocchini, P., Mesa-Barrameda, E., Santoro, N.: Uniform scattering of autonomous mobile robots in a grid. In: IPDPS, pp. 1–8 (2009)
4. Chand, P.K., Kumar, M., Molla, A.R., Sivasubramaniam, S.: Fault-tolerant dispersion of mobile robots. In: Bagchi, A., Muthu, R. (eds.) CALDAM, pp. 28–40 (2023)
5. Cohen, R., Fraigniaud, P., Ilcinkas, D., Korman, A., Peleg, D.: Label-guided graph exploration by a finite automaton. ACM Trans. Algorithms **4**(4), 42:1–42:18 (Aug 2008)
6. Cybenko, G.: Dynamic load balancing for distributed memory multiprocessors. J. Parallel Distrib. Comput. **7**(2), 279–301 (1989)
7. Das, A., Bose, K., Sau, B.: Memory optimal dispersion by anonymous mobile robots. In: Mudgal, A., Subramanian, C.R. (eds.) CALDAM 2021. LNCS, vol. 12601, pp. 426–439. Springer, Cham (2021). https://doi.org/10.1007/978-3-030-67899-9_34
8. Das, S., Flocchini, P., Prencipe, G., Santoro, N., Yamashita, M.: Autonomous mobile robots with lights. Theor. Comput. Sci. **609**, 171–184 (2016)
9. Dereniowski, D., Disser, Y., Kosowski, A., Pajak, D., Uznański, P.: Fast collaborative graph exploration. Inf. Comput. **243**(C), 37–49 (2015)
10. Elor, Y., Bruckstein, A.M.: Uniform multi-agent deployment on a ring. Theor. Comput. Sci. **412**(8–10), 783–795 (2011)
11. Flocchini, P., Prencipe, G., Santoro, N.: Distributed Computing by Oblivious Mobile Robots. Synthesis Lectures on Distributed Computing Theory. Morgan & Claypool Publishers, San Rafael (2012)
12. Flocchini, P., Prencipe, G., Santoro, N.: Distributed Computing by Mobile Entities, Theoretical Computer Science and General Issues, vol. 1. Springer, Cham (2019). https://doi.org/10.1007/978-3-030-11072-7
13. Fraigniaud, P., Ilcinkas, D., Peer, G., Pelc, A., Peleg, D.: Graph exploration by a finite automaton. Theor. Comput. Sci. **345**(2–3), 331–344 (2005)
14. Gorain, B., Mandal, P.S., Mondal, K., Pandit, S.: Collaborative dispersion by silent robots. In: Devismes, S., Petit, F., Altisen, K., Di Luna, G.A., Fernandez Anta, A. (eds.) Stabilization, Safety, and Security of Distributed Systems. SSS 2022. LNCS, vol. 13751, pp. 254–269. Springer, Cham (2022). https://doi.org/10.1007/978-3-031-21017-4_17
15. Hsiang, T.R., Arkin, E.M., Bender, M.A., Fekete, S., Mitchell, J.S.B.: Online dispersion algorithms for swarms of robots. In: SoCG, pp. 382–383 (2003)
16. Hsiang, T., Arkin, E.M., Bender, M.A., Fekete, S.P., Mitchell, J.S.B.: Algorithms for rapidly dispersing robot swarms in unknown environments. In: WAFR, pp. 77–94 (2002)
17. Italiano, G.F., Pattanayak, D., Sharma, G.: Dispersion of mobile robots on directed anonymous graphs. In: Parter, M. (ed.) Structural Information and Communication Complexity. SIROCCO 2022. LNCS, vol. 13298, pp. 191–211. Springer, Cham (2022). https://doi.org/10.1007/978-3-031-09993-9_11
18. Kaur, T., Mondal, K.: Distance-2-dispersion: dispersion with further constraints. In: Mohaisen, D., Wies, T. (eds.) Networked Systems, pp. 157–173 (2023)
19. Kshemkalyani, A.D., Ali, F.: Efficient dispersion of mobile robots on graphs. In: ICDCN, pp. 218–227 (2019)
20. Kshemkalyani, A.D., Molla, A.R., Sharma, G.: Fast dispersion of mobile robots on arbitrary graphs. In: Dressler, F., Scheideler, C. (eds.) ALGOSENSORS 2019. LNCS, vol. 11931, pp. 23–40. Springer, Cham (2019). https://doi.org/10.1007/978-3-030-34405-4_2

21. Kshemkalyani, A.D., Molla, A.R., Sharma, G.: Dispersion of mobile robots on grids. In: Rahman, M.S., Sadakane, K., Sung, W.-K. (eds.) WALCOM 2020. LNCS, vol. 12049, pp. 183–197. Springer, Cham (2020). https://doi.org/10.1007/978-3-030-39881-1_16
22. Kshemkalyani, A.D., Molla, A.R., Sharma, G.: Efficient dispersion of mobile robots on dynamic graphs. In: ICDCS, pp. 732–742 (2020)
23. Kshemkalyani, A.D., Molla, A.R., Sharma, G.: Dispersion of mobile robots using global communication. J. Parallel Distrib. Comput. **161**, 100–117 (2022)
24. Kshemkalyani, A.D., Sharma, G.: Near-optimal dispersion on arbitrary anonymous graphs. In: Bramas, Q., Gramoli, V., Milani, A. (eds.) OPODIS. LIPIcs, vol. 217, pp. 8:1–8:19 (2021)
25. Menc, A., Pajak, D., Uznanski, P.: Time and space optimality of rotor-router graph exploration. Inf. Process. Lett. **127**, 17–20 (2017)
26. Molla, A.R., Moses, W.K.: Dispersion of mobile robots: the power of randomness. In: Gopal, T.V., Watada, J. (eds.) TAMC 2019. LNCS, vol. 11436, pp. 481–500. Springer, Cham (2019). https://doi.org/10.1007/978-3-030-14812-6_30
27. Molla, A.R., Mondal, K., Moses Jr, W.K.: Byzantine dispersion on graphs. In: IPDPS, pp. 942–951. IEEE (2021)
28. Molla, A.R., Mondal, K., Moses Jr, W.K.: Optimal dispersion on an anonymous ring in the presence of weak byzantine robots. Theor. Comput. Sci. **887**, 111–121 (2021)
29. Pattanayak, D., Sharma, G., Mandal, P.S.: Dispersion of mobile robots tolerating faults. In: WDALFR, pp. 17:1–17:6 (2021)
30. Poudel, P., Sharma, G.: Time-optimal uniform scattering in a grid. In: ICDCN, pp. 228–237 (2019)
31. Shibata, M., Mega, T., Ooshita, F., Kakugawa, H., Masuzawa, T.: Uniform deployment of mobile agents in asynchronous rings. In: PODC, pp. 415–424 (2016)
32. Shintaku, T., Sudo, Y., Kakugawa, H., Masuzawa, T.: Efficient dispersion of mobile agents without global knowledge. In: Devismes, S., Mittal, N. (eds.) SSS 2020. LNCS, vol. 12514, pp. 280–294. Springer, Cham (2020). https://doi.org/10.1007/978-3-030-64348-5_22
33. Subramanian, R., Scherson, I.D.: An analysis of diffusive load-balancing. In: SPAA, pp. 220–225 (1994)

Brief Announcement: Asynchronous Gathering of Finite Memory Robots on a Circle Under Limited Visibility

Satakshi Ghosh(✉), Avisek Sharma, Pritam Goswami, and Buddhadeb Sau

Jadavpur University, 188, Raja S.C. Mallick Rd, Kolkata 700032, India
{satakshighosh.math.rs,aviseks.math.rs, pritamgoswami.math.rs,buddhadeb.sau}@jadavpuruniversity.in

Abstract. In this paper, we consider a set of mobile entities, called robots, located in distinct locations and operating on a continuous circle of fixed radius. The gathering problem asks for the design of a distributed algorithm that allows the robots to assemble at a single point on the circle. Robots have limited visibility π, i.e., each robot can only see the points of the circle, which are at an angular distance strictly less than π from the robot. Di Luna *et al.* [1] provided a deterministic gathering algorithm of oblivious and silent robots on a circle under a semi-synchronous scheduler with π visibility. Now, considering the asynchronous scheduler, to the best of our knowledge, there is no work that solves this problem. So, here in this work, we have proposed a deterministic algorithm that gathers any number of robots on a circle having π visibility and finite memory under an asynchronous scheduler.

Keywords: Gathering · Asynchronous · Circle · Limited visibility · Robots · Finite memory

1 Introduction

In swarm robotics, robots achieving some tasks with minimum capabilities are the main focus of interest. If a swarm of robots with minimum capabilities can do the same task, then it is more effective to use swarm robots rather than robots with many capabilities, as designing the robots in the swarm is much cheaper and simpler than making robots with many capabilities. The gathering problem requires n robots that are initially positioned arbitrarily must meet at a single point within a finite time. Note that the meeting point is not fixed initially. In this work, we investigate the gathering of robots on a circle, and they are on the perimeter of a circle of fixed radius R. They can only move along the perimeter of that circle. Here the robots have limited visibility, which means each robot can see only the points on the circle that have an angular distance strictly smaller than a constant θ from the robot's current location, where $0 < \theta \leq \pi$. Here,

S. Dolev and B. Schieber (Eds.): SSS 2023, LNCS 14310, pp. 430–434, 2023.
https://doi.org/10.1007/978-3-031-44274-2_32

angles are expressed in radians. This problem becomes trivial if a unique leader can be chosen who remains the leader throughout the algorithm. But even with chirality, electing a unique leader is not trivial, even when the robots can not see only one point on the circle. Also, even if a unique leader is elected, making sure that the leader remains the leader throughout the execution of the algorithm is another challenge that has to be taken care of. This challenge makes this problem quite nontrivial and interesting.

Here we have proposed an algorithm for solving the gathering of robots on a circle with a finite memory robot model under ASYNC scheduler and visibility π. The work that is most related to our work is done by Di Luna *et al.* [1]. In their paper, they have shown that robots on a circle cannot gather if the visibility is less or equal to $\frac{\pi}{2}$ and provided an algorithm under SSYNC scheduler with oblivious robots considering a robot's having π visibility. In this paper, our main achievement is that, by equipping the robots with finite memory, we have gained a deterministic gathering algorithm that works under an asynchronous scheduler.

2 Robot Model

In the problem, we are considering the $\mathcal{FSTA}$ robot model. The robots are anonymous and identical, but not oblivious. Robots have a finite persistent memory. Robots cannot communicate with each other. Robots have weak multiplicity detection capability, i.e., robots can detect a multiplicity point, but cannot determine the number of robots present at a multiplicity point. All robots are placed on a circle of fixed radius. The robots agree on a global sense of handedness. All robots move at the same speed, and their movement is rigid. Robots operate in LOOK-COMPUTE-MOVE cycle. In each cycle, a robot takes a snapshot of the positions of the other robots according to its own local coordinate system (LOOK); based on this snapshot, it executes a deterministic algorithm to determine whether to stay put or to move to another point on the circle (COMPUTE); and based on the algorithm, the robots either remain stationary or make a move to a point (MOVE). In fully asynchronous adversarial scheduler (ASYNC), the robots are activated independently, and each robot executes its cycles independently. This implies the amount of time spent in LOOK, COMPUTE, MOVE, and inactive states are finite but unbounded, unpredictable, and not necessarily the same for different robots. We do not consider a general asynchronous scheduler. Precisely, we assumed that in the LCM cycle of a robot, it takes a non-zero time (non instantaneous) to finish its look and compute phase together. The robots have no common notion of time. Here, the initial configuration is asymmetric. Robots have limited visibility, which means they cannot see the entire circle. Let a and b be two points on a circle $\mathcal{C}$, then the angular distance between a and b is the measure of the angle subtended at the centre of $\mathcal{C}$ by the shorter arc with endpoints a and b. A robot has visibility π, which means that it can see all the other robots that have an angular distance less than π.

3 Definitions and Preliminaries

Before discussing the algorithm, we first introduce some definitions. A configuration with no multiplicity point is said to be *rotationally symmetric* if there is a nontrivial rotation with respect to the center which leaves the configuration unchanged. Let r be a robot in a given configuration with no multiplicity point and let $r_1, r_2, \ldots, r_n$ be the other robots on the circle in clockwise order. Then the *angular sequence* for robot r is the sequence

$$(cwAngle(r, r_1), cwAngle(r_1, r_2), cwAngle(r_2, r_3), \ldots, cwAngle(r_n, r)).$$

We denote this sequence as $\mathcal{S}(r)$. Further, we call $cwAngle(r, r_1)$ as the leading angle of r. A robot r is said to be an *antipodal robot* if there exists a robot r' on the angular distance π of the robot. In such a case, r and r' are said to be antipodal robots to each other. Note that a robot that is not antipodal is said to be a non antipodal robot. Also, as the configuration is initially rotationally asymmetric, based on the results from the paper [1] we can say that all the robots have distinct angle sequences. In a configuration, a robot with the lexicographically smallest angular sequence is called a *true leader.* If the configuration is rotationally asymmetric and contains no multiplicity point, there exists exactly one robot that has strictly the smallest lexicographic angle sequence. Hence, there is only one true leader in such a configuration. Since a robot on the circle cannot see whether its antipodal position is occupied by a robot or not. So a robot can assume two things: 1) the antipodal position is empty, let's call this configuration $C_0(r)$ 2) the antipodal position is nonempty, let's call this configuration $C_1(r)$. So a robot r can form two angular sequences. One considering $C_0(r)$ configuration and another considering $C_1(r)$. The next two definitions are from the viewpoint of a robot. There may be the following possibilities. Possibility-1: $C_0(r)$ configuration has rotational symmetry, so $C_1(r)$ is the only possible configuration. Possibility-2: $C_1(r)$ configuration has rotational symmetry, so $C_0(r)$ is the only possible configuration. Possibility-3: Both $C_0(r)$ and $C_1(r)$ has no rotational symmetry, so both $C_0(r)$ and $C_1(r)$ can be possible configurations.

A robot r in a rotationally asymmetric configuration with no multiplicity point is called *sure leader* if r is the true leader in $C_0(r)$ and $C_1(r)$ configurations. Note that, the Sure leader is definitely the true leader of the configuration. Hence at any time if the configuration is asymmetric and contains no multiplicity point, there is at most one Sure leader. A robot r in a rotationally asymmetric configuration with no multiplicity point is called a *confused leader* if both $C_0(r)$ and $C_1(r)$ are possible configurations and r is a true leader in one configuration but not in another. A robot in an asymmetric configuration with no multiplicity point is said to be a *follower* robot if it is neither a sure leader nor a confused leader. Suppose r is a confused leader, and s is the first clockwise neighbour of r. The robot s is said to be a *safe neighbour* of r if the first clockwise neighbour of the true leader of the $C_1(r)$ configuration is not antipodal to s.

Note that the above definitions are set in such a way that the sure leader (or, a confused leader or, a follower robot) can recognise itself as a sure leader (or, a confused leader or, a follower robot). One result that holds for any asymmetric configuration is:

Result 1. *For any given rotationally asymmetric configuration with no multiplicity point, there can be at most one confused leader other than the true leader.*

The Fig. 1 and Fig. 2 give the existence of all four above cases.

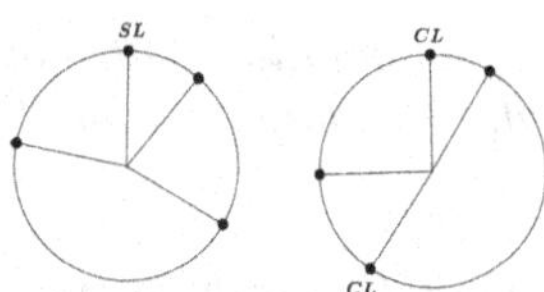

Fig. 1. Only one sure leader (SL) and two confused leaders (CL)

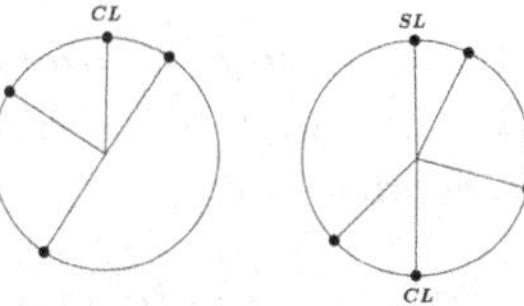

Fig. 2. Only one confused leader (CL) and one sure leader (SL) and one confused leader (CL).

4 Discussion of the Algorithm and Correctness

Each robot has four states that are `off`, `moveHalf`, `moveMore`, and `terminate`. A sure leader always moves to its neighbour's position and makes a multiplicity point. But a confused leader cannot always move to its neighbour's position. If a confused leader has a safe neighbour, then it will move to its neighbour's position and make a multiplicity point. But if the neighbour is not safe, then a confused leader will not always move to its neighbour's position. If the first clockwise neighbour of the confused leader (say, r) is not safe and the $C_0(r)$ configuration has another confused leader other than r, then r does nothing. But if the neighbour is not safe and there is no other confused leader in the $C_0(r)$ configuration, then r first changes its state to `moveHalf` and moves to the midpoint of the leading angle with the first clockwise neighbour. After this move, if r sees the sure leader of the initial configuration, then r changes its state `terminate` and moves counter clockwise to its initial position. So r will not move to its clockwise first neighbour position. But if the confused leader cannot see any robot, then it changes its state to `moveMore` and moves the midpoint of its leading angle with the clockwise neighbour. As the scheduler is non-standard asynchronous, after this move, r will know if its antipodal has a robot or not. So either it changes its state `terminate` or moves to the clockwise first neighbour position by changing its state `off` and makes a multiplicity point. So in all the cases, at least one and at most two multiplicity points will form. When a robot sees a multiplicity point and it is the first clockwise or counterclockwise neighbour of the multiplicity point, it will move to that multiplicity point. In this way, when all robots gather at any one multiplicity point between two multiplicity points, robots from one multiplicity point at a smaller clockwise distance from the other multiplicity point will move to the other multiplicity point. In this way, all robots will gather at a point and no longer move.

We have proved that, if all robots are initially placed in a rotationally asymmetric configuration with no multiplicity point, the execution of the algorithm ensures that all robots eventually meet at a point within a finite time and no longer move under the asynchronous scheduler. First, we demonstrate that, starting from the initial configuration, robots will produce at least one and a maximum of two multiplicity points during the algorithm's finite execution.

Theorem 1. *Let C be a rotationally asymmetric configuration with no multiplicity point, then after finite execution of Algorithm at least one multiplicity point will be created.*

Lemma 1. *From any rotationally asymmetric configuration with no multiplicity point, within finite execution of Algorithm, the robots can form at most two multiplicity points, and then all robots gather at a point on the circle.*

Hence, we can conclude the following theorem.

Theorem 2. *There exists a gathering algorithm that gathers any set of robots with finite memory and π visibility from any initial rotationally asymmetric configuration under asynchronous scheduler.*

Details results and proofs are available in the full version of the paper [2].

5 Conclusion

In this paper, we present a gathering algorithm for robots with finite memory on a circle under an asynchronous scheduler with visibility π. Robots are initially in distinct positions on the circle, forming any rotationally asymmetric configuration. We assume that each robot has finite persistent memory. For future studies on this problem, it will be interesting if one can give a gathering algorithm when robots are oblivious or the visibility is less than π.

Acknowledgement. The first author is supported by the West Bengal State Government Fellowship Scheme. The Second and third authors are supported by UGC, the Government of India.

References

1. Luna, G.A.D., Uehara, R., Viglietta, G., Yamauchi, Y.: Gathering on a circle with limited visibility by anonymous oblivious robots. In: DISC 2020, pp. 12:1–12:17 (2020)
2. Ghosh, S., Sharma, A., Goswami, P., Sau B.: Asynchronous gathering of robots with finite memory on a circle under limited visibility. CoRR abs/2302.07600 (2023)

Wait-Free Updates and Range Search Using Uruv

Gaurav Bhardwaj[1(✉)], Bapi Chatterjee[2], Abhay Jain[1], and Sathya Peri[1]

[1] Indian Institute of Technology Hyderabad, Hyderabad, India
CS19RESCH11003@iith.ac.in

[2] Indraprastha Institute of Information Technology Delhi, Delhi, India

Abstract. CRUD operations, along with range queries make a highly useful abstract data type (ADT), employed by many dynamic analytics tasks. Despite its wide applications, to our knowledge, no fully wait-free data structure is known to support this ADT. In this paper, we introduce Uruv, a proactive linearizable and practical wait-free concurrent data structure that implements the ADT mentioned above. Structurally, Uruv installs a balanced search index on the nodes of a linked list. Uruv is the first wait-free and proactive solution for concurrent B^+tree. Experiments show that Uruv significantly outperforms previously proposed lock-free B^+trees for dictionary operations and a recently proposed lock-free method to implement the ADT mentioned above.

Keywords: Wait-Free · Lock-Free · Range Search · B+ Tree

1 Introduction

With the growing size of main memory, the in-memory big-data analytics engines are becoming increasingly popular [25]. Often the analytics tasks are based on retrieving keys from a dataset specified by a given range. Additionally, such applications are deployed in a streaming setting, e.g., Flurry [12], where the dataset ingests real-time updates. Ensuring progress to every update would be attractive for many applications in this setting, such as financial analytics [21]. The demand for real-time high-valued analytics, the powerful multicore CPUs, and the availability of large main memory together motivate designing scalable concurrent data structures to utilize parallel resources efficiently.

It is an ever desirable goal to achieve *maximum progress* of the concurrent operations on a data structure. The maximum progress guarantee – called *wait-freedom* [14] – ensures that each concurrent non-faulty thread completes its operation in a finite number of steps. Traditionally, wait-freedom has been known for its high implementation cost and subsided performance. Concomitantly, a weaker guarantee that some non-faulty threads will finitely complete their operations – known as *lock-freedom* – has been a more popular approach. However, it has been found that the lock-free data structures can be transformed to *practical* wait-free [16] ones with some additional implementation and performance overhead. Progress promises of wait-free data structures make their development

S. Dolev and B. Schieber (Eds.): SSS 2023, LNCS 14310, pp. 435–450, 2023.
https://doi.org/10.1007/978-3-031-44274-2_33

imperative, to which a practical approach is to co-design them with their efficient lock-free counterpart. While a progress guarantee is desirable, consistency of concurrent operations is a necessity. The most popular consistency framework is *linearizability* [15], i.e., every concurrent operation emerges taking effect at an atomic step between its invocation and return.

In the existing literature, the lock-free data structures such as k-ary search trees [7], and the lock-based key-value map KiWi [3] provide range search. In addition, several generic methods of concurrent range search have been proposed. Chatterjee [9] presented a lock-free range search algorithm for lock-free linked-lists, skip-lists, and binary search trees. Arbel-Raviv and Brown [1] proposed a more generic approach associated with memory reclamation that fits into different concurrency paradigms, including lock-based and software transactional memory-based data structures. Recently, two more approaches – bundled-reference [19] and constant time snapshots [24] – were proposed along the same lines of generic design. Both these works derive from similar ideas of expanding the data structure with versioned updates to ensure linearizability of scans. While the former stores pointers with time-stamped updates, the latter adds objects to nodes time-stamped by every new range search. Moreover, bundled-reference [19] design requires locks in every node.

In most cases, for example [3,9,19,24], the range scans are unobstructed even if a concurrent modification (addition, deletion, or update) to the data structure starves to take even the first atomic step over a shared node or pointer. A reader would perceive, indeed for good reasons, that once the modifications are made wait-free the entire data structure will become wait-free. However, to our knowledge, none of these works actually investigates how trivial or non-trivial it would be to arrive at the final implementation of concurrent wait-free CRUD and range-search. This is exactly where our work contributes.

Proposed Wait-Free Linearizable Proactive Data Structure

In principle, Uruv's design derives from that of a B$^+$Tree [10], a self-balancing data structure. However, we need to make the following considerations:

Wait-Freedom: Firstly, to ensure wait-freedom to an operation that needs to perform at least one `CAS` execution on a shared-memory word, it must *announce* its invocation [16]. Even if delayed, the announcement has to happen on realizing that the first `CAS` was attempted a sufficient number of times, and yet it starved [16]. The announcement of invocation is then followed by a *guaranteed help* by a concurrent operation at some finite point [16].

Linearizability: Now, to ensure linearizability of a scan requires that its output reflects the relevant changes made by every update during its lifetime. The technique of repeated multi-scan followed by validation [7], and collecting the updates at an augmented object, such as RangeCollector in [9], to let the range search incorporate them before it returns, have been found scaling poorly [7,9]. Differently, multi-versioning of objects, for example [19], can have a (theoretical) possibility to stockpile an infinite number of versioned pointers between two nodes. Interestingly, [1] exploits the memory reclamation mechanism to synchronize the range scans with delete operations via logically deleted nodes. However, for lock-freedom, they use a *composite primitive* double-compare-single-swap (DCSS). In comparison, [24] uses only single-word CAS. However, managing the announcement by a starving updater that performs the first CAS to introduce a versioned node to the data structure requires care for a wait-free design.

Node Structure: The "fat" (array-based) data nodes, for example Kiwi [3], improve traversal performance by memory contiguity [17]. However, the benchmarks in [24] indicate that it does not necessarily help as the number of concurrent updates picks up. Similarly, the lock-free B+trees by Braginsky and Petrank [5] used memory chunks, and our experiments show that their method substantially underperforms. Notwithstanding, it is wise to exploit memory contiguity wherever there could be a scope of "slow" updates in a concurrent setting.

Proactive Maintenance: Finally, if the number of keys in a node exceeds (falls short of) its maximum (minimum) threshold after an insertion (deletion), it requires splitting (merging). The operation splitting the node divides it into two while adding a key to its parent node. It is possible that the split can percolate to the root of the data structure if the successive parent nodes reach their respective thresholds. Similarly, merging children nodes can cause cascading merges of successive parent nodes. With concurrency, it becomes extremely costly to tackle such cascaded split or merge of nodes from a leaf to the root. An alternative to this is a *proactive approach* which checks threshold of nodes whiles traversing down a tree every time; if a node is found to have reached its threshold, without waiting for its children, a pre-emptive split or merge is performed. As a result, a restructure remains localized. To our knowledge, no existing concurrent tree structure employs this proactive strategy.

With these considerations, we introduce a key-value store **Uruv** (or, Uruvriksha[1]) for wait-free updates and range search. More specifically,

(a) Uruv stores keys with associated values in leaf nodes structured as linked-list. The interconnected leaf nodes are indexed by a balanced tree of fat nodes, essentially, a classical B+ Tree [10], to facilitate fast key queries (Sect. 2).
(b) The key-nodes are augmented with list of versioned nodes to facilitate range scans synchronize with updates (Sect. 3).
(c) Uruv uses single-word CAS primitives. Following the fast-path-slow-path technique of Kogan and Petrank [16], we *optimize* the helping procedure for wait-freedom (Sect. 4). We prove linearizability and wait-freedom and present the upper bound of step complexity of operations (Sect. 5).
(d) Our C++ implementation of Uruv significantly outperforms existing similar approaches – lock-free B+tree of [5], and OpenBWTree [23] for dictionary operations. It also outperforms a recently proposed method by Wei et al. [24] for concurrent workloads involving range search (Sect. 6).

A full version of the paper is available at http://arxiv.org/abs/2307.14744 [4]. Please refer to the full version for detailed pseudocode.

[1] Uruvriksha is the Sanskrit word for a wide tree.

2 Preliminaries

We consider the standard shared-memory model with atomic `read`, `write`, `FAA` (fetch-and-increment), and `CAS` (compare-and-swap) instructions. Uruv implements a key-value store $(\mathcal{K}, \mathcal{V})$ of keys $K \in \mathcal{K}$ and their associated values $V \in \mathcal{V}$.

The Abstract Data Type (ADT): We consider an ADT $\mathcal{A}$ as a set of operations: $\mathcal{A}$ = {INSERT(K, V), DELETE(K), SEARCH(K), RANGEQUERY ($K1, K2$)}

1. An INSERT(K, V) inserts the key K and an associated value V if $K \notin \mathcal{K}$.
2. A DELETE(K) deletes the key K and its associated value if $K \in \mathcal{K}$.
3. A SEARCH(K) returns the associated value of key K if $K \in \mathcal{K}$; otherwise, it returns -1. It does not modify $(\mathcal{K}, \mathcal{V})$.
4. A RANGEQUERY(K_1, K_2) returns keys $\{K \in \mathcal{K} : K_1 \leq K \leq K_2\}$, and associated values without modifying $(\mathcal{K}, \mathcal{V})$; if no such key exists, it returns -1.

2.1 Basics of Uruv's Lock-Free Linearizable Design

Uruv derives from a B$^+$Tree [10], a self-balancing data structure. However, to support linearizable range search operations, they are equipped with additional components. The key-value pairs in Uruv are stored in the *key nodes*. A *leaf node* of Uruv is a sorted linked-list of key nodes. Thus, the leaf nodes of Uruv differ from the array-based leaf nodes of a B$^+$Tree. The *internal nodes* are implemented by arrays containing ordered set of keys and pointers to its descendant children, which facilitate traversal from the root to key nodes. A search path in Uruv is shown in Fig. 1.

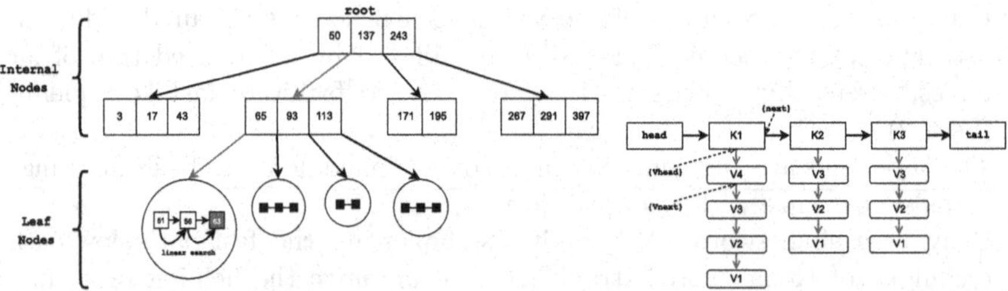

Fig. 1. Example of Uruv's design. In this example, a search operation is being performed wherein the red arrows indicate a traversal down Uruv, and we find the key, highlighted red, in the linked-list via a linear search. (Color figure online)

Fig. 2. Versioned key nodes

Unlike an array in a B+Tree's leaf node, the key nodes making leaf nodes of Uruv contain lists of versioning nodes mainly to ensure linearizability of range search operations. The mechanism of linearizable range search derives from that of Wei et al. [24] – every range search increments a data structure-wide version counter whereby concurrent addition and removal operations determine their versions. A range search returns the keys and corresponding values only if its version is at most the version of the range search. Thus the linearization point of range search coincides with the atomic increment of version counter.

The associated values to a key are stored in the versioning nodes, see Fig. 2. The creation of a key-value pair, its deletion, and addition back to the key-value store updates the version list with a version and associated value. With this design, Uruv supports concurrent linearizable implementation of the ADT operations as described above.

3 Lock-Free Algorithm

3.1 The Structures of the Component Nodes

Here we first describe the structure of the nodes in Uruv. See Fig. 3. A versioning node is implemented by the objects of type Vnode. A key node as described in the last section, is implemented by the objects of the class llNode. Nodes of type llNode make the linked-list of a leaf-node which is implemented by the class VLF_LL.

The leaf and internal nodes of Uruv inherit the Node class. See Fig. 4. An object of class Node of Uruv, hereafter referred to as a node object, keeps count of the number of keys. A node object also stores a boolean to indicate if it is a leaf node. A boolean variable 'frozen' helps with "freezing a node" while undergoing a split or merge in a lock-free updatable setting. A thread on finding that a node is frozen helps the operation that triggered the freezing.

```
Vnode{
    value_t value;
    int ts;
    Vnode* nextv;
}

llNode{
    key_t key;
    Vnode* vhead;
    llNode* next;
}

VLF_LL{
    llNode* head;
}
```

Fig. 3. Versioned Lock-Free Linked-List Data Structure

Every leaf node has three pointers *next*, *newNext* and a pointer to version list *ver_head* and one variable *ts* for the timestamp. The *next* pointer points to the next adjacent leaf node in Uruv. When a leaf node is split or merged, the *newNext* pointer ensures leaf connection. A new leaf node is created to replace it when a leaf node is balanced. Using the *newNext* pointer, we connect the old and new leaf nodes. When traversing the leaf nodes for RangeQuery with *newNext* set, we follow *newNext* instead of *next* since that node has been replaced by a newer node, ensuring correct traversal. The initial *ts* value is associated with the construction of the leaf node.

```
Uruv{
    Node* root;
}
InternalNode: Node{
    long key[MAX]
    Node* ptr[MAX+1]
    helpidx
}
LeafNode: Node{
    VLF_LL* ver_head;
    LeafNode* next;
    LeafNode* newNext;
    int ts
}
Node{
    long count;
    bool isLeaf;
    bool frozen;
}
```

Fig. 4. The details of object structures

3.2 Versioned Linked-List

The description of lock-free linearizable implementation of the ADT operations RangeQuery, Insert, and Delete requires detailing the versioned linked list. A versioned list holds the values associated with the key held at various periods. Each versioned node (`Vnode`) in the versioned list has a value, the time when the value was modified, and a link to the previous version of that key. Versioned linked-list information may be seen in Fig. 2 and Fig. 3. The versioned list's nodes are ordered in descending order by the time they have been updated. Compared to the [13], there is no actual delinking of nodes; instead, we utilise a tombstone value (a special value not associated with any key) to indicate a deleted node. Moreover, deleting a node requires no help since there is no delinking. Although, for memory reclamation, we retain a record of active RangeQuery and release nodes that are no longer needed. Any modification to the versioned linked list atomically adds a version node to the `vhead` of `llNode` using `CAS`.

3.3 Traversal and Proactive Maintenance in Uruv

We traverse from root to leaf following the order provided by the keys in the internal nodes. In each internal node, a binary search is performed to determine the appropriate child pointer. While traversal in Insert and Delete operations, we follow the proactive approach as described earlier. Essentially, if we notice that a node's key count has violated the maximum/minimum threshold, we instantly conduct a split/merge action, and the traversal is restarted. The proactive maintenance is shown in Fig. 5.

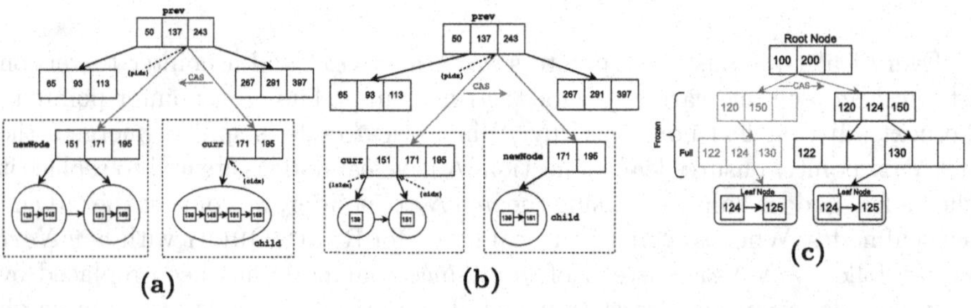

Fig. 5. (a) Split Leaf, (b) Merge Leaf, (c) Split Internal

3.4 ADT Operations

```
1:  Insert(key, value)
2:     retry:
3:     Node* curr := root
4:     if curr = nullptr then
5:        Node* nLeaf →insLeaf(key, value)
6:        if !root.CAS(curr, nLeaf) then
7:           goto retry
8:        else return
9:     curr := balanceRoot(curr)
10:    if !curr then goto retry
11:    Node* prev, child := nullptr
12:    int pidx, cidx
13:    while !curr → isLeaf do
14:       if curr → helpIdx ≠ −1 then
15:          Node* res := help(prev, pidx, curr)
16:          if res then curr := res
17:          else goto retry
18:       cidx is set to the index of appropriate child based on key using Binary Search
19:       child := curr → ptr[cidx]
20:       if child → isLeaf && child → frozen then
21:          curr → freezeInternal()
22:          if !curr →setHelpIdx(cidx) then
23:             goto retry
24:          Node*newNode := child → balanceLeaf(prev, pidx, curr, cidx)
25:          if newNode then
26:             then curr := newNode
27:          else goto retry
28:       else if !child → isLeaf && child → count ≥ MAX then
29:          curr → freezeInternal()
30:          if !curr →setHelpIdx(cidx) then
31:             goto retry
32:          Node* newNode := child → splitInternal(prev, pidx, curr, cidx)
33:          if newNode then
34:             then curr := newNode
35:          else goto retry
36:       prev := curr
37:       curr := child
38:       pidx := cidx
39:    res := curr → insertLeaf(key, value)
40:    if res = Failed then
41:       goto retry
42:    else return res
```

Fig. 6. Pseudocode of INSERT operation

An Insert operation starts with performing a traversal as described above to locate the leaf node to insert a key and its associated value. It begins with the root node; if it does not exist, it builds a new leaf node and makes it the root with a CAS. If it cannot update the root, another thread has already changed it, and it retries insertion. Method balanceRoot splits the root if needed and replaces it with a new root using CAS. If CAS fails, then some other thread must have changed the root, and it returns null. If there is no need to split the root, it will return the current root (Fig. 6).

Lines 14–17 describe the helping mechanism, which makes the data structure lock-free. If any node helpIdx is set to a value other than −1, then the child node at helpIdx is undergoing the split/merge process. In that case, it will help that child finish its split/merge operation. Method help helps *child* node in split/merge operation and returns the new *curr* node if it successfully replaces it using *CAS*; otherwise, it returns null. Then, it performs a binary search over *curr*'s keys at line 18 to find the correct child pointer. It copies the child pointer into *child* and stores its index in the pointer array as *cidx*.

If the child node is a frozen leaf node or an internal node that has reached the threshold, it performs a split/merge operation. It starts by freezing its parent, *curr*, at line 21 by setting a special freezing marker on every child pointer, so that no other thread can change the parent node and cause inconsistency. After freezing the parent, it stores the index of the child pointer in helpIdx of the parent node using *CAS* so that other threads can help in split/merge operation. If setHelpIdx fails, that means some other thread has already set the helpIdx, and it retries.

Restructuring a *child* is performed at line 24 and 32 using balanceLeaf and splitInternal respectively. balanceLeaf performs the split/merge operation on the leaf node based on the number of elements and returns the node replaced by the parent node using CAS. Similarly, splitInternal splits the internal node and returns the new parent node. If in any of the above methods, CAS is failed, then some other thread must have replaced it, and it will return nullptr and retries at line 31 and 35. It repeats the same process until it reaches the leaf node. Once it reaches the leaf node, it performs the insert operation in the leaf node at line 39. It returns on success, otherwise it retries.

Insert into a Leaf. In the leaf node, all the updates occur concurrently in the versioned linked list. It first checks if the leaf node is frozen. If it is, it returns "Failed", realizing that another thread is trying to balance this node. If the node's count has reached the maximum threshold, it freezes it and returns "Failed". Leaf node is frozen by setting a special freezing mark on llnode *next* pointer and the *vhead* pointer. In both the cases, when it returns "Failed" insertion will be retried after balancing it. Otherwise, it would insert the key into the versioned lock-free linked list. If another thread is concurrently freezing the leaf node, the insertion into the linked list might fail. If it fails, it will again return "Failed" and retries the insertion. If the key is already present in the linked list, it updates that key's version by adding a new version node in the version list head with a new value. Else it will create a new node in the linked list containing the key and its value in the version node. After the key is inserted/updated in the linked list, its timestamp is set to the current timestamp, which is the linearization point for insertion in the tree.

A Delete operation follows a similar approach as INSERT. It traverses the tree to the leaf node, where the key is present. The difference in traversal with respect to INSERT operation is that at line 28, instead of checking the max threshold, it checks for the minimum threshold. Instead of splitting the internal node at line 32, it merges the internal node. Once a leaf node is found, it checks whether the key is in the linked list. If it is in the linked list, it will update a tombstone value in the version list to mark that key as deleted. If the key is absent, it returns "Key not Present".

Delete from Leaf. If the key is present, this operation creates a versioned node with a tombstone value to set it as deleted. Just like inserting the new versioned node its timestamp is set to the current timestamp. If the key is not present in the linked list it simply returns "Key Not Present".

Search Operation. Traversal to a leaf node in case of searching doesn't need to perform any balancing. After finding the leaf node, it checks the key in the linked list; if it is present, it returns the value from the version node from the head of the list; otherwise, it simply returns "Key not Present". Before reading the value from the versioned node it checks if the timestamp is set or not. If it is not set, it sets the timestamp as the current timestamp before reading the value.

RangeQuery. A range query returns keys and their associated values by a given range from the data. Uruv supports a linearizable range query employing a multi-version linked list augmented to the nodes containing keys. This approach draws from Wei et al. [24]'s work. A global timestamp is read and updated every time a range query is run. The leaf node having a key larger than or equal to the beginning of the supplied range is searched after reading the current time. Then, it chooses a value for the relevant key from the versioned list of values. Figure 5(c) depicts a versioned linked list, with the higher versions representing the most recent modifications.

By iterating over each versioned node individually, it selects the first value in the list whose timestamp is smaller than the current one. This means that the value was changed before the start of the range query, making it consistent. It continues to add all keys and values that are less than or equal to the end of the given range. Because all of the leaf nodes are connected, traversing them is quick. After gathering the relevant keys and values, the range query will produce the result.

As a leaf node could be under split or merge, for every leaf node that we traverse, we first check whether their *newNext* is set. If it is and the leaf pointed to by *newNext* has a timestamp lower than the range query's timestamp, it traverses the *newNext* pointer. This ensures that our range query collects data from the correct leaf nodes. Were the timestamp not part of the leaf node, there is a chance that the range query traverses *newNext* pointers indefinitely due to repeated balancing of the leaf nodes.

4 Wait-Free Construction

We now discuss a wait-free extension to the presented lock-free algorithm above. Wait-freedom is achieved using fast-path-slow-path method [22]. More specifically, a wait-free operation starts exactly as the lock-free algorithm. This is termed as the *fast path*. If a thread cannot complete its operation even after several attempts, it enters the *slow path* by announcing that it would need help. To that effect, we maintain a global `stateArray` to keep track of the operations that every thread currently needs help with. In the slow path, an operation first publishes a `State` object containing all the information required to help complete its operation.

For every thread that announces its entry to the slow path, it needs to find helpers. After completing some fixed number of fast path operations, every thread will check if another thread needs some help. This is done by keeping track of the thread to be helped in a thread-local `HelpRecord` object presented in Fig. 7. After completing the *nextCheck* amount of fast path operations, it will assist the *currTid*. Before helping, it checks if *lastPhase* equals *phase* in *currTid*'s `stateArray` entry. If it does, the fast path thread will help execute the wait-free implementation of that operation; otherwise, *currTid* doesn't require helping as its entry in the `stateArray` has changed, meaning the operation has already been completed. In the worst case, if the helping thread also faces massive contention, every available thread will eventually execute the same operation, ensuring its success.

```
State* stateArray[totalThreads]

class HelpRecord{
    long currTid;
    long lastPhase;
    long nextCheck;
}
```

```
class State{
    long phase;
    bool finished;
    Vnode* vnode;
    long key;
    long value;
    llNode* searchNode
}
```

Fig. 7. Data structures used in wait-free helping

Notice that when data and updates are uniformly distributed, the contention among threads is low, often none. Concomitantly, in such cases, a slow path by any thread is minimally taken.

Wait-Free Insert. Traversal in Wait-free INSERT is the same as that in the lock-free INSERT as mentioned in Sect. 3. While traversal a thread could fail the `CAS` operation in a split/merge operation of a node and would need to restart traversal from the root again. At first glance, this would appear to repeat indefinitely, contradicting wait-freedom, but this operation will eventually finish due to helping. If a thread repeatedly fails to traverse Uruv due to such failure, every other thread will eventually help it find the leaf node. Once we reach the leaf node, we add the key to the versioned linked list as described below. There are two cases - either a node containing the key already exists, or a node does not exist.

In the former case, we need to update the linked list node's *vhead* with the versioned node, *vnode*, containing the new value using `CAS`. The significant difference between both methods is the usage of a shared `Vnode` from the `stateArray` in wait-free versus a thread local `Vnode` in lock-free. Every thread helping this insert will take this *vnode* from the `stateArray` and first checks the variable finished if the operation has already finished. They then check if the phase is the same in the `stateArray`, and *vnode*'s timestamp is set or not. If either is not true, some other thread has already completed the operation, and they mark the operation as finished. Else, they will try to update the *vhead* with *vnode* atomically. After inserting the *vnode*, it initialises the timestamp and sets the finished to be true.

In the latter case, we create a linked list node, *newNode*, and set its *vhead* to the *vnode* in the `stateArray` entry. It tries adding *newNode* like the lock-free linked list's insert. If it is successful, the timestamp of *vnode* is initialized, and the finished is set to true in the `stateArray`.

Wait-Free Delete. DELETE operation follows the same approach as INSERT. If the key is not present in the leaf node, it returns "Key Not Present" and sets the finished to be true. Otherwise, it will add the *vnode* from `stateArray` similar to wait-free INSERT. The only difference is that the *vnode* contains the tombstone value for a deleted node.

Search and RangeQuery. Neither operation modifies Uruv nor helps any other operation; hence their working remain as explained in Sect. 3.

5 Correctness and Progress Arguments

To prove the correctness of Uruv, we have shown that Uruv is linearizable by describing *linearization points* (LPs) that map any concurrent setting to a sequential order of said operations. We discuss them in detail below.

5.1 Linearization Points

As explained earlier, we traverse down Uruv to the correct leaf node and perform all operations on the linked list in that leaf. Therefore, we discuss the LPs of the versioned linked list.

Insert: There are two cases. If the key does not exist, we insert the key into the linked list. However, the timestamp of the `vnode` is not set, so the LP for INSERT operation is when the timestamp of `vnode` is set to the current timestamp. This can be executed either just after the insertion of the key in the linked list or by some other thread before reading the value from `vnode`.

If the key already exists, we update its value by atomically replacing a new versioned node by its current *vhead*. After successfully changing the *vhead*, the node's timestamp is still not set. It can be set just after adding the new versioned node or by some other thread before reading the value from the newly added versioned node. In both the cases the LP is when the timestamp of the versioned node is set to the current timestamp.

Delete. There are two cases. If the key does not exist, then there is no need to delete the key as it does not exist. Therefore, the LP would be where we last read a node from the linked list. Instead, if the key exists, the LP will be same as INSERT when we set the timestamp of the versioned node.

Search. There are two cases, first if the key doesn't exist in the linked list, the SEARCH LP would be when we first read the node whose key is greater than the key we are searching for in the linked list. Second, if the key is present in the linked list it reads the value in the versioned node at `vhead`. So the LP is when we atomically reads the value from the versioned node. If a concurrent insert/delete leads to a split/merge operation, then there is a chance that the search will end up at a leaf node that is no longer a part of Uruv. In that case, the search's LP would have happened before insert/delete's LP. Search's LP remains the same as above.

RangeQuery. RANGEQUERY method reads the global timestamp and increment it by 1. So the LP for range query would be the atomic read of global timestamp. The range query's LP will remain the same regardless of any other concurrent operation.

6 Experiments

In this section, we benchmark Uruv against (a) previous lock-free variants of the B$^+$Tree for updates and search operations (to our knowledge, there are no existing wait-free implementations of the B$^+$Tree, and lock-free B$^+$Trees do not implement range search), and (b) the lock-free VCAS-BST of [24], which is the best-performing data structure in their benchmark. The code of the benchmarks is available at https://github.com/PDCRL/Uruv.git.

Experimental Setup. We conducted our experiments on a system with an IBM Power9 model 2.3 CPU packing 40 cores with a minimum clock speed of 2.30 GHz and a maximum clock speed of 3.8 GHz. There are four logical threads for each core, and each has a private 32 KB L1 data cache and L1 instruction cache. Every pair of cores shares a 512 KB L2 cache and a 10 MB L3 cache. The system has 240 GB RAM and a 2 TB hard disk. The machine runs Ubuntu 18.04.6 LTS. We implement Uruv in C++. Our code was compiled using g++ 11.1.0 with -std = c++17 and linked the pthread and atomic libraries. We take the average of the last seven runs out of 10 total runs, pre-warming the cache the first three times. Our average excludes outliers by considering results closest to the median.

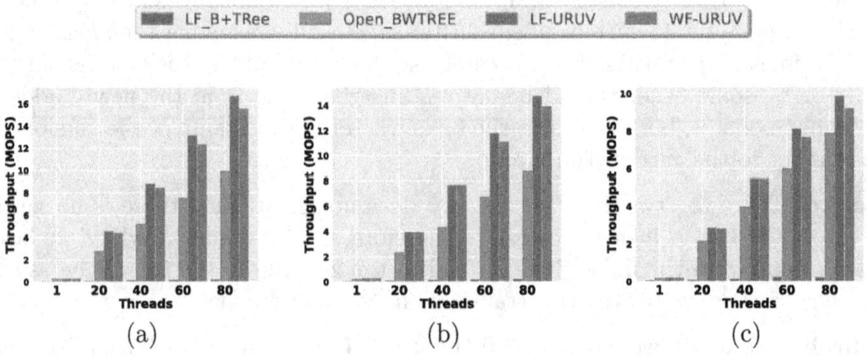

Fig. 8. The performance of **Uruv** when compared to **LF_B+Tree** [5] and **Open_BwTree** [23]. Higher is better. The workload distributions are (a) Reads - 100% (b) Reads - 95%, Updates - 5%, and (c) Reads - 50%, Updates - 50%

Benchmark. Our benchmark takes 7 parameters - read, insert, delete, range query, range query size, prefilling size, and dataset size. Read, insert, delete, and range queries indicate the percentage of these operations. We use a uniform distribution to choose between these four operations probabilistically. We prefill each data structure with 100 million keys, uniformly at random, from a universe of 500 million keys ranging [1, 500M].

Performance for Dictionary Operations. Results of three different workloads - Read-only (Fig. 8a), Read-Heavy (Fig. 8b), and a Balanced workload (Fig. 8c) are shown in Fig. 8. Across the workloads, at 80 threads, Uruv beats LF_B$^+$Tree [5] by **95**×, **76**×, and **44**× as it replaces the node with a new node for every insert.

Uruv beats OpenBwTree [23] by **1.7**×, **1.7**×, and **1.25**×. The performance of LF-URUV and WF-URUV correlates since WF-URUV has a lower possibility of any thread taking a slow path. In all three cases, the gap between Uruv and the rest increases as the number of threads increases. This shows the scalability of the proposed method. As we move from 1 to 80 threads, Uruv scales **46**× to **61**× in performance, LFB$^+$Tree scales **2.4**× to **5**× and OpenBw-Tree scales **39**× to **42**×. These results establish the significantly superior performance of Uruv over its existing counterpart.

Performance for Workloads Including Range Search. We compare Uruv against VCAS-BST in various workloads in Fig. 9. Figures 9a–9c are read-heavy workloads and Fig. 9d–9f are update-heavy workloads. Across each type of workload, we vary the range query percentage from 1% to 10%. At 80 threads, we beat VCAS-BST by **1.38**× in update-heavy workloads and **1.68**× in read-heavy workloads. These set of results demonstrate the efficacy of Uruv's wait-free range search.

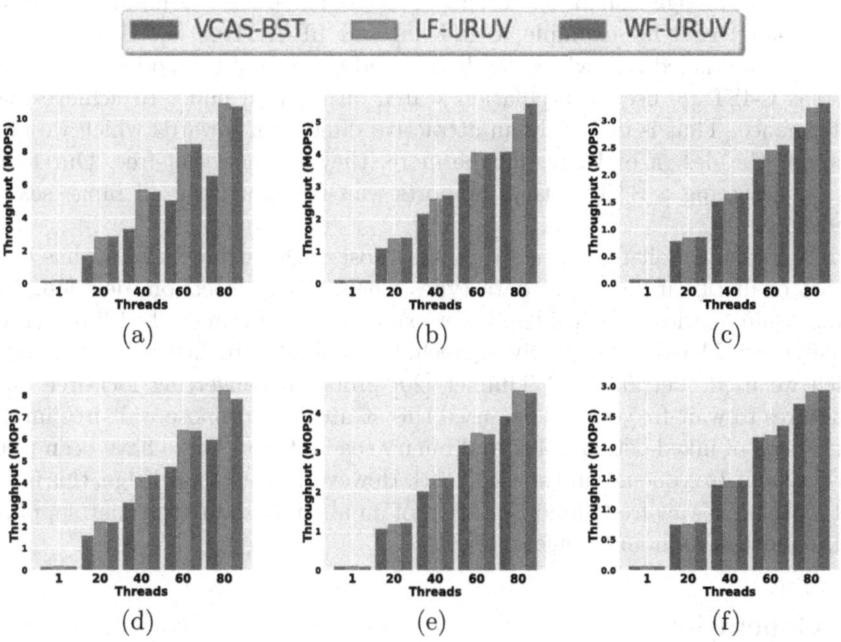

Fig. 9. The performance of **Uruv** when compared to **VCAS-BST**. The workload distributions are (a) Reads - 94%, Updates - 5%, Range Queries of size 1K - 1%, (b) Reads - 90%, Updates - 5%, Range Queries of size 1K - 5%, (c) Reads - 85%, Updates - 5%, Range Queries of size 1K - 10%, (d) Reads - 49%, Updates - 50%, Range Queries of size 1K - 1%, (e) Reads - 45%, Updates - 50%, Range Queries of size 1K - 5%, and (f) Reads - 40%, Updates - 50%, Range Queries of size 1K - 10%

7 Related Work

We have already discussed the salient points where Uruv differs from existing techniques of concurrent range search. In particular, in contrast to the locking method of bundled references [19] and the lock-free method of constant time snapshots [24], Uruv guarantees wait-freedom. The architecture ensuring wait-freedom in Uruv, i.e., its `stateArray`, has to accommodate its multi-versioning. The existing methods did not have to consider this.

Anastasia et al. [5] developed the first lock-free B^{+}Tree. In their design, every node implements a linked-list augmented with an array. This ensures that each node in the linked-list is allocated contiguously. It slows down updates at the leaf and traversal down their tree. Uruv's design is inspired by their work, but, does away with the arrays in the nodes. As the experiments showed, it clearly benefits. Most importantly, we also support linearizable wait-free range search, which is not available in [5]. OpenBw-Tree [23] is an optimized lock-free B^{+}tree that was designed to achieve high performance under realistic workloads. However, again, it does not support range search.

We acknowledge that other recently proposed tree data structures could be faster than Uruv, for example, C-IST [8] and LF-ABTree [6]. However, LF-ABTree is a relaxed tree where the height and the size of the nodes are relaxed whereas C-IST [8] uses interpolation search on internal nodes to achieve high performance. That is definitely an attractive dimension towards which we plan to adapt the design of Uruv. Furthermore, they are not wait-free. Our focus was on designing a B^{+}Tree that supports wait-free updates and range search operations.

In regards to wait-free data structures, most of the attempts so far has been for Set or dictionary abstract data types wherein only insertion, deletion, and membership queries are considered. For example, Natarajan et al. [18] presented wait-free red-black trees. Applying techniques similar to fast-path-slow-path, which we used, Petrank and Timmet [20] proposed converting lock-free data structures to wait-free ones. They used this strategy to propose wait-free implementations of inked-list, skip-list and binary search trees. There have been prior work on wait-free queues and stacks [2,11]. However, to our knowledge, this is the first work on a wait-free implementation of an abstract data type that supports add, remove, search and range queries.

8 Conclusion

We developed an efficient concurrent data structure Uruv that supports wait-free addition, deletion, membership search and range search operations. Theoretically, Uruv offers a finite upper bound on the step complexity of each operation, the first in this setting. On the practical side, Uruv significantly outperforms the existing lock-free B^{+}Tree variants and a recently proposed linearizable lock-free range search algorithm.

References

1. Arbel-Raviv, M., Brown, T.: Harnessing epoch-based reclamation for efficient range queries. ACM SIGPLAN Not. **53**(1), 14–27 (2018)
2. Attiya, H., Castañeda, A., Hendler, D.: Nontrivial and universal helping for wait-free queues and stacks. J. Parallel Distrib. Comput. **121**, 1–14 (2018)
3. Basin, D., et al.: KiWi: a key-value map for scalable real-time analytics. In: PPOPP, pp. 357–369 (2017)
4. Bhardwaj, G., Jain, A., Chatterjee, B., Peri, S.: Wait-free updates and range search using Uruv (2023). arXiv:2307.14744
5. Braginsky, A., Petrank, E.: A lock-free B+ tree. In: Proceedings of the Twenty-Fourth Annual ACM Symposium on Parallelism in Algorithms and Architectures, pp. 58–67 (2012)
6. Brown, T.: Techniques for constructing efficient lock-free data structures. CoRR, abs/1712.05406 (2017). arXiv:1712.05406
7. Brown, T., Avni, H.: Range queries in non-blocking k-ary search trees. In: Baldoni, R., Flocchini, P., Binoy, R. (eds.) OPODIS 2012. LNCS, vol. 7702, pp. 31–45. Springer, Heidelberg (2012). https://doi.org/10.1007/978-3-642-35476-2_3
8. Brown, T., Prokopec, A., Alistarh, D.: Non-blocking interpolation search trees with doubly-logarithmic running time. In: PPOPP, pp. 276–291 (2020)
9. Chatterjee, B.: Lock-free linearizable 1-dimensional range queries. In: Proceedings of the 18th International Conference on Distributed Computing and Networking, pp. 1–10 (2017)
10. Comer, D.: Ubiquitous B-tree. ACM Comput. Surv. (CSUR) **11**(2), 121–137 (1979)
11. Fatourou, P., Kallimanis, N.D.: A highly-efficient wait-free universal construction. In: Proceedings of the Twenty-Third Annual ACM Symposium on Parallelism in Algorithms and Architectures, pp. 325–334 (2011)
12. Flurry. Flurry Analytics (2022). https://www.flurry.com/. Accessed May 2022
13. Harris, T.L.: A pragmatic implementation of non-blocking linked-lists. In: Welch, J. (ed.) DISC 2001. LNCS, vol. 2180, pp. 300–314. Springer, Heidelberg (2001). https://doi.org/10.1007/3-540-45414-4_21
14. Herlihy, M., Shavit, N.: On the nature of progress. In: OPODIS, pp. 313–328 (2011)
15. Herlihy, M.P., Wing, J.M.: Linearizability: a correctness condition for concurrent objects. ACM Trans. Program. Lang. Syst. (TOPLAS) **12**(3), 463–492 (1990)
16. Kogan, A., Petrank, E.: A methodology for creating fast wait-free data structures. ACM SIGPLAN Not. **47**(8), 141–150 (2012)
17. Kowalski, T., Kounelis, F., Pirk, H.: High-performance tree indices: locality matters more than one would think. In: 11th International Workshop on Accelerating Analytics and Data Management Systems (2020)
18. Natarajan, A., Savoie, L.H., Mittal, N.: Concurrent wait-free red black trees. In: Higashino, T., Katayama, Y., Masuzawa, T., Potop-Butucaru, M., Yamashita, M. (eds.) SSS 2013. LNCS, vol. 8255, pp. 45–60. Springer, Cham (2013). https://doi.org/10.1007/978-3-319-03089-0_4
19. Nelson, J., Hassan, A., Palmieri, R.: Bundled references: an abstraction for highly-concurrent linearizable range queries. In: PPOPP, pp. 448–450 (2021)
20. Petrank, E., Timnat, S.: A practical wait-free simulation for lock-free data structures (2017)
21. Tian, X., Han, R., Wang, L., Gang, L., Zhan, J.: Latency critical big data computing in finance. J. Finance Data Sci. **1**(1), 33–41 (2015)

22. Timnat, S., Braginsky, A., Kogan, A., Petrank, E.: Wait-free linked-lists. In: OPODIS, pp. 330–344 (2012)
23. Wang, Z., et al.: Building a bw-tree takes more than just buzz words. In: Proceedings of the 2018 International Conference on Management of Data, pp. 473–488 (2018)
24. Wei, Y., Ben-David, N., Blelloch, G.E., Fatourou, P., Ruppert, E., Sun, Y.: Constant-time snapshots with applications to concurrent data structures. In: PPOPP, pp. 31–46 (2021)
25. Zhang, H., Chen, G., Ooi, B.C., Tan, K.-L., Zhang, M.: In-memory big data management and processing: a survey. IEEE Trans. Knowl. Data Eng. **27**(7), 1920–1948 (2015)

Stand-Up Indulgent Gathering on Lines

Quentin Bramas[1], Sayaka Kamei[2], Anissa Lamani[1](✉), and Sébastien Tixeuil[3]

[1] University of Strasbourg, ICube, CNRS, Strasbourg, France
alamani@unistra.fr
[2] Hiroshima University, Higashihiroshima, Japan
[3] Sorbonne University, CNRS, LIP6, IUF, Paris, France

Abstract. We consider a variant of the crash-fault gathering problem called stand-up indulgent gathering (SUIG). In this problem, a group of mobile robots must eventually gather at a single location, which is not known in advance. If no robots crash, they must all meet at the same location. However, if one or more robots crash at a single location, all non-crashed robots must eventually gather at that location. The SUIG problem was first introduced for robots operating in a two-dimensional continuous Euclidean space, with most solutions relying on the ability of robots to move a prescribed (real) distance at each time instant.

In this paper, we investigate the SUIG problem for robots operating in a discrete universe (i.e., a graph) where they can only move one unit of distance (i.e., to an adjacent node) at each time instant. Specifically, we focus on line-shaped networks and characterize the solvability of the SUIG problem for oblivious robots without multiplicity detection.

Keywords: Crash failure · fault-tolerance · LCM robot model

1 Introduction

1.1 Context and Motivation

Mobile robotic swarms recently received a considerable amount of attention from the Distributed Computing scientific community. Characterizing the exact hypotheses that enable solving basic problems for robots represented as disoriented (each robot has its own coordinate system) oblivious (robots cannot remember past action) dimensionless points evolving in a Euclidean space has been at the core of the researchers' goals for more than two decades. One of the key such hypotheses is the scheduling assumption [14]: robots can execute their protocol fully synchronized (FSYNC), in a completely asynchronous manner (ASYNC), of having repeatedly a fairly chosen subset of robots scheduled for synchronous execution (SSYNC).

Among the many studied problems, the *gathering* [22] plays a benchmarking role, as its simplicity to express (robots have to gather in finite time at the exact

This paper was supported by JSPS KAKENHI No. 23H03347, 19K11828, and project SAPPORO (Ref. 2019-CE25-0005-1).

S. Dolev and B. Schieber (Eds.): SSS 2023, LNCS 14310, pp. 451–465, 2023.
https://doi.org/10.1007/978-3-031-44274-2_34

same location, not known beforehand) somewhat contradicts its computational tractability (two robots evolving assuming SSYNC scheduling cannot gather, without additional hypotheses).

As the number of robots grows, the probability that at least one of them fails increases, yet, relatively few works consider the possibility of robot failures. One of the simplest such failures is the *crash* fault, where a robot unpredictably stops executing its protocol. In the case of gathering, one should prescribe the expected behavior in the presence of crash failures. Two variants have been studied: *weak* gathering expects all correct (that is, non-crashed) robots to gather, regardless of the positions of the crashed robots, while *strong* gathering (also known as stand-up indulgent gathering – SUIG) expects correct robots to gather at the (supposedly unique) crash location. In continuous Euclidean space, weak gathering is solvable in the SSYNC model [1,3,6,13], while SUIG (and its variant with two robots, stand up indulgent rendezvous – SUIR) is only solvable in the FSYNC model [4,5].

A recent trend [14] has been to move from the continuous environment setting to a discrete one. More precisely, in the discrete setting, robots can occupy a finite number of locations, and move from one location to another if they are neighboring. This neighborhood relation is conveniently represented by a graph whose nodes are locations, leading to the "robots on graphs" denomination. This discrete setting is better suited for describing constrained physical environments, or environments where robot positioning is only available from discrete sensors [2]. From a computational perspective, the continuous setting and the discrete setting are unrelated: on the one hand, the number of possible configurations (that, the number of robot positions) is much more constrained in the discrete setting than in the continuous setting (only a finite number of configurations exists in the discrete setting), on the other hand, the continuous setting offers algorithms designers more flexibility to solve problematic configurations (e.g., using arbitrarily small movements to break a symmetry).

In this paper, we consider the discrete setting, and aim to characterize the solvability of the SUIR and SUIG problems: in a set of locations whose neighborhood relation is represented by a line-shaped graph, robots have to gather at one single location, not known beforehand; furthermore, if one or more robots crash anytime at the same location, all robots must gather at this location.

1.2 Related Works

In graphs, in the absence of faults, mobile robot gathering was primarily considered for ring-shaped graphs [10,11,15–17,19,20]. For other topologies, gathering problem was considered, e.g., in finite grids [12], trees [12], tori [18], complete cliques [9], and complete bipartite graphs [9]. Most related to our problem is the (relaxed) FSYNC gathering algorithm presented by Castenow et al. [8] for grid-shaped networks where a single robot may be stationary. The main differences with our settings are as follows. First, if no robot is stationary, their [8] robots end up in a square of 2×2 rather than a single node as we require. Second, when one robot is stationary (and thus never moves), all other robots gather at the stationary robot location, *assuming a stationary robot can be detected as such when on the same node* (instead, we consider that a crashed robot cannot be detected), and assuming a stationary robot never moves from the beginning of the execution (while we consider anytime crashes). Third, they assume that initial positions are neighboring (while we characterize which patterns of initial positions are solvable).

In the continuous setting, the possibility of a robot failure was previously considered. As previously stated, the weak-gathering problem in SSYNC [1,3,6,13], and the SUIR and SUIG problems in FSYNC [4,5] were previously considered. In particular, solutions to SUIR and SUIG [4,5] make use of a level-slicing technique, that mandates them to move by a fraction of the distance to another robot. Obviously, such a technique cannot be translated to the discrete model, where robots always move by exactly one edge.

Works combining the discrete setting and the possibility of robot failures are scarce. Ooshita and Tixeuil [21] considered transient robot faults placing them at arbitrary locations, and presented a probabilistic self-stabilizing gathering algorithm in rings, assuming SSYNC, and that robots are able to exactly count how many of them occupy a particular location. Castaneda et al. [7] presented a weaker version of gathering, named edge-gathering. They provided a solution to edge-gathering in acyclic graphs, assuming that any number of robots may crash. On the one hand, their scheduling model is the most general (ASYNC); on the other hand, their robot model makes use of persistent memory (robots can remember some of their past actions, and communicate explicitly with other robots).

Overall, to our knowledge, the SUIR and SUIG problems were never addressed in the discrete setting.

1.3 Our Contribution

In this paper, we initiate the research on SUIG and SUIR feasibility for robots on line-shaped graphs, considering the vanilla model (called OBLOT [14]) where robots are oblivious (that is, they don't have access to persistent memory between activations), are *not* able to distinguish multiple occupations of a given location, and can be completely disoriented (no common direction). More precisely, we focus on both of finite/infinite lines, and study conditions that preclude or enable SUIG and SUIR solvability. As in the continuous model, we first prove that SUIG and SUIR are impossible to solve in the SSYNC model, so we concentrate on the FSYNC model. It turns out that, in FSYNC, SUIR is solvable if and only if the initial distance between the two robots is even, and that SUIG is solvable if only if the initial configuration is not edge-symmetric. Our positive results are constructive, as we provide an algorithm for each case and prove it correct. As expected, the key enabling algorithmic constructions we use for our protocols are fundamentally different from those used in continuous spaces [4,5], as robots can no longer use fractional moves to solve the problem, and can be of independent interest to build further solutions in other topologies.

The rest of the paper is organized as follows. Section 2 presents our model assumptions, Sect. 3 is dedicated to SUIR, and Sect. 4 is dedicated to SUIG. We provide concluding remarks in Sect. 5.

2 Model

The line consists of an infinite or finite number of nodes $u_0, u_1, u_2, \ldots$, such that a node u_i is connected to both $u_{(i-1)}$ and $u_{(i+1)}$ (if they exist). Note that in the case where the line is finite of size n, two nodes of the line, u_0 and u_{n-1} are only connected to u_1 and u_{n-2}, respectively.

Let $R = \{r_1, r_2, \ldots, r_k\}$ be the set of $k \geq 2$ autonomous robots. Robots are assumed to be anonymous (i.e., they are indistinguishable), uniform (i.e., they all execute the same program, and use no localized parameter such as a particular orientation), oblivious (i.e., they cannot remember their past actions), and disoriented (i.e., they cannot distinguish left and right). We assume that robots do not know the number of robots k. In addition, they are unable to communicate directly, however, they have the ability to sense the environment including the positions of all other robots, i.e., they have infinite view. Based on the snapshot resulting of the sensing, they decide whether to move or to stay idle. Each robot r executes cycles infinitely many times, *(i)* first, r takes a snapshot of the environment to see the positions of the other robots (LOOK phase), *(ii)* according to the snapshot, r decides whether it should move and where (COMPUTE phase), and *(iii)* if r decides to move, it moves to one of its neighbor nodes depending on the choice made in COMPUTE phase (MOVE phase). We call such cycles LCM (LOOK-COMPUTE-MOVE) cycles. We consider the *FSYNC* model in which at each time instant t, called round, each robot r executes an LCM cycle synchronously with all the other robots, and the *SSYNC* model where a non-empty subset of robots chosen by an adversarial scheduler executes an LCM cycle synchronously, at each t.

A node is considered *occupied* if it contains at least one robot; otherwise, it is *empty*. If a node u contains more than one robot, it is said to have a *tower* or *multiplicity*. The ability to detect towers is called *multiplicity detection*, which can be either *global* (any robot can sense a tower on any node) or *local* (a robot can only sense a tower if it is part of it). If robots can determine the number of robots in a sensed tower, they are said to have *strong* multiplicity detection. In this work, we assume that robots do not have multiplicity detection and cannot distinguish between nodes with one robot and those with multiple robots.

As robots move and occupy nodes, their positions form the system's *configuration* $C_t = (d(u_0), d(u_1), \ldots)$ at time t. Here, $d(u_i) = 0$ if node u_i is empty and $d(u_i) = 1$ if it is occupied.

Given two nodes u_i and u_j, a segment $[u_i, u_j]$ represents the set of nodes between u_i and u_j, inclusive. No assumptions are made about the state of the nodes in $[u_i, u_j]$. Any node $u \in [u_i, u_j]$ can be either empty or occupied. The number of occupied nodes in $[u_i, u_j]$ is represented by $\|[u_i, u_j]\|$. In Fig. 1, each node u_i, where $i \in \{2, 3, \ldots, 9\}$, is part of the segment $[u_2, u_9]$. Note that $\|[u_2, u_9]\| = 3$ since nodes u_2, u_5, and u_9 are occupied.

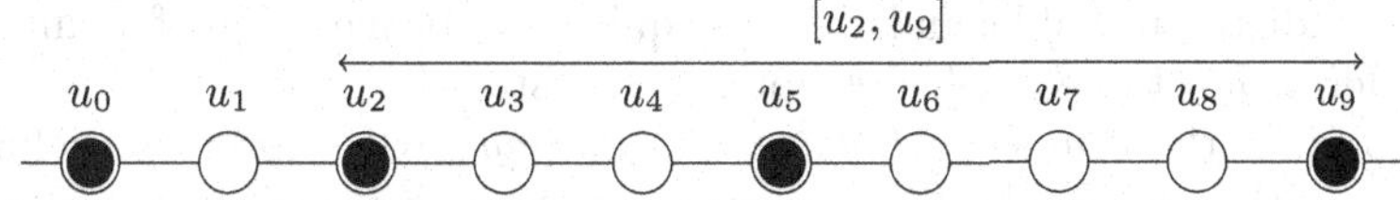

Fig. 1. Instance of a configuration in which the segment $[u_2, u_9]$ is highlighted.

For a given configuration C, let u_i be an occupied node. Node u_j is considered an *occupied neighboring node* of u_i in C if it is occupied and if $|[u_i, u_j]| = 2$. A *border node* in C is an occupied node with only one occupied neighboring node. A robot on a border node is referred to as a *border robot*. In Fig. 1, when $k = 4$, nodes u_0 and u_9 are border nodes.

The *distance* between two nodes u_i and u_j is the number of edges between them. The distance between two robots r_i and r_j is the distance between the two nodes occupied by r_i and r_j, respectively. We denote the distance between u_i and u_j (resp. r_i and r_j) $dist(u_i, u_j)$ (resp. $dist(r_i, r_j)$). Two robots or two nodes are *neighbors* (or adjacent) if the distance between them is one. A sequence of consecutive occupied nodes is a *block*. Similarly, a sequence of consecutive empty nodes is a *hole*.

An *algorithm* A is a function mapping the snapshot (obtained during the LOOK phase) to a neighbor node destination to move to (during the MOVE phase). An *execution* $\mathcal{E} = (C_0, C_1, \ldots)$ of A is a sequence of configurations, where C_0 is an initial configuration, and every configuration C_{t+1} is obtained from C_t by applying A.

Let r be a robot located on node u_i at time t and let $S^+(t) = d(u_i), d(u_{i+1}), \ldots, d(u_{i+m})$ and $S^-(t) = d(u_i), d(u_{i-1}), \ldots d(u_{i-m'})$ be two sequences such that $m, m' \in \mathbb{N}$. Note that $m = n-i-1$ and $m' = i$ in the case where the line is finite of size n, $m = m' = \infty$ in the case where the line is infinite. The view of robot r at time t, denoted $View_r(t)$, is defined as the pair $\{S^+(t), S^-(t)\}$ ordered in the increasing lexicographical order.

Let C be a configuration at time t. Configuration C is said to be *symmetric* at time t if there exist two robots r and r' such that $View_r(t) = View_{r'}(t)$. In this case, r and r' are said to be symmetric robots. Let C be a symmetric configuration at time t then, C is said to be *node-symmetric* if the distance between two symmetric robots is even (i.e., if the axis of symmetry intersects with the line on a node), otherwise, C is said to be *edge-symmetric*. Finally, a non-symmetric configuration is called a *rigid* configuration.

Problem Definition. A robot is said to be *crashed* at time t if it is not activated at any time $t' \geq t$. That is, a crashed robot stops execution and remains at the same position indefinitely. We assume that robots cannot identify a crashed robot in their snapshots (i.e., they are able to see the crashed robots but remain unaware of their crashed status). A crash, if any, can occur at any round of the execution. Furthermore, if more than one crash occurs, all crashes occur at the same location. In our model, since robots do not have multiplicity detection capability, a location with a single crashed robot and with multiple crashed robots are indistinguishable, and are thus equivalent. In the sequel, for simplicity, we consider at most one crashed robot in the system.

We consider the *Stand Up Indulgent Gathering* (SUIG) problem defined in [5]. An algorithm solves the SUIG problem if, for any initial configuration C_0 (that may contain multiplicities), and for any execution $\mathcal{E} = (C_0, C_1, \dots)$, there exists a round t such that all robots (including the crashed robot, if any) gather at a single node, not known beforehand, for all $t' \geq t$. The special case with $k = 2$ is called the *Stand Up Indulgent Rendezvous* (SUIR) problem.

3 Stand Up Indulgent Rendezvous

We address in this section the case in which $k = 2$, that is, the SUIR problem. We show that SSYNC solutions do not exist when one seeks a deterministic solution (Corollary 1), and that even in FSYNC, not all initial configurations admit a solution (Theorem 1). By contrast, all other initial configurations admit a deterministic SUIR solution (Theorem 2).

Theorem 1. *Starting from a configuration where the two robots are at odd distance from each other on a line-shaped graph, the SUIR problem is unsolvable in FSYNC by deterministic oblivious robots without additional hypotheses.*

Proof. Let us first observe that in any configuration, both robots must move. Indeed, if no robot moves, then no robot will ever move, and SUIR is never achieved. If one robot only moves, then the adversary can crash this robot, and the two robots never move, hence SUIR is never achieved.

In any configuration, two robots can either: *(i)* move both in the same direction, *(ii)* move both toward each other, or *(iii)* move both in the opposite direction. Assuming an FSYNC scheduling and no crash by any robot, in the case of *(i)*, the distance between the two robots does not change, in the case of *(ii)*, the distance decreases by two, and in the case of *(iii)*, it increases by two. Since the distance between the two robots is initially odd, then any FSYNC execution of a protocol step keeps the distance between robots odd. As a result, the distance never equals zero, and the robots never gather. □

Corollary 1. *The SUIR problem is unsolvable on a line in SSYNC without additional hypotheses.*

Proof. For the purpose of contradiction, suppose that there exists a SUIR algorithm A in SSYNC. Consider an SSYNC schedule starting from a configuration where exactly one robot is activated in each round. Since any robot advances by exactly one edge per round, and that A solves SUIR, every such execution reaches a configuration where the two robots are at distance $2i + 1$, where i is an integer, that is, a configuration where robots are at odd distance from one another. From this configuration onward, the schedule becomes synchronous (as a synchronous schedule is still allowed in SSYNC). By Theorem 1, rendezvous is not achieved, a contradiction. □

By Theorem 1, we investigate the case of initial configurations where the distance between the two robots is even. It turns out that, in this case, the SUIR problem can be solved.

Theorem 2. *Starting from a configuration where the two robots are at even distance from each other, the SUIR problem is solvable in FSYNC by deterministic oblivious robots without additional hypotheses.*

Proof. Our proof is constructive. Consider the simple algorithm "go to the other robot position".

When no robot crashes, at each FSYNC round, the distance between the two robots decreases by two. Since it is initially even, it eventually reaches zero, and the robots stop moving (the other robot is on the same location), hence rendezvous is achieved.

If one robot crashes, in the following FSYNC rounds, the distance between the two robots decreases by one, until it reaches zero. Then, the correct robot stops moving (the crashed robot is on the same location), hence rendezvous is achieved. □

Observe that both Theorems 1 and 2 are valid regardless of the finiteness of the line network.

4 Stand Up Indulgent Gathering

We address the SUIG problem ($k \geq 2$) on line-shaped networks in the following. Section 4.1 first derives some impossibility results, and then Sect. 4.2 presents our algorithm; finally, the proof of our algorithm appears in Sect. 4.3.

4.1 Impossibility Results

Theorem 3 ([20])**.** *The gathering problem is unsolvable in FSYNC on line networks starting from an edge-symmetric configuration even with strong multiplicity detection.*

Corollary 2. *The SUIG problem is unsolvable in FSYNC on line networks starting from an edge-symmetric configuration even with strong multiplicity detection.*

Proof. Consider a FSYNC execution without crashes, and apply Theorem 3. □

As a result of Corollary 2, we suppose in the remaining of the section that initial configurations are *not* edge-symmetric.

Lemma 1. *Even starting from a configuration that is not edge-symmetric, the SUIG problem is unsolvable in SSYNC without additional hypotheses.*

Proof. The proof is by induction on the number X of occupied nodes. Suppose for the purpose of contradiction that there exists such an algorithm A.

If $X = 2$, and if the distance between the two occupied nodes is 1, consider an FSYNC schedule. All robots have the same view, so either all robots stay on their locations (and the configuration remains the same), or all robots go to the other location (and the configuration remains with $X = 2$ and a distance of 1 between the two locations). As this repeats forever, in both cases, the SUIG is not achieved, a contradiction. If $X = 2$, and if the distance between the two occupied nodes, u_i and u_j, is at least 2, consider a schedule that either *(i)* executes all robots on u_i, or *(ii)* executes all robots at u_j, at every round. So, the system behaves (as robots do not use additional hypotheses such as multiplicity detection) as two robots, initially on distinct locations separated by distance at least 2. As a result, the distance between the two occupied nodes eventually becomes odd. Then, consider an FSYNC schedule, and by Theorem 1, A cannot be a solution, a contradiction.

Suppose now that for some integer X, the lemma holds. Let us show that it also holds for $X + 1$. Consider an execution starting from a configuration with $X+1$ occupied nodes. Since A is a SUIG solution, any execution of A eventually creates at least one multiplicity point by having a robot r_1 on one occupied node moved to an adjacent occupied node. Consider the configuration C_b that is immediately before the creation of the multiplicity point. Then, in C_b, *all* robots at the location of r_1 make a move (this is possible in SSYNC), so the resulting configuration has X occupied nodes. By the induction hypothesis, algorithm A cannot solve SUIG from this point, a contradiction.

So, for all possible initial configurations, algorithm A cannot solve SUIG, a contradiction. □

As a result of Lemma 1, we suppose in the sequel that the scheduling is FSYNC.

4.2 Algorithm $\mathcal{A}_L$

In the following, we propose an algorithm $\mathcal{A}_L$ in FSYNC such that the initial configuration is not edge-symmetric.

Before describing our strategy, we first provide some definitions that will be used throughout this section. In given configuration C, let d_C be the largest even distance between any pair of occupied nodes and let U_C be the set of occupied nodes at distance d_C from another occupied node. If C is node-symmetric, U_C consists only of the two border nodes ($|U_C| = 2$). Then, let u and u' be nodes in U_C. By contrast, if C is rigid, then $|U_C| \geq 2$ (refer to Lemma 2). Since each robot has a unique view in a rigid configuration, let $u \in U_C$ be the node that hosts the robots with the largest view among those on a node of U_C and let u' be the occupied node at distance d_C from u. Observe that if there are two candidate nodes for u', using the view of the robots again, we can uniquely elect one of the two which are at distance d_C from u (by taking the one with the largest view). That is, u and u' can be identified uniquely in C. We refer to $[u, u']$ by

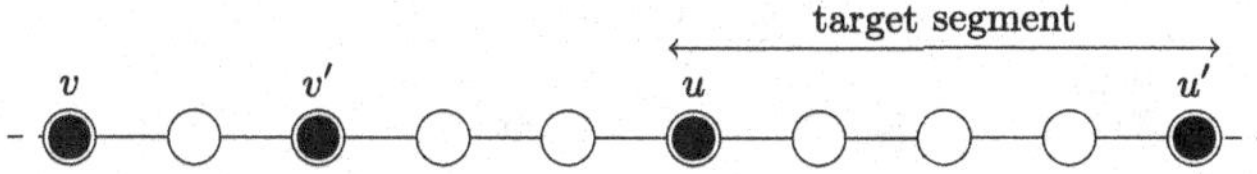

Fig. 2. Instance of a configuration in which $[u, u']$ is the target segment. Nodes v and v' are both in $O_{[u,u']}$.

the target segment in C, and denote the number of occupied nodes in $[u, u']$ by $|[u, u']|$. Finally, the set of occupied nodes which are not in $[u, u']$ is denoted by $O_{[u,u']}$. Refer to Fig. 2 for an example.

We first observe that in any configuration C in which there are at least three occupied nodes, there exist at least two occupied nodes at an even distance.

Lemma 2. *In any configuration C where there are at least three occupied nodes, there exists at least one pair of robots at an even distance from each other.*

Proof. Assume by contradiction that the lemma does not hold and let u_1, u_2, and u_3 be three distinct occupied nodes such that u_2 is located between u_1 and u_3. Assume w.l.o.g. that $d_1 = dist(u_1, u_2)$ and $d_2 = dist(u_2, u_3)$. By the assumption, both d_1 and d_2 are odd. That is, there exist $q, q' \in \mathbb{N}$, $d_1 = 2q+1$ and $d_2 = 2q'+1$. Hence, $d_1 + d_2$ is even since $d_1 + d_2 = 2(q + q' + 1)$. A contradiction. □

We propose, in the following, an algorithm named $\mathcal{A}_L$ that solves the SUIG problem on line-shaped networks. The main idea of the proposed strategy is to squeeze the robots by reducing the distance between the two border robots such that they eventually meet on a single node. To guarantee this meeting, robots aim to reach a configuration in which the border robots are at an even distance. Note that an edge-symmetric configuration can be reached during this process. However, in this case, we guarantee that not only one robot has crashed but also, eventually, when there are only two occupied adjacent nodes, the crashed robot is alone on its node ensuring the gathering. Let C be the current configuration. In the following, we describe robots' behavior depending on C:

1. C is edge-symmetric. The border robots move toward an occupied node.
2. Otherwise. Let $[u, u']$ be the target segment in C, and let $O_{[u,u']}$ be the set of robots located on a node, not part of $[u, u']$. Robots behave differently depending on the size of $O_{[u,u']}$:
   (a) $|O_{[u,u']}| = 0$ (u and u' host the border robots). In this case, the border robots are the ones to move. Their destination is their adjacent node toward an occupied node (refer to Fig. 3 for an example).
   (b) $|O_{[u,u']}| = 1$. Let u_v be the unique occupied node in $O_{[u,u']}$. Assume w.l.o.g. that u_v is closer to u than to u'. We address only the case in which $dist(u, u_v)$ is odd. (Note that if $dist(u, u_v)$ is even, the border nodes are at an even distance and $|O_{[u,u']}| = 0$.)
      i. If the number of occupied nodes is three and u_v and u are two adjacent nodes, robots on both u and u' are the ones to move. Their destination is their adjacent node toward u_v (refer to Fig. 4).

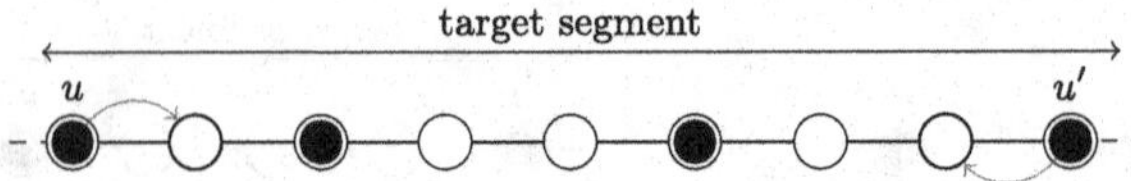

Fig. 3. Instance of a configuration in which $|O_{[u,u']}| = 0$. Robots at the border move toward an occupied node as shown by the red arrows. (Color figure online)

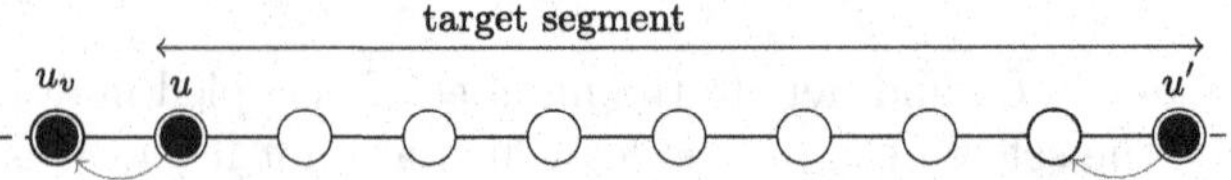

Fig. 4. Instance of a configuration of the special case in which $|O_{[u,u']}| = 1$ with only three occupied nodes. Robots on u and u' move to their adjacent node toward the node in $O_{[u,u']}$, node u_v, as shown by the red arrows. (Color figure online)

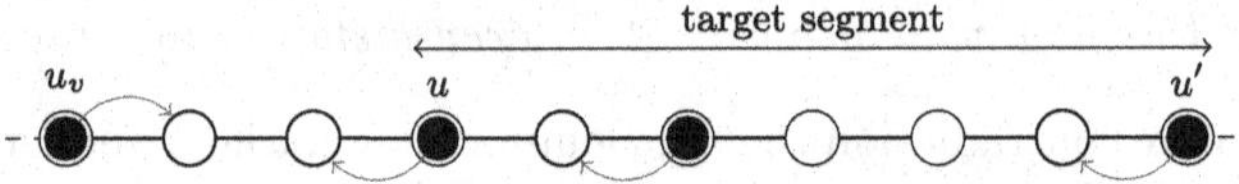

Fig. 5. Instance of a configuration in which $|O_{[u,u']}| = 1$. Robots in $[u, u']$ move to their adjacent node toward the robot in $O_{[u,u']}$ while the robots in $O_{[u,u']}$ move toward the target segment as shown by the red arrows. (Color figure online)

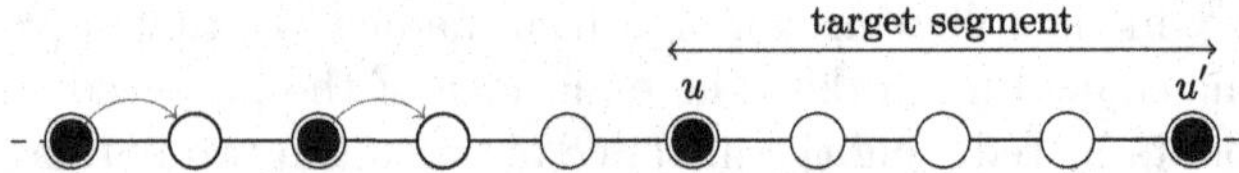

Fig. 6. Instance of a configuration in which $|O_{[u,u']}| > 1$. Robots in $O_{[u,u']}$ move to their adjacent node toward the target segment as shown by the red arrows. (Color figure online)

   ii. Otherwise, all robots are ordered to move. More precisely, robots on a node of $[u, u']$ move to an adjacent node toward u_v while the robots on u_v move to an adjacent node toward u (refer to Fig. 5).

(c) $|O_{[u,u']}| > 1$. In this case, the robots that are in $O_{[u,u']}$ move toward a node of $[u, u']$ (refer to Fig. 6).

4.3 Proof of the Correctness

We prove in the following the correctness of $\mathcal{A}_L$.

Lemma 3. *Let C be a non-edge-symmetric configuration, and let $[u, u']$ be the target segment. If $|O_{[u,u']}| > 1$, then all nodes in $O_{[u,u']}$ are located on the same side of $[u, u']$.*

Proof. Assume by contradiction that the lemma does not hold and assume that there exists a pair of nodes $u_1, u_2 \in O_{[u,u']}$ such that u_1 and u_2 are on different sides of $[u, u']$. Assume w.l.o.g. that u_1 is the closest to u and u_2 is the closest to u'. Let $dist(u_1, u) = d_1$ and $dist(u_2, u') = d_2$. If d_1 and d_2 are both even or both odd, $dist(u_1, u_2)$ is even. Since $dist(u_1, u_2) > dist(u, u')$, $[u, u']$ is not the target segment, a contradiction. Otherwise, assume w.l.o.g. that d_1 is even and d_2 is odd, then $dist(u_1, u')$ is even. Since $dist(u_1, u') > dist(u, u')$, $[u, u']$ is not the target segment, a contradiction. □

Lemma 4. *Starting from a non-edge-symmetric configuration C, if no robot crashes, all robots gather without multiplicity detection in $O(\mathcal{D})$ by executing $\mathcal{A}_L$, where $\mathcal{D}$ denotes the distance between the two borders in C.*

We focus in the following on the case in which a single robot crashes.

Lemma 5. *Starting from a configuration C where there are only two occupied nodes at distance $\mathcal{D} > 1$, one hosting the crashed robot, gathering is achieved in $\mathcal{D}$ rounds, where $\mathcal{D}$ denotes the distance between the two borders in C.*

Proof. First observe that if the crashed robot is not collocated with a non-crashed robot, after one round the robots on the other border move towards the crashed robot location, and gathering is achieved after $\mathcal{D}$ rounds.

Now assume that the crashed robot is collocated with at least one non-crashed robot. If $\mathcal{D} = 2$, then after one round, all non-crashed robots are located at the same node, adjacent to the crashed robot location, and after one more round, gathering is achieved. If $\mathcal{D} > 3$ is even, then after one round the crashed robot is alone, and the non-crashed robots form two multiplicity points and are the extremities of the target segment. So, after one more round, they both move towards the crashed robot location, and we reach a configuration with two occupied nodes, and the distance between them has decreased by two. By induction and the previous case, gathering is eventually achieved. If $\mathcal{D} = 3$, then similarly, one can show that in three rounds, gathering is achieved. If $\mathcal{D} > 3$ is odd, then similarly, one can show that after three rounds we reach configuration with two occupied nodes, and their distance has decreased by 3 (so, the distance is now even and we can apply one of the previous even cases). □

Lemma 6. *Let C be a configuration where $[u, u']$ is the target segment with $O_{[u,u']} = \{v\}$, and w.l.o.g. u' is a border. Let $\mathcal{D}$ be the distance between the two border nodes u' and v. If u' hosts a crashed robot and $dist(v, u) = 1$, then gathering is achieved in $O(\mathcal{D})$ rounds.*

Lemma 7. *Let C be a configuration where $[u, u']$ is the target segment, $|O_{[u,u']}| = 1$ and w.l.o.g. $dist(u, v) < dist(u', v)$ where $v \in O_{[u,u']}$. Let $\mathcal{D}$ be the distance between the two border nodes u' and v in C. If u' hosts a crashed robot, then gathering is achieved in $O(\mathcal{D})$ rounds.*

Proof. Recall that, since $v \in O_{[u,u']}$, $dist(u', v)$ is odd in C. If the distance m between u and v is 1, the we apply Lemma 6, otherwise, by $\mathcal{A}_L$, the robots in v move to an empty node toward u, and all the other robots move towards v. Thus, after one round, we reach a configuration C_1 where the robots on v becomes at an even distance from u', the crashed robot location. Since the robots on u are also ordered to move toward v, the distance between the robots at v and u decreases by two.

Again, as u' hosts a crashed robot, after one more round, a configuration C_2 in which the borders are at an odd distance is reached again, and the distance between the robots at u and v is again decreased by two (or stay the same if they are adjacent in C_2 as they just swap their positions).

As the distance m between v and u is odd in C (otherwise, the border robots are at an even distance in C), we can repeat the same 2-round process ($\lceil m/4 \rceil$ times) until we reach a configuration in which the robots at u and v are at distance 1 so, by Lemma 6, gathering is achieved. □

Lemma 8. *Starting from a configuration C where the crashed robot is at a border, and the border robots are at an even distance $\mathcal{D}$, by executing $\mathcal{A}_L$, after $O(\mathcal{D})$ rounds, gathering is achieved.*

Lemma 9. *Starting from a non-edge-symmetric configuration C with one crashed robot, all robots executing $\mathcal{A}_L$ eventually gather without multiplicity detection in $O(\mathcal{D})$ rounds, where $\mathcal{D}$ denotes the distance between the two borders in C.*

Proof. First, let us consider the case where $\mathcal{D}$ is even.

1. If the crashed robot is at an equal distance from both borders, by $\mathcal{A}_L$, the border robots move toward each other. As they do, the distance between them remains even. Hence, the border robots remain the only ones to move. Eventually, all robots which are not co-located with the crashed robot become border robots and hence move. Thus, the gathering is achieved in $\frac{\mathcal{D}}{2}$ rounds.
2. If the crashed robot is a border, by Lemmas 8, we can deduce that the gathering is achieved in $O(\mathcal{D})$ rounds.
3. Otherwise, as the border robots move toward each other by $\mathcal{A}_L$, the crashed robot eventually becomes at the border. We hence retrieve case 2..

From the cases above, we can deduce that the gathering is achieved whenever a configuration in which the borders are at an even distance, is reached.

Let us now focus on the case where $\mathcal{D}$ is odd. By $\mathcal{A}_L$, two occupied nodes u and u' at the largest even distance are uniquely identified to set the target segment $[u, u']$ (recall that C is, in this case, rigid, and each robot has a unique view since the initial configuration cannot be edge-symmetric). The robots behave differently depending on the size of $O_{[u,u']}$, the set of occupied nodes outside the segment $[u, u']$. By Lemma 3, all nodes in $O_{[u,u']}$ are on the same side. Assume w.l.o.g. that for all $u_i \in O_{[u,u']}$, u_i is closer to u than u'. Two cases are possible:

1. $|O_{[u,u']}| > 1$. Let $u_f, u_{f'} \in O_{[u,u']}$ be the two farthest nodes from u such that $dist(u, u_f) > dist(u, u_{f'})$. Note that u_f is a border robot. Let u_{f+1} be u_f's adjacent node toward u'_f. If u_f does not host a crashed robot, then as the robots on u_f move toward u and those on u' remain idle by $\mathcal{A}_L$, after one round, the border robots become at an even distance and we are done. By

contrast, if u_f hosts a crashed robot, then either u_f hosts other non-crashed robots, and hence after one round, we retrieve a configuration C' in which $[u_{f+1}, u']$ is the target segment and $|O_{[u_{f+1},u']}| = 1$ or a configuration C' in which $[u_{f'}, u']$ is the target segment and $|O_{[u_{f'},u']}| = 1$ as robots on $u_{f'}$ also move toward u by $\mathcal{A}_L$. In both cases, we retrieve the following case.

2. $|O_{[u,u']}| = 1$. Let u_f be in $O_{[u,u']}$ and assume w.l.o.g. that $dist(u, u_f) < dist(u', u_f)$ (observe that u_f is a border node). If u_f hosts the crashed robot, then, after one round, the border robots are at an even distance as robots on u' move toward u_f by $\mathcal{A}_L$. Similarly, if u' hosts the crashed robot, then by Lemmas 6 and 7 after $O(\mathcal{D})$ rounds, a configuration in which the border robots are at an even distance is reached. If neither u_f nor u' hosts the crashed robot, then when the border robots move by $\mathcal{A}_L$ (other robots also move, but we focus for now on the border robots), either the distance between the two borders becomes even after one round (in the case where u_f is adjacent to u as the robots simply exchange their respective positions) or the distance between the border robots remains odd but decreases by two. Observe that in the later case, the border robots keep moving toward each other by $\mathcal{A}_L$ until one of them becomes a neighbor to a crash robot.
Let C' be the configuration reached once a border robot becomes adjacent to a crashed robot. Let u_b be the border node that is adjacent to crashed robot, and let $u_{\overline{b}}$ be the other border node. We refer to the node that hosts the crashed robot by u_c. Since $dist(u_b, u_c) = 1$ and $dist(u_b, u_{\overline{b}})$ is odd, $dist(u_{\overline{b}}, u_c)$ is even. Hence, $|O_{[u_{\overline{b}},u_c]}| = 1$. Two cases are possible:
   - If C' hosts only three occupied nodes, then, after one round, the distance between the border robots becomes even, and we are done (recall that robots on $u_{\overline{b}}$ and u_c move toward u_b by $\mathcal{A}_L$.
   - If there are more than 3 occupied nodes and u_c hosts also non-crashed robots in C', then after one round, the distance between the border robots becomes even as the robots on $u_{\overline{b}}$ move toward u_c, those on u_b move to u_c and the non-crashed robots on u_c move toward u_b by $\mathcal{A}_L$. Hence, we are done.
   - Otherwise, after one round, the distance between the two borders remains odd as both borders move toward each other by $\mathcal{A}_L$. In the configuration reached C'', u_c becomes a new border occupied by a crashed robot and non-crashed robots. If there are only two occupied nodes in C'', by $\mathcal{A}_L$, the border robots move toward each other. That is, in the next round, the border robots become at an even distance, and we are done. If there are more than two occupied nodes in C'', by Lemmas 2 and 3, a configuration with a new target segment $[o, o']$ which includes one border node is reached. Let us first consider the case in which $u_c \in [o, o']$. If $|O_{[o,o']}| > 1$, then after one round, the border robots become at an even distance, and we are done. By contrast, if $|O_{[o,o']}| = 1$, then we are done by Lemmas 6 and 7. Next, let us consider the case where $u_c \notin [o, o']$. Let o_f be the closest occupied node of u_c. Without loss of generality, $dist(o, u_c) < dist(o', u_c)$ holds. If $|O_{[o,o']}| > 1$, then after one round, a configuration in which $[o', o_f]$ is the target segment and $u_c \in O_{[o',o_f]}$ is

reached. After one additional round, we are done. Finally, if $|O_{[o,o']}| = 1$, then robots on the nodes in $[o, o']$ move toward u_c, and we are done.

From the cases above, we can deduce that the theorem holds. □

From Lemmas 4 and 9, we can deduce:

Theorem 4. *Starting from a non-edge-symmetric configuration C, algorithm $\mathcal{A}_L$ solves the SUIG problem on line-shaped networks without multiplicity detection in $O(\mathcal{D})$ rounds, where $\mathcal{D}$ denotes the distance between the two borders in C.*

5 Concluding Remarks

We initiated the research about stand-up indulgent rendezvous and gathering by oblivious mobile robots in the discrete model, studying the case of line-shaped networks. For both rendezvous and gathering cases, we characterized the initial configurations from which the problem is impossible to solve. In the case of rendezvous, a very simple algorithm solves all cases left open. In the case of gathering, we provide an algorithm that works when the starting configuration is not edge-symmetric. Our algorithms operate in the vanilla model without any additional hypotheses, and are asymptotically optimal with respect to the number of rounds to achieve rendezvous or gathering. Open questions include:

1. Is it possible to circumvent impossibility results in SSYNC using extra hypotheses (e.g., multiplicity detection)?
2. Is it possible to solve SUIR and SUIG in other topologies?

References

1. Agmon, N., Peleg, D.: Fault-tolerant gathering algorithms for autonomous mobile robots. SIAM J. Comput. **36**(1), 56–82 (2006)
2. Balabonski, T., Courtieu, P., Pelle, R., Rieg, L., Tixeuil, S., Urbain, X.: Continuous *vs.* discrete asynchronous moves: a certified approach for mobile robots. In: Atig, M.F., Schwarzmann, A.A. (eds.) NETYS 2019. LNCS, vol. 11704, pp. 93–109. Springer, Cham (2019). https://doi.org/10.1007/978-3-030-31277-0_7
3. Bouzid, Z., Das, S., Tixeuil, S.: Gathering of mobile robots tolerating multiple crash faults. In: IEEE 33rd International Conference on Distributed Computing Systems (ICDCS), pp. 337–346 (2013)
4. Bramas, Q., Lamani, A., Tixeuil, S.: Stand up indulgent rendezvous. In: Devismes, S., Mittal, N. (eds.) SSS 2020. LNCS, vol. 12514, pp. 45–59. Springer, Cham (2020). https://doi.org/10.1007/978-3-030-64348-5_4
5. Bramas, Q., Lamani, A., Tixeuil, S.: Stand up indulgent gathering. In: Gąsieniec, L., Klasing, R., Radzik, T. (eds.) ALGOSENSORS 2021. LNCS, vol. 12961, pp. 17–28. Springer, Cham (2021). https://doi.org/10.1007/978-3-030-89240-1_2
6. Bramas, Q., Tixeuil, S.: Wait-free gathering without chirality. In: Scheideler, C. (ed.) SIROCCO 2014. LNCS, vol. 9439, pp. 313–327. Springer, Cham (2015). https://doi.org/10.1007/978-3-319-25258-2_22

7. Castaneda, A., Rajsbaum, S., Alcántara, M., Flores-Penaloza, D.: Fault-tolerant robot gathering problems on graphs with arbitrary appearing times. In: 2017 IEEE International Parallel and Distributed Processing Symposium (IPDPS), pp. 493–502 (2017)
8. Castenow, J., Fischer, M., Harbig, J., Jung, D., auf der Heide, F.M.: Gathering anonymous, oblivious robots on a grid. Theor. Comput. Sci. **815**, 289–309 (2020)
9. Cicerone, S., DiStefano, G., Navarra, A.: Gathering robots in graphs: the central role of synchronicity. Theoret. Comput. Sci. **849**, 99–120 (2021)
10. D'Angelo, G., Navarra, A., Nisse, N.: A unified approach for gathering and exclusive searching on rings under weak assumptions. Distrib. Comput. **30**(1), 17–48 (2017)
11. D'Angelo, G., Stefano, G.D.: AlfredoNavarra: gathering on rings under the look-compute-move model. Distrib. Comput. **27**(4), 255–285 (2014)
12. D'Angelo, G., Stefano, G.D., Klasing, R., Navarra, A.: Gathering of robots on anonymous grids and trees without multiplicity detection. Theoret. Comput. Sci. **610**, 158–168 (2016)
13. Défago, X., Potop-Butucaru, M., Raipin-Parvédy, P.: Self-stabilizing gathering of mobile robots under crash or byzantine faults. Distrib. Comput. **33**, 393–421 (2020)
14. Flocchini, P., Prencipe, G., Santoro, N. (eds.): Distributed Computing by Mobile Entities, Current Researchin Moving and Computing, vol. 11340. Springer, Cham (2019). https://doi.org/10.1007/978-3-030-11072-7
15. Izumi, T., Izumi, T., Kamei, S., Ooshita, F.: Time-optimal gathering algorithm of mobile robots with local weak multiplicity detection in rings. IEICE Trans. **96-A**(6), 1072–1080 (2013)
16. Kamei, S., Lamani, A., Ooshita, F., Tixeuil, S.: Asynchronous mobile robot gathering from symmetric configurations without global multiplicity detection. In: Kosowski, A., Yamashita, M. (eds.) SIROCCO 2011. LNCS, vol. 6796, pp. 150–161. Springer, Heidelberg (2011). https://doi.org/10.1007/978-3-642-22212-2_14
17. Kamei, S., Lamani, A., Ooshita, F., Tixeuil, S.: Gathering an even number of robots in an odd ring without global multiplicity detection. In: Rovan, B., Sassone, V., Widmayer, P. (eds.) MFCS 2012. LNCS, vol. 7464, pp. 542–553. Springer, Heidelberg (2012). https://doi.org/10.1007/978-3-642-32589-2_48
18. Kamei, S., Lamani, A., Ooshita, F., Tixeuil, S., Wada, K.: Asynchronous gathering in a torus. In: 25th International Conference on Principles of Distributed Systems (OPODIS 2021), vol. 217, pp. 9:1–9:17 (2021)
19. Klasing, R., Kosowski, A., Navarra, A.: Taking advantage of symmetries: gathering of many asynchronous oblivious robots on a ring. Theoret. Comput. Sci. **411**(34–36), 3235–3246 (2010)
20. Klasing, R., Markou, E., Pelc, A.: Gathering asynchronous oblivious mobile robots in a ring. Theoret. Comput. Sci. **390**(1), 27–39 (2008)
21. Ooshita, F., Tixeuil, S.: On the self-stabilization of mobile oblivious robots in uniform rings. Theoret. Comput. Sci. **568**, 84–96 (2015)
22. Suzuki, I., Yamashita, M.: Distributed anonymous mobile robots: formation of geometric patterns. SIAM J. Comput. **28**(4), 1347–1363 (1999)

Offline Constrained Backward Time Travel Planning

Quentin Bramas[1(✉)], Jean-Romain Luttringer[1], and Sébastien Tixeuil[2,3]

[1] ICUBE, Strasbourg University, CNRS, Strasbourg, France
bramas@unistra.fr
[2] Sorbonne University, CNRS, LIP6, Paris, France
[3] Institut Universitaire de France, Paris, France

Abstract. We model transportation networks as dynamic graphs and introduce the ability for agents to use Backward Time-Travel (BTT) devices at any node to travel back in time, subject to certain constraints and fees, before resuming their journey.

We propose exact algorithms to compute travel plans with constraints on BTT cost or the maximum time that can be traveled back while minimizing travel delay (the difference between arrival and starting times). These algorithms run in polynomial time. We also study the impact of BTT device pricing policies on the computation of travel plans with respect to delay and cost and identify necessary properties for pricing policies to enable such computation.

1 Introduction

Evolving graphs (and their many variants) are graphs that change over time and are used to model real-world systems that evolve. They have applications in many fields in Computer Science, where they arise in areas such as compilers, databases, fault-tolerance, artificial intelligence, and computer networks. To date, such graphs were studied under the hypothesis that time can be traveled in a single direction (to the future, by an action called waiting), leading to numerous algorithms that revisit static graph notions and results.

In this paper, we introduce the possibility of Backward time travel (BTT) (that is, the ability to go back in time) when designing algorithms for dynamic graphs. In more details, we consider the application of BTT devices to transportation networks modeled by evolving graphs. In particular we focus on the ability to travel from point A to point B with minimal delay (that is, minimizing the time difference between arrival and start instants), taking into account meaningful constraints, such as the cost induced by BTT devices, or their span (how far back in time you are allowed to go).

To this paper, BTT was mostly envisioned in simple settings (with respect to the cost associated to time travel or its span). For example, the AE model [12] considers that a single cost unit permits to travel arbitrarily in both space and time, trivializing the space-time travel problem entirely. Slightly more constrained models such as TM [11] and BTTF [16] consider devices that either: *(i)*

S. Dolev and B. Schieber (Eds.): SSS 2023, LNCS 14310, pp. 466–480, 2023.
https://doi.org/10.1007/978-3-031-44274-2_35

only permit time travel [11] (but remain at the same position), or *(ii)* permit either time travel or space travel, but not both at the same time [16]. However, the cost involved is either null [11], or a single cost unit per time travel [16].

Instead, we propose to discuss BTT in a cost-aware, span-aware context, that implies efficiently using BTT devices within a transportation system (from a simultaneous delay and cost point of view), and the computation of the corresponding multi-modal paths. More precisely, in this paper, we address the problem of space-time travel planning, taking into account both the travel delay of the itinerary and the cost policy of BTT device providers. The context we consider is that of transportation systems, where BTT devices are always available to the agents traveling. Using each BTT device has nevertheless a cost, decided by the BTT device provider, and may depend on the span of the backward time jump. Although BTT devices are always active, the ability to go from one location to another (that is, from one BTT device to another) varies across time. We consider that this ability is conveniently modeled by a dynamic graph, whose nodes represent BTT devices, and whose edges represent the possibility to instantly go from one BTT device to another. Given a dynamic graph, we aim at computing travel plans, from one BTT device to another (the closest to the agent's actual destination), considering not only travel delay and induced cost, but also schedule availability and common limitations of BTT devices.

In the following, we study the feasibility of finding such travel plans, depending on the pricing policy. It turns out that when the schedule of connections is available (that is, the dynamic graph is known), very loose conditions on the pricing policy enable to devise optimal algorithms (with respect to the travel delay and induced cost) in polynomial time, given a cost constraint for the agents, or a span constraint for the BTT devices.

Related Work. Space-Time routing has been studied, but assuming only forward time travel, *i.e.*, waiting, is available. The idea of using dynamic graphs to model transportation network was used by many studies (see *e.g.* Casteigts et al. [2] and references herein), leading to recently revisit popular problems previously studied in static graphs [1,4,10]. In a dynamic (or temporal) graph, a journey represents a temporal path consisting in a sequence of edges used at given non-decreasing time instants. The solvability of a problem can depend on whether or not a journey can contain consecutive edges occurring at the same time instant. Such journeys are called *non-strict*, as opposed to *strict* journey where the sequence of time instants must be strictly increasing. In our work, we extend the notion of non-strict journey to take into account the possibility to go back in time at each node, but one can observe that our algorithm also work with the same extension for strict journey by adding one time unit to the arrival of each edge in our algorithms.

The closest work in this research path is due to Casteigts et al. [3], who study the possibility of discovering a temporal path between two nodes in a dynamic network with a waiting time constraint: at each step, the traveling agent cannot wait more than c time instants, where c is a given constant. It turns out that finding the earliest arriving such temporal path can be done in polynomial time. Perhaps surprisingly, Villacis-Llobet et al. [14] showed that if one allows to go several times through the same node, the obtained temporal path can arrive earlier, and finding it can be done in linear time. As previously mentioned, this line of work only considers *forward* time travel: a temporal path cannot go back in time.

Constrained-shortest-paths computation problems have been extensively studied in the context of static graphs [5]. Although these problems tend to be NP-Hard [7] (even when considering a single metric), the ones considering two additive metrics (commonly, the delay and a cost) gained a lot of traction over the years due to their practical relevance, the most common use-case being computer networks [8,9]. In this context, each edge is characterized by a weight vector, comprising both cost and delay. Path computation algorithms thus have to maintain and explore all non-comparable paths, whose number may grow exponentially with respect to the size of the network. To avoid a worst-case exponential complexity, most practical algorithms rely on either approximation schemes [13] or heuristics. However, these contributions do not study multi-criteria path computation problems within a time travel context. Conversely, we study and provide results regarding the most relevant time-traveling problems while considering the peculiarities of this context (in particular, the properties of the cost function). In addition, we show that most of these problems can be solved optimally in polynomial-time.

Contributions. In this paper, we provide the following contributions:

- An in-depth analysis of the impact of the BTT device providers pricing policies on the computation of low-latency and low-cost paths. In particular, we show that few features are required to ensure that the efficient computation of such paths remains possible.
- Two exact polynomial algorithms able to compute travels with smallest delay to a given destination and minimizing the cost of traveling back in time. The first algorithm also supports the addition of a constraint on the backward cost of the solution. The other one supports a constraint on how far back in the past one can go at each given time instant.

2 Model

In this section, we define the models and notations used throughout this paper, before formalizing the aforementioned problems.

We represent the network as an evolving graph, as introduced by Ferreira [6]: a graph-centric view of the network that maps a dynamic graph as a sequence of static graphs. The *footprint* of the dynamic graph (that includes all nodes and edges that appear at least once during the lifetime of the dynamic graph), is fixed. Furthermore, we assume that the set of nodes is fixed over time, while the set of edges evolves.

More precisely, an evolving graph G is a pair $(V, (E_t)_{t\in\mathbb{N}})$, where V denotes the finite set of vertices, $\mathbb{N}$ is the infinite set of time instants, and for each $t \in \mathbb{N}$, E_t denotes the set of edges that appears at time t. The *snapshot* of G at time t is the static graph $G(t) = (V, E_t)$, which corresponds to the state, supposedly fixed, of the network in the time interval $[t, t+1)$. The *footprint* $\mathcal{F}(G)$ of G is the static graph corresponding to the union of all its snapshots, $\mathcal{F}(G) = \left(V, \bigcup_{t\in\mathbb{N}} E_t\right)$. We say $((u, v), t)$ is a temporal edge of graph G if $(u, v) \in E_t$. We say that an evolving graph is *connected* if its footprint is connected.

Space-Time Travel. We assume that at each time instant, an agent can travel along any number of adjacent consecutive communication links. However, the graph may not be connected at each time instant, hence it may be that the only way to reach a particular destination node is to travel forward (*i.e.*, wait) or backward in time, to reach a time instant where an adjacent communication link exists. In more detail, an agent travels from a node s to a node d using a *space-time travel* (or simply travel when it is clear from the context).

Definition 1. *A* space-time travel *of* length k *is a sequence* $((u_0, t_0), (u_1, t_1), \ldots, (u_k, t_k))$ *such that*

- $\forall i \in \{0, \ldots k\}$, $u_i \in V$ *is a node and* $t_i \in \mathbb{N}$ *is a time instant,*
- $\forall i \in \{0, \ldots k-1\}$, *if* $u_i \neq u_{i+1}$, *then* $t_i = t_{i+1}$ *and* $(u_i, u_{i+1}) \in E_{t_i}$ i.e., *there is a temporal edge between* u_i *and* u_{i+1} *at time* t_i.

By extension, the *footprint* of a travel is the static graph containing all edges (and their adjacent nodes) appearing in the travel. Now, the *itinerary* of a travel $((u_0, t_0), (u_1, t_1), \ldots, (u_k, t_k))$ is its projection $(u_0, u_1, \ldots, u_k)$ on nodes, while its *schedule* is its projection $(t_0, t_1, \ldots, t_k)$ on time instants.

Definition 2. *A travel* $((u_0, t_0), (u_1, t_1), \ldots, (u_k, t_k))$ *is* simple *if for all* $i \in \{2, \ldots, k\}$ *and* $j \in \{0, \ldots, i-2\}$, *we have* $u_i \neq u_j$.

Intuitively, a travel is simple if its footprint is a line (*i.e.*, a simple path) and contains at most one time travel per node (as a consequence, no node appears three times consecutively in a simple travel).

Definition 3. *The* delay *of a travel* $T = ((u_0, t_0), (u_1, t_1), \ldots, (u_k, t_k))$, *denoted* $delay(T)$ *is defined as* $t_k - t_0$.

The Backward Cost of a Travel

Definition 4. *The* backward-cost *is the cost of going to the past. The backward-cost function* $\mathfrak{f} : \mathbb{N}^* \to \mathbb{R}^+$ *returns, for each* $\delta \in \mathbb{N}$, *the backward-cost* $\mathfrak{f}(\delta)$ *of traveling* δ *time instants to the past. As we assume that there is no cost associated to forward time travel (that is, waiting), we extend* $\mathfrak{f}$ *to* $\mathbb{Z}$ *by setting* $\mathfrak{f}(-\delta) = 0$, *for all* $\delta \in \mathbb{N}$. *In particular, the backward-cost of traveling* 0 *time instants in the past is zero. When it is clear from context, the backward-cost function is simply called the cost function.*

Definition 5. *The* backward-cost *(or simply cost) of a travel* $T = ((u_0, t_0), (u_1, t_1), \ldots, (u_k, t_k))$, *denoted* $cost(T)$ *is defined as follows:*

$$cost(T) = \sum_{i=0}^{k-1} \mathfrak{f}(t_i - t_{i+1})$$

Definition 6. *Let* $T_1 = ((u_0, t_0), (u_1, t_1), \ldots, (u_k, t_k))$ *and* $T_2 = ((u'_0, t'_0), (u'_1, t'_1), \ldots, (u'_{k'}, t'_{k'}))$ *be two travels. If* $(u_k, t_k) = (u'_0, t'_0)$*, then the* concatenated travel $T_1 \oplus T_2$ *is defined as follows:*

$$T_1 \oplus T_2 = ((u_0, t_0), (u_1, t_1), \ldots, (u_k, t_k), (u'_1, t'_1), \ldots, (u'_{k'}, t'_{k'}))$$

Remark 1. One can easily prove that $cost(T_1 \oplus T_2) = cost(T_1) + cost(T_2)$. In the following, we sometimes decompose a travel highlighting an intermediate node: $T = T_1 \oplus ((u_i, t_i)) \oplus T_2$. Following the definition, this means that T_1 ends with (u_i, t_i), and T_2 starts with (u_i, t_i), so we also have $T = T_1 \oplus T_2$ and $cost(T) = cost(T_1) + cost(T_2)$.

Our notion of space-time travel differs from the classical notion of *journey* found in literature related to dynamic graphs [6] as we do *not* assume time instants monotonically increase along a travel. As a consequence, some evolving graphs may not allow a journey from A to B yet allows one or several travels from A to B (See Fig. 3).

We say a travel is cost-optimal if there does not exist a travel with the same departure and arrival node and times as T having a smaller cost. One can easily prove the following Property.

Property 1. Let T be a cost-optimal travel from node u to node v arriving at time t, and T' a sub-travel of T *i.e.*, a travel such that $T = T_1 \oplus T' \oplus T_2$. Then T' is also cost-optimal. However, this is not true for delay-optimal travels.

Problem Specification. We now present the problems that we aim to solve in this paper. First, we want to arrive at the destination as early as possible, *i.e.*, finding a time travel that minimizes the delay. Among such travels, we want to find one that minimizes the backward cost.

In the remaining of this paper, we consider a given evolving graph $G = (V, (E_t)_{t \in \mathbb{N}})$, a given a cost function $\mathfrak{f}$, a source node *src* and a destination node *dst* in V. *Travels*(G, src, dst) denotes the set of travels in G starting from *src* at time 0 and arriving at *dst*.

Definition 7. *The* Optimal Delay Optimal Cost space-time travel planning *(ODOC) problem consists in finding, among all travels in* $Travels(G, src, dst)$*, the ones that minimize the travel delay and, among them, minimize the cost. A solution to the ODOC problem is called an ODOC travel.*

One can notice that this problem is not very hard as there is a single metric (the cost) to optimize, because a travel with delay zero always exists (if the graph is temporally connected). But in this paper we study the two variants defined thereafter (see the difference in bold).

Definition 8. *The* ***C-cost-constrained*** *ODOC problem consists in finding among all travels in* $Travels(G, src, dst)$ ***with cost at most*** $C \geq 0$*, the ones that minimize the travel delay and, among them, one that minimizes the cost.*

Definition 9. *The* $\mathcal{H}$***-history-constrained*** *ODOC problem consists in finding among all travels in Travels(G, src, dst)* ***satisfying,***

$$\forall u, u', t, t',\ \text{if}\ T = T_1 \oplus ((u,t)) \oplus T_2 \oplus ((u',t')) \oplus T_3,\ \text{then}\ t' \geq t - \mathcal{H},$$

the ones that minimize the travel delay and, among them, one that minimizes the cost (Fig. 3).

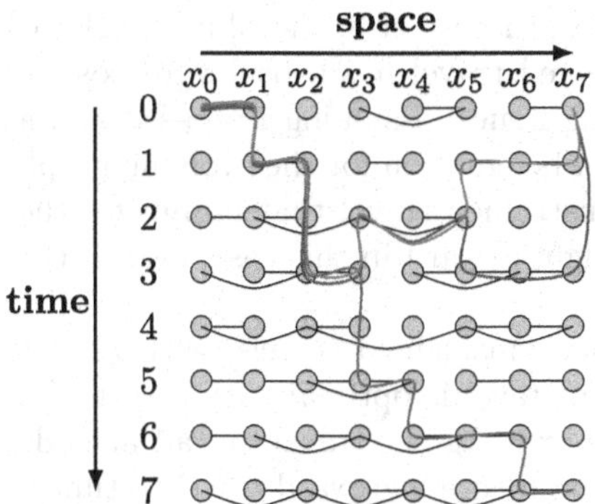

Fig. 1. Possible representation of an evolving graph. Possible travels from x_0 to x_7 are shown in red, green and blue. Note that the blue and green travels require to send an agent to the past (to a previous time instant). (Color figure online)

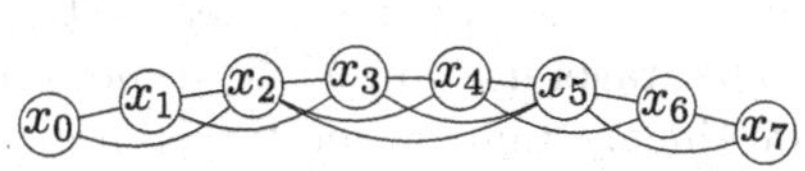

Fig. 2. Footprint of the evolving graph represented in Fig. 1.

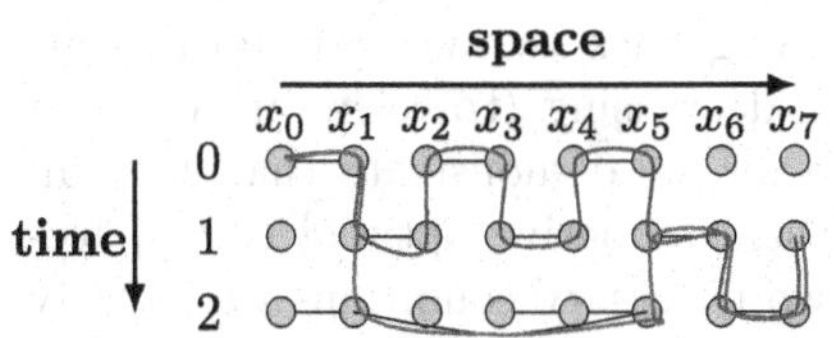

Fig. 3. Example of an evolving graph for which there exists no journey, yet there exists several travels from x_0 to x_7. The two travels, in blue and green, are 1-history-constrained. (Color figure online)

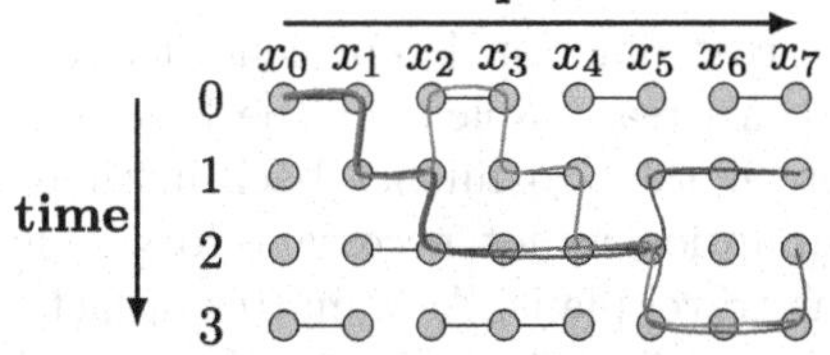

Fig. 4. Example of an evolving graph for which there exist at least three travels from x_0 to x_7 with a cost constraint of 1 (assuming $\mathfrak{f} : d \mapsto d$). The blue travel has optimal delay. (Color figure online)

Visual Representation of Space-Time Travels. To help visualize the problem, consider a set of $n+1$ nodes denoted $x_0, x_1, x_2, \ldots, x_n$. Then, the associated evolving graph can be seen as a vertical sequence of graphs mentioning for each time instant which edges are present. A possible visual representation of an evolving graph can be seen in Fig. 1. One can see the evolution of the topology (consisting of the nodes x_0 to x_7) over time through eight snapshots performed from time instants 0 to 7. Several possible travels are shown in red, green and blue. The red travel only makes use of forward time travel (that is, waiting) and is the earliest arriving travel in this class (arriving at time 7). The green and blue travels both make use of backward time travel and arrive at time 0, so they have minimal travel delay. Similarly, the red travel concatenated with $((x_7, 7), (x_7, 0))$ (*i.e.*, a backward travel to reach x_7 at time 0) also has minimal travel delay. However, if we assume that the cost function is the identity ($\mathfrak{f} : d \mapsto d$) then the green travel has a backward cost of 3, the blue travel has a backward cost of 4, and the concatenated red travel has a backward cost of 7. Adding constraints yields more challenging issues: assuming $\mathfrak{f} : d \mapsto d$ and a maximal cost $\mathcal{C}$ of 1, at least three travels can be envision for the evolving graph depicted in Fig. 4, but finding the 1-cost-constrained travel that minimizes the delay (that is, the blue travel) is not as straightforward in this case, even if the footprint of the evolving graph is a line.

Similarly, in Fig. 3 we show two $\mathcal{H}$-history-constrained travels, with $\mathcal{H} = 1$ (assuming $\mathfrak{f} : d \mapsto d$). Here, clearly, the green travel is optimal with a cost of 2 (the blue travel has cost 3). The choice made by the green travel to wait at node x_1 two time instants is good, even if it prevents future backward travel to time 0 since $\mathcal{H} = 1$; because it is impossible to terminates at time 0 anyway. So it seems like the choice made at node x_1 is difficult to make before knowing what is the best possible travel. If we add more nodes to the graph and repeat this kind of choice, we can create a graph with an exponential number of 1-history-constraint travel and finding one that minimizes the cost is challenging. Surprisingly, we show that it remains polynomial in the number of nodes and edges.

3 Backward-Cost Function Classes

The cost function $\mathfrak{f}$ represents the cost of going back to the past. Intuitively, it seems reasonable that the function is non-decreasing (travelers are charged more it they go further back in time), however we demonstrate that such an assumption is not necessary to enable travelers to derive optimal cost space-time travel plans. As a matter of fact, the two necessary conditions we identify to optimally solve the ODOC space-time travel planning problem are $\mathfrak{f}$ to be non-negative and that it attains its minimum (not just converge to it). These conditions are shown to be sufficient by construction, thanks to the algorithm presented in the next section (and Theorem 2). Due to space constrains, proofs are omitted.

Definition 10. *A cost function* $\mathfrak{f}$ *is* user optimizable *if it is non-negative, and it attains its minimum when restricted to any interval* $[C, \infty)$*, with* $C > 0$*. Let* $\mathcal{UO}$ *be the set of user optimizable cost functions.*

Theorem 1. *If the cost function* $\mathfrak{f}$ *is not in* $\mathcal{UO}$*, then there exist connected evolving graphs where no solution exists for the ODOC space-time travel planning problem.*

Proof. First, it is clear that if $\mathfrak{f}(d) < 0$ for some $d \in \mathbb{N}^*$, then we can construct travels with arbitrarily small cost by repeatedly appending $((y,t),(y,t+d),(y,t))$ to any travel arriving at node y at time t (*i.e.*, by waiting for d rounds and going back in time d rounds), rendering the problem unsolvable.

Now, let $C \in \mathbb{N}^*$ and $\mathfrak{f}$ be a non-negative function that does not attain its minimum when restricted to $[C,\infty)$. This implies that there exists an increasing sequence $(w_i)_{i\in\mathbb{N}}$ of integers $w_i \geq C$, such that the sequence $(\mathfrak{f}(w_i))_{i\in\mathbb{N}}$ is decreasing and converges towards the lower bound $m_C = \inf_{t\geq C}(\mathfrak{f}(t))$ of $\mathfrak{f}_{|[C,\infty)}$. Consider a graph with two nodes x_0 and x_1 that are connected by a temporal edge after time C and disconnected before. Since a travel from x_0 to x_1 arriving at time 0 must contain a backward travel to the past of amplitude at least C, its cost is at least equal to m_C. Since m_C is not attained, there is no travel with cost exactly m_C. Now, assume for the sake of contradiction that a cost-optimal travel T to x_1 arriving at time 0 has cost $m_C + \varepsilon$ with $\varepsilon > 0$. Then, we can construct a travel with a smaller cost. Let i_ε such that $\mathfrak{f}(w_{i_\varepsilon}) < m_C + \varepsilon$ (this index exists because the sequence $(\mathfrak{f}(w_i))_{i\in\mathbb{N}}$ converges to m_C).

Let $T' = ((x_0,0),(x_0,C),(x_1,C),(x_1,w_{i_\varepsilon}),(x_1,0))$. Then we have

$$cost(T') = \mathfrak{f}(w_{i_\varepsilon}) < m_C + \varepsilon = cost(T),$$

which contradicts the optimality of T. □

We now present the set of *user friendly* cost functions that we use in the sequel to ease proving optimization algorithms, as they allow *simple* solutions to the ODOC problem (Lemma 1). We prove in Theorem 2 that we do not lose generality since an algorithm solving the ODOC problem with user friendly cost functions can be transformed easily to work with any user optimizable ones.

Definition 11. *A cost function* $\mathfrak{f}$ *is* user friendly *if it is user optimizable, non-decreasing, and sub-additive*[1]. *Let* $\mathcal{UF}$ *be the set of user friendly cost functions.*

Lemma 1. *If the cost function* $\mathfrak{f}$ *is in* $\mathcal{UF}$ *and there exists a solution to the ODOC space-time travel planning problem in an evolving graph* G*, then there also exists a* simple *travel solution.*

Proof. Let T be a solution to the ODOC space-time travel planning problem. If there exists a node x_i and two time instants t_1 and t_2, such that $T = T_1 \oplus ((x_i,t_1)) \oplus T_2 \oplus ((x_i,t_2)) \oplus T_3$, then we construct T' as follows

$$T' = T_1 \oplus ((x_i,t_1),(x_i,t_2)) \oplus T_3$$

and we show that $cost(T') \leq cost(T)$. Indeed, it is enough to show (thanks to Remark 1) that

$$cost(((x_i,t_1),(x_i,t_2))) \leq cost(T_2).$$

By definition $cost(((x_i,t_1),(x_i,t_2))) = \mathfrak{f}(t_1 - t_2)$. If $t_1 < t_2$, then the cost is null by convention and the Lemma is proved. Otherwise $t_1 > t_2$. On the right hand side, we have:

[1] sub-additive means that for all $a,b \in \mathbb{N}$, $\mathfrak{f}(a+b) \leq \mathfrak{f}(a) + \mathfrak{f}(b)$.

$$cost(T_2) = \sum_{i=1}^{k} \mathfrak{f}(d_i)$$

where $d_1, d_2, \ldots, d_k$ is the sequence of differences between the times appearing in T_2. Since T_2 starts at time t_1 and ends at time t_2, then $\sum_{i=1}^{k} d_i = t_1 - t_2$. Since the function is sub-additive and increasing, we obtain:

$$\mathfrak{f}(t_1 - t_2) < \sum_{i=1}^{k} \mathfrak{f}(d_i)$$

By repeating the same procedure, we construct a time-travel with the same destination and same backward-cost as T but that does not contain two occurrences of the same node, except if they are consecutive. □

Theorem 2. *If an algorithm A solves the optimal cost space-time travel planning problem for any cost function in $\mathcal{UF}$, then there exists an algorithm A' solving the same problem with any $\mathfrak{f}$ in $\mathcal{UO}$.*

Proof. We consider an algorithm A as stated. Let $\mathfrak{f}$ be an arbitrary cost function in $\mathcal{UO}$, that is, $\mathfrak{f}$ is non-negative, and always attains its minimum.

From $\mathfrak{f}$, we now construct a cost function $\mathfrak{f}_{inc}$ as follows:

$$\mathfrak{f}_{inc}(t) = \min_{j \geq t} (\mathfrak{f}(j))$$

By construction, $\mathfrak{f}_{inc}$ is non-decreasing. Moreover, since $\mathfrak{f}$ is in $\mathcal{UO}$, it always attains its minimum, and we have:

$$\forall d, \ \exists d_m \text{ such that } \mathfrak{f}_{inc}(d) = \mathfrak{f}(d_m). \tag{1}$$

Then, we construct $\widetilde{\mathfrak{f}}$ as follows:

$$\widetilde{\mathfrak{f}}(t) = \min_{a \in \alpha(t)} \left(\sum_{a_i \in a} \mathfrak{f}_{inc}(a_i) \right)$$

where $\alpha(t)$ is the set of all the non-negative sequences that sum to t. Now, $\widetilde{\mathfrak{f}}$ is sub-additive by construction, hence $\widetilde{\mathfrak{f}} \in \mathcal{UF}$. Since $\alpha(t)$ is finite, the minimum is attained.

Also, $\forall t \geq 1$, $\widetilde{\mathfrak{f}}(t) \leq \mathfrak{f}(t)$, so that for any travel, its backward cost with respect to $\mathfrak{f}$ is at least equal to its backward cost with respect to $\widetilde{\mathfrak{f}}$.

Let G be a dynamic graph. Our goal is to construct an algorithm A' finding a cost-optimal (with respect to $\mathfrak{f}$) space-time travel in G. The algorithm A' works as follows. Let $\widetilde{T}$ be an optimal solution found by algorithm A on G assuming function $\widetilde{\mathfrak{f}}$ is used. A' now constructs, from $\widetilde{T}$, a time-travel T that is a cost-optimal (with respect to $\mathfrak{f}$) on G.

The travel T is constructed from $\widetilde{T}$ by replacing any sub-space-time travel $((x_i, t_i), (x_i, t_i - t))$, with $t \geq 0$, by the following sub space-time travel: $((x_i, t_i - a_1), (x_i, t_i - a_1 - a_2), \ldots, (x_i, t_i - \sum_{j=1}^{k} a_j))$ satisfying:

$$a \in \alpha(t) \quad \wedge \quad \widetilde{\mathfrak{f}}(t) = \sum_{j=1}^{\text{length of } a} \mathfrak{f}_{inc}(a_j)$$

Then, each $((u,t),(u,t-d))$, with $d \geq 0$, is replaced by $((u,t),(u,t-d+d_m),(u,t-d))$ such that:

$$d_m \geq d \quad \wedge \quad \mathfrak{f}_{inc}(d_m) = \mathfrak{f}(d)$$

We know that d_m exists thanks to Eq. 1. The space-time travel T uses the same temporal edges as $\widetilde{T}$, so it is well defined. Moreover, by construction $\mathfrak{f}(T) = \widetilde{\mathfrak{f}}(\widetilde{T})$, and T is optimal with respect to $\mathfrak{f}$ because the backward-cost of a travel with respect to $\mathfrak{f}$ is at least equal to its backward-cost with respect to $\widetilde{\mathfrak{f}}$, as observed earlier. Hence, if a better solution exists for $\mathfrak{f}$, it is also a solution with the same, or smaller, cost with $\widetilde{\mathfrak{f}}$, contradicting the optimality of $\widetilde{T}$. The above procedure defines an algorithm, based on A, that solves the ODOC problem with function $\mathfrak{f}$. □

4 Offline $\mathcal{C}$-Cost-Constrained ODOC Algorithm

In this section, we present Algorithm 1 that solves the $\mathcal{C}$-cost-constrained ODOC problem in time polynomial in the number of edges. More precisely, since the number of edges can be infinite, we only consider edges occurring before a certain travel (see the end of the section for a more precise description of the complexity). Algorithm 1 is different from existing shortest path algorithms because we need to efficiently take into account the cost and the delay of travels. It is well-known that constrained shortest path algorithms are exponential when considering two additive metrics [15] but surprisingly, our algorithm is polynomial by using the specificity of the time travel. Our algorithm works as follows. At each iteration, we extract the minimum cost to reach a particular node at a particular time and we extend travels from there by updating the best-known cost of the next node. We reach the next nodes either by using the next temporal edge that exists in the future (we prove that considering only the next future edge is enough) or using each of the past temporal edge.

We first prove that our algorithm terminates, even if the graph is infinite and if there is no solution.

Lemma 2. *Algorithm 1 always terminates.*

Proof. Assume for the sake of contradiction that it does not terminates. First, we observe that, for any $u \in V$, `minCost`$[u]$ is non-increasing (using the lexicographical order), so it must reach a minimum value $(c_{u,\min}, t_{u,\min})$, which represent, for a node u, the minimum cost a travel towards u can have and the minimum time such a travel can arrive. Moreover, the cost associated with a pair (u,t) extracted in Line 4 is non-decreasing (because we always extract a pair with minimum cost), so either this cost reach a maximum or tends to

Algorithm 1: Offline $\mathcal{C}$-cost-constrained ODOC Algorithm (input: $G, \mathfrak{f}, \mathcal{C}, src, dst$)

/* `nodeCost[u,t]` stores the current best cost of travels from node src to node u arriving at time t. `minCost`$[u]$ stores a pair (c,t) where c is the current known minimum cost of a travel towards u, and t the smallest time where such travel arrives. `pred`$[u,t]$ stores the suffix of an optimal travel to u arriving at t. */

1 $\forall u \in V, \forall t,$ `nodeCost`$[u,t] = \infty$ `minCost`$[u] = (\infty, \infty)$;
2 `nodeCost`$[src, 0] \leftarrow 0$; done $\leftarrow \emptyset$;
3 **while** $\exists (u,t) \notin$ done such that `nodeCost`$[u,t] < \infty$ **do**
4   $(u,t) \leftarrow \text{argmin}_{(u,t)\notin \text{done}}($`nodeCost`$[u,t])$;
5   done $\leftarrow$ done $\cup \{(u,t)\}$;
6   $c \leftarrow$ `nodeCost`$[u,t]$;
7   **for** *each neighbor v of u* **do**
8   let t_{future} the smallest time after (or equal to) t where edge $((u,v), t_{future})$ exists;
9   let $(c_{min}, t_{min}) =$ `minCost`$[v]$;
10   **if** `nodeCost`$[v, t_{future}] > c$ and $(c < c_{min}$ or $t_{future} < t_{min})$ **then**
11   `nodeCost`$[v, t_{future}] \leftarrow c$;
12   `pred`$[v, t_{future}] \leftarrow ((u,t), (u, t_{future}), (v, t_{future}))$;
13   **if** $(c, t_{future}) <_{lexico}$ `minCost`$[v]$ **then** `minCost`$[v] \leftarrow (c, t_{future})$;
14   **for** each t_{past} such that $(u,v) \in E_{t_{past}}$ **do**
15   let $c_{past} = c + \mathfrak{f}(t - t_{past})$;
16   **if** $c_{past} \leq \mathcal{C}$ and `nodeCost`$[v, t_{past}] > c_{past}$ **then**
17   `nodeCost`$[v, t_{past}] \leftarrow c_{past}$;
18   `pred`$[v, t_{past}] \leftarrow ((u,t), (u, t_{past}), (v, t_{past}))$;
19 let $t_{\min}$ be the minimum time instant such that $\exists t$, `nodeCost`$[dst, t] + \mathfrak{f}(t - t_{\min}) \leq \mathcal{C}$;
20 **if** $t_{\min}$ *exists* **then return** `ExtractTimeTravel`$(dst, t_{\min},$ `nodeCost`, `pred`$)$;
21 **else return** $\perp$;

infinity. In the former case, let $c_{\max}$ be that maximum *i.e.*, after some time, every time a pair (u,t) is extracted, `nodeCost`$[u,t] = c_{\max}$. Since a pair is never extracted twice, pairs are extracted with arbitrarily large value t. Some, at some point in the execution, for every pair (u,t) extracted, we have $t > t_{u,\min}$. Moreover, $c_{\max} \geq c_{u,\min}$. So, every time a pair is extracted, condition Line 10 is false. Hence, $c_{\max}$ is not added into `nodeCost` anymore, which contradicts the fact that $c_{\max}$ is associated with each extracted pair after some time. So the latter case occurs *i.e.*, the cost associated with extracted pairs tends to infinity. After some time, this cost is greater than any $c_{u,\min}$. Again, since a pair is never extracted twice, pairs are extracted with arbitrarily large value t. Some, at some point in the execution, for every pair (u,t) extracted, we have $t > t_{u,\min}$, and the condition Line 10 is always false. Hence, from there, every time a value is added into `nodeCost`, it is according to Line 17, so the associated time smaller than the time extracted, which contradicts the fact that arbitrarily large value t are added to nodeCost. □

We now prove the correctness of our algorithm, starting with the main property we then use to construct a solution. Let $\delta_\mathcal{C}$ be the function that returns, for each pair (u, t) where u is a node and t a time, the best backward-cost smaller or equal to $\mathcal{C}$, from *src* to u, for travels arriving at time t.

Lemma 3. *When a pair (u, t) is extracted from* nodeCost *at line 4, then*

$$\delta_\mathcal{C}(u, t) = \texttt{nodeCost}[u, t]$$

Proof. Assume for the sake of contradiction that this is not true, and let (u, t) be the first tuple extracted such that the property is false. Let $c_{u,t} = \texttt{nodeCost}[u, t]$. Let T be a $\mathcal{C}$-cost-constrained backward-cost-optimal travel to u arriving at time t (hence $cost(T) < c_{u,t}$ by assumption).

Let T' be the longest prefix of T, to (x, t') (*i.e.*, such that $T = T' \oplus (x, t') \oplus T''$, for some T''), such that (x, t') was extracted from nodeCost and satisfies $\delta_\mathcal{C}(x, t') = \texttt{nodeCost}[x, t']$. Now, T' is well defined because the first element in T is $(src, 0)$ and, by Line 2, $(src, 0)$ is the first extracted pair, and satisfies $\texttt{nodeCost}[src, 0] = 0 = \delta_\mathcal{C}(src, 0)$. Hence, prefix $((src, 0))$ satisfies the property, so the longest of such prefixes exists. Observe that T', resp. T'', ends, resp. starts, with (x, t'), by the definition of travel concatenation.

When (x, t') is extracted from nodeCost, it is extended to the next future edge (Lines 8 to 11), and all past edges (Lines 14 to 17). T'' starts either (a) with $((x, t'), (x, t_a), (y, t_a))$, with $t_a < t'$, (b) with $((x, t'), (x, t_a), (y, t_a))$ with $t_a > t'$, or (c) with $((x, t'), (y, t'))$, where $y \in N(x)$.

In case (a), this means that the temporal edge $((x, y), t_a)$ exists, hence, by Line 17, we know that $\texttt{nodeCost}[y, t_a] \leq \texttt{nodeCost}[x, t'] + \mathfrak{f}(t' - t_a)$. However, since T' is a sub-travel, $cost(T') = \delta_\mathcal{C}(x, t') = \texttt{nodeCost}[x, t']$, hence

$$\texttt{nodeCost}[y, t_a] \leq cost(T' \oplus ((x, t'), (x, t_a), (y, t_a))) = \delta_\mathcal{C}(y, t_a),$$

and (y, t_a) must have been extracted before (u, t), otherwise

$$\delta_\mathcal{C}(u, t) < \texttt{nodeCost}[y, t] \leq \texttt{nodeCost}[y, t_a] = \delta_\mathcal{C}(y, t_a)$$

which is a contradiction (a sub-travel of a cost-optimal travel cannot have a greater cost, see Property 1). So, $T' \oplus ((x, t'), (x, t_a), (y, t_a))$ is a longer prefix of T with the same property as T', which contradicts the definition of T'.

In case (b), this means that the temporal edge $((x, y), t_a)$ exists, hence, by Line 11, we know that $\texttt{nodeCost}[y, t_a] \leq \texttt{nodeCost}[x, t']$. Again, we have $cost(T') = \delta_\mathcal{C}(x, t') = \texttt{nodeCost}[x, t']$, hence

$$\texttt{nodeCost}[y, t_a] \leq cost(T' \oplus ((x, t'), (x, t_a), (y, t_a))) = \delta_\mathcal{C}(y, t_a),$$

which contradicts the definition of T'.

In case (c), this means that the edge $((x, y), t')$ exists, which implies, using a similar argument, a contradiction. □

The previous lemma says that nodeCost contains correct information about the cost to reach a node, but actually, it does not contain all the information. Indeed, a node u can be reachable by a travel at a given time t and still nodeCost$[u, t] = \infty$. This fact helps our algorithm to be efficient, as it does not compute all the optimal costs for each possible time (in this case, the complexity would depend on the duration of the graph, which could be much higher than the number of edges). Fortunately, we now prove that we can still find all existing travel using nodeCost.

Lemma 4. *For all $u \in V$, $t \in \mathbb{N}$, there exists a C-cost-constrained travel T from src to u arriving at time t, if and only if there exists $t' \in \mathbb{N}$ such that nodeCost$[u, t'] + \mathfrak{f}(t' - t) \leq C$.*

Theorem 3. *If the cost function $\mathfrak{f}$ is in $\mathcal{UF}$, Algorithm 1 outputs a travel T if and only if T is a solution of the C-cost-constrained ODOC problem.*

Let us now analyze the complexity of Algorithm 1. We assume that retrieving the next or previous edge after or before a given time takes $O(1)$ time. For example, the graph can be stored as a dictionary that maps each node to an array that maps each time to the current, previous, and next temporal edges. This array can be made sparser with low complexity overhead to save space if few edges occur per time-instant.

Since each temporal edge is extracted from nodeCost at most once and the inner *for* loop iterates over a subset of edges, the time complexity is polynomial in the number of temporal edges. We must also consider the time to extract the minimum from nodeCost, which is also polynomial. If there are an infinite number of temporal edges[2], Lemma 2 shows that our algorithm always terminates, even if no solution exists. Therefore, its complexity is polynomial in the size of the finite subset of temporal edges extracted from nodeCost.

Let $\mathcal{E}$ be the set of temporal edges $((u, v), t)$ such that (u, t) or (v, t) is extracted in Line 4 of our algorithm during its execution.

Theorem 4. *If the cost function $\mathfrak{f}$ is in $\mathcal{UF}$, then Algorithm 1 terminates in $O(|\mathcal{E}|^2)$.*

5 Offline $\mathcal{H}$-History-Constrained ODOC Algorithm

Section 4 made the assumption that a given agent was able to go back to *any* previous snapshot of the network. However, this hypothesis might not hold as the difficulty to go back in time may depend on how far in the future we already reach. Hence, we consider in this section that $\mathcal{H}$ denotes the maximum number of time instants one agent can travel back to. In more detail, once an agent reaches time instant t, it cannot go back to $t' < t - \mathcal{H}$, even after multiple jumps.

[2] An evolving graph with an infinite number of edges can exist in practice even with bounded memory, e.g., when the graph is periodic.

Algorithm 2: Offline $\mathcal{H}$-history-constrained ODOC Algorithm

/* $c[i, t-h, t]$ stores the cost of a cost optimal travel to node x_i, arriving before or at time $t-h$, that is $\mathcal{H}$-history-constrained, and never reaches a time instant greater than t.
pred$[u, t-h, t]$ stores the suffix of an optimal travel to u arriving at $t-h$ that never reaches a time greater than t. */

$c[*] \leftarrow \infty$; $c[src, *] \leftarrow 0$ pred$[*] \leftarrow \bot$;
$t_{\max} \leftarrow$ upper bound on the time reached by a cost-optimal travel to dst;
for $t = 0, 1, 2, \ldots, t_{\max}$ **do**
  /* for simplicity, we assume $c[u, t-h, t] = \infty$ if $t-h < 0$ */
  for $u \in V$ **do**
    $c[u, t-h, t] \leftarrow \min(c[u, t-h, t-1], c[u, t-h-1, t-1])$;
  repeat $|V|$ **times**
    for $u \in V$ **do**
      for $h = \mathcal{H}, \mathcal{H}-1, \ldots, 0$ **do**
        $m \leftarrow \min_{\substack{t' \in [t-\mathcal{H}, t] \\ (u,v) \in E_{t'}}} (c[v, t', t] + \mathfrak{f}(t' - (t-h)))$;
        if $c[u, t-h, t] < m$ **then**
          $c[u, t-h, t] \leftarrow m$;
          pred$[u, t-h, t] \leftarrow (v, t')$ (with the corresponding min arguments);
  if the minimum time instant $t_{\min}$ such that $c[dst, t_{\min}, t_{\min} + \mathcal{H}] < \infty$ exists **then**
    return ExtractHistoryConstrainedTravel$(dst, t_{\min}, t_{\min} + \mathcal{H}, c)$;
return $\bot$;

In this section, it is important to notice that the capability of BTT devices does not depend on the time when the agent uses it but rather on the largest time reached by the agent.

We present Algorithm 2 that solve the $\mathcal{H}$-history-constrained ODOC problem. The algorithm uses dynamic programming to store intermediary results. At each iteration, we update the optimal cost based on the best cost of previous nodes. For each node x_i and time t we need to store the best cost depending on the maximum time reached by the agent.

Theorem 5. *If the cost function* $\mathfrak{f}$ *is in* $\mathcal{UF}$*, then Algorithm 2 solves the* $\mathcal{H}$*-history-constrained ODOC problem and has* $O(n^2\mathcal{H}(t_{\min} + \mathcal{H}))$ *complexity, with* $t_{\min}$ *the delay of a solution.*

6 Conclusion

We presented the first solutions to the optimal delay optimal cost space-time constrained travel planning problem in dynamic networks, and demonstrated that the problem can be solved in polynomial time, even in the case when backward time jumps can be made up to a constant, for any sensible pricing policy. It would be interesting to investigate the online version of the problem, when the future of the evolving graph is unknown to the algorithm.

References

1. Casteigts, A., Flocchini, P., Mans, B., Santoro, N.: Shortest, fastest, and foremost broadcast in dynamic networks. Int. J. Found. Comput. Sci. **26**(4), 499–522 (2015). https://doi.org/10.1142/S0129054115500288
2. Casteigts, A., Flocchini, P., Quattrociocchi, W., Santoro, N.: Time-varying graphs and dynamic networks. Int. J. Parallel Emergent Distrib. Syst. **27**(5), 387–408 (2012). https://doi.org/10.1080/17445760.2012.668546
3. Casteigts, A., Himmel, A., Molter, H., Zschoche, P.: Finding temporal paths under waiting time constraints. Algorithmica **83**(9), 2754–2802 (2021). https://doi.org/10.1007/s00453-021-00831-w
4. Casteigts, A., Peters, J.G., Schoeters, J.: Temporal cliques admit sparse spanners. J. Comput. Syst. Sci. **121**, 1–17 (2021). https://doi.org/10.1016/j.jcss.2021.04.004
5. Chen, S., Nahrstedt, K.: An overview of QoS routing for the next generation high-speed networks: problems and solutions. IEEE Netw. **12**, 64–79 (1998). https://doi.org/10.1109/65.752646
6. Ferreira, A.: On models and algorithms for dynamic communication networks: the case for evolving graphs. In: Quatrièmes Rencontres Francophones sur les Aspects Algorithmiques des Télécommunications (ALGOTEL 2002), Mèze, France, pp. 155–161. INRIA Press (2002)
7. Garey, M.R., Johnson, D.S.: Computers and Intractability: A Guide to the Theory of NP-Completeness. W. H. Freeman & Co., San Francisco (1990)
8. Garroppo, R.G., Giordano, S., Tavanti, L.: A survey on multi-constrained optimal path computation: exact and approximate algorithms. Comput. Netw. **54**(17), 3081–3107 (2010). https://doi.org/10.1016/j.comnet.2010.05.017
9. Guck, J.W., Van Bemten, A., Reisslein, M., Kellerer, W.: Unicast QoS routing algorithms for SDN: a comprehensive survey and performance evaluation. IEEE Commun. Surv. Tutor. **20**(1), 388–415 (2018). https://doi.org/10.1109/COMST.2017.2749760
10. Luna, G.A.D., Flocchini, P., Prencipe, G., Santoro, N.: Black hole search in dynamic rings. In: 41st IEEE International Conference on Distributed Computing Systems, ICDCS 2021, Washington DC, USA, 7–10 July 2021, pp. 987–997. IEEE (2021). https://doi.org/10.1109/ICDCS51616.2021.00098
11. Pal, G.: The time machine (1960)
12. Russo, A., Russo, J.: Avengers: Endgame (2019)
13. Thulasiraman, K., Arumugam, S., Brandstädt, A., Nishizeki, T.: Handbook of Graph Theory, Combinatorial Optimization, and Algorithms (2016)
14. Villacis-Llobet, J., Bui-Xuan, B.M., Potop-Butucaru, M.: Foremost non-stop journey arrival in linear time. In: Parter, M. (ed.) SIROCCO 2022. LNCS, vol. 13298, pp. 283–301. Springer, Cham (2022). https://doi.org/10.1007/978-3-031-09993-9_16
15. Wang, Z., Crowcroft, J.: Quality-of-service routing for supporting multimedia applications. IEEE J. Sel. Areas Commun. **14**(7), 1228–1234 (1996). https://doi.org/10.1109/49.536364
16. Zemeckis, R.: Back to the future (1985)

Machine Learning-Based Phishing Detection Using URL Features: A Comprehensive Review

Asif Uz Zaman Asif[1(✉)], Hossein Shirazi[2], and Indrakshi Ray[1]

[1] Colorado State University, Fort Collins, CO 80523, USA
{asif09,indrakshi.ray}@colostate.edu

[2] San Diego State University, San Diego, CA 92182, USA
hshirazi@sdsu.edu

Abstract. Phishing is a social engineering attack in which an attacker sends a fraudulent message to a user in the hope of obtaining sensitive confidential information. Machine learning appears to be a promising technique for phishing detection. Typically, website content and Unified Resource Locator (*URL*) based features are used. However, gathering website content features requires visiting malicious sites, and preparing the data is labor-intensive. Towards this end, researchers are investigating if *URL*-only information can be used for phishing detection. This approach is lightweight and can be installed at the client's end, they do not require data collection from malicious sites and can identify zero-day attacks. We conduct a systematic literature review on *URL*-based phishing detection. We selected recent papers (2018 –) or if they had a high citation count (50+ in Google Scholar) that appeared in top conferences and journals in cybersecurity. This survey will provide researchers and practitioners with information on the current state of research on *URL*-based website phishing attack detection methodologies. In this survey, we have seen that even though there is a lack of a centralized dataset, algorithms like Random Forest, and Long Short-Term Memory with appropriate lexical features can detect phishing *URL*s effectively.

Keywords: Phishing · social engineering · URL-based · survey · cybersecurity · machine learning · feature extraction · data repository

1 Introduction

Phishing is a social engineering attack intended to deceive the victim and attempt to obtain sensitive data with the ultimate goal of stealing the victim's valued possessions. Although phishing has persisted since the mid 90's [22], such attacks have escalated in recent times due to the increased use of online activities. According to reports provided by the Anti-Phishing Working Group (*APWG*), more than a million phishing attacks were recorded in the First Quarter (*Q*1) of 2022. With 23.6% of all attacks, the financial sector was the one most commonly

S. Dolev and B. Schieber (Eds.): SSS 2023, LNCS 14310, pp. 481–497, 2023.
https://doi.org/10.1007/978-3-031-44274-2_36

targeted by phishing in $Q1$ [9]. Attackers are constantly adapting their strategies which makes phishing detection particularly hard.

Typically, the attacker attempts to redirect users to a phishing site using a malicious *URL*. *URL* manipulation is often the first stage in building phishing websites. Attackers work on various means through which a malicious *URL* can be represented. Since the representation of *URL* keeps on changing, even professionals cannot correctly identify phishing *URLs*. Past approaches for phishing detection use signature-based and rule-based mechanisms. However, these approaches are ineffective against zero-day attacks which are referred to as vulnerabilities that are exploited as soon as they are discovered or even before anyone is aware of them.

Machine learning researchers have used *URL*-based features and content-based features (website images, HTML, and JavaScript code) to distinguish phishing from genuine websites. In this survey, we focussed only on *URL*-based features. A number of reasons motivated this choice. First, machine learning algorithms focusing on lexical characteristics of *URL* are lightweight and more efficient than those using both content-based and *URL*-based features. Second, this approach can thwart phishing attacks at the very initial stage when a user stumbles into a potentially harmful *URL* or phishing campaign. Third, the use of *URL* only features does not require one to visit malicious websites to download content-based features. Visiting malicious websites may cause malware to be loaded which may lead to future attacks. Fourth, *URL*-based classifiers can be installed on clients' mobile devices as they are lightweight – the clients' browsing habits are abstracted from the servers – making them more privacy-preserving.

In this survey, we produced a comprehensive review of the research on *URL*-based phishing detectors using machine learning. We looked into the feature extraction procedure, the datasets, the algorithms, the experimental design, and the results for each work. We looked at the crucial steps in creating a phishing detector, and after analyzing several different approaches, we gave our conclusions regarding the features that may be used, the ideal algorithms, the dataset's current state, and some recommendations. We used two criteria for the paper selection process in this survey. First, we looked into the articles on *URL*-based phishing detection that has been published in the past five years (2018 onwards) in journals having an impact factor of 2.0 or higher and in conferences from Tier (1, 2, and 3)[1]. We also examined papers having at least 50 citations in Google Scholar. We found 26 papers satisfying our criteria.

The rest of the paper is organized as follows. The anatomy of an *URL* is explained in Sect. 2. Feature extraction techniques used by researchers are illustrated in Sect. 3. Section 4 of the paper discusses machine learning algorithms that are used. The numerous data sources that are used by researchers are covered in Sect. 5. Section 6 contains the experimental results and presents an overview of the survey findings. Finally, Sect. 7 concludes the paper.

---

[1] We used the following sources for conference rankings: https://people.engr.tamu.edu/guofei/sec_conf_stat.htm.

2 Malicious URLs

The anatomy of an *URL* is critical for understanding how attackers manipulate it for launching phishing attacks. An attacker may manipulate any segment of the URL to create a malicious link that can be used to launch a phishing attack.

The *URL* of a website is made up of three major components: scheme, domain, and path. The scheme specifies the protocol used by the *URL*. The domain name identifies a specific website on the internet. The paths are then used to identify the specific resource that a web client is attempting to access.

An attacker often uses social engineering to trick a victim so that the malicious *URL* goes undetected. To accomplish this goal, the attacker will employ various obfuscation techniques. In this case, the attacker may obfuscate the hostname with the IP address, and the phished domain name is placed in the path, for example, http://159.203.6.191/servicepaypal/. Furthermore, an attacker can obfuscate a domain name that is unknown or misspelled, such as http://paypa1.com, which is misspelled and unrelated to the actual domain.

The most important details in the above *URLs* are the techniques used to redirect a victim to a malicious site and entice them to provide sensitive information to the attacker. PayPal is incorporated in the malicious *URL* in all of these cases, creating a sense of urgency for the victim and making them vulnerable to judgemental errors. To prevent *URL*-based website phishing attacks, an automated approach is needed.

3 Feature Extraction

Manual feature extraction is required for *URL*-based website phishing attack detection when using machine-learning; this is generally known as using handcrafted features. However, when a deep learning approach is employed, the feature extraction procedure is done automatically and does not require domain expertise.

Researchers have often used *URL* lexical features alongside domain features to create a better ML model. Table 1 provides a list of features used by the algorithms.

URL Lexical Features: Information that is directly connected to a website's *URL* components is referred to as *URL* lexical features. *URL*-based characteristics include lexical features that keep track of the attributes of the *URL*, such as its length, domain, and subdomain. Popular lexical elements of *URLs* include the use of the Hypertext Transfer Protocol Secure (*HTTPS*) protocol, special characters and their counts (for a dot, a hyphen, and at symbol), numerical characters, and IP addresses.

Domain Features: Information about the domain on which a website is hosted is included in the domain features. The age of the domain and free hosting is generally included in this feature set as it is a crucial signal for distinguishing between a legitimate website and a phishing website. Typically, a newly hosted website serves as a warning sign for a phishing site.

Word Features: These prevent a typical user from becoming suspicious. Attackers utilize words like secure, support, safe, and authentic within the *URL* itself to make it appear real. To make the *URL* appear legitimate, they also include well-known brand names, such as PayPal and Amazon inside the *URL*.

Character Features: Phishing sites often use suspicious characters. The length of the *URL*, the usage of uncommon letters or symbols, and misspelled words are a few examples of character-based indicators that are frequently used to identify phishing websites.

Search Index Based Features: These include website page ranking, Google index, and website traffic information. The average lifespan of a phishing website is quite short, and it typically produces no statistics.

Table 1. Combination of features used in the literature

Ref.	[19]	[37]	[11]	[24]	[21]	[2]	[35]	[13]	[6]	[34]	[14]	[17]	[42]	[40]	[7]	[39]	[45]	[41]	[44]	[4]	[3]	[5]	[8]	[29]	[12]	[20]
Automatic Features													✓	✓							✓					
Hand-Crafted Features	✓	✓	✓	✓	✓	✓	✓	✓	✓	✓	✓	✓			✓	✓		✓				✓	✓	✓		✓
URL Lexical Features	✓	✓	✓	✓	✓	✓	✓	✓	✓	✓	✓	✓			✓	✓						✓	✓	✓	✓	✓
Domain Features	✓	✓	✓		✓	✓					✓				✓								✓			
Word Features	✓	✓	✓		✓		✓	✓		✓							✓									
Character Features																	✓	✓	✓	✓						
Search Index Features						✓																				
Total Features	**17**	–	**46**	**51**	**14**	**35**	**104**	**12**	**42**	**93980**	**17**	–	–	–	**95+**	**87**	–	**9**	–	–	–	**111**	**30**	**30**	–	**48**

4 Algorithms

The parts that follow provide a description of the machine learning and deep learning algorithms used for *URL*-based phishing detection.

4.1 Classification Using Machine Learning

Logistic Regression (*LR*) is a common statistical machine-learning method for binary classification problems or for predicting an outcome with two possible values and this is specifically required for phishing detection because *URL* might either be legitimate or fraudulent [6,7,14,29,34,37,41]. *LR* can process a lot of *URLs* as it is a computationally efficient technique and can handle big datasets with high-dimensional feature spaces [7,29]. In order to select the most crucial aspects for phishing *URL* detection, feature selection can be done using *LR* models. In addition to increasing the model's effectiveness, this can decrease the input space's dimensionality and works with word-based features [37], character-based features [7] and bi-gram-based features which is, contiguous pairs of words [41]. Additionally, when given a balanced dataset, *LR* can learn the decision boundary that best discriminates between positive and negative samples without favoring either class [14,34]. However, in order to train the model, *LR* needs labeled data. This can be a problem in phishing detection because acquiring labeled data can be challenging [6].

Decision Tree (*DT*) is a type of supervised machine learning method for classification and regression tasks. It works by iteratively segmenting the input data into subsets based on the values of the input attributes in order to discriminate between the various classes or forecast the target variable. *DT* is commonly used by researchers for phishing detection problems [5,6,13,20,29,34,35,40]. Phishing *URLs* frequently exhibit traits that set them apart from real *URLs*. *DT* algorithm learns to distinguish between legal and phishing *URLs* using these properties as input to the features needed to train the algorithm. For detecting *URL*-based phishing, *DT* is advantageous because it is a highly interpretable model that makes it possible for human specialists to determine the reasoning behind a choice. Given the large potential for feature density in *URLs*, the feature space is highly dimensional. Without suffering dimension problems, *DT* can handle this type of data [29]. Moreover, *DT* that use lexical features can produce a better result, it creates a set of rules based on lexical properties that are simple for human specialists to comprehend [34,35,40]. When working with massive datasets, decision trees offer outcomes with good performance [5,40]. However, overfitting is common in *DT*, especially in small or significantly unbalanced datasets. A model may as a result perform well on training data but badly on the newly collected information [13].

Random Forest (*RF*) is another machine learning method used for classification, regression, and feature selection tasks [4,6,7,11,13,20,24,29,34,35,39,40,42]. Because *RF* can manage large and complex datasets and has the capability to deal with noisy data it is well-adapted for *URL*-based phishing detection [40]. To make predictions, the ensemble learning method of *RF*, combines data from various decision trees, reducing the possibility of overfitting while improving the model's generalization capabilities [7,29,34,35,39]. A measure of feature importance can also be provided by *RF*, which means that this algorithm can be used to understand the key features that contribute to phishing detection, improving the algorithm's overall accuracy [11,24,29]. *RF* is better for the real-time detection of phishing *URLs* because it is computationally efficient and can be trained on big datasets rapidly as it requires minimal parameter tuning [11]. We also observed that using the lexical features of the *URL*, *RF* can produce good performance accuracy [35]. However, the *RF* algorithm may not work well with imbalanced datasets but it can be observed that on a balanced dataset, it gives better performance [4,39,42]. Another disadvantage of using *RF* is that the model produces better results at the cost of both training and prediction time [13].

Naive Bayes (*NB*) algorithm is a probabilistic algorithm used in machine learning for classification purposes which is based on Bayes' theorem, to identify *URL*-based website phishing [7,11,13,14,20,21,29,35,39–41]. *NB* can manage high-dimensional data, which means the algorithm can handle a large number of features in the *URL* [7]. *NB* is susceptible to the model's feature selection, though the model's accuracy may suffer if essential features are excluded [41]. It can therefore work better on small feature sets with important features [29]. Additionally, it was discovered that applying only word-based features to *NB* does not yield better results [35]. The *NB* algorithm also has the benefit of learning the underlying patterns in the data with a small quantity of labeled training data, given how difficult it can be to acquire labeled data, this is especially helpful for *URL*-based phishing detection [39,40]. When there are an uneven amount of samples in each class, *NB* may not perform well. This could lead to a model that is biased in support of the dominant class [21]. On a balanced sample, however, this algorithm performance improves [11].

Gradient Boosting (*GB*) is a machine learning technique that creates a sequence of decision trees, each of which aims to fix the flaws of the one previous to it. The combined forecasts of all the trees result in the final prediction [7,20,29,34,39]. Since *GB* can be used to train models on huge datasets, it is especially suitable for large-scale phishing attack detection [39]. Additionally, the balanced dataset makes sure that the accuracy of the model is not biased towards one class over another and forces the model to equally understand the underlying patterns of the data for each class. As a result, the model becomes more accurate and generalizable [20,34,39]. Moreover, *GB* is effective when more attributes are considered [7,34] as well as on character-based features [29,39]. The model may be less accurate or may not perform well on new, untested data if the training data is biased or insufficient. However, on a balanced dataset, the algorithm performs better [20]. To ensure that the model is able to extract the most informative features from the data, *GB* necessitates thorough feature engineering. When dealing with complicated and diverse information like *URLs*, this can be a time-consuming and difficult operation [7,34].

Adaptive Boosting (*AdaBoost*) is a machine learning algorithm that is a member of the ensemble learning technique family. This approach for supervised learning can be applied to classification and regression tasks and is also used for *URL*-based website phishing detection [29,35,39,40]. As an ensemble approach it combines several weak learners to provide a final prediction, *AdaBoost* is a powerful algorithm that can be a viable choice for *URL*-based phishing detection [29]. *AdaBoost* can predict outcomes more precisely when it has access to a larger training dataset. The algorithm can produce predictions that are more accurate by better capturing the underlying relationships and patterns in the data [39,40]. However, *AdaBoost* may not be the best option for datasets with a lot of irrelevant or redundant features because it does not directly do the feature selection. This may lead to longer training times and poor results [35].

K-Nearest Neighbour ($K-NN$) is an algorithm where a prediction is made based on the labels of the k data points that are closest to an input data point in the training set. In the context of *URL*-based phishing detection, this means that the algorithm may compare a new *URL* to a list of known phishing and legitimate *URLs* and find the ones that are most similar to the new *URL* and thus are used for *URL*-based website phishing detection [2,4,6,20,29,34,35,39]. High-dimensional feature vectors, such as those found in *URLs*, might be challenging to process. However, the $K-NN$ technique can efficiently detect similarities across *URLs* and is well-suited to high-dimensional data [39]. Even with imbalanced datasets, where the proportion of samples in one class is significantly higher than the other, the $K-NN$ approach can perform well [20,34]. Additionally, $K-NN$ works well with word-based features [2,34,35]. In $K - NN$ when producing predictions, an algorithm that has a bigger value of k will take into account more neighbors and improves performance [4]. However, the number of nearest neighbors taken into account or the distance measure utilized can have an impact on how well the $K - NN$ method performs. These hyperparameters may need a lot of effort to be tuned [29]. The $K - NN$ method is susceptible to adversarial attacks, in which a perpetrator creates *URLs* on purpose to avoid being detected by the system [6,34].

Support Vector Machine (SVM), a form of supervised learning algorithm used in classification and regression analysis, was commonly used by researchers [2,4,6,11,13,14,20,21,24,29,34,39,42]. SVM is good for detecting *URL*-based website phishing because it can handle high-dimensional data and identify intricate connections between features [39]. Numerous characteristics, including the lexical features of the *URL*, and the existence of specific keywords, can be used to detect phishing when analyzing *URLs*. These characteristics can be used by SVM to recognize trends in phishing *URLs* and separate them from real *URLs*. It can be observed that only using the lexical features of the *URL* does not yield good results [34]. However, hybrid features like a combination of text, image, and web page content work better for SVM [2]. Hence to achieve optimum performance, SVM requires fine-tuning of several parameters, SVMs additionally can require a lot of computational power, especially when working with big datasets [13]. This may slow down training and prediction times and necessitate the use of powerful hardware [4]. Moreover, the ratio of legitimate *URLs* to phishing *URLs* is very uneven, which can result in unbalanced data that will degrade the performance of SVM [11]. However, on a balanced dataset, SVM performs better [42]. Additionally, if there is a lack of training data, SVM's accuracy is likely to decline [21].

4.2 Classification Using Deep Learning

Neural Network (*NN*) uses complex patterns and correlations between input features can be learned. By finding patterns that are suggestive of phishing attempts, *NN* can learn to differentiate between legitimate and phishing *URLs* in the context of *URL*-based phishing detection [5,7,20]. The ability of *NN* to acquire intricate patterns and connections between the characters in a sequence makes them effective for character-based characteristics [7]. Additionally, because the algorithm can learn from the data and produce predictions for each class with nearly equal importance, neural networks can perform well on balanced datasets [20]. However, to perform well, *NN* needs a lot of high-quality training data. Especially in rapidly changing phishing contexts, collecting and identifying a sufficiently large and diverse array of *URL*s might be difficult [5].

Multi-Layer Perceptron (*MLP*) is another type of *NN* that has been found to be successful in *URL*-based phishing detection [13,14,39]. A class imbalance may significantly affect several other algorithms, however, because *MLP*s employ numerous hidden layers and may thus identify more complex patterns in the data, they are less prone to this problem [13,14]. However, it can be computationally expensive to train *MLP*s, especially for larger datasets or more intricate network designs. Long training periods may result from this, which may slow down the deployment of phishing detection systems [39].

Convolutional Neural Network (*CNN*) is a class of neural networks that are frequently employed in computer vision, but recently it has emerged to be a great tool for phishing detection [3,4,7,8,12,40–42,45]. When labeled training data is limited, *CNN*s can benefit from pre-trained models and transfer learning to enhance performance in detecting phishing *URL*s. *CNN* is capable of handling variations in the input data, including changes to the *URL*'s length and the existence of unexpected letters or symbols. This is because the pooling layers can downsample the feature maps to lessen the influence of variances, while the convolutional filters used in *CNN* can recognize patterns in various regions of the *CNN* [7,45]. Without manual feature engineering, *CNN* can automatically extract high-level features from the data that comes in. This is because the filters in the convolutional layers are trained to identify the most important data patterns [4,7,8,41]. Additionally, the *CNN* performs well on a balanced dataset [12,42]. It is possible to train more sophisticated *CNN* architectures that can recognize subtler patterns and correlations in the data with a larger dataset which can increase the model's capacity to correctly categorize new phishing samples [3,4,40]. However, if a *CNN* model fits the training data too closely and cannot generalize to new, untested data, the problem of overfitting arises. This can be prevented by using batch normalization and dropout techniques [3]. Additionally, *CNN*s can require a lot of processing power, particularly when employing deep structures with numerous layers, therefore, this can need a lot of computing power and hardware resources [4,8,41].

Recurrent Neural Network (*RNN*) are a type of neural network that excels at processing sequential data such as text or time series data. Because *URL*s may be represented as a sequence of characters, and because *RNN*s can learn to recognize patterns and characteristics in this sequence, they can be utilized for *URL*-based phishing detection [40,41]. Each character or characteristic in a *URL* is built sequentially, depending on the ones that came before. These sequential relationships can be observed by *RNN*s, which can then utilize to forecast whether a *URL* is genuine or phishing. *RNN* performance on balanced datasets depends on the particular task at hand as well as the network's architecture. For tasks requiring capturing long-term dependencies and temporal correlations between the input features, *RNN*s are especially well-suited [41]. To properly learn to recognize patterns in sequential data, such as *URL*s, *RNN*s need a lot of training data. This implies that *RNN*s may not be used efficiently for phishing detection for enterprises with limited access to training data [40]. *RNN*s can be challenging to understand, particularly when working with massive data sets. *RNN*s can only be as effective as the training set that they are given. The *RNN* may struggle to accurately identify new and emerging dangers if the training data is not representative of all the threats that an organization might encounter [40].

Long Short-Term Memory (*LSTM*) is a specific type of *RNN* that was developed to address the issue of vanishing gradients that *RNN* frequently encounter and thus this algorithm is used by researchers for phishing detection [3,8,14,19,40,42,44,45]. The long-term dependencies and sequential patterns in *URLs* can be captured by *LSTM*, making it a good choice for *URL*-based website phishing detection. In order to detect tiny variations and patterns in phishing *URLs* that could otherwise go undetected, *LSTM* networks are particularly good at identifying sequential data and hence is a good choice for *URL*-based website phishing attack [3,14]. *LSTM*s can function well even when trained on minimal amounts of data [40]. These models are perfect for dealing with imbalanced datasets because they can find long-term correlations in the data. For identifying trends in the minority class, these dependencies can be very important [44,45]. Additionally, *LSTM* performs poorly for small datasets [8] but performs well on large datasets [19]. However, particularly when using vast data sets, training *LSTM* models can be computationally and memory-intensive [42]. Overfitting is a possibility with *LSTM* models, especially when working with limited data. When a model develops a proficiency at recognizing trends in training data but is unable to generalize that skill to fresh, untried data, overfitting occurs. This issue can be solved by using dropout in *LSTM* [3]. *LSTM* is complex in nature but the number of parameters needed for an *LSTM* model can be decreased by using pre-trained word embeddings like Word2Vec [19].

Bidirectional Long Short-Term Memory (*BiLSTM*) is a form of machine learning-based *RNN* architecture that is used to detect *URL*-based website phishing attacks [12,19,41,44]. *BiLSTM* is a form of neural network design that is effective at detecting data's sequential patterns. The capacity of *BiLSTM* algorithms is to examine the complete *URL* string in both ways, i.e., from the beginning to the end and from the end to the beginning, which makes them particularly useful for *URL*-based phishing detection [12,19,41]. Positive instances are often more scarce in imbalanced datasets than negative examples. *BiLSTM* may simultaneously learn from both phishing and legitimate instances, which may aid in improving its ability to distinguish between the two classes [19,44]. It can be costly computationally to train *BiLSTM* networks, especially if the input sequences are large and complex. The algorithm's capacity to scale for very big datasets may be constrained by this [19,44].

Gated Recurrent Units (*GRU*) is a sort of recurrent neural network that has been found to be useful for *URL*-based phishing detection [19,44]. *GRU*s are more memory-efficient and require fewer parameters than other recurrent neural network types. They are thus well suited for use in contexts with limited resources, such as those seen in cloud-based systems or on mobile devices [19]. Additionally, on imbalance datasets, *GRU*s can perform well [19,44].

Bidirectional Gated Recurrent Units (*BiGRU*) is a *GRU* version that captures sequential dependencies in both forward and backward directions. *BiGRU* is useful for detecting *URL*-based phishing [19,44]. There are two layers in *BiGRU*, one of which moves the input sequence forward and the other which moves it backward. This gives the network the ability to record dependencies that happen both before and after a certain input feature, which is helpful for identifying intricate patterns in *URL*s. Additionally, on imbalance datasets, *BiGRU*s can perform well [19,44].

5 Dataset

The availability and quality of data are essential for the performance of machine learning-based phishing detection algorithms. To detect phishing attacks, algorithms need to be trained on large and diverse datasets. It is also important to keep the data up-to-date to reflect the latest trends and techniques used by attackers. This section will explore various data sources available for both phishing and legitimate websites and the detailed overview is shown in Table 3.

Phishing data sources are collections of *URL*s used to identify and block phishing websites and train a machine-learning model to detect new samples of phishing websites.

PhishTank.com is a community-based repository where contributors work to sanitize data and information pertaining to online phishing. The data is available in CSV or XML formats. In addition, an Application programming interface (*API*) is also available for research purposes [32].

OpenPhish.com is a live repository of phishing *URL*s, obtained from security researchers, government agencies, and other organizations. It uses automated and manual verification methods to ensure the sites are phishing sites [31].

Researchers also use websites like **MalwareUrl** [26], **MalwareDomain** [33], and **MalwareDomainList** [25] to collect malicious *URL*s. These community-driven tools are used to combat cyber threats.

Researchers collect legitimate *URL*s by compiling a list of popular websites, using web crawling sources, and online directories.

Common Crawl is a large-scale web crawl that is made up of petabytes of data that have been collected since 2008. It includes raw web page data, extracted metadata, and text extractions. This repository's material is maintained in Web ARChive (*WARC*) format, which contains *URL*-related data [15].

DMOZ.org was a large, open directory of the web, created and maintained by a volunteer editor community. It was one of the largest and most comprehensive directories on the web, with millions of websites listed and organized into thousands of categories. However, the project was discontinued in 2017 due to a decline in editor participation and the dominance of search engines [16].

Yandex.XML as a search engine provides API to submit queries and receive answers in XML format [43].

Alexa Web Crawl. Alexa is used to collect authentic *URLs* through the Internet Archive starting from 1996 [10].

In addition to data sources of phishing and legitimate *URLs*, there are existing ready-to-use datasets.

ISCXURL2016 is a dataset that includes both authentic and phishing *URLs*. There are 35,300 benign *URLs* in this dataset that was gathered from the top Alexa websites using the Heritrix web crawler. For phishing, this dataset also contains 12,000 *URLs* from the WEBSPAM-UK2007 dataset, 10,000 *URLs* from OpenPhish, 11,500 *URLs* from DNS-BH, and 45,450 *URLs* from Defacement *URLs*; a total of more than 78,000 *URLs* [38].

MillerSmiles Archives is a collection of phishing emails compiled by security researcher Paul Miller. The archives have not been updated since 2013 and the domain name millersmiles.co.uk is inactive [28].

Phishstorm is a dataset that contains both legitimate and phishing *URLs*. 48,009 legitimate *URLs* and 48,009 phishing *URLs* are included in this dataset's total of 96,018 *URLs* [27].

Ebbu2017 dataset comprises 36,400 valid *URLs* and 37,175 phishing *URLs*. The legitimate *URLs* were collected from Yandex.XML and the phishing data was collected from PhishTank [18].

UCI-15 dataset defined 30 different attributes for phishing *URLs* and extracted values of those attributes for each phishing URL. Data were collected mainly from PhishTank, MillerSmiles, and from Google search operator and the total number of instances in this dataset is 2456 [30].

UCI-16 dataset containing 1353 examples of both legitimate and phishing *URLs*, is also used by researchers. It comprises 10 distinct features. Phishing *URL* data are gathered from PhishTank and legitimate *URLs* as collected from Yahoo and using a crawler [1].

MDP-2018 dataset, which was downloaded between January and May 2015 and May and June 2017, has 48 features that were taken from 5000 legitimate *URLs* and 5000 phishing *URLs*. This dataset includes details on both legal and fraudulent *URLs*. Sources of fraudulent websites include PhishTank, OpenPhish, and legitimate websites like Alexa and Common Crawl [36].

6 Experimental Evaluations and Survey Findings

The findings reported in the phishing literature are important because they will aid in the identification of the algorithms that will be used to detect phishing in *URL*. Detailed information is provided in Table 2 where the best-performing algorithms are reported. Additionally, the metrics are briefly explained in the appendix.

Table 2. Performance evaluation by researchers with metrics: [Acc]uracy, [P]recision, [Rec]all, [F1]-Score. Studies [6,24,37] used other metrics.

Ref	Best Performing Algorithm	P	Rec	Acc	F1
[5]	*DT*			97.40	96.30
[39]	Gradient Tree Boosting (*GTB*)			97.42	
[29]	eXtreme Gradient Boosting (*XGBoost*)	95.78	96.77	96.71	96.27
[11]	*RF*	94.00	94.00	94.05	93.20
[35]	*RF*	97.00		97.98	
[13]	*RF*	97.40		99.29	98.22
[21]	*SVM*			91.28	
[42]	*CNN*	99.57	100.00	99.80	99.78
[8]	*CNN*	99.00	99.20	99.20	99.20
[4]	*CNN*	96.53	95.09	95.78	95.81
[41]	*CNN*	97.33	93.78	95.60	95.52
[45]	*CNN*			98.30	94.95
[7]	*CNN*	92.35	98.09	99.02	95.13
[40]	*LSTM*	99.88	99.82	99.97	99.85
[3]	*GRU*	98.00		97.56	
[19]	*BiGRU*	99.40	99.50	99.50	99.40
[44]	*BiGRU*	99.64	99.43	95.55	99.54
[20]	Transformer			96+	
[17]	LURL			97.40	
[34]	EXPOSE			97+	
[12]	GramBedding	97.59	98.26	98.27	99.73
[2]	Adaptive Neuro-Fuzzy Inference System (*ANFIS*)			98.30	
[14]	Multi-Modal Hierarchical Attention Model (*MMHAM*)	97.84	96.66	97.26	97.24

We now list our observations on automated *URL*-based website phishing detection strategies employing machine learning algorithms.

Feature Selection process has a significant impact on the performance of an automated website phishing detector. The specific features must be chosen before the classification process can begin for both machine learning and deep learning approaches. However, if a deep learning-based approach is used, the feature extraction process can be done automatically because these algorithms are capable of identifying the key characteristics on their own; as a result, deep learning features can also be used if researchers are attempting to come up with new sets of features. For a *URL*-based website phishing attack detector to operate well, a combination of features directly connected to the *URL* is required. For instance, combining Domain Name System (*DNS*), domain, and lexical elements of the *URL* will improve the detector's accuracy. There is one thing to keep in mind, though, and that is to avoid using too many features for classification as this could lead to bias and over-fitting, both of which would impair the detector's effectiveness.

Algorithms from the fields of machine learning and deep learning used by researchers to combat the problem of phishing. Researchers initially employed heuristic-based approaches to tackle these issues, but as machine learning models advanced, this strategy was swiftly supplanted. The manual feature extraction was a vital component of the machine learning-based method because it influenced how well the algorithms worked. Deep learning-based approaches, however, are currently quite popular because the models can now automatically infer the semantics of the *URL*, eliminating the need for manual extraction. Although the essence of these works has been simplified, the underlying architecture is still a conundrum. As a result of this survey, we can see that developing a *URL*-based detector using deep learning-based algorithms yields better results. Additionally, someone who has little prior domain expertise about what features to choose for categorization purposes may benefit from a deep learning method because this can be done automatically.

Based on the classification accuracy of these algorithms in this domain, it can be suggested that RF algorithms in the area of machine learning perform the best with an accuracy of 99.29% with DT being another excellent machine learning algorithm that comes in second place with an accuracy of 97.40%. $LSTM$ is an algorithm that is the best choice (accuracy 99.96%) and *CNN* is the second-best-performing algorithm with accuracy of 99.79% for the deep learning-based approaches.

Datasets utilized were not from a single source, and each researcher used a separate dataset to develop their system. As a result, the lack of a shared dataset can be a concern because one dataset may contain certain phishing site data while the other one does not. Furthermore, because phishing *URL* databases are not open-source, many academics do not use them. This is advantageous because attackers may acquire publicly accessible datasets and use them to extract key attributes and tailor their assaults accordingly. The drawback of that is that it might be laborious and time-consuming for a researcher to create a dataset.

7 Conclusions

We discussed *URL*-based phishing detection approaches, focusing on the features, algorithms, and datasets used by researchers. We observed that lexical analyzers are effective tools for detecting *URL*-based phishing since they can detect phishing on the fly (real-time detection), and they can also correctly identify newly constructed malicious websites. However, more effort needs to be put into making the detector more robust because attackers are always coming up with new ways to use phishing attacks to evade the defenses. One approach to do this is to use adversarial phishing samples to train the model, and these samples can be produced using an Generative Adversarial Network (GAN).

Google Sites is increasingly used to create websites, and fraudsters use it to build phishing websites and conduct phishing attacks. The problem, in this case, is that because sites created with Google Sites disclose less information in the *URL*, the approaches covered in this survey may not be adequate to thwart phishing attempts made using Google Sites. For such websites, a combination of *URL*-based and content-based features need to be used to make the detection techniques effective.

Acknowledgements. This work was supported in part by funding from NSF under Award Numbers CNS 1715458, DMS 2123761, CNS 1822118, NIST, ARL, Statnett, AMI, NewPush, and Cyber Risk Research.

Appendix

The metrics used to assess the performance of the algorithms are described below. We use N to represent the number of legitimate and phishing websites, with P denoting phishing and L denoting legitimate.

Precision is the proportion of phishing attacks ($N_{P \to P}$) classified correctly as phishing attacks to the total number of attacks detected ($N_{L \to P} + N_{P \to P}$). $Precision = \frac{N_{P \to P}}{N_{L \to P} + N_{P \to P}}$

Recall is the proportion of phishing attacks ($N_{P \to P}$) classified correctly to total phishing attacks ($N_{P \to P} + N_{P \to L}$). $Recall = \frac{N_{P \to P}}{N_{P \to P} + N_{P \to L}}$

Accuracy is the proportion of phishing and legitimate sites that have been correctly classified ($N_{L \to L} + N_{P \to P}$) to the total number of sites $Accuracy = \frac{N_{L \to L} + N_{P \to P}}{TotalSites}$

F1-Score is a widely used evaluation metric that combines the model's recall and precision into a single score for binary classification models. $F1 - score = \frac{2 * (Precision * Recall)}{Precision + Recall}$

Table 3. Dataset sources and the size of the data used for experiments in the literature

Ref	Dataset				
	Dataset source		Dataset size		Total Samples
	Legitimate	Phishing	Legitimate	Phishing	
[19]	Common Crawl	PhishTank	800k	759k	1,500k
[37]	DMOZ	PhishTank	55k	55k	100k
[11]	DMOZ	PhishTank	100k	15k	115k
[24]	Alexa	PhishTank	110k	32k	142k
[21]	Yahoo directory, DMOZ	PhishTank	2k	32k	34k
[2]	Google Search Operator	PhishTank, MillerSmiles	6k	6.8k	12.8k
[35]	Yandex.XML	PhishTank	36k	37k	73k
[13]	Kaggle [23]	PhishTank	40k	60k	100k
[6]	DMOZ	PhishTank, MillerSmiles	54k	52.8k	106.8k
[34]	DMOZ, Alexa, Phish-storm	PhishTank, OpenPhish, Phish-storm	96k	96k	192k
[14]	DMOZ	PhishTank	4k	4k	8k
[17]	Alexa	PhishTank	7k	6k	13k
[42]	Common Crawl	PhishTank	10.6k	10.6k	21.2k
[40]	Alexa, DOMZ	PhishTank, OpenPhish, MalwareURL, MalwareDomain, MalwareDomainList	79k	62k	141k
[7]	Alexa, Yandex, Common Crawl	PhishTank, OpenPhish, MalwareDomain	278k	278k	556k
[39]	Google Search Operator, Yahoo, Alexa, Common Crawl	PhishTank, MillerSmiles, OpenPhish	10.4k	11.9k	22.3k
[45]	Alexa	PhishTank	343k	70k	413k
[41]	Alexa	PhishTank	245k	245kk	490k
[44]	Common Crawl	PhishTank	800k	759kk	1559k
[4]	Common Crawl	PhishTank	1140k	1167kk	2307k
[3]	Common Crawl	PhishTank	2220k	2353k	4573k
[5]	Alexa	PhishTank	85k	60k	145k
[8]	Alexa	PhishTank	10k	9.7k	19.7k
[29]	Kaggle (Source not mentioned)	Kaggle (Source not mentioned)	-	-	11k
[12]	Custom Crawler developed	PhishTank, OpenPhish	400k	400k	800k
[20]	Alexa, Common Crawl	PhishTank, OpenPhish	25.96k	25.96k	51.9k

References

1. Abdelhamid, N.: UCI Machine Learning Repository (2016). https://archive.ics.uci.edu/ml/datasets/Website+Phishing
2. Adebowale, M.A., Lwin, K.T., Sanchez, E., Hossain, M.A.: Intelligent web-phishing detection and protection scheme using integrated features of images, frames and text. Expert Syst. Appl. **115**, 300–313 (2019)
3. Al-Ahmadi, S., Alotaibi, A., Alsaleh, O.: PDGAN: phishing detection with generative adversarial networks. IEEE Access **10**, 42459–42468 (2022)
4. Al-Alyan, A., Al-Ahmadi, S.: Robust URL phishing detection based on deep learning. KSII Trans. Internet Inf. Syst. (TIIS) **14**(7), 2752–2768 (2020)
5. Al-Haija, Q.A., Al Badawi, A.: URL-based phishing websites detection via machine learning. In: 2021 International Conference on Data Analytics for Business and Industry (ICDABI), pp. 644–649. IEEE (2021)
6. AlEroud, A., Karabatis, G.: Bypassing detection of URL-based phishing attacks using generative adversarial deep neural networks. In: Proceedings of the Sixth International Workshop on Security and Privacy Analytics, pp. 53–60 (2020)

7. Aljofey, A., Jiang, Q., Qu, Q., Huang, M., Niyigena, J.P.: An effective phishing detection model based on character level convolutional neural network from URL. Electronics **9**(9), 1514 (2020)
8. Alshingiti, Z., Alaqel, R., Al-Muhtadi, J., Haq, Q.E.U., Saleem, K., Faheem, M.H.: A deep learning-based phishing detection system using CNN, LSTM, and LSTM-CNN. Electronics **12**(1), 232 (2023)
9. APWG: phishing activity trends report (2021). https://apwg.org/trendsreports/. Accessed 14 Nov 2021
10. ARossi: Alexa crawls. https://archive.org/details/alexacrawls?tab=about
11. Aung, E.S., Yamana, H.: URL-based phishing detection using the entropy of non-alphanumeric characters. In: Proceedings of the 21st International Conference on Information Integration and Web-based Applications & Services, pp. 385–392 (2019)
12. Bozkir, A.S., Dalgic, F.C., Aydos, M.: GramBeddings: a new neural network for URL based identification of phishing web pages through n-gram embeddings. Comput. Secur. **124**, 102964 (2023)
13. Butnaru, A., Mylonas, A., Pitropakis, N.: Towards lightweight URL-based phishing detection. Future Internet **13**(6), 154 (2021)
14. Chai, Y., Zhou, Y., Li, W., Jiang, Y.: An explainable multi-modal hierarchical attention model for developing phishing threat intelligence. IEEE Trans. Dependable Secure Comput. **19**(2), 790–803 (2021)
15. Common crawl. https://commoncrawl.org/
16. Curlie. https://curlie.org/
17. Dutta, A.K.: Detecting phishing websites using machine learning technique. PLoS ONE **16**(10), e0258361 (2021)
18. Ebubekirbbr: Pdd/input at master · ebubekirbbr/pdd (2019). https://github.com/ebubekirbbr/pdd/tree/master/input
19. Feng, T., Yue, C.: Visualizing and interpreting RNN models in URL-based phishing detection. In: Proceedings of the 25th ACM Symposium on Access Control Models and Technologies, pp. 13–24 (2020)
20. Haynes, K., Shirazi, H., Ray, I.: Lightweight URL-based phishing detection using natural language processing transformers for mobile devices. Procedia Comput. Sci. **191**, 127–134 (2021)
21. Jain, A.K., Gupta, B.B.: PHISH-SAFE: URL features-based phishing detection system using machine learning. In: Bokhari, M.U., Agrawal, N., Saini, D. (eds.) Cyber Security. AISC, vol. 729, pp. 467–474. Springer, Singapore (2018). https://doi.org/10.1007/978-981-10-8536-9_44
22. KnowBe4: History of phishing. https://www.phishing.org/history-of-phishing. Accessed 24 June 2022
23. Kumar, S.: Malicious and benign URLs (2019). https://www.kaggle.com/datasets/siddharthkumar25/malicious-and-benign-urls
24. Lee, J., Ye, P., Liu, R., Divakaran, D.M., Chan, M.C.: Building robust phishing detection system: an empirical analysis. In: NDSS MADWeb (2020)
25. Malware domain list. https://www.malwaredomainlist.com/. Accessed 03 Apr 2023
26. MalwareURL: Fighting malware and cyber criminality. http://www.malwareurl.com/. Accessed 03 Apr 2023
27. Marchal, S.: Phishstorm - phishing/legitimate URL dataset (2014). https://research.aalto.fi/fi/datasets/phishstorm-phishing-legitimate-url-dataset
28. MillerSmiles.co.uk: Phishing scams and spoof emails at millersmiles.co.uk. http://www.millersmiles.co.uk/

29. Mithra Raj, M., Arul Jothi, J.A.: Website phishing detection using machine learning classification algorithms. In: Florez, H., Gomez, H. (eds.) ICAI 2022. CCIS, vol. 1643, pp. 219–233. Springer, Cham (2022). https://doi.org/10.1007/978-3-031-19647-8_16
30. Mohammad, R.M.A.: UCI Machine Learning Repository (2015). https://archive.ics.uci.edu/ml/datasets/phishing+websites
31. OpenPhish: Phishing intelligence. https://openphish.com/
32. PhishTank: Join the fight against phishing. https://phishtank.com/
33. RiskAnalytics: Not all threat intel is created equal. https://riskanalytics.com//. Accessed 03 Apr 2023
34. Sabir, B., Babar, M.A., Gaire, R.: An evasion attack against ml-based phishing URL detectors. arXiv preprint arXiv:2005.08454 (2020)
35. Sahingoz, O.K., Buber, E., Demir, O., Diri, B.: Machine learning based phishing detection from URLs. Expert Syst. Appl. **117**, 345–357 (2019)
36. Tan, C.L.: Phishing dataset for machine learning: feature evaluation (2018). https://data.mendeley.com/datasets/h3cgnj8hft/1
37. Tupsamudre, H., Singh, A.K., Lodha, S.: Everything is in the name – a URL based approach for phishing detection. In: Dolev, S., Hendler, D., Lodha, S., Yung, M. (eds.) CSCML 2019. LNCS, vol. 11527, pp. 231–248. Springer, Cham (2019). https://doi.org/10.1007/978-3-030-20951-3_21
38. UNB. https://www.unb.ca/cic/datasets/url-2016.html
39. Vaitkevicius, P., Marcinkevicius, V.: Comparison of classification algorithms for detection of phishing websites. Informatica **31**(1), 143–160 (2020)
40. Vinayakumar, R., Soman, K., Poornachandran, P.: Evaluating deep learning approaches to characterize and classify malicious URL's. J. Intell. Fuzzy Syst. **34**(3), 1333–1343 (2018)
41. Wang, W., Zhang, F., Luo, X., Zhang, S.: PDRCNN: precise phishing detection with recurrent convolutional neural networks. Secur. Commun. Netw. **2019**, 1–15 (2019)
42. Wei, W., Ke, Q., Nowak, J., Korytkowski, M., Scherer, R., Woźniak, M.: Accurate and fast URL phishing detector: a convolutional neural network approach. Comput. Netw. **178**, 107275 (2020)
43. Yandex. https://yandex.com/dev/
44. Yuan, L., Zeng, Z., Lu, Y., Ou, X., Feng, T.: A character-level BiGRU-attention for phishing classification. In: Zhou, J., Luo, X., Shen, Q., Xu, Z. (eds.) ICICS 2019. LNCS, vol. 11999, pp. 746–762. Springer, Cham (2020). https://doi.org/10.1007/978-3-030-41579-2_43
45. Zheng, F., Yan, Q., Leung, V.C., Yu, F.R., Ming, Z.: HDP-CNN: highway deep pyramid convolution neural network combining word-level and character-level representations for phishing website detection. Comput. Secur. **114**, 102584 (2022)

Workflow Resilience for Mission Critical Systems

Mahmoud Abdelgawad(✉), Indrakshi Ray(✉), and Tomas Vasquez(✉)

Department of Computer Science, Colorado State University, Fort Collins, CO 80523, USA
{M.Abdelgawad,Indrakshi.Ray,Tomas.Vasquez}@colostate.edu

Abstract. Mission-critical systems, such as navigational spacecraft and drone surveillance systems, play a crucial role in a nation's infrastructure. Since these systems are prone to attacks, we must design resilient systems that can withstand attacks. Thus, we need to specify, analyze, and understand where such attacks are possible and how to mitigate them while a mission-critical system is being designed. This paper specifies the mission-critical system as a workflow consisting of atomic tasks connected using various operators. Real-world workflows can be large and complex. Towards this end, we propose using Coloured Petri Nets (CPN), which has tool support for automated analysis. We use a drone surveillance mission example to illustrate our approach. Such an automated approach is practical for verifying and analyzing the resiliency of mission-critical systems.

Keywords: Mission-critical Systems · Workflow · Coloured Petri Nets

1 Introduction

A mission-critical system is one whose failure significantly impacts the mission [8,16]. Examples of mission-critical systems include navigational systems for a spacecraft and drone surveillance systems for military purposes. These systems are prone to attacks because they can cripple a nation [6]. Mission-critical systems must fulfill survivability requirements so that a mission continues in the face of attacks. Thus, this requires specifying and analyzing a mission before deployment to assess its resilience and gauge what failures can be tolerated.

A mission can be described in the form of a workflow consisting of various tasks connected via different types of control-flow operators. Researchers have addressed workflow resiliency in the context of assigning users to tasks [7,12–15,19,21]. However, active attackers can compromise the capabilities of various entities. The destruction of the capabilities may cause the mission to abort or fulfill only a subset of its objectives. Analyzing resiliency considering attacker actions for mission-critical systems is yet to be explored.

Our work aims to fill this gap. We formally specify a mission in the form of a workflow, the definition of which is adapted from an earlier work [20]. A mission is often complex, and manually analyzing the workflow is tedious and error-prone. We demonstrate how such a workflow can be transformed into a Coloured Petri Net (CPN). CPN has automated tool support [17] that can be used for formal analysis.

Formal analysis may reveal deficiencies in the mission specification. Addressing such deficiencies improves the cyber-resiliency posture of the mission. We demonstrate

S. Dolev and B. Schieber (Eds.): SSS 2023, LNCS 14310, pp. 498–512, 2023.
https://doi.org/10.1007/978-3-031-44274-2_37

our approach using a mission-critical drone surveillance system. We provide a divide-and-conquer approach that helps decompose a complex workflow and shows how to analyze the sub-parts and obtain the analysis results for the total workflow.

The rest of the paper is organized as follows. Section 2 provides the formal definitions for workflow and Coloured Petri Nets. Section 3 describes a motivating example and formally represents the workflow for mission-critical systems. Section 4 defines the transformation rules from workflow to CPN along with the development of the CPN hierarchy model. Section 5 focuses on verifying the CPN so-generated and analyzing resiliency. Section 6 enumerates some related work. Section 7 concludes the paper and points to future directions.

2 Background

2.1 Workflow Definition

Typically, a workflow consists of tasks connected through operators [1–5,20]. The syntax of the workflow adapted from [20] is defined as follows.

Definition 1 (Workflow). *A workflow is defined recursively as follows.*
$W = t_i \otimes (t|W_1 \otimes W_2|W_1\#W_2|W_1\&W_2|if\{C\}\,W_1\,else\,W_2|\,while\{C\}\{W_1\}W_2) \otimes t_f$
where

- *t is a user-defined atomic task.*
- *t_i and t_f are a unique initial task and a unique final tasks respectively.*
- *$\otimes$ denotes the sequence operator. $W_1 \otimes W_2$ specifies W_2 is executed after W_1 completes.*
- *# denotes the exclusive choice operator. $W_1\#W_2$ specifies that either W_1 executes or W_2 executes but not both.*
- *& denotes the and operator. $W_1\&W_2$ specifies that both W_1 and W_2 must finish executing before the next task can start.*
- *$if\{C\}\,W_1\,else\,W_2$ denotes the conditioning operator. C is a Boolean valued expression. Either W_1 or W_2 execute based on the result of evaluating C but not both.*
- *$while\{C\}\{W_1\}$ denotes iteration operator. If C evaluates to true W_1 executes repeatedly until the expression C evaluates to false.*

Definition 2 (Simple and Complex Operators). *A simple operator is an operator that imposes one single direct precedence constraint between two tasks. The only simple operator is the sequence operator. All other operators are referred to as complex operators.*

Definition 3 (Simple and Compound Workflows). *A* simple workflow *is a workflow that consists of at most one single complex operator and finitely many simple operators. All other workflows are* compound workflows. *A compound workflow can be decomposed into* component workflows, *each of which may be a simple or a compound one.*

Definition 4 (Entities). *The tasks of a workflow are executed by active entities, referred to as* subjects. *The entities on which we perform tasks are referred to as* objects. *An entity has a set of typed variables that represents its attributes.*

Definition 5 (State of an Entity). *The values of the attributes of an entity constitute its* state. *The state of a subject determines whether it can execute a given task. The state of an object determines whether some task can be performed on it.*

In the remainder of this paper we abstract from objects and only consider critical systems specified as subjects.

Definition 6 (Mission). *A mission is expressed as a workflow with a control-flow, a set of subjects, a subject to task assignment relation, and some initial conditions and objectives. Formally,* $\mathcal{M} = (W, \mathcal{S}, \mathcal{ST}, I, O)$ *where W is the control-flow corresponding to the mission,* $\mathcal{S}$ *is a set of subjects,* $\mathcal{ST} \subseteq S \times Tasks(W)$ *is the set of subject to task assignments, I is the set initial conditions, and O is the set of mission objectives. The subject to task assignment should satisfy the access control policies of the mission. The conditions and objectives are expressed in predicate logic.*

2.2 Coloured Petri Nets (CPN)

A Colored Petri Net (CPN) is a directed bipartite graph, where nodes correspond to places P and transitions T. Arcs A are directed edges from a place to a transition or a transition to a place. The input place of transition is a place for which a directed arc exists between the place and the transition. The set of all input places of a transition $r \in T$ is denoted as $\bullet r$. An output place of transition is a place for which a directed arc exists between the transition and the place. The set of all output places of a transition $r \in T$ is denoted as $r\bullet$. Note that we distinguish between tasks and transitions by using the label r for transitions. CPNs operate on multisets of typed objects called tokens. Places are assigned tokens at initialization. Transitions consume tokens from their input places, perform some action, and output tokens on their output places. Transitions may create and destroy tokens through their executions. The distribution of tokens over the places of the CPN defines the state, referred to as marking, of the CPN. Formally, a Non-Hierarchical CPN is defined [9,10] as $CPN = (P, T, A, \Sigma, V, C, G, E, I)$, where P, T, A, Σ, and V, are sets of places, transitions, arcs, colors, variables, respectively. C, G, E, I are functions that assign colors to places, guard expressions to transitions, arc expressions to arcs, tokens at initialization expression respectively.

Definition 7 (Simple Workflow CPN). *A simple workflow CPN is a CPN that models a simple workflow. A simple workflow CPN has a unique input place i and a unique output place o.*

Definition 8 (CPN Module). *A CPN Module consists of a CPN, a set of substitution transitions, a set of port places, and a port type assignment function. The set of port places defines the* interface *through which a module exchanges tokens with other modules. Formally a CPN module is defined as in [10] as:* $CPN_M = (CPN, T_{sub}, P_{port}, PT)$ *where (i) CPN is a Colored Petri Net (ii)* $T_{sub} \subseteq T$ *is a set of substitution transitions (iii)* $P_{port} \subseteq P$ *is a set of port places (iv)* $PT : P_{port} \rightarrow \{IN, OUT, IN \backslash OUT\}$

Definition 9 (Simple CPN Module). *A Simple CPN Module is a CPN module in which the CPN is a Simple Workflow CPN and the interface of the module is defined by a single input port place* i' *and a single output port place* o'.

Definition 10. Hierarchical CPN *A* Hierarchical CPN *is defined by the authors in [10] as:* $CPN_H = (S, SM, PS, FS)$ *where (i) S is a finite set of modules. ces and transitions must be disjoint from all other modules' places and transitions. For a module* $s \in S$ *we use the notation* P^s *to denote the set of places of the module s. Similarly, for each of the other elements of the module s. (ii)* $SM \subseteq T_{sub} \times S$ *is a relation that maps each substitution transition to a sub- module. Note that [9, 10] defines* $SM : T_{sub} \rightarrow S$ *as a function. However, it is easier to compute SM if defined as a set. (iii)* $PS(t) \subseteq P_{sock}(t) \times P_{port}^{SM(t)}$ *is a port-socket relation function that assigns a port-socket relation to each substitution transition. (iv)* $FS \subseteq 2^P$ *is a set of non-empty fusion sets. A fusion set is a set of places that are functionally equivalent. (v) We additionally define global sets of places, transitions, arcs, colors, and variables as the union of the places, transitions, arcs, colors, and variables of each module. Furthermore, we define global initialization, arc expression, guard expression functions to be consistent with the functions defined for each module. We refer to these global elements by omitting the superscript in the notation.*

Definition 11 (Module Hierarchy). *A Module Hierarchy is a directed graph where each module* $s \in S$ *is a node; and for any two modules* $s_1, s_2 \in S$*, there exists a directed arc from* s_1 *to* s_2 *if and only if there is a substitution transition in* s_1 *that is mapped to the module* s_2*. As represented in [10], the module hierarchy is formally defined as:* $MH = (N_{MH}, A_{MH})$ *where (i)* $N_{MH} = S$ *is the set of nodes, and (ii)* $A_{MH} = \{(s_1, r, s_2) \in N_{MH} \times T_{sub} \times N_{MH} \mid r \in T_{sub}^{s_1} \wedge s_2 = SM(r)\}$
A module with no incoming arcs in the module hierarchy is refereed to as a prime module.

3 Motivating Example

We shall refer to the surveillance drone mission example to illustrate the transformation framework. Let $\mathcal{M}_{drone}$ be a mission specification that models a drone performing some data collection tasks over a region of interest. The drone has a camera that can take pictures at high and low altitudes and sensors capturing heat signals and radiation levels. The sensors are only accurate at low altitudes. There are three regions of interest: Regions A, B, and C. Region A is where the drone is regularly scheduled to perform surveillance; this region is large but close to the deployment point. Regions B and C are smaller but are further away from the deployment point. The drone is likely to be detected at low altitudes when it is in Region A. Therefore, the drone can only fly at high altitudes from where it can only use its camera. The drone may fly over regions B or C at high or low altitudes. However, due to the lack of visibility over the regions, only the heat and radiation sensors can capture meaningful data. Therefore, the drone can only collect data with its sensors over regions B and C. The mission succeeds if the drone collects data and returns to the deployment point. The control-flow of this mission is described by the task graph in Fig. 1 and given as control-flow expression below:

$$W = Init \otimes Check\_Status \otimes Deploy \otimes if(instruction)\{(Fly\_to\_Region_B \# Fly\_to\_Region_C) \otimes (Measure\_Radiation\_level \# Measure\_Heat\_Signal)\}else\{Fly\_to\_RegionA \otimes while\{battery\_level > 1\} \{Scan\_Vehicles \& Scan\_Construction\}\} \otimes Return\_to\_Base \otimes Final$$

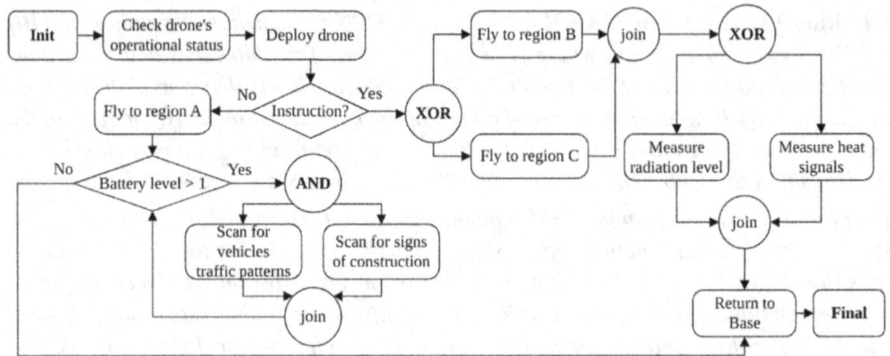

Fig. 1. Workflow of Surveillance Drone Mission.

This mission has a single entity called $drone_1$ of type *Drone*, that is, $\mathcal{S} = \{drone_1 : Drone\}$. The attributes of type *Drone*, denoted as *Drone.Attributes*, are given as: $Drone.Attributes = \{type : string;\ location : string;\ fly\_enabled : bool;\ battery\_level \in \{1,2,3,4\};\ instruction\_issued : bool;\ camera\_enabled : bool;\ sensors\_enabled : bool;\ data\_collected : bool\}$

We define functions that return the values of various attributes. For example, $location(drone_1)$ returns the location of $drone_1$. Every task can be performed by $drone_1$. Therefore, the subject task assignment function assigns $drone_1$ to each task. $\mathcal{ST} = \{(drone_1, transition)\ |t \in Tasks(W)\}$. Let I be a predicate logic formula giving the initialization conditions as:

$$I = \exists s \in \mathcal{S} \,|\, (type(s) = Drone) \wedge (location(s) = \text{“}base\text{”})$$
$$\wedge (fly\_enabled(s) = true) \wedge (battery\_level(s) = 4) \wedge (instruction\_issued(s) = false) \wedge$$
$$(camera\_enabled(s) = true) \wedge (sensors\_enabled(s) = true) \wedge (data\_collected = false)$$

Let O be a predicate logic formula that defines the mission objectives as:
$O = \exists s \in \mathcal{S} \,|\, (type(s) = Drone) \wedge (location(s) = \text{“}base\text{”}) \wedge (data\_collected(s) = true)$
If an attribute of the subject s is not explicitly constrained by the initial conditions or the objective, then that attribute can take on any value in its domain. Mission specification is as follows: $\mathcal{M}_{drone} = (W, \mathcal{S}, \mathcal{ST}, I, O)$.

4 Workflow to CPN Transformation Rules

Our approach maps a Mission-Specification $\mathcal{M} = (W, \mathcal{S}, \mathcal{ST}, I, O)$ to a Hierarchical Colored Petri Net $CPN_H = (S, SM, PS, FS)$. The approach follows six processes as shown in Fig. 2. The first two processes deal with the decomposition and simplification of the control-flow. The decomposition procedure partitions the control-flow into a set of disjoint expressions that each model a workflow component. Each component is either a simple or compound workflow. The simplification procedure then iterates each component substituting any nested components with tasks. A task substituting a nested workflow in another workflow is *substitution task*. A workflow that has had all of its components substituted for tasks is said to be *simplified*. The simplification process outputs a set of simple workflows, a set of substitution tasks for each component, and a substitution relation that tracks which component was substituted by which task. The formalization process extracts from the simple workflow the sets of workflow tasks, substitution tasks, begin and end tasks, and precedence constraints over all tasks. These sets are collectively called a *formalized component*.

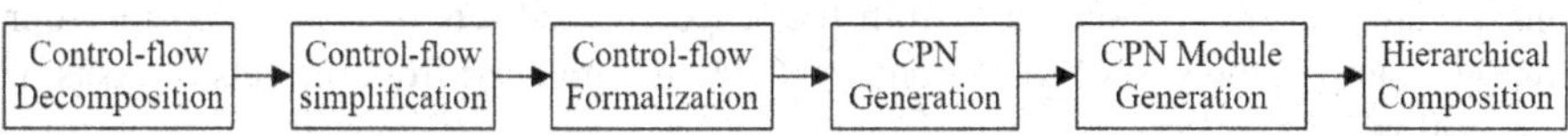

Fig. 2. Workflow to CPN Transformation Framework

The fourth process applies 7 rules to each component that, together with the remaining elements of the mission, are mapped to a Non-Hierarchical Colored Petri Net. The structure of each Non-Hierarchical CPN (places, transitions, and arcs) is semantically equivalent to the component. The fifth process generates a CPN module by adding an interface to each Non-Hierarchical CPN. The sixth process relates each module through relationships between substitution transitions, sub-modules, and port and socket places. The final output is a Hierarchical CPN representing a complete model of the original mission. Table 1 illustrates the notation used to decompose, simplify and formalize the control-flow. Note that the sets $Task(W)$, $Tasks_S(W)$, and $Task_U(W)$ are disjoint subsets of the set of all tasks $Tasks_W$. i.e. $Task(W) \cap Tasks_S(W) \cap Task_U(W) = \emptyset$

Table 1. Control-flow Notation Table

Symbol	Description
$Tasks_W$	Set of all tasks in a workflow
$Tasks(W) \subseteq Tasks_W$	Set of all workflow tasks in W
$Components$	Set of component workflows
$Tasks_S(W) \subseteq Tasks_W$	Set of substitution tasks of W
$Tasks_U(W) \subseteq Tasks_W$	Set of support tasks of W
$Tasks_B(W) \subseteq Tasks_W$	Set of begin tasks of W
$Tasks_E(W) \subseteq Tasks_W$	Set of end tasks of W
$Prec(W)$	The set of precedence constraints in W
$Substitutions$	Relation between component workflows and substitution tasks of W

Transformation Rules. The structure of the Non-Hierarchical CPN is made up of the places P', transitions T', and arcs A'. We define the structure of Non-Hierarchically CPNs in a similar manner as a workflow-net or process net [1,2,18]. A workflow-net is a Petri Net with a unique input place i and a unique output place o. A workflow-net has the additional property that when the output place o is connected to the input place i by a transition r', the resulting *extended net* is strongly connected.

Rule 1: Transition Set Generation: Tasks are modeled as transitions in the Non-Hierarchical CPN. Our algorithm maps each task $t_k \in Tasks_{W'}$ to a unique transition $r_k \in T'$. Let T'_{map} be a relation between the set of tasks and the set of transitions. The pair $(t_k, r_k) \in T'_{map}$ indicates that the transition r_k is mapped from the task t_k. Through the remainder of the paper, we maintain this indexing convention. That is, r_k denotes the transition mapped from the task t_k. Let T'_{sub}, T'_U, T'_B and T'_E be subsets of T'. The set T'_{sub} is the set of substitution transitions such that $T'_{sub} = \{r_s \mid (t_s, r_s) \in T'_{map} \wedge t_s \in Tasks_S(W')\}$. The sets of support transitions T'_U, begin transitions T'_B, and end transitions T'_E are constructed similarly from the respective subsets of tasks. Consider our running example, the sets of transitions for CPN' are mapped from the sets of tasks of W' as follows:
$Tasks'_W \rightarrow T' = \{r_1, r_{s1}, r_{s5}, r_5, r_c\}$, $Tasks_U(W') \rightarrow T'_U = \{r_c\}$, $Tasks_S(W') \rightarrow T'_S = \{r_{s1}, r_{s5}\}$, $Tasks_B(W') \rightarrow T'_B = \{r_1\}$, and $Tasks_E(W') \rightarrow T'_E = \{r_5\}$. The relation between tasks and transitions is $T'_{map} = \{(t_1, r_1), (t_{s1}, r_{s1}), (t_{s5} r_{s5}), (t_5, r_5), (t_c, r_c)\}$.

Rule 2: Place and Arc Set Generation: The set of places P' is initialized with a unique input place i and a unique output place o. The set of arcs is initialized to the empty set. For each begin transition $r_b \in T'_B$ the algorithm adds a directed arc connecting the input place i and the transition r_b to A', i.e. $A' \leftarrow (i, r_b)$. Similarly, for each end transition $r_e \in T'_E$, the algorithm adds a directed arc connecting the transition r_b and the input place i to A', i.e. $A' \leftarrow (r_e, o)$. Consider our running example, $r_1 \in T'_B$ implies that $A' \leftarrow (i, r_1)$ and $r_5 \in T'_E$ implies $A' \leftarrow (r_5, o)$. For each (t_k, t_j) in $Prec(W')$, we create a new place m and add the arcs (r_k, m) and (m, r_j) to A'. That is, $P' \leftarrow m$, and $A' \leftarrow (t_k, m), (m, t_j)$. If one task has two direct successors i.e. $(t_q, t_j), (t_q, t_k) \in Prec(W')$, then this denotes a point at which a split occurs. If a task has two direct predecessors, i.e. $(t_j, t_q), (t_k, t_q) \in Prec(W')$, then this denotes a point at which a join occurs. There are two types of splits and joins. There are or-splits/joins and there are and-splits/joins [18]. Or-splits should always be joined by an or-join. Similarly, an and-split should always be joined by an and-join. The or-split/join only occurs in control-flows that contain the exclusive-or operator or the conditioning operator. When an or-split is imposed by the exclusive-or operator and there is task t_q that directly precedes $t_j \# t_k$, such as $t_q \otimes (t_j \# t_k)$, the transition r_q should output to a single place m that is the input to both r_j and r_k. Then the either transition r_j or r_k will execute by consuming the output of r_q, but not both. We thus leverage the fact that given a place m that is input to two transitions, then either transition may consume the token in the place m. When an or-split is imposed by the conditioning operator, then the split is modeled by the support transition r_c- where r_c routs the execution based on the evaluation of a Boolean expression. Therefore, $(t_q, t_j), (t_q, t_k) \in A'$ and an exclusive-or operator in the control-flow implies that $P' \leftarrow m$, $P' \leftarrow m'$, and $A' \leftarrow (r_q, m), (r_q, m'), (m, r_j), (m', r_k))$, however, $m = m'$. Similarly, when an or-join is imposed by the exclusive-or operator or the conditioning operator, and there is task t_q that directly succeeds $t_j \# t_k$, such as $(t_j \# t_k) \otimes t_q$, then the output place of r_j and r_k should be a single place that is the input to r_q. Therefore, $(t_j, t_q), (t_k, t_q) \in A'$ and the conditioning operator or exclusive-or is in the control-flow implies that $P' \leftarrow m$ and $P' \leftarrow m'$, and $A' \leftarrow (r_j, m), (r_k, m'), (m, r_q), (m', r_1)$, however, $m = m'$. The and-split/join only occurs in control-flows that contain the parallel-split operator. The and-split is modeled by the support transition r_g. The and-join is modeled by the support transition r_s. The structure of CPN' is formally described as:

$P' = \{i, o, p_1, p_2, p_3, p_4\}$
$T' = \{r_1, r_{s1}, r_{s5}, r_5, r_c\}$
$A' = \{(i, r_1), (r_1, p_1), (p_1, r_c), (r_c, p_2), (r_c, p_3), (p_2, r_{s1}), (p_3, r_{s5}), (r_{s1}, p_4), (r_{s5}, p_4), (p_4, r_5), (r_5, o)\}$

Thus far we have addressed five of the six well-behaved building blocks proposed by the Workflow Management Coalition [18] to model any control-flow. That is, the and-split, and-join, or-split, or-join, and sequence. The final building block is iteration. In the special case that the simple workflow contains the iteration operator, our algorithm adds two additional arcs to the set of arcs. One directed arc going from the support transition r_{c1} to the output place o models the iteration never executing. One directed arc going from the support transition r_{c2} to the output place of r_{c1} models the iteration continuing. One can see that our model can implement all six well-behaved building blocks proposed by the Workflow Management Coalition [18] and can therefore model any control-flow. Furthermore, we will later show that the manner in which we connect our CPN modules forms well behaved control structures [18].

Rule 3: Colors and Variable Set Generation: The color set of a simple workflow CPN consists of the different types of entities in the Simple CPN model. The types can be primitive types such as *Bool*, *Int*, or *String* or more complex user-defined types. In the drone surveillance example, there is only one subject of type *Drone*. The data type *Drone* is mapped to a record color set labeled *Drone*. Each attribute of the type *Drone* becomes a label in the record color set as:

$$color\,Drone = \textbf{ record } \{type : String; location : String; fly\_enabled : Bool;$$
$$detected : bool; battery\_level : Int \in \{1,2,3,4\}; instruction\_issued : Bool;$$
$$sensors\_enabled : Bool; camera\_enabled : Bool; data\_collected : Bool\}$$

Set of colors Σ' is constructed by adding any compound color sets and declaring the primitives that compose them. $\Sigma' = \{Bool, String, Int, Drone\}$ Set of variables V is declared such that there is variable for each color in Σ. $V' = \{instruction : Bool; y : String, i : Int, drone : Drone\}$.

Rule 4: Assigning Colors to Places: Each task can be performed by a drone. Therefore, each place $p \in P'$ is assigned the color $Drone \in \Sigma'$.

Rule 5: Assigning Guard Expressions: For each workflow task $t_k \in Tasks_{W'}$, we assign to the transition r_k a guard expression $G'(r_k)$ equivalent to $Pre(t_k)$. In other words, the guard expression evaluates to true if and only if the conjunction of the preconditions of t_k evaluates to true. The empty set of pre conditions is equivalent to the pre condition that always evaluates to true. Support and substitution tasks always have an empty set of pre conditions, therefore the guards of the respective transitions always evaluate to true. The only tasks of W' that have non-empty sets of pre conditions are t_1 and t_5 such that $Pre(t_1) = \{fly\_enabled(drone_1) = true\}$ and $Pre(t_5) = \{fly\_enabled(drone_1) = true, battery\_level(drone_1) \geq 1\}$. Therefore, the guard expression function is $G'(r_1) = g_1 = fly\_enabled(drone) = true$ and $G'(r_5) = g_5 = fly\_enabled(drone) = true \wedge battery\_level(drone) \geq 1$. Where $drone \in V'$ takes on the value of the instance of $drone_1$ when r_1 and r_2 are enabled. For all other cases in *CPN*' the guard expression is always true.

Rule 6: Assigning Arc Expressions: Each transition is assigned an input arc expression that evaluates to a token of the same color as the input place of the transition. Each transition is assigned an output arc expression that updates the token received over the input arc, such that the post conditions of the corresponding task evaluate to true. Substitution transitions can neither be enabled nor occur. Therefore, the arc expressions over their connected arcs have no semantic meaning. Support transitions route the execution of the workflow. For sequential and parallel executions, the output arc expressions are identical to the input arc expressions. For support transitions that evaluate a condition, each output arc models a case of the condition. The output arc of these transitions, should output the token received over the input arc only if the case evaluates to true. Otherwise, they output the empty set.

For example, for the arc $(r_c, p_2) \in A'$, is given the arc expression $E'((r_c, p_1)) = c_1 = if(instruction\_issued(drone) = true)\{drone\}else\{empty\}$. The arc (r_5, o) is given the arc expression $E'((r_5, o)) = e_5 = \{(location(drone) = \text{"}deployment\_point\text{"}) \wedge (battery\_level(drone) = battery\_level(drone) - 1)\}$. Note that the syntax we use for the arc expressions is based on function notation that is easy to understand. CPN Tools has its own modeling language which we avoid using for simplicity.

Rule 7: Initialization: The initialization function I' sets the initial state of the model by assigning a multiset of tokens to each place $p \in P'$. I must satisfy the initial conditions of the mission. Recall, I calls for a subject s with the following valuation: $(type(s) = Drone) \wedge (location(s) = \text{"}deployment\_point\text{"}) \wedge (fly\_enabled(s) = true) \wedge (battery\_level(s) = 4) \wedge (instruction\_issued(s) = false)) \wedge (camera\_enabled(s) = true) \wedge (sensors\_enabled(s) = true) \wedge (data\_collected = false)$

Over the input place i, the initialization function $I'(i)$ evaluates to a multiset of size one that satisfies the initial conditions of the workflow. For every other place, the initialization function evaluates to the empty set of tokens. It is important to note that for our analysis we are considering a single drone in isolation. Therefore, the initialization function of every other CPN in our final hierarchical model will evaluate to the empty set for every place. The result of applying rules 1–7 to our example W' is CPN' as described by Fig. 3. We have omitted writing each arc expression explicitly into the diagram to maintain readability.

We construct a hierarchical CPN (CPN_H) from the set of modules S and their original relationships in the workflow. Recall that a Hierarchical Colored Petri Net $CPN_H = (S, SM, PS, FS)$ consists of a set of modules S, an assignment of substitution transitions to modules SM, a relation between port places and socket places PS -where the pair $(p, p') \in PS$ signifies that p is a socket place of a substitution transition t that has been mapped to a a sub module s such that p' is a port place of the same type as p; and a set of fusion places FS. We have already defined and computed the set of modules S. The set of fusion places is empty e.g. $FS = \emptyset$. Therefore, the task is now to compute SM and PS. The module CPN'_M is the prime module (top level of the hierarchy) and every other module is a sub-module with respect to CPN'. The initial marking M_0 always evaluates to a non-empty set of tokens at the input port $i' \in P'$; and every other place is empty. The place i' has a single output arc connected to the transition r_i. Thus, all execution sequences must begin at r_i. The model has a single final transition r_f

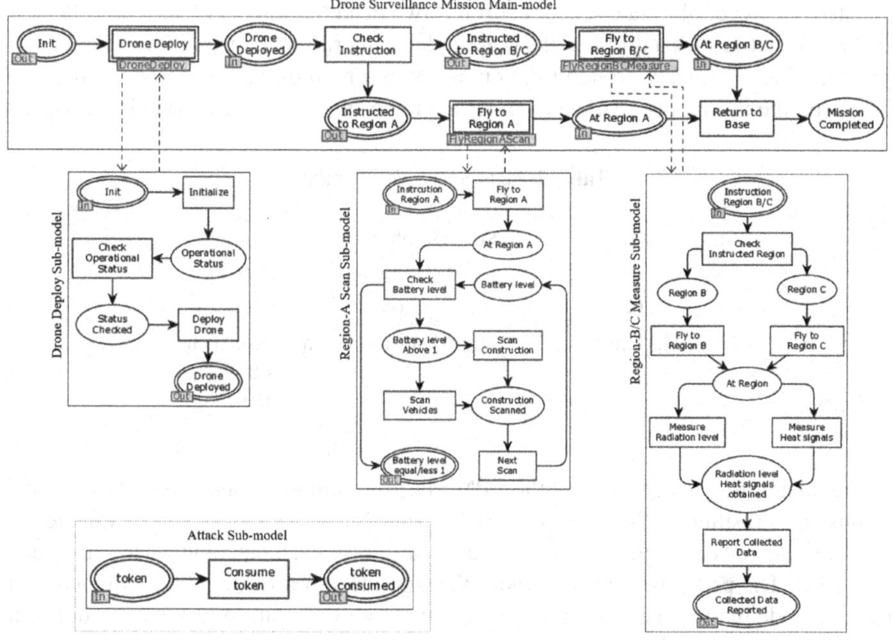

Fig. 3. CPN Models of Surveillance Drone Mission.

with a single output place o'. Therefore, any execution sequence that is complete must terminate with the transition r_f and a token in the place o'. The initial transition $r_i \in T'$ and final transition $r_f \in T'$ model the begin and end tasks of the original workflow.

5 Resiliency Analysis

An attack is an action taken by an adversary that changes the state of a subject in a way that renders it unable to perform a task it has been assigned. An attack scenario consists of the target of the attack. The set of attributes of the target, which are attackable, an attack task, and an integer limit on the number of times the attack may occur. A mission workflow is resilient to an attack scenario if, after the attack occurs, there exists a successful execution from the point at which the attack occurred.

There are various scenarios of workflow resilience, including static, decremental, and dynamic resilience [19] (see Sect. 6). In this paper, we investigate static resilience. Static resilience describes a situation where a subset of users become unavailable before the execution of the workflow. Once a subset of users is made unavailable, no user of this subset may become available again.

The analysis examines the state space of the CPN model with the attack scenario where the drone's camera fails while scanning region A since we know that it is the only location where the drone uses its camera. Table 2 reports 57 nodes and 65 arcs that are strongly connected components (SCC). It also reports that model transitions are fully executed. However, the state space report has two dead markings (42 and 57). The first dead marking (42) has a drone in the output place and received instruction. The second dead marking (57) has a drone in the output place and did not receive an instruction. Therefore, the mission is guaranteed to terminate in success under an attack scenario.

Table 2. State Space Verification

State Space		SCC Graph		Status
#Nodes 57	#Arcs 65	#Nodes 57	#Arcs 65	Full
Dead Markings [42, 57]		Dead Transition None		Live Transition None

We then write a program using the CPN-ML programming language [11] to analyze the mission's resilience. We then use the CPN State Space Analysis Tool to evaluate the program functions and return an execution sequence for each outcome where the attack succeeded. The program then backtracks through the shortest execution sequence and finds the node in the state space representing the state where the attack occurred. From that state, it searches for an execution sequence that results in a successful outcome (attack failure). If it finds one, it returns the execution sequence. Otherwise, it returns an empty list. The program also returns information about the set of dead markings and partitions the set into three subsets. The dead markings represent outcomes where the attack did not occur, the attack occurred, and the mission failed, and where the attack occurred, and the mission succeeded.

Table 3 summarizes the resiliency analysis result. The first column describes the scanning iteration of Region A. The first row shows 37 total dead markings (DM), 2 dead markings that represent outcomes where the attack did not occur (DNA), 10 dead markings that represent outcomes where the attack occurred but failed (DAF), 25 dead markings that represent outcomes where the attack occurred and succeeded (DAS). The algorithm found paths that reach only 4 of the 25 DAS markings (RDAS).

Table 3. Static Resilience Analysis Results

Scan Iteration Number	Dead Markings (DM)	Attack Didn't Occur (DNA)	Attack Occurred but Failed (DAF)	Attack Occurred and Succeede (DAS)	Reachable DAS (RDAS)
1	37	2	10	25	4
2	33	2	10	21	0
3	16	2	9	5	0
4	12	2	10	0	0

The program inspects the set of DNA markings and returns that the mission is correct and valid. The DNA markings represent the original outcomes of the mission. The size of this set should be the same as the original set of dead markings. For the 25 failed outcomes, the program found a successful execution sequence for four outcomes. We compare the successful execution sequence with the failed execution sequence for each of these four outcomes. It leads us to find the state where the execution sequences diverge and, from that state, ensure that the transition and binding element that leads to success always occur. For instance, node 42 corresponds to a failed outcome where the attack happened at node 3. From node 3, our program found a path to node 57 - a successful outcome. We now compare the path from node 3 to node 57 and the path from node 3 to node 42. We find that the execution sequences diverge at node 5. From node 5, proceeding to node 10 or node 9 is possible. The change in state from node 5 to node 10 results from the transition with the variable instruction bound to the value *false*. The change in state from node 5 to node 9 results from the transition with the variable instruction bound to the value *true*. We now know that the attack succeeds if the drone's battery is less than 3 units in the state represented by node 5, where transition *receiveinstruction* is enabled. Transition receive instruction models the workflow routing based on an instruction issued.

In Iteration 2, the state space is re-calculated, and the analysis is repeated. The second row of Table 3 describes the statistics generated by the program's second iteration. The result is four fewer outcomes where the attack succeeded. The program returns a set of nodes representing the states where the attack occurred, and no path to a successful outcome exists. Note that these are not dead markings. From each of these nodes, there is a path to a dead marking that represents the failure of the mission (success of the attack).

In Iteration 3, the state space is re-calculated, and the analysis is repeated. The third row of Table 3 summarizes the statistics generated by the program's second iteration. We expected the set of outcomes where the attack failed to remain at 10, now 9. The reduced size of the failed attack set means the outcome is lost because the drone is initialized with its instruction set to *false*. Thus the attack at node 3, which was found to be resilient, never executes. We focus on the 5 markings where the attack occurred and succeeded. After inspecting all five markings, we find the attack succeeds because it is delivered when the drone has just enough battery to perform one additional pass over Region A. We can eliminate these failed outcomes by increasing the requirement on the loop over Region A from more than one unit of battery to more than two units of battery. It turns out that the drone always has some reserve battery if it is attacked.

In Iteration 4, the state space is re-calculated, and the analysis is repeated. The third row of Table 3 summarizes the statistics generated by the program's second iteration. Since the set of attack successes is empty, we can be confident that the attack can not succeed under the restricted workflow.

In summary, we have shown how to assess a mission's resilience and find the conditions required for the mission to succeed. We have also shown how to restrict a workflow to improve its resilience.

6 Related Work

The literature on workflow resiliency problems introduces solutions to address the unavailability [13, 15, 19]. Our work argues that the workflow resiliency problem can sometimes be viewed as unavailability and degradation. In other words, attacks do not permanently remove subjects from service; they decrease their capabilities. Consider the drone surveillance example; a failure in the drone's camera affects the termination and success of the workflow. Regarding resilience based on availability, one can assume whether the camera's loss is critical enough to remove the drone from the workflow. The drone should be kept since its other sensors can complete the workflow.

Wang *et al.* [19] introduce three types of resilience, static, decremental, and dynamic resilience. Static resilience refers to a situation in which users become unavailable before the workflow executes, and no users may become available during the execution. Decremental resiliency expresses a situation where users become unavailable before or during the execution of the workflow, and no previously unavailable users may become available during execution, while dynamic resilience describes the situation where a user may become unavailable at any time; a previously unavailable user may become available at any time. The different types of resilience formulations capture various types of attack scenarios.

Mace *et al.* [13,15] propose a quantitative measure of workflow resiliency. They use a Markov Decision Process (MDP) to model workflow to provide a quantitative measure of resilience. They refer to binary classification, such as returning an execution sequence if one exists and declaring the workflow resilient; or returning false and declaring the workflow not resilient. The authors show that the MDP models give a termination rate and an expected termination step.

7 Conclusion

This paper emphasizes the workflow resiliency of the task degradation problem, specifically for mission-critical cyber systems. We presented a set of rules that formally transforms workflow represented by a mission into Coloured Petri Nets (CPNs). We then solved various analysis problems related to the resiliency of mission-critical such as cyber-attacks. We developed an approach based on formalization rules that address the complexity of mission workflows, simplify them, and transform them into simple CPNs. These simple CPNs are then modulated and combined as a hierarchy CPN model.

We applied the approach to a drone surveillance system as an illustrative example. We used the CPN tools to run verification and reachability analysis. The results showed that the workflow resiliency problem could sometimes be unavailability and degradation. A workflow subject is not permanently removed from service when an attack occurs; it decreases its capabilities. However, the mission can continue, and the workflow can be completed. We have shown how to assess a mission's resilience and find the conditions to succeed. We have also shown how to restrict a workflow to improve its resilience.

Future work will focus on extending the generated model to account for multiple subjects and investigating decremental and dynamic resilience. We will design a set of algorithms corresponding to the transformation rules. Our end goal is to automate the process of verification and resilience analysis of workflows.

Acknowledgements. This work was supported in part by funding from NSF under Award Numbers CNS 1715458, DMS 2123761, CNS 1822118, NIST, ARL, Statnett, AMI, NewPush, and Cyber Risk Research.

References

1. Aalst, W.M.P.: Verification of workflow nets. In: Azéma, P., Balbo, G. (eds.) ICATPN 1997. LNCS, vol. 1248, pp. 407–426. Springer, Heidelberg (1997). https://doi.org/10.1007/3-540-63139-9_48
2. van der Aalst, W.: Structural characterizations of sound workflow nets (1996)
3. Arpinar, I.B., Halici, U., Arpinar, S., Doğaç, A.: Formalization of workflows and correctness issues in the presence of concurrency. Distrib. Parallel Databases **7**(2), 199–248 (1999). https://doi.org/10.1023/A:1008758612291
4. Bride, H., Kouchnarenko, O., Peureux, F.: Verifying modal workflow specifications using constraint solving. In: Albert, E., Sekerinski, E. (eds.) IFM 2014. LNCS, vol. 8739, pp. 171–186. Springer, Cham (2014). https://doi.org/10.1007/978-3-319-10181-1_11
5. Bride, H., Kouchnarenko, O., Peureux, F., Voiron, G.: Workflow nets verification: SMT or CLP? In: ter Beek, M.H., Gnesi, S., Knapp, A. (eds.) FMICS/AVoCS -2016. LNCS, vol. 9933, pp. 39–55. Springer, Cham (2016). https://doi.org/10.1007/978-3-319-45943-1_3
6. Chong, J., Pal, P., Atigetchi, M., Rubel, P., Webber, F.: Survivability architecture of a mission critical system: the DPASA example. In: 21st Annual Computer Security Applications Conference (ACSAC 2005), pp. 10–pp. IEEE (2005)
7. Fong, P.W.L.: Results in workflow resiliency: complexity, new formulation, and ASP encoding, pp. 185–196. Association for Computing Machinery, New York (2019)
8. Houliotis, K., Oikonomidis, P., Charchalakis, P., Stipidis, E.: Mission-critical systems design framework. Adv. Sci. Technol. Eng. Syst. J. **3**(2), 128–137 (2018)
9. Jensen, K., Kristensen, L., Wells, L.: Coloured Petri Nets and CPN Tools for modelling and validation of concurrent systems. STTT **9**, 213–254 (2007). https://doi.org/10.1007/s10009-007-0038-x
10. Jensen, K., Kristensen, L.M.: Coloured Petri Nets: Modelling and Validation of Concurrent Systems, 1st edn. Springer, Heidelberg (2009). https://doi.org/10.1007/b95112
11. Jensen, K., Kristensen, L.M.: CPN ML programming. In: Jensen, K., Kristensen, L.M. (eds.) Coloured Petri Nets, pp. 43–77. Springer, Heidelberg (2009). https://doi.org/10.1007/b95112_3
12. Mace, J., Morisset, C., van Moorsel, A.: Modelling user availability in workflow resiliency analysis. In: Proceedings of the 2015 Symposium and Bootcamp on the Science of Security, HotSoS 2015, pp. 1–10. ACM (2015)
13. Mace, J.C., Morisset, C., van Moorsel, A.: Quantitative workflow resiliency. In: Kutyłowski, M., Vaidya, J. (eds.) ESORICS 2014. LNCS, vol. 8712, pp. 344–361. Springer, Cham (2014). https://doi.org/10.1007/978-3-319-11203-9_20
14. Mace, J.C., Morisset, C., van Moorsel, A.: WRAD: tool support for workflow resiliency analysis and design. In: Crnkovic, I., Troubitsyna, E. (eds.) SERENE 2016. LNCS, vol. 9823, pp. 79–87. Springer, Cham (2016). https://doi.org/10.1007/978-3-319-45892-2_6
15. Mace, J.C., Morisset, C., Moorsel, A.: Impact of policy design on workflow resiliency computation time. In: Campos, J., Haverkort, B.R. (eds.) QEST 2015. LNCS, vol. 9259, pp. 244–259. Springer, Cham (2015). https://doi.org/10.1007/978-3-319-22264-6_16
16. Ponsard, C., Massonet, P., Molderez, J.F., Rifaut, A., van Lamsweerde, A., Van Tran, H.: Early verification and validation of mission critical systems. Formal Methods Syst. Des. **30**(3), 233–247 (2007). https://doi.org/10.1007/s10703-006-0028-8

17. Ratzer, A.V., et al.: CPN tools for editing, simulating, and analysing coloured Petri nets. In: van der Aalst, W.M.P., Best, E. (eds.) ICATPN 2003. LNCS, vol. 2679, pp. 450–462. Springer, Heidelberg (2003). https://doi.org/10.1007/3-540-44919-1_28. http://cpntools.org
18. van der Aalst, W.M., ter Hofstede, A.H.: Verification of workflow task structures: a Petri-net-baset approach. Inf. Syst. **25**(1), 43–69 (2000). https://doi.org/10.1016/S0306-4379(00)00008-9. https://www.sciencedirect.com/science/article/pii/S0306437900000089
19. Wang, Q., Li, N.: Satisfiability and resiliency in workflow authorization systems. ACM Trans. Inf. Syst. Secur. **13**(4), 1–35 (2010)
20. Yang, P., Xie, X., Ray, I., Lu, S.: Satisfiability analysis of workflows with control-flow patterns and authorization constraints. IEEE Trans. Serv. Comput. **7**(2), 237–251 (2014). https://doi.org/10.1109/TSC.2013.31
21. Zavatteri, M., Viganò, L.: Last man standing: static, decremental and dynamic resiliency via controller synthesis. J. Comput. Secur. **27**(3), 343–373 (2019)

Invited Paper: How Do Humans Succeed in Tasks Like Proving Fermat's Theorem or Predicting the Higgs Boson?

Leonid A. Levin(✉)

Boston University, Boston, MA 02215, USA
https://www.cs.bu.edu/fac/Lnd/

Abstract. I discuss issues of inverting feasibly computable functions, optimal discovery algorithms, and the constant overheads in their performance.

Keywords: Search problems · Optimal algorithm · Inductive inference

Our computers do a huge number of absolutely wonderful things. Yet most of these things seem rather mechanical. Lots of crucial problems that do yield to the intuition of our very slow brains are beyond our current computer arts.

Great many such tasks can be stated in the form of inverting easily computable functions, or reduced to this form. (That is, finding inputs/actions that could produce a given result in a given realistic process.)

We have no idea about intrinsic difficulty of these tasks. And yet, traveling salesmen do get to their destinations, mathematicians do find proofs of their theorems, and physicists do find patterns in transformations of their bosons and fermions! How is this done, and how could computers emulate their success?

Of course, these are collective achievements of many minds engrossed in a huge number of papers. But today's computers can easily search through all math and physics papers ever written. The limitation is not in physical capacity.

And insects solve problems of such complexity and with such efficiency, as we cannot dream of. Yet, few of us would be flattered by comparison to the brain of an insect. What advantage do we humans have?

One is the ability to solve **new** problems on which evolution did not train zillions of our ancestors. We must have some pretty universal methods, not dependent on the specifics of focused problems. Of course, it is hard to tell how, say, mathematicians find their proofs. Yet, the diversity and dynamism of math achievements suggest that some pretty universal mechanisms must be at work.

Let me now focus on a specific technical problem: Consider, for instance, algorithms that 3-color given graphs[1]. Is it true that every such algorithm can be sped-up 10 times on **some** infinite set of graphs?

Or, *there is a "perfect" algorithm, that cannot be outsped 10 times even on a* **subset** *of graphs?*

[1] This is a complete problem, i.e. all other inversion problems are reducible to it.

S. Dolev and B. Schieber (Eds.): SSS 2023, LNCS 14310, pp. 513–517, 2023.
https://doi.org/10.1007/978-3-031-44274-2_38

Note, there is a 3-coloring algorithm that cannot be outsped by more than constant factors on **any** subset. The question is, must these constants get really big?

***

But before further discussion, some history:

In the 50s, in the Russian math community there was much interest in the works of Claude Shannon. But many of Shannon's constructions required exhaustive search of all configurations. There was an intense interest in whether these exponential procedures could be eliminated (see [9]).

And Sergey Yablonsky wrote a paper that he interpreted as showing that no subexponential method could work on a problem that is, in today's terms, co-NP. It is a problem of finding a boolean function of maximal circuit complexity.

Kolmogorov saw this claim as baseless since the proof considered only a specific type of algorithms. Unhappy with such misleading ideas being promoted, Kolmogorov advocated the need for efforts to find valid proofs for common beliefs that complexities of some popular problems are indeed unavoidable.

This task required a convincing definition of the running time. But Turing Machines were seen as too restricted to use for meaningful speed lower bounds. Kolmogorov formulated (see [6]) a graph-based model of algorithms that had time complexities as they are understood today.

He also ran a seminar where he challenged mathematicians with quadratic complexity of multiplication. And an unexpected answer was soon found by Anatoly Karatsuba, and improved by Andrei Toom: multiplication complexity turned out nearly linear.

This was an impressive indication that common sense is an unreliable guide for hardness of computational problems, and must be verified by valid proofs.

***

I, at that time, was extremely excited by some other work of Kolmogorov. He (and independently Ray Solomonoff) used the Turing's Universal Algorithm for an optimal definition of informational complexity, randomness, and some other related concepts.

I noted that similar constructions yield an optimal up to a constant factor algorithm for a problem now called Tiling, and thus for any search problem, as they all have a straightforward reduction to Tiling.

To my shagreen, Kolmogorov was not impressed with the concept of optimality, saw it as too abstract for the issue at hand. (Indeed, finding specific bounds did not look as hopeless then as it now does.) But he was much more interested in my remark that Tiling allows reduction to it of all other search problems. He thought I should publish **that** rather than the optimal search.

I thought it would only be worth publishing if I can reduce it to some popular problems. My obstacle was that combinatorics was not popular in Russia, and my choice of problems that might impress the math community was rather limited. I saw no hope for something like factoring, but spent years in naive attempts on things like graph isomorphism, finding small circuits for boolean tables, etc.

Meanwhile an interesting angle was added to the issues. In 1969 Michael Dekhtiar, a student of Boris Trakhtenbrot, published a proof [3] that under some oracles inverting simple functions has exponential complexity. In the US, Baker, Gill, and Solovay did this independently [1].

Later I ran into problems with communist authorities. And friends advised me to quickly publish all I have while the access to publishing is not yet closed to me. So I submitted several papers in that 1972, including the one about search [7] (where Kolmogorov agreed to let me include the optimal search). I guess I must thank the communists for this publication.

But the greatest developments by far were going on in the United States. S. Cook [2], R. Karp [5], and Garey and Johnson [4] made a really revolutionary discovery. They found that 3-SAT reduces to great many important combinatorics problems.

Combinatorics received much attention in the West and these results became a coup!

***

Kolmogorov asked several questions at that time, still open and interesting. One was: Are there polynomial time algorithms that have no **linear** size circuits? We knew that some slow polynomial time algorithms cannot be replaced by faster **algorithms**. But can linear-sized circuits families replace **all** of them?

His other interesting comment was a bit more involved. We proved at that time that mutual information between strings is roughly symmetric. The proof involved exponential search for short programs transforming a strings x into y. Kolmogorov wondered if such search for short fast (meant in robust terms, tolerating $+O(1)$ slacks in length and in log time) programs would not be a better candidate than my Tiling to see if search problems are exponentially hard.

He said that, often, a good candidate to consider is one that is neither too general, nor too narrow. Tiling, being universal, may be too general, lacking focus. Some other problems (say, factoring) – too narrow. And search for fast short programs looked like a good middle bet to him. It still does to me! :-)

Such search is involved in another type of problems that challenge our creativity: extrapolating the observed data to their whole natural domains. It is called by many names, “Inductive Inference”, “passive learning”, and others. Occam Razor is a famous principle of extrapolation. A version attributed to Einstein suggests: hypothesis need be chosen as simple as possible, but no simpler :-).

***

Ray Solomonoff gave it a more formal expression: The likelihoods of various extrapolations, consistent with known data, decrease exponentially with the length of their shortest descriptions. Those short programs run about as fast as the process that had generated the data.

There have been several technical issues that required further attention. I will stay on a simple side, not going into those details. Most of them have been clarified by now, **if** we ignore the time needed to find such short fast programs. This may be hard. Yet, this is still an inversion task, bringing us back to the issues of optimal search. I have a little discussion of such issues in [8].

***

Now, back to my focus. The concept of optimal algorithm for search problems ignores constant factors **completely**. So, it is tempting to assume that they must be enormous.

However, this does not seem so to me. Our brains have evolved on jumping in trees, not on writing math articles. And yet, we prove Fermat's Theorems, design nukes, and even write STOC papers. We must have some quite efficient and quite universal guessing algorithms built-in.

So, I repeat a formal question on these constants:

Can every algorithm for complete search problems be outsped 10 times on an infinite subset? OR, there is a "perfect" one that cannot be, even on a subset?

Of course, careless definitions of time can allow fake speed-ups. For instance if we ignore the alphabet size and reduce the number of steps just by making each step larger due to the larger alphabet. Or if we exclude the required end testing of the input/output relation, and choose a relation that itself allows a non-constant speed-up. But it is easy to carefully define time to preclude such cheating.

***

Let me now go into some little technicalities to see what issues are involved in understanding these constant factors. We look at the optimal search for an inverse w of a fast algorithm f, given the output x that f must produce from w.

We refine Kolmogorov Complexity with **time**, making it computable. The time-refined complexity **Kt** of w given x considers all prefixless programs p by which the universal algorithm U generates w from x in time T. (T includes running $f(w)$ to confirm it is x.) $\mathbf{Kt}(w|x)$ is the minimum of length of p, plus $\log T$.

The Optimal Inverter searches for solutions w in increasing order of this complexity **Kt** of w given x, **not** of length of w. For instance, shorter proofs may be much harder to find, having higher complexities. The Inverter generates and checks in time 2^k all w up to complexity k.

Btw, the optimal search makes the concept of complexity applicable to individual instances of search tasks, not just to families of instances which we now call "problems" and complexities of which we study. So we can ask how hard is, say, to find a short proof for Fermat's theorem, not for theorems in general. Would not this notion fit tighter?

The big **catch** here is that **each** wasteful bit U requires of p **doubles** the time. We would need a **very** "pure" U, frugal with wasting bits. Do our brains have such a one built-in? It seems so to me. We do seem to have little disagreement on what is "neat" and what is cumbersome. There are differences in our tastes, but they are not so huge that we could not understand each other's aesthetics. But this is just a feeling. The formal question remains:

Is there an algorithm for a complete search problem that cannot be outsped ten times, even on an infinite subset?

(Of course, this 10 is a bit arbitrary, can be replaced with your favorite reasonable constant.)

References

1. Baker, T.P., Gill, J., Solovay, R.: Relativizations of the P = NP question. SIComp **4**(4), 431–442 (1975)
2. Cook, S.: The complexity of theorem proving procedures. In: STOC-1971, pp. 151–158 (1971)
3. Dekhtiar, M.: On the impossibility of eliminating exhaustive search in computing a function relative to its graph. Russ. Proc. USSR Acad. Sci. **14**, 1146–1148 (1969)
4. Garey, M.R., Johnson, D.S.: Computers and Intractability: A Guide to the Theory of NP-Completeness. W.H. Freeman (1979)
5. Karp, R.M.: Reducibility among combinatorial problems. In: Miller, R.E., Thatcher, J.W. (eds.) Complexity of Computer Computations, pp. 85–103. Plenum (1972)
6. Kolmogorov, A.N., Uspenskii, V.A.: On the definition of an algorithm. Uspekhi Mat. Nauk **13**(4), 3–28 (1958). AMS Transl. 1963. 2nd ser. 29:217–245
7. Levin, L.A.: Универсальные Задачи Перебора (1973). (in Russian) [Universal search problems]. Probl. Inf. Transm. **9**(3), 115–116. English Translation in [9]
8. Levin, L.A.: Universal heuristics: how do humans solve "unsolvable" problems? In: Dowe, D.L. (ed.) Algorithmic Probability and Friends. Bayesian Prediction and Artificial Intelligence. LNCS, vol. 7070, pp. 53–54. Springer, Heidelberg (2013). https://doi.org/10.1007/978-3-642-44958-1_3. Also in a CCR/SIGACT Workshop Report "Visions for Theoretical Computer Science"
9. Trakhtenbrot, B.A.: A survey of Russian approaches to perebor (brute-force search) algorithms. Ann. Hist. Comput. **6**(4), 384–400 (1984)

Self-stabilizing Byzantine-Tolerant Recycling

Chryssis Georgiou[1], Michel Raynal[2], and Elad M. Schiller[3](✉)

[1] Computer Science, University of Cyprus, Nicosia, Cyprus
chryssis@cs.ucy.ac.cy

[2] IRISA, Univ. Rennes 1, Rennes, France
michel.raynal@irisa.fr

[3] Computer Science and Engineering, Chalmers University of Technology, Gothenburg, Sweden
elad@chalmers.se

Abstract. Numerous distributed applications, such as cloud computing and distributed ledgers, necessitate the system to invoke asynchronous consensus objects for an unbounded number of times, where the completion of one consensus instance is followed by the invocation of another. With only a constant number of objects available, object reuse becomes vital. We investigate the challenge of object recycling in the presence of *Byzantine* processes, which can deviate from the algorithm code in any manner. Our solution must also be *self-stabilizing*, as it is a powerful notion of fault tolerance. Self-stabilizing systems can recover automatically after the occurrence of *arbitrary transient-faults*, in addition to tolerating communication and (Byzantine or crash) process failures, provided the algorithm code remains intact. We provide a recycling mechanism for asynchronous objects that enables their reuse once their task has ended, and all non-faulty processes have retrieved the decided values. This mechanism relies on synchrony assumptions and builds on a new self-stabilizing Byzantine-tolerant synchronous multivalued consensus algorithm, along with a novel composition of existing techniques.

Glossary:

BC	Byzantine-tolerant Consensus;
BDH	Ben-Or, Dolev, and Hoch [5];
BFT	non-self-stabilizing Byzantine fault-tolerant solutions;
COR	Consensus Object Recycling (Definition 1);
DPS	Dolev, Petig, and Schiller [9];
MMR	Mostéfaoui, Moumen, and Raynal [22];
RCCs	random common coins;
SSBFT	self-stabilizing Byzantine fault-tolerant;
κ**–SGC**	κ-state global clock.

S. Dolev and B. Schieber (Eds.): SSS 2023, LNCS 14310, pp. 518–535, 2023.
https://doi.org/10.1007/978-3-031-44274-2_39

1 Introduction

We study the problem of recycling asynchronous consensus objects. We propose a more robust solution than the state-of-the-art solution to achieve this goal.

Fault Model. We study solutions for message-passing systems. We model a broad set of failures that can occur to computers and networks. Our model includes up to t process failures, *i.e.*, crashed or Byzantine [19]. In detail, the adversary completely controls any Byzantine node, *e.g.*, the adversary can send a fake message that the node never sent, modify the payload of its messages, delay the delivery of its messages, or omit any subset of them. We assume a known maximum number, t, of Byzantine processes. For solvability's sake, we also restrict the adversary from letting a Byzantine process impersonate a non-faulty one, *i.e.*, as in [27], we assume private channels between any pair of nodes.

Self-stabilization. In addition to the failures captured by our model, we also aim to recover from *arbitrary transient-faults*, *i.e.*, any temporary violation of assumptions according to which the system was designed to operate. This includes the corruption of control variables, such as the program counter, packet payload, and indices, *e.g.*, sequence numbers, which are responsible for the correct operation of the studied system, as well as operational assumptions, such as that at least a distinguished majority of processes never fail. Since the occurrence of these failures can be arbitrarily combined, we assume that these transient-faults can alter the system state in unpredictable ways. In particular, when modeling the system, Dijkstra [7] assumes that these violations bring the system to an arbitrary state from which a *self-stabilizing system* should recover. Dijkstra requires recovery after the last occurrence of a transient-fault and once the system has recovered, it must never violate the task specifications. *I.e.*, there could be any finite number of transient faults before the last one occurs, which may leave the system in an arbitrary state. Moreover, recovery from an arbitrary system state is demonstrated once all transient faults cease to happen, see [3,8]

Memory Constraints. In the absence of transient faults, one can safely assume that the algorithm variables, such as a counter for the message sequence number, are unbounded. This assumption can be made valid for any practical setting by letting each counter use enough bits, say, 64, because counting (using sequential steps) from zero to the maximum value of the counter will take longer than the time during which the system is required to remain operational. Specifically, if each message transmission requires at least one nanosecond, it would take at least 584 years until the maximum value can be reached. However, in the context of self-stabilization, a single transient fault can set the counter value into one that is close to the maximum value. Thus, any self-stabilizing solution must cope with this challenge and use only bounded memory and communication.

Self-stabilization via Algorithmic Transformation. This work is dedicated to designing a generic transformer, which takes an algorithm as input and systematically redesigns it into its self-stabilizing variation as output. Existing transformers differ in the range of input algorithms and fault models they can transform, see Dolev [8, 2.8], Katz and Perry [17], Afek *et al.* [2], and Awerbuch *et al.* [4].

Dolev, Petig, and Schiller [9] (DPS in short) proposed a transformer of crash-tolerant algorithms for asynchronous message-passing systems into ones that also recover from transient faults.Lundström *et al.* show DPS's applicability to various communication abstractions, such as atomic snapshot [12], consensus [15, 21], reliable broadcast [20], and state-machine replication [16]. DPS mandates that (DPS.i) the input algorithm guarantees, after the last transient fault occurrence, the completion of each invocation of the communication abstraction, *i.e.*, it should eventually terminate regardless of the starting state. This condition facilitates the eventual release of resources used by each invocation. Additionally, (DPS.ii) it associates a sequence number with each invocation to differentiate the resources utilized by different invocations. This enables the recycling of resources associated with obsolete invocations through a sliding window technique, along with a global restart once the maximum sequence number is reached.

Recently, DPS was utilized by Duvignau *et al.* [11] for converting Byzantine fault-tolerant (BFT) reliable broadcast proposed by Bracha and Toueg [6] into a Self-Stabilizing BFT (SSBFT) variation. This solution recycles reliable broadcast objects using synchrony assumptions. It also relies on the fact that the process may allocate independent local memory and sequence numbers per sender. However, consensus objects often use shared sequence numbers, and thus, parts of their local memories are codependent. Therefore, we use another approach.

Problem Description. This work studies an important building block that is needed for the SSBFT implementation of asynchronous consensus objects. With only a bounded number of consensus objects available, it becomes essential to reuse them robustly. We examine the case in which the repeated invocation of consensus needs to reuse the same memory space and the $(k+1)$-th invocation can only start after the completion of the k-th instance. In an asynchronous system that uses only a bounded number of objects, ensuring the termination of the k-th instance before invoking the $(k+1)$-th might be crucial, *e.g.*, for total order broadcasting, as in some blockchains. Thus, we require SSBFT consensus objects to eventually terminate regardless of their starting state, as in (DPS.i).

We focus on addressing the challenge of recycling asynchronous consensus objects after they have completed their task and delivered their decision to all non-faulty processes. This task becomes complex due to the presence of asynchrony and Byzantine failures. Utilizing the joint sequence numbers of (DPS.ii) for recycling consensus objects is not straightforward, because it requires ensuring that all non-faulty processes have delivered the decided value (for the k-th consensus invocation) as well as agreeing that such collective delivery occurred before incrementing the sequence number counter (that is going to be used by the $(k+1)$-th invocation). To overcome this chicken-and-egg problem, we relax the problem requirements by allowing the recycling mechanism to depend on synchrony assumptions. To mitigate the impact of these assumptions, a single recycling action can be performed for a batch of δ objects, where δ is a predefined constant determined by the available memory. Thus, our approach facilitates asynchronous networking in communication-intensive components, *i.e.*, the consensus objects, while Asynchronous recycling actions are performed according to a load parameter, δ.

Our Solution in a Nutshell. Our solution aims to emulate (DPS.ii) by incorporating synchrony assumptions specifically for the recycling service, while keeping the consensus object asynchronous to handle intensive message exchange.

To begin, we maintain an index that points to the most recently invoked object in a constant-size array. In order to ensure that all non-faulty processes agree on the value of the index, we utilize a novel technique called *simultaneous increment-or-get indexes* (SGI-index). When recycling an object, we increment the index, but this increment is performed only after an agreement among the non-faulty processes that the relevant object has made its decision and delivered it to all non-faulty processes. Thus, we use a new SSBFT multivalued consensus before each increment, ensuring that consensus is reached before the increment. *I.e.*, all needed deliveries had occurred before the increment.

Additionally, our solution answers how an SSBFT asynchronous consensus object can provide an indication that at least one non-faulty process has made a decision and delivered. We utilize this indication as input to trigger the recycling action, effectively incorporating it into the SSBFT multivalued consensus.

Related Work. Object recycling was studied mainly in the context of crash-tolerant (non-BFT) systems [25,29]. There are a few (non-self-stabilizing) implementations of garbage collection in the presence of Byzantine processes, *e.g.*, [23].

Non-self-stabilizing BFT Consensus. Rabin [26] offers a solution to BFT *consensus* (cf. Sect. 2 for definitions). It assumes the availability of *random common coins* (RCCs), allowing for a polynomial number of communication steps and optimal resilience, *i.e.*, $t < n/3$, where n is the number of participating processes. Mostéfaoui, Moumen, and Raynal [22], or MMR in short, is a signature-free BFT binary consensus solution. MMR is optimal in resilience, uses $O(n^2)$ messages per consensus invocation, and completes within $O(1)$ expected time.

Non-self-stabilizing Synchronous BFT Multivalued Consensus. The proposed recycling mechanism uses an SSBFT multivalued consensus, which is based on a non-self-stabilizing BFT multivalued consensus. Kowalski and Mostéfaoui [18] proposed the first multivalued optimal resilience, polynomial communication cost, and optimal $t+1$ rounds, but without early stopping. Abraham and Dolev [1] advanced the state of the art by offering also optimal early stopping. Unlike the above BFT solutions, our SSBFT multivalued solution adds self-stabilization.

SSBFT Consensus. To the best of our knowledge, the only SSBFT RCCs construction is the one by Ben-Or, Dolev, and Hoch [5], in short BDH, for synchronous systems with private channels. BDH uses its SSBFT RCCs construction as a building block for devising an SSBFT clock synchronization solution. Recently, Georgiou, Marcoullis, Raynal, and Schiller [13], or GMRS in short, presented an SSBFT variation on MMR, which offers a BFT binary consensus. GMRS preserves MMR's optimality, and thus, we use GMRS in this work. AGMRS follows the design criteria of loosely self-stabilizing systems, ensuring task completion but with rare safety violation events. In the context of the studied problem, the former guarantee renders the latter one irrelevant.

Our Contribution. We propose an important building block for reliable distributed systems: a new SSBFT mechanism for recycling SSBFT consensus objects. The proposed mechanism stabilizes within expected $\mathcal{O}(\kappa)$ synchronous rounds, where $\kappa \in \mathcal{O}(t)$ is a predefined constant (that depends on synchrony assumptions) and t is an upper bound on the number of Byzantine processes. We also present, to the best of our knowledge, the first SSBFT synchronous multivalued consensus solution. The novel composition of (i) SSBFT recycling and (ii) SSBFT recyclable objects has a long line of applications, such as replication and blockchain. Thus, our transformation advances the state of the art by facilitating solutions that are more fault-tolerant than the existing implementations, which cannot recover from transient faults.

For convenience, a Glossary appears after the References. Due to the page limit, the full correctness proof appear in the Acomplementary technical report [14].

2 Basic Result: Recyclable SSBFT Consensus Objects

In this section, we define a recyclable variation on the consensus problem, which facilitates the use of an unbounded number of consensus instances via the reuse of a constant number of objects (as presented in Sect. 4). Then, we sketch Algorithm 1, which presents a recyclable variation on an SSBFT asynchronous consensus algorithm (such as GMRS). Towards the end of this section, Theorem 1 demonstrates that Algorithm 1 constructs recyclable SSBFT consensus objects.

Algorithm 1: A recyclable variation on GMRS; p_i's code.

```
local variables: /* the algorithm's local state is defined here.                */
  delivered[P] := [False, ..., False] delivery indications; delivered[i] stores the local
  indication and delivered[j] stores the last received indication from p_j ∈ P;
constants: initState := (•, [False, ..., False]);
interfaces: recycle() do (local state, delivered) ← initState; /* also
    initialize all attached communication channels [8, Ch. 3.1]                 */
  wasDelivered() do {if ∃S ⊆ P : n−t ≤ |S| : ∀p_k ∈ S : delivered[k] = True then
    return 1 else return 0;}
operations: propose(v) do {implement the algorithm logic};
result() do begin
    if there is a decided value then {delivered[i] ← True; return v};
    else if an error occurred then {delivered[i] ← True; return ↯};
    else return ⊥;
do forever begin
    if result() = ⊥ then delivered[i] ← ⊥;/* consistency test */
    /* implementation of the algorithm's logic                                  */
    foreach p_j ∈ P do send EST(•, delivered[i]) to p_j;
upon EST(•, deliveredJ) arrival from p_j begin
    delivered[j] ← deliveredJ;
    /* merge arriving information with the local one                            */
```

Byzantine-Tolerant Consensus (BC). This problem requires agreeing on a value from a given set V, which every A(non-faulty) node inputs via propose(). It requires *BC-validity*, *i.e.*, if all non-faulty nodes propose the same value $v \in V$, only v can be decided, *BC-agreement*, *i.e.*, no two non-faulty nodes can decide different values, and *BC-completion*, *i.e.*, all non-faulty nodes decide a value. When the set, V, from which the proposed values are taken is $\{0, 1\}$, the problem is called *binary consensus*. Otherwise, it is referred to as *multivalued consensus*.

Recyclable Consensus Objects. We study systems that implement consensus objects using storage of constant size allocated at program compilation time. Since these objects can be instantiated an unbounded number of times, it becomes necessary to reuse the storage once consensus is reached and each non-faulty node has received the object result via result(). To facilitate this, we assume that the object has two meta-statuses: *used* and *unused*. The *unused* status represents both objects that were never used and those that are no longer in current use, indicating they are available (for reuse). Our definition of recyclable objects assumes that the objects implement an interface function called wasDelivered() that must return 1 anytime after the result delivery. Recycling is triggered by the recycling mechanism (Sect. 4), which invokes recycle() at each non-faulty node, thereby setting the meta-status of the corresponding consensus object to *unused*. We specify the task of recyclable object construction as one that requires eventual agreement on the value of wasDelivered(). In detail, if a non-faulty node p_i reports delivery (*i.e.*, $\mathsf{wasDelivered}_i() = 1$), then all non-faulty nodes will eventually report delivery as well. We clarify that during the recycling process, *i.e.*, when at least one non-faulty node invokes recycle(), there is no need to maintain agreement on the values of wasDelivered().

Algorithm Outline. Algorithm 1's boxed code lines highlight the code lines relevant to recyclability. AThe set of nodes is denoted by $\mathcal{P}$. We avoid the restatement of the algorithm, and to focus on the parts that matter in this work, the other parts are given in words (cf. GMRS [13] for full details). The code uses the symbol • to denote any sequence of values. We assume that the object allows the proposal of v via propose(v) (line 7). As in result() (line 8), once the consensus algorithm decides, one of the decided value is returned (line 9). Since the algorithm tolerates transient faults, the object may need to indicate an internal error via the return of the (transient) error symbol, $\lightning$ (line 10). In all other cases, the $\bot$-value is returned (line 11). GMRS uses a do-forever loop that broadcasts the protocol messages (line 14). Any node that receives this protocol message, merges the arriving information with the one stored by the local state (line 16).

Recyclable Variation. Algorithm 1 uses the array $delivered[\mathcal{P}]$ (initialized to [False, ..., False]) for delivery indications, where $delivered_i[i] : p_i \in \mathcal{P}$ stores the local indication and $delivered_i[j] : p_i, p_j \in \mathcal{P}$ stores the indication that was last received from p_j. This indication is set to True whenever result() returns a non-$\bot$ value (lines 9 to 10). Algorithm 1 updates $delivered[j]$ according to the arriving values from p_j (lines 14 and 16). The interface function wasDelivered() (line 6) returns 1 if at least $n - t$ entries in $delivered[]$ hold True. The interface function recycle() (line 5) allows the node to restart its local state w.r.t. Algorithm 1.

Theorem 1. *Algorithm 1 offers a recyclable asynchronous consensus object.*

Proof Sketch of Theorem 1. If $\exists i \in \mathit{Correct} : \mathsf{wasDelivered}_i() = 1$, then $\mathsf{result}_i() \neq \bot$ (line 13). By BC-completion, eventually $\forall j \in \mathit{Correct} : \mathsf{result}_j() \neq \bot \wedge \mathsf{wasDelivered}_j() = 1$ (lines 9 and 10). $\square_{Theorem\ 1}$

3 System Settings for the Recycling Mechanism

This model considers a synchronous message-passing system. The system consists of a set, $\mathcal{P}$, of n *nodes* (sometimes called *processes* or *processors*) with unique identifiers. At most $t < n/3$, out of the n nodes, are faulty. Any pair of nodes $p_i, p_j \in \mathcal{P}$ has access to a bidirectional reliable communication channel, $channel_{j,i}$. In the *interleaving model* [8], the node's program is a sequence of *(atomic) steps*. Each step starts with (i) the communication operation for receiving messages that is followed by (ii) an internal computation, and (iii) finishes with a single *send* operation. The *state*, s_i, of node $p_i \in \mathcal{P}$ includes all of p_i's variables and $channel_{j,i}$. The term *system state* refers to the tuple $c = (s_1, s_2, \cdots, s_n)$. Our model also assumes the availability of a κ-state global clock, reliable communications, and random common coins (RCCs).

A κ-State Global Clock. We assume that the algorithm takes steps according to a common global pulse (beat) that triggers a simultaneous step of every node in the system. Specifically, we denote synchronous executions by $R = c[0], c[1], \ldots$, where $c[x]$ is the system state that immediately precedes the x-th global pulse. And, $a_i[x]$ is the step that node p_i takes between $c[x]$ and $c[x+1]$ simultaneously with all other nodes. We also assume that each node has access to a κ-state global clock via the function $clock(\kappa)$, which returns an integer between 0 and $\kappa - 1$. Algorithm 3 of BDH [5] offers an SSBFT κ-state global clock that stabilizes within a constant time.

Reliable Communication. Recall that we assume the availability of reliable communication. Also, any non-faulty node $p_i \in \mathcal{P}$ starts any step $a_i[x]$ with receiving all pending messages from all nodes. And, if p_i sends any message during $a_i[x]$, it does so only at the end of $a_i[x]$. We require (i) any message that a non-faulty node p_i sends during step $a_i[x]$ to another non-faulty node p_j is received at p_j at the start of step $a_j[x+1]$, and (ii) any message that p_j received during step $a_j[x+1]$, was sent at the end of $a_i[x]$.

Random Common Coins (RCCs). As mentioned, BDH presented a synchronous SSBFT RCCs solution. Algorithm $\mathcal{A}$, which has the output of $rand_i \in \{0, 1\}$, is said to provide an RCC if $\mathcal{A}$ satisfies the following:

- **RCC-completion:** $\mathcal{A}$ completes within $\Delta_{\mathcal{A}} \in \mathbb{Z}^+$ synchronous rounds.
- **RCC-unpredictability:** Denote by $E_{x \in \{0,1\}}$ the event that for any non-faulty process, p_j, $rand_j = x$ holds with constant probability $p_x > 0$. Suppose either E_0 or E_1 occurs at the end of round $\Delta_{\mathcal{A}}$. We require that the adversity can predict the output of $\mathcal{A}$ by the end of round $\Delta_{\mathcal{A}} - 1$ with a probability that is not greater than $1 - \min\{p_0, p_1\}$. Following [22], we assume that $p_0 = p_1 = 1/2$.

Our solution depends on the existence of a self-stabilizing RCC service, *e.g.*, BDH. BDH considers *(progress) enabling* instances of RCCs if there is $x \in \{0, 1\}$ such that for any non-faulty process p_i, we have $rand_i = x$. BDH correctness proof depends on the consecutive existence of two enabling RCCs instances.

Legal Executions. The set of *legal executions* (LE) refers to all the executions in which the requirements of task T hold. In this work, T_{recycl} denotes the task of consensus object recycling (specified in Sect. 4), and LE_{recycl} denotes the set of executions in which the system fulfills T_{recycl}'s requirements.

Arbitrary Node Failures. As explained in Sect. 1, Byzantine faults model any fault in a node including crashes, arbitrary behavior, and malicious behavior [19].

For the sake of solvability [19,24,28], our fault model limits only the number of nodes that can be captured by the adversary. That is, the number, t, of Byzantine failure needs to be less than one-third of the number, n, of nodes. The set of non-faulty nodes is denoted by *Correct*.

Arbitrary Transient-Faults. We consider any temporary violation of the assumptions according to which the system was designed to operate. We refer to these violations and deviations as *arbitrary transient-faults* and assume that they can corrupt the system state arbitrarily (while keeping the program code intact). Our model assumes that the last transient fault occurs before the system execution starts [3,8]. Also, it leaves the system to start in an arbitrary state.

Self-stabilization. An algorithm is *self-stabilizing* for the task of LE, when every (unbounded) execution R of the algorithm reaches within a finite period a suffix $R_{legal} \in LE$ that is legal. Namely, Dijkstra [7] requires $\forall R : \exists R' : R = R' \circ R_{legal} \wedge R_{legal} \in LE \wedge |R'| \in \mathbb{Z}^+$, where the operator $\circ$ denotes that $R = R' \circ R''$ is the concatenation of R' with R''. The part of the proof that shows the existence of R' is called the *convergence* (or recovery) proof, and the part that shows that $R_{legal} \in LE$ is called the *closure* proof. We clarify that once the execution of a self-stabilizing system becomes legal, it stays legal due to the property of closure. The main complexity measure of a self-stabilizing system is its stabilization time, which is the length of the recovery period, R', which is counted by the number of its synchronous rounds.

4 SSBFT Recycling Mechanism

We present an SSBFT recycling mechanism for recyclable objects (Sect. 2). The mechanism is a service that recycles consensus objects via the invocation of recycle() by all (non-faulty) nodes. The coordinated invocation of recycle() can occur only after the consensus object has terminated and the non-faulty nodes have delivered the result, via result(), as indicated by wasDelivered().

Consensus Object Recycling (COR). Definition 1 specifies the COR problem for a single object. COR-validity-1 is a safety property requiring that recycle() is invoked only if there was at least one reported delivery by a non-faulty node. COR-validity-2 is a liveness property requiring that eventually recycle() is invoked. COR-agreement is a safety property requiring that all non-faulty nodes simultaneously set the object's status to unused. This allows any node p_i to reuse the object immediately after the return from $\mathsf{recycle}_i()$.

Definition 1 (Consensus Object Recycling).

- ***COR-validity-1:*** *If a non-faulty node, p_j, invokes* $\mathsf{recycle}_j()$, *then at least one non-faulty node, p_i, reported delivery.*
- ***COR-validity-2:*** *If all non-faulty nodes report delivery, then at least one non-faulty node, p_j, eventually invokes* $\mathsf{recycle}_j()$.
- ***COR-agreement:*** *If a non-faulty node invokes* recycle(), *then all non-faulty nodes, p_i, invoke* $\mathsf{recycle}_i()$ *simultaneously.*

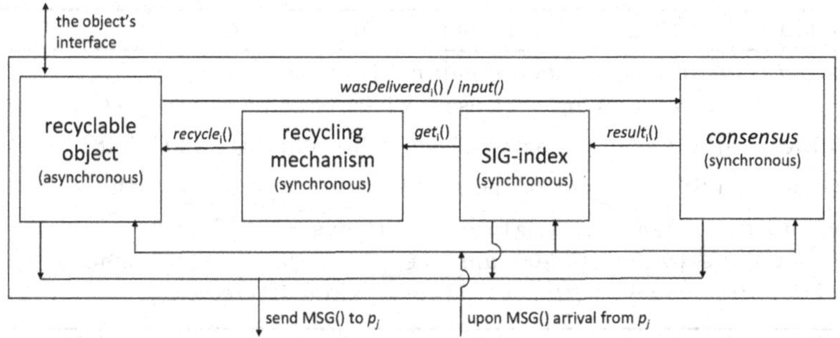

Fig. 1. The solution uses recyclable objects (Algorithm 1), a recycling mechanism (Algorithm 2), multivalued consensus (Algorithm 3), and SIG-index (Algorithm 4). Algorithms 1 and 3 solve the BC problem (Sect. 2) for asynchronous, and resp., synchronous settings. Algorithms 2 and 4 solve the COR, resp., SGI-index problems (Sect. 4).

Multiple Objects. We also specify that the recycling mechanism makes sure that, at any time, there are at most a constant number, $logSize$, of active objects, *i.e.,* objects that have not completed their tasks. Once an object completes its task, the recycling mechanism can allocate a new object by moving to the next array entry as long as some constraints are satisfied. Specifically, the proposed solution is based on a synchrony assumption that guarantees that every (correct) node retrieves (at least once) the result of a completed object, x, within $logSize$ synchronous rounds since the first time in which at least $t + 1$ (correct) nodes have retrieved the result of x, and thus, x can be recycled.

Solution Overview. The SSBFT recycling solution is a composition of several algorithms, see Fig. 1. Our recycling mechanism is presented in Algorithm 2. It allows every (correct) node to retrieve at least once the result of any object that is stored in a constant-size array and yet over time that array can store an unbounded number of object instances. The proposed service mechanism (Algorithm 2) ensures that every instance of the recyclable object, which is implemented by Algorithm 1, is guaranteed that every (correct) node calls result() (line 6) at least once before all (correct) nodes simultaneously invoke recycle() (line 5). This aligns with the solution architecture (Fig. 1).

We consider the case in which the entity that retrieves the result of object *obj* might be external (and perhaps, asynchronous) to the proposed solution. The proposed solution does not decide to recycle *obj* before there is sufficient evidence that, within $logSize$ synchronous cycles, the system is going to reach a state in which *obj* can be properly recycled. Specifically, Assumption 1 considers an event that can be locally learned about when wasDelivered() returns '1' (line 6).

Assumption 1 (A bounded time result Aretrieval) *Let us consider the system state,* $c[r]$*, in which the result of object obj was retrieved by at least* $t+1$ *(correct) nodes. We assume, within* $logSize$ *synchronous cycles from* $c[r]$*, the*

Algorithm 2: SSBFT synchronous recycling; p_i's code

```
constants: indexNum number of indices of recyclable objects;
logSize ∈ {0, ..., indexNum − 2} user-defined bound on the object log size;
variables: obj[indexNum] : array of recyclable objects, e.g., GMRS;
ssbftIndex : an SSBFT index of the current object in use (Algorithm 4);
upon pulse /* signal from global pulse system */ begin
    foreach x ∉ {y mod indexNum : y ∈ {z − logSize, ..., z}} where
      z = indexNum + ssbftIndex.getIndex() do obj[x].recycle();
```

system reaches a state, $c[r + logSize]$, *in which all* $n - t$ *(correct) nodes have retrieved the result of obj at least once.*

Algorithm 2's recycling guarantees are facilitated by an SSBFT multivalued consensus object (Algorithm 3). It helps to decide on a single piece of evidence from all collected ones (regarding recyclability) and Algorithm 4 uses the agreed evidence for updating the index that points to the current entry in the object array. We later add details on Algorithm 2 before proving its correctness (Theorem 4).

Evidence Collection Using an SSBFT (Multivalued) Consensus (Algorithm 3). The SSBFT multivalued consensus protocol returns within $t + 1$ synchronous rounds an agreed non-$\perp$ value as long as at least $t + 1$ nodes proposed that value, *i.e.*, at least one (correct) node proposed that value. As mentioned, wasDelivered() (line 6) provides the input to this consensus protocol. Thus, whenever '1' is decided, at least one (correct) node gets an indication from at least $n - t$ nodes that they have retrieved the results of the current object. This implies that by at least $t + 1$ (correct) nodes have retrieved the results, and, by Assumption 1, all $n - t$ (correct) nodes will retrieve the object result within a known number of synchronous rounds. Then, the object could be recycled. We later add details on Algorithm 3 before proving its correctness.

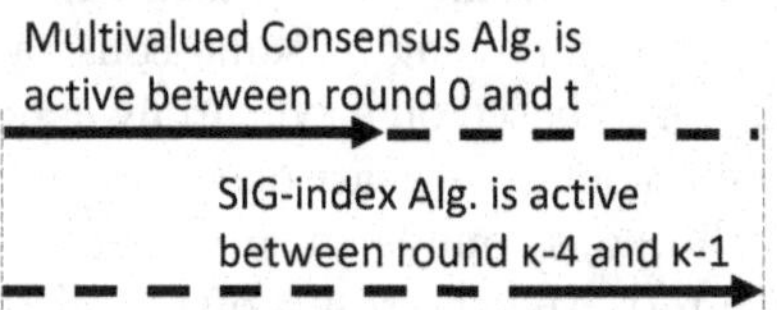

Fig. 2. The solution schedule uses a cycle of $\kappa = \max\{t + 1, logSize\}$ synchronous rounds.

SSBFT Simultaneous Increment-or-Get Index (SIG-Index). Algorithm 4 allows the proposed solution to keep track of the current object index that is currently used as well as facilitate synchronous increments to the index. We call this task *simultaneous increment-or-get index* (SIG-index). During legal executions of Algorithm 4, the (correct) nodes assert their agreement on the index value and update the index according to the result of the agreement on wasDelivered()'s value. We later add details on Algorithm 4 before proving its correctness (Theorem 3).

Algorithm 3: SSBFT synchronous multivalued consensus; p_i's code

```
variables: currentResult stores the most recent result of co;
co a (non-self-stabilizing) BFT (multivalued) consensus object;
interface required:
input() : source of (the proposed values) of the given consensus protocol;
interface provided:
result(): do return(currentResult) // most recent co's decided value;
message structure: ⟨appMsg⟩, where appMsg is the application message, i.e.,
    a message sent by the given consensus protocol;
upon pulse /* signal from global pulse system */ begin
    let M be a message that holds at M[j] the arriving ⟨appMsg_j⟩ messages
        from p_j for the current synchronous round and M' = [⊥, ..., ⊥];
    if clock(κ) = 0 then
        currentResult ← co.result();
        co.restart();
        M' ← co.propose(input()) // for recycling input() ≡ wasDelivered()
    else if clock(cycleSize) ∈ {1, ..., t} then M' ← co.process(M);
    foreach p_j ∈ P do send ⟨M'[j]⟩ to p_j;
```

Scheduling Strategy. As mentioned, our SSBFT multivalued consensus requires $t+1$ synchronous rounds to complete and provide input to Algorithm 4 and $\kappa-(t+1)$ synchronous rounds after that, any (correct) node can recycle the current object (according to the multivalued consensus result), where $\kappa = \max\{t+1, logSize\}$. Thus, Algorithm 4 has to defer its index updates until that time. Fig. 2 depicts this scheduling strategy, which considers the schedule cycle of κ. That is, the SIG-index and multivalued consensus starting points are 0 and $\kappa-4$, respectively. Note that Algorithm 2 does not require scheduling since it accesses the index only via Algorithm 4's interface of SIG-index, see Fig. 1.

Communication Piggybacking and Multiplexing. We use a piggybacking technique to facilitate the spread of the result (decision) values of the recyclable objects. As Fig. 1 illustrates, all communications are piggybacked. Specifically, we consider a meta-message $MSG()$ that has a field for each message sent by all algorithms in Fig. 1. That is, when any of these algorithms is active, its respective field in $MSG()$ includes a non-$\perp$ value. With respect to GMRS's field, $MSG()$ includes the most recent message that GMRS has sent (or currently wishes to send). This piggybacking technique allows the multiplexing of timed and reliable communication (assumed for the recycling mechanism) and fair communication (assumed for the recyclable object).

SSBFT Recycling (Algorithm 2). As mentioned, Algorithm 2 has an array, *obj*[] (line 19), of *indexNum* recyclable objects (line 17). The array size needs to be larger than *logSize* (line 18 and Assumption 1). Algorithm 2's variable set also includes *ssbftIndex*, which is an integer that holds the entry number of the latest object in use. Algorithm 2 accesses the agreed current index via

Algorithm 4: SSBFT synchronous SIG-index; p_i's code

```
constants: I : bound on the number of states an index may have;
variables: index ∈ {0, ..., I − 1} : a local copy of the global object index;
ssbftCO : an SSBFT multivalued consensus object (Algorithm 3) used for
    agreeing on the recycling state, i.e., 1 when there is a need to recycle
    (otherwise 0);
interfaces provided: getIndex() do return index;
message structure: ⟨index⟩: the logical object index;
upon pulse /* signal from global pulse system */ begin
    let M be the arriving ⟨index_j⟩ messages from p_j;
    switch clock(κ) /* consider clock() at the pulse beginning */ do
        case κ − 4 do broadcast ⟨index = getIndex()⟩;
        case κ − 3 do
            let propose := ⊥;
            if ∃v ≠ ⊥ : |{⟨v⟩ ∈ M}| ≥ An − t then propose ← v;
            broadcast ⟨propose⟩;
        case κ − 2 do
            let bit := 0; save ← ⊥;
            if ∃s ≠ ⊥ : |{⟨s⟩ ∈ M}| > n/2 then save ← s;
            if |{⟨save ≠ ⊥⟩ ∈ M}| ≥ An − t then bit ← 1;
            if save = ⊥ then save ← 0;
            broadcast ⟨bit⟩;
        case κ − 1 do
            let inc := 0;
            if ssbftCO.result() then inc ← 1;
            if |{⟨1⟩ ∈ M}| ≥ An − t then index ← (save + inc) mod I;
            else if |{⟨0⟩ ∈ M}| ≥ An − t then index ← 0;
            else index ← rand(save + inc) mod I;
```

ssbftIndex.getIndex(). This lets the code to nullify any entry in *obj*[] that is not *ssbftIndex.getIndex*() or at most *logSize* older than *ssbftIndex.getIndex*(). Theorem 4 shows Algorithm 2's correctness.

SSBFT Synchronous Multivalued Consensus. Algorithm 3 assumes access to a deterministic (non-self-stabilizing) BFT (multivalued) consensus object, *co*, such as the ones proposed by Kowalski and Mostéfaoui [18] or Abraham and Dolev [1], for which completion is guaranteed to occur within $t+1$ synchronous rounds. We list our assumptions regarding the interface to *co* in Definition 2. *Required consensus object interface.* Our solution uses the technique of recomputation of *co*'s floating output [8, Ch. 2.8], where *co* is specified in Definition 2.

Definition 2 (Synchronous BFT Consensus). *Let co be a BFT (non-self-stabilizing) synchronous multivalued consensus that implements the following.*

- *restart() sets co to its initial state.*

- *propose(v) proposes the value v when invoking (or re-invoking) co. The returned value is a message vector, M[], that includes all the messages, M[j], that co wishes to send to node p_j for the current synchrony round.*
- *process(M) runs a single step of co. The returned value is a message vector that includes all the messages that co wishes to send for the current round.*
- result() *returns a non-⊥ results after the completion of co.*

Detailed Description. Algorithm 3's set of variables includes *co* itself (line 24) and the current version of the result, *i.e.*, *currentResult* (line 23). This way, the SSBFT version of *co*'s result can be retrieved via a call to result() (line 28). Algorithm 3 proceeds in synchronous rounds. At the start of any round, node p_i stores all the arriving messages at the message vector M (line 31).

When the clock value is zero (line 32), it is time to start the re-computation of *co*'s result. Thus, Algorithm 3 first stores *co*'s result at $currentResult_i$ (line 33). Then, it restarts *co*'s local state and proposes a new value to *co* (lines 34 and 35). For the recycling solution presented in this paper, the proposed value is retrieved from wasDelivered() (line 6). For the case in which the clock value is not zero (line 36), Algorithm 3 simply lets *co* process the arriving messages of the current round. Both for the case in which the clock value is zero and the case it is not, Algorithm 3 broadcasts *co*'s messages for the current round (line 37).

Correctness Proof. Theorem 2 shows that Algorithm 3 stabilizes within 2κ rounds.

Theorem 2. *Algorithm 3 is an SSBFT deterministic (multivalued) consensus solution that stabilizes within* 2κ *synchronous rounds.*

Proof of Theorem 2. Let R be an execution of Algorithm 3 Within κ synchronous rounds, the system reaches a state $c \in R$ in which $clock(\kappa) = 0$ holds. Immediately after c, every (correct) node, p_i, simultaneously restarts co_i and proposes the input (lines 34 and 35) before sending the needed messages (line 37). Then, for the $t < \kappa$ synchronous rounds that follow, all (correct) nodes simultaneously process the arriving messages and send their replies (line 36 and 37). Thus, within 2κ synchronous rounds from R's start, the system reaches a state $c' \in R$ in which $clock(\kappa) = 0$ holds. Also, in the following synchronous round, all (correct) nodes store *co*'s results. These results are correct due to Definition 2. $\square_{Theorem\ 2}$

SSBFT Simultaneous Increment-or-Get Index. The task of *simultaneous increment-or-get index* (SGI-index) requires all (correct) nodes to maintain identical index values that all nodes can independently retrieve via $getIndex()$. The task assumes that all increments are performed according to the result of a consensus object, *ssbftCO*, such as Algorithm 3. Algorithm 4 presents an SGI-index solution that recovers from disagreement on the index value using RCCs. That is, whenever a (correct) node receives $\mathrm{A}n - t$ reports from other nodes that they have each observed $\mathrm{A}n - t$ identical index values, an agreement on the index value is assumed and the index is incremented according to the most recent result of *ssbftCO*. Otherwise, a randomized strategy is taken for guaranteeing recovery from a disagreement on the index value. Our strategy is inspired by BDH [5].

Detailed Description. Algorithm 4 is active during four clock phases, *i.e.*, $\kappa - 4$ to $\kappa - 1$. Each phase starts with storing all arriving messages (from the previous round) in the array, M (line 44). The first phase broadcasts the local index value (line 46). The second phase lets each node vote on the majority arriving index value, or $\bot$ in case such value was not received (lines 48 to 50). The third phase resolves the case in which there is an arriving non-$\bot$ value, *save*, that received sufficient support when voting during phase two (lines 52 to 55). Specifically, if $save \neq \bot$ exists, then $\langle bit = 1\rangle$ is broadcast. Otherwise, $\langle bit = 0\rangle$ is broadcast. On the fourth phase (lines 58 to 62), the (possibly new) index is set either to be the majority-supported index value of phase two plus *inc* (lines 58 to 60), where *inc* is the output of *ssbftCO*, or (if there was insufficient support) to a randomly chosen output of the RCC (lines 61 and 62).

Correctness Proof. Theorem 3 bounds Algorithm 4's Astabilization time.

Theorem 3. *Algorithm 4 is an SSBFT SGI-index implementation that stabilizes within expected* $\mathcal{O}(1)$ *synchronous rounds.*

Proof Sketch of Theorem 3. Lemma 1 implies that, within $O(1)$ of expected rounds, all (correct) nodes have identical *index* values. Recall that $c[r] \in R$ is *(progress) enabling* if $\exists x \in \{0,1\} : \forall i \in Correct : rand_i = x$ holds at $c[r]$ (Sect. 3). Due to the page limit, the Closure proof appears in [14].

Lemma 1 (Convergence). *Let* $r > \kappa$. *Suppose* $c[r] \in R$ *is (progress) enabling system state (Sect. 3) for which* $clock(\kappa) = \kappa - 1$ *holds. With probability at least* $\min\{p_0, p_1\}$, *all (correct) nodes have the same index at* $c[r+1]$.

Proof Sketch of Lemma 1. The proof is implied by Claims 1, 2, 3 and 4.

Claim 1. *Suppose no (correct)* $p_i \in \mathcal{P}$ *receives* $\langle x\rangle$ *from at least* $An - t$ *different nodes at* $a_i[r]$. *With probability* p_0, *any (correct)* p_j *assigns* 0 *to* $index_j$ *at* $a_j[r]$.

Proof of Claim 1 The proof is implied directly from lines 59 to 62. $\square_{Claim 1}$

Claim 2. *Suppose* $p_i : i \in Correct$ *receives* $\langle 0\rangle$ *from at least* $An - t$ *different nodes at* $a_i[r]$. *Also,* $p_j : j \in Correct$ *receive* $\langle x\rangle$ *from at least* $An - t$ *different nodes at* $a_j[r]$, *where* $i = j$ *may or may not hold. The step* $a_j[r]$ *assigns* 0 *to* $index_j$.

Proof Sketch of Claim 2. Line 61 implies the proof since $x = 0$. $\square_{Claim 2}$

Claim 3. *Suppose* p_i *receives* $\langle 1\rangle$ *from at least* $An - t$ *different nodes at* $a_i[r]$. *At* $c[r]$, $(ssbftCO_i.\mathsf{result}(), save_i) = (ssbftCO_j.\mathsf{result}(), save_j) : i, j \in Correct$.

Proof Sketch of Claim 3. At $c[r]$, $ssbftCO_i$.result() $=$ $ssbftCO_j$.result() holds (BC-agreement). There is $p_k : k \in \mathit{Correct}$ that has sent $\langle 1 \rangle$ at $a[r-1]$. By lines 52 to 54, p_j receives at $a_j[r-1]$ the message $\langle x \rangle$ from at least $An - t$ different nodes, where $x = save_j \neq \bot$. Any (correct) node broadcasts (line 50) either $\bot$ or x at $a[r-2]$. At $a[r-1]$, (correct) nodes receive at most $f < n - 2f$ values that are neither $\bot$ nor $x \neq \bot$. Thus, $save_i = save_j$. $\square_{Claim}3$

Claim 4. *Let* $i, j \in \mathit{Correct}$*. Suppose* p_i *receives* $\langle 1 \rangle$ *from at least* $An-t$ *different nodes at* $a_i[r]$ *and* p_j *receives* $\langle x \rangle$ *from at least* $An - t$ *different nodes at* $a_j[r]$*. With a probability of at least* $\min\{p_0, p_1\}$*,* $a_i[r]$ *and* $a_j[r]$ *assign the same value to* $index_j$*, and resp.,* $index_j$*.*

Proof Sketch of Claim 4. Steps $a[r-1]$ and $a[r]$ independently assign x, and resp., *rand*. With a probability of at least $\min\{p_0, p_1\}$, all (correct) nodes update *index* to 0 or $save + inc$ (Claim 3). $\square_{Claim}$ 4 $\square_{Lemma}1$ $\square_{Theorem}$ 3

Theorem 4. *Algorithm 2 is an SSBFT recycling mechanism (Definition 1) that stabilizes within expected* $\mathcal{O}(\kappa)$ *synchronous rounds.*

Proof of Theorem 4. COR-validity-1 and COR-validity-2 are implied by arguments 1 and 2, respectively. COR-agreement is implied by Argument 3. The stabilization time is due to the underlying algorithms.

Argument 1. *During legal executions, if the value of index is incremented (line* 60*),* $\exists i \in \mathit{Correct}$: wasDelivered() $= 1$ *holds.* By the assumption that wasDelivered() provides the proposed values used by the SSBFT multivalued consensus. The value decided by this SSBFT consensus is used in line 59 determines whether, during legal executions, the value of *index* is incremented module I (line 60), say, from ind_1 to ind_2.

Argument 2. *During legal executions, if* $\forall i \in \mathit{Correct}$: wasDelivered$_i$() $= 1$ *holds, index is incremented.* Implied by Argument 1 and BC-validity.

Argument 3. *During legal executions, the increment of index is followed by the recycling of a single object,* $obj[x]$*, the same for all (correct) nodes.* Line 21 (Algorithm 2) uses the value of *index* as the returned value from *ssbftIndex.getIndex*() when calculating the set $S(ind) = \{y \bmod indexNum : y \in \{indexNum + ind - logSize, \ldots, indexNum + ind\}\}$, where $ind \in \{ind_1, ind_2\}$. For every $x \notin S(ind)$, $obj[x]$.recycle() is invoked. Since $ind_2 = ind_1 + 1 \bmod I$, during legal executions, there is exactly one index, x, that is in $S(ind_1)$ but not in $S(ind_2)$. *I.e.*, $x = (indexNum + ind_1 - logSize) \bmod indexNum$ and only $obj[x]$ is recycled by all (correct) nodes (BC-agreement of the SSBFT consensus). $\square_{Theorem}$ 4

5 Conclusion

We have presented an SSBFT algorithm for object recycling. Our proposal can support an unbounded sequence of SSBFT object instances. The expected stabilization time is in $\mathcal{O}(t)$ synchronous rounds. We believe that this work is preparing the groundwork needed to construct SSBFT Blockchains. As a potential avenue for future research, one could explore deterministic recycling mechanisms, say by utilizing the Dolev and Welch approach to SSBFT clock synchronization [10], to design an SSBFT SIG-index. However, their solution has exponential stabilization time, making it unfeasible in practice.

Acknowledgments. Supported by VINNOVA, the CyReV project (2019-03071).

References

1. Abraham, I., Dolev, D.: Byzantine agreement with optimal early stopping, optimal resilience and polynomial complexity. In: STOC, pp. 605–614. ACM (2015)
2. Afek, Y., Kutten, S., Yung, M.: Memory-efficient self stabilizing protocols for general networks. In: van Leeuwen, J., Santoro, N. (eds.) WDAG 1990. LNCS, vol. 486, pp. 15–28. Springer, Heidelberg (1991). https://doi.org/10.1007/3-540-54099-7_2
3. Altisen, K., Devismes, S., Dubois, S., Petit, F.: Introduction to Distributed Self-Stabilizing Algorithms. Morgan & Claypool Publishers (2019)
4. Awerbuch, B., Patt-Shamir, B., Varghese, G., Dolev, S.: Self-stabilization by local checking and global reset. In: Tel, G., Vitányi, P. (eds.) WDAG 1994. LNCS, vol. 857, pp. 326–339. Springer, Heidelberg (1994). https://doi.org/10.1007/bfb0020443
5. Ben-Or, M., Dolev, D., Hoch, E.N.: Fast self-stabilizing Byzantine tolerant digital clock synchronization. In: PODC, pp. 385–394. ACM (2008)
6. Bracha, G., Toueg, S.: Resilient consensus protocols. In: PODC, pp. 12–26. ACM (1983)
7. Dijkstra, E.W.: Self-stabilizing systems in spite of distributed control. Commun. ACM **17**(11), 643–644 (1974)
8. Dolev, S.: Self-stabilization. MIT Press, Cambridge (2000)
9. Dolev, S., Petig, T., Schiller, E.M.: Self-stabilizing and private distributed shared atomic memory in seldomly fair message passing networks. Algorithmica **85**(1), 216–276 (2023)
10. Dolev, S., Welch, J.L.: Self-stabilizing clock synchronization in the presence of Byzantine faults. J. ACM **51**(5), 780–799 (2004)
11. Duvignau, R., Raynal, M., Schiller, E.M.: Self-stabilizing Byzantine fault-tolerant repeated reliable broadcast. Theor. Comput. Sci. **114070** (2023)
12. Georgiou, C., Lundström, O., Schiller, E.M.: Self-stabilizing snapshot objects for asynchronous failure-prone networked systems. In: PODC, pp. 209–211. ACM (2019)
13. Georgiou, C., Marcoullis, I., Raynal, M., Schiller, E.M.: Loosely-self-stabilizing byzantine-tolerant binary consensus for signature-free message-passing systems. In: Echihabi, K., Meyer, R. (eds.) NETYS 2021. LNCS, vol. 12754, pp. 36–53. Springer, Cham (2021). https://doi.org/10.1007/978-3-030-91014-3_3
14. Georgiou, C., Raynal, M., Schiller, E.M.: Self-stabilizing Byzantine-tolerant recycling. CoRR, arXiv:2307.14801 (2023)
15. Lundström, O., Raynal, M., Schiller, E.M.: Self-stabilizing multivalued consensus in asynchronous crash-prone systems. In: EDCC, pp. 111–118. IEEE (2021)
16. Lundström, O., Raynal, M., Schiller, E.M.: Brief announcement: self-stabilizing total-order broadcast. In: Devismes, S., Petit, F., Altisen, K., Di Luna, G.A., Fernandez Anta, A. (eds.) SSS 2022. LNCS, vol. 13751, pp. 358–363. Springer, Cham (2022). https://doi.org/10.1007/978-3-031-21017-4_27

17. Katz, S., Perry, K.J.: Self-stabilizing extensions for message-passing systems. In: PODC, pp. 91–101. ACM (1990)
18. Kowalski, D.R., Mostéfaoui, A.: Synchronous Byzantine agreement with nearly a cubic number of communication bits. In: PODC, pp. 84–91. ACM (2013)
19. Lamport, L., Shostak, R.E., Pease, M.C.: The Byzantine generals problem. ACM Trans. Program. Lang. Syst. **4**(3), 382–401 (1982)
20. Lundström, O., Raynal, M., M. Schiller, E.: Self-stabilizing uniform reliable broadcast. In: Georgiou, C., Majumdar, R. (eds.) NETYS 2020. LNCS, vol. 12129, pp. 296–313. Springer, Cham (2021). https://doi.org/10.1007/978-3-030-67087-0_19
21. Lundström, O., Raynal, M., Schiller, E.M.: Self-stabilizing indulgent zero-degrading binary consensus. In: ICDCN, pp. 106–115 (2021)
22. Mostéfaoui, A., Moumen, H., Raynal, M.: Signature-free asynchronous Byzantine consensus with $t < n/3$, $O(n^2)$ messages. In: PODC, pp. 2–9. ACM (2014)
23. Oliveira, T., Mendes, R., Bessani, A.N.: Exploring key-value stores in multi-writer Byzantine-resilient register emulations. In: OPODIS, vol. 70, pp. 30:1–30:17 (2016)
24. Pease, M.C., Shostak, R.E., Lamport, L.: Reaching agreement in the presence of faults. J. ACM **27**(2), 228–234 (1980)
25. Plainfossé, D., Shapiro, M.: A survey of distributed garbage collection techniques. In: Baler, H.G. (ed.) IWMM 1995. LNCS, vol. 986, pp. 211–249. Springer, Heidelberg (1995). https://doi.org/10.1007/3-540-60368-9_26
26. Rabin, M.O.: Randomized Byzantine generals. In: FOCS, pp. 403–409 (1983)
27. Raynal, M.: Fault-Tolerant Message-Passing Distributed Systems. Springer, Heidelberg (2018). https://doi.org/10.1007/978-3-319-94141-7
28. Toueg, S.: Randomized Byzantine agreements. In: PODC, pp. 163–178. ACM (1984)
29. Veiga, L., Ferreira, P.: Asynchronous complete distributed garbage collection. In: IPDPS. IEEE Computer Society (2005)

Do Not Trust in Numbers: Practical Distributed Cryptography with General Trust

Orestis Alpos(✉) and Christian Cachin

University of Bern, Bern, Switzerland
{orestis.alpos,christian.cachin}@unibe.ch

Abstract. In *distributed cryptography* independent parties jointly perform some cryptographic task. In the last decade distributed cryptography has been receiving more attention than ever. Distributed systems power almost all applications, blockchains are becoming prominent, and, consequently, numerous practical and efficient distributed cryptographic primitives are being deployed.

The failure models of current distributed cryptographic systems, however, lack expressibility. Assumptions are only stated through numbers of parties, thus reducing this to *threshold cryptography*, where all parties are treated as identical and correlations cannot be described. Distributed cryptography does not have to be threshold-based. With *general distributed cryptography* the *authorized sets*, the sets of parties that are sufficient to perform some task, can be arbitrary, and are usually modeled by the abstract notion of a general *access structure*.

Although the necessity for general distributed cryptography has been recognized long ago and many schemes have been explored in theory, relevant practical aspects remain opaque. It is unclear how the user specifies a trust structure efficiently or how this is encoded within a scheme, for example. More importantly, implementations and benchmarks do not exist, hence the efficiency of the schemes is not known.

Our work fills this gap. We show how an administrator can intuitively describe the access structure as a Boolean formula. This is then converted into encodings suitable for cryptographic primitives, specifically, into a tree data structure and a monotone span program. We focus on three general distributed cryptographic schemes: *verifiable secret sharing*, *common coin*, and *distributed signatures*. For each one we give the appropriate formalization and security definition in the general-trust setting. We implement the schemes and assess their efficiency against their threshold counterparts. Our results suggest that the general distributed schemes can offer richer expressibility at no or insignificant extra cost. Thus, they are appropriate and ready for practical deployment.

Keywords: Distributed cryptography · Monotone span programs · Digital signature · Verifiable secret sharing · Common coin

1 Introduction

1.1 Motivation

Throughout the last decade, largely due to the advent of blockchains, there has been an ever-increasing interest in distributed systems and practical cryptographic primitives.

S. Dolev and B. Schieber (Eds.): SSS 2023, LNCS 14310, pp. 536–551, 2023.
https://doi.org/10.1007/978-3-031-44274-2_40

Naturally, the type of cryptography most suitable for distributed systems is distributed cryptography: independent parties jointly hold a secret key and perform some cryptographic task. Many deployments of distributed cryptography exist today. Threshold signature schemes [8, 17] distribute the signing power among a set of parties. They have been used in state-machine replication (SMR) protocols, where they serve as unique and constant-size vote certificates [33,47]. Furthermore, random-beacon and common-coin schemes [11, 15] provide a source of reliable and distributed randomness. Multiparty computation (MPC) is a cryptographic tool that enables a group of parties to compute a function of their private inputs. As it finds applications in private [7] and sensitive computations [30], security is of paramount importance.

One can thus say that we are in the era of distributed cryptography. However, all currently deployed distributed-cryptographic schemes express their trust assumptions through a number, with a threshold, hence reducing to the setting of *threshold cryptography*, where all parties may misbehave with the same probability. Distributed cryptography does not have to be threshold-based. In *general distributed cryptography* the *authorized sets*, the sets of parties sufficient to perform the task, can be arbitrary. Our position is that general distributed cryptography is essential for distributed systems.

Increasing Systems Resilience and Security. First, general distributed cryptography has the capacity to increase the resilience of a system, as failures are, in practice, always correlated [46]. Cyberattacks, exploitation of specific implementation vulnerabilities, zero-day attacks, and so on very seldom affect all parties in an identical way—they often target a specific operating systems or flavor of it, a specific hardware vendor, or a specific software version. In another example, blockchain nodes are typically hosted by cloud providers or mining farms, hence failures are correlated there as well. Such failure correlations are known and have been observed; they can be expressed in a system that supports general trust, significantly increasing resilience and security.

Facilitating Personal Assumptions and Sybil Resistance. Some works in the area of distributed systems generalize trust assumptions in yet another dimension: they allow each party to specify its own. The consensus protocol of Stellar [29] allows each party to specify the access structure of its choice, which can consist of arbitrary sets and nested thresholds. Similarly, the consensus protocol implemented by Ripple [41] allows each party to choose who it trusts and communicates with. In both networks, the resulting representation of trust in the system, obtained when the trust assumptions of all parties are considered together, can only be expressed as a generalized structure. Hence, current threshold-cryptographic schemes cannot be integrated or used on top of these networks.

1.2 State of the Art

We focus on three important distributed-cryptographic primitives for distributed protocols.

Verifiable secret sharing. *Secret sharing* [42] allows a dealer to share a secret in a way that only authorized sets can later reconstruct it. *Verifiable Secret Sharing (VSS)* [23,37] additionally allows the parties to verify their shares against a malicious dealer.

Common coin. A *common coin* [11,38] scheme allows a set of parties to calculate a pseudorandom function $\mathcal{U}$, mapping coin names C to uniformly random bits $\mathcal{U}(C) \in \{0, 1\}$ in a distributed way.
Distributed signatures. We additionally describe, implement, and benchmark a general distributed-signature scheme [8,17] based on BLS signatures [9]. However, due to space limitations, this scheme and its evaluation are shown only in the full version of this paper [3].

The generalization of threshold-cryptographic schemes to any linear access structure is known and typically employs Monotone Span Programs (MSP) [27], a linear-algebraic model of computation. General schemes using the MSP have already been described in theory [14,22,32]. However, no implementations exist, despite the merit of general distributed cryptography. In our point of view, the reasons are the following.

- Essential implementation details are missing, and questions related to the usability of general schemes have never been answered in a real system. How can the trust assumptions be efficiently encoded? Previous general distributed schemes assume the MSP is given to all algorithms, but how is this built from the trust assumptions?
- Some distributed cryptographic schemes, such as VSS and common-coin schemes, have been described in models weaker than the MSP. Can we describe and prove all schemes of interest in a unified language?
- Most importantly, implementations and benchmarks do not exist, hence the efficiency of general schemes is not known. What is the concrete efficiency of the MSP? How does a generalized scheme compare to its threshold counterpart? How much efficiency needs to be "sacrificed" in order to support general trust?

1.3 Contributions

The goal of this work is to bridge the gap between theory and practice by answering the aforementioned questions.

- We explore intuitive ways for an administrator to specify the trust assumption. This is then converted into two different encodings, a tree and an MSP, the former used for checking whether a set of parties is authorized and the latter for all algebraic operations. An algorithm and its efficiency are shown for building the MSP.
- We first recall a general VSS scheme, and then extend the common-coin construction of Cachin, Kursawe, and Shoup [11] into the general-trust model. The schemes are in the MSP model, and we provide security definitions and proofs that are appropriate for the general-trust setting.
- We implement and benchmark the aforementioned schemes, both threshold and general versions. We assess the efficiency of the general schemes and provide insights on the observed behavior. The benchmarks include multiple trust assumptions, thereby exploring how they affect the efficiency of the schemes.

1.4 Related Work

General Distributed Cryptography. Secret sharing over arbitrary access structures has been extensively studied in theory. The first scheme is presented by Ito, Saito, and Nishizeki [26], where the secret is shared independently for every authorized set. Benaloh and Leichter [6] use monotone Boolean formulas to express the access structure and introduce a recursive secret-sharing construction. Gennaro presents a general VSS scheme [22], where trust is specified as Boolean formulas in disjunctive normal form. Choudhury presents general asynchronous VSS and common-coin schemes secure against a computationally-unbounded adversary [13].

Later, the *Monotone Span Program (MSP)* is introduced [27] as a linear-algebraic model of computation. In the information-theoretic setting, Cramer, Damgård, and Maurer [14] construct a VSS scheme that uses MSPs. A general VSS scheme is also presented by Mashhadi, Dehkordi, and Kiamari [32], which requires multiparty computation for share verification. A different line of work encodes the access structure using a *vector-space secret-sharing scheme* [10], a special case of an MSP where each party owns exactly one row. Specifically, Herranz and Sáez [24] construct a VSS scheme based on Pedersen's VSS [37]. Distributed key generation schemes have also been described on vector-space secret sharing [16].

Common Coin Schemes. Common coin schemes (or *random beacons* [15,18]) model randomness produced in a distributed way. Multiple threshold schemes have been proposed in the literature [11,15,38] and are used in practice [18]. Raikwar and Gligoroski [39] present an overview. Our work extends the common-coin scheme of Cachin, Kursawe, and Shoup [11]. The same threshold construction appears in DiSE [1, Figure 6], where it is modeled as a DPRF [34]. The scheme outputs an unbiased value.

Lower Bounds for General Secret Sharing. Superpolynomial lower bounds are known for MSPs [4,40] and general secret sharing [28]. As the focus of this work is on practical aspects, we assume that the administrator can, in the first place, efficiently describe the trust assumptions, either as a collection of sets or as a Boolean formula. Arguably, access structures of practical interest fall in this category. Moreover, it is known that MSPs are more powerful than Boolean formulas and circuits. Babai, Gál, and Wigderson [4] prove the existence of monotone Boolean functions that can be computed by a linear-size MSP but only by exponential-size monotone Boolean formulas. In those cases the MSP can be directly plugged into a generalized scheme.

2 Background and Model

Notation. A bold symbol $\boldsymbol{a}$ denotes a vector. We avoid distinguishing between $\boldsymbol{a}$ and $\boldsymbol{a}^\intercal$, that is, $\boldsymbol{a}$ denotes both a row and a column vector. Moreover, for vectors $\boldsymbol{a} \in \mathcal{K}^{|a|}$ and $\boldsymbol{b} \in \mathcal{K}^{|b|}$, where $\mathcal{K}$ is a field, $\boldsymbol{a} \| \boldsymbol{b} \in \mathcal{K}^{|a|+|b|}$ denotes concatenation, and a_i is short for $\boldsymbol{a}[i]$. Notation $x \xleftarrow{\$} S$ means x is chosen uniformly at random from set S. The set of all parties is $\mathcal{P} = \{p_1, \ldots, p_n\}$. E.w.n.p. means "except with negligible probability".

Adversary Structures and Access Structures. An *adversary structure* $\mathcal{F}$ is a collection of all *unauthorized* subsets of $\mathcal{P}$, and an *access structure (AS)* $\mathcal{A}$ is a collection of all *authorized* subsets of $\mathcal{P}$. Both are monotone. Any subset of an unauthorized set is unauthorized, i.e., if $F \in \mathcal{F}$ and $B \subset F$, then $B \in \mathcal{F}$, and any superset of an authorized set is authorized, i.e., if $A \in \mathcal{A}$ and $C \supset A$, then $C \in \mathcal{A}$. As in the most general case [25] we assume that any set not in the access structure can be corrupted by the adversary, that is, the adversary structure and the access structure are the complement of each other. We say that $\mathcal{F}$ is a Q^2 *adversary structure* if no two sets in $\mathcal{F}$ cover the whole $\mathcal{P}$.

In all schemes we assume that the adversary structure $\mathcal{F}$, implied by the access structure $\mathcal{A}$, is a Q^2 adversary structure. The adversary is Byzantine and static, and corrupts a set $F \in \mathcal{F}$ which is, w.l.o.g, maximally unauthorized, i.e., there is no $F' \in \mathcal{F}$ such that $F' \supset F$.

Monotone Span Programs [27]. Given a finite field $\mathcal{K}$, an MSP is a tuple (M, ρ), where M is an $m \times d$ matrix over $\mathcal{K}$ and ρ is a surjective function $\{1, \dots, m\} \rightarrow \mathcal{P}$ that labels each row of M with a party. We say that party p_i *owns* row $j \in \{1, \dots, m\}$ if $\rho(j) = p_i$. The *size* of the MSP is m, the number of its rows. The fixed vector $\mathbf{e}_1 = [1, 0, \dots, 0] \in \mathcal{K}^d$ is called the *target vector*. For any set $A \subseteq \mathcal{P}$, define M_A to be the $m_A \times d$ matrix obtained from M by keeping only the rows owned by parties in A, i.e., rows j with $\rho(j) \in A$. Let $M_A^{\intercal}$ denote the transpose of M_A and $Im(M_A^{\intercal})$ the span of the rows of M_A. We say that the MSP *accepts* A if the rows of M_A span $\mathbf{e}_1$, i.e., $\mathbf{e}_1 \in Im(M_A^{\intercal})$. Equivalently, there is a *recombination vector* $\boldsymbol{\lambda}_A$ such that $\boldsymbol{\lambda}_A M_A = \mathbf{e}_1$. Otherwise, the MSP *rejects* A. For any access structure $\mathcal{A}$, we say that an MSP *accepts* $\mathcal{A}$ if it accepts exactly the authorized sets $A \in \mathcal{A}$. It has been proven that each MSP accepts exactly one monotone access structure and each monotone access structure can be expressed in terms of an MSP [5,27].

Algorithm 1 (Linear secret-sharing scheme). *A linear secret-sharing scheme (LSSS) over a finite field $\mathcal{K}$ shares a secret $x \in \mathcal{K}$ using a* coefficient vector $\boldsymbol{r}$, *in such a way that every share is a linear combination of x and the entries of $\boldsymbol{r}$. Linear secret-sharing schemes are equivalent to monotone span programs [5,27]. We formalize an LSSS as two algorithms, Share() and Reconstruct().*

1. *Share(x). Choose uniformly at random $d-1$ elements $r_2, \dots, r_d$ from $\mathcal{K}$ and define the* coefficient vector $\boldsymbol{r} = (x, r_2, \dots, r_d)$. *Calculate the secret shares $\boldsymbol{x} = (x_1, \dots, x_m) = M\boldsymbol{r}$. Each x_j, with $j \in [1, m]$, belongs to party $p_i = \rho(j)$. Hence, p_i receives in total m_j shares, where m_j is the number of MSP rows owned by p_i.*
2. *Reconstruct($A, \boldsymbol{x}_A$). To reconstruct the secret given an authorized set A and the shares $\boldsymbol{x}_A$ of parties in A, find the recombination vector $\boldsymbol{\lambda}_A$ and compute the secret as $\boldsymbol{\lambda}_A \boldsymbol{x}_A$.*

Computational Assumptions. Let $G = \langle g \rangle$ be a group of prime order q and $x_0 \xleftarrow{\$} \{0, \dots, q-1\}$. The *Discrete Logarithm (DL)* assumption is that no efficient probabilistic algorithm, given $g_0 = g^{x_0} \in G$, can compute x_0, e.w.n.p. The *Computational Diffie-Hellman (CDH)* assumption is that no efficient probabilistic algorithm, given $g, \hat{g}, g_0 \in G$, where $\hat{g} \xleftarrow{\$} G$ and $g_0 = g^{x_0}$, can compute $\hat{g}_0 = \hat{g}^{x_0}$, e.w.n.p.

3 Specifying and Encoding the Trust Assumptions

An important aspect concerning the implementation and deployment of general distributed cryptography is specifying the Access Structure (AS). We require a solution that is intuitive, so that users or administrators can easily specify it, that facilitates the necessary algebraic operations, such as computing and recombining secret shares, and in the same time offers an efficient way to check whether a given set is authorized.

The administrator first specifies the access structure as a monotone Boolean formula, which consists of *and*, *or*, and *threshold* operators. A *threshold* operator $\Theta_k^K(q_1,\ldots,q_K)$ specifies that any subset of $\{q_1,\ldots,q_K\}$ with cardinality at least k is authorized, where each q_i can be a party identifier or a nested operator (observe that the *and* and *or* operators are special cases of this). This is an intuitive format and can be easily specified in JSON format, as shown in the examples that follow.

The next step is to internally encode the access structure within a scheme. For this we use two different encodings. First, the Boolean formula is encoded as a tree, where a node represents an operator and its children are the operands. The size of the tree is linear in the size of the Boolean formula, and checking whether a set is authorized takes time linear in the size of the tree. The second is a an MSP, which is the basis for all our general distributed cryptographic primitives. The MSP is directly constructed from the JSON-encoded Boolean formula, using the following algorithm.

Building the MSP from a Monotone Boolean Formula [2,35]. We now describe how an MSP can be constructed given a monotone Boolean formula. The details of the algorithm can be found in the full version of this paper [3]. We use a recursive insertion-based algorithm. The main observation is that the t-of-n threshold access structure is encoded by an MSP $\mathcal{M} = (M,\rho)$ over finite field $\mathcal{K}$, with M being the $n \times t$ Vandermonde matrix $V(n,t)$. The algorithm parses the Boolean formula as a sequence of nested *threshold* operators (*and* and *or* are special cases of *threshold*). Starting from the outermost operator, it constructs the Vandermonde matrix that implements it and then recursively performs *insertions* for the nested threshold operators. In a high level, an *insertion* replaces a row of M with a second MSP M' (which encodes the nested operator) and pads with 0 the initial matrix M, in case M' is wider than M. If the Boolean formula includes in total c operators in the form $\Theta_{d_i}^{m_i}$, then the final matrix M of the MSP that encodes it has $m = \sum_1^c m_i - c + 1$ rows and $d = \sum_1^c d_i - c + 1$ columns, hence size linear in the size of the formula.

Example 1. Recent work [20] presents the example of an *unbalanced-AS*[1], where n parties in $\mathcal{P}$ are distributed into two organizations $\mathcal{P}_1$ and $\mathcal{P}_2$, and the adversary is expected to be within one of the organizations, making it easier to corrupt parties from that organization. They specify this with two thresholds, t and k, and allow the adversary to corrupt at most t parties from $\mathcal{P}$ and in the same time at most k parties from $\mathcal{P}_1$ or $\mathcal{P}_2$. For example, we can set $t = \lfloor n/2 \rfloor$ and $k = \lfloor t/2 \rfloor - 1$. Let $n = 9$, $\mathcal{P}_1 = \{p_1,\ldots,p_5\}$, $\mathcal{P}_2 = \{p_6,\ldots,p_9\}$, $t = 4$, and $k = 1$. The access structure (taken as the complement of the adversary structure) is $\mathcal{A} = \{A \subset \mathcal{P} : |A| > 4 \vee (|A \cap \mathcal{P}_1| > 1 \wedge |A \cap \mathcal{P}_2| > 1)\}$. In terms of a monotone Boolean formula, this can be written as

[1] This is a special case of bipartite AS [36].

```
{ "select": 6,
  "out-of": [
    {"select": 2, "out-of": ["Blockdaemon1", "Blockdaemon2", "Blockdaemon3"]},
    {"select": 2, "out-of": ["SDF1", "SDF2", "SDF3"]},
    {"select": 2, "out-of": ["WirexSingapore", "WirexUK", "WirexUS"]},
    {"select": 2, "out-of": ["CoinqvestFinland", "CoinqvestHongKong", "CoinqvestGermany"]},
    {"select": 2, "out-of": ["SatoshiPayUS", "SatoshiPaySG", "SatoshiPayDE"]},
    {"select": 2, "out-of": ["FranklinTempleton1", "FranklinTempleton2", "FranklinTempleton3"]},
    {"select": 3, "out-of": ["LOBSTR1", "LOBSTR2", "LOBSTR3", "LOBSTR4", "LOBSTR5"]},
    {"select": 2, "out-of": ["Hercules", "Lyra", "Boötes"]}
]}
```

Fig. 1. A JSON file that specifies the access structure of the SDF1 validator in the live Stellar blockchain (we use the literals returned by Stellar as party identifiers).

$F_{\mathcal{A}} = \Theta_5^9(\mathcal{P}) \vee \big(\Theta_2^5(\mathcal{P}_1) \wedge \Theta_2^4(\mathcal{P}_2)\big)$. The MSP constructed with the given algorithm has $m = 2n$ rows and $d = t + 2k + 2 = n - 1$ columns.

Example 2. Another classical general AS from the field of distributed systems is the *M-Grid* [31]. Here $n = k^2$ parties are arranged in a $k \times k$ grid and up to $b = k - 1$ Byzantine parties are tolerated. An authorized set consists of any t rows and t columns, where $t = \lceil \sqrt{b/2 + 1} \rceil$. Let us set $n = 16$ and, hence, $k = 4$, $b = 3$, and $t = 2$. This means that and any two rows and two columns (twelve parties in total) make an authorized set. The Boolean formula that describes this AS is $F_{\mathcal{A}} = \Theta_2^4\left(\Theta_4^4(R_1), \Theta_4^4(R_2), \Theta_4^4(R_3), \Theta_4^4(R_4)\right) \wedge \Theta_2^4\left(\Theta_4^4(C_1), \Theta_4^4(C_2), \Theta_4^4(C_3), \Theta_4^4(C_4)\right)$, where R_ℓ and C_ℓ denote the sets of parties at row and column ℓ, respectively. We call this access structure the *grid-AS*.

Example 3. The Stellar blockchain supports general trust assumptions for consensus [29]. Each party can specify its own access structure, which is composed of nested threshold operators. We extract[2] the AS of one Stellar validator and show in Fig. 1 a JSON file that can be used in our general schemes. It can be directly translated into an MSP, enabling general distributed cryptography in or on top of the blockchain of Stellar. The MSP constructed with the presented algorithm has $m = 25$ rows and $d = 15$ columns.

4 Verifiable Secret Sharing

In this section we recall a general Verifiable Secret Sharing (VSS) scheme [24]. It generalizes Pedersen's VSS [23,37] to the general setting.

Security. The security of a general VSS scheme is formalized by the following properties (in analogy with the threshold setting [23,37]).

1. Completeness. If the dealer is not disqualified, then all honest parties complete the sharing phase and can then reconstruct the secret.

[2] https://www.stellarbeat.io/, https://api.stellarbeat.io/docs/.

2. Correctness. For any authorized sets A_1 and A_2 that have accepted their shares and reconstruct secrets z_1 and z_2, respectively, it holds that $z_1 = z_2$, e.w.n.p. Moreover, if the dealer is honest, then $z_1 = z_2 = s$.
3. Privacy. Any unauthorized set F has no information about the secret.

The Scheme. The scheme is synchronous and uses the same communication pattern as the standard VSS protocols [23,37]. Hence complaints are delivered by all honest parties within a known time bound, and we assume a broadcast channel, to which all parties have access. Let $G = \langle g \rangle$ be a group of large prime order q and $h \overset{\$}{\leftarrow} G$.

1. *Share(x).* The dealer uses Algorithm 1 to compute the *secret-shares* $\boldsymbol{x} = (x_1, \ldots, x_m) = LSSS.Share(x)$. The dealer also chooses a random value $x' \in \mathbb{Z}_q$ and computes the *random-shares* $\boldsymbol{x}' = (x'_1, \ldots, x'_m) = LSSS.Share(x')$. Let $\boldsymbol{r} = (x, r_2, \ldots, r_d)$ and $\boldsymbol{r}' = (x', r'_2, \ldots, r'_d)$ be the corresponding coefficient vectors. The dealer computes commitments to the coefficients $C_1 = g^x h^{x'} \in G$ and $C_\ell = g^{r_\ell} h^{r'_\ell} \in G$, for $\ell = 2, \ldots d$, and broadcasts them. The *indexed share* (j, x_j, x'_j) is given to party $p_i = \rho(j)$. Index j is included because each p_i may receive more than one such tuples, if it owns more than one row in the MSP. We call a *sharing* the set of all indexed shares $X_i = \{(j, x_j, x'_j) \mid \rho(j) = p_i\}$ received by party p_i.
2. *Verify(j, x_j, x'_j).* For each indexed share $(j, x_j, x'_j) \in X_i$, party p_i verifies that
$$g^{x_j} h^{x'_j} = \prod_{\ell=1}^{d} C_\ell^{M_{j\ell}}, \tag{1}$$
where M_j is the j-th row-vector of M and $M_{j\ell}$, for $\ell \in \{1, \ldots d\}$, are its entries.
3. *Complain().* Complaints are handled exactly as in the standard version [23]. Party p_i broadcasts a *complaint* against the dealer for every invalid share. The dealer is disqualified if a complaint is delivered, for which the dealer fails to reveal valid shares.
4. *Reconstruct(A, X_A).* Given the sharings $X_A = \{(j, x_j, x'_j) \mid \rho(j) \in A\}$ of an authorized set A, a combiner party first verifies the correctness of each share. If a share is found to be invalid, reconstruction is aborted. The combiner constructs the vector $\boldsymbol{x}_A = [x_{j_1}, \ldots, x_{j_{m_A}}]$, consisting of the m_A secret-shares of parties in A, and, using Algorithm 1, returns $LSSS.Reconstruct(A, \boldsymbol{x}_A)$.

Theorem 1. *Under the discrete logarithm assumption for group G, the above* general VSS *scheme is secure (satisfies completeness, correctness, and privacy).*

A proof can be found in the full version of this paper [3]. Completeness holds by construction of the scheme, while correctness reduces to the discrete-log assumption. For the privacy property, we pick arbitrary secrets x and $\tilde{x}$ and show that the adversary cannot distinguish between two executions with secret x and $\tilde{x}$.

5 Common Coin

The scheme extends the threshold coin scheme of Cachin, Kursawe, and Shoup [11] to accept any general access structure. It works on a group $G = \langle g \rangle$ of prime order q and uses the following cryptographic hash functions: $H : \{0,1\}^* \rightarrow G$, $H' : G^6 \rightarrow \mathbb{Z}_q$, and $H'' : G \rightarrow \{0,1\}$. The first two, H and H', are modeled as random oracles. The idea is that a secret value $x \in \mathbb{Z}_q$ uniquely defines the value $\mathcal{U}(C)$ of a publicly-known coin name C as follows: hash C to get an element $\tilde{g} = H(C) \in G$, let $\tilde{g}_0 = \tilde{g}^x \in G$, and define $\mathcal{U}(C) = H''(\tilde{g}_0)$. The value x is secret-shared among $\mathcal{P}$ and unknown to any party. Parties can create coin shares using their secret shares. Any party that receives enough coin shares can then obtain $\tilde{g}_0$ by interpolating x in the exponent.

Security. The security of a general common-coin scheme is captured by the following properties (analogous to threshold common coins [11]).

1. Robustness. The adversary cannot produce coin C and valid coin shares for an authorized set, s.t. and their combination outputs value different from $\mathcal{U}(C)$, e.w.n.p.
2. Unpredictability. It is defined through the following game. The adversary corrupts, w.l.o.g, a maximally unauthorized set F. It interacts with honest parties according to the scheme and in the end outputs a coin C, which was not submitted for coin-share generation to *any* honest party, as well as a coin-value prediction $b \in \{0,1\}$. The probability that $\mathcal{U}(C) = b$ should not be significantly different from $1/2$.

The Scheme. It consists of the following algorithms.

1. *KeyGen()*. A dealer chooses uniformly an $x \in \mathbb{Z}_q$ and shares it among $\mathcal{P}$ using the MSP-based LSSS from Algorithm 1, i.e., $\boldsymbol{x} = (x_1, \ldots, x_m) = LSSS.Share(x)$. The secret key x is destroyed after it is shared. We call a *sharing* the set of all key shares $X_i = \{(j, x_j) \mid \rho(j) = p_i\}$ received by party p_i. The verification keys $g_0 = g^x$ and $g_j = g^{x_j}$, for $1 \leq j \leq m$, are made public.
2. *CoinShareGenerate(C)*. For coin C, party p_i calculates $\tilde{g} = H(C)$ and generates a coin share $\tilde{g}_j = \tilde{g}^{x_j}$ for each key share $(j, x_j) \in X_i$. Party p_i also generates a *proof of correctness* for each coin share, i.e., a proof that $\log_{\tilde{g}} \tilde{g}_j = \log_g g_j$. This is the Chaum-Perdersen proof of equality of discrete logarithms [12] collapsed into a non-interactive proof using the Fiat-Shamir heuristic [21]. For every coin share $\tilde{g}_j$ a valid proof is a pair $(c_j, z_j) \in \mathbb{Z}_q \times \mathbb{Z}_q$, such that

$$c_j = H'(g, g_j, h_j, \tilde{g}, \tilde{g}_j, \tilde{h}_j), \text{ where } h_j = g^{z_j}/g_j^{c_j} \text{ and } \tilde{h}_j = \tilde{g}^{z_j}/\tilde{g}_j^{c_j}. \quad (2)$$

   Party p_i computes such a proof for coin share $\tilde{g}_j$ by choosing s_j at random, computing $h_j = g^{s_j}$, $\tilde{h}_j = \tilde{g}^{s_j}$, obtaining c_j as in (2), and setting $z_j = s_j + x_j c_j$.
3. *CoinShareVerify($C, \tilde{g}_j, (c_j, z_j)$)*. Verify the proof above.
4. *CoinShareCombine()*. Each party sends its coin sharing $\{(j, \tilde{g}_j, c_j, z_j) \mid \rho(j) = p_i\}$ to a designated combiner. Once valid coin shares from an authorized set A have been received, find the recombination vector $\boldsymbol{\lambda}_A$ for set A and calculate $\tilde{g}_0 = \tilde{g}^x$ as

$$\tilde{g}_0 = \prod_{j \mid \rho(j) \in A} \tilde{g}_j^{\boldsymbol{\lambda}_A[j]}, \quad (3)$$

   where the set $\{j \mid \rho(j) \in A\}$ denotes the MSP indexes owned by parties in A. The combiner outputs $H''(\tilde{g}_0)$.

Theorem 2. *In the random oracle model, the above* general common coin *scheme is secure (robust and unpredictable) under the assumption that CDH is hard in G.*

The proof is presented in the full version of this paper [3]. In a high level, we assume an adversary that can predict the value of a coin with non-negligible probability and show how to use this adversary to solve the CDH problem in G. The proof handles specific issues that arise from the general access structures. Specifically, the simulator, given the shares of F, has to create valid shares for other parties. As opposed to the threshold case, it can be the case that the shares of F, together with the secret x, do not fully determine all other shares.

6 Evaluation

In this section we compare the polynomial-based and MSP-based encodings, and benchmark the presented schemes on multiple general trust assumptions. To this goal, we benchmark each scheme on four configurations, resulting from different combinations of encoding and access structure (AS), as seen in Table 1. Notice that the first two describe the same threshold AS, encoded once by a polynomial and once an MSP. With the first two configurations we investigate the practical difference between polynomial-based and MSP-based encoding of the same access structure. The last three configurations measure the efficiency we sacrifice for more powerful and expressive AS.

Table 1. Evaluated configurations and corresponding MSP dimensions. Configurations with general AS encode it as an MSP (necessary for algebraic operations, such as sharing and reconstruction) and as a tree (for checking whether a set of parties is authorized).

Configuration	Encoding	Access Structure	MSP dimensions	
			m	d
polynomial $(n+1)/2$	polynomial	$\lceil\frac{n+1}{2}\rceil$-of-$n$	–	–
MSP $(n+1)/2$	MSP+tree	$\lceil\frac{n+1}{2}\rceil$-of-$n$	n	$\lceil\frac{n+1}{2}\rceil$
MSP Unbalanced	MSP+tree	*unbalanced-AS*, Example 1	$2n$	$n-1$
MSP Grid	MSP+tree	*grid-AS*, Example 2	$2n$	$2(n+t-k)\approx 2n$

We implement all presented schemes in C++. The benchmarks only consider CPU complexity, by measuring the time it takes a party to execute each algorithm. Network latency, parallel share verification, and communication-level optimizations are not considered, as they are independent to the encoding of the AS. All benchmarks are made on a virtual machine running Ubuntu 22.04, with 16 GB memory and 8 dedicated CPUs of an AMD EPYC-Rome Processor at 2.3 GHz and 4500 bogomips. The number of parties n is always a square, for *grid-AS* to be well-defined, and we report mean values and standard deviation over 100 runs with different inputs.

6.1 Benchmarking Basic Properties of the MSP

We first measure the size of authorized sets. Authorized sets are obtained in the following way. Starting from an empty set, add a party chosen uniformly from the set of all parties, until the set becomes authorized. This simulates an execution where shares arrive in an arbitrary order, and may result in authorized sets that are not minimal, in the sense that they are supersets of smaller authorized sets, but contain redundant parties. We repeat this experiment 1000 times and report the average size in Fig. 2a. For the $\lceil\frac{n+1}{2}\rceil$-of-$n$ AS, of course, authorized sets are always of size $\lceil\frac{n+1}{2}\rceil$. For the *unbalanced-AS* they slightly smaller, and for the *grid-AS* they are significantly larger, as they contain full rows and columns of the grid.

We next measure the bit length of the recombination vector. This is relevant because the schemes involve interpolation in the exponent, exponentiation is an expensive operation, and a shorter recombination vector results in fewer exponentiations. We observe in Fig. 2b that the complexity of the AS does not necessarily affect the bit length of the recombination vector. There are two important observations to explain Fig. 2b. First, each entry of the recombination vector that corresponds to a redundant party is 0, as that share does not contribute to reconstruction. Second, we observe through our benchmarks that, when the MSP is sparse and has entries with short bit length, then the recombination vector also has a short bit length.

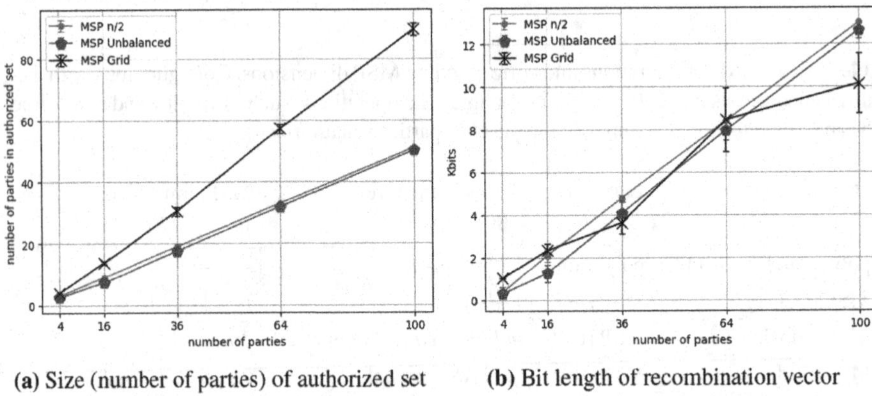

(a) Size (number of parties) of authorized set **(b)** Bit length of recombination vector

Fig. 2. Benchmarking basic properties of the MSP, for a varying number of parties.

6.2 Running Time of Verifiable Secret Sharing

We implement and compare the MSP-based scheme of Sect. 4 with Pedersen's VSS[3] [37]. For *Share()* we report the time it takes to share a random secret $s \in \mathbb{Z}_q$,

[3] Polynomial evaluation is done without the DFT optimization.

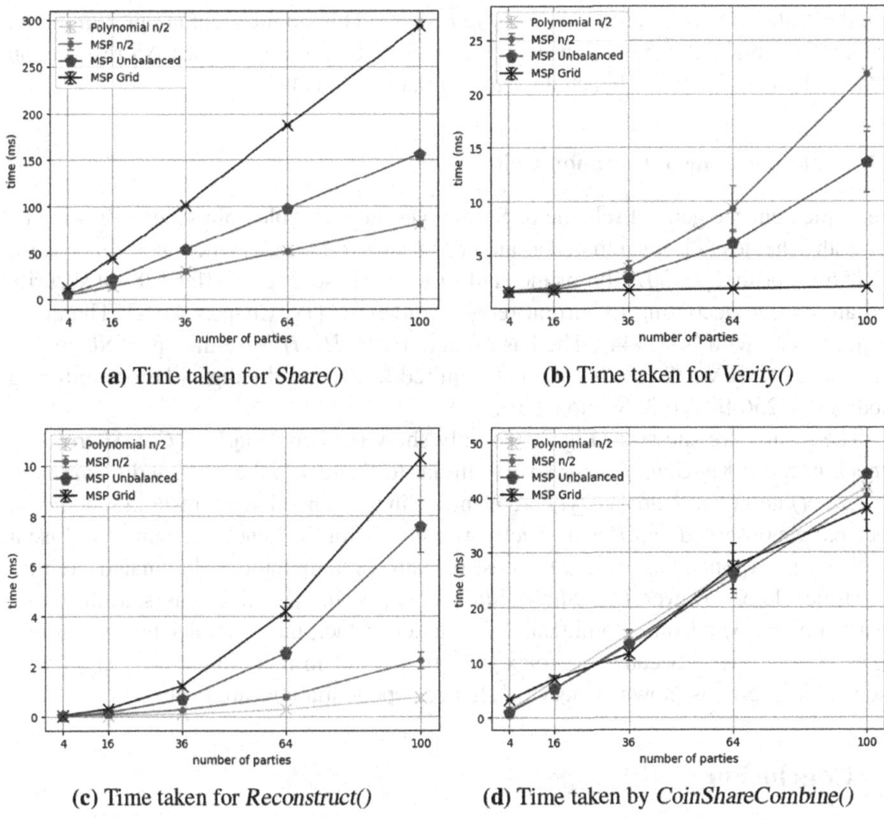

(a) Time taken for *Share()*

(b) Time taken for *Verify()*

(c) Time taken for *Reconstruct()*

(d) Time taken by *CoinShareCombine()*

Fig. 3. Time taken by each algorithm in the threshold and general VSS (3a–3c), and in the threshold and general coin (3d) for a varying number of parties.

for *Verify()* the average time it takes a party to verify *one* of its shares and for *Reconstruct()* the time to reconstruct the secret from an authorized group. The results are shown in Fig. 3.

The first conclusion (comparing the first two configurations in Figs. 3a and 3b) is that the MSP-based and polynomial-based operations are equally efficient, when instantiated with the same AS. The only exception is the *Reconstruct()* algorithm, shown in Fig. 3c, where general VSS is up to two times slower. This is because computing the recombination vector employs Gaussian elimination, which has cubic time complexity.

The second conclusion (comparing the last three configurations) is that general VSS is moderately affected by the complexity of the AS. For *Share()*, shown in Fig. 3a, more complex AS incur a slowdown because a larger number of shares and commitments have to be created. *Reconstruct()*, in Fig. 3c, is also slower with more complex AS, because it performs Gaussian elimination on a larger matrix. We conclude this is the only part of general VSS that cannot be made as efficient as in threshold VSS. On the other hand, *Verify()*, in Fig. 3b, exhibits an interesting behavior: the more complex the

AS, the faster it is on average to verify *one* share. This might seem counter-intuitive, but can be explained from the observations of Sect. 6.1; more complex AS result in an MSP with many 0-entries, hence the exponentiations of (1) are faster.

6.3 Running Time of Common Coin

We implement the general scheme of Sect. 5 and the threshold coin scheme from [11]. For both schemes G is instantiated as an order-q subgroup of $\mathbb{Z}_p$, where $p = qm+1$, for q a 256-bit prime, p a 3072-bit prime, and $m \in \mathbb{N}$. These lengths offer 128-bit security and are chosen according to current recommendations [19, Chapter 4.5.2]. The arithmetic is done with NTL [44]. The hash functions H, H', H'' use the openSSL implementation of SHA-512 (so that it's not required to expand the digest before reducing modulo the 256-bit q [43, Section 9.2]).

The results are shown in Fig. 3. We only show the benchmark of *CoinShareCombine()*, because *KeyGen()* behaves very similar to *Share()* in the VSS, and *CoinShareGenerate()* and *CoinShareVerify()* are identical in the general and threshold scheme. In Sect. 6.2 we observed that *Reconstruct()* was slower for the general scheme, because it involved no exponentiations and the cost of matrix manipulations dominated the running time. Here, however, *CoinShareCombine()* runs similarly in all cases, as the exponentiations in (3) become dominant. As a matter of fact, the general scheme is sometimes faster. This is because complex AS often result in recombination vectors with shorter bit length, as shown in Sect. 6.1, hence exponentiations are faster.

7 Conclusion

In this work we provide the first implementation and practical assessment of distributed cryptography with general trust. We fill all gaps on implementation details and show how a system can be engineered to support general distributed cryptography. We describe, implement, and benchmark distributed cryptographic schemes, specifically, a verifiable secret-sharing scheme, a common-coin scheme, and a distributed signature scheme (as a generalization of threshold signatures), all supporting general trust assumptions. For completeness, we also present the security proofs for all general schemes and handle specific cases that arise from the general trust assumptions (see Theorem 2). Our results suggest that practical access structures can be used with no significant efficiency loss. It can even be the case (VSS share verification, Fig. 3b) that operations are on average faster with complex trust structures encoded as Monotone Span Programs (MSP). We nevertheless expect future optimizations, orthogonal to our work, to make MSP operations even faster. Similar optimizations have already been discovered for polynomial evaluation and interpolation [45]. We expect that our work will improve the understanding and facilitate the wider adoption of general distributed cryptography.

Acknowledgments. This work has been funded by the Swiss National Science Foundation (SNSF) under grant agreement Nr. 200021_188443 (Advanced Consensus Protocols).

References

1. Agrawal, S., Mohassel, P., Mukherjee, P., Rindal, P.: DiSE: distributed symmetric-key encryption. In: CCS, pp. 1993–2010. ACM (2018)
2. Alpos, O., Cachin, C.: Consensus beyond thresholds: generalized Byzantine quorums made live. In: SRDS, pp. 21–30. IEEE (2020)
3. Alpos, O., Cachin, C.: Do not trust in numbers: practical distributed cryptography with general trust. IACR Cryptology ePrint Archive, p. 1767 (2022). https://eprint.iacr.org/2022/1767
4. Babai, L., Gál, A., Wigderson, A.: Superpolynomial lower bounds for monotone span programs. Combinatorica **19**(3), 301–319 (1999)
5. Beimel, A.: Secure schemes for secret sharing and key distribution. Ph.D. thesis, Technion (1996)
6. Benaloh, J., Leichter, J.: Generalized secret sharing and monotone functions. In: Goldwasser, S. (ed.) CRYPTO 1988. LNCS, vol. 403, pp. 27–35. Springer, New York (1990). https://doi.org/10.1007/0-387-34799-2_3
7. Benhamouda, F., et al.: Can a public blockchain keep a secret? In: Pass, R., Pietrzak, K. (eds.) TCC 2020. LNCS, vol. 12550, pp. 260–290. Springer, Cham (2020). https://doi.org/10.1007/978-3-030-64375-1_10
8. Boldyreva, A.: Threshold signatures, multisignatures and blind signatures based on the Gap-Diffie-Hellman-Group signature scheme. In: Desmedt, Y.G. (ed.) PKC 2003. LNCS, vol. 2567, pp. 31–46. Springer, Heidelberg (2003). https://doi.org/10.1007/3-540-36288-6_3
9. Boneh, D., Lynn, B., Shacham, H.: Short signatures from the Weil pairing. J. Cryptol. **17**(4), 297–319 (2004)
10. Brickell, E.F.: Some ideal secret sharing schemes. In: Quisquater, J.-J., Vandewalle, J. (eds.) EUROCRYPT 1989. LNCS, vol. 434, pp. 468–475. Springer, Heidelberg (1990). https://doi.org/10.1007/3-540-46885-4_45
11. Cachin, C., Kursawe, K., Shoup, V.: Random oracles in constantinople: practical asynchronous Byzantine agreement using cryptography. J. Cryptol. **18**(3), 219–246 (2005)
12. Chaum, D., Pedersen, T.P.: Wallet databases with observers. In: Brickell, E.F. (ed.) CRYPTO 1992. LNCS, vol. 740, pp. 89–105. Springer, Heidelberg (1993). https://doi.org/10.1007/3-540-48071-4_7
13. Choudhury, A.: Almost-surely terminating asynchronous Byzantine agreement against general adversaries with optimal resilience. In: ICDCN, pp. 167–176. ACM (2023)
14. Cramer, R., Damgård, I., Maurer, U.: General secure multi-party computation from any linear secret-sharing scheme. In: Preneel, B. (ed.) EUROCRYPT 2000. LNCS, vol. 1807, pp. 316–334. Springer, Heidelberg (2000). https://doi.org/10.1007/3-540-45539-6_22
15. Das, S., Krishnan, V., Isaac, I.M., Ren, L.: SPURT: scalable distributed randomness beacon with transparent setup. In: IEEE Symposium on Security and Privacy, pp. 2502–2517. IEEE (2022)
16. Daza, V., Herranz, J., Sáez, G.: On the computational security of a distributed key distribution scheme. IEEE Trans. Comput. **57**(8), 1087–1097 (2008)
17. Desmedt, Y.: Society and group oriented cryptography: a new concept. In: Pomerance, C. (ed.) CRYPTO 1987. LNCS, vol. 293, pp. 120–127. Springer, Heidelberg (1988). https://doi.org/10.1007/3-540-48184-2_8
18. Drand: A distributed randomness beacon daemon (2022). https://drand.love
19. ECRYPT-CSA: Algorithms, key size and protocols report. H2020-ICT-2014 - Project 645421 (2018). https://www.ecrypt.eu.org/csa/documents/D5.4-FinalAlgKeySizeProt.pdf
20. Eriguchi, R., Nuida, K.: Homomorphic secret sharing for multipartite and general adversary structures supporting parallel evaluation of low-degree polynomials. In: Tibouchi, M., Wang, H. (eds.) ASIACRYPT 2021. LNCS, vol. 13091, pp. 191–221. Springer, Cham (2021). https://doi.org/10.1007/978-3-030-92075-3_7

21. Fiat, A., Shamir, A.: How to prove yourself: practical solutions to identification and signature problems. In: Odlyzko, A.M. (ed.) CRYPTO 1986. LNCS, vol. 263, pp. 186–194. Springer, Heidelberg (1987). https://doi.org/10.1007/3-540-47721-7_12
22. Gennaro, R.: Theory and practice of verifiable secret sharing. Ph.D. thesis, Massachusetts Institute of Technology, Cambridge, MA, USA (1996)
23. Gennaro, R., Jarecki, S., Krawczyk, H., Rabin, T.: Secure distributed key generation for discrete-log based cryptosystems. J. Cryptol. **20**(1), 51–83 (2007)
24. Herranz, J., Sáez, G.: Verifiable secret sharing for general access structures, with application to fully distributed proxy signatures. In: Wright, R.N. (ed.) FC 2003. LNCS, vol. 2742, pp. 286–302. Springer, Heidelberg (2003). https://doi.org/10.1007/978-3-540-45126-6_21
25. Hirt, M., Maurer, U.M.: Complete characterization of adversaries tolerable in secure multi-party computation (extended abstract). In: PODC, pp. 25–34. ACM (1997)
26. Ito, M., Saito, A., Nishizeki, T.: Secret sharing scheme realizing general access structure. Electron. Commun. Jpn. **72**, 56–64 (1989)
27. Karchmer, M., Wigderson, A.: On span programs. In: Computational Complexity Conference, pp. 102–111. IEEE Computer Society (1993)
28. Larsen, K.G., Simkin, M.: Secret sharing lower bound: either reconstruction is hard or shares are long. In: Galdi, C., Kolesnikov, V. (eds.) SCN 2020. LNCS, vol. 12238, pp. 566–578. Springer, Cham (2020). https://doi.org/10.1007/978-3-030-57990-6_28
29. Lokhava, M., et al.: Fast and secure global payments with stellar. In: SOSP, pp. 80–96. ACM (2019)
30. Lu, D., Yurek, T., Kulshreshtha, S., Govind, R., Kate, A., Miller, A.K.: HoneyBadgerMPC and AsynchroMix: practical asynchronous MPC and its application to anonymous communication. In: CCS, pp. 887–903. ACM (2019)
31. Malkhi, D., Reiter, M.K., Wool, A.: The load and availability of Byzantine quorum systems. SIAM J. Comput. **29**(6), 1889–1906 (2000)
32. Mashhadi, S., Dehkordi, M.H., Kiamari, N.: Provably secure verifiable multi-stage secret sharing scheme based on monotone span program. IET Inf. Secur. **11**(6), 326–331 (2017)
33. Miller, A., Xia, Y., Croman, K., Shi, E., Song, D.: The honey badger of BFT protocols. In: CCS, pp. 31–42. ACM (2016)
34. Naor, M., Pinkas, B., Reingold, O.: Distributed pseudo-random functions and KDCs. In: Stern, J. (ed.) EUROCRYPT 1999. LNCS, vol. 1592, pp. 327–346. Springer, Heidelberg (1999). https://doi.org/10.1007/3-540-48910-X_23
35. Nikov, V., Nikova, S.: New monotone span programs from old. IACR Cryptology ePrint Archive, p. 282 (2004)
36. Padró, C., Sáez, G.: Secret sharing schemes with bipartite access structure. IEEE Trans. Inf. Theory **46**(7), 2596–2604 (2000)
37. Pedersen, T.P.: Non-interactive and information-theoretic secure verifiable secret sharing. In: Feigenbaum, J. (ed.) CRYPTO 1991. LNCS, vol. 576, pp. 129–140. Springer, Heidelberg (1992). https://doi.org/10.1007/3-540-46766-1_9
38. Rabin, M.O.: Randomized Byzantine generals. In: FOCS, pp. 403–409. IEEE Computer Society (1983)
39. Raikwar, M., Gligoroski, D.: SoK: decentralized randomness beacon protocols. In: Nguyen, K., Yang, G., Guo, F., Susilo, W. (eds.) ACISP 2022. LNCS, vol. 13494, pp. 420–446. Springer, Cham (2022). https://doi.org/10.1007/978-3-031-22301-3_21
40. Robere, R., Pitassi, T., Rossman, B., Cook, S.A.: Exponential lower bounds for monotone span programs. In: FOCS, pp. 406–415. IEEE Computer Society (2016)
41. Schwartz, D., Youngs, N., Britto, A.: The Ripple protocol consensus algorithm. Ripple Labs (2014). https://ripple.com/files/ripple_consensus_whitepaper.pdf
42. Shamir, A.: How to share a secret. Commun. ACM **22**(11), 612–613 (1979)

43. Shoup, V.: A Computational Introduction to Number Theory and Algebra Version 2. Cambridge University Press (2009). https://shoup.net/ntb/ntb-v2.pdf
44. Shoup, V.: Number Theory Library for C++ version 11.5.1 (2020). https://shoup.net/ntl
45. Tomescu, A., et al.: Towards scalable threshold cryptosystems. In: IEEE Symposium on Security and Privacy, pp. 877–893. IEEE (2020)
46. Vogels, W.: Life is not a State-Machine (2006). https://www.allthingsdistributed.com/2006/08/life_is_not_a_statemachine.html
47. Yin, M., Malkhi, D., Reiter, M.K., Golan-Gueta, G., Abraham, I.: Hotstuff: BFT consensus with linearity and responsiveness. In: PODC, pp. 347–356. ACM (2019)

Synergistic Knowledge

Christian Cachin, David Lehnherr(✉), and Thomas Studer

University of Bern, Bern, Switzerland
{christian.cachin,david.lehnherr,thomas.studer}@unibe.ch

Abstract. In formal epistemology, group knowledge is often modelled as the knowledge that the group would have if the agents shared all their individual knowledge. However, this interpretation does not account for relations between agents. In this work, we propose the notion of synergistic knowledge, which makes it possible to model those relationships. As examples, we investigate the use of consensus objects and the problem of the dining cryptographers. Moreover, we show that our logic can also be used to model certain aspects of information flow in networks.

Keywords: Distributed Knowledge · Synergy · Modal Logic

1 Introduction

A simplicial interpretation of the semantics of modal logic has gained recent interest, due to the success of applying topological methods to problems occurring in distributed systems. The topological approach to distributed computing, exemplified by Herlihy, Kozlov and Rajsbaum [10], interprets the configurations of a distributed system as a simplicial complex. The vertices of a simplicial complex represent local states of different agents and an edge between two vertices means that the two local states can occur together.

Modal logic has various applications to problems in distributed computing, such as agreement (c.f. Halpern and Moses [8]). Models for modal logic are usually based on a possible worlds approach where the operator $\Box$ is evaluated on Kripke frames. In a world w, a formula ϕ is known, denoted by $\Box\phi$, if and only if ϕ is true in each world indistinguishable from w. These frames can be extended to multi-agent systems by introducing an indistinguishability relation for each agent. A formula ϕ is distributed knowledge of a group, first introduced by Halpern and Moses [8], if and only if ϕ is true in all worlds that cannot be distinguished by any member of the group.

Given a set of agents, van Ditmarsch, Goubault, Ledent and Rajsbaum [2] define a simplicial model for settings in which all agents are present at any point in time. This semantics is shown to be equivalent to the modal logic $\mathsf{S5}_n$. In the same setting, Goubault, Ledent and Rajsbaum [5] look at distributed task computability through the lens of dynamic epistemic logic (c.f. van Ditmarsch, van der Hoek and Kooi [3]). Using dynamic epistemic logic makes it possible to model the relationship between input and output configurations of tasks, which is one

S. Dolev and B. Schieber (Eds.): SSS 2023, LNCS 14310, pp. 552–567, 2023.
https://doi.org/10.1007/978-3-031-44274-2_41

of the core objectives of the classical topological approach to distributed systems (c.f. Herlihy and Shavit [11]). Work regarding models where some agents might not be present in a configuration was conducted independently by van Ditmarsch and Kuznets [4] and Goubault, Ledent and Rajsbaum [6]. The latter work shows the equivalence between their simplicial models and Kripke models for the logic $\mathsf{KB4}_n$, whereas van Ditmarsch and Kuznets [4] deal with crashed agents by letting formulas be undefined and show that their logic is sound. Randrianomentsoa, van Ditmarsch and Kuznets [12] show in a follow up work that the route taken by van Ditmarsch and Kuznets [4] leads to a sound and complete semantic for their axiom system. Both works remark that impure complexes cannot capture the information of improper Kripke frames, i.e. models in which some worlds cannot be distinguished from others by all agents. They point out the need for extending the interpretation of simplicial complexes to simplicial sets, i.e. simplicial complexes that may contain the same simplex arbitrarily often. Furthermore, the latter work also shed light on a new notion of group knowledge which differs from the usual definition of distributed knowledge. Their example is depicted in Fig. 1 in which the agents a and b individually cannot distinguish the worlds X and Y, i.e. the two solid triangles, since the vertices labelled with a and b belong to both X and Y. However, a and b together can distinguish between X and Y since the worlds do not share an edge between vertices a and b. In a follow up work, Goubault, Kniazev, Ledent and Rajsbaum [7] provide, among various results, a semantics for such simplicial sets and provide a higher order interpretation of distributed knowledge for a set of agents.

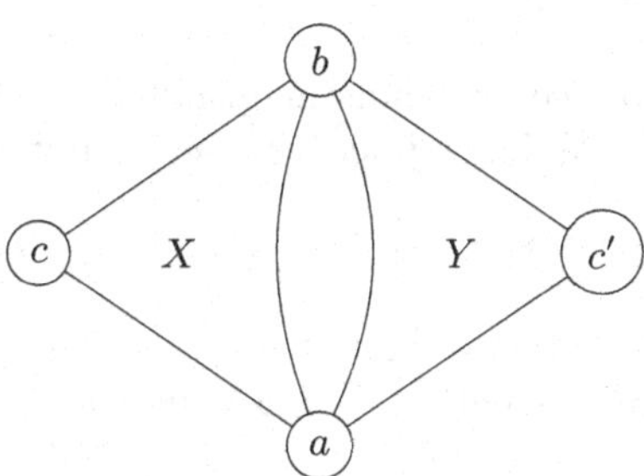

Fig. 1. A model in which two agents a and b can together distinguish between the worlds X and Y. However, they cannot do so individually.

In this paper, we propose the notion of synergistic knowledge, which allows a group of agents to know more than just the consequences of their pooled knowledge. That is, our newly introduced epistemic operator $[G]$ supports a principle that could be paraphrased as *the sum is greater than its parts*, hence the name synergistic knowledge. Different to the higher order interpretation of distributed knowledge by Goubault, Kniazev, Ledent and Rajsbaum [7], which analyses the knowledge of a set of agents, we interpret G as a simplicial complex over the set of agents. Hence, we refer to G as an agent pattern instead of a group.

The operator $[G]$ allows us to model relations between subgroups of agents and how they interact with each other. Hence, two agent patterns G and H may contain the same agents, but differ in the relations among them. For example, in Fig. 1, we can distinguish the pattern $\{\{a\},\{b\}\}$, which cannot distinguish between X and Y because the two worlds share vertices labelled with a and with b, from the pattern $\{\{a,b\}\}$, which can distinguish X and Y due to X and Y not sharing an edge. As applications for synergistic knowledge, we investigate the use of consensus objects (c.f. Herlihy [9]) and the problem of the dining cryptographers (c.f. Chaum [1]).

Our main contribution consists in i) providing a novel simplicial set semantics for modal logic that is simpler than previous approaches as it does not refer to category theory or make use of chromatic maps, and ii) the introduction of a new knowledge operator $[G]$ that allows us to express distributed knowledge in a more fine grained way, as well as iii) presenting a new notion of indistinguishability, called componentwise indistinguishability, which models the flow of information in networks. All points mentioned are accompanied by examples.

In Sect. 2, we introduce our new simplicial set model together with a corresponding indistinguishability relation. Section 3 studies the logic induced by our model. In Sect. 4, we present examples that illustrate the use of our logic. In Sect. 5, we adapt our notion of indistinguishability and show how it can be used in order to model the information flow in a network. Lastly, we draw a conclusion of our work in Sect. 6.

2 Indistinguishability

In this section, we introduce the indistinguishability relation that is used to model synergistic knowledge. Let Ag denote a set of finitely many agents and let

$$\mathsf{Agsi} = \{(A,i) \mid A \subseteq \mathsf{Ag} \text{ and } i \in \mathbb{N}\}.$$

We may think of a pair $(\{a\},i) \in \mathsf{Agsi}$ as representing agent a in local state i. Further, let $S \subseteq \mathsf{Agsi}$. An element $(A,i) \in S$ is *maximal in* S if and only if

$$\forall (B,j) \in S. |A| \geq |B|, \text{ where } |X| \text{ denotes the cardinality of the set } X.$$

Definition 1 (Simplex). *Let* $\emptyset \neq S \subseteq \mathsf{Agsi}$. *$S$ is a* simplex *if and only if*

S1*: The maximal element is unique, i.e.*

$$\text{if } (A,i) \in S \text{ and } (B,j) \in S \text{ are maximal in } S \text{ then, } A = B \text{ and } i = j.$$

The maximal element of S is denoted as $\max(S)$.

S2*: S is uniquely downwards closed, i.e. for all $(B,i) \in S$ and $\emptyset \neq C \subseteq B$*

$$\exists! j \in \mathbb{N}.(C,j) \in S, \text{ where } !\exists j \text{ means that there exists exactly one } j.$$

S3: *S contains nothing else, i.e.*

$$(B, i) \in S \text{ and } (A, j) = \max(S) \text{ implies } B \subseteq A.$$

Definition 2 (Complex). *Let* $\mathbb{C}$ *be a set of simplices.* $\mathbb{C}$ *is a* complex *if and only if*

C: *For any* $S, T \in \mathbb{C}$*, if there exist* A *and* i *with* $(A, i) \in S$ *and* $(A, i) \in T$*, then*

$$\text{for all } B \subseteq A \text{ and all } j \quad (B, j) \in S \iff (B, j) \in T.$$

Condition C guarantees that the maximal element of a simplex uniquely determines it within a given complex.

Lemma 1. *Let* $\mathbb{C}$ *be a complex and* $S, T \in \mathbb{C}$*. We find*

$$\max(S) = \max(T) \text{ implies } S = T.$$

Proof. We show $S \subseteq T$. The other direction is symmetric. Let $(A, i) = \max(S)$. Assume $(B, j) \in S$. Because of S3, we have $B \subseteq A$. By Condition C, we conclude $(B, j) \in T$. □

Whenever it is clear from the context, we abbreviate $(\{a_1, ..., a_n\}, i)$ as $a_1...a_n i$ in order to enhance readability. Furthermore, we may use a row (or a mixed row-column) notation to emphasize simplices. For example,

$$\left\{ \begin{Bmatrix} ab0 \\ a0 \\ b0 \end{Bmatrix}, \begin{Bmatrix} ab1 \\ a0 \\ b1 \end{Bmatrix} \right\}$$

is a complex that contains 2 simplices. Whenever we refer to a simplex within a complex, we write $\langle Ai \rangle$ for the simplex with maximal element (A, i). Condition C guarantees that this notation is well-defined.

Oberserve that Condition C ensures that neither

$$\left\{ \begin{Bmatrix} ab0 \\ a0, b0 \end{Bmatrix}, \begin{Bmatrix} ab0 \\ a1, b1 \end{Bmatrix} \right\} \quad \text{nor} \quad \left\{ \begin{Bmatrix} abc0 \\ ab0, ac0, bc0 \\ a0, b0, c0 \end{Bmatrix}, \begin{Bmatrix} ab0 \\ a1, b1 \end{Bmatrix} \right\}$$

is a complex, although each individual simplex is well-formed.

Definition 3 (Indistinguishability). *Let* $S \subseteq \mathsf{Agsi}$*, we define*

$$S^\circ = \{A \mid \exists i \in \mathbb{N} : (A, i) \in S\}.$$

An agent pattern G *is a subset of* $\mathsf{Pow}(\mathsf{Ag}) \setminus \{\emptyset\}$*. An agent pattern* cannot distinguish *between two simplices* S *and* T*, denoted by* $S \sim_G T$*, if and only if* $G \subseteq (S \cap T)^\circ$*.*

Definition 4 (Partial equivalence relation (PER)). *A relation* $R \subseteq S \times S$ *is a partial equivalence relation if and only if it is symmetric and transitive.*

Lemma 2 (PER). *$\sim_G$ is a PER.*

Proof. Symmetry immediately follows from the fact that set intersection is commutative. To show transitivity, let S, T, U be simplices with $S \sim_G T$ and $T \sim_G U$, i.e.

$$G \subseteq (S \cap T)^\circ \tag{1}$$

$$G \subseteq (T \cap U)^\circ \tag{2}$$

Let $A \in G$. Because of (1), there exists i with

$$(A, i) \in S \quad \text{and} \quad (A, i) \in T. \tag{3}$$

Because of (2), there exists j with

$$(A, j) \in T \quad \text{and} \quad (A, j) \in U. \tag{4}$$

From (3), (4), and Condition S2 we obtain $i = j$. Thus by (3) and (4), we get $A \in (S \cap U)^\circ$. Since A was arbitrary in G, we conclude $G \subseteq (S \cap U)^\circ$. □

Lemma 3. *Let $G \subseteq \mathsf{Pow}(\mathsf{Ag})$ be an agent pattern and*

$$\mathsf{noSym}(G) := \{\{a\} \mid \exists A \in G \text{ and } a \in A\}.$$

Let $\mathcal{S}_G$ be a set of simplices such that for any $S \in \mathcal{S}_G$ we have $\mathsf{noSym}(G) \subseteq S^\circ$. The indistinguishability relation $\sim_G$ is reflexive on $\mathcal{S}_G \times \mathcal{S}_G$ and empty otherwise.

Proof. We first show reflexivity. If $G = \emptyset$, then trivially $G \subseteq (S \cap S)^\circ$ for any S. Assume $G \neq \emptyset$. Let $S \in \mathcal{S}_G$. For each $B \in G$, we have to show that $B \in (S \cap S)^\circ$, i.e. that

$$\text{there exists } i \text{ with } (B, i) \in S. \tag{5}$$

Let $(A, i) := \max(S)$. Let $b \in B$. Because of $\mathsf{noSym}(G) \subseteq S^\circ$, there exists l such that $(\{b\}, l) \in S$. By S3 we get $b \in A$. Since b was arbitrary in B, we get $B \subseteq A$. By S2 we conclude that (5) holds and symmetry is established.

We now show that $\sim_G$ is empty otherwise. Let S be a simplex such that $\mathsf{noSym}(G) \nsubseteq S^\circ$ and let T be an arbitrary simplex. Then there exists a, A with $a \in A \in G$ and $\{a\} \notin S^\circ$, i.e.

$$\text{for all } i, (\{a\}, i) \notin S. \tag{6}$$

Suppose towards a contradiction that

$$G \subseteq (S \cap T)^\circ \tag{7}$$

Because of $A \in G$ we get $A \in (S \cap T)^\circ$. Hence $A \in S^\circ$, i.e. there exists l with $(A, l) \in S$. With S2 and $\{a\} \subseteq A$ we find that there exists j with $(\{a\}, j) \in S$. This is a contradiction to (6). Thus (7) cannot hold. □

Corollary 1. *$\sim_G$ is an equivalence relation on $\mathcal{S}_G \times \mathcal{S}_G$.*

The following two lemmas establish basic properties of the indistinguishability relation.

Lemma 4 (Anti-Monotonicity). *$G \subseteq H$ implies $\sim_H \subseteq \sim_G$.*

Proof. Assume $G \subseteq H$. For any two simplices S and T with $S \sim_H T$, we have $G \subseteq H \subseteq (S \cap T)^\circ$ by definition and hence $S \sim_G T$, which concludes the proof. □

Lemma 5 (Downward closure). *Let $\mathbb{C}$ be a complex and $S, T \in \mathbb{C}$. Further, let $A \in (S \cap T)^\circ$ and $B \subseteq A$. We find $B \in (S \cap T)^\circ$.*

Proof. From $A \in (S \cap T)^\circ$, we obtain that there exists i such that $(A, i) \in S$ and $(A, i) \in T$. From S2 we find that there exists j such that $(B, j) \in S$. Thus by C, we get $(B, j) \in T$ and we conclude $B \in (S \cap T)^\circ$. □

From the previous two lemmas we immediately obtain the following:

Corollary 2. *Let G be an agent pattern. Let $A, B \subseteq \mathsf{Ag}$ such that $A \subseteq B \in G$. We have*

$$\sim_{G \cup \{A\}} = \sim_G .$$

The next lemma states that adding synergy to an agent pattern makes it stronger in the sense that it can distinguish more simplices. This is shown in Example 1 where the pattern $\{\{a\}, \{b\}\}$ cannot distinguish $\langle abc0 \rangle$ and $\langle abc1 \rangle$ but $\{\{a, b\}\}$ can distinguish these two simplices.

Lemma 6. *Let $H_1, H_2, \ldots, H_n \subseteq \mathsf{Ag}$ with $n \geq 2$ We have*

$$\sim_{\{H_1 \cup H_2, \ldots, H_n\}} \subseteq \sim_{\{H_1, H_2, \ldots, H_n\}} .$$

Proof. From the Lemma 5 and Lemma 4 we find that

$$\sim_{\{H_1 \cup H_2, \ldots, H_n\}} = \sim_{\{H_1 \cup H_2, H_1, H_2, \ldots, H_n\}} \subseteq \sim_{\{H_1, H_2, \ldots, H_n\}} .$$

□

In traditional Kripke semantics, distributed knowledge of a set of agents is modeled by considering the accessibility relation that is given by the intersection of the accessibility relations of the individual agents. The following lemma states that in our framework, this intersection corresponds to the agent pattern consisting of singleton sets for each agent.

Lemma 7. *Let $G \subseteq \mathsf{Ag}$ and $H = \bigcup_{a \in G} \{\{a\}\}$. We have*

$$\bigcap_{a \in G} \sim_{\{\{a\}\}} = \sim_H .$$

Proof. $(S, T) \in \bigcap_{a \in G} \sim_{\{\{a\}\}}$ iff for each $a \in G$, we have $\{a\} \in (S \cap T)^\circ$ iff (by the definition of H) $H \subseteq (S \cap T)^\circ$ iff $S \sim_H T$. □

3 Logic

The logic of synergistic knowledge is a normal modal logic that includes a modality $[G]$ for each agent pattern G. It is closely related to the logic of distributed knowledge but has some additional validities concerning the pattern-based modalities, see, e.g., (Sub) and (Clo) below.

Let Prop be a countable set of atomic propositions. Formulas of the language of synergistic knowledge $\mathcal{L}_{\mathsf{Syn}}$ are inductively defined by the following grammar:

$$\phi ::= p \mid \neg\phi \mid \phi \wedge \phi \mid [G]\phi$$

where $p \in \mathsf{Prop}$ and G is an agent pattern. The remaining Boolean connectives are defined as usual. In particular, we set $\bot := p \wedge \neg p$ for some fixed $p \in \mathsf{Prop}$.

Definition 5 (Model). *A model $\mathcal{M} = (\mathbb{C}, V)$ is a pair where*

1. *$\mathbb{C}$ is a complex and*
2. *$V : \mathbb{C} \to \mathsf{Pow}(\mathsf{Prop})$ is a valuation.*

Definition 6 (Truth). *Let $\mathcal{M} = (\mathbb{C}, V)$ be a model, $w \in \mathbb{C}$, and $\phi \in \mathcal{L}_{\mathsf{Syn}}$. We define $\mathcal{M}, w \Vdash \phi$ inductively by*

$$\begin{array}{lll} \mathcal{M}, w \Vdash p & \textit{iff} & p \in V(w) \\ \mathcal{M}, w \Vdash \neg\phi & \textit{iff} & \mathcal{M}, w \nVdash \phi \\ \mathcal{M}, w \Vdash \phi \wedge \psi & \textit{iff} & \mathcal{M}, w \Vdash \phi \textit{ and } \mathcal{M}, w \Vdash \psi \\ \mathcal{M}, w \Vdash [G]\phi & \textit{iff} & w \sim_G v \textit{ implies } \mathcal{M}, v \Vdash \phi \quad \textit{for all } v \in \mathbb{C}. \end{array}$$

We write $\mathcal{M} \Vdash \phi$ if $\mathcal{M}, w \Vdash \phi$ for all $w \in \mathbb{C}$. A formula ϕ is valid *if $\mathcal{M} \Vdash \phi$ for all models $\mathcal{M}$.*

The following formulas are valid:

$$[G](\phi \to \psi) \to ([G]\phi \to [G]\psi) \tag{K}$$

$$[G]\phi \to [G][G]\phi \tag{4}$$

$$\phi \to [G]\neg[G]\neg\phi \tag{B}$$

$$[G]\phi \to [H]\phi \quad \text{if } G \subseteq H \tag{Mono}$$

Let G be an agent pattern. We define, as usual, the formula $\mathsf{alive}(G)$ to be $\neg[G]\bot$. For a single agent a we write $\mathsf{alive}(a)$ instead of $\mathsf{alive}(\{a\})$. The expected equivalences hold:

$$\mathcal{M}, w \Vdash \mathsf{alive}(G) \quad \text{iff} \quad G \subseteq w^\circ \quad \text{iff} \quad w \sim_G w. \tag{8}$$

Indeed, we have $\mathcal{M}, w \Vdash \neg[G]\bot$ iff it is not the case that for all v with $w \sim_G v$, it holds that $\mathcal{M}, v \Vdash \bot$. This is equivalent to there exists v with $w \sim_G v$, which is equivalent to there exitsts v with $G \subseteq (w \cap v)^\circ$. This is equivalent to $w \sim_G w$ and also to $G \subseteq w^\circ$.

Related to $\mathsf{alive}(\cdot)$, the following formulas are valid:

$$\mathsf{alive}(G) \land \mathsf{alive}(H) \to \mathsf{alive}(G \cup H) \qquad \text{(Union)}$$

$$\mathsf{alive}(G) \to \mathsf{alive}(\{B\}) \quad \text{if there is } A \text{ with } A \in G \text{ and } B \subseteq A \qquad \text{(Sub)}$$

$$\mathsf{alive}(G) \to \mathsf{alive}(\{A \cup B\}) \quad \text{if } A, B \in G \qquad \text{(Clo)}$$

(Union) is an immediate consequence of (8). For (Sub), assume $w \sim_G w$, $A \in G$, and $B \subseteq A$. We have $A \in (w \cap w)^\circ$. By Lemma 5 we find $B \in (w \cap w)^\circ$. Hence $w \sim_{\{B\}} w$, which yields (Sub). To show Clo, assume $w \sim_G w$ and $A, B \in G$. Hence $A \in (w \cap w)^\circ$. That is $A \in w^\circ$, i.e. there exists i with $(A, i) \in w$. Let C, j be such that $(C, j) = \max(w)$. By S3, we get $A \subseteq C$. Similarly, we find $B \subseteq C$, and thus $A \cup B \subseteq C$. Using S2, we obtain $A \cup B \in w^\circ$. Therefore, $w \sim_{\{A \cup B\}} w$ and (Clo) is estabished.

Further, note that axiom (T) holds when restricted to groups of agents that are alive:

$$\mathsf{alive}(G) \to ([G]\phi \to \phi) \qquad \text{(T)}$$

Question 1. Do the axioms (K), (4), (B), (Mono), (Union), (Sub), and (Clo) together with all propositional tautologies and the rules of modus ponens and [G]-necessitation provide a complete axiom system for our notion of validity?

Lemma 7 motivates the following abbreviation. Let $G \subseteq \mathsf{Ag}$ be a set of agents and set $H := \bigcup_{a \in G}\{\{a\}\}$. Then we let D_G be the modality $[H]$. We call this the distributed knowledge modality and let $\mathcal{L}_\mathsf{D}$ be the restriction of $\mathcal{L}_\mathsf{Syn}$ that contains distributed knowledge D_G as the only modality. Note that the usual axioms for the logic of distributed knowledge, formulated in $\mathcal{L}_\mathsf{D}$, hold with respect to synergistic models.

Question 2. Is the logic of synergistic knowledge a conservative extension (with respect to $\mathcal{L}_\mathsf{D}$) of the logic of distributed knowledge?

4 Examples

In this section, we present some examples that illustrate possible applications of our logic to distributed systems. Example 1 highlights one of the main characteristics of synergetic knowledge. That is, the agents a and b can together distinguish between the worlds $\langle abc0\rangle$ and $\langle abc1\rangle$ although they cannot do so individually. Hence, our logic can express the difference between the patterns $\{\{a\}, \{b\}\}$ and $\{\{a, b\}\}$.

Regarding the notation, we will omit the set parentheses for agent patterns whenever it is clear from the context and write for example $[abc, ab, ac]$ instead of $[\{\{a, b, c\}, \{a, b\}, \{a, c\}\}]$.

Example 1 (Two triangles). Let $\mathsf{Ag} = \{a, b, c\}$, $p \in \mathsf{Prop}$, and consider the model $\mathcal{M} = (\mathbb{C}, V)$ in Fig. 2 which is given by the complex

$$\mathbb{C} = \left\{ \left\{ \begin{matrix} abc0 \\ ab0, bc0, ac0 \\ a0, b0, c0 \end{matrix} \right\}, \left\{ \begin{matrix} abc1 \\ ab1, bc1, ac1 \\ a0, b0, c1 \end{matrix} \right\} \right\}$$

and by a valuation V such that $p \in V(\langle abc0 \rangle)$ and $p \notin V(\langle abc1 \rangle)$. We find

$$\mathcal{M}, \langle abc0 \rangle \Vdash [ab]p \text{ and } \mathcal{M}, \langle abc1 \rangle \Vdash [ab]\neg p,$$

because the worlds $\langle abc0 \rangle$ and $\langle abc1 \rangle$ can be distinguished due to

$$\{\{a, b\}\} \nsubseteq (\langle abc0 \rangle \cap \langle abc1 \rangle)^{\circ} = \{\{a\}, \{b\}\}.$$

However, for the pattern $H = \{\{a\}, \{b\}\}$ it holds that

$$H = \{\{a\}, \{b\}\} \subseteq (\langle abc0 \rangle \cap \langle abc1 \rangle)^{\circ},$$

and hence $\mathcal{M}, \langle abc0 \rangle \nVdash [H]p$. Lastly, if we add c to H, the agents know p:

$$\mathcal{M}, \langle abc0 \rangle \Vdash [a, b, c]p.$$

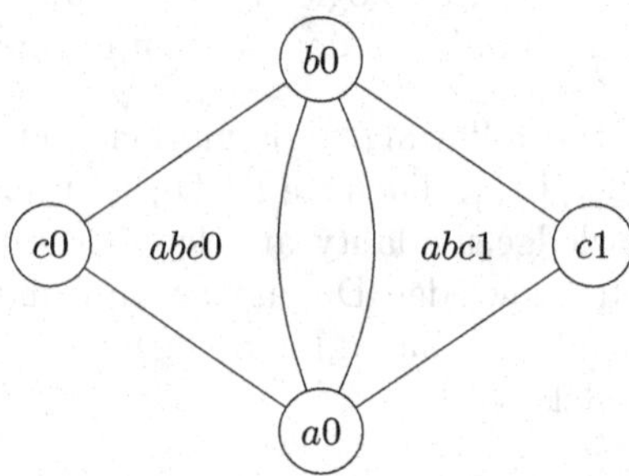

Fig. 2. A model in which two agents a and b can together distinguish between the worlds X and Y. However, they cannot do so individually.

Another motivation for simplicial sets is that we can model how agents can reason about each others death. As remarked by van Ditmarsch and Kuznets [4] as well as by Goubault, Ledent and Rajsbaum [6], simplicial complexes are not enough to model a setting where an agent considers it possible to be the only one alive. Such scenarios are important, because they arise in failure detection protocols. Example 2 shows such a model.

Example 2 (Two-agents). Let $\mathsf{Ag} = \{a, b\}$, and consider the model $\mathcal{M} = (\mathbb{C}, V)$ in Fig. 3 which is given by an arbitrary valuation and the complex

$$\mathbb{C} = \left\{ \left\{ \begin{matrix} ab0 \\ a0, b0 \end{matrix} \right\}, \{a0\} \right\}$$

It is straightforward to verify that $\mathcal{M}, \langle ab0 \rangle \Vdash \mathsf{alive}(a)$ and $\mathcal{M}, \langle ab0 \rangle \Vdash \mathsf{alive}(b)$. However, $\mathcal{M}, \langle a0 \rangle, \nVdash \mathsf{alive}(b)$ because $\{b\} \not\subseteq \langle a0 \rangle^{\circ}$ and hence $\mathcal{M}, \langle a0 \rangle \Vdash [b]\bot$. Moreover, a alone does not know whether $\mathsf{alive}(b)$ because a cannot distinguish $\langle a0 \rangle$ from $\langle ab0 \rangle$ due to $\{\{a\}\} \subseteq (\langle a0 \rangle \cap \langle ab0 \rangle)^{\circ}$.

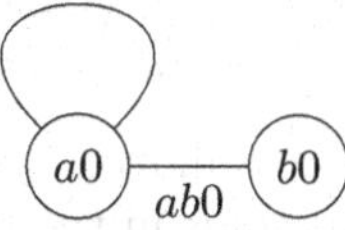

Fig. 3. A model in which a considers it possible that it is the only agent alive.

In Examples 3 and 4 we interpret synergy as having access to some shared primitives. Given three agents, Example 3 captures the idea that for some applications, the agent pattern must include the area of the triangle and not just its edges. Example 4 demonstrates that the patterns $\{\{a,b\},\{a,c\}\}$, $\{\{a,b\},\{b,c\}\}$, and $\{\{b,c\},\{a,c\}\}$ are weaker than the pattern $\{\{a,b\},\{a,c\},\{b,c\}\}$.

Example 3 (Consensus number). A n-consensus protocol is implemented by n processes that communicate through shared objects. The processes each start with an input of either 1 or 0 and must decide a common value. A consensus protocol must ensure that

1. Consistency: all processes must decide on the same value.
2. Wait-freedom: each process must decide after a finite number of steps.
3. Validity: the common decided value was proposed by some process.

Herlihy [9] defines the consensus number of an object O as the largest n for which there is a consensus protocol for n processes that only uses finitely many instances of O and any number of atomic registers. It follows from the definition that no combination of objects with a consensus number of $k < n$ can implement an object with a consensus number of n.

We can represent the executions of a n-consensus protocol as a tree in which one process moves at a time. By validity and wait-freedom, the initial state of the protocol must be bivalent (i.e. it is possible that 0 or 1 are decided), and there must exist a state from which on all successor states are univalent. Hence, the process that moves first in such a state decides the outcome of the protocol. This state is called the critical state.

In order to show that an object has a consensus number lower than k, we derive a contradiction by assuming that there is a valid implementation of a k-consensus protocol. Next, we maneuver the protocol into a critical state and show that the processes will not be able to determine which process moved first. Therefore, for some process P, there exist two indistinguishable executions in which P decides differently. However, if the object has a consensus number of k, the processes will be able to tell who moved first.

Synergetic knowledge is able to describe the situation from the critical state onwards. We interpret an element $\{p_1, ..., p_k\}$ of a synergy pattern G as the processes p_1 up to p_k having access to objects with a consensus number of k. For each process p_i, we define a propositional variable move_i that is true if p_i moved first at the critical state. Furthermore, we define

$$\varphi_i := \mathsf{move}_i \wedge \bigwedge_{1 \leq j \leq n \text{ and } j \neq i} \neg \mathsf{move}_j,$$

i.e., if φ_i is true, then the i-th process moved first. Let $\mathcal{M} = (\mathbb{C}, V)$ be a model, if $\mathcal{M} \Vdash [G]\varphi_1 \vee [G]\varphi_2 \vee \cdots \vee [G]\varphi_n$ holds in the model, then it is always possible for the processes in G to tell who moved first. Lastly, if G has n agents, we have for any G' with less than n agents

$$\mathcal{M} \nVdash [G']\varphi_1 \vee [G']\varphi_2 \vee \cdots \vee [G']\varphi_n,$$

which means that the access to objects with a consensus number of n is required.

For three agents a, b and c, the model $\mathcal{M} = (\mathbb{C}, V)$ is given by

$$\mathbb{C} = \left\{ \left\{ \begin{matrix} abc0 \\ ab0 \\ bc0 \\ ac0 \\ a0, b0, c0 \end{matrix} \right\}, \left\{ \begin{matrix} abc1 \\ ab0 \\ bc0 \\ ac0 \\ a0, b0, c0 \end{matrix} \right\}, \left\{ \begin{matrix} abc2 \\ ab0 \\ bc0 \\ ac0 \\ a0, b0, c0 \end{matrix} \right\} \right\}$$

with a valuation V that represents that someone moved first, i.e.

$$\mathcal{M}, \langle abc0 \rangle \Vdash \varphi_a \qquad \mathcal{M}, \langle abc1 \rangle \Vdash \varphi_b \qquad \mathcal{M}, \langle abc2 \rangle \Vdash \varphi_c.$$

It is easy to check that $\langle abc0 \rangle \sim_{ab,ac,bc} \langle abc1 \rangle$ and hence, having access to an object with consensus number 2 is not enough in order to distinguish those worlds. However,

$$\mathcal{M} \Vdash [abc]\varphi_a \vee [abc]\varphi_b \vee [abc]\varphi_c$$

is true and shows that access to objects with consensus number 3 suffices.

Example 4 (Dining cryptographers). The dining cryptographers problem, proposed by Chaum [1], illustrates how a shared-coin primitive can be used by three cryptographers (i.e. agents) to find out whether their employer or one of their peers paid for the dinner. However, if their employer did not pay, the payer wishes to remain anonymous.

For lack of space, we do not give a full formalisation of the dining cryptographers problem. Instead, we solely focus on the ability of agreeing on a coin-flip and the resulting knowledge. In what follows, we will provide a model in which the agents a, b and c can determine whether or not their employer paid if and only if they have pairwise access to a shared coin.

Let the propositional variable p denote that their employer paid. We interpret an agent pattern $G = \{\{a, b\}\}$ as a and b, having access to a shared coin. Our model $\mathcal{M} = (\mathbb{C}, V)$, depicted in Fig. 4, is given by the complex

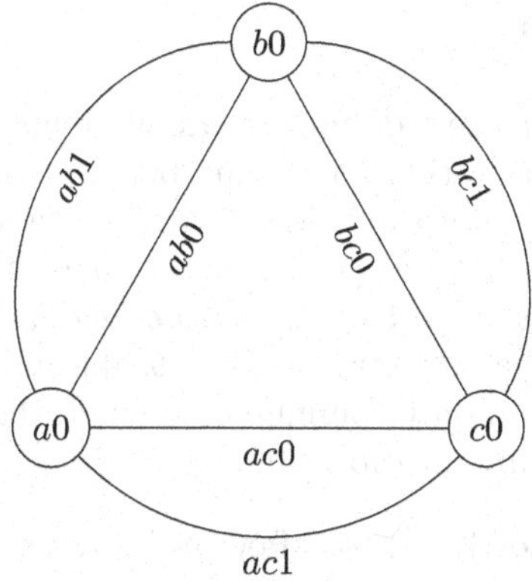

Fig. 4. Dining cryptographers model.

$$\mathbb{C} = \left\{ \begin{array}{c} \left\{ \begin{array}{c} abc0 \\ ab0 \\ bc0 \\ ac0 \\ a0, b0, c0 \end{array} \right\}, \left\{ \begin{array}{c} abc1 \\ ab1 \\ bc0 \\ ac0 \\ a0, b0, c0 \end{array} \right\}, \left\{ \begin{array}{c} abc2 \\ ab0 \\ bc1 \\ ac0 \\ a0, b0, c0 \end{array} \right\}, \left\{ \begin{array}{c} abc3 \\ ab0 \\ bc0 \\ ac1 \\ a0, b0, c0 \end{array} \right\}, \\ \left\{ \begin{array}{c} abc4 \\ ab1 \\ bc1 \\ ac0 \\ a0, b0, c0 \end{array} \right\}, \left\{ \begin{array}{c} abc5 \\ ab1 \\ bc0 \\ ac1 \\ a0, b0, c0 \end{array} \right\}, \left\{ \begin{array}{c} abc6 \\ ab0 \\ bc1 \\ ac1 \\ a0, b0, c0 \end{array} \right\}, \left\{ \begin{array}{c} abc7 \\ ab1 \\ bc1 \\ ac1 \\ a0, b0, c0 \end{array} \right\} \end{array} \right\}$$

and the valuation V is chosen such that

$$\begin{array}{llll} p \in V(\langle abc0 \rangle), & p \notin V(\langle abc1 \rangle), & p \notin V(\langle abc2 \rangle), & p \notin V(\langle abc3 \rangle), \\ p \in V(\langle abc4 \rangle), & p \in V(\langle abc5 \rangle), & p \in V(\langle abc6 \rangle), & p \notin V(\langle abc7 \rangle). \end{array}$$

Consider the agent pattern $G = \{\{a, b\}, \{a, c\}, \{b, c\}\}$, then

$$\mathcal{M} \Vdash [G]p \vee [G]\neg p, \tag{9}$$

i.e. in any world, if all agents have pairwise access to shared coins, they can know the value of p. Furthermore, for each $H \subsetneq G$ and each $w \in \mathbb{C}$

$$\mathcal{M}, w \nVdash [H]p \vee [H]\neg p. \tag{10}$$

Notice that (10) states that there is no world, where an agent pattern H can know whether p or $\neg p$, and hence, it is stronger than $\mathcal{M} \nVdash [H]p \vee [H]\neg p$.

5 Communication

In this section, we will explore a different reading of agent patterns, namely as a description of the communication happening between the agents. Let G be the pattern $\{\{a\}, \{b, c\}\}$. We interpret this as *b and c communicate with each other* but *there is no communication between a and b or c*. A formula $[G]\phi$ will thus be interpreted as *a knows ϕ* ***and*** *the group b,c has distributed knowledge of ϕ*. We can also distinguish the patterns $\{\{a, b\}, \{b, c\}\}$ and $\{\{a, b\}, \{b, c\}, \{a, c\}\}$. In the first one, a and c can only communicate via b whereas in the second one, a and c have a direct communication channel.

Definition 7 (Connected). *Let $C \subseteq \mathsf{Pow}(\mathsf{Ag})$, we call two elements $X, Y \in C$* connected in C *if and only if there exist $Z_0, ..., Z_k \in C$ with $Z_i \cap Z_{i+1} \neq \emptyset$ for $0 \leq i < k$ and $Z_0 = X$ and $Z_k = Y$.*

Definition 8 (Connected Component). *Let $C \subseteq \mathsf{Pow}(\mathsf{Ag})$, we call C a* connected component *if and only if for any $X, Y \in C$ with $X \neq Y$ it holds that X and Y are connected in C.*

Let $G \subseteq \mathsf{Pow}(\mathsf{Ag})$. We call H a maximal connected component of G *if and only if $H \subseteq G$ and there is no connected component $H' \subseteq G$ such that H is a proper subset of H'.*

We can represent an agent pattern G as the union of its maximal connected components. Let $C_1, \ldots, C_k$ be the maximal connected components of G. We have $G = \bigcup_{i=1}^{k} C_i$ and if $X \in C_i$ and $Y \in C_j$ with $i \neq j$, then X and Y are not connected in G.

Definition 9 (Componentwise indistinguishability). *Let $G = \bigcup_{i=1}^{k} C_i$ be an agent pattern with k maximal connected components C_i. We say that G cannot distinguish componentwise two simplices S and T, denoted by $S \mathsf{E}_G T$, if and only if*

$$\exists 1 \leq j \leq k.\ S \sim_{C_j} T,$$

i.e. there is some maximal component of G that cannot distinguish S and T.

We use the notation E_G since this relation is used to model something like *every component of G knows that.* For this section, we adapt the truth definition as follows:

$$\mathcal{M}, w \Vdash [G]\phi \quad \text{iff} \quad w \mathsf{E}_G v \text{ implies } \mathcal{M}, v \Vdash \phi \quad \text{for all } v \in \mathbb{C}.$$

Let $G := \{\{a\} \mid a \in \mathsf{Ag}\}$. Then we can read $[G]\phi$ as everybody knows that ϕ.

We immediately obtain the following properties:

Lemma 8. *Let $G = \bigcup_{i=1}^{k} C_i$ be an agent pattern with k maximal connected components C_i. Then E_G is symmetric. Moreover, let $\mathcal{S}_G$ be a set of simplices such that for any $S \in \mathcal{S}_G$ we have $\mathsf{noSym}(C_i) \subseteq S^{\circ}$ for some $1 \leq i \leq n$. Then the indistinguishability relation E_G is reflexive on $\mathcal{S}_G \times \mathcal{S}_G$.*

Note that E_G is not transitive. Also, anti-monotonicity does not hold in general. It does, however, hold componentwise.

Lemma 9 (Anti-monotonicity). *Let $G = \bigcup_{i=1}^{k} C_i$ be an agent pattern with k maximal connected components C_i. Let C be a connected component with $C \supseteq C_i$ for some $1 \leq i \leq k$ and let $H := G \cup C$. We find that $\mathsf{E}_H \subseteq \mathsf{E}_G$.*

Lemma 10 (Link). *Let $F, G, H \subseteq \mathsf{Pow}(\mathsf{Ag})$ be connected components such that $F \cup G$ is connected and $F \cup H$ is connected. The following formula is valid:*

$$[G]A \wedge [H]B \rightarrow [F \cup G \cup H](A \wedge B).$$

Proof. First, observe that $F \cup G \cup H$ is connected. Thus, by Lemma 9, $[G]A$ implies $[F \cup G \cup H]A$ and $[H]B$ implies $[F \cup G \cup H]B$. Since $[F \cup G \cup H]$ is a normal modality, we conclude $[F \cup G \cup H](A \wedge B)$. □

Example 5 (Missing link). Two networks G and H, each modelled as a connected component, both know that if malicious activity is detected, certain services must be stopped. Let mact be a propositional variable that indicates whether an intruder has been spotted and let stop indicates that the services are disabled. Since the procedure is known to both networks, we have

$$[G](\mathsf{mact} \rightarrow \mathsf{stop}) \wedge [H](\mathsf{mact} \rightarrow \mathsf{stop}) \text{ as well as } [G \cup H](\mathsf{mact} \rightarrow \mathsf{stop}).$$

Suppose now that G detects malicious activity, i.e. $[G]\mathsf{mact}$. Thus, G will stop certain services, i.e. $[G]\mathsf{stop}$. If the networks cannot communicate with each other, i.e. $G \cup H$ is not connected, then H will not stop the services. Hence, G and H as a whole are not following the security protocol, i.e. $\neg[G \cup H]\mathsf{stop}$, and might leave the system in a vulnerable state. However, if a coordinating node relays messages from G to H, then H could shut down its services as well. By Lemma 10 we find that for some network F, such that $F \cup G$ as well as $F \cup H$ is connected, it holds that

$$([G \cup H](\mathsf{mact} \rightarrow \mathsf{stop}) \wedge [G]\mathsf{mact}) \rightarrow [F \cup G \cup H]\mathsf{stop}.$$

6 Conclusion

In this paper we present a semantics for epistemic reasoning on simplicial sets and introduce the synergistic knowledge operator $[G]$. Synergistic knowledge describes relations among agents of a group and enables us to reason about what the group can know beyond traditional distributed knowledge. For example, in Example 4, the pattern $\{\{a, b\}, \{a, c\}\}$ differs from $\{\{a, b\}, \{a, c\}, \{b, c\}\}$, although both contain the same agents.

Furthermore, we develop a logic based on our model and study some of its validities. We show that classical distributed knowledge, as introduced by Halpern and Moses [8], can be expressed with the operator $[G]$, if G is a set of singleton sets.

Moreover, we provide various examples of how our logic can be used to describe problems that arise in distributed computing. In Example 2 we illustrate how to model scenarios that arise in failure detection protocols, and in Examples 3 and 4 we showcase how synergistic knowledge may occur in distributed systems, if agents access shared primitives.

Lastly, we discussed a new notion of indistinguishability that accounts for the connectivity of the agent pattern G. Componentwise indistinguishability seems fruitful for analysing knowledge in networks with respect to their underlying topology.

Acknowledgments. This work has been funded by the Swiss National Science Foundation (SNSF) under grant agreement Nr. 200021_188443 (Advanced Consensus Protocols).

References

1. Chaum, D.: The dining cryptographers problem: unconditional sender and recipient untraceability. J. Cryptol. **1**(1), 65–75 (1988). https://doi.org/10.1007/BF00206326
2. van Ditmarsch, H., Goubault, É., Ledent, J., Rajsbaum, S.: Knowledge and simplicial complexes. In: Lundgren, B., Nuñez Hernández, N.A. (eds.) Philosophy of Computing, vol. 143, pp. 1–50. Springer, Cham (2022). https://doi.org/10.1007/978-3-030-75267-5_1
3. van Ditmarsch, H., van der Hoek, W., Kooi, B.: Dynamic Epistemic Logic, 1st edn. Springer, Dordrecht (2007). https://doi.org/10.1007/978-1-4020-5839-4
4. van Ditmarsch, H., Kuznets, R.: Wanted dead or alive: epistemic logic for impure simplicial complexes. J. Log. Comput. (to appear)
5. Goubault, É., Ledent, J., Rajsbaum, S.: A simplicial complex model for dynamic epistemic logic to study distributed task computability. Inf. Comput. **278**, 104597 (2021). https://doi.org/10.1016/j.ic.2020.104597
6. Goubault, É., Ledent, J., Rajsbaum, S.: A simplicial model for $KB4_n$: epistemic logic with agents that may die. In: Berenbrink, P., Monmege, B. (eds.) 39th International Symposium on Theoretical Aspects of Computer Science, STACS 2022. LIPIcs, Marseille, France, 15–18 March 2022 (Virtual Conference), vol. 219, pp. 33:1–33:20. Schloss Dagstuhl - Leibniz-Zentrum für Informatik (2022). https://doi.org/10.4230/LIPIcs.STACS.2022.33
7. Goubault, É.G., Kniazev, R., Ledent, J., Rajsbaum, S.: Semi-simplicial set models for distributed knowledge (2023)
8. Halpern, J.Y., Moses, Y.: Knowledge and common knowledge in a distributed environment. In: Kameda, T., Misra, J., Peters, J.G., Santoro, N. (eds.) Proceedings of the Third Annual ACM Symposium on Principles of Distributed Computing, Vancouver, B.C., Canada, 27–29 August 1984, pp. 50–61. ACM (1984). https://doi.org/10.1145/800222.806735
9. Herlihy, M.: Wait-free synchronization. ACM Trans. Program. Lang. Syst. **13**(1), 124–149 (1991). https://doi.org/10.1145/114005.102808
10. Herlihy, M., Kozlov, D.N., Rajsbaum, S.: Distributed Computing Through Combinatorial Topology. Morgan Kaufmann (2013). https://store.elsevier.com/product.jsp?isbn=9780124045781

11. Herlihy, M., Shavit, N.: The topological structure of asynchronous computability. J. ACM **46**(6), 858–923 (1999). https://doi.org/10.1145/331524.331529
12. Randrianomentsoa, R.F., van Ditmarsch, H., Kuznets, R.: Impure simplicial complexes: complete axiomatization. Log. Methods Comput. Sci. (to appear)

Post-quantum Secure Stateful Deterministic Wallet from Code-Based Signature Featuring Uniquely Rerandomized Keys

Pratima Jana(✉) and Ratna Dutta

Department of Mathematics, Indian Institute of Technology Kharagpur, Kharagpur 721302, India
pratimajanahatiary@kgpian.iitkgp.ac.in, ratna@maths.iitkgp.ac.in

Abstract. The deterministic wallet is a promising cryptographic primitive used in cryptocurrencies to protect users' wealth where a key derivation process enables the creation of any number of derived keys from a master key. A general architecture of a deterministic wallet using a signature with rerandomizable keys was introduced by Das et al. in CCS'19. A signature scheme with rerandomizable keys allows independently but consistently rerandomizing the master private key and the master public key. The deterministic wallet from rerandomizable signatures by Das et al. was instantiated from the signature scheme of Boneh-Lynn-Shacham (BLS) and Elliptic Curve Digital Signature Algorithm (ECDSA) which do not provide security against quantum computers. Designing a deterministic wallet is a difficult task and there are only a limited number of deterministic wallet constructions. In this paper, we focus on designing a post-quantum secure code-based deterministic wallet as code-based public key cryptosystem is a promising alternative in the post-quantum era. We first develop a post-quantum secure signing technique with key rerandomizability property that relies on the hardness of *Restricted Decision General Decoding problem* (RDGDP), *Decisional Syndrome Decoding Problem* (DSDP), *General Decision Syndrome Decoding problem* (GDSDP) and *Syndrome Decoding Problem* (SDP). In addition, our scheme exhibits the feature of uniquely rerandomizable keys. We present a thorough security proof and show that our design is secure against existential unforgeability under chosen-message attacks using honestly rerandomized keys. Finally, we employ the property of uniquely rerandomizable keys of our construction to develop a deterministic wallet that achieves security against wallet unlinkability and wallet unforgeability under the hardness of RDGDP, DSDP, GDSDP and SDP problems. We support the conjectured security of our deterministic wallet with regional security analysis.

Keywords: Post-quantum Cryptography · Stateful Deterministic Wallet · Rerandomized Signature · Code-based Cryptography · Cryptocurrency

S. Dolev and B. Schieber (Eds.): SSS 2023, LNCS 14310, pp. 568–582, 2023.
https://doi.org/10.1007/978-3-031-44274-2_42

1 Introduction

Blockchain technology has become quite popular in the last ten years since it offers a distributed architecture that makes it possible to execute applications securely in addition to making straightforward payments. It gets further promoted by Bitcoin [15], the first cryptocurrency to gain widespread adoption. Cryptocurrency is a digital asset that is also recognized as a digital currency and is primarily built on blockchain technology. The money transferred in decentralized cryptocurrencies is managed by a network of miners. Most cryptocurrencies use transactions to update their balances. A cryptocurrency transaction is the transmission of information between specified blockchain addresses. Let us consider two users *Alice* and *Bob* with private-public key pairs $(\mathsf{sk}_A, \mathsf{pk}_A)$ and $(\mathsf{sk}_B, \mathsf{pk}_B)$. The public address of a user is generated by taking the hash of the corresponding user's public key. Let *Alice* want to transfer the amount *amt*, to *Bob*'s address (which is the hash of Bob's public key pk_B). These transfers have to be signed with *Alice*'s private key sk_A on the message that informally says "The amount *amt* is transferring from pk_A to pk_B". Signed transactions are broadcast to a network of nodes and active computers that validate transactions according to a set of criteria. Valid transactions need to be confirmed by being included in blocks through the process of mining which is done by the miner. Since only *Alice* knows the private key sk_A corresponding to pk_A, only she can compute a valid signature. Thus possession of sk_A implies complete control over the funds corresponding to address pk_A. As a result, attacks against private keys are extremely tempting. Naturally, there are several instances of remarkable cyberattacks in which the attacker stole millions of dollars by getting into a system and obtaining the private key [5,19]. In 2018, attackers were able to steal more than $1 billion worth of Bitcoin according to the cryptocurrency research firm CipherTrace [11].

In general, storing just a small quantity of bitcoin in a *hot wallet* and moving bigger sums of money to a *cold wallet* can help ones prevent this attack. A *hot wallet* is software with a direct Internet connection that operates on a PC or a smartphone and a *cold wallet* is one that is frequently not linked to the network. A hot/cold wallet can be easily constructed by creating a key pair $(\mathsf{pk}_{\mathsf{cold}}, \mathsf{sk}_{\mathsf{cold}})$ and keeping the appropriate public key $\mathsf{pk}_{\mathsf{cold}}$ on the *hotwallet*, while the corresponding private key $\mathsf{sk}_{\mathsf{cold}}$ is kept on the *cold wallet*. By broadcasting that the user is giving money to $\mathsf{pk}_{\mathsf{cold}}$ on the blockchain a user can transfer money to the *coldwallet*. The *cold wallet* never needs to turn on as long as the owner doesn't wish to use his or her money. There is a significant flaw in this basic strategy. All transactions are publicly visible as blockchain is transparent. Therefore, it is simple to link all transactions to a particular public address to a *hot wallet* that has the public key $\mathsf{pk}_{\mathsf{cold}}$ (whose hash is that particular public address). Since the same public key $\mathsf{pk}_{\mathsf{cold}}$ is used for all transactions that target the cold wallet which consists the private key $\mathsf{sk}_{\mathsf{cold}}$, a significant sum of money may eventually accrue in the cold wallet. As a result, the next time when the wallet goes online, $\mathsf{pk}_{\mathsf{cold}}$ is a tempting target for an attack. The primary reason for this kind of attack is the linkability between the transaction. Creating as many new key pairs as there are transactions is a common technique for making the transactions unlinkable. This method, however, is limited to a priori set of transactions and requires a sizable hot/cold wallet that expands linearly in storage as transactions increase.

The bitcoin improvement proposal (BIP32) [23] for the well-known cryptocurrency Bitcoin has solved these two concerns of linkability and large storage space and the method is frequently referred to as deterministic wallets [7] in the literature on cryptocurrencies. The definition of stateful deterministic wallets in the context of hot/cold was first formalized by Das et al. [8]. For deterministic wallets, one creates a single master public key and master private key in an initialization phase and stores them in the hot and cold wallets respectively. Instead of creating new key pairs each time, two session key derivation algorithms are used in deterministic wallets to produce session public keys and session private keys from the master public and the master private keys respectively. In addition to the master public and master private keys, the deterministic public key derivation algorithm and the private key derivation algorithm also maintain some state information to generate session public keys and session private keys respectively. This allows one to produce an unlimited number of session keys while only requiring the storage of a single (master) key. Deterministic wallet schemes must satisfy unlinkability property in addition to the basic idea of unforgeability to make sure that it is impossible for a third party to connect two transactions made to the same wallet. According to the notion of forward security in unlinkability, a transaction transmitted to session public keys generated before the hot wallet attack cannot be connected to the master public key.

1.1 Related Works

Many cryptocurrencies leverage the idea of hot and cold wallets to give their users additional security assurances. The deterministic wallet mechanism proposed in BIP32 [23] that is utilized for Bitcoin has many flaws as identified by Gutoski and Stebila [12] in 2015. They investigated the well-known attacks against deterministic wallets [7] and after just one session key has been exposed it enables the recovery of the master private key. Instead of taking into account the conventional model of unforgeability where the adversary attempts to forge a signature, they have adopted a significantly weaker model where the adversary's goal is to obtain the master private key. In 2018, Fan et al. [10] examined the security of hot/cold by addressing "privilege escalation attacks" which lacks any formal security analysis. Later, in 2016, Turuani et al. [22] investigated the Bitcoin Electrum wallet in the Dolev-Yao model [9].

Das et al. [8] formally proposed the concept of a stateful deterministic wallet in 2019, taking into account the two desirable security properties of wallet unforgeability and wallet unlinkability. Perfectly rerandomizable keys are the foundation for their stateful deterministic wallet. They proposed a general model for a stateful deterministic wallet that makes use of signature techniques with keys that are perfectly rerandomizable. The discrete logarithm-based Elliptic

Curve Digital Signature Algorithm (ECDSA) signature system is used to implement all widely used cryptocurrencies and Das et al. instantiated a provably secure ECDSA-based deterministic wallet in [8]. In addition, they have shown how Boneh-Lynn-Shacham (BLS) signatures [6] can be used to construct signatures using rerandomizable keys and thus can be a possible candidate for instantiating their deterministic wallet.

The aforementioned deterministic wallet scheme offers an efficient way to improve the security of users' money, but none are resistant to quantum attacks as they are built on the discrete logarithm problem and its variants, which is vulnerable to quantum attack due to Shor's algorithm [18]. Alkadri et al. [1] presented a construction from a generic lattice-based Fiat-Shamir signature scheme to develop the first post-quantum secure signature technique with only public key is rerandomizable. They showed how to implement the wallet scheme suggested by Das et al. [8] based on the qTESLA signature [2]. However, they offered security using a weaker model than that in Das et al. [8].

1.2 Our Contributions

The somewhat unsatisfactory state-of-affairs inspires our search for a code-based construction of a stateful deterministic wallet. The difficulty arises from the need for an efficient code-based signature scheme with uniquely rerandomizable keys. [8] and [1] are the closest related works to ours. The two stateful deterministic wallets presented by Das et al. [8] relied on the *Discrete Logarithm Problem* (DLP) and *Computational Diffie-Hellman* (CDH) problem and do not guarantee security in the quantum world due to Shor's algorithm [18]. Alkadri et al. [1] introduced the first post-quantum secure signature scheme with rerandomizable public keys by presenting a construction from the lattice settings which is secure under the *Module Learning With Errors* (MLWE) assumption and *Module Shortest Integer Solution with infinity norm* (MSIS^∞) assumption. Our contribution in this paper can be summed up as follows:

- We initiate the study of the signature scheme with rerandomized keys in code-based settings and develop the first code-based signature scheme Code-RSig with rerandomized keys. Furthermore, our scheme satisfies the property of uniquely rerandomizable keys. It is proven to achieve existential unforgeability under chosen message attack assuming the hardness of *Restricted Decision General Decoding problem* (RDGDP), *Decisional Syndrome Decoding Problem* (DSDP), *General Decision Syndrome Decoding problem* (GDSDP) and *Syndrome Decoding Problem* (SDP) which is supported by a concrete security analysis.
- We exploit the feature of uniquely rerandomizable keys of Code-RSig to develop a code-based stateful deterministic wallet against wallet unlinkability and wallet unforgeability under the hardness of RDGDP, DSDP, GDSDP and SDP.

Table 1 compares our code-based signature scheme Code-RSig with rerandomized keys to existing works in relation to the size of the key, the size of

Table 1. Comparative analysis of signature scheme with rerandomized keys with respect to key size, signature size and quantum security

Scheme	Quantum secure	Key Size $\vert\mathsf{sk}\vert$	$\vert\mathsf{pk}\vert$	Signature $\vert\sigma\vert$	Security
REC [8]	No	1 in $\mathbb{Z}_p$	1 in $\mathbb{G}$	2 in $\mathbb{Z}_p$	DLP
RBLS [8]	No	1 in $\mathbb{Z}_p$	1 in $\mathbb{G}$	1 in $\mathbb{G}$	CDH
Lattice-RSig [1]	Yes	1 in $R_q^{k_1+k_2}$, 1 in $\{0,1\}^{\ell_G}$	1 in $R_q^{k_1}$	1 in $R_q^{k_1+k_2}$, 1 in $\mathbb{T}_\kappa^m$	MLWE, MSIS$^\infty$
Code-RSig	Yes	1 in $\mathbb{F}_2^{s\times n}$	1 in $\mathbb{F}_2^{(n-k)\times s}$	1 in $\mathbb{F}_2^n$, 1 in $\mathbb{F}_2^s$	RDGDP, DSDP, GDSDP, SDP

$\vert\mathsf{sk}\vert$ is the size of the private key, $\vert\mathsf{pk}\vert$ is the size of the public key, Com. Cost is Computation Cost, Sig. Gen. is Signature generation cost, Sig. Ver. is the Signature Verification cost. $\mathbb{G}$ be a group with prime order, $R = \mathbb{Z}[x]/(f(x))$ = polynomial ring and $R_q = \mathbb{Z}_q[x]/(f(x))$ where q is prime and $f(x)$ is a monic polynomial of degree m, $R_q = R/q$ for prime q. $\mathbb{T}_\kappa^m$ represents the subset of R_q include all polynomials Hamming weight κ and coefficients are from $\{-1, 0, 1\}$. n, k, s, k_1, k_2 are integers. CDH = Computational Diffie-Hellman, DLP = Discrete Logarithm Problem, MSIS$^\infty$ = Module Shortest Integer Solution with infinity norm, MLWE = Module Learning With Errors Problem, RDGDP = Restricted Decision General Decoding problem, DSDP = Decisional Syndrome Decoding Problem, GDSDP = General Decision Syndrome Decoding problem, SDP = Syndrome Decoding Problem.

the signature and quantum security. We compare our scheme with two Diffie-Hellman based constructions REC and RBLS proposed by Das et al. [8] as well as lattice-based construction given by Alkadri et al. [1]. In contrast to [8], our scheme Code-RSig enjoys post-quantum security similar to the lattice-based signature scheme with rerandomized public keys Lattice-RSig [1]. However, Lattice-RSig necessitates a large key length and signature size compared to our candidate. Besides, this lattice-based scheme is proven to be secure in the weak security model in the sense that the Lattice-RSig scheme only achieved indistinguishability between session public keys distribution and the master public key distribution but session private keys distribution are not indistinguishable from the distribution of the master private key. Our code-based key rerandomizable signature scheme is secure in the strong security model proposed in [8] where the randomized session private key and randomized session public key are identically distributed to the master private key and the master public key respectively.

As exhibited in Table 2 our scheme outperforms Lattice-RSig in terms of computation cost since Lattice-RSig scheme requires $2k_1k_2$ multiplication over R_q and our scheme requires $2n(n+s-k)-ks$ multiplication over $\mathbb{F}_2$. Although, in terms of computational cost the schemes of [8] are efficient compared to our scheme but these are not quantum secure.

2 Preliminary

An overview of the underlying mathematics is given in this section, along with some recalls of the fundamental cryptographic building blocks.

Table 2. Comparative analysis of the computational cost of the signature scheme with rerandomized keys

Scheme	Computational Cost	
	Signature Generation	Signature Verification
REC [8]	1 exponential in $\mathbb{G}$, 2 mul in $\mathbb{G}$, 1 add in $\mathbb{G}$, 1 inverse in $\mathbb{Z}_p$	2 exponential in $\mathbb{G}$, 2 mul in $\mathbb{G}$, 1 add in $\mathbb{G}$,1 inverse in $\mathbb{Z}_p$
RBLS [8]	1 exponential in $\mathbb{G}$	2 pairing
Lattice-RSig [1]	$k_1 k_2$ mul in R_q, $k_2(k_1+2)$ add in R_q	$k_1 k_2$ mul in R_q, $k_2(k_1+1)$ add in R_q
Code-RSig	$n(n+s-k)$ mul in $\mathbb{F}_2$, $n(n+s-k-1)+k$ add in $\mathbb{F}_2$	$(n-k)(n+s)$ mul in $\mathbb{F}_2$, $(n-k)(n+s-1)$ add in $\mathbb{F}_2$

Here $\mathbb{G}$ be a group with prime order, $R = \mathbb{Z}[x]/(f(x))$ = polynomial ring, $R_q = \mathbb{Z}_q[x]/(f(x))$ where q is prime and $f(x)$ is a monic polynomial of degree m, $\mathbb{T}^m_\kappa$ represent the subset of R_q include all polynomials Hamming weight κ and coefficients are from $\{-1, 0, 1\}$.n, k, s, k_1, k_2 are integers. n, k, s, k_1, k_2 are integers.

2.1 Notations

For an unambiguous presentation of the paper, we adopt the notations described in Table 3.

Table 3. Notations used

Symbol	Description
λ	: security parameter
$a \xleftarrow{\$} A$	: uniformly sampling any random a from the set A
$\mathcal{S}^n_w \subseteq \mathbb{F}^n_2$	: All binary vectors with weight w and length n are included in this set
$\mathsf{wt}(\mathbf{x})$	: denotes Hamming weight of $\mathbf{x}$, which is the number of 1 in the binary vector $\mathbf{x}$
$N(R)$	: the highest Hamming weight that each row of matrix R can have
d_{GV}	: Gilbert-Varshamov (GV) bound
$S_1 \| S_2$	: concatenation of matrices S_1 and S_2

Definition 2.11. The function $\epsilon(\cdot)$ is said to be *negligible*, if for every positive integer n, there exists an integer N_n such that for all $x > N_n$, $|\epsilon(x)| < 1/x^n$.

2.2 Basic Definition of Coding Theory

Given integers n and k, a binary linear $[n, k]$ *code* $\mathcal{C}$ is a k-dimensional subspace of $\mathbb{F}^n_2$. Each element of $\mathcal{C}$ is called a *codeword.* A matrix $G \in \mathbb{F}^{k\times n}_2$ is a generator matrix of a linear code $\mathcal{C}$ if $\mathcal{C} = \{\mathbf{m}G : \mathbf{m} \in \mathbb{F}^k_2\}$. A matrix $H \in \mathbb{F}^{(n-k)\times n}_2$ is a *parity check matrix* of $\mathcal{C}$ if $\mathcal{C} = \{\mathbf{c} \in \mathbb{F}^n_2 : H\mathbf{c}^{\mathrm{T}} = 0\}$. The *syndrome* of a vector $\mathbf{e} \in \mathbb{F}^n_2$ under H is defined as $\mathbf{s} = H\mathbf{e}^{\mathrm{T}}$ where $\mathbf{s} \in \mathbb{F}^{n-k}_2$. Given an $[n, k]$-linear code $\mathcal{C}$ over $\mathbb{F}_2$, the generator matrix G is under systematic form if and only if it is of the form $[I_k || P]$. For every $\mathbf{x} = (x_1, \ldots, x_n) \in \mathbb{F}^n_2$ the Hamming weight $\mathsf{wt}(\mathbf{x})$ equals the number of 1 in binary vector $\mathbf{x}$. $N(R)$ denotes the row sum norm of a matrix R in $\mathbb{F}^{s\times n}_2$.

In [17], Pierce proved that the Gilbert-Varshamov (GV) bound is a strict bound for almost every linear code. The lemma below comes from Tilburg [21].

Lemma 2.21 (Gilbert-Varshamov (GV) bound [21]). *Consider $\mathcal{C}$ to be an $[n,k]$-linear code over $\mathbb{F}_q$. The GV bound d_{GV} is the minimum is the smallest d that ensures*

$$\sum_{i=0}^{d-2} \binom{n}{i} (q-1)^i \geq q^{n-k}.$$

Furthermore, it says

$$d_{GV} = nH_q^{-1}\left(1 - \frac{k}{n}\right) + O(n), [\textit{for large } n]$$

in which $H_q(x) = -x\log_q(x) - (1-x)\log_q(1-x) + x\log_q(q-1)$ denotes the q-ary entropy function and it is invertible when restricted to $[0, 1-\frac{1}{q}]$.

In the following, we recall some hard problems of coding theory.

Definition 2.22 (Syndrome Decoding Problem (SDP) [14]). Let n, k, w_H be integers. Given a parity check matrix $H \in \mathbb{F}_2^{(n-k)\times n}$ and a syndrome $\mathbf{s} \in \mathbb{F}_2^{n-k}$, the SDP asks to find a vector $\mathbf{e} \in \mathbb{F}_2^n$ such that $H\mathbf{e}^{\mathrm{T}} = \mathbf{s}$ and $\mathsf{wt}(\mathbf{e}) \leq w_H$.

Definition 2.23 (Decisional Syndrome Decoding Problem (DSDP) [20]). Let n, k, w_H be integers. Given a parity check matrix $H \in \mathbb{F}_2^{(n-k)\times n}$, the DSDP asks to distinguish the pair $(H, H\mathbf{e}^{\mathrm{T}})$ from $(H, \mathbf{s})$ with $\mathbf{s} \xleftarrow{\$} \mathbb{F}_2^{n-k}$ and $\mathsf{wt}(\mathbf{e}) \leq w_H$.

The syndrome decoding problem is proven to be NP-complete by Berlekamp, McEliece and Tilborg in [4]. If w_H is less than the $Gilbert-Varshamov$ bound then the solution to the SDP is ensured to be unique and SDP is NP hard. The DSDP has been shown to be hard by Applebaum, Ishai and Kushilevitz in [3].

Definition 2.24 (General Decoding problem(GDP) [20]). Let w_H, n, and k all be positive integers. Given a generator matrix $G \in \mathbb{F}_2^{k\times n}$ of random $[n,k]$-linear codes over $\mathbb{F}_2$ and $\mathbf{y} \in \mathbb{F}_2^n$, the GDP asks to find $\mathbf{m} \in \mathbb{F}_2^k$ and $\mathbf{e} \in \mathbb{F}_2^n$ such that $\mathsf{wt}(\mathbf{e}) \leq w_H$ and $\mathbf{y} = \mathbf{m}G + \mathbf{e}$.

Lemma 2.25 ([13]). *Let n and k be positive integers. Let $G \in \mathbb{F}_2^{k\times n}$ be a generator matrix and $H \in \mathbb{F}_2^{(n-k)\times n}$ be a parity check matrix of random $[n,k]$-linear codes over $\mathbb{F}_2$, then GDP is as hard as the SDP.*

Definition 2.26 (Decision General Decoding problem(DGDP) [20]). Let w_H, n and k all be positive integers. Given a generator matrix $G \in \mathbb{F}_2^{k\times n}$ of random $[n,k]$-linear code over $\mathbb{F}_2$, $\mathbf{m} \in \mathbb{F}_2^k$ and $\mathbf{e} \in \mathbb{F}_2^n$ with $\mathsf{wt}(\mathbf{e}) \leq w_H$, the DGDP asks to distinguish the pair $(G, \mathbf{m}G + \mathbf{e})$ from $(G, \mathbf{y})$ with $\mathbf{y} \xleftarrow{\$} \mathbb{F}_2^n$.

In [13], Li et al. proved that the McEliece cryptosystems and Niederreiter cryptosystems are equivalent. This, in turn, implies the GDP and the SDP are also equivalent. In [16], the DGDP is proved as an NP-hard problem by Persichetti.

Song et al. [20] introduced the following problems and showed a reduction to prove that these problems are as hard as some well-known hard problems in code-based cryptography.

Definition 2.27 (General Syndrome Decoding problem (GSDP) [20]). Let w_H, n and k all be positive integers. Given a parity check matrix $H \in \mathbb{F}_2^{(n-k)\times n}$ of a random $[n,k]$-linear codes and $T \in \mathbb{F}_2^{(n-k)\times s}$ a random matrix, the GSDP asks to find a matrix $R \in \mathbb{F}_2^{s\times n}$ such that $N(R) \leq w_H$ and $HR^{\mathrm{T}} = T$.

Lemma 2.28 ([20]). *Let w_H, n and k all be positive integers. Given a parity check matrix $H \in \mathbb{F}_2^{(n-k)\times n}$ of a random $[n,k]$-linear codes and a random matrix $T \in \mathbb{F}_2^{(n-k)\times s}$, the GSDP is as hard as the SDP problem.*

Definition 2.29 (General Decision Syndrome Decoding problem (GDSDP) [20]). Let w_H, n and k all be positive integers. Given a parity check matrix $H \in \mathbb{F}_2^{(n-k)\times n}$ of a random $[n,k]$-linear codes and a random matrix $R \in \mathbb{F}_2^{s\times n}$ and $N(R) \leq w_H$, the GDSDP asks to distinguish the pair (H, HR^{T}) from (H, Y) with $Y \xleftarrow{\$} \mathbb{F}_2^{(n-k)\times s}$.

Lemma 2.210 ([20]). *Let w_H, n and k all be positive integers. Given a parity check matrix $H \in \mathbb{F}_2^{(n-k)\times n}$ of a random $[n,k]$-linear codes and a random matrix $R \in \mathbb{F}_2^{s\times n}$ and $N(R) \leq w$, the GDSDP is as hard as the DSDP problem.*

Definition 2.211 (Restricted Decision General Decoding problem (RDGDP) [20]). Let G be a generator matrix of a random $[n,k]$-linear codes and w'_H a positive integer. If $\mathsf{wt}(\mathbf{m}G + \mathbf{e}) \leq w'_H$ always holds for $\mathbf{m} \xleftarrow{\$} \mathbb{F}_2^k$ and $\mathbf{e} \xleftarrow{\$} \mathcal{S}_{w_H}^n$, then the RDGDP asks to distinguish the pair $(G, \mathbf{m}G + \mathbf{e})$ from $(G, \mathbf{y})$ with $\mathbf{y} \xleftarrow{\$} \mathbb{F}_2^n$ and $\mathsf{wt}(\mathbf{y}) \leq w'_H$.

Lemma 2.212 ([20]). *Let G be a generator matrix of a random $[n,k]$-linear codes and w'_H a positive integer. If $\mathsf{wt}(\mathbf{m}G + \mathbf{e}) \leq w'_H$ always holds for $\mathbf{m} \xleftarrow{\$} \mathbb{F}_2^k$ and $\mathbf{e} \xleftarrow{\$} \mathcal{S}_{w_H}^n$, then RDGDP is as hard as DGDP.*

3 Our Code-Based Signature Scheme with Perfectly Rerandomizable Keys

3.1 Protocol Description

We describe below our code-based signature scheme with perfectly rerandomizable keys Code-RSig leveraging the code-based Fiat-Shamir signatures scheme of Song et al. [20] Code-Sig.

Code-RSig.Setup$(1^\lambda) \rightarrow \mathsf{pp}_{\mathsf{sgn}}$: This algorithm is run by a trusted party on input 1^λ and returns the public parameter $\mathsf{pp}_{\mathsf{sgn}}$ as follows.

i. Chooses positive integers $(n, k, r, s, \ell, w_1, w_2) \in \mathbb{N}^7$ such that $n = \ell r$ and $\ell(w_1 + r - s) + w_2 \leq d_{GV}$ where w_1 and w_2 represent the Hamming weight and let d_{GV} be the *Gilbert – Varshamov* bound of random $[n,k]$-linear codes over $\mathbb{F}_2$.

ii. Samples uniformly a parity check matrix H from $\mathbb{F}_2^{(n-k)\times n}$ and a keyed weight restricted hash function $\mathcal{H} : \mathbb{F}_2^{n-k} \times \{0,1\}^* \rightarrow \mathcal{S}_{w_1}^s$.
iii. Publishes $\mathsf{pp}_{\mathsf{sgn}} = (n, k, r, s, \ell, w_1, w_2, d_{GV}, H, \mathcal{H})$.

$\mathsf{Code\text{-}RSig.KeyGen}(\mathsf{pp}_{\mathsf{sgn}}) \rightarrow (\mathsf{sk}, \mathsf{pk})$: On input $\mathsf{pp}_{\mathsf{sgn}}$, a user executes this algorithm below and generates a private key sk and public key pk:

i. Chooses randomly systematic generator matrices $E_1, \ldots, E_\ell$ of ℓ distinct random $[r, s]$-linear codes over $\mathbb{F}_2$ where each $E_i = [I_s||R_i]$, I_s is the identity matrix of order s and R_i is a random matrix from $\mathbb{F}_2^{s\times(r-s)}$ for $i = 1, \ldots, \ell$, sets $E = [E_1|| \ldots ||E_\ell] \in \mathbb{F}_2^{s\times n}$ and samples permutation matrices $P_1 \in \mathbb{F}_2^{s\times s}$ and $P_2 \in \mathbb{F}_2^{n\times n}$.
ii. Computes $U = P_1 E P_2 \in \mathbb{F}_2^{s\times n}$ and $V = HU^{\mathrm{T}} \in \mathbb{F}_2^{(n-k)\times s}$.
iii. Sets $\mathsf{sk} = U$ and $\mathsf{pk} = V$.
iv. Publishes pk and keeps sk secret to himself.

$\mathsf{Code\text{-}RSig.Sign}(\mathsf{pp}_{\mathsf{sgn}}, \mathsf{sk}, m) \rightarrow \sigma$: By running this algorithm, a signer generates a signature σ on a message $m \in \{0,1\}^*$ using public parameter $\mathsf{pp}_{\mathsf{sgn}}$ and his private key $\mathsf{sk} = U$ by working as follows:

i. Samples $\mathbf{e}$ from $\mathcal{S}_{w_2}^n$.
ii. Computes syndromes $\mathbf{y} = H\mathbf{e}^{\mathrm{T}} \in \mathbb{F}_2^{n-k}$ and the challenge $\mathbf{c} = \mathcal{H}(\mathbf{y}, m) \in \mathcal{S}_{w_1}^s$.
iii. Computes the response $\mathbf{z} = \mathbf{c}U + \mathbf{e} \in \mathbb{F}_2^n$.
iv. Outputs the signature $\sigma = (\mathbf{z}, \mathbf{c})$.

$\mathsf{Code\text{-}RSig.Verify}(\mathsf{pp}_{\mathsf{sgn}}, \mathsf{pk}, m, \sigma) \rightarrow \mathsf{Valid/Invalid}$: Employing the public parameter $\mathsf{pp}_{\mathsf{sgn}}$ and signer's public key $\mathsf{pk} = V$, a verifier verifies the signature σ on m by checking the following steps.

i. Parses $\sigma = (\mathbf{z}, \mathbf{c}) \in \mathbb{F}_2^n \times \mathcal{S}_{w_1}^s$.
ii. If $\mathsf{wt}(\mathbf{z}) \leq \ell(w_1 + r - s) + w_2$ and $\mathcal{H}((H\mathbf{z}^{\mathrm{T}} - V\mathbf{c}^{\mathrm{T}}), m) = \mathbf{c}$ then returns Valid, otherwise returns Invalid. Note that, this $\mathbf{z}$ and a random vector $\mathbf{z}'$ of weight $\leq \ell(w_1 + r - s) + w_2$ in $\mathbb{F}_2^n$ are indistinguishable.

$\mathsf{Code\text{-}RSig.Randsk}(\mathsf{pp}_{\mathsf{sgn}}, \mathsf{sk}, \rho) \rightarrow \mathsf{sk}'$: This deterministic private key randomization algorithm is run by a user who takes as input the public parameter $\mathsf{pp}_{\mathsf{sgn}} = (n, k, r, s, \ell, w_1, w_2, d_{GV}, H, \mathcal{H})$, his own private key $\mathsf{sk} = U$ and a randomness matrix $\rho = [\rho_1'|| \ldots ||\rho_\ell'] \in \mathbb{F}_2^{s\times n}$ where each $\rho_i' = [O_s||R_i']$, O_s is the zero matrix of order s and R_i' is a random matrix from $\mathbb{F}_2^{s\times(r-s)}$ for $i = 1, \ldots, \ell$ and generates a rerandomized private key $\mathsf{sk}' = \mathsf{sk} + \rho = U + \rho \in \mathbb{F}_2^{s\times n}$.

$\mathsf{Code\text{-}RSig.Randpk}(\mathsf{pp}_{\mathsf{sgn}}, \mathsf{pk}, \rho) \rightarrow \mathsf{pk}'$: A user runs this deterministic public key rerandomization algorithm, on input the public parameter $\mathsf{pp}_{\mathsf{sgn}} = (n, k, r, s, \ell, w_1, w_2, d_{GV}, H, \mathcal{H})$, a public key $\mathsf{pk} = V$ and a randomness matrix $\rho = [\rho_1'|| \ldots ||\rho_\ell'] \in \mathbb{F}_2^{s\times n}$ where each $\rho_i' = [O_s||R_i']$, O_s is the zero matrix of order s and R_i' is a random matrix from $\mathbb{F}_2^{s\times(r-s)}$ for $i = 1, \ldots, \ell$ and generates a rerandomized public key $\mathsf{pk}' = V' = V + H\rho^{\mathrm{T}} \in \mathbb{F}_2^{(n-k)\times s}$.

Remark 3.11. Let $U = P_1 E P_2 \in \mathbb{F}_2^{s\times n}$ where $P_1 \in \mathbb{F}_2^{s\times s}$, $P_2 \in \mathbb{F}_2^{n\times n}$ are permutation matrices, $E = [E_1|| \ldots ||E_\ell] \in \mathbb{F}_2^{s\times n}$ with $E_i = [I_s||R_i]$, I_s is the identity matrix of order s and $R_i \in \mathbb{F}_2^{s\times(r-s)}$ is a random matrix for $i = 1, \ldots, \ell$.

Also assume that, $\rho = [\rho'_1||\dots||\rho'_\ell] \in \mathbb{F}_2^{s\times n}$ where each $\rho'_i = [O_s||R'_i]$, O_s is the zero matrix of order s and $R'_i \in \mathbb{F}_2^{s\times(r-s)}$ is a random matrix for $i = 1, \dots, \ell$. Then, $U+\rho = P_1[E'_1||\dots||E'_\ell]P_2$ where $E'_i = [I_s||R_i+P_1^{-1}R'_iP_2^{-1}]$ for $i = 1, \dots, \ell$.

Since R_i and R'_i both are uniformly random matrix in $\mathbb{F}_2^{s\times(r-s)}$, implies that $R_i + P_1^{-1}R'_iP_2^{-1}$ is also a uniformly random matrix in $\mathbb{F}_2^{s\times(r-s)}$. Hence, $U+\rho = P_1[E'_1||\dots||E'_\ell]P_2$ where $E'_i = [I_s||R_i + P_1^{-1}R'_iP_2^{-1}]$ for $i = 1, \dots, \ell$ and $R_i+P_1^{-1}R'_iP_2^{-1}$ is uniformly random matrix in $\mathbb{F}_2^{s\times(r-s)}$. This implies $U+\rho$ and U have the same distribution.

Remark 3.12. Let the signature $\mathbf{z} = \mathbf{c}U + \mathbf{e}$ be generated by the above signature scheme where $\mathbf{c} \in \mathcal{S}^s_{w_1}$ and $\mathbf{e} \in \mathcal{S}^n_{w_2}$ and $U = P_1EP_2 \in \mathbb{F}_2^{s\times n}$, $P_1 \in \mathbb{F}_2^{s\times s}$, $P_2 \in \mathbb{F}_2^{n\times n}$ are permutation matrices, then $\mathsf{wt}(\mathbf{z}) \leq \ell(w_1 + r - s) + w_2$.

Correctness: Our proposed scheme is correct as it satisfies the following three requirements:

i. For all $\mathsf{pp_{sgn}} = (n, k, r, s, \ell, w_1, w_2, d_{GV}, H, \mathcal{H}) \leftarrow$ Code-RSig.Setup(1^λ), all ($\mathsf{sk} = U$, $\mathsf{pk} = V$) $\leftarrow$ Code-RSig.KeyGen ($\mathsf{pp_{sgn}}$), all message $m \in \{0,1\}^*$ and all signature $\sigma = (\mathbf{z}, \mathbf{c}) \leftarrow$ Code-RSig.Sign($\mathsf{pp_{sgn}}$, sk, m) we have Code-RSig.Verify ($\mathsf{pp_{sgn}}$, pk, m, σ) = Valid which follows from the correctness of signature scheme Code-Sig.

ii. For all $\mathsf{pp_{sgn}} = (n, k, r, s, \ell, w_1, w_2, d_{GV}, H, \mathcal{H}) \leftarrow$ Code-RSig.Setup(1^λ), all ($\mathsf{sk} = U$, $\mathsf{pk} = V$) $\leftarrow$ Code-RSig.KeyGen($\mathsf{pp_{sgn}}$), all message $m \in \{0,1\}^*$, all randomness matrix $\rho \in \mathbb{F}_2^{s\times n}$ and signature $\sigma' = (\mathbf{z}', \mathbf{c}') \leftarrow$ Code-RSig.Sign($\mathsf{pp_{sgn}}$, sk$'$, m) where sk$' = U + \rho \leftarrow$ Code-RSig.Randsk($\mathsf{pp_{sgn}}$, sk, ρ), it holds that Code-RSig.Verify($\mathsf{pp_{sgn}}$, pk$'$, m, σ) = Valid where pk$' = V' = V + H\rho^{\mathrm{T}} = H(U^{\mathrm{T}} + \rho^{\mathrm{T}}) \leftarrow$ Code-RSig.Randpk($\mathsf{pp_{sgn}}$, pk, ρ) as $\mathbf{z}' = \mathbf{c}'(U+\rho) + \mathbf{e}'$ with $\mathbf{e}' \leftarrow \mathcal{S}^n_{w_2}, \mathbf{y}' = H(\mathbf{e}')^T, \mathbf{c}' = \mathcal{H}(\mathbf{y}'||m)$ and therefore,

$$\begin{aligned}\mathcal{H}(H(\mathbf{z}')^{\mathrm{T}} - V'(\mathbf{c}')^{\mathrm{T}}), m) &= \mathcal{H}((H(\mathbf{c}'(U+\rho) + \mathrm{e}')^{\mathrm{T}} - V'(\mathrm{c}')^{\mathrm{T}}, m)\\ &= \mathcal{H}(H((U^{\mathrm{T}} + \rho^{\mathrm{T}})(\mathbf{c}')^{\mathrm{T}}) + H(\mathbf{e}')^{\mathrm{T}} - V'(\mathbf{c}')^{\mathrm{T}}, m)\\ &= \mathcal{H}((V'(\mathbf{c}')^{\mathrm{T}} + \mathbf{y}' - V'(\mathbf{c}')^{\mathrm{T}}), m)\\ &= \mathcal{H}(\mathbf{y}', m)\\ &= \mathbf{c}'\end{aligned}$$

and from Remarks 3.11 and 3.12, it follows that $\mathsf{wt}(\mathbf{z}') \leq \ell(w_1 + r - s) + w_2$.

iii. Consider a randomized private-public key pair (sk$' = U + \rho$, pk$' = V + H\rho^{\mathrm{T}}$) which is a randomization of private-public key pair (sk $= U$, pk $= V$) $\leftarrow$ Code-RSig.KeyGen($\mathsf{pp_{sgn}}$). Here $U = P_1EP_2 \in \mathbb{F}_2^{s\times n}$, $P_1 \in \mathbb{F}_2^{s\times s}$, $P_2 \in \mathbb{F}_2^{n\times n}$ are permutation matrices and $E = [E_1||\dots||E_\ell] \in \mathbb{F}_2^{s\times n}$ with $E_i = [I_s||R_i]$ for $i = 1, \dots, \ell$ and randomness matrix $\rho = [\rho'_1||\dots||\rho'_\ell] \in \mathbb{F}_2^{s\times n}$ where each $\rho'_i = [O_s||R'_i]$, O_s is the zero matrix of order s and $R'_i \in \mathbb{F}_2^{s\times(r-s)}$ is a random matrix for $i = 1, \dots, \ell$. Hence, $U+\rho = P_1[E'_1||\dots||E'_\ell]P_2$ where $E'_i = [I_s||R_i + P_1^{-1}R'_iP_2^{-1}]$ for $i = 1, \dots, \ell$ and set $E' = E'_1||\dots||E'_\ell$. Consider a freshly generated key pair $(\mathsf{sk}'', \mathsf{pk}'') \leftarrow$ Code-RSig.KeyGen$(\mathsf{pp}_{\mathsf{sgn}})$ where $\mathsf{sk}'' = U_1 \in \mathbb{F}_2^{s\times n}$ and $\mathsf{pk}'' = V_1 = HU_1^{\mathrm{T}}$ and let $U_1 = Q_1FQ_2 \in \mathbb{F}_2^{s\times n}$ and $Q_1 \in \mathbb{F}_2^{s\times s}$, $Q_2 \in \mathbb{F}_2^{n\times n}$ are permutation matrices and $F = [F_1||\dots||F_\ell] \in \mathbb{F}_2^{s\times n}$ with $F_i = [I_s||A_i]$, A_i is $s \times (r-s)$ random matrix for $i = 1,\dots,\ell$. Hence, $\mathsf{sk}' = U + \rho = P_1E'P_2$ and $\mathsf{sk}'' = U_1 = Q_1FQ_2$ are identically distributed by Remark 3.12. Also both $\mathsf{pk} = V$ and $\mathsf{pk}' = V_1$ are indistinguishable from random $Y \xleftarrow{\$} \mathbb{F}_2^{(n-k)\times s}$ under the hardness of GDSDP 2.29. Then in turn implies that pk' and pk'' are identically distributed. Thus the distribution of $(\mathsf{sk}', \mathsf{pk}')$ and $(\mathsf{sk}'', \mathsf{pk}'')$ is identical.

3.2 Security

Lemma 3.21. *The proposed code-based rerandomizable signature scheme* Code-Rsig *has uniquely rerandomizable public keys.*

Proof. Due to page restrictions, the proof of Lemma 3.21 will appear in the full version of the paper.

Theorem 3.22. *The proposed signature scheme Code-RSig with perfectly rerandomizable keys is secure against unforgeability under chosen message attack with honestly rerandomized keys (UF-CMA-HRK) as the code-based signature scheme Code-Sig is secure against existential unforgeability under adaptive chosen message attack (UF-CMA).*

Proof. The proof of Theorem 3.22 will appear in the full version of the paper.

4 Our Code-Based Stateful Deterministic Wallet

4.1 Protocol Description

This section contains the construction of a stateful deterministic wallet SDW = (SDW.Setup, SDW.MGen, SDW.SKDer, SDW.PKDer, SDW.Sign, SDW.Verify) leveraging our code-based signatures with key rerandomization Code-RSig presented in Sect. 3.

SDW.Setup$(1^\lambda) \rightarrow \mathsf{pp}_{\mathsf{wsgn}}$: A trusted party executes this algorithm on input 1^λ and returns the public parameter $\mathsf{pp}_{\mathsf{wsgn}}$ as follows.

i. Choose positive integers $(n, k, r, s, \ell, w_1, w_2) \in \mathbb{N}^7$ such that $n = \ell r$ and $\ell(w_1+r-s)+w_2 \leq d_{GV}$ where w_1 and w_2 represent the Hamming weight and let d_{GV} be the Gilbert-Varshamov(GV) bound of random $[n, k]$-linear codes over $\mathbb{F}_2$.
ii. Samples uniformly H from $\mathbb{F}_2^{(n-k)\times n}$ and a keyed weight-restricted hash function $\mathcal{H} : \mathbb{F}_2^{n-k} \times \{0,1\}^* \rightarrow \mathcal{S}_{w_1}^s$ and $\mathcal{H}_1 : \{0,1\}^\kappa \times \Lambda \rightarrow \mathbb{F}_2^{s\times n} \times \{0,1\}^\kappa$ where κ is polynomially depended on the security parameter λ and H is a parity check matrix.

iii. Publishes $\mathsf{pp}_{\mathrm{wsgn}} = (\mathsf{pp}_{\mathrm{sgn}}, \mathcal{H}_1)$ where $\mathsf{pp}_{\mathrm{sgn}} = (n, k, r, s, \ell, w_1, w_2, d_{GV}, H, \mathcal{H})$.

$\mathsf{SDW.MGen}(\mathsf{pp}_{\mathrm{wsgn}}) \rightarrow (\mathsf{msk}, \mathsf{mpk}, St_0)$: On input $\mathsf{pp}_{\mathrm{wsgn}}$, a user runs this algorithm to generate a master private-public key pair $(\mathsf{msk}, \mathsf{mpk})$ and an initial state St_0 as follows:

i. Samples uniformly an initial state $St_0 \xleftarrow{\$} \{0,1\}^{\kappa}$.
ii. Executes the $\mathsf{Code\text{-}RSig.KeyGen}(\mathsf{pp}_{\mathrm{sgn}})$ algorithm (see Sect. 3) to compute the master private-public key pair as follows:
   - Chooses randomly systematic generator matrices $E_1, \ldots, E_\ell$ of ℓ distinct random $[r, s]$-linear codes over $\mathbb{F}_2$ where each $E_i = [I_s||R_i]$, I_s is $s \times s$ identity matrix and R_i is $s \times (r-s)$ matrix for $i = 1, \ldots, \ell$, sets $E = [E_1|| \ldots ||E_\ell] \in \mathbb{F}_2^{s \times n}$ and samples permutation matrices $P_1 \in \mathbb{F}_2^{s \times s}$, $P_2 \in \mathbb{F}_2^{n \times n}$ and computes $U = P_1 E P_2 \in \mathbb{F}_2^{s \times n}$ and $V = HU^{\mathrm{T}} \in \mathbb{F}_2^{(n-k) \times s}$.
   - Sets $\mathsf{msk} = U$ and $\mathsf{mpk} = V$.
iii. Publishes mpk and keeps msk and St_0 secret to himself.

$\mathsf{SDW.SKDer}(\mathsf{pp}_{\mathrm{wsgn}}, \mathsf{msk}, \mathsf{id}, St) \rightarrow (\mathsf{sk}_{\mathsf{id}}, St')$: This randomize private key derivation algorithm is invoked by a user on input the public parameter $\mathsf{pp}_{\mathrm{wsgn}}$ along with his master private key $\mathsf{msk} = U$, his identity $\mathsf{id} \in \Lambda$ and current state St and generates a session private key $\mathsf{sk}_{\mathsf{id}}$ and an updated state St' as follows:

i. Computes $\mathcal{H}_1(St, \mathsf{id}) = (\rho_{\mathsf{id}}, St')$ where $\rho_{\mathsf{id}} \in \mathbb{F}_2^{s \times n}$ and $St' \in \{0,1\}^*$.
ii. Computes a session private key by executing $\mathsf{Code\text{-}RSig.Randsk}(\mathsf{pp}_{\mathrm{sgn}}, \mathsf{msk}, \rho_{\mathsf{id}})$ presented in Sect. 3 as follows:
   - Parses the randomness matrix $\rho_{id} = [E'_1|| \ldots ||E'_\ell] \in \mathbb{F}_2^{s \times n}$ where each $E'_i = [O_s||R'_i]$, O_s is $s \times s$ zero matrix and R'_i is $s \times (r-s)$ matrix for $i = 1, \ldots, \ell$.
   - Sets the rerandomized private key $\mathsf{sk}_{\mathsf{id}} = \mathsf{msk} + \rho_{\mathsf{id}} = U_{\mathsf{id}}$ (say).
iii. Keeps the session private key $\mathsf{sk}_{\mathsf{id}} = U_{\mathsf{id}}$ and an updated state St' secret to himself.

$\mathsf{SDW.PKDer}(\mathsf{pp}_{\mathrm{wsgn}}, \mathsf{mpk}, \mathsf{id}, St) \rightarrow (\mathsf{pk}_{\mathsf{id}}, St')$: This probabilistic public key rerandomization algorithm is invoked by a user who takes as input the public parameter $\mathsf{pp}_{\mathrm{wsgn}}$, his master public key $\mathsf{mpk} = V \in \mathbb{F}_2^{(n-k) \times s}$, his identity id $\in \Lambda$, and a current state $St \in \{0,1\}^{\kappa}$ and generates a session public key $\mathsf{pk}_{\mathsf{id}}$ and an updated state St' as follows:

i. Computes $\mathcal{H}_1(St, \mathsf{id}) = (\rho_{\mathsf{id}}, St')$ where $\rho_{\mathsf{id}} \in \mathbb{F}_2^{n \times s}$ and $St' \in \{0,1\}^*$.
ii. Sets the session public key by executing $\mathsf{Code\text{-}RSig.Randpk}(\mathsf{pp}_{\mathrm{sgn}}, \mathsf{mpk}, \rho_{\mathsf{id}})$ described in Sect. 3 as follows:
   - Parses the randomness matrix $\rho_{\mathsf{id}} = [E'_1|| \ldots ||E'_\ell] \in \mathbb{F}_2^{s \times n}$ where each $E'_i = [O_s||R'_i]$, O_s is the zero matrix of order s and $R'_i \in \mathbb{F}_2^{s \times (r-s)}$ is a random matrix for $i = 1, \ldots, \ell$.
   - Sets the rerandomized public key $\mathsf{pk}_{\mathsf{id}} = V + H\rho_{\mathsf{id}}^{\mathrm{T}} = HU^{\mathrm{T}} + H\rho_{\mathsf{id}}^{\mathrm{T}} = H(U + \rho_{\mathsf{id}})^{\mathrm{T}} = V_{\mathsf{id}}$ (say).

iii. Publishes the session public key $\mathsf{pk}_{\mathsf{id}} \in \mathbb{F}_2^{(n-k)\times s}$ and keeps the updated state $St' \in \{0,1\}^\kappa$ secret to himself.

$\mathsf{SDW.Sign}(\mathsf{pp}_{\mathsf{wsgn}}, \mathsf{sk}_{\mathsf{id}}, \mathsf{pk}_{\mathsf{id}}, m) \rightarrow \sigma$: In this algorithm, a signer generates a signature σ on the message $m \in \{0,1\}^*$ using his session private key $\mathsf{sk}_{\mathsf{id}} = U_{\mathsf{id}} \in \mathbb{F}_2^{s\times n}$ and session public key $\mathsf{pk}_{\mathsf{id}} = V_{\mathsf{id}} \in \mathbb{F}_2^{(n-k)\times s}$ corresponding to his identity id. By proceeding as follows:

i. Sets $\overline{m} = (\mathsf{pk}_{\mathsf{id}}, m)$.
ii. Computes a signature σ on the message $\overline{m}$ by executing the algorithm $\mathsf{Code\text{-}RSig.Sign}(\mathsf{pp}_{\mathsf{sgn}}, \mathsf{sk}_{\mathsf{id}}, \overline{m})$ described in Sect. 3 as follows:
   - Samples $\mathbf{e} \xleftarrow{\$} \mathcal{S}_{w_2}^n$.
   - Computes syndrome $\mathbf{y} = H\mathbf{e}^{\mathrm{T}} \in \mathbb{F}_2^{n-k}$ and the challenge $\mathbf{c} = \mathcal{H}(\mathbf{y}, \overline{m}) \in \mathcal{S}_{w_1}^s$.
   - Computes the response $\mathbf{z}_{\mathsf{id}} = \mathbf{c}U_{\mathsf{id}} + \mathbf{e} \in \mathbb{F}_2^n$.
   - Sets the signature $\sigma = (\mathbf{z}_{\mathsf{id}}, \mathbf{c})$
iii. Returns the signature σ.

$\mathsf{SDW.Verify}(\mathsf{pp}_{\mathsf{wsgn}}, \mathsf{pk}_{\mathsf{id}}, m, \sigma) \rightarrow \mathsf{Valid/Invalid}$: Employing the session public key $\mathsf{pk}_{\mathsf{id}} = V_{\mathsf{id}} \in \mathbb{F}_2^{(n-k)\times s}$ of signer with identity $\mathsf{id} \in \Lambda$, a verifier verifies the signature σ on $m \in \{0,1\}^*$. It proceeds as follows:

i. Set $\overline{m} = (\mathsf{pk}_{\mathsf{id}}, m)$.
ii. Verifies the signature σ on the message $\overline{m}$ by running the algorithm $\mathsf{Code\text{-}RSig.Verify}(\mathsf{pp}_{\mathsf{sgn}}, \mathsf{pk}_{\mathsf{id}}, \overline{m}, \sigma)$ is presented in Sect. 3 as follows:
   - Parse $\sigma = (\mathbf{z}_{\mathsf{id}}, \mathbf{c}) \in \mathbb{F}_2^n \times \mathcal{S}_{w_1}^s$ where $\mathbf{c} = \mathcal{H}(\mathbf{y}, \overline{m})$, $\mathbf{y} = H\mathbf{e}^{\mathrm{T}}$ and $\mathbf{z}_{\mathsf{id}} = \mathbf{c}U_{\mathsf{id}} + \mathbf{e}$.
   - If $\mathsf{wt}(\mathbf{z}_{\mathsf{id}}) \leq \ell(w_1 + r - s) + w_2$ and $\mathcal{H}(H\mathbf{z}_{\mathsf{id}}^{\mathrm{T}} - V_{\mathsf{id}}\mathbf{c}^{\mathrm{T}}, \overline{m}) = \mathbf{c}$ then returns Valid, otherwise returns $\mathsf{Invalid}$.

Correctness: The correctness of our stateful deterministic wallet from code-based cryptography derives from the correctness of the code-based signature scheme with perfectly rerandomizable keys described in Sect. 3.

4.2 Security

Theorem 4.21. *Let $\mathcal{A}$ be an adversary that plays with the challenger $\mathcal{C}$ in the experiment $\mathsf{Exp}_{\mathsf{SDW},\mathcal{A}}^{\mathsf{WAL\text{-}UNL}}(\lambda)$ against our construction of code-based stateful deterministic wallet SDW = (SDW.Setup, SDW.MGen, SDW.SKDer, SDW.PKDer, SDW.Sign, SDW.Verify) presented above. Then*

$$\mathsf{Adv}_{\mathsf{SDW},\mathcal{A}}^{\mathsf{WAL\text{-}UNL}}(\lambda) \leq \frac{Q_{\mathcal{H}_1}(Q_{PK}+2)}{2^\kappa}$$

where Q_{PK} denotes the number of queries to oracle $\mathcal{O}_{\mathsf{PK}}(\cdot)$ and $Q_{\mathcal{H}_1}$ denotes the number of random oracle queries to the $\mathcal{H}_1$ by $\mathcal{A}$.

Proof. The proof of Theorem 4.21 will appear in the full version of the paper.

Theorem 4.22. *Let $\mathcal{A}$ be an adversary that plays in the wallet unforgeability experiment* $\mathsf{Exp}_{\mathsf{SDW},\mathcal{A}}^{\mathsf{WAL\text{-}UNF}}(\lambda)$ *against our construction of a code-based stateful deterministic wallet* SDW = ($\mathsf{SDW.Setup}$, $\mathsf{SDW.MGen}$, $\mathsf{SDW.SKDer}$, $\mathsf{SDW.PKDer}$, $\mathsf{SDW.Sign}$, $\mathsf{SDW.Verify}$) *presented above. Let $\mathcal{B}$ is an adversary that plays the UF-CMA-HRK experiment* $\mathsf{Exp}_{\mathsf{RSig},\mathcal{A}}^{\mathsf{UF\text{-}CMA\text{-}HRK}}(\lambda)$ *against the code-based signature Code-RSig scheme with uniquely rerandomizable keys presented in Sect. 3. Then*

$$\mathsf{Adv}_{\mathsf{SDW},\mathcal{A}}^{\mathsf{WAL\text{-}UNF}}(\lambda) \leq \mathsf{Adv}_{\mathsf{Code-RSig},\mathcal{B}}^{\mathsf{UF\text{-}CMA\text{-}HRK}}(\lambda) + \frac{Q_{\mathcal{H}_1}^2}{N}$$

where $Q_{\mathcal{H}_1}$ denotes the number of random oracle queries to $\mathcal{H}_1$ made by $\mathcal{A}$ and $N = 2^{ns}$.

Proof. The proof of Theorem 4.22 will appear in the full version of the paper.

5 Conclusion

Throughout this paper, we developed a secure stateful deterministic wallet scheme from code-based cryptography. In terms of key size and signature size our scheme Code-RSig seems well as compared to some other existing works on the signature scheme with rerandomized keys as shown in Table 1. As compared to the lattice-based scheme [1], our code-based key rerandomizable signature technique is shown to be secure in the strong security model. In the near future, it would be preferable to design constructs that are more practical and secure by employing appropriate signature techniques from code-based cryptography.

Acknowledgements. This work is supported by the University Grants Commission, Government of India under Grant No. 1223/(CSIRNETJUNE2019).

References

1. Alkeilani Alkadri, N., et al.: Deterministic wallets in a quantum world. In: Proceedings of the 2020 ACM SIGSAC Conference on Computer and Communications Security, pp. 1017–1031 (2020)
2. Alkim, E., Barreto, P.S.L.M., Bindel, N., Krämer, J., Longa, P., Ricardini, J.E.: The lattice-based digital signature scheme qTESLA. In: Conti, M., Zhou, J., Casalicchio, E., Spognardi, A. (eds.) ACNS 2020. LNCS, vol. 12146, pp. 441–460. Springer, Cham (2020). https://doi.org/10.1007/978-3-030-57808-4_22
3. Applebaum, B., Ishai, Y., Kushilevitz, E.: Cryptography with constant input locality. J. Cryptol. **22**(4), 429–469 (2009)
4. Berlekamp, E., McEliece, R., Van Tilborg, H.: On the inherent intractability of certain coding problems (corresp.). IEEE Trans. Inf. Theory **24**(3), 384–386 (1978)
5. BLOOMBERG: "How to Steal \$500 Million in Cryptocurrency". http://fortune.com/2018/01/31/coincheck-hack-how/
6. Boneh, D., Lynn, B., Shacham, H.: Short signatures from the weil pairing. J. Cryptol. **17**, 297–319 (2004)

7. Buterin, V.: Deterministic Wallets, Their Advantages and Their Understated Flaws. http://bitcoinmagazine.com/technical/deterministic-wallets-advantages-flaw-1385450276
8. Das, P., Faust, S., Loss, J.: A formal treatment of deterministic wallets. In: Proceedings of the 2019 ACM SIGSAC Conference on Computer and Communications Security, pp. 651–668 (2019)
9. Dolev, D., Yao, A.: On the security of public key protocols. IEEE Trans. Inf. Theory **29**(2), 198–208 (1983)
10. Fan, C.I., Tseng, Y.F., Su, H.P., Hsu, R.H., Kikuchi, H.: Secure hierarchical bitcoin wallet scheme against privilege escalation attacks. Int. J. Inf. Secur. **19**, 245–255 (2020)
11. Forgang, G.: Money laundering through cryptocurrencies (2019)
12. Gutoski, G., Stebila, D.: Hierarchical deterministic bitcoin wallets that tolerate key leakage. In: Böhme, R., Okamoto, T. (eds.) FC 2015. LNCS, vol. 8975, pp. 497–504. Springer, Heidelberg (2015). https://doi.org/10.1007/978-3-662-47854-7_31
13. Li, Y.X., Deng, R.H., Wang, X.M.: On the equivalence of McEliece's and Niederreiter's public-key cryptosystems. IEEE Trans. Inf. Theory **40**(1), 271–273 (1994)
14. Li, Z., Xing, C., Yeo, S.L.: A new code based signature scheme without trapdoors. Cryptology ePrint Archive (2020)
15. Nakamoto, S.: Bitcoin: a peer-to-peer electronic cash system. Decentralized Bus. Rev., 21260 (2008)
16. Persichetti, E.: Improving the efficiency of code-based cryptography. Ph.D. thesis, University of Auckland (2012)
17. Pierce, J.: Limit distribution of the minimum distance of random linear codes. IEEE Trans. Inf. Theory **13**(4), 595–599 (1967)
18. Shor, P.W.: Polynomial-time algorithms for prime factorization and discrete logarithms on a quantum computer. SIAM Rev. **41**(2), 303–332 (1999)
19. Skellern, R.: Cryptocurrency hacks: More than $2 b USD lost between 2011–2018 (2018)
20. Song, Y., Huang, X., Mu, Y., Wu, W., Wang, H.: A code-based signature scheme from the lyubashevsky framework. Theor. Comput. Sci. **835**, 15–30 (2020)
21. van Tilburg, J.: Security-analysis of a class of cryptosystems based on linear error-correcting codes (1994)
22. Turuani, M., Voegtlin, T., Rusinowitch, M.: Automated verification of electrum wallet. In: Clark, J., Meiklejohn, S., Ryan, P.Y.A., Wallach, D., Brenner, M., Rohloff, K. (eds.) FC 2016. LNCS, vol. 9604, pp. 27–42. Springer, Heidelberg (2016). https://doi.org/10.1007/978-3-662-53357-4_3
23. Wiki, B.: Bip32 proposal (2018). http://en.bitcoin.it/wiki/BIP_0032

Square Attacks on Reduced-Round FEA-1 and FEA-2

Amit Kumar Chauhan[1], Abhishek Kumar[2,3(✉)], and Somitra Kumar Sanadhya[4]

[1] QNu Labs Private Limited, Bengaluru, India
akcindia.macs@gmail.com
[2] Indian Institute of Technology Ropar, Rupnagar, India
[3] Bosch Global Software Technologies Private Limited, Bengaluru, India
abhishekk.iitrpr@gmail.com
[4] Indian Institute of Technology Jodhpur, Jodhpur, India
somitra@iitj.ac.in

Abstract. FEA-1 and FEA-2 are the South Korean Format-Preserving Encryption (FPE) standards. In this paper, we discuss the security of FEA-1 and FEA-2 against the square attacks. More specifically, we present a three-round distinguishing attack against FEA-1 and FEA-2. The data complexity of this three-round distinguisher is 2^8 plaintexts. We use this three-round distinguisher for key recovery against four rounds of FEA-1. The time complexity of this key recovery attacks is $2^{137.6}$, for both 192-bit and 256-bit key sizes.

In addition, we extend the three-round distinguisher to a five-round distinguisher for FEA-2 using the tweak schedule. We use this distinguisher to mount six round key recovery attack with complexity $2^{137.6}$, for 192-bit and 256-bit key sizes.

Keywords: Format-preserving encryption · FEA · Square attacks · FEA-1 · FEA-2

1 Introduction

1.1 Format-Preserving Encryption (FPE)

A block cipher is a cryptographic algorithm that transforms a message to ensure its confidentiality. In principle, the modern days block ciphers work on some fixed-size binary strings, for example, the domain size of AES [10] and DES [8] are 128-bit and 64-bit, respectively. In other words, these ciphers permute the binary string data for a chosen key. The block cipher modes [13] of operations play an important role if the message size is other than the block size.

In many practical applications, such as encryption of Credit Card Number (CCN) or Social Security Number (SSN), the data itself is treated as an integer. Considering the efficiency and ease of handling these data, it is preferable to encrypt these arbitrarily domain sized data onto the same set, i.e., treating

S. Dolev and B. Schieber (Eds.): SSS 2023, LNCS 14310, pp. 583–597, 2023.
https://doi.org/10.1007/978-3-031-44274-2_43

such data as string of digits/letters rather that string of bits. Unfortunately, the conventional block ciphers and their modes, such as ECB, CBC, or CTR [13] are not able to cater this purpose.

Format-Preserving Encryption (FPE) refers a symmetric-key cryptographic primitive that transforms data of a predefined domain into itself. In other words, FPF encrypts a sequence digits/letters into another sequence of digits/letters. Moreover, the encrypted data has the same length as the original data. Many financial or e-commerce applications store fixed format financial data like CCN and such formatted data should be encrypted and treated as same format data only for practical reasons. It implies that an encryption algorithm which works for these applications must be a permutation over the same field. Since a conventional block cipher can not fulfill this purpose, FPE schemes are in use for this purpose.

1.2 Related Work

The history of FPE starts with the introduction of *data-type preserving encryption* by Brightwell and Smith [5] from the database community. The first notable FPE solution from the cryptographic community is by Black and Rogaway [3]. This work introduced the use of Feistel construction and usability of cycle walking technique for designing a FPE schemes. Most of the popular FPE schemes including NIST standard FF1 and FF3-1 follow the design principle of combining cycle walking with Feistel network [1,4,14,17]. On the other hand, the feasibility of designing substitution-permutation network (SPN) based FPE construction is explored in [6,7,12,15].

In 2014, two different Feisel based FPE schemes FEA-1 and FEA-2 were proposed by Lee *et al.* [16]. Currently, these schemes are the South-Korean FPE standards (TTAK.KO-12.0275). The lighter round function of these schemes results in almost double efficiency than FF1 and FF3-1 despite of more number of rounds. The first third party analysis of FEA-1 and FEA-2 is reported by Dunkelman *et al.* [11]. These attacks exploit the fact that the smallest domain size of these schemes is 8-bit only. In this work, the authors proposed full round distinguishing attacks for all versions of FEA-1 and FEA-2 and full round key-recovery attacks on FEA-1 and FEA-2 with 192-bit and 256-bit key-sizes. For a domain size N^2 and number of rounds r, the time and data complexity of these attacks are $O(N^{r-3})$ and $O(N^{r-4})$, respectively. The second analysis is based on linear cryptanalysis of FEA-1 and FEA-2 by Tim Beyne [2]. For FEA-1, the time and data complexity are $O(N^{r/2-1.5})$ for both distinguishing as well as message recovery attacks. For FEA-2, distinguishing and message-recovery attack needs $O(N^{r/3-1.5})$ and $O(N^{r/3-0.5})$ time and data, respectively.

To the best of our knowledge, apart from the above-mentioned attacks on FEA algorithms, there does not exist any other third party analysis on FEA. In [16], the designers analyzed the security against the square attack and claimed: "*Square attacks are not effective against the TBCs since the KSP-KSP function with MDS diffusion layers do not admit good integral characteristics. There are 3-round integral characteristics for our TBCs for some block bit-lengths. But there do not seem to exist useful characteristics when the number of rounds is greater than 4.*"

1.3 Our Contribution

In this work, we present new distinguishing and key recovery attacks for FEA-1 and FEA-2. To the best of our knowledge, this is the first third-party analysis of FEA-1 and FEA-2 based on square attacks. For FEA-1, the proposed distinguisher covers up to three rounds, i.e., six layers of SP functions. For FEA-2, the proposed distinguisher can distinguish up to five rounds, i.e., ten layers of SP functions. The data and time complexity of both distinguishers are 2^8 plaintexts and encryptions, respectively. Note that we explain these distinguishing attacks for 128-bit blocks only, but these distinguishers are valid for all block lengths more than 16-bit long.

Moreover, we use these proposed distinguishers to mount the key recovery attacks for both FEA-1 and FEA-2. Since both FEA-1 and FEA-2 use 128-bit key material in each round function, this implies that the key recovery attack can't be extended for 128-bit key size. For 192-bit and 256-bit key sizes, only one round extension is possible for both the FEA-1 and FEA-2. For all block lengths equal or greater thant 16-bit, the complexities of a four round FEA-1 and six round FEA-2 key recovery attacks are $2^{137.6}$. In Table 1, we summarize the results of square attacks for both FEA-1 and FEA-2.

Table 1. Summery of square attacks on reduced-round FEA-1 and FEA-2.

Algorithm	Rounds	Key Size	Attack Type	Complexity	Ref.
FEA-1	3	-	Distinguisher	2^8	Sect. 4.1
FEA-1	4	192/256	Key Recovery	$2^{137.6}$	Sect. 5.2
FEA-2	5	-	Distinguisher	2^8	Sect. 4.2
FEA-2	6	192/256	Key Recovery	$2^{137.6}$	Sect. 5.1

It is interesting to note that for selected parameters (domain size and number of rounds), attacks presented in this paper are more efficient than the attacks explained in [11]. For example, the time complexity of key recovery attack of six round FEA-2 for domain size 128-bit is 2^{192} as per [11]. The time complexity of our attack for same parameters is $2^{137.6}$ (Table 1). Moreover, this work confirms that square attacks are not really a threat for considered ciphers as the number of rounds attacked are less than 30% of the total rounds, in all cases. However, our analysis proves that the number of round that can be attacked using square attack certainly goes beyond the designer's claim for FEA-2.

1.4 Organization of the Paper

In Sect. 2, we explain the notations followed by brief introduction of square attack. Section 3 of this paper explains brief details of FEA-1 and FEA-2. In

Sect. 4, we propose the three rounds square distinguishers for FEA-1 and five rounds square distinguishers for FEA-2. Section 5 describes the key recovery attacks on FEA-2 and FEA-1. Finally, we conclude our work and discuss future works in Sect. 6.

2 Preliminaries

2.1 Notations

Throughout the paper, we will use the following notations.

- $|x|$: Length of bit-string x.
- $X[i]$: $(i+1)^{\text{th}}$ byte of string X.
- $X_R^{(r-1)}$: Right half input of the rth round.
- $X_L^{(r-1)}$: Left half input of the rth round.
- $Rk_a^{(r)}$ and $Rk_b^{(r)}$: The rth round subkeys.
- T_r : Tweak input for the rth round.

2.2 Square Attack

For a byte oriented cipher, the square attack starts with a Λ-set that are all different for some of the state bytes and all equal for the remaining state bytes. The all different byte and the equal bytes are termed as 'active' (A) bytes and 'passive' (C) bytes, respectively. Further, a byte is called 'balanced' (B) if the sum of all 256 values of a byte is 0 and if it is not possible to make any prediction about the sum of all 256 values of a byte, we call it an 'unknown' (?) byte.

The main operations used by FEA-1 and FEA-2 are substitution layer (S), diffusion layer (P), Key addition layer (K), tweak addition and xor ($\oplus$). Applying the substitution layer and key addition layer results over an active/passive byte as input, outputs an active/passive bytes. In other words, given a Λ-set as input to substitution layer and key addition layer results in a Λ-set.

The permutation layer (P) of FEA-1 and FEA-2 is an 8×8 MDS matrix. Every output byte of the permutation layer is a linear combination of all eight input bytes. Application of permutation layer over a all passive byte input, outputs all passive byte outputs. An input Λ-set with a single active byte results an output with all active bytes. Moreover, an input Λ-set with more than a single active byte results in a all byte balanced output.

The xor of an active byte with a balanced byte results in a balanced byte. The xor of an active byte with an active byte definitely results in a balanced byte. Furthermore, Table 2 represents the properties of xor operation. Note that for the tweak addition, if the tweak is a constant value an input active/passive byte, outputs active/passive byte. For the distinguisher, we choose round tweak as Λ-sets where one byte of the tweak is active. In such situations, if the tweak byte as well as the state byte are active such that $\Lambda_i \oplus t_i = c$ for $0 \leq i \leq 255$ for each i, the byte becomes a constant byte after tweak addition.

Table 2. Properties of XOR operation. Here, A, B and C denotes active bytes, balanced bytes and passive bytes respectively [18].

$\oplus$	A	B	C
A	B	B	A
B	B	B	B
C	A	B	C

3 Specification of FEA

FEA is a format-preserving encryption algorithm and follows the Feistel structure with tweaks. There are two variants of FEA, namely FEA-1 and FEA-2 which support the domain size in $[2^8, \ldots, 2^{128}]$ and key bit-lengths 128, 192, and 256. Both FEA-1 and FEA-2 specifies two different families of tweakable block ciphers (TBC). Table 3 represents the number of rounds defined according to the key bit-lengths and TBC types.

Table 3. Number of rounds according to the key bit-lengths and TBC types.

Key Length	FEA-1	FEA-2
128	12	18
192	14	21
256	16	24

There are three main components of both FEA-1 and FEA-2 families: the key schedule, the tweak schedule, and the round function. In subsequent subsections, we briefly describe these components.

3.1 Key Schedule

FEA-1 and FEA-2 both use the same key schedule. The key schedule takes the secret key K and the block size n as inputs. Each iteration of the key schedule outputs four 64-bit round keys. Each round of the encryption/decryption needs two 64-bit sub-keys. i.e., these four round keys are used in two consecutive rounds.

3.2 Tweak Schedule

Let n denote the block bit-length of TBC, and let $n_1 = \lceil n/2 \rceil$ and $n_2 = \lfloor n/2 \rfloor$. The tweak schedule for each type TBC is described next.

For FEA-1, the tweak T of bit-length $(128-n)$ is divided into two sub-tweaks T_L and T_R of length $64 - n_2$ and $64 - n_1$, respectively. Then, we let $T_a^i = 0$ for every round, and define T_b^i for the i-th round by

$$T_b^i = \begin{cases} T_L & \text{if } i \text{ is odd} \\ T_R & \text{if } i \text{ is even} \end{cases}$$

For FEA-2, the tweak T of bit-length 128 is divided into two sub-tweaks T_L and T_R of 64-bit each. Here, T_L is the first 64 consecutive bits of T and T_R is the next 64 consecutive bits. Then, T_a^i and T_b^i for i-th round are determined as

$$T_a^i || T_b^i = \begin{cases} 0 & \text{if } i \equiv 1 \pmod 3 \\ T_L & \text{if } i \equiv 2 \pmod 3 \\ T_R & \text{if } i \equiv 0 \pmod 3 \end{cases}$$

3.3 Round Function

As defined in [16], the round functions are composition of Tw-KSP-KSP-Tr functions. Here, Tw and Tr define round tweak addition and truncation, respectively. The KSP defines composition of round key addition (K), substitution layer (S) and diffusion layer (P). The substitution layer is defined as the eight parallel same 8-bit S-boxes. The diffusion layer is defined as multiplication with an 8×8 MDS matrix $\mathcal{M}$ defined over the field $\mathsf{GF}(2^8)$. The round function supports input/output bit-length in $[4 \dots 64]$.

A complete description of the round function is depicted in Fig. 1.

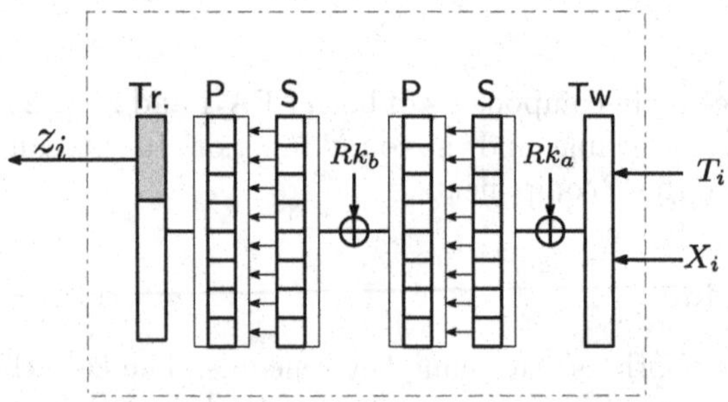

Fig. 1. Round function of FEA algorithm.

4 Distinguishers for FEA Algorithms

In this section, we present three round distinguishers for both FEA-1 and FEA-2. Additionally, we present an improved five round distinguisher for FEA-2 using the tweak schedule. The distinguishers presented in this section are based on the square attack, originally demonstrated for block cipher Square [9].

4.1 Three Round Distinguishers for FEA-1 and FEA-2

Here, we present a basic three round distinguishing attack for both FEA-1 and FEA-2. For simplicity, the block size n, chosen for the following attacks are 128-bits for both FEA-1 and FEA-2. The corresponding tweak lengths are 0-bit for FEA-1 and 128-bits for FEA-2 (considering the design specifications).

As shown in Fig. 2, we start with a Λ-set of 256 plaintexts such that only first byte is active and other bytes are constant values. We then run three rounds of FEA-1 or FEA-2, and observe that all the bytes of the left half of the third round output are balanced.

Let $X_L^{(r-1)}$ and $X_R^{(r-1)}$ be the right and left inputs of the state for the rth round, respectively. Let T_r be the tweak input for the rth round and $\mathbf{R}$ represents one round of FEA-1/FEA-2. We now provide a three round distinguisher for FEA-1/FEA-2, which is described as follows:

1. Choose a set of 256 plaintexts $\mathbf{P} = \{(X_{L,i}^{(0)}, X_{R,i}^{(0)}) \mid 0 \leq i \leq 255\}$ such that the first byte of $\mathbf{P}$ is active and all other bytes are constant.
2. Set round tweaks $T_2 = T_3 = 0$ and by design specification $T_1 = 0$ for FEA-2. The round tweak length for FEA-1 is 0 (refer Sect. 3.2).
3. For $0 \leq i \leq 255$:
   (a) For $0 \leq j \leq 2$:
      i. Compute $(X_{L,i}^{(j+1)}, X_{R,i}^{(j+1)})$ from $(X_{L,i}^{(j)}, X_{R,i}^{(j)}, T_j)$:
      $$(X_{L,i}^{(j+1)}, X_{R,i}^{(j+1)}) \leftarrow \mathbf{R}(X_{L,i}^{(j)}, X_{R,i}^{(j)}, T_j).$$
4. Check that all bytes of $X_L^{(3)}$ are balanced.

We further describe the details of the three round distinguisher attack procedure. Start with choosing plaintexts $X_L^{(0)}$ and $X_R^{(0)}$ which are as follows:

$$X_L^{(0)} = (A, \beta_2, \beta_3, \beta_4, \beta_5, \beta_6, \beta_7, \beta_8) \tag{1}$$
$$X_R^{(0)} = (\alpha_1, \alpha_2, \alpha_3, \alpha_4, \alpha_5, \alpha_6, \alpha_7, \alpha_8), \tag{2}$$

where the byte A takes all 256 values for making a Λ-set, and other bytes α_i for $1 \leq i \leq 8$ and β_j for $1 \leq j \leq 8$ are fixed arbitrary constants.

After executing the first round on inputs $(X_L^{(0)}, X_R^{(0)})$, the second round inputs $X_L^{(1)}$ and $X_R^{(1)}$ becomes

$$X_L^{(1)} = (\alpha_1, \alpha_2, \alpha_3, \alpha_4, \alpha_5, \alpha_6, \alpha_7, \alpha_8) \tag{3}$$
$$X_R^{(1)} = (A, \gamma_2, \gamma_3, \gamma_4, \gamma_5, \gamma_6, \gamma_7, \gamma_8). \tag{4}$$

After applying the second round function to $X_R^{(1)}$, we expect that each byte right output of the second round are balanced.

$$X_L^{(2)} = (A, \gamma_2, \gamma_3, \gamma_4, \gamma_5, \gamma_6, \gamma_7, \gamma_8) \quad (5)$$

$$X_R^{(2)} = (B_1, B_2, B_3, B_4, B_5, B_6, B_7, B_8). \quad (6)$$

We then apply the third round, and it can be easily observed that all the bytes of the left half of third round output are balanced. Thus, we obtain a three round distinguisher for both FEA-1 and FEA-2.

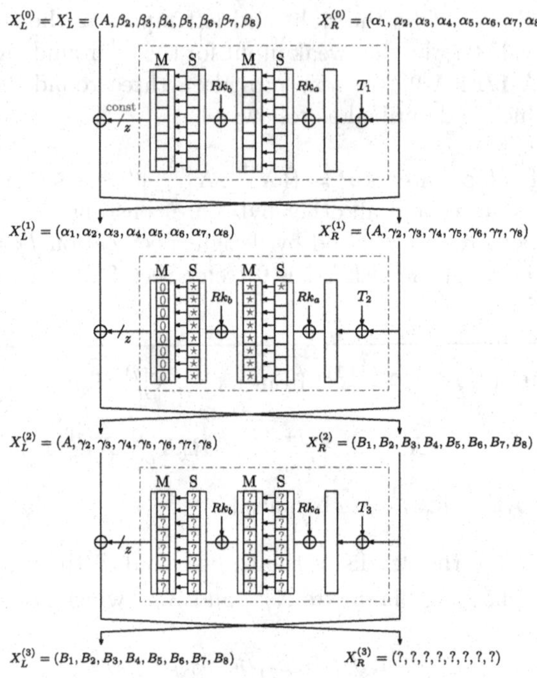

Fig. 2. Three round distinguisher for FEA-1.

Note that the distinguisher presented above is valid for all the domain size in between 16-bit to 128-bit. An attacker just need to choose the tweak length accordingly.

4.2 Five Round Distinguisher for FEA-2

We now present a five round distinguisher for FEA-2 (Fig. 2), by exploiting the tweak scheduling algorithm. As specified in design, the tweak T is always a 128-bit value and the process of round tweak generation is explained in Sect. 3. We explain the attack for 128-bit block size, i.e., $n = 128$. However, this attack is valid for all domain size of 16-bit or more.

Let $X_L^{(r-1)}$, $X_R^{(r-1)}$ and T_r be the right input, left inputs, and tweak for the rth round, respectively. Now, we can construct a five round distinguisher by suitably choosing $X_L^{(0)}$, $X_R^{(0)}$, and T_2. The round tweaks T_1, T_3 and T_4 are passive ($T_1 = T_4 = 0$ and T_3 is constant) for all 256 plaintexts. Let $\mathbf{R}$ represents one round of FEA-2. We now provide a five round distinguisher for FEA-2, which is described as follows:

1. Choose a set of 256 plaintexts $\mathbf{P} = \{(X_{L,i}^{(0)}, X_{R,i}^{(0)}) \mid 0 \le i \le 255\}$ such that the first byte of $\mathbf{P}$ is active and all other bytes are constant.
2. Set round tweak $T_3 = 0$. By design specification $T_1 = T_4 = 0$ and $T_2 = T_5$.
3. Set seven bytes of T_2 $(T_2[1], T_2[2], \ldots, T_2[7])$ as constants.
4. For $0 \le i \le 255$:
   (a) Compute $(X_{L,i}^{(1)}, X_{R,i}^{(1)})$ from $(X_{L,i}^{(0)}, X_{R,i}^{(0)}, T_1)$ (by applying one round of FEA-2):
   $$(X_{L,i}^{(1)}, X_{R,i}^{(1)}) \leftarrow \mathbf{R}(X_{L,i}^{(0)}, X_{R,i}^{(0)}, T_1).$$
   (b) Choose $T_{2,i}[0]$ such that $(X_{R,i}^{(1)}[0] \oplus T_{2,i}[0])$ a constant (all other bytes of T_2 are set as constants in Step 3).
   (c) For $1 \le j \le 4$:
      i. Compute $(X_{L,i}^{(j+1)}, X_{R,i}^{(j+1)})$ from $(X_{L,i}^{(j)}, X_{R,i}^{(j)}, T_j)$:
      $$(X_{L,i}^{(j+1)}, X_{R,i}^{(j+1)}) \leftarrow \mathbf{R}(X_{L,i}^{(j)}, X_{R,i}^{(j)}, T_j).$$
5. Check that all bytes of $X_L^{(5)}$ are balanced.

A detailed description of the five round distinguising attack is provided below: We start with a Λ-set of 256 plaintexts as input, where the first byte is active and all other bytes are arbitrary constants, i.e.,

$$X_L^{(0)} = (A, \beta_2, \beta_3, \beta_4, \beta_5, \beta_6, \beta_7, \beta_8) \tag{7}$$
$$X_R^{(0)} = (\alpha_1, \alpha_2, \alpha_3, \alpha_4, \alpha_5, \alpha_6, \alpha_7, \alpha_8) \tag{8}$$

After executing the first round, the first byte of $X_R^{(1)}$, i.e., $X_R^{(1)}[0]$ is active and remaining bytes are still constant values.

$$X_L^{(1)} = (\alpha_1, \alpha_2, \alpha_3, \alpha_4, \alpha_5, \alpha_6, \alpha_7, \alpha_8) \tag{9}$$
$$X_R^{(1)} = (A, \gamma_2, \gamma_3, \gamma_4, \gamma_5, \gamma_6, \gamma_7, \gamma_8) \tag{10}$$

Here, we choose the round tweaks T_2, such that the xor of the round tweaks and the corresponding round inputs are always a constant value. Since, only the first byte of $X_R^{(1)}$ is an active byte, the corresponding tweak byte $T_2[0]$ (the first byte of T_2) is chosen active such that $(X_R^{(1)}[0]_i \oplus T_2[0]_i)$ is passive (constant value) for $0 \leq i \leq 255$. This implies that the second round function is not active and the left half of the output of the second round is constant, i.e., the input of the third round is constant.

Now we extend this distinguisher for three more rounds (Fig. 3), i.e., total five rounds, and observe that all the bytes of the left half of the fifth round output are balanced. Thus, we obtain a distinguisher for five rounds of FEA-2. Note that similar to the three round distinguisher, only one round function is effectively active for five round distinguisher.

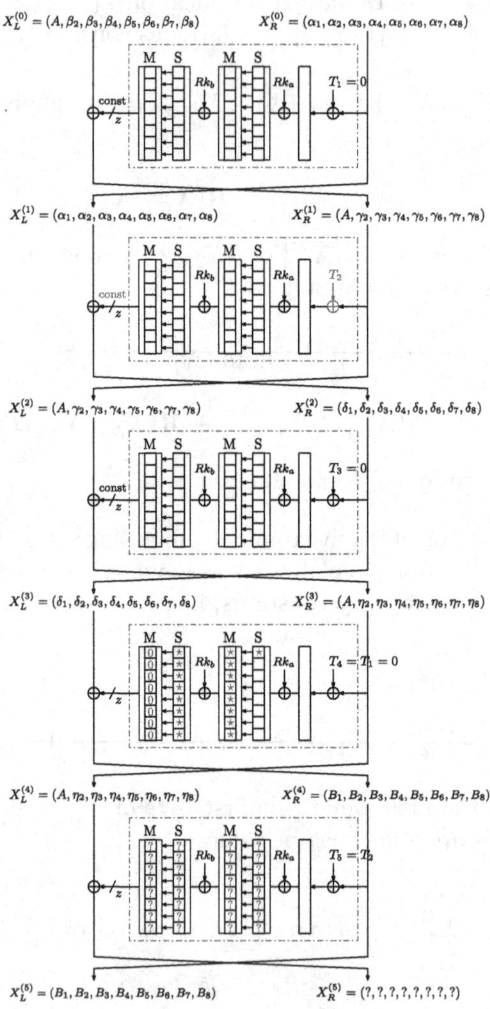

Fig. 3. Five round distinguisher for FEA-2.

5 Key Recovery Attacks

In this section, we describe key recovery attacks on FEA-2 using the distinguishers presented in the Subsect. 4.2. Firstly, we describe six round key recovery attacks for FEA-2 using the five round distinguisher. This attack works for 192-bit and 256-bit key-sizes of FEA-2. Further, we present a four round attack for both 192-bit and 256-bit key-sizes of FEA-1.

5.1 Six Round Key Recovery Attack on FEA-2

We describe six round key recovery attacks for FEA-2 by using the five round distinguisher, described in Subsect. 4.2.

5.1.1 Extension by a Round at the Beginning In order to construct this six round key recovery attack, we append an extra round at the start of five round distinguisher described in Subsect. 4.2. The key idea for this six round attack is based on choosing a collection of plaintexts such that the first round output forms a Λ-set as described in Eqs. (7) and (8). The attack is demonstrated in Fig. 4.

In the specification of FEA-2, it is given that T_1 is always 0, while we choose $T_2 = 0$ and T_3 such that $T_3 \oplus X_R^{(2)}$ is constant for every 256 values of $X_R^{(2)}$.

Step 1. Guess the all eight byte of $Rk_a^{(1)}$ and $Rk_b^{(1)}$ of the first round key. That is, guess total 16-bytes of the key.

Step 2. Choose input plaintexts as

$$\mathbf{I} = \{(X_L^{(0)}(i), X_R^{(0)}(i)) \mid 0 \leq i \leq 255\},$$

where $X_R^{(0)}(i) = (i, \beta_1, \beta_2, \beta_3, \beta_4, \beta_5, \beta_6, \beta_7)$ for arbitrarily chosen constants $(\beta_1, \ldots, \beta_7)$ and $X_L^{(0)}(i) = (z_j(i) \oplus \alpha_j)$ for $0 \leq j \leq 7$, where α_j are arbitrary constant values for $0 \leq i \leq 7$ and $z_0(i)$ is defined as

$$\begin{aligned} z_0(i) = 28 \cdot S(y_0(i) \oplus Rk_b^{(1)}[0]) \oplus 1a \cdot S(y_1(i) \oplus Rk_b^{(1)}[1]) \\ \oplus 7b \cdot S(y_2(i) \oplus Rk_b^{(1)}[2]) \oplus 78 \cdot S(y_3(i) \oplus Rk_b^{(1)}[3]) \\ \oplus c3 \cdot S(y_4(i) \oplus Rk_b^{(1)}[4]) \oplus d0 \cdot S(y_5(i) \oplus Rk_b^{(1)}[5]) \\ \oplus 42 \cdot S(y_6(i) \oplus Rk_b^{(1)}[6]) \oplus 40 \cdot S(y_7(i) \oplus Rk_b^{(1)}[7]). \end{aligned} \tag{11}$$

In Eq. 1, $y_0(i), y_1(i), y_2(i), y_3(i), y_4(i), y_5(i), y_6(i), y_7(i)$ are defined as

$$\begin{aligned} y_0(i) &= 28 \cdot S(i \oplus Rk_a^{(1)}[0]) \oplus C_0; & y_4(i) &= c3 \cdot S(i \oplus Rk_a^{(1)}[0]) \oplus C_4 \\ y_1(i) &= 1a \cdot S(i \oplus Rk_a^{(1)}[0]) \oplus C_1; & y_5(i) &= d0 \cdot S(i \oplus Rk_a^{(1)}[0]) \oplus C_5 \\ y_2(i) &= 7b \cdot S(i \oplus Rk_a^{(1)}[0]) \oplus C_2; & y_6(i) &= 42 \cdot S(i \oplus Rk_a^{(1)}[0]) \oplus C_6 \\ y_3(i) &= 78 \cdot S(i \oplus Rk_a^{(1)}[0]) \oplus C_3; & y_7(i) &= 40 \cdot S(i \oplus Rk_a^{(1)}[0]) \oplus C_7, \end{aligned}$$

here $C_0, C_1, C_2, C_3, C_4, C_5, C_6, C_7$ values depend upon the constants and other seven key bytes of Rk_a.

Similarly, we can compute $z_j(i)$'s for $1 \leq j \leq 7$. Basically, $z_j(i)$'s values are the output of the round function corresponding to the inputs $X_R^{(0)}(i)$, $Rk_a^{(1)}$ and $Rk_b^{(1)}$.

Step 3. If the guessed keys are the correct keys, then the right half of the second round input ($X_R^{(1)}$) consists of constant bytes α_j for $0 \leq j \leq 7$, i.e., $X_R^{(1)} = (\alpha_0, \alpha_1, \alpha_2, \alpha_3, \alpha_4, \alpha_5, \alpha_6, \alpha_7)$.

Step 5. Use the five round distinguisher as described previously.

Step 6. Let $X_L^{(6)}$ and $X_R^{(6)}$ be outputs corresponding to the inputs in the set **I** (see Step 2) after 6 rounds of FEA-2. If all bytes of $X_L^{(6)}$ are balanced, then we can accept guessed key as the correct key. Otherwise, go back to Step 1, and guess another key and repeat the process.

In Step 1, we guess all eight bytes of $RK_a^{(1)}$ and $RK_b^{(1)}$. That is, we guess all 16 bytes of the round key in Step 1. A wrong key can pass this test with a probability 2^{-64}. In order to filter the wrong key, we need three Λ-sets of plaintexts as inputs. We require 2^8 number of six round encryptions for each guessed key. Therefore, the time complexity of six round attack is $3 \times 2^8 \times (2^8)^{16} \approx 2^{137.6}$ (Fig. 4).

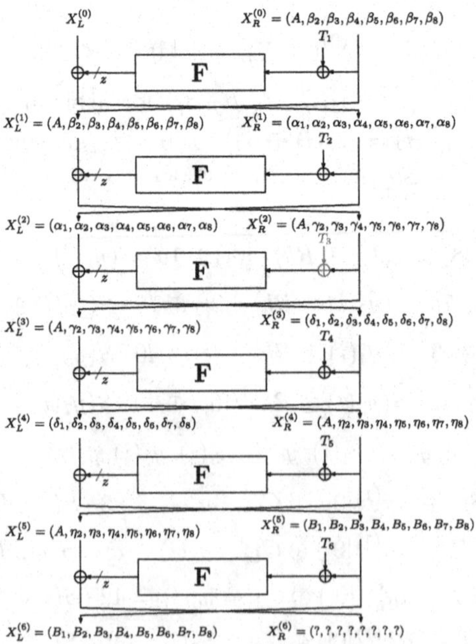

Fig. 4. Six round key recovery attacks on FEA-2 by adding a round in the beginning.

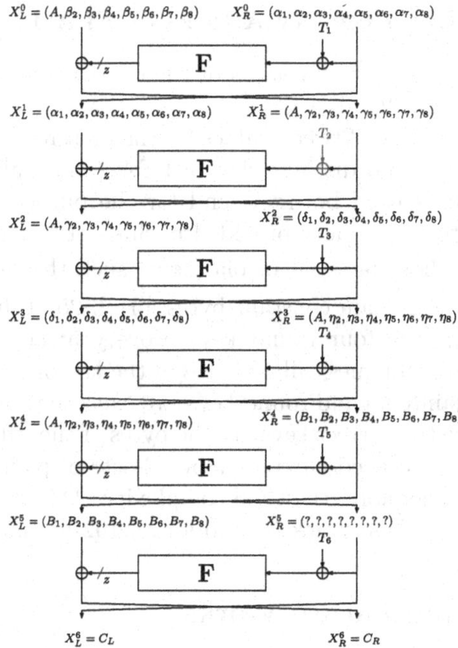

Fig. 5. Six round key recovery attack of FEA-2 by extending a round at the end.

5.1.2 Extension by a Round at the End In order to construct this six round key recovery attack, we extend the five rounds distinguisher presented in Subsect. 4.2 by adding an extra round at the end. The attack is demonstrated in Fig. 5.

This six round attack initiates with choosing a collection of plaintexts such that the first round input forms a Λ-set as described in Eqs. (7) and (8). The tweak value T_1 is always 0 (by design specification), while we choose T_2 such that $(T_2 \oplus X_R^{(1)})$ is constant for every 256 values of $X_R^{(1)}$ and $T_3 = 0$. After choosing plaintexts and the round tweaks, run six rounds of FEA-2. Let Y_L, Y_R represents the left and right halves of six round output, respectively, i.e., $X_L^{(6)} = Y_L$ and $X_R^{(6)} = Y_R$.

In order to check the balance property at the end of the 5th round, we decrypt the ciphertext Y_L, Y_R, by one round by guessing all the 16-bytes of round keys $Rk_a^{(6)}$ and $Rk_b^{(6)}$ for all 256 ciphertexts of the set. After decrypting, check whether the XOR of all 256 values of $x_L^{(5)}$ equals zero, i.e., $X_L^{(5)}$ is balanced. If $X_L^{(5)}$ is not balanced, then the guessed round key is a wrong key. Otherwise, the guessed key is the correct key.

A wrong key can pass this test with a probability 2^{-64}. To filter the wrong key, we need three Λ-sets of plaintexts as inputs. We require 2^8 number of six round encryptions for each guessed key. Therefore, the time complexity of six round attack is $3 \times 2^8 \times (2^8)^{16} \approx 2^{137.6}$.

5.2 Four Round Key Recovery Attacks on FEA-1

The key recovery attacks on four rounds of FEA-1 is based on the three round distinguisher given in Fig. 2.

Note that there is no role of tweak values for the presented three round distinguisher unlike the five round distinguisher of FEA-2. This allows the flexibility of extending the rounds from both the end for the purpose of the key recovery attacks. Similar to the attacks provided in Subsect. 5.1.1, the key recovery attacks are based on choosing a set of plaintexts such that all the $X_L^{(0)}$ form a Λ-set while all the $X_R^{(0)}$ remain constant bytes for all 256 values.

In order to mount the four round key recovery attack, we append extra round at the beginning and guess all 16 bytes of the key of the first round. After choosing the set of plaintexts and round keys, we execute three round of FEA-1. If the guessed keys are the correct keys, all the bytes of the left half of the output are balanced. Further, we need three or more Λ-sets of plaintexts as inputs to filter the wrong key. Therefore, the time complexity of the four round attack is $3 \times 2^8 \times (2^8)^{16} \approx 2^{137.6}$. This attack is valid for all 192-bit and 256-bit key-sizes.

6 Conclusion and Future Works

We presented two new distinguishers for FEA-1 and FEA-2 and extended these distinguishers to mount key-recovery attacks. In particular, we showed that the reduced round FEA-2 is vulnerable to square cryptanalysis beyond the author's claims. Increasing the number of rounds or improving the efficiency of presented distinguishing as well as key recovery attacks are open problems in this domain. Moreover, analyzing the security strength of FEA-1/FEA-2 against other cryptanalytic techniques are interesting line of work.

References

1. Bellare, M., Ristenpart, T., Rogaway, P., Stegers, T.: Format-preserving encryption. In: Jacobson, M.J., Rijmen, V., Safavi-Naini, R. (eds.) SAC 2009. LNCS, vol. 5867, pp. 295–312. Springer, Heidelberg (2009). https://doi.org/10.1007/978-3-642-05445-7_19
2. Beyne, T.: Linear cryptanalysis of FF3-1 and FEA. In: Malkin, T., Peikert, C. (eds.) CRYPTO 2021. LNCS, vol. 12825, pp. 41–69. Springer, Cham (2021). https://doi.org/10.1007/978-3-030-84242-0_3
3. Black, J., Rogaway, P.: Ciphers with arbitrary finite domains. In: Preneel, B. (ed.) CT-RSA 2002. LNCS, vol. 2271, pp. 114–130. Springer, Heidelberg (2002). https://doi.org/10.1007/3-540-45760-7_9
4. Brier, E., Peyrin, T., Stern, J.: BPS: a format-preserving encryption proposal. Submission to NIST (2010)
5. Brightwell, M., Smith, H.: Using datatype-preserving encryption to enhance data warehouse security. In: 20th National Information Systems Security Conference Proceedings (NISSC), pp. 141–149 (1997)

6. Chang, D., et al.: SPF: a new family of efficient format-preserving encryption algorithms. In: Chen, K., Lin, D., Yung, M. (eds.) Inscrypt 2016. LNCS, vol. 10143, pp. 64–83. Springer, Cham (2017). https://doi.org/10.1007/978-3-319-54705-3_5
7. Chang, D., Ghosh, M., Jati, A., Kumar, A., Sanadhya, S.K.: A generalized format preserving encryption framework using MDS matrices. J. Hardw. Syst. Secur. **3**(1), 3–11 (2019)
8. Coppersmith, D., Holloway, C., Matyas, S.M., Zunic, N.: The data encryption standard. Inf. Secur. Tech. Rep. **2**(2), 22–24 (1997)
9. Daemen, J., Knudsen, L., Rijmen, V.: The block cipher square. In: Biham, E. (ed.) FSE 1997. LNCS, vol. 1267, pp. 149–165. Springer, Heidelberg (1997). https://doi.org/10.1007/BFb0052343
10. Daemen, J., Rijmen, V.: The Design of Rijndael: AES - The Advanced Encryption Standard. Springer, Information Security and Cryptography. Springer, Heidelberg (2002). https://doi.org/10.1007/978-3-662-04722-4
11. Dunkelman, O., Kumar, A., Lambooij, E., Sanadhya, S.K.: Cryptanalysis of feistel-based format-preserving encryption. IACR Cryptol. ePrint Arch., p. 1311 (2020)
12. Durak, F.B., Horst, H., Horst, M., Vaudenay, S.: FAST: secure and high performance format-preserving encryption and tokenization. In: Tibouchi, M., Wang, H. (eds.) ASIACRYPT 2021. LNCS, vol. 13092, pp. 465–489. Springer, Cham (2021). https://doi.org/10.1007/978-3-030-92078-4_16
13. Dworkin, M.: NIST Special Publication 800–38A: recommendation for block cipher modes of operation-methods and techniques (2001)
14. Dworkin, M.: Recommendation for block cipher modes of operation: methods for format-preserving encryption. NIST Special Publication SP 800–38G Rev. 1, 800–38G (2019)
15. Granboulan, L., Levieil, É., Piret, G.: Pseudorandom permutation families over abelian groups. In: Robshaw, M. (ed.) FSE 2006. LNCS, vol. 4047, pp. 57–77. Springer, Heidelberg (2006). https://doi.org/10.1007/11799313_5
16. Lee, J.-K., Koo, B., Roh, D., Kim, W.-H., Kwon, D.: Format-preserving encryption algorithms using families of tweakable blockciphers. In: Lee, J., Kim, J. (eds.) ICISC 2014. LNCS, vol. 8949, pp. 132–159. Springer, Cham (2015). https://doi.org/10.1007/978-3-319-15943-0_9
17. Spies, T.: Feistel Finite Set Encryption. NIST submission (2008). https://csrc.nist.gov/groups/ST/toolkit/BCM/modes-development.html
18. Yeom, Y., Park, S., Kim, I.: On the security of CAMELLIA against the square attack. In: Daemen, J., Rijmen, V. (eds.) FSE 2002. LNCS, vol. 2365, pp. 89–99. Springer, Heidelberg (2002). https://doi.org/10.1007/3-540-45661-9_7

Asynchronous Silent Programmable Matter: Line Formation

Alfredo Navarra(✉) and Francesco Piselli

Dipartimento di Matematica e Informatica, Università degli Studi di Perugia, Perugia, Italy
alfredo.navarra@unipg.it, francesco.piselli@unifi.it

Abstract. Programmable Matter (PM) has been widely investigated in recent years. It refers to some kind of matter with the ability to change its physical properties (e.g., shape or color) in a programmable way. One reference model is certainly Amoebot, with its recent canonical version (DISC 2021). Along this line, with the aim of simplification and to better address concurrency, the SILBOT model has been introduced (AAMAS 2020), which heavily reduces the available capabilities of the particles composing the PM. In SILBOT, in fact, particles are asynchronous, without any direct means of communication (silent) and without memory of past events (oblivious). Within SILBOT, we consider the *Line formation* primitive in which particles are required to end up in a configuration where they are all aligned and connected. We propose a simple and elegant distributed algorithm – optimal in terms of number of movements, along with its correctness proof.

Keywords: Programmable Matter · Line Formation · Asynchrony · Stigmergy

1 Introduction

The design of smart systems intended to adapt and organize themselves in order to accomplish global tasks is receiving more and more interest, especially with the technological advance in nanotechnology, synthetic biology and smart materials, just to mention a few. Among such systems, main attention has been devoted in the recent years to the so-called *Programmable Matter* (PM). This refers to some kind of matter with the ability to change its physical properties (e.g., shape or color) in a programmable way. PM can be realized by means of weak self-organizing computational entities, called *particles.*

In the early 90s, the interest in PM by the scientific community was mostly theoretical. In fact, the ideas arising within such a context did not find support in technology that was unprepared for building computational devices at

A brief announcement about the results contained in this paper appears in the proceedings of the 37th International Symposium on Distributed Computing (DISC) 2023 [17]. The work has been supported in part by the Italian National Group for Scientific Computation (GNCS-INdAM).

S. Dolev and B. Schieber (Eds.): SSS 2023, LNCS 14310, pp. 598–612, 2023.
https://doi.org/10.1007/978-3-031-44274-2_44

micro/nanoscale. Nowadays, instead, nano-technology has greatly advanced and the pioneering ideas on PM could find a practical realization. The production of nano units that integrate computing, sensing, actuation, and some form of motion mechanism are becoming more and more promising. Hence, the investigation into the computational characteristics of PM systems has assumed again a central role, driven by the applied perspective. In fact, systems based on PM can find a plethora of natural applications in many different contexts, including smart materials, ubiquitous computing, repairing at microscopic scale, and tools for minimally invasive surgery. Nevertheless, the investigation on modeling issues for effective algorithm design, performance analysis and study on the feasibility of foundational tasks for PM have assumed a central and challenging role. Various models have been proposed so far for PM. One that deserves main attention is certainly Amoebot, introduced in [10]. By then, various papers have considered that model, possibly varying some parameters. Moreover, a recent proposal to try to homogenize the referred literature has appeared in [8], with the intent to enhance the model with concurrency.

One of the weakest models for PM, which includes concurrency and eliminates direct communication among particles as well as local and shared memory, is SILBOT [6]. The aim has been to investigate on the minimal settings for PM under which it is possible to accomplish basic global tasks in a distributed fashion. Actually, with respect to the Amoebot model, in SILBOT particles admit a 2 hops distance visibility instead of just 1 hop distance. Even though this does not seem a generalization of SILBOT with respect to Amoebot, the information that can be obtained by means of communications (and memory) in Amoebot may concern particles that are very far apart from each other. Moreover, there are tasks whose resolution has been shown to require just 1 hop distance visibility even in SILBOT (see, e.g. [18]), perhaps manipulating some other parameters. Toward this direction of simplification and in order to understand the requirements of basic tasks within PM, we aim at studying in SILBOT the *Line formation* problem, where particles are required to reach a configuration where they are all aligned (i.e., lie on a same axis) and connected.

1.1 Related Work

The relevance of the Line formation problem is provided by the interest shown in the last decades within various contexts of distributed computing. In graph theory, the problem has been considered in [13] where the requirement was to design a distributed algorithm that, given an arbitrary connected graph G of nodes with unique labels, converts G into a sorted list of nodes. In swarm robotics, the problem has been faced from a practical point of view, see, e.g. [14]. The relevance of line or V-shape formations has been addressed in various practical scenarios, as in [1,3,23], based also on nature observation. In fact, ants form lines for foraging activities whereas birds fly in V-shape in order to reduce the air resistance. In robotics, line or V-shape formations might be useful for exploration, surveillance or protection activities. Most of the work on robots considers direct communications, memory, and some computational power. For application underwater or in the outerspace, instead, direct communications are rather unfeasible and this motivates the investigation on removing such a capability, see, e.g. [15,21]. Concerning more theoretical models, the aim has been usually to study the minimal settings under which it is possible to realize basic primitives like Line formation. In [2,20], for instance, Line formation has been investigated for (semi-)synchronized robots (punctiform or not, i.e., entities occupying some space) moving within the Euclidean plane, admitting limited visibility, and sharing the knowledge of one axis on direction. For synchronous robots moving in 3D space, in [22], the plane formation has been considered, which might be considered as the problem corresponding to Line formation for robots moving in 2D. In [16], robots operate within a triangular grid and Line formation is required as a preliminary step for accomplishing the Coating of an object. The environment as well as the movements of those robots remind PM. Within Amoebot, Line formation has been approached in [11], subject to the resolution of Leader Election, which is based, in turn, on communications and not on movements.

1.2 Outline

In the next section, we provide all the necessary definitions and notation, along with the formalization of the Line formation problem. In Sect. 3, we give some preliminary results about the impossibility to resolve Line formation within SILBOT. Then, in Sect. 4, we provide a resolution algorithm for the case of particles sharing a common orientation. In Sect. 5, we show a possible running example about the proposed algorithm. In Sect. 6, we prove the correctness as well as the optimality in terms of number of moves of the proposed algorithm. Finally, in Sect. 7, we provide some conclusive remarks and possible directions for future work.

2 Definitions and Notation

In this section, we review the SILBOT model for PM introduced in [5,6], and then we formalize the Line formation problem along with other useful definitions.

In SILBOT, particles operate on an infinite triangular grid embedded in the plane. Each node can contain at most one particle. Each particle is an automaton with two states, CONTRACTED or EXPANDED (they do not have any other form of persistent memory). In the former state, a particle occupies a single node of the grid while in the latter, the particle occupies one single node and one of the adjacent edges, see, e.g. Figure 1. Hence, a particle always occupies one node, at any time. Each particle can sense its surrounding up to a distance of 2 hops, i.e., if a particle occupies a node v, then it can see the neighbors of v, denoted by $N(v)$, and the neighbors of the neighbors of v. Hence, within its visibility range, a particle can detect empty nodes, CONTRACTED, and EXPANDED particles.

Any positioning of CONTRACTED or EXPANDED particles that includes all n particles composing the system is referred to as a *configuration*. Particles alternate between active and inactive periods decided by an adversarial schedule, independently for each particle.

In order to move, a particle alternates between EXPANDED and CONTRACTED states. In particular, a CONTRACTED particle occupying node v can move to a neighboring node u by expanding along edge (v, u), and then re-contracting on u. Note that, if node u is already occupied by another particle then the EXPANDED one will reach u only if u becomes empty, eventually, in a successive activation. There might be arbitrary delays between the actions of these two particles. When the particle at node u has moved to another node, the edge between v and u is still occupied by the originally EXPANDED particle. In this case, we say that node u is *semi-occupied.*

A particle commits itself into moving to node u by expanding in that direction. At the next activation of the same particle, it is constrained to move to node u, if u is empty. A particle cannot revoke its expansion once committed.

The SILBOT model introduces a fine grained notion of asynchrony with possible delays between observations and movements performed by the particles. This reminds the so-called ASYNC schedule designed for theoretical models dealing with mobile and oblivious robots (see, e.g. [4,7,12]). All operations performed by the particles are non-atomic: there can be delays between the actions of sensing the surroundings, computing the next decision (e.g., expansion or contraction), executing the decision.

The well-established fairness assumption is included, where each particle must be activated within finite time, infinitely often, in any execution of the particle system, see, e.g., [12].

Particles are required to take deterministic decisions. Each particle may be activated at any time independently from the others. Once activated, a particle looks at its surrounding (i.e., at 2 hops distance) and, on the basis of such an observation, decides (deterministically) its next *action.*

If two CONTRACTED particles decide to expand on the same edge simultaneously, exactly one of them (arbitrarily chosen by the adversary) succeeds.

If two particles are EXPANDED along two distinct edges incident to a same node w, toward w, and both particles are activated simultaneously, exactly one of the particles (again, chosen arbitrarily by the adversary) contracts to node w, whereas the other particle does not change its EXPANDED state according to the commitment constraint described above.

A relevant property that is usually required in such systems concerns connectivity. A configuration is said to be *connected* if the set of nodes occupied by particles induce a connected subgraph of the grid.

Definition 1. *A configuration is said to be* initial, *if all the particles are* CONTRACTED *and connected.*

Definition 2. *[Line formation] Given an initial configuration, the* Line formation *problem asks for an algorithm that leads to a configuration where all the particles are* CONTRACTED, *connected and aligned.*

Definition 3. *Given a configuration C, the corresponding* bounding box *of C is the smallest parallelogram with sides parallel to the West–East and SouthWest–NorthEast directions, enclosing all the particles.*

See Fig. 1b for a visualization of the bounding box of a configuration. Note that, in general, since we are dealing with triangular grids, there might be three different bounding boxes according to the choice of two directions out of the three available. As it will be clarified later, for our purposes we just need to define one by choosing the West–East and SouthWest–NorthEast directions. In fact, as we are going to see in the next section, in order to solve Line formation in SILBOT, we need to add some capabilities to the particles. In particular, we add a common orientation to the particles. As shown in Fig. 2a, all particles commonly distinguish among the six directions of the neighborhood that by convention are referred to as the cardinal points $\mathbb{NW}$, $\mathbb{NE}$, $\mathbb{W}$, $\mathbb{E}$, $\mathbb{SW}$, and $\mathbb{SE}$.

Furthermore, in order to describe our resolution algorithm, we need two further definitions that identify where the particles will be aligned.

Definition 4. *Given a configuration C, the line of the triangular grid containing the southern side of the bounding box of C is called the* floor.

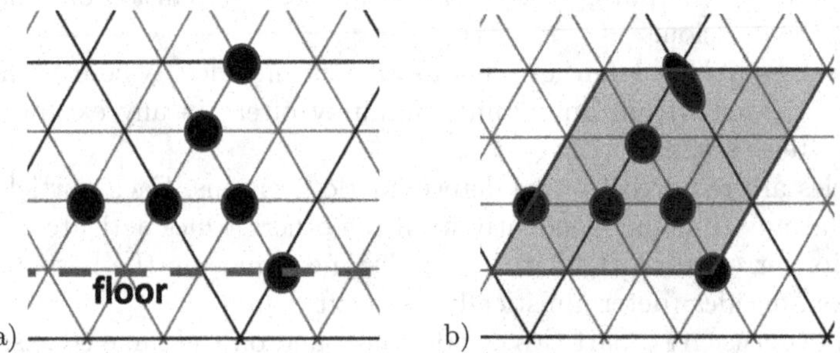

Fig. 1. (*a*) A possible initial configuration with emphasized the *floor* (dashed line); (*b*) a possible evolution of the configuration shown in (a) with an expanded particle. The shaded parallelogram is the minimum bounding box containing all the particles.

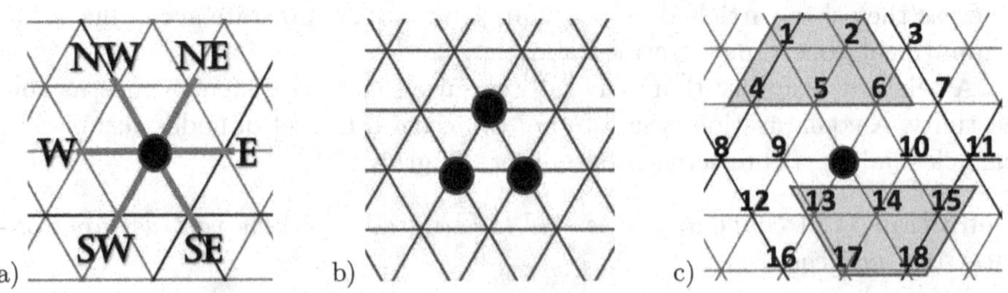

Fig. 2. (*a*) A representation of the orientation of a particle; (*b*) An initial configuration where Line formation is unsolvable within SILBOT; (*c*) Enumerated visible neighborhood of a particle; the two trapezoids emphasize two relevant areas for the definition of the resolution algorithm.

Table 1. Literature on SILBOT.

Problem	*Schedule*	*View*	*Orientation*	*Reference*
Leader Election	ASYNC	2 hops	no	[5]
Scattering	ED-ASYNC	1 hop	no	[18]
Coating	ASYNC	2 hops	chirality	[19]
Line formation	ASYNC	2 hops	yes	**this paper**

Definition 5. *A configuration is said to be* final *if all the particles are* CONTRACTED*, connected and lie on floor.*

By the above definition, a final configuration is also initial. Moreover, if a configuration is final, then Line formation has been solved. Actually, it might be the case that a configuration satisfies the conditions of Definition 2 but still it is not final with respect to Definition 5. This is just due to the design of our algorithm that always leads to solve Line formation on floor.

3 Impossibility Results

As shown in the previous section, the SILBOT model is very constrained in terms of particles capabilities. Since its first appearance [6], where the Leader Election problem has been solved, the authors pointed out the need of new assumptions in order to allow the resolution of other basic primitives. In fact, due to the very constrained capabilities of the particles, it was not possible to exploit the election of a leader to solve subsequent tasks. The parameters that can be manipulated have concerned the type of schedule, the hop distance from which particles acquire information, and the orientation of the particles. Table 1 summarizes the primitives so far approached within SILBOT and the corresponding assumptions. Leader Election was the first problem solved when introducing SILBOT [5]. Successively, the Scattering problem has been investigated [18]. It asks for moving the particles in order to reach a configuration where no two particles are neighboring to each other. Scattering has been solved by reducing the visibility range to just 1 hop distance but relaxing on the schedule which is not ASYNC. In fact, the ED-ASYNC schedule has been considered. It stands for Event-Driven Asynchrony, i.e., a particle activates as soon as it admits a neighboring particle, even though all subsequent actions may take different but finite time as in ASYNC. For Coating [19], where particles are required to surround an object that occupies some connected nodes of the grid, the original setting has been considered apart for admitting chirality, i.e., a common handedness among particles.

In this paper, we consider the Line formation problem, where particles are required to reach a configuration where they are all aligned and connected. About the assumptions, we add a common orientation to the particles to the basic SILBOT model. The motivation for endowing the particles with such a capability comes by the following result:

Theorem 1. *Line formation is unsolvable within* SILBOT, *even though particles share a common chirality.*

Proof. The proof simply comes by providing an instance where Line formation cannot be accomplished within the provided assumptions. By referring to Fig. 2b, we note that even if particles share chirality, they are all indistinguishable. No matter the algorithm designed for solving Line formation, an adversary may activate all particles synchronously so that they all behave symmetrically to each other. Hence, any action performed by a particle will be applied by all of them in a symmetric way. It means that any reachable configuration maintains the initial symmetry. Since a configuration solving Line formation for the provided instance requires to distinguish a particle which lies between the other two, we conclude that such a solution cannot be achieved. □

Note that, the arguments provided in the proof of Theorem 1 can be extended to any configuration where the initial symmetry is 'not compatible' with the formation of a line.

Motivated by Theorem 1, we assume a common orientation to the particles. Consequently, each particle can enumerate its neighborhood, up to distance of 2 hops, as shown in Fig. 2c. This will be useful for the definition of the resolution algorithm. Actually, it remains open whether it is possible to design an algorithm even when particles share just one direction instead of the full orientation.

4 Algorithm *WRain*

The rationale behind the name *WRain* of the proposed algorithm comes by the type of movements allowed. In fact, the evolution of the system on the basis of the algorithm mimics the behavior of particles that fall down like drops of rain subject to a westerly wind. The Line formation is then reached on the lower part of the initial configuration where there is at least a particle – what we have called *floor*.

In order to define the resolution Algorithm *WRain*, we need to define some functions, expressing properties related to a node of the grid. We make use of the enumeration shown in Fig. 2c, and in particular to the neighbors enclosed by the two trapezoids.

Definition 6. *Given a node v, the next Boolean functions are defined:*

- Upper(v) *is* true *if at least one of the visible neighboring nodes from v at positions* $\{1, 2, 4, 5, 6\}$ *is occupied by a particle;*
- Lower(v) *is* true *if at least one of the visible neighboring nodes from v at positions* $\{13, 14, 15, 17, 18\}$ *is occupied by a particle;*
- Pointed(v) *is* true *if there exists a particle p occupying a node $u \in N(v)$ such that p is* EXPANDED *along edge (u, v);*
- Near(v) *is* true *if there exists an empty node $u \in N(v)$ such that* Pointed(u) *is true.*

For the sake of conciseness, sometimes we make use of the above functions by providing a particle p as input in place of the corresponding node v occupied by p.

We are now ready to formalize our Algorithm *WRain*.

Algorithm 1. *WRain.*

Require: Node v occupied by a CONTRACTED particle p.
Ensure: Line formation.
1: **if** $\neg Near(v)$ **then**
2:     **if** $Pointed(v)$ **then**
3:         p expands toward $\mathbb{E}$
4:     **else**
5:         **if** $\neg Upper(v) \wedge Lower(v)$ **then**
6:             p expands toward $\mathbb{SE}$

It is worth noting that Algorithm *WRain* allows only two types of expansion, toward $\mathbb{E}$ or $\mathbb{SE}$. Moreover, the movement toward $\mathbb{E}$ can happen only when the node v occupied by a particle is intended to be reached by another particle, i.e., $Pointed(v)$ holds. Another remarkable property is that the algorithm only deals with expansion actions. This is due to the constraint of the SILBOT model that does not permit to intervene on EXPANDED particles, committed to terminate their movement. An example of execution of *WRain* starting from the configuration of Fig. 1a is shown in the next section.

5 Running Example

In this section, we show a possible execution of Algorithm *WRain*, starting from the configuration shown in Fig. 1a (or equivalently by starting directly from the configuration shown in Fig. 3a). Being in an asynchronous setting, there are many possible executions that could occur. In our example, we consider the case where all the particles that can move according to the algorithm apply the corresponding rule. It is basically an execution subject to the fully synchronous schedule (which is a special case of ASYNC).

From the considered configuration of Fig. 1a, Algorithm *WRain* allows only the particle on top to move. In fact, considering the node v occupied by such a particle, we have that $Near(v)$, $Pointed(v)$ and $Upper(v)$ are all *false*, whereas $Lower(v)$ is true. Note that, none of the nodes occupied by the other particles imply function *Upper* to be true but the leftmost for which function *Lower* is false. Hence, the configuration shown in Fig. 1b is reached, eventually. After the movement of the EXPANDED particle, see Fig. 3a, the configuration is basically like an initial one with CONTRACTED and connected particles. The only movement occurring in initial configurations is given by Line 6 of Algorithm *WRain*. In fact, when there are no EXPANDED particles, only Line 6 can be activated, as Line 3 requires function *Pointed* to be true for a node occupied by a CONTRACTED particle. From the configuration of Fig. 3a, there are two particles – the top ones, that can move according to the algorithm. If both are activated, configuration of Fig. 3b is obtained. Successively, the rightmost EXPANDED particle is free to move, whereas the other EXPANDED particle allows the pointed particle to expand, as shown in Fig. 3c, by means of Line 3 of the algorithm.

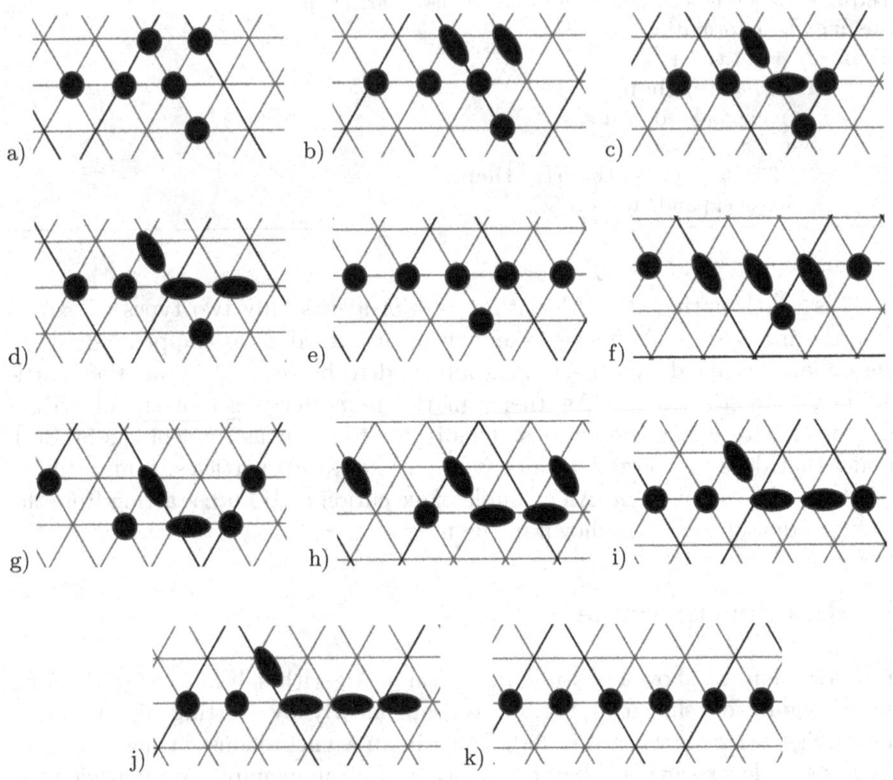

Fig. 3. A possible execution when starting from the configuration shown in Fig. 1a.

As already observed, the movement toward $\mathbb{SE}$ is generated by the rule at Line 6 of Algorithm *WRain*, whereas the movement toward $\mathbb{E}$ can only be induced by EXPANDED particles as specified by the rule at Line 3. By keep applying the two rules among all particles, the execution shown in the subsequent Figs. 3d–k is obtained, hence leading to the configuration where all particles are CONTRACTED and aligned along *floor*. It is worth noting that the configuration shown in Fig. 3g is disconnected. However, as we are going to show, the possible disconnections occurring during an execution are always recovered. In particular, in the specific example, connectivity is recovered right after as shown in Fig. 3i.

6 Correctness and Optimality

In this section, we prove the correctness of Algorithm *WRain* as well as its optimality in terms of number of moves performed by the particles.

We prove the correctness of Algorithm *WRain* by showing that the four following claims hold:

Claim 1 - Configuration Uniqueness. Each configuration generated during the execution of the algorithm is unique, i.e., non-repeatable, after movements, on the same nodes nor on different nodes;

Claim 2 - Limited Dimension. The extension of any (generated) configuration is confined within a finite bounding box of sides $O(n)$;

Claim 3 - Evolution guarantee. If the (generated) configuration is connected and not final there always exists at least a particle that can expand or contract;

Claim 4 - Connectivity. If two particles initially neighboring to each other get disconnected, they recover their connection sooner or later (not necessarily becoming neighbors).

The four claims guarantee that a final configuration is achieved, eventually, in finite time, i.e., Line formation is solved. In fact, by assuming the four claims true, we can state the next theorem.

Theorem 2. *Given n* CONTRACTED *particles forming a connected configuration, Algorithm WRain terminates in a connected configuration where all the particles are aligned along* floor.

Proof. By Claim 3 we have that from any non-final configuration reached during an execution of *WRain* there is always at least one particle that moves. Hence, by Claim 1, any subsequent configuration must be different from any already reached configuration. However, since Claim 2 states that the area where the particles move is limited, then a final configuration must be reached as the number of achievable configurations is finite. Actually, if we imagine a configuration made of disconnected and CONTRACTED particles, all lying on *floor*, then the configuration is not final according to Definition 5 but none of the particles would move. However, by Claim 4, we know that such a type of configurations cannot occur, and in particular, if two particles initially neighboring to each other get disconnected, then they recover their connection, eventually. Since the initial configuration is connected, then we are ensured that also the final configuration is connected as well. □

We now provide a proof for each of the above claims.

Proof (of Claim 1 - Configuration Uniqueness).

Since the movements allowed by the algorithm are toward either $\mathbb{E}$ or $\mathbb{SE}$ only, then the same configuration on the same nodes cannot arise during an execution as it would mean that some particles have moved toward $\mathbb{W}$, $\mathbb{NW}$, or $\mathbb{NE}$. Concerning the case to form the same configuration but on different nodes, it is sufficient to note that a particle lying on a node v of *floor* can only move toward $\mathbb{E}$ (since *Lower*(v) is false, cf. Line 6 of Algorithm *WRain*). Hence, either none of the particles on *floor* move, in which case the same configuration should appear on the same nodes – but this has been already excluded; or the same configuration may appear if all the particles move toward $\mathbb{E}$. However, based on the algorithm, the only movement that can occur from an initial configuration is toward $\mathbb{SE}$, hence the claim holds. □

Proof (of Claim 2 - Limited Dimension).

From the arguments provided to prove Claim 1, we already know that any configuration obtained during an execution of *WRain* never overpasses *floor*, defined by the initial configuration. Moreover, since the movements are toward either $\mathbb{E}$ or $\mathbb{SE}$ only, then the northern and the western sides of the bounding box of the initial configuration are never overpassed as well. Concerning the eastern side, we show that this can be shifted toward east in the generated configurations at most n times

About movements toward $\mathbb{SE}$ that overpass the eastern side, they cannot happen more than $n-1$ times according to Algorithm *WRain*. In fact, each time it happens, the northern side moves toward south.

About the movement toward $\mathbb{E}$, it requires a pushing-like process by another particle that either comes from $\mathbb{W}$ or from $\mathbb{NW}$. The claim then follows by observing that a particle can be pushed at most $n-1$ times, one for each other particle. In fact, if a particle p is pushed toward $\mathbb{E}$, then the pushing particle p' either comes from $\mathbb{W}$ or from $\mathbb{NW}$, i.e., after the pushing p and p' are on the same WestEast axis. Hence, in order to push again p toward $\mathbb{E}$, it is necessary that a third particle, p'' pushes p' that in turn pushes p. This may happen, for instance, if initially the particles are all aligned along the western side of the bounding box. Hence, by making the union of the bounding boxes of all the configurations obtained during an execution of *WRain*, the obtained box has the sides of size upper bounded by n. □

Proof (of Claim 3 - Evolution guarantee).

Let us assume the configuration does contain a particle p, occupying node v, EXPANDED toward node u. If u is empty, then p (or possibly another particle) will reach u, eventually. If u is occupied, then the particle p' in u – if not already EXPANDED, will be pushed to move toward $\mathbb{E}$. In any case, there must be a particle at the end of a chain of EXPANDED particles that either expands itself or moves toward the empty node toward which it is expanded. In any case, the configuration evolves.

Let us consider then the case where all the particles are CONTRACTED and connected. If all the particles lie on *floor*, then the configuration is final. Hence, if the configuration is not final, there must exist a particle p occupying a node v which is not on *floor* such that, $\neg Near(v) \wedge \neg Pointed(v) \wedge \neg Upper(v) \wedge Lower(v)$ holds, i.e., according to Algorithm *WRain*, p expands toward $\mathbb{SE}$. The existence of p is guaranteed by the fact that $\neg Near(v) \wedge \neg Pointed(v)$ clearly holds since none of the particles are EXPANDED, whereas $\neg Upper(v) \wedge Lower(v)$ holds for at least one of the topmost particles that of course does not admit neighboring particles on top, but admits particles below, due to connectivity. □

Proof (of Claim 4 - Connectivity).

Let us consider two neighboring particles p and p' of the initial configuration. Without loss of generality, let us assume that the two particles become disconnected due to the movement of p from node v to node u. In fact, expansions do not cause disconnections as an EXPANDED particle still maintains the node occupied. If the movement is toward $\mathbb{E}$, then we are sure there is another particle EXPANDED toward v, i.e., v remains semi-occupied. Consequently, either p' moves and recovers its connection with p or another particle moves to v, again recovering the connection between p and p'. Moreover, after its movement, p cannot move again as long as v remains semi-occupied since $Near(p)$ is true during that time; whereas, if p' moves during that time (necessarily toward $\mathbb{E}$ or $\mathbb{SE}$), it becomes neighbor of p again.

Then, the movement of p must be toward $\mathbb{SE}$. According to Algorithm *WRain*, p has decided to move toward $\mathbb{SE}$ because: $Near(v)$ is false, i.e., none of the nodes in $N(v)$ is semi-occupied; $Pointed(v)$ is false; $Upper(v)$ is false and in particular the are no particles in positions $\{4, 5, 6\}$ according to the enumeration of its neighborhood shown in Fig. 2c; whereas there is at least one particle p'' among positions $\{13, 15, 17, 18\}$. In fact, 14 must be empty as p is moving there. Hence, the movement toward 14 makes p neighboring p''. It follows that, if the movement of p has caused a disconnection from p', then p' is in position 9, with respect to v, that represents the connection to p before the movement. In fact, we know that positions $\{5, 6\}$ are empty, whereas the movement to 14 maintains p neighboring with $\{10, 13\}$, i.e., only the connection to 9 can get lost. Hence, p' makes $Upper(p)$ true, and p makes $Lower(p')$ true. It follows that p won't move anymore unless another particle $\overline{p}$ (possibly arriving successively) pushes it from v or from 13. In either cases, $\overline{p}$ connects p with p'. If p doesn't move before p', then p' must move, eventually. In fact, this happens as soon as either it is pushed or the *Upper* function evaluated from 9 becomes false. By Claims 1, 2 and 3, this must happen, eventually, since the configuration is not final. □

We are now ready to prove the optimality of Algorithm *WRain* in terms of number of total moves performed by the robots.

Lemma 1. *Given n CONTRACTED particles forming a connected configuration, Algorithm WRain terminates within $O(n^2)$ movements.*

Proof. In order to prove the lemma, it suffices to remark that any particle moves at most $n-1$ times toward $\mathbb{E}$ and $n-1$ times toward $\mathbb{SE}$, hence obtaining a number of total movements upper bounded by $O(n^2)$. □

Theorem 3. *Algorithm WRain is asymptotically optimal in terms of number of movements.*

Proof. As proven in [11], Line formation requires $\Omega(n^2)$ movements. That proof simply comes by assuming the initial configuration formed by n particles composing a connected structure of diameter at most $2\sqrt{n}+2$ (e.g., if they form a hexagonal or square shape), and then summing up all the necessary movements required to reach a configuration where particles form a line. Hence, by combining such a result with Lemma 1, the claim holds. □

7 Conclusion

We investigated on the Line formation problem within PM on the basis of the SILBOT model. With the aim of considering the smallest set of assumptions, we proved how chirality was not enough for particles to accomplish Line formation. We then endowed particles with a common sense of direction and we proposed *WRain*, an optimal algorithm – in terms of number of movements, for solving Line formation. Actually, it remains open whether by assuming just one common direction is enough for solving the problem. Furthermore, although in the original paper about SILBOT [5] it has been pointed out that 1 hop visibility is not enough for solving the Leader Election, it is worth investigating what happens for Line formation.

Other interesting research directions concern the resolution of other basic primitives, the formation of different shapes or the more general pattern formation problem. Also variants on the original SILBOT model deserve main attention. As shown in Table 1, small modifications to the original model may allow the resolution of challenging tasks. It would be interesting, for instance, to understand what might change if EXPANDED particles are allowed to revoke from their commitment on moving forward, i.e., if algorithms could deal also with EXPANDED particles.

Furthermore, adding a few bits of visible memory like allowing the particles to assume different states other than CONTRACTED and EXPANDED, or being endowed with visible lights similar to those studied in robot systems as in [9], might reveal higher potentials for PM.

References

1. Cai, H., Guo, S., Gao, H.: A dynamic leader-follower approach for line marching of swarm robots. Unmanned Syst. **11**(01), 67–82 (2023)
2. Castenow, J., Götte, T., Knollmann, T., Meyer auf der Heide, F.: The max-line-formation problem. In: Johnen, C., Schiller, E.M., Schmid, S. (eds.) SSS 2021. LNCS, vol. 13046, pp. 289–304. Springer, Cham (2021). https://doi.org/10.1007/978-3-030-91081-5_19
3. Chaudhuri, S.G.: Flocking along line by autonomous oblivious mobile robots. In: Hansdah, R.C., Krishnaswamy, D., Vaidya, N.H., (eds.) Proceedings of the 20th International Conference on Distributed Computing and Networking (ICDCN), pp. 460–464. ACM (2019)
4. Cicerone, S., Di Stefano, G., Navarra, A.: A structured methodology for designing distributed algorithms for mobile entities. Inf. Sci. **574**, 111–132 (2021)

5. D'Angelo, G., D'Emidio, M., Das, S., Navarra, A., Prencipe, G.: Asynchronous silent programmable matter achieves leader election and compaction. IEEE Access **8**, 207619–207634 (2020)
6. D'Angelo, G., D'Emidio, M., Das, S., Navarra, A., Prencipe, G.: Leader election and compaction for asynchronous silent programmable matter. In: Proceedings of the 19th International Conference on Autonomous Agents and Multiagent Systems (AAMAS), pp. 276–284. International Foundation for Autonomous Agents and Multiagent Systems (2020)
7. D'Angelo, G., Di Stefano, G., Navarra, A., Nisse, N., Suchan, K.: Computing on rings by oblivious robots: a unified approach for different tasks. Algorithmica **72**(4), 1055–1096 (2015)
8. Daymude, J.J., Richa, A.W., Scheideler, C.: The canonical Amoebot model: algorithms and concurrency control. In: 35th International Symposium on Distributed Computing, DISC 2021, vol. 209 of LIPIcs, pp. 20:1–20:19 (2021)
9. D'Emidio, M., Di Stefano, G., Frigioni, D., Navarra, A.: Characterizing the computational power of mobile robots on graphs and implications for the Euclidean plane. Inf. Comput. **263**, 57–74 (2018)
10. Derakhshandeh, Z., Dolev, S., Gmyr, R., Richa, A.W., Scheideler, C., Strothmann, T.: Brief announcement: Amoebot - a new model for programmable matter. In: Proceedings of the 26th ACM Symposium on Parallelism in Algorithms and Architectures, (SPAA), pp. 220–222. ACM (2014)
11. Derakhshandeh, Z., Gmyr, R., Strothmann, T., Bazzi, R., Richa, A.W., Scheideler, C.: Leader election and shape formation with self-organizing programmable matter. In: Phillips, A., Yin, P. (eds.) DNA 2015. LNCS, vol. 9211, pp. 117–132. Springer, Cham (2015). https://doi.org/10.1007/978-3-319-21999-8_8
12. Flocchini, P., Prencipe, G., Santoro, N. (eds.): Distributed computing by mobile entities, current research in moving and computing, vol. 11340. Springer, Cham (2019). https://doi.org/10.1007/978-3-030-11072-7
13. Gall, D., Jacob, R., Richa, A.W., Scheideler, C., Schmid, S., Täubig, H.: A note on the parallel runtime of self-stabilizing graph linearization. Theory Comput. Syst. **55**(1), 110–135 (2014)
14. Jeong, D., Lee, K.: Dispersion and line formation in artificial swarm intelligence. In: Proceedings of the 20th International Conference on Collective Intelligence (2014)
15. Jiang, Z., Wang, X., Yang, J.: Distributed line formation control in swarm robots. In: IEEE International Conference on Information and Automation (ICIA), pp. 636–641. IEEE (2018)
16. Kim, Y., Katayama, Y., Wada, K.: Pairbot: a novel model for autonomous mobile robot systems consisting of paired robots (2020)
17. Navarra, A., Piselli, F.: Line formation in silent programmable matter. In: Proceedings of the 37th International Symposium on Distributed Computing (DISC), LIPIcs (2023)
18. Navarra, A., Prencipe, G., Bonini, S., Tracolli, M.: Scattering with programmable matter. In: Barolli, L. (ed.) AINA 2023. LNCS, vol. 661, pp. 236–247. Springer, Cham (2023). https://doi.org/10.1007/978-3-031-29056-5_22
19. Piselli, F.: Silent programmable matter: Coating. Master's thesis, University of Perugia, Italy (2022)
20. Sil, A., Chaudhuri, S.G.: Formation of straight line by swarm robots. In: Mandal, J.K., Mukherjee, I., Bakshi, S., Chatterji, S., Sa, P.K. (eds.) Computational Intelligence and Machine Learning. AISC, vol. 1276, pp. 99–111. Springer, Singapore (2021). https://doi.org/10.1007/978-981-15-8610-1_11

21. Sousselier, T., Dréo, J., Sevaux, M.: Line formation algorithm in a swarm of reactive robots constrained by underwater environment. Expert Syst. Appl. **42**(12), 5117–5127 (2015)
22. Yamauchi, Y., Uehara, T., Kijima, S., Yamashita, M.: Plane formation by synchronous mobile robots in the three-dimensional Euclidean space. J. ACM, **64**(3), 16:1–16:43 (2017)
23. Yang, J., Wang, X., Bauer, P.: Line and V-shape formation based distributed processing for robotic swarms. Sensors **18**(8), 2543 (2018)

Author Index

S. Dolev and B. Schieber (Eds.): SSS 2023, LNCS 14310, pp. 613–614, 2023.
https://doi.org/10.1007/978-3-031-44274-2

Printed in the United States
by Baker & Taylor Publisher Services